Public Law and Public Administration

FOURTH EDITION

PHILLIP J. COOPER
Mark O. Hatfield School of Government
Portland State University

THOMSON

WADSWORTH

Australia • Brazil • Canada • Mexico • Singapore
Spain • United Kingdom • United States

Public Law and Public Administration
Fourth Edition
Phillip J. Cooper

Executive Editor: David Tatom
Associate Development Editor: Rebecca Green
Editorial Assistants: Eva Dickerson, Paige Fillipp
Technology Project Manager: Inna Fedoseyeva
Senior Marketing Manager: Janise Fry
Senior Marketing Assistant: Teresa Jessen
Project Manager, Editorial Production: Marti Paul
Creative Director: Rob Hugel
Art Director: Maria Epes
Print Buyer: Karen Hunt

Permissions Editor: Bob Kauser
Production Service: International Typesetting
  and Composition
Copy Editor: Lunaea Weatherstone
Illustrator: International Typesetting and Composition
Cover Designer: Bartay Studio
Cover Printer: Thomson West
Compositor: International Typesetting
  and Composition
Printer: Thomson West

Library of Congress Control Number: 2006927616

ISBN 0-495-00755-2

Thomson Higher Education
10, Davis Drive Belmont,
CA 94002-3098 USA

For more information about our products, contact us at:
Thomson Learning Academic Resource Center
1-800-423-0563

For permission to use material from this text or product, submit a request online at
http://www.thomsonrights.com.
Any additional questions about permissions can be submitted by e-mail to
thomsonrights@thomson.com.

*Dedicated to Professor Chester A. Newland who has demonstrated
for many years by quiet example what it truly means to be a public service professional
in practice and in the classroom.*

Contents

Preface to the Fourth Edition

Many books on law and courts begin with Alexis de Tocqueville's familiar observation that almost all important political problems in America sooner or later are recast as legal problems. But if Tocqueville had visited this country at the dawn of the twenty-first century rather than early in the nineteenth, he might have changed the observation to something like: "Sooner or later most important political problems in America are transformed into administrative problems which, in turn, find their way into the courts." In our country, there is a complex, ongoing interaction between matters legal and administrative. This book is about that interaction. Its premise is that public law problems confronting public managers are not merely legal but are also administrative and political. Those problems and the means by which they are addressed are key not only to those in government but also to the nonprofit organizations, for-profit firms, and individuals who interact with government.

It has now been more than twenty years since this book was published in its first edition. It is gratifying to know that teachers and students of law and public management continue to find it valuable as it has evolved over time. They have said that its approach to the subject and its concern with the perspectives of both public administrators and consumers of administrative decisions are valuable and still not generally available in other texts in the field. For all those comments any author would be grateful; and I am.

The fourth edition of the book retains its core design and chapter format. However, a variety of important themes have been woven into the chapters and the material and examples have been updated. Beginning with the third edition, an important change was made in the book as issues associated with the increase in contracting out—not just for the purchase of goods, but for the acquisition of services—were incorporated throughout. Whether it is contracting for services by state or local governments, contracting for temporary personnel in federal or state agencies, the use of nonprofit or for-profit organizations to deliver services and manage programs, as well as the increasing reliance on interjurisdictional agreements to accomplish public purposes more efficiently and effectively, it is essential to consider contracting in all elements of public law and public administration. While, for reasons that will become clear in the text, the law of government contracts is separate from administrative law, it is no longer reasonable to ignore the reality that the public law of public administration must pay attention to contract operations. Moreover, contractual relationships are by definition legal relationships. Any suggestion that contracting is an alternative to legal approaches to public management sets up a false dichotomy that is dangerous to public service professionals, whether they work in government units or nonprofit organizations. Contracts are legal devices and have been since the Code of Hammurabi. Contracting out is a matter of public law in public administration. Contracting issues were integrated throughout and have been updated since the publication of the third edition.

Second, another of the significant forces that has changed so much of the work of public managers is the increasing sophistication and centrality of technology. In particular, the dramatic growth of the Internet and the increasing penetration of computer usage has, along with other forces, led to the rise of e-government at all levels. For these reasons, revisions were done with attention to important technological developments in the field as a whole and in the particular topics addressed in each of the chapter. That said, the use of Internet sites and other key technological features was included with care for the fact that so much changes so rapidly in cyberspace.

Third, intergovernmental relations continues to grow as a central fact of life in public management. Now, more than ever before, states and local governments are responsible for a wide range of services and regulatory administration, including programs originally created by the Congress. That is true despite many reductions in budgets, human resources, and assistance from Washington over the past quarter century. At the same time, governance has become a particularly important conceptual and practical approach to accomplishing public goals even if there continues to be considerable debate as to exactly what that concept means. Working hand-in-hand with the expanded use of contracting and the increasing importance of both nonprofit and for-profit organizations in the development and operation of public programs, governance is one of the points of connection between those who focus on public policy creation and those who focus on public management. This edition attempts to highlight issues and challenges that arise from the governance concept and to explain the areas where existing law works effectively in governance regimes and where there are either conflicting characteristics or simply requirements for new law to address these evolving techniques of serving the public interest.

There is another factor that is more important now than in earlier eras in American public administration, and that is the dynamic impact of globalization on life virtually everywhere in the world. And while its effects may be more or less subtle in certain circumstances, they are nonetheless real. Whether it is international agreements that condition domestic regulation of the environment or trade agreement restrictions on state or local policymaking, it is now necessary for administrators at all levels to be alert to the presence of international issues and to be alert to their possible importance. Those issues have influenced such wide-ranging administrative challenges as efforts to deal with sewage treatment problems in Nogales, Arizona, to attempts by the State of Washington to protect the Puget Sound ecosystem from pollution by oil tankers, to Massachusetts' efforts to follow its collective values at it purchases goods and services in the marketplace. This global impact theme appears in several areas of the text in an attempt to increase awareness and consider critical issues that are raised by these forces.

The last three decades have also been years in which law and legal process have been blamed for most of the ills in the public arena by leaders of both parties. From the attack on the Washington that brought President Carter to office, through the Reagan years of pointing to government as the problem and not the solution, to the Clinton years in which the National Performance Review and reinventing government were grounded in an attack on rules and administrative law processes, to the George W. Bush years in which outsourcing has been a driving theme throughout the federal government, this has been a difficult period. These administrations, and many at the state level that have taken similar approaches, have found themselves with a host of serious difficulties—in no small part because of their tendency to blame their governments and public servants for the states' or the national government's difficulties and because of their failure to comprehend the central role of public law and public administration in governance. Ends and means matter. When possibly laudable goals are pursued without a sensitivity to the forces that have brought about a body of public law, as part of our commitment to the rule and supremacy of law, bad things often happen to good people and good ideas. To the working public manager, those trends have resulted in a variety of statutes and executive orders that have significantly affected many of the aspects of law and administration. This edition seeks to integrate these changes throughout with explanations of the their sources, operation, and consequences. Where they present serious difficulties, the attempt has been made to signal the problems and alert professionals to how they are being addressed.

One of the ironies of this period is that the attack on regulation has been at the heart of the politics of both of the nation's leading political parties and at all levels of government. Even so, it has been a era in which everything from international environmental accords, to airline safety, to concern with unsafe foods and drugs, to serious issues in health care organizations, to abuses of financial services and communications industries have brought demands for more, not less, regulation and more sophisticated accountability processes. It was in part for these reasons that the third edition added a new case study to the appendices. It is a study of the controversy surrounding the efforts by the Environmental Protection Agency to respond to calls that it ensure environmental justice. It adds a regulatory case study to accompany the social service *Mathews v. Eldridge* case study. It is also a case that evolved in the setting of the love/hate relationship with regulation that characterizes contemporary politics. The elements of these newer approaches to regulation are woven throughout the book's chapters.

The other purpose of the environmental justice case study is to provide a consideration of the concept of equity which is so important to public law and public administration. This edition highlights issues of equity in each of the areas of the field. It can be challenging for some students of the public administration to engage the concept of equity in large part because the term is used with too little care and almost no attention to the origins or the theory of equity in so much literature as well as in contemporary political and management debates.

Last, but most assuredly not least, the dramatic effects of September 11, 2001 have conditioned so many aspects of public life in the contemporary world that it seems difficult to recall what life was like before what we now refer to simply as 9/11. There have been so many new policies, new agencies, and changes to longstanding laws and organizations that we are not yet really clear as to the full meaning of the events of that fateful day for public law and public administration. With that caveat in mind, the fourth edition includes consideration of those changes that are apparent as of this writing and suggests some observations, within the limits of prudence, as to other issues likely to arise in the near term.

It should be said, though, that while every effort has been made to address contemporary trends, I regard the grounding of this text in the history and fundamentals of the field to be one of the strengths of the volume. This fourth edition seeks to address the new but with a firm grounding in mainstream. I hope that I have achieved a successful balance.

And speaking of balance, one of the important questions over the years about Public Law and Public Administration was how to integrate case law into the courses in which this text is used. A small but carefully selected and edited set of cases has been published by Thomson Learning as a companion casebook for this text. Its chapters are keyed to chapters in the core text. It also contains a selection of classic foundation cases in public law. This revision has taken into consideration matters presented in that casebook and has not duplicated them.

ACKNOWLEDGMENTS

It goes without saying that a book that has a history also has a long list of colleagues who have contributed to it in ways great and small. Years ago, Professors Dwight Waldo, Michael 0. Sawyer, John Clarke Adams, and Spencer Parratt encouraged my work in the area of law and administration and suggested the need for this book. Since then, colleagues at several universities have provided feedback on the volume in its various versions and editions. They include Professor Douglas Morgan at Portland State University, Howard Ball of the University of Vermont; Robert S. Gilmour then of the University of Connecticut; A. Lee Fritschler then at the Brookings Institution; Thomas Lauth of University of Georgia; William Richardson of the University of South Dakota, John A. Rohr of Virginia Polytechnic

Institute and State University, and Rick Green currently at the University of Utah. Their help and encouragement are sincerely appreciated.

I am particular grateful to Claudia who has helped in the development of this volume in more ways than I can say.

Phillip J. Cooper
Portland, Oregon

Credits

This page constitutes an extension of the copyright page. We have made every effort to trace the ownership of all copyrighted material and to secure permission from copyright holders. In the event of any question arising as to the use of any material, we will be pleased to make the necessary corrections in future printings. Thanks are due to the following authors, publishers, and agents for permission to use the material indicated.

Chapter 2. 30: From Federal Reporter, Third Series, West Publishing 1998. **48:** From West Law Finder, Third Series, West Publishing 1978.

Chapter 5. 158: From Congressional Control of Administrative Regulation: A Case Study of Legislative Votes, 90 *Harvard L. Rev.*, 1376-77 (1977). © 1977 by the Harvard Law Review Association. Used by permission of Harvard Law Review Association.

Chapter 6. 205: Cracks in 'The New Property': Adjudicative Due Process in the Administrative State, 62 *Cornell Law Rev.* 445, 489-90 (1977). © Cornell Law Review (1977). Used by permission of the Cornell Law Review.

Chapter 7. 267: The Honorable Carl McGowan, "Reflections on Rulemaking Review," originally published in 53 *Tul. L. Rev.* 681-96 (1979). Reprinted with permission of the Tulane Law Rev. Assn., which holds the copyright.

Chapter 9. 311: Discretionary Clemency: Mercy at the Prosecutor's Option, 1976 *Utah L. Rev.* 57, 59, 60, 64 (1976). Used by permission of the Utah Law Review. **312:** Abraham D. Sofaer, "Judicial Control of Informal Discretionary Adjudication and Enforcement," 72 *Colum. L. Rev.* 1296-97, 1300-1, 1313, 1374 (1972). © 1972 by the Directors of the Columbia Law Rev. Assn, I nc. Portions reprinted by permission of the review and the author. **318:** Richard B. Stewart, "The Reformation of American Administrative Law," 88 *Harv. Law Rev.*, 1667, 1695, 1676 n.25 (1975). © 1975 by the Harvard Law Review and the author. **342:** Richard B. Stewart, "The Reformation of American Administrative Law," 88 *Harv. Law Rev.*, 1667, 1695, 1676 n.25 (1975). © 1975 by the Harvard Law Review and the author.

Chapter 10. 362: James Q. Wilson, "The Politics of Regulation," in Wilson, ed., *The Politics of Regulation*, Basic Books, 1980, pp. 362-63, 366, 368, 369. Used by permission of James Q. Wilson. **375:** James Q. Wilson, "The Politics of Regulation," in Wilson, ed., *The Politics of Regulation*, Basic Books, 1980, pp. 362-63, 366, 368, 369. Used by permission of James Q. Wilson. **390:** Abraham Ribicoff, "Congressional Oversight and Regulatory Reform," 28 *Ad. L. Rev.*, 415, 418 (1976). Reprinted by permission from Administrative Law Review 1976. © The American Bar Association. All rights reserved. This information or any portion thereof may not be copied or disseminated in any form or by any means or downloaded or stored in an electronic database or retrieval system without the express written consent of the American Bar Association. **396:** The Threat of a Rulemaking Nightmare: What Proposed Legislation Might Have Done. Used by permission of Congressman Henry A. Waxman.

Chapter 11. 434: Remedies for Improper Disclosure of Genetic Data from Leonard L. Riskin and phililp J. Reilly, 8 *Rutgers Camden L. J.* 480, 483 (1977). © Rutgers Camden Law Journal. Used by permission.

1

Introduction: Defining the Field

Public law and public administration is an intensely practical field and perhaps the best way to begin to understand it is to consider a number of scenarios and the questions posed by each. Each presents a real situation and all will be discussed later in the text.

Suppose that you are a staff member in the office of the head of the U.S. Food and Drug Administration. One day you receive a request for guidance concerning a petition received from prisoners on death row in Texas. The inmates allege that the use of death by lethal injection poses a grave risk of cruel and unusual punishment. Specifically, they contend, based upon claims in British medical publications, that the lack of knowledge concerning the precise use and impact of drugs employed in the executions presents a real danger that prisoners would remain conscious but paralyzed while they died through asphyxiation. Indeed, researchers writing in the prestigious journal *The Lancet* wrote in 2005 that:

> Anaesthesia during lethal injection is essential to minimise suffering and to maintain public acceptance of the practice.... Protocol information from Texas and Virginia showed that executioners had no anaesthesia training, drugs were administered remotely with no monitoring for anaesthesia, ... and no peer-review was done. Toxicology reports from Arizona, Georgia, North Carolina, and South Carolina showed that post-mortem concentrations of thiopental in the blood were lower than that required for surgery in 43 of 49 executed inmates (88%); 21 (43%) inmates had concentrations consistent with awareness. Methods of lethal injection anaesthesia are flawed and some inmates might experience awareness and suffering during execution.[1]

The prisoners argue that, given the current state of knowledge, the use of the pharmaceuticals involved is not safe and effective. This use of the drugs involved would be safe and effective only if the drugs caused a quick and painless death. The statutes governing FDA operations clearly require the agency to ensure that drugs are both safe and effective for the uses to which they are applied. Therefore, the prisoners assert, the FDA has an obligation to institute an investigation into execution by lethal injection and to support their petition for an injunction against further executions until the FDA process is concluded.[2]

How should the agency respond? Would you do nothing? If you did, would you be vulnerable to a liability judgment? Worse, would your boss face a barrage of media pressure when this matter goes public, as it most assuredly would? Would you call the state? What would happen if the Texas Attorney General said that it was none of your business because crimes and punishments are questions for the state under the Tenth Amendment to the United States Constitution? How would such a claim relate to your own statutory responsibilities under federal law? Would it make a difference to you if the inmate cited precedents from the United States Circuit Courts of Appeals that said the FDA has authority over state use of experimental drugs in prisons and that it has jurisdiction to regulate the use of drugs to euthanize laboratory animals? To what degree is your agency implicated in the possible Eighth Amendment violation arising from a potentially cruel and unusual punishment if the prisoners' allegations proved to be correct in light of the published research?

Or consider a very different scenario.[3] Tennessee contracted operation of some of its prisons with the for-profit Corrections Corporation of America (CCA). Ronnie Lee McKnight, an inmate in one of the facilities, brought an action under 42 U.S.C. §1983 (a very important federal civil rights law that allows those whose constitutional or statutory rights were violated by state or local authorities to seek redress in federal courts) against prison guards employed by CCA. McKnight claimed that their use of excessively tight physical restraints violated his constitutional rights.

The guards claimed a qualified immunity from suit, the same sort of protection from liability that would be available to a guard working in a state prison as a public employee. The federal district court rejected the private guards' claims of qualified immunity from suit and the United States Circuit Court of Appeals for the Sixth Circuit affirmed.

Suppose that you were a justice of the United States Supreme Court. Would you find that private employees working for a contract provider of correctional services enjoys the same immunity from suit or would you see them as different from standard public employees? Does it matter that there are other mechanisms of accountability available in the case of civil servants but not for the employees of private contractors? If you would find a distinction, what would be the basis for it? If there is no difference between the public and private employees, what are the possible implications of such a ruling? If the situation involved a federal government contractor, would the firm be liable in a comparable situation? If so, under what kind of law?[4]

Think of yourself as a member of the Federal Communications Commission (FCC), the independent regulatory commission charged with regulating broadcasting on the airwaves in the public interest. More than 25 years ago, a man drove into New York City with his eight-year-old son at two o'clock in the afternoon and set in motion a policy process that has reverberated to this day. The radio was tuned to a public broadcasting station. For various reasons, the driver did not take note of the program currently being aired. Suddenly, to the surprise of the boy and the consternation of the father, a long string of profanity issues from the radio. The program on the air was playing a monologue recorded by a nightclub comedian concerning "seven dirty words." The monologue focused on words that, according to the comedian in question, "you couldn't say on the public airwaves, the ones you definitely wouldn't say ever." The recording was played as a part of program on the use and abuse of language in American culture. When the man arrived home, he promptly phoned the field office of the Federal Communications Commission (FCC) to complain. Such language, he said, should not be broadcast over the public airwaves and, in any case, it certainly should not be aired during the middle of the day when the audience was likely to contain large numbers of children.

The FCC agreed, issuing rules prohibiting the broadcasting of indecent materials—language not extreme enough to qualify as obscene under the tests set forth by the U.S. Supreme Court.

While objections were raised by free speech advocates on the basis of the First Amendment to the U.S. Constitution, the Court nevertheless upheld the FCC action.[5]

Fast-forward to the halftime entertainment at the Super Bowl on February 1, 2004. The buildup to this event had been substantial, with advertising led by Viacom and its subsidiary MTV and aired on some 20 CBS television stations. On January 28, MTV carried a posting on its website with the headline "Janet Jackson's Super Bowl Show Promises 'Shocking Moments.'"

> As the big game approaches, one of the top questions along with "Who's going to win?" is "What will Janet Jackson be doing at the halftime show?" It quotes choreographer Dulduleo as saying, "I don't think the Super Bowl has ever seen a performance like this. The dancing is great. She's more stylized, she's more feminine, she's more a woman as she dances this time around. *There are some shocking moments in there too.*" (Emphasis added.)[6]

And indeed, it turned out that there were a large number of shocked viewers in the audience of some 140 million watching this prime-time event that Sunday evening, enough to file more complaints with the FCC regarding a television program—some 540,000—than ever before in that agency's long history.[7]

What brought all those comments was, to be sure, the overall nature of the performances, but most especially a duet by Ms. Jackson and Justin Timberlake. The commission summarized what took place:

> She was soon joined by Justin Timberlake for a duet of "Rock Your Body," during which he urged her in the song to allow him to "rock your body" and "just let me rock you 'til the break of day" while following her around the stage and, on several occasions, grabbing and rubbing up against her. At the close of the song, immediately after singing the lyrics "gonna have you naked by the end of this song," Mr. Timberlake pulled off the right portion of Ms. Jackson's bustier, exposing her breast.[8]

An hour later, MTV posted an ad for the rebroadcast of the Super Bowl halftime show, under the headline "Janet Gets Nasty... Jaws across the country hit the carpet at exactly the same time. You know what we're talking about . . . Janet Jackson, Justin Timberlake and a kinky finale that rocked the Super Bowl to its core."[9] It then invited viewers to tune in for the rebroadcast.

Viacom, CBS, and others named in the complaint answered that they were not aware that the two performers had decided to use what they referred to as a "costume reveal." However, critics responded that rehearsal tapes revealed that while that particular action in the performance may not have been known to the broadcasters, they were very much aware, as their advertising indicated, that the presentation was deliberately designed to be sexually provocative and even "shocking."

As a member of the commission, what would you do? What means would you employ in investigating the complaint? Would you sanction the broadcasters or would you merely warn its management? If you would fine the broadcasters, how large a fine would be needed to get their attention considering the fact that each 30-second commercial on that Super Bowl program cost the advertiser some $2 million?[10] Would you argue that the issue should be left to the marketplace to resolve? How is a concept like "indecency" to be defined for purposes of decisionmaking in this case? How would you decide?

Consider now the situation in which the U.S. Department of Agriculture (USDA) found itself at the end of 2003. It was just two days before Christmas, and the Safeway stores in the Seattle area were running a door-buster special on standing rib roasts of beef, a traditional holiday favorite. Happy shoppers had returned home to show off their appetizing purchases when the television news stations carried a news conference called by the USDA. It was called to announce that: "Today we received word from USDA's National Veterinary Services Laboratories in Iowa that a single Holstein cow from Washington State has tested as presumptive positive for BSE or what is widely known as mad cow disease."[11] The matter involved one Holstein cow that had been on a ranch in eastern Washington State. This was the first cow with BSE (bovine spongeform encephalopathy) identified in the United States. This disease was bad enough among cattle, but it was all the more feared because it was linked to Creutzfeldt-Jacob disease in humans.

In addition to the most critical possibility of spread of a life-threatening disease, the presence of BSE in U.S. cattle also represented a major economic threat. The British cattle industry had been dramatically shaken by BSE, and, more recently, Canadian cattle ranchers faced closure of borders in the U.S. and elsewhere when cattle with BSE were detected in Canadian herds earlier in 2003.

There was an immediate public reaction, but not only because of the presence of BSE. It was learned that the cow in question was a so-called "downer animal," which meant that it was not physically healthy when it was taken for slaughter. Second, the animal was slaughtered at a small local facility and parts of the cow were then sent on to two distribution plants, Midway Meats and Interstate Meat in Washington State. While broad assurances were offered as to the safety of the meat, concerns mounted immediately as to whether those assurances were adequately supported by science and medicine.

What should the USDA do? If new regulations for the handling and processing of cattle are needed, it will take time to develop them. Should the agency have alternative mechanisms to deal with a serious health threat like this, different from its normal policy development techniques? If so, how is it possible to ensure that steps taken in the immediate aftermath of an emergency are later considered in greater detail when the initial threat passes? Does it matter that the agency that is acting in this instance is one that is primarily oriented to agricultural production and marketing as compared for example to the Centers for Disease Control, the National Institutes of Health, or other units of the U.S. Department of Health and Human Services?

Suppose you just began work in a new community as a city manager. All seems well as you settle into your new job, until the second week. On Monday morning your secretary asks to speak to you after the staff meeting. She asks if you know how it was that she came to work for you. While you knew that she was new to the office, though not to the city government, you shake your head and ask if she wants to share that information.

She explains that she had worked for a popular city department head who, she says, sexually harassed her. Immediately on edge, you wait for the rest of the story. She explains that she has not filed a complaint, but she applied for and got the new position as your secretary.

Your secretary tells you that she was not aware at the time that the city had a policy prohibiting sexual harassment and establishing a process for processing a complaint. She now feels that she needs to vindicate herself in light of rumors circulating within the organization and out of a sense of duty to others who may have to work with the same man. She politely but firmly insists that you are obligated to reopen the matter and take vigorous action. Further, she warns that if prompt action is not taken, she may have to seek damages from members of the city council and possibly from you as well.

What are your obligations, both legally and as a manager? What happens if you fail to act? Are you and the members of the council liable? What would the situation be if another employee later experiences harassment? What are your responsibilities in terms of due process for the accused? Are there privacy issues and, if so, what are they? What is your obligation, if any, in terms of your secretary's complaints about the process? How do you view the relationship between your potential legal liability and your obligations as a manager?[12]

Finally, assume you are an official in a Department of Veterans Affairs hospital (historically known as the VA). A gravely ill man comes to your facility suffering from terminal cancer. He insists that he contracted his illness as a result of exposure to various toxic substances while serving with the U.S. Army in Desert Storm, the 1991 Middle East conflict.[13] He demands that your facility provide him with medical care and that the VA and other government agencies provide financial and counseling services to his wife and children.

Checking with your superiors, you find that while the VA has not taken a final position on how to deal with all aspects of what is being called Gulf War Syndrome, the Department's preliminary position is that there is no clear basis for finding that any exposure to the combat arena in the Iraq conflict resulted in a service-related disability requiring VA support.

What do you do? Do you turn the man away? Do you admit him for testing, knowing that you are sidestepping agency policy? Do you admit him for treatment but disavow any responsibility for family problems related to the premature death of the relatively young father and husband? How would you begin to assess your own authority and obligations? Would you try to get around the law? If you can make the judgment that it is acceptable to break the law for what you regard as a good cause, what are the limits of that behavior? To what extent is this an issue of ethics as compared to a question of law, and what is the difference?

FOUNDATIONS AND PERSPECTIVES: PUBLIC LAW, POLICY PROBLEMS, AND THE NATURE OF ADMINISTRATIVE LAW

These are only some of the important problems of public law and public administration that will be addressed in this book. The situations that will be considered are problems of public law as opposed to private civil conflicts. Private law conflicts are the types of disputes that arise following the Saturday morning "fender bender" in the local shopping center parking lot or when the neighbors chop down the half of your cherry tree that happens to hang over their property line. Public law conflicts, on the other hand, involve the government more directly, as a party in the dispute and not merely as the provider of a forum for dispute resolution. The term *public administration* is a part of this book's title because governmental actions are defined and controlled by special provisions of the Constitution and laws. As such, government actions must be accomplished in particular ways. The need for responsiveness and responsibility in government agencies requires that legal guidelines be carefully drawn in cases where government acts. This remains true despite efforts at deregulation and privatization. Indeed, these questions are even more challenging in an era in which it is common to think not of focused action by a unit of government alone, but of what is termed governance. Governance is complex concept that assumes that key decisions and implementation today are often the product of a set of nonprofit, for-profit, and governmental organizations at several levels.

It is useful to bear in mind the fact that disputes involving public administrators can be of two general types, policy or status. The largest number of cases arise because someone seeks a social service benefit such as disability benefits, a license or permit for which they have applied such as a business permit, or a determination of status, as in the case of a claim for refugee status handled by U.S.

Citizenship and Immigration Services, a part of the Department of Homeland Security (formerly the Immigration and Naturalization Service [INS]). More of these kinds of cases are handled every year than are faced by all of the lawsuits brought in all of the federal courts in the nation.

On the other hand, there are cases that are brought that are intended to change policy rather than just to provide a benefit or compensation to an applicant. Consider the case of a suit brought by parents of young people committed to mental health facilities by the state to enforce a right to treatment claim or seeking an order compelling the state to maintain safe and humane conditions in the facility.[14] The nature and dynamics of these policy-oriented disputes are obviously different and more complex than compensatory or status claims. It helps to be alert to whether a particular situation involves a policy challenge as compared to a status claim. Of course, a case can begin as a status claim and escalate into a policy dispute over time (see the *Mathews v. Eldridge* case study in Appendix 1). Once that point is reached, the nature and dynamics of the case are transformed for reasons that will become clear in the chapters to come.

The body of law that is concerned with actions by administrative agencies is known as administrative law. To ensure that this term (which in this book serves as shorthand for public law and public administration) is properly understood, it is necessary to spend some time on the problem of definition. In surveying a number of the most influential works over the years of the field's development,[15] one finds that "administrative law" has been defined in two senses. On the one hand, the concept has a broad sense that includes "not only administrative powers, their exercise, and remedies but also such subjects as the various forms of administrative agencies; the exercise of and limitations upon regulatory power; the law of the civil service; the acquisition and management of governmental property; public works; and administrative obligations."[16] Having recognized this broad sense, however, most legal practitioners tend to dismiss that perspective in favor of a narrower conception.

There are at least two reasons why much of the literature has tended toward the narrow view. First, much of what has been written in this area is intended to provide guidance primarily to attorneys, and they often demand clearly defined and narrowly drawn categories. Second, some authors, such as Bernard Schwartz, have flatly stated that the broad definition exceeds the range of questions appropriately addressed by lawyers:

> To the American lawyer, these are matters for public administration, not administrative law; they are primarily the concern of the political scientist. In this country, administrative law is not regarded as the law relating to public administration, the way commercial law is the law relating to commerce, or land law the law relating to land. It is limited to powers and remedies and answers the questions: (1) What powers may be vested in administrative agencies? (2) What are the limits of those powers? (3) What are the ways in which agencies are kept within these limits?[17]

Despite the fact that some authors in the legal community began to take a broader view in the 1980s,[18] the tendency to focus on the narrow procedural approach remains dominant among practitioners and many law school faculty. There is also no small amount of irony in the fact that administrative law is not even a required subject in law school despite the fact that the vast majority of people are far more likely to be involved some kind of administrative dispute than they are to be a party to a civil lawsuit or a criminal prosecution. And it remains equally clear that the vast majority of public servants are provided with little education by their colleagues in the legal profession about how they are to be represented if they are challenged.[19]

Since the purpose of this book is to understand a number of perspectives on the administrative justice system, including those of lawyers, public administrators, benefit claimants, regulated groups, courts, legislators, and political scientists, we will proceed by using a broad definition of administrative law.

The authors, who work from a narrow view of administrative law, base their definition on a number of specific distinctions that should not be quickly or uncritically made and one key omission that has become increasingly important. Indeed, it will become apparent that much of administrative law started from this set of premises, assumptions that do not reflect the reality of public administration in some important respects. The reader may be uncertain at the outset precisely why it is so important to understand these seemingly formalistic distinctions, but it will become increasingly clear as later chapters unfold just how these factors present difficulties for public managers and others involved in the administrative justice system.

First, there is the oft-repeated assumption that administrative law is procedural and not substantive. According to this view, neither the substantive decisions made by the agencies involved nor the substantive mandate directed to the agencies by the legislature are administrative law.[20] Martin Shapiro, a political scientist, correctly observed that "such a procedural focus tended to leave in some sort of nonlegal limbo the substantive policies and decisions of administrative agencies."[21] Administrative law questions do not arise without reference to substantive administrative decisions, to the legislation that controls the administrative action, and to the complex fact pattern that gave rise to the governmental decision.[22]

A second distinction on which the narrow definition rests concerns what is sometimes called the internal versus external dichotomy. This view asserts that the proper scope of administrative law is limited to agency actions that affect the rights of private parties.[23] The legal relationships among governmental officers, government departments, or different levels of government are excluded. The view is that the "administrative lawyer is not concerned with administrative powers as such; only when administrative power is turned outward against the person or property of private citizens does he deem it a proper subject of administrative law."[24] Given the historically complex set of intergovernmental relations that influences public policy,[25] this view is myopic. In light of the current reality, such a view is just plain dangerous. As an academic characterization, this view dramatically distorts the reality that public managers see every day and that citizens encounter when they engage with the public sector.

More attention will be given to the concept of intergovernmental relations and administrative law in later chapters.[26] Now that the supersonic passenger liner Concorde has gone out of service, it is interesting to look back on the controversy over the effort by the British and French to gain landing rights in the United States for their cooperative, then leading-edge venture in aviation. Concorde was a controversial airplane from its inception. Designed to fly at more than twice the speed of sound, Concorde began its record-breaking flights in 1969 and 1970. The British and French concluded that the craft would be economical only if it could fly the transatlantic air routes from London and Paris to New York, Washington, and other American cities. Air France and British Airways applied to the United States for landing rights.

Two and a half years after Concorde made its first friendship flight to this country, Secretary of Transportation William Coleman authorized a test period of 16 months, which permitted one flight daily into Dulles Airport in Washington and Kennedy Airport in New York.[27] That decision, announced on February 4, 1976, intensified the existing conflict among federal authorities, British Airways, Air France, the state of New York, the state of New Jersey, residents in the area of Kennedy Airport, and the Port Authority of New York, which operates the airport. The controversy centered on anticipated noise, not from supersonic flight, but from takeoff and landing of the craft. The foreign governments were pressuring the United States to permit landings on pain of losing some of this country's routes abroad. The federal government was pressuring the Port Authority to cooperate in the experimental landing period, but the residents were protesting. Their protests took the forms of political pressure on state lawmakers and demonstrations, the most significant of which were long, slow automobile caravans that blocked entrances and exits to and from the airport.

On February 28, 1976, the New York legislature voted to bar landings of the Concorde.[28] The Port Authority issued a ban, beginning March 11, against landings at the airport pending the outcome of a study of approximately six months' duration of the probable impact of Concorde traffic into Kennedy. During the following year, Secretary Coleman's original order permitting the Concorde landings was challenged by one side in the controversy and upheld in the Supreme Court, test flights into Dulles began, and the Port Authority ban was also challenged by the organizations on the other side of the debate.

In March 1977, a federal district court found that the Port Authority order was discriminatory and vacated it. The Port Authority appealed but was unsuccessful in the Second Circuit Court of Appeals. The case went to the United States Supreme Court, which in October 1977 formally refused to review the findings of the lower court.

This case clearly shows how major public policy questions that are "internal" are classic administrative law questions. In fact, many administrative law questions cannot be fully understood without a proper respect for the significance of intergovernmental relations. As will become clear through this book, intergovernmental complexity has only increased over time and no simple attempt to impose a sharp internal versus external classification will be adequate to address the law and administrative problems that arise in such contexts. Also for reasons that will be developed later in this chapter and throughout the book, there is a tendency today not to rely on government agencies at any level to implement policy within government. Instead, policymakers increasingly rely on governance regimes that include not only local, state, and federal governmental units but also nonprofit and even for-profit organizations. This trend has further rendered the internal versus external dichotomy obsolete.

A third distinction that has been employed as the basis for narrow definition of administrative law is the dichotomy between so-called quasi-legislative action and quasi-judicial action. Louis L. Jaffe and Nathaniel L. Nathanson suggested that "it will serve our purposes to identify the administrative process as rulemaking when not done by the legislature and adjudication when not done by the courts."[29] As will be indicated in Chapters 4 through 7, it is often difficult in specific cases to determine whether an agency action is legislative or adjudicatory in nature.[30] This is an important classificatory device. It was at the heart of the enactment of the Administrative Procedure Act, with which the reader will become familiar in later chapters.[31] Even so, it does not easily explain or accommodate many agency activities or processes. It should not and will not limit our inquiry into administrative law.

Finally, traditionally administrative law has specifically excluded from its consideration situations involving the use of contracts as compared with administrative activities based upon regulations or adjudicative rulings.[32] One of the historical reasons for that separation was that in the late 1940s, when several important pieces of legislation were passed to address administrative processes and institutions, separate statutes were adopted to cover administrative procedure and what was then called procurement, now referred to as contracting or (in federal government language) acquisitions or competitive sourcing.[33] There were many factors that led to the separate laws (which will be addressed later in the text), and it would be problematic at this stage of legal development to claim that public contract law is a part of what we call administrative law, though there clearly should be movement in that direction. Even so, most social service programs as well as many other government activities long considered as inherently governmental are now provided by contracts at all levels of government. Given that fact and the reality that government could not do without those contractors given current levels of funding and institutional support, one cannot realistically contemplate administrative law today without maintaining an awareness of the degree to which it is influenced by the law and practice of government contracts.[34] Sadly, there are still those public managers who regard contract management issues as somehow outside their policy or line of management activities even when they are less and less directly involved in policy operations and far more engaged in the implementation and operation of policy through contractors. It is untenable to continue to act as though these are totally separate and unrelated bodies of law. The distinction may work for some lawyers and judges, but, increasingly, not for public administrators.

For purposes of this study, then, administrative law is the branch of law that deals with public administration, providing the authority on which administrative agencies operate as well as the limits necessary to control them. The term is broadly defined to include both substantive and procedural concerns, internal as well as external issues, and aspects of the legal environment of administration that exceed simple quasi-legislative and quasi-judicial categories. Though recognizing critical distinctions, this view also acknowledges the intimate interaction of the law of public contracts with many other key aspects of the administrative law.

AN ORIENTATION TO THE ADMINISTRATIVE
JUSTICE SYSTEM

The institutions, actors (referred to here as repeat players and single shot players), and processes that together produce administrative law decisions may be thought of as the administrative justice system. Before one can begin to deal in depth with the details of law, politics, and administration, it is necessary to acquire a rudimentary understanding of the parts of the system and interrelationships among them.

Institutions

Administrative agencies differ greatly in form and responsibility. Since each agency is created by statute or executive order to respond to unique needs at different periods in history, it is natural that they vary considerably. For present purposes there are two commonly accepted ways to conceptualize the nature and operation of administrative agencies: functional and institutional approaches. Using a functional classification, there are regulatory bodies, social service agencies, second generation regulatory agencies, and administrative service agencies.

Functional Classification of Agencies

The functional classifications are significant and will be discussed in greater detail in Chapters 5, 6, and 10. After World War II, legal literature about the administrative justice system has tended to emphasize the major independent regulatory commissions, while scholars of public administration have paid particular attention to social service agencies. Fortunately, that situation has changed somewhat, but the tendency remains. That is in part not surprising since attorneys are most often retained by regulated firms or agencies engaged in regulatory enforcement. From the public manager's perspective, the largest agencies and programs are oriented toward providing services of one kind or another rather than regulation.

Regulatory Commissions   Until the 1980s, the Interstate Commerce Commission,[35] created in 1887, was generally referred to as the prototype for the medium-size independent regulatory commissions. These commissions used to be referred to in the literature on regulation as the "Big Seven" or "Big Ten" (depending on who was counting) federal commissions. These agencies were created by Congress as collegial bodies with a great deal of independence from the executive branch and Congress to protect the agencies from political interference. A list of the most important of the commissions in modern history would have to include:

Nuclear Regulatory Commission (NRC): Nuclear safety enforcement

Federal Communications Commission (FCC): Regulation of broadcasting

Federal Energy Regulatory Commission, part of the Department of Energy: Pricing and allocation of oil and gas

Federal Trade Commission: Elimination of unfair or deceptive trade practices and antitrust enforcement

Securities and Exchange Commission: Regulation of stock and bond markets

National Labor Relations Board: Regulation of labor/management relations

Federal Maritime Commission: Regulation of shipping[36]

The list changed rapidly during the 1970s and 1980s as deregulation bills moved through Congress. It was a fascinating and ironic political period (discussed further in Chapter 10) in which a conservative Republican President supported budget deficits and liberal Democrats cosponsored deregulation bills in Congress. For example, the Civil Aeronautics Board (CAB) and the Interstate Commerce Commission (ICC) went out of business, providing at least a partial response to the question: *Are government organizations immortal?*[37]

However, since the 1990s there have been renewed discussions about whether it might be useful to return to the use of independent commissions to address criticisms of some existing regulatory bodies that seem to have been politicized, such as the Federal Aviation Administration (FAA).[38] There have been concerns about the need for greater independence and more in-house capacity for the Food and Drug Administration as concerns have been expressed about such challenges as drug approval and oversight. Indeed, that criticism led Health and Human Services Secretary Michael Leavitt to launch reforms internally even as the threat of congressional action loomed. In taking these steps, he said: "The public has spoken and they want more oversight and openness. . . . They want to know what we know, what we do with the information and why we do it. We will address their concerns by cultivating openness and enhanced independence."[39] This latest round of calls for action, including possible legislation, came following testimony by FDA scientist David Graham regarding efforts by the agency to block testimony on Vioxx and other drugs that were later the center of attention because of unrevealed dangers.[40] Demanding an independent drug safety office, even so conservative a Republican as Senator Charles Grassley (R-IA) insisted: "The Food and Drug Administration has to be a vigilant watchdog. Some say we need a rottweiler as opposed to a chihuahua. . . . The goal of today's initiative, then, by Senator Dodd and me is to place drug safety front and center at the Food and Drug Administration once and for all."[41] Similarly, there were calls for enhancement of the independence of and demands for more effective action by the Securities and Exchange Commission well before the Enron and Global Crossing scandals broke.[42]

Independent commissions are usually headed by three to seven commissioners appointed for fixed terms by the president with the advice and consent of the Senate. At the federal level, terms of commissioners are often staggered with terms long enough to reduce the likelihood that a one-term president would be able to replace the entire commission. The commissioners are protected against arbitrary removal by the president except for just cause such as illegal or unethical actions.

Independent commissions are found at the state and local levels as well. Probably the leading example is the state public utilities commission. While it appeared for a time that the political drive for utilities deregulation might send that kind of body the way of the Interstate Commerce Commission (ICC), scandals such as the Enron debacle have led to renewed expectations of effective state PUC oversight. Some state constitutions give independent status to agencies that are executive branch organizations in other states.

Regulatory agencies perform a number of functions. They occasionally control access to a particular industry or profession, usually by some form of licensing. For example, for obvious technical reasons there is a limit to the number of radio or television stations or other communications services that can broadcast over standard broadcast frequencies in a particular geographic area without causing interference. Since the airwaves are a national resource, an agency was created to grant licenses in the public interest to broadcast various kinds of programming. The Federal Communications Commission grants the licenses and conducts renewal proceedings on a regular basis to determine whether the broadcaster deserves to retain the license. Even with deregulation and privatization of some aspects of the communications field,[43] there is still regulation in the operation of broadcasters. In fact, recent efforts to address problems with respect to cable TV (under the Cable Television Consumer Protection and Competition Act of 1992)[44] and the Internet (under the Communications Decency Act of 1996)[45] have raised new questions about the nature of communications regulation. And, as the brief discussion of the Super Bowl case at the beginning of the chapter demonstrated, while this may be a period of significant deregulation in communications, one television program still produced the largest number of citizen complaints in history and demands for regulation.

Watchdog agencies, as they are sometimes called, also establish and enforce standards of fair market or professional practice. Federal Trade Commission (FTC) actions against deceptive or false advertising are obvious examples. Medical and bar association enforcement of professional codes of ethics are further illustrations.[46] At the local level, common examples include regulation of taxicabs or restaurants. The power to regulate in this fashion has been called by Ernst Freund, a leading scholar on the subject, the power of corrective intervention.[47] Regulatory bodies are frequently called on to set routes and rates where market forces do not appear to operate effectively, as in the case of local utility companies, which have traditionally been monopolies within their service areas. The problem in such cases is to determine what is a fair rate, where fair is defined as an amount that covers costs plus a reasonable return on investment, in order to ensure the continued availability of capital needed by the utility.

Social Service Agencies   Despite the high visibility of the major regulatory agencies they are, in terms of personnel and dollars, small by comparison with social service agencies such as the Social Security Administration (SSA) and the Department of Veterans Affairs (VA). The Social Security Administration processes several times the combined number of cases listed on the dockets of all the federal courts in the nation, deciding 8 million new claims in 2004, resolving more than 1 million appeals, and processing over 1.6 million periodic continuing disability reviews.[48] The VA employs several times more people than all of the major federal regulatory agencies combined with more than 235,000, and operating "157 hospitals, 869 outpatient clinics, 134 nursing homes, 42 domiciliaries, 206 readjustment counseling centers, 57 veterans benefits regional offices, and 120 national cemeteries."[49] By contrast, despite its visibility and daunting number of programs and commitments, the U.S. Environmental Protection Agency had at the time of this writing only "17,511 full-time-equivalent employees."[50] The budget of the Occupational Safety and Health Administration is $464 million compared to a budget for the Medicaid program in the U.S. Department of Health and Human Services of $194 billion.[51] The same reality of the relative scale of social service versus regulatory programs is true at the state level where social service agencies far outpace regulatory bodies in size and fiscal significance.

Social service agencies generally respond to requests for benefits or services. The claims are generally made by individuals who know little about government. The problem of the government is to give aid provided for by law with sensitivity to individual problems while simultaneously guarding the public treasury against fraud and maintaining sufficient professional distance and rules of general applicability so that arbitrariness is avoided. Of course, social service programs do not just include those traditionally perceived as welfare operations. Education and health care programs are among the largest and most complex of social service operations and involve a host of administrative law issues.

Social service agencies have a heavy intergovernmental component.[52] Programs such as Social Security disability and community development were designed to involve several levels of government. Not surprisingly, that interconnection among governmental units involves complex communication and coordination problems. That arrangement is becoming even more complicated as efforts are being made to move away from what have been termed entitlement programs and toward greater state-by-state discretionary operation of these programs under block grant arrangements. For example, the so-called welfare reform legislation of 1996 authorized transfer of greater responsibility for programs to the states with federal support coming in the form of a grant allowing states to make choices as to levels of program support. Under this approach, states that choose to provide more benefits or allow a wider range of applicants to qualify for assistance must assume the increased costs. For its part, the federal government is no longer legally obligated to provide a minimum level of support from year to year. Thus, while this approach offers greater flexibility, it also means a much more complex system for any applicant to navigate and one that is likely to present a good deal of variability from one state to the next.

It is also characteristic of social service agencies that they increasingly rely on contractors, often not-for-profit organizations, to do the actual service delivery for many kinds of programs. That is particularly true at the state level and for those programs funded directly by the federal government, but also increasingly for programs at the county level. In fact, for nonprofit organizations, government contracts and grants are the most important revenue sources.[53] Into this mix has come increasing competition by for-profit firms for service delivery, which has not only created new dynamics for the governmental agencies who are responsible for the programs and contract for the services, but also for nonprofits who find themselves more frequently in competition with for-profit firms.[54] That has had important consequences for those organizations.[55] Certainly health care is one policy domain in which these dynamics have been evident.

Second-Generation Regulators   Some agencies, especially a number of those created from the 1970s on, perform both regulatory and social service functions. The Occupational Safety and Health Administration (OSHA), the Environmental Protection Agency (EPA), the Consumer Product Safety Commission (CPSC), and the Equal Employment Opportunity Commission (EEOC) are examples. These agencies have varying degrees of regulatory power. In addition to their watchdog roles, they provide direct services to individuals or communities. The EPA provides various programs of assistance with respect to water quality and waste disposal efforts in local communities. The EEOC clears civil suits by individuals or brings litigation itself on behalf of those who feel that they have been discriminated against in hiring and promotions in violation of Title VII of the Civil Rights Act of 1964 and its many subsequent amendments. On occasion these agencies may be negotiators, and at other times they may act as the enforcement arm of government. In contemporary terms, we say that they are implementing policy mixes rather than independent policies. That is, they administer a range of tools that a legislature has decided should be available to attack a problem, from grants to regulation to market-based alternatives to regulation to informational programs.

These so-called second-generation regulators also differ from older regulatory agencies in terms of the legislative mandates on which they operate. For many years the Congress and regulatory commissions were criticized on grounds that these agencies were given broad delegations of authority, little guidance as to how to use that discretion, and a vague responsibility that amounted to little more than an admonition to regulate in the public interest.[56] However, beginning in the 1970s, that changed. Statutes became more complex in both their procedural and substantive requirements. Also, the tendency to place what are termed "sunset" clauses in legislation (a requirement that a program or policy be reauthorized every five or seven years or go out of existence) led legislatures at both the federal and state levels to add more elements to statutes each time they reauthorized programs.

Administrative Service Agencies   Another type of organization that used to receive little attention but has become more significant over the years can be termed an administrative service agency. These agencies are often known by a generic title, like the General Services Administration (GSA) of the federal government. States and even some larger local governments have similar agencies.

At an earlier time, such organizations were viewed as essentially ancillary bodies and given very little attention. They procured light bulbs and other ordinary supplies and were seen as little more than purchasing agents. However, in the past two decades, as the way government does business has changed, these agencies have become more important.[57] They now lease and manage property, contract for a host of services as well as products, provide support and guidance for other contracting units or government, and often set the terms for the purchase and management of such critical systems such as computers. The GSA, for example, now operates the single point of entry online portal for contracting.[58] It has also reorganized its operations in order to play an even greater role in Internet-based contracting, an important field of work in light of efforts to increase competitive sourcing. Indeed, state or local government organizations are often told by commercial firms that the government rate means the GSA rate and conditions. In some settings, these service agencies are expected to play important parts in capacity building for other agencies and to ensure that the infrastructure other agencies need is in place and functioning properly. Thus, while these organizations often receive relatively little attention, it is important to be aware of their presence and their increasingly diverse and significant roles.

Institutional Types

From the perspective of traditional governmental institutions, one can think of agencies as traditional executive branch agencies, independent commissions that report primarily to the legislature and yet retain a great deal of independence, independent agencies within the executive branch, municipal corporations, special purpose units, and government surrogates and governance regimes.

Executive Branch Agencies   Executive branch agencies, of course, are those that function at the national or state level in the executive branch, usually headed by a political appointee, and generally considered to be the operating arms of the presidential or gubernatorial administration. The qualifying term "usually" is included because in some state governments heads of key agencies such as the Superintendent of Public Instruction or the Attorney General are independently elected, a fact that is often extremely important in shaping the role their agencies play and the politics of the state.

Independent Regulatory Commissions   These bodies were described earlier. They are intended to ensure independence from attempts at political interference. That is why their commissioners are appointed for fixed terms that often span more than the four years of a presidential or gubernatorial administration and also explains why they can only be removed from office for cause—that is, for what amounts to a dereliction of duty or a violation of legal or ethical constraints. While legislators often see these bodies as accountable to them, they still possess considerable legal independence. Nevertheless, they must operate in a complex political environment in which both the executive and legislature seek to influence the behavior of independent organizations.

Independent Regulatory Agencies Within the Executive Branch   This effort to achieve influence has led most modern presidents to appoint committees to study the operation of government and, not surprisingly, their presidentially appointed members usually advise that greater control should be given to the president over executive agencies and greater influence over the independent commissions as well.

Thus, during the Richard Nixon administration, an effort was undertaken to fold independent regulatory bodies into existing executive branch agencies. The argument was that the commissions would retain their legal independence and be protected from interference but be placed within the executive departments just for administrative and managerial efficiency. Therefore, the Federal Aviation Administration (FAA) is now within the Department of Transportation (DOT) and the Occupational Safety and Health Administration (OSHA) operates from within the Department of Labor (DOL).

Of course, it was clear that placing these bodies within the executive departments would influence their operations in many ways, and that has happened. For example, there has been ongoing criticism that the FAA has been unduly influenced by the White House and the Secretary of Transportation many times since the reorganization, ranging from delays in acting to ground aircraft following the crash of a DC-10 at Chicago's O'Hare airport in the late 1970s, to the handling of the Professional Air Traffic Controllers' strike in the 1980s, to the failure to take precautions in connection with newly emerging airlines that might have prevented the Valujet crash of the 1990s, to more recent arguments, eerily similar to the Valujet critique, of a failure to address the growing practice by airlines of contracting out their major maintenance tasks to private firms in other countries.[59]

Municipal Corporations and County Governments   Still, of the more than 80,000 units of government in the United States, the vast majority are neither federal nor state agencies, but units of local government. Of these, the most important are municipal governments and counties. It is important to note that these structures differ around the country. In many parts of the nation, counties are very important local government players, providing educational, health, social service, judicial, and correctional services. The cities and other municipalities provide the infrastructure of streets, water, sewerage, communications, public safety, and other standard services. However, in some northeastern states, the primary operating unit is the town government for most local government services with what would be the remaining county services provided by state agencies.

In any case, local governments are municipal corporations that derive their existence and their authority from the state.[60] Some states have home rule provisions in their law that allow local government substantial independence and ordinance writing authority. Others are not home rule states; which means that local governments are limited to the authority provided in their charter and under state statutes. Local governments can sue and be sued as municipal corporations.

On the other hand, modern debates over intergovernmental relations have raised questions that are still being addressed about the precise status of particular units and officers at the local level. Thus, county sheriffs have been considered to be state rather than county officers for some purposes[61] but could not be forced to accept a federal role when the federal government sought to enlist their participation in the Brady Bill gun purchase clearance process.[62] As the federal government sends more functions and programs back to the states and as the states, in their turn, devolve more of those program responsibilities to the local levels, though not necessarily with commensurate legal or fiscal decision-making authority appropriate to the task, these questions become more important.[63]

Special Purpose Governmental Units   There are many units at the local level that are special purpose units, such as special districts, authorities, or councils of government.[64] There is an increasing number of special units that have come from a growing number of interstate compacts. These are agreements among states that are sanctioned by the Congress. The decisions of the bodies created by these compacts bind the states that are parties to the compact.[65]

There is also a variety of special purpose units at the national level. They are special purpose in the sense that they were deliberately constructed outside of the normal categories discussed to this point. Referred to by Ronald Moe as "quasi-crypto-pseudo governmental organizations," government corporations are created to carry out particular tasks, such as the protection of the mortgage market, the administration of student loans, the insurance of banks and saving and loan institutions, and many more.[66] The Government Corporation Control Act provides a listing of those entities that are wholly owned by the federal government and those that have mixed public and private ownership.

> "Government corporation" means a mixed-ownership Government corporation and a wholly owned Government corporation.
>
> (2) "mixed-ownership Government corporation" means—
> (A) the Central Bank for Cooperatives.
> (B) the Federal Deposit Insurance Corporation.
> (C) the Federal Home Loan Banks.
> (D) the Federal Intermediate Credit Banks.
> (E) the Federal Land Banks.
> (F) the National Credit Union Administration Central Liquidity Facility.
> (G) the Regional Banks for Cooperatives.
> (H) the Rural Telephone Bank when the ownership, control, and operation of the Bank are converted under section 410(a) of the Rural Electrification Act of 1936 (7 U.S.C. 950(a)).
> (I) the Financing Corporation.
> (J) the Resolution Trust Corporation.
> (K) the Resolution Funding Corporation.
> (L), (M) [Redesignated]
> (3) "wholly owned Government corporation" means—
> (A) the Commodity Credit Corporation.
> (B) the Community Development Financial Institutions Fund.
> (C) the Export-Import Bank of the United States.
> (D) the Federal Crop Insurance Corporation.
> (E) Federal Prison Industries, Incorporated.
> (F) the Corporation for National and Community Service.
> (G) the Government National Mortgage Association.
> (H) the Overseas Private Investment Corporation.

(I)   the Pennsylvania Avenue Development Corporation.

(J)   the Pension Benefit Guaranty Corporation.

(K)   the Rural Telephone Bank until the ownership, control, and operation of the Bank are converted under section 410(a) of the Rural Electrification Act of 1936 (7 U.S.C. 950(a)).

(L)   the Saint Lawrence Seaway Development Corporation.

(M) the Secretary of Housing and Urban Development when carrying out duties and powers related to the Federal Housing Administration Fund.

(N)   the Tennessee Valley Authority.

(O)   [Deleted]

(P)   the Panama Canal Commission.

(Q)   the Millennium Challenge Corporation.[67]

While these organizations are often well out of the public eye most of the time, one or another of them will surface now and again when serious difficulties are seen. One of the primary reasons for their significance is the fact that they often manage what is termed contingent liability such as loan guarantees that will have to be paid as in the case of the savings and loan debacle of the 1980s. More recently, the Pension Benefit Guarantee Corporation drew attention when United Airlines, in serious financial distress, sought to transfer its pension obligations to the corporation. The corporation, created to assist retirees whose former employers went out of business, is funded by a modest premium paid by employers that is not sufficient even to address the commitments that the PBGC must address presently. Indeed, at the time of the United Airlines proposal in 2005, the corporation was under-funded by some $21 billion. Not only would acceptance of the airline's obligations have added dramatically to that set of commitments, but it appeared likely to trigger a string of efforts by firms seeking to rid themselves of defined benefit pension obligations with the primary costs off-loaded onto the public sector.

These are interesting problems for students and practitioners of public law because they were designed, in part at least, in an effort to make them look more like private sector organizations and to be exempt from most of the administrative law that applies to all other agencies. Yet they place the government in the position of facing their contingent liability should the bill come due.

Government Surrogates and Governance Regimes: A Complex Field Largely Undeveloped

Increasingly, many of the questions that arise in the field of public law and public administration reach beyond the work of specific governmental entities and engage nongovernmental organizations. In some situations contractors operate on behalf of the government in the implementation and operation of programs charged to a particular government agency, as in the example of the prison guards at beginning of this chapter. These people who carry out governmental functions and the organizations for which they work are, to this point at least, operating in an area that provides more questions than answers as to their status, relationship to legal authority, and accountability. A number of these unresolved issues will be addressed in the chapters that follow.

In a wider sense, though, the past two decades have witnessed an increasing tendency to speak of governance rather than government and seek to solve problems not by assigning them to a unit of government but by developing a coalition of governmental institutions at several levels together with nongovernmental organizations of various types to assess a problem, develop solutions, and work together to implement those policies. The term governance, which had previously been used simply to refer to the process of governing, has become very important both to scholars and policymakers, but there is currently little agreement on its precise meaning. In a synthesis of the works on governance, Frederickson concluded that:

> [G]overnance is now everywhere and appears to mean anything and everything. Because governance is a power word, a dominant descriptor, and the current preference of academic tastemakers, there has been a rush to affix to it all of the other fashions of the day. Governance is the structure of political institutions. Governance is the shift from the bureaucratic state to

the hollow state or to third-party government. Governance is market-base approaches to government. Governance is the development of social capital, civil society, and high levels of citizen participation. Governance is the work of empowered, muscular, risk-taking public entrepreneurs. Governance is the new public management or managerialism. Governance is public sector performance. Governance is interjurisdictional cooperation and network management. Governance is globalization and rationalization. Governance is corporate oversight, transparency and accounting standards. (Citations omitted.)[68]

Agranoff and McGuire observe that: "[T]he term 'governance' is often used to describe a wide range of organization types that are linked together and engaged in public activities, enlarging (and changing) the domain of government. Governance connotes that more than public agencies are involved in the formulation and implementation of policy.... [W]e look to current governance as involving multiple organizations and connections that are necessary to carry out public purposes."[69] This approach to the concept, as Agranoff and McGuire explain, emphasizes collaboration.

Lynn, Heinrich, and Hill note that: "The definitions of governance in public-sector literature reflect institutional and network concepts.... Even more numerous are uses that refer to multi-agency partnerships, self-governing networks, and the blurring of responsibilities between the public and private sectors...."[70] They add: "In its broadest sense, then, governance in the public sector concerns relationships between authoritative decisions and government performance.... [W]e define the term governance as regimes of laws, rules, judicial decisions, and administrative practices that constrain, prescribe, and enable the provision of publicly supported goods and services."[71] Yehezkel Dror reaches beyond the problem-solving approach to consider a more proactive concept of governance that is "the ability to build the future as an expression of collective human will and choice, based on the human freedom to try and influence evolving history."[72] And the debate continues.[73]

Most of the scholarship emphasizes the development of governance regimes, which are collaborations of governmental and nongovernmental organizations. The concept often includes informal as well as formally constituted governance regimes, many of which are developed, break down, and are reformulated over time as circumstances and challenges dictate. The tendency is toward collaboration as compared to hierarchical mandates with accountability based on performance rather than formal mandates and legal responses.[74]

Unlike the more or less well-developed law and procedures of grants and contracts, governance regimes are even less uniform and more complex. For reasons that will become clear as we move along, the operation of these collaborative networks and other structures present a host of challenges that are ever more complex than traditional public administration operations.[75] However, whatever may be the intent and expectations, to the degree that government agencies, funds, or legal authority are involved, there are public law issues and processes to be considered. In order to understand and address those public law issues, it is necessary first to map the particular governance regime in question to identify the participating organizations, identify key norms such as provisions of memoranda of understanding or contracts used to create the coalition, the policies in whatever form they may be that are at the core of the system's work, and the processes by which it performs its responsibilities. In sum, it is important to recognize government surrogates and governance regimes as types of institution that present unique types of public law challenges.

Repeat Players and Single-Shot Players: Very Different Parties in the System

Just as the types of administrative organizations differ, so too do the kinds of individuals and groups that deal with the agencies. In particular, it is useful to distinguish two significantly different categories of parties who place demands on the administrative justice system—single-shot players and repeat players. The terms are borrowed from analyses of the criminal justice process.[76] Single-shot players are generally individuals who rarely deal with government agencies. Examples include those who apply for benefits from the Department of Veterans Affairs or the Social Security Administration. They are not usually represented by legal counsel, are generally under pressure to get a response quickly, and may know very little about the agencies and programs with which they are dealing.

Repeat players, on the other hand, are often organizations with more or less continuous, long-term relationships with particular agencies. They generally have in-house or outside counsel to represent them. These firms or groups frequently have substantial financial and technical resources at their command and consequently operate with comparatively greater flexibility in their dealings with the agencies. Repeat players are perhaps best typified by regulated businesses such as drug companies or manufacturing firms.

Nonprofit organizations (often referred to as nongovernmental organizations [NGOs]) and government contractors represent a particular type of repeat player. They often become quite expert at interacting with relevant governmental bodies, but they remain outside government. Governmental agencies sometimes seem to have the upper hand in these relationships, but the truth is that public officials and agencies are often dependent upon these groups for support or even for the delivery of services in the case of the contractors.[77]

It is important to note very clearly in any analysis of a problem in law and administration what kinds of parties are involved in both sides of the debate. The assumption that most agencies or most parties before the agencies are alike will distort a consideration of the operation of the administrative justice system.

Administrative Processes: A Simple Descriptive Model of the Administrative Process

It is useful to bring the definitions and categories together into a simple descriptive model of administrative processes. Figure 1.1 outlines the relationships among the various actors and institutions in the administrative justice system. Each agency differs somewhat in its method of dealing with administrative law problems, but this general description provides a kind of road map.

Single-shot and repeat players place demands on the system. The demands of the former may be nothing more than a telephone call to the Department of Veterans Affairs requesting information on the procedure to apply for educational benefits, or it may be something much more complex. Repeat players frequently seek different kinds of information. Whatever the demand, it is usually passed through an informal process filter, in which an attempt is made to resolve problems short of formal legal actions. Chapter 8 explains how and why most administrative law questions are resolved informally rather than in the more formal stages of the administrative justice system.

A common first step in cases requiring more formal process is consideration of the matter by a hearing examiner, generally known as an administrative law judge (ALJ).[78] The ALJ develops a record containing pertinent documents, written submissions, and in some cases transcripts of oral testimony, decides questions of fact, and makes preliminary conclusions as to the disposition of the matter under consideration. If an appeal is needed, it will usually be an administrative appeal in which the record will be examined by other officers within the agency. In rulemaking proceedings, the record developed by the ALJ moves up to agency heads for a final decision on whether and in what form to issue a regulation. Given the number and complexity of the decisions that department heads or commissions are called on to make, the work of agency staff members in aiding the decisionmakers is crucial. They frequently prepare digests of hearing records and highlight important questions or problems in the records that allow the decisionmakers to focus quickly on the most relevant considerations. Because the decisions that issue from agencies involve so many individuals and because they are, unlike judicial opinions, rarely signed by the author of the opinion, the term *institutional decision* is often used to describe them.

Some form of review of agency decisions can be sought in the courts, although there are significant limits on the scope and nature of judicial review. These constraints are considered in Chapter 7. If a case presents important legal questions, there may be appeals within the judicial system leading to a

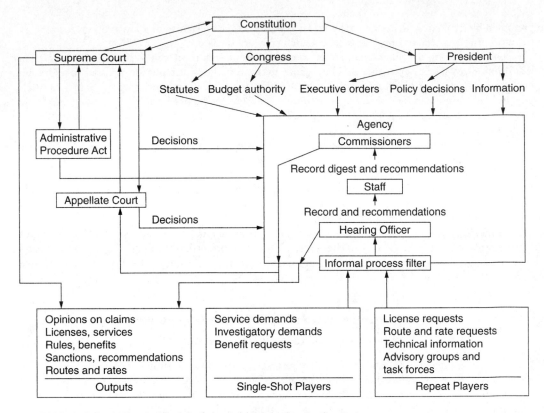

FIGURE 1.1 A Simple Model of the Administrative Justice System

possible—though extremely rare—hearing in the U.S. Supreme Court or in the states by the state supreme court.

There are also institutional inputs to the administrative justice system. Congress creates, empowers, funds, and conducts oversight of the agencies, as do the state legislatures at that level. The statutes are vital because they define and limit the authority of an agency. Any action taken that exceeds the statutory authority is by definition unlawful and is referred to as *ultra vires* action.[79] After all, nothing in the U.S. Constitution requires administrative agencies or grants them any authority. Most are created by statutes under the Article 1, Section 8, powers of the Congress. Budget authority is, of course, also critical since an agency without the funds necessary to use its statutory authority is a paper tiger. The same is true of state agencies, though there are some exceptional cases in which a few state constitutions do establish a limited number of commissions or agencies usually headed by an independently elected official who is therefore not subject to the control of the governor.

The executive branch, aside from its general policymaking and management functions, provides specific inputs. Specific policy directives to agencies are of obvious importance. Examples of such directives include executive orders, presidential memoranda, national security directives, and presidential signing statements.[80] More will be said about these instruments in Chapter 2. Governors and even mayors in some strong-mayor cities also issue executive orders.

Another major input, discussed in detail in Chapter 11, is information that is supplied to the administrative unit by other agencies.

The judiciary provides both inputs and feedback. The agency receives as inputs the decisions of courts interpreting the Constitution, statutes related to its operations, and the agency's enabling act, which is the statute that establishes the agency and defines its authority. The courts also provide

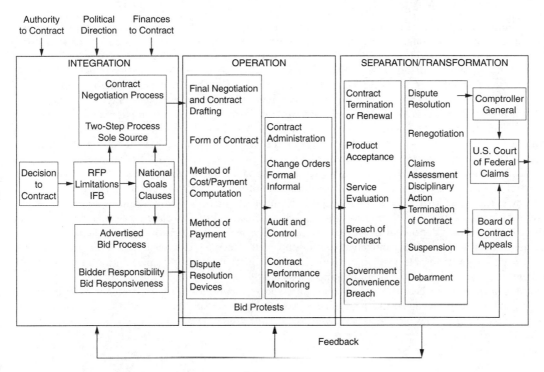

FIGURE 1.2 Public Contract Process Model

feedback by responding in cases brought for review to questions about the accuracy of agency interpretations of statutes and also to the adequacy of the agency's procedures. The key source of law on fair
and adequate administrative procedure is the Administrative Procedure Act (APA).[81]

Administrative Process and Public Contract Process:
Similarities and Differences

When governments call upon contractors to play key roles as service providers for public programs,
public managers and the consumers of administrative decisions are plunged into a significantly different
set of processes. The contract process starts from the basically hierarchical administrative process
described above, but also involves a more horizontal process (see Figure 1.2), starting from the point at
which a decision is made to use a contractual relationship to accomplish a public purpose. The irony of
public contract administration is that while basic governance relationships are about authority, and are
in their nature vertical, contractual relationships are horizontal in character and operate from a base
mutual commitment in which, theoretically at least, the parties are equals. Thus, for example, in a
regulatory relationship, government establishes the rules and determines when and how they are to be
enforced. In the contractual context, both parties set the rules and either can trigger enforcement of the
contract's requirements. It is this tension between the vertical and horizontal models that provides the
essential tension in public contract administration. In an earlier time, this issue was addressed by making
public contracts what are termed contracts of adhesion in which government sets the rules and contractors were willing to either accept them or not do business. However, in more recent years the
argument has been precisely that the contracting process should be made to look less like a standard
process of regulation and control and more like a business contract with its horizontal relationship and
negotiated character.

The horizontal model is based upon the three core aspects of the contract relationship. They are: (1) integration of the nongovernmental organizations (whether nonprofit or for-profit) or other agency with the primary government unit; (2) operation of the joint endeavor; and (3) separation or transformation of the relationship when a contract ends.[82]

The integration stage is concerned with the development of the working partnership and involves the decision to contract, the formation of the contract management team and empowerment of the contracting officer, and the selection of processes for choosing a contractor whether by a standard bidding mechanism or by negotiation. The operation phase involves the period of the working relationship between the contracting agency and the contractor, beginning with contract negotiations, continues through contract drafting, and extends through the management of operations. Despite the fact that most discussions about contracting tend to emphasize the bidding process, the most important parts of the contract process really occur in the operation phase.[83] That is particularly true for service contracts that tend to continue for long periods and for which there are often limited numbers of competitors available or where government lacks the capability for direct service delivery and is therefore essentially dependent upon the contractor. The separation/transformation stage occurs when a decision is made to end a contractual relationship or to fundamentally change it. This stage involves contract close-out, dispute resolution, and management of the political and administrative tensions inherent in the transition out of an existing partnership.

It is important to bear these two rather different—though clearly interrelated—models in mind. Especially in a time when so much of what is done, particularly at the state and local level is actually accomplished through contracts, it is dangerous to ignore the contract model.

PRODUCER AND CONSUMER PERSPECTIVES
ON ADMINISTRATIVE DECISIONS

How one evaluates the success or failure of one agency or the entire administrative justice system, as in most other fields, depends on one's perspective of the system. Consumers of administrative decisions, whether they are single-shot or repeat players, necessarily perceive the system differently from producers of administrative decisions. The case of *Mathews v. Eldridge,* presented in Appendix 1, describes the plight of a man who had a series of misfortunes in his personal life and faced a long, difficult legal battle with the Social Security Administration over his claim for disability benefits. It is easy to be sympathetic to one who appears to have suffered grievously at the hands of the bureaucracy. From the producer's side in that case, administrators must try to clear more than a million and a quarter disability claims in a year as rapidly, fairly, and cost-effectively as possible and still meet demands from the general public to cut costs, reduce the size of social service payment roles, and implement enough checks in the system to guard the public treasury against unwarranted claims.

A complicating factor in the attempt to develop a balanced perspective on questions of law and administration is that, at various times, the producer becomes a consumer and vice versa. States that operate education programs for children with special needs under the Individuals with Disabilities Education Act (IDEA) or health care programs under Medicaid are themselves consumers of decisions by the federal agencies that administer those programs in the form of regulations. They then become producers of decisions for those seeking services at the state and local level as they issue their own regulations and make decisions on individuals claims for services.

Our form of government presupposes that all citizens are both producers and consumers of government decisions. Clearly, government officials are often more directly involved in the production process, but citizen participation in political and administrative matters, to the degree that the two differ, also affects decisionmaking. Additionally, a Department of Energy official may be simultaneously a decisionmaker on solar power technology development programs and a consumer of decisions before the Department of Veterans Affairs in search of educational benefits to support college courses in public administration. For all these reasons and more, the reader should not confuse the term *consumer* as it is used here with the contemporary tendency to speak of citizens as customers.[84]

Contractual relationships, networks, and other forms of what were described earlier as governance regimes also complicate the question. One of the central ideas of collaboration-driven governance arrangements, involving not only government units of several levels but also nonprofit and even for-profit organizations, is that there is and should be a movement away from hierarchy. Contemporary governance models urge that decision processes should be more consensus-based—more negotiated than mandated—and that authority should be more horizontal than vertical in its nature and exercise. The notion that there are producers and consumers of decisions appears contrary to that conception of collaboration. That is not the case.

Where a group works together to produce decisions together, the group or its governing body is the decisionmaker and each constituent group or member is the consumer. Where government contracts for services or awards grants to facilitate community programs, the agency involved decides who will receive the funds. Where service networks are established by nonprofit organizations or for-profit firms, they often operate through the awarding of subcontracts under contracts or grants provided by the federal or state governments. In these situations, as in the others described to this point in the chapter, there is some locus of decision, some point of action that we can identify and analyze. Similarly, there are organizations and individuals who then must work with those decisions.

Careful analysis and decision in any problem of law and administration requires the attempt to deal with both the producer and the consumer perspectives on the matter. That is not to say that everything is relative or that there is no such thing as an erroneous or unfair output from the administrative justice system. These comments merely advise caution when intuition pushes one to choose sides quickly and uncritically.

A SIX-PART APPROACH TO PROBLEMS
IN PUBLIC LAW AND PUBLIC ADMINISTRATION

The development of a useful conceptual framework with which to approach problems raised in the administrative justice system is a continuing challenge. A helpful rule of thumb, however, is that one should always test a problem at the outset for the presence of each of the following types of issues: (1) constitutional, (2) statutory, (3) procedural, (4) factual, (5) contractual, and (6) supranational. Most administrative law problems contain more than one of these elements.

Constitutional questions concern such matters as whether the due process clause of the Fifth or Fourteenth Amendments requires that an individual be afforded the opportunity to appear in person to argue his or her case before benefit payments are terminated. Statutory questions ask for explanations of legislation as applied to particular problems and often, either explicitly or implicitly, present inquiries as to the scope of administrative discretion in a particular policy area.

Procedural questions focus not on what the agency has done or proposes to do, but highlight the manner in which the agency goes about its actions. A challenge to a regulation issued by an agency may rest on the assertion that the agency did not provide adequate opportunity for interested parties to make their criticisms known before the rule was published in its final form. Factual matters are of major significance because problems of law and administration are frequently highly technical and complex. For example, the attempt to determine questions regarding regulations on air quality involves scientific, economic, and medical considerations. Though actors in the administrative justice system prefer to leave such matters to the experts, some understanding is needed to deal with air quality questions at any level.

To these four traditional questions, it is now necessary to add two more. In contemporary public administration it is essential to ask whether there are contractual issues. There are four types of contractual concerns. First, there are internal and often personnel-related contracts. Many agencies have collective bargaining agreements that specify a wide range of substantive and procedural obligations for public managers in dealing with their employees. In the state and federal contexts, for example, employees who are facing disputes with their employers may elect either to proceed according to procedures set forth in collective bargaining agreements or under processes available under civil service laws. Second, there are external contracts like the many agreements under which state and local governments pay private sector firms to provide goods and services. In most states, for example, much of the health care and mental-health care supported by the government is actually delivered by for-profit or not-for-profit organizations under contract. Third, there are interjurisdictional contracts, agreements under which, for example, one community agrees to provide ambulance service to a neighboring city in return for police services or perhaps for cash. Fourth, there interorganizational governance agreements that extend beyond government to include nongovernmental actors, not as traditional contractors expected provide a service for government but as what are often called public/private partnerships.

While it is true that such public sector contracts must conform to relevant federal or state law, they add a very important dimension to decisionmaking. They are different both substantively and procedurally from more traditional direct service provided by administrative agencies. Thus, for example, public administrators may make management changes by working in new ways with their employees, but in a contractual situation such decisions are made by the contracting firm and not by the government. Normally, such decisions are within the discretion of the contracting firm so long as they deliver the promised service at the established price within the agreed time limit. So why should public administrators care as long as those results are achieved? They must care because citizens have certain rights, not only about the substance of the service they receive but also with respect to the processes that govern how those services are provided. If they are to address such questions, government managers must then be concerned about what authority they retain over the contractor under the terms of the agreement. In a governance regime, contracts provide a kind of constitution of that body, setting forth the structure of the relationships, the authority and jurisdiction it possesses, and the processes by which key decisions are to be made. Indeed, service networks are made up of sets of contracts. Thus, it is critically important when confronting a problem in law and administration to consider whether there are contractual issues involved.

The final question is whether there are any supranational issues. It is increasingly common to find that a particular area of policy is not only affected by state or national law but also by regional agreements—such as the North American Free Trade Agreement (NAFTA)—that involve a number of countries or global agreements—such as the General Agreement on Tariffs and Trade (GATT)—that involve many nations. Treaties have the force of law under our Constitution and are superior to state law under its supremacy clause.[85] The United States Environmental Protection Agency (EPA), for example, has responsibility for implementing and complying with more than a hundred international agreements that affect EPA's domestic policymaking and administration. Even states and localities are affected both directly and indirectly by international accords.[86] Thus, while there may very well be no supranational issue involved in an particular case, it is increasingly a good idea to ask the question.

This six-part approach departs significantly from the traditionally narrow procedural method discussed earlier and presents a more accurate picture of contemporary administrative law problems.

SUMMARY

The resolution of problems of public law and public administration involves the attempt to deal with difficult questions under conditions of pressure. In general, the field of law that deals with these problems is called administrative law. For purposes of this study, administrative law is defined broadly. It includes substantive as well as procedural problems. It is concerned with the intergovernmental problems of law and administration and applies to other kinds of matters in addition to the traditional quasi-legislative and quasi-judicial types of decisions, including the relationship of public contracting to other administrative operations.

Agencies exist within a loosely defined system, often called the administrative justice system. Different types of individuals and groups, referred to here as single-shot players and repeat players, make demands on the system for several different kinds of decisions. The demands are resolved through a number of processes and institutions.

In the contemporary context, in which government often shares authority with collaborative groups (sometimes called governance regimes), there are not fewer administrative law questions, but more and more complex questions than ever before. The fact that one of the realities of that contemporary context is the growing role of globalization similarly adds both new questions and increased complexity. Neither of these important forces can be ignored.

In approaching problems of administrative law, one must be alert to both consumer and producer perspectives. A careful consideration of the elements of decisions in each case begins with a search for constitutional questions, factual issues, statutory problems, procedural matters, contractual questions, and supranational dimensions.

In order to be able to operate in this administrative justice system, it is necessary to understand both the law as it is written and what that law looks like in operation. These are the topics considered in Chapters 2 and 3.

NOTES

1. Leonidas G. Koniaris, Teresa A. Zimmers, David A. Lubarsky, and Jonathan P. Sheldon, "Inadequate Anaesthesia in Lethal Injection for Execution," 365 *The Lancet* 1412 (2005). The actual case on which this mini-case study is based is from the mid-1980s, but the issue was, as this quote indicates, still in doubt as of 2005.

2. See *Heckler v. Chaney*, 470 U.S. 821 (1985). The opinion below may be found at 718 F.2d 1174 (D.C.Cir. 1983). Chapter 2 will explain how to read this citation and find the report in the library or on the Internet.

3. See *Richardson v. McKnight*, 521 U.S. 399 (1997).

4. See *Correctional Services Corporation v. Malesko*, 534 U.S. 61 (2001).

5. *Federal Communications Commission v. Pacifica*, 438 U.S. 726 (1978).

6. *In the Matter of Complaints Against Various Television Licensees Concerning Their February 1, 2004, Broadcast of the Super Bowl XXXVIII Halftime Show*, File No. EB-04-IH-0011, "Notice of Apparent Liability for Forfeiture," August 31, 2004, p. 19, at http://www.fcc.gov/eb/Orders/2004/FCC-04-209A1.html, as of April 3, 2006.

7. "Statement of Chairman Michael K. Powell," *In the Matter of Complaints Against Various Television Licensees Concerning Their February 1, 2004, Broadcast of the Super Bowl XXXVIII Halftime Show*, File No. EB-04-IH-0011, August 31, 2004, 1.

8. *In the Matter of Complaints Against Various Television Licensees Concerning Their February 1, 2004, Broadcast of the Super Bowl XXXVIII Halftime Show*, p. 6.

9. *In the Matter of Complaints Against Various Television Licensees Concerning Their February 1, 2004, Broadcast of the Super Bowl XXXVIII Halftime Show*, p. 20.

10. "Statement of Commissioner Michael J. Coops," *In the Matter of Complaints Against Various Television Licensees Concerning Their February 1, 2004, Broadcast of the Super Bowl XXXVIII Halftime Show*, File No. EB-04-IH-0011, August 31, 2004, 1.

11. U.S. Department of Agriculture, "Transcript of News Conference with Agriculture Secretary Ann M. Veneman on BSE," December 23, 2003, p. 1. at http://www.usda.gov/wps/portal/!ut/p/_s.7_0_A/ 7_0_1OB/.cmd/ad/.ar/sa.retrievecontent/.c/6_2_1UH/.ce/7_2_5JM/.p/5_2_4TQ/.d/3/_th/J_2_9D/ _s.7_0_A/7_0_1OB?PC_7_2_5JM_contentid=2003/12/0433.html&PC_7_2_5JM_navtype= RT& PC_7_2_5JM_parentnav=TRANSCRIPTS_SPEEC, as of April 3, 2006.

12. See *Faragher v. City of Boca Raton,* 524 U.S. 775 (1998).

13. For a comparable problem involving Vietnam-era veterans, see Peter Schuck, *Agent Orange in Court* (Cambridge: Belknap, 1986).

14. See *Pennhurst State School & Hospital v. Halderman,* 451 U.S. 1 (1981); *Wyatt v. Stickney,* 325 F.Supp. 781 (MDAL 1971). Discussed in greater detail in Phillip J. Cooper, *Hard Judicial Choices* (New York: Oxford University Press, 1988).

15. The following works were surveyed for a definition of administrative law: Frank Goodnow, *The Principles of the Administrative Law of the United States* (New York: Putnam, 1905); James M. Landis, *The Administrative Process* (New Haven: Yale University Press, 1938); James Hart, *An Introduction to Administrative Law with Selected Cases* (New York: Crofts, 1940); Roscoe Pound, *Administrative Law: Its Growth, Procedure and Significance* (Pittsburgh: University of Pittsburgh Press, 1942); Frank E. Cooper, supra note 6; J. Forrester Davison and Nathan D. Grundstein, *Administrative Law: Cases and Readings* (Indianapolis: Bobbs-Merrill, 1952); Morris D. Forkosch, *A Treatise on Administrative Law* (Indianapolis: Bobbs-Merrill, 1956); E. Blythe Stason and Frank E. Cooper, *The Law of Administration Tribunals: A Collection of Judicial Decisions, Statutes, Administrative Rules and Orders and Other Materials,* 3rd ed. (Chicago: Callaghan, 1957); Kenneth Culp Davis, *Administrative Law Treatise* (St. Paul: West, 1958); David L. Sills, ed., *International Encyclopedia of the Social Sciences* (New York: Macmillan, 1968); Robert S. Lorch, *Democratic Process and Administrative Law* (Detroit, Mich.: Wayne State University Press, 1969); Ernest Gellhorn, *Administrative Law and Process in a Nutshell* (St. Paul: West, 1972); Walter Gellhorn and Clark Byse, *Administrative Law: Cases and Comments* (Mineola, NY: Foundation Press, 1974); Edwin W. Tucker, *Text-Cases-Problems on Administrative Law, Regulation of Enterprise and Individual Liberties* (St. Paul: West, 1975); Louis L. Jaffee and Nathaniel L. Nathanson, *Administrative Law: Cases and Materials* (Boston: Little, Brown, 1976); and Bernard Schwartz, *Administrative Law* (Boston: Little, Brown, 1976).

16. Schwartz, *supra* note 15, at pp. 2.

17. *Id.*

18. See e.g., William F. Funk, Sidney Shapiro, and Russell L. Weaver, eds., *Administrative Procedure and Practice,* 2nd ed. (St. Paul: West Publishing, 2001).

19. See generally Cornell W. Clayton, "Government Lawyers: Who Represents Government and Why Does It Matter?" in Phillip J. Cooper and Chester A. Newland, eds., *Handbook of Public Law and Administration* (San Francisco: Jossey-Bass, 1997).

20. "Administrative law is not, by this definition, the substantive rules made by administrators, nor is it the adjudicative decisions they make." Robert S. Lorch, *Democratic Process and Administrative Law* (Detroit.: Wayne State University Press, 1969), pp. 59. See also Kenneth Culp Davis, *Administrative Law Treatise* (St. Paul: West, 1958), §1.01, and Schwartz, *supra* note 15, at pp. 3.

21. Martin Shapiro, *The Supreme Court and Administrative Agencies* (New York: Free Press, 1968), pp. 106.

22. For an example of how the nature, form, and purpose of legislation and agency action blend with complex facts and policy issues, see *Volkswagen Aktiengesellschaft v. Federal Maritime Commission,* 390 U.S. 261, 309–10 (1968), Justice Douglas dissenting.

23. Davis, *supra* note 20, at §1.01.

24. Bernard Schwartz in David L. Sills, ed., *International Encyclopedia of the Social Sciences* (New York: Macmillan, 1968), pp. 68.

25. See generally Paul E. Peterson, *The Price of Federalism* (Washington, DC: Brookings, 1995); Alice M. Rivlin, *Reviving the American Dream: The Economy, the States, and the Federal Government.* Washington, DC: Brookings, 1992; Deil S. Wright, *Understanding Intergovernmental Relations,* 3rd ed. (Pacific Grove, CA: Brooks/Cole Publishing, 1988).

26. See Chapters 4, 7, and the *Eldridge* case in Appendix 1.

27. See the *New York Times,* Tuesday, October 18, 1977, pp. 1, and Thursday, October 13, 1977.

28. *Id.,* October 18, pp. 28.

29. Louis L. Jaffee and Nathaniel L. Nathanson, *Administrative Law: Cases and Materials* (Boston: Little, Brown, 1976), pp. 2.

30. This is not a new problem. For some indication of the difficulties encountered over the years, see *United States v. Florida East Coast Railroad,* 410 U.S. 224 (1973), and *United States v. Allegheny-Ludlum Steel Corp.,* 406 U.S. 742 (1972).

31. "The basic scheme underlying the legislation is to classify all proceedings into two categories, namely, "rulemaking" and "adjudication." Attorney General Tom C. Clark to Bureau of the Budget Director Harold D. Smith, June 3, 1946, Truman Papers, Truman Library.

32. See e.g., 5 U.S.C. §553(a)(2).

33. See U.S. Government Accountability Office, *Improving the Sourcing Decisions of the Government* (Washington, DC: GAO, 2003). See also W. Noel Keyes, *Government Contracts,* 4th ed. (St. Paul: West, 2005).

34. The author has addressed a number of these issues in much greater detail in Phillip J. Cooper, *Governing by Contract* (Washington, DC: CQ Press, 2002).

35. See generally Isaiah Sharfman, *The Interstate Commerce Commission* (New York: The Commonwealth Fund, 1937), and Robert Fellmeth, *The Interstate Commerce Commission* (New York: Grossman, 1970).

36. The list changed rapidly during the 1970s and 1980s as deregulation bills moved through Congress.

37. Washington, DC: Brookings Institution, 1976. While some of the functions of these agencies survived and were transferred elsewhere, the commissions themselves died.

38. See e.g., the criticisms by former FAA Inspector General Mary Schiavo, *Flying Blind, Flying Safe* (New York: Avon Books, 1997).

39. Press release, U.S. Department of Health and Human Services, Food and Drug Administration, February 15, 2005, at http://www.hhs.gov/news/press/2005pres/20050215.html, as of April 3, 2006.

40. Testimony of Dr. David Graham, before a hearing of the U.S. Senate Finance Committee, *FDA, Merck, and Vioxx,* 108th Cong., 2d Sess. (2004).

41. News conference at http://proxy.lib.pdx.edu:2067/congcomp/document?_m=f61cc381097374ffab 964485238bc8e4&_docnum=15&wchp=dGLzVzz-zSkSA&_md5=60c4a9919356e3d2e61259dda5f7cb67, as of September 7, 2005.

42. See e.g., Steven A. Ramirez, "Depoliticizing Financial Regulation," 41 *William & Mary Law Review* 503 (2000).

43. See Telecommunications Act of 1996, P.L. 104-104, 110 Stat. 56.

44. See *Denver Area Educational Telecommunications Consortium v. F.C.C.,* 518 U.S. 727 (1996).

45. See *Reno v. American Civil Liberties Union,* 138 L.Ed.2d 874 (1997).

46. See e.g., *Withrow v. Larkin,* 421 U.S. 35 (1975) and *Bates v. State Bar,* 433 U.S. 350 (1977).

47. Ernest Freund, *Administrative Powers Over Persons and Property* (Chicago: University of Chicago Press, 1928), ch. 1.

48. Social Security Administration, *SSA's Performance and Accountability Report for Fiscal Year (FY) 2004* (Baltimore: Social Security Administration, 2005), pp. 45. At http://www.ssa.gov/finance/, as of October 1, 2005, pp. 45. As the *Eldridge* case study indicates, even in 1974 the disability program had 1,250,400 filings. U.S. House of Representatives, Subcommittee on Social Security of the Committee on Ways and Means, *Delays in Social Security Appeals,* 94th Cong., 1st Sess. (1975), pp. 34. In that year the combined total of major federal court filings was less than 200,000. See *Management Statistics for United States Courts* (Washington, DC: Administrative Office of U.S. Courts, 1975).

49. Department of Veterans Affairs, *Organizational Briefing Book, May 2005* (Washington, DC: Department of Veterans Affairs, 2005, pp. 1. Also available at http://www.va.gov/ofcadmin/orgbrfbook.pdf, as of October 1, 2005. This comparison in size and scope was noted long ago in Kenneth Culp Davis, *Administrative Law: Cases-Text-Problems,* 6th ed. (St. Paul: West, 1977), pp. 2.

50. U.S. Environmental Protection Agency, *Fiscal Year 2004 Annual Report,* (Washington, DC: U.S. EPA, 2005), pp. 2.

51. See U.S. Office of Management and Budget, *The Budget for FY 2006,* (Washington, DC: OMB, 2005), pp. 216 and 149 respectively.

52. "The service polity is a formidable political administrative entity, characterized by pressures upon public budgets by clients and public employees; demands for humane, equitable, and responsive service by clients;

demands for evidence of productivity by politicians and the public; a challenge to the nature of professionalism and administrative expertise in face-to-face relations; and related factors. Questions of collective bargaining by public employees, of productivity and equity in the provision of services, and of the political rights and responsibilities of public employees as a large segment of the public are the heart of the service polity." James D. Carroll, "Service, Knowledge, and Choice: The Future as Post-Industrial Administration," 35 *Public Administration Rev.* 578 (1975).

53. Lester M. Salamon, *Resilient Sector: The State of Nonprofit America* (Washington, DC Brookings Institution Press, 2003).

54. A. Burton Weisbrod, "The Future of the Nonprofit Sector: Its Entwining with Private Enterprise and Government,"16 *Journal of Policy Analysis and Management* 541 (1997).

55. See Salamon, *supra* note 53 and Weisbrod, *supra* note 54.

56. Theodore Lowi, *The End of Liberalism* (New York: Norton, 1969).

57. These issues are addressed in greater detail in Phillip J. Cooper, *Governing by Contract: Challenges and Opportunities for Public Managers* (Washington, DC: CQ Press, 2003).

58. "Federal Business Opportunities, FedBizOpps, at http://www.fbo.gov/ as of May 12, 2006.

59. See Mary Schiavo, *Flying Blind, Flying Safe* (New York: Avon Books, 1997) and Paul Eddy, Elaine Potter, and Bruce Paige, *Destination Disaster* (New York: Ballentine Books, 1976).

60. *Reynolds v. Sims,* 377 U.S. 533, 575 (1964).

61. *McMillan v. Monroe County,* 520 U.S. 781 (1997).

62. *Printz v. United States,* 521 U.S. 898 (1997).

63. See e.g., *Wisconsin Public Intervenors v. Mortier,* 501 U.S. 597 (1991).

64. Consider the complex situation when Congress tried to have the operating control over Washington, D.C., airports operated by a an airport authority and simultaneously put in place a board of members of Congress with the power to veto decisions made by the authority. See *Metropolitan Washington Airports Authority v. Citizens for the Abatement of Aircraft Noise,* 501 U.S. 252 (1991).

65. See *Lake Country Estates v. Tahoe Regional Planning Agency,* 440 U.S. 391 (1979).

66. See Ronald C. Moe and Robert S. Gilmour, "Rediscovering Principles of Public Administration: The Neglected Foundation of Public Law," 55 *Public Administration Review* 135 (1995); Ronald C. Moe and Thomas H. Stanton, "Government-Sponsored Enterprises as Federal Instrumentalities: Reconciling Private Management with Public Accountability," 49 *Public Administration Rev.* 321 (1989); Ronald C. Moe, "'Law' Versus 'Performance' as Objective Standard," 48 *Public Administration Rev.* 675 (1988); "Exploring the Limits of Privatization," 47 *Public Administration Rev.* 453 (1987).

67. 31 U.S.C. §9101.

68. H. George Frederickson, "Whatever Happened to Public Administration? Governance, Governance Everywhere," at http://www.rhul.ac.uk/Management/News-and-Events/seminars/HGeorgeFrederickson 11.2.04%20Paper.pdf, as of September 10, 2005, pp. 5–6. Advanced copy provided by author. Forthcoming in Ewan Ferlie, Laurence E. Lynn, and Christopher Pollitt, eds., *The Oxford Handbook of Public Management* (London: Oxford University Press, 2006).

69. Robert Agranoff and Michael McGuire, *Collaborative Public Management: New Strategies for Local Governments* (Washington, DC: Georgetown University Press, 2003), pp. 20–21.

70. Laurence E. Lynn, Jr., Carolyn J. Heinrich, and Carolyn J. Hill, *Improving Governance: A New Logic for Empirical Research* (Washington, DC: Georgetown University Press, 2001), pp. 6.

71. Id.

72. Yehezkel Dror, *The Capacity to Govern* (London: Routledge, 2001), pp. 7.

73. See Patricia W. Ingraham and Laurence E. Lynn, Jr., eds., *The Art of Governance: Analyzing Management and Administration* (Washington, DC: Georgetown University Press, 2004).

74. H. George Frederickson and Kevin B. Smith, *The Public Administration Theory Primer* (Boulder, Colo.: Westview Press, 2002), Ch. 9.

75. See Agranoff and McGuire, *supra* note 69. See also Laurence J. O'Toole, Jr., "Different Public Managements? Implications of Structural Context in Hierarchies and Networks," in Jeff Brudney, Laurence J. O'Toole, and

Hal Rainey, eds., *Advancing Public Management: New Directions in Theory, Methods, and Practice* (Washington, DC: Georgetown University Press, 2000); Phillip J. Cooper, "Canadian Refugee Services: The Challenges of Network Operations," 18 *Refuge* 14 (2000).

76. See e.g., Marc Galanter, "Why the Haves Come Out Ahead: Speculations on the Limits of Legal Change," 9 *Law & Society Rev.* 95 (1974).

77. Burton A. Weisbrod, "The Future of the Nonprofit Sector: Its Entwining with Private Enterprise and Government," 16 *Journal of Policy Analysis and Management* 541 (1997).

78. 37 *Federal Register* 16787 (1972).

79. The term *ultra vires* comes from corporate law. It derives from the idea that corporate ownership and control rest not with management but with the owners. Some of that control is delegated to management, but actions beyond those delegated are not binding on the corporation as a body or on the owners of the corporation. The relationship of citizens, legislators, and administrators is analogous to the corporate example.

80. See Phillip J. Cooper, *By Order of the President: The Use and Abuse of Presidential Direct Action* (Lawrence, KS: University Press of Kansas, 2002).

81. 5 U.S.C. §551 et seq.

82. For a more complete development of this model, see Cooper, *Governing by Contract, supra* note 57.

83. See e.g., U.S. Office of Management and Budget, *Summary Report of the SWAT Team on Civilian Agency Contracting* (Washington, DC: Office of Management and Budget, 1992), pp. I. See also Donald F. Kettl, *Sharing Power* (Washington, DC: Brookings Institution, 1993) and Phillip J. Cooper, "Government Contracts in Public Administration: The Role and Environment of the Contracting Office," 40 *Public Administration Review* 459 (1980).

84. On the complexities and problems of this use of the citizen as customer concept, see Jon Pierre, "The Marketization of the State: Citizens, Consumers, and the Emergence of the Public Market," in B. Guy Peters and Donald Savoie, eds., *Governance in a Changing Environment* (Montreal: McGill-Queen's University Press, 1995).

85. Article I, §2.

86. See *Missouri v. Holland,* 252 U.S. 416 (1920) and *Ware v. Hylton,* 3 U.S. (3 Dall.) 199 (1796) for historic examples.

2

The Law in Books: An Introduction to Legal Research

T hat's the law!" When people make such a claim they mean at least two things. First, they are asserting that the law as it is written requires or prohibits some action. This is a reference to the law in books or, as it is frequently referred to, the "black letter law." Second, the claim of legality suggests implicitly or explicitly that the courts will interpret and apply the written law in a predictable manner. This is a reference to the law in action. Chapter 3 will deal with those aspects of legal theory and judicial policymaking that comprise the law in action. This chapter will address the problem of locating and using the law in books.

Legal research is not simple, but neither is it magical or exotic. Techniques of legal research are based on the need to find the most authoritative statements, rulings, and commentaries on specific problems in the shortest possible time. Like most other skills—for example, using a computer—the only way to learn legal research is through practice. In fact, like many other types of research, computers have made legal research considerably easier than it used to be and have provided means for public managers to access important information even in small communities and a long distance from a law library. However, the online legal research systems assume that the searcher understands how to use the traditional tools of legal research. It is therefore necessary to learn those basics before moving on to discuss contemporary technological shortcuts.

SOURCES OF LAW AND TYPES OF LEGAL AUTHORITY

To set the stage for working with the law in books, we must first consider the sources of the law and the process through which the law is developed. When the television or newspaper media report major legal decisions affecting public policy, the cases discussed are frequently disputes that have been decided by the United States Supreme Court. However, the Supreme Court deals with only a handful of the thousands of cases that are pending at any given time. Most of the major interpretations that guide administrative action at any level of public sector action come from lower federal courts or state tribunals. For all these reasons, it is important to begin with some comment on the manner in which legal disputes work their way through the legal system and which sources of law are used to resolve them.

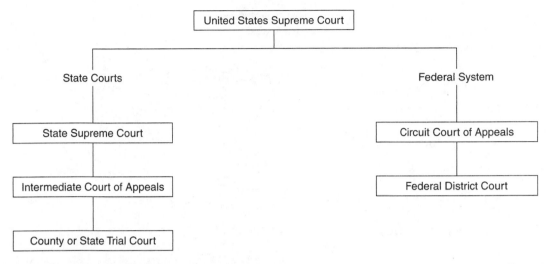

FIGURE 2.1 The Dual Court System

The Dual Court System

Most potential legal disputes never go to court. They are resolved through discussion and compromise. Increasingly, those that appear to present the likelihood of litigation are dispatched through some form of alterative dispute resolution, a type of procedure that will be addressed in detail in Chapters 6 and 8.

Of the controversies that do develop into formal legal cases, most are dealt with in the state courts. Most criminal and domestic relations problems, for example, are judged in state courts according to state rules. For the most part, local government issues are addressed in those courts as well as challenges brought against state administrative agencies. With this caveat in mind, let us turn briefly to a description of the American dual system of courts (see Figure 2.1).

Cases that come from state courts usually begin in a county court with a trial before a judge and, in some cases, a jury. The jury is the trier of fact whose duty it is to determine whether, for example, Mary Smith really punched Harry Jones in the nose. The judge must interpret the law to determine how the law should be applied in the particular case before the court. Thus, if Smith admits that she hit Jones but claims that it was in self-defense, the judge must interpret the meaning of self-defense under state law. This is done at the point at which the judge instructs the members of the jury as to the law they are to apply. Hence, in the Smith case, the problem for the jury would be to take the instructions from the judge as to what facts must exist in order for self-defense to apply. The jury then determines whether those conditions existed. The judge also makes interpretations of law in the process of the trial as she rules on due process claims or evidentiary objections made by the attorneys.

If the parties agree to a bench trial with no jury, then the judge is the trier of both fact and law.

If the case is lost at the trial court level, an appeal to an intermediate appellate court may be made on questions of law. Normally, the appeals court will not review questions of fact decided by the jury. The primary reason is that the judge and jury were present to see the testimony of witness and to assess the demeanor of the witnesses, which provides a much more complete picture of the evidence than the cold written record—which is all that is available to an appellate court. The facts on appeal are taken directly from the trial court record.

Should the decision at the appellate level be found unsatisfactory, one may have recourse to the state supreme court, which is the highest authority on the law of that state.[1] The decision of the U.S. Supreme Court in the 2000 presidential election case, *Bush v. Gore,* was so controversial in part because

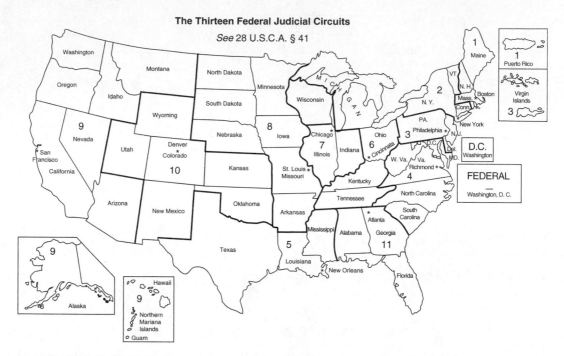

FIGURE 2.2 The Federal Judicial Circuits
SOURCE: 1-58 F.3d (1998).

it was such a departure from that norm.[2] At its core, the dispute in that case was about the meaning of Florida elections law, and the state supreme court had spoken on the point. Nevertheless, a sharply divided U.S. Supreme Court stepped away from the normal rule of deference to state supreme court interpretations of state law. By contrast, in a later case from Colorado concerning a woman's right to sue law enforcement officials for failure to protect her as required by a state court domestic protection order, the Supreme Court sent the woman back to state court for a reading on whether state law gave her a right to that protection.[3] In many cases, the state supreme court also has administrative responsibility for the operation of the entire state court system. If one asserts a question of federal law, even in a case that comes through the state courts, there may be an opportunity to have the case reviewed in the United States Supreme Court.[4]

Cases that come up through the federal court system begin in the federal district courts.[5] There are 94 federal district courts staffed by 678 judges.[6] Each district court interprets the federal law within its district; and most states have a number of such districts within their borders.[7]

Appeals from decisions made in the federal district courts are taken to the United States Circuit Courts of Appeals. There are 11 numbered judicial circuits and the D.C. Circuit (see Figure 2.2).

An additional appellate tribunal known as the Circuit Court of Appeals for the Federal Circuit was also created to combine special purpose courts located in the nation's capital. The Federal Circuit has become better known in recent years in part because of the many patent disputes that arisen in an era of burgeoning technological development.

The circuit courts rule over activities within their respective circuits. Judges in the circuit courts sit in three-judge panels; a majority vote is needed to decide a case. Obviously, given the number of different panels within the circuits and the number of circuits within the United States, there are bound to be conflicting interpretations of law. Within a circuit, such conflicts are resolved by having all of the judges sit together to review a case *en banc*. Of course, it is extremely expensive to have a dozen or more judges spend time on a single case. Thus, circuits try to discourage *en banc* proceedings and some have implemented what is termed a partial *en banc* process in which a majority of the judges within that circuit (not all of them) sit to resolve the conflicts.

Conflicts among circuits arise frequently, and are often initiated by policy changes issued by federal agencies. For example, the Secretary of Health and Human Services in the Reagan administration issued what has come to be known as the abortion "gag rule," which prohibited federally funded family planning clinics from providing patients with information concerning abortion services though they could provide information about services associated with childbirth. Not surprisingly, suits were filed in several federal courts around the nation that resulted in differing opinions in the First, Second, and Tenth Circuits.[8] Conflicts among the circuits must be resolved by the Supreme Court, which was what ultimately happened with the gag rule case.[9]

Cases come to the Supreme Court in one of three forms. Disputes may be taken on appeal from state supreme courts,[10] circuit courts of appeals,[11] or other special courts.[12] Most cases come to the Court on a writ of *certiorari*.[13] The decision to grant a writ of certiorari is purely discretionary and is reached through what has come to be known as "the rule of four." If four of the nine justices vote to hear the case, the writ is issued to the lower court directing that the record in the case be sent up for review.

Although it is common to hear some angry litigant declare that he or she intends to take a case "all the way to the Supreme Court," the chances that the Court will actually hear the case and render a full-dress opinion on it are remote. In the 2004–05 term of the Court, for example, there were a total of 8,588 cases on the docket at one point or another, 1,092 of which were cases carried over from the previous term. The other 7,496 cases were new. Of that number, 6,590 cases were either refused review or withdrawn. Some 826 cases were decided summarily—that is, without an oral argument or full-dress opinion. There were only 87 cases actually heard in oral argument and only 85 of those produced full signed opinions.[14]

Second, cases are taken to the Court on certification.[15] In this situation, a lower court certifies a particular question of law to the Supreme Court in an effort to get a clear interpretation of an ambiguous area of the law.

In reading opinions, a researcher will also encounter cases that have been taken to the Supreme Court as appeals as a matter of right.[16] The idea behind this type of appeal was that there are certain kinds of cases of such significance that Congress made a guaranteed appeal available. As a practical matter, the Supreme Court found a way around this requirement by refusing to note probable jurisdiction. That means that the Court does not agree that the case in question really fits the category of cases that deserve to come before the court on appeal as of right. Beyond that, Chief Justice Warren Burger spent much of his tenure in what turned out to be a successful effort to get Congress to eliminate many of the statutory provisions that required the Court to take cases on appeal.

Repositories of the Black Letter Law

The decisions of appellate courts are, under the Anglo-American system of precedent, the law within their respective jurisdictions. But precedent is only one of a number of sources of black letter law. There are several:

- Constitutions
- Treaties
- Statutes
- Ordinances
- Executive orders

- Administrative regulations
- Appellate court decisions
- Contracts

Constitutions are by definition fundamental laws and are superior to any other legal enactment whether in the form of a statute or a joint resolution. Treaties are negotiated by the president and ratified by the Senate. There are also other forms of international agreements that, though they are not ratified by the Senate, have the force of law. Executive agreements or diplomatic protocols are examples.[17] In case of a conflict, the provisions of a treaty are superior to state law.[18]

Statutes are enactments of the Congress or the state legislatures. The general types of legislation and their characteristics are discussed at the beginning of Chapter 5. There is sometimes in the contemporary context a tendency among public managers not to pay as much attention to legislation as might be the case. Administrative agencies depend on statutes for their authority—not only the enabling act that creates the agency, but also the authorization legislation that creates or changes specific policies the agency is to administer and appropriations acts that not only provide funds for administrative work but also often set forth mandates or indicate actions that are to be prohibited. Ordinances are the local government equivalent of legislation.[19]

Executive orders are directives issued by the president[20] or, in the states, by the governor to officials in the executive branch.[21] There have been more than 13,000 such orders issued by presidents, extending back to earliest days of the republic. (For an example of a complete executive order, see Appendix 4.) Presidents since Jimmy Carter, both Democratic and Republican, have found these very attractive devices, particularly in the face of recalcitrant legislatures controlled by the opposition party. Indeed, Vice President Gore's National Performance Review process recommended that the president should use such orders in preference to seeking legislation whenever possible.[22] Certainly President George W. Bush made wide use of executive orders, ranging from creation of the administration's Faith-Based Initiative, encouraging contracting with faith-based organizations,[23] to the order mandating trial by military commission of persons designated by the administration as illegal combatants.[24]

Governors, too, have found executive orders increasingly attractive and for similar reasons.[25] A few of these have attracted considerable attention, such as orders issued by California governor Pete Wilson, concerned with blocking services to undocumented immigrants, and Florida governor Jeb Bush's orders against affirmative action.[26] More recently, Governor Kathleen Babineaux Blanco of Louisiana issued a series of executive orders in the wake of Hurricane Katrina (see Figure 2.3).

Even mayors in a number of cities who have the authority to issue orders have done so in both visible and less well-publicized contexts. Examples include orders issued by former New York mayor Rudolph Giuliani following the 9/11 attacks and New Orleans mayor C. Ray Nagin in conjunction with Hurricane Katrina. Less well known are significant management policy orders such as those issued by Chicago mayor Richard Daley on hiring and contracting issues.[27]

Chief executives have issued executive orders either on the basis of statutory authority or on the basis of their constitutional authority. In many instances, particularly those associated with war or other emergencies, Congress has retroactively ratified the presidential actions.[28] In fact, courts have gone so far as to imply congressional ratification from the fact that the legislature continued funding for the policy created by the order.[29] Of course, chief executives may not issue orders that exceed their authority or violate provisions of the Constitution or statutes.[30] One of the best-known examples concerned the Supreme Court ruling against President Truman's order seizing steel mills during a labor dispute. More recent examples include the ruling against President Clinton's order prohibiting contracts with firms that hire permanent replacements for striking employees.[31]

Presidential proclamations are also authoritative legal statements and can be important, though they are most often used for ceremonial purposes such as designation of special days of recognition. Unlike executive orders, which are directed to officials in government, proclamations are more general statements to the public such as proclamations issued by presidents George H. W. Bush and Bill Clinton intended to address efforts by large numbers of Haitians to come to the U.S., many of whom were killed

EXECUTIVE DEPARTMENT

EXECUTIVE ORDER NO. KBB 2005 - 27

EMERGENCY PROCEDURES FOR CONDUCTING STATE BUSINESS

WHEREAS,   pursuant to the Louisiana Homeland Security and Emergency Assistance and Disaster Act, R.S. 29:721, *et seq.*, a state of emergency was declared through Proclamation No. 48 KBB 2005;

WHEREAS,   Hurricane Katrina has caused unprecedented and extensive damage in the state of Louisiana and this tragic event has significant consequences on the financial conditions of the state; and

WHEREAS,   the Louisiana Homeland Security and Emergency Assistance and Disaster Act, R.S. 29:721, *et seq.*, confers upon the governor of the state of Louisiana emergency powers to deal with emergencies and disasters, including those caused by fire, flood, earthquake or other natural or man-made causes, to ensure that preparations of this state will be adequate to deal with such emergencies or disasters, and to preserve the lives and property of the citizens of the state of Louisiana;

NOW THEREFORE I, KATHLEEN BABINEAUX BLANCO, Governor of the state of Louisiana, by virtue of the authority vested by the Constitution and laws of the state of Louisiana, do hereby order and direct as follows:

SECTION 1:   Cabinet members, statewide elected officials, and state agency heads are authorized and empowered to use their best judgment in purchasing necessary goods and services to satisfy the situation caused by this emergency and shall maintain, as much as practicable, documentation which includes vendors names and addresses, goods or services purchased, prices paid, invoices and the emergency related reasons for those purchases. Strict compliance with R.S. 39:1490, et seq., and 39:1551, et seq. shall not be required.

SECTION 2:   The inspector general is directed and authorized to monitor those transactions conducted outside the scope of regulatory statutes, orders, rules and regulations to insure that those transactions are directly related to the emergency situation and are prudently handled and if any inappropriate transactions are noted, those situations shall be reported directly to the governor.

SECTION 3:   All cabinet members, statewide elected officials and department heads are authorized to transfer the directions, job assignments, personnel, and functions of their departments for the purpose of performing or facilitating emergency services as necessary.

SECTION 4:   All available resources of state government should be utilized as reasonably necessary to cope with this emergency.

SECTION 5:   Subject to any applicable requirements for compensation, private property may be utilized or commandeered in those areas of the state directly affected by Hurricane Katrina. However, no private property shall be utilized or commandeered under this authority without prior consultation and approval by the Office of the Governor.

FIGURE 2.3 Louisiana Executive Order *(Continued)*

SECTION 6:   Evacuations and limits on ingress and egress to the disaster area are hereby authorized to be ordered as necessary by the Office of Homeland Security and Emergency Preparedness.

SECTION 7:   This Order is effective upon signature and shall continue in effect until amended, modified, terminated, or rescinded by the governor, or terminated by operation of law.

IN WITNESS WHEREOF, I have set my hand officially and caused to be affixed the Great Seal of Louisiana, at the Capitol, in the city of Baton Rouge, on this 3rd day of September, 2005.

/S/ Kathleen Babineaux Blanco
GOVERNOR OF LOUISIANA

**ATTEST BY
THE GOVERNOR**

/S/ Al Ater
SECRETARY OF STATE

FIGURE 2.3 (Continued)

in the attempt. Both presidents issued executive orders to the U.S. Coast Guard as to how that agency was to respond, but both presidents also issued proclamations warning Americans not to attempt to facilitate illegal entries.[32] Such proclamations are more than mere admonitions. They can be and have been the basis for criminal prosecution.[33]

Recent presidents have increasingly employed another device, known as a presidential signing statement, in an effort to influence the interpretation of statutes and to shape the implementation of new legislation. These are statements prepared for the White House by the Department of Justice and issued at the time a new piece of legislation is signed into law. The statements interpret the legislation and often assert limits on the way it is to be understood and administered by executive branch officials based on assertions by the president that the language of the statute intrudes upon the constitutional powers of the president. These statements have been used by presidents as a kind of line item veto to set aside the language of legislation without providing a formal veto that could be overridden by Congress.[34] Although efforts have been made, beginning with Attorney General Edwin Meese during the Reagan administration, to have the president's interpretations at the time legislation is signed accorded an important status, these statements do not carry the force of law. That is not to say that they are without significance. These statements instruct the heads of administrative agencies that they are to implement the new law in accordance with the president's signing statement and that process of shaping the initial implementation of the policy can have little-seen but significant impacts over the long term.

Administrative regulations are promulgated by an administrative agency within the area of authority delegated to the agency by the legislature. They will be the subject of extensive consideration in Chapter 5. It is a common and significant problem that many Americans do not understand that many administrative regulations do carry the force of law.

Finally, contracts are sources of law. A contract is the law governing a relationship. Unlike legislation and regulations that are enacted and enforced by government, a contract is created as a meeting of the minds in which both parties shape the law that will establish and govern their specific relationship.[35] Either party can trigger enforcement and each is accountable to the other, usually in the form of damages, for a breach of the contract. Indeed, even the manner of resolution of disputes can be and often is made part of the contract. While there was a time when government contracts were described as contracts of adhesion in which the nongovernmental party accepted or rejected the terms offered by the government and was then bound by them, today's contracts are far more likely to contain a host of fully negotiated terms in addition to those that are required to be included by statute or agency regulations.[36] That is true even at the federal government level under what is termed the Federal Acquisition Regulation (FAR), but it is even more the case at the state and local level. Government is increasingly contracting for services rather than merely purchasing common products, and those service contracts are extending well beyond services that were more or less routine (such as janitorial services) to the actual day-to-day operations of sophisticated governmental programs. This has made public contracts far less standard in character and more complex in operation.

BEGINNING LEGAL RESEARCH

Legal materials are published by official sources at various levels of government and by private commercial houses. In doing legal research work, the researcher must frequently move from materials prepared by one private publisher to those of the government or another publisher. Unfortunately, the reference systems do not cross-refer well in all cases. Therefore, the discussion to follow will be somewhat redundant so that users will be able to understand the resources and problems of each system of books.

After one has developed a familiarity with the tools of legal research, it is normal to select favorite research strategies for different types of research problems. In general, though, most students of the craft agree that there are three parts to legal research: (1) finding the law; (2) reading the law; and (3) supplementing the law.

FINDING THE LAW

Every year Congress enacts many new laws; the Supreme Court hands down more than 80 full opinions in major cases; U.S. Circuit Courts of Appeals disposes of some 56,000 cases;[37] the district courts more than 240,000 cases;[38] state appellate courts add almost 300,000 more;[39] administrative agencies produce hundreds of regulations; and legislatures, courts, and agencies in all 50 states add their share to the law already "on the books." The problem then is to locate the law on the specific topic about which one wishes to learn.

First, one must be aware that words are important. The researcher must get into the habit of searching for key words. Therefore, learning the language of the area of law that one is investigating is one of the first steps. Do not be put off by legalisms or exotic words. No one can know all areas of the law, or even the language or jargon currently in vogue in a particular specialty. Attempt to discover clear descriptive terms in the study of a subject to aid in the law-finding process.

Suppose, for example, that one wanted information on the topic of discrimination in employment. "Discrimination" and "employment" are two obvious words that one would use to find material on the topic, but there are any number of other possible terms. One might check various indexes under "sex discrimination," "age discrimination," "race discrimination," "aliens," "equal protection," "labor," "equal opportunity," "affirmative action," or "employment tests."

Make a list of the terms that come to mind or words that are mentioned in titles or early reading in the research area. It will not be long before one finds certain terms repeated in research sources. Using these words, the researcher will be able to focus on his or her specific interest and save time.

Indexes, Dictionaries, and Encyclopedias

Finding the law starts much like any other kind of research. The beginning researcher will need to refer to dictionaries for definitions of new terms. Two of the most commonly available comprehensive legal dictionaries are *Black's Law Dictionary*[40] and *Ballentine's Law Dictionary*.[41] Many people, particularly those who do not have a frequent need for a complete legal dictionary, tend to use an online legal dictionary such as the one provided by FindLaw.com.[42] In law, unlike some other fields, words usually have an authoritative definition derived directly from the definition given to the words by courts that have considered them. Legal dictionaries provide the reader with the definitions and references to cases in which those definitions were developed.

If one knew nothing about a topic of general interest in any field, an encyclopedia could be a first stop, though encyclopedias are less commonly used than they once were. In the social sciences, for example, one might refer to the *International Encyclopedia of the Social and Behavioral Sciences*.[43] In legal research, the researcher would go to West's *Corpus Juris Secundum*[44] ("second body of law") or to the Lawyers Cooperative's *American Jurisprudence, Second Series* (frequently referred to as Am. Jur. 2d).[45] Despite their somewhat forbidding titles, both sets are encyclopedias in that they do two things: (1) they present the beginning researcher with an encyclopedic article on major topics like any other encyclopedia; and (2) they footnote almost every statement of any consequence in the article to legal cases that discuss the point. Increasingly, the tendency of non-lawyers is to turn to the Internet and such sites as Findlaw.com or Cornell University Law School's Legal Information Institute (LII) "Law About" page.[46] One of the great problems of using Internet sources that are not as well established as those mentioned here is that there is no assurance of what is authoritative and what is not. The Findlaw.com and LII sites are useful and generally well-regarded sites, but many websites are neither substantively helpful nor authoritative.

Most law reference books, including indexes and encyclopedias, are much too expensive to republish each year as new developments occur in the law. To accommodate changes, many research volumes contain a "pocket part," so named because it is a paperback part added by means of a pocket in the binding on the inside back cover. Whenever using a legal volume, be certain to check for a pocket part updating the material from the main body of the book. One of the attractions of online databases or authoritative websites is that, unlike bound volumes, the updates can be easily and rapidly updated. Of course, one of the problems with websites is that some are kept current while others are not well maintained.

If one knows there is a statute or regulation on a given subject, there are online sites that can assist in finding a reference and indeed in locating the full text of the document. For example, the federal government maintains an Internet service called GPO Access (GPO stands for Government Printing Office).[47] It is a vehicle for accessing a range of federal government publications, including statutes and regulations. It is a simple way to access the *Federal Register*. Most states publish their statutes on the state legislature's website which can be reached through the state government's site. Indeed, the legislative websites for many states make it possible to track pending legislation during the legislative session as well as to access the state code.

One of the most common mistakes made by beginning legal researchers is to overlook the obvious. The card catalog, which is most often now available on computer terminals in the library and may be accessed by modem from elsewhere, may well contain a reference to a legal treatise or summary monograph of the topic under consideration. That said, there are at least three reasons why many public managers will look to law journals (also known as law reviews) rather than treatises or monographs. First, there is the obvious point that one can read two or three journal articles in the time it takes to move through a larger volume. Second, law review articles can be selected that are more narrowly tailored to the subject about which a researcher seeks information. Third, while book-length treatments are more comprehensive, law reviews may be more current.

Law journals constitute some of the most important legal research tools, especially for a public administration student or practitioner. The Wilson *Index to Legal Periodicals and Books*[48] and LexisNexis provide access to law review articles referenced by subject, author, case title, and book review title.

Of the two, the Wilson *Index* is sometimes available in college or larger public libraries without special access accounts. It is increasingly common to find that individual journals or authors will make available articles in full text on their websites and these articles may be located using standard search engines.

Law Review Articles as Law Finders

From a social scientist's or administrator's point of view, law review articles are some of the best law finders. They accomplish a number of goals. Articles on the topic under study frequently provide the neophyte in a particular area of law with several types of useful information. First, a law review offers an introduction to the field of interest. The introductions usually provide a helpful start for the uninitiated and are structured from a quite general introduction to more specific detail. Along the way, a law review piece often provides a basic familiarization with the jargon in use in a given area of law and policy. Most such articles set forth a survey of the major statutes and leading cases in the field under study as well as references to leading treatises, government reports, and other journal articles on the topic. They also commonly set out one or more conceptual frameworks for understanding the major issues and conflicts in a particular policy area. Finally, most such pieces provide, directly or indirectly, a brief who's who in the field and indicate the major actors' positions on the policy or legal issue under consideration. In short, they provide a good deal more than just an argument on a particular issue and are relatively user-friendly.

When using the law reviews as law finders, try scanning the introduction, the first footnote (which identifies the credentials of the author), the conclusion (which is usually a survey paragraph), the section headings in the body of the article, and the footnotes. After reading the body of the article, read the footnotes separately. The footnotes are checked by the law review editorial staff, and so can generally be relied upon as accurate references.

A law review, dictionary, or encyclopedia is not cited as a primary legal source. They are secondary sources—the Constitution, cases, statutes, treaties, or agency regulations are the primary references. A second caveat is that one should not simply adopt the point of law noted in a secondary source without carefully examining the primary source. These research tools are intended to assist the researcher in finding the law, not to present the law itself.

READING THE LAW

We turn now to an examination of the manner of presentation of the law by the government and private publishers. However, to get from the law finder to the black letter law, one must understand the use of legal citations. It is relatively easy to understand the basic form for legal citations, but there are readily available sources when questions arise. The most commonly used guide is published jointly by the Harvard, Columbia, Yale, and University of Pennsylvania Law Reviews and is known as *The Blue Book: A Uniform System of Citation.*[49] The Cornell University School of Law Legal Information Institute has published Professor Peter M. Martin's *Introduction to Basic Legal Citation (LII 2003 ed.)* on their website.[50]

The citation consists for present purposes of two parts: the case or article title and the reference. The following example uses *Rust v. Sullivan,* 500 U.S. 173 (1991). A title is italicized as a proper title. The reference indicates where the cited case or article may be found. It begins with the volume number in which the item is found. The initials abbreviate the name of the publication in which the item is printed. The second number indicates the page on which the case or article begins. Finally, the date in parentheses tells the reader the year in which the case or article was published. *Rust,* then, may be found in volume 500 of the *United States Reports* (the official reporter for the U.S. Supreme Court), beginning on page 173, decided in 1991.[51]

Lower court citations must contain an indication as to which court rendered the opinion because, unlike U.S. Supreme Court opinions, a lower court's ruling is only binding within its jurisdiction. Hence *St. Johnsbury Academy v. D.H., 20 F.Supp.2d 675 (DVT 1998)*, refers to an opinion rendered by the United States District Court for the District of Vermont and is reported in Volume 20 of the *Federal Supplement, Second Series*. The *Federal Supplement* reports opinions of federal district courts. *St. Johnsbury Academy v. D.H., 240 F.3d 163 (2nd Cir. 2001)* refers to an opinion rendered in the same case by the United States Circuit Court of Appeals for the Second Circuit reported in the *Federal Reporter, Third Series*. The third circuit covers a larger area than Vermont, but still only includes a portion of the Northeast. The *Federal Reporter* reports the opinions of the United States Circuit Court of Appeals.

The same general form is used for most important citations in law. In the case of statutes, for example, codes are cited first by title number, which refers to the topical section of the body of law, the published title of the code as in U.S.C. (for United States Code), then by the section (abbreviated § or in the plural §§) followed by the year of publication of the version of the code involved. Regulations are reported in the *Code of Federal Regulations,* abbreviated C.F.R., but until they are codified, one will often encounter them as published in the *Federal Register,* abbreviated Fed. Reg. A similar form is used for law review citations, with the volume of the law review first, the name of the publication, the year on which it begins, and the year in which it was published.

Legislative Enactments

During a given year, Congress may enact several hundred statutes. There are also 50 state legislatures more or less continuously engaged in enacting laws. Using statutes is not particularly difficult once the researcher understands the various forms in which a piece of legislation appears as it moves from introduction through passage and into use in legal disputes.

When a member of the House of Representatives or a senator introduces a legislative proposal, it is assigned a bill number.[52] Thus, the bill to create the Department of Homeland Security began as H.R. 5005. Once the bill has been enacted into law, it is assigned a public law number. For example, the Homeland Security Act of 2002 is Public Law 107-296, which means that the statute was the 296th law enacted by the 107th Congress. Each year the statutes are compiled chronologically by public law number into the *Statutes at Large*. Again, the Homeland Security Act can be found at 116 Stat. 2135 (2002), which, as shown in the preceding paragraphs, means that the legislation can be found in Volume 116 of the *Statutes at Large* beginning on page 2135 (2002).

As the new laws emerge, the West series *U.S. Code Congressional and Administrative News* (often referred to by its abbreviation, USCCAN) reports the text of the statute and the legislative history of the new law, including the background of the law, changes made during the legislative process, and interpretations suggested during the enactment process.

Volumes of chronologically arranged laws would be very difficult to use by themselves. For this reason, statutes are codified, which means that they are arranged by subject and then incorporate any amendments that have been adopted by the legislature since the legislation was originally enacted. Thus, the Administrative Procedure Act that appears in Title 5 of the United States Code (and reproduced in Appendix 3 of this text) not only contains the original version of the statute, but all amendments since then, including, for example, the addition of amendments to APA made in 1996 by the Small Business Growth and Fairness Act, P.L. 104-121.

The official government version of this compilation is the United States Code, abbreviated U.S.C.[53] Private publishers have developed annotated codes, e.g., the *United States Code Annotated* (West) and the *United States Code Service* (Lawyers Cooperative). The annotated codes contain the same verbatim statement of the legislation, but they also give additional references to the background of the legislation and to the interpretations of the various sections of the statute made over the years by courts. If one is using a bound volume as opposed to an online version of the document, remember to check for recent changes in the pocket part of the volume.

One may wonder why it is necessary to have something like the *Statutes at Large* to retain the public laws as passed if there is a code that is current and more comprehensive. The reason is that the ability to access a public law demonstrates what a particular piece of legislation contained at the time it was enacted. One can then look at each new public law that amended the earlier legislation to follow the way that the law developed in a particular field. The code only contains the current version of the law with all of the amendments integrated into the text. The same logic applies to the publication of rules as they are issued by agencies in the *Federal Register* and then codified in the *Code of Federal Regulations*. The development of the regulations can be traced through the *Federal Register* while the C.F.R. provides the current version.

State legislative enactments are reported in a similar fashion. Compilations of statutes enacted annually are often referred to as "session laws." Then, like the federal government practice, the states place these new statutes into their state code. The state may not publish an official code, but instead may recognize a commercial code as having official status or contract with a code service to publish the material. Increasingly, most states publish their statutes on the state legislature's website, which can be reached through the state government's site. Indeed, the websites for some states make it possible to track pending legislation during the legislative session as well as to access the state code. In order to look backward, states retain their session laws in the same way that the federal government retains the public laws published in the *Statutes at Large*.

The process of locating municipal ordinances is more complex. Some municipal codes are locally produced and may be, but usually are not, placed on the city's website. Many communities have their codes published and maintained by commercial code services, which have the current codes in their computer systems and provide hard copy, CD-ROM, or online access with passwords to the municipality. These contractors take new ordinances and integrate them with the existing code and may also provide periodic reviews of the codes along with legal advice to the governing bodies of the city as to the need to consider updates or incorporate recent judicial rulings. While these municipal code services will do searches of ordinance provisions for a fee or sometimes as a part of a community's service contract, they generally treat their databases as valuable proprietary information and do not make them available on the Internet.

However they are located, statutes and ordinances may be difficult to interpret in specific cases. Chapters 3 and 5 will discuss the process of statutory interpretation in greater detail. For the moment, it is useful to remember that the words of a statute may necessarily be vague because the legislature, among other reasons, must enact laws that are general enough to cover a range of problems and future circumstances. In consequence, courts and administrators must frequently attempt to find evidence of exactly what the legislators had in mind at the time the bill was enacted. The search for this legislative intent is known as legislative history, which includes a consideration of the reasons that prompted the legislation, the form of the measure as it was initially introduced and its sponsors, amendments made during the process as well as the reasons advanced to support them, conference committee changes during efforts to resolve differences between the houses of the legislature on different versions of the bill, debates on the floor, and statements made at the executive bill signing ceremony.[54]

The *U.S. Code Congressional and Administrative News* has attempted to aid the researcher in finding recent legislative histories. For some major pieces of legislation, Congress will carefully compile and publish a one-volume sourcebook on a bill. One example that has been used over the years to assist in understanding the very important Privacy Act is the U.S. Senate Committee on Government Operations and House Committee on Government Operations, *Sourcebook on Privacy, Legislative History of the Privacy Act of 1974,* S. 3413 (Public Law 93-579), 94th Cong., 2d Sess. (1976). Some histories are cataloged as separate volumes within the card catalog general collection. Finally, another finding tool for legislative histories is the *Union List of Legislative Histories*.[55]

The Law Librarians Society of Washington, D.C., has provided a variety of useful material for researching federal legislative histories, including a step-by-step guide which is published on the Internet.[56] The site also publishes McKinney and Sweet's *Federal Legislative History: A Practitioner's Guide to Compiling the Documents and Sifting for Legislative Intent*.[57] The guide makes reference to a variety of materials that are available without the need for subscriptions to proprietary research databases such as LexisNexis.

Public sources available on the Internet may be found through the Government Printing Officer website, called GPO Access.[58] The other major public access for legislative history is the website operated by Congress known as "Thomas."[59] The Thomas site uses congressional documents and links to the GPO sites for bill tracking and legislative history materials.

The task of researching state legislative history is often considerably more challenging than tracing congressional work. Many state governments have unique processes or limited legislative reporting systems. For these and other reasons, it is often very difficult to do legislative history research at the state level.[60] There is frequently little more available than the bill jacket (the materials accompanying the legislation as it moved through the process) and the session laws that demonstrated the older version of the law and the precise changes that were made by the new legislation. There are rarely transcripts of committee hearings or other proceedings. The Indiana University Law Library has provided a great deal of assistance by creating a website that provides links to resources for state legislative history state-by-state.[61]

Executive Lawmaking

In most cases, statutes are implemented through the use of administrative regulations that have the force of law. Until 1935, there was no uniform system for reporting regulations and other official executive branch rulings. After a major New Deal decision in the Supreme Court illustrated the fact that only a handful of people may have had access to regulations affecting the entire nation,[62] Congress enacted the Federal Register Act.[63]

The federal government is required by the Federal Register Act to publish in the *Federal Register* administrative orders and regulations, executive department announcements, presidential proclamations and executive orders, and any other announcements or material that Congress may require be publicized in the *Register*. The *Federal Register* is published daily and distributed throughout the country to U.S. depository libraries (e.g., most large universities), and other subscribers. It is also published on the Internet through the GPO pages.

The *Register* is like the *Statutes at Large* in that it is chronologically arranged. As with legislative enactments, the regulations are later arranged by subject, or codified, and appear as the *Code of Federal Regulations,* abbreviated C.F.R. The C.F.R. is updated completely once each year. In the interim, of course, new regulations are constantly in publication. These interim changes are reported in the "C.F.R. Parts Affected" pamphlet located with the index at the end of the C.F.R. volumes. These parts-affected tables send the researcher to the *Federal Register* pages published since the last C.F.R. revision that contain additions or deletions.

Like most legal reference tools, the C.F.R. index is very detailed. Along with the regular title and subject portion, the index contains tables by United States Code section number, which tell the reader where to find regulations interpreting specific statutes.

Because the C.F.R. prints only the language of the regulation, the researcher must return to the *Federal Register* for background material published at the time the regulation was announced. This shuffling among regulations, when coupled with the myths and fears that abound concerning regulations, can trigger mild panic in someone who is told to find the regulations on a particular subject. Believe it or not, regulations really are written by human beings who speak and write English. On the other hand, one should not expect regulations governing, for example, the licensing of nuclear power plants to read like a newspaper article. The attempt by those who draft regulations to walk the fine line between loose overgeneralized prose and bureaucratic legalese is a constant battle.

One who must deal with administrative agencies on a regular basis should also be aware of two general sources. The first is the *U.S. Government Manual,* which is extremely easy to use (see Figure 2.4) and is available both in hard copy and through the GPO Access website. The entries are organized by agency. The section on each agency begins with a list of officers. Then follows a background statement on the mission of the agency and the legislation that brought it into existence, as well as other statutes the agency is assigned to administer. Most entries include an organization chart. Finally, the entries comment on specific departments or task groups and frequently list telephone numbers and addresses to contact for further information. Information of this sort can also be found by accessing a federal or state agency's home page. Similar information is sometimes available on a state or local government's home page as well.

Second, most agencies publish annual reports. The reports contain the same type of information as the *U.S. Government Manual,* but in much greater detail. Additionally, the reports generally contain budgetary information, human resource data, workload analysis in terms of type and quantity, and current problems and issues. These reports can be found through the card catalog in government depository libraries or by the use of indexes of government publications, or on the Internet.

The president and governors issue a variety of directives that are becoming increasingly important. Executive orders and proclamations are published in the *Federal Register* both in hard copy and online. Unfortunately, these directives are not codified, or at least they have not been since the late 1980s, so it can be difficult to access them by subject. The National Archives operates a website that is quite helpful. It is known as the "Executive Order Disposition Tables" and allows a researcher to select a president, choose a year, and then search for orders.[64] The entries indicate the subject, provide links to the *Federal Register* site for full text copies, and notes the status of the order such as whether it supersedes or amends an existing order. If so, the page provides links to the previous orders affected by the new directive. Executive orders, proclamations, some presidential memoranda to agency heads, and presidential signing statements are also published in the *Weekly Compilation of Presidential Documents,* published in hard copy and on the GPO website.

Another type of presidential directive is known under the generic term National Security Directive, though several presidents have changed the name slightly, in part at least to stay one step ahead of frustrated members of Congress who have tried on a few occasions to write legislation that would require chief executives to inform Congress of the existence and content of these directives.[65] These directives began as policy papers prepared by the staff of the National Security Council, which would be signed by the president if he concurred in the recommendations and issued for action by the appropriate agencies. Most of these were and are issued as classified documents. While they were created to govern foreign policy matters, they have often had a great deal of impact domestically. Some presidents wish to have some of the directives made public. Indeed, the George W. Bush administration created a series of such directives, which it called Homeland Security Directives, that are used to issue policy in that field. The Federation of American Scientists operates a website that has links to those NSDs that are declassified and publicly available, listed by president.[66]

Locating state level executive orders is often more complex. Some states integrate the orders into their state code. Others publish the orders as in a series of documents. Still others simply have a link from the governor's website to executive orders. Finding such orders issued by mayors is even more challenging, since only a few of the largest cities have any direct link to such orders.

Judicial Decisions

Since our courts work on a system of precedent, it is extremely important that case reports be widely available. That is easier said than done in a nation with so many legal disputes resolved in diverse forums. To meet the challenge, case reports are organized by type of tribunal and by type of controversy.

The decisions of the United States Supreme Court apply nationally. They are reported officially in the *United States Reports,* published by the federal government in both hard copy and on the Internet at the U.S. Supreme Court website.[67] The major private systems also print Supreme Court decisions. West Publishing Company prepares the *Supreme Court Reporter,* abbreviated S.Ct. The S.Ct. is designed to cross-refer to the West research tools. The Lawyers Cooperative Publishing Company distributes the *U.S. Supreme Court Reports, Lawyers Edition* (Second Series), abbreviated L.Ed.2d. Like the materials originally developed by West, L.Ed.2d cross-refers to other Lawyers Cooperative works. The text of the opinion reported in all three reporters is exactly the same. In fact, the two private reporters even show

FEDERAL TRADE COMMISSION   **425**

For further information, contact the Director of External Affairs, Federal Retirement Thrift Investment Board, 1250 H Street NW., Washington, DC 20005. Phone, 202–942–1640. Internet, www.tsp.gov.

FEDERAL TRADE COMMISSION

600 Pennsylvania Avenue NW., Washington, DC 20580
Phone, 202–326–2222. Internet, www.ftc.gov.

Chairman	DEBORAH P. MAJORAS
Chief of Staff	MARYANNE KANE
Commissioners	PAMELA JONES HARBOUR, THOMAS B. LEARY, JONATHAN LEIBOWITZ, ORSON SWINDLE
Executive Director	JUDITH BAILEY, *Acting*
Deputy Executive Director	JUDITH BAILEY
Chief Information Officer	STEPHEN WARREN
Chief Financial Officer	HENRY HOFFMAN
Director, Bureau of Competition	SUSAN A. CREIGHTON
Deputy Directors	JEFFREY SCHMIDT
	BARRY NIGRO
Director, Bureau of Consumer Protection	LYDIA B. PARNES, *Acting*
Deputy Directors	LYDIA B. PARNES
	C. LEE PEELER
Director, Bureau of Economics	LUKE FROEB
Deputy Directors	MARK FRANKENA
	PAUL A. PAUTLER
General Counsel	WILLIAM BLUMENTHAL
Principal Deputy General Counsel	JOHN D. GRAUBERT
Director, Office of Congressional Relations	ANNA H. DAVIS
Director, Office of Public Affairs	NANCY NESS JUDY
Director, Office of Policy Planning	MAUREEN K. OHLHAUSEN, *Acting*
Secretary of the Commission	DONALD S. CLARK
Chief Administrative Law Judge	STEPHEN J. MCGUIRE
Inspector General	ADAM R. TRZECIAK, *Acting*

[For the Federal Trade Commission statement of organization, see the *Code of Federal Regulations,* Title 16, Part 0]

The Federal Trade Commission has jurisdiction to enhance consumer welfare and protect competition in broad sectors of the economy. The Commission enforces the laws that prohibit business practices that are anticompetitive, deceptive, or unfair to consumers; promotes informed consumer choice and public understanding of the competitive process; and seeks to accomplish its mission without impeding legitimate business activity.

The Federal Trade Commission was established in 1914 by the Federal Trade Commission Act (15 U.S.C. 41–58). The Commission is composed of five members appointed by the President, with the advice and consent of the Senate, for a term of 7 years. Not more than three of the Commissioners may be members of the same political party. One Commissioner is designated by the President as Chairman of the Commission and is responsible for its administrative management.

FIGURE 2.4 Typical Pages from the *U.S. Government Manual*

SOURCE: Administrative Conference of the United States, *U.S. Government Manual,* (Washington, DC: U.S. Government Printing Office, 2005, pp. 425--428).

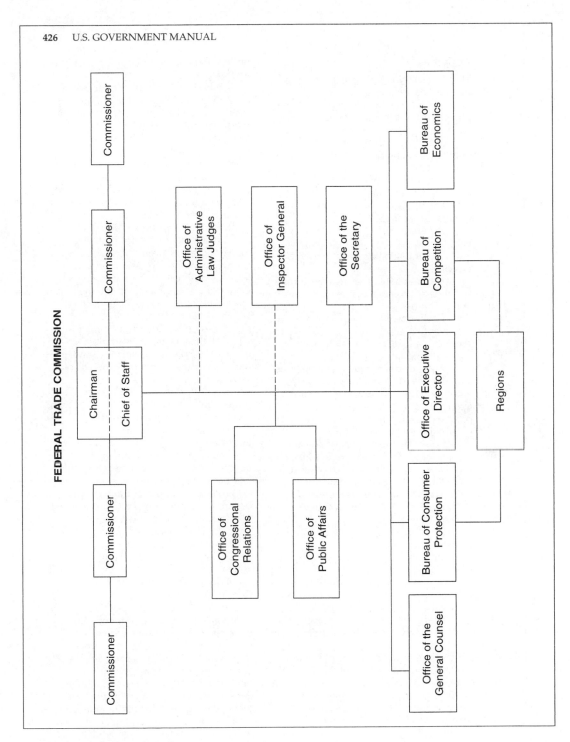

FIGURE 2.4 (*Continued*)

Activities

The Commission's principal functions include the following:

—promoting competition through the prevention of general trade restraints such as price-fixing agreements, boycotts, illegal combinations of competitors, and other unfair methods of competition;

—stopping corporate mergers, acquisitions, or joint ventures that may substantially lessen competition or tend to create a monopoly;

—preventing pricing discrimination, exclusive dealing, tying arrangements, and discrimination among competing customers by sellers;

—preventing interlocking directorates or officers' positions that may restrain competition;

—preventing the dissemination of false or deceptive advertisements of consumer products and services as well as other unfair or deceptive practices;

—promoting electronic commerce by stopping fraud on the Internet and working with other domestic and foreign agencies to develop and promote policies to safeguard online privacy of personal information;

—protecting the privacy of consumers' personal information to prevent illegal or unwanted use of financial or other data;

—stopping various fraudulent telemarketing schemes and protecting consumers from abusive, deceptive, or unwanted telephone tactics; and enforcing the National Do Not Call Registry;

—ensuring truthful labeling of textile, wool, and fur products;

—requiring creditors to disclose in writing certain cost information, such as the annual percentage rate, before consumers enter into credit transactions, as required by the Truth in Lending Act;

—protecting consumers against circulation of inaccurate or obsolete credit reports and ensuring that credit bureaus, consumer reporting agencies, credit grantors, and bill collectors exercise their responsibilities in a manner that is fair and equitable;

—educating consumers and businesses about their rights and responsibilities under Commission rules and regulations; and

—gathering factual data concerning economic and business conditions and making it available to the Congress, the President, and the public.

Competition   One of the two major missions of the Commission is to encourage competition in the American economy. The Commission seeks to prevent unfair practices that undermine competition and attempts to prevent mergers of companies if the result may be to lessen competition. Under some circumstances, companies planning to merge must first give notice to the Commission and the Department of Justice's Antitrust Division and provide certain information concerning the operations of the companies involved.

The Commission also enforces the provisions of the Robinson-Patman Act, a part of the Clayton Act prohibiting companies from discriminating among their customers in terms of price or other services provided.

Consumer Protection   Consumer protection is the second of the two main missions of the Commission. The Commission, therefore, works to accomplish the following:

—increase the usefulness of advertising by ensuring that it is truthful and not misleading;

—reduce instances of fraudulent, deceptive, or unfair marketing practices;

—prevent creditors from using unlawful practices when granting credit, maintaining credit information, collecting debts, and operating credit systems; and

—educate the public about Commission activities.

The Commission initiates investigations in areas of concern to consumers. It has issued and enforces many trade regulation rules in areas important to consumers, including health and nutrition claims in advertising; environmental advertising and labeling; general advertising issues; health care, telemarketing and electronic commerce, business opportunity, and franchise and investment fraud; mortgage lending and discrimination; enforcement of

F I G U R E   2.4   (*Continued*)

428 U.S. GOVERNMENT MANUAL

Commission orders; and enforcement of credit statutes and trade regulation rules.

Competition and Consumer Advocacy
To promote competition, consumer protection, and the efficient allocation of resources, the Commission also advocates consumer interest in a competitive marketplace by encouraging courts, legislatures, and government administrative bodies to consider efficiency and consumer welfare as important elements in their deliberations. The Commission uses these opportunities to support procompetitive means of regulating the Nation's economy, including the elimination of anticompetitive restrictions that reduce the welfare of consumers and the implementation of regulatory programs that protect the public and preserve as much as possible the discipline of competitive markets.

Compliance Activities   Through systematic and continuous review, the Commission obtains and maintains compliance with its cease-and-desist orders. All respondents against whom such orders have been issued are required to file reports with the Commission to substantiate their compliance. In the event compliance is not obtained, or if the order is subsequently violated, civil penalty proceedings may be instituted.

Cooperative Procedures   In carrying out the statutory directive to prevent unfair methods of competition or unfair or deceptive practices, the Commission makes extensive use of voluntary and cooperative procedures. Through these procedures, business and industry may obtain authoritative guidance and a substantial measure of certainty as to what they may do under the laws administered by the Commission.

The Commission issues administrative interpretations in plain language of laws enforced by the Commission. Guides provide the basis for voluntary abandonment of unlawful practices by members of a particular industry or by an industry in general. Failure to comply with the guides may result in corrective action by the Commission under applicable statutory provisions.

Enforcement   The Commission's law enforcement work falls into two general categories: actions to foster voluntary compliance with the law, and formal administrative or Federal court litigation leading to mandatory orders against offenders.

Compliance with the law may be obtained through voluntary and cooperative action by private companies in response to nonbinding staff advice, formal advisory opinions by the Commission, and guides and policy statements delineating legal requirements as to particular business practices.

Formal litigation is instituted either by issuing an administrative complaint or by filing a Federal district court complaint charging a person, partnership, or corporation with violating one or more of the statutes administered by the Commission. If the charges in an administrative matter are not contested or if the charges are found to be true after an administrative hearing in a contested case, an order may be issued requiring discontinuance of the unlawful practices.

Investigations   Investigations by the Commission may originate through complaint by a consumer or a competitor, the Congress, or from Federal, State, or municipal agencies. Also, the Commission itself may initiate an investigation into possible violations of the laws it administers. No formality is required in submitting a complaint. A letter giving the facts in detail, accompanied by all supporting evidence in possession of the complaining party, is sufficient. The Commission also maintains electronic complaint systems that are accessible through its Web site. It is the general policy of the Commission not to disclose the identity of any complainant, except as required by law or Commission rules.

Upon receipt of a complaint, various criteria are applied in determining whether the particular matter should be investigated.

An order issued after an administrative proceeding that requires the respondent to cease and desist or take other corrective action may be appealed.

FIGURE 2.4   *(Continued)*

Appeals processes may go as far as the Supreme Court.

In addition to or in lieu of the administrative proceeding initiated by a formal complaint, the Commission may request that a U.S. district court issue a preliminary or permanent injunction to halt the use of allegedly unfair or deceptive practices, to prevent an anticompetitive merger or unfair methods of competition from taking place, or to prevent violations of any statute enforced by the Commission.

Reports The Commission prepares studies of conditions and problems affecting the marketplace. Such reports may be used to inform legislative proposals in response to requests of the Congress and statutory directions, or for the information and guidance of the Commission, the executive branch of the Government, and the public. Such reports have provided the basis for significant legislation and have also led to voluntary changes in the conduct of business, with resulting benefits to the public.

Regional Offices—Federal Trade Commission

Region	Address	Director
East Central (DC, DE, MD, MI, OH, PA, VA, WV)	Suite 200, 1111 Superior Ave., Cleveland, OH 44114	John Mendenhall
Midwest (IA, IL, IN, KS, KY, MN, MO, ND, NE, SD, WI)	Suite 1860, 55 E. Monroe St., Chicago, IL 60603	C. Steven Baker
Northeast (CT, MA, ME, NH, NJ, NY, RI, VT, PR, VI)	Suite 318, One Bowling Green, New York, NY 10004	Barbara Anthony
Northwest (AK, ID, MT, OR, WA, WY)	Suite 2896, 915 2d Ave., Seattle, WA 98174	Charles A. Harwood
Southeast (AL, FL, GA, MS, NC, SC, TN)	Suite 1500, 225 Peachtree St., NE., Atlanta, GA 30303	Andrea Foster
Southwest (AR, LA, NM, OK, TX)	Suite 2150, 1999 Bryan St., Dallas, TX 75201	Bradley Elbein
Western (AZ, CA, CO, HI, NV, UT)	Suite 570, 901 Market St., San Francisco, CA 94103	Jeffrey A. Klurfeld
	Suite 700, 10877 Wilshire Blvd., Los Angeles, CA 90024	

Sources of Information

Contracts and Procurement Persons seeking to do business with the Federal Trade Commission should contact the Assistant CFO for Acquisitions, Federal Trade Commission, Washington, DC 20580. Phone, 202–326–3068. Fax, 202–326–3529. Internet, www.ftc.gov.

Employment Civil service registers are used in filling positions for economists, accountants, investigators, and other professional, administrative, and clerical personnel. The Federal Trade Commission employs a sizable number of attorneys under the excepted appointment procedure. All employment inquiries should be directed to the Director of Human Resources

Management, Federal Trade Commission, Washington, DC 20580. Phone, 202–326–2021. Fax, 202–326–2328. Internet, www.ftc.gov.

General Inquiries Persons desiring information on consumer protection or restraint of trade questions, or to register a complaint, should contact the Federal Trade Commission (phone, 202–326–2222 or 877–382–4357) or the nearest regional office. Complaints may also be filed on the Internet at www.ftc.gov.

Publications Consumer and business education publications of the Commission are available through the Consumer Response Center, Federal Trade Commission, Washington, DC 20580. Phone, 877–382–4357. TTY, 866–653–4261. Internet, www.ftc.gov.

For further information, contact the Office of Public Affairs, Federal Trade Commission, 600 Pennsylvania Avenue NW., Washington, DC 20580. Phone, 202–326–2180. Fax, 202–326–3366. Internet, www.ftc.gov.

FIGURE 2.4 (Continued)

the *United States Reports* page numbers at corresponding points in the text of the decision. When taking notes on Supreme Court cases, always use the *U.S. Reports* pagination to avoid confusion.

There are really three reasons why researchers tend to work with the private reporters. First, they are generally available sooner in both the advance sheets, which present very recent opinions, and in the full bound volumes. This has been less of a factor since the Court began publishing its opinions on its website as the rulings are announced. Second, the private editions are slightly less cumbersome because they generally print two or three *U.S. Reports* pages per page of L.Ed.2d or S.Ct. Finally, the private reporters provide more introductory material and headnotes as well as the cross-referencing capability.

Official reporters are also available for many other courts, but the private reporters, including the online proprietary databases, are more widely used. As a matter of form, however, where there is an official reporter, that publication is cited alone, or is cited first if it is cited with a private reporter.[68] Here again, the lower federal courts and state courts now commonly release their opinions on their websites, and most of these can be located through Cornell's LII site or Findlaw.com for those who do not have access to proprietary databases.

Most of the major opinions of the U.S. Circuit Courts of Appeals are reported in West's *Federal Reporter*, now in its third series and cited F.3d. The courts do not consider all decisions significant enough to warrant adding more volumes of reports to already large and expensive libraries. As was noted earlier in the discussion of citations form, it is important when reading the decisions of courts other than the U.S. Supreme Court to take care to record which court rendered the ruling.

Federal district court opinions are reported in the *Federal Supplement, Second Series,* cited as F.Supp.2d. District court opinions are usually rendered by only one judge, but in a few instances the researcher will encounter older decisions prepared by a three-judge district court.[69] This goes back to a time when legislation provided for certain types of cases, such as those challenging the constitutional validity of state statutes, to go directly to a three-judge federal court. An appeal from a three-judge court would go directly to the U.S. Supreme Court.

West's National Reporter System also publishes opinions by state supreme courts and, on occasion, state appeals courts. For purposes of the system, the country is divided into seven reporting regions. These regions were established in the late nineteenth century based on economic rather than political similarity. Hence, some of the states seem intuitively out of line with the name of the volume that reports their opinions. However, the states reported are listed on the title page of each volume (see Figure 2.5).

Other Case Reporters

Occasionally one encounters a reference to the F.R.D., which refers to a West series called the *Federal Rules Decisions*. The F.R.D. series contains opinions interpreting federal rules of civil and criminal procedure issued by any of the federal courts. An administrator might, for example, encounter a case concerning consumer or environmental class action suits in this reporter.

Many administrative agencies also publish opinions to support their findings in adjudicatory proceedings. Like court cases, the agencies often publish an official reporter. The *National Labor Relations Board Decisions* is an example. The Commerce Clearing House (CCH) and the Bureau of National Affairs (BNA) are two of the major private publishers that print administrative reporters. Many of these reporters can now be accessed through online services like LexisNexis. Agencies such as the Nuclear Regulatory Commission now commonly publish their opinions online as well.[70]

SUPPLEMENTING THE LAW

Supplementing legal research involves at least two distinct kinds of work. First, one must ensure that materials are current. Second, the researcher must round out the research or place it in proper context. Failure to follow through in legal research by supplementing materials, as in most other things, can nullify the hard work expended in finding and reading the law.

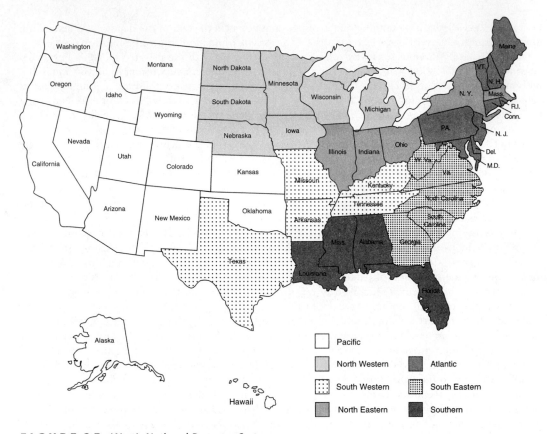

FIGURE 2.5 West's National Reporter System

SOURCE: *The West Law Finder* (St. Paul: West, 1978), p. 2. Used by permission of West Publishing Company.

Updating Knowledge

This chapter began by defining legal research in terms of access to the most authoritative and most recent statement of law by the highest possible decisionmaker. Given the great number of courts that deliver opinions every day, this seems an almost impossible task. Fortunately, there are a number of tools specifically designed to help the researcher ensure that currency is maintained.

Shepard's Citations is the primary tool to use in updating case materials. The citator is organized by the citation of the case under consideration. It indicates where the researcher can go to find other cases in any major court in the country that has rendered a decision that mentions the researcher's case. *Shepard's* also notes whether the more recent decisions explained the earlier option, overruled it, or followed the earlier holding as a statement of controlling law. *Shepard's* seems a bit intimidating on first glance, but it is easy to use, and particularly so now that it is available online.[71] Consider the following example.

San Antonio Independent School District v. Rodriguez, 411 U.S. 1 (1973), was a major case on the responsibilities of states and local school districts versus individual rights in the area of public school financing. Suppose an administrator desired to know whether the holding in *San Antonio* was still current and what more recent case materials might be available that show how that case has been applied and interpreted.

Turn first to *Shepard's U.S. Citations,* which is the citator for decisions of the United States Supreme Court. (All the citators indicate on the binding the type of material cited.) Turn to the part of the book with the *United States Reports* designation at the top of the page. The volume numbers are noted in the upper-right corner of the page. Where volume 411 is indicated, look down the page until there appears a boldface number I with a line under it. This volume, page, and title format is used in all the case citators.

The initial entry is the history of the case, followed by a long list of citations to the *U.S. Reports,* the *Federal Reporter,* the *Federal Supplement,* and other case reporters in the states. These are pages in various cases in which the *San Antonio* decision has been mentioned. The context in which the case was mentioned is indicated by the small letters to the left of the case citations. The abbreviations are explained fully at the beginning of each volume. An "o," for example, indicates that the case being researched was overruled. An "f," on the other hand, shows that the ruling was cited as the controlling law in a more recent case. In addition to indicating whether a case is still "good" law, the citator can be used as a law finder to locate more recent cases that cited the basic case as controlling (f), explained it (e), or harmonized that case with what appeared to be conflicting rulings (h).

Most people who need to use citators today have access to online services and can do a cite check almost instantly using those tools. Even so, like all online tools, it is necessary to understand the basic tool in order to understand the most modern version.

Loose-Leaf Services, Websites, and Listservs:
A Constantly Developing Set of Tools

For many years, commercial publishers made a business out of carving out specific areas of law and public policy that are of interest to professionals who want rapid updating on that law in the shortest possible time. These tools have been referred to as loose-leaf services; the name was derived from the loose-leaf format in which the reporters were traditionally distributed. Commerce Clearing House and the Bureau of National Affairs were the two leaders in that field, with general publications such as *CCH Supreme Court* and BNA's *United States Law Week.* These firms also developed a number of more specialized loose-leafs for particular subject areas, such as the *Media Law Reporter,* the *Criminal Law Reporter,* and the *Environmental Law Reporter.*

However, many of these loose-leaf services have been being replaced or acquired by subscription services on the Internet or even by free alternative websites. These materials can sometimes be accessed through online services like LexisNexis or in other cases by direct subscription. There are any number of ways to use the Internet to access recent rulings in summary or in full text without charge. For example, Cornell Law School's Legal Information Institute (LII) operates pages that not only access U.S. Supreme Court information, but also provide summaries of important and newsworthy cases from the past year from around the country in an easy to use summary format with links to full opinions.

There are specialized law journals or annual surveys in standard law reviews for those who have little time to keep up with the major developments across the nation over the year. In the general area of administrative law, for example, the Section on Administrative Law of the American Bar Association publishes the *Administrative Law Review.* For a general review of the U.S. Supreme Court's most recent term, the *Harvard Law Review* November survey issue is first rate. The *Duke Law Journal* produces an annual administrative law survey.

There are now any number of websites and listservs operated by universities, nonprofit organizations or trade associations in particular policy domains, or governmental units, including tribal governments. The key to using loose-leafs, specialized journals, or online sites and listservs is to select one or a few of them and develop a routine for reviewing those chosen. The two continuing problems with respect to online sources are inundation and reliability. It has often been said that doing research on the Internet is a bit like trying to take a drink of water from a fire hose. There is simply so much material available in so many forms that it can be overwhelming. There is also the tendency to spend one's time locating interesting sites on the Web rather than doing the seemingly less interesting and more difficult careful reading and analysis of the materials found. Further, if the task is to keep current, web surfing is simply too unsystematic to accomplish the task.

Rounding Out Research

For law and public administration practitioners or scholars, the great strength of legal research is paradoxically also its great weakness. Legal research tools and techniques are designed to methodically narrow the study to a very small part of a massive body of law. Tunnel vision is always dangerous, and particularly so in public law and public administration problems.

Administrative law problems arise from and are affected by a wide range of factors. There are statutory problems, which are continually dealt with in one way or another by Congress or the state legislature. Financial matters affect an agency's ability to investigate, to litigate, and to counsel. Appropriations hearings in the legislature often deal with more substantive policy questions than the protection of the public fisc. Interest groups lobby in all branches of government, including the judiciary. New scientific, economic, and administrative developments are always in progress. For all these reasons, it is wise for anyone who is doing research in law and administration to step back after completing the problem-oriented research in case law and take notice of the larger environment in which the problem exists.

The easiest tools for this purpose are periodicals aimed at the informed public. Two of the most commonly used periodicals at the national level are the *Congressional Quarterly* and the *National Journal*. At the state and local level, *Public Management* and *Governing* are two of the most widely read. Both can be found in most major libraries. A relatively brief look at these publications will tell the researcher whether the topic under study is currently a matter of significant debate in government. This kind of scanning also tends to provide some sense of context. Some states, such as California and Illinois, have similar publications.

Government publications can be useful, offering valuable information that is both timely and carefully prepared. More important, the person who does not round out research with government documents may fail to accurately perceive a law and policy conflict. The *Eldridge* case study in Appendix 1 provides a case in point. A check of congressional documents in the months leading up to the argument before the U.S. Supreme Court would have shown that the government had no intention of arguing the case on grounds of precedent, but focused instead on financial and policy problems. It would also have demonstrated contradictions in the government's case.

A specific example of a generally useful and widely respected set of materials is the Government Accountability Office (GAO, formerly known as the General Accounting Office) reports. These reports are the result of analyses conducted by GAO teams at the request of members of Congress or congressional committees. The GAO reports provide current useful data on a wide range of subjects. One free copy of any GAO report is available to anyone who requests it. These reports may also be retrieved in full text on the Web through the GAO home page. The GAO produces something called the daybook, which is a listserv that contains very brief summaries of reports and testimony produced each days with links to executive summaries or the full documents. One can subscribe on the GAO website.[72]

One of the things that has changed with the growing importance of the Internet and what is termed e-government is that there is less need for broad-based indexes, since agencies commonly publish key documents on their websites. However, virtually all agencies have their own systems and structures for their websites. There is a general government portal, known as Firstgov.gov, that is designed as a base search engine for federal agencies.[73] That said, a number of the standard Internet search engines seem to be effective for purposes of rounding out research so long as the researcher uses a time boundary.

SUMMARY

The law in books, or black letter law, is important and available to most students and practitioners of public law and public administration. Hands-on experience is necessary to learn this skill well, but time, practice, and persistence will demonstrate that legal research is not particularly difficult. The goal is to find current, high-level authority on the specific points of law under study. The process begins with the use of law finders to locate statutes, regulations, and cases. One then reads the law itself and supplements the law through any of a number of devices. Finally, the researcher places the research in a larger context through consulting public documents and public affairs journals, which note whether and to what extent the law and policy problem under study is currently on the public agenda.

While the growth in computer-based research tools has provided a great deal of quickly available and helpful information, it is still necessary to learn the traditional tools first in order to understand the electronic sources. The computer-based work is most often done by attorneys using online legal research services which may or may not be available to public managers because of the cost. They may still use the many Internet-based sources either to access the law or for purposes of rounding out research in light of recent developments. And in any event, the publicly available sites are rapidly coming to provide many of the types of information formerly available only on proprietary databases.

Ultimately, however, the task is not merely compiling a set of sources, but requires the next step, which is to consider those materials with care with an understanding of how legal decisions are made and how the documents setting forth those decisions can be understood by those public managers whose job it is to implement and operate public programs and agencies. These challenges go to the need to understand not only the law in books, but the law in action, which is the subject of Chapter 3.

NOTES

1. See *Arizonans for Official English v. Arizona,* 520 U.S. 43, 48 (1997); *Johnson v. Fankel,* 520 U.S. 911, 917 (1997). There are a host of interesting comparisons between the federal and state systems in Frank M. Coffin, *On Appeal: Courts, Lawyering, and Judging* (New York: W.W. Norton, 1994).

2. *Bush v. Gore,* 531 U.S. 98 (2000).

3. *Town of Castle Rock, Colorado v. Gonzales,* 162 L. Ed. 2d 658 (2005).

4. The types of cases and methods for getting them to the Supreme Court are nicely set forth in David O'Brien, *Storm Center,* 3rd ed. (New York: W.W. Norton, 1993). See also Phillip J. Cooper and Howard Ball, *The United States Supreme Court: From the Inside Out* (Englewood Cliffs, NJ: Prentice Hall, 1996), Ch. 5.

5. For an in-depth discussion of the nature of the federal judicial system, see Lawrence Baum, *American Courts: Process and Policy,* 4th ed. (Boston: Houghton Mifflin, 1998), p. 3.

6. Administrative Office of U.S. Courts, "U.S. District Court – Judicial Caseload Profile," at http://www.uscourts.gov/cgi-bin/cmsd2005.pl as of April 28, 2006.

7. The numbers of courts, their staffing, jurisdiction, and caseloads are published annually by the Administrative Office of U.S. Courts. See http://www.uscourts.gov/.

8. *Massachusetts v. Secretary of HHS,* 899 F.2d 53 (1st Cir. 1990); *Planned Parenthood v. Sullivan,* 913 F.2d 1492 (10th Cir. 1990); and *New York v. Sullivan,* 889 F.2d 401 (2nd Cir. 1989).

9. *Rust v. Sullivan,* 500 U.S. 173 (1991).

10. 28 U.S.C. §1257.

11. 28 U.S.C. §1254 or §1252.

12. These include the Court of Claims, 28 U.S. C.2 §1252; Court of Customs and Patent Appeals, 28 U.S.C. §1251; Customs Court, §1251; or in some circumstances three-judge federal district courts, 28 U.S.C. §§1253, 1284.

13. State supreme courts, 28 U.S.C. §1257, courts of appeals, 28 U.S.C. §1254, and Court of Claims, 28 U.S.C. §1255.

14. David B. Sweet, "Statistical Information for 2004–2005 Term," 162 L.Ed.2d 315, C-1 (2005). Issued in Advance Sheets, August 16, 2005.

15. U.S. Circuit Courts of Appeals, 28 U.S.C. §1254, or Court of Claims, 28 U.S.C.§1255.

16. The Court may still avoid most of these cases if it wishes by refusing to note probable jurisdiction.

17. See generally *United States v. Pink,* 315 U.S. 203 (1942); *United States v. Belmont,* 301 U.S. 324 (1937); *United States v. Curtiss-Wright,* 299 U.S. 309 (1936); *B. Altman & Co. v. United States,* 224 U.S. 583 (1912).

18. Laurence Tribe, *American Constitutional Law* (Mineola, NY: Foundation Press, 1978), pp. 167–72.

19. David L. Corliss, "Ordinances, Statutes, and Democratic Discipline: A Local Perspective on Drafting Laws," in Phillip J. Cooper and Chester A. Newland, eds., *Handbook of Public Law and Administration* (San Francisco: Jossey-Bass, 1997).

20. I have addressed this issue in greater detail in Phillip J. Cooper, *By Order of the President: The Use & Abuse of Executive Direct Action* (Lawrence, KS: University of Kansas Press, 2002). See also William G. Howell, *Power without Persuasion: The Politics of Direct Presidential Action* (Princeton: Princeton University Press, 2003); Kenneth R. Mayer, *With the Stroke of a Pen* (Princeton: Princeton University Press, 2001); Louis Fisher, *The Constitution Between Friends: Congress, the President and the Law* (New York: St. Martin's Press, 1978), pp. 128–32.

21. See e.g., "Note: Gubernatorial Executive Orders as Devices for Administrative Direction and Control," 50 *Iowa Law Rev.* 78 (1964).

22. Al Gore, *From Red Tape to Results: Creating a Government that Works Better and Costs Less,* Report of the National Performance Review (Washington, DC: Government Printing Office, 1993).

23. Executive Order 13198, "Agency Responsibilities with Respect to Faith-Based and Community Initiatives," 66 Fed. Reg. 8497 (2001); Executive Order 13199, "Establishment of White House Office of Faith-Based and Community Initiatives," 66 Fed. Reg. 8499 (2001).

24. Military Order of November 13, 2001, "Detention, Treatment, and Trial of Certain Non-Citizens in the War Against Terrorism," 66 Fed. Reg. 57833 (2001).

25. See e.g., Governor Pete Wilson's order barring affirmative action programs in state government. Executive Order W-124-95, June 1, 1995.

26. See Florida governor Jeb Bush, Executive Order 99-281, http://www.state.fl.us/eog/executive_orders/1999/November/eo99-281, July 30, 2001; California governor Pete Wilson, Executive Orders W-136-95, W-136-96. See *Coalition for Economic Equity v. Wilson,* 946 F.Supp. 148 (NDCA 1996), vacated and remanded, 122 F.3d 692 (9th Cir. 1997).

27. Office of the Mayor, "Mayor Unveils Ethics Reform Aims to Strengthen Integrity of City Government," October 27, 1997, http://w5.ci.chi.il.us./Mayor/SpecialNotices/html/Ethics.97.10.27.html, as of 4/14/01.

28. *In re Wilson,* 140 U.S. 575 (1891).

29. See *Isbrandtsen-Moller v. United States,* 300 U.S. 139 (1937); *Fleming v. Mohawk Wrecking & Lumber,* 331 U.S. 111 (1947); *Swayne v. Hoyt,* 300 U.S. 297, 300–301 (1937).

30. *Youngstown Sheet & Tube v. Sawyer,* 343 U.S. 579 (1952); *Cole v. Young,* 351 U.S. 536 (1956); *United States v. Symonds,* 120 U.S. 46 (1887); *Kendall v. United States,* 37 U.S. (12 Pet.) 524 (1838).

31. *Chamber of Commerce v. Reich.* 74 F.3d 1322 (D.C.Cir. 1996).

32. See the discussion of these actions in *Sale v. Haitian Centers Council,* 509 U.S. 155 (1993).

33. See e.g., *United States v. Wayte,* 710 F.2d 1385 (9th Cir. 1983).

34. Further explanation and examples of the signing statements are provided in Phillip J. Cooper, "George W. Bush, Edgar Allan Poe, and the Use and Abuse of Presidential Signing Statements," 35 *Presidential Studies Quarterly* 515 (2005) and Cooper, *By Order of the President,* Ch. 7.

35. The character of the relationship is explained in greater detail in Phillip J. Cooper, *Governing by Contract* (Washington, DC: CQ Press, 2002).

36. See generally W. Noel Keyes, *Government Contracts: Under the Federal Acquisition Regulation,* 2nd ed. (St. Paul: West Publishing, 1996) and W. Noel Keyes, *Government Contracts,* 4th ed. (St. Paul: West Publishing, 2004).

37. Administrative Office of U.S. Courts, "Table B. U.S. Courts of Appeals—Appeals Commenced, Terminated, and Pending During the 12-Month Periods Ending March 31, 2003 and 2004," at http://www.uscourts.gov/caseload2004/tables/B00Mar04.pdf, as of October 1, 2005. Frank M. Coffin, *On Appeal: Courts, Lawyering, and Judging* (New York: W.W. Norton, 1994).

38. Administrative Office of U.S. Courts, "Table C. U.S. District Courts—Civil Cases Commenced, Terminated, and Pending During the 12-Month Periods Ending March 31, 2003 and 2004," http://www.uscourts.gov/caseload2004/tables/C00Mar04.pdf, as of October 1, 2005.

39. As of this writing, the most recent number was 298,224, National Center for State Courts, "Table 1. Reported National Caseload for State Appellate Court 2001," http://www.ncsconline.org/D_Research/csp/2002_Files/2002_Tables_1-4.pdf, as of October 1, 2005. See generally Coffin, *supra* note 37, at pp. 53.

40. *Black's Law Dictionary,* 5th ed. (St. Paul: West, 1979).

41. William S. Anderson, ed., *Ballentine's Law Dictionary,* 3rd ed. (Rochester, NY: Lawyers Cooperative, 1969).

42. http://dictionary.lp.findlaw.com/, as of September 17, 2005.

43. N.J. Smelser and P.B. Baltes, eds., *International Encyclopedia of the Social and Behavioral Sciences* (New York: Elsevier, 2001).

44. *Corpus Juris Secundum* (St. Paul: West, 1952).

45. *American Jurisprudence, 2d series* (Rochester, NY: Lawyers Cooperative, 1970).

46. http://www.law.cornell.edu/topics/ as of September 17, 2005.

47. At http://www.gpoaccess.gov/databases.html, as of September 17, 2005.

48. *Index to Legal Periodicals and Books* (Bronx, NY: Wilson, 2005).

49. *Harvard Law Review, Columbia Law Review, University of Pennsylvania Law Review,* and *Yale Law Journal, The Bluebook: A Uniform System of Citation,* 18th ed. (Cambridge: Harvard, Columbia, Yale, and University of Pennsylvania Law Reviews, 2005).

50. At http://www.law.cornell.edu/citation/, as of September 17, 2005.

51. For a complete list of legal citation forms and their uses, see *A Uniform System of Citations,* 13th ed. (Cambridge: Harvard Law Review Association, 1981).

52. On the specifics of the legislative process, see Charles J. Zinn, *How Our Laws Are Made* (Washington, DC: Government Printing Office, 1971).

53. References to parts of a code are made by title and section number. Note, for example, that the Civil Rights Act provision presented is Title 42 of the U.S. Code at Section (§) 1983.

54. Robert Goehlert, *Congress and Law-Making: Researching the Legislative Process* (Santa Barbara, CA: CLIO Books, 1979).

55. Law Librarians' Society of Washington, D.C., *Union List of Legislative Histories,* 3rd ed. (Vienna, VA: Coiner, 1967).

56. http://www.llsdc.org/sourcebook/index.html, at September 18, 2005.

57. Richard J. McKinney and Ellen A. Sweet, *Federal Legislative History: A Practitioner's Guide to Compiling the Documents and Sifting for Legislative Intent* (Washington, DC: Law Librarians' Society of Washington, D.C., 2005), at http://www.llsdc.org/sourcebook/fed-leg-hist.htm, as of September 18, 2005.

58. http://www.gpoaccess.gov/, as of September 18, 2005.

59. http://thomas.loc.gov/, September 29, 2005.

60. See generally Gwendolyn B. Folsum, *Legislative History: Research for the Interpretation of Laws* (Charlottesville: University of Virginia Press, 1972).

61. Jennifer Bryan, "State Legislative History Research Guides on the Web," Indiana University School of Law Library – Bloomington, http://www.law.indiana.edu/library/services/sta_leg.shtml, as of September 18, 2005.

62. *Panama Refining Co. v. Ryan,* 293 U.S. 388 (1935).

63. 49 Stat. 500 (1935).

64. National Archives, Disposition Tables from Dwight W. Eisenhower to George W. Bush, http://www.archives.gov/federal-register/executive-orders/disposition.html, as of September 18, 2005.

65. See Cooper, *By Order of the President,* Ch. 6.

66. Federation of American Scientists, "Nation Security Directives," http://www.fas.org/irp/offdocs/direct.htm, as of September 18, 2005.

67. http://www.supremecourtus.gov/, as of September 29, 2005.

68. For example, the following opinion was published in both the official reporter of New York and the commercial West edition. In either case, it should be cited as *Fresh Meadows Medical Associates v. Liberty Mutual Insurance Co.,* 49 N.Y. 2d 98, 400 N.E. 2d 3030 (NY 1979).

69. See e.g., *J.L. v. Parham,* 412 F. Supp. 112 (M.D.Ga. 1976). The three-judge district courts provided an expedited way of getting important cases from trial through appeal to the Supreme Court in cases like challenges to the constitutionality of state statutes, as was true in this Georgia case, discussed in Chapter 6.

70. See e.g., the NRC ruling, rejecting challenges to the licensing of a high level nuclear waste disposal facility in Utah. "Memorandum and Order," *In the Matter of Private Fuel Storage,* at http://www.nrc.gov/reading-rm/doc-collections/commission/orders/2005/2005-19cli.html, as of September 9, 2005.

71. On *Shepard's* generally, see *How to Use Shepard's Citations* (Colorado Springs: Shepard's Citations, 1971).

72. http://www.gao.gov/, as of September 19, 2005.

73. http://www.firstgov.gov/index.shtml, as of September 19, 2005.

3

The Law in Action

Chapters 1 and 2 defined the field of public law and public administration and demonstrated the role of the administrative justice system as a subset of the larger American legal system. The essential institutions and black letter law provisions of the government have been discussed. However, anyone who reads newspaper accounts of important legal controversies or has been personally involved in one quickly learns that law is not simply a mechanical process into which one feeds elements of a legal conflict and from which one draws an automatic response. This chapter addresses those elements of jurisprudence, legal reasoning, and judicial policymaking that, together with the law in books, make up the law in action.

PROBLEMS OF JUDICIAL DECISIONMAKING: "THE CASE OF THE SPELUNCEAN EXPLORERS"

In 1949 Professor Lon Fuller developed a hypothetical case that affords students of law an opportunity to deal with some of the complexities involved in deciding hard cases. The case, entitled "The Case of the Speluncean Explorers,"[1] is outlined below. Come to a decision in the matter and consider arguments on both sides of that conclusion.

As developed at trial, the facts that gave rise to the case occurred in the spring of the year 4299 in the nation of Newgarth. Five members of a cave-exploring club, the Speluncean Society, set out to explore a cavern recently discovered by one of the club's members. The five were all in good physical condition and properly outfitted for their foray into the cave. In accordance with society rules, the group left an outline of their planned exploration with the society's secretary and each member left information with his family.

Not long after entering the cave, the spelunkers felt a severe earth tremor. They retraced their steps to the cave entrance, but found that it had been blocked by a massive rock slide. The five sat down near the cave entrance to assess their supplies and await rescue. They hoped for a quick rescue since, although all were in good physical condition and unharmed by the slide, they had little food and only a moderate amount of water.

When the group did not return home at the appointed time, the society officers initiated a rescue effort. It did not take long for the experts called to the scene to determine that extricating the trapped explorers would be a major undertaking. Engineers, medical personnel, troops, police officials, and others were summoned to the site. During the second week of excavation, ten rescuers were killed when a new rock slide caught them by surprise. Along with the death toll, the costs of the effort rose alarmingly.

Twenty days after the spelunkers had entered the cave, it was learned that the group had a small radio transceiver in the cave. Radio contact was established and, to the delight of the rescuers, it was learned that the men in the cave, though weak, were all alive. The initial elation soon gave way to fear and frustration. The engineers in charge of the rescue informed the men in the cave that an additional 12 days would be the minimum time required to break through based on the view from outside and the description from within the cave. After a brief consultation with a team of doctors concerning their conditions and supplies, it was determined that the men could not survive for the required 12 days. The doctors conveyed the information to the spokesman for the trapped men, a fellow named Roger Whetmore. Whetmore asked for any suggestions or instructions from the rescuers. There were none.

Communication ceased for several hours. Then Whetmore made contact with the rescue team, and asked whether it would be possible for four members to survive if they drew sustenance from the flesh of one of their own number. The doctors answered reluctantly that it would be possible. Whetmore and his colleagues inquired whether anyone on the outside would advise them how the victim should be selected. The doctors refused to respond. The men asked for a legal opinion. No legal officials would answer. They asked for moral guidance. None of the ministers on hand would reply. Radio contact was terminated.

The rescuers broke through to the men in the cave after the predicted total of 32 days. They found four men suffering from exposure and shock, but alive. Roger Whetmore had provided the necessary nourishment for his colleagues.

The Newgarth criminal law clearly states that "whoever shall willfully take the life of another shall be punished by death." It has no other provisions regarding homicide. After they recovered in a hospital from their ordeal, the four survivors were tried for the murder of Roger Whetmore.

At trial, it was determined that it had been Whetmore's suggestion that the men should survive at the expense of one of their number. After much discussion, his fellow prisoners agreed to the plan. When authorities on the outside refused to provide guidance as to the manner of selection, it had been Whetmore who advanced the idea of rolling dice. And it had been Whetmore who produced the dice, which he always carried as good luck pieces. But when it had come time to roll the dice and carry out the plan, Whetmore changed his mind, arguing that it was too drastic a solution. The others refused his desire to withdraw since it was he who had developed the plan and convinced the others of its necessity. They rolled the dice for him, but permitted him an opportunity to object if he thought the manner of rolling the dice was unfair. He raised no objection. He lost and the others carried out the plan.

The jury asked to be allowed to issue a finding of facts, but wished the judge to apply the law to those facts and render the final verdict. All parties agreed to this arrangement. The jury found the facts as described above and the judge concluded on those facts that the four were guilty of a violation of the statute. He added that the death sentence was, of course, the only possible sentence under the statute. As soon as the trial ended, the judge and the members of the jury jointly prepared a letter requesting executive clemency for the four condemned men.

When the decision and the sentence were reported in the press, there was a massive public outcry against what was perceived to be a gross miscarriage of justice. Speculation ran rampant concerning the possibility of a reversal of the ruling in the Supreme Court. Some reporters concentrated on information which seemed to indicate that the president would not grant clemency.

If the case came to the Supreme Court and the reader were a member of it, how should it deal with the case? Would one say that the words of the statute of murder are clear and must be applied exactly as they are written? Should the Court decide the case by a verbatim application of the law, but unofficially join the petition for executive clemency?

Or would one reverse, arguing that, under the conditions in the cave, the men were in a state of nature in which the ordinary laws of Newgarth were inapplicable? If so, would the social contract entered into willingly by all the members of the group be binding? Could they demand specific performance from Whetmore as the contract law might provide?

What of the argument that the seemingly clear and absolute law of murder was not all that clear? If self-defense is not a willful taking of life, were these men guilty given the inevitable death they faced in the cave? Would enforcement of the death penalty in this case fit the spirit of the law as well as the letter?

If the Court overturned the ruling, would it appear that the law of contract was more important than laws regarding murder? If the view that a social contract had been made in the cave was accepted, how remote from ordinary circumstances must one be to declare the accepted laws of the community inapplicable? Could a plan as carefully developed as this one was, and which had been discussed over a lengthy period of time, realistically not be understood to be a willful taking of life?

Should the court be permitted to make one official ruling and join in an unofficial communication to another branch of government? Is this a responsible position? Assuming that the judge is aware that the law will cause an obvious injustice if applied as written, should he or she ignore the harm to be done and apply the law strictly? Is it the business of the judge to make decisions on the rightness or wrongness of the law?

Is the problem here less a question of dogmatic applications of strongly held judicial philosophies on either side and more a matter of how to handle these particular defendants, since the uniqueness of the facts in this case make it unlikely that any precedent that emerges from the decision will ever be applied in the future? Should the judges give any consideration to the clear statements of public opinion on the matter?

To be sure, a decision in a case like this requires an explicit understanding of the law involved and of the facts, but it also demands at least an implicit set of beliefs about the nature and purpose of law.[2] Decisions in cases that have considerable legal and political significance also require that the judge understand his or her own role in the judicial process. Jurisprudence is the study of the philosophy that provides these underpinnings for legal decisionmaking.

PURPOSES OF LAW AND APPROACHES TO LEGAL THEORY

A decision in the case of the Speluncean explorers could depend on the view one has of the purpose of the law. If the purpose is to have justice done between parties involved in litigation, the decision might hold for the defendants. On the other hand, if the purpose of law is primarily to preserve civil society by maintaining order, one may wish to treat these four men more harshly. One who reads in the Anglo-American legal tradition can readily identify a number of purposes of law that appear to coexist, although different authors have emphasized different goals at various times in history.

Purposes of Law

For many, the law exists to provide justice in the society as a whole and for the specific participants in the case at issue. The problem is to define justice as a concept and then to apply it in a particular case.

Another commonly accepted purpose is the management of change. For example, laws that govern credit cards, computer credit records, and Internet transactions help to facilitate economic change, and ensure that the change is orderly and under some measure of control. The ability to perform *in vitro* fertilization produced disputes over whether surrogate mothers who bore children produced by sperm donated by the husband of a married couple had parental rights or lost them by virtue of signing a surrogacy agreement.[3] Some time later the question arose concerning parental rights and obligations of a same-sex couple who used available medical techniques to have a child.[4] The contemporary capabilities of medical science to prolong life for terminally ill patients have raised questions about the right of patients to seek the assistance of physicians to die what they consider a dignified death.[5] In all of these cases the need to solve real problems came long before state legislatures or the Congress enacted statutes to address them.

The flexibility of the legal process permits change through judicial interpretation of existing law. During the debate over ratification of the United States Constitution, critics argued that the new charter of government was too vague. To be useful, they asserted, the fundamental law should be specific and clearly applicable to particular situations. James Madison, generally regarded as the father of the Constitution, rejected that notion. Writing in *Federalist Paper* No. 44, Madison argued that a set of laws, especially a constitution, that attempted to completely codify every aspect of the legal system would be both under- and overinclusive.[6] It would be underinclusive because no lawmaker, however prescient, could draft laws that would cover every possible contingency that might arise in the future. Yet the body of law would also be overinclusive because it would be rigid, and would freeze the norms and problems of one period into the law that would be imposed in the future when circumstances had changed.

A third purpose of law is to maintain stability. One of the benefits of the legal system that permits us to live and work together in civil society is a certain predictability. While the law does allow for change, it is also, especially in the Anglo-American tradition, inherently conservative. *Stare decisis,* the rule that precedent should govern new cases, is strong. One learns, for example, that a driver of an automobile that strikes another vehicle from the rear will generally be held responsible for the accident. One can guide his or her actions in the future based on the knowledge that the same rule of liability will likely be applied if he or she is involved in a similar accident.

At the same time, there are debates about whether and when courts might consider overturning previous precedents. Thus, in the confirmation hearings for President George W. Bush's nomination of Judge John Roberts to succeed William Rehnquist as Chief Justice of the United States, a number of Democrats and the Republican Chair of the Senate Judiciary Committee pressed the nominee to interpret *stare decisis* in a way that would resist efforts to overturn the *Roe v. Wade* decision on abortion, while others worked just as intently to get Roberts to suggest an approach to *Roe* that would offer an avenue for the reversal of that ruling. Chairman Arlen Specter (R-PA) began his questioning of Roberts with this discussion.

> SPECTER: Judge Roberts, there are many subjects of enormous importance that you will be asked about in this confirmation hearing, but I start with the central issue which perhaps concerns most Americans, and that is the issue of the woman's right to choose and *Roe v. Wade.*
>
> And I begin collaterally with the issue of *stare decisis* and the issue of preceden[ts]. *Black's Law Dictionary* defines *stare decisis* as, "Let the decision stand," to adhere to precedence and not unsettle things which are established. Justice Scalia articulated, quote, "The principal purpose of *stare decisis* is to protect reliance interest and further stability in the law...."
>
> SPECTER: Justice Frankfurter articulated the principle, quote, "We recognize that *stare decisis* embodies an important social policy that represents an element of continuity in law and is rooted in the psychological need to satisfy reasonable expectations." Justice Cardozo, in a similar vein, quote, "No judicial system could do society's work if each issue had to be decided afresh in every case which raised it." In our initial conversation, you talked about the stability and humility in the law. Would you agree with those articulations of the principles of *stare decisis,* as you had contemplated them, as you said you looked for stability in the law?
>
> ROBERTS: Yes, Mr. Chairman, I would. I would point out that the principle goes back even farther than Cardozo and Frankfurter. Hamilton, in *Federalist* No. 78, said that, "To avoid an arbitrary discretion in the judges, they need to be bound down by rules and precedents." So, even that far back, the founders appreciated the role of precedent in promoting evenhandedness, predictability, stability, adherence of integrity in the judicial process.[7]

Chairman Specter pressed Roberts to agree that because of this need for settled expectations and planning of lives based on settled law, *Roe v. Wade* should not be overturned. Roberts recognized those interests, but kept open his opportunity to vote as he wished in future cases by indicating that sometimes precedents are overruled and the principal of *stare decisis* is not absolute.

ROBERTS: Well, I feel the need to stay away from a discussion of particular cases. I'm happy to discuss the principles of *stare decisis*. And the court has developed a series of precedents on precedent, if you will. They have a number of cases talking about how this principle should be applied. And as you emphasized, in *Casey,* they focused on settled expectations. They also looked at the workability and the erosion of precedents.[8]

Thus, the debate over just how much stability the law should provide and when and under what conditions the rule of *stare decisis* should give way to the need to reconsider prior precedents continues.[9]

A fourth purpose of the law is to provide for orderly and peaceful resolution of disputes. If there is an accident, one need not jump from the car to have it out with the other party in the middle of the street. Instead, we generally retain an attorney to resolve the dispute in the accepted forum, a court. The society provides the courts and sets rules for their operation to provide a fair forum in which grave controversies may be resolved on the basis of reason. It is clear that this system is not perfectly fair or absolutely unbiased. Even so, we know that there is a systematic civilized means to settle disputes.

Law is also a means of facilitating private arrangements. Adoption is an example. Through legal process we make someone, to all intents and purposes, a child of a mother and father when they are not biologically related. The law allows the creation of unique legal entities to help those who wish to accomplish personal goals. For example, through incorporation, several people can join together for business purposes in a way that protects their personal property and limits their individual liability to the amount invested in the corporation. There are many similar examples of situations in which the law provides support for private endeavors.

Finally, the law is a mechanism that maintains a sense of historical continuity in the society. For example, the American way of life as it has developed in this century is reflected in our laws. One can trace changes in social and legal norms and relate them to the circumstances that brought them about. These long-term trends and historical connections in the law help the society develop for the future.

These are just some of the many purposes of law.[10] Over the centuries, various legal scholars have developed substantial theories of law based on one or more of these purposes. Such bodies of theory and the writings of those associated with each are often referred to as "schools of jurisprudence."

SCHOOLS OF JURISPRUDENCE: THEORETICAL APPROACHES TO LEGAL DECISIONMAKING

In addition to offering theories about the purpose of law, schools of jurisprudence differ as to the role of the legal process in the state, the role of the judge, and the relationship between the law and the society it serves. A judge's jurisprudence provides a general approach to legal decisionmaking. Scholars who have studied approaches to legal theory generally have classified them into a number of philosophical schools.[11] Among the most commonly acknowledged schools are natural law, analytic jurisprudence, historical, sociological, realist/behavioralist, political jurisprudence, and deterministic jurisprudence.

Natural Law Jurisprudence

One of the oldest of the approaches to the law, the natural law school of jurisprudence is represented in its various manifestations by such people as Aristotle, Cicero, Hugo Grotius, Saint Thomas Aquinas, John Locke, and a more contemporary legal scholar, Lon Fuller. Natural law jurisprudence has been of major importance to western law in general and to American law in particular.[12] At its heart, this body of theory rests heavily on the proposition that human beings are part of a natural order of things and should act in harmony with that order. Particularly in its more modern manifestations, the theory suggests that while people's relationship to their environment is a matter of natural order, their relationship with others is in large part a matter of social contract.

Our ability to live together under such a social compact stems from the fact that people are both rational and social beings who, under the right conditions, can govern themselves. But the social contracts under which the society operates, such as the U.S. Constitution, must be in harmony with the law of nature and the natural rights of all citizens. At the time of the American Revolution, these natural rights were known as the rights of Englishmen. As developed in our Constitution, they were in general terms those rights to life, liberty, and property referred to by Locke and discussed by Jefferson in the Declaration of Independence.[13]

Judges who operate within a natural law context share one or more of the following decision principles in resolving cases. There does exist a natural law that is prior to law created by people. There is some conception from natural law of truth and justice. The true and just decision can be found by reasonable people if they have access to information and search for the right decision. There should be some relationship between the law that is and what ought to be. Judges, rather than making law, should discover the law from principles of natural law and reason.

Like most such philosophies, natural law has adherents who range from ardent apostles, such as Saint Thomas Aquinas,[14] who developed a complete typology of law based on the relationship between man and his creator and man and his fellows, to Lon Fuller,[15] who merely suggested that there are some moral principles that come before man-made laws and must be considered in any legal system. In part, Fuller was reacting to the analytical school of jurisprudence.

Analytical Jurisprudence

The scholars of analytical jurisprudence include such writers as Thomas Hobbes, John Austin, and Hans Kelsen, who rejected the idea that anything apart from manmade law is of concern to the jurisprudential scholar.[16] Law is positive, a product of human beings. Natural order is not expected. The analytical approach has a more pessimistic view of human nature. Hobbes assumed that life outside a powerful government, in a state of nature, would be the "war of all against all," in which life would be "solitary, poor, nasty, brutish and short."

Under the analytical approach, people are not presumed to be especially rational. They are not basically very good in any moral sense, but obey laws because the laws are backed by sanctions. For whatever reason, the analytical scholars insist that it is the *logic* of positive laws that is important.

From these premises John Austin launched his attempt to develop a fully articulated logical system of law. He began with the idea that law is the command of the sovereign backed by a sanction. The task is to develop from that premise a system that is logically coherent and consistent. Hans Kelsen began from what he called a "grund norm," a basic principle, to do the same.

Under this approach to jurisprudence the task of the lawyer and the judge is not to find the law in a natural law sense, but to maintain the logical integrity of the legal fabric. This process of rationalizing rules is a continuous one. The concern is not for historical continuity, but rather for consistency among the pronouncements of the lawgiver.

Historical Jurisprudence

Historical jurisprudential scholars reject the idea that the law can be understood either as an analytical system or as an enduring reflection of the natural order. They insist that law is the product of the custom and history of a people. The two leading scholars of this persuasion are Sir Henry Maine and Friedrich Karl von Savigny.[17] Maine demonstrated that existing English law was in fact primarily a product of the historical development of legal principles from the Roman period to the British nation state era. Savigny, studying German law, made the point that the law consists of the "volksgeist," the spirit of the people, and the "zeitgeist," spirit of the times. The changing patterns of societies are the underpinnings of the law as it exists in any single time and place. Hence, it should not be surprising that nineteenth-century German law and twentieth-century American law differ in major ways. Although Maine and

Savigny developed their theories from quite different directions, both concluded that history is the primary factor in the development of law. It is the task of the judge to apply the law in light of this historical dynamic.

Sociological Jurisprudence

The sociological approach to jurisprudence is concerned with the spirit of the people, but in a different sense. Probably the most influential of the modern writers in this area was Roscoe Pound.[18] Pound summarized the approach as follows:

Comparing sociological jurists with jurists of other schools, we may say:

1. They look more to the working of the law than to its abstract content.
2. They regard law as a social institution which may be improved by intelligent human effort, and hold it their duty to discover the best means of furthering and directing such effort.
3. They lay stress upon the social purposes which law subserves rather than upon sanction.
4. They urge that legal precepts are to be regarded more as guides to results which are socially just and less as inflexible molds.
5. Their philosophical views are diverse.[19]

In other words, the law is, and ought to be, concerned with the maximization of social wants and needs and the minimization of social tensions and costs. That courts are engaged in balancing important interests is basic to this approach. It is eclectic in origin and method, but clearly normative in its actual operation.[20]

Realist-Behavioralist Tradition of Law

The legal realists also reject the mechanical notion of clear response from clearly analyzed principles of law. Three major groups writing at different periods during the last century have developed a body of writings that are best understood as the realist-behavioralist tradition.

The first group wrote at about the turn of the century. Justice Oliver Wendell Holmes is the leading figure.[21] Holmes rejected the idea that the law was some "brooding omnipresence in the sky" that can be discovered through pure reason. The life of the law, he said, is experience. Holmes asserted that scholars of analytical jurisprudence were guilty of the "fallacy of logical form," those of the historical approach faced the "pitfall of antiquarianism," and the natural law philosophers were operating "in that naive state of mind that accepts what has been familiar and accepted by them and their neighbors as something that must be accepted by all men everywhere."[22] However, unlike the scholars of sociological jurisprudence, Holmes was less concerned with the relationship between the moral or social "ought" and the legal "is." "The prophecies of what the courts will do in fact, and nothing more pretentious, are what I mean by the law."[23]

Holmes, along with such other writers as John Chipman Gray,[24] acknowledged that judges make law. For various reasons, the judges, at least in a nation [with a] common law heritage like America's, cannot avoid issuing decisions that are the law. The important thing, according to these writers, is to understand how judges make law so that we may understand the law better and improve it in the future.

A second group of legal realists came along during the 1930s and includes such writers as Jerome Frank and Karl Llewellyn.[25] They added at least two dimensions to their predecessors' work. First, they suggested that the process of legal decisionmaking is important for understanding what the law is and why judges are important. A fact skeptic, Jerome Frank argued that a legal decision is more than a product of a legal rule applied to a specific set of facts. The processes through which we determine facts, most notably the "fight theory of law" and the jury system as presently used, add several variables that affect the final determination of the facts in a case. Frank acknowledged others who, like Llewellyn, suggested that the interpretation of rules was far more complicated than a simple clean analytical process. Second, they argued that judges make decisions on a wide range of bases, only some of which are conscious, rational, and analytic. Other elements of decisionmaking are more complex and less obvious.

Glendon Schubert and other behaviorialists took the importance of the judge and the significance of nonrational aspects of decisionmaking and legal process as the starting point for their work. They went further to suggest, working from a political science perspective, that the study of law should emphasize process rather than product. "The orientation is Bentleyan, behavioristic, actional and non-motivational."[26] What matters is the law in action, and that should be studied scientifically to understand the nonrational aspects of legal decisions.

In a very general sense the basic assumptions of the realist-behavioralist scholars are as follows. Law consists of a set of decisions made by persons in power. These decisions are not necessarily rational. Judges have preferences and values, and their decisions, for good or ill, are affected by the inherited and acquired traits that they bring to the bench. The behavior of judges is also affected, especially in appellate courts, by the fact that such courts are collegial bodies that operate with all the strengths and weaknesses imposed by small group dynamics.

Political Jurisprudence

Another group of scholars is closely related to the judicial realists in the Jerome Frank tradition. These people may be referred to as students of political jurisprudence. Martin Shapiro, Walter Murphy, and J. Woodford Howard are authors in this tradition.[27] In many respects, they are like the behavioralists, but they tend to emphasize the study of political relationships that affect the law. Judges are important as individual actors, as are legal institutions and interest groups that affect the court, internally and from the outside. These authors' works evidence a concern for policy-oriented judges.[28] They assume that judges are policymakers and they ask questions about how the judges actually make the policy and the implications of that policy for other parts of government.

Deterministic Jurisprudence

Over the years, a number of writers have suggested that law is deterministic. Some, like Michael Parenti,[29] assert that since all law is designed to preserve the status quo, judicial decisions are not especially important. The Marxist critique of modern legal systems is the clearest example. In that perspective the law exists to keep those in power in place and those out of power subservient.

Justice Cardozo's Eclecticism

Several authors have been cited whose work can be classified loosely into various schools of jurisprudential thought. But many of us approach legal problems from a more eclectic perspective. Justice Cardozo explained this process well in a lecture that was later published as *The Nature of the Judicial Process*.[30] Asked to give an address on the subject of how he decided cases, Cardozo found it to be a very difficult task. Up to a point, it was easy enough to comment on statutory interpretation and common law development, but he had to acknowledge that the judge must also play a significant role in the development of the law.

> Where does the judge find the law which he embodies in his judgment? There are times when the source is obvious . . . [but] codes and statutes do not render the judge superfluous, nor his work perfunctory and mechanical. There are gaps to be filled.[31]

He recognized "judge-made laws as one of the existing realities of life."[32] The problem is to understand the direction that a judge takes in deciding a case that will doubtless make new law. Cardozo gave the following summary:

> The directive force of a principle may be exerted along the line of logical progression, this I will call the rule of analogy or the method of philosophy; along the line of historical development, this I will call the method of evolution; along the line of customs of the community, this I will call the method of tradition; along the line of justice, Morals and Social Welfare, the mores of the day, and this I will call the method of sociology.[33]

Cardozo concluded that he and other judges use most of these methods depending on the kind of case and the nature of the facts.

Whether one has developed an eclectic view of law, as did Justice Cardozo, or one that is more exclusive, such as one of those advanced in one of the schools of thought discussed above, it is important to understand the philosophical base from which one approaches a legal controversy. Assumptions about the purposes of law and approaches to legal decisions set limits on decisionmaking. Failure to deal with the theoretical underpinnings of legal disputes can, as Justice Holmes suggested, be deadly to one who must deal with the law.

> Theory is the most important part of the dogma of the law, as the architect is the most important man who takes part in the building of the house. . . . It is not to be feared as impractical, for, to the competent, it simply means going to the bottom of the subject. For the incompetent, it sometimes is true, as has been said, that an interest in general ideas means an absence of particular knowledge.[34]

With this survey of legal thought as a basis, let us turn to a consideration of the specific skills used in making legal decisions. The collection of analytical techniques employed to resolve legal controversies is known as legal reasoning.

LEGAL REASONING

Recognizing the need to protect the integrity of the judicial process as much as possible from the potential arbitrariness of judges and others, members of the legal community have developed a body of procedures and rules to govern legal decisionmaking. These constraints on the decisionmaking process seek to regularize the process of legal problem solving to permit orderly development of the law and at the same time maintain stability in the legal system. Most of these decision rules and rules of self-restraint are imposed by courts on themselves and are policed by the judges. The legal community has a number of methods for reminding the judges of their limitations and criticizing decisionmakers who breach those professional norms. One of the most effective of these is criticism and praise in law reviews. Consider some of the following professional guidelines for judges.

Institutional Influences on Decisionmaking

One of the more significant characteristics of the courts as decisionmakers is that they are not self-starters. They must wait for cases to be brought before them at the proper time and in the appropriate manner for resolution. When a case is brought to a court, it must be dealt with as it stands, not as the judge would like it to be presented.

For example, it was clear to the legal community that the U.S. Supreme Court would be called on in the mid-1970s to decide whether affirmative action programs for admission to graduate and professional schools violated either the equal protection clause of the Constitution or the Civil Rights Act of 1964. The case that finally reached the Court, *Regents v. Bakke*,[35] was a complicated one, involving a challenge by a California man to the affirmative action program of the University of California Medical School at Davis. The facts of this particular suit were even more complex than the usually complicated fact patterns of affirmative action cases. In part because of the difficult issues in the case, but also partly because of the facts that caused this particular man to sue, the Supreme Court was badly split in its decision.[36] The Court rendered six opinions in the case with no more than five judges joining in any one part of Court's opinion, and then only with respect to those two parts of the opinion prepared by Justice Powell.

It is perhaps ironic, though not particularly surprising, that a case brought some 20 years after *Bakke* to test whether affirmative action would be struck down by the Rehnquist Court was actually diverted to avoid a problematic decision. In this case, originating in Piscataway, New Jersey, a white female teacher had been terminated during a budget cutback and an African-American colleague retained on grounds, according to the school district, of a need for diversity. Because they were so similarly qualified and possessed comparable seniority, the case seemed likely to move the Supreme Court in search of a direct ruling on the permissibility of an affirmative action decision. Given the fact that recent rulings in the Supreme Court suggested that the Court may be headed in that direction,[37] civil rights organizations came together in late 1997 to provide support for a financial settlement that would remove the case before it was heard in the Supreme Court.

Thus, in the *Bakke* case, the fact issues led to fragmentation while in the New Jersey case, the clarity of the case threatened a very different kind of outcome. Eventually, after repeated efforts by various parties from around the nation to force the issues, the Court decided two cases from the University of Michigan, striking down the undergraduate admissions program but upholding the law school affirmative action process.[38]

Another example of the problems of reactive decisionmaking is the body of case law in which courts have ordered school desegregation or intervened in the operation of prisons and mental health facilities.[39] Many judges attempted to dodge decisions in these cases, but found themselves faced with cases properly before their courts that required decisions. They faced the dilemma of telling a deserving litigant that he or she, though advancing a just claim, was not entitled to a legal remedy, or else producing a remedy that was certain to bring down an avalanche of political criticism and social outrage.

Another factor that influences judicial decisionmaking is "equity," which has a rich heritage extending back at least as far as Aristotle. There are difficulties involved in writing law that make it highly likely that some laws will fall with undue and unintended harshness on citizens. The Speluncean Explorers situation is an example. Most people react with horror at the idea of sacrificing a life only to execute the men who were saved from the cave. On the other hand, it seems undesirable to appear to give official approval to the actions taken by the men in the cave. One option for the judge is to argue that equity dictates that, while the men must receive some punishment since society cannot condone the taking of life, the statute was never intended to cover a situation like the one at bar and the full weight of its sanction should not fall on these defendants.

Equity, then does not mean equality, though the two terms are often used interchangeably in contemporary social science. Equity is deliberately unequal treatment of some people before the law for some very limited purposes where equal application would be unjust. In even simpler terms, equity is deliberate inequality in the interest of justice.

As a formal institutionalized practice, equity reaches back to the time when it was believed that the sovereign was possessed of a sense of perfect justice. When the king no longer dispensed justice but delegated that task to judges there were bound to be difficulties. Some cases were brought on appeal to the king acting in equity to ameliorate the harsh judgments of the courts. Eventually, even this task overwhelmed the Crown and the task of decisionmaking concerning equity was delegated to the Lord High Chancellor, who came to be known as "my Lord Keeper" for his role as the keeper of the king's conscience. Since then, equity law has become much more formal and limited, but the idea of equity remains a major factor in judicial decisions. For a more in-depth discussion of equity, see Appendix 2.

Another long-standing concept of major importance is the "legal fiction." It permits one to make assumptions about the world that are not real in an empirical sense for legal purposes. The practice of permitting a corporation to sue or be sued in its own name is one such fiction. The personality of a ship is another example. Justice William O. Douglas cited this practice in a discussion about who should represent some environmental interests.

> Our case law has personified vessels: "A ship is born when she is launched, and lives so long as her identity is preserved. Prior to her launching she is a mere congeries of wood and iron.... In the baptism of launching she receives her name, and from the moment her keel touches water she is transformed. She acquires a personality of her own."[40]

When such fictions are involved in litigation, they may cause the decisionmaker difficulties in matching the fictional concepts to real outcomes in the law. For example, a bank brought a case to the Supreme Court in which it claimed that the First Amendment of the Constitution, which protects freedom of speech, barred the state of Massachusetts from restricting its expenditure of corporate funds to defeat a tax measure then pending on the ballot.[41] If a corporation can sue and be sued, can it claim protection under the First Amendment?

In general, Anglo-American legal decisionmaking is guided by the doctrine of *stare decisis,* or the rule of precedent. More will be said about this approach to legal decisionmaking. For the present, it is important to understand that the idea that previous rulings should govern new cases makes the law inherently conservative. A judge attempts to decide whether actions taken at some point in the past by a person or persons now involved in a legal dispute violated the law. The decision is predicated on the existing rules of law at or before the time the actions were taken.

As each new decision of a court of record is rendered in the form of a judicial opinion, new law is, in a very real sense, made by the judge. Consider again the cave explorers. A judge could decide the case any number of ways. Two possible approaches are:

1. The agreement to take one life to save the lives of the rest when all were under clear threat of death, if entered into voluntarily by all parties, is lawful, and enforcement of that agreement is not a willful taking of life within the meaning of the statute.

2. Even if the taking of one life will save the lives of a substantial number of others who face imminent death, a homicide is a willful taking of life under the law.

Whichever decision is adopted, there is an official interpretation that will be presumed to be the law. In the first approach, the judge is interpreting the actions in the cave as a form of self-defense that has not traditionally been considered a "willful" action as required by the murder statutes. In the second, the interpretation may mean that the law makes no allowance for life-threatening situations except for traditional notions of self-defense. Hence, when a judge renders an opinion, no matter how much he or she may attempt to circumscribe the ruling of law, it will be treated as the new interpretation of law to guide the actions of those who may in the future face a similar or even a related legal situation. Even a decision not to take a case often produces a precedent on such subjects as standing to bring suit, jurisdiction, or the ripeness of a case for review.

Since all such opinions are new law, courts are generally expected to seek to resolve legal problems on the narrowest principle available. This self-imposed rule, sometimes honored as much in the breach as in the observance, is important to the maintenance of that critical balance between change and stability in the law.

Rules of Self-Restraint in Federal Courts

Over the years the United States Supreme Court has developed a set of rules governing legal decisionmaking in federal courts. These rules, sometimes referred to in general terms as the *Ashwander* rules (from a case that attempted to synthesize and describe rules of self-restraint),[42] describe the kinds of controversies that the courts will resolve and caveats to be observed by judges in dealing with them. We shall come to these rules again in our discussion of judicial review of administrative actions in Chapter 7, but it is necessary to touch on them briefly here since they so heavily condition the law in action.

Though there are a number of specific rules of self-restraint, but most fall into two categories. The first concerns the Article III authorization for federal courts to decide actual "cases and controversies" that arise under the Constitution or federal law. Thus, the first question is, does the court have jurisdiction to hear the case? Second, is it the kind of case that the courts can hear and do something about? This category of questions is often discussed under the concept of justiciability. Writing for the Supreme Court in *Baker v. Carr,* Justice Brennan described the concept as follows:

> The distinction between the two grounds is significant. In the instance of nonjusticiability, consideration of the cause is not wholly and immediately foreclosed; rather, the Court's inquiry necessarily proceeds to the point of deciding whether the duty asserted can be judicially identified and its breach judicially determined, and whether protection for the right asserted can be judicially molded. In the instance of a lack of jurisdiction the cause either does not "arise under" the Federal Constitution, laws or treaties (or fall within one of the other enumerated categories of Art. 111, §2), or is not a "case or controversy" within the meaning of that section; or the cause is not one described by any jurisdictional statute.[43]

Whether a particular case presents legal questions that are within the jurisdiction of the court and justiciable must be decided before the court reaches any decision on the substance of the claims made by those involved in the case.

Among the rules by which the courts make such determinations is the rule that the person who brings a lawsuit must have legal standing to do so. He or she must have been injured or stand in imminent danger of being injured by the party being sued.[44] The idea is that the people who bring suits should be the right parties to get the case before the court. Under an adversary system such as ours, the appropriate person is one who stands to win or lose something significant in the resolution of the case. Our "fight theory" of law operates on the premise that those who stand to be seriously affected will put forward the best case for their respective positions.[45] With both sides advancing the best arguments, the judge sees the case with the legal issues carefully defined and the various alternatives properly arrayed. The judge is then able to focus the decision process on the narrow aspects that must be decided to resolve the problem at hand. Standing, then, has to do with the persons or groups bringing a suit and not with the nature of the questions of law those people would like the court to resolve.

Related, in some respects, to the problem of standing is the rule that federal courts will not decide collusive suits or provide advisory opinions.[46] Agencies and private individuals would like to avoid taking actions that might later open them to a lawsuit. Similarly, legislatures would sometimes like to get some reaction on the constitutionality of a new measure before time and money are wasted on implementing a law that will fall before a court order. Thus, for example, when Congress adopted the line item veto statute in early 1996 that gave the president the power to "cancel" certain items in appropriations legislation, it was clear that there would be challenges. Congress provided for such challenges and for an expedited appeal to the Supreme Court to get a prompt constitutional opinion on this new device. However, the Supreme Court denied standing in the case, saying that a resolution of the constitutional question would have to wait until the president made use of the item veto authority and a case could be brought by someone who demonstrate a clear injury as a result.[47] The Court's ruling came as a surprise to many observers because it had agreed to review the Gramm-Rudman-Holling budget deficit reduction act under very similar circumstances in a 1986 case.[48] However, President Clinton did use the item veto authority on a variety of spending programs in the fall of 1997 only to be challenged by governmental units and other groups who were affected by the cuts. This time the Court took the matter up and ultimately declared the item veto unconstitutional in June 1998.[49]

These types of efforts by legislatures and chief executives to get what amount to advisory opinions have given rise to what are known as collusive suits in which the parties at interest agree to a legal action in an attempt to get a legal opinion clarifying their respective positions under the law. In general terms, collusive suits are not considered actual cases or controversies within the meaning of Article III of the Constitution.[50] There is no "concrete adversity" as required under our judicial rules. Although some state courts do provide advisory opinions (see Figure 3.1), most state courts and all federal courts refuse to produce such decisions. If, for example, one wishes an opinion on the legality of an agency action before an actual suit is instituted in court, the standard procedure is to ask the U.S. Attorney General (or the state AG at that level) for an advisory opinion on the matter.

Courts generally refuse to hear cases that do not present live issues. Such cases are rejected as moot. *De Funis v. Odegaard* provides an example. Marco De Funis sought admission to the University of Washington School of Law. He was unsuccessful on his initial application to the school, but other students with lower test scores and grade-point averages were admitted through a special admissions program. De Funis sued, claiming discrimination in violation of the equal protection clause. But by the time his suit reached the United States Supreme Court, his situation had changed. He had been admitted to the school the next year and was in his final term of law school when the case came before the Court. The school indicated that De Funis would not be dismissed from the school even if he lost his appeal. The Court held that De Funis no longer had a live controversy or case against the school.[51]

Before one's case is heard in appellate courts, all remedies in lower courts and agencies must have been exhausted. This doctrine serves a number of purposes. First, it helps to clear the docket of higher courts.[52] Second, it discourages needless opinion production in higher courts that would add to the already massive body of law. Third, it protects the integrity of the decision processes in lower courts and agencies. These tribunals are afforded the opportunity to shape litigation as needed and to correct their own errors before matters are taken up on review. Finally, where there is federal court review of state action, exhaustion permits state officials to resolve problems short of federal court action that might raise important questions of federalism.

Appellate courts generally limit their review to questions of law and accept lower court findings on questions of fact.[53] There are some exceptions, but in most cases a reviewing court limits its inquiry to whether the law was properly interpreted and applied in lower courts or agencies. This rule of restraint is based in part on the idea that the "cold record" that comes up to a reviewing court of appeal is not sufficiently complete to determine the facts of a case. Appellate judges cannot see or hear the responses of witnesses. The transcripts contain their words but not their inflections or facial expressions, which may be quite helpful to the decisionmaker.

Judges will refuse to decide some legal issues because they are "political questions" and therefore nonjusticiable. There are at least two important aspects to the political question doctrine. First, the courts use the doctrine to restrain themselves in cases where an issue should not be resolved by the judiciary. Second, from a practical standpoint, the political question is a device by which courts can escape making decisions they would rather avoid for the present. From a doctrinal perspective, the Supreme Court has held that there are some cases in which the decisions involved were constitutionally committed to someone other than the judiciary. This is a matter of respect for the separation of powers. On the other hand, there are some cases that the courts have found intrinsically unfit for judicial resolution. Justice Brennan has written one of the most succinct descriptions of the doctrine.

> Prominent on the surface of any case held to involve a political question is found a textually demonstrable constitutional commitment of the issue to a coordinate political department; or a lack of judicially discoverable and manageable standards for resolving it; or the impossibility of deciding without an initial policy determination of a kind clearly for nonjudicial discretion; or the impossibility of a court's undertaking independent resolution without expressing lack of respect due coordinate branches of government; or an unusual need for unquestioning ad-herence to a political decision already made; or the potentiality of embarrassment from multifarious pronouncements by various departments on one question.[54]

The Court has always had some practical concern for its position in the polity. Since the Court has neither the "power of the purse nor the sword,"[55] it depends on support from the other branches of government and a strong sense of legitimacy of judicial actions from the general public to gain

SUPREME COURT OF FLORIDA

ADVISORY OPINION TO THE GOVERNOR-1996
AMENDMENT 5 (EVERGLADES)
No. 90,042

November 26, 1997

The Honorable Lawton Chiles
Governor, State of Florida
The Capitol
Tallahassee, Florida 32301

Dear Governor Chiles:

We acknowledge receipt of your communication March 6, 1997, requesting our advice pursuant to section 1(c), article IV of the Florida Constitution....

In accordance with our rules, we made a preliminary determination that your request is properly within the purview of article IV, section 1(c), in that Amendment 5 directly affects your duty as governor to see that the law is faithfully executed (by providing the South Florida Water Management District and the Department of Environmental Protection with direction as to their enforcement responsibilities) and to report on the state's progress in restoring the Everglades System. To ensure full and fair consideration of the issues raised, we permitted interested persons to file briefs and to present oral argument before the Court....

As to your first question, that is, whether Amendment 5 is self-executing, ... we conclude that Amendment 5 is not self-executing and cannot be implemented without the aid of legislative enactment because it fails to lay down a sufficient rule for accomplishing its purpose. As you suggest in your letter, "too many policy determinations remain unanswered".... Thus, we answer the first part of your first question in the negative.

The second part of your first question asks whether legislative action is required in light of the pre-existing Everglades Forever Act. We answer in the affirmative. In a case where the constitutional provision is not self-executing, such as the instant case, "all existing statutes which are consistent with the amended Constitution will remain in effect until repealed by the Legislature"....

Your second question asks us to construe the phrase "primarily responsible" as used in Amendment 5. The touchstone for determining the meaning of a constitutional amendment adopted by initiative is the intent of the voters who adopted it, and it is well settled that the words and terms of a Constitution are to be interpreted in their most usual and obvious meaning., unless the text suggests that they have been used in a technical sense. The presumption is in favor of the natural and popular meaning in which the words are usually understood by the people who have adopted them.... Voters reading the ballot summary or the entire amendment would most likely understand that the words "primarily responsible" would be applied in accordance with their ordinary meaning to require that individual polluters, while not bearing the total burden, would bear their share of the costs of abating the pollution found to be attributable to them.

In conclusion, we answer your inquiries by finding that (1) Amendment 5 is not self-executing; (2) the amendment requires implementing legislation, notwithstanding the existence of the Everglades Forever Act; and (3) the words "primarily responsible" require those in the EAA who cause water pollution in the EPA or EAA to bear the costs of abating that pollution.

Respectfully,

Gerald Kogan
Chief Justice

FIGURE 3.1 A Florida Supreme Court Advisory Opinion

compliance with its judgments. For this and other reasons, the Court occasionally uses rules of self-restraint, especially the political question doctrine, to avoid cases the majority considers should be avoided. On this use of the doctrine, John P. Frank has written:

> The term "political question" is a magical formula which has the practical result of relieving a court of the necessity of thinking further about a particular problem. It is a device for transferring the responsibility for decision of questions to another branch of the government; and it may sometimes operate to leave a problem in mid-air so that no branch decides it.[56]

Examples of problems considered political questions include decisions to call out the militia, determinations regarding general foreign policy, and internal disciplinary rules in Congress. In the final analysis, a political question is anything the Court says it is.

Another rule of self-restraint relating to the concern for respect among the branches and the effective operation of the government is the presumption in favor of government action. Normally, a court will presume that a statute passed by a legislature, a regulation issued by an agency, or a decision of a government official is lawful and any challenger carries the burden to prove the contrary. (The qualifying term "normally" is added because there are limited circumstances under which the presumption is reversed, such as in cases where there is evidence that people were treated differently on the basis of race.[57]) That presumption of validity does not depend on an assumption about the wisdom or fairness of government officials.

The narrowest principle approach to legal decisionmaking applies with even greater force to decisions that may involve interpretation of the Constitution. Since the Constitution is the basic charter of government, decisions about its meaning are not to be taken lightly or unnecessarily. The Court will attempt to avoid deciding a case on constitutional grounds. If it is necessary to reach a constitutional question, the Court will generally attempt to limit the breadth of the decision.[58]

The Process of Hearing a Case

At this point we have a court made up of judges each of whom approaches legal decisionmaking with some sort of jurisprudential view of his or her role, and each of whom has an understanding of institutional factors that influence the resolution of cases as well as an explicit commitment to a flexible but significant set of rules of self-restraint. Chapter 2 detailed the procedure through which a case winds its way up on appeal. What happens when the case comes before a major appeals court, e.g., the United States Supreme Court? There are a number of procedures involved in getting a case from the docket to a decision published as an opinion in the Court's reports.

The first problem is getting a case on the docket. If the Court finally accepts a case for review on the merits, there has already been extensive development of the suit in the lower courts and agencies. That material is made available to the Court. Given the nature of the crowded docket that the Court faces, acceptance of the case generally means that the questions raised in the case are important. Even so, the Court has a relatively small amount of time to deal with each dispute. Consequently, the process of argument is fairly standardized.

The parties in the case file written briefs that identify the issues, develop the law on the subject as it presently exists, apply that law to the facts established in the lower court or agency, and recommend a specific disposition of the case by the Court. The briefs ask for an interpretation of the Constitution, a statute, or one of the Court's prior opinions. In addition to case law, historical evidence, legislative histories, and sociological or other forms of data, the advocates may offer commentaries published in law reviews or treatises as support for their views. These briefs are considered along with the record and whatever *amicus curiae* (friend of the court) briefs are accepted in the case. The docket information along with links to the briefs on the merits can be found on the U.S. Supreme Court website.[59]

Some, but not all, cases brought before the Supreme Court are then set down for oral argument before the Court. Unless the case is of major importance, the Court rarely gives the advocates in a case more than an hour to present all arguments. Unlike the trial before a jury, an appellate argument is more of an interchange between advocates and judges than a lecture by a lawyer.[60] The advocates begin with a brief restatement of the facts and issues and move on to emphasize or clarify important points raised in the briefs submitted to the Court.

The justices have had an opportunity to read the briefs and to do some research into the case prior to the argument. They come to the argument with different perspectives. Some will have strong views about a case based on their reading of it, consideration of previous decisions, or for jurisprudential reasons. Others may be concerned about the public policy implications involved in attempting to resolve the case. Still others will be uncommitted and may be swayed by the oral presentation.

At argument the justices question the advocates about their briefs, the public policy implications of their positions, and the applicability of the Court's prior decisions. Often the questions come in the form of hypothetical situations in which the advocates are asked to project the results of their reading of the law into possible future circumstances. A judge who has grave doubts, to put it mildly, about a position may ask what is known as the "jugular question," which seeks to go to the heart of the argument with a strong challenge to the position presented by an attorney.[61] Some of the questions are raised with an eye toward a justice's desire to persuade other members of the Court to his or her point of view. Another motivation for questioning is an attempt by some judges to probe the arguments in search of promising directions for an opinion they may have to write in the case. In any event, when the Chief Justice indicates that "the case is submitted," the arguments by attorneys end and consideration by the judges begins. The Supreme Court now publishes transcripts of the oral arguments on its website.[62] It is often interesting, and can be revealing as to the likely direction of a ruling, to examine the oral arguments.

There are often questions about whether oral arguments, like *amicus curiae* briefs, really matter. Every now and again, it becomes clear that sometimes they may indeed matter. Perhaps one of the clearest contemporary examples arose in the University of Michigan affirmative action admissions case mentioned earlier. When the Court accepted the case, the university sought supporting arguments from a wide variety of sources. It appeared probable that the decisions in those cases were from a divided court and every vote would count. One of the friend of the court briefs in support of the university's position was filed by what appeared on first glance to be an unlikely source. It was a group of retired generals and admirals who argued that affirmative action programs were extremely important in their efforts to diversify the officer corps after having learned hard lessons about the consequences of the lack of such diversity in the Vietnam War era. It was clear at oral argument that these arguments, coming as they did from such a surprising group, gave some of the justices pause. They made it a point to question those challenging the university, including the Solicitor General's representative, with reference to the officers' arguments, and those attorneys had difficulty providing effective responses.

The arguments were important because the case turned in significant part on whether ensuring a diverse student body constituted a compelling interest that would justify using race as a factor in the admissions process. Writing for the Court, Justice O'Connor noted:

> What is more, high-ranking retired officers and civilian leaders of the United States military assert that, "based on [their] decades of experience," a "highly qualified, racially diverse officer corps . . . is essential to the military's ability to fulfill its principle mission to provide national security." The primary sources for the Nation's officer corps are the service academies and the Reserve Officers Training Corps (ROTC), the latter comprising students already admitted to participating colleges and universities. . . . At present, "the military cannot achieve an officer corps that is both highly qualified and racially diverse unless the service academies and the ROTC used limited race-conscious recruiting and admissions policies." . . . To fulfill its mission, the military "must be selective in admissions for training and education for the officer corps, and it must train and educate a highly qualified, racially diverse officer corps in a racially diverse setting." . . . We agree that "it requires only a small step from this analysis to conclude that our country's other most selective institutions must remain both diverse and selective."[63] (Citations removed.)

Appellate courts hold conferences at which the cases are discussed and votes taken on the disposition of the dispute. In the Supreme Court, the standard practice is for the Chief Justice to assign the drafting an opinion to a member of the majority in the case if he or she is part of the majority. If the Chief Justice is not with the majority, that task falls to the senior member of the majority.

After the case is assigned, the judge prepares a draft of an opinion and circulates it for consideration by his or her colleagues. The idea is to attract as many members of the court to one's position as possible. A unanimous opinion is the most powerful statement a court can make. The members of the court can make changes in their voting posture at any time before the decision is rendered. Thus, there is always a chance that one can win over votes cast on the other side of the case at conference. Of course, there is also the possibility of losing votes. Hence, one must be concerned about drafting an opinion that will gain the support of the court, receive the support or at least the acquiescence of the public, and be accepted by the legal community as providing a well-crafted and cogent statement of the law.

In addition to changing votes, members of a court have other options in responding to the draft opinion. If a judge wishes to agree with the actual outcome of a case but for different reasons from those advanced in the majority opinion, he or she may enter a concurring opinion or join in a concurring opinion written by another member of the court. Those who disagree with the majority may enter dissenting opinions individually or as a group. Judges who write separate opinions enjoy greater latitude in what they write and in the manner in which their argument is presented, since they speak only for themselves and not for the court as a whole. These opinions provide a certain dynamic in the law. They may be drawn upon by future jurists and commentators in drafting new opinions.

However, if several opinions are issued in a case, although they may be interesting and helpful in understanding the views of particular members of the Court, it is difficult to know which direction the Court will take in the future.

There are two reasons for emphasizing the processes of appellate courts in this chapter. First, television and other media have, for good or ill, provided most Americans with a good deal of information about the way that trial courts operate and there is no reason to repeat it here. Second, in many cases, particularly where courts are called upon to review policymaking by administrative agencies in the form of rulemaking, the process is generally a challenge in an appellate court. The reasons are several, but in large part this mode is used because the agency itself acts like a trial-level court. It collects evidence, develops a record, often after a hearing, and produces a reasoned opinion, precisely the kinds of steps and factors that come out of a trial-level court.

Logic in the Law

The techniques of decisionmaking that judges employ to arrive at a determination of the meaning of the law in a particular case are known collectively as "legal reasoning."[64] As the leading author on the subject, Edward Levi, notes, there are really three different sets of techniques within the general rubric of legal reasoning. They are application of constitutional principles, statutory interpretation, and common law development.[65]

Legal Reasoning for Constitutional Questions: Complex Considerations for Fundamental Questions   In the early years of national development, Chief Justice John Marshall explained the Court's view on the nature of constitutional decisionmaking. In *Marbury v. Madison,* the Court declared an act of Congress, section 13 of the Judiciary Act of 1789, unconstitutional.[66] In the opinion, Chief Justice Marshall indicated that the Constitution is a "superior paramount law, unchangeable by ordinary means." It is, he wrote, "emphatically the province and duty of the judicial department" to say what that fundamental law means.

The primary difficulty in understanding the meaning of the Constitution is that a fundamental law designed to remain useful over a long period must be rather general in its terms. One of the criticisms leveled by those who opposed ratification was that the document was vague. Writing in *The Federalist,*

James Madison noted that an attempt to write a basic charter of government would become impossible if narrow specificity and precision were to be the benchmarks of draftsmanship. It would, he said, be necessary to develop a fully detailed code of all rights, duties, and privileges for all time to come. Such an undertaking would destroy the purpose of a Constitution and would, in any case, be impossible since no set of framers could have such prescience as to predict all possible developments that would call for special interpretations by the Congress.

Interpretation of the Constitution involves, at the least, a consideration of the language of the document, consideration of the intent of the framers to the degree that it is possible to discern it, the circumstances that have given rise to the problem under consideration, and the possible need for change in the law of the Constitution.

An interpretation of the language of the Constitution begins with a reading of the document, but it continues through a reading of the gloss the courts have placed on those words during the history of American constitutional development. For example, the Constitution gives the president the power to make treaties by and with the advice and consent of the Senate.[67] But does the word "treaties" mean executive agreements and diplomatic protocols? Does the language mean that if any agreement is made by the executive branch, it must be ratified by the Senate? The Supreme Court has held that, although executive agreements are for some purposes like treaties and may therefore be made by the president under Article II, they are not exactly the same and do not require Senate approval in all cases.[68]

Even if the language of a constitutional provision appears to provide a simple answer, judges often look further to the spirit or intent of the provision in question where it is possible to determine that intent. The First Amendment is one of the best examples of this problem. The language is seemingly clear and absolute: "Congress shall make no law" abridging freedoms of religion, speech, press, and peaceful assembly. As Justice Black was so fond of pointing out, it does not say "may make no bad laws" or "unfair laws," but no law. However, Justice Black was virtually alone in reading the language literally, since it is clear that the framers of the Constitution were well aware of existing law which proscribed or at least punished some kinds of expression. The Court has summarized these restrictions as matters of defamation, obscenity, or fighting words.[69]

There are a number of sources to which one may refer on the intent of the framers, including Madison's *Notes on Debates in the Federal Convention of 1787*,[70] Max Farrand's *The Framing of the Constitution*,[71] Robert Rutland's *The Birth of the Bill of Rights 1776–1791*,[72] Jonathan Elliott's *Debates. . . on the Adoption of the Federal Constitution . . .*[73] and *The Federalist Papers*.[74] There is also a substantial body of historical material on the Constitution and early national period that is helpful.[75] That said, it is often extremely difficult to reach a clear and unambiguous understanding of the intent of the framers. For one thing, one must ask whose intent is to count. Is it the majority of those attending the constitutional convention who spoke or voted for a particular interpretation? Does intent include those who debated and voted on the provision in the state ratifying conventions? Does it include the arguments rendered in *The Federalist Papers* written to support ratification of the document? These are frequently debated topics and there is only limited agreement among judges. There are times when it is possible to discern a relatively consistent line of reasoning during the convention and during the ratification debates, such as the decision to move away from a Constitution as a treaty among states like the previous Articles of Confederation, but most often there is a good deal of room for disagreement as to whether there really was a coherent statement of the framers' intent.

Often, although the language does not speak directly to a particular problem and there is no specific mention of the purpose of a particular provision so clear as to resolve a dispute, the circumstances in which a case arises are helpful to an understanding of a case. This was the situation facing the Supreme Court in one of its early cases, *McCulloch v. Maryland*.[76] The Congress had chartered the Bank of the United States as its central financial institution based on its understanding of the powers granted under Article I of the Constitution. But Article I says nothing of the power of the legislature to charter a bank. We know from the history of the framing of the Constitution that Congress was given a number of specifically enumerated powers—particularly including financial authority—in Section 8 of Article I to remedy some of the problems that had caused the downfall of the Articles of Confederation.

This did not settle the question whether the so-called "necessary and proper" clause gave Congress power to incorporate a bank. Marshall wrote for the Court, reminding critics that "it is a constitution we are expounding." Such a frame of government must be flexible. In this case, Marshall went into a lengthy consideration of the circumstances in which the bank had been created and the logical connections between the creation of the bank and the accomplishment of some of the matters specifically delegated to Congress by the Constitution to demonstrate that the chartering of the bank was constitutional.

Finally, courts do consider the need for change in interpretation. The framers of the Constitution made no mention of privacy either in the document itself or in the amendments later enacted. Does that mean there is no right to privacy under the Constitution? The Ninth Amendment states: "The enumeration in the Constitution, of certain rights, shall not be construed to deny or disparage others retained by the people." There is little else to which one can point as a direct source. The Supreme Court held in 1965 that there was indeed a constitutionally protected right to privacy, which was a "penumbral" right flowing from the First, Third, Fourth, Fifth, and Ninth amendments.[77] The decision in *Griswold* and others delivered since make clear the view of the justices that it is necessary for a document that protects liberty in modern America to include that protection. Interesting, even those who have been critical of the *Griswold* recognition of the right to privacy hasten to add that they would not now consider reversing it.

Statutory Interpretation: A Conversation Between Branches   Statutes are different. They may be altered whenever the legislature—state or federal—wishes to change them. In part for this reason, the courts have generally held that one should read them and apply them more literally than is possible or desirable with constitutional provisions.[78] As with constitutional interpretation, statutory language must be read with an eye toward the judicial gloss that language has received since its enactment. Additionally, it is a convention that one should also look to contemporaneous administrative interpretation of the language of a statute.[79] This deference comes from the view that administrators charged with implementing pieces of legislation are usually given the authority to administer the laws because they are considered experts in the general field dealt with by the legislation. For this and other reasons, the courts often defer to interpretations made by those administrators, though a good deal more will be said about this topic in Chapter 7.

The spirit of the law or the intent of the writers of the statute is an important issue in statutory interpretation. The Supreme Court ruling in *United Steelworkers v. Weber*[80] is a case in point. This case arose when a white employee of the Kaiser Aluminum Gramercy Works sued, claiming that an affirmative action plan developed voluntarily as a part of a contract between the company and the union was discriminatory on the basis of race and therefore unlawful under Title VII of the Civil Rights Act of 1964. The program established a craft training plan in the plant that would accept applicants who wished to participate, with selections based on seniority. Within the overall plan was the requirement that 50 percent of those selected were to be minority group members until the level of participants met some approximation of the local population. The language of Title VII makes clear that, absent a finding of past discrimination, hiring quotas cannot be imposed on a business, but there was some question whether voluntary programs were also prohibited.

The case turned on the intent of the statute. The law had undergone a lengthy debate and a number of compromises during its development. Was the statute meant to bring an end to discrimination on the basis of race against minority groups and to permit voluntary efforts to eliminate the effects of past discrimination? Or was the statute meant to cut off any consideration of race in the future unless there was a specifically proven violation, in which case a race-conscious equitable remedy could be imposed by a court? Justice Brennan, writing for the Court, argued the former. Justice Rehnquist wrote for himself and Chief Justice Burger, arguing the latter view of the purpose of the statute.

In some instances, of course, the other branches may conclude that the courts have misinterpreted the intent of legislation and may reverse those judicial rulings with new statutes. For example, the Supreme Court issued a number of rulings in 1989, interpreting the Civil Rights Act of 1964 in ways that would have made it extremely difficult to use the statute to identify and remedy discrimination. Although there was a Congress with Democratic majority and a Republican president, George H. W. Bush, there was broad agreement that the Court had erred. A process was quickly launched that resulted in the Civil Rights Act of 1990 which was vetoed by the president with a request for further negotiations that could produce an acceptable bill. Congress obliged and the next year the Civil Rights Act of 1991 was signed into law. Congress announced in Section 2 its finding that "the decision of the Supreme Court in *Wards Cove Packing Co. v. Atonio,* 490 U.S. 642 (1989) has weakened the scope and effectiveness of Federal civil rights protections" and declared in Section 3 that its intention was "to respond to recent decisions of the Supreme Court by expanding the scope of relevant civil rights statutes in order to provide adequate protection to victims of discrimination."[81]

Some recent presidents have contended that they too should have a voice in discussions of legislative history. While many presidents have used signing statements or veto messages to air their approval of or disagreement with legislation action, some have tried to take a more systematic approach. The Reagan administration worked diligently to have a careful process of detailed presidential signing statements and then to seek to have those published along with other legislative history information in U.S. Code Congressional and Administrative news, and the Bush administration continued that practice. These presidents did not, however, succeed in obtaining any kind of legal force for their interpretations of legislative intent. However, it would be a mistake to underestimate the importance of these presidential signing statements. Consider the following examples.

President George H. W. Bush signed P.L. 102-104, the Energy and Water Development Appropriations Act of 1992. But in so doing, he issued a signing statement that reads in part:

> Sections 304 and 506 of the Act raise constitutional concerns. Section 304 would direct the Secretary of Energy, "to the fullest extent possible," to ensure that 10% of the funds for the Superconducting Super Collider go to various institutions that are defined by their racial composition. To the extent that important governmental objectives are not clearly identified as the basis for such designations, they may raise constitutional concerns. I therefore direct the Secretary, as part of his obligation, to implement section 304 "to the fullest extent possible," to administer the section in a constitutional manner.[82]

Although couched in guarded language, it is clear that the president has declared the affirmative action contracting provisions of the statute unconstitutional and has directed the Secretary of Energy not to implement these presumptively unconstitutional provisions. In other statutes where the interpretations are not quite as stark, the interpretations and instructions given by the president will shape the initial implementation of a statute. Since such early actions become part of a pattern and practice of agency behavior over time, there is every likelihood that such presidential wishes indirectly become a factor in what the courts understand to be contemporaneous administrative construction.

President George W. Bush's administration took a cue from his predecessors', but made even more frequent and wide-ranging use of signing statements. He also used signing statements to attack provisions with which he disagreed, such as affirmative action policies. It became standard during Bush's first term for his signing statements to signal opposition to such programs with a reference to the Fifth Amendment's due process clause. For example, in the Export-Import Bank Reauthorization Act of 2002 statement, the president used what was to become formulaic language for rejection of affirmative action provisions. Referring to Section 7(b) of the legislation, the statement announced that: "The executive branch shall carry out Section 7(b) . . . in a manner consistent with the requirements of equal protection under the Due Process Clause of the Fifth Amendment to the Constitution."[83] The Supreme Court had determined as far back as 1954 that the Fifth Amendment due process clause incorporated the concept of equal protection of the law and therefore prohibited discrimination.[84] Since the Bush administration had made clear its view that affirmative action programs were a violation of equal protection of the laws, the use of the language about the Fifth Amendment meant that the administration would treat legislative provisions requiring or suggesting affirmative action accordingly. It employed this formula 15 times during the first Bush term of office.

Actually, the George W. Bush administration issued some 108 signing statements during its first term, which contained no less than 505 constitution challenges to various provisions of legislation adopted by Congress even though the president chose to sign the bills into law rather than issue a formal veto.[85] In one signing statement on the Consolidated Appropriations Act of 2004, the White House issued 32 constitutional objections and indicated that the administration would implement the statute in a manner consistent with its interpretation of what was constitutionally appropriate. The president said: "Many provisions of the CAA are inconsistent with the constitutional authority of the President to conduct foreign affairs, command the Armed Forces, protect sensitive information, supervise the unitary executive branch, make appointments, and make recommendations to the Congress. Many other provisions unconstitutionally condition execution of the laws by the executive branch upon approval by congressional committees."[86] The administration also repeatedly rejected mandates in legislation to provide certain kinds of information and reports, indicating that it would consider such language as requests for information rather than requirements.[87]

The Clinton administration went so far as to issue its own interpretation of a statute even though it posed no constitutional objection. This unusual reach by a president in signing a bill came in October of 1999 as Clinton signed the Defense Authorization Act for Fiscal Year 2000. The Congress had expressed repeated frustration with security lapses at nuclear facilities and particularly in connection with the operation of the Los Alamos nuclear facility with its responsibility for research and readiness of America's nuclear weapons. In the end, Congress required in the legislation the creation of the National Nuclear Security Administration, which was to work with the Secretary of Energy but have independence from that office. In no case, said the Congress, was there to be what was termed "double-hatting" in which existing DOE officials would also perform the new duties. President Clinton made it clear that he was not going to implement the law as the Congress had written it and his signing statement engaged in the very "double-hatting" Congress had prohibited when Clinton said: "Until further notice, the Secretary of Energy shall perform all duties and functions of the Under Secretary for Nuclear Security.... The Secretary is instructed to guide and direct all personnel of the National Nuclear Security Administration by using his authority, to the extent permissible by law, to assign any Departmental officer or employee to a concurrent office within the NNSA."[88] Only a few months later, further revelations came to light concerning lost laptop computers with highly classified information in them. The administration capitulated. There followed a blistering set of hearings before the Senate Armed Services committee in June 2000.[89]

While presidential signing statements have been important in a number of respects, and despite the best efforts of a number of recent presidents to have more impact, these declarations are not formally part of the legislative history in a legal sense. These statements have rarely been cited by a court in its efforts to interpret a particular statute.[90]

Even though statutes may be more easily changed than constitutional provisions, it is still impossible for those who draft legislation to foresee all the problems that might arise under the administration of a statute in the future. Neither is it possible to get a change in a statute every time a new situation develops during the implementation of a legislative enactment. For this reason, changing circumstances may also be considered in matters of statutory interpretation. The development of cable and community antenna television service provides an example. The law that established the jurisdiction of the Federal Communications Commission was enacted long before commercial television in any form was available. When the earliest cable technology was ready to put into service, the question arose whether the FCC could regulate cable under the law. The Commission concluded that the regulation of the new technology was reasonably ancillary to its other specifically defined duties and fell within its jurisdiction. The Supreme Court agreed.[91]

Common Law: A Form of Reasoning and a Body of Law   Case law or common law development is a somewhat different problem. The techniques of common law analysis are used in all judicial decisionmaking in an Anglo-American legal system, but primarily these methods developed when there were no statutes or legislative enactments to apply to new cases. Common law decisionmaking involves the classification of facts and the application of rules found in existing law and applied through a process of analogy either directly or with some changes to fit the different circumstances of a particular set of facts.

As a judge prepares to hear a case, he or she looks to the briefs to determine whether there is a specifically applicable statute or court precedent that might be applied to the present case. In some instances, referred to as "cases of first impression," there is no precedent that is sufficiently helpful in resolving the case before the court. For example, there was reference earlier in the chapter to the first case in which there was a contest over parental rights in a case involving a surrogate mother. The woman signed a contract with a couple to be paid a fee plus her medical expenses in return for which she would be artificially inseminated, carry the fetus to term, deliver the baby, and then surrender her parental rights to the couple. However, after the baby was born, the woman decided that she did not wish to relinquish her rights, and a long series of very difficult and contentious events led the surrogate mother and the couple into a New Jersey courtroom to resolve the question of who would have custody and parental rights for a child who was referred to in the litigation as "Baby M."[92] There was no statute that addressed the problem and no precedent. It was a case of first impression. In such cases, the judge must develop a rule based on the law as it is applied in other jurisdictions or other related but different areas of the law.

At argument the advocates attempt to convince the judge that a favorable case is the appropriate precedent. Thus, in the Baby M case, the attorney for the couple argued in favor of the use of contract law. The surrogate mother had entered into an agreement as a competent and informed adult, they contended, and was therefore obligated to adhere to its terms. The surrogate mother's attorney answered that this was a case that clearly ought to be treated as a custody case, using the well-established best interest of the child standard that is normally applied in such cases. Besides, they argued, to apply contract law would be tantamount to legalizing the practice of selling babies. The trial court rejected the surrogate's argument, but attempted to combine the legal standards at least to some extent.

> [T]his court concludes and holds that the surrogate-parenting agreement is a valid and enforceable contract pursuant to the laws of New Jersey. The rights of the parties to contract are constitutionally protected under the 14th Amendment of the United States Constitution. This court further finds that Mrs. Whitehead has breached her contract in two ways: 1) by failing to surrender to Mr. Stern the child born to her and Mr. Stern and 2) by failing to renounce her parental rights to that child....
>
> An agreement between parents is inevitably subservient to the considerations of best interests of the child. The welfare of a child cannot be circumscribed by an agreement of the parents.... It must follow that "best interests" are paramount to the contract and this court must answer a best interests inquiry if it is to specifically perform the surrogate-parenting agreement.[93]

The trial court issued a judgment and opinion which relied heavily on the contract aspect:

1. The surrogate parenting agreement of February 6, 1985, will be specifically enforced.

2. The prior order of the court giving temporary custody to Mr. Stern is herewith made permanent. Prior orders of visitation are vacated.

3. The parental rights of defendant Mary Beth Whitehead are terminated.

4. Mr. Stern is formally adjudged the father of Melissa Stern.[94]

The state supreme court overturned that ruling. "We invalidate the surrogacy contract because it conflicts with the law and public policy of this State."[95] That court found that such a contract does indeed amount to the selling of babies and is not valid. Moreover, the Supreme Court concluded that it was also against good policy. The only valid way to treat the case, then, was as a matter of custody law under the best interest of the child standard. The surrogate mother's rights were restored though custody might remain with the father. Visitation issues would have to be worked out by the trial court after further hearings.

In a later California case, however, the factual situation was different. In that case, a surrogate mother was not artificially inseminated, but instead agreed to have an embryo implanted and then carry the fetus to term. In that case, the California court concluded that the question that had to be answered before any other law could be applied was whether the surrogate was the mother of the child. The court applied existing paternity law in the state and concluded that since blood tests demonstrated that the surrogate was not the biological mother under the existing law applied to determine parental responsibility, she had no parental rights.[96]

It should be clear from these examples that cases of first impression can be very difficult. The task is made all the more challenging where there is no statute that was truly designed for the type of problem before the court. There was a baby in the courtroom who needed to go home with someone and the judge had to make that determination.

Basically, common law reasoning requires the judge to undertake a process of discovery, synthesis, and analogy. The facts of various precedents advanced by the parties in the case are studied to determine whether they are sufficiently like the pending case to be appropriate precedents. The motivating theory is that the law should treat like parties similarly in like situations. If a judge determines that a particular case is applicable, he or she must analyze that case to synthesize from the opinion what is known as the rule of the case. That is, he or she must determine a specific rule or test that was the basis of the decision in the precedent case.

Such analysis can be quite difficult, for a number of reasons. Among them, one must recall that judges frequently compromise or add explanatory materials in their opinions to get approval of colleagues and the acquiescence of the parties to the case. Thus, some of the material in the opinion is necessary to the holding in the case while the remainder of the opinion is extra information. The former is known in the law as the *ratio decidendi* and the latter as *obiter dictum*. Much of the discussion in legal cases and law review literature concerns differences of opinion about just what parts of the opinion are essential and therefore applicable as precedent and which are mere *dicta*.

Having developed the rule of the precedent case, the judge must apply that rule by analogy to the case at hand. Sometimes the fit is a good one and the answer to the problem before the court is easily resolved. However, it is rare that there is an exact fit. In the first place, if there is a clear precedent, a competent attorney would advise a client of that fact and advise against litigation. Second, no two cases are ever exactly alike. Hence, one frequently finds legal decisions resting on the ability of one side to differentiate existing precedents from the case at hand. If the rule of the earlier case does not easily fit, the judge must decide whether the earlier rule can be modified to apply to the new case. If not, the judge must craft a new rule and justify it. If a modification is necessary, it is incumbent on the judge to justify that change in approach.

Consider the following simple example. Assume that one was a judge when the first automobile rear-end collision occurred. There is no statutory guidance with which to determine which party in the accident will be held responsible for any damages in the collision. From an examination of other areas of law, one concludes that a driver should be in control of his or her vehicle and that a vehicle that approaches from the rear is required to avoid the accident or face a presumption of liability for failure to control the car. Assume that a similar case arises later. Unlike the first incident, this does not involve a stopped vehicle being struck from the rear by an approaching car. Instead, a driver backs out of a driveway that is partially obstructed by shrubbery in the early evening. The car has defective backup lights and is struck from behind by another car. The differences between the two situations are important. In the second abstract case, there are several possible options. One might still apply the rule that the driver approaching from the rear should have had the last clear chance to avoid the accident and is therefore liable. The judge might hold that the rule of the first case does not apply because there both vehicles were clearly in the mainstream of traffic, whereas here one vehicle failed to exercise due care in entering the roadway. Another option would be to find the driver approaching from the rear responsible, but hold that that driver's responsibility should be mitigated by the contributory negligence of the driver whose defective vehicle improperly blocked the roadway.

Reading Judicial Opinions: A Search for Reasoning, Not Just Reasons

The institutional, legal reasoning, opinion-crafting, and jurisprudential factors come together in the judicial opinion. For the beginner, there are several points to consider in approaching opinions. At the end of the day, the core concern will be the reasoning that the author of the opinion employed to get from the issue that was presented to the conclusion the court reached. That is important because we expect that the same logic will be used in a similar case in the future and can govern our behavior accordingly.

The first task in reading the opinion is to attempt to understand the precise facts that gave rise to the suit and the stages of legal action through which the case has moved on its way to its present position. Second, consider the issues in the case. More precisely, what questions has the court been asked to address in the case and which questions has it answered? What was the court's response to each of those questions? We then seek to understand and outline the court's logic. We look for the premise from which the judge proceeded and then try to follow the links in the chain of reasoning that takes the judge from that point to the statement of the particular standard, test, or rule that is to be applied. We then read to determine how the court applied that standard to the current case. As the reader moves through this analytic process, part of the task is to understand what is essential to the holding in the case and what may be classified as *dicta*. It is important to be clear about the distinction between a holding in the case—that is, the ruling on the key point of law—and the disposition—what is to happen with the case after the ruling. Look for doctrinal development: Are there tests or rules used or developed that seem relatively detailed and fit into a pattern of cited precedents? Finally, consider the judge's view of the policy implications in a particular opinion.

THE JUDICIARY AS A POLICYMAKING BRANCH OF GOVERNMENT

Thus far we have approached the law in action from the perspective of a particular judge on a specific court attempting to resolve a case. It is also important to consider courts from a more general perspective as parts of the judiciary and the judiciary as part of the government. That is, it is important to understand some of the relationships among courts as well as between courts and other branches of government at the federal, state, and local levels.

Intercourt Relations

Judges are important political actors in government. The decisions delivered by courts are exercises in policymaking.[97] The ideological rhetoric and political games that are played by politicians and lawyers who roundly condemn judges for making law, but get paid professionally for attempting to get the judges to do precisely that on behalf of their clients is not useful. While it is true that judges have a task different from that of legislators or executive officers, it is nevertheless true, particularly in Anglo-American legal systems, that judges make law, which means they make policy.

That said, the judiciary is not a monolith, nor is it a neatly defined hierarchy in which the lines of authority are clearly defined and well separated.[98] Different courts have different procedures for the appointment of judges,[99] serve widely diverse communities,[100] and approach decisionmaking from different practical if not jurisprudential perspectives. The case load and case mix faced by various courts influence the conditions in which the judges in that court work. Some judges are secure in what amounts to life tenure, legally enforced institutional independence, and stable, if sometimes inadequate, support budgets. Other judges must stand for reelection, are staffed by patronage appointees who may or may not be professionally competent and who are not necessarily stable occupants of an office, and face budgets that are affected by county governments, disputes in the state legislature, and the vagaries of property tax policy. These political and administrative factors shape the politically complex relations among judges and courts. For the present, consider the following two aspects of judicial politics.

The decision regarding the judge or court with which one files suit is not necessarily a neutral or narrow legal question. Two important major determinants of forum selection are political in nature. First, interest groups have learned that litigation can be an effective tactic to achieve their ends where appeal to a legislative body or an administrative agency appears unlikely to be successful.[101] To improve the chances of a favorable outcome, an interest group—such as an environmental group, a civil rights organization, or a business group—may select a particular jurisdiction because of certain political conditions in the area or special legal factors that operate there.[102] If a case can be shaped in a favorable manner, the likelihood of a particular outcome may be considerably enhanced. Second, there is outright forum shopping by many groups, businesses, and institutions. Forum shopping—the selection of a forum in which to raise a suit—is based on analyses of the personal or jurisprudential proclivities of the judges sitting in a particular court and the political forces in the environment that operate to dispose judges favorably toward the party bringing the suit.[103] It was no accident that tobacco companies challenged Environmental Protection Agency findings regarding the dangers of secondhand smoke in a court in North Carolina. There is no allegation of bias on the part of judges there, but there is an awareness of the political environment. Another example is the selection of some Bible Belt locations for major prosecutions of obscenity charges.[104] The classic example in administrative law has been the tendency of petrochemical groups to challenge federal government regulations in New Orleans.[105]

Of course, there is another and very different aspect to the forum issue. State legislatures and the Congress sometimes require that challenges to agency policymaking be brought at a court in the capital. That is convenient in a number of respects, but it also means that a farmer or small business owner from a distant community may be at a disadvantage compared to well-organized interest groups who operate in the capital. The costs and inconvenience of coming to the capital are not small matters, even in some states, let alone at the national level.

In addition to the problems of forum selection, important questions arise in the area of what is called "impact analysis."[106] As one scholar of the judiciary has said, "The Constitution may mean what the Supreme Court says it does, but Supreme Court opinions mean what the district court judges say they mean."[107] When the Supreme Court renders a decision, the case is not at an end. Appellate courts do not speak to the individuals in the case as much as they do to the lower courts. The decision directs a lower court to correct an error or to take some further action. Not all Supreme Court decisions have the impact they were expected to produce. Lower courts can use a number of tactics to evade higher court rulings.[108] One of the best-known problems of impact has been evasion of school desegregation rulings.[109]

As Louis Fisher has explained, a ruling by a court does not necessarily signal an end to a dispute. It may simply be one step in an ongoing "constitutional dialogue."[110] Fisher's point is that the legislature may very well respond to a court ruling by adopting a revised statute and a president may react by instructing executive agencies to proceed according to the administration's interpretation of that new law. That is precisely what happened, for example, when the Congress reacted to a number of Supreme Court rulings under civil rights statutes in the late 1980s, as noted earlier in this chapter. Congress and the president, including members from both political parties, conducted negotiations for nearly two years, ultimately producing the Civil Rights Act of 1991, deliberately designed to reverse by statute those Supreme Court rulings. However, President Bush, frustrated by his inability to get all that he wanted from Congress, attempted to reinterpret the statute with a presidential signing statement at the time he signed the legislation into law.[111] And the process goes on!

The Judiciary and Other Parts of Government

For these and other reasons, it is clear that judicial policymaking is also very much affected by the relationships among courts and other branches and levels of government. Federal courts, for example, are part of the political process.[112]

A host of federal district court rulings on school busing to remedy racial segregation and intervention in unequal provision of government services at the state and local levels indicate just how political an environment these judges face.[113] Circuit Courts of Appeals must attempt to resolve some of the differences among circuits and deal with other problems, such as appeals from rulings made by the president or by administrative agencies.[114] State supreme courts are the ultimate arbiters of the law of their respective states, but they must also deal with various branches of the federal government when there is alleged to be a conflict between federal law and state law.[115] Finally, the local courts often face the most direct effect of the political environment since they are not afforded the isolation and academic calm of the appellate courts.[116] Judges at the local level must face highly charged issues of fact and law in an emotion-laden and politically volatile atmosphere. Whether the political relationships between these judicial tribunals and other actors on the political scene are major open conflicts or subtle pressures, they are factors that mold the cases and the decision environment within which the law develops.

SUMMARY

When legal challenges are launched, the law in books is debated. But the debate becomes a product of other factors in addition to the letter of the law. These influences on the law shape the law in books into the law in action. Among the influences one must consider is the jurisprudential perspective of the judges who decide the case. There are many views on the nature and purpose of the law and each jurist is influenced, often unconsciously, by his or her own approach to these conceptions of law. The analytical tools and rules used by judges to resolve cases also shape the law in action. Some of the constraints on decisionmaking are institutional, such as rules of self-restraint. Other tools are conventions on the manner in which judges are to interpret constitutions, statutes, and cases. In addition to the techniques of legal reasoning, there are other factors to be considered, such the need to develop consensus in support of a decision among a judge's colleagues.

Finally, decisionmaking in court does not take place in a political vacuum. Complex and delicate political factors are part of the decision environment. Some of these result from the problem of maintaining cooperation among courts at various levels of government and in different parts of the nation. Still other political variables result from the important and sometimes fragile relationships between courts and other actors in the political environment at all levels of government. An understanding of public law and public administration requires a sensitivity for both the law in books and the law in action.

NOTES

1. Lon Fuller, "The Case of the Speluncean Explorers," 62 *Harvard L. Rev.* 616 (1949).

2. Another case raises a number of these questions and adds a variety of others. See Lon Fuller, "The Case of the Grudge Informer." in Fuller, *The Morality of Law* (New Haven: Yale University Press, 1969), p. 245–53.

3. *In re Baby M,* 525 A.2d 1128 (NJ 1987), rev'd 537 A.2d 1227 (NJ 1988).

4. *K.M. v. E.G.,* 37 Cal. 4th 130; 117 P.3d 673 (CA 2005); *Elisa B. v. Superior Court of ElDorado County,* 37 Cal. 4th 108; 117 P.3d 660 (CA 2005); *Kristine H. v. Lisa R.,* 37 Cal. 4th 156; 117 P.3d 690 (CA 2005).

5. *Washington v. Glucksberg,* 521 U.S. 702 (1997).

6. Alexander Hamilton, James Madison, and John Jay, *The Federalist Papers* (New York: Mentor, 1961), p. 284–88.

7. "Transcript: Day Two of the Roberts Confirmation Hearings," *Washington Post,* September 13, 2005, at http://www.washingtonpost.com/wp-dyn/content/article/2005/09/13/AR2005091300876.html, as of September 25, 2005.

8. *Id.*

9. See generally *Lawrence v. Texas,* 539 U.S. 558 (2003); *Planned Parenthood of Southeastern Pennsylvania v. Casey,* 505 U.S. 833 (1992).

10. For a further discussion of the purposes of law, see Harold Berman and William Greiner, *The Nature and Functions of Law* (Mineola, NY: Foundation Press, 1972).

11. These schools are described differently by various scholars of jurisprudence. Anyone wishing to pursue this line of inquiry would do well to survey some of the leading texts in jurisprudence, including George W. Paton and David P. Derham, *A Textbook of Jurisprudence,* 4th ed. (London: Oxford University Press, 1972); Julius Stone, *The Province and Function of Law* (Cambridge: Harvard University Press, 1950); Carl J. Friedrich, *The Philosophy of Law in Historical Perspective,* 2nd ed. (Chicago: University of Chicago Press, 1963); George C. Christie, *Text and Readings on Jurisprudence—The Philosophy of Law* (St. Paul: West Publishing, 1973); and Roscoe Pound, *An Introduction to the Philosophy of Law* (New Haven: Yale University Press, 1954), particularly the bibliography, p. 169–87.

12. An edited collection of the most apropos writings by these authors is Clarence Morris, ed., *The Great Legal Philosophers* (Philadelphia: University of Pennsylvania Press, 1971).

13. See e.g., E. S. Corwin, "The 'Higher Law' Background of American Constitutional Law," 42 *Harvard L. Rev.* 149 (1928–29) and Carl L. Becker, *The Declaration of Independence: A Study in the History of Political Ideas* (New York: Vintage Books, 1958).

14. Morris, *supra* note 12, at p. 56–79.

15. Fuller, *supra* note 2.

16. Morris, *supra* note 12, at p. 335–63. See also Pound, *supra* note 5.

17. *Id.,* at p. 289–300. Maine's major contribution was *Ancient Law* (London: Dent, 1972). Savigny's works were *Law of a People as an Emanation of Its Common Consciousness* (1814), *History of the Roman Law in the Middle Ages* (1815–31), and *The System of Roman Law* (1840–48).

18. Morris, *supra* note 12, at p. 532–37. See also Pound, *supra* note 11.

19. Roscoe Pound, "The Scope and Purpose of Sociological Jurisprudence," 25 *Harvard L. Rev.* 487, 516 (1912).

20. Like any aspect of a philosophical school, the quasi-economic rationality operating in Pound's sociological school can be taken to extremes. See e.g., Gordon Tullock, *The Logic of the Law* (New York: Basic Books, 1971).

21. Oliver Wendall Holmes, Jr., "The Path of the Law," 10 *Harvard L. Rev.* 457 (1918).

22. Oliver Wendall Holmes, Jr., "Natural Law," 32 *Harvard L. Rev.* 40, 41 (1918).

23. Holmes, *supra* note 21, at p. 460–61.

24. John Chipman Gray, *The Nature and Sources of Law* (New York: Macmillan, 1927), Ch. 4.

25. Jerome Frank's leading jurisprudential works include *Law and the Modern Mind* (New York: Coward-McCann Brentanos, 1930) and *Courts on Trial* (New York: Atheneum, 1971). Karl Llewellyn's most widely known work is *The Bramble Bush* (New York: Oceana, 1951).

    On the neorealists generally, see Julius Paul, *The Judicial Realism of Jerome Frank* (The Hague: Mertinus Nijhoff, 1959), and Wilfred E. Rumble, Jr., *American Legal Realism* (Ithaca, NY: Cornell University Press, 1968).

26. Jack W. Peltason, *Federal Courts in the Political Process* (Garden City, NY: Doubleday, 1955), p. 1.

27. See e.g., Walter F. Murphy, *Elements of Judicial Strategy* (Chicago: University of Chicago Press, 1964); J. Woodford Howard, *Mr. Justice Murphy: A Political Biography* (Princeton, NJ: Princeton University Press, 1968); and Martin Shapiro, "Political Jurisprudence," 52 *Kentucky L.J.* 294 (1964).

28. Walter Murphy defined a policy-oriented judge or justice as follows: "By this term I mean a Justice who is aware of the impact which judicial decisions can have on public policy, realizes the leeway for discretion which his office permits, and is willing to take advantage of this power and leeway to further particular policy aims." Murphy, *supra* note 27, at p. 4.

29. Michael Parenti, *Democracy for the Few* (New York: St. Martin's Press, 1977). On class theory relating to law, see generally Renzo Sereno, *The Rulers* (New York: Harper & Row, 1968).

30. Benjamin N. Cardozo, *The Nature of the Judicial Process* (New Haven: Yale University Press, 1921).

31. *Id.*, at p. 14.

32. *Id.*, at p. 10.

33. *Id.*, at p. 30.

34. Holmes, supra note 21, at p. 477.

35. 438 U.S. 265 (1978).

36. There were two special problems in Bakke's situation. First, while his grades and test scores were higher than some students admitted through the affirmative action program, it is not clear that he would have been admitted on the scholastic basis even if there had been no such program. Second, many medical schools might have considered his age a problem.

37. See *Adarand v. Pena,* 515 U.S. 200 (1995); *Richmond v. Croson,* 488 U.S. 469 (1989).

38. *Gratz v. Bolling,* 539 U.S. 244 (2003) and *Grutter v. Bollinger,* 539 U.S. 306 (2003).

39. On desegregation, see *Brown v. Board of Education of Topeka, Kansas, I,* 347 U.S. 483 (1954); *Brown v. Board of Education of Topeka, Kansas, II,* 349 U.S. 294 (1955); *Cooper v. Aaron,* 358 U.S. 1 (1958); *Green v. County School Bd.,* 391 U.S. 430 (1968); *Alexander v. Holmes County, Mississippi,* 396 U.S. 1218 (1969); *Swann v. Charlotte-Mechlenburg Board of Education,* 402 U.S. 1 (1970); *Milliken v. Bradley,* 418 U.S. 717 (1974); *Board of Ed. of Oklahoma City v. Dowell,* 498 U.S. 237 (1991); *Freeman v. Pitts,* 503 U.S. 467 (1992); *Missouri v. Jenkins,* 515 U.S. 70 (1995). On prisons and mental health, see *Helling v. McKinney,* 509 U.S. 25 (1993); *Holt v. Sarver,* 300 F.Supp. 825 (EDAR 1969); *J.L. v. Parham,* 412 F.Supp. 112 (MDGA 1976); *Pennhurst State School and Hospital v. Halderman,* 451 U.S. 1 (1981); *Rhodes v. Chapman,* 452 U.S. 337 (1981); *Wyatt v. Stickney,* 325 F.Supp. 781 (MDAL 1971). I have dealt with these situations at length in Cooper, *Hard Judicial Choices* (New York: Oxford, 1988). See also Frank M. Johnson, Jr., "The Role of the Judiciary with Respect to the Other Branches of Government," in Walter F. Murphy and C. Herman Prichett, eds., *Courts, Judges, and Politics: An Introduction to the Judicial Process,* 3rd ed. (New York: Random House, 1979), p. 66–71.

40. *Sierra Club v. Morton,* 405 U.S. 727, 742, n. 2 (1972), Justice Douglas dissenting.

41. *First National Bank v. Bellotti,* 435 U.S. 765 (1978).

42. *Ashwander v. Tennessee Valley Authority,* 297 U.S. 288 (1936), Justice Brandeis concurring.

43. *Baker v. Carr,* 369 U.S. 186, 198 (1962). See also Laurence H. Tribe, *American Constitutional Law* (Mineola, NY: Foundation Press, 1978), §§3-7-3-27.

44. "The fundamental aspect of standing is that it focuses on the party seeking to get his complaint before a federal court and not on the issues he wishes to have adjudicated. The 'gist of the question of standing' is whether the party seeking relief has 'alleged such a personal stake in the outcome of the controversy as to assure that concrete adverseness which sharpens the presentation of issues upon which the court so largely depends for illumination of difficult constitutional questions.' ... In other words, when standing is placed in issue in a case, the question is whether the person whose standing is challenged is a proper party to request an adjudication of a particular issue and not whether the issue itself is justiciable." *Flast v. Cohen,* 392 U.S. 83, 99 (1968).

45. Frank, *Courts on Trial, supra* note 25, Ch. 6.

46. *Muskrat v. United States,* 219 U.S. 346 (1911). See also Tribe, *supra* note 43, at §3-10.

47. *Raines v. Byrd,* 521 U.S. 811 (1997).

48. *Bowsher v. Synar,* 478 U.S. 714 (1986).

49. *Clinton v. City of New York,* 524 U.S. 417 (1998).

50. An exception to this rule in the judicial proceeding is a declaratory judgment, under which it is sometimes possible to obtain from a judge a declaration of the rights and obligations of people before the court. 28 U.S.C. §2201. This is true even though as of the time of the suit there has been no direct legal injury. But declaratory judgments are exceptions to the general rule and usually require a showing that there will be irreparable harm to the person before the court if declaratory relief is not granted.

51. *DeFunis v. Odegaard,* 416 U.S. 312 (1974).

52. See generally, *McCarthy v. Madigan,* 503 U.S. 140 (1992); *Coit Independent Joint Venture v. FSLIC,* 489 U.S. 561 (1989); *McKart v. United States,* 395 U.S. 185 (1969).

53. On the appellate process generally, see Frank M. Coffin, *On Appeal: Courts, Lawyering, and Judging* (New York: W.W. Norton, 1994).

54. *Baker v. Carr,* 369 U.S. 186, 217 (1962).

55. Hamilton, Madison, and Jay, *Federalist 78, supra* note 6, at p. 465. See also Alexander M. Bickel, *The Least Dangerous Branch* (Indianapolis: Bobbs-Merrill, 1975), Ch. 1.

56. John P. Frank, "Political Questions," in Edmund Cahn, ed., *Supreme Court and Supreme Law* (New York: Simon & Schuster, 1971), p. 37. See also Charles G. Post, *The Supreme Court and Political Questions* (New York: Da Capo Press, 1969).

57. See *Gratz v. Bolling* and *Grutter v. Bollinger, supra* note 38. On the origins of what has sometimes been called the two-tier test, see *San Antonio Independent School District v. Rodriguez,* 411 U.S. 1 (1973).

58. See e.g., *Rescue Army v. Municipal Court,* 331 U.S. 549 (1947).

59. http://www.supremecourtus.gov/, as of September 23, 2005. The link from the Supreme Court site for briefs is to the American Bar Association's Preview of U.S. Supreme Court Cases site, at http://www.abanet.org/publiced/preview/briefs/home.html, as of September 23, 2005.

60. For in-depth consideration of this process prepared for a wide audience, see Anthony Lewis, *Gideon's Trumpet* (New York: Random House, 1964), and Alan F. Westin, *The Anatomy of a Constitutional Law Case* (New York: Macmillan, 1958). To see the process more from the vantage point of the judge, see Leon Friedman, ed., *United States v. Nixon: The President Before the Supreme Court* (New York: Chelsea House, 1974).

61. Excerpts from arguments before the Court were published in *United States Law Week – Supreme Court* (Washington, DC: Bureau of National Affairs, 1958–date).

62. At http://www.supremecourtus.gov/oral_arguments/argument_transcripts.html, as of September 23, 2005.

63. *Grutter v. Bollinger, supra* note 38, at 333–334.

64. For a comprehensive treatment of legal reasoning, see Lief Carter, *Reason in Law* (Boston: Little, Brown, 1979).

65. Edward Levi, *An Introduction to Legal Reasoning* (Chicago: University of Chicago Press, 1949).

66. *Marbury v. Madison,* 5 U.S. (1 Cranch) 137 (1803).

67. U.S. Constitution, Article II, §2.

68. See e.g., *Dames & Moore v. Regan,* 453 U.S. 654 (1981); *United States v. Pink,* 315 U.S. 203 (1942); *United States v. Belmont,* 301 U.S. 324 (1937); and *B. Altman & Co. v. United States,* 224 U.S. 583 (1912).

69. *Chaplinsky v. New Hampshire,* 315 U.S. 568 (1942).

70. James Madison, *Notes on Debates in the Federal Convention of 1787* (Athens: Ohio University Press, 1966).

71. Max Farrand, *The Framing of the Constitution of the United States* (New Haven: Yale University Press, 1913), and Max Farrand, ed., *Records of the Federal Convention of 1787, rev. ed., 4 vols.* (New Haven: Yale University Press, 1966).

72. Robert A. Rutland, *The Birth of the Bill of Rights, 1776–1791* (Chapel Hill: University of North Carolina Press, 1955).

73. Jonathan Elliott, *Debates in the Several States on the Adoption of the Federal Constitution as Recommended by the General Convention at Philadelphia in 1787,* 2nd ed. (New York: Burt Franklin, 1888).

74. Hamilton, Madison, and Jay, *supra* note 6.

75. See e.g., Robert Wood, *The Creation of the American Republic, 1776–1787* (Chapel Hill: University of North Carolina Press, 1969).

76. *McCulloch v. Maryland,* 17 U.S. (4 Wheat.) 316 (1819).

77. *Griswold v. Connecticut,* 381 U.S. 479 (1965).

78. See Levi, *supra* note 65, and Carter, *supra* note 64. See also William O. Douglas, "Judges and Legislators," in Alan F. Westin, ed., *The Supreme Courts: Views from Inside* (New York: Norton, 1961).

79. *Chevron U.S.A. v. Natural Resources Defense Council,* 467 U.S. 837, 844 (1984); *United States v. Rutherford,* 442 U.S. 544, 553-54 (1979).

80. *United Steelworkers v. Weber,* 443 U.S. 193 (1979).

81. P.L.102-166, 105 Stat. 1071 (1991).

82. "Statement by President George Bush upon Signing H.R. 2427, August 17, 1991," 27 *Weekly Compilation of Presidential Documents* 1142 (1991).

83. 38 *Weekly Compilation of Presidential Documents* 1014 (2002).

84. *Bolling v. Sharpe,* 347 U.S. 497 (1954).

85. Phillip J. Cooper, "George W. Bush, Edgar Allan Poe, and the Use and Abuse of Presidential Signing Statements," 35 *Presidential Studies Quarterly* 515, 521 (2005).

86. 40 *Weekly Compilation of Presidential Documents* 137 (2004).

87. Cooper, *supra* note 85.

88. William Jefferson Clinton, "Statement on Signing the National Defense Authorization Act for Fiscal Year 2000," 35 *Weekly Compilation of Presidential Documents* 1927, 1928 (1999).

89. U.S. Senate, Hearing Before the Armed Services Committee, *Security Failures at Los Alamos National Laboratory,* 106th Cong., 2nd Sess. (2000). This and other disputes regarding presidential signing statements are discussed further in Phillip J. Cooper, *By Order of the President: The Use & Abuse of Executive Direct Action* (Lawrence, KS: University Press of Kansas, 2002), Ch. 7.

90. For an example of a case in which the statements were used, see *Southern Offshore Fishing Association v. Daley,* 995 F. Supp. 1411, 1427 n. 23 (MDFL 1998).

91. *United States v. Southwestern Cable Co.,* 392 U.S. 157 (1968) and a later related case, *United States v. Midwest Video,* 406 U.S. 649 (1972).

92. *In re Baby M,* 525 A.2d 1128 (NJ 1987), rev'd 537 A.2d 1227 (NJ 1988).

93. 525 A.2d, at 1166-1167.

94. *Id.,* at 1175.

95. *In the Matter of Baby M,* 537 A.2d 1227, 1234 (NJ 1988).

96. *Anna J. v. Mark C.,* 286 Cal. Rptr. 369 (CalApp 1991).

97. See generally Glendon Schubert, *Judicial Policy Making,* rev. ed. (Glenview, IL: Scott, Foresman, 1974).

98. Sheldon Goldman and Thomas P. Jahnige, *The Federal Courts as a Political System,* 2nd ed. (New York: Harper & Row, 1976), Ch. 2.

99. See Burt Neuborne, "The Myth of Parity," 90 *Harvard L. Rev.* 1105 (1977); Kenneth Dolbeare, *Trial Courts in Urban Politics* (New York: Wiley, 1967); Richard J. Richardson and Kenneth L. Vines, *The Politics of Federal Courts* (Boston: Little, Brown, 1970); and John R. Schmidhauser, *Judges and Justices* (Boston: Little, Brown, 1979).

100. See e.g., S. Sidney Ulmer, *Courts, Law and Judicial Processes* (New York: Free Press, 1981); James Eisenstein and Herbert Jacob, *Felony Justice* (Boston: Little, Brown, 1977); and James R. Klonoski and Robert I. Mendelsohn, *The Politics of Local Justice* (Boston: Little, Brown, 1970).

101. See e.g., Clement E. Vose, *Caucasians Only: The Supreme Court, the NAACP, and the Restrictive Covenant Cases* (Berkeley: University of California Press, 1959). See also Jack W. Peltason, *Fifty-Eight Lonely Men* (Urbana: University of Illinois Press, 1971).

102. For example, a challenge to petrochemical industry regulation was brought in the Fifth Circuit Court of Appeals, headquartered in New Orleans, Louisiana. See *Industrial Union Department, AFL-CIO v. American Petroleum Institute,* 448 U.S. 607 (1980).

103. See Robert Ash, "Forum Shopping Has Distinct Advantages in Seeking Declaratory Judgments on Exemptions," 51 *Journal of Taxation* 112 (1979), and Comment, "Forum Shopping in the Review of NLRB Orders," 28 *U. Chicago L. Rev.* 552 (1961).

104. See Ted Morgan, "United States versus the Princes of Porn," *New York Times Magazine,* March 6, 1977, p. 16.

105. See the discussion of *American Petroleum Institute* case in Chapter 7.

106. See Charles A. Johnson and Bradley C. Canon, *Judicial Policies: Implementation and Impact,* 2nd ed. (Washington, DC: CQ, 1995); Stephen L. Wasby, *The Impact of the United States Supreme Court* (Homewood, IL: Dorsey, 1970); and Theodore L. Becker and Malcolm Feeley, *The Impact of Supreme Court Decisions,* 2nd ed. (New York: Oxford, 1973).

107. Jack W. Peltason, *Federal Courts in the Political Process* (Garden City, NY: Doubleday, 1955), p. 14.

108. See Walter F. Murphy, "Lower Court Checks on Supreme Court Power," 53 *American Political Science Rev.* 1017 (1959); Jerry K. Beatty, "State Court Evasion of United States Supreme Court Mandates During the

Last Decade of the Warren Court," 6 *Valparaiso U. L. Rev.* 260 (1970); Bradley C. Cannon, "Reactions of State Supreme Courts to U.S. Supreme Court Civil Liberties Decisions," 8 *Law and Society Rev.* 109 (1973); and Donald E. Wilkes, Jr., "The New Federalism in Criminal Procedure: State Court Evasion of the Burger Court," 62 *Kentucky L. J.* 421 (1973).

109. See *supra* note 39.

110. Louis Fisher, *Constitutional Dialogues* (Princeton: Princeton University Press, 1988).

111. "Statement of President of the United States George Bush on Signing S. 1745, November 21, 1991," 27 *Weekly Compilation of Presidential Documents* 1701 (1991).

112. See Richardson and Vines, *supra* note 99.

113. I have dealt with these at length in *Hard Judicial Choices, supra* note 39.

114. Many administrative agency statutes permit appeals from agency rulings to the U.S. Circuit Court of appeals in Washington, D.C., or in the circuit in which one's business is headquartered.

115. See e.g., *Hodel v. Virginia Surface Mining and Reclamation Ass'n,* 452 U.S. 264 (1981).

116. See Dolbeare, *supra* note 99.

4

A History of Law
and Administration

Mr. Withers was a commissioner of sewers. During a routine inspection, Withers discovered a defect in a flood control wall that protected a small farm next to a river. The commissioner had considerable discretion in assessing a repair fee. Withers chose to assess the fee against the farm, but the resident of that property sued, claiming that the fee should have been assessed against all property owners who benefited from the flood control wall. The court held that although Withers had a great deal of latitude in performing his duties, this levy against the single property owner was an abuse of administrative discretion. The river was the Thames, the tribunal was the Court of Common Pleas, and the date was 1599.[1]

The point of the reference to *Rooke's Case,* of course, is that problems of law and administration did not begin with the creation of the Department of Homeland Security in 2002, the Environmental Protection Agency or Occupational Safety and Health Administration in the 1970s, President Johnson's Great Society programs, the expansion of social services during the 1950s, the enactment of the Administrative Procedure Act in 1946, the rise of the New Deal, the Progressive Era's reform movements, or even with the creation of the Interstate Commerce Commission in 1887. Similarly, concern over abuses of administrative discretion, efficiency and effectiveness in administration, and fear of judicialization of the administrative processes of government are not new phenomena.

There are at least two reasons for devoting attention to the historical foundations of public law and public administration. First, students and practitioners of administration ignore the historical underpinnings of their field at the risk of Santayana's dictum that those who ignore history are doomed to repeat it. Second, and of much more immediate concern for this discussion, is the fact that administrative law has evolved in an ad hoc fashion over the years without a clear understanding of its theoretical underpinnings. The developing concepts and approaches to administrative law have not been synthesized and integrated with the larger legal and governmental literature. In part, the ad hoc development of the field is a function of important historical events that have changed both theories and practices in administration.

Writing in 1941, Walter Gellhorn described the pragmatic origins of administrative law: "The striking fact is that new agencies have been created or old ones expanded not to satisfy an abstract governmental theory, but to cope with problems of recognized public concern."[2] An understanding of the concepts and practices that together comprise administrative law requires a study of the historical roots of the subject.

The history of administrative law will be divided into five periods during which practical and theoretical problems influenced the growth and development of this field of law. The first period extends from the founding of the republic to 1928. The second period is the so-called "Golden Age of Administrative Tribunals"[3]—the New Deal, World War II with its monumental administrative operations, and the postwar period, including the enactment of the Administrative Procedure Act, which remains the basic statute governing the operation of the administrative law process. The third period extends from 1950 to 1969. The fourth period begins at the end of the Johnson administration. At that time the literature on administrative law and court rulings experienced a marked change. The change was also reflected in popular responses to the energy crisis and other events of the 1970s. The final period includes the Carter administration and after, a period that can be described as a counter-bureaucracy challenge, an attack on administrative law, and the rise of new governance models with new public law and public administration challenges.

A number of significant themes and conceptual conflicts flow through these periods of development. In broad compass, one might map them as follows. During the first hundred years of the republic, we came to the realization that powerful administrative agencies were essential and turned our attention to the important problems of ensuring that administrative activities took place within an administrative justice system governed by the rule of law. During the New Deal years, theoretical discussions gave way to the practical problems of the moment. Concern for the rule of law was resolved as procedural protections against arbitrary administrative activities were developed and buttressed by increased judicial review of agency activity. In the third period, we realized that procedural regularity, general requirements for some kind of due process, and the availability of judicial review had not resolved some very basic problems of law and administration. The fourth period was marked by attempts to respond to some of the problems of the administrative justice system, with varying degrees of success. Efforts during the final period have been primarily directed toward dismantling programs and organizations rather than fixing problems and blaming administrative law and the administrative justice process for public sector problems. Ironically, even as this attack on administrative law has proceeded, the development and implementation of new policy instruments, the increasing attention to governance regimes as mechanisms to address problems and operate programs, and the character of the contemporary administrative environment have demanded more innovative and effective law and public management efforts. They have made public law issues more rather than less important.

LAW AND ADMINISTRATION IN AMERICA TO 1928

A history of administrative law is a story both of the unfolding of events and of the development of ideas. It is also an effort to meet the need for more effective process with which to govern and the simultaneous need to address issues of the legitimacy of public administration. Many of the important ideas and events that would shape the rise of administrative law in the years following the industrial revolution were products of forces that guided the early years of our nation. It is to those early foundation years that we now turn.

The Early Years: More Foundations for Modern Public Law than Most Realize

Public administration in America can be traced back to the first colonial settlements. Indeed, John Winthrop, governor of the Massachusetts Bay Colony, had been a justice of the peace in England before his departure for the New World.[4] At that time, justices of the peace in England were as much administrative officers as judicial officials.[5] The problems of administering the colonies involved both public and private matters: public insofar as the colonies were, by and large, societies of free people who entered into social compacts, and private inasmuch as they were communities founded on the authority and financing of joint stock companies or proprietors. As the colonies grew in numbers and population, it became necessary to develop structures and processes for their governance.

About 1763, following the French and Indian War, the British began to strengthen their administrative system in the colonies. Indeed, some of the reaction against British rule had to do with the scope and methods of administration by British governors and administrators, rather than their form of government.[6]

The years during which America functioned under the Articles of Confederation were administrative disasters in part because of a lack of power on which to construct an effective administrative operation.

> The government of the Confederation had run steadily down until its movements almost ceased. . . .When [Washington] entered New York late in April 1789, to become the first President under the new Constitution, he took over almost nothing from the dying confederation. There was, indeed, a foreign office with John Jay and a couple of clerks to deal with correspondence from John Adams in London and Thomas Jefferson in Paris; there was a Treasury Board with an empty treasury; there was a "Secretary at War" with an authorized army of 840 men; there were a dozen clerks whose pay was in arrears, and an unknown but fearful burden of debt, almost no revenue, and a prostrate credit.[7]

Alexander Hamilton and John Marshall experienced this dearth of administration during the Revolutionary War and under the Articles of Confederation.[8] Both became strong advocates of an effective structure for public administration during the debates over the ratification of the Constitution and in the years that followed. In fact, Hamilton, with James Madison and John Jay, wrote the leading campaign document for the Constitution, *The Federalist Papers.*[9] The argument advanced in the *Federalist,* reduced to its most basic form, was that the people needed a strong, effective government, and the proposed Constitution promised to provide such a government while establishing sufficient safeguards to ensure against abuses of power by those in positions of authority.

When the officials of the new government took office, they lost no time in constructing the various governmental units necessary to remedy the defects of the Articles of Confederation.

> In 1789, the first Congress established a complete administrative machinery for the collection of customs and duties, necessitating administrative adjudication of disputes; it provided for the payment of pensions to disabled soldiers "under such regulations as the President of the United States may direct"; granted power to the Secretary of State, the Secretary for the Department of War, and the Attorney General or any two of them to grant patents "if they shall deem the invention or discovery sufficiently useful and important"; and provided that persons trading with Indians must procure a license, and that such license shall be governed in all things touching upon said trade and intercourse by such rules and regulations as the President shall prescribe.[10]

By 1790 there was a federal regulatory statute "for protecting seamen against unseaworthy ships," with judicial action as the primary means of enforcement until a substantial administrative structure was established to deal with the problem in the mid-nineteenth century.[11] In 1797 and 1798 New York established a pair of statutes for New York City to regulate "noxious trades" that were believed to be dangerous to health, with enforcement responsibility vested in the commissioner of health, the mayor, and a judicial tribunal.[12] In sum: "Of the fifty-one major federal agencies which the Attorney General's Committee on Administrative Procedure selected for its study of the administrative process in 1941, eleven traced their beginnings to statutes enacted prior to the close of the Civil War."[13]

Chief Justice John Marshall led the Supreme Court into the nineteenth century with opinions in important cases that established the judiciary as a coequal third branch of government.[14] Two Marshall Court decisions are particularly important in the development of administrative law. *McCulloch v. Maryland,* which gave a broad interpretation to the "necessary and proper clause" of the legislative article of the Constitution, provided clear constitutional authority for Congress to create a wide variety of administrative institutions.[15] *Gibbons v. Ogden* and later cases maintained that the Article 1, §8, power to regulate interstate commerce was also to be read broadly.[16] Taken together, these two constitutional provisions provide the authority for most of the federal agencies in existence.

The Industrial Revolution and the Progressive Era:
Public Administration as Reform

Presidential leadership in public administration floundered during the term of President Andrew Jackson, whose philosophy was that no task of government was so complex that it could not be performed by the average citizen.[17] Expertise was of no value. He also held that the best administration of the people's business resulted from frequent rotation in office. These simplistic notions fell before the demands of national development and events brought about by the Civil War.

The mobilization of the nation for war and the accompanying administrative nightmares transformed the public administration. Difficulties of communication, transportation, and management of resources afflicted both North and South. One of the major results of the Civil War was increased industrialization, particularly the dramatic growth of the railroads.

The importance of public administration underwent a quantum leap in the closing decades of the nineteenth and early decades of the twentieth century. The industrial revolution brought not only new technology, but also the destruction of the insular agricultural community, the burgeoning growth of urban areas, and an increasingly complex, interrelated, and machine-oriented economy.

The Populist and Progressive reform movements were in part reactions to the social, economic, and political upheavals of the postwar period; it was the beginning of the end of what Richard Hofstadter has termed "the Agrarian Myth."[18] The Granger movement's battle with the railroads brought about state regulation of some aspects of the grain trade. It gave rise to the regulation of public utilities and the independent commissions designed to carry out that function. That, in turn, was a major factor in the creation of the Interstate Commerce Commission (ICC) in 1887.[19] The ICC is generally acknowledged to be the prototype for the several major independent regulatory commissions established in the twentieth century.

Even though the first three decades of the twentieth century were the time of laissez faire economics, public administration assumed proportions and objectives never before attempted. Market manipulations by large corporations, monopolies, and holding companies brought about a number of investigations and were instrumental in the creation of the Federal Trade Commission (FTC) in 1914.[20] World War I brought a blurring of the lines between the public and private sectors of the economy with massive war contracting and mobilization.[21] The 1920s were prosperous years for some Americans, but they were also years of turmoil and unstable economic development.[22] The 1920s witnessed the onset of severe agricultural depression.[23]

Progressive reformers worked at all levels to rectify political corruption and to deal with the social spillovers of the new industrial age. Their efforts were based on two fundamental principles that are of continuing importance to administrative law. The first was an emerging social conscience, which required that the society through government had an obligation to deal with social problems that developed as the nation grew and industrialization increased.[24] Not content with Herbert Spencer's social Darwinism, the Progressives argued that someone must deal with the problems that the marketplace did not resolve. The second important idea that emerged from this movement was a new faith in professionalism and expertise. At the local government level, this led to the rise of the City Manager movement. This was a reform driven in significant part by corruption in contracting by local officials. The growth of the professions was seen as a promising means of applying newly discovered scientific and technological knowledge to social and economic problems.

During the years before the crash of 1929, many of the problems of law and administration that were to be of importance in the next decade were recognized. Investigations of market manipulations and other financial chicanery were undertaken.[25] Utilities began to develop, and with them came problems of regulating the companies (necessarily monopolies at that point) formed to deliver utility services.[26] Power generation policies became increasingly important with a new statute, the Federal Water Power Act,[27] created to be administered by the Federal Power Commission.

The law in general was not well structured to meet new controversies brought to court over administrative decisions. That fact was recognized as early as 1915 by Elihu Root:

> There is one special field of law development which has manifestly become inevitable. We are entering upon the creation of a body of administrative law quite different in its machinery, its remedies, and its necessary safeguards from the old methods of regulation by specific statutes enforced by the courts. As any community passes from simple to complex conditions the only way in which government can deal with the increased burdens thrown upon it is by the delegation of power to be exercised in detail by subordinate agents, subject to the control of general directions prescribed by superior authority. The necessities of our situation have already led to an extensive employment of that method. The Interstate Commerce Commission, the state public service commissions, the Federal Trade Commission, the powers of the Federal Reserve Board, the health departments of the states, and many other supervisory offices and agencies are familiar illustrations.... There will be no withdrawal from these experiments. We shall go on; we shall expand them, whether we approve theoretically or not, because such agencies furnish protection to rights and obstacles to wrongdoing which under our new social and industrial conditions cannot be practically accomplished by the old and simple procedure of legislatures and courts in the last generation. Yet the powers that are committed to these regulating agencies, and which they must have to do their work, carry with them great and dangerous opportunities of oppression and wrong. If we are to continue a government of limited powers these agencies must themselves be regulated. The limits of their powers must be fixed and determined. The rights of the citizen against them must be made plain. A system of administrative law must be developed, and that with us is still in its infancy, crude and imperfect.[28]

Some efforts were already under way to establish those principles and to deal with the problems Root noted. Indeed, the year 1928 was chosen as the end point for this period in part because it saw the publication of Ernst Freund's *Administrative Powers over Persons and Property*,[29] which was the last major work in the first phase of literature development in the area of public administration and law.

The Literature of Public Law and Public Administration Emerges:
Can We Have an Administrative Law and If So, What Must It Include?

The important authors of this period presented an agenda of problems and set the terms of political and legal discourse for years to come. They were concerned with three major questions. First, could there legitimately be such a thing as administrative law in the United States, given our Anglo-American jurisprudential heritage? Second, are these administrative bodies legitimate or are they products of constitutionally illegitimate delegations of power? Third, assuming they are constitutional, how does one go about setting limits on them such that they can be said to comport with the rule of law?

The authors of particular importance who addressed these questions were A. V. Dicey, Frank Goodnow, John Dickinson, and Ernst Freund.

The British scholar A. V. Dicey examined the British legal and constitutional tradition and concluded that: "There can be with us nothing really corresponding to administrative law."[30] By this injunction Dicey meant that the rule of law requires that any action that results in injury to the liberty or property interests of a citizen or any challenge to actions of government officials is subject to final determination in the ordinary courts according to common law.[31] Clearly, the purposes of administration and administrative law, among which were interests in the establishment of tribunals better suited than ordinary courts for resolving special administrative problems, required a different form of operation than the strict regime demanded by Dicey. He eventually abandoned that "extravagant version of the rule of law," but it was an important interpretation and had significant consequences for administrative law in the years to come.[32]

Frank Goodnow is often referred to as the father of American administrative law. Writing at the turn of the century, Goodnow dismissed Dicey's extreme argument and asserted that administrative law and major administrative agencies are not only possible but necessary.[33] The problem, according to Goodnow, is how to limit appropriately some of the discretionary authority necessarily exercised by administrators.

Any attempt to deal with possible abuses of authority by administrators must be addressed, in Goodnow's view, with a sensitivity for the complex environment within which administration takes place. Administrators execute the will of the state. When the will of the state is expressed as "unconditional commands" specifically stated and narrowly defined by the legislature, the administrator need do no more than seek out violators of the law and enforce the statute.[34] The room for administrative arbitrariness in such circumstances is small. Goodnow then attempted to come to grips with a problem not recognized by Dicey.

> There are many duties which the government is called upon to perform in a complex civilization which cannot be performed under a system of unconditional commands. No legislature has such insight or extended vision as to be able to regulate all the details in the administrative law, or to put in the form of unconditional commands rules which will in all cases completely and adequately express the will of the state. It must abandon the system of unconditional commands and resort to conditional commands which vest in the administrative officer large powers of a discretionary character. The legislature, therefore, enacts a series of general rules of administrative law which in distinction from those we have just considered may be called relative or conditional statutes.[35]

Under conditional statutes, administrators are called on to interpret the "will of the state." "In the case of conditional statutes, the administration has not merely to execute the state's will, but has as well to participate in its expression as to the details which have not been regulated by the legislature."[36]

Goodnow feared that abuses of discretion might be a problem even with efforts to control them, but he was willing to concede that at some point the requirements of administration are sufficiently important to justify some inconvenience to individuals in their dealings with administrators. Government, after all, involves the balancing of priorities. For Goodnow, the priorities were: (1) efficient operation of the people's business; (2) the protection of individual rights and interests; and (3) efforts to achieve the general goals of social welfare.

John Dickinson, writing some years later, arrayed the priorities somewhat differently than Goodnow.[37] He suggested that the law is an instrument designed to protect the individual from government.[38] Hence, individual rights and liberties are prior to administrative convenience or efficiency. Dickinson understood that there must be a significant number of administrative bodies and that these agencies will make determinations that affect the liberty and property interests of individuals. Nevertheless, he found several major aspects of the developing administrative law in need of reform.

First, he found that the existing administrative structure lacked a clear set of regular procedures sufficient to satisfy even the most charitable view of the requirements of the rule of law. "Summarizing, we can say that a regime of law requires a logically coherent system of general rules based on precedent and accepted principles of justice."[39] He saw no such logically coherent system in administrative law. Second, where he found something that approximated due process protections, Dickinson viewed the protections for the citizen to be less acceptable than those available in law courts. Common law rules of evidence and authority did not apply in a formal sense.[40] Jury trials were not available. The rules by which disputes were to be governed were often developed in the course of the resolution of the matter rather than before the fact. Third, unlike judges, administrators who drafted rules and decided cases enjoyed little independence from government or politics. Finally, the very expertise that made administrators effective rendered them myopic when it came time to draft rules of general applicability.[41]

After a long and careful analysis, Dickinson recognized the legitimacy of agencies and the administrative justice system subject to certain conditions. Administrative procedure must be regularized. Minimum due process protections must be available. A full judicial review of agency decisions must always be available as a check. "Administrative justice exists in defiance of the supremacy of law only insofar as administrative adjudications are final or conclusive and not subject to corrections by a law court."[42]

Writing in 1928, Ernst Freund suggested that administrative law was necessary, but that the problem of its inclusion in the American system of justice was the need to find and maintain appropriate grants of and limitations on administrative power.[43] In his works, Freund was interested in setting limits on discretion while allowing sufficient latitude to ensure the effective operation of government. He was primarily concerned that the legislature should be the body to limit power by ensuring the preparation of statutes that would structure and limit discretion.

In a major study published in 1917, *Standards of American Legislation,* Freund discussed some of the events and problems that required Congress to become more active in drafting new measures for regulatory purposes and to meet demands for social welfare programs.[44] In the early days it was possible for neighbors or businessmen to obtain relief in court through common law suits for fraud or nuisance.[45] But as the society changed and grew individual remedies became less feasible and legislatures were called on for regulatory legislation that required administrators for enforcement. Freund argued that the courts' inability or unwillingness to come to grips with changing social, political, and economic reality added to the pressure on the legislatures.[46] But Freund was also aware that the legislatures faced the problem of drafting major legislation in a period of laissez faire economics, when many judges would carefully scrutinize regulatory or social welfare statutes for weaknesses that would lead to their demise.

In his *Administrative Powers over Persons and Property,* Freund went further to suggest that legislatures had to construct statutes carefully to ensure that the necessary power granted to administrators would not be abused. He recognized two types of administrative powers—control and service—and two means of exercising those powers—with and without discretion. Control powers could be subdivided into enabling powers and directing powers. Enabling powers are exemplified by licensing and the like. Directing powers, or "powers of corrective intervention," are those normally ascribed to regulatory administration. Freund touched only lightly on service powers, but at that time government services and problems associated with providing them were limited compared to contemporary administrative functions.

Freund used this typology of administrative powers as a framework to deal with uses and abuses of administrative discretion. He understood that administrative discretion must be viewed as a continuum, with one end marked by a rigid impersonal system of rules bound to work hardship on those who are affected by them.[47] At the other end, one finds complete administrative arbitrariness—what Freund refers to as the "principle of unfreedom."[48] Some discretion is necessary.

> The plausible argument in favor of administrative discretion is that it equalizes the exercise of public power over private interests, permitting adjustment of varying circumstances, and avoiding undesirable standardization of restraints, disqualifications, and particularly of government.[49]

By understanding the types of power and the methods of their use and abuse, legislators can draft laws that will meet the needs for which they are created and will be administered with the appropriate degree of properly exercised discretion.

In summary, the early period of administrative law and administration presented the problems and the terms of political, social, and economic discourse for the years to come. Dicey's denial of the possibility of administrative law gave way to Dickinson's demand for justice with law through procedural reform and judicial review in administration. Goodnow and Freund made clear the reasons for the new body of law, but also raised some of the important theoretical problems that must be dealt with in constructing an acceptable administrative justice system. All recognized the need to deal with administrative discretion. However, just as the theoretical development of the field began to gain momentum, the Great Depression diverted attention to day-to-day problems of administration.

THE GOLDEN AGE OF ADMINISTRATIVE
TRIBUNALS: 1928–1950

The years from the onset of the Great Depression through the early post–World War II period were marked by a veritable explosion of administrative activity. This dramatic increase, coupled with problems noted by the authors of the earlier period, brought attempts at reform and development in administrative law. Those efforts gave rise to sharp disagreements in the literature over the new, decidedly pragmatic, approach to administrative law.

The New Deal and Administrative Law Problems: Challenges
for Those Inside Government and Criticism from Those Outside

The stock market crash of 1929 was of seminal importance for law and administration for a variety of reasons. It demonstrated the complexity and interrelatedness of the society that, until then, had prided itself on rugged individualism. Hard-working, conscientious men and women lost everything just as quickly and painfully as did the market manipulators and others who had engaged in what has been termed "predatory finance."[50] The crash also showed that while the market system did many things very well, it required some policing to ensure that the competition was indeed fair and open.[51] By the time Franklin Roosevelt took office, President Hoover's assurances that this was merely a temporary downturn in the economy, a time of market correction, were unacceptable. The government was expected to do something about the state of the economy and the social consequences of the depression.[52] President Roosevelt felt an obligation to try new techniques to meet these demands: "The country needs, and unless I mistake its temper, the country demands bold, persistent experimentation. It is common sense to take a method and try it: If it fails, admit it frankly and try another. But above all, try something."[53]

The Roosevelt administration moved on two fronts. It sought to stabilize the marketplace through several types of legislative programs including bank regulation, market regulation, agricultural incentives and controls, codes of competition developed by members of the business community under provisions of the National Industrial Recovery Act (NIRA) and related policies. President Roosevelt and his colleagues also moved on the social welfare front with jobs programs and other techniques designed to realize more personal security for individuals than could be provided within the twentieth-century American market economy.[54]

Many of the statutes enacted by the Congress during the New Deal, such as the Securities and Exchange Act, the Public Utility Holding Company Act, the Federal Power Commission legislation, and agricultural market legislation, were products of the investigations conducted and policies advocated during the twenties. But there is no doubt that the broad jurisdiction given administrative agencies of the New Deal marked a new era in public administration by virtue of the size and scope of operations.

The New Deal is properly understood as two related though distinct periods, the first and second New Deals. The dividing point is roughly set at the 1936 presidential campaign. During the first part of the New Deal there was a relatively high degree of cooperation between the federal government and the business community. After the markets stabilized and economic recovery was under way, private sector groups became disenchanted with programs and agencies established after the crash. They were no happier about other regulatory programs that had their beginnings in earlier years but were implemented during the New Deal, such as the Securities and Exchange Commission (SEC). The decline of cooperative spirit turned into outright conflict by 1936, with Roosevelt building his campaign around opposition to those he referred to as "economic royalists."[55]

The breakpoint is also important because it marked a turning point in the relationship between the Supreme Court, the New Deal administration, and Congress. Before the so-called "switch in time that saved nine," the Court had been dominated by a group of justices trained and appointed at the high point of laissez faire economic and political fervor. Citing abuses of the commerce power, the taxing and spending powers, and other provisions of the Constitution, the Court struck down several major New Deal programs.[56] However, two members of the Court switched their positions on some of the powers of the Congress and FDR was able, during the latter years of the New Deal, to appoint a majority of the members of the Court, making it a much more philosophically favorable forum for New Deal programs.[57]

The onset of World War II meant mobilization of the entire nation. Such a task required administration on an unprecedented scale. Mobilization further blurred the lines between the public and private sectors of the economy. Government contracting and government-supported scientific research and development became major areas of growth.

The end of the war, however, did not mean the end of the administrative programs created to deal with the conflagration. Education, housing, and employment were needed for thousands of returning veterans. The arrival of the United States on the scene of international politics brought with it demands for American aid in restoring the nations ravaged by war. The birth of the nuclear age created an awesome responsibility to administer peacetime uses of fissionable materials. As the nation entered the 1950s, the questions presented for discussion were whether the administrative branches of government were equal to the tasks before them and whether the law provided sufficient safeguards to ensure that a government powerful enough to meet modern needs could be controlled.

In Search of a Coherent Body of Administrative Law

In May 1933, the Executive Committee of the American Bar Association created the Special Committee on Administrative Law to come to grips with the administration explosion. Louis G. Caldwell, chairman of the committee, opened his remarks to the first session of the Special Committee by observing: "The first Session of the 73rd Congress. . .left more than the usual quota of footprints in the field assigned to our committee. In fact, last spring witnessed a more formidable legislative output than has ever before found its way into the statutes at large in time of peace."[58]

As Caldwell and his colleagues went to work, it became clear that the overriding theme of the gathering was the fear of burgeoning administrative power without clear constraints on that power sufficient to ensure responsiveness and responsibility of those in administrative positions. It was recognized that one reason for the increase in administrative tribunals was dissatisfaction with orthodox judicial proceedings and legislative actions and the need for continuity and expertness in administration.[59] Caldwell announced his intention that the committee should place the bridle of the rule of law on government agencies.[60] The conference began a study of the administrative process to be used as a basis for regularizing administrative procedure and clarifying standards for judicial review of agency decisions.

Progress in reforming the administrative justice system was slow for the next several years. Pressure for change increased with the change in the political and economic climate of the second New Deal. The Brownlow Commission criticized the agencies as a "headless fourth branch of government."[61] Roosevelt rejected that assessment and directed the Attorney General to appoint a study commission to perform a complete analysis on the state of the administrative justice system and provide recommendations. The Attorney General's Committee on Administrative Procedure was created in February 1939.[62] The committee, like other groups studying the topic, approached the subject with the assumption that the most effective way to deal with public law and public administration problems was by examining and modifying administrative procedures used in adjudications done by agencies, the procedural aspects of administrative rulemaking, and problems of judicial review of agency actions.[63]

The report of the Attorney General's Committee was published in 1941.[64] The most extensive and authoritative study produced during this period, the report had three major consequences. First, it suggested that the administrative system could be usefully and adequately dealt with by a statutory formulation of administrative procedure, which would: (1) regularize policymaking by providing orderly rulemaking procedures that allowed public participation; (2) ensure minimum due process protections where agencies adjudicate disputes (including guaranteed independence for administrative adjudicators); and (3) provide guidance for the conduct of judicial review adequate to ensure that administrative law decisions would be integrated with the larger body of law. Those suggestions were enacted into law as the McCarren-Summers Bill, now more commonly known as the Administrative Procedure Act.[65]

Although the committee never claimed that its recommendations would solve all the problems of law and administration, the statute that resulted was the only source of law that specifically applied to most areas of administrative decisionmaking by most agencies of the federal government. The APA has, unfortunately, come to be thought of as a kind of constitution of administrative law and the report itself as an administrative treatise analogous to Farrand's Records of the Federal Convention of 1787.[66] In any event, the report was a superior piece of work on law and administration and as such deserves consideration as one of the most important pieces of literature in law and administration of that period.

Also in the early postwar period, Congress adopted two key pieces of legislation that cover federal government contracting, the Armed Services Procurement Act of 1947 (ASPA)[67] and the Federal Property and Administrative Services Act of 1949 (FPASA).[68] The APA exempted contracting from its coverage. Of course, in those days, the focus of public administration was not primarily on intergovernmental service delivery. There was more focus on regulation or direct government action at the federal level. Contracting was primarily focused on purchase of goods rather than services. These characteristics would change dramatically in the years to come.

Literary Conflict Over Administrative Law Development

The efforts to develop an adequate system of administrative justice were carried out amidst a hard-fought conflict, much of it conducted in the legal literature and court opinions. The disagreement reflected the political and economic tensions of the New Deal years. Surprisingly, the discussion tended to ignore much of the literature published earlier and the history of administration before the creation of the Interstate Commerce Commission in 1887.[69] Also rather surprising was the fact that most of the arguments on both sides were fairly narrowly drawn, with a certain pragmatism, explicit in some works and implicit but still present in others. Perhaps these characteristics can be explained by the fact that the debate over the legitimacy of administrative agencies and the proposed methods to control their activities was literally a battle of professional advocates.

In general terms, the critics of administrative law as it existed during this period made two major arguments.[70] The first was that administrative agencies with the power to make rules that carried the force of law were unconstitutional because they operated on the basis of unconstitutional delegations of legislative power. The intensity of this argument varied from those who said that any authorization of rulemaking power to non-elected civil servants and political appointees exceeded the legislative power of Congress, to those who grudgingly accepted the need to delegate some authority to fill in the ambiguous terms of statutes enacted by Congress, but refused to accept broad standardless delegations of authority to administer a particular field of policy with no more direction to the agency than an admonition to act in "the public interest."

The nondelegation arguments ran along the following lines. An administrative agency exists by virtue of the statute that created it. The powers delegated by the legislature define the boundaries of agency activity. Similarly, the legislature has only the powers delegated to it by the people through the Constitution. A long-standing legal maxim holds that a person who possesses a delegated power may not delegate that power away to someone else. The people delegated the power to make laws to the legislature and that power may not be delegated away to an administrative agency. In addition to being an abuse of the legislative power, such a grant of authority to the agency would violate the separation of powers since the agency would have the power to make and enforce the law.[71] The less strident nondelegation partisans admitted some delegation was necessary because the legislature could not make sufficiently detailed statutes for all future circumstances, but they could and should do more than give administrators a blank check.

The second major attack on the rise of administrative law focused on a perceived violation of the rule of law arising from a lack of court-like protections in administrative adjudications and the so-called "combination-of-functions" problem.[72] Combination-of-functions referred to the fact that many of the agencies made rules, enforced the rules, and then adjudicated disputes arising from enforcement of the rules.

Criticism hit a high point with the "headless fourth branch" condemnation by the Brownlow Commission. James M. Landis, a leading New Dealer and member of the Securities and Exchange Commission, entered the lists in defense of administrative processes.[73] Landis began with the premise that administrative powers grew in part because of the deficiencies of the judiciary and the legislature. "Without much political theory but with a keen sense of the practicalities of the situation, agencies were created whose functions embraced the three aspects of government."[74] Specifically, Landis argued that efficient and effective responses to problems of administering the people's business could only be achieved by experts with an ongoing interest in particular policy areas. These expert administrators must have some discretion to accomplish their tasks.[75] Responding to the argument against delegation of authority, he asserted that there are tasks that government must perform. As the society becomes more complex, those tasks multiply. When legislators identify a matter that requires government action, one of two factors may result in a rather broad grant of discretion to administrators to deal with the problem. First, the issue (e.g., health code administration) may be so complex that legislators cannot possibly understand at the outset the many specific problems involved in administering a policy. Alternatively, competing interests within the legislature may agree that some kind of policy and administrative mechanism is necessary, but they may not be able to achieve consensus on details. Rather than do nothing, the legislature settles on a general statute and vests the agency involved with considerable discretion to fill in the details.

In the end, Landis seemed satisfied that the existing checks were sufficient to prevent administrative arbitrariness. He argued that because agencies specialize in rather narrow fields, they can be checked fairly quickly. Their discretion within that narrow range of activity is limited by statutes and subject to judicial review. Because judicial review is available, he asserted, administrators will take care to provide reasoned opinions in support of their decisions.

The next major defense of administrative justice came with the publication of the report of the Attorney General's Committee in 1941. On the way to its conclusions about regularization of procedures, the report noted several important aspects of law and administration worthy of further consideration. First, the committee recognized a central dilemma of administrative law. There is a basic conflict between those who demand complete standardization of procedures, such as that expected in the judicial system, and those who argue for more flexibility so that administrators may use their expertise in the changing administrative environment to accomplish the purposes for which their agencies were created. The committee recognized that neither extreme was acceptable.

Second, the committee emphasized a generally unstated fact. Most cases that arise in administrative law are disposed of informally rather than by formal procedures. The committee went so far as to label informal procedures the "lifeblood of the administrative process."[76] Third, and somewhat related to the prevalence of informal proceedings, administrative disputes involve more than two parties. It is one thing for an administrator to produce a decision satisfactory to the person or group before an agency as well as the administrator himself or herself, but quite another if the finding comes at the expense of the public interest. Since most such decisions are not made in public proceedings, it is difficult to ensure that all interests are adequately protected. Procedural regularity should help check abuses, as should judicial review, but both are better devices to ensure protection for individual participants in a dispute than they are controls to ensure that agencies are sufficiently vigorous in administering policy.[77] Ultimately, the committee sought refuge from administrative arbitrariness in the time-honored legal command-ments of procedural regularity, due process, and judicial review.

Probably the strongest defense of the contemporary administrative system was written by the director of the study for the Attorney General's Committee, Walter Gellhorn.[78] Gellhorn, like Landis, began with the premise that the large-scale administrative state exists because circumstances and existing weaknesses in traditional government structures require it.[79] The developing approach to administration and law offered expertise, continuity (which he preferred to call "specialization"), and understanding or sympathetic administration.[80] It also made possible the processing of the huge volume of disputes before the government.

Gellhorn saw contemporary administrative law in the third phase of its development. The first phase was a struggle over the legitimacy of administrative law as a field of law. The second was an inevitable growth of administration, accompanied by a call for strict judicial review. The third phase was the development of administrative procedure. He thought that development had gone well and he defended it with vigor.

Gellhorn contended that the greatest danger was that critics of administration would succeed in over-judicializing the administrative process. He argued that courts and agencies perform different governmental roles and should have different procedures tailored to their respective functions. Speci-fically, he argued in favor of informal proceedings and for flexible elements in formal proceedings. He asserted that most of the combination-of-functions arguments concerning rulemaking, enforce-ment, and adjudication were based on gross generalizations. In the first place, Gellhorn wrote, most agencies have no prosecutorial powers, and those that do rarely use them. Even where such cases arise, he insisted that there was no more reason to suspect administrators of bias or arbitrariness than judges. Beyond that, the combination-of-functions argument assumed that agencies are monoliths when in fact they are highly complex structures with many parts and some structure and operational separations among their various divisions.[81] Gellhorn summarized his view nicely as follows:

> I have attempted to show that neither the existence nor the form of the Federal administra-tive machinery is in itself an alarming phenomenon. To be sure, there is a danger that any power, once granted, may be abused by its possessor. Having recognized that fact, however, we need not conclude that power must be wholly withheld. In each instance we must decide whether the intended objective Federal control is important enough to warrant assuming the inherent risks of misgovernment....What is needed today is alert determination that the agencies shall in purpose and in method prove themselves to be efficient instruments of democratic government.[82]

Like Gellhorn, Jerome Frank was fearful of over-judicialization of the administrative process. The government and the critics of administration might "substitute a 'lawyercracy' for democracy, to turn our entire government into a government of lawyers, or a government solely by the judiciary."[83] He took issue with the idea that rigid procedural requirements would be helpful. Those who demanded rigorous checks and denied the validity of the role performed by agencies on grounds that they threatened the rule of law were, in Frank's view, infatuated with the words "a government of laws, and not of men."[84] What is needed, he wrote was "a government of laws administered by the right kind of men."[85]

> Curiously, it often happens that the very men who one day stress that truth [that public officers are human], the next day help to obscure it, by distorting the real truth contained in the phrase "a government of laws, and not of men." . . .Hypnotized by those words, we picture as an existing reality—or at least as a completely achievable ideal—a government so contrived that it matters not at all what men, at any given moment, constitute government. Such an idea is a narcotic. It is bad medicine. It does not protect us from bad government. On the contrary, it invites bad government.[86]

He argued that when one examines specific operations of particular agencies, it becomes clear that administrators are no more or no less trustworthy than judges. To the degree that the discussion focuses on the discretion used by administrators, Frank argued that it was often not the administrator who sought to exercise his or her own discretion, but rather the agency's clientele who wanted individual, differential treatment for each case. In his view, the federal government was in fact fairly meeting the requirements of basic democratic values, maintaining a balance between government power sufficient to accomplish its tasks and limits on government adequate to the maintenance of individual liberty.[87]

> It is imperative that in a democracy it should never be forgotten that public office is, of necessity, held by mere men who have human frailties.. . .To pretend, then, that government, in any of its phases, is a machine—that it is not a human affair; that the language of statutes—if only they are adequately worded—plus appeals to the upper courts, will alone do away with the effect of human weaknesses in government officials is to worship illusion. And it is a dangerous illusion.[88]

The eminent jurisprudential scholar Roscoe Pound responded to such arguments in his *Administrative Law: Its Growth, Procedure and Significance*.[89] Dean Pound set out to bury the debate over whether there can be such a thing as a powerful administrative system within a democracy. He was willing to dispose of the separation-of-powers arguments about delegation of power. Administrative agencies had "very real grievances against the common law and judicial review as developed under the common law in the United States." The imposition of overly strict rules of evidence in some areas and complete retrials on judicial review had placed intolerable burdens on administrative actions. Pound agreed that there was a need for flexibility and expertise, but he was not prepared to allow the relative youth of the field and the need for flexibility to excuse the denial of basic justice. "I am not here to preach a going back to eighteenth-century doctrines of natural rights and natural law as such. But I do insist upon the role of ideals."[90] Any body of law must be based on "a set of received ideals." The primary problem lay not in the argument over details on how to provide instrumental checks on administrators, but rather in that there was no consensus on the ideals for administrative law. In Pound's view, the nation was experiencing a "time of transition when men are struggling to adapt the machinery of justice to new conditions imperfectly grasped. . .seek[ing] short cuts through a reversion to justice without law—not without a judicial or administrative process, of course, but without authoritative precepts or an authoritative technique of applying them."[91] Until such a theoretical foundation could be established, Pound argued that judicial review would have to be used carefully and effectively to guard against abuses in the name of efficiency or expertise.

> I am not attacking administration as a means of government in the society of today nor deploring the rise of administrative justice and delegation to standards, or determinations of fact necessary to the exercise of their functions. But administration is not all of the ordering of human relations. We may pay too high a price for efficiency. We must pay a certain price for freedom; and a reasonable balance between efficiency and individual rights is that price. If the balance does not leave absolute power to administrative agencies, it does not follow that it may

not leave them enough power to function intelligently and efficiently under a government of laws and not men. I grant that a government of law must yet be a government of men. Laws govern as they are applied by men. But they may and should be applied by men according to law.[92]

The years from 1928 to 1950 may have been golden years for administrative tribunals, but a great deal of heat was engendered by the process by which the gilt was polished. The views of the efficacy of administrative law and means necessary to accomplish public purposes within the bounds of law ranged from those who rejected outright the legitimacy of the administrative justice system, notwithstanding the significant body of literature developed in the earlier years, to those who were afraid that needed discretion and flexibility would be strangled by rigid procedural requirements and exhaustive judicial review.

The ardent foes of administration were doomed from the outset. The delegation-of-powers argument had been settled years before. The first Congress gave the president authority to administer benefits to veterans of the Revolutionary War under such regulations as he saw fit to issue. In 1813, in the case of *The Brig Aurora,* the Supreme Court sanctioned the principle of delegation by the Congress.[93] Since the early years, the delegation doctrine had been tested repeatedly.[94] Administrative actions were sustained in all but three major cases, two involving the National Industrial Recovery Act: *Panama Refining Co. v. Ryan*[95] and *Schechter Poultry Corp. v. United States.*[96] The other case was in the area of coal mining.[97] The combination-of-functions argument was met in the Administrative Procedure Act by including protection for the independence of hearing examiners. Procedural regularity, due process provisions, and some availability of judicial review, although not as much as such critics as Pound would have liked, were also provided by the APA.

But the Administrative Procedure Act was a limited starting point for administrative law development. Narrow and procedural, it lacked the kind of consensus on larger ideals sought by Pound. With its enactment a new concern arose: whether the APA would be interpreted in such a manner as to render administrative agencies impotent.[98] Would the APA be sufficient to protect against abuses of power or would it prevent agencies from accomplishing the tasks for which they were designed?

FROM THE NEW DEAL TO THE NEW FEDERALISM: LAW AND ADMINISTRATION, 1950–1969

The years from early post–World War II demobilization through the decades of the 1950s and the turbulent 1960s were years of important development in law and administration. They were years of testing the Administrative Procedure Act approach to problems facing administrators in a complex administrative environment and those facing individuals and groups attempting to deal with those administrators. By 1969, the APA approach would be found wanting and the search would be underway for new answers. The evaluation of the operation of the administrative justice system during this period was affected by a reordering of academic priorities and methodologies. In government and in the larger legal community, authors who were once ardent defenders of existing administrative law became its strongest critics.

Toward a New Administrative Environment: Post-War Challenges and Responses

In his history of the years 1945 to 1960, Eric Goldman wrote:

Beneath everything, two critically important questions were pressing to be answered. One of the questions concerned affairs inside the United States: would America continue through extensions of the welfare state and welfare capitalism and through a variety of other techniques, the economic and social revolution which had marked the previous decades? The other question concerned foreign affairs: would the United States keep moving along the path marked out in the early Truman Years, a path suggested by the words "containment" and "coexistence" and one which represented a sharp departure from deep-seated American traditions?[99]

The attempt to answer these two questions shaped the environment of administration.

The war ended, but international concerns still demanded the nation's attention. The Cold War was beginning. A somewhat warmer conflict was brewing in Washington, where President Truman found himself battling congressional opponents.[100] For Truman, it was one crisis after another: Alger Hiss, Israel, China, the Berlin blockade, Joe McCarthy, and Korea.[101] When these issues captured the national limelight, administrative problems declined in importance on the policy agenda. Truman attempted to make some headway on the administrative front by calling on Herbert Hoover. The president, who had great respect for Mr. Hoover, called for a commission to study the federal administrative establishment. Congress, with a unanimous vote for the Lodge-Brown Act[102] in July 1947, created the President's Commission on Organization of the Executive Branch of Government, more popularly known as the Hoover Commission.[103] The commission's report, delivered in February 1949, called for a more streamlined administration organized to be more responsive to presidential direction.[104] Although it deferred to the 1941 Report of the Attorney General's Committee on most matters of administrative law, the report concluded: "Administrative justice today unfortunately is not characterized by economy, simplicity, and dispatch. It remains, however, a necessity in our complex economic system."[105] The commission recommended an administrative conference for further study.

By 1953, when President Eisenhower took office, there had been a number of calls for a conference on administrative law problems. As a result, questions of law and administration were included in the second Hoover Commission report, the result of the commission's work from 1953-1955.[106] The commission established the Task Force on Legal Services and Procedures staffed by leading legal scholars, several of whom had served on the Attorney General's Committee and had been instrumental in the enactment of the APA.[107] The second report, which will be treated in more detail later, was highly critical of the administrative justice system and issued 74 separate recommendations for change. Among these was a call for a major administrative conference. Congress was not generally receptive to the recommendations of the second Hoover Commission, and those advanced by the Task Force on Legal Services and Procedures fared no better than the rest.[108] The American Bar Association seemed content with the status quo; reports of meetings during this period suggest that the bar was more interested in settling into practice under the APA than in major change.[109]

The 1950s were marked by a plethora of important political, economic, and social developments. Major Supreme Court desegregation rulings were as controversial as they were necessary.[110] Joe McCarthy did not last long as a Senate power, but others on the House Un-American Activities Committee carried on the campaign of fear and intimidation with loyalty programs and strained security investigations threatening government workers.[111] In addition to foreign policy crises in Europe and the Middle East, Eisenhower was faced with a vexing administrative problem in this country: control over the growth of technology. When he left office, the president warned of the problems of administering a burgeoning military-industrial complex.

Part of that complex was a set of international relations and national security institutions that had to be managed. While many Americans were busy getting on with life in the postwar world, there was much that was changing in public affairs at all levels. The National Security Act of 1947 had produced a broad reconfiguration of foreign policy and security administration.[112] The reorganization of the military, development of the Atomic Energy Commission (AEC), creation of the Central Intelligence Agency (CIA), growing importance of the National Security Council (NSC), and a new approach to State Department operations were not items about which most Americans were interested, but the effect was to reshape and expand an entire dimension of public administration, a domain that was to become increasingly important throughout the Cold War and after as the effects of globalization penetrated into even small communities in the United States and others around the globe.

What was to become more obvious sooner was the dramatic shift in importance in administration from regulatory administration to social service delivery. Development of health, safety, and other social services had begun earlier at the local level with the Progressive era providing a particular impetus for urban reform. But social service problems during the Great Depression and the two wars that followed were national in scope and required national assistance. Suburban housing development became important. New parts of the country experienced growing pains as returning veterans relocated families to the West Coast and other places they had seen during their service days.[113] Veterans' housing, health, and educational benefits created administrative problems that were complex and numerous. By the late 1950s the baby boom came to schools, and the need for capital expenditures for schools, costs of training teachers, and attempts to ensure some uniformity in education practices added to the strain on public administration. During this period the Social Security Administration also began to experience an increase in its workload with the implementation of the Social Security Disability program and expansion in other federal programs.[114]

John F. Kennedy assumed office with the best intentions of examining and responding to problems of law and administration, as indicated first by his call for a major study with specific recommendations and later by his appointment of an administrative conference. Unfortunately, attention was again diverted by events abroad. It was post time for the space race. Kennedy's international relations skills were tested by the Soviet Union. The world went to the brink of nuclear war in the Cuban missile crisis. Other important issues during Kennedy's administration included the intensification of civil rights efforts, the Bay of Pigs fiasco, and growing involvement in the conflict in Southeast Asia.

The Johnson years saw dramatic increases in administrative activity. In particular, the "War on Poverty," which Johnson pursued as one of several routes to the Great Society, was waged in part by the use of grants and contracts that increased the complexity of intergovernmental relations.[115] The war in Vietnam, enactment and implementation of the Civil Rights Act, domestic unrest, and continued strain on human services in all areas added task after task to an already strained administrative state. Again, many of these tasks were as controversial and as difficult as they were necessary. For example, although the U.S. Commission on Civil Rights had been created in the 1950s, it was only a very limited first step in what was needed to turn the promise of equal rights for all into reality. The 1960s saw enactment of the Civil Rights Act of 1964, the Voting Rights Act of 1965, the Fair Housing Act of 1968, and a number of executive orders issued by the Kennedy and Johnson administrations that would require new organizations, such as the Equal Employment Opportunity Commission, but also less well-known developments in existing institutions, such as the Civil Rights Division of the U.S. Department of Justice and Fair Housing and Credit Section of the U.S. Department of Housing and Urban Development. As in the case of the foreign and national security arena, this was a developing field of public administration with new methods and responsibilities.

Americans were becoming more mobile and expecting basic standards of education, health care, and other services when they moved around the nation. However, different states either could not or would not provide minimum safety net standards. The national government became involved with such policies as the Elementary and Secondary Education Act of 1965 and the enactment of the Medicare program. The fact that these policy domains were traditionally and constitutionally under the control of the states meant that federal policies would depend upon a system of grants. Thus, in addition to the increasing intergovernmental and service character of government policies, the period also saw the need for administration of a range of different types of policy tools.

The burgeoning growth in science and technology, spurred by the goal of placing a man on the moon before the decade ended, and war mobilization had positive and negative consequences. Among the positive results was development of electronic technology, which advanced the state of the art in a variety of areas, but none so dramatically as the field of automated data processing. But that progress had disadvantages as well. The increased use of computers meant the development of massive data banks with information about all aspects of one's life.[116] The decade came to an end with growing political and social turmoil. The future was very much in doubt.

Intellectual Fragmentation on Administrative Law Development

Writing in 1950, James Hart asserted:

> The relationship of administrative justice to the supremacy of law is, however, but the lawyer's way of expressing the central problem not only of administrative law, but of political science as a whole. In abstract terms, that problem is the adjustment of authority and liberty. At the relatively concrete level of administrative law, it may be called the adjustment of the public and the private interest. The student who fails to approach administrative law in terms of this problem will fail to see the subject as part of political science and hence will be unable to make intelligent administrative law judgments.[117]

The relationship between practice and theory, problems of making day-to-day adjustments of the public and private interests in administration, and the interconnections among law, public administration, and political science are all important ingredients of a balanced and comprehensive perspective on the problems of public law and public administration. Unfortunately, for a variety of reasons, that synthesis of views and concepts broke down, with important consequences for the manner in which the administrative justice system operated, was evaluated, and ultimately was modified.

The attempts to meld theory and practice of administrative law development had already begun to break down during the 1930s, as Gellhorn, Landis, and others insisted that practice, not theory, should shape and must control the administrative process. Despite the criticisms of writers such as Dean Pound, many observers felt that the practical or instrumental view of administrative law prevailed and was enacted into law as the Administrative Procedure Act. Problems of adjustment of authority and liberty, or of adjustment between public and private interests, had been remedied as much as they were going to be by regularizing procedures, specifying rules of due process, and making judicial review available in some areas of administrative activity. The task for someone proceeding from an analytical jurisprudence base was to carefully develop a logically coherent system of rules and categories for problem solving from the initial set of statutory requirements. That task, and establishing its own role in the administrative justice system, is precisely what the legal community turned to during the 1950s and 1960s.

Political science had no such unity of purpose or perspective in the postwar years. The two subfields of that discipline most concerned with administrative law were experiencing major changes that took both in directions that meant a break with the lawyers and an abandonment of important administrative law questions.

Public administration was undergoing an "identity crisis."[118] For a number of reasons, public administrators wanted to establish the field as a unique area of practice and study. In the preface to his now famous work, *Introduction to the Study of Public Administration,* Leonard D. White asserted that "the study of administration should start from the base of management rather than the foundation of law."[119] His attitude was at least in part a response to the existing overemphasis on law by those interested in the study and practice of public administration. It was also a reaction to the domination of the public service by those with legal training.[120] After all, efficiency was the new end of administration since the scientific management movement had appeared on the scene.[121] The need for change became apparent following postwar publication of the seminal works by Dwight Waldo[122] and Herbert Simon,[123] which sought to bring public administration to a more mature level. Based on the work of Simon and others, administration grew as a generic area of study that sought to avoid exclusive identification with either public administration or business administration. The result was that public administrators had little time or page space for administrative law matters during the 1950s and 1960s. An additional influence was the fact that schools that continued to teach administrative law (and over the years the number at which the subject was required dwindled) tended to use law school materials or to favor books on the regulatory environment of business. By 1968, Waldo concluded that the antilaw bias had gone too far:

> Perhaps I have been subverted by two years of association with the Continental administration, but I am of the opinion that we now suffer from lack of attention to constitutional-legal matters. Our early antilegal and antilawyer bias is understandable and forgivable, but it is dangerously obsolete and self-defeating.[124]

Political science, as a discipline, was also undergoing a postwar change. The new direction was oriented toward process and based on a behavioral methodology and conceptual framework that avoided normative concerns. More predictive research was favored, focused on political activity by groups rather than substantive policy decisions made by specific individuals or issued by particular institutions. In the subfield known as public law there were two important developments. First, public law declined in popularity, compared with other subfields.[125] Second, it followed the track of the larger discipline by becoming "Bentleyan, behavioristic, actional and nonmotivational."[126] As a result, questions on the substantive development of law and administration attracted little scholarly attention.[127]

In summary, much of the literature on law and administration during these years was written by legal practitioners and some government investigators. It tended to take an analytical approach that stressed the need to clarify categories, concepts, and procedures in the APA.

The Administrative Procedure Act Under Pressure: Commentary and Criticism of the APA

The report of the Task Force on Legal Services and Procedure is important in part because of the substantive findings it presented and also because the task force was staffed by people who had been instrumental in administrative law during the 1950s and 1960s. After examining nearly a decade of operation under the Administrative Procedure Act, the task force concluded that the administrative justice system was not operating satisfactorily.

The task force examined the effectiveness of legal procedures under the Administrative Procedure Act enacted by Congress in 1946. It found that the statute had not always been implemented and followed by agencies in the executive branch to the extent intended by Congress and concluded that substantial amendments should be made to the act to strengthen it as the charter of due process of law in administration.[128]

The task force began with the premise that efficiency in administration requires efficient and effective legal practices with regard to relationships between one agency and another and between the agency and the citizens served by that agency. But at each stage of the report where the need for efficiency and effectiveness is stressed, an admonition is added: "Economy in Federal Government operations through improvements in legal procedures is an end earnestly sought by this task force. Procedural safeguards cannot be sacrificed to economy or efficiency."[129] The goal was efficiency, effectiveness, and fundamental fairness in administrative justice.

The report specifically rejected the conventional wisdom among administrators that wide discretion permits flexibility in administration, which in turn yields efficiency. On the contrary, discretionary authority may in fact result in inefficiency:

> Positive limitations should be imposed by statute upon the exercise of administrative powers, authority, or discretion, to the end that statutes are faithfully executed, the rights of the parties are fully protected, and the administration of matters committed to agency action is prompt, fair and efficient.[130]

The task force also lamented the ad hoc manner in which agencies were established. Lack of planning and coordination had led to conflicts among federal agencies and between federal and state agencies.

Even where no jurisdictional controversies arose, agency authority was vague because of the lack of standards in many of the statutes that created the agencies.[131]

The group saw the need for long-range congressional action to correct deficiencies in the administrative justice system, but urged self-help by administrators as the first step in the needed reform. Most urgent was the need for administrators to define the means by which their agencies planned to exercise their authority. The Administrative Procedure Act was constructed on the theory that agencies promulgate future policies through rulemaking or quasi-legislative procedures, and apply existing policies to current problems using quasi-judicial adjudicatory procedures. In practice, the task force found, agencies were not carefully articulating policy through rulemaking, but were loosely using adjudications to make policy and to resolve contemporary disputes. This common law-development approach to administration might be less of a problem if the rule of *stare decisis,* or the binding effect of precedent, was followed as rigorously in administration as it was in the judiciary, but the task force found that agencies often took advantage of the less strenuous concept of precedent often applied to agencies:

> It is a manifest hardship to subject an individual to a penalty, or other sanction, for continuing to do that which for long was considered by him, and others, to be permissible under the law. Unfortunately, situations have arisen where, as a result of an adjudicatory proceeding initiated by an agency, a sanction has been imposed upon an individual for engaging in such conduct, even though no statute or rule had been enacted or promulgated specifically condemning it....A clear inequity arises when persons rely in good faith upon authoritative agency opinions, only to be informed in subsequent proceedings that the opinion is not binding upon the agency.[132]

In sum, agencies should use rulemaking as much as possible to guide the public and should avoid policymaking through adjudications.[133]

Where agencies do adjudicate, they have a burden to ensure prompt action primarily because the expense of protracted administrative proceedings may effectively deny due process and fundamental fairness to the person before the agency. The task force urged that more be done to ensure that persons appearing before agencies be made more aware of their options and the nature of the process they are confronting.[134]

The task force also took note of some of the special problems of law and administration in the areas of social services and benefits. In 1941, Gellhorn had written that this might be a problem in administrative law, but that benefit claims only required a claimant to carry the burden of proving that he or she was eligible for the benefit claimed.[135] The task force, with the benefit of a study of several years of practice and a clearer perspective on postwar social programs, concluded that there was more at stake than proof by a claimant. There was more involved, they wrote, than the question of whether the claimant had a legal right to a benefit or was merely granted the benefit as a matter of privilege by the government. The report argued that the fairness and effectiveness of benefit claims case processing was a concern of citizens generally and not merely of those with claims. Benefit programs are based on legislative determinations of the public interest, and are funded from tax revenues. Therefore the people have a right to ensure that administrators execute the programs for the purpose and in the manner prescribed by the legislature.[136]

Given their observations of existing practices, the members of the task force concluded that, at least in the short term, judicial review would have to be relied on to ensure proper operation of the administrative justice system. "A plain, simple and prompt judicial remedy should be available for every legal wrong because of agency action or failure to act. Judicial controls over administrative action should be expanded and strengthened."[137]

James M. Landis was a member of the task force of the second Hoover Commission. In fact, Landis had been the leading defender of the faith, administrator, and a member of most of the major study groups that had examined administrative law since the 1930s. So it came as no surprise when President-elect Kennedy asked Landis to prepare a report on the state of administrative justice and make recommendations for upgrading existing practices. The Landis report was an indictment of the administrative justice system: "Effective procedural solutions, so necessary to the proper functioning of the administrative agencies, have admittedly not been achieved despite the sweeping studies which culminated in the Administrative Procedure Act of 1946 and the many studies which have followed."[138]

The *Report on Regulatory Agencies to the President-Elect* did not mince words.[139] Landis recognized the need for the agencies, the complexity of their work environment, and the stakes involved in the cases and policies with which they dealt. Even so, he was angry at the conduct, bordering on influence peddling, practiced by attorneys.[140] He was dissatisfied with the manner in which agencies had implemented procedural requirements. He concluded that administrative law problems had effectively halted administrative planning and policy formulation. "Inordinate delay characterizes the disposition of adjudicatory proceedings before substantially all of our regulatory agencies."[141] If administrative law procedures had been developed to save time and money, they had failed.[142] Even with all of the complex procedures, Landis was not satisfied that agency decisions were characterized by fundamental fairness. In addition to political interference or unethical *ex parte* contacts with agency decisionmakers, he saw an increasing tendency toward institutional decisionmaking.

> Generalizations as to the organization of administrative agencies are not only difficult but dangerous to make. Unlike the judges of the federal judiciary, members of administrative commissions do not do their own work....But, worse than this, it is a general belief founded on considerable evidence, that briefs of counsel, findings of hearing examiners, relevant portions of the basic records, are rarely read by the individuals theoretically responsible for the ultimate decisions.[143]

Landis made a number of suggestions to the president on ways to deal with some of the problems noted in his survey. But the more important result of this report was the complete reversal of one of the major proponents of the administrative procedure solution as to the problems of administrative justice. He had come full circle to the conclusion that much remained to be done before we could rest satisfied with the state of administrative law.[144]

Peter Woll was one of the few political scientists writing on law and administration during this period.[115] In his *Administrative Law: The Informal Process,*[146] Woll concentrated on the point made by the Attorney General's Committee in 1941, largely ignored since then, that informal procedures are "the lifeblood" of the administrative process. With some of the earlier writers, Woll acknowledged the key words of administrative law from the administrators' perspective: speed, flexibility, cost effectiveness, continuity, expertise, and sympathetic administration.[147] "Congress and the judiciary have voluntarily relinquished power and permitted the broad exercise of discretion on the part of administrators."[148]

Woll asserted that "requirements of public policy, expertise, and speed have rendered administrative adjudication today primarily informal in nature."[149] Even in cases where agencies are involved in adversary processes or adjudications, Woll argues, "full-fledged legal procedure is rarely employed."[150] His survey of agency workloads suggested that informal conferences and other devices had become alternatives to formal procedures. Even where formal procedures were used, informal agreements that were developed in prehearing conferences were used to limit the scope of the formal proceedings. He concluded that the gradual increase in the use of informal processes had been accepted because it was assumed that a person dissatisfied with agency actions would have recourse to all the protections of the formal process. But Woll found that for reasons of cost and time there was some doubt about the availability of alternatives; indeed, informal process had "replaced" formal procedures.[151] "Because of the widespread use of informal procedures in the administrative process, it is no longer possible to say that private parties subject to the jurisdiction of administrative agencies have recourse to traditional adjudicative procedure to settle their cases."[152]

He was critical of those who had spent so much time on problems of administrative law without understanding that the majority of administrative justice activity is informal and has little to do with narrow debates over close interpretation of the Administrative Procedure Act. To those who would propose reforms for administrative law, Woll advised a balanced perspective that recognized the complaints of those before agencies, but also included concern for the problems faced by administrators.[153]

Dissatisfaction expressed by many with the implementation of the APA, the apparent unwillingness of Congress to develop innovative reforms for administrative law, and the ambiguity of the contemporary administrative environment led many writers in the 1950s and 1960s to focus on judicial review as the centerpiece of administrative justice.[154] Judges continued to defer to the expertise of administrators, imposing relatively mild forms of review on agency decisions.[155] The debate over whether that situation should change was the focus of much of the literature in law reviews during this period.

One of the most prominent authors writing on administrative law was Kenneth Culp Davis, whose first major work was his 1951 treatise, *Administrative Law*.[156] In that path-breaking work, Davis set out to develop a body of administrative law based on the Administrative Procedure Act with elaborations that sought to give guidance to judges and attorneys in this developing area of the law. By the late 1950s, Davis's categories of administrative process, based on the APA, court decisions, and his own thinking, had grown into the multi-volume *Administrative Law Treatise,* later updated by regular supplements.[157]

Davis was relatively satisfied with the APA approach to operation of the administrative justice system and was engaged in the task of refining that body of law. Among other things, this work led Davis to conclude that there were areas of administrative law activity that were not subject to judicial review "even for arbitrariness or abuse of discretion."[158] Davis's assertions touched off a decade of debate with such writers as Louis Jaffe,[159] who argued that public administration depended for its legitimacy on judicial review as well as regular procedures and minimal due process protections. Davis's leading adversary was Raoul Berger. Davis based his argument primarily on statutory grounds, but it was precisely that narrowness that drew Berger's fire.[160] Berger argued that no statute could justify arbitrary government action, prohibited in his view by the Constitution and principles of justice.

The debate reflects some of the larger problems of this period. Davis made a great many contributions to the day-to-day development of the guidelines needed to deal with ongoing problems that could not await the promulgation of a new administrative law. Berger and others, dissatisfied by what they saw as the narrow APA approach to administrative justice, recognized that a broader approach was necessary if administrative law was to succeed in the long run in integrating emerging law into the larger legal and governmental system. For both practical and theoretical reasons, the administrative justice system had been found wanting. But all agreed that administrative law had to grow. After 1969 there was a search for incremental reforms and attempts at experimentation with those reforms.

ADMINISTRATIVE JUSTICE
IN THE MODERN CONTEXT: 1969–1976

The decade of the 1970s was a period of rapid change in law and administration. In part the changes resulted from a number of historic events that followed in quick succession. Other developments arose from deliberate attempts to deal with problems vividly demonstrated during the 1960s. Like most changes in law and politics, these changes will affect "who gets what, where, when, how," as Lasswell put it in his definition of politics.[161] It is too early to tell what the results of the wave of renewed attention to problems of law and administration will be, but one can at least note the trends and the criticisms.

Administrative Environment Shaped by Conflict

Richard Nixon came to the White House at a turbulent time. The mood of the population alternated between fear and anger, aroused by both foreign and domestic concerns. There was an unpopular war in Vietnam as well as social activism in the streets at home. United States prestige declined abroad.

In this country, citizens locked and bolted doors, installed burglar alarms, and armed themselves in an unprecedented manner. The fear of violent crime brought cries for tougher law enforcement, which resulted in more policy for government to implement, such as the Omnibus Crime Control and Safe Streets Act and the creation of the Law Enforcement Assistance Administration.[162]

In addition, a number of political movements were growing. Environmental interests, women's groups, Hispanics, African-Americans, and poverty organizations came to the seat of government on some occasions, took to the streets on others, and became increasingly sophisticated in the use of litigation as another forum for interest group conflict. Soon it could be said that legal challenge and response was a predictable part of any major policy activity. And during the decades of the 1970s and 1980s, conservatives once again became active interest group litigators, challenging the more liberal groups of the preceding decade.[163]

The Nixon administration pronounced the Great Society a failure and substituted for it the New Federalism, which purported to return decisionmaking in social programs and other policy areas to states and local governments.[164] The dismantling of the Great Society meant transfer of essential services to other levels of government, and with this came revenue sharing and other complex grant programs.

While the president's men were engaged in eliminating some agencies, Congress and the administration itself were responding to new demands for regulation in consumer product safety, occupational health and safety, and environmental quality with the establishment of new agencies. It comes as a surprise to many students now that not only was the Environmental Protection Agency created during the Nixon administration, but it was based not upon a statute pressed by Congress but by a presidential reorganization plan developed at the White House.

The problems of administration had changed. The government faced an increasingly complicated intergovernmental environment and heavy social service demands. The nation had become predominantly an urban and suburban society, and both the problems of the cities and the tensions between them and the suburbs as well as rural communities were growing. Administrative programs, services, regulatory devices, and benefit claims processes had all become politicized. Even so, it might have been possible to employ new techniques of administration to reduce governmental confusion—but for Watergate and the energy crisis.

The nation was badly shaken by the events that led to the downfall of the Nixon administration. Aftershocks continued to rock Washington, including revelations on domestic and foreign misdeeds of the CIA and on improper use of income tax records by the White House, attempts to influence regulatory decisions affecting those perceived to be enemies of the administration, and FBI violations of civil liberties. These tremors seriously damaged an image that had long been important to the efficacy of modern administration.

The picture that has emerged, correct or not, was that of government against the people. Those who remembered the days when the "best and the brightest" went to Washington to fight the Depression were shaken.[165] Cynics, on the other hand, felt vindicated. It must be recalled that administration had grown up largely based on faith: first, the faith born in the Progressive era that professionals in different disciplines could solve national problems and, second, that these people were committed to the common good.

There had never been any particular love of bureaucracy, but after Watergate the level of distrust increased dramatically. Ironically, the people convicted for Watergate violations were not career civil servants but political appointees, mostly lawyers. For the administrator in the 1970s, the problem became—and as the nation moved into the twenty-first century, remained—how to carry out difficult and necessary administrative tasks in a hostile environment; particularly when that hostility is exploited for political gain by elected officials. Indeed, the level of violence against public officials has increased dramatically, of which the best-known example is the Oklahoma City Federal Building bombing.

The energy crisis that had its first effects in 1973 continues to influence policy in ways few would previously have imagined. Among other things, the energy crisis clearly destroyed the myth that experts can solve society's problems without drastic alterations in standards and modes of living. The day of the administrative quick fix is at an end. However, the first thought that occurred to many in dealing with the energy crisis was to create new administrative agencies to meet regulatory needs and to develop innovative policies. At the same time that national demands to decrease the size and role of government generally were heard, equally strident demands were made for the government to solve the energy problem, with each interest group claiming first priority in whatever policy would be developed in Washington.

The judiciary also changed during this period. By 1975, the Supreme Court had changed its identity from the Warren Court to the Nixon-appointed Burger Court.[166] The views of the Warren Court majority, coupled with the demands to make civil rights a reality in daily life for minorities, women, persons with disabilities, and other groups sometimes termed "public interest" lobbies such as environmental groups, had resulted in an expanding sphere of activity for the federal courts. The Burger Court was appointed with the definite purpose of reducing that involvement, and the new majority, in several areas, did just that.[167]

In the academic community, problems of law and administration have again been recognized as significant by public administration scholars and some political scientists. Among the reasons for this resurgence of interest were the increased number of law and policy conflicts, the high visibility of some law and administration problems, such as detailed orders to administrators on operation of prison health facilities following suits by inmates and patients,[168] and the increasing importance of policy studies as a popular part of these disciplines. Policy studies attempts to apply some of the methods and concepts of the 1950s and 1960s to the substance of government policy as well to as the processes of government.[169] This shift to policy studies involved both methodological developments in and, more important, attention to what is studied. Attention to the substance of policy, with more interest in what came to be known as policy domains or policy tracks, as well as to the processes that produced it indicated a need for attention to public law questions.

Reform Efforts in Action and in Literature

On the positive side, the 1970s witnessed attempts to ameliorate problems noted in earlier years. Attempts at reform were, at first, relatively limited and largely incremental, but even those initial efforts were significant. Each year Congress considered a variety of bills, at least one of which was entitled something like "The Administrative Procedure Reform Act of 19__." Most were efforts to patch deficiencies in the APA. There were few attempts to go beyond this kind of adjustment to a more comprehensive attempt to construct a coherent administrative law on which to build specific procedures and institutions. In fact, one may view some of the failures of the APA in light of Sir Henry Maine's warning that premature codification of developing areas of law may be dangerous.[170]

Some experimental reforms were attempted. Many such efforts were intended by the interest groups who supported them to advance their own goals, but that was, of course, no reason to reject suggestions or experiments out of hand. Executive experiments included reorganization of agencies, attempts to reduce interagency conflicts through the use of interagency working groups, limited deregulation initiatives, civil service reform, and proposals to deal with privacy and freedom-of-information problems. Despite the fact that it has now been some time since these initiatives were launched, the jury is still out on these efforts and much more will be said about them in future chapters.

Congress was extremely active during the 1970s with efforts to come to grips with administrative problems. Ironically, one of the methods used by Congress was its own counterbureaucracy—administrative offices designed to prepare research and monitor activities of other administrative agencies on behalf of Congress. Some of the statutes enacted in the 1970s reacted to earlier criticisms about vague and open-ended wording in laws that left administrators free to roam in a given policy area. An example is the Education for All Handicapped Children Act,[171] later reauthorized and renamed the Individuals with Disabilities Education Act (IDEA),[172] which some observers consider may even have gone too far in the direction of procedural specificity.[173] Congress appointed a number of study groups that have, unlike some of their predecessors, seemingly had a very real policy impact. For example, the Commission on Procurement's efforts led to substantial changes in the system of grants and contracts administration. The Ribicoff Committee *Study on Federal Regulation* figured prominently in regulatory reform efforts, well before the deregulation movement that began in the late 1970s. Congress also had the benefit of recommendations from the Administrative Conference of the United States (ACUS), a prestigious body of experts from several areas of scholarship and practical experience in administration (which was unfortunately killed off by later administrations). Although the statute creating the conference was enacted at the request of President Kennedy and signed into law by President Johnson, it did not become effective until after staffing began in 1968.[174]

One of the most controversial of the experiments was the legislative veto concept. Legislative veto provisions were attached to a variety of bills, permitting Congress by various means to veto a rule promulgated by an administrative agency.[175] Congress enacted a series of information laws that provide for protection of privacy and for access to government documents. A related package of statutes includes the Government in the Sunshine Act,[176] which responds to some of the complaints on the difficulty many individuals and groups encounter in participating in rulemaking processes, and the Federal Advisory Committee Act,[177] which attempts to meet criticisms made since the Landis Report about the dangers of off-the-record contacts by regulated groups and special access by interest groups to administrators.

The courts were also part of this period of experimentation, although different courts approached the subject differently. On the basis of the criticisms of the earlier period and the experiences of the courts with agencies, some judges were less willing to grant wide deference with only cursory review of administrative decisions. Judge David Bazelon summarized the concern of these judges.

> We stand on the threshold of a new era in the history of the long and fruitful collaboration of administrative agencies and reviewing courts. For many years, courts have treated administrative policy decisions with great deference, confining judicial attention primarily to matters of procedure. On matters of substance, the courts regularly upheld agency action, with a nod in the direction of the "substantial evidence" test, and a bow to the mysteries of administrative expertise. Courts occasionally asserted, but less often exercised, the power to set aside agency action on the ground that an impermissible factor had entered into the decision, or a crucial factor had not been considered. Gradually, however, that power has come into more frequent use, and with it, the requirements that administrators articulate factors on which they base their decisions.[178]

Judges at all levels became more willing than before to send opinions or rules back to agencies (the term is to "remand" them) for clarification and for a demonstration that the procedures of the APA had been followed in letter and in spirit. One device developed to meet that set of concerns was hybrid rulemaking (discussed in detail in Chapter 5).[179] It is perhaps ironic that, looking back at these developments from a twenty-first century perspective, the institution of hybrid rulemaking which is ubiquitous now was so controversial at the time of its inception. The process was developed in response to calls by scholars on judges to press administrators for guidelines and assurances of a careful hearing of the information offered by those who came before agencies engaged in rulemaking, what Judge Bazelon and others referred to as a thorough ventilation of the issues. Hybrid rulemaking requires a minimum level of material in records supporting agency rules to show that administrators made decisions based on some kind of evidence and did not arbitrarily reject evidence offered by citizens or groups to the agency.

While the Supreme Court was less willing during this period than before to grant automatic deference to administrative agencies, it was also not well disposed toward some of the new techniques, such as hybrid rulemaking, if they were imposed by courts as opposed to the legislature.[180] On another front, the Court limited the authority of federal courts to interfere with administrative action in progress by pressing lower courts to limit the use of remedial orders that involved the courts in specific requirements for change in administrative operations. It also expanded opportunities to sue administrators and units of government after the fact to recover damages in the event of maladministration or violations of constitutional or statutory rights.[181]

As these experiments got underway, a number of authors continued to probe for new directions in the reform of law and administration. One reason for selecting 1969 as the break point between this period and preceding decades was the change in presidential administrations, but a major intellectual rationale is that 1969 is the year in which Kenneth Culp Davis published his *Discretionary Justice: A Preliminary Inquiry*[182] and a related article, "A New Approach to Delegation."[183] A long-standing supporter of conventionally defined administrative law, he had arrived at the conclusion that much remained to be done before it could be said that the administrative justice system was functioning properly. Davis made a strong case that discretion is widespread and open to abuse. The dangers of abuse were exacerbated, in his view, by the lack of public proceedings and by the burdens placed on those who attempt to get judicial review of agency actions.[184] Davis, confident that the discretion could be controlled, structured, and limited with relative ease,[185] preferred to rely primarily on self-help by administrators. He asked only that they expand the use of rulemaking to announce their own view of agency discretion and means for its use,[186] and that agencies avoid interposing technical defenses in cases where a citizen decided to seek judicial review.[187] If agencies would not take these steps, Davis suggested that courts should encourage them to do so."[188] Davis recognized that "our system is the result of long-term, rudderless drift,"[189] but he argued that by avoiding massive efforts at reform—given the major conflicts implied in such reform campaigns—important and effective incremental changes could be achieved.[190]

Louis Jaffe and Judge J. Skelly Wright, two of the many who reacted to Davis's work, agreed with his assessment of the problems of the administrative justice system, but disagreed with his call for voluntary change by administrators.[191] Both concluded that careful judicial review would likely be necessary until congressional action was taken.[192]

Abraham Sofaer is another critic of the position that administrators would voluntarily make rules to control their own discretion.[193] In his study of the Immigration and Naturalization Service (since reorganized and integrated into the Department of Homeland Security), an agency with perhaps the widest range of discretionary authority of any federal administrative body, Sofaer agreed with the dangers of discretion noted by Davis and others. Based on his study (discussed further in Chapter 9), Sofaer concluded that not only was such broad discretionary authority dangerous to those who might suffer from arbitrary agency action, but it also led to major inefficiencies and high reversal rates on appeal.[194] He did not assume that administrators were likely to divest themselves of discretion, and reported an attempt by the Administrative Conference to convince INS officials to promulgate rules defining their own discretion. The INS officials responded that they were not going to limit their own flexibility by issuing standards.[195] Sofaer suggested that courts should prod legislatures and executives to mandate agency rulemaking and other reforms.[196]

Ernest Gellhorn and Glen O. Robinson were in general agreement with the idea that agencies were unlikely to limit their own discretion,[197] as was Richard B. Stewart.[198] Stewart summarized the several suggestions with the most support during this period, including "deregulation and abolition of agencies; enforcement of the doctrine against delegation of legislative power; a requirement that agencies crystallize their exercise of discretion through standards and adoption of allocational efficiency as a substitute yardstick for agency decisions."[199] He concluded that none of these alone would solve the problems, and that experimentation ought to continue. These authors had concluded that it was time to stop asking whether the APA was in good health and begin treatment for the difficult, but probably curable, ailments that all could readily diagnose.

CARTER AND AFTER: THE COUNTERBUREAUCRACY CHALLENGE AND THE ATTACK ON ADMINISTRATIVE LAW

At about the time the Carter administration came to Washington, however, a significant change occurred. It was a shift that was maintained and indeed intensified from about 1977 through the Reagan years, with varying levels of intensity, through the George H. W. Bush administration, in a particular form, through the Clinton administration, and with increased vigor in the George W. Bush years.

The approach of these presidents and substantial numbers of members of Congress in this period was not primarily in the direction of reform or analytic critique of public administration as much as it was a more or less direct attack on the bureaucracy and in many respects on important aspects of administrative law. Whether one agrees or disagrees with the ideological or partisan underpinnings of those efforts, they were in approach and results qualitatively different from earlier reform movements. Indeed, the term "reform" is a misnomer that has been applied to activities not directed toward improvement but toward radical change, reduction, or elimination. At the core of the debate and activity surrounding these changes one finds several key factors, including: (1) promotion of a mythology of bureaucracy, (2) a deliberate politicization of the public service, (3) the use of reform to cloak ideological challenges to the idea of a public service, (4) a dramatic deregulation movement, (5) a problematic reshaping of intergovernmental relations, (6) a shift in response by courts to administrative responsibility, (7) the effects of fiscal stress, (8) a growing impact of globalization on domestic public administration, and (9) an increasing reliance on governance models to meet contemporary challenges.

Presidential and congressional candidates of both parties in campaigns from 1976 through 1984 pressed a "government is the problem" theme with great success. Starting with the 1992 election, the slogan for the so-called "New Democrats," led by Bill Clinton and his running mate, Al Gore, shifted to a slightly different line—that the problem was one of good people stuck in a bad system.[200] Hence, following on the title of a book published soon after the new administration took office, the task was to "reinvent government."[201]

At the core of many of these campaigns was a set of generalizations with some elements of fact but otherwise so overblown as to amount to a mythology of bureaucracy. The picture that emerged was that of a public administration that had reputedly grown at an alarming rate (particularly during the 1970s); that government was becoming a much greater consumer of national resources; that that was the cause of the economic woes of the nation; that the number of bureaucrats had grown like Cabbage Patch dolls; that they were isolated in the bloated puzzle palaces of Washington, D.C. and completely disconnected from the rest of the country; that they were generally incompetent, inefficient, irresponsible, and unresponsive to the people; that the bureaucracy was engaged in profligate spending, throwing away money in Washington that had been wrested from the taxpayers of various states and localities around the nation; that those spending decisions were made without participation by states and localities; that mechanisms of accountability were all but nonexistent, and that the government—and principally the bureaucracy—was rife with fraud, abuse, and waste of a sort that could only be resolved by executive appointees who were, as one president described them, "meaner than junk yard dogs."

Granting that governments, including the federal government, have a host of problems of one sort or another and that administrators and their agencies are in the thick of some of them, the reality was far different from the myth. Government was not growing at anything like the pace that was suggested either in terms of percentage of GNP (or percentage of GNP as compared to our major global trading competitors) or in numbers of employees per thousand population.

> While political rhetoric and a considerable body of academic research continue to picture the federal government as a rapidly expanding behemoth growing disproportionally in both scope and size relative to the rest of the society in order to handle a steadily growing range of responsibilities, in fact something considerably more complex has been underway. For, while the range of federal responsibilities has indeed increased dramatically, the relative size of the federal enterprise, in terms of both budget and employment, has paradoxically remained relatively stable. Between 1954 and 1979, for example, the rate of growth of the federal budget just barely exceeded that of the Gross National Product (GNP), so that the budget's share of GNP increased only from 19.4 to 20.9 percent. Even more important, the rate of growth of federal civilian employment lagged far behind the real growth of the budget, so that the number of federal employees per 1,000 people in the population registered a decline during this twenty-five-year period of more than 10 percent.[202]

The federal non-defense civil service all but stopped growing in the 1970s and it was anything but Washington-based. In fact, less than 20 percent of federal employees were stationed in the nation's capital. While it was true that as many as one in six jobs were public sector related, more than 80 percent were state and local government positions in the labor-intensive fields of education, public safety, and health care, and the ratio of federal to state and local employees has continued to decline since then. That was not surprising given that these are the areas where the demands for services were most directly felt. It should be noted that some have argued that the "true size of government" has in fact grown, primarily because of the number of contractors that have been used to substitute for work formerly done by government agencies.[203] To be sure, there have indeed been large numbers of contractors employed in part as a way to reduce public employees while maintaining services, but contractors are different from civil service employees both legally and in management terms.[204] They are not simply extensions of existing administrative agencies.

When asked about their views of bureaucracy, the public continued to insist that they would as soon have their sons and daughters selling used cars as have them in public service. But when asked about how well particular agencies responded to their requests, the reactions were generally positive.[205]

The overwhelming percentage of non-defense expenditures were actually made by states and localities through various pass-through and intergovernmental financing schemes.[206] Ironically, it was the Reagan administration that proclaimed a "new federalism" that was responsible for the elimination of revenue sharing, an extremely important support for state and local governments during the 1970s and for cutting funding levels for block grants, another critical element in fiscal federalism.[207] "Thus, federal grants financed 25 percent of state and local expenditures in 1980. However, by 1988, they were financing only 18.2 percent."[208] Indeed, it was during an era dominated by politicians of both parties who ran against Washington's bureaucratic controls that there was a burgeoning growth in what came to be called unfunded mandates.

Accountability had been enhanced through judicial rulings that made available damage suits against individual officers or units of government. Changes in substantive legislation and administrative procedure enhanced opportunities for participation and accountability. Certainly, many in the bureaucracy said, career administrators were much more amenable to accountability than the president, who could run for reelection only once and who would not be defeated because someone had been mistreated by an agency or by members of Congress, who represent on average more than half a million citizens each. There was no credible evidence that government was demonstrably fraught with more fraud, abuse, and waste than private sector organizations.[209]

The fact that presidents, governors, state legislators, and many congressional candidates of both political parties promoted the myths to a public already prepared to believe the worst did not improve working relationships among administrators and elected officials. Still, many administrators applauded the concern with improving productivity and accountability, and supported candidates who called for change.

However, a number of actions taken during the late 1970s and 1980s politicized public administration and turned recognition of a need for improvement into tension over whether it would be possible to maintain a truly professional public administration in the contemporary political environment.

The Carter administration was adamant about its perceived need to get control of the bureaucracy. With that in mind, the administration launched its effort to replace the existing Civil Service Commission with a new arrangement that gave the White House greater leverage. The Civil Service Reform Act moved the adjudicative functions of the old commission to the Merit System Protection Board (MSPB) and vested all other powers over the civil service in the Office of Personnel Management (OPM). The legislation created a Senior Executive Service (SES), allowing more flexible use and control of top-level career civil servants. The same devices that gave the chief executive more control also meant less security for senior career staff. They could be transferred out of agencies and fields in which they had spent a professional lifetime. They could be removed from SES positions without standard civil service protections in ways that would make it extremely difficult, if not as a practical matter impossible, for them to return to normal career status positions.

The Carter administration also used executive orders to enhance the role of the Office of Management and Budget (OMB) by authorizing OMB to monitor proposed rulemaking in order to discourage unnecessary regulation and encouraging cost/benefit analysis of rules that were to be promulgated.

The Reagan administration took the tools provided by its predecessor and moved well beyond the policies of the Carter administration. Reagan installed an extremely controversial director of OPM who began his tenure with a chastening address to the American Society for Public Administration in which he informed the membership that he and the administration intended to put public administrators in their place. The OPM took a variety of actions widely perceived to have politicized the federal executive civil service. In addition, political appointments were expanded in scope and in reach down into lower levels of agencies through the use of temporary appointments and by other means, allowing a greater penetration of lower ranks of the bureaucracy. There were OPM policies aimed at the personal lives or health decisions of civil servants and the modification of charitable contributions options by inclusion or removals of groups from the Combined Federal Campaign that increased tension within the bureaucracy.[210] Dramatic budget cutbacks in domestic and regulatory agencies resulted in reductions in force and a sense that the civil service was under attack. The authority of the Office of Management and Budget to inhibit rulemaking was dramatically enhanced as cost/benefit requirements were expanded and made mandatory. The OMB director was provided with more specific control authority in preclearance of regulation. The enhanced demand for privatization, the move to transfer government functions to the private sector, and to increase contracts with private firms to avoid direct public service delivery, played on the bureaucratic mythology. The administration's use of outside consultants with very strong ideological positions with respect to the civil service added to the stress. The Grace Commission Report and the Heritage Foundation's *Mandate for Leadership II* are examples.[211]

On the other hand, the defense agencies saw substantial increases in personnel and expenditures. In fact, several Department of Defense units found themselves in trouble because they could not efficiently meet the need for dramatically expanded contract development and administration, resulting in a number of widely publicized problems.

The rhetoric concerning decentralization of programs and functions to states or localities added to the stress in the bureaucracy because resources did not come with the responsibilities. Revenue sharing was halted and various other grants and forms of financial assistance were dramatically reduced, while federal mandates for service remained. In the states, reduction of federal aid often meant a reduction in state assistance to localities which, in many instances, came at the worst possible time given dramatic downturns in the economy. That resulted in decreased income and sales tax revenues and a general resistance to property and local option sales tax increases, the only viable mechanisms for local revenue enhancement.

The term "reform" was frequently employed by a variety of elected officials. While some meant improvement of the public service, others used the concept of reform for an ideologically based attack on public administration. Although some of the efforts at deregulation were based on rational policy analysis considerations, others were ideological and had little to do with better government or policymaking. The rhetoric of ideology, whether it comes from the left or the right, and however it is masked, usually contributes to increased tension.

Courts appeared to be part of the assault on public administration. Federal courts backed away from the expanding trend during the Warren Court years of enhanced due process and free speech protections for public employees. While the Supreme Court did reduce the authority of district courts to issue wide-ranging injunctions mandating changes in the operation of education, public safety, and health care agencies, it expanded the ability of citizens to launch suits for money damages against officials and their agencies.

The Clinton campaign criticized the Reagan and George H. W. Bush administrations on grounds that their attacks on public service and interference with regulatory and social service agency processes in such areas of the blocking of rulemaking had jeopardized the environment and public safety. The Clinton era theme of reinventing government came with promises that the process would empower public employees and free them from needless constraints. The reality turned out to be different, in part because of positions taken by the administration, in part because of the behavior of the federal courts, and in part because of the 1994 sweep of congressional elections led by soon-to-be Speaker of the House Newt Gingrich (R-GA) and his so-called "Contract with America."[212]

While the rhetoric of the White House, the Congress, and many state administrations may have been different, many of the attitudes and trends were the same. Notwithstanding their rhetoric, the common measuring rod for both the Republicans and Democrats was cost savings, largely achieved by eliminating public employees. This was true despite the fact that, except for political appointees and senior executives, the federal civil service was already in several important respects in significant decline.[213]

The press for deregulation by administrative agencies in the form of elimination of rules intensified. It is no accident that the title of the report of the National Performance Review headed by Vice President Gore was *From Red Tape to Results*.[214] Indeed, following similar political waves in other countries, Washington insiders found a new four-letter word, "command and control." There were several problems and a number of ironies in this seemingly obvious criticism of regulatory excesses. The first was that the Clinton administration not only kept many of the executive orders that had been imposed during the Reagan years that piled requirements on administrative agencies, making their regulatory processes less efficient, but it added its own generation of executive mandates that added even more constraints and workload to understaffed agencies. Chapters 5, 9, and 10 will discuss these orders in detail, but they added a host of unfunded mandates. For the administration's part, there was no recognition that many of the regulations that had been written had been mandated by the Congress.[215] The burdens that were added to agency rulemaking put many agencies in the position of violating statutory obligations to issue regulations within a particular time because of burdens on rulemaking mandated by the White House and Capitol Hill.

Despite rhetoric about devolution and decentralization, both Congress and the White House have been more than willing to attempt to interfere in ongoing agency operations, and both have been willing to intervene in state and local matters. The legislation outlawing unfunded mandates by the federal government was not made retroactive and seems, in any event, to have had little effect.

The Clinton administration's emphasis was clearly on policy formulation rather than implementation. And where possible, the preferred designs were those that seemed to promise alternatives to public administration. In particular, privatization or contracting out, the use of market-oriented strategies in place of regulation, and negotiated strategies to avoid enforcement or legal decisions were to be preferred. Not surprisingly, some of the difficulties that emerged in the use of these approaches have had to do with the failure to develop the legal infrastructure and train the people needed to manage more contracted operations and other market-oriented policy tools.[216] On the one hand, decentralization and the effort to resolve problems by negotiating on an individual basis is attractive, but such approaches lead to the kind of lack of standards, risk of arbitrariness, and lack of wider accountability that led to the pressure during the 1950s and 1960s for more rulemaking.

Indeed, the Clinton years marked the beginning of a general trend away from legal accountability and toward political accountability (which will be discussed in Chapter 13), without any attempt by the legislature or the chief executive to remove the existing legal obligations, both substantive and procedural, that agencies must honor. Despite the demand that accountability should be focused on performance rather than law or legal process, there have been few periods in modern history in which there has been a greater demand by the opposition party and the public for traditional legal responsibility. The pressure by Congress for more and broader investigations under the provisions of the Special Counsel statute[217] and the Supreme Court's ruling that the president had to deal while in office with the suit brought against him by a former Arkansas employee[218] are only two of the many examples.

On a related point, the full court press against regulation has itself encountered somewhat of a backlash. Private firms have warned against excessively broad deregulation efforts. A number of Wall Street firms have even called for enhancement of Securities and Exchange Commission authority and budgets in the wake of major insider trading scandals. Demands have been made, in the wake of illnesses and deaths related to tainted or improperly prepared meats, for stronger regulatory efforts by the Food and Drug Administration. On the other hand, a recent FDA Administrator received nationwide praise for his vigorous pursuit of tobacco firms. The Federal Aviation Administration has received repeated criticism for relaxing its oversight of airlines and aircraft manufacturers in a string of incidents ranging from inadequate airport security to the failure to regulate new low-cost carriers such as Valujet.[219] State Attorneys General have cooperated in their efforts to ensure regulation in some fields where the federal government had deregulated or where it appeared that Washington was not getting results quickly enough.[220]

Although the renewed attention to contracting has resulted in some efficiencies in some areas,[221] it had become clear even before George W. Bush came to office that contracting is not a way to simply or completely replace many public officers and agencies. Indeed, some of the experiments in contracting out large public operations lost a measure of their luster after experience and close examination revealed shortcomings.[222] Not only has it not always been clear how much is saved in some service contracting efforts,[223] but Government Accountability Office (GAO) studies have demonstrated that contracting out of services has sometimes implicated the government in such problems as unfair labor practices.[224] Thus, while contracting is a valuable tool and there have been a number of interesting innovations in that field, it was and is important for public managers to develop better techniques of contract administration, which also requires improvements in the law of public contracts.[225]

While George W. Bush came to office after a successful campaign to convince the electorate that his would be a pragmatic and moderate administration, the Bush team took office with a strong sense of ideological purpose and a program of action, much like the Reagan administration years earlier. And like the Reagan White House, the Bush administration moved to take advantage of tools and programs of the previous Democratic administration and also went well beyond its predecessor's initiatives in pursuit of its own agenda. The Bush administration moved quickly to implement what was termed the President's Management Agenda, published by the Office of Management and Budget.[226] The agenda identified nine program areas that the administration intended to address, starting with its controversial Faith-Based Initiative intended to increase contracting with faith-based organizations and to encourage those contractors to feel free to employ elements of their faith in the operation of contracted programs.[227]

A number of those program priorities certainly carried significant consequences for public managers and perhaps because of their visibility, there was not as much attention to the five items that were identified in the agenda as "Government-wide Initiatives." Those government-wide initiatives included:

- Strategic Management of Human Capital
- Competitive Sourcing
- Improved Financial Performance
- Expanded Electronic Government
- Budget and Performance Integration[228]

For those who read the document, it was clear that the administration wanted to move beyond performance-based management of previous administrations, of the sort enacted in the Government Performance and Results Act, and toward a model that was far more closely aligned with private sector corporate management.

While some of the terminology was very close to what had been employed in the Clinton administration's reinventing government policies, the approach went beyond that effort. For one thing, the administration intended to make good on its promise to ensure that the budget process would be used to reward or sanction performance or the lack of it. That had been a claim of numerous administrations in the past, but the Bush White House moved quickly to implement a system of performance evaluation based on what it terms the Program Assessment Rating Tool (PART). It published the results of the PART evaluations program-by-program within agencies on the Internet. However, it would also be clear that the criteria and methods of evaluations had strong ideological dimensions.

The competitive sourcing initiative also went well beyond previous administrations' efforts. The administration moved forcefully to encourage a reexamination of the so-called A-76 process, named for the circular published by the OMB which sets policy for how it is to be determined whether activities currently performed by agencies should go to contract bid and how those bids should be managed. Since agencies were scored on the degree to which each of the government-wide initiatives was implemented, there was pressure to move more programs to bid, and with them would come reductions in government employees. There were a range of complexities in all of this, but perhaps one of the most important was the lack of adequate contract management capacity to handle the competitive sourcing program and its consequences.

The administration also launched its own antiregulatory drive through a number of means, from the appointment of executive leaders who would press for deregulation to the administration's own program that stressed that the burden would be placed on agencies not only to meet cost-benefit requirements with more evidence, but also to shift the burden of proof to those who wanted to generate new rules (or for that matter any significant policy initiatives) instead of affording a presumption of validity to agency regulatory efforts based on respect for the agency's expertise and experience. In fact, the administration in mid-2002 rejected the long-standing presumptions of agency expertise and called for external "peer review" of agency findings in support of regulatory programs.[229]

The other prong of the agenda that has had major significance for public law and public administration is the strategic management of human capital. Here again, the administration sought to move away from the version of civil service as it had been revised over the previous two decades and toward a model that is clearly drawn from corporate management in the private sector. In addition to the day-to-day development of human resource policy, the administrative moved to obtain congressional support and then to launch rulemaking processes to develop completely new human resource management policies separate and different from civil service requirements. At the time of this writing, those two systems have been promulgated but are still in litigation and the early stages of implementation.[230] Finally, and in broad scope, the administration consistently asserted what it called the exclusive power of the president to "supervise the unitary executive."[231] This assertion was a broad-based claim to exclusive control and its full significance was not understood by many of those to whom the language was directed, such as members of the Congress.[232]

At this point, it is essential to underscore a date, September 11, 2001, that is now indelibly etched in American history, in the minds of those who experienced that day in New York City or elsewhere, and in public policy. It will be some years before distance and emerging information will permit a full understanding of the implications of the attacks on the World Trade Center and the Pentagon, and the attempted additional strike against Washington, foiled by the courageous passengers of United Airlines Flight 93 in the skies over Pennsylvania.[233]

With respect to public law and public administration, however, two points are clear. First, the president took the position that the attacks marked the beginning of a war against terrorism. Congress, as it commonly does in times of conflict, granted the president broad authority in several respects, including the use of military action and other means to address not only the specific attackers, but also to act more broadly. Most Americans and indeed most public managers were perhaps not clear as to the scope of that congressional action. Public Law 107-40 provided:

> That the President is authorized to use all necessary and appropriate force against those nations, organizations, or persons he determines planned, authorized, committed, or aided the terrorist attacks that occurred on September 11, 2001, or harbored such organizations or persons, in order to prevent any future acts of international terrorism against the United States by such nations, organizations or persons.[234]

The president employed a variety of executive orders and other directives, including one that created a White House Office of Homeland Security.[235] The Congress quickly adopted what has since become the very controversial USA Patriot Act.[236] In 2002 the Congress passed the another broad delegation of authority and major reorganization of the executive branch known as the Homeland Security Act, which combined some 22 agencies into the new department.[237] There has been considerable debate since 2001 about some of these pieces of legislation and their broad grants of authority as well as the authority claimed by the president under Article II of the Constitution. One of the important aspects of this debate is the fact that the war against terrorism is not a conflict with a specific traditional adversary and there is little to indicate when, if ever, that conflict will end. The question then arises just how long the U.S. will function under wartime statutes and presidential authority.

The second set of actions has not been as well recognized, but it is also very important. Whether one agrees or disagrees with the policies in question, the Bush administration has clearly used the conflict and the related concern with homeland security to leverage several of the priorities central to the president's agenda. For example, the Homeland Security Act granted authority to the Department of Homeland Security (DHS) to create a new human resource management system outside the existing civil service process. Beyond that specific action, the legislation provided in Title XIII, entitled "Federal Workforce Improvements," that all executive branch agencies would be required to create an office of Chief Human Capital Officers. It went on to create a government-wide council of such officers and directed those officers to move forward on a series of strategic human capital management initiatives with OMB oversight and guidance. Section 1311 of the act provided for "inclusion of agency human capital strategic planning in performance plans and programs performance reports." The Homeland Security Act also provided for a range of exemptions from existing human resource management policies, contracting policy, and information access and privacy requirements.

Similarly, the disaster of Hurricanes Katrina and Rita in 2005 also provided opportunities to obtain more authority and employ more exemptions from existing requirements. Thus, even lobbyists for contractors were surprised when the "Second Emergency Supplemental Appropriates Act to Meet Immediate Needs Arising from the Consequences of Hurricane Katrina, 2005" was discovered to have a concluding "General Provision" that raised the exemption from standard procurement require-ments from purchases of $2,500 or less to $250,000 or less.[238] After that policy development surfaced, the criticism caused OMB to roll back the $250,000 limit even though Congress had authorized it.

Even as all of these expansions in executive authority were developing, there were expressions of frustration and concern with some of the results of earlier deregulation. These came on the heel of scandals such as Enron and Global Crossing, among others, that resulted in new legislation known as Sarbanes-Oxley Act of 2002 to increase regulation on financial reporting.[239] Concerns about reported political interference in Food and Drug Administration regulation led to congressional regulations (discussed in Chapter 1) and ultimately to the resignation of the FDA administrator in 2005. Impacts of globalization and on domestic workforce size and compensation, including key fringe benefits, coupled with dramatic increased in health care costs have led to increased expectations for more active policy efforts by all levels of government. The loss of retirement funds from failing businesses, including not only those (such as Enron) involved in financial scandals but also such large firms as major airlines, have brought renewed expectations for government action to address the problems, particularly as the so-called baby boom generation moves toward its retirement years.

In a number of interesting respects, these are trends that follow similar concerns in other countries, both developed and developing, whether they have been headed by conservative or liberal leaders. Indeed, even international institutions that provided some of the sharpest attacks on public administra-tion and public service, such as the World Bank, have now begun advocating the rebuilding of capacity for the implementation and management of public policy.[240]

The Continuing Development of the Scholarly Underpinnings of Public Law and Public Administration: From Public Administration to the New Public Management to Governance

Speaking of international institutions, global forces have played an important role in the development of both the practice and theory of public law and public administration throughout this period. Moreover, there is every reason to expect that they will continue to do so. Rapid political, social, and economic change were among the key forces at play in the public policy arena of the mid-1970s. Two of the most important factors shaping the domestic situation were the rise of such international trading blocs as OPEC (the Organization of Petroleum Exporting Countries) and the oil boycott that they imposed. Petroleum prices shot up 400 percent and those increases flowed rapidly through economies around the world, fueling worldwide inflation. The United States had been in economic trouble since the early 1970s with the beginnings of the post–Vietnam War economic hangover. These and other factors dramatically affected all aspects of public policy around the world.

In Great Britain and several other countries, the forces described were among the factors that laid the groundwork for a major political shift to the right as Margaret Thatcher came to power as Britain's prime minister. Thatcher's lead was later followed by a range of conservative leaders in other countries from Canada to Australia, including Ronald Reagan in the United States. However, well before Reagan, Thatcher and the others had identified government as the problem they wanted to attack, economics and particularly neoliberal market theories as a driving force behind the changes, and the broad social programs that had been growing since World War II as a major target for elimination or at least dramatic reduction.[241] Not all of the countries that moved in this direction did so because of ideological shifts. In some cases, such as those of the Scandinavian nations, there were pressures from developing regionalization and global business competition. There were also moves in these directions in the developing countries, in some instances because of political changes but also because international donor organizations such as the World Bank and the International Monetary Fund made these kinds of changes conditions of assistance during the 1980s and into the 1990s.

In addition to the macro-level political changes and the ideological argument that raged around them, there was a range of scholars and practitioners of public administration who pieced together elements of these changes into what has become known as the "new public management."[242] Both scholarship and government reports emerged through the late 1970s and the 1980s that laid out the elements of this new framework.[243] Indeed, American scholars were in many cases well behind the trend.

The common elements to this new approach included downsizing (of the public sector overall and of individual organizations), deregulation, decentralization, delayering, right-sizing, reinventing, and re-engineering.[244] New public management advocates sought to focus on performance measured in various ways, but at its best by the customer. The citizen is viewed as a customer. Wherever possible, the new public managers contend, the move should be away from anything that resembles command and control regulation or direct service delivery and toward market-oriented tools that utilize incentives and disincentives, supply and demand pressures, and privatization. Thus, user fees, fines, marketable permits, special taxes, insurance programs, special funds, and competitive contracting are preferred to regulation or direct service delivery. The term "public administration" is displaced by public management and governance.

There was one other international trend that came to have a major impact. Ironically, it was based on ideas that came originally from the West but gained success and notoriety in Japan and then came back to the United States as American scholars looked to the emerging "Asian Miracle" in the business world to provide management techniques that could be borrowed. This was the Total Quality Management movement.[245] While it shared some of the premises of the new public management movement, it was less oriented toward efficiency and more toward effectiveness, customer satisfaction, and organizational learning. The learning organization is one that is engaged in an effort to maintain a culture of continuous improvement. While there were tensions between TQM and the new public management,[246] referred to in the United States as reinventing government, elements of TQM (later known simply as quality management) principles have been absorbed into the thinking of most new public management scholars.

In addition to these global trends, there were forces in the United States developing throughout this period that have affected progress and the lack of it in law and public administration. The movement toward what has come to be called public choice has reinforced the tendencies toward market logic and away from a public law perspective. Coming out of welfare economics, reactions against great society programs of the 1960s, the growing power of the national government, and a generally neoconservative/libertarian political wave, critics such as Vincent Ostrum called for dramatic change in the public sector.[247] Ostrum attacked national policymaking, calling for decentralization and the use of market-oriented policy implements. Ostrum was but one voice in a larger and longer conversation that sought to replace much of political thinking with economic logic or at least to redefine politics in economic terms. In this view, the political arena is a kind of marketplace in which rational choices are not achieved by political consensus in governmental bodies but by individual decisions expressed in market terms. Whatever emerges from that set of choices represents collective action or public choice. In such a model, whatever policy option allows the greatest individual choice is by definition the best alternative. Therefore, public choice advocates go beyond the new public managers in their responsiveness to the customer and argue for voucher programs that give program beneficiaries the ability to choose their program providers as well as making private sector choices readily available in place of, or at least in competition with, public organizations.[248]

But public choice advocates were not the only ones to attack the traditional distinctions between the public and the private sectors. The new public managers increasingly came to adopt the view that organizations should be seamless,[249] and the boundaries among organizations both public and private are and should increasingly be porous.[250] In this context, public management is increasingly a problem of creating and managing networks to accomplish tasks and solve problems with a studied disregard for traditional public law concerns about jurisdiction, procedural regularity, claims to legal rights, or concern with equity or equality. The issue is efficiency and customer satisfaction, with a very definite preference for a utilitarian perspective. If an approach solves a problem, then it ought to be seriously considered regardless of its tendency to break the mold—indeed perhaps precisely because it promises to break the traditional institutional or legal model.

What all of these approaches had in common was a reaction against an orientation toward law and legal process in favor of reliance on the dynamics of the marketplace, on participation and consensus in organizational life, and with a preference for process-oriented policy designs as opposed to traditional administration based upon formally delegated authority backed by sanctions. Indeed, process and policy innovation were rapidly displacing much of traditional public administration theory and practice.

But there was also an emerging critique of excess concern with process and inadequate attention to institution that quickly became known as the new institutionalism.[251] The political scientists who identified with rational choice approaches to public policy seized on this new institutionalism but adapted it to the rational choice framework by viewing public organizations as relationships of principals and agents, operating in a contractual manner. Behavior of these organizational players and their political superiors was then to be understood in terms of game theory and economics.[252]

There have also been challenges to these trends in public administration, political science, economics, and business administration. At the operational level, critics began to note that the management of contracts was more complex and problematic than privatization and marketization advocates suggested,[253] and that network management using a private sector model popularized by a well-known athletic shoe company presented a host of complexities.[254] From a public law perspective, Ronald Moe, Robert Gilmour, and others have rejected the Bozeman argument and the effort to transform public administration from a public law base into an enterprise of applied economics.[255] Indeed, they suggest that the effort to expand the use of devices such as government corporations and privatization, in part to circumvent administrative law processes and accountability mechanisms, has resulted in significant problems.

These reactions have not been limited to the United States. In preparation for the 50th Resumed Session of the United Nations General Assembly, a session focused on the role of public administration in sustainable development, the experts group on public administration asserted that:

> A primary distinction between public administration and other endeavors is that officers of government are created by and act within the authority of law. Thus the legal framework offers the basis of public administration. It also ensures rights, security, and stability. It is both the

means by which governments regulate and provide services to citizens and the means by which those citizens may protect their rights. It is also a vehicle with which to address problems of corruption or abuse of power....It provides means for controlling the public sector in the sense of providing mechanisms of accountability and responsibility.[256]

A further set of criticisms has come from another perspective but is very much consistent with a restoration of attention to public law foundations of contemporary governance. These commentaries go to the importance of understanding institutions as embodiments of fundamental values and to the relationships among institutions, fundamental principles of the republic, contemporary desires for an awareness of public morality, and public sector ethics. At the root of this conversation is a recognition that institutions are not mere functional mechanisms. As Michael Sandel put it, "Political institutions are not simply instruments that implement ideas independently conceived; they are themselves embodiments of ideas."[257] Moreover, they are not merely the preferences of the moment, emphasizing the question of popularity in the political marketplace but the result of fundamental premises and ongoing contemporary debate.[258] And, again, this is not just a domestic debate but one that is taking place even in the emerging democracies.[259]

The point is not that these critics reject the many efforts to achieve innovations in public administration. Indeed, a number of these critics are relatively conservative politically and certainly not opposed to the use of privatization or the effort to reform regulatory and social service law and procedures. They recognize that, for example, there is every reason to develop incentives to ensure better service, but they do not accept simplistic efforts to picture citizens as customers.[260] They recognize that contracting involves important elements common to the business world, but they recognize as well that negotiators on the public sector side of the table come with special challenges and responsibilities.[261]

While this set of debates has been in progress, there has been a focus on the concept of governance and the management of governance regimes, as described in Chapter 1. The governance models have incorporated much of the agenda of the new public management, but have in some respects gone beyond it. The emphasis on negotiated structures consisting of nonprofit, for-profit, and governmental organizations at all levels along with creative use of policy tools to address new or even seemingly intractable long-standing problems has become a focus of a good deal of scholarly attention. However, for reasons pointed out by Gilmour, Moe, Louis Fisher, and others, these governance regimes have not only not reduced the importance of public law, but they have in many respects created new and even more complex issues arising out of the agreements on which these networks are constructed and operated. As Lester Salamon, one of the leading advocates of what he terms "the new governance," recognized:

> Contrary to the hopeful assumptions of some, 'third party government' poses immense management challenges, perhaps far more immense than those posed by traditional public administration. With power dispersed and numerous semiautonomous entities involved in the operation of public programs, even straightforward tasks become difficult. Indirect tools require advanced planning of far more operation details than is the case with more direct tools. Matters that could be dealt with internally on an ad hoc basis in direct government have to be settled in advance through legally binding contracts under "third party government."[262]

In sum, this is a time of real challenges for public law in public management, but it is also a time when the discussion of the emerging problems and innovations is robust and creative.[263] The challenge developed in part because of the need to respond to the legitimate criticisms that have been leveled at regulatory and social service administration over the past two decades while maintaining those essential administrative law fundamentals that have merged over the two centuries of our national existence. At the same time, it is necessary to create the tools and capabilities needed to implement new types of policy instruments and to work across sectors, throughout the intergovernmental system, and with supranational organizations both regional and global.

SUMMARY

One of the weaknesses of much of the literature and law in public law and public administration is the lack of consideration of the historical underpinnings of the present administrative justice system. That system can be traced back to the very beginning of our country. Certainly, it is inaccurate to assume that our problems in law and administration have sprung full blown from the New Deal, the Great Society, or the New Federalism.

An examination of the history of law and administration in the United States may conveniently be divided into five major periods defined by important political and economic events, problems of governmental administration and attempts to remedy them, and the literature that has provided a continuous record of ongoing problems and possible solutions. From the founding of the republic to about 1928 we experienced the development of public administration, the contest over the legitimacy of broad administrative authority in light of the requirements of the rule of law, and thoughtful theoretical consideration of bases from which to develop a coherent body of administrative law.

Attempts at theory building gave way to the practical needs that arose during the Great Depression, requiring immediate solutions to pressing problems. A compromise solution was adopted with the agreement in government and the legal community that basic due process protections, regular procedure, and the availability of judicial review would provide sufficient protection from administrative arbitrariness. That compromise was enacted into law as the Administrative Procedure Act.

The third period of administrative law development indicated that the APA was no substitute for a coherent theory of administrative law or for more comprehensive techniques of ensuring necessary flexibility for administrators while simultaneously providing safeguards against arbitrariness. The 1970s marked the beginning of specific attempts at significant change. Although highly controversial and admittedly politicized, a number of incremental changes in the operation of the administrative justice system were attempted in several areas of government.

The current period is a time of significant change as efforts such as the new public management and more recently the governance approach have challenged traditional administrative law processes. Whether it is the attack on rulemaking, the rise in the use of presidential direct action through the use of executive orders, the increase in contracted-out operations, or the advocacy of alternative dispute resolution as opposed to formal enforcement and adjudication, it seems clear, as we settle into the twenty-first century, that a host of forces are at place that will render administrative law quite different than it has been over the past 50 years.

NOTES

1. *Rooke's Case,* 5 Co. Rep. 996, 77 Eng. Rep. 209.

2. Walter Gellhorn, *Federal Administrative Proceedings* (Baltimore: John Hopkins, 1941), p. 5.

3. Louis G. Caldwell, "Remarks to the ABA Convention," 58 *Rep. ABA* 197, 201 (1933).

4. Edmund S. Morgan, *The Puritan Dilemma: The Story of John Winthrop* (Boston: Little, Brown, 1958).

5. Frank Goodnow, *Comparative Administrative Law* (New York: Putnam, 1893), Vol. 2, Book 5, Ch. 3.

6. See generally Bernard Bailyn, *The Ideological Origins of the American Revolution* (Cambridge: Harvard University Press, 1967).

7. Leonard D. White, *The Federalists: A Study in Administrative History* (New York: Macmillan, 1959), p. 1. See also Leonard D. White, *The Jeffersonians: A Study in Administrative History, 1801–1829* (New York: Macmillan, 1959).

8. John C. Miller, *Alexander Hamilton and the Growth of the New Nation* (New York: Harper & Row, 1959), and Albert Beveridge, *The Life of John Marshall* (Boston: Houghton Mifflin, 1916–1919).

9. Alexander Hamilton, James Madison, and John Jay, *The Federalist Papers* (New York: Mentor, 1961).

10. Milton M. Carrow, *The Background of Administrative Law* (Newark, NJ: Associated Lawyers, 1948), p. 6.

11. Ernst Freund, *Administrative Powers over Persons and Property: A Comparative Survey* (Chicago: University of Chicago Press, 1928), p. 145.

12. *Id.,* at pp. 143–44.

13. Carrow, *supra* note 10, at p. 6.

14. *Marbury v. Madison,* 5 U.S. (1 Cranch) 137 (1803); *Cohens v. Virginia,* 19 U.S. (6 Wheat.) 264 (1821); *Fletcher v. Peck,* 10 U.S. 87 (1810); and *United States v. Judge Peters,* 9 U.S. (5 Cranch) 115 (1809).

15. *McCulloch v. Maryland,* 17 U.S. (4 Wheat.) 316 (1819). The necessary and proper clause is found in Article 1, §8, clause 18, of the U.S. Constitution.

16. *Gibbons v. Ogden,* 22 U.S. (9 Wheat.) 1 (1824) and *The Daniel Ball,* 77 U.S. (10 Wall.) 557 (1871).

17. See Robert Remini, *Andrew Jackson* (New York: Harper & Row, 1966), and G. Van Deusen, *The Jacksonian Era* (New York: Harper & Row, 1959).

18. Richard Hofstadter, *The Age of Reform* (New York: Random House, 1955), Ch. 1.

19. Carrow, *supra* note 10, at pp. 7–9. See also Isaiah Sharfman, *The Interstate Commerce Commission* (New York: Commonwealth Fund, 1937).

20. Gerald C. Henderson, *The Federal Trade Commission: A Study in Administrative Law and Procedure* (New Haven: Yale University Press, 1924).

21. F. Trowbridge vom Bauer, "Fifty Years of Government Contract Law," 29 *Federal Bar Journal* 305 (1970).

22. William Leuchtenburg, *The Perils of Prosperity* (Chicago: University of Chicago Press, 1958).

23. See generally John Kenneth Galbraith, *The Great Crash of 1929* (Boston: Houghton Mifflin, 1961).

24. Hofstadter, *supra* note 18, Ch. 5.

25. Galbraith, *supra* note 23.

26. See e.g., U.S. Senate, *Report of the Federal Trade Commission on Utility Corporations,* Sen. Doc. no. 92, 70th Cong., 1st Sess., 1935, pt. 73A.

27. 41 Stat. 1063 (1920).

28. Elihu Root, "Public Service by the Bar," in Robert Bacon and James B. Scott, eds., *Elihu Root: Addresses on Government and Citizenship* (Cambridge: Harvard University Press, 1916), pp. 534–35.

29. Freund, *supra* note 11.

30. A. V. Dicey, *Introduction to the Study of the Law of the Constitution* (London; Macmillan, 1965), p. 203.

31. "When we say that the supremacy or the rule of law is characteristic of the English constitution, we generally include at least three distinct though kindred conceptions....We mean, in the first place, that no man is punishable or can be lawfully made to suffer in body or goods except for a distinct breach of law established in the ordinary legal manner before the ordinary courts of the land. In this sense the rule of law is contrasted with every system of government based on the exercise by persons in authority of wide or arbitrary discretionary powers of constraint. We mean in the second place, when we speak of the 'rule of law' as a characteristic of our country, not only that with us no man is above the law, but (what is a different thing) that here every man, whatever be his rank or condition, is subject to the ordinary tribunals....There remains yet a third and a different sense in which the 'rule of law' or the predominance of the legal spirit may be described as a special attribute of English institutions. We may say that the constitution is pervaded by the rule of law on the ground that the general principles of the constitution are with us the result of judicial decisions determining the right of private persons in particular cases brought before the courts." *Id.,* at pp. 188–196.

32. Dicey, in 1915, responded with regret but understanding when the King's Bench Division and the House of Lords handed down their opinions in *Board of Education v. Ria,* A.C. 179, 80 L.J.K.B. 796 (1911), and *Local Government Board v. Arlidge,* A.C. 120, 84 L.J.K.B. 72 (1915). He stated (p. 497): "There remain two checks upon the abuse of judicial or quasi-judicial powers by a government department. In the first place, every department in the exercise of any power possessed by it must conform precisely to the language of any statute by which the power is given to the department, and if any department fails to observe this rule the courts of justice may treat its action as a nullity....In the second place, a Government department must exercise any power in the spirit of judicial fairness."

Thus, Dicey still defended the English system based on his belief that administrative discretion would be carefully limited and that agencies would be required to act like courts in the disposition of cases.

For a discussion of the "extravagant version of the rule of law," see Jerome Frank, *If Men Were Angels: Some Aspects of Government in a Democracy* (New York: Harper & Brothers, 1942), and Kenneth Culp Davis, *Discretionary Justice: A Preliminary Inquiry* (Baton Rouge: Louisiana State University Press, 1969).

33. See Goodnow, *supra* note 5, and his *The Principles of Administrative Law in the United States* (New York: Putnam, 1905).

34. *Id.,* at pp. 323–24.

35. *Id.*

36. *Id.,* at p. 325.

37. John Dickinson, *Administrative Justice and the Supremacy of Law in the United States* (New York: Russell & Russell, 1927). "In Anglo-American jurisprudence, government and law have always in a sense stood opposed to one another; the law has been rather something to give the citizen a check on government than an instrument to give the government control over the citizen. There is a famous passage, which was long attributed to Bracton, to the effect that the king has a superior, to wit, the law; and if he be without a bridle, a bridle ought to be put on him, namely, the law." *Id.,* at p. 32.

38. *Id.,* at p. 113.

39. "The crucial qualities of a common-law court which are absent from administrative tribunals are at least three, two of them being procedural and one substantive. Administrative tribunals are not bound by procedural safeguards which would mould the outcome of an action at law; more specifically they are, in the first place, not bound by the common law rules of evidence and in the second place, parties to proceedings before them do not have the benefit of jury trial. The substantive differences between the administrative procedure and the procedure at law is that the administrative tribunal decides controversies coming before them, not by fixed rules of law, but by the application of governmental discretion or policy." *Id.,* at pp. 35–36.

40. *Id.,* at p. 234.

41. *Id.,* at p. 234.

42. *Id.,* at pp. 37–38.

43. Freund, *supra* note 11.

44. Ernst Freund, *Standards of American Legislation* (Chicago: University of Chicago Press, 1917).

45. *Id.,* Ch. 3.

46. "First, its standards had failed to keep pace with advancing or changing ideals; it was most emphatic in maintaining order and authority, least emphatic in relieving social weakness and inferiority; it developed no principles of reasonableness regarding economic stands or equivalents . . .; its ideal of public policy was too exclusively the advantage of the many and not sufficiently the regard for claims of individual personality; equity was absorbed with property interest to the neglect of nonmaterial human rights." *Id.,* at p. 70.

47. Freund, *supra* note 11, at p. 72.

48. *Id.,* at p. 74.

49. *Id.,* at p. 97.

50. William O. Douglas, "Address to the International Management Congress" in James Allen, ed., *Democracy and Finance: The Addresses and Public Statements of William O. Douglas as a Member and Chairman of the Securities and Exchange Commission* (New Haven: Yale University Press, 1940), p. 56.

51. The confession of a former president of the stock exchange to misappropriation of clients' securities was one of the most devastating examples. Memorandum, William O. Douglas to Stephen A. Early, October 27, 1938, OF 1060 Whitney Folder, Franklin Delano Roosevelt Papers, Franklin Delano Roosevelt Library. See also Louis D. Brandeis, *Other People's Money* (New York: Harper & Row, 1967).

52. See generally James MacGregor Burns, *Roosevelt: The Lion and the Fox* (New York: Harcourt, Brace & World, 1956); William E. Leuchtenburg, *Franklin D. Roosevelt and the New Deal, 1932–1940* (New York: Harper & Row, 1963); and Arthur M. Schlesinger, *The Coming of the New Deal* (Boston: Houghton Mifflin, 1958).

53. Franklin D. Roosevelt, speaking at Oglethorpe University, in Howard Zinn, ed., *New Deal Thought* (Indianapolis: Bobbs-Merrill, 1966), p. 83. See also Jerome Frank, "Experimental Jurisprudence," 78 *Congressional Record* 12412 (1934).

54. Franklin D. Roosevelt, addressing the Commonwealth Club in San Francisco, in Zinn, *supra* note 53. See also Leuchtenburg, *supra* note 52, p. 165.

55. Burns, *supra* note 52, Ch. 14.

56. *Panama Refining Co. v. Ryan,* 293 U.S. 388 (1935); *Schechter Poultry v. United States,* 295 U.S. 995 (1935); *Carter v. Carter Coal Co.,* 298 U.S. 238 (1936); and *United States v. Butler,* 297 U.S. 1 (1936).

57. See generally Fred Rodell, *Nine Men: A Political History of the Supreme Court of the United States from 1790 to 1955* (New York: Random House, 1955).

58. Louis G. Caldwell, "Remarks to ABA Convention," 58 *Reports of the ABA* 197, 197 (1933).

59. *Id.*

60. "A little later I may attempt partially to define an administrative tribunal; for the present let us assume that it is something that looks like a court and acts like a court, but somehow escapes being classified as a court whenever you attempt to impose any limitation on its powers." *Id.*

61. Brownlow Commission, *Report of the President's Committee on Administrative Management* (Washington, DC: Government Printing Office, 1937).

62. The committee was a distinguished body chaired by Dean Acheson with Walter Gellhorn as executive director. Other members were Francis Biddle, Ralph F. Fuchs, Lloyd K. Garrison, Lawrence Groner, Harry M. Hart, Jr., Carl McFarland, James W. Morris, Harry Schulman, E. Blythe Stason, and Arthur T. Vanderbilt.

63. The committee specifically rejected any suggestion that it should consider the wisdom, propriety, or correctness of legislation or administration. See the report cited in note 64, pp. 1–2.

64. U.S. Senate, Report of the Attorney General's Committee on Administrative Procedure, *Administrative Procedure in Government Agencies,* Sen. Doc. no. 8, 77th Cong., 1st Sess. (1941).

65. 5 U.S.C. §551 et seq.

66. Max Farrand, ed., *Records of the Federal Convention of 1787,* rev. ed., 4 Vols. (New Haven: Yale University Press, 1911).

67. 62 Stat. 21, 10 U.S.C. §2303 et seq.

68. 63 Stat. 393.

69. Even the Attorney General's Committee Report focused on relatively recent problems and did not reflect a particularly strong concern for historical continuity.

70. In later years Kenneth Culp Davis would argue that these debates of the thirties over narrow, albeit significant, topics sapped much of the creative energy available to build a new and better administrative jurisprudence. Davis, *supra* note 32, pp. 50–51.

71. Carrow, *supra* note 10, Ch. 7, "The So-Called Rule Against Delegation."

72. Frank, *supra* note 32, Ch. 12, and later Davis, *supra* note 32, pp. 28–42, argued that these concerns stemmed from a belief in an "extravagant version of the rule of law."

73. James M. Landis, *The Administrative Process* (New Haven: Yale University Press, 1938).

74. *Id.,* at p. 2.

75. *Id.,* at p. 24.

76. "Enough [examples] have been given, however, to make clear that even where formal proceedings are fully available, informal procedures constitute the vast bulk of administrative adjudication and are truly the lifeblood of the administrative process. No study of administrative procedure can be adequate if it fails to recognize this fact and focus attention upon improvement at these stages." Attorney General's Committee Report, *supra* note 64, at p. 35.

77. On judicial review, the committee observed: "In the whole field of administrative law the functions that can be performed by judicial review are fairly limited. Its objective, broadly speaking, is to serve as a check on the administrative branch of government's check against excess of power and abusive exercise of power in derogation of private right. But that relates only to one or two more or less equally important aspects of administration. From the point of view of public policy and public interest, it is important not only that the administrator should not encroach on private rights but also that he should effectively discharge his statutory obligations. Excessive favor of private interest may be as prejudicial as excessive encroachment." *Id.,* at p. 76.

78. Gellhorn, *supra* note 2; this work is taken from his James Schouler Lectures at Johns Hopkins, delivered in May 1941, just after publication of the report of the Attorney General's Committee.

79. *Id.*, at p. 5.

80. By "sympathetic administration" Gellhorn meant effective administration carried out by people who know enough about the special problems of the regulated industry or the group seeking services to be sensitive to practical problems.

81. Gelhorn, *supra* note 2, at p. 25.

82. *Id.*, at pp. 39–40.

83. Frank, *supra* note 32, at p. 181.

84. That phrase found its way into American constitutional law in *Marbury v. Madison,* 5 U.S. 137,163 (1803).

85. *Id.*, at p. 9.

86. *Id.*, at p. 3.

87. "It has been widely said that the first problem of today is to reconcile the Expert State and the Free State. Our American democracy, while accommodating itself to new factors heretofore unknown, will have to achieve a balance—which wise political thinkers have always regarded as the chief task of sound government—between two opposed tendencies: enough power to make the government effective but enough liberty to leave the citizens a free agent; it must mediate between absolute dependence and absolute independence for its citizens. In new and difficult circumstances, we must solve the age-old fundamental problem of government, that of reconciling liberty and authority." *Id.*, at p. 18.

88. *Id.*, at pp. 3–7.

89. Roscoe Pound, *Administrative Law: Its Growth, Procedure and Significance* (Pittsburgh: University of Pittsburgh Press, 1942).

90. *Id.*, at p. 113.

91. *Id.*, at pp. 19–20.

92. *Id.*, at p. 55.

93. *The Brig Aurora,* 11 U.S. (7 Cranch) 382 (1813).

94. See e.g., *Field v. Clark,* 143 U.S. 649 (1892); *United States v. Grimaud,* 220 U.S. 506 (1911); *Butterfield v. Stranahan,* 192 U.S. 470 (1904); and *J.W. Hampton, Jr., & Co. v. United States,* 276 U.S. 394 (1928).

95. *Panama Refining Co. v. Ryan,* 293 U.S. 388 (1935).

96. *Schecter Poultry Corp. v. United States,* 295 U.S. 495 (1935).

97. *Carter v. Carter Coal Co.,* 298 U.S. 238 (1936).

98. See e.g., F. Blachly, "Critique of the Federal Administrative Procedure Act," in G. Warren, ed., *The Federal Administrative Act and the Administrative Agencies: Proceedings of an Institute Conducted by the New York University School of Law on February 1–8, 1947* (New York: New York University School of Law, 1947).

99. Eric Goldman, *The Crucial Decade—And After: America, 1945–1960* (New York: Vintage, Books, 1960), p. vi.

100. *Id.* See also Robert Griffin, *The Politics of Fear: Joseph B. McCarthy and the Senate* (New York: Hayden, 1970), and Merle Miller, *Plain Speaking: An Oral Biography of Harry S Truman* (New York: Putnam, 1973).

101. See generally, David McCulloch, *Truman* (New York: Simon and Schuster, 1992).

102. 97 Stat. 246 (1947).

103. Commission members included Herbert Hoover (chairman), Dean Acheson (vice chairman), Arthur S. Flemming, James Forrestal, George H. Mead, George D. Aiken, Joseph P. Kennedy, James K. Pollock, Clarence J. Brown, Carter Monasco, and James H. Rowe, Jr.

104. Commission on Organization of the Executive Branch of Government, *The Hoover Commission Report on the Organization of the Executive Branch of Government* (New York: McGraw-Hill, Inc., 1949).

105. *Id.*, at p. 436.

106. For an excellent commentary on the work of the Hoover Commission and its reports, see Neil MacNeil and Harold W. Metz, *The Hoover Commission Report, 1953–1955: What It Means to You as Citizens and Taxpayers* (New York: Macmillan, 1956). Mr. MacNeil served as editor-in-chief for the commission's report.

107. Task Force members included James March Douglas (chairman), Herbert W. Clark, Cody Fowler, Albert J. Harne, James M. Landis, Carl McFarland, Ross L. Malone, Jr., David F. Maxwell, Harold R. Medina, David W. Peck, Reginald H. Smith, E. Blythe Stason, Elbert Par Tuttle, and Edward L. Wright. Consultants were former justice Robert H. Jackson, George Roberts, and Arthur T. Vanderbilt.

108. There is speculation that the reason that the second Hoover Commission report recommendations were not followed relates to perceptions in Congress that the second round of Commission efforts went beyond efficiency-oriented reorganization proposals to more substantive policy criticisms.

109. See the reports of the ABA Administrative Law Section in 80-84 *Reports of the ABA* (1955–1959).

110. Jack W. Peltason, *Fifty-Eight Lonely Men* (Urbana: University of Illinois Press, 1971). See also Richard Kluger, *Simple Justice* (New York: Knopf, 1976).

111. See generally Griffin, *supra* note 100.

112. P.L. 80-253, 61 Stat. 495 (1947).

113. See e.g., John R. Owens, Edmond Costantini, and Louis F. Weschler, *California Politics and Parties* (London: Macmillan, 1970), Ch. 1.

114. Robert G. Dixon, *Social Security Disability and Mass Justice: A Problem in Welfare Adjudication* (New York: Praeger, 1973).

115. Michael D. Reagan, *The New Federalism* (New York: Oxford University Press, 1972).

116. Alan F. Westin, *Privacy and Freedom* (New York: Atheneum, 1967).

117. James Hart, *Introduction to Administrative Law with Selected Cases,* 2nd ed. (New York: Appleton-Century-Crofts, 1950), p. 23.

118. Dwight Waldo, *The Enterprise of Public Administration: A Summary View* (Novato, CA: Chandler & Sharp, 1980), p. 69.

119. Leonard D. White, *Introduction to the Study of Public Administration,* 4th ed. (New York, Macmillan 1955), p. xvi.

120. Frederick C. Mosher, *Democracy and the Public Service* (New York: Oxford University Press, 1968), Ch. 2–4, and Dwight Waldo, *The Administrative State* (New York: Ronald Press, 1948), pp. 79–80.

121. Waldo, *supra* note 118, Ch. 10. See also Henri Fayol and Frederick W. Taylor, in D.S. Pugh, ed., *Organization Theory* (Baltimore: Penguin, 1971).

122. Waldo, *supra* note 118.

123. Herbert Simon, *Administrative Behavior,* 3rd ed. (New York: Free Press, 1976).

124. Dwight Waldo, "Scope of the Theory of Public Administration" in James C. Charlesworth, ed., *Theory and Practice of Public Administration: Scope, Objectives, and Methods, monograph no. 8, Annals of the American Academy of Political and Social Science* (1968), pp. 14–15.

125. See C. Herman Pritchett, "Public Law and Judicial Behavior," 30 *Journal of Politics* 480 (1968).

126. See the discussion of this trend in Chapter 3.

127. That is, they attracted little attention from the leading public law scholars.

128. U.S. House of Representatives, Task Force on Legal Services and Procedure, *Report on Legal Services and Procedure Prepared for the Commission on Organization of the Executive Branch,* House Doc. no. 1128, 84th Cong., 1st Sess. (1955), p. 2.

129. *Id.,* at p. 19.

130. *Id.,* at p. 30.

131. "Administrative agencies exercise powers delegated to them by Congressional enactment. The scope and meaning of these powers are sometimes inadequately formulated in the legislation. Vague and general statutory terms confer an unnecessarily broad range of discretionary authority upon the administrative officials entrusted to carry out legislative objectives. Such grants of authority, inadequately limited by statutory safeguards and standards are encountered throughout the administrative process." *Id.,* at p. 22.

132. *Id.,* at p. 31.

133. "The primary method which agencies should use to effectuate legislative provisions is the adoption of implementing rules which will give information and guidance to the public. In principle, agencies should not

proceed by adjudication where the subject matter permits the determination and statement of a policy by a rule of general applicability." *Id.,* at p. 24.

134. "All persons should be able to understand administrative processes and to protect their just rights before administrative agencies. They should have reasonable notice of regulations, information concerning the manner in which they defend their position, and knowledge of the means and extent of judicial relief from administrative error." *Id.,* at p. 19.

135. Gellhorn, *supra* note 2, at p. 104.

136. Task Force report, *supra* note 128, at p. 209.

137. *Id.,* at p. 28.

138. U.S. Senate, *Report on Regulatory Agencies to the President-Elect,* 86th Cong., 2d Sess. (1960). (Hereafter referred to as Landis Report).

139. Landis's description of the situation at the Federal Power Commission is an excellent example of the tenor of the Landis Report: "The Federal Power Commission without question represents the outstanding example in the federal government of the breakdown of the administrative process. The complexity of its problems is no answer to its more patent failures." *Id.,* at p. 54.

140. "One of the worst phases of this situation is the existence of groups of lawyers in Washington itself, who implicitly hold out to clients that they have means of access to various agencies off the record that are more important than those that can be made on the record." *Id.,* at p. 14.

141. *Id.,* at p. 5.

142. *Id.,* at p. 9.

143. For an interesting commentary on the Landis Report, see Carl McFarland, "Landis' Report: The Voice of One Crying in the Wilderness," 47 *Virginia L. Rev.* 373 (1961).

144. *Id.,* at pp. 19–20.

145. Another notable political scientist at work in this area was Martin Shapiro, *The Supreme Court and Administrative Agencies* (New York: Free Press, 1968).

146. Peter Woll, *Administrative Law: The Informal Process* (Berkeley: University of California Press, 1963).

147. "The raison d'etre of the administrative process is the increasing need for more flexibility than is provided by either Congress or the courts. Modern regulation requires specialization, expertise, continuity of service, and flexibility for utilization of a variety of skills which would not be possible operating within a strict common-law framework. Even the formal administrative process was intended to be more flexible than a court of law, and the courts half permitted this utilization of more flexible procedure; however, it is actually the informal administrative process that epitomizes those characteristics for which there was a felt need at the time of the creation: of the administrative agency as a regulators device." *Id.,* at p. 188.

148. *Id.,* at p. 5.

149. *Id.,* at p. 2.

150. *Id.,* at pp. 29–30.

151. *Id.,* at p. 34.

152. *Id.,* at p. 61.

153. "Present day criticism of the independent regulatory agencies by the American Bar Association and some of its representatives concentrates upon administrative proceeding through proper use of formal judicial techniques. Criticism from the administrative standpoint, on the other hand, focus upon the importance of proper policy formulation and coordination, and upon the need for greater efficiency in handling the adjudicative and legislative tasks of agencies. The orientation of each group I reflected in their respective proposals for administrative law reform." *Id.,* at p. 177.

154. See e.g., Louis L. Jaffe, *Judicial Control of Administrative Action* (Boston: Little, Brown, 1965).

155. Chapter 7 describes this tradition of deference.

156. Kenneth Culp Davis, *Administrative Law* (St. Paul: West Publishing, 1951).

157. Kenneth Culp Davis, *Administrative Law Treatise* (St. Paul: West Publishing, 1958).

158. *Id.,* §28-16.

159. Jaffe, *supra* note 154.

160. Raoul Berger, "Administrative Arbitrariness and Judicial Review," 65 *Columbia L. Rev.* 55 (1965); Davis, *Administrative Law Treatise, 1965 Supplement,* §28.16; Berger, "Administrative Arbitrariness – A Reply to Professor Davis," 114 *U. Pennsylvania L. Rev.* 783 (1966); Davis, "A Final Word," 14 *U. Pennsylvania L. Rev.* 814 (1966); Berger, "Rejoinder," 114 *U. Pennsylvania L. Rev.* 816 (1966); Davis, "Postscript," 114 *U. Pennsylvania L. Rev.* 823 (1966); Berger, "Sequel," 51 *Minnesota L. Rev.* 601 (1967); Davis, "Not Always," 51 *Minnesota L. Rev.* 643 (1967); Berger, "Synthesis," 78 *Yale L. J.* 965 (1969).

161. Harold D. Lasswell, *Politics Who Gets What, When and How* (New York: McGraw-Hill, 1936).

162. See generally "Report of the Twentieth Century Fund Task Force on the Law Enforcement Assistance Administration," *Law Enforcement: The Federal Role* (New York: McGraw-Hill, 1976).

163. See e.g., Lee Epstein, *Conservatives in Court* (Knoxville: University of Tennessee Press, 1985); Karen O'Connor and Lee Epstein, "The Rise of Conservative Interest Group Litigation," 45 *Journal of Politics* 479 (1983).

164. Reagan, *supra* note 115.

165. The phrase "the best and the brightest" is best known today as the title of a best-selling book by David Halberstam (New York: Random House, 1972), but it was a New Deal term long before that.

166. See James F. Simon, *In His Own Image: The Supreme Court in Richard Nixon's Era* (New York: McKay, 1973).

167. See U.S. House of Representatives, Hearings Before the Subcommittee on Courts, Civil Liberties, and the Administration of Justice of the Committee on the Judiciary, *The State of the Judiciary and Access to Justice,* 95th Cong., 1st. Sess. (1977). See also R. A. Sedler and A. W. Houseman, eds., "Symposium: Access to Federal Courts: Rights Without Remedies," 30 *Rutgers L. Rev.* 841 (1977).

168. See *Rhodes v. Chapman,* 452 U.S. 337 (1981).

169. See Yezekel Dror, *Design for the Policy Sciences* (New York: American Elsevier Pub. Co., 1971) and, later, *Public Policymaking Reexamined* (San Francisco, Chandler Pub. Co., 1968).

170. Sir Henry Maine, *Ancient Law* (New York; Everyman Press, 1972), Ch. 1.

171. P.L. 94-142, 89 Stat. 773, 20 U.S.C. §§1232, 1401, 1405, 1406, 1411-1420, 1453 (1976). See Erwin L. Levine and Elizabeth M. Wexler, *PL94-142: An Act of Congress* (New York: Macmillan, 1981).

172. 20 U.S.C. §1400 *et seq.*

173. Stephen R. Chitwood, "Legalizing American Public Administration—Practical and Theoretical Implications for the Field," unpublished paper presented at 1978 annual meeting of the American Society for Public Administration.

174. From that time on, the ACUS published annual recommendations with supporting scholarly Studies. Unfortunately, it fell victim to the budget crunch of the 1990s and went out of existence. There has been an effort to reauthorize it with the support of a wide variety of legal scholars and even justices of the U.S. Supreme Court, but the future is uncertain. See P.L.108-401, 118 Stat. 2255 (2004).

175. See the legislative veto provision of the Federal Trade Commission Improvement Act of 1980, reproduced in Chapter 5.

176. P.L. 94-409, 90 Stat. 1241, 5 U.S.C. §5526.

177. 5 U.S.C. App. 1. See the discussion of the Act in Chapter 11. The Act is reproduced in Appendix 3.

178. *Environmental Defense Fund v. Ruckelshaus,* 439 F. 2d. 584, 597 (D.C.Cir. 1971).

179. See e.g., Ralph F. Fuchs, "Development and Diversification in Administrative Rule Making," 72 *Northwestern U. L. Rev.* 83 (1977), and Stephen Williams, "'Hybrid Rulemaking' under the Administrative Procedure Act: A Legal and Empirical Analysis," 42 *U. Chicago L. Rev.* 401 (1975).

180. *Vermont Yankee Nuclear Power Corp. v. Natural Resources Defense Council,* 435 U.S. 519 (1978). See Antonin Scalia, "Vermont Yankee: The APA, the D.C. Circuit, and the Supreme Court," 1979 *Supreme Court Rev.* 345 (1979), and "*Vermont Yankee Nuclear Power Corp. v. Natural Resources Defense Council, Inc.*: Three Perspectives," 91 *Harvard L. Rev.* 1805 (1978).

181. *Rizzo v. Goode,* 423 U.S. 362 (1976); *Maine v. Thiboutot,* 448 U.S. 1 (1980); *Owen v. City of Independence,* 445 U.S. 622 (1980); *Butz v. Economou,* 438 U.S. 478 (1978); *Monell v. New York City Dep't of Social Service,* 436 U.S. 658 (1978); and *Wood v. Strickland,* 420 U.S. 308 (1975).

182. Davis, *supra* note 32.

183. Kenneth Culp Davis, "A New Approach to Delegation," 36 *U. Chicago L. Rev.* 713 (1969).

184. Davis, *supra* note 32, at p. 113. Several statutes have been enacted in this area since Davis wrote his criticism, but the critique remains valid a decade after it was originally published.

185. *Id.*, Ch. 3–5.

186. *Id.*, Ch. 3.

187. *Id.*, at pp. 159–61.

188. *Id.*, at pp. 57–59.

189. *Id.*, at p. 159.

190. "My opinion is, paradoxically, today's excessive discretionary power is largely attributable to the zeal of those who a generation ago were especially striving to protect against discretionary power. If they had been less zealous they would have attempted less, and if they had attempted less they might have succeeded. They attempted too much—so much that they could not possibly succeed—and they were decisively defeated. They tended to oppose all discretionary power; they should have opposed only unnecessary discretionary power." *Id.*, at pp. 27–28.

191. Louis L. Jaffe, "Book Review," 14 *Villanova L. Rev.* 773 (1969), and J. Skelly Wright, "Beyond Discretionary Justice," 81 *Yale L. J.* 575 (1972).

192. See e.g., Wright, *supra* note 191, at p. 595.

193. Abraham Sofaer, "Judicial Control of Informal Discretionary Adjudication and Enforcement," 72 *Columbia L. Rev.* 1293 (1972).

194. "The call for greater control of informal discretionary action deserves sympathetic attention. Ample evidence has accumulated of the need for legislative, judicial, and administrative reform to narrow discretionary power in numerous areas. Broad discretion in adjudication and enforcement at INS causes inconsistency, arbitrariness, and inefficiency." *Id.*, at p. 1374.

195. *Id.*, at pp. 1313.

196. *Id.*, at pp. 1358.

197. Ernest Gellhorn and Glen O. Robinson, "Perspectives on Administrative Law," 75 *Columbia L. Rev.* 771 (1975).

198. Richard B. Stewart, "The Reformation of American Administrative Law," 88 *Harvard L. Rev.* 1667 (1975).

199. *Id.*, at pp. 1688.

200. Al Gore, Report of the National Performance Review, *From Red Tape to Results: Creating a Government That Works Better & Costs Less* (Washington, DC: Government Printing Office, 1993).

201. David Osborne and Ted Gaebler, *Reinventing Government* (New York: Penguin, 1992).

202. Lester M. Salamon, *Partners in Public Service: Government-Nonprofit Relations in the Modern Welfare State* (Baltimore: Johns Hopkins University Press, 1995), p. 19.

203. Paul C. Light, *The True Size of Government* (Washington, DC: Brookings Institution, 1999).

204. On the convergence and tensions between the government, private, and nonprofit sectors, see Lester M. Salamon, *The Resilient Sector: The State of Nonprofit America* (Washington, DC: Brookings Institution Press, 2003); A. Burton Weisbrod, "The Future of the Nonprofit Sector: Its Entwining with Private Enterprise and Government," 16 *Journal of Policy Analysis and Management* 541 (1997). I have discussed the legal criteria that go to the differences in Phillip J. Cooper, *Governing by Contract* (Washington, DC: CQ Press, 2002), pp. 71–76.

205. Charles Goodsell, *The Case for Bureaucracy,* 3rd ed. (Chatham, NJ: Chatham House, 1994).

206. See Donald F. Kettl, *Sharing Power* (Washington, DC: Brookings Institution, 1993); *Government by Proxy* (Washington, DC: CQ Press, 1988).

207. See U.S. General Accounting Office, *Block Grants: Characteristics, Experience, and Lessons Learned* (Washington, DC: General Accounting Office, 1995).

208. Phillip J. Cooper, Albert Hyde, J. Steven Ott, Linda Brady, Harvey White, and Olivia Hidalgo-Hardeman, *Public Administration for the Twenty-First Century* (Fort Worth: Harcourt, Brace, 1998), p. 129.

209. See generally, George W. Downs and Patrick D. Larkey, *The Search for Government Efficiency* (New York: Random House, 1986).

210. See e.g., *Cornelius v. NAACP*, 473 U.S. 788 (1985).

211. On the Report of the President's Private Sector Survey on Cost Control (better known as the Grace Commission Report), see Charles Goodsell, "The Grace Commission: Seeking Efficiency for the Whole People," 44 *Public Administration Rev.* 196 (1984). Stuart M. Butler, Michael Sanera, and W. Bruce Weinrod, *Mandate for Leadership II* (Washington, DC: Heritage Foundation, 1984).

212. See generally, John J. DiIulio, Jr., and Donald F. Kettl, *Fine Print: The Contract with America, Devolution, and the Administrative Realities of American Federalism* (Washington, DC: Brookings Institution, 1995).

213. *Id.,* p. 15.

214. Report of the National Performance Review, *From Red Tape to Results: Creating a Government That Works Better & Costs Less* (Washington, DC: Government Printing Office, 1993).

215. Cornelius M. Kerwin, *Rulemaking* (Washington, DC: CQ Press, 1994).

216. See e.g., U.S. Office of Management and Budget, *Summary Report of the SWAT Team on Civilian Agency Contracting* (Washington, DC: Office of Management and Budget, 1992) and Donald F. Kettl, *Sharing Power* (Washington, DC: Brookings Institution, 1993).

217. See Katy Harrigar, *Independent Justice: The Federal Special Prosecutor in American Politics* (Lawrence, KS: Kansas University Press, 1992). See also Cornell W. Clayton, ed., *Government Lawyers: The Federal Legal Bureaucracy and Presidential Politics* (Lawrence, KS: Kansas University Press, 1995). Leaders of both parties were more than happy to let the special prosecutor statute lapse when it came time for reauthorization.

218. *Clinton v. Jones,* 520 U.S. 681 (1997).

219. Mary Schiavo, *Flying Blind, Flying Safe* (New York: Avon Books, 1997) and Paul Eddy, Elaine Potter, and Bruce Paige, *Destination Disaster* (New York: Ballentine Books, 1976).

220. See e.g., *Morales v. TWA,* 504 U.S. 374 (1992).

221. See e.g., U.S. General Accounting Office, *Acquisition Reform: Purchase Car Use Cuts Procurement Costs, Improves Efficiency* (Washington, DC: General Accounting Office, 1996).

222. See e.g., Carol Ascher, Norm Fruchter, and Robert Berne, *Hard Lessons: Public Schools and Privatization* (New York: Twentieth Century Fund, 1996) and Craig Richards, Rima Shore, and Max. B. Sawicky, *Risky Business: Private Management of Public Schools* (Washington, DC: Economic Policy Institute, 1996).

223. U.S. General Accounting Office, *Private and Public Prisons: Studies Comparing Operational Costs and/or Quality of Service* (Washington, DC: General Accounting Office, 1996).

224. See U.S. General Accounting Office, *Worker Protection: Federal Contractors and Violations of Labor Law* (Washington, DC: General Accounting Office, 1995) and U.S. General Accounting Office, *Occupational Safety and Health: Violations of Safety and Health Regulations by Federal Contractors* (Washington, DC: General Accounting Office, 1996).

225. See e.g., U.S. Office of Management and Budget, *Summary Report of the SWAT Team on Civilian Agency Contracting* (Washington, DC: Office of Management and Budget, 1992).

226. U.S. Office of Management and Budget, *The President's Management Agenda* (Washington, DC: OMB, 2001).

227. See Executive Order 13198, "Agency Responsibilities with Respect to Faith-Based and Community Initiatives," 66 Fed. Reg. 8497 (2001); Executive Order 13199, "Establishment of White House Office of Faith-Based and Community Initiatives," 66 Fed. Reg. 8499 (2001).

228. OMB, President's Management Agenda, *supra* note 226, contents.

229. U.S. Office of Management and Budget, Office of Information and Regulatory Affairs, "Peer Review and Information Quality: Proposed Bulletin Under Executive Order 12866 and Supplemental Information Quality Guidelines," at http://www.whitehouse.gov/omb/pubpress/2003-34.pdf, as of October 4, 2005.

230. See e.g., *National Treasury Employees Union v. Chertoff,* 2005 U.S. Dist. LEXIS 17216 (D.D.C. 2005).

231. See e.g., "Statement on Signing the Consolidated Appropriations Resolution in February 2003," 39 *Weekly Compilation of Presidential Documents* 226 (2003); "Statement on Signing the Intelligence Authorization Act for FY2004," 39 *Weekly Compilation of Presidential Documents* 1778 (2003). See also Executive Order 13361, 69

Fed. Reg. 67633 (2004); Executive Order 13346, 69 Fed. Reg. 41905 (2004); Executive Order 13302, 68 Fed. Reg. 27429 (2003); Executive Order 13257, 67 Fed. Reg. 7259 (2002).

232. On the concept of the unitary control of the executive, see Christopher S. Yoo, Steven G. Calabresi, and Laurence D. Nee, "The Unitary Executive During the Third Half-Century, 1889–1945," 80 *Notre Dame Law Review* 1 (2004; Steven G. Calabresi, "The Virtues of Presidential Government." 18 *Constitutional Commentary* 51 (2001); Neal Devins and Michael Herz, "Velazquez and Beyond: The Uneasy Case for Department of Justice Control of Federal Litigation, 5 *University of Pennsylvania Journal of Constitutional Law* 558 (2003); Lawrence Lessig and Cass Sunstein, "The President and the Administration," 94 *Columbia Law Review* 2 (1994).

233. National Commission on Terrorist Attacks Upon the United States, *The 9/11 Commission Report: Final Report of the National Commission on Terrorist Attacks Upon the United States* (Washington, DC: Government Printing Office, 2003), p. 14

234. 115 Stat. 224 (2001).

235. Executive Order 13228, 66 Fed. Reg. 51812 (2001)

236. P.L. 107-56, 115 Stat. 272 (2001).

237. P.L. 107-296, 116 Stat. 2135 (2002).

238. P.L. 109-62, 119 Stat. 1991 (2005), §101.

239. P.L.107-204, 116 Stat. 745 (2002).

240. World Bank, *World Development Report 1997* (New York: Oxford University Press, 1997).

241. Donald J. Savoie, *Thatcher, Reagan, Mulroney: In Search of a New Bureaucracy* (Toronto: University of Toronto Press, 1994).

242. See B. Guy Peters and Donald Savoie, eds., *Governance in a Changing Environment.* (Montreal: McGill/Queens University Press, 1995).

243. See Christopher Pollitt in Peters and Savoie, ibid. See also Paul M. Tellier, *Public Service 2000: A Report on Progress* (Ottawa: Minister of Supply and Services, 1992) and Management Advisory Board and Management Improvement Advisory Committee, *Accountability in the Public Sector* (Canberra: Australian Government Publishing Service, 1993).

244. See Peters and Savoie, *supra* note 242. See also James Perry, ed., *The Handbook of Public Administration,* 2nd ed. (San Francisco: Jossey-Bass, 1996).

245. W. Edwards Deming, *Out of the Crisis: Quality, Productivity and Competitive Position* (Cambridge, UK: Cambridge University Press, 1988). See also Mary Walton, *The Deming Management Method* (New York: Dodd, Mead, 1986).

246. See Patricia Ingraham in Peters and Savoie, *supra* note 242.

247. Vincent Ostrum, *The Intellectual Crisis in American Public Administration,* 2nd ed. (Tuscaloosa: University of Alabama Press, 1989).

248. See e.g., John E. Chubb and Terry More, *Politics, Markets, & America's Schools* (Washington, DC: Brookings Institution, 1990).

249. Russel M. Linden, *Seamless Government: A Practical Guide to Reengineering the Public Sector* (San Francisco: Jossey-Bass, 1994).

250. See Barry Bozeman, *All Organizations Are Public* (San Francisco: Jossey-Bass, 1987); "Exploring the Limits of Public and Private Sectors: Sector Boundaries as Maginot Line," *Public Administration Review* 48 (Mar./Apr. 1988): pp. 672–74.

251. See James G. March and Johan P. Olsen, *Rediscovering Institutions: The Organizational Basis of Politics* (New York: Free Press, 1990).

252. *Id.,* p. 3. See also Terry M. Moe, "The Economics of Organization," 26 *American Journal of Political Science* 739 (1984).

253. Donald F. Kettl, *Sharing Power: Public Governance and Private Markets* (Washington, DC: Brookings, 1993).

254. See H. Brinton Milward "Implications of Contracting Out: New Roles for the Hollow State," in Patricia W. Ingraham and Barbara S. Romzek, eds., *New Paradigms for Government* (San Francisco: Jossey-Bass, 1994).

255. Ronald C. Moe and Robert S. Gilmour, "Rediscovering Principles of Public Administration: The Neglected Foundation of Public Law," 55 *Public Administration Rev.* 135 (1995); Ronald C. Moe, "'Law' Versus 'Performance' as Objective Standard," 48 *Public Administration Rev.* 675 (1988); "Exploring the Limits of Privatization," 47 *Public Administration Rev.* 453 (1988).

256. United Nations Experts Group on Public Administration and Finance, "Draft Report of the Twelfth Meeting of Experts on the United Nations Programme in Public Administration and Finance to the Resumed 50th General Assembly Session on Public Administration and Development," August 11, 1995, p. 48.

257. Michael J. Sandel, *Democracy's Discontent* (Cambridge: Harvard University Press, 1996), p. ix

258. See John Rohr, *Ethics for Bureaucrats: An Essay on Law and Values* (New York: Marcel Dekker, 1978); Rohr, *To Run a Constitution: The Legitimacy of the Administrative State* (Lawrence, KS: Kansas University Press, 1986); William D. Richardson, *Democracy, Bureaucracy, & Character* (Lawrence, KS: University of Kansas Press, 1997); William D. Richardson and Lloyd G. Nigro, "Administrative Ethics and Founding Thought: Constitutional Correctives, Honor, and Education," 47 *Public Administration Rev.* 367 (1987).

259. Vaclav Havel, *The Art of the Impossible: Politics as Morality in Practice* (New York: Alfred A. Knopf, 1994). See also James Q. Wilson, *The Moral Sense* (New York: The Free Press, 1993).

260. See Jon Pierre, "The Marketization of the State: Citizens, Consumers, and the Emergence of the Public Market," in Peters and Savoie, *supra* note 242.

261. Lloyd Burton, "Ethical Discontinuities in Public-Private Sector Negotiation," 9 *Journal of Policy Analysis and Management* 23 (1990).

262. Lester M. Salamon, *The Tools of Government: A Guide to the New Governance* (New York: Oxford University Press, 2002), p. 38.

263. See e.g., the essays in Phillip J. Cooper and Chester A. Newland, eds., *Handbook of Public Law and Administration* (San Francisco: Jossey-Bass, 1997).

5

Agency Rulemaking

The chapters in Part I have considered the operation of the administrative justice system as a whole. Particular attention has been given to the need for a broad understanding of administrative law, a concern for producer and consumer perspectives on administrative decisionmaking, a multifaceted approach to administrative law problems that recognizes the growing importance of supranational factors and contract-based governance arrangements, the need for sensitivity to the relationship between the law in books and the law in action. The next several chapters will be more particular in orientation, focusing on specific elements of administrative justice. There are also problems of informal process, discretion, and power law to be considered in Chapters 8–13, but first we turn to the formal processes of administrative law that have developed, as Chapter 4 indicated, out of several decades of administrative practice and legal challenge. This is sometimes referred to as the black letter law of public administration.

These formal procedures are agency rulemaking, administrative adjudication, and judicial review of administrative activity. This chapter focuses on the methods by which rules are adopted. As Chapter 4 suggested, rulemaking is a process that has been evolving over time, even though its basic elements have been well established for years. Each new president and congressional majority, as well as governors and state legislatures, place their own new ideas and, to be sure, their frustrations with rules and rulemaking into policies that continue to reshape the process and the product. Controversies over such policies as the Food and Drug Administration's (FDA) rules seeking to ban dietary supplements containing ephredrine alkaloids,[1] the Department of Agriculture's and FDA's rulemaking in response to the discovery of a cow with bovine spongiform encephalopathy (also known as "Mad Cow" disease),[2] and the EPA's decision under the Bush administration to reverse course and withdraw its rules on arsenic in drinking water are only a few of the contemporary battles over agency rulemaking.[3] This chapter will consider both the well-established foundation principles of rulemaking and also more recent trends and shifts in emphasis. As these examples demonstrate, the importance of rulemaking has not diminished even in an era dominated by advocates of deregulation and the increased use of governance arrangements that involve a host of governmental and nongovernmental organizations. The dynamics of globalization have in some respects added to the need for rulemaking rather than reducing it.

Before considering the formal aspects of administrative law, it is necessary to gain at least a general understanding of the statutory foundations of administrative law and, in particular, to develop a familiarity with the Administrative Procedure Act (APA), which governs administrative practice in federal agencies. Most states have a similar statute intended to ensure a degree of uniformity in agency operations.[4]

THE STATUTORY FOUNDATIONS OF ADMINISTRATIVE LAW

Since administrative agencies are primarily creatures of statute, and most of what they do is authorized or constrained by statute, it is important to be aware of the legislative foundations on which public administrators function. That is true regardless of the level of government. It is even important for executives in not-for-profit organizations. A knowledge of statutes not only tells these consumers of administrative decisions how agencies and communities can operate but also addresses such specific concerns as the structure and operation of programs that nonprofit organizations wish to engage as well as the processes for grants, contracts, and other forms of partnerships that governmental bodies may use. Indeed, statutes (and ordinances, which are the local government analog of legislation) are the way that the judgments of democracy are moved through the constitutional process and transformed into policy in the streets. More specifically, it is important for public sector executives to understand the basic types of statutes and their significance.

Enabling Acts, Authorization Statutes, and Appropriations Legislation

Generally speaking, there are three types of statutes that are commonly employed in public administration. They are enabling acts, authorization statutes, and appropriations laws. A true statutory picture of an agency can be painted only with all of these taken together.

Enabling acts are used to create public agencies. At the local level, many communities function on the basis of charters issued by the state legislature, which illustrate another type of enabling act. Enabling laws establish organizations and define their basic powers as well as their jurisdiction, the settings within which those powers can be used. It is important to remember the distinction between having legal authority and possessing the jurisdiction to use it in any given situation. Both are prescribed by statute.

Of course, enabling acts rarely stand alone. Agencies usually acquire additional program responsibilities from what are termed authorization statutes. As the name suggests, authorizations statutes are legislation that is used to present a new policy or to require an agency to undertake new responsibilities. Agencies often acquire many such new programs and duties over the years.

There are several sources for these statutes, and their importance varies with circumstances of their enactment and depends upon the office a public administrator occupies. During the 1960s and 1970s, it sometimes seemed as though everything of significance, in terms of legislation at least, was coming from Washington. That was not true, of course, but it was the case that Congress was launching a wide range of important and expansive programs in a variety of fields. State and local governments have been very active since the 1980s, in part because they had to be and in part because states have been attempting to assert their own authority to address local needs while simultaneously responding to federal requirements.[5] Still, to a city manager, the willingness of legislatures at all levels to develop new programs, often without adequate resources to support them, means just one unfunded mandate after another. Congress enacted an unfunded mandates statute, but it was not made retroactive, nor does it prohibit the states from placing such mandates on local governments.[6]

However, one of the increasingly important types of authorization statute is the growing number of statutes that are passed to implement international agreements, such as the Ocean Dumping Convention and many other environmental or health accords. In these situations, the legislation may be of a peculiar form, requiring unusual action or a different process from what is often employed in standard domestic legislation. Thus, the Coast Guard found itself facing a difficult squeeze in attempting to develop regulations to comply with the international ocean dumping restrictions. The problem was that the Coast Guard, a unit of the U.S. Department of Transportation, had to meet the deadlines of the international agreement and related legislation but had as well to comply with U.S. domestic administrative procedure requirements. The same is true of many other agencies that find themselves more engaged in international issues than most Americans would expect. The U.S. Environmental Protection Agency's (EPA) role in NAFTA implementation issues and the Nuclear Regulatory Commission's (NRC) obligations to reconcile U.S. rules with those of the International Atomic Energy Agency (discussed later in this chapter) provide examples.

A number of these statutes also implement international accords that establish border governance arrangements, commercial agreements, or, more recently, national and international security agreements designed to address threats from international terrorism. These agreements are often broader in scope than some of the earlier agreements and address not just specific fields of public policy, but are cross-cutting, affecting a wide range of issues and policies. These statutes, following the design of the treaties they are intended to implement, often combine elements of enabling acts, as when they set up a governing body with representatives from two or more nations, and authorization legislation, since they contain specific policy-oriented material in one or more fields. Certainly, the legislation and executive orders implementing the North American Free Trade Agreement provide examples.[7]

There are also budget bills and related fiscal legislation often classified under the heading of appropriations statutes. What is referred to as "the federal budget" really consists of 13 separate appropriations bills. There are also often continuing resolutions, used to keep funds flowing when the budget bills have not been passed by the beginning of the new fiscal year (a common contemporary phenomenon and one that arises in a slightly different form at the state level as well as in the federal process). Then there is what is called budget reconciliation legislation, which is passed when the budget process is complete and the levels of continuation funding must be adjusted to final funding levels. In many years, there is also a need for debt limit extension legislation at the national level, usually needed to allow the federal government to borrow to address increasing debt.

Also common in recent years has been the tendency to miss the beginning of the fiscal year with most appropriations bills and later to enact something often called a Consolidated Appropriations Act for the fiscal year. These pieces of legislation may be more than a thousand pages long and, because they are essential pieces of legislation, it is common to load a variety of different kinds of provisions onto them.[8] Debt limit extension bills also attract the tendency to hang ornaments on the legislation, leading to a tendency to refer to these types of must-pass bills as Christmas tree statutes.

Theoretically, these statutes have only to do with spending limits. However, they are often used to make substantive law, affecting the way a particular agency operates by creating new policies and programs or by specifying the ways in which funds must, may, or may not be used. For example, Congress adopted a very controversial set of policies known collectively as "The Real ID Act of 2005" as Division B of the "Emergency Supplemental Appropriations Act for Defense, the Global War on Terror, and Tsunami Relief, 2005."[9] The Real ID Act made significant changes in the law governing those who claim refugee status in the United States, authorized significant border protection actions by the Department of Homeland Security, and established a variety of requirements for state governments in issuing driver's licenses.

Management Laws

These fiscal bills are sometimes used to implement government-wide statutes that fit under the heading of management laws. Thus, the debt limit extension bill in 1996 was used to adopt significant revisions to the Administrative Procedure Act.[10] Management laws provide tools for managing and controlling agencies. In addition to the federal APA and its state-level equivalents, there are civil service statutes at all levels of government that define public employment, prescribe rights for employees, and set procedures for supervision and discipline. Civil service statutes are modified in operation by collective bargaining agreements entered into by government units and employee bargaining units. While the contracts may not violate civil service law, they may add requirements beyond those listed in the statute.

Another set of statutes controls government contracting. Historically, these laws have been separate from the APAs. They were adopted with a concern for preventing corruption and often focus on the processes by which bids are accepted and contracts are awarded. The 1990s witnessed attempts at the federal level to modify these laws using both statutes and executive orders.[11] Most states have not yet given adequate attention to their contracting laws. Even at the federal level, the statutes are still in need of a great deal of work.

Overall, there is a need to update these contracting statutes to address growing trends to contract for services rather than merely for the purchase of goods (the traditional conceptual framework for most contracting laws). The statutes also need to better integrate government contract law with other general management statutes. When so much of what is done by government at all levels is carried out through contract, it is inappropriate to have such a lack of integration between government contract laws and other management statutes such as the APAs.

There is also a significant body of legislation concerned with maintaining accountability. Among these is the federal Ethics in Government Act (for which virtually every state has adopted some related policy), which prohibits conflicts of interest and sets other protections against abuse of office. There are also investigative and auditing statutes such as the federal government's Inspector General Act.[12] Inspectors general are officers who hold special independence and exercise investigative and reporting authority.[13]

The Civil Rights Framework

A large body of statutes was created and amended from the late 1950s into the 1990s that sought to address the wide-ranging issues associated with civil rights. It is true that there are constitutional provisions in the Fourteenth Amendment that require states, and by extension local governments, to ensure that all persons receive the equal protection of the laws. It is also true that the Supreme Court has read the Fifth Amendment to require similar guarantees from the federal government.[14] However, Congress has for a variety of reasons adopted more specific sets of statutory protections that prohibit discrimination on the basis of race, gender, age, pregnancy, and physical disability. The most pervasive statute in this field is the Civil Rights Act of 1964, with its numerous amendments, which prohibits discrimination in the terms or conditions of employment, in programs funded by the federal government, and in places of public accommodation. Since that statute was adopted, other protections have been added, including the Age Discrimination in Employment Act (ADEA),[15] Pregnancy Disability Amendments,[16] Individuals with Disabilities Education Act,[17] and the Americans with Disabilities Act (ADA).[18] At the federal level, the Civil Service Reform Act of 1978 attempted to integrate a number of these statutes into a coherent framework covering federal civil servants against discrimination.[19]

The most often used statute to enforce civil rights with respect to state and local government is a post–Civil War law codified as 42 U.S.C. §1983. That statute permits a citizen whose rights under the Constitution or laws of the United States are violated to sue state or local employees and units of local government.[20]

THE ADMINISTRATIVE PROCEDURE ACT

Of course, for public administration, one of the most important elements in the statutory framework is the Administrative Procedure Act (APA) and its state-level equivalents. Before addressing particular aspects of formal administrative law, however, it is important to block out the statute as a whole. This is a useful practice for anyone approaching a statute (or an administrative rule) for the first time. Begin by examining the introductory paragraphs, including the section on definitions. For reasons that will become clear later in this chapter, it is important to be aware that the decisions about the meaning of key concepts that are used in a statute, as well as decisions about what activities might be listed as exempt from the statute's provisions, often represent important political judgments. They should not be ignored or glossed over in an effort to get at what seems to be the more important substantive portion of a piece of legislation.

The next aspect of blocking a statute is the task of considering the key headings of the major portions of the law. These titles can provide a good deal of information and an overall sense of the nature of a statute even before the reader has considered any of its detailed provisions. In the case of the APA, such a blocking exercise makes it quite clear just how directly this law responds to the kinds of issues that had emerged over the history of the field, as considered in Chapter 4, and not from some coherent theory of administrative law.

The APA can be understood by observing in some detail its basic components, which include: (1) an introduction, (2) fair information practices rules, (3) rulemaking, (4) adjudications, (5) qualifications and conduct of the presiding officer in administrative proceedings, (6) special regulatory flexibility provisions for small organizations, (7) judicial review of administrative decisions, and (8) regulatory analysis and review requirements. These components correspond to concerns about the need to establish general guidelines for federal agencies with: (1) due process protections in adjudications, (2) open, orderly, and participative rulemaking, and (3) judicial review as the cornerstones of administrative law. The sections concerned with regulatory flexibility analysis and congressional review were added later to address particular political attacks on regulation.

In the search for a conceptual framework to use as an organizing tool for the statute, the framers of the APA emphasized the idea that most matters of administrative law (as the term was understood in the 1940s when the statute was enacted) could be classified as quasi-legislative, which resulted in the making of rules, or quasi-judicial, which, like court decisions, produced orders governing particular cases or licenses awarded to applicants.[21] It was around this dichotomy that the act was structured.[22]

Thus, a lengthy definition is provided for what constitutes a rule. Rulemaking is defined as the process for producing a rule. An order is defined basically as a decision other than a rule, and adjudication is defined as the process for issuing an order. Licensing is defined as a particular species of adjudication. This set of conceptual relationships both explains the importance of the definitions section of a statute and illustrates just how the rule/order distinction provides the basis for the statute. It also recalls the discussion in Chapter 1 about the limiting dichotomies that were built into administrative law (the internal/external distinction, the process/substance problem, and the quasi-legislative/quasi-judicial classifications).

With these organizing principles in mind, let us turn to a brief introduction to the APA provisions. Follow the discussion using the copy of the APA reprinted in Appendix 3.

The Introduction Section

Title 5 of the United States Code contains statutes that control the internal operations of government in general and administrative concerns, e.g., government personnel laws, in particular. The APA begins with §551 of that title.[23] As indicated above, the APA has a substantial introduction that contains a lengthy list of definitions. This lexicon represents an effort by the legislature to work out a common language for administrative law from the many conflicting interpretations that had grown up around court decisions and agency practices.

One of the first problems was to define the actors and institutions in the administrative process. Just what is an administrative agency? Are all government organizations "agencies" within the meaning of the APA? From a brief look at the statute, one can see that the Congress exempted its own internal operations, those of the judiciary, some aspects of military activity, and a few other organizations from the coverage of the APA.[24] Section 551 defines "agency" as "each authority of the Government of the United States whether or not it is within or subject to review by another agency." But is a government corporation to be governed by the strictures of the APA? What of the Executive Office of the President?

These important ambiguities led to amendment of the act in 1974. The new section [§552(3)] indicates that, at least for the information practices portion, the definition of agency "includes any executive department or military department, Government corporation, Government controlled corporation, or other establishment in the executive branch of the Government (including the Executive Office of the President), or any other regulatory agency."[25]

Another major point of confusion defined in the introduction concerns the processes or types of actions taken by agencies that are to be covered. Categories of agency action are not easily divided up, since they overlap. Therefore, some convention on the meaning of terms is necessary. In particular, the framers of the APA wanted to clarify, to a limited extent at least, the difference between quasi-legislative activities or rulemaking, which produce rules, and quasi-judicial activities or adjudications, which yield orders. This process of definition began with the nature of a rule [§551(4)]. In general terms, the act defines as orders any final agency decisions that are not rules [§551(6)]. The definitions of rulemaking and adjudication were then simply stated in terms of the processes for making rules and orders [§551(5) and (7)]. There are, however, a variety of administrative activities that are neither simply rulemaking nor adjudication. Two examples are ratemaking and licensing, discussed later in this chapter. When a television station requests a license to operate from the Federal Communications Commission, is it seeking an adjudication of a dispute in the hope of receiving an order or is it asking the agency to engage in rulemaking? When a public utility requests that electrical user rates be increased, is it asking the Public Service Commission to engage in rulemaking or is it requesting an adjudication of its claim to increased revenues? The convention that resulted defined ratemaking within the rule definition and set special descriptive terms for licensing [§551(9)], but treated it as a species of adjudication.

It is worth repeating that, for reasons that should be clear by this point, the definitions or introduction section of the Administrative Procedure Act, as for any other statute, is an important section. Its provisions are more than cold definitions. This section represents a continuing attempt to work out a common language for the administrative justice system.

Fair Information Practices

The longest of the provisions of the APA is the set of rules governing fair information practices. These amendments were developed as separate pieces of legislation and enacted over a 30-year period from the 1960s through the 1990s. Section 552 is the Freedom of Information Act[26] (FOIA), which, along with the earlier Federal Register Act, establishes the policy that government documents and materials should be available to the public, prescribes the means by which requests for information are to be processed, and fixes methods of redress for those who are, for one reason or another, denied access to requested information. Section 552(b) sets out a number of types of materials that are exempt from these open access rules.

The APA §552a is the Privacy Act of 1974,[27] which seeks to protect against unwarranted or inaccurate reporting of information about individuals that the government may have collected for any of several purposes. The Privacy Act makes a significant number of exceptions to the general rule against disclosure of information about an individual, which allows for criminal investigations and other particularly sensitive types of proceedings. Like the FOIA, the Privacy Act sections of the APA establish procedures and remedies for abuses by administrators.

There are two other parts to the fair information practices part of the APA. These two provisions focus on the need to encourage openness in proceedings undertaken by agencies as well as to provide for a better opportunity for interested groups or individuals to participate in agency activities. Related provisions attempt to ensure that participation is equally available to all significant groups and not merely to a limited set of special interest organizations. The Government in the Sunshine Act[28] (§552b) performs the first task. The Federal Advisory Committee Act[29] (5, U.S.C. App. 2) accomplishes the second goal. In both cases, the sections of the APA provide a set of procedures for monitoring compliance and remedial steps that may be taken to redress violations.

Rulemaking

Section 553 of the APA describes the basic processes an agency must perform to make a rule. Discussion of these requirements will occupy much of the remainder of this chapter. For the present, it is important to note again that the statute exempts some activities from its provisions. In particular, the rulemaking section exempts military or foreign affairs [§553(a)(1)]; "a matter relating to agency management or personnel or to public property, loans, grants benefits, or contracts" [§553(a)(2)]; activities such as internal agency reorganizations and the like [§553(b)(A)]; and cases where there are emergency circumstances of a special nature that require some deviation from the normal requirements for rulemaking [§553(b)(B)].

Section 553 goes on to describe procedures to ensure that rulemaking will be based on proper legal authority; that it is within the power granted by the legislature; that there is some opportunity in one form or another for public participation in the process; and that the rule is properly and clearly stated by the agency and is promulgated in a manner that will afford interested people a fair opportunity to know what the rule will require and to have some advance warning when the new rule will be implemented.

Adjudication

Section 554 describes the nature of administrative adjudication. Specifically, §554 requires the minimum procedures necessary to guarantee that those who have a case adjudicated by the government are afforded the basic due process requirements of notice, an opportunity to be heard in some form, and a decision by an impartial decisionmaker.

Qualifications and Conduct of the Presiding
Officer in Administrative Proceedings

The APA and related civil service laws speak to two problems regarding the administrative law judge (ALJ, an official who has often been referred to as a hearing examiner) or others who might conduct hearings for an administrative agency. First, it states the authority and responsibility of the ALJ for the manner in which a hearing is conducted and the form in which the initial findings are rendered. Sections 556 and 557 provide relatively detailed procedures for formal hearings; these rules are applicable when a formal adjudicative hearing is to be conducted or when the statute that guides the agency's work requires that a rule or decision be made "on the record after an opportunity for an agency hearing," as required by §§553(c) and 554(c) and (d).[30] Sections 556 and 557 prescribe the methods of proceeding and the means for taking evidence during the hearing.

Second, the statute provides in §§554(d), 557(d)(1) and, in other parts of Title 5, §§3105, 7521, 5362, 3344, and 1305, for means of ensuring the independence of hearing examiners from inappropriate influences from outside the agency and from pressure from within the agency, whether directly applied in a particular case or even indirectly exercised by pay judgments, threats to job security, or possible job assignments.

Judicial Review of Agency Decisions

Sections 701 through 706 prescribe the scope and method of judicial review of agency proceedings. They attempt to provide a structure for judicial review of agency actions that preserves an opportunity for a judicial check on possible arbitrary actions or abuses of discretion, and at the same time maintains some warnings against premature or excessive intervention by courts into areas properly the business of the agency.

The Regulatory Flexibility Act, Regulatory Analysis, and Regulatory Review Sections

Two portions were added to the APA in the 1970s and 1990s, respectively, that were aimed at perceived regulatory excesses in situations where small businesses, small units of government, and not-for-profit organizations are concerned. Sections 600 et seq. (an abbreviation of *et sequitur*, meaning "and following") are the pieces of the Regulatory Flexibility Act. This statute was adopted during the Carter administration in an effort to make certain that, when administrative agencies issue rules that have a significant effect on small businesses, small units of government, and NGOs (nongovernmental organizations, generally nonprofits), they have seriously considered the regulatory burden that will be imposed by the new rules and any flexibility that might be extended in the rules to facilitate compliance and reporting under the new policy in order to reduce undue costs.

The provisions of the Reg. Flex. Act were extended and strengthened in 1996 with the passage of three statutes that were adopted as part of the debt limit extension bill.[31] These bills also adopted a legislative review process, known as the Congressional Review Act, for rulemaking that allows Congress time to adopt a resolution of disapproval for proposed regulations.[32] The details of these procedures will be addressed later in this chapter.

Congress supported the trend toward creative governance processes and structures that provide negotiated alternatives to standard formal administrative procedures with the passage of the Negotiated Rulemaking Act[33] and the Alternative Dispute Resolution Act.[34]

Each of the parts of the Administrative Procedure Act noted above will be discussed in detail in future chapters. Two caveats should be observed in order to understand administrative law and the operation of the APA. First, its provisions should not be read in splendid isolation. The Administrative Procedure Act is always applied in conjunction with a particular statute or set of statutes and discussions of its provisions arise in the context of a particular problem or set of facts and may involve constitutional questions. Recall as well that it is increasingly common for such cases to have reference to international agreements or contractual obligations. Second, the Administrative Procedure Act is not a constitution of administrative law. It is merely one statute with a variety of sections and particular provisions. The provisions are quite likely to change. Therefore, it is useful to think of the statute in terms of its major sections rather than particular provisions. The remainder of this chapter will focus on the rulemaking segment of the act.

RULEMAKING IN CONTEXT

Because rulemaking occurs in connection with particular problems confronted by one or more agencies acting under some statutory authority, it is useful to come to the black letter law of rulemaking with a sense of the context in which this sort of administrative action takes place. This chapter will employ very different types of rulemaking problems for that purpose.

First, assume that Congress responds to the continuing controversy over rapidly rising energy prices and concerns about U.S. dependence on foreign oil sources and calls by administration officials to reinvigorate the nuclear power industry. However, given concerns about the scandals in some major energy firms and suspicion about the transparency and accountability of nuclear power policy and management in the past, the Congress adopts a requirement that rejects all existing statutes that govern the licensing of nuclear power facilities. In a new statute, the Congress states that, notwithstanding the problematic history of nuclear power in this country, it will be the policy of the United States to make prudent use of nuclear power at least through the next several decades, recognizing that this course poses a number of major difficulties. It proposes that the Nuclear Regulatory Commission completely rewrite all its regulations on nuclear-powered electrical generating facilities within the next 180 days. The statute contains a provision that will force complete review of the nuclear use policy and all agency regulations made to implement it in five years.[35] The NRC is directed to establish separate systems of regulation for (1) medical or scientific uses of nuclear energy and (2) commercial purposes. Decisions on licensing of commercial nuclear power plants will be made in two parts, with the first clearance to be made for construction and the final permit decision to be rendered prior to operation of the facility.[36] The commission's statute directs it to produce a uniform system of licensing rules.

How should the commission proceed? What information do the commissioners need to know? Should they develop a list of descriptive factors that applicants for licenses will be asked to provide? If not, where should they begin?

If the commissioners chose first to array the important questions about proposed plants, they might proceed as follows. They might say that what is involved, in reality, is the design of the application forms that will bring information to the commission from would-be plant developers needed to make decisions about licensing for construction and operation of proposed facilities. Perhaps it would help to conceptualize a fictional plant and ask questions about it. In that way, the commissioners may be able to focus on just what information they need to make future licensing decisions. Where should the description of the plant begin? A physical description of the facility might be a useful starting point. How should the location and structure be discussed? If the commissioners want to begin with the location of the plant, what is meant by location: the address, the geographical coordinates, or the location on a local road map? Or perhaps it is more important to describe the location in terms of its proximity to a population center. In that case, do the commissioners wish to know the distance from the plant to the center of the nearest city, or the distance to the nearest residential area, whether it is the center of the nearest city or not? Are these materials sufficient to describe the location and physical nature of the facility? If not, what other information is needed?

Another important factor in licensing decisions might be the security of the facility, in terms of both its physical integrity and its plans for defense against internal and external threats to the safety of the plant and its environs. The commissioners would perhaps like to have materials that describe the reputation and capabilities of the applicant who will build and operate the plant. But how much do they wish to know? In addition, in security questions, what information should be demanded? The commissioners could request data on the size and training of the security force, alarm systems, and other physical security devices to be employed. Some of those involved in the construction and operation of the plant might be required to have security clearances. If so, what level of clearance would be required and for which employees? After all, security clearances are expensive to perform. Would the contractors be required to obtain clearances? If so, would subcontractors be included? There might be real dangers in having subassemblies made by uncleared workers in plants away from the construction site itself that would later lead to catastrophic failure of the entire facility. As the list lengthens, the costs in time and money increase dramatically.

The applications would certainly contain a separate section for technical assessments. A major area of interest here could be the fuel cycle and its possible impact on the safety of the plant and the environment. As generalists selected through a political process rather than technical experts, are the commissioners capable of assessing the data they might receive from the applicants? Unsuccessful applicants might very well argue that the commission lacks sufficient expertise to make technical assessments. If there is a problem, can the members of the commission adequately evaluate claims made by the applicants and operators of the facility? The commission will doubtless call on its staff for help here. Of course, judgments about such requirements also mandate that the availability of resources for commission operations be carefully considered. What will happen if the rules that are put in place commit the organization to evaluations and decisionmaking processes that they simply cannot afford or cannot accomplish within a reasonable period of time?

Thus far, the focus of the discussion has been on substantive questions about proposed plants for which licenses may be sought. But what of the procedures by which the applications will be processed and their contents evaluated? If a construction permit is issued, does it follow that an operating permit will more or less automatically issue in due course unless specific and serious problems arise during construction?[37] If not, and the operations certification can be kept completely separate from the construction permit process, what appeal will the would-be operator have from an initial adverse finding? After all, by the time the operations certification process arises, millions will have been spent on the project with no hope of recovery.[38] If, on the other hand, the second part of the licensing process is more or less automatic, barring some major problem, what procedure will be available for groups claiming to represent the public interest to intervene if they assert that a major problem does indeed exist that justifies terminating the project?[39]

Finally, will any means be provided by which those planning future projects can obtain interpretive guidelines to clarify agency rules after they are issued? If so, how will the guidelines be formulated and promulgated? To what degree will the commission be bound to the guidelines in its future decisionmaking?

In all this, the NRC will have to reconcile whatever rules it creates with the rules issued by the International Atomic Energy Agency (IAEA) to which the U.S. is committed by treaty obligations.

This example suggests some of the concerns with which an administrator must deal in developing rules within the modern governmental context. Such problems as developing sufficiently precise language, adherence to a systematic method in considering a large variety of detailed issues, a practical yet sensitive feel for the scope and impact of the proposed rules, an understanding of the political forces that operate with respect to a particular policy problem, and the ever-present issue of costs of the new rules are all significant. Note also how the kinds of questions raised in the development of rules take the administrator across several levels of information, from the very detailed to the very general and from the intensely technical to broad inquiries that concern wide-ranging policy considerations. That ability to move across levels and to remain aware of exactly where one is focused at any given point is an important skill for public administrators.

From the perspective of the formal administrative law, rulemaking is a process that is governed by the Administrative Procedure Act along with the statutes that establish the agency involved and grant it authority. This process may be understood through responses to the following questions: (1) What is a rule? (2) What are the specific types of rules? and (3) By what procedure are rules promulgated?

WHAT IS A RULE? WHERE DEFINITIONS MATTER A GREAT DEAL

To understand what the APA requires in any particular agency action, it is necessary first to determine whether the action is a rulemaking activity or an adjudication. When an administrator makes rules, he or she is acting as a policymaker, not unlike a legislator, albeit with a limited range of authority. When one contemplates an adjudication, however, the appropriate image is of a court-like proceeding. There are no due process rights involved in a quasi-legislative procedure. After all, one has no rights of any significance to get a policy enacted by a legislature or to play an active role in that process. Rights are associated with court-like proceedings, which have an adversarial cast to them. In the latter situation, one takes a very active personal or group role in the decision process. The Administrative Procedure Act incorporates that difference in perspective and process.

Of course, as Chapter 1 noted, many administrative activities do not fit neatly into either of the two categories. Two of the most obvious examples of ambiguous proceedings are rate-setting problems and licensing processes. Rate requests by utility companies appear to be requests for some decisionmaker to sit in judgment on the merits of the company's immediate case, but policy decisions for the future are also involved. The former is a court-like activity, but the latter more closely resembles the work of a legislature. In the case of broadcasting, licensing looks to the future public interest of the community served by the station, but it also settles a claim—often disputed—over control of a valuable business enterprise for particular companies or individuals, often on the basis of past events. The former resembles a policymaking decision and the latter has the characteristics of a court proceeding. For these and other reasons, classification of administration activity within the APA categories is important.

Administrative Procedure Act Definitions Set the Foundation

Section 551(4) of the APA states that the term "rule" means

> the whole or part of agency statement of general or particular applicability and future effect designed to implement, interpret, or prescribe law or policy or describing the organization, procedure, or practice requirements of an agency and includes the approval or prescription for the future of rates, wages, corporate or financial structures or reorganization thereof, prices, facilities, appliances, services or allowances thereof or of valuations, costs, or accounting, or practices bearing on any of the foregoing.

This definition describes what a rule is, the types of rules noted in the APA, and resolves the question about rate-setting decisions. Rates are developed as rules. Rulemaking is described as the "agency process for formulating, amending, or repealing a rule."[40]

As indicated earlier, the act continues to employ the rule definition as the base for other terms by defining an "order" as the final disposition "of an agency in a matter other than rulemaking but including licensing."[41] The licensing problem is settled in general terms. "Adjudication" is then, not surprisingly, an "agency process for the formulation of an order."[42]

General Characteristics of Rules and Rulemaking

When one refers to rules and rulemaking, one usually means that the action being taken by the administrator is quasi-legislative in that the agency is acting more like a legislature than a court. Rules are usually general in scope. They are made to govern all those under the authority of an agency or that are targeted by a particular piece of legislation rather than one particular individual or business firm. Like legislation, rules are made to cover a class of people and a class of actions, for example, all school bus drivers or all generators of hazardous waste. Rules, again like legislation, are intended to guide future actions rather than to evaluate actions that have already taken place. Conversely, adjudications are quasi-judicial. They are most often specific, applying to particular named parties involved in a case. Finally, the purpose of adjudication is to resolve a dispute over a set of facts that has already occurred (though an adjudication may result in orders that prohibit or require some kind of conduct in the future, as with those mandating correction of unconstitutional prison conditions).

The U.S. Constitution does not grant power to any administrative agencies (though some state constitutions do establish a limited number of state agencies). Public organizations are created by the Congress and, in the states, by the state legislatures. The authority the agency possesses is defined and limited by the provisions of the legislation creating it (the enabling act) plus the authorization statutes that have been added to the agency's portfolio. Whatever actions the agency takes in excess of the authority delegated to it by the legislature are by definition unlawful.

It is one thing for an agency to have statutory authority to act, as in the Food and Drug Administration's ability to regulate drugs and drug delivery devices. It is another for the agency to have jurisdiction to apply its regulatory authority in a given situation. Statutory authority is concerned with what an agency may do, while questions of jurisdiction go to where, when, and under what conditions the agency may exercise that authority. The importance of jurisdiction was underscored in a very high visibility case concerning tobacco advertising.

There was a great deal of public approval for the work of the FDA when in 1996 it issued rules banning advertising by tobacco companies aimed at minors on grounds that cigarettes and smokeless tobacco were, and were intended to be, drug delivery devices that supplied nicotine to the user's system.[43] In deciding the challenge to the FDA rules brought by the tobacco companies, the Supreme Court recognized that:

> [T]he FDA quite exhaustively documented that "tobacco products are unsafe," "dangerous," and "cause great pain and suffering from illness."....It found that the consumption of tobacco

products "presents extraordinary health risks," and that "tobacco use is the single leading cause of preventable death in the United States.". . .It stated that "more than 400,000 people die each year from tobacco-related illnesses, such as cancer, respiratory illnesses, and heart disease, often suffering long and painful deaths," and that "tobacco alone kills more people each year in the United States than acquired immunodeficiency syndrome (AIDS), car accidents, alcohol, homicides, illegal drugs, suicides, and fires, combined.". . .Indeed, the FDA characterized smoking as "a pediatric disease,". . .because "one out of every three young people who become regular smokers . . . will die prematurely as a result."[44]

And to all of these damaging findings, the agency added that some 82 percent of adults who smoke began as minors. Moreover, in the early 1990s, the agency had found clear evidence that the industry had intended nicotine to be used as a drug and that cigarettes would be effective delivery devices.[45]

Given all of that evidence and the agency's statutory authority, it might seem clear that FDA had both the authority to act and the jurisdiction to do so with respect to cigarette advertising directed to minors. However, the regulation of tobacco had long been a controversial matter with great sums expended by the industry and lobbying by the farmers who produced tobacco and their political representatives.[46] While the Congress had not specifically prohibited the FDA from taking the kind of action it took in these rules, the Supreme Court concluded that, when existing legislation was interpreted in light of the Court's understanding of legislative purpose and the full array of tobacco-related legislation was considered, "Congress ha[d] clearly precluded the FDA from asserting jurisdiction to regulate tobacco products."[47]

If a court finds that an agency has adopted a regulation that exceeds statutory authority, the regulation is held to be *ultra vires* and therefore unlawful.[48] That is to say, the authority of the government will not be available to enforce the rule. The concept of *ultra vires* action comes from corporation law, which holds that the owners of a firm cannot be called to answer for actions taken by officers who acted beyond their proper range of authority. Similarly, since administrators function on the basis of authority delegated to them by the legislature, the government should not be held responsible and cannot be made to support actions taken by officials who exceed their proper authority. Similarly, even if an agency had the authority to act, its actions are not valid if the agency exceeds its jurisdiction or if it is prohibited by the legislature from exercising jurisdiction in a particularly area. As the APA explains, rules may not be "in excess of statutory jurisdiction, authority, or limitations, or short of statutory rights."[49]

The APA also requires judges to strike down agency rules that are "arbitrary, capricious, an abuse of discretion, or otherwise not in accordance with law,"[50] or those made "without observance of procedure required by law."[51] In simple terms, these provisions require that: (1) administrative actions generally should have some reasonable basis for the decision based upon the record developed in the rulemaking; (2) they should be related to the purposes the administrator is intended to accomplish; and (3) they should be made according to the procedures for rulemaking prescribed by the APA and the enabling statute of the agency.[52]

TYPES OF RULES: LEGISLATIVE VERSUS NONLEGISLATIVE RULES AND WHY IT MATTERS

Agencies make different kinds of regulations, each of which carries different requirements for making the rule and varying degrees of legal force. The categories come from the APA. The first category is referred to as substantive or legislative rules. The other types are collectively termed nonlegislative rules, a category that includes procedural rules, interpretive rules, and policy statements.

Substantive or Legislative Rules

Substantive or legislative rules are those rules, described in the definition of a rule in §551(4), that "implement,...or prescribe law or policy." Legislative rules, to return to the nuclear power plant example, cover such matters as the safety requirements for construction of the generating facility or the regulations governing transportation of the fuel to and from the plant. Another example is the attempt by the FDA to regulate tobacco advertising directed at minors discussed earlier.

Legislative or substantive regulations are legally binding and can be enforced in court.[53] As long as the rules are properly enacted and published in the *Federal Register,* organizations and individuals must obey substantive rules as they would a statute enacted by Congress and published in the *Statutes at Large*. State-level administrative procedures acts provide for substantive rules at that level as well.

The amount of authority given different agencies to promulgate substantive rules varies with the statute that guides the agency's actions. Historically, some organizations were given a virtual carte blanche to issue such regulations as are needed to accomplish the purposes assigned by Congress. If those purposes included, for example, the obligation to ensure that broadcasting was conducted in accordance with the public interest, the rulemaking authority was broad indeed. In more recent years, the Congress and many state legislatures have adopted statutes that are much more detailed both in their substantive and procedural obligations. In fact, it might not be surprising to learn that in an era of deregulation, statutes may also carry prohibitions against the issuance of new rules. Thus, Section 209 of the Help America Vote Act of 2002 provided: "The Commission shall not have any authority to issue any rule, promulgate any regulation, or take any other action which imposes any requirement on any State or unit of local government, except to the extent permitted under section 9(a) of the National Voter Registration Act of 1993."[54] Of course, the courts are the final arbiters of the meaning of a statute and the limits of agency statutory authority.[55]

Procedural Rules

Procedural rules "describe the organization, procedure, or practice requirements of an agency."[56] The APA and the agency enabling act may establish procedures for an agency, but the organization may go beyond such recommendations to add additional processes. In general, agencies have inherent powers to promulgate procedural rules.[57] Indeed, they are encouraged to establish such rules. Good management requires some flexibility in agency procedures, but standardization and publication of procedures lend an air of fairness and impartiality to agency interactions with individuals, groups, and other agencies. Although agencies may not be required to issue procedural rules, and need not follow APA rulemaking requirements if they do make procedural rules,[58] the rules of procedure the agency *does* choose to issue must be published in the *Federal Register*.[59] Once procedural rules are promulgated, the normal rule is that agencies are required to honor them particularly where they confer a procedural benefit on those before the agency.[60]

Interpretive Rules

The third variety of administrative rule is the interpretative (or interpretive) rule. (The APA, §553 uses the term "interpretative," but the term "interpretive" is often employed in practice.) Interpretive rules are statements issued by agencies that present the agency's understanding of the meaning of the language in its regulations or the statutes it administers. These rules are not legislative or substantive rules. They are specifically exempted from the normal rulemaking processes required by the APA,[61] although they must be published in the *Federal Register* if they are enacted.[62] Three important questions remain. First, what is the difference between an interpretive rule and a substantive or legislative rule? Second, if interpretive rules do not carry complete binding legal force, why have them at all? Third, since by claiming that a regulation it issues is interpretive rather than substantive an agency can avoid costly and time-consuming rulemaking procedures, who is to determine the appropriate category for any particular rule?

Interpretive rules are not intended to add to or subtract from the existing body of statutory law or regulations in any particular field. They are merely explanatory statements that provide guidance on the understanding that an administrator has of existing law. It is helpful to think of an interpretive rule as a quasi-legislative analog of the advisory opinion.[63]

Suppose one wished to know whether it would be lawful to deduct from one's income tax the price of a new automobile as a business expense. The Internal Revenue Service provides answers to some tax questions by telephone or on a walk-in basis at IRS offices. If an IRS adviser indicated that one was correct in interpreting the code to allow the price of the car to be written off as a business expense, should one accept the advice? If called in for an audit at a future date, should one be able to hold the auditor to the advice given by the agency employee?

Consider another example. Suppose a struggling farm community receives word from the Department of Agriculture that the federal government will underwrite loans for financially pressed farmers suffering the combined effect of high interest rates and drought. The loan programs begin and the farmers are assured that they will continue. They plan their finances and plant accordingly, but a new administration is elected and determines that the loan program must be substantially cut back to eliminate abuses in the program. If a farmer who had previously been assured of help at the local office is told that he will not receive the promised loan, does he have any way to hold the government to the earlier promise? Should he have?

The tension between the desire to ensure that citizens receive prompt assistance and the need to make certain that they receive accurate information is often greatest in emergency situations. The very nature of the human needs in cases of natural disaster, for example, seems to require that agencies be held to advice given by their employees. Unfortunately, these are the conditions most likely to generate a host of difficulties over time. Certainly the many terrible events surrounding the devastation wrought by Hurricane Katrina provided examples of the inadequacy of federal assistance and unwillingness or inability to provide answers to the thousands left homeless. However, in the period after the immediate threat had passed when people were attempting to put their lives back together, a host of questions arose with a wide range of long-term implications not only for the citizens but also for the agencies designed to serve them.

In such cases one is tempted to demand enforcement of advisory opinions or interpretative rules on the ground that citizens acted in good faith on the basis of what they believed to be an authoritative statement of government policy. On the other hand, these are useful examples of why one who would understand the administrative justice system must deal with the perspective of the producers of administrative decisions as well as the consumers of those rulings. Can agencies be held to every comment or promise allegedly made by any employee at any level of an organization? It is in everyone's best interest to have agency employees give accurate information on particular problems and interpretations of more general policies. Such information or advice will likely save the agency lengthy disputes later.

This matter gets to be especially challenging in a time when so many government programs for which administrative agencies are responsible are actually operated by contractors. Thus, it became a matter of embarrassment—and no small amount of political controversy—when some recipients of social service programs in New England called to get guidance on problems with their benefit cards and found themselves speaking with a call center in India. Seven Northeast states contracted with Citibank to operate their social service benefit card programs. The card contractor had subcontracted with a Wisconsin firm that operated call centers in India.[64] The programs that provided the resources for the benefit cards were state programs with federal involvement. There are obvious complexities when a call center that is not even located in the U.S. is providing information on domestic U.S. programs operated under both federal and state law. There are sufficient complexities involved in holding the contractor and subcontractor accountable, without taking into account the people on the other end of the telephone on the other side of the globe.

Many of the kinds of difficulties with advisory opinions are also true of interpretive rules. A published interpretation guides all who deal with an agency, but should interpretations be treated like substantive rules, as binding on agency officials? If so, the administrator faces a system that would discourage any rulemaking beyond that which is absolutely necessary, since any additional interpretations would be treated to all intents and purposes as substantive binding rules. This exacerbates the misguided tendency by some people in public agencies to warn their colleagues: "Don't put it in writing!" After all, in such circumstances, the interpretive rules would presumably be binding on the agency, but would only be guidelines to anyone else. Why then should an administrator issue guidelines or provide advice? Why limit one's own flexibility with nothing in return? And if, from an administrator's viewpoint at least, interpretive rules are going to be treated like substantive rules, why not call as much of the necessary rulemaking interpretive rather than substantive, thereby avoiding the work and cost of APA-mandated substantive rulemaking processes?

For these and other reasons, while interpretive as opposed to substantive rules are not supposed to be binding, there is ambiguity about just what will be treated as an interpretive rule and what will be found by a court to be a legislative rule.[65] In the near term, consumers of administrative decisions in or out of government would probably be wise to assume that interpretive rules do not bind the agency. However, in drafting interpretive rules, producers of such decisions should consider at least the possibility that a court will give the rule binding force against the agency.

Interpretive rules are useful devices even if their binding force is questionable. In the years since enactment of the APA, several reports and studies have urged agencies to use rulemaking as much as possible and avoid adjudication as a mode of policymaking.[66] In this way, consumers of agency decisions can get information ahead of time on what agency policy is and the probable direction of future agency decisions. Interpretive rules offer administrators a simple method of conveying information on current agency thinking without complex procedures. The idea is to give guidance and to avoid, as much as possible, future conflict. From the standpoint of consumers, interpretive rules provide information from an authoritative source to guide their actions.

Finally, either because an administrator perceives the effect of an interpretive rule as indistinguishable or because he or she sees a possibility of saving time and effort, an administrator may be tempted to treat what is really a substantive rule as an interpretive rule. Consider the following example.

The Occupational Safety and Health Act provides for inspections of workplaces in search of safety hazards, and also prohibits employers from discriminating against employees who exercise their rights under the act. The agency issued a rule saying that employers who refused to pay a worker representative who accompanied the OSHA inspector during the time required to complete the walk-around inspection would be in violation of the antidiscrimination provisions of the statute. The National Chamber of Commerce contested the rule on the ground that OSHA had not followed the requirements of the APA and its enabling act in promulgating the walk-around rule. The agency countered that the rule was merely interpretive, defining employer discrimination as the concept was used in the statute. Since the rule was interpretive, OSHA argued, it was exempt from standard procedures. The D.C. Circuit Court of Appeals disagreed. The court held that: "A rule is interpretive, rather than legislative, if it is not issued under statutory authority to make rules having the force of law or if the agency intends the rule to be no more than an expression of its construction of a statute."[67] The walk-around rule was, in the court's view, clearly intended to be a rule promulgated under the OSHA authority to make rules having the force of law that did more than merely clarify an agency understanding of statutory language. Therefore, the agency was required to follow normal rulemaking procedures.

The courts will decide on judicial review whether a rule is interpretive or substantive regardless of the label the administrator prefers to apply.[68] Whatever the agency may call it, a court will term it a legislative rule rather than an interpretive rule or policy statement:

> If an agency acts as if a document issued at headquarters is controlling in the field, if it treats the document in the same manner as it treats a legislative rule, if it bases enforcement actions

on the policies or interpretations formulated in the document, if it leads private parties or State permitting authorities to believe that it will declare permits invalid unless they comply with the terms of the document, then the agency's document is for all practical purposes "binding."[69]

A court will also likely reject an agency's claim that it is issuing an interpretative rather than a substantive rule if "the rule effectively amends a prior legislative rule"[70] or "if an agency's present interpretation of a regulation is a fundamental modification of a previous interpretation."[71]

HOW ARE RULES MADE?

The manner in which rules are made by administrative agencies is important for many of the same reasons that the processes by which a bill is enacted into law by the Congress are significant. Both are lawmaking activities. But the activities of the legislature are somewhat more visible than those of administrative agencies and are subject to the judgment of the ballot box. The authority to issue rules with relatively limited checks on that power was one of the reasons why those worried about possible administrative arbitrariness referred to administrative agencies as a "headless fourth branch of government." Among the cures for this potentially dangerous situation was the establishment of regular procedures for rulemaking, included in the Administrative Procedure Act.

Consider the process step by step, following Figure 5.1. Let us take as an example the case of the discovery in late 2003 of a BSE-infected cow in Washington, outlined in Chapter 1. It may only have been one Holstein cow, but it triggered a range of issues that affected the entire nation and the processes for addressing them. First, it must be determined which agency at what level of government should take action. In this case, it is relatively obvious that the U.S. Department of Agriculture (USDA) would be at the center of efforts to address the BSE, and within USDA, the Food Safety and Inspection Service (FSIS) is the responsible agency. However, there can be more at issue in such a situation than may be readily apparent. Thus, the Food and Drug Administration also had a role to play, since there was concern that some of the kinds of materials taken from cattle might find their way into cosmetics as well as human food, and the FDA administers the Food, Drug, and Cosmetic Act. Because there is a concern that humans might contract Creutzfeldt-Jakob disease (a fatal disease for which there no cure at present), the Centers for Disease Control (CDC) also have issues to consider.[72]

The fact that more than one agency may be involved is an increasingly common phenomenon and it often means that there will be parallel rulemaking processes in operation, stemming from the same problem at the same time. The additional fact the agencies involved may have different missions driven by different statutory mandates can be significant as well. On the other hand, different agencies may engage in a joint rulemaking effort. That was one of the steps taken in the mad cow matter, as the Animal and Plant Health Inspection Service and the Food Safety and Inspection Service, both agencies within the USDA, and the Food and Drug Administration, a unit in the Department of Health and Human Services, published notice of proposed rulemaking together to consider additional measures to be taken beyond what each of these offices had done individually.[73]

Once it is determined which organization (or organizations) is responsible, there is a question whether the agency will take action at all—one of the most important decisions that any administrator must make. One may voluntarily decide to take action either because someone has petitioned for agency intervention in a particular situation or because it simply seems like the appropriate step to take. On the other hand, action may be mandated either by legislation or because the situation is so serious that it demands action. That is certainly the case in the BSE example. Indeed, as it became clear that little had been done to ensure that sick animals were not taken for slaughter and processing, and that testing was limited and sporadic, there were demands from around the nation for immediate action and criticism for past failures that had left the nation so vulnerable.

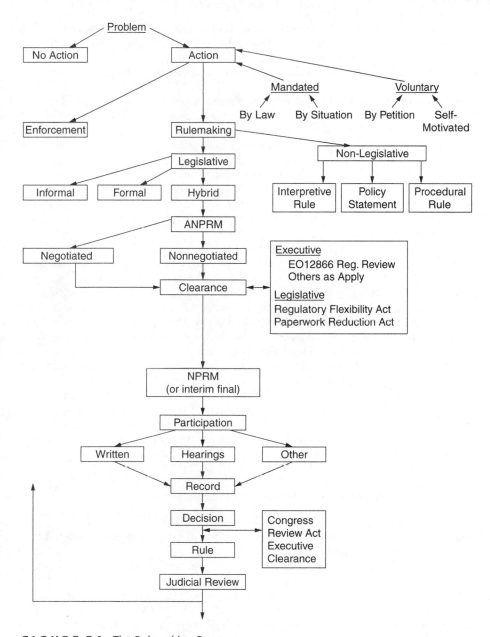

FIGURE 5.1 The Rulemaking Process

The question then is what kind of action should be taken? One possible approach is to pursue an enforcement action, seeking to apply existing statutes and regulations. The USDA moved to locate the meat products from the infected animal, which had gone to two different processors, and to determine whether any of those products had been shipped from the distributors to supermarkets—even as some of those markets in the Seattle area were reassuring customers that their beef had come from processors in the Midwest and there was no problem. It soon became apparent that indeed some of those stores did receive products from at least one of the two distributors involved in the BSE investigation. In the process of the effort to identify the cow, its origin, the character of the feed eaten by the cow, the handling of the animal at slaughter, and the distribution of the animal products, it became clear that simply enforcing existing rules was not even close to adequate in confronting the range of problems posed by the BSE situation.

Given that information, the agency must decide whether to begin the process to develop substantive (legislative) rules or to take action through nonlegislative mechanisms such as interpretative or procedural rules. As soon as USDA officials explained at news conferences what policies were in place, it was obvious that mere changes in interpretation of existing rules or new procedural rules would not be adequate to address a problem that was rapidly growing in significance. As the global 24-hour news cycle focused attention on the BSE matter, other countries moved to restrict imports, an extremely important set of markets for U.S. growers. Even domestically, consumers were becoming frightened by the evidence of a lack of protections that they had assumed were in place and were changing their shopping habits. The question then became, what process was needed to issue the substantive rules required to address the BSE problem?

The APA, enabling legislation enacted since the APA, executive branch policies, and various court decisions have given us essentially three types of processes through which substantive administrative regulations are made: informal, formal, and hybrid rulemaking procedures. Informal rulemaking is referred to as a "notice and comment" procedure and is governed by §553 of the APA. Formal rulemaking is so named because it involves a formal hearing that looks very much like a court proceeding. It is governed by §§556 and 557 of the APA. A hybrid procedure, as the term implies, is a compromise between the formal and informal processes and is governed by the requirements of the agency's enabling act and, in the case of executive branch agencies, by executive orders.

Before discussing the types of rulemaking, it is necessary to clarify the potentially confusing use of the terms "formal" and "informal." Chapter 1 discussed the very important fact that much of what is done by administrative agencies is done through informal discussions and exchanges of information. These activities are guided by no particular set of processes except habit, individual and group interaction, and circumstance. But the term "informal" as it is used in rulemaking does not mean without standards or procedures. One might be well advised to think of informal rulemaking as simplified rulemaking. Both formal and informal rulemaking are standardized processes.

Notice and Comment Rulemaking

Informal or simplified rulemaking is generally governed by APA §553. This section identifies those few sorts of rulemaking that are exempt from the act and describes the steps that most administrative agencies must accomplish in order to promulgate a rule.

The rulemaking section exempts military and foreign affairs functions of the federal government, for rather obvious reasons.[74] It also exempts matters relating to "agency management or personnel or to public property, loans, grants, benefits or contracts."[75] At about the same time that the APA was enacted, another set of statutory provisions—the Federal Property and Administrative Services Act, among others—were enacted to deal with some of these problems.[76] As more functions at all levels of government are performed by contract, this separation has become increasingly problematic. It is no longer the case that government contracts are primarily concerned with the purchase of goods. As more of the contracts concern ongoing service delivery efforts, the need to better integrate contracting law with administrative procedure statutes increases. Unfortunately, that has not happened to date and we must function under the segregated framework until such changes are legislated. Indeed, there has been some discussion over the years about whether it would be advisable to include rulemaking in a number of formerly exempted areas in the APA requirement, and eliminate overlap and confusion.[77]

Procedural and interpretive rules are not required to be made in accordance with the APA procedures.

Finally, emergency rulemaking may sometimes be required, particularly in matters involving threats to life, health, or safety, and is also exempted. Consider the following example. Nuclear materials processor Babcock and Wilcox was proposing to ship a load of fissile materials related to work it was doing under contract for the Navy. Although its proposed shipment complied with existing U.S. Nuclear Regulatory Commission (NRC) and Department of Transportation (DOT) rules, the company's calculations suggested that the combination of materials could go critical and there was a clear potential for a serious nuclear accident. The company notified the NRC of its concerns and volunteered that it would not move forward with the shipment.

Transportation of materials in the field of nuclear power and nuclear fuels processing is one of those sectors in which there is a complex regulatory structure, involving not only more than one domestic agency but also international institutions. The NRC, which cooperates with DOT under a memorandum of understanding, has been more or less continually working to update nuclear shipping safety standards and also to maintain compliance with U.S. commitments to IAEA rules, using standard rulemaking techniques under the APA.[78] However, when NRC specialists checked the Babcock and Wilcox calculations, they decided an emergency rule was needed to deal with it the problem that had been discovered. The announcement of the rule would have to respond to the APA requirement that an agency could only use emergency rulemaking "when the agency for good cause finds (and incorporates the finding and a brief statement of reasons therefor in the rules issued) that notice and public procedure thereon are impracticable, unnecessary, or contrary to the public interest."[79] The NRC rule included just such a statement:

Good Cause for Immediate Adoption

The Commission is promulgating this emergency final rule because the problem of regulatory safety limits over quantities and concentrations of fissile material and moderators, which has been demonstrated to permit criticality in at least one proposed shipment, is an important safety issue meriting immediate corrective action. An accidental nuclear criticality in the public domain would very likely involve fatalities, health effects from the resulting radiations, and extensive clean-up costs. . . ..

Moreover, the nature of the materials being imported and shipped domestically has recently changed due to initiatives with the States of the former Soviet Union to reduce weapons usable material such as high-enriched uranium. The materials B&W had intended to ship were byproducts from processing this type of material. Shipments made under 10 CFR 71.18, 71.22 or 71.53 are made without specific NRC approval and the possibility exists that a licensee could unwittingly make an unsafe shipment in reliance upon the present rules. Thus, the Commission must amend its rules quickly to prevent unsafe shipments from occurring.

For the reasons stated above, the Commission finds good cause, pursuant to Section 553(b)(B) of the Administrative Procedure Act (APA) (5 U.S.C. 553(b)(B)), to dispense with notice and prepromulgation public comment as being impracticable and contrary to the public interest. Further, the Commission finds, pursuant to Section 553(d)(3) of the APA (5 U.S.C. 553(d)(3)), that good cause exists for making these amendments immediately effective because the need to have these regulations in place outweighs the inconvenience, if any, to licensees who may need to alter shipping plans.[80]

In its emergency rulemaking action, the NRC indicated that it would accept comments on the rule for 30 days even though the rule would go into force immediately. The NRC then entered into a contract with the Oak Ridge National Laboratory to conduct hazard studies on the kind of problem that NRC addressed in its emergency rule, the results of which were used in developing later rules issued by NRC. At about the same time, the IAEA was also making changes to its rules at the international level. Thus, in 2004, the U.S. Department of Transportation had to issue new rules to ensure that its hazardous materials rules were compatible with the IAEA changes and, in the process, incorporated the NRC rules as well.[81]

This brief case study not only demonstrates how emergency rules can be used but shows as well the importance of remaining alert to possible supranational issues in administration. It also highlights the way in which the activities of governance regimes (as compared to action by a single government agency) are at the center of some of the most important policymaking and administration that one finds in the contemporary environment. In this case, a for-profit contractor alerted a regulatory agency to a problem that prompted rulemaking by that independent regulatory commission that regulates nuclear materials transport under a memorandum of agreement with an executive branch agency. The NRC then contracted with a Department of Energy laboratory, currently managed by the University of Tennessee and Battelle, to carry out research used to support future rulemaking. Battelle describes itself as "a charitable trust organized as a non-profit corporation under the laws of the State of Ohio.... exempt from federal taxation under Section 501(c)(3) of the Internal Revenue Code because it is organized for charitable, scientific and educational purposes."[82] That said, Battelle boasts that: "Battelle, with the labs it manages and co-manages, oversees a staff of 19,000 scientists, engineers and support specialists. Each year, Battelle is involved in thousands of technology projects for nearly 1,000 companies and government agencies. Battelle conducts $2.9 billion in annual research and development, which results in 50 to 100 patented inventions each year."[83] It also claims that it engages in "$2.9 billion in annual research and development. Battelle provides solutions and develops innovative products, helping commercial customers leverage technology into a competitive advantage. We also team with more than 800 federal, state and local government agencies, providing cost-effective science and technology in the areas of national security, homeland defense, health and life sciences, energy, transportation and environment."[84] The DOT then incorporated the work of the other organizations and the NRC rules that resulted into its own revised rules.

Emergency rulemaking is also done at the state level. Unlike the federal APA, though, many state administrative procedure acts contain a requirement that emergency rules are to be treated as temporary rules and that the agency that issued them must act within a specified period to replace the emergency action with a full rulemaking process. Thus, in the fall of 2004, the governor of Oregon, responding to a number of serious events involving the use of the drug known simply as "meth," (methamphetamine) called upon the state pharmacy board to issue rules that would make it more difficult for those who made the street drug to obtain the necessary ingredients. The Oregon Board of Pharmacy issued a temporary rule, requiring retailers of over-the-counter products containing pseudoephedrine (often cold and flu medications) to remove the products from open shelves and to require photo identification for those who wished to purchase the drugs. In order to justify the exemption from normal rulemaking requirements under the Oregon Administrative Procedure Act, the board was required to file a "Statement of Need and Justification" to accompany the temporary rule. In explaining its actions, the board noted:

> The Board finds that failure to act promptly will result in serious prejudice to the public interest. Specifically, the Board is persuaded that the manufacture of methamphetamine in small labs in Oregon creates substantial public health and public safety problems. These labs are easily set up in kitchens, garages, apartments and even hotel rooms. The use of pseudoephedrine in the manufacture of methamphetamine creates toxic pollution in the lab and greatly increases the danger of fire and explosions. Small labs pose a serious danger to children living with the meth cooks, including exposure to toxic chemicals. Recently, the state of Oklahoma has restricted the sale of pseudoephedrine and required identification from purchasers. Preliminary information from Oklahoma shows that similar restrictions have drastically cut the number of meth labs in Oklahoma.
>
> This rule, by limiting the availability of pseudoephedrine, is expected to reduce the number of meth labs in Oregon and to alleviate the associated public health and safety problems. [85]

Under the Oregon APA, like other states, the temporary rule can remain in effect for 180 days.[86] Hence, the Board of Pharmacy published notice of final rules on May 1, 2005.[87]

While it is true that there are obvious and important cases, such as the NRC rules above, in which emergency rulemaking is justified, courts will be on guard to ensure that agencies do not simply seek to use the emergency exemption to avoid the burdens of normal rulemaking requirements.[88] Thus, there were efforts during the early Reagan years to justify changes in agency regulations without APA procedures on grounds that the nation was in a period of serious economic stress.

Not surprisingly, though, the USDA Food Safety and Inspection Service (FSIS) moved quickly to issue three sets of rules in early January 2004, utilizing the emergency rulemaking exemption for normal procedural requirements.[89] One set of rules was designed to prohibit the use of high-risk materials in human food and to limit the use of so-called downer cattle (animals too sick to enter the slaughterhouse on their own power). A second set of rules aimed at "Meat Produced by Advanced Meat/Bone Separation Machinery and Meat Recovery (AMR) Systems," and a third targeted "Use of Certain Stunning Devices Used to Immobilize Cattle During Slaughter." The issue was to ensure that the products considered most likely to carry a danger of transmitting disease from BSE to humans were blocked from entry into the human food chain. That said, the FDIS simultaneously announced a request for comments on these rules and indicated its intention to move forward with a variety of full-blown rulemaking procedures beyond the emergency actions.

The remaining variation on the non-legislative rule is what is referred to as a policy statement.

> A general statement of policy...does not establish a "binding norm." It is not finally determinative of the issues or rights to which it is addressed. The agency cannot apply or rely upon a general statement of policy as law because a general statement of policy only announces what the agency seeks to establish as policy. A policy statement announces the agency's tentative intentions for the future.[90]

Policy statements are increasingly common, in part because such statements of general policy are, like interpretative and procedural rules, exempt from the rulemaking requirements of §553. While the courts have evolved a criteria for determining what the nature and constraints of a policy statement are, they have also acknowledged that differentiating among these types of rules in practice can sometimes be "enshrouded in considerable smog,"[91] "fuzzy,"[92] "tenuous," "blurred," and "baffling."[93] In spite of the ambiguity, courts continue to work to ensure that the distinctions among the types of rules are maintained as much as possible for the simple reason that they recognize such devices can be used to evade the notice and participation requirements of the APA. "In light of the obvious importance of these policy goals of maximum participation and full information, we have consistently declined to allow the exceptions itemized in §553 to swallow the APA's well-intentioned directive."[94] This was a danger that the framers of APA foresaw and the courts have therefore concluded that "exceptions to section 553 will be narrowly construed and only reluctantly countenanced."[95] There are indications of some degree of frustration by judges who see evidence of attempts to evade those rulemaking requirements by labeling what are in fact substantive rules as policy statements. "[T]he agency's characterization of its own action is not controlling if it self-servingly disclaims any intention to create a rule with the 'force of law,' but the record indicates otherwise."[96]

The criteria that are generally used by a court to determine whether an agency statement is a policy statement are as follows: "A policy statement is one that first, does not have a present-day binding effect, that is, it does not impose any rights and obligations, and second, genuinely leaves the agency and its decision-makers free to exercise direction."[97] If a policy statement applies in the present or if the agency is stating a clear commitment rather than leaving itself a range of discretion, then its action does not qualify as a policy statement. If a statement applies currently but "merely clarif[ies] or explain[s] existing law or regulations" but does not add anything new, it is an interpretative rule.[98] If it does add something and is considered binding by the agency involved, it is a substantive or legislative rule and must meet the APA requirements.[99] Thus, when the U.S. Environmental Protection Agency (EPA) issued a press release concerning its controversial use of third-party research data to determine whether the use of certain pesticides was harmful, its claim that the press release was merely a policy statement was challenged. The release said that: "the Agency will not consider or rely on any such human studies in its regulatory decisionmaking, whether previously or newly submitted."[100] The D.C.Circuit concluded that: "This clear and unequivocal language, which reflects an obvious change in established agency practice, creates a 'binding norm' that is 'finally determinative of the issues or rights to which it is addressed.'"[101] It therefore ruled against the agency on grounds that this was a substantive rule that was required to be issued in accordance with the requirements of the APA.

For all substantive rules made under §553, the administrative agency must proceed as follows. (See Figure 5.1.) First, a notice of proposed rulemaking is published in the *Federal Register*. The notice must contain: "(1) a statement of the time, place, and nature of public rulemaking proceedings: (2) reference to the legal authority under which the rule is proposed; and (3) either the terms or substance of the proposed rule or a description of the subjects and issues involved."[102] The agency must give individuals and groups "an opportunity to participate in the rulemaking."[103] Participation can be made available in any of several forms, but the most common is simply the presentation of a name and address of someone in the agency designated to receive public comment on the proposed rule. There is usually a name, address, and telephone number for the contact person and a date by which all comments are to be in the hands of agency decisionmakers.[104]

Under the provisions of the E-Government Act (discussed further in Chapter 11), federal agencies are required to "accept submissions under section 553(c) of title 5, United States Code, by electronic means."[105] That same legislation required creation of a unified Internet portal for federal agencies, which is operated by the General Services Administration (GSA). With respect to the development of regulation, GSA operates RegInfo.gov. This website has a link for "Public Comment on Rulemaking" which takes the user to Regulations.gov,[106] a site where visitors may "Find, review, and submit comments on proposed regulations."[107] The RegInfo.gov site also provides access to the current version of the federal government's regulatory agenda and regulatory plan as well as regulatory reviews done under Executive Order 12866 (issued by President Clinton and amended by executive order issued by President George W. Bush).

The E-Government Act also requires agencies to operate electronic dockets that contain rulemaking materials and comments that are submitted. Those agencies have websites for the agency and websites for their pending rulemaking dockets. As a result, many no longer accept comments simply by e-mail submission to a particular address, though paper submissions are still possible. Consider, for example, the following standard language from a FDA rulemaking that is part of the ongoing effort to develop rules to response to the mad cow disease issue.

> To ensure more timely processing of comments, FDA is no longer accepting comments submitted to the agency by email. FDA encourages you to continue to submit electronic comments by using the Federal eRulemaking Portal or the agency Web site, as described in the Electronic Submissions portion of this paragraph.
>
> *Instructions*: All submissions received must include the agency name and Docket No(s). or Regulatory Information Number (RIN) for this rulemaking. All comments received may be posted without change to *http://www.fda.gov/ohrms/dockets/default.htm,* including any personal information provided. For detailed instructions on submitting comments and additional information on the rulemaking process, see the "Comments" heading of the SUPPLEMENTARY INFORMATION section of this document.
>
> *Docket*: For access to the docket to read background documents or comments received, go to *http://www.fda.gov/ohrms/dockets/default.htm,* and insert the docket number(s), found in brackets in the heading of this document, into the "Search" box and follow the prompts and/ or go to the Division of Dockets Management, 5630 Fishers Lane, rm. 1061, Rockville, MD 20852.[108]

The FDA docket site contains a button for comments. That takes the reader to a list of pending rules and the visitor then moves down through the site levels to find where the comment may be submitted.[109]

While there are a variety of relatively obvious advantages to the online participation opportunities, it should also be clear from this information that, notwithstanding the language of the E-Government Act, there are likely to be issues of the so-called digital divide that arise from the move to a focus on electronic Internet-based participation.[110] It takes some degree of knowledge and effort beyond what the average Internet user may bring to the task to be able to navigate the new process. On the positive side of the ledger, smaller nonprofit organizations scattered across the nation can find this a much less expensive and more timely method for providing their response to agency proposals than before.

After giving notice of the proposed rulemaking and a general opportunity for comment, the agency is free to produce its final version of the new regulation. The final rule must be published in the *Federal Register* 30 days before its effective date. Presumably, those concerned will have an opportunity within that time to learn of the issuance of the regulation and bring themselves into conformity with it. The final rule must contain, in addition to the actual text of the rule, a "concise general statement" setting forth the purpose of the rule and the legal basis on which it was issued.[111]

Until the late 1970s, the notice and comment procedure was relatively simple. No more was required of an agency issuing a rule, unless the specific statutes that governed its operation mandated more or if the enabling act required that rules be "made on the record after an agency hearing."[112] If the language "on the record after...hearing" is used, the agency involved must use formal rulemaking procedures rather than the notice and comment technique just described unless the statute says otherwise.

Formal Rulemaking Under the APA

While there are only a handful of statutes in federal administrative law that require formal rulemaking processes, it is important to understand what this type of rulemaking is, why it has been used, and why it has generally been rejected in modern legislation. Food and drug regulatory matters provided examples of the formal approach, though even here efforts have been made to eliminate the formal approach with few exceptions. The arguments in favor of formalized procedures are: (1) they ensure that all aspects of the development of a new regulation are spelled out in detail on the record; (2) full opportunity is given to all interested groups to participate at length in the deliberations over the proposed new rule; (3) they provide careful limits on the information used in the decisionmaking process to ensure that every bit of evidence can be tested in a hearing; (4) all objections to findings of law or fact in the development of the rule can be decided and reasoned opinions provided; and (5) the burden-of-proof requirement ensures that those likely to be adversely affected by the new rule can be assured that it is necessary and justified by clear evidence on the record developed at hearing.

The arguments against formalized rulemaking, which resembles a full dress trial-type hearing, are not difficult to guess. Such procedures are tremendously costly and involve extensive delay. The great dispute over 3 percent limits on non-peanut products in peanut butter stretched on for approximately 12 years.[113] Formalized procedures leave little administrative flexibility within which expert administrators can perform the functions for which their agencies were created. There is a great danger that the administrative process will be replaced by a heavily judicialized decision process not well suited to policymaking.[114]

But there are still some areas of administration where the consequences of the risks of poor quality or arbitrary rulemaking by administrative agencies are so great that legislatures have been hesitant to dispense with the admittedly burdensome formal process. One example of this problem has arisen with respect to the rules governing approval of new drugs or medical devices for the treatment of AIDS. The complaint that FDA procedures take too long and cost too much is not new. Besides, the argument runs, when the issue is treatment for a terminal illness, the decision as to whether to take medication should belong to the patient. This dispute erupted in the 1960s and 1970s with regard to a variety of treatments for cancer, the best known of which was Laetrile.[115] In the 1990s, efforts to deal with HIV/AIDS brought pressure for fast-track approval processes and for other simplified processes and policies.

However, following initial experiments with such fast-track procedures, FDA found itself under attack because the fact that it had not required more complex procedures for approval had meant that there had not been sufficient information recorded to provide necessary baseline data so that it could be determined whether various treatment modalities were in fact efficacious. Also, the fact that what testing was done generally involved men meant that the use of pharmaceuticals for women with HIV/AIDS resulted in unexpected side effects and different results. These kinds of tensions continue despite the fact that President Clinton signed legislation in November 1997 designed to streamline the FDA processes.

In a formal §§556 and 557 rulemaking proceeding, where such an approach is required, the administrative law judge (ALJ) or members of the regulatory commission involved hold a formal trial-type hearing. It is an adversary proceeding with many, although not all, of the requirements of a formal civil trial. On completion of the proceeding, the ALJ makes findings of fact, decides questions of law raised during the hearing, and issues a preliminary opinion. All the material developed at hearing is sent to the members of the commission or to the secretary, if it is a single head cabinet department, for a final decision. That decisionmaker examines the record, or a digest of the record prepared by agency staff personnel, and considers the recommendations of the ALJ. The decision of the ALJ is not binding on the policymaker, but it must be considered. Any final rule must be substantial evidence on the record before the agency at the time of the decision.[116]

The informal process, by contrast, offers maximum administrative flexibility, permits the use of a wide variety of information drawn from diverse sources, and involves no presumed rights of individuals or groups who would like to influence the rulemaking process. On the other hand, notice and comment rulemaking does not, at least on the face of the statute, guarantee that comments offered by the public will be considered in any particular manner, that information used will not be biased, or that evidence and method of evaluating data used by the agency will be open to challenge. The formal process does safeguard the integrity of the evidence by permitting some degree of testing through the use of cross-examination or the submission of contradictory evidence. The formal process insulates the fact-finding process from unseen or unchallenged influence and establishes a strong record that can be used to determine whether the administrator was acting arbitrarily or not. It does presume a need for fairness to contending parties in a policy dispute. However, the formal process is unmercifully burdensome, expensive, and constraining to an administrator.

Hybrid Rulemaking: The Contemporary Standard for Rulemaking

Given the existing choices between an excessively formal procedure and a weak informal process, it was natural that a compromise third alternative would be developed. Hybrid rulemaking is now favored by Congress, the president, and the courts, but the prime mover behind the early development of the hybrid process from the late 1960s through the mid-1970s was the judiciary. The principal catalyst was the growing number of disputes over regulations issued by various agencies that involved a significant and complex scientific or technological debate. One who would understand more recent trends in the administrative process must understand the reasons for the process of hybrid rulemaking development.

Two of the most commonly heard criticisms of the administrative process, especially following the report of the Task Force on Legal Services and Procedures of the second Hoover Commission from the mid-1950s through the 1960s, were (1) that administrative agencies ought to make policy decisions through rulemaking proceedings rather than in case-by-case adjudications,[117] and (2) for a variety of reasons, effective judicial review would be necessary to ensure the responsiveness and responsibility of administrators.[118] Rulemaking did increase during the late 1960s, perhaps in part because of the demands for it, but certainly also because the number of agencies and the scope of administration also increased. In particular, regulation of the environment, implementation of the civil rights laws, and changes in the marketplace brought rapid administrative policy generation and saw legal challenges and responses increase. Many of these policies involved complex technical issues. In such an environment the problem for judges is how to respond to the call for effective judicial review while at the same time respecting the well-understood doctrine of deference to administrative expertise. One must keep administrators within the law without second-guessing their policy judgments.

In a series of cases, several courts worked out solutions.[119] The general line of reasoning ran somewhat as follows. The APA and other statutes and common law doctrines required courts, on judicial review of agency action, to ensure that the agency was not acting in violation of constitutional provisions, was acting within the authority granted to the agency by statute, and was not acting in a way that was "arbitrary, capricious, an abuse of discretion or otherwise not in accordance with law."[120] In terms of a policy promulgated in the form of a rule, what does it mean to ask whether the rulemaking was arbitrary, capricious, or an abuse of discretion? There are several possibilities. First, an administrator might have included some factors in the decisionmaking process that were impermissible, e.g., whether a certain racial or religious group would be advantaged or disadvantaged. Second, since the APA requires an opportunity for some form of public participation, an administrator might be acting arbitrarily if he or she refused to consider obviously relevant and important information offered in response to notice and comment announcements. Finally, and in the most general sense, arbitrary action is commonly thought of as action without a basis in reason. But how is a reviewing court to determine whether the rule was issued as a matter of fiat or as a reasoned determination? Probably the best way is to examine the record, or more generally the set of information in whatever form that was before the administrator when he or she made the decision to issue the rule and inquire as to how the decision was reached.[121] More generally, without second-guessing the substance of the decision, the judges wanted to make sure that when the APA required notice, the information provided was adequate to allow real participation; that when the statute called for participation, that opportunity was meaningful and adequate to ensure a full consideration of the issues and not merely *pro forma;* and that when the APA called for consideration of the comments submitted by participants in the rulemaking process, there was some evidence that the agency did in fact seriously consider that information and did not merely put the material into a box somewhere.

The processes required came to be known as hybrid rulemaking.[122] From the judges' point of view, it was a workable way of meeting their responsibilities without interference with the operation of government. If, after all, presumptions are made in judicial review of the rulemaking record in favor of the validity of agency action and the review is indeed limited to that record, one can perhaps ensure against administrative arbitrariness and at the same time avoid judicial usurpation of administration authority by emphasizing the requirements of an adequate record.

The cornerstone of hybrid rulemaking is the rulemaking record. One of those involved in the development of the hybrid process, Judge David L. Bazelon, commenting on the Vermont Yankee ruling,[123] summarized his views on the usefulness and appropriateness of this form of rulemaking:

> Courts do not have resources to get deeply into the area of agency expertise. The court can make sure the agency did its task by ensuring that a good rulemaking record is established. Such a record provides for:
>
> (1) Judicial review — because the judge understands what was considered and how it was considered;
>
> (2) Peer review — because it gets all the material out where the professional scientific community can see the record and respond to it;
>
> (3) Legislative oversight — so that we can learn from [agency performance];
>
> (4) An adhesive force in public opinion in that there is no sense of secrecy or cover up;
>
> (5) Reconsideration of policy — because as values change we can reconsider policy. We can look back five months, five years, fifty years, or two hundred years to judge the bases for decisions to know how to evaluate them in light of changing values.[124]

Gellhorn and Bruff summarized the nature and purposes of this hybrid form as follows:

Several purposes are discernible in these new statutory and judicial requirements. One is to assure fair treatment of persons submitting comments by requiring actual agency consideration and response. A second is to foster reasoned agency decisionmaking by exposing thinking within the agency to public criticism and by requiring reasoned resolution of the issues. A third is to facilitate judicial review by providing a record to justify a final rule. Obviously, these purposes are closely intertwined.[125]

In general terms, hybrid rulemaking involves the §553 process plus such specific procedures as are needed to establish that when a rule is promulgated it will be supported by a rulemaking record, which:

1. Gives a statement of the basis and purpose of the rule and cites supporting documentation;
2. Sets forth the data on which the agency relied in developing the rule;
3. Describes the methodology the agency employed in analyzing its data and developing the final policy;
4. Provides evidence that there was adequate notice to those who might be interested in commenting on the proposed rule;
5. Shows that a sufficient amount of time was provided so that comments could be prepared and submitted to the agency;
6. Indicates that comments could challenge the data admittedly relied on by the agency, either on paper or by some form of oral argument;
7. Gives evidence that the agency did examine relevant significant public comments and responded, albeit perhaps in a limited way, to those criticisms and suggestions.[126]

But these judicially imposed reforms quickly became controversial.[127] Were the judges really simply demanding substantial compliance with the provisions of the APA and agency enabling acts as opposed to rubber-stamping agency decisions, or were they second-guessing the requirements actually imposed by the legislature and substituting judicial policy views for the discretion that was properly the province of the expert administrator? Although this was an interesting topic for debate, some of the significance of the controversy was rendered moot by the fact that Congress and the president have since imposed a hybrid rulemaking process on almost all agencies since the technique was first launched in judicial opinions. Many states have also imposed all or most of the hybrid requirements through modifications in state APAs. Congress has included some additional requirements above the basic §553 notice and comment process in almost all major pieces of legislation enacted since the early 1970s that contained significant rulemaking authority.[128]

For example, the Toxic Substances Control Act[129] includes hybrid or §553-plus requirements for rulemaking by the Environmental Protection Agency in the area of hazardous substances regulation. That is why hybrid rulemaking is sometimes referred to as "553-plus" rulemaking. The TSCA requires the kinds of items generally included in demands for hybrid rulemaking in situations in which the EPA either promulgates a rule for the testing of a substance or in which the agency decides actually to regulate the manufacture or distribution of particular substances found through the testing process to be toxic (see Figure 5.2).

The trend toward hybrid procedures has not been limited to the courts and the legislature. President Carter issued Executive Order 12044 on March 23, 1978. Among other things, this order required executive branch agencies not otherwise required to do so to employ the additional requirements of adequate notice, openness, participation, and development of a rulemaking record usually included in hybrid rulemaking. Thus, the Carter order required that advanced notice be given of the agency's intention to issue a rule so that interested parties could become involved early in the process rather than after insiders and agency personnel had already reached preliminary conclusions about the content of the rule. Since then, sixty to ninety days prior to publication of a notice of proposed rulemaking, executive branch agencies have been required to provide an advanced notice of proposed rulemaking (ANPRM). It required that notice be published in sources other than the *Federal Register* where it was more likely to

SEC. 6 REGULATION OF HAZARDOUS CHEMICAL SUBSTANCES AND MIXTURES.

(a) SCOPE OF REGULATION.—If the Administrator finds that there is a reasonable basis to conclude that the manufacture, processing, distribution in commerce, use, or disposal of a chemical substance or mixture, or that any combination of such activities, presents or will present an unreasonable risk of injury to health or the environment, the Administrator shall by rule apply one or more of the following requirements to such substance or mixture to the extent necessary to protect adequately against such risk using the least burdensome requirements: . . . .

(c) PROMULGATION OF SUBSECTION (a) RULES.—

(1) In promulgating any rule under subsection (a) with respect to a chemical substance or mixture, the Administrator shall consider and publish a statement with respect to—

(A) the effects of such substance or mixture on health and the magnitude of the exposure of human beings to such substance or mixture,

(B) the effects of such substance or mixture on the environment and the magnitude of the exposure of the environment to such substance or mixture,

(C) the benefits of such substance or mixture for various uses and the availability of substitutes for such uses, and

(D) the reasonably ascertainable economic consequences of the rule, after consideration of the effect on the national economy, small business, technological innovation, the environment, and public health.

If the Administrator determines that a risk of injury to health or the environment could be eliminated or reduced to a sufficient extent by actions taken under another Federal law (or laws) administered in whole or in part by the Administrator, the Administrator may not promulgate a rule under subsection (a) to protect against such risk of injury unless the Administrator finds, in the Administrator's discretion, that it is in the public interest to protect against such risk under this Act. In making such a finding the Administrator shall consider

(i) all relevant aspects of the risk, as determined by the Administrator in the Administrator's discretion, (ii) a comparison of the estimated costs of complying with actions taken under this Act and under such law (or laws) and (iii) the relative efficiency of actions under this Act and under such law (or laws), and (iv) the relative efficiency of actions under this Act and under such law (or laws) to protect against such risk of injury.

(2) When prescribing a rule under subsection (a) the Administrator shall proceed in accordance with section 553 of title 5, United States Code (without regard to any reference in such section to sections 556 and 557 of such title), and shall also

(A) publish a notice of proposed rulemaking stating with particularity the reason for the proposed rule;

(B) allow interested persons to submit written data, views, and arguments, and make all such submissions publicly available;

(C) provide an opportunity for an informal hearing in accordance with paragraph (3);

(D) promulgate, if appropriate, a final rule based on the matter in the rulemaking record (as defined in section 19(a)); and

(E) make and publish with the rule the finding described in subsection (a).

(3) Informal hearings required by paragraph (2)(C) shall be conducted by the Administrator in accordance with the following requirements:

(A) Subject to subparagraph (B), an interested person is entitled—

(i) to present such person's position orally or by documentary submissions (or both), and

(ii) if the Administrator determines that there are disputed issues of material fact it is necessary to resolve, to present such rebuttal submissions and to conduct (or have conducted under subparagraph (B)(ii) such cross-examination of persons as

F I G U R E 5.2 A Sample Hybrid Rulemaking Requirement[130] (*Continued*)

the Administrator determines (I) to be appropriate, and (II) to be required for a full and true disclosure with respect to such issues.

(B) The Administrator may prescribe such rules and make such rulings concerning procedures in such hearings to avoid unnecessary costs or delay. Such rules or rulings may include (i) the imposition of reasonable time limits on each interested person's oral presentations, and (ii) requirements that any cross-examination to which a person may be entitled under subparagraph (A) be conducted by the Administrator on behalf of that person in such manner as the Administrator determines (I) to be appropriate, and (II) to be required for a full and true disclosure with respect to disputed issues of material fact.

(C) (i) Except as provided in clause (ii), if a group of persons each of whom under subparagraphs (A) and (B) would be entitled to conduct (or have conducted) cross-examination and who are determined by the Administrator to have the same or similar interests in the proceeding cannot agree upon a single representative of such interests for purposes of cross-examination the Administrator may make rules and rulings (I) limiting the representation of such interest for such purposes, and (II) governing the manner in which such cross-examination shall be limited.

(ii) When any person who is a member of a group with respect to which the Administrator has made a determination under clause (i) is unable to agree upon group representation with the other members of the group, then such person shall not be denied under the authority of clause (i) the opportunity to conduct (or have conducted) cross-examination as to issues affecting the person's particular interests if (I) the person satisfies the Administrator that the person has made a reasonable and good faith effort to reach agreement upon group representation with the other members of the group and (II) the Administrator determines that there are substantial and relevant issues which are not adequately presented by the group representative.

(D) A verbatim transcript shall be taken of any oral presentation made, and cross-examination conducted in any informal hearing under this subsection. Such transcript shall be available to the public.

(4) (A) The Administrator may, pursuant to rules prescribed by the Administrator, provide compensation for reasonable attorneys' fees, expert witness fees, and other costs of participating in a rulemaking proceeding for the promulgation of a rule under subsection (a) to any person—

(i) who represents an interest which would substantially contribute to a fair determination of the issues to be resolved in the proceeding, and

(ii) if—

(I) the economic interest of such person is small in comparison to the costs of effective participation in the proceeding by such person, or

(II) such person demonstrates to the satisfaction of the Administrator that such person does not have sufficient resources adequately to participate in the proceeding without compensation under this subparagraph.[62]

FIGURE 5.2 (*Continued*)

be read by those affected. It called for expanded opportunities for participation and development of a solid rulemaking record. Presidents Reagan and Clinton not only maintained the requirements imposed by Carter but added to them significantly.[131]

Ever since the Carter order, and the various innovations that have been implemented since then, rulemaking has looked very different than the picture presented in §553. Indeed, it now looks more like Figure 5.1.

Once the decision is made that substantive rules will be needed and a hybrid process is selected as the means for promulgating the rule, several steps are taken. First, assuming there is time to do so, the agency publishes its intention to develop rules on a particular subject in the regulatory agenda (accessed through Reg.Info.gov) and the agency then publishes an Advance Notice of Proposed Rulemaking (ANPRM), which signals the beginning of the public process. One of the next decisions to be made is whether to engage in negotiated rulemaking process. Obviously, in the BSE example, there were clear reasons why these steps were bypassed.

Negotiated Rulemaking

Like most relatively new developments, there are three important questions to be asked of the innovation known as negotiated rulemaking. What is this process? What benefits does it offer? And what potential problems does it pose?

Negotiated rulemaking grew out of the same trends that have encouraged the use of alternative dispute resolution techniques in adjudicative processes. The basic explanation is that all of the creative policymaking in the world will be meaningless if the rule that results is either overturned by a court or becomes hopelessly enmeshed in ongoing litigation brought by a variety of frustrated interest groups or regulated firms. And there has seemingly been an increasing tendency to intensify legal challenges to agency action.[132] The idea of negotiated rulemaking is to avoid that problem or to reduce the scope and intensity of conflict that might result.

Professors Lawrence Susskind and Gerard McMahon provided a helpful description of the process well before it became popular:

> In negotiated rulemaking, an agency and other parties with a significant stake in a rule participate in facilitated face-to-face interactions designed to produce a consensus. Together the parties explore their shared interests as well as differences of opinion, collaborate in gathering and analyzing technical information, generate options, and bargain and trade across these options according to their differing priorities. If a consensus is reached, it is published in the *Federal Register* as the agency's notice of proposed rulemaking, and then the conventional review and comment process takes over.[133]

The process involves selection of a facilitator to assemble a negotiated rulemaking committee, consisting of representatives of relevant stakeholders. The information about the process and the means by which the committee is to be selected is published in the *Federal Register* (see Figure 5.3). The selection process is obviously important because it is necessary to keep the size of the committee down to approximately 20 to 25 members.[134] More participants would make it extraordinarily difficult to conclude a successful negotiation.

A second consultant may then be brought in to facilitate the actual work of the committee once the members of the group have been chosen. The use of a second party is intended to avoid any actual or apparent conflicts of interest between the naming of the members of the negotiating committee and the group's operations. The parties begin with an agreement to work together as equal participants in negotiations until consensus is reached. Technically, of course, the agency representative is not legally bound by the negotiations, but if he or she walks away, immediate conflict is likely. On the other hand, the longer the agency—and for that matter, the other parties—remains in the negotiations, the more difficult it will be to break off the talks. The product of the committee's negotiation is a notice of proposed rulemaking which is then subject to the normal notice and participation requirements of the APA.

Department of Labor

Occupational Safety and Health Administration

29 CFR Part 1926

[Docket No. S–775]
RIN No. 1218–AA65

Safety Standards for Steel and Other Metal and Non-Metal Erection

AGENCY: Occupational Safety and Health Administration (OSHA), U.S. Department of Labor.
ACTION: Announcement of Intent To Establish Negotiated Rulemaking Committee; Request for Representation.

SUMMARY: The Occupational Safety and Health Administration is announcing its intent to estblish a Steel Erection Negotiated Rulemaking Advisory Committee under the Negotiated Rulemaking Act (NRA) and the Federal Advisory Committee Act (FACA). The Committee will negotiate issues associated with the development of a proposed revision of the existing safety provisions in its construction standards for steel erection (29 CFR part 1926, subpart R). The Committee will include representatives of identified parties who would be significantly affected by the final rule. OSHA solicits interested parties to nominate representatives for membership for representation on the Committee.
DATES: OSHA must receive written comments and requests for membership or representation by March 29, 1993.
ADDRESSES: All written comments should be sent, in quadruplicate, to the following address: Docket Office, Docket S–775, Room N–2625, 200 Constitution Ave., N.W., Washington, D.C., 20210; Telephone (202) 219–7894.

II. Proposed Negotiation Procedures

The following proposed procedures and guidelines may be augmented as a result of comments received in response to this document or during the negotiation process

A. Committee Formation

This negotiated rulemaking Committee will be formed and operated in full compliance with the requirements of the Federal Advisory Committee Act (FACA) in a manner consistent with the requirements of the Negotiated Rulemaking Act (NRA)

B. Interests Involved

The Agency intends to conduct negotiated rulemaking proceedings with particular attention to ensuring full and adequate representation of those interests that may be significantly affected by the proposed rule. Section 562 of the NRA defines the term "interest" as follows:

(5) "interest" means, with respect to an issue or matter, multiple parties which have a similar point of view or which are likely to be affected in a similar manner

The following interests have been tentatively identified as "significantly affected" by the matters that may be included in the proposed rule:

--Architectural, design and engineering firms;
--Developers, property owners and general contractors;
--Erection contractors using steel and erection contractors using materials other than steel;
--Fabricators of structural steel and non-steel metal products;
--Insurance organizations and public interest groups;
--Labor organizations representing employees who perform erection work;
--Manufacturers and suppliers of fall protection safety equipment;
--Manufacturers and suppliers of structural members and pre-engineered components; and
--Government entities.

One purpose of this document is to determine whether a standard regulating erection operations associated with steel and/or other metal and non-metal material members would significantly affect interests that are not listed above. OSHA invites comment and suggestions on this list of "significantly affected" interests.

In this regard, the Department of Labor recognizes that the regulatory actions it takes under its programs may at times affect various segments of society in different ways, and that this may in some cases produce unique "interests" in a proposed rule based on income, gender, or other such factors. Particular attention will be given by the Department to ensure that any unique interests which have been identified in this regard, and which it is determined will be significantly affected by the proposed rule are fully represented.

C. Members

The negotiating group should not exceed 25 members, and 15 would be preferable. The Agency believes that more than 15 members would make it difficult to conduct effective negotiations.

OSHA is aware that there are many more potential participants, whether they are listed here or not, than there are membership slots on the Committee. The Agency does not believe, nor does the NRA contemplate, that each potentially affected group must participate directly in the negotiations; nevertheless, each affected interest will hopefully be adequately represented. In order to have a successful negotiation, it is importatnt for interested parties to identify and form coalitions that adequately represent significantly affected interests. These coalitions, in order to provide adequate representation, must agree to support, both financially and technically, a

member to the Committee whom they will choose to represent their "interest"

FIGURE 5.3 Notice of Negotiated Rulemaking

SOURCE: 57 Fed. Reg. 61860, 61863 (1992).

Of course, given this complex set of processes, even the most ardent supporters of negotiated rulemaking recognize that it is appropriate only for a limited number of situations that present the right kinds of characteristics. Probably the best-known advocate of negotiated rulemaking, Philip J. Harter, has provided a list of criteria for judging whether an agency should seek to use negotiated rulemaking:

[T]here need to be a limited number of interests that will be significantly affected by the rule, and they have to be organized sufficiently so that you can select individuals to represent them.

[T]he issues have to be known and ripe for a decision. . .. [T]he issues need to be crystallized—you know what you are talking about, not necessarily the solution, but you know what the problem is, and it is ready for you. . . .

[T]he issues have to be such that no party—no individual or representative of an interest—will have to compromise, give in on, something of fundamental value.

There have to be a number of issues in the rulemaking. The whole purpose of the negotiation is kind of the Jack Sprat theory. What one person values the other person does not value as much, and you can trade and optimize everybody's satisfaction because people look at this differential value on the issues.

The agency has to be willing to use the process and participate in it. . . .Everyone knows that every agency can find enormously creative ways to sabotage something it does not like. . ..

[I]t is important for the agency to participate actively in the process itself, just like anybody else in the rough and tumble and give and take of the deliberations.[135]

For all these reasons, the tendency has been to provide this option to agencies and then permit its leaders to use their discretion as to whether the particular rulemaking process that is pending is a good candidate for the negotiated approach.[136] Indeed, the Negotiated Rulemaking Act presumes against judicial review of the decision to use the negotiated process. "Any agency action relating to establishing, assisting, or terminating a negotiated rulemaking committee under this subchapter shall not be subject to judicial review. Nothing in this section shall bar judicial review of a rule if such judicial review is otherwise provided by law."[137] That said, the Congress has adopted some legislation, such as the No Child Left Behind Act, that mandates the use of negotiated rulemaking.[138]

Even so, there are limits to the circumstances in which the technique should be employed. In addition to its limited utility, negotiated rulemaking has been subject to a variety of other criticisms. By definition, negotiated rulemaking involves moving a process that was intended to be open to broad participation into meeting rooms, most often in Washington, occupied by a very limited number of people, usually not more than two dozen. The responses to such concerns are two. First, the idea is that the negotiating committee must be constructed so that it is representative of all the interests involved. Second, when the committee has finished its work, the result is a notice of proposed rulemaking which must then go through the APA mandated comment process.

However, the simple claim that the committee will be representative and inclusive is a large assertion. In the contemporary environment, the effort to achieve agreement about which groups can represent which positions and what groups of people is very complex. Many of the major interest groups in such areas as the environment or education are not in agreement on positions with respect to a host of policies. Indeed, they continue to exist in significant part because they define themselves as distinct from other interest groups in the same policy arena. From the limited amount of case law available on the subject, it seems clear that it can be difficult for those left out of the process to challenge the construction of the negotiated rulemaking committee for several reasons. These problems include the argument that the choice of members of the committee is not final agency action that would allow judicial review and the fact that is will be extremely difficult for challengers to demonstrate standing to sue since they will have to show a connection between the fact that they were omitted from the committee and a specific outcome of the rules at the end of the process of a sort that violates a properly established legal right in which they have a concrete interest.[139]

Further, since these proceedings generally take place in one place in the nation, most commonly Washington, D.C., there is a clear limitation as to who will be included. That is not helped by the fact that Congress does not appropriate funds for the purpose of bringing representatives to Washington to participate in such activities. These are not simple, one-shot sessions. Most complex negotiations take a considerable period of time and numerous meetings. Clearly, there are strong biases in this kind of process toward established and financially well-off Washington-based political players.

One answer is that under the Federal Advisory Committee Act (FACA), these sessions must be open. Of course, would-be participants could only attend if they knew of the meetings in the first place. Moreover, by definition, although they may attend, such visitors are not participants. Beyond that, while the meetings of the whole committee at which formal decisions are taken are open, the same is not necessarily true of meetings held by caucuses or subcommittees created to work on particular aspects of the overall problem.[140]

The contention is equally problematic that these difficulties can be mitigated by the fact that the results of the committee's work becomes a notice of proposed rulemaking that must then be subjected to the APA comment process. While it is theoretically possible for the agency or any party to the negotiation to walk away from the process at any point, the fact is that by the time any consensus is reached, there are heavy costs by all parties, including the government. If a consensus achieved through such a complex were then to be significantly altered during a notice and comment process after the committee concluded its work, the entire point of the negotiated rulemaking process would be undermined. Thus, the question must be asked whether any such comment process is meaningful and whether there is any likelihood that such input as is received will be seriously considered and used by the agency to alter the proposed rule.

On the other hand, it is not all that clear that those who participate in a negotiated rulemaking committee can be sure that their understanding of the consensus reached in that process will survive once the rulemaking moves through the notice and comment process, the rule becomes final, and is implemented. Thus, the D.C. Circuit rejected a challenge by the Association of American Railroads to an interpretation given to a rule made through a negotiated process in which the association participated. The interpretation came in a technical bulletin that the DOT claimed was an interpretative rule and was not required to be made in a full rulemaking proceeding under the APA. The association specifically asserted that this interpretation was a major change in the rule because it ran counter to assurances provided by agency representatives during the negotiations of the committee that had produced the earlier rule. Indeed, the association asserted that: "[T]he railroads' agreement with the outcome of the negotiated rulemaking was 'critically dependent on their ability (consistent with the regulations) to use red flags [alone] to demarcate working limits.'" However, the court rejected that argument, noting that: "[T]he AAR points to no evidence to support this assertion; all evidence in the record is post-negotiated rulemaking. Even if true, moreover, agreement to a negotiated rulemaking based on a presumptive interpretation of ambiguous language" was hardly sufficient to justify the claim that a later interpretation was a completely new rule.[141]

Chief Judge Posner of the Seventh Circuit went even farther in warning those who participate in such procedures not to assume that their agreements will be honored. A group that serviced student loans concluded when a rule emerged after the notice and comment process that the U.S. Department of Education had negotiated in bad faith during the negotiated part of the process before the proposed rule went to notice and comment. Posner warned:

> The servicers argue that the Department negotiated in bad faith with them. Neither the 1992 amendment nor the Negotiated Rulemaking Act specifies a remedy for such a case, and the latter act strongly implies there is none. 5 U.S.C. § 570....
>
> During the negotiations, an official of the Department of Education promised the servicers that the Department would abide by any consensus reached by them unless there were compelling reasons to depart. The propriety of such a promise may be questioned. It sounds like an

abdication of regulatory authority to the regulated, the full burgeoning of the interest-group state, and the final confirmation of the "capture" theory of administrative regulation....

We have doubts about the propriety of the official's promise to abide by a consensus of the regulated industry, but we have no doubt that the Negotiated Rulemaking Act did not make the promise enforceable.... The practical effect of enforcing it would be to make the Act extinguish notice and comment rulemaking in all cases in which it was preceded by negotiated rulemaking; the comments would be irrelevant if the agency were already bound by promises that it had made to the industry. There is no textual or other clue that the Act meant to do this. Unlike collective bargaining negotiations...the Act does not envisage that the negotiations will end in a binding contract. The Act simply creates a consultative process in advance of the more formal arms' length procedure of notice and comment rulemaking.[142]

In sum, negotiated rulemaking is a tool that some have found useful in relatively limited numbers of situations with the right kinds of characteristics to address well-focused but contentious issues. Indeed, Congress adopted the Negotiated Rulemaking Act in 1990[143] to encourage, though not require, the use of negotiated rulemaking. President Clinton incorporated support for this approach in his executive order on rulemaking, E.O. 12866 (see Appendix 4A). Even so, its difficulties are obvious and significant. It will be some time before the future of this particular rulemaking technique becomes clear. Those developments will be all the more important to watch in light of the fact that Congress has taken to requiring the technique in some statutes.

Regulatory Analysis and Executive Preclearance

If it is assumed that the mad cow problem is not appropriate for a negotiated rulemaking and the agencies involved move to a wide-ranging process for gathering information and produces a notice of proposed rulemaking (NPRM), they must then move through the related processes of regulatory analysis and executive preclearance in order to move the process along.

Several recent presidents have been concerned that agencies were not taking sufficient care in rulemaking to ensure that a new regulation was necessary and that its probable economic impact had been considered. The requirement that agencies perform a regulatory analysis prior to issuance of a new rule calls for essentially three types of information: (1) the agency is expected to show that the new regulation is really necessary; (2) the administrator is to indicate what other alternative policy instruments were available and why they were rejected in favor of the regulation. Finally, (3) the agency is generally expected to show that it has considered the likely costs and benefits of the proposed regulation.

President Ford issued Executive Order 11821 in 1974, authorizing the Office of Management and Budget to require inflation-impact assessments by agencies that wished to promulgate new rules. President Carter expanded on the theme dramatically in his regulatory improvement policy order of 1978 Executive Order 12044, shown in Figure 5.4.

President Reagan used the Carter order as a basis for his own executive order on rulemaking procedure, E.O. 12291, issued just after he took office in 1981.[144] The Reagan order expanded dramatically on the Carter mandate and granted the Office of Management and Budget significant authority to use the process to constrain agency rulemaking.[145]

The Reagan order required agencies to go much further than the Carter order in terms of their regulatory analyses. Where the Carter order merely sought to ensure that impacts had been considered, that there was an assessment of the relationship between potential costs and benefits, and that alternatives to standard regulation had been considered, the Reagan order mandated a far more sweeping analysis and authorized the Office of Management and Budget to play a more active role in the process. Executive order 12291 required that:

As President of the United States of America, I direct each Executive Agency to adopt procedures to improve existing and future regulations.

Section 1. Policy. Regulations shall be as simple and clear as possible. They shall achieve legislative goals effectively and efficiently. They shall not impose unnecessary burdens on the economy, on individuals, on public or private organizations, or on State and local governments.

To achieve these objectives, regulations shall be developed through a process which ensures that:

(a) the need for and purposes of the regulation are clearly established;

(b) heads of agencies and policy officials exercise effective oversight;

(c) opportunity exists for early participation and comment by other Federal agencies, State and local governments, businesses, organizations and individual members of the public;

(d) meaningful alternatives are considered and analyzed before the regulation is issued; and

(e) compliance costs, paperwork and other burdens on the public are minimized.

Sec. 2. Reform of the Process for Developing Significant Regulations. Agencies shall review and revise their procedures for developing regulations to be consistent with the policies of this Order and in a manner that minimizes paperwork.

Agencies' procedures should fit their own needs but, at a minimum, these procedures shall include the following:

(a) Semiannual Agenda of Regulations. To give the public adequate notice, agencies shall publish at least semiannually an agenda of significant regulations under development or review. On the first Monday in October, each agency shall publish in the FEDERAL REGISTER a schedule showing the times during the coming fiscal year when the agency's semiannual agenda will be published. Supplements to the agenda may be published at other times during the year if necessary, but the semiannual agendas shall be as complete as possible. The head of each agency shall approve the agenda before it is published. At a minimum, each published agenda shall describe the regulations being considered by the agency, the need for and the legal basis for the action being taken, and the status of regulations previously listed on the agenda.

(b) Agency Head Oversight. Before an agency proceeds to develop significant new regulations, the agency head shall have reviewed the issues to be considered, the alternative approaches to be explored, a tentative plan for obtaining public comment, and target dates for completion of steps in the development of the regulation.

(c) Opportunity for Public Participation. Agencies shall give the public an early and meaningful opportunity to participate in the development of agency regulations. They shall consider a variety of ways to provide this opportunity, including (1) publishing an advance notice of proposed rulemaking; (2) holding open conferences or public hearings; (3) sending notices of proposed regulations to publications likely to be read by those affected; and (4) notifying interested parties directly. Agencies shall give the public at least 60 days to comment on proposed significant regulations. in the few instances where agencies determine this is not possible the regulation shall be accompanied by a brief statement of the reasons for a shorter time period.

(d) Approval of Significant Regulations. The head of each agency, or the designated official with statutory responsibility, shall approve significant regulations before they are published for public comment in the FEDERAL REGISTER. At a minimum, this official should determine that:

(1) the proposed regulation is needed;

(2) the direct and indirect effects of the regulation have been adequately considered;

(3) alternative approaches have been considered and the least burdensome of the acceptable alternatives has been chosen;

FIGURE 5.4   Executive Order 12044: Improving Government Regulations

(4) public comments have been considered and an adequate response has been prepared;

(5) the regulation is written in plain English and is understandable to those who must comply with it;

(6) an estimate has been made of the new reporting burdens or recordkeeping requirements necessary for compliance with the regulation;

(7) the name, address and telephone number of a knowledgeable agency official is included in the publication; and

(8) a plan for evaluating the regulation after its issuance has been developed.

(e) Criteria for Determining Significant Regulations. Agencies shall establish criteria for identifying which regulations are significant. Agencies shall consider among other things: (1) the type and number of individuals, businesses, organizations, State and local governments affected; (2) the compliance and reporting requirements likely to be involved; (3) direct and indirect effects of the regulation including the effect on competition; and (4) the relationship of the regulations to those of other programs and agencies. Regulations that do not meet an agency's criteria for determining significance shall be accompanied by a statement to that effect at the time the regulation proposed.

Sec. 3. Regulatory Analysis. Some of the regulations identified as significant may have major economic consequences for the general economy, for individual industries, geographical regions or levels of government. For these regulations, agencies shall prepare a regulatory analysis. Such an analysis shall involve a careful examination of alternative approaches early in the decision-making process.

The following requirements shall govern the preparation of regulatory analyses:

(a) Criteria. Agency heads shall establish criteria for determining which regulations require regulatory analyses. The criteria established shall:

(1) ensure that regulatory analyses are performed for all regulations which will result in (a) an annual effect on the economy of $100 million or more; or (b) a major increase in costs or prices for individual industries, levels of government or geographic regions; and

(2) provide that at the agency head's discretion, regulatory analysis may be completed on any proposed regulation.

(b) Procedures. Agency heads shall establish procedures for developing the regulatory analysis and obtaining public comment.

(1) Each regulatory analysis shall contain a succinct statement of the problem; a description of the major alternative ways of dealing with the problems that were considered by the agency; an analysis of the economic consequences of each of these alternatives; and a detailed explanation of the reasons for choosing one alternative over the others.

(2) Agencies shall include in their public notice of proposed rules an explanation of the regulatory approach that has been selected or is favored and a short description of the other alternatives considered. A statement of how the public may obtain a copy of the draft regulatory analysis shall also be included.

(3) Agencies shall prepare a final regulatory analysis to be made available when the final regulations are published.

Regulatory analyses shall not be required in rulemaking proceedings pending at the time this Order is issued if an Economic Impact Statement has already been prepared in accordance with Executive Orders 11821 and 11949.

FIGURE 5.4 (*Continued*)

Section 2. General Requirements. In promulgating new regulations, reviewing existing regulations, and developing legislative proposals concerning regulations, all agencies, to the extent permitted by law, shall adhere to the following requirements:

(a) Administrative decisions shall be based on adequate information concerning the need for and consequences of proposed government action;

(b) Regulatory action shall not be undertaken unless the potential benefits to society for the regulation outweigh the potential costs to society;

(c) Regulatory objectives shall be chosen to maximize the net benefits to society;

(d) Among alternative approaches to any given regulatory objective, the alternative involving the least net cost to society shall be chosen; and

(e) Agencies shall set regulatory priorities with the aim of maximizing the aggregate net benefits to society, taking into account the condition of the particular industries affected by regulations, the condition of the national economy, and other regulatory actions contemplated for the future.

Failure to satisfy these and the other provisions of the order meant in a number of cases that the OMB prohibited the agency from moving to the next step and publishing the NPRM.

The George H. W. Bush administration continued the Reagan regulatory analysis and review orders but added some twists in terms of how the reviews were to be managed, including creation of a council on competitiveness headed by the vice president, intended to catch issues that the regular OMB review might miss. (Just how these reviews were handled within the White House and their political implications will be addressed in Chapter 10.)

But the Reagan and Bush administrations thought that they could achieve some of the policy goals they had not been able to attain in Congress using this type of constraint on rulemaking. They proceeded by mandating through executive orders that agencies include in their preliminary rulemaking efforts such matters as impacts on intergovernmental relations (E.O. 12372),[146] federalism (E.O. 12612),[147] the family (E.O. 12606),[148] the taking of private property (E.O. 12630),[149] and mandating inclusion of elements of civil justice reform (E.O. 12778).[150]

These issues were addressed publicly by expanding the beginning section of the publication in the *Federal Register* of the Notice of Proposed Rulemaking (known as the preamble) beyond what it had been even under hybrid rulemaking. A series of statements was added indicating how each of the orders had been complied with or why a particular order or statutory requirement did not apply (see Figure 5.5). The twin dangers were that serious consideration of each of these sets of requirements could be quite burdensome to understaffed and underfunded agencies. Even so, there was simultaneously a relatively cynical view that these things were essentially pro forma and not to be taken seriously unless a key player raised the issue. Thus, the requirements seemed to be both too much and not enough.

Although, as candidates, Bill Clinton and Al Gore criticized the Reagan/Bush regulatory analysis review processes on grounds that they were intended to, and did in fact, handcuff environmental and health agencies in their efforts to protect the public and the environment, Clinton did not lift the burdens once elected. In fact, as Chapter 4 explained, the Clinton administration's National Performance Review blamed administrative rules and the rulemaking process itself for posing barriers to effective governance. Moreover, the administration, like its predecessors, promptly posed for pictures on the White House lawn next to stacks of regulations and vowed that it would measure its success in part by the number of such rules that it eliminated.[151] Further, the administration insisted that agencies needed to demonstrate greater flexibility in their approaches and to avoid what it termed "one size fits all" policy solutions.

Thus, President Clinton issued Executive Order 12866 (reproduced in full in Appendix 4A) which in many respects went beyond the Reagan/Bush era requirements on agency rulemaking.[152] For example, to the previous requirement for a positive cost/benefit calculation, the Clinton order added a mandate for risk assessments that would demonstrate that the agency had considered options adequate

33835

Rules and Regulations

Federal Register

Vol. 63, No. 119

Monday, June 22, 1998

This section of the FEDERAL REGISTER contains regulatory documents having general applicability and legal effect, most of which are keyed to and codified in the Code of Federal Regulations, which is published under 50 titles pursuant to 44 U.S.C. 1510.

The Code of Federal Regulations is sold by the Superintendent of Documents. Prices of new books are listed in the first FEDERAL REGISTER issue of each week.

DEPARTMENT OF AGRICULTURE

Federal Crop Insurance Corporation

7 CFR Parts 447 and 457

RIN 0563–AB48

Popcorn Crop Insurance Regulations; and Common Crop Insurance Regulations, Popcorn Crop Insurance Provisions

AGENCY: Federal Crop Insurance Corporation, USDA.

ACTION: Final rule.

SUMMARY: The Federal Crop Insurance Corporation (FCIC) finalizes specific crop provisions for the insurance of popcorn. The provisions will be used in conjunction with the Common Crop Insurance Policy, Basic Provisions, which contain standard terms and conditions common to most crops. The intended effect of this action is to provide policy changes to better meet the needs of the insured, include the current popcorn crop insurance regulations with the Common Crop Insurance Policy for ease of use and consistency of terms, and to restrict the effect of the current popcorn crop insurance regulations to the 1998 and prior crop years.

EFFECTIVE DATE: July 22, 1998.

FOR FURTHER INFORMATION CONTACT: Linda Williams, Insurance Management Specialist, Research and Development, Product Development Division, Federal Crop Insurance Corporation, United States Department of Agriculture, 9435 Holmes Road, Kansas City, MO 64131, telephone (816) 926–7730.

SUPPLEMENTARY INFORMATION:

Executive Order 12866

This rule has been determined to be exempt for the purposes of Executive Order 12866 and, therefore, has not been reviewed by the Office of Management and Budget (OMB).

Paperwork Reduction Act of 1995

Pursuant to the Paperwork Reduction Act of 1995 (44 U.S.C. chapter 35), the collections of information have been approved by the Office of Management and Budget (OMB) under control number 0563–0053 through October 31, 2000.

Unfunded Mandates Reform Act of 1995

Title II of the Unfunded Mandates Reform Act of 1995 (UMRA), Public Law 104–4, establishes requirements for Federal agencies to assess the effects of their regulatory actions on State, local, and tribal governments and the private sector. This rule contains no Federal mandates (under the regulatory provisions of title II of the UMRA) for State, local, and tribal governments or the private sector. Therefore, this rule is not subject to the requirements of sections 202 and 205 of the UMRA.

Executive Order 12612

It has been determined under section 6(a) of Executive Order 12612, Federalism, that this rule does not have sufficient federalism implications to warrant the preparation of a Federalism Assessment. The provisions contained in this rule will not have a substantial direct effect on States or their political subdivisions or on the distribution of power and responsibilities among the various levels of government.

Regulatory Flexibility Act

This regulation will not have a significant economic impact on a substantial number of small entities. The amount of work required of the insurance companies will not increase because the information used to determine eligibility is already maintained at their office and the other information now required is already being gathered as a result of the present policy. No additional actions are required as a result of this action on the part of either the insured or the insurance companies. Additionally, this regulation does not require any greater action on the part of small entities than is required on the part of large entities. Therefore, this action is determined to be exempt from the provisions of the Regulatory Flexibility Act (5 U.S.C. 605), and no Regulatory Flexibility Analysis was prepared.

Federal Assistance Program

This program is listed in the Catalog of Federal Domestic Assistance under No. 10.450.

Executive Order 12372

This program is not subject to the provisions of Executive Order 12372 which require intergovernmental consultation with State and local officials. See the Notice related to 7 CFR part 3015, subpart V, published at 48 FR 29115, June 24, 1983. ¯

Executive Order 12988

This rule has been reviewed in accordance with Executive Order 12988 on civil justice reform. The provisions of this rule will not have a retroactive effect. The provisions of this rule will preempt State and local laws to the extent such State and local laws are inconsistent herewith. The administrative appeal provisions published at 7 CFR part 11 must be exhausted before any action for judicial review of any determination made by FCIC may be brought.

Environmental Evaluation

This action is not expected to have a significant impact on the quality of the human environment, health, and safety. Therefore, neither an Environmental Assessment nor an Environmental Impact Statement is needed.

National Performance Review

This regulatory action is being taken as part of the National Performance Review Initiative to eliminate unnecessary or duplicative regulations and improve those that remain in force.

Background

On Wednesday, April 9, 1997, FCIC published a notice of proposed rulemaking in the **Federal Register** at 62 FR 17103 to add to the Common Crop Insurance Regulations (7 CFR part 457), a new section, 7 CFR 457.126, Popcorn Crop Insurance Provisions. The new provisions will be effective for the 1999 and succeeding crop years. These provisions will replace and supersede the current provisions for insuring popcorn found at 7 CFR part 447 (Popcorn Crop Insurance Regulations). FCIC also amends 7 CFR part 447 to limit its effect to the 1998 and prior crop years.

Following publication of the proposed rule, the public was afforded 30 days to

---

F I G U R E   5.5 A Typical Rule Preamble

SOURCE: 63 Fed. Reg. 33835 (1998).

to protect health and safety within acceptable limits given the context as opposed simply to mandating the most extensive or more costly action without regard to actual the risks posed by less extensive regulatory approaches (see Chapter 10).

Following its predecessors, the Clinton administration mandated that agencies prepare a regulatory plan outlining the areas in which they intend to issue significant rules in addition to providing the clearance material in its NPRM. It also mandated that agencies were immediately to begin a review of existing regulations:

> In order to reduce the regulatory burden on the American people, their families, their communities, their State, local, and tribal governments, and their industries; to determine whether regulations promulgated by the executive branch of the Federal Government have become unjustified or unnecessary as a result of changed circumstances; to confirm that regulations are both compatible with each other and not duplicative or inappropriately burdensome in the aggregate; to ensure that all regulations are consistent with the President's priorities and the principles set forth in this Executive order, within applicable law; and to otherwise improve the effectiveness of existing regulations.[153]

Supervision over the agenda, preclearance, and periodic rule review functions were placed in the Director of the Office of Information and Regulatory Affairs (OIRA) of the Office of Management and Budget (OMB).

The standards and scope of the regulatory analyses to be provided was expanded significantly over earlier practice. The Clinton order sets forth the following principles to govern agency rulemaking:

Section 1. Statement of Regulatory Philosophy and Principles.

(a) The Regulatory Philosophy. Federal agencies should promulgate only such regulations as are required by law, are necessary to interpret the law, or are made necessary by compelling public need, such as material failures of private markets to protect or improve the health and safety of the public, the environment, or the well-being of the American people. In deciding whether and how to regulate, agencies should assess all costs and benefits of available regulatory alternatives, including the alternative of not regulating. Costs and benefits shall be understood to include both quantifiable measures (to the fullest extent that these can be usefully estimated) and qualitative measures of costs and benefits that are difficult to quantify, but nevertheless essential to consider. Further, in choosing among alternative regulatory approaches, agencies should select those approaches that maximize net benefits (including potential economic, environmental, public health and safety, and other advantages, distributive impacts; and equity), unless a statute requires another regulatory approach.

(b) The Principles of Regulation. To ensure that the agencies' regulatory programs are consistent with the philosophy set forth above, agencies should adhere to the following principles, to the extent permitted by law and where applicable.

   (1) Each agency shall identify the problem that it intends to address (including, where applicable, the failures of private markets or public institutions that warrant new agency action) as well as assess the significance of that problem.

   (2) Each agency shall examine whether existing regulations (or other law) have created, or contributed to, the problem that a new regulation is intended to correct and whether those regulations (or other law) should be modified to achieve the intended goal of regulation more effectively.

   (3) Each agency shall identify and assess available alternatives to direct regulation, including providing economic incentives to encourage the desired behavior, such as user fees or marketable permits, or providing information upon which choices can be made by the public.

(4) In setting regulatory priorities, each agency shall consider, to the extent reasonable, the degree and nature of the risks posed by various substances or activities within its jurisdiction.

(5) When an agency determines that a regulation is the best available method of achieving the regulatory objective, it shall design its regulations in the most cost-effective manner to achieve the regulatory objectives. In doing so, each agency shall consider incentives for innovation, consistency, predictability, the costs of enforcement and compliance (to the government, regulated entities, and the public), flexibility, distributive impacts, and equity.

(6) Each agency shall assess both the costs and the benefits of the intended regulation and, recognizing that some costs and benefits are difficult to quantify, propose or adopt a regulation only upon a reasoned determination that the benefits of the intended regulation justify its costs.

(7) Each agency shall base its decisions on the best reasonably obtainable scientific, technical, economic, and other information concerning the need for, and consequences of, the intended regulation.

(8) Each agency shall identify and assess alternative forms of regulation and shall, to the extent feasible, specify performance objectives, rather than specifying the behavior or manner of compliance that regulated entities must adopt.

(9) Wherever feasible, agencies shall seek views of appropriate State, local, and tribal officials before imposing regulatory requirements that might significantly or uniquely affect those governmental entities. Each agency shall assess the effects of Federal regulations on State, local, and tribal governments, including specifically the availability of resources to carry out those mandates, and seek to minimize those burdens that uniquely or significantly affect such governmental entities, consistent with achieving regulatory objectives. In addition, as appropriate, agencies shall seek to harmonize Federal regulatory actions with related State, local, and tribal regulatory and other governmental functions.

(10) Each agency shall avoid regulations that are inconsistent, incompatible, or duplicative with its other regulations or those of other Federal agencies.

(11) Each agency shall tailor its regulations to impose the least burden on society, including individuals, businesses of differing sizes, and other entities (including small communities and governmental entities), consistent with obtaining the regulatory objectives, taking into account, among other things, and to the extent practicable, the costs of cumulative regulations.

(12) Each agency shall draft its regulations to be simple and easy to understand, with the goal of minimizing the potential for uncertainty and litigation arising from such uncertainty.

What may have come as somewhat of a surprise to White House watchers was the fact that when George W. Bush succeeded Clinton he chose to retain the Clinton order with some amendments. The amendments were extremely limited and focused on removing the vice president as a participant in the regulatory review process. The responsibilities that had previously been lodged in the office of the vice president in previous administrations were divided between the OMB director and, in some instances, the president's office. The Clinton order as amended by the George W. Bush's Executive Order 13258[154] is provided in Appendix 4A. However, the G. W. Bush administration chose to add its new requirements for regulatory analysis by OMB Circular rather than in an executive order. The basic process remained, but the requirements for the analysis changed as set forth in OMB Circular A-4 published in 2003.[155]

Thus, currently federal agencies must provide preclearance information to the White House in the form of the expanded regulatory analyses mandated by the Clinton/Bush executive order and circular.

Then they must—as with the situation in the Reagan and Bush years—address issues raised by other presidential executive orders that call for agencies to address other impacts.

In addition, agencies must comply with legislatively mandated regulatory analysis requirements such as the Regulatory Flexibility Act, calling for special attention to impacts on small governments, small businesses, and not-for-profit organizations.[156] There is also a requirement found in the Paperwork Reduction Act of 1995 to address impacts of proposed rules in terms of requirements that might exist in the planned regulation that the agencies involved collect new, more, or different kinds of information.[157] If there is the possibility of a significant environmental impact, the federal agency must provide an environmental impact statement under the provisions of the National Environmental Policy Act.[158] Finally, there is an obligation under the Unfunded Mandates Reform Act of 1995 to assess the possible impacts on states, local governments, and tribal governments in the form of requirements for action for which no funds are provided by the federal government.[159]

The process has become sufficiently complex that agencies now use fairly extensive flow charts, containing reporting requirements and time lines to guide those responsible for a particular rulemaking through the maze. In addition, the status of clearance and materials produced for that process are posted on Regulation.gov and on the agency's Internet Docket site.

The Notice of Proposed Rulemaking and Participation Processes

At this point, the agency has satisfied preclearance requirements and is about to issue a Notice of Proposed Rulemaking. It will then select various means to gather feedback on the substance of a proposed rule. Remember that hybrid rulemaking encourages agencies to use expanded notice and opportunities for participation. It is common, particularly in complex and controversial areas for agencies, both state and federal, to go well beyond simple publication of notice in the federal or state register. Agencies that are seriously seeking input often encourage coverage in newspapers, trade journals, on the Internet, and in the broadcast media. They also tend to maintain notification lists or more often listservs containing the names of organizations and individuals who wish to be informed of all of the agency's official pronouncements. Indeed, some state APAs require agencies to maintain such lists, subject to periodic requirements that subscribers renew their statements of interest.

Similar efforts have been employed by agencies seeking to ensure adequate and effective opportunities for participation. Obviously, a decision by an agency to solicit only written comments is likely to produce a limited range of responses, and usually just from well-established interest groups that track notices in the *Federal Register* and have inside information on agency policymaking. Thus, it is common for federal and state agencies to hold hearings. Here, again, a hearing held in Washington or even in the state capital during normal business hours is most likely to ensure participation primarily by the usual suspects. Hence, many agencies have in cases of very significant rules taken to holding hearings outside the capital or even a number of hearings in the parts of the state or nation particularly affected by the proposed rule. Hearings held in the evenings or on weekends and in convenient locations offer the opportunity for wider participation. It is important to remember that a hearing in a hybrid rulemaking process is not an adjudication. It is like a legislative hearing, held to gather information, and does not imply due process rights on any would-be participant.

As this chapter has noted at various points, there are now means of providing notice and opportunity on the Internet. While the Internet certainly provides low-cost options for participation relative to more traditional approaches, successful use of the online approach to participation will require both education for public awareness and in terms of how to access and respond. There is also a concern about the degree to which there may develop a two-tier system in which the information-rich are better able than ever before to make their voices heard while the information-poor may become even further estranged from the policymaking process than they are today. It seems clear that, at least until the technology and knowledge of its use are better distributed with the polity, this equity issue will require attention.

Clearly, such expanded notification and participation efforts place burdens on agencies. On the other hand, they can help to reach out to relevant publics, both to obtain serious feedback and to defeat possible claims made later that the agency was behaving in an arbitrary and capricious manner in its rulemaking.

In that respect, the use of expanded participation mechanisms is seen by experienced administrators as a way to defuse potential opposition and to begin to encourage later compliance even while a new policy is in its early stages of development.

Unfortunately, there are still agencies that, to be charitable, do not really encourage full participation by the range of individuals, groups, and institutions who will be affected by important rules changes. For example, the Individuals with Disabilities Education Act (IDEA) required reauthorization when the George W. Bush administration came into office. In early October 2001, unbeknownst to most people in the special education community, the *Federal Register* carried the announcement that the president had issued Executive Order 13227, creating the President's Commission on Special Education. The members were to be appointed by the president and were given the task of making a major study of issues and problems in the IDEA with a report to be produced by April 30, 2002, a period of only six months.[160] The Commission was not provided with its own staff or its own website but was managed by and communications controlled through the U.S. Department of Education.

Given the events of September 11 and its aftermath, it was a complex time in the nation's history for any policymaking effort that truly sought to be participative, but there were indications that this process did little to encourage serious engagement. The commission held its first meeting on January 15, 2002, but notice of that meeting was not published until December 19, less than a week before Christmas, and those with disabilities who required accommodations to participate were required to notify the agency no later than January 8.[161] The commission was required to publish notice of the meeting under the Federal Advisory Committee Act, but given the timing and circumstances, the notice provided was hardly calculated to ensure openness and engagement of relevant representatives of the public. The commission held its remaining meetings in several cities over the next few months, but unless one knew what was in progress, was watching the *Federal Register,* and was able to respond very quickly, it was unlikely that he or she would be in a position to attend. The Commission issued its report, entitled *A New Era: Revitalizing Special Education for Children and their Families,* in July 2002, having received a brief extension.[162] The recommendations, if enacted, would indeed bring about a "new era," for the report contained a variety of controversial findings and recommendations. The problem was that its existence was not well known, even among clinicians and others who work with families who have children with special needs.

A significantly amended version of IDEA was adopted by Congress as the Individuals with Disabilities Education Improvement Act in December 2004.[163] Three days before the new year, the Department of Education did not publish an Advanced Notice of Proposed Rulemaking (ANPRM), but rather something the agency termed a "Notice of request for comments and recommendations on regulatory issues under the Individuals with Disabilities Education Act (IDEA), as amended by the Individuals with Disabilities Education Improvement Act of 2004."[164] Assuming that parents, school district officials, and clinicians who work regularly in this field were paying attention to the *Federal Register* between Christmas and New Year's Day and that they understood what this document was, they would also have seen that they only had until February 28 to provide their input. The document indicated that comments could be provided via Regulation.gov, but there was no Regulation Identifier Number (RIN) that is used to navigate Regulation.gov and RegInfo.gov, nor was there a Department of Education docket number, which is the other standard mode of indexing. The "notice" document indicated that there would be public meetings in six cities, but it did not say when they were scheduled and instead simply said: "We will notify you through notices published in the *Federal Register* of the specific dates and locations of each of these meetings."

The reasons why participation was so important in this case would be apparent to anyone involved in special education, to the families with children who have special needs, and to the clinicians who work with children, families, and school-based teams. The IDEA is a complex statute with multiple programs and a host of procedural elements. Indeed, while the statute requires a free and appropriate public education in the least restrictive environment for each qualified child, the manner in which it is determined just what is appropriate is a process involving a variety of key participants, including the family. The statute at the state level is implemented not only through the statute and rules issued by the U.S. Department of Education, but also in accordance with state regulations. For all these reasons, any effort to ensure real notice and effective and adequate participation would have required time and robust publication efforts.

The agency eventually published a notice of proposed rulemaking, but not until June 21, after almost all school districts had concluded operations for the year, and teachers and parents were engaged in other pursuits. The NPRM announced six meetings in six cities, but all were to be completed by July 7, with one final meeting set for Washington, D.C., on July 12. One of the meetings had already taken place by the time the NPRM was published, one was to take place in Sacramento two days after the publication, another two days after that in Las Vegas, another three days later in New York, another two days after that in Chicago, and the sixth three days after the Fourth of July holiday.[165] Then, just to add insult to injury, the NPRM stated: "To be considered, comments must be received at one of the addresses provided in the ADDRESSES section no later than 5 p.m. Washington, DC Time on September 6, 2005. Comments received after this time will not be considered."[166] The idea that an agency would publish its notice of proposed rulemaking after the end of the school year and then select an absolute closing date at the beginning of September when schools and parents were attempting to get the academic year started sends an unmistakable message that participation was neither seriously sought nor really desired. While there was a RIN number on the NPRM, there was no Department of Education docket number, which is the usual device used for accessing the online docket information about rulemaking in most agencies. Yes, the agency had provided more than 60 days for comments, but it is surely unlikely that anyone knowledgeable of the operations of IDEA and familiar with the operation of schools and their relationships with families would conclude that the agency was seriously attempting to engage those most directly affected by their pending rules. To add to that impression, the agency proceeded to publish on its website a series of guidance papers on its interpretations of the changes from the former operation of IDEA even before the final rules were announced.[167]

It is well to remember when managing a rulemaking process that the groups and individuals who are alienated because the process was not seen to be open, orderly, and participative may very well take their frustrations to court and tie the rules up in litigation for an extended period. But even more important is the fact that agencies depend upon those affected by significant rulemaking to ensure implementation and collaboration for the future.

A Decision Whether to Issue an Interim Final Rule

The twin difficulties of addressing the complexities of modern rulemaking and the simultaneous need to produce agency action—and, ultimately, compliance—have encouraged the use of a tool known as the interim final rule. The interim final rule is an announcement by an agency that it anticipates implementation of a particular rule by a specific point in time (sometimes immediately if it is an emergency), but that the rule may later be changed subject to input that the agency may receive as the notice and participation processes are completed. This device is nowhere to be found in the APA and indeed is found in very few statutes, but it has become increasingly common, particularly at the federal level.

The exact origins of the interim final rule are unclear, but it seems to have emerged in the Federal Aviation Administration (FAA) with efforts to address relatively technical rule changes in situations in which it was important that all affected participants have as much advanced notice of an impending change to ensure maximum compliance when the change was formally mandated. In some situations, the interim final rule was treated like what the APA refers to as emergency rulemaking, situations in which an agency states that there was good cause to short-circuit the normal notice and comment process. More often, the claim was that there was every intention to comply with the full notice and comment process, even in its expanded hybrid rulemaking form, but that an interim final rule was intended to help those involved to ready themselves for compliance with a new policy. It was to be understood, however, that adjustments might very well be made between the time that the interim final rule was issued and the promulgation of the final rule based upon testimony or other information received during that period.

For these reasons, it should not be surprising that the USDA and the FDA used the interim final option to issue rules rapidly in response to the mad cow situation. In that case, the first set of three major rules was generated in less than a month after the single Holstein had been identified in Washington State. In fact, in a rolling rulemaking process after that, the two lead agencies generated several sets of interim final rules, and final rules have not been issued at the time of this writing.

12/23/2003 USDA Announces diagnosis of one Holstein cow in Washington with BSE.

1/12/2004 USDA "Prohibition of the Use of Specified Risk Materials for Human Food and Requirements for the Disposition of Non-Ambulatory Disabled Cattle"[168]

1/12/2004 USDA "Meat Produced by Advanced Meat/Bone Separation Machinery and Meat Recovery (AMR) Systems"[169]

1/12/2004 USDA "Prohibition of the Use of Certain Stunning Devices Used to Immobilize Cattle During Slaughter"[170]

7/14/2004 FDA Use of Materials Derived from Cattle in Human Food and Cosmetics[171]

9/7/2005 FDA Use of Materials Derived from Cattle in Human Food and Cosmetics[172]

Clearly, efforts to use the interim final rule to evade APA requirements and the mandates imposed by executive orders could be challenged either in court or politically by the White House. In the more conservative version, however, the agencies claim to be following all of the requirements but merely providing as much information about the agency's intentions as possible.

There is a certain attractiveness to the interim final idea. For the agency, it signals a strong intention to act in a particular direction by a date certain while retaining some degree of flexibility that might allow for adjustments in policy during the interim period. To those affected by the rules, it sends a strong message that it would be wise to begin to bring their organizations into compliance even as they work with the agency to seek favorable modifications of the proposal. Even some legislators have been favorably disposed because this seems to be a way to cut through all of the politically loaded complexities of rulemaking and get action, even if it is only tentative. Hence, when President George H. W. Bush and the Congress responded to the national furor over hypodermic needles on East Coast beaches with the passage of the Medical Waste Tracking Act[173] the legislation authorized the Environmental Protection Agency (EPA) to promulgate interim final rules: "The Administrator may promulgate such regulations in interim final form without prior opportunity for public comment, but the Administrator shall provide an opportunity for public comment on the interim final rule." Indeed, the legislation and the EPA rulemaking process set nothing short of a blistering pace with the legislation passed in less than 90 days and the subsequent interim final rules issued 90 days after that.

The downsides of the interim final rule approach bear some similarities to the potential problems with negotiated rulemaking. The nature of the process intensifies the likelihood that insiders will be the only stakeholders with knowledge of what is happening and any kind of realistic opportunity to be involved before the agency has become relatively committed. True, the notice and participation processes continue, but the probability is not strong that an agency that has publicly announced its policy in the form of an interim final rule will significantly change course later as a result of public input. To many critics, including those in the executive branch, the expanded use of the interim final device seemed more like an effort to evade the burdens of rulemaking processes and White House control rather than an effort to enhance efficiency and effectiveness.

On the other hand, with so many burdens placed upon rulemaking processes by both the chief executive and the legislature, it is hardly surprising to find that agencies are using devices like interpretative rules, policy statements, or interim final rules. After all, the same elected officials in both branches who have placed the burdens on the agencies have continued to issue policies that required either directly or by implication that more rules be issued. And even though the Congress adopted the Unfunded Mandates law, it did not make it retroactive, leaving in place all of the existing rulemaking obligations that agencies must satisfy.

The Final Rule

Assuming that an agency has moved its rulemaking process through the various stages described above, it can now publish notice of its final rule. The APA only requires that the rule be published 30 days before it is to become effective. Agencies are aware that it often takes a considerably longer period for those affected to bring themselves into compliance. At the same time, it is common for Congress to mandate rulemaking and to require it to be completed within 180 days. Given the process that has been described to this point, and the level of complexity of many subjects about which agencies are called upon to issue rules, it is not surprising that administrators feel constrained to cut the time lines as close as possible. This problem of notice at the point of publication of the final rule is another factor that tends to make interim final rules attractive.

The Legislative Veto

Despite all of these pressures, however, Congress (and state legislators at that level) has repeatedly sought to be involved even at this late stage of the rulemaking process through something that has come to be called the legislative veto. It is an opportunity for the legislature to block a rule once an agency has decided upon a course of action. The legislative veto has emerged in several forms over time. The past two decades have witnessed the rise, fall, and recently a reemergence of the legislative veto.

The legislative veto device has been extremely controversial since its use increased dramatically during the 1970s.[174] The reasons for the controversy will be discussed in the consideration of regulation in Chapter 10. For the present, it is important to note what the legislative veto is and how it works. Despite the fact that the veto has been ruled unconstitutional in federal law, it is nevertheless still a significant factor in rulemaking. In fact, in 1996, Congress found a way to adopt a form of legislative review that would give it a kind of veto option but one that would survive the kinds of legal challenges that had brought down earlier procedures.

The legislative veto requires that agencies submit proposed rules to the legislature before they are issued. In its classic form, the veto allowed the legislature to vote to prevent the publication of the rule. The agency enabling act, or in some instances program authorization legislation, indicated whether a legislative veto process was required. Attempts to require a government-wide (or generic) veto as an amendment to the APA were not successful during the 1970s and 1980s despite numerous efforts to adopt one.

There have historically been three basic types of vetoes in use. The first was a veto by concurrent resolution, in which a resolution must pass both houses of the legislature to veto the rule. In a concurrent resolution the president is not permitted a veto. The second type of legislative veto was the one-house veto in which either house of the legislature could reject a rule by simple resolution. Finally, there was what was known as the committee veto, which by various means permitted a legislative committee to kill a proposed rule.

Early debates over the legislative veto ranged widely from the efficacy of the veto as a legislative oversight technique, to the political impact of the device, to the constitutionality of the tool, to the burdens on administrators of compliance with the manifold coordination and review requirements imposed by the veto.[175] However, those discussions appeared to be short-circuited by several judicial opinions holding the legislative veto unconstitutional.

The first major ruling came in a case that was not about rulemaking at all, *Immigration and Naturalization Service v. Chadha*.[176] *Chadha* was a challenge to a statutory device by which members of one house of Congress could veto names of aliens who had been granted exemptions from deportation, and thereby permitted to apply for permanent resident status. This process was more a veto of an adjudicative-type decision than a rulemaking proceeding. Nevertheless, the U.S. Circuit Court of Appeals for the Ninth Circuit used the case as an occasion to consider the constitutionality of the legislative veto. The appeals court found the device in violation of the separation of powers and the U.S.

Supreme Court agreed. Unfortunately, most commentators, regardless of their perspective on the veto, found the Supreme Court's opinion poorly done, providing little explanation or guidance.

The D.C. Circuit issued a much stronger opinion in *Consumer Energy Council v. Federal Energy Regulatory Commission,* which did concern a veto of rulemaking.[177] The court found violations of separation of powers in that the Congress interfered with executive authority and usurped the judicial role in statutory interpretation. It also found that the one-house veto violated the principle of bicameralism and breached the presentment clause of Article I under which the Congress is required to submit legislation to the chief executive for a possible veto. The court confirmed that assessment some months later in a case involving a congressional veto of a Federal Trade Commission rule that would have required used car dealers to reveal to prospective buyers those defects which they knew existed in vehicles they presented for sale.[178] The Supreme Court affirmed both D.C. Circuit decisions without opinion.[179]

These rulings did not, however, put an end to the significance of the legislative veto. In the first place, many states have adopted legislative veto provisions in particular substantive legislation or as a part of the state APA. The federal court rulings do not affect the status of state laws under state constitutions. In Washington, Congress continued to enact statutes with legislative veto provisions. In fact, Louis Fisher, examining the situation one year after the 1983 *Chadha* decision, found that 30 additional legislative vetoes had been adopted.[180] Administrators operating in ambiguous situations must consider the advisability of conforming to such requirements rather than fighting them unless the chief executive is prepared to risk severe legislative relations difficulty with an all-out interbranch battle. There had been reticence to take a strident position, in part because Congress has threatened to counter with a range of limitations in enabling legislation that would make life difficult for many administrators. The G. W. Bush White House has taken an adamant position, but it has also had a Congress controlled by its own political party.

The legislative attack on rulemaking continued throughout the 1980s and into the 1990s even as presidents pursued simultaneous efforts to curtail rulemaking within their own branch. In 1996, Congress included amendments to the APA in the debt limit extension legislation that created a variation on the legislative veto theme commonly known as a report and wait provision. These amendments added Section 800 et seq. to the APA entitled Congressional Review of Agency Rulemaking.

The review process works as follows. Agencies are required before a rule takes effect to submit a report to each of the two houses of Congress and to the Comptroller General of the United States (the head of the Government Accountability Office). In addition to the rule and related descriptive materials, the report must include:

(i) a complete copy of the cost-benefit analysis of the rule, if any;

(ii) the agency's actions relevant to sections 603, 604, 605, 607, and 609 [Regulatory Flexibility Act]

(iii) the agency's action relevant to sections 202, 203, 204, and 205 of the Unfunded Mandates Reform Act of 1995; and

(iv) any other relevant information or requirements under any other Act and any relevant Executive orders.[181]

The GAO then has 15 calendar days to provide an assessment of the materials provided by the agency as well as its compliance with rulemaking procedural requirements. At the time of this writing, the GAO General Counsel has been posting the GAO reports on rules on its website. Once the GAO report signals that what is at issue is a major rule, the statute delays implementation of the rule for an additional 60 days to give Congress time to take action to block the rule.

Congress may then move to block the regulation by voting out a joint resolution. The reason for the choice of a joint resolution is that it avoids several of the constitutional problems that led to the demise of earlier legislative veto provisions. It is an action of both houses of Congress and it does go to the President unlike the committee, one-house, or concurrent resolution approaches previously struck by the courts.

There has been one very public use of the Legislative Review Act to strike a rule. That came in the case of the so-called ergonomics rules issued by the Occupational Safety and Health Administration, which were designed to prevent injuries, medical costs, and employee absenteeism that stemmed from repetitive stress injuries.[182] The George W. Bush administration came to office, as did a number of new members of Congress, with a announced intention to attack what they regarded as unnecessary or unduly costly regulations. The Congress promptly adopted Senate Joint Resolution 6, which became Public Law 107-5 when it was signed by President Bush on March 26, 2001.

IN DEFENSE OF RULES

Clearly, many of the procedural burdens, including the manifold analyses and clearance processes imposed in recent decades, were intended to discourage rulemaking. Indeed, they have succeeded. It should come as no surprise that many administrators have tried a variety of tactics to avoid these burdens. It is also not surprising that politicians have seen attacks on rules and regulation in general as a winning tactic. And while no one will defend excessive and poorly developed rules, it is entirely appropriate to recall just why we have come to the use of rules and carefully structured techniques of rulemaking.

Functional and Historical Arguments

There were several reasons why administrative agencies were encouraged during the 1950s and 1960s to do more rulemaking. None of those arguments began from the idea that anyone likes a proliferation of regulations. Instead, the reasons included a combination of management interests and concern about maintenance of the legitimacy of public administration.

On one level, the promulgation of rules enhances efficiency. Rules provide standard policy statements which can be broadly and uniformly applied. The rulemaking process develops records and aids in long-term policy development as opposed to ad hoc methods, which leave an agency without memory of what worked and what did not.

From a very different perspective, the use of rulemaking reduces the likelihood of arbitrariness and supports a general sense of fairness in administration. One of the complaints against policymaking by adjudication that was prevalent before serious implementation of the APA was precisely that it amounted to making up the rules in the middle of the game. When rules exist, those inside and outside of the agency may bring their behavior into compliance. Without such rules, it is very difficult to provide due process to anyone eventually called to answer before an agency.

Rules also provide protections for the society quite apart from the individuals who must deal with an agency on a day-to-day basis. Rules bind administrators, facilitate oversight, and provide predictability about agency behavior. Without these characteristics, it may be impossible to ensure any kind of effective accountability. Thus, it is self-defeating for politicians and even for professional administrators to mount broad attacks on rules. It can very easily be the case that proudly proclaiming that one has eliminated hundreds of meddlesome rules and therefore cut the power of bureaucracies to interfere in our lives is a completely false picture. Often, simply eliminating rules, or discouraging their issuance in the first place, means that agencies are left unchecked, unguided, and relatively unaccountable. The same problem exists with such declarations when made by public employees, since rules bind their employer as well as the employees themselves.

In sum, properly used, rules and effective processes for rulemaking can provide better government, advance administrative efficiency, and help ensure fundamental fairness in the process.

Contracting as Rulemaking

There is another very real irony in the arguments about deregulation, which begins from the premise that eliminating rules is a good in its own right. In the past two decades, there has been an often repeated call to eliminate direct government action based upon rules in favor of a wider use of contracting out for services. One of the fundamental fallacies at the heart of that contention is the failure to recognize that contracting is a process for rulemaking. It is simply a different kind of rulemaking, one in which the rules are set between the parties to an agreement for purposes of governing their relationship as compared to the more traditional notion of creating general rules for a wider array of individuals, firms, or groups. Hence, the use of literally thousands of contracts at all levels of government means thousands of uncoordinated rulemaking processes that do not involve participation opportunities for the public, with significant amounts of information about parties withheld from public view to protect the proprietary interests of contractors who are in fact rulemakers in this world of deal-by-deal rule generation.

While it is true that governments, at all levels, sometimes try to ensure common provisions in contracts, the very nature of contracting is about setting specific terms for particular relationships that often differ from contract to contract in both technical and broader senses. This phenomenon is readily apparent to anyone who studies the many state contracts with not-for-profit organizations for social service delivery. An even more common example exists at the local government level where public managers may work in a context in which there are five or more collective bargaining agreements covering employees. Although there are commonly efforts at pattern bargaining to obtain as much consistency as possible across contracts, it is typically the case that there are significant differences in work rules, disciplinary procedures, training requirements, and supervisory relationships from one agreement to the next.

Efforts to ensure accountability, and more often to prevent fraud, mean that there is tremendous pressure to so constrain the nature and process of contracting, particularly at the federal government level, that many elements of government contracting have lost their flexible nature and seem more like alternative systems of regulation. Thus, to be a truly useful and effective management and service delivery tool, contracts must be permitted to have the characteristics that make them what they are. At the same time, that flexibility undermines their usefulness as a substitute for systems of rules.

The point is not that contracting for services is bad, but merely that it is no substitute for the sound use of rulemaking to produce needed systems of rules. Indeed, simplistic ideas about substituting contracting for government action based on rules are not realistic and may be self-defeating.

The Perverse Encouragement of More Litigation

Another ironic feature of the anti-rule movement in the years since the 1980s is that this dynamic encourages the reemergence of old form of regulation based upon lawsuits rather than open, orderly, and participative public rulemaking. Before regulation developed as a modern tool of governance individuals took action to constrain behavior by others that they considered harmful largely through private lawsuits such as suits in nuisance law or various kinds of property cases. As Chapter 4 explained, it was in part in reaction to this state of affairs that modern administrative law practices were developed.

It should not be surprising to find that, in an era when these systems of regulation have been under attack, there have been indications of the reemergence of this case-by-case private lawsuit approach to addressing important problems. Thus, we have seen numerous major lawsuits regarding the tobacco industry, firearms manufacturers, managed care organizations, airlines, pharmaceutical manufacturers, medical device suppliers, and automobile manufacturers, to name but a few. These are often not primarily compensatory suits, but often policy-oriented cases with individual or group plaintiffs stepping in to change behavior by lawsuit when the government seems unable or unwilling to take on a problem through standard rulemaking techniques. These cases are frequently private suits, brought by large numbers of individual plaintiffs, but increasingly state attorneys general are learning to use similar techniques to regulate corporate conduct, as in the case of the huge tobacco litigation that produced a nationwide settlement.

Historically, it was the chaos of numerous suits brought by individuals to conduct what would by any object assessment be considered regulation that helped to create administrative law as we know it today (see Chapter 4). The reasons why are well known to anyone who has studied the history of the late nineteenth and early twentieth century. First, if anyone thinks that regulation by rulemaking is a lengthy and costly process, they have not begun to consider how much more costly and burdensome it is to reach the same goals by numerous large lawsuits. Second, those who want to bring the suits and those who must defend against them have much less predictability in this common law oriented regulation than they do in a situation of rules. The judge, after all, is normally ruling on something that has happened in the past, not generally focused on making rules for the future, though injunctive relief is in a sense a kind of rulemaking. Of course, federal courts at least have been strongly encouraged by the U.S. Supreme Court not to use injunctive relief but to be more forthcoming with damages for those injured in a particular course of conduct.

In the world of regulation by litigation, the parties do not have good reason to know what is acceptable and unacceptable until the case and the appeals that stem from it are completed. That is one of the most important reasons why it was considered necessary to move away from regulation by common law process in the first place. Related to this problem of unpredictability is the fact that regulation by litigation creates a maddeningly complex lack of uniformity that is neither in the interest of regulated firms nor of those who are supposed to be protected.

From very different perspectives, such numerous, complex, and widespread cases burden the courts and ask judges to do what administrative agencies were designed to accomplish. The irony is that this last concern is often expressed by attorneys for the same industries that are attacking the rules and the agencies that were created to develop and administer them.

These are some of the reasons why the attack on rules and rulemaking is so counterproductive. There is one more: many statutes require both that rules be issued and that they be made according to a lawful process.

SUMMARY

Rulemaking is one of the primary devices through which administrative agencies make authoritative policy statements. There is some regularity to the rulemaking process, although the starting point for an understanding of any particular agency's work is the agency-enabling act. The Administrative Procedure Act sets forth the standard procedures, based on understandings of the nature of a rule, the type of rule involved in specific situation, and the manner in which that type of rule must be promulgated. The determination of the rule type, whether substantive, procedural, or interpretative, determines the formality involved in rulemaking and the degree of legal force involved in any rulemaking procedure. Those procedures may be formal, informal (simplified), or hybrid processes. The hybrid procedure is a compromise form developed from a variety of sources, most notably the courts.

While it is true that for much of the past two decades there has been a concerted attack waged against rules and rulemaking, they remain critical features of modern public administration.

The standardization of rulemaking as a process was one of the cornerstones of formal judicial process developed in earlier years and codified in the Administrative Procedure Act. Judicial review is a second fundamental concept. The regularization of adjudications to provide for fundamental fairness in decisionmaking by agencies is the third basic element, and it is to this subject that we turn in Chapter 6.

NOTES

1. *Nutraceutical Corp. v. Crawford,* 364 F. Supp. 2d 1310 (D.Utah 2005).
2. See e.g., U.S. Department of Agriculture, Food Safety and Inspect Service, "Prohibition of the Use of Specified Risk Materials for Human Food and Requirements for the Disposition of Non-Ambulatory

Disabled Cattle AGENCY," Interim Final Rule, 69 Fed. Reg. 1862 (2004); U.S. Department of Health and Human Services, Food and Drug Administration, "Use of Materials Derived from Cattle in Human Food and Cosmetics," Interim Final Rule, 69 Fed. Reg. 42256 (2004).

3. U.S. Environmental Protection Agency, "EPA to Propose Withdrawal of Arsenic in Drinking Water Standard," March 20, 2001 at http://yosemite.epa.gov/opa/admpress.nsf/0/ 77e59dbb919fdf4785256a150063d6a0?OpenDocument, as of October 22, 2005.

4. For material on specific areas of state administrative law, see Appendix 5.

5. See Carl Stenberg, "Engines of Change: Leading from the States" and Beverly Cigler, "Adjusting to Changing Expectations at the Local Level," in James L. Perry, ed., *Handbook of Public Administration,* 2nd ed. (San Francisco: Jossey-Bass, 1996).

6. See Unfunded Mandates Reform Act, P.L. 104-4, 109 Stat. 48 (1995).

7. North American Free Trade Implementation Act, Pub. L. 103-182, 107 Stat. 2057; Executive Order 12915, 59 Fed. Reg. 25775 (1994).

8. See e.g., Consolidated Appropriations Act, 2005, P.L. 108-447, 118 Stat. 2809 (2004).

9. P.L. 109-13; 119 Stat. 231 (2005).

10. P.L. 104-121; 110 Stat. 847 (1996), Also known as the Contract with America Advancement Act of 1996.

11. Examples include the Federal Acquisition Streamlining Act of 1994, P.L. 103-355, 108 Stat. 3243 (1994), and E.O. 12931, 59 Fed. Reg. 52387 (1994).

12. Inspector General Act, P.L. 95-452, 92 Stat. 1101 (1978).

13. See generally, "IGNet, Federal Inspectors General," http://www.ignet.gov/, as of October 11, 2005.

14. *Bolling v. Sharpe,* 347 U.S. 497 (1954).

15. P.L. 90-202, 81 Stat. 607 (1967).

16. 42 U.S.C.§2000e(k).

17. P.L. 108-446; 118 Stat. 2647 (2004).

18. P.L. 101-336; 104 Stat. 327 (1990).

19. 5 U.S.C. §7101 et seq.

20. See *Maine v. Thiboutot,* 448 U.S. 1 (1980); *Owen v. City of Independence,* 445 U.S. 622 (1980).

21. "The basic scheme underlying the legislation is to classify all proceedings into two categories, namely, 'rulemaking' and 'adjudication.'" U.S. Attorney General Tom C. Clark to Director Harold D. Smith, Bureau of the Budget, June 3, 1946, Truman Papers, Truman Library.

22. But see the discussion of this dichotomy in Chapter 1.

23. 5 U.S.C. §551 et seq. Because there have been a number of amendments to the act over the four decades since its passage, and because some of the APA provisions, such as those governing hearing examiners, have several overlapping areas of importance, the sections of the APA are not all numbered in sequence.

24. 5 U.S.C. §551 (a)(A)-(E).

25. The debate came to the boiling point during the Nixon administration when the Executive Office of the President was expanded into a counterbureaucracy. Congress may have granted some deference to internal executive branch operations, but the claims by the White House against requests for information by Watergate investigators and the liberal use of security classification stamps prompted Congress to add the clarification during their strengthening amendments to the Freedom of Information Act (see note 23 *supra*).

26. P.L. 89-554, 80 Stat. 383 (1966); P.L. 90-23, 81 Stat. 54 (1967); P.L. 93-502, 88 Stat. 1561-1564 (1974); P.L. 94-409, 90 Stat. 1247 (1976).

27. P.L. 93-579, 88 Stat. 1896 (1974).

28. P.L. 94-409, 90 Stat. 1241 (1976).

29. P.L. 92-463, 86 Stat. 770 (1972); P.L. 94-409, 90 Stat. 1241 (1976).

30. The Supreme Court has held that for a statute to be interpreted to require the formal process it must contain precisely the correct language. It must require that rules be made "on the record after an agency hearing." Merely stating that rules be made "after a hearing" is not sufficient to trigger the form §§556-557 process. *United States v. Florida East Coast Ry. Co.,* 410 U.S. 224, 234-38 (1973).

31. P.L. 104-121, 110 Stat. 847. (1996).

32. *Id.*, Sec. 251, Congressional Review of Agency Rulemaking, which adds §§800 et seq. outlining the process for legislative review.

33. 5 U.S.C. §561 et seq.

34. 5 U.S.C. §571 et seq.

35. This type of statutory provision is referred to as a "sunset" clause, so named because it will set on the policy unless specific action is taken to reenact it within a specified period. For an explanation of origins and operation of sunset reviews, see "Zero Base Sunset Review," 14 *Harvard Journal on Legislation* 505 (1977).

36. This format approximates existing requirements. See Donald W. Sever, Jr., *Seabrook and the Nuclear Regulatory Commission: The Licensing of a Nuclear Power Plant* (Hanover, NH: University Press of New England, 1980).

37. See generally, *Power Reactor Dev. Co. v. International Union of Electrical Radio and Machine Workers,* 367 U.S. 396 (1961).

38. *Id.*, Justice Douglas dissenting. This problem is discussed in detail in Chapter 10.

39. See *supra* note 30 and *Northern Public Service Co. v. Porter County Chapter of the Izaak Walton League of America,* 423 U.S. 12 (1975), particularly Justice Douglas, concurring.

40. 5 U.S.C. §551(5).

41. *Id.*, at §551(6).

42. *Id.*, at §551(7).

43. 61 Fed. Reg. 44397 (1996).

44. *Food and Drug Administration v. Brown & Williamson Tobacco Corp.,* 529 U.S. 120, 134-135 (2000).

45. *Id.*, at 171-174.

46. See A Lee Fritschler and James M. Hoefler, *Smoking and Politics: Politics and the Federal Bureaucracy,* 5th Ed. (Upper Saddle River, NJ: Prentice Hall, 1995).

47. *Food and Drug Administration v. Brown & Williamson Tobacco Corp, supra* note 44, at 126.

48. On the delegation of power doctrine and its limits, see Bernard Schwartz, *Administrative Law* (Boston: Little, Brown, 1976), pp. 151–52. See also Walter Gellhorn, Clark Byse, and Peter Strauss, *Administrative Law: Cases and Comments,* 7th ed. (Mineola, NY: Foundation Press, 1979), pp. 52–77.

49. 5 U.S.C. §706(2)(C).

50. *Id.*, at §706(2)(A).

51. *Id.*, at §706(2)(D).

52. Schwartz, *supra* note 48, at pp. 152–53.

53. *Chrysler Corp. v. Brown,* 441 U.S. 281, 301-302 (1979); *United States v. Nixon,* 418 U.S. 683, 695-96 (1974). See Kenneth Culp Davis, *Administrative Law Treatise,* 2nd ed. Vol. 2 (San Diego, CA: Kenneth Culp Davis, 1979), §7:21.

54. Help America Vote Act of 2002, P.L. 107- 252, 116 Stat. 1666 (2002).

55. *International Brotherhood of Teamsters v. Daniel,* 439 U.S. 551, 566-67 (1979); *Securities and Exchange Commission v. Sloan,* 436 U.S. 103, 117-19 (1978); *United States v. Nixon,* 418 U.S. 683, 704-706 (1974); *Halperin v. Kissinger,* 606 F.2d 1192, 1211 (D.C.Cir. 1979); *National Treasury Employees Union v. Nixon,* 492 F.2d 587, 604, 612-16 (D.C.Cir. 1974); *National Automatic Laundry and Cleaning Council v. Schultz,* 443 F.2d 687, 695 (D.C.Cir. 1971).

56. 5 U.S.C. §551(4).

57. Schwartz, *supra* note 48, at p. 153.

58. *Chao v. Rothermel,* 327 F.3d 223, 227 (3rd Cir. 2003).

59. 5 U.S.C. §553(b)(A) exempts procedural and interpretive rules from standard rulemaking proceedings, but §552(a)(1)(C) requires that such procedural rules as an agency does promulgate must be published.

60. *Ballard v. Commissioner of Internal Revenue,* 161 L. Ed. 2d 227, 243 (2005); *United States v. Caceres,* 440 U.S. 741, 752 n. 14 (1979); *Morton v. Ruiz,* 415 U.S. 199, 235 (1974); *Vitarelli v. Seaton,* 359 U.S. 539 (1959); and

Service v. Dulles, 354 U.S. 363, 388 (1957). While the Court in *American Farm Lines v. Black Ball Freight Service,* 397 U.S. 532, 538-539 (1970), recognized that "it is always within the discretion of a court or an administrative agency to relax or modify its procedural rules adopted for the orderly transaction of business before it when in a given case the ends of justice require it," that ruling did not swallow the long-standing obligations of agencies to honor their procedures, particularly where those procedures confer an important procedural benefit on the party before the agency.

61. 5 U.S.C. §§553(b)(A), 553(d)(2).

62. *Id.,* at §552(a)(1)(D).

63. It is helpful, but it is no substitute for further development of the law. See *Chrysler Corp. v. Brown, supra* note 53, at pp. 301–302.

64. B.J. Roche, "When the Buck Stops in India," *Boston Globe,* March 28, 2004, p. B4; Associated Press State & Local Wire, "State Responds to Discovery of Outsourcing Contract," March 23, 2004.

65. See Robert A. Anthony, "Interpretative Rules, Policy Statements, Guidances, Manuals, and the Like — Should Federal Agencies Use Them to Bind the Public?" 41 *Duke L.J.* 1311 (1992). For some sense of the long-standing nature of this debate, compare Davis, *supra* note 53, vol. 2 §§7:13 and 7:21, with Schwartz, *supra* note 48, at pp. 160–61.

66. See generally Henry J. Friendly, *The Federal Administrative Agencies: The Need for Better Definition of Standards* (Cambridge: Harvard University Press, 1962), and Kenneth Culp Davis, *Discretionary Justice: A Preliminary Inquiry* (Baton Rouge: Louisiana State University Press, 1969). See also the discussion of the findings of the Task Force on Legal Services and Procedure of the second Hoover Commission in Chapter 4.

67. *Chamber of Commerce v. Occupational Safety and Health Agency,* 636 F.2d 464, 488 (D.C.Cir. 1980).

68. See generally *General Motors v. Ruckelshaus,* 724 F.2d 979, 985 (D.C.Cir. 1983); *Citizens to Save Spencer County v. United States Environmental Protection Agency,* 600 F.2d 844, 879 n. 171 (D.C.Cir. 1979); *Citizens Communication v. FCC,* 447 F.2d 1201, 1204 n.5 (D.C.Cir. 1971.) *Id.,* at p. 468.

69. *Appalachian Power Co. v. Environmental Protection Agency,* 208 F.3d 1015, 1021 (D.C.Cir. 2000).

70. *American Mining Congress v. Mine Safety & Health Administration,* 995 F.2d 1106, 1112 (D.C.Cir. 1993).

71. *Paralyzed Veterans of America v. D.C. Arena, L.P.,* 117 F.3d 579, 586 (D.C.Cir. 1997). See also *SBC v. Federal Communications Commission,* 414 F.3d 486, 497-498 (3rd Cir. 2005).

72. Centers for Disease Control, "Creutzfeldt-Jakob Disease – Nationwide Education and Communication," 70 Fed. Reg. 34183 (2005).

73. 69 Fed. Reg. 42288 (2004).

74. 5 U.S.C. §553(a)(1).

75. *Id.,* at §553(a)(2).

76. These laws are discussed in Phillip J. Cooper, "Government Contracts in Public Administration: The Role and Environment of the Contracting Officer," 40 *Public Administration Rev.* 459 (1980).

77. Congress adopted amendments to the Office of Federal Procurement Policy Act in, P.L. 98-577, in 1984 that contains provisions describing the process for making contracting regulations (see 98 Stat. 3067), which roughly mirror the notice and comment procedures outlined in section 553 of the APA. However, this does not solve the problems described above.

78. "Currently, DOT and NRC jointly regulate the transportation of radioactive material in the United States in accordance with a July 2, 1979, Memorandum of Understanding (MOU; 44 FR 38690)." 69 Fed. Reg. 3632 (2004).

79. 5 U.S.C. §553(b)(B).

80. 62 Fed. Reg. 5907, 5910 (1997).

81. 69 Fed. Reg. 3634 (2004).

82. "About Battelle," at http://www.battelle.org/more/default.stm, as of November 4, 2005.

83. *Id.*

84. *Id.*

85. Board of Pharmacy, "Statement of Need and Justification in the Matter of: The amendment of OAR 855-050-0035," at http://www.leds.state.or.us/Pharmacy/pdf/1004_need-justification_div050_amend.pdf, as of November 4, 2005.

86. O.R.S. 183.335(6)(a).

87. Rules 855-050-0037, 855-050-0038, 855-050-0039, 855-050-0041, 855-050-0042, 855-050-0043 were published in the *Oregon Bulletin*, May 1, 2005, at http://arcweb.sos.state.or.us/rules/0505_Bulletin/0505_ch855_bulletin.html, as of April 24, 2006.

88. *Jifry v. Federal Aviation Administration,* 370 F.3d 1174, 1179 (D.C.Cir. 2004); *Natural Resources Defense Council v. Evans,* 316 F.3d 904, 911 (9th Cir. 2003); *Utility Solid Waste Activities Group v. EPA,* 236 F.3d 749, 754-755 (D.C.Cir. 2001); *Tennessee Gas Pipeline Co. v. FERC,* 969 F.2d 1141, 1144 (D.C.Cir. 1992); *American Federal of Government Employees v. Block,* 655 F.2d 1153, 1156 (D.C.Cir. 1981).

89. 69 Fed. Reg. 1862, 1874, and 1885 (2004).

90. *American Bus Association v. United States,* 627 F.2d 525, 529 (D.C.Cir. 1980), quoting *Pacific Gas & Electric Co. v. FPC,* 506 F.2d 33, 38 (D.C.Cir. 1974).

91. *Id.*

92. *American Hospital Association v. Bowen,* 834 F.2d 1037, 1046 (D.C.Cir. 1987).

93. *Community Nutrition Institute v. Young,* 818 F.2d 943, 946 (D.C.Cir. 1987).

94. *American Hospital Association v. Bowen, supra* note 92, at pp. 1044. See also *Alcaraz v. Block,* 746 F.2d 593, 612 (D.C.Cir. 1984).

95. *National Association of Home Health Agencies v. Schweiker,* 690 F.2d 932, 949 (D.C.Cir. 1982). See also *American Hospital Association v. Bowen, supra* note 92, at 1044.

96. *Croplife American v. Environmental Protection Agency,* 329 F.3d 876, 883 (D.C.Cir. 2003), citing *General Electric v. EPA,* 290 F.3d 377, 383-85 (D.C.Cir. 2002); *Sugar Cane Growers Coop. of Fla. v. Veneman,* 289 F.3d 89, 95-96 (D.C.Cir. 2002).

97. *McLouth Steel Products Corporation v. Thomas,* 838 F.2d 1317, 1320 (D.C.Cir. 1988).

98. *American Hospital Association v. Bowen, supra* note 92, at p. 1045.

99. But see *Lincoln v. Vigil,* 508 U.S. 182 (1993) in which the Court concluded: "Whatever else may be considered a 'general statemen[t] of policy,' the term surely includes an announcement like the one before us, that an agency will discontinue a discretionary allocation of unrestricted funds from a lump-sum appropriation." *Id.,* at 197. This usage plainly does not fit the nonbinding nature and future possible effect criteria generally accepted in the other case law. The Court in *Vigil* did not even address this problem.

100. Environmental Protection Agency, press release, "Agency Requests National Academy of Sciences Input on Consideration of Certain Human Toxicity Studies; Announces Interim Policy," December 14, 2001, cited in *Croplife American v. Environmental Protection Agency, supra* note 96, at 878.

101. *Croplife American v. EPA, supra* note 96, at 881.

102. *Id.,* at §553(b)(1), (2), (3).

103. *Id.,* at §553(c).

104. The APA does not establish any minimum required time between publication of the notice of proposed rulemaking and the date of the publication of the final rule. In a number of instances serious questions have been raised regarding the adequacy of the notice.

105. P.L. 107-347; 116 Stat. 2899 (2002), Section 206(c).

106. At http://www.regulations.gov/fdmspublic-bld61/component/main, as of November 8, 2005.

107. At http://www.reginfo.gov/public/, as of November 8, 2005.

108. 70 Fed. Reg. 58570 (2005).

109. At http://www.fda.gov/ohrms/dockets/default.htm, as of November 8, 2005.

110. See the E-Government Act, *supra* note 100, Section 202(c).

111. 5 U.S.C. §553(c).

112. *Id.* See note 30 *supra.*

113. Mark J. Green, *The Other Government,* rev. ed. (New York: Norton, 1978), pp. 137–45.

114. See e.g., Jerome Frank, *If Men Were Angels: Some Aspects of Government in a Democracy* (New York: Harper & Brothers, 1942), p. 181, and Walter Gellhorn, *Federal Administrative Proceedings* (Westport, CT: Greenwood Press, 1941), Ch. 2.

115. See *United States v. Rutherford,* 442 U.S. 544 (1979).

116. See e.g., *American Textile Manufacturers Institute v. Donovan,* 452 U.S. 490 (1981). The need for substantial evidence to support a rule is rather confusing. The letter of the APA, 5 U.S.C. §706(2)(E), requires only substantial evidence justification in formal rulemaking but for several reasons, discussed in detail in Chapter 7, the substantial evidence concept in rulemaking is more broadly applied than a narrow reading of the APA would suggest.

117. U.S. House of Representatives, Task Force on Legal Services and Procedure, *Report on Legal Services and Procedure Prepared for the Commission on Organization of the Executive Branch,* House Doc. no. 128, 84th Cong, 1st Sess. (1955), p. 24.

118. See e.g., J. Skelly Wright, "Beyond Discretionary Justice," 81 *Yale L. J.* 575 (1972), and Louis Jaffe, "Book Review," 14 *Villanova Law Rev.* 773 (1969).

119. Some of the most widely discussed of these cases were *Mobil Oil v. Federal Power Commission,* 483 F.2d 1238 (D.C.Cir. 1973); *International Harvester Co. v. Ruckelshaus,* 478 F. 2d 615 (D.C.Cir. 1973); *Appalachian Power Co. v. Environmental Protection Agency,* 477 F.2d 495 (4th Cir. 1973); *Walter Holm & Co. v. Hardin,* 449 F.2d 1009 (D.C.Cir 1971); *American Airlines v. Civil Aeronautics Board,* 359 F.2d 624 (D.C.Cir. 1966).

120. 5 U.S.C. §706(2)(A).

121. *Citizens to Preserve Overton Park v. Volpe,* 410 U.S. 402 (1971).

122. See e.g., Stephen Williams, "Hybrid Rulemaking Under the Administrative Procedure Act: A Legal and Empirical Analysis," 42 *University of Chicago L. Rev.* 401 (1975).

123. *Natural Resources Defense Council v. Nuclear Regulatory Commission,* 547 F.2d 633 (D.C.Cir. 1976), rev'd sub nom. *Vermont Yankee Nuclear Power Corp. v. NRDC,* 435 U.S. 519 (1978).

124. This particular quotation comes from an interview of Judge Bazelon by the author. The NRDC opinion contains his views on this subject, *supra* note 123, 547 F.2d, at pp. 644–646.

125. Harold H. Bruff and Ernest Gellhorn, "Congressional Control of Administrative Regulation: A Study of Legislative Vetoes," 90 *Harvard L. Rev,* 1369, 1376–77 (1977).

126. This summary is taken from the cases cited at note 119 *supra*; Richard B. Stewart, "Vermont Yankee and the Evolution of Administrative Procedure," 91 *Harvard L. Rev.* 10 (1978); Bruff and Gellhorn, *supra* note 125; and William Pederson, "Formal Records and Informal Rulemaking," 85 *Yale L. J.* 38 (1975).

127. See generally Stewart, *supra* note 126; Charles Byse, "Vermont Yankee and the Evolution of Administrative Procedure: A Somewhat Different View," 91 *Harvard L. Rev.* 1823 (1978); Stephen Breyer, "Vermont Yankee and the Courts' Rule in the Nuclear Energy Controversy," 91 *Harvard L. Rev.* 1833 (1978); and Antonin Scalia, "Vermont Yankee: The APA, the D.C.Circuit and the Supreme Court," 1978 *Supreme Court Rev.* 345.

128. See e.g., Occupational Safety and Health Act of 1970, 29 U.S.C. §651 et seq. and the Consumer Product Safety Act of 1972, 15 U.S.C. §2051 et seq. See also Consumer Product Safety Commission Improvement Act of 1974, 15 U.S.C. § 1193 et seq.

129. Toxic Substances Control Act of 1976, 15 U.S.C. §2601.

130. 15 U.S.C. §§2603, 2605.

131. See generally, Cornelius M. Kerwin, *Rulemaking: How Government Agencies Write Law and Make Policy* (Washington, DC: Congressional Quarterly Press, 1994).

132. See e.g., Rosemary O'Leary, *Environmental Change: Federal Courts and the EPA* (Philadelphia: Temple University Press, 1993).

133. Lawrence Susskind and Gerard McMahon, "The Theory and Practice of Negotiated Rulemaking," 3 *Yale Journal on Regulation* 133, 136–37 (1985).

134. Chip Cameron, Philip J. Harter, Gail Bingham, and Neil R. Eisner, "Alternative Dispute Resolution with Emphasis on Rulemaking Negotiations," 4 *Administrative Law Journal* 83, 87 (1990).

135. *Id.,* at 87–88.

136. 5 U.S.C. §563.

137. 5 U.S.C. §570.

138. 20 U.S.C. §6571(b)(3)(A).

139. *Center for Law and Education v. Department of Education,* 396 F.3d 1152 (D.C.Cir. 2005).

140. Cameron, Harter, Bingham, and Eisner, *supra* note 134, at 90.

141. *Association of American Railroads v. Department of Transportation,* 198 F.3d 944, 950 (D.C.Cir. 1999).

142. *USA Group Loan Services v. Riley,* 82 F.3d 708, 714-715 (7th Cir. 1996).

143. P.L. 101-648 amended the APA by adding sections 581 et seq. Originally, the statute required periodic reauthorization, but it was made permanent by P.L. 104-320, 110 Stat. 3870 (1996).

144. 46 Fed. Reg. 13193 (1981).

145. The administration later issued E.O. 12498, 50 Fed. Reg. 1036 (1985), which expanded OMB authority to regulate the regulators even further.

146. 47 Fed. Reg. 30959 (1982).

147. 52 Fed. Reg. 41685 (1987).

148. 52 Fed. Reg. 34188 (1987).

149. 53 Fed. Reg. 8859 (1988).

150. 56 Fed. Reg. 55195 (1991).

151. See E.O. 12861 entitled "Elimination of One-Half of Executive Branch Internal Regulations," 58 Fed. Reg. 48255 (1993).

152. 58 Fed. Reg. 51735 (1993).

153. E.O. 12866, Section 5.

154. 67 Fed. Reg. 9385 (2002).

155. Office of Management and Budget, Office of Information and Regulatory Affairs, "Circular A-4, Regulatory Analysis," September 17, 2003, at http://www.whitehouse.gov/omb/circulars/a004/a-4.pdf, as of November 13, 2005.

156. Chapter 10 discusses the regulatory analysis movement in general and the Regulatory Flexibility Act of 1980 and the amendments of it in the Small Business Regulatory Enforcement Fairness Act of 1996 in particular. This act mandates analyses for virtually all agencies when the rules involved will have a significant impact on small businesses or small units of government.

157. P.L. 104-13, 109 Stat. 163 (1995).

158. 42 U.S.C. §4321 et seq.

159. P.L. 104-4, 109 Stat. 48 (1995).

160. 66 Fed. Reg. 51287 (2001).

161. 66 Fed. Reg. 65473 (2001).

162. At http://www.ed.gov/inits/commissionsboards/whspecialeducation/reports/pcesefinalreport.pdf, as of November 12, 2005.

163. P.L. 108-446; 118 Stat. 2647 (2004).

164. 69 Fed. Reg. 77968 (2005).

165. Yes, the agency had published a set of dates, but without additional information, in the *Federal Register* on April 1 and then modified one of the dates and provided locations in the federal register on May 31, assuming, of course, that one happened to be looking for that information in the *Register* on those dates.

166. 70 Fed. Reg. 35782 (2005).

167. U.S. Department of Education, Office of Special Education & Rehabilitative Services, IDEA 2004 Resources, at http://www.ed.gov/policy/speced/guid/idea/idea2004.html, as of November 12, 2005.

168. 69 Fed. Reg. 1862 (2004).

169. 69 Fed. Reg. 1874 (2004).

170. 69 Fed. Reg. 1885 (2004).

171. 69 Fed. Reg. 42256 (2004).

172. 70 Fed. Reg. 53063 (2005).

173. P.L. 100-582, 102 Stat. 2950 (1988).

174. See e.g., Robert G. Dixon, "The Congressional Veto and Separation of Powers: The Executive on a Leash," 56 *North Carolina L. Rev.* 423 (1978).

175. See e.g., Barbara Hinckson Craig, *The Legislative Veto* (Boulder, CO: Westport, 1983); Ernest Gellhorn and Harold Bruff, "Congressional Control of Administrative Regulation: A Study of Legislative Vetoes," 90 *Harvard L. Rev.,* 1369; and Dixon, *supra* note 174.

176. 462 U.S. 919 (1983).

177. 673 F. 2d 425 (D.C.Cir. 1982).

178. *Consumers Union v. FTC,* 691 F.2d 575 (D.C.Cir. 1982).

179. *Process Gas Consumers v. Consumer Energy Council,* 463 U.S. 1216 (1983); *United States Senate v. FTC,* 463 U.S. 1216 (1983).

180. Louis Fisher, "One Year After *INS v. Chadha:* Congressional and Judicial Developments," (Washington, DC: Congressional Research Service, 1984), p. ii. See also Fisher, "Judicial Misjudgments About the Lawmaking Process: The Legislative Veto Case," 45 *Public Administration Rev.* 705 (1985).

181. 5 U.S.C. §801 (a)(1)(B).

182. 65 Fed. Reg. 68262 (2000).

6

Administrative Adjudications

Notwithstanding popular concern about administrative power, which focuses on the profusion of government regulations, agencies make far more quasi-judicial decisions than they do rulemaking judgments. Is an industrial plant in violation of air quality standards? Should a specific coal miner be entitled to benefits under the black lung compensation rogram?[1] In some situations, the decisionmaker is attempting to resolve a particular case according to existing rules or standards, while in others the agency is engaged in policymaking through adjudication following an administrative analog of the common law process of legal development. In any event, the administrator is making decisions that matter, judgments that determine rights or status under the law. The consequences of administrative decisions can be of major importance, and therefore the means by which they are made are also significant. Consider the following examples.

Mr. Greene was general manager of the Engineering Research Corp (ERCO), a company that developed and produced electronic devices under contract to the federal government and the U.S. Navy in particular. Greene had been with the firm from 1937 to 1951, when ERCO received a communication from the Army-Navy-Air Force Personnel Security Board. Greene had been cleared for security three times by the services during World War II and after. But on November 21, 1951, his firm was informed that the company could lose its access to classified materials because Greene was considered a risk. In December, Greene was formally notified that his clearance had been revoked because his associations and activities from 1942 to 1947 suggested that he was a Communist or a Communist sympathizer.

In January 1952, Greene was granted a hearing before the Industrial Employment Review Board at which he presented a substantial amount of evidence and testimony himself, and through former associates at ERCO and in the military, which indicated that Greene's contacts with Soviet embassy personnel during the war and immediately after were official visits on behalf of ERCO as a representative to sell materials to an ally. Greene's witnesses testified that they knew Greene to be a trustworthy citizen with an impeccable record of contribution to American military efforts in both World War II and the Korean War. No testimony was offered by the government. Evidence was taken from reports compiled by various investigators, none of whom were members of the deciding body. None of the sources of the information testified before the board. Greene requested an opportunity to know and face his accusers, which request was denied on security grounds. The board reinstated Greene's clearance.

Just over a year later, ERCO was again contacted about Greene's security clearance—this time by the Secretary of the Navy. The loyalty-security program for defense industries had been reorganized. The Secretary had reviewed the earlier decision of the Industrial Employment Review Board on his own motion without further hearings or other notice to Greene and had determined that he would recommend that the Secretary of Defense reverse the board's decision. In the interim, ERCO was advised to remove Greene from any area of the plant's activities in which he might come in contact with Navy projects. Since their operation was based on defense department contracts, ERCO had no choice but to terminate Greene's employment, although both the president of the firm and the chairman of the board wrote the Secretary of the Navy protesting the Navy's actions and lauding Greene's 16-plus years of service to the company and the Navy. The company asked for some process through which the decision might be discussed or reconsidered, to which the Navy replied that "as far as the Navy Department is concerned, any further discussion on this problem at this time will serve no useful purpose."[2]

It was not until fall 1953 that Greene's attorney was able to get the Navy to produce a statement of the charges against Greene from the Eastern Industrial Personnel Board, which had been given jurisdiction in the case. The allegations were of the same general nature as the charges first leveled in 1951, with no additional material. In April 1954, Greene was given another hearing at which he again presented a great deal of personal testimony and supporting material from others. Greene also testified that since he had been terminated by ERCO, he had been unable to obtain employment as an engineer in the aircraft industry and had finally landed a job as an architectural draftsman, at a much lower pay scale. The board, offering no reasons for its decision and again without permitting Greene to examine the evidence against him, or to face the investigators who had gathered the evidence or the witnesses who had given the evidence, upheld the determination by the Secretary of the Navy. Greene protested the decision and asked for a review. The Industrial Personnel Security Review Board reviewed the record in the case, but gave Greene no opportunity to present arguments. It affirmed the earlier decision, again without reasons, only restating the generalized assertions about his associations and his questionable veracity.

The ruling came in 1954. Greene sought judicial review in the District Court for the District of Columbia, which dismissed his petition without a hearing. That lower court decision was upheld by the Circuit Court of Appeals. The case was finally decided in Greene's favor by the United States Supreme Court in 1959.

What had Greene done to deserve all this? What was the evidence introduced against him? Given the testimony of his supervisors at ERCO and military officials, why did the process ever go as far as it did? What was the nature of the evidence that was so sensitive that the names of the informants could not be made available to Greene and his attorney?

The following excerpts are taken from the Supreme Court's opinions *Greene v. McElroy*.[3] The bracketed language is that of the Supreme Court.

> The specifications were contained in a letter to petitioner's council dated April 9, 1954, which was sent nineteen days before the hearing. That letter provided in part:
> "Security considerations permit disclosure of the following information that has thus far resulted in the denial of clearance to Mr. Greene:
> 1. "During 1942 subject was a member of the Washington Book Shop Association, an organization that has been cited by the Attorney General of the United States as Communist and subversive.*

---

*In 1942 no justification was required to place an organization on that list. This process was later overturned in *Joint Anti-Fascist Refugee Committee v. McGrath*, 341 U.S. 123 (1951).

2. "Subject's first wife, Jean Hinton Greene, to whom he was married from approximately December 1942 to approximately December 1947, was an ardent Communist during the greater part of the period of the marriage.

3. "During the period of Subject's first marriage he and his wife had MM Communist publications in their home including...Karl Marx's *Das Kapital*.

4. "Many apparently reliable witnesses have testified that during the period of Subject's first marriage his personal sympathies were in general accord with those of his wife, in that he was sympathetic towards Russia; followed the Communist Party 'line'; presented 'fellow traveller arguments'; was apparently influenced by 'Jean's wild theories'; etc. "[Nothing in the record established that any witnesses "testified" at any hearing on these subjects and everything in the record indicates that they could have done no more than make such statements to investigative officers.]

5. "In about 1946 Subject invested approximately $1000 in the Metropolitan Broadcasting Corporation and later became a director of its Radio Station WQQW. It has been reliably reported that many of the stockholders of the Corporation were Communists or pro-Communists and that the news coverage and radical programs of Station WQQW frequently paralleled the Communist Party 'line.' [This station is now Station WGMS, Washington's "Good Music Station." Petitioner stated that he invested money in the station because he liked classical music and he considered it a good investment.]

6. "On 7 April 1947 Subject and his wife jean attended the Third Annual Dinner of the Southern Conference for Human Welfare, an organization that has been officially cited as a Communist front." [This dinner was also attended by many Washington notables, including several members of this Court.]

7. "Beginning about 1942 and continuing for several years thereafter Subject maintained sympathetic associations with various officials of the Soviet Embassy." [High-level executives of ERCO, as above noted, testified that these associations were carried on to secure business for the corporation.][4]

As the Court indicated, none of this "evidence" was submitted by witnesses under oath subject to cross-examination. Greene, of course, provided several notable witnesses who did testify under oath and were therefore subject to cross-examination by the government. The opinion of the Court describes their experience:

> And the following questions were asked of various witnesses presented by the petitioner evidently because the Board had confidential information that petitioner's ex-wife was "eccentric."
>
> Q. Now you were in Bill's home, that red brick house that you're talking about.....
>
> Q. Was there anything unusual about the house itself, the interior of it, was it dirty?...
>
> Q. Were there any beds in their house which had no mattresses on them?...
>
> Q. Did you ever hear it said that Jean slept on a board in order to keep the common touch?...
>
> Q. When you were in Jean's home did she dress conventionally when she received her guests?...
>
> Q. Let me ask you this, conventionally when somebody would invite you for dinner at their home, would you expect them, if they were a woman, to wear a dress and shoes and stockings and the usual clothing of the evening or would you expect them to appear in overalls?[5]

The Court later describes the cross-examination to which Greene was subjected in the government's attempt to show that the evidence introduced against his ex-wife was applicable to him.

Q. I'd like to read to you a quotation from the testimony of a person who had identified himself as having been a very close friend of yours over a long period of years. He states that you, as saying to him one day that you were reading a great deal of pro–Communist books and other literature. Do you wish to comment on that?. . .

Q. Incidentally this man's testimony was entirely favorable in one respect. He stated that he didn't think you were a Communist but he did state that he thought that you had been influenced by Jean's viewpoints and that he had received impressions definite that it was your wife who was parlor pink and that you were going along with her.. . .

Q. This same friend testified that he believed that you were influenced by Jean's wild theories and he decided at that time to have no further association with you and your wife.[6]

The Court struck down this process, developed by administrators, which permitted citizens to be deprived of the opportunity to pursue a lawful occupation without the opportunity to confront witnesses against them and to cross-examine those witnesses.

The second situation was quite different from that faced by Mr. Greene. A suit on behalf of two boys, aged 12 and 13, was brought against the commissioner of the Georgia Department of Human Services, officials of department responsible for mental health treatment, and the office in charge of Family and Children's Services. Attorneys for the boys argued that the state law that gave minors who were committed to mental health facilities, by their parents or by the state, no right to a hearing to determine whether they should be confined was an unconstitutional denial of due process in violation of Fourteenth Amendment. The facts that gave rise to the case as it reached United States Supreme Court are as follows:

J.R. was born on August 14, 1962. Approximately three months after birth, a juvenile court, because of severe parental neglect, removed him from his parents' home and placed him in a foster home under the supervision of the Georgia Department of Family and Children Services. After having lived in a total of seven different foster homes, when he was almost eight years of age he was admitted by the defendant on June 25, 1970, to Georgia's oldest and largest mental hospital, called Central State Hospital at Milledgeville, Georgia. In each foster home it seemed that he had lost his place to a more favored child. On October 27, 1966, a juvenile court order had given "permanent custody for the purpose of placing said child for adoption" to the Georgia Department of Family and Children Services. Adoption did not materialize, and without hearing or order J.R. remained in the custody of the Department of Family and Children Services in said foster homes until that department applied directly to said mental hospital for his admission to said mental hospital pursuant 88-503.1. Upon admission he was found by hospital personnel to be mentally ill, and his mental illness was described as "1. Borderline mental retardation 310.90- 2. Unsocialized aggressive reaction of childhood. 308.40." Exhibit 7. In early 1973, hospital personnel began requesting the Department of Family and Children Services to remove J.R. from hospital confinement and place him in long-term foster or adoptive home because of the feeling that he "will only regress if he does not get a suitable home placement, and as soon as possible." Exhibit 9-2-A. On August 9, 1973, hospital personnel "felt that efforts to obtain placement should be primary at this time, lest [J.R.] become institutionalized child." Exhibit 10-A-2. A foster home was not obtained for J.R. and he remained in confinement. On October 24, 1975, when this lawsuit was filed, he had been confined for five years and four months of his thirteen years, two months of life.[7]

J.L. at birth on October 1, 1963, was adopted. His parents divorced when he was three, and he went to live with his mother. She remarried and gave birth to a child. On May 15, 1970, his mother and stepfather, pursuant to the previously quoted state law §88-503.1, applied for his admission to what is now Central State Hospital; he was admitted. Hospital personnel found that J.L. was mentally ill and diagnosed his illness as "Hyperkinetic Reaction of C 308.00." On September 8, 1972, he was discharged to his mother, but she brought him back to the hospital and readmitted him ten days later. He then remained in the hospital in confinement, and at the time this lawsuit commenced had been in confinement for five years and five months of his twelve years, one month of life. In 1973 hospital personnel indicated to the Department of Family and Children Services that J.L. needed to be removed from hospital confinement and placed in specialized foster care. His records show that the Department of Family and Children Services indicated that the department could not pay for institutionalized (private) foster care unless J.L. was eligible for such paid for by A.F.D.C. [Aid to Families with Dependent Children] or Social Security funds. He was not an A.F.D.C. eligible child. See Exhibit 1. Specialized foster care was not obtained for J.L. by the defendants.[8]

Under the state's voluntary commitment law, the child generally remains confined without a hearing unless the parents, or the state in the case of a ward of the state, ask for the release. It is then up to the adult or the state to find appropriate care outside the institution. The district court found that although many parents commit their children with all the right intentions and motives, there are problems.

While parents generally make such applications with the best of intentions and with the sincere desire to seek help for their child, the defendants nevertheless recognize what society knows but had rather not admit— "there are a lot of people who still treat [mental hospitals] as dumping grounds." [Dr. John P. Filley, Director, Child and Adolescent Mental Health Services, deposition at 48].[9]

The court also found that once children are sent to a facility, it is likely that a reason can be found for confining them.

Then the statutory concept is that "if found to show evidence of mental illness and to be suitable for treatment, such person may be given care and treatment...and...may be detained by such facility for such period and under such conditions as may be authorized by law."...In practice the language "evidence of mental illness and to be suitable for treatment" is as indefinite and elusive to the psychiatrists employed by the state as it is to a layman. Note the...following deposition of Dr. John Filley, Director, Child and Mental Health Services:...In sum and substance Dr. Filley testified that the decision to hospitalize for care and treatment comes about in the following manner: "The parent may come in saying, 'I can't handle it any more; do something.' And, they say at the hospital or it might be the psychiatrist who says, 'I think hospitalization is indicated.' The parent would agree and that would decide it."[10]

The state often commits a juvenile for whom adoptive parents cannot be found or adequate foster placement secured.

The district court received testimony from employees and supervisors of Georgia's mental hospitals that a substantial portion of the non-psychotic older juveniles being held in confinement were there solely because funds had not been made available for suitable placement or because the families would not take the children for whom discharge had been recommended.

The three-judge district court concluded that the Georgia voluntary commitment statute was unconstitutional insofar as it permitted children to be held without an opportunity for a hearing at which the state would show cause why the children should be confined.

> By this statute the state gives to parents the power to arbitrarily admit their children to a mental hospital for an indefinite period of time. "Where the state undertakes to act in parens patriae, it has the inescapable duty to vouchsafe due process," . . . and this necessarily includes procedural safeguards to see that even parents do not use the power to indefinitely hospitalize children in an arbitrary manner. . . .
>
> It is thus apparent that this statute supplies not the flexible due process that the situation of the plaintiff children demands, but, instead, absolutely no due process. It is also apparent that it affords to parents, guardians, the Department of Human Resources as Custodian, and super-intendents the "unchecked and unbalanced power over [the] essential liberties" . . . of these children that is universally mistrusted by our "whole scheme of American government." The double check that is needed is that which is guaranteed by the Fourteenth Amendment—due process of law. There being none the statute in question violates the Due Process Clause of the Fourteenth Amendment and is unconstitutional.[11]

In 1979, the United States Supreme Court reversed the district court ruling and held that the initial screening process at the hospital along with the good intentions of the parents and the state were sufficient protection for the child's rights to due process of law.[12]

The *Greene* case, the juvenile commitment suit, and the *Mathews v. Eldridge* Social Security dis-ability benefits conflict, presented in Appendix 1, all involved decisions by government officials or agencies of an adjudicatory nature that carried important consequences. These cases are all unusual in that they were addressed by the United States Supreme Court, but they do illustrate several of the major recurring aspects of administrative law that guide administrators in making decisions about individual claims and disputes. *Parham* concerned a demand that children be afforded a hearing on their hospi-talization and, in effect, confinement. The case of the government employee discharged for allegedly accusing his superior of improprieties and the *Eldridge* case both involved demands for a hearing before, rather than after, government acted against the individuals concerned. Eldridge argued that a hearing should be available before the disability benefit checks were cut off. Mr. Greene was able to present his case in a hearing, but he argued that the hearing was not a fair proceeding because he was not accorded certain of the elements of due process, namely, the right to confront his accusers and to test the veracity of their testimony by cross-examination, generally required by the concept that one should have a fair hearing before being injured by a government action.

THE ESSENCE OF THE DUE PROCESS CLAIM

Administrative justice rules governing the conduct of adjudicatory proceedings make up the second major category of formal administrative law. They result from the understanding that, despite a number of ambiguities in definition, in making adjudicatory decisions agencies act rather like courts. They are required to employ the traditional elements of fair decisionmaking that fall under the rubric of due process of law. The due process protections ensure not that one will win a dispute, but that the dispute will be resolved fairly through a regular procedure. The centerpiece of the Anglo-American concept of due process of law is that before suffering injury one is entitled to a fair hearing at which one may present arguments and evidence in one's behalf.[13] Unlike the discussion of rulemaking procedures, which were more legislative, albeit by degrees, adjudicatory procedures that are quasi-judicial involve assertions of rights. Due process rights are protected by the Constitution, statutes, regulations, contracts and judicial interpretations. The requirements of administrative adjudication may be understood through consideration of questions that have to do with a fair hearing. One can ask: (1) Is a hearing required in a particular situation? (2) If so, at what point in an administrative action is the hearing required? (3) What kind of hearing is required? (4) What are the essential elements of an administrative hearing?

The responses to these questions will be more understandable if the discussion is informed by an understanding of the procedural due process model of administrative justice.

PROCEDURAL DUE PROCESS MODEL OF ADMINISTRATIVE JUSTICE

The rules that govern administrative adjudications are very much products of the historical developments detailed in Chapter 4. They represent compromises between the recognized need that administrators must function with some flexibility and dispatch and the fear of administrative arbitrariness, which has grown as government has become more involved in day-to-day life. In much the same way that rulemaking requirements developed in an attempt to control nonelected officials who could make rules that had the force of law, so the adjudication requirements developed in an effort to limit judicial-type decisions having the force of law made without some of the formalities normally available in a court of law.

Due Process and the Rule of Law

Notwithstanding the numerous dangers inherent in the "extravagant version of the rule of law," the United States is, and prides itself on being, a nation committed to the rule of law. On the need to control abuses of administrative discretion, J. Skelly Wright observed:

> If that consensus is properly marshalled and the legal tactics carefully planned, King Rex [an administrator who would like unbounded authority] can indeed be turned into a constitutional monarch. Failing that, we may still be able to pull off a bloodless coup d'etat and send the King packing to a land that does not purport to govern its affairs by rules of law.[14]

Reminding administrators that administrative law is but one aspect of the American governmental system and, like the others, functions under the rule of law, Louis L. Jaffe wrote:

> An agency is not an island entire of itself. It is one of the many rooms in the mansion of the law. The very subordination of the agency to judicial jurisdiction is intended to proclaim the premise that each agency is to be brought into harmony with the totality of the law; the law as it is found in the statute at hand, the statute book at large, the principles and conceptions of the "common law" and the ultimate guarantees associated with the Constitution.[15]

By almost any standard, the concept that government should not take any action that seriously injures an individual without providing at least some of the elements of due process of law is at the heart of the Anglo-American definition of the rule of law. The idea of due process can be traced at least as far back as the Magna Carta. "King John promised that 'no free man shall be taken or imprisoned or exiled or in any way destroyed, nor will we go upon him nor send upon him, except by the lawful judgment of his peers or by the law of the land.' "[16] The "law of the land," of course, included all the protections afforded by the entire fabric of the law.[17] The term "due process of law" was first used in England in 1354. "No man of what state or condition he be, shall be put out of his lands or tenements nor taken, nor disinherited, nor put to death, without he be brought to answer by due process of law."[18]

During the colonial period and early nationhood, many of the state governments adopted statements in their constitutions or laws requiring due process protections.[19] In part to bolster the principles of fair and independent adjudications, the framers of the U.S. Constitution established a co-equal judiciary as opposed to the subordinate status accorded that branch of government in England. The Fifth Amendment to the new Constitution included a protection against the deprivation of life, liberty, or property without due process of law. But that provision only protected citizens against abuses of authority by the national government and not the governments of the states or localities.[20] Experience before and after the Civil War indicated that the states were as capable of abusing citizens as were officials in Washington and in some respects were more dangerous simply because citizens dealt far more often with state and local officials than with federal authorities.[21] Hence, when the Fourteenth Amendment was drafted, it included an admonition that no state shall "abridge the privileges or immunities of citizens,...nor deprive any person of life, liberty, or property without due process of law, nor deny to any person the equal protection of the laws."

Of course, although "supremacy of law" and "due process of law" are important symbolic terms and concepts praised and ascribed to by all, their precise requirements can be difficult to define in individual cases. This is true even of criminal law, where one would think the precepts of due process of law would be most clearly understood.

Defined stringently enough, due process would require any government official to proceed with a formal court trial in any situation in which the citizen involved might suffer a loss, for example, in bringing a business into compliance with a regulation. Some authors who were writing about the developing administrative state at the end of the nineteenth and the beginning of the twentieth centuries defined the term exactly that way, with A. V. Dicey leading the attack on any adjudication not conducted in an "ordinary court" under the rules of ordinary common law.[22] The debate over just what due process required was a cornerstone of the entire argument over whether administrative law was or was not legitimate.[23] As Chapter 4 indicated, some of those anxieties were exacerbated as administrative activities increased during the New Deal.

However, courts were not well equipped to deal with administrative adjudications. Indeed, it was the failure of the courts in the regulatory arena that was one of the strongest reasons for the development of administrative law.[24] The courts provided a scrupulously fair forum, but their rules were much better suited to civil cases between individuals, to be argued before juries, than for the complex problems of regulation and social service. There was no way that judges could acquire the expertise that was needed to resolve expeditiously some of the problems agencies faced.

The courts, in a number of decisions, and the Congress, in enacting the APA, reached a compromise on administrative adjudications by ensuring that those processes would be regular, would be guided by the basic principles of due process, and could be reviewed by a court to ensure that the agency had indeed fulfilled the technical requirements of due process of law and, in a larger way, also fulfilled the fundamental fairness demanded by due process and the concept of supremacy of law.

Procedural versus Substantive Due Process

It is important to note some of the limits that the concept of due process imposes on administrators. First, there is in American constitutional law a recognition of the difference between substantive and procedural due process.

Procedural due process permits government to take action that may have grave consequences for a person (or a group) as long as it follows fair procedures. Thus, the Fifth Amendment requires that one may not be deprived of life, liberty, or property without due process. But if all the procedures needed to ensure a fair decision process are followed, the government may take property, it may sentence citizens to jail, and it may even mandate execution. Procedural due process does not mean that a person before a government organization is entitled to win a dispute, but only that the government must deal with the case fairly and in accordance with all the requirements of law.

The idea that due process prevents government from taking some actions against an individual regardless of the procedural protections provided is frequently referred to as substantive due process. The classic example of substantive due process in action was *Lochner v. New York,* an early twentieth century case challenging a New York law that limited the working hours of bakery employees to no more than 60 hours in a week or ten hours per day.[25] The law was a health and safety statute to protect workers in what the legislature deemed to be an unsafe work environment. The Supreme Court found that the law interfered with the liberty of bakery workers and owners to enter into contracts to sell or purchase labor on any terms they might set. The opinion for the divided Court, written by Justice Peckham, ruled that the legislature had no authority in that area. "There is no reasonable ground for interfering with the liberty of person or the right of free contract, by determining hours of labor, in the occupation of a baker."[26] That line of decisions was later overturned.

Although judges have been wary of venturing into substantive due process interpretations, given the criticisms of the *Lochner* era rulings, there have been a few situations in which the Court has been willing to take a substantive due process position in barring government actions late in the twentieth and even into the twenty-first century. Thus, the Court in 1977 struck down an action by East Cleveland, Ohio, to convict a grandmother of a criminal offense because she had her son and his children living with her for a time. Believe it or not, the son's stepchild did not meet the city's zoning code definition of the grandmother's "family."[27] She was therefore in violation of the ordinance. More recently, in 2003, the Court struck down a Texas statute barring sexual relations between persons of the same sex on grounds that:

> Liberty protects the person from unwarranted government intrusions into a dwelling or other private places. In our tradition the State is not omnipresent in the home. And there are other spheres of our lives and existence, outside the home, where the State should not be a dominant presence. Freedom extends beyond spatial bounds. Liberty presumes an autonomy of self that includes freedom of thought, belief, expression, and certain intimate conduct. The instant case involves liberty of the person both in its spatial and more transcendent dimensions.[28]

Such cases have been rare and are generally concerned with disputes over the constitutionality of legislation and not the administration of a policy.

As early as the 1930s the Supreme Court spoke to the limits on the kinds of requirements that judges should require in administrative adjudications.

> [T]he courts will not substitute their discretion for [the administrator's]....If he is authorized to determine questions of fact, his decision must be accepted unless he exceeds his authority by making a determination which is arbitrary or capricious or unsupported by evidence..., or by failing to follow a procedure which satisfied elementary standards of fairness and reasonableness essential to due conduct of the proceeding which Congress has authorized.[29]

In general, then, when someone refers to due process in connection with an administrative adjudication, procedural due process is what is meant. But even these requirements of minimal court-like procedures are not required in everything that looks like a quasi-judicial action.

Investigations versus Adjudications

Agencies may hold hearings on individual problems that appear to be court-like or adjudicatory procedures, but are in fact merely investigatory activities. In such situations people who may see themselves as being injured by the administrative procedure are nevertheless not entitled to participate in the same manner or with the same procedural protections that one normal thinks of in a court-like proceeding.

The Supreme Court dealt with the problem in *Withrow v. Larkin*.[30] Its opinion began with the recognition that "concededly, a 'fair trial in a fair forum is a basic requirement of due process.'... This applies to administrative agencies which adjudicate as well as to courts. *Gibson v. Berryhill,* 411 U.S. 564, 579...(1973)."[31] In the end, however, the Court found that the fact that the administrative body was merely engaged in an investigative process rather than an actual adjudication was enough to justify the decision not to allow the doctor whose activities were at issue in the proceeding to participate as fully as he might in a full-scale adjudication. The Court held that the investigatory hearing was rather like a grand jury proceeding, in that the board was merely determining whether a formal proceeding to discipline the physician should be pursued just as a grand jury would decide whether there was probable cause to conclude that a crime had been committed, that the individual accused may have committed it, and that a formal procedure for determining guilt or innocence should be instituted.

This is a somewhat simplified, and indeed clarified, interpretation of the Court's decision. Dr. Larkin was a Michigan physician who was licensed in Wisconsin under a reciprocal licensing agreement. Dr. Larkin allegedly performed abortions in his office in Wisconsin. The Wisconsin licensing authorities informed Larkin that they would hold "uncontested" hearings to determine whether there was probable cause to follow through with a formal administrative procedure looking toward a revocation of his license and possibly a recommendation that the public prosecutor should institute a criminal prosecution. Larkin and his attorney were permitted to attend the hearing, but not to present a case directly or indirectly by cross-examining witnesses against Larkin. At the end of the hearing, Larkin was allowed to "explain" the evidence presented against him.

The board decided to launch a formal hearing to remove his license. Larkin brought suit in a federal district court, claiming that the hearing was in violation of due process for several reasons. Most prominent among the abuses, he asserted, was the board's refusal to permit him to participate in the uncontested hearing and the fact that the same body that had heard evidence against him without benefit of cross-examination and had made a preliminary finding that his license should be revoked would be judging his fitness to practice medicine. It was, in Larkin's view, an unfair procedure conducted by a biased decisionmaking body.

The Court concluded that the hearing was investigative and not adjudicative. The *Withrow* decision points up the fact that agencies are not courts and not every administrative procedure that looks like an adjudication will be treated like one. Additionally, the decision supports the proposition that administrative due process is allowed to be considerably less formal than the judicial variety.

Administrative versus Judicial Due Process

What are some of the differences between due process in court and the limits of due process in agency adjudications? Specific elements of administrative due process will be considered in detail later in this chapter, but consider the problem, for the moment at least, in broad compass.

What is meant by due process in a judicial proceeding? In general, Anglo-American jurisprudence requires that a citizen should not be called upon to appear before a court unless a violation of a properly enacted law is alleged. The person summoned has a right to expect that he or she will be notified of the purpose of the proceeding and the nature of the charges being asserted in order to prepare an adequate defense. He or she is entitled to be represented by an attorney who will present the case. He or she may call witnesses and present evidence in his or her own behalf and challenge the evidence presented on the other side by cross-examination. The judge who presides should be unbiased and independent. In serious matters, a trial by jury is available. The process should result in a reasoned decision supported by the evidence developed at trial in accordance with interpretations of law that are explained by the decisionmaking judge. The citizen should be entitled to at least one appeal on the correctness of the interpretation to a higher tribunal.

In administrative adjudications, some of these procedures are slightly different from those expectations. First, there is no recourse to a trial by jury. Second, the procedures for presentation of evidence are slightly less formal than in a court trial since there is no jury to be deceived by inappropriate offers of proof. While there is a right to representation, there is no obligation for government to provide counsel to those who cannot afford to hire their own lawyer. Third, the decisionmaker is not totally independent. He or she is employed by the agency involved, although there are provisions to ensure that the administrative law judge has some protection against attempts at pressure. Indeed, the fact that the judge is a part of the agency permits him or her to bring an expertise to the case and to maintain continuity in decisions. One is entitled to an appeal from an administrative decision, but it is necessary to accomplish all stages of administrative appeal before moving to a totally separate tribunal.

ADMINISTRATIVE DUE PROCESS: A DEVELOPING PROCESS

Administrative adjudications became increasingly significant as the nineteenth century ended and the twentieth began. Decisions that affected the railroads and other businesses were appealed to the highest courts, which led to a significant body of judicial opinions explaining the minimum requirements of due process. State and local administrative rulings in zoning decisions and a host of other areas of regulation contributed to this growing body of law.[32]

These early cases, while granting considerable deference to the substance of administrative rulings, reminded officials that the Constitution does "not mean to leave room for the play and action of purely personal and arbitrary power."[33] Actions by government that cause serious harm to an individual require an opportunity for a hearing.[34] Due process protections extend to all who live under the jurisdiction of American law, whether they are citizens or aliens (though for reasons that will become clear shortly that guarantee has not always been honored in the post-9/11 context).[35] Rejecting the idea that a hearing to satisfy the due process requirements should consist merely of an opportunity to submit written objections to the administrative authority, the Supreme Court held: "Many requirements essential in strictly judicial proceedings may be dispensed with in proceedings of this nature. But even here a hearing in its very essence demands that he who is entitled to it shall have the right to support his allegations by argument, however brief; and, if need be, by proof, however informal."[36] The case law required that administrative orders would be voided if no hearing was afforded the individual or firm involved, if the hearing was not fair or adequate, if there was no reasoned decision, or if that decision was not supported by the evidence acquired during the adjudication.[37]

The second period was, as the commentary in Chapter 4 noted, significant for the growth in administrative activity because of New Deal activities and wartime mobilization. It was a period of debate over what to do about administrative law. To one examining the decisions of the Supreme Court, however, there is an apparent agreement that while there may have been arguments concerning what Congress could authorize agencies to do, there was no disputing the fact that when administrators conduct court-like proceedings, they must obey the general requirements of due process of law.[38] Rules of due process law were slowly developing which sought to avoid second-guessing on the substance of decisions but did mandate minimal requirements for a fair hearing in a fair forum decided by a fair decisionmaker. The adjudications sections and the requirements and procedures for hearing examiners section of the APA were drafted in an attempt to codify the requirements laid down in the judicial opinions.[39]

In the third period, also described in Chapter 4, several factors led to increased procedural due process protections for consumers of administrative decisions and concomitant burdens on administrators. The growth in administrative activity was one of the most important influences on the refinement of due process requirements for administrative adjudications. Increases in social services, e.g., education, the administration of New Deal and postwar social welfare programs, and the responsibilities of the major regulatory agencies meant more quasi-judicial activities in more areas raising new problems.

Another aspect of the increasing importance of due process was growing awareness of the fact that in an increasingly interdependent society, with no frontiers to escape to for a new start and diminishing privacy, an adverse governmental decision regarding a job or a benefit claim could have profoundly harmful consequences.

> Employability is the greatest asset most people have. Once there is a discharge from a prestigious federal agency, dismissal may be a badge that bars the employee from other federal employment. The shadow of that discharge is cast over the area where private employment may be available. And the harm is not eliminated by the possibility of reinstatement, for in many cases the ultimate absolution never catches up with the stigma of the accusation.... Unlike a layoff or discharge due to fortuitous circumstances such as a so-called energy crisis, a discharge on the basis of the captious or discriminatory attitudes of a superior may be a cross to carry the rest of an employee's life. And we cannot denigrate the importance of one's social standing or the status of social stigma as legally recognized harm....
>
> There is no frontier where the employee may go to get a new start. We live today in a society that is closely monitored. All of our important acts, our setbacks, the accusations made against us go into the data banks, instantly retrieved by the computer.[40]

In a commuter society, the loss of a driver's license may have more severe consequences than a short jail sentence. In an urban society with a highly mobile workforce, in which the extended family is for many people no longer in place to care for the aged or the infirm, the responsibilities of the state becomes complex and the pressures on the individual greater than ever before. When disability benefits are terminated, residents of a public housing project are evicted, a young person is expelled from school, or subsidies or government guaranteed loans to a business person are canceled, the administrator involved is making decisions that will have profound effects on the consumer of the decision. And through all of this there is the now ubiquitous computer record that follows one across distance and time.

Another point obvious to all, including judges, was the critical literature that indicated that administrative adjudications under the early years of implementation of the APA left much to be desired. In particular, the Task Force on Legal Services and Procedures of the second Hoover Commission and the Landis Report expressed concern about arbitrariness and breaches of fundamental due process protections.

Finally, the excesses brought about by the Cold War, particularly those associated with the various loyalty and security programs, made a mockery of the concept of due process. The programs never succeeded in locating subversives in government who were proven to be Communists. They did drive nearly 2,000 men and women from government work, and many more from work in private industry. The courts were, or became, concerned about violations of substantive rights such as freedom of speech and association,[41] but they were equally concerned about the arbitrariness and lack of procedural fairness involved in government treatment of those accused of disloyalty, whether in public employment or in the private sector. The case of *Greene v. McElroy* is one example. There were others.

Groups were listed by the Attorney General as subversive or Communist organizations with no evidence or opportunity for their members to respond until the Supreme Court barred the practice.[42] Those who were members of the organizations so listed were treated as outcasts. State governments enacted laws barring the state treasurer from paying employees who did not, within a specified period, sign vague loyalty oaths that required one to assure that one had not been a member of any subversive group. In one such situation, college professors refused to sign for several reasons, among which was the fact that they could not know which groups were acceptable and which were not. In the course of the litigation, the state supreme court ruled that the proscribed organizations were only those named on the Attorney Generals list. Given that explanation, the professors requested another opportunity to take the oath. It was denied. The Supreme Court struck down the state law, finding:

> There can be no dispute about the consequences visited upon a person excluded from public employment on disloyalty grounds. In the view of the community, the stain is a deep one;

indeed, it has become a badge of infamy. Especially is this so in a time of cold war and hot emotions when "each man begins to eye his neighbor as a possible enemy!"...

We need not pause to consider whether an abstract right to public employment exists. It is sufficient to say that constitutional protection does extend to the public servant whose exclusion pursuant to a statute is patently arbitrary or discriminatory.[43]

Some who were harmed by these abuses were later vindicated in the courts, but other stories had no happy ending. Judge Henry Edgerton described one case.

Without trial by jury, without evidence, and without even being allowed to confront the accusers or to know their identity, a citizen of the United States has been found disloyal to the government of the United States.

For her supposed disloyal thoughts she had been punished by dismissal from a wholly nonsensitive position in which her efficiency rating was high. The case received nationwide publicity. Ostracism inevitably followed.[44]

Dorothy Bailey was terminated from her administrative job and barred from reapplying for three years. The only specific allegation against her was that 15 years earlier she had attended a Communist Party meeting. She answered that a professor had required her and other undergraduate students in a political science seminar at Bryn Mawr to visit different groups to gather information about party platforms.

The Loyalty Board's decision was affirmed in part by the Circuit Court of Appeals in a split decision. Bailey appealed to the Supreme Court, which deadlocked with four votes to affirm and four to reverse.[45] Her dismissal stood.

In his dissent from the Circuit Court decision, Judge Edgerton discussed in detail some of the more gross abuses involved in the loyalty cases. After noting that Bailey had presented several witnesses and some 70 affidavits from character references, Edgerton turned to the government's case.

Appellant sought to learn the names of the informants, or if their names were confidential, then at least whether they had been active in appellant's union, in which there were factional quarrels. The Board did not furnish or even have this information. Chairman Richardson said: "I haven't the slightest knowledge as to who they were or how active they might have been in anything. All that the Board knew or we know about the informants is that unidentified members of the Federal Bureau of Investigation, who did not appear before the Board, believed them to be reliable."[46]

Edgerton found evidence to indicate that the evidence in the record had not been taken under oath and that there was no information about the credibility of the reports. Speaking to the kind of evidence often used in such "proceedings," Edgerton wrote:

In loyalty hearings the following questions have been asked of employees against whom charges have been brought....."Do you read a good many books?" "What books do you read?" "What magazines do you buy or subscribe to?" "Do you think that Russian Communism is likely to succeed?" "How do you explain the fact that you have an album of Paul Robeson records in your home?" "Do you ever entertain Negroes in your home?. . . Is it not true. . .that you lived next door to and therefore were closely associated with a member of the I.W.W.?"...A woman employee was accused of disloyalty because, at the time of the siege of Stalingrad, she collected money for Russian war relief (she also collected money for British and French Relief). A record filed in this court shows that an accused employee was taken to task for membership in the Consumers Union and for favoring legislation against racial discrimination.[47]

To some readers, the discussion of a red scare era loyalty/security case may seem out of date, and some have even found it laughable to think that such processes and evidence could actually have existed in U.S. policy and could have found their way to the U.S. Supreme Court. However, there were cases in which officials took shortcuts through the requirements of due process in order get perceived radicals or subversives throughout the 1960s and into the 1970s. Few young Americans today are aware of the Nixon administration's domestic surveillance program that led to a variety of consequences for those whose names or group affiliations found their way into files on those who were considered subversive.[48] Then there was updated red scare effort of the late 1970s and early 1980s, which involved circulation of lists of groups and individuals who were supposedly linked to subversives or Communists. That project burst into the public spotlight when Senator Jeremiah Denton verbally attacked the wife of Senator Dale Bumpers (D-AK) on the floor of the Senate in October 1982.[49] Since 2001, there have also been a series of arrests and detentions without trial, in many instances without charges, of many people for extended periods of time without even access to legal counsel. In addition, there have been changes in immigrations proceedings to make the hearings secret, excluding all except the specific parties to the adjudication and their lawyer (discussed later in this chapter).[50]

As the Supreme Court moved into the 1960s, the increasing ability of administrators to make important and harmful adjudicative decisions became more apparent. The effects appeared to be wide-ranging. There was evidence, from the most flagrant abuses of the loyalty security programs to less widespread but equally dangerous practices, of a tendency toward administrative arbitrariness.[51] The courts, with the Supreme Court leading the way, responded with several types of rulings that afforded more individuals in more situations more procedural protections. Much of the case law on this subject is discussed in the *Eldridge* case study in Appendix 1, but it is useful to consider the kinds of administrative problem situations that the Court addressed and its approach to solving these difficulties.

The Right/Privilege Dichotomy

As the *Eldridge* case study notes,[52] one of the developments in the due process area was the Warren Court's elimination of the remnants of the so-called right versus privilege dichotomy.[53] This dichotomy was based on the idea that government has different responsibilities in its quasi-judicial activities depending on whether an agency decision affects a right or a privilege. A right is protected against government intervention by law—for example, one's right to acquire, use, and dispose of property. This right, or legal claim, is based on the Constitution, which limits the government's ability to interfere with the exercise of one's property interests. In such situations, due process protections clearly apply. But there are other situations in which an individual or group may be seriously affected by an adjudicative decision and yet be unable to identify a basic legal right that is clearly being endangered. For example, it was argued that since there is no *per se* right to a government job, one who does not agree with limitations that go with the position—for example, rules that limit political speech—should simply resign. Alternatively, he or she may be terminated without any particular due process limitations.[54] Similarly, it was argued that welfare programs were merely gifts of public largesse which, by definition, could be granted under any conditions or requirements that the society promulgates. Since these are privileges, one can make no legal demand on the state for any particular mode of administration of the program, whether it is arbitrary or not.

But the lessons of the loyalty-security programs and the changing social, economic, and political circumstances were understood. The Supreme Court rejected the right versus privilege dichotomy and held that government may not impose unconstitutional or arbitrary conditions on public employment or the receipt of public benefits.[55] Nor may government deny procedural due process protections to those whose benefits are terminated or denied on the ground these benefits are mere privileges. The protections apply across a broad range of adjudicatory decisions that cause serious harm to the affected individuals.[56]

The Demise of Irrebuttable Presumptions

For various reasons, generally having to do with administrative convenience, some laws have been written with so-called irrebuttable presumptions. These are assumptions about one's status or situation that are part of an enacted policy about which one may not argue. Consider the following example.

Reverend Bell was a circuit-riding minister in Georgia. One Sunday following services he joined a parishioner's family for dinner, leaving his automobile parked in front of the house at the curb. While the reverend was enjoying his dinner, a five-year-old girl named Sherry Capes "rode her bicycle into the side of his automobile."[57] The girl's parents filed an accident report, alleging injury to Sherry in the amount of $5,000. Reverend Bell was not covered by liability insurance. Under existing Georgia law, he was required to file a bond equal to claimed damage regardless of the possibility of his innocence and also to provide proof of continuing financial resources against future claims or face a suspension of his license. Bell argued that deprivation of his license would mean an extreme hardship and, further, that there was no way that he could be found liable for the girl's injuries. He called for a hearing to contest his possible liability. However, the state code made fault, guilt, or innocence irrelevant to the suspension of the license. In effect, the Georgia law presumed that an uninsured motorist involved in an accident would be held liable for the total amount of damages claimed regardless of the facts in the case. The state supreme court upheld the code, but the United States Supreme Court reversed, holding that:

> [O]nce licenses are issued, as in petitioner's case, their continued possession may become essential in the pursuit of a livelihood. Suspension of issued licenses thus involves state action that adjudicates important interests of the licensees. In such cases the licenses are not to be taken away without procedural due process required by the Fourteenth Amendment.[58]

The absolute presumption of liability is unacceptable. Before the state can suspend the minister's license, he must at least be given the opportunity to argue that he could not possibly be found liable. The question was not whether there was any state ban on issuance of licenses without insurance, but rather that, given the fact that the state did not require insurance, it could not deprive the driver of an important interest without an opportunity to be heard.

A second case that reached the Supreme Court was that of a woman who contested a Connecticut statute, alleging due process violations on the ground that the statute contained an irrebuttable presumption.[59] The state law was that a student who began study in the university as an out-of-state resident would be considered, for tuition purposes, an out-of-state student throughout the period of his or her education in the state. A woman who came to the state university as a nonresident later married a lifelong Connecticut resident and became a citizen of the state with respect to taxes, voting registration, driver's license, and the like. She argued that due process required that she at least be given an opportunity to argue her *bona fides* as a Connecticut resident and citizen. The Court agreed. The Court recognized that a state has a legitimate interest in protecting its taxpayers against undue burdens on the educational system, but maintained that such concerns do not justify blanket presumptions about individual situations. Administrative convenience does not justify depriving residents who are apparently citizens in all other respects of the opportunity to argue against administrative classifications that make them academic nonresidents.

The Court has struck down other irrebuttable presumptions that served the general purpose of administrative convenience and efficiency. The Court struck down a state law that held that servicemen stationed or claiming citizenship in the state would be presumed to be nonresidents,[60] a law that required school teachers to take maternity leave five months before the projected delivery date, whether it was medically necessary or not,[61] and an Illinois law that presumed that all fathers of illegitimate children— even if they had lived with the mother and provided support as did other, married fathers—were unfit parents and hence were unable to receive custody of the children in the event of the death of the mother.[62] The Court's opinion in the Illinois case well summarizes its reasons for rejecting irrebuttable presumptions:

> Illinois has declared that the aim of the juvenile Court Act is to protect "the moral, emotional, mental, and physical welfare of the minor and the best interest of the community" and to strengthen the minor's family ties whenever possible, removing him from the custody of his

parents only when his welfare or safety, or the protection of the public cannot be adequately safeguarded without removal....These are legitimate interests, well within the power of the State to implement. We do not question the assertion that neglectful parents may be separated from their children.

But we are not asked to evaluate the legitimacy of the state ends, rather, to determine whether the means used to achieve these ends are constitutionally defensible. What is the state interest in separating children from fathers without a hearing designed to determine whether the father is unfit in a particular disputed cases...Illinois...[argues] that Stanley and all other unmarried fathers can reasonably be presumed to be unqualified to raise their children.

It may be, as the State insists, that most unmarried fathers are unsuitable and neglectful parents. It may also be that Stanley is such a parent and that his children should be placed in other hands. But all unmarried fathers are not in this category; some are wholly suited to have custody of their children. This much the state readily concedes, and nothing in this record indicates that Stanley is or has been a neglectful father who has not cared for his children. Given the opportunity to make his case, Stanley may have been seen to be deserving of custody of his offspring....

Despite *Bell* and *Carrington,* it may be argued that unmarried fathers are so seldom fit that Illinois need not undergo the administrative inconvenience of inquiry in any case, including Stanley's. The establishment of prompt efficacious procedures to achieve legitimate state ends is a proper state interest worthy of cognizance in constitutional adjudication. But the Constitution recognizes higher values than speed and efficiency. Indeed, one might fairly say of the bill of rights in general, and the Due Process Clause in particular, that they were designed to protect the fragile values of a vulnerable citizenry from the overbearing concern for efficiency and efficacy that may characterize praiseworthy government officials no less, and perhaps more, than mediocre ones.

Procedure by presumption is always cheaper and easier than individual determination. But where, as here, the procedure forecloses the determinative issues of competence and care, when it explicitly disdains present realities in deference to past formalities, it needlessly risks running roughshod over the important interests of both parent and child. It therefore cannot stand.[63]

Other Areas of Due Process Development

In addition to these two broad doctrinal areas, the Court found in a number of particular policy areas that government must afford some kind of hearing to those injured by government action. Cases requiring a hearing included termination of benefits to welfare recipients,[64] parole and probation revocation and prison disciplinary actions,[65] school disciplinary actions, e.g., suspensions for more than a limited period,[66] driver's license suspension,[67] the use of government institutions for debt collection through such mechanisms as garnishment of wages and repossession and sequestration of property,[68] protection of reputation from public branding by authorities as an alcoholic,[69] and termination of tenured public employees or termination of nontenured public employees where the manner of termination holds the employee up to public scorn or ridicule and threatens the possibility of future employment.[70]

In sum, due process was for many years seen as requisite to protect individuals from arbitrary governmental action, particularly by unelected officials. The ever-changing environment, which citizens cannot escape and in which they are more vulnerable than ever before to government excesses is acknowledged, and the view that administrative convenience is sufficient ground to override protections is rejected. Finally, the opinions were written from well-documented experience, which showed that administrative arbitrariness was a continuing problem and resulted in severe hardships on those who must deal with agencies (particularly single-shot players). The opinions maintain that administrative quasi-judicial procedures must be carefully watched to ensure that they are fair in substance as well as in form, that fair process requires a hearing of some kind at which a party may present a case, and that the hearing should be accorded before and not after governmental action which harms the citizen.

The Burger Court and After: The Reformulation
of Administrative Due Process

By 1974 and 1975, however, the environment of administrative law was again changing. The composition and philosophy of the Supreme Court had also changed.[71] In several cases agencies had adopted fair hearing regulations in one form or another.[72] Questions were now being raised about how far what was being termed the due process explosion would go. Critics of more and earlier hearing opportunities for agency clients focused on the fact that more hearings meant increased administrative burdens, higher costs from maintaining benefit recipients on programs pending hearings, reduced administrative flexibility in handling agency decision processes, and the potential for agency proceedings to become so formalized that all individual decisions would take on the trappings of a court trial.[73] These reactions and other factors led to two significant developments. First, there was a significant shift in the manner in which administrative due process was conceptualized. Second, cases arose in several of the specific areas in which due process requirements had been expanding that either marked an end to expansion or the beginning of actual relaxation of due process requirements.

The Burger and later the Rehnquist Courts' rulings on administrative adjudications marked a significant shift in general approach to the concept of procedural due process. The Court moved away from a view of due process as protection against government arbitrariness and toward due process as a tool for fact-finding in disputes involving specifically, and relatively narrowly, defined legal rights. This distinction is aptly described in Laurence Tribe's discussion of the intrinsic and instrumental approaches to due process.[74] The intrinsic approach uses relatively specific procedures not merely to protect the interests of a particular individual in a specific case in a correct decision regarding well-established liberty or property rights but also to provide a sense of legitimacy in quasi-judicial decisions by permitting those adversely affected by a government decision to participate in the process by which their situation is determined. More generally, the procedures are used to provide a mechanism as a check on government to prevent arbitrariness. The instrumental approach holds that due process is properly understood as a set of techniques used to arrive at accurate decisions in a particular type of decision, namely, one in which a citizen can demonstrate particular injury to a well-defined legal right, specifically, a liberty or property right. In fact, these two approaches are different poles on a continuum along which different justices would quite likely space themselves. The movement of the Court from the intrinsic side to the instrumental took some time, but can be considered to have begun with *Board of Regents v. Roth* in 1972 and became firm around 1975, when the Burger Court was fully established.[75] It was established as a new standard for due process requirements in *Mathews v. Eldridge* in 1976, a standard which continues to be controlling some three decades later.[76]

David Roth was an assistant professor of political science at Wisconsin State University at Oshkosh. Like most young professors, he was hired on a year-to-year contract until he was able to qualify for tenure. Before the end of his first year, however, Roth was informed that he would not be rehired. Roth claimed that the refusal to grant another contract, which was to all intents and purposes termination of his employment, was based on Roth's criticism of the university and in particular of its summary suspension of a number of minority students. Under university rules, the college was not required to tell Roth why his contract would not be renewed or to give him a hearing at which he could present his arguments. He sued the state authorities, contending that the due process clause of the Fourteenth Amendment gave him a right to a hearing at which he could show that he had been terminated for exercising his First Amendment right to freedom of speech. If he could establish that this was indeed the cause, previous cases barred the university from terminating him. The federal district court agreed with Roth's request for a hearing, and its decision was affirmed by the court of appeals. The Supreme Court was divided but reversed the lower courts. In a five-to-three decision (Justice

Powell did not participate), the Court concluded that Roth had not identified a liberty or property right that entitled him to a hearing.

The Court held that there are two parts to judging a case that involves a procedural due process claim to a hearing. First, it must be determined that the plaintiff has a liberty or property interest sufficient to demonstrate that he or she is entitled to procedural due process. Only if that initial finding is made does one get to the question of what kind of process is due.

> The requirements of procedural due process apply only to the deprivation of interests encompassed by the Fourteenth Amendment's protection of liberty and property. When protected interests are implicated, the right of some kind of prior hearing is paramount. But the range of interests protected by procedural due process is not infinite.[77]

Notwithstanding its recognition that the definition of the interests that are constitutionally protected is difficult, and given the fact "that the property interests protected by procedural due process extend well beyond ownership of real estate, chattels, or money,"[78] the Court set limits on these concepts of protected rights as they applied to Roth and, ultimately, others in future cases.

Given past precedents, Roth's liberty interests might have been implicated if, for example, the state made "any charge against him that might seriously damage his standing and associations in the community. It did not base the nonrenewal of his contract on a charge, for example, that he had been guilty of dishonesty or immorality. Had it done so this would be a different case."[79] And, the Court added, "there is no suggestion that the State, in declining to re-employ the respondent, imposed on him a stigma or other disability that foreclosed his freedom to take advantage of other employment opportunities."[80] Since Roth could not show such an injury, he was not entitled to due process.

But if he were able to identify a property right, he might qualify:

> Certain attributes of "property" interests protected by procedural due process emerge from these decisions. To have a property interest in a benefit, a person clearly must have more than a unilateral expectation of it. He must, instead, have a legitimate claim of entitlement to it....
>
> Property interests, of course, are not created by the Constitution. Rather, they are created and their dimensions are defined by existing rules or understandings that stem from an independent source such as state law-rules or understandings that secure certain benefits and that support claims of entitlement to those benefits.
>
> Just as the welfare recipients' "property" interest in welfare payments was created and defined by statutory terms, so the respondent's "property" interest in employment at Wisconsin State University–Oshkosh was created and defined by the terms of his appointment....In these circumstances, the respondent surely had an abstract concern in being rehired, but he did not have a property interest sufficient to require the university authorities to give him a hearing when they declined to renew his contract of employment.[81]

Thus Roth had no right to a hearing. The narrower instrumental approach to procedural due process has guided most of the Court's decisions since 1974–75.

The dissenters in *Roth,* Justices Brennan, Douglas, and Marshall, argued that the narrow instrumental approach misunderstands the meaning and importance of due process. William Van Alstyne summarized the criticisms of *Roth* and later rulings:

> The two-step inquiry of Mr. Justice Stewart in *Roth* may seem to have the advantage of settled authority, but only to those who started reading cases in 1972. The fact is...that *Roth* was itself a wholly unprecedented case—no case prior to that time had even hinted at *Roth's* wizened view that liberty in a free society can be conceived as something having nothing to do with fundamental fairness of how facts are determined and standards applied in the Administrative State. Indeed, as others have noted, the *Roth* approach is shot through with anomalies.
>
> First, the plaintiff must overcome the often insurmountable burden of *Roth-Arnett-Bishop* challenge to show in what sense he was vested with a substantive property interest greater than

that circumscribed by the procedural restrictions laid upon it. He may utterly fail in this endeavor . . . although it be true, even as the Court will concede, that the administrative decision mistaken and the loss to the individual is grievous. Yet failing at this stage amount of grievous loss and no degree of probable mistake entitle him to even trivial adjudicative due process. Anomalously, however, no matter how trivial the loss in fact may be, if the litigant is able to meet the vested property test, then he will be able to have the matter reconsidered according to due process of law, although under the circumstances that due process may be minimal.*,[82]

A Reemerging Right/Privilege Distinction and the Return of the Irrebuttable Presumption

Parallel, and in some respects related, to the shift in the Supreme Court away from broad readings of the due process hearing requirement is a shift toward reinstituting the right/privilege dichotomy. Two examples make the point. The first concerns a person claiming due process rights against an irrebuttable presumption. Mrs. Salfi was married to her husband for only a month before he suffered a heart attack. He was by all accounts well before they were married, with no history of heart disease or any other significant malady. He was hospitalized for several months following the attack and died, leaving his wife and her two children by a previous marriage. Mrs. Salfi applied for Social Security survivor's benefits, but her claim was rejected on the basis of an irrebuttable presumption that a spouse married to an insured person than nine months before the death of the insured married solely to take advantage of the benefits. Salfi demanded a hearing, under the due process clause of the Fifth Amendment, at which she might prove that there was no possible way that she could have known of her husband's impending demise when they were married.

Writing for the Court, Justice Rehnquist upheld the presumption. "Unlike the claim in *Stanley* [the claim of deprivation of parental rights without a hearing] . . . a noncontractual claim to receive funds from the treasury enjoys no constitutionally protected status."[83] If Salfi has a claim to a hearing, it must be because of a deprivation of liberty or property. *Roth* had defined liberty narrowly so as not to include the idea that any arbitrary government action that meant grievous harm to a particular citizen required a hearing. Therefore, if Salfi had a claim it must be because of a property interest. But *Roth* had ruled that property interests are created and defined by statute and this statute authorized no hearing. With regard to irrebuttable presumptions, the argument is obviously circular.

Both the affirmation of the presumption and the statement that benefit claims enjoy "no constitutionally protected status" were significant departures from earlier rulings. The effect was to treat the Salfi claim more in the nature of a request for a privilege rather than as a request by a citizen for rectification of arbitrary government action.

Bishop v. Wood[84] was another example that suggested the reemergence of the right/privilege dichotomy. The language of the case is quite similar to the old overruled view that employment is a privilege. The case was also important because it further limited the meaning of liberty under the due process clause, holding that harm to one's reputation may not be sufficient to require a hearing.

Carl Bishop, a policeman who was classified as "a permanent employee" (as opposed to a probationary employee), was fired by the city manager of Marion, North Carolina. Though he was later informed that he had been fired for alleged "failure to follow certain orders, poor attendance at police training classes, causing low morale, and conduct unsuited to an officer,"[85] he was not accorded a hearing. Bishop and other policemen filed affidavits denying the allegations. Bishop argued that under

---

*From William Van Alstyne, "Cracks in 'The New Property': Adjudicative Due Process in the Administrative State," *62 Cornell L. Rev. 489–90 (1977)*. Copyright © 1977 by Cornell University; all rights reserved. Used by permission of *Cornell Law Review,* William Van Alstyne, and Fred B. Rothman and Company.

Roth and other cases he had a property interest and a liberty interest that supported his claim to be heard.

Bishop claimed that his firing for cause would bring him into disrepute and severely injure his chances for future employment as a police officer. Whether the reasons had been made public or not, he would be known as having been fired from the police department. Further, any potential employer would be informed of the reasons for his termination. Since he had had no opportunity to defend himself, the charges would be accepted as true. The Supreme Court ruled against Bishop.

By 1976, the Court had shifted its approach to such issues dramatically since 1971, when it decided *Wisconsin v. Constantineau.*[86] Under a Wisconsin statute a local sheriff had posted a notice at all establishments selling liquor in his county that Norma Grace Constantineau was not to be sold any liquor, under penalty of law. She had been given no hearing at which to learn the basis for this action, which presumably would be taken by all to mean that she abused alcohol, nor had she been given any opportunity to defend herself. The Court wrote:

> Where a person's good name, reputation, honor, or integrity is at stake because of what the government is doing to him notice and an opportunity to be heard are essential. "Posting" under the Wisconsin Act may to some be merely the mark of an illness, to others it is a stigma, an official branding of a person. The label is a degrading one. Under the Wisconsin Act, a resident of Hartford is given no process at all. This appellee was not afforded a chance to defend herself. She may have been the victim of an official's caprice. Only when the whole proceedings leading to the pinning of an unsavory label on a person are aired can oppressive results be prevented.[87]

That broad protection against official labeling changed in 1976 when the Court decided *Paul v. Davis.*[88] A local sheriff circulated flyers to merchants identifying Davis and others of being "active shoplifter[s]." Davis had never been convicted of such a crime. His employer told him to get the problem straightened out or lose his job. Davis sued, claiming that he had been deprived of liberty without due process. The Court disagreed:

> While we have in a number of our prior cases pointed out the frequently drastic effect of the "stigma" which may result from defamation by the government, this line of cases does not establish the proposition that reputation alone, apart from some more tangible interests such as employment, is either "liberty" or "property" by itself sufficient to invoke the procedural protection of the Due Process Clause.[89]

Justice Stevens, writing for a five-to-four majority in *Bishop,* concluded that although the statements made about the policeman were damaging, they were not publicly disclosed. Therefore, no name-clearing hearing was required for the protection of liberty interests. The claim to a property interest was rejected because neither Bishop's contract nor state law guaranteed the policeman a right to a hearing.

The four dissenters argued that this decision misinterpreted previous decisions, undermined the protections of liberty by permitting an employer to stigmatize an employee in future job opportunities as long as the reasons for the firing were not made public, and, finally, undermined protected property interests of non-probationary public employees by dramatically limiting the definition of property interests to the statutory language. As Justice Brennan correctly observed, "the Court's approach is a resurrection of the discredited rights/privileges distinction."[90]

In a much later ruling, the Court rejected a claim by a clinical psychologist who had resigned from a position that a supervisor had, allegedly with malicious intent, written a letter to his future employer undermining his employment opportunity. He ultimately lost his job because of it. Even so, the Court, relying on *Paul v. Davis,* found that there was no due process protection available though he might possibly be able to sue the author of the letter for defamation.[91] The dissenters found the Court's position absurd since not only was there a possible loss of the ability to gain employment but a loss of government employment job that the man then held. Justice Marshall wrote: "The loss in Siegert's case is particularly tragic because his professional specialty appears to be one very difficult to practice outside of government institutions. The majority's callous disregard of the real interests at stake in this case is profoundly disturbing."[92]

The Supreme Court pressed the new approach to due process rights in a variety of cases after the shift of the mid-1970s. Several rulings cut back on previously recognizing hearing requirements or halted the expansion of such requirements. They included: a decision upholding an Illinois law permitting drivers' licenses to be revoked without a hearing after three suspensions;[93] an opinion that permits removal of a medical student from a state university without a hearing for reasons other than grades,[94] a decision that school disciplinary actions need not allow any particular protections;[95] and opinions rejecting claims to hearings of particular kinds in prison discipline or transfers,[96] claims for pretermination hearings in disability benefits cases,[97] and demands for pretermination hearings by tenured federal employees and others.[98]

These rulings did not purport directly to overturn the earlier decisions. Indeed, the Court continues to assert that that doctrine of unconstitutional conditions is still very much alive and that it has not reinstated the right/privilege dichotomy. However, at least one of the justices has called upon the Court to admit what any candid observer of the Court's due process rulings of the past two decades would clearly know. By 1990, Justice Scalia thought the trend had gone far enough to state what he regarded as the obvious conclusion:

> I am not sure, in any event, that the right-privilege distinction has been as unequivocally rejected as Justice Stevens supposes. It certainly has been recognized that the fact that the government need not confer a certain benefit does not mean that it can attach any conditions whatever to the conferral of that benefit. But it remains true that certain conditions can be attached to benefits that cannot be imposed as prescriptions upon the public at large. If Justice Stevens chooses to call this something other than a right-privilege distinction, that is fine and good—but it is in any case what explains the nonpatronage restrictions upon federal employees that the Court continues to approve.[99]

Scalia thought that this was a positive development, at least with respect to public employees, and Chief Justice Rehnquist and he were prepared to say so directly. Five years earlier, Rehnquist had written that one who accepts government entitlements of any kind must agree to the conditions that come with them.[100]

Just how far the Court will go in narrowing the range of constitutionally protected interests that will trigger due process rights is unclear. In one of the more recent contributions to the discussion, Justice Scalia once again wrote for the Court. While Chief Justice Rehnquist is gone now, there were echoes of his views on protected interests in Scalia's opinion. He wrote:

> The procedural component of the Due Process Clause does not protect everything that might be described as a "benefit": "To have a property interest in a benefit, a person clearly must have more than an abstract need or desire" and "more than a unilateral expectation of it. He must, instead, have a legitimate claim of entitlement to it." *Board of Regents of State Colleges v. Roth,* .... Such entitlements are "'of course, . . . not created by the Constitution. Rather, they are created and their dimensions are defined by existing rules or understandings that stem from an independent source such as state law.'" *Paul v. Davis.* . . . Our cases recognize that a benefit is not a protected entitlement if government officials may grant or deny it in their discretion.

In a 2005 case, the U.S. Circuit Court of Appeals for the Tenth Circuit, generally regarded as one of the two most conservative circuits in the nation, found that Jessica Gonzales had a protected interest in the enforcement of a restraining order issued by a Colorado court under the authority of a stringent state statute against her former husband sufficient to allow her to pursue an action based on procedural due process.[101] State law had made clear, according to the district and circuit courts, that she had a due process protected interest in the enforcement of the order. It was not enforced and she was not afforded an opportunity even to be seriously heard on the need for its enforcement. The result was tragic in that the man murdered Gonzales's three daughters. Nevertheless, the Supreme Court reversed, finding no protected interest cognizable under the due process clause.[102]

As the discussion of the *Salfi* case earlier suggested, the Burger and Rehnquist Courts have indicated a greater willingness than before to allow the use of irrebuttable presumptions and the circuit courts have generally applied that narrowed test to any cases that do not specifically raise a constitutionally protected fundamental right.[103] The approach is to require only that the classification be rationally related to a legitimate state purpose and not be invidiously discriminatory.[104]

These developments should not be understood to mean that due process is any less important in public administration than before, whether it involves citizens affected by governmental decisions or employees facing critical decisions about their career. Notwithstanding the efforts by the Supreme Court to limit the legal requirements of due process significantly since the mid-1970s, it remains important both because of the need for effective fact-finding processes and because there is a need to address the wider legitimacy issues that were so much a part of the evolution of administrative law. These changes in legally mandated standards of due process should not signal a retreat from the proposition that administrative adjudicative decisions ought to embody fundamental fairness, which is generally obtained by using at least minimal procedural due process techniques.

Apart from these fundamental questions, administrative adjudications are mandated by a host of provisions. Even though constitutional claims to due process protections have been discouraged, there remain many statutes, regulations, and contracts that require various elements of procedural due process. It therefore remains important to address the questions raised at the beginning of the chapter about the nature and management of administrative adjudications.

IS A HEARING DUE?

In general, a person facing an adjudicative or quasi-judicial decision is entitled to a hearing if a statute, a regulation, a contract, a properly implemented treaty,[105] or the Constitution requires it. If the enabling act of the agency or the particular statute in question and the associated regulations do not specifically require a hearing, if the person who is the target of agency action contends the hearing comes too late in the decision process, or if he or she finds the hearing inadequate, he or she may argue that the due process clause of the Constitution requires more procedural protections from the agency.

If the argument is that the due process clause of the Fifth Amendment (for federal government action) or the Fourteenth Amendment (for state or local proceedings) requires more procedural protections than are provided by the statutes involved or agency regulations that go beyond the statutory requirements, the next step is to apply the *Mathews v. Eldridge* balancing test. Under the *Eldridge* standard, in order to determine whether more, different, or earlier due process protections are required, a reviewing court is to consider:

> . . . first, the private interest that will be affected by the official action; second, the risk of an erroneous deprivation of such interest through the procedure used, and the probable value, if any, of additional or substitute safeguards; and, finally, the Government's interest, including the function involved and the fiscal and administrative burdens that the additional or substitute procedural requirements would entail.[106]

As the previous discussion of the trends in the Burger and Rehnquist era indicated, the types of interest considered adequate to demand constitutional protection have narrowed over time. Traditionally, one could claim a due process right to a hearing under the Constitution of one were "condemned to suffer grievous loss" to protected interests.[107] But, as the Court held in *Roth,* "the requirements of procedural due process apply only to the deprivation of interests encompassed by the Fourteenth Amendment's protection of liberty and property."[108] Therefore, the claimed interests must be defined in each case. Property interests are perhaps broader than standard views of real property, and may include such matters as receipt of public benefits once one has qualified or, in some cases, public employment where statutes, regulations, or contracts establish tenure rights. In general, however, such property interests are limited as defined by the statutes involved.[109] Liberty interests may be asserted as the basis of a demand for a hearing where one claims protection of specific Bill of Rights guarantees, such as protection against having children removed from one's custody,[110] or where liberty is deprived by holding a person up to public scorn or ridicule[111] or acting in a manner that injures the person's opportunities to find future employment.[112]

If the court determines that the liberty or property interest for which protection is claimed is adequately supported, it will seek to determine how much and what kind of protections are necessary and how much such procedures will improve the accuracy of decisionmaking. This second part of the Eldridge standard addresses "the risk of an erroneous deprivation of such interest through the procedure used" and, if it appears that the fact-finding process is flawed, "the probable value, if any, of additional or substitute safeguards."

When and if a challenger establishes a protected interest and the importance of added protection, the balancing portion of the *Eldridge* test is triggered which entails a consideration of "the Government's interest, including the function involved and the fiscal and administrative burdens that the additional or substitute procedural requirements would entail." Since a requirement for a hearing, or for more formal procedures where some kind of hearing is already available, almost always means increased costs and administrative burdens, it is clear that the balance will most often tend to weigh in favor of the administrator.

However, there are several problems with balancing tests, as Justice Hugo Black was fond of pointing out, such that while public managers may be pleased at the move to a less expansive approach to the requirements for hearings, they should not assume that they will prevail in any given situation. Black pointed to two ongoing problems with balancing tests.[113] The first is the fact that the balance is often incorrectly set. As Black noted, the appropriate question is often not the burdens or dangers to the society versus the burdens or constraints on the individual. The real balance is between the burdens on society from additional safeguards versus the danger to society from the lack such safeguards. The second reality is that one cannot know the outcome of a judicial balancing test until a court has decided the case. Nevertheless, the *Eldridge* test has remained the constitutional standard for more than three decades.

WHEN IS A HEARING DUE?

The American theory of procedural due process requires that one be accorded notice and a hearing before and not after one suffers at the hands of government. But how does one know when that point is reached? Frequently, the right to a hearing is presented in terms of entitlement to hearing before final action by the government. But what is final agency action? There are at least two answers, one practical and one legally defined. In practical terms, the government has acted when the consumer of administrative action is actually affected, e.g., when his paycheck stops or his disability payments cease. In legal terms, the action is final when the decision process in the agency, which may involve a number of steps, is completed. The *Eldridge* case study discussed this problem in detail, but consider one example.

Consider the case of a tenured public employee who concluded that his supervisor was engaged in illegal practices. In fact, he charged him with extortion on grounds that the employee believed the supervisor had threatened a group with denial of a federal grant unless they assisted him politically and financially. He made his charges known to agency officials. The official sent a letter indicating that he was to be dismissed for the "efficiency of the service." The employee was told that he had 30 days to respond in writing to the dismissal and that he could speak with the supervisor concerning the termination. He wrote a letter objecting to being fired, but the supervisor indicated that he would not change his mind. He indicated that the employee was free, after termination, to pursue an administrative appeal that might eventually culminate in a hearing before an administrative law judge or panel. In this case, the employee was fired for cause, including allegedly false and abusive accusations. No one doubted that, as a tenured public employee, he was entitled to be heard at some point; the question was whether he had to be accorded a hearing before his pay and benefits were terminated. The government argued that its decision in his case would not come to the hearing stage until a number of other administrative steps had been taken. He had been informed by his superior in writing of the allegations against him, to which he could respond in writing. Following that, he could be terminated although a review of the decision would continue. At the end of the agency review process, the terminated employee could obtain a full hearing before an independent decisionmaker. If he prevailed, he would be reinstated with back pay. The employee answered that since the government average for reaching the hearing stage was approximately 11 months, he and his family would be deprived of income and health care benefits as well as be saddled with the stigma of being fired without having an opportunity to be heard. A fragmented Supreme Court managed to get five justices to agree that so long as the employee got a hearing at some point before the final decision to terminate him was made, due process was satisfied, even though that decision came after his paycheck stopped.[114] Although the Court indicated that if a delay was long enough there might come a point at which due process would mandate action, no guidance was provided as to just how long that would be and, given the facts in the case, it would clearly be more than a year.

This case arose early in the process in which the Court was reversing the earlier trend toward greater due process protection. After a decade of decisions in that direction, a similar case came to the Court known as *Cleveland Bd. of Ed. v. Loudermill*.[115] While Justice White, writing for the Court, was unwilling to acknowledge a reimposition of the right/privilege dichotomy, he did maintain that the Court would impose a broad balancing process to determine whether and what kind of process was due. Moreover, the Court left no doubt that the balance was to be made with particular sensitivity to the needs of government supervisors.

> Here, the pretermination hearing need not definitively resolve the propriety of the discharge. It should be an initial check against mistaken decisions—essentially, a determination of whether there are reasonable grounds to believe that the charges against the employee are true and support the proposed action....The essential requirements of due process, and all that respondents seek or the Court of Appeals required, are notice and an opportunity to respond. The opportunity to present reasons, either in person or in writing, why proposed action should not be taken is a fundamental due process requirement....The tenured public employee is entitled to oral or written notice of the charges against him, an explanation of the employer's evidence, and an opportunity to present his side of the story....To require more than this prior to termination would intrude to an unwarranted extent on the government's interest in quickly removing an unsatisfactory employee.[116]

The Court was willing to allow such an informal pretermination proceeding on grounds that at some point there would be an opportunity for a post-termination hearing. However, while the Court recognized that "at some point, a delay in the post-termination hearing would become a constitutional violation,"[117] it gave no guidance as to when that point would be reached. In the *Loudermill* case, the employee did not receive a post-termination hearing until two and a half months after he made his appeal and did not receive a decision for another six and a half months. The Ohio statute under which that process was conducted contained no time limit of any kind.[118] Nevertheless, the Court found that the nine month delay did not violate due process requirements.[119]

These cases, the *Eldridge* decision, and others rendered after the shift in the Court's approach to administrative due process make it clear that in deciding at what point in the administrative decision process a hearing is required, the Court will weigh the cost, administrative burden, and possible harm to the government against the cost and harm to the consumer of the decision. For example, the Court would not require pretermination hearings for Social Security benefits in *Eldridge* or for the non-probationary employee in *Arnett,* but it refused to overturn a requirement for pretermination hearings for welfare recipients on the grounds that their loss outweighs the increased cost in time and money to the government since they may very well have no resources to press their claim through the entire decision process.

WHAT KIND OF HEARING IS NEEDED?

Assuming one is entitled to a hearing at some point in the decision process, what does a hearing look like? The answer is in three parts. First, what are the various forms of hearings? Second, what kind of hearing must be accorded in a particular agency? Third, will these hearing processes be preempted by some form of alternative dispute resolution technique?

The forms in which consumers of administrative decisions may be heard vary from what have been referred to as "full-blown trial-type hearings" to "paper hearings." One might classify administrative hearings into four types, ranging from the least to the most formal. All are directed to the resolution of a dispute over a decision that has government sanction and that decides the legal status or entitlements of a specific citizen or group.

First, there are alternative dispute resolution (ADR) techniques. These techniques will be addressed in more detail in Chapter 8. For the present, however, ADR is based on the idea that agreements voluntarily arrived at and mutually agreed on are preferable to adversary proceedings, in which there is a winner on whose behalf an edict is imposed on the loser.[120] Government officials and those in the private sector have for more than two decades pressed for the increased use of negotiation, conciliation, arbitration, ombudsmen, restorative justice programs, and other alternatives to standard adjudications.[121] Even where there will be a more or less formal adjudication, prehearing conferences are often held to attempt to reach settlement or at least to limit the range of disagreements. The APA encourages such practices: "The agency shall give all interested parties opportunity for. . .the submission and consideration of facts, arguments, offers of settlement, or proposals of adjustment when the time, the nature of the proceedings, and the public interest permit."[122] Indeed, both Congress and the White House formally advocated increased use of ADR with the adoption of the Administrative Dispute Resolution Act.[123]

Second, in some areas it is acceptable to use a procedure known as a paper hearing.[124] All the evidence and arguments are submitted in writing, with no oral arguments contemplated. Paper hearings are like the process known as summary judgment in other areas of the law. Where there is no material dispute over the facts or the facts can be adequately determined by an examination of documentary evidence, actual hearings may not be considered necessary. Arguments on questions of law may be resolved by submission of legal briefs, memoranda, or even simple letters. The chief advantage of a paper hearing is the saving of both time and expense for the agency and the consumer.

There are many problems with paper adjudications, a few of which are examined in detail in the *Eldridge* case study in Appendix 1. That is particularly true when the consumer of the decision is without legal counsel. Other difficulties arise when, for one reason or another, the record in matter is poorly prepared (examples of which are discussed in the *Eldridge* case study.) It is also true when questions that appear at the outset to be clear and relatively simple turn out to be very complex. For example, in a disability case, like that discussed in *Eldridge,* the claimant's physician is required to submit his or her findings on the claimant's disability. This has often been done with a letter or summary statement stating that, in the doctor's view, the claimant is unable to perform his normal occupation. But the agency requires detailed clinical findings describing the specific problems that render the claimant completely disabled and unfit to perform any gainful employment. A further complicating factor has in some cases related to the fact that a number of foreign-born and trained physicians practice in rural communities in the United States and some have sometimes had difficulty communicating their findings and conclusions in the kind of specialized administrative terminology, sometimes referred to derisively as *Bureauspeak,*[125] that the agency requires. For these and many other reasons, it should not be surprising that each time Mr. Eldridge filed and paper submissions were reviewed, his claim was denied, but each time he was afforded an oral hearing at which he could appear and give testimony, he prevailed.

Discussions about the usefulness and difficulties of paper hearings generally take an instrumental approach to due process. That is, given the savings in time and money, is it possible to avoid oral hearings and still make accurate adjudicative decisions? The results of such analyses are mixed, but there is still more to be considered. The intrinsic importance of providing a measure of face-to-face due process exists both because the courts have recognized the changing governmental context and the history of abuses when adequate due process protections were not provided and because the legitimacy of government action is strengthened when a citizen is permitted, even in very informal proceedings, to tell his or her story before the decisionmaker.

The third type of hearing might be referred to as a simple oral hearing, not necessarily in a trial-like setting, perhaps no more than an opportunity to be told by an administrator why some particular action is being taken and given a chance to object and provide reasons. Such a process gives the consumer of the decision the opportunity to convince the decisionmaker, provides the cathartic effect of telling one's story, and preserves the option for later redress since the exchange can be the basis for a later dispute to recompense the consumer for injury.[126]

An example of the need for this type of due process came about when several children were suspended from school for allegedly participating in an illegal assembly at another school. They were not afforded an opportunity to tell their side of the story even though they asserted that they were nowhere near the other school at the time and could prove it. Their loss of education, possible harm to grade averages, public embarrassment, and potential harm based on school records showing a suspension were deemed sufficient to require some kind of due process. The Supreme Court held that the Constitution requires some minimal due process protection for children suspended from school for ten days or more, or for other similarly stern disciplinary measures. Fears that the Court would require formal trial-type hearings have been rejected in later decisions.

> In *Goss v. Lopez,*...we held that due process requires, in connection with the suspension of a student from public school for disciplinary reasons, "that the student be given oral or written notice of charges against him and, if he denies them, an explanation of the evidence the authorities have and an opportunity to present his side of the story....All that Goss required was an informal give-and-take between the student and the administrative body dismissing him that would, at least, give the student the opportunity to characterize his conduct and put it in what he deems the proper context.[127]

Finally, the Court had for many years concluded that important actions that could inflict grievous loss require trial-type hearings, which, although not nearly as formal as court trials, require the standard minimum elements of due process.[128] In the last analysis, the *Mathews v. Eldridge* three-part standard is invoked to determine the adequacy of hearing processes where someone claims that the requirements of relevant statutes and regulations do not provide sufficient procedural protections.

WHAT ARE THE ESSENTIAL ELEMENTS OF AN ADMINISTRATIVE HEARING?

As this chapter has indicated, just what process is due in any particular case, when it is due, and what general form it must take vary considerably. So, too, the elements of a hearing vary from agency to agency, depending on the requirements of the agency's enabling legislation, treaty obligations, the particular act being enforced, agency regulations, contractual obligations, and judicial interpretations of the Constitution and statutes applicable to the agency. However, under the APA (and its state-level counterparts), a number of general characteristics of administrative adjudicatory hearings apply broadly and are required of most federal and state agencies. These provide the traditional due process requirements of notice, an opportunity to be heard, to submit evidence on one's behalf, and to challenge opposing evidence, and a hearing before an impartial decisionmaker who will render a reasoned decision on the record that may be challenged on appeal.

Notice

The APA describes the basic requirements of a hearing in §§554, 555, 556, and 557. The first requirement of an adjudication is that the person involved should be notified of the nature and progress of the proceeding. "An elementary and fundamental requirement of due process in any proceeding which is to be accorded finality is notice reasonably calculated, under all the circumstances, to appraise interested parties of the pendency of the action and afford them an opportunity to present their objections."[129]

Of particular importance are the adequacy of the notice, the timeliness of the information, and the proper distribution of the notice. As to adequacy, the APA requires that: "Persons entitled to notice of an agency hearing shall be timely informed of: (1) the time, place, and nature of the hearing; (2) the legal authority and jurisdiction under which the hearing is to be held; and (3) the matters of fact and law asserted."[130] Notice must be "timely," that is, it must afford interested parties sufficient time to prepare. How much time is required may vary considerably. Perhaps the most difficult question is the proper distribution of notice. Who must be notified and in what form? The named parties must be personally informed, usually by mail. Other interested parties may be sufficiently notified by constructive notice, or by notice in newspapers of general circulation.

For many years, the assumption has been that notice is the least problematic part of due process, since it is a well-understood concept and the means for providing legal notice have been used regularly for so long. Perhaps ironically, there is a tension at work that cautions against taking notice requirements lightly. For the average person, the danger is that, in the flood of information that he or she receives in many forms on a daily basis, it is easy to mistake or misunderstand a form or perhaps just a postcard that arrives in the mail. Many Americans assume that before anything serious can be done to them, they will be contacted in person. Unless they are educated about what it means to be notified by an agency and how that kind of notice arrives, the people affected may not recognize or understand what the notice means or what it requires. Indeed, some have the mistaken idea that government agencies must prove that the individual who faces an adjudication actually received the notice and understands their specific legal obligations. However, as the Supreme Court explained in a case brought by a person who claimed he could have been easily notified since he was in custody, far less is often required:

> We note that none of our cases. . .has required actual notice in proceedings such as this. Instead, we have allowed the Government to defend the "reasonableness and hence the constitutional validity of any chosen method. . .on the ground that it is in itself reasonably certain to inform those affected." . . .
>
> . . . Undoubtedly the Government could make a special effort in any case (just as it did in the movie "Saving Private Ryan") to assure that a particular piece of mail reaches a particular individual who is in one way or another in the custody of the Government. . . . But the Due Process Clause does not require such heroic efforts by the Government; it requires only that the Government's effort be "reasonably calculated" to apprise a party of the pendency of the action. . . .[131]

Perhaps ironically, this lack of awareness of official communications by many citizens can also be a difficulty for the agency involved, since those affected may not respond with the necessary information in a timely fashion, leading to later misunderstandings and disputes. Yet another difficulty is that programs such as Medicare, Social Security disability, or veterans' benefits involve large numbers of participants, including some people who have physical, developmental, or mental health challenges, including a large number of elderly senior citizens such that standard methods of notification are not adequate. For example, a Vietnam veteran with serious physical and mental health challenges, including schizophrenia, applied for and received Social Security disability benefits for some time before he was sent a notification that those benefits were going to be terminated. The man did not have any legal representation or legal guardian who would have understood what had to be done to appeal the decision. It was years later that those helping the man discovered what had happened to him and took action to restore benefits as well as to recover the benefits the man had lost over time. The Social Security Administration had since destroyed the records in the case and ultimately denied the claim for recovery of the past benefits. However, the circuit court of appeals overturned that decision: "[W]e hold that Udd has established that he lacked the mental capacity. . .to understand the cessation of his disability benefits and to take the steps necessary to pursue an appeal. The termination of his benefits without meaningful notice thus constituted a denial of due process."[132] It is therefore important for administrators to consider the population they serve in order to ensure effective and adequate notice.

Additionally, notice questions arise when others may be involved in an administrative adjudication apart from the agency and the particular party with a case pending. In licensing proceedings, e.g., those involving broadcasters[133] or power plant facilities,[134] there may be others who assert a sufficiently strong interest in the outcome of the decision to be included in the hearing process. Notice that is not adequately distributed to ensure that all parties with protected interests are made aware of the hearing can jeopardize the integrity of the proceeding. That is particularly true where the resolution of the claims of one party may be dispositive of the claims of others who have not been specifically included in the process. Where an agency seeks to resolve an issue through settlement with a party who is potentially in dispute with that agency, there is a risk that the desire for a settlement may tempt those directly involved not to complicate matters by providing notice to others. Congress was sufficiently aware of this problem when it enacted the Alternative Dispute Resolution Act that the statute indicated ADR was not appropriate where "the matter significantly affects persons or organizations who are not parties to the proceeding."[135]

Interested parties who wish to participate but are not the primary or named parties are generally referred to as "intervenors." In general, federal agencies have come to deal with the problem of notice to intervenors by maintaining notification lists that contain the names of likely participants in actions pending on an agency's docket. Given contemporary technology, agencies often operate e-mail listservs for the purpose.

Of course, the discussion of the use of e-mails as a means of notice raises as many questions as it solves for both legal and technological reasons. There is currently an ongoing discussion about the increasing tendency to seek judicial approval to use electronic notice as a primary mechanism of notice. In an article with the e-age title: "You've Got Mail: The Modern Trend Towards Universal Electronic Service of Process," Jeremy Colby explained the foundations and directions of the use of e-mail to provide notice.[136] He noted that the first federal court approval of the use of e-mail notice came in a bankruptcy case in Georgia in 2000[137] and the first circuit court of appeals decision to uphold the practice came later that same year.[138] Since then, there have been a number of rulings at the district court level to uphold the process, but the case law on electronic notice in administrative law is still to be developed.[139] It is as yet still not certain how widely electronic notice will be used in the public law context or what safeguards will be put in place to address a host of obvious problems from the digital divide. Possible problems range from unequal access to the Internet and e-mail to the use of electronic signatures to verify delivery of the notice, as well as the simple fact that so many people and organizations change their e-mail addresses and Internet URL locations so often that ensuring accurate information for communications may be difficult.

This set of notice issues has already been significantly shaped by the fact that the Internet is one of the key forces of globalization. Internet businesses and firms doing business in the United States but located elsewhere have already prompted new concerns about how to issue notice to such organizations from those in the U.S. bringing one or another type of legal action.[140]

The Hearing

An oral hearing allows one to present evidence, to challenge adverse evidence, to present an argument as to the proper interpretation of the evidence and the law, and to petition for particular kinds of relief. The Administrative Procedure Act and other sources of administrative law acknowledge and seek to implement these objectives. The APA provides that where parties are unable to reach a conclusion to the proceeding "by consent, a hearing is to be held in accordance with §§556 and 557 of the act."[141] Further, "in fixing the time and place for hearings, due regard shall be had for the convenience and necessity of the parties or their representatives."[142] "A party is entitled to present his case or defense by oral or documentary evidence, to submit rebuttal evidence, and to conduct such cross-examination as may be required for a full and true disclosure of the facts."[143] Recognizing the complexity of the adjudicatory process, the APA provides that: "A person compelled to appear in person before an agency or representative therefore is entitled to be accompanied, represented, and advised by or with counsel or other duly qualified representative. A party is entitled to appear in person or by or with counsel or other duly qualified representative in an agency proceeding."[144] The government is not, however, required to provide counsel at the public expense.[145] In fact, there have even been rulings that have upheld obvious attempts to discourage the use of attorneys.[146]

If the agency has subpoena authority granted by statute, "agency subpoenas authorized by law shall be issued to a party on request and, when required by rules of procedure, on a statement or showing of general relevance and reasonable scope of the evidence sought."[147] That is, one may seek the agency's help under its power to issue subpoenas in order to prepare one's case. However, since agencies do not have the power to hold someone in contempt, which is the normal manner in which subpoenas are enforced, they must go to court to ask the court to enforce a subpoena if cooperation is not immediately forthcoming from a person or organization holding evidence.[148] If it comes to that, the APA provides that: "On contest, the court shall sustain the subpoena or similar process or demand to the extent that it is found to be in accordance with law."[149]

At the heart of the hearing process is the presentation of evidence. There are at least two aspects to discussion of evidence in administrative adjudications.[150] First, what evidence is to be admitted into the record for consideration by the decisionmaker? The administrative adjudicatory process was deliberately designed to be more flexible and less formal than a court trial. In particular, because there is no jury, it was intended to allow much less formality in the presentation of evidence. The decisionmaker is a properly trained and experienced evaluator of evidence who is less likely than members of a jury to be misled by weak or improperly presented evidence. For these reasons, the APA provides that: "Any oral or documentary evidence may be received, but an agency as a matter of policy shall provide for the exclusion of irrelevant, immaterial, or unduly repetitious evidence."[151] In general, administrative law judges tend to admit most of the evidence that is offered since his or her decision is less likely to be overturned if proffered evidence is accepted than if evidence was offered and rejected.

The second problem, then, is to determine how all the evidence that is collected is to be evaluated. The APA states: "Except as otherwise provided by statute, the proponent of a rule or order has the burden of proof."[152] "A sanction may not be imposed or rule or order issued except on consideration of the whole record or those parts thereof cited by a party and supported by and in accordance with the reliable, probative, and substantial evidence."[153] The requirement that one consider the whole record is intended to ensure that the decisionmaker consider all the evidence and not merely portions of it that would favor one side. "Substantial evidence" has been interpreted to mean "the kind of evidence on which responsible persons are accustomed to rely in serious affairs."[154] "Probative" evidence is evidence that tends to prove, which is nicely circular.[155] The term "substantial evidence" has been interpreted to require that a decision be supported by a "scintilla" of evidence.[156] To cut the point more carefully, the

Tenth Circuit noted: "This is something more than a mere scintilla but something less than the weight of the evidence....Evidence is generally substantial under the APA if it is enough to justify, if the trial were to a jury, refusal to direct a verdict on a factual conclusion."[157] As Justice Scalia explained the standard for the majority in *Allentown Mack Sales and Service v. National Labor Relations Board*: "[W]e must decide whether on this record it would have been possible for a reasonable jury to reach the Board's conclusion."[158]

It is also important to understand what substantial evidence is not. The Sixth Circuit explained that: "[O]ur review of the ALJ's factual determinations is limited to determining whether those determinations are supported by substantial evidence on the record as a whole—not whether there was substantial evidence in the record for a result other than that arrived at by the ALJ."[159]

In the end, whether the weight of evidence is adequate to support is a matter of judgment. That judgment may be tested on appeal.

Judgment exercised by the administrative law judge in the evaluation of evidence is most severely tested when the decisionmaker must weigh different types of evidence. Probably the best example of this problem arose in *Richardson v. Perales*.[160] To make an extraordinarily long story short, Mr. Perales applied for disability insurance, claiming a back injury. Government physicians examined him and found no disability. Perales sought an agency hearing. Accompanied by his attorney and Dr. Morales, one of his physicians, Perales sought to prove the disability. The government introduced medical reports from the government doctors who did not appear at the hearing. Instead, a physician who had not examined Perales appeared for the government as a consultant to interpret the reports submitted by the other government physicians. Since the reports of the government physicians who had examined Perales were interpreted by another person who had not examined him, the evidence was hearsay rather than direct evidence.

One of the main reasons why hearsay evidence is such a problem is that the sources of evidence are not on hand to be cross-examined. The decisionmaker cannot observe the demeanor of the witness as a key to judging his or her veracity, and no questions can be asked to round out the cold reports. On the other hand, Perales's doctor was present and prepared to face cross-examination.

Perales's attorney argued two points. First, the government's medical consultant should not be permitted to testify since he had no direct knowledge of Perales's condition and hence could not corroborate the hearsay evidence offered by the government in the medical reports. Second, he argued that the government's case was strictly hearsay while Perales offered direct evidence. Therefore, Perales's offers of proof should outweigh the government's.

The Supreme Court held in favor of the government:

> We conclude that a written report by a licensed physician who has examined the claimant and who sets forth his medical findings in his area of competence may be received as evidence in a disability hearing and, despite its hearsay character and an absence of cross-examination, and despite the presence of opposing direct medical testimony and testimony by the claimant himself, may constitute substantial evidence supportive of a finding by the hearing examine adverse to the claimant, when the claimant has not exercised his right to subpoena the reporting physician and thereby provide himself with the opportunity for cross-examination of the physician.[161]

The Court simply stated that it is the duty of the trier of fact, the ALJ in this case, to weigh the evidence and his or her actions are to be guided by the general concern for fundamental fairness.[162]

The Presiding Officer

Some formal hearings are conducted by members of regulatory commissions or high-ranking administrators, but most are done by administrative law judges (ALJ), about whom more will be said in later chapters. Whoever conducts the hearing has essentially four responsibilities: (1) management of the hearing; (2) development of an adequate and properly prepared record; (3) preservation of the integrity of the proceedings; and (4) the rendering of a reasoned decision that is based on the record and is responsive to the claims and arguments of the parties involved.[163] A primary obligation that affects all of the other aspects of the hearing is the protection of the integrity of the proceeding. To aid the decisionmaker in this effort, he or she is granted certain protections by the Administrative Procedure Act against attempts to influence the development of the record or to coerce his or her decision.

The attempt by one party to a case to communicate arguments or information to an ALJ (or other adjudicator) outside the normal hearing process is referred to as an *ex parte* communication. The APA provides procedures for dealing with such attempts at influence and states that the "agency may, to the extent consistent with the interests of justice and the policy of the underlying statutes administered by the agency, consider a violation of section 557 (d) [the *ex parte* communication rules] of this title sufficient grounds for a decision adverse to a party who has knowingly committed such violation or knowingly caused such violation to occur."[164]

The debate over just what kind of remedy courts should impose in *ex parte* communications cases developed out of the strike by the *Professional Air Traffic Controllers' Organization (PATCO)* and the Reagan administration's reaction to it. The government moved to decertify the controllers' union as a legitimate bargaining representative, a matter assigned for decision to the Federal Labor Relations Authority (FLRA). While the case was pending before the FLRA there were two alleged *ex parte* contacts.

The first alleged contact came when Secretary of Transportation Drew Lewis called one of the members of the FLRA. The court later found:

> Secretary Lewis stated that he was not calling about the substance of the PATCO case but wanted Member Frazier to know that, contrary to some news reports, no meaningful efforts to settle the strike were underway. Secretary Lewis also stated that the Department of Transportation would appreciate expeditious handling of the case.[165]

The Secretary later called another member of the FLRA. What the members did not know at the time was that the union was preparing to argue for more time to prepare its case with respect to a number of critical issues. While the Secretary claimed that his call was merely a request for the status of the decision and not an attempt to influence the FLRA, the union charged that it was a blatant and damaging *ex parte* communication.

The complaint on the other side did not involve PATCO directly but the behavior of another labor leader. Another FLRA member, Mr. Applewhaite, was invited to dinner by Albert Shanker, a New York–based labor activist in the educational field. The court described the meeting as follows:

> Although he did not inform Member Applewhaite of his intentions when he made the arrangements, Mr. Shanker candidly admitted that he wanted to communicate directly to Member Applewhaite his sentiments, previously expressed in his public statements, that PATCO should not be severely punished for its strike.[166]

According to the court, toward the end of the dinner, Shanker expressed his view to Applewhaite though he made no threat or promise regarding the outcome of the case.

There was no doubt in the minds of the judges later asked to review the FLRA decertification decision that there had been *ex parte* contact, but the question was what should be done about it. Writing for a three-judge panel of the D.C. Circuit, Judge Edwards concluded that:

> Congress sought to establish common-sense guidelines to govern ex parte contacts in administrative hearings, rather than rigidly defined and woodenly applied rules. The disclosure of ex parte communications serves two distinct interests. Disclosure is important in its own right to prevent the appearance of impropriety from secret communications in a proceeding that is required to be decided on the record. Disclosure is also important as an instrument of

fair decisionmaking; only if a party knows the arguments presented to a decisionmaker can the party respond effectively and ensure that its position is fairly considered.[167]

However, there was also the complex problem of how to fashion a corrective if these principles were violated. The court fashioned the following standard:

> In enforcing this standard a court must consider whether, as a result of improper ex parte communications, the agency's decisionmaking process was irrevocably tainted so as to make the ultimate judgment of the agency unfair, either to an innocent party or to the public interest that the agency was obliged to protect. In making this determination, a number of considerations may be relevant: the gravity of the ex parte communications; whether the contracts may have influenced the agency's ultimate decision; whether the party making the improper contacts benefitted from the agency's ultimate decision; whether the contexts of the communications were unknown to opposing parties, who therefore had no opportunity to respond; and whether vacation of the agency's decision and remand for new proceedings would serve a useful purpose.[168]

Though all three judges expressed their outrage at the kind of conduct that had been displayed in the case, the court applied the above criteria and upheld the FLRA decertification decision. However, while later courts have continued to apply the PATCO ruling as the guiding standard, they have reached very different conclusions on the facts of other cases.[169]

It is commonly the case that a decisionmaker who is the subject of an attempted *ex parte* communication will disqualify himself or herself from participation in the case and will inform appropriate authorities, which might include the Department of Justice in the federal government or the State Attorney General at that level.

As do courts, agencies sometimes go outside the evidence produced by the parties at the hearing for information. This is referred to as taking "official notice" of some well-established fact that is commonly known. However, in such cases the parties do have the right to enter rebuttals to this kind of "official notice."[170]

That said, agencies are not free to use concepts such as official notice or general information gathering processes to avoid the prohibitions against *ex parte* contacts. Consider, for example, the case of the Federal Energy Regulatory Commission's (FERC) creation in 2003 of an exemption in its regulations concerning *ex parte* communications for market monitors. In 2000, the FERC had required all firms involved with transmission of power to join regional transmission organizations (RTOs) and assigned to those RTOs market monitoring responsibilities. They were to provide information to the FERC to

> [E]nsure that markets within the region covered by an RTO do not result in wholesale transactions or operations that are unduly discriminatory or preferential or provide opportunity for the exercise of market power....RTOs can choose to perform the monitoring function themselves or use an independent contractor....Market monitors must report to the Commission objective information about RTO markets, evaluate the behavior of market participants, and recommend how markets can operate more competitively and efficiently....[171]

However, these monitors were clearly private sector actors and they were not managed by the agency. The 2003 changes exempted the monitors from the *ex parte* regulations. The FERC indicated that it would place the market monitor recommendations on the record if and when they had an actual effect on an FERC decision and not otherwise. The agency's efforts amounted to a regulatory amendment of the statutory prohibition against *ex parte* contacts. The D.C. Circuit reversed the FERC action, concluding that: "The Commission is powerless to override Congress' directive banning *ex parte* communications relevant to pending on-the-record proceedings between decisional staff and interested persons outside the agency."[172]

The other area of concern with respect to the integrity of the proceeding is to ensure against efforts by government to pressure decisionmakers or punish them for ruling in favor of claimants. Unlike the *ex parte* contact, which takes place in the context of a particular case, this problem is more general in nature and concerns wider efforts to influence not one case, but types of decisionmaking. This issue produced dramatic clashes during the 1980s and focused on actions taken against Social Security ALJs who were thought to be ruling too frequently in favor of claimants, overturning the initial decisions made by state vocational rehabilitation agencies. A policy was instituted that required such ALJs to be brought in for retraining. The administration argued that this was nothing more than an effort to ensure the proper management of ALJs and provide some kind of accountability. The Association of Administrative Law Judges countered that the administration move was nothing less than a flagrant attempt to intimidate ALJs out of ruling in favor of claimants. They clearly had the better of the case, since it was the declared intention of the administration to reduce the number of persons receiving various social service benefits, including disability, given that specific quotas of adverse decisions were used to trigger adverse actions, and in light of the fact that there were clear justifications for high reversal rates at that time as explained in the *Mathews v. Eldridge* case study. To drive home their point, the ALJs retained no less a Republican luminary and HHS expert than former cabinet secretary Elliot Richardson.

While the case was pending, the administration rescinded the critical elements of the program. For that reason, Judge Green did not enter judgment for the plaintiffs. However, the court concluded:

> [D]efendants unremitting focus on allowance rates. . .created an untenable atmosphere of tension and unfairness which violated the spirit of the APA, if no specific provision there-of. Defendants' insensitivity to that degree of decisional independence the APA affords to administrative law judges and the injudicious use of phrases such as "targeting," "goals," and "behavior modification" could have tended to corrupt the ability of administrative law judges to exercise that independence in the vital cases they decide.[173]

There is authority for the appropriate administrators "to adopt reasonable measures in order to improve the decisionmaking process."[174] On the other hand, "To coerce ALJs into. . .deciding more cases against claimants—would, if shown, constitute. . .'a clear infringement of decisional independence.'"[175]

Finally, it is the obligation of the ALJ to prepare a reasoned decision setting forth the findings of fact and conclusions of law according to the requirements of §557 of the APA. If no appeal is taken from the ALJ ruling, it becomes final.

Administrative Appeal

A hearing will often be conducted by an ALJ on behalf of commissioners or other high agency officials. In that case there may be either an opportunity for one to appeal the decision of the ALJ or, in other situations, an automatic review of his or her decision. The agency may affirm, modify, or reject the ruling, but it must at least consider the ALJ's findings.[176] The reason for this requirement is that the ALJ actually heard the presentation of the case and saw the witnesses. The initial decision was based on more than the cold record. Therefore, while the ALJ ruling is not binding, it is a matter to be considered even by agency heads.

CONTRACTING, CONTEMPORARY GOVERNANCE
TECHNIQUES, AND ISSUES OF ADJUDICATION

Many of these core principles that make up the hearing process and set forth the responsibilities of the decisionmaker, whether it is an ALJ, a licensing board, or the members of an independent regulatory commission, are well established and have been for many years. The basic concern with ensuring fundamental fairness, providing a process that not only is fair but is also seen to be fair has been present for more than a century. However, there are a number of more recent developments above and beyond the trends discussed to this point in the chapter that are often associated with the kinds of contemporary governance models described in Chapter 1. Many of these approaches to disputes involve negotiated or at least less formal alternatives to the adjudicative model described in the APA. Several of these will be discussed in Chapter 8 and concern the various tools of alternative dispute resolution (ADR). Others have to do with the involvement of nongovernmental participants in decisionmaking that is adjudicative in nature, efforts merely to streamline adjudicative processes through movement away from standard requirements expected in procedural due process, or actions taken in what are considered to be emergency situations, such as post-9/11 homeland security matters. Consider first some of the issues associated with contracting and adjudications and then some of the other adjudicative issues related to contemporary governance models.

One of the most important areas of adjudicative change has to do with expansion of government contracting, particularly contracting for services. In addition to the obvious, but nevertheless complex area of disputes that arise between government and its contractors, there have also been developments in such activities as contracted-out adjudications, due process issues related to contract employees of government agencies, and problems arising with respect to due process in contracted-out activities, from day care centers to prisons.[177]

Contractors Adjudicating for the Government

It is increasingly common for agencies to outsource adjudicative decisions. The Congress has sanctioned this practice in such measures as the Personal Responsibility and Work Opportunity Reconciliation Act of 1996, which permitted states to contract out welfare policy implementation to include eligibility determinations.[178] The United States Supreme Court unanimously approved the contracting out by governmental agencies of adjudicative processes, even in a situation in which there was no right of further appeal from the ruling of the private decisionmaker. The *Schweiker v. McClure*[179] case arose out of a challenge to Medicare decisions. Congress authorized the Department of Health and Human Services to contract out Medicare Part B claims adjudications to private insurance carriers.

The company would decide a claim and either pay the requested amount from the Medicare Insurance Trust Fund or deny the claim. If the claimant disputed the decision, another claims person would review the case. In the event that the claimant was still rejected, the person could request a hearing to be held by another employee of the company. No further review, internal or external, was authorized by statute or rules.

The district court found that this process did not provide an impartial decisionmaker and in fact created a situation in which there was "pecuniary interest" by the contractor in selecting hearing officers.[180] The court also challenged the fact that there was not a provision for an external review.

One of the challenges that gave rise to modern administrative law, discussed in Chapter 4, grew out of complaints levied by critics from A. V. Dicey to John Dickinson that important decisions were being made by government about individuals without an opportunity for them to obtain due process in a court of law. These commentators had grave concerns about the dangers to the rule of law and to basic concepts of justice that flowed from placing adjudicative decisions in the hands of administrators rather than judges, people trained to protect individual rights. Instead, these decisions were to be made by people who worked for the very agencies that made the rules and enforced the rules under which the adjudicative proceedings were brought, what Chapter 4 referred to as the combination-of-functions problem. Modern administrative law addressed this issue by (1) creating special protections for administrative law judges' independence and civil service status; (2) encouraging the availability of administrative appeals; and (3) providing external judicial review. The other support was that these public servants were bound by various accountability laws that apply to the public sector and to elected officials in the legislature and the executive branch.

Mandating that citizens submit their disputes with government to decision by private employees, hired and paid by a for-profit contractor and not subject to the accountability laws that apply to public sector officials, presents a range of serious issues. It also raises the very real danger that contractors will see it as in their interest to reduce the number of claims granted to demonstrate their effectiveness on behalf of their contract partner.[181] The fact that no external appeal was available in the Medicare case provides support for those concerns. That these kinds of behaviors can occur has been raised in high relief by the bipartisan support in Congress and the White House for reform of health maintenance organization (HMO) decisionmaking, particularly with respect to a need to address perverse incentives and the lack of independent review of decisions.[182]

Notwithstanding all of these difficulties, the Supreme Court, in an extremely brief opinion, rejected the lower court ruling and upheld the contractor adjudication. It began by admitting that: "The hearing officers involved in this case serve in a quasi-judicial capacity, similar in many respects to that of administrative law judges."[183] And, clearly, "due process demands impartiality on the part of those who function in judicial or quasi-judicial capacities."[184] However, the Court made two assertions. First, if an individual had a claim against a particular decisionmaker, he or she might seek disqualification of that adjudicator on grounds of bias.[185] Second, using the second element of the *Mathews v. Eldridge* standard, the Court found that there was no "risk of erroneous decision" under the contracted system because the contractor would presumably appoint well-qualified people to hear the cases. Therefore, even though the Court was willing to accept that "the additional cost and inconvenience of providing administrative law judges would not be unduly burdensome,"[186] such a step was not required to ensure due process.

Of course, the challenge was not to a particular decisionmaker in the case, but to the process itself. The issue was not simply that a particular hearing officer might be biased but that there are manifold systemic biases in a process where a for-profit firm hired employees at will ("at will" is a term of art that means at the discretion of the hiring authority and without guarantees against termination) with no protections to ensure independence or prevent retribution for rendering decisions the contractor might regard as unfavorable. Besides, since the people hired to be hearing officers were not government employees, there was no way that a claimant can be reasonably expected to have access to information about the possible biases of the decisionmaker. They are not subject to Freedom of Information requests or any other form of ethics law or disclosure requirements. In effect, that Court's ruling said that citizens should trust the contractor.

The Court also indicated that the claimants had not adequately demonstrated that the current decisionmakers were rendering incorrect rulings. That assertion adopted a very narrow instrumental view of due process, one that was developed against a background that assumed all of the other accountability protections available to address decisions made by public agencies. It was also circular, since the fact that there was no independent administrative or judicial review of the claims adjudications meant that there was little or no way to obtain evidence that the Court would ever see as adequate to engage the issue.[187] And there was no discussion of any form of oversight that could be expected to produce evidence as to the possible abuses.

Contracted Activities and Citizens' Claims

The issue of the availability of oversight of the behavior of these private sector contract adjudicators illustrates another dimension of government contracting and due process. It is in many respects unclear just how, when, and to what extent government officials can reach into a contractor's organization to correct abuses by the contractor or discipline inappropriate conduct by the contractor's employees. After all, the advantage of contracting is presumably that government buys the services of the contractor, who is then responsible both for delivering the service and managing its own operations, including the behavior of its employees.

This issue is not limited to the U.S. context. Consider the following two examples, one of which is drawn from a Latin American neighbor and another from a northeastern state in this country.

The central government provides funds for contracts to provide child care services. The contractors are mostly nonprofit organizations of various kinds and sizes spread around the country. One of the contractors was a child care center operated in a local church. During the course of the contract, some parents complained that some of the personnel at the center were in various subtle and not so subtle ways attempting to inculcate their beliefs in the children. Who has responsibility for hearing the parents' grievance, rendering judgment, and implementing remedies? Would it be the manager of the center, the contract agency of the national government, or someone else? What would be the situation if there was no provision in the contract that established complaint procedures or that specifically permitted the government to intervene in the supervision of the center's personnel? In fact, there is nothing in the contract that addresses the kind of conduct criticized by the parents. Is the government required either to wait until the contract period has run or must it take action to terminate the contract before it can act? Who has what adjudicative rights and obligations in this setting?

A northeastern state contracts with various providers that operate facilities for juvenile offenders with psychiatrist disorders. A young man committed to such a facility demanded that he be taken off-site to attend religious services for his particular faith. A manager at the facility refused on grounds that the expense and other difficulties involved in providing security and transportation as well as supervision were not within the contract. The facility also argued that it was not required to provide on-site services for every religious group that might be demanded. The young man and his family contend that the free exercise clause of the First Amendment trumps the contract and someone, somewhere is responsible for meeting his religious needs. Where does the young man's complaint get filed and decided? What kind of process is involved? Does the contractor have adjudicative rights in such a case as well? It is clear that a court would have jurisdiction in a case brought by the parents for violation of the First Amendment, but what authority does the state have to intervene in the operation of the contractor, and what adjudicative process would be required before that could happen? This is, of course, a related but separate issue from the question of differences in the liability of contract employees as compared to civil servants doing the same job, which will be discussed in Chapter 13.[188]

Clearly, these kinds of issues suggest that agencies need to take care in drafting service contracts to address situations in which there may be adjudicative claims. It also means that such contracts need to be as clear as possible about the circumstances and the processes by which the government can intervene in the operation of the contract organization to correct problems. While these demands are important in their own right, they must be addressed against the backdrop of a broader issue. The dilemma is that to the degree that government remains actively involved in the day-to-day operations of the contract organization, including the specific behaviors of its employees, it loses the advantages that contracting was intended to provide. The contract agency then not only must incur the costs and burdens of contract administration, but it must also maintain a direct and detailed involvement in precisely the service it thought it was off-loading to the contractor. Pushed far enough, the contracting organization can lose its independence and the flexibility, which form the basis for its ability to manage efficiently and presumably deliver higher quality service at a lower price than government itself could offer. If that happens, the contractor can become little more than a collection of individual contract employees who have become adjuncts to the government agency, and the contract organization becomes essentially a shell that government uses to house and pay the employees.

Contract Employees and Adjudication

Indeed, many governmental units at all levels have chosen, rather than contracting out to a private organization, simply to hire individuals as contract employees rather than regular civil servants. The private sector initiated this trend in the early 1990s as firms increasingly decided that rather than hiring permanent staff, they would hire the talent they needed as they needed it. In addition to the fact that they did not need to retain large staffs, they also found that hiring individuals as contractors rather than regular employees permitted them to save substantial sums in terms of fringe benefits. They did not have to address medical care or retirement programs, two of the most expensive benefit programs in any organization.

Of course, in the private sector context, the hiring of contract employees is relatively simple, whereas it is much more complex in the public sector context. Public contract law was never designed to be used in such a manner. Even so, it is increasingly common for state agencies to hire individual contractors. The question then arises as to when and whether these contractors are performing functions that implicate adjudicative rights and processes.

Contract Disputes

In addition to all of these relatively recent developments regarding adjudicative implications of contracted out government, there remains the long-standing issue of adjudications in cases of contract disputes. Related tensions go well back in time. Even in the earliest years of the republic, there were debates over how to simultaneously ensure efficiency and protect accountability. In the early disputes, the argument was that efforts to ensure adequate accountability often resulted in late payments to contractors involving not just months but years. The level of complexity and possible litigation expenses also present potential risk factors that private sector organizations must include in their decisionmaking about whether to contract and how to build the added expenses and risk into cost estimates for bid purposes.

There is a separate body of statutes that address contract disputes.[189] However, the separate systems are holdovers from an earlier time in which contracting was primarily focused on the purchasing of goods and where these activities were not closely integrated with direct service delivery to citizens. Now that there is so much contractor involvement in services, the existence of the older dispute processes pose as many difficulties as they solve. The best that can be said at this point is that it will be some time before the law becomes settled in this area.

Contemporary Governance Arrangements
and the Management of Adjudication

As complex as these contract-based adjudications are, the growing use of a wide range of flexible governance arrangements (see Chapter 1) are even more complex than the contract issues alone. Consider the new and significantly different manner in which Medicare adjudications are to be managed, and then brief descriptions of the streamlined Nuclear Regulatory Commission licensing process for nuclear plants and the new process for administering immigration hearings in the post-9/11 context.

Outsourced and Expedited: Centralized, High Technology Adjudication of Medicare Disputes   In April 2005, Robert Pear published a story in the *New York Times* entitled "Medicare Change Will Limit Access to Claim Hearing," which was promptly picked up by a few major newspapers across the nation, but received surprisingly little attention apart from that coverage.[190] Pear reported that the Department of Health and Human Services was about to publish new rules that make it more challenging to obtain a hearing before an ALJ in cases where Medicate claims were rejected. "For years, hearings have been held at more than 140 Social Security offices around the country. In July, the Department of Health and Human Services will take over the responsibility, and department officials said all judges would then be located at just four sites—in Cleveland; Miami; Irvine, Calif.; and Arlington, Va."[191] Anyone who wanted to avoid the videoconference or telephone hearing to obtain a face-to-face hearing would have to meet special requirements and waive the normal 90-day requirement for a decision.

What Pear was reporting was a process that had been underway for some time. Congress required, as part of the Medicare Prescription Drug, Improvement, and Modernization Act of 2003, that adjudications and administrative appeals processes for Medicare claims be moved from the Social Security Administration to the Department of Health and Human Services by October 1, 2005.[192] The idea was to streamline the adjudications process through the use of a limited number of key contract adjudicators and case managers, the widespread use of technology to replace dozens of field offices and individual hearings, and carefully monitored performance standards for those involved in adjudicating claims to ensure efficiency. It also required HHS to prepare a plan for this process that was to be evaluated by the Government Accountability Office so that critical evaluation would be available before HHS moved forward with implementation in 2005.

The GAO issued a critical report in the fall of 2004, laying out the many challenge for HHS and finding that the department's plans were far from complete.[193] It had to hire contractors to handle the basic case adjudications. It also would have to hire and train a core of ALJs who could handle the roughly 122,000 cases a year that were taken from initial claims denial to a hearing process. Although it is referred to as an appeals process, this is an administrative hearing that is the only opportunity for a face-to-face decision process. The so-called appeals process is required to produce a decision within 90 days under the 2003 legislation. Even more complex was the expectation that efficiencies would be realized by having claimants file on the Internet and then resolve their hearings through video-conferences or teleconferences (VTC) that would allow the agency to avoid having its ALJs travel extensively. However, HHS had not fully explained how it was going to ensure the availability of enough videoconferencing facilities throughout the nation to handle the caseload. Neither had it made clear how it would handle the demand for face-to-face hearings. The SSA had more than 140 locations around the country where it could conduct hearings, but HHS did not have such a system.

> Moreover, no analysis has been done to determine what proportion of appellants would actually be interested in having their appeals heard using videoconferences or teleconferences. Several ALJs told us that beneficiaries are often uncomfortable using videoconference facilities and prefer to have their cases heard face-to-face. While appellants have the right to request in-person hearings, the plan does not include an assessment of HHS's capacity to conduct such hearings. There is no contingency provision to facilitate in-person hearings, should this be appellants' preference. Further, as a result of changes to the appeals process due to BIPA, hearings by ALJs will provide an appellant's sole opportunity to be heard in person, making access to them all the more important.[194]

On June 30, 2005, with the transfer to HHS set by statute to begin on July 1, the GAO issued a follow-up report on the process.[195] It found a number of serious shortcomings, particularly from the point of view of the nearly 5 million people who would be processing appeals and of the more than 110,000 who would press their appeals through to the adjudicative hearing stage. The department proposed to solve many of its facilities and management problems by maintaining only four facilities where hearings would be conducted, to be located in Arlington, Virginia; Miami, Florida; Cleveland, Ohio; and Irvine, California. The GAO update found that HHS was operating on the assumption that some 90 percent of challengers would use VTC technology. It had not, as of May 2005, determined whether there would be any travel funds available for those who had to travel to receive an in-person hearing.[196] The department was planning experiments on the use of the VTC technology and expected that it would have to enter into contracts with commercial videoconferencing firms, but had not resolved that matter. The caseload data were unclear since it was not certain how many cases the new prescription drug benefit would produce.

Notwithstanding the lack of data, HHS was estimating that it could handle the full hearing load with 54 ALJs by virtue of efficient case management and performance standards.[197] However, the GAO and others had expressed concerns earlier that there were no clear protections in place to ensure the independence of the ALJs, and the pressures and expectations set up by the agency suggested cause for concern.

Finally, and perhaps most importantly, the GAO found, when it presented its draft 2005 report, that HHS corrected the document to make clear that the statute did not require a specific form of hearing and that the claimants would have to request an in-person hearing and show good cause to support that request, which would be granted as a matter of management discretion. The GAO replied, "However, our concern extends beyond legal requirements and encompasses a variety of reasons why appellants may be uncomfortable with VTC hearings. For example, beneficiary appellants may be intimidated by the unfamiliar technology or may be concerned that a lack of personal contact with the ALJ may put them at a disadvantage. It is this type of information—the beneficiary appellants' perspective on the use of VTCs as opposed to in-person hearings—that HHS has not provided."[198]

HHS published its new policies as interim final rules on March 8, 2005, with an effective date of May 1, but indicated that it would keep a comment period open.[199] However, those wishing to have their comments considered needed to submit them no later than May 9.

Those who work with Medicare beneficiaries and experienced ALJs saw these changes as serious threats to their ability to obtain a fundamentally fair and accurate resolution of their claims. Pear quoted Nancy M. Coleman, director of the ABA-affiliated Commission on Law and Aging: "'It's a travesty, what's happening to the appeal rights of Medicare beneficiaries.'" Finally, he quoted Ronald G. Bernoski, president of the Association of Administrative Law Judges, who summarized the dangers of this creative governance arrangement: "'Video teleconferences will undermine the judges' ability to assess the credibility and demeanor of witnesses, . . . and it could reduce the beneficiaries' confidence in the proceedings. The intrinsic value of a Medicare hearing is that citizens have an opportunity to sit down in front of a high-ranking official and tell their story to someone who listens carefully and makes a reasoned decision.'"[200] But, of course, this is a governance arrangement that very clearly responds to the instrumental view of due process and not its intrinsic values as explained earlier in this chapter. It remains to be seen what administrative due process will be under this new Medicare system.

Streamlined Nuclear Power Plant Licensing   There are many efforts to find streamlined adjudicative processes that value efficiency and effectiveness highly in contexts in which other values may have to be adjusted. The United States Circuit Court of Appeals for the First Circuit was asked to deal with just such a situation when it was asked in 2004 to determine the validity of the U.S. Nuclear Regulatory Commission's streamlined licensing process for nuclear plants.[201]

The controversy over the new reactor licensing policy began in 1998. The NRC staff knew that they were facing applications to renew licenses from most of the current operating nuclear facilities, which were built in the 1960s and operating under 40-year licenses.[202] To that point, reactor hearings had been considered formal hearings under the requirements of §§554, 556, and 557 of the APA. However, the NRC responded to its pending workload and the trend toward using less formal and more instrumental processes to manage its adjudications. The commission indicated its future direction in its 1998 policy statement: "In its review, the Commission has considered its existing policies and rules governing adjudicatory proceedings, recent experience and criticism of agency proceedings, and innovative techniques used by our own hearing boards and presiding officers and by other tribunals. Although current rules and policies provide means to achieve a prompt and fair resolution of proceedings, the Commission is directing its hearing boards and presiding officers to employ certain measures described in this policy statement to ensure the efficient conduct of proceedings."[203] The commission called upon its licensing boards to use electronic filings and other new technologies that could increase the efficiency and promptness of the proceedings. It made it clear that hearing officers were to take greater control over the schedules for those hearings and hold any would-be participants to those deadlines.

Late in 1998, the NRC general counsel issued a memorandum supporting the commission's authority for its streamlining efforts. "OGC reached the conclusion that except for a very limited set of hearings—those associated with the licensing of uranium enrichment facilities—the Atomic Energy Act did not mandate the use of a 'formal on-the-record' hearing within the meaning of the APA, 5 U.S.C. 554, 556, and 557, and that the Commission enjoyed substantial latitude in devising suitable hearing processes that would accommodate the due process rights of participants."[204]

In 2001, the NRC published a notice of proposed rulemaking for changes in its adjudicatory proceedings for licensing, which began from the premise that "the use of formal adjudicatory procedures is not essential to the development of an adequate hearing record; yet all too frequently their use resulted in protracted, costly proceedings."[205] The commission set forth its legal position based upon the memorandum issued earlier by the general counsel and announced its intentions to move forward with its rulemaking to effectuate the new streamlined adjudicative process.

The NRC issued its final rule in January 2004, following its announced intentions in the NPRM in 2001.[206] It kept its range of adjudicative procedural options in reserve, but announced that the less formal model was the appropriate approach for licensing adjudications. The new rule gave the NRC greater latitude in determining who should conduct a hearing, eliminated much of what had been standard discovery procedures before (to be replaced by general filing requirements), and gave the presiding officer of the adjudication considerable discretion as to time limits and milestones for the hearing process that were to be observed by all parties. As Judge Selya of the First Circuit later noted, the commission also changed the operation of the hearing itself.

> [T]he presumption is that all interrogation of witnesses will be undertaken by the hearing officer, not the litigants. . . . Parties are allowed to submit proposed questions in advance of the hearing, but the presiding officer is under no compulsion to pose them. . . . Parties are not allowed to submit proposed questions during the hearing unless requested to do so by the presiding officer. . . . Cross-examination is not available as of right, although a party may request permission to conduct cross-examination that it deems "necessary to ensure the development of an adequate record for decision." . . . A party seeking leave to conduct cross-examination must submit a cross-examination plan, which will be included in the record of the proceeding regardless of whether the request is allowed.[207]

A number of public interest groups sought judicial review of the new procedures and were supported by the attorneys general of five states who filed an *amicus curiae* brief in the case. The First Circuit panel affirmed the NRC position that while the applicable statute required a hearing, it did not specify precisely the kind of hearing that was needed. Therefore the court rejected the argument that NRC had acted beyond its authority and in violation of its statutory obligation when it issued the streamlined adjudication rules. It also upheld the changes and rejected the claim that the NRC action was arbitrary and capricious. Judge Selya concluded: "Though the Commission's new rules may approach the outer bounds of what is permissible under the APA, we find the statute sufficiently broad to accommodate them."[208]

Judge Lipez concurred in Selya's opinion, but wrote to explain a host of significant difficulties with the way NRC had proceeded. In summary, he wrote:

> It is striking that so many smart people at the NRC could be so wrong for so long about the requirements of the APA. Although this history does not affect the outcome of this case, it . . . serves to explain some of the legitimate frustrations of the petitioners, who felt that they were dealing with a moving target as the NRC tried to justify its new regulations. With so much at stake in these nuclear reactor licensing proceedings, the rulemaking process should have followed a steadier course. For reasons I shall explain, this was not the rulemaking process at its best.[209]

But, of course, the question whether what the NRC did was adjudication (and not just rulemaking) at its best is a significant one, given, as Judge Lipez correctly noted, that there is "so much at stake in nuclear reactor licensing proceedings." While the reasons for the NRC desire to avoid standard adjudicative procedures under the APA seem obvious, the long-term implications of agency departures from basic APA norms is much harder to predict, not only with respect to nuclear power plants, but for public law and public administration more generally. Once again, the instrumental approach to due process has been vindicated, but there are significant questions that remain for the legitimacy of administrative decisionmaking that APA adjudication requirements were created to support.

Secret Immigration Hearings in the Contemporary Context   Just over a week after the terrorist attacks on September 11, 2001, the nation's Chief Immigration Judge, Michael Creppy, issued a directive via e-mail to all immigration judges based upon instructions from Attorney General John Ashcroft.[210] Upon notification from Creppy's office that a particular case involved a person of "special interest" on national security grounds, the judge was to immediately close the proceedings to anyone except the individual involved and his or her attorney. No family members, friends, or reporters were to be permitted into the hearing. Further, they were not to provide any information to anyone about the case, including the fact of its existence. By later Justice Department directive, the judges were authorized to prohibit the parties to the case or their attorneys from disclosing, indefinitely, any information on the case.[211]

It became clear in a relatively short period that this process would not be reserved for a few very serious terrorism cases. Instead, an estimated 600 secret proceedings were conducted pursuant to the Creppy memorandum and later Department of Justice rules by the middle of 2003.[212] And as David Cole explained with careful documentation:

> The government has selectively subjected foreign nationals to interviews, registration, automatic detention, and deportation based on their Arab or Muslim national origin; detained thousands of them, here and abroad; tried many of them in secret, and refused to provide any trials or hearings whatsoever to others; interrogated them for months on end under highly coercive, incommunicado conditions and without access to lawyers; authorized their exclusion based on pure speech; made them deportable for wholly innocent political associations with disfavored groups; and authorized their indefinite detention on the attorney general's say-so.[213]

Many of those detained on grounds that they had some ostensible connection with the investigation into terrorism and the attacks of 9/11 were housed in correctional facilities (operated by contractors) that the U.S. Department of Justice Inspector General found deplorable. The IG report found a variety of abuses of detainees' rights after September 11, ranging from physical and verbal abuse to inadequate protection for lawyer and social visits, to harassment such as leaving the lights on in detainee cells 24 hours a day for months.[214] Few of these individuals were ever charged, much less tried and convicted, with terrorism. There has been an ongoing legal battle that has involved the United States Supreme Court in the question of how long persons can be held without charge and without the ability to confer with counsel or have a hearing on their confinement.[215]

Step back to the Creppy memorandum and consider a Detroit case that evolved from it. Judge Elizabeth Hacker was scheduled to hold a hearing for Rabih Haddad, a citizen of Lebanon, who had overstayed his tourist visa in December 2002. When Haddad, his attorney, family members, Congressman John Conyers, and media representatives arrived for the hearing, they were informed that the hearing was to be closed and none of them, except Haddad and his attorney, would be permitted. At the end of the hearing, he was denied bail and taken into custody. Subsequent hearings in January 2003 were also closed and Haddad was later removed from Detroit to Chicago. However, the *Detroit Free Press* and other local newspapers, Congressman Conyers, and Haddad brought suit against Creppy, Hacker, and Ashcroft, challenging the constitutional validity of the Creppy memorandum.

Judge Nancy Edmunds of the United States District Court for the Eastern District of Michigan issued a preliminary injunction against any further secret immigration proceedings under the Creppy memorandum. While there were several grounds presented in the case, including the APA, the due process clause of the Fifth Amendment, and immigrations statutes, the focus in this preliminary injunction proceeding was on the First Amendment argument advanced by the newspapers.[216]

The Sixth Circuit affirmed Edmunds's decision. Judge Keith began his opinion by recognizing the terrible losses of the 9/11 attack, but quickly noted that governmental attempts to respond to that situation could not sweep away the constraints of the Constitution. He also recognized the broad powers of the executive branch in matters of immigration, but refused to accept the government's argument that its authority was virtually unlimited and unreviewable.

> Today, the Executive Branch seeks to take this safeguard away from the public by placing its actions beyond public scrutiny. Against non-citizens, it seeks the power to secretly deport a class if it unilaterally calls them "special interest" cases. The Executive Branch seeks to uproot people's lives, outside the public eye, and behind a closed door. Democracies die behind closed doors. The First Amendment, through a free press, protects the people's right to know that their government acts fairly, lawfully, and accurately in deportation proceedings. When government begins closing doors, it selectively controls information rightfully belonging to the people. Selective information is misinformation. The Framers of the First Amendment "did not trust any government to separate the true from the false for us."...They protected the people against secret government.[217]

The panel was obviously concerned by the sweep of the claim to unrestricted authority in the name of national security offered by counsel for the government.

> [T]here seems to be no limit to the Government's argument. The Government could use its "mosaic intelligence" argument as a justification to close any public hearing completely and categorically, including criminal proceedings. The Government could operate in virtual secrecy in all matters dealing, even remotely, with "national security," resulting in a wholesale suspension of First Amendment rights. By the simple assertion of "national security," the Government seeks a process where it may, without review, designate certain classes of cases as "special interest cases" and, behind closed doors, adjudicate the merits of these cases to deprive non-citizens of their fundamental liberty interests.... This, we simply may not countenance. A government operating in the shadow of secrecy stands in complete opposition to the society envisioned by the Framers of our Constitution.[218]

And the panel also rejected the idea that there was somehow less basis for a claimed right to an open hearing because this was an administrative adjudication rather than a criminal trial. Keith quoted the Supreme Court's 1938 ruling in the *Morgan* case: "[I]n administrative proceedings of a quasi-judicial character the liberty and property of the citizen shall be protected by the rudimentary requirements of fair play. These demand 'a fair and open hearing,' – essential alike to the legal validity of the administrative regulation and to the maintenance of public confidence in the value and soundness of this important governmental process. Such a hearing has been described as an 'inexorable safeguard.'"[219]

The panel decision then moved through the existing standards that have been employed in cases demanding open adjudicative proceedings and concluded that both elements of the existing standard for First Amendment–based access were met. However, the court was concerned that this matter should be understood not only in instrumental and technical terms, but also for the danger to intrinsic approaches to due process discussed earlier, questions of legitimacy of public action.

> A true democracy is one that operates on faith—faith that government officials are forth-coming and honest, and faith that informed citizens will arrive at logical conclusions. This is a vital reciprocity that America should not discard in these troubling times. Without question, the events of September 11, 2001, left an indelible mark on our nation, but we as a people are united in the wake of the destruction to demonstrate to the world that we are a country deeply committed to preserving the rights and freedoms guaranteed by our democracy. Today, we

reflect our commitment to those democratic values by ensuring that our government is held accountable to the people and that . . . rights are not impermissibly compromised. Open proceedings, with a vigorous and scrutinizing press, serve to ensure the durability of our democracy.[220]

Just two months after the Sixth Circuit ruling, the United States Circuit Court of Appeals for the Third Circuit, deciding a different case about the Creppy memorandum, rejected the Sixth Circuit's reasoning and ruled against challenges to the Creppy memorandum closing of immigration proceedings in a case coming from New Jersey. The U.S. Supreme Court refused to take the cases to resolve the conflict.[221] The problems remain.

There is no doubt that the United States has a long and troubled history of abuses of due process in times of real and presumed emergency. However, the tendency to move away from well-established due process protections toward an increasingly constrained instrumental view of administrative due process across a wide range of activities raises serious questions for the future. Particularly, these are questions not primarily of efficiency but rather of legitimacy.

THE UTILITY OF DUE PROCESS

The complexities of due process—along with the perceived delays and costs of ensuring fundamentally fair decisionmaking in matters that affect the rights, duties, employment, or status of individuals inside or outside an agency—lead to frustration. They also cause many administrators to applaud the Supreme Court's decisions reversing the earlier trend toward more and more extensive due process protections. However, just as there are strong arguments in support of rules and rulemaking, so too there are important reasons for administrators to value due process and fundamentally fair adjudicative decisionmaking.

Although much more will be said about the matter in Chapter 12, management with a strong basis in due process is essential to effective internal agency management. Clearly, organizational morale is significantly better where there is a sense that managers operate fairly. In fact, scholars of organizational behavior and management are increasingly writing on organizational justice and organizational due process.[222] To the degree that employees understand that the basic concepts of notice, an opportunity to be heard, a fair decisionmaker, and a reasoned decision are honored in decisionmaking, there is likely to be greater attention to mission performance and less time spent focused on battles over conspiracies real or imagined.

Similarly, the expectation that some kind of due process is available to those who must interact with an agency from the outside supports the idea that fundamental fairness is a guiding value. It also enhances the expectation of equal treatment and reduces the likelihood that decisions will be regarded as discriminatory or arbitrary.

It is also likely that a habit of applying the basic concepts of due process and the principle of fundamental fairness will improve decisionmaking. These principles help to keep the decisionmaker sensitive to the individual nature of the decision and its impact on the people involved. It should be remembered that the due process requirements of administrative law were not incorporated merely because they were techniques for improved decisions, but also because of the need to address basic issues of the legitimacy of administrative decisionmaking.

For those administrators who find these arguments too amorphous or idealistic, it is worth remembering that there is a very immediate and real danger in failing to attend to the requisites of due process. Because the Supreme Court's decisions do not set forth a clear standard but instead rely upon a case-by-case balancing test, a decisionmaker cannot be certain whether a failure to provide fulsome due process protections in any given case will ultimately be upheld in a civil rights suit brought later.

SUMMARY

Administrative adjudications are attempts to ensure not only that there are effective fact-finding techniques available to producers and consumers of administrative decisions but also that the basic American values of fairness and due process of law are maintained in administrative agency operations. The rules governing what process an agency must provide are prescribed by the Constitution, treaty obligations, relevant agency statutes, agency regulations, contract requirements, and court decisions interpreting all of these.

Administrative adjudications are more flexible and informal than court trials. To understand them, one must consider the development of the concept of administrative due process and be mindful of the concepts that together make up procedural due process in administration. With regard to particular kinds of adjudications, one must ask a series of questions to understand what is required. Is a hearing required? At what point in an administrative action is a hearing required? What kind of a hearing is required? What are the essential elements of an administrative hearing?

The dramatically increased use of contracting by governments at all levels for service delivery—to provide goods and technology as well as the use of a range of other contemporary governance regimes that involve government with nonprofit and for-profit organizations—has created added dimensions to the general discussion of administrative adjudications. It is a conversation which is, in many respects, only beginning and it raises many questions for which the answers are as yet unclear. Whether the concern is the contracting out of adjudicative processes, the administration of important public programs and institutions by contract employees, or the situation facing the public manager whose organizations include contract workers as well as public servants, the role and character of adjudicative processes in the evolving public sector is an area in need of continued attention. Another area of concern is the use of contractors as adjudicators in public administration fields.

In the end, administrative decisionmakers are required to exercise a great deal of judgment and discretion because of the nature of the controversies they decide and also because of the flexible and informal nature of the administrative adjudicatory process. The developers of administrative law have been optimistic that this relative flexibility and informality are necessary and workable, given the availability of access to judicial review in courts of law to correct mistakes made in agency activities. We turn to the process of judicial review in the next chapter.

NOTES

1. See J. Randolph and R. Humphreys, "Black Lung Benefits Reform: Mirage or Reality?" 19 *Labor L. J.* 555 (1977), and Brit Hume, *Death and the Mines* (New York: Grossman, 1971), Ch. 3, 4.

2. *Greene v. McElroy,* 360 U.S. 474, 483 (1959).

3. *Id.*

4. *Id.,* at p. 484.

5. *Id.,* at p. 487.

6. *Id.,* at p. 498.

7. *J.L. v. Parham,* 412 F. Supp. 112, 116–17 (MDGA 1976).

8. *Id.,* at p. 117.

9. *Id.,* at p. 133.

10. *Id.,* at p. 134

11. *Id.,* at pp. 138–39.

12. *Parham v. J.R.,* 442 U.S. 584 (1979).

13. "The fundamental requisite of due process is the opportunity to be heard." *Grannis v. Ordean,* 234 U.S. 385, 394 (1914).

14. J. Skelly Wright, "Beyond Discretionary Justice," 81 *Yale L. J.* 575, 597 (1972).

15. Louis L. Jaffe quoted in Wright, *Id.,* at p. 596.

16. U.S. House of Representatives, *Constitution of the United States of America: Analysis and Interpretation,* 92d Cong., 2d Sess. (1973), pp. 1137–38.

17. The Supreme Court has traced our concept of due process to that British tradition. "As we have said on more than one occasion, it may be difficult, if not impossible, to give the term 'due process of law' a definition which will embrace every permissible exertion of power affecting private rights and exclude such as are forbidden. They come to us from the law of England, from which country our jurisprudence is to a great extent derived, and their requirement was there designed to secure the subject against the arbitrary action of the Crown and place him under the protection of the law. They were deemed to be equivalent to 'the law of the land.' In this country, the requirement is intended to have a similar effect against legislative power, that is, to secure the citizen against any arbitrary deprivation of his rights, whether relating to his life, his liberty, or his property." *Dent v. West Virginia,* 129 U.S. 114, 123-24 (1889).

18. Constitution, *supra* note 16, at p. 1138.

19. Robert A. Rutland, *The Birth of the Bill of Rights, 1776–1791* (Chapel Hill: University of North Carolina Press, 1955), Ch. 2, 3.

20. *Barron v. Mayor and City Council of Baltimore,* 32 U.S. (7 Pet.) 243 (1883).

21. Rutland, *supra* note 19, at p. 222.

22. See Chapter 4, notes 29–31 and accompanying text.

23. See the commentary on Dicey, Goodnow, Freund, Dickinson, Landis, and Gellhorn in Chapter 4.

24. See e.g., Walter Gellhorn, *Federal Administrative Proceedings* (Westport, CT: Greenwood Press, 1941), pp. 6–14.

25. *Lochner v. New York,* 198 U.S. 45 (1905).

26. *Id.,* at p. 57.

27. See e.g., *Moore v. East Cleveland,* 431 U.S. 494 (1977).

28. *Lawrence v. Texas,* 539 U.S. 558, 562 (2003).

29. *Dismuke v. United States,* 297 U.S. 167, 172 (1936).

30. *Withrow v. Larkin,* 421 U.S. 35 (1975).

31. *Id.,* at pp. 46–47.

32. As noted in Chapter 4, it was during this period that federal suits were being brought against state and local government action under the Fourteenth Amendment. It was the time of the rise of the large corporations able to sustain long-term large-scale litigation against government actions viewed as hostile. Also during this period, the newer statutes tended to provide for enforcement by administrative adjudication rather than through private suits in civil courts. Finally, the courts were growing into the judicial system as we now know it. The bar was developing and providing a group of attorneys who would attempt to answer Elihu Root's call to develop a sophisticated body of administrative law. Frank Goodnow, Ernst Freund, Woodrow Wilson, and John Dickinson were teaching them how this might be accomplished.

33. *Yick Wo v. Hopkins,* 118 U.S. 356, 369 (1886). *Yick Wo* was decided primarily on equal protection grounds, but the Court related both equal protection and due process to the central problem of administrative arbitrariness that could render a statutory program unconstitutional. Though the statute was lawful as written, it would be void if administered in an arbitrary manner.

34. *Grannis v. Ordean,* 234 U.S. 385 (1914) and *Dent v. West Virginia,* 129 U.S. 114 (1889).

35. *Yamataya v. Fisher,* 189 U.S. 86 (1903).

36. *Londoner v. Denver,* 210 U.S. 373, 386 (1908).

37. "A finding without evidence is arbitrary and baseless. And even if the government's contention is correct, it would mean that the Commissioner had a power possessed by no other officer, administrative body, or tribunal under our government. It would mean that, where rights depended upon facts, the Commission could disregard all rules of evidence, and capriciously make findings by administrative fiat. Such authority,

however beneficently exercised in one case, could be injuriously exerted in another, is inconsistent with rational justice, and comes under the Constitution's condemnation of all arbitrary exercise of power.

In the comparatively few cases in which such questions have arisen it has been distinctly recognized that administrative orders, quasi-judicial in character, are void if a hearing was denied; if that granted was inadequate or manifestly unfair; if the finding was contrary to the 'indisputable character of the evidence' [cities]; or if the facts found do not as a matter of law, support the order made." *Interstate Commerce Commission v. Louisville & Nashville Ry. Co.,* 227 U.S. 88. 91–92 (1913). See also *Crowell v. Benson,* 285 U.S. 22, 50 (1932).

38. *Morgan v. United States,* 304 U.S. 1 (1938); *St. Joseph Stock Yards v. United States,* 298 U.S. 38 (1936); and *Dismuke v. United States ,* 297 U.S. 167 (1936).

39. See generally the discussion of the act in *Wong Yang Sung v. McGrath,* 339 U.S. 33 (1950).

40. *Sampson v. Murray,* 415 U.S. 61, 95–97 (1974), Justice Douglas dissenting.

41. *Keyishian v. Board of Regents,* 385 U.S. 589 (1967), and *United States v. Robel,* 389 U.S. 258 (1967).

42. *Joint Anti-Facist Refugee Committee v. McGrath,* 341 U.S. 123 (1951).

43. *Wieman v. Updegraff,* 344 U.S. 184, 191–92 (1952).

44. *Bailey v. Richardson,* 182 F.2d 46, 66 (D.C.Cir. 1950).

45. *Bailey v. Richardson,* 341 U.S. 918 (1951).

46. *Bailey v. Richardson, supra* note 44.

47. *Id.,* at pp. 72–73.

48. See e.g., the facts surrounding *Laird v. Tatum,* 408 U.S. 1 (1972).

49. See Mary McGrory, "In the Senate, Echoes of McCarthy Over the Issue of Peace," *Washington Post,* October 5, 1982, p. A3; Donnie Radcliffe, "Women, War and Peace Links: Betty Bumpers Fends Off a Senator's Red Scare," *Washington Post,* October 7, 1982, p. D1.

50. David Cole, *Enemy Aliens: Double Standards and Constitutional Freedoms in the War on Terrorism* (New York: The New Press, 2003).

51. See e.g., *U.S. ex rel. Accardi v. Shaughnessy,* 347 U.S. 260 (1954).

52. See Appendix 1.

53. William Van Alstyne, "The Demise of the Right-Privilege Distinction in Constitutional Law," 81 *Harvard L. Rev.* 1439 (1968).

54. This theory is generally traced to an opinion written by Justice Holmes while he was a member of the Massachusetts Supreme Court. "The petitioner may have a constitutional right to talk politics, but he has no constitutional right to be a policeman. There are few employments for hire in which the servant does not agree to suspend his constitutional right of free speech, as well as of idleness, by the terms of his contract." *McAuliffe v. Mayor of New Bedford,* 155 Mass. 216, 220 (Mass. 1892).

55. *Slochower v. Board of Higher Education,* 350 U.S. 55 (1956); *Speiser v. Randall,* 357 U.S. 513 (1958); *Sherbert v. Verner,* 347 U.S. 398 (1963); *Keyishian v. Board of Regents,* 385 U.S. 589 (1967); *Pickering v. Board of Education ,* 391 U.S. 563 (1968); *Shapiro v. Thompson,* 394 U.S. 618 (1969); *Goldberg v. Kelly,* 397 U.S. 254 (1970); *Perry v. Sinderman,* 408 U.S. 593 (1972); *Mt. Healthy Board of Education v. Doyle,* 429 U.S. 274 (1977); and *Givhan v. Board of Education of Western Line Consolidated School Dist.,* 439 U.S. 410 (1979).

56. *Goldberg v. Kelly,* 397 U.S. 254, 263 (1970).

57. *Bell v. Burson,* 402 U.S. 535, 537 (1971).

58. *Id.,* at p. 539.

59. *Vlandis v. Kline,* 412 U.S. 441 (1973).

60. *Carrington v. Rash,* 380 U.S. 89 (1965).

61. *Cleveland Board of Education v. LaFleur,* 414 U.S. 632 (1974).

62. *Stanley v. Illinois,* 405 U.S. 645 (1972).

63. *Id.,* at pp. 652–57.

64. *Goldberg v. Kelly, supra* note 56.

65. *Wolf v. McDonnell,* 418 U.S. 539 (1974); *Gagnon v. Scarpelli,* 411 U.S. 778 (1973); and *Morrissey v. Brewer,* 408 U.S. 471 (1972). But see *Sandin v. Conner,* 515 U.S. 472 (1995).

66. *Goss v. Lopez,* 419 U.S. 565 (1975). See also *Wood v. Strickland,* 420 U.S. 308 (1975), and *Carey v. Piphus,* 435 U.S. 247 (1978).

67. *Bell v. Burson, supra* note 57.

68. *North Georgia Finishing v. Di-Chem,* 419 U.S. 601 (1975); *Fuentes v. Shevin,* 407 U.S. 67 (1972); and *Sniadach v. Family Finance,* 395 U.S. 337 (1969).

69. *Wisconsin v. Constantineau,* 400 U.S. 433 (1971).

70. *Board of Regents v. Roth,* 408 U.S. 564 (1972). See also *Wieman v. Updegraff, supra* note 43, at p. 191.

71. See the discussion in the *Eldridge* case study in Appendix 1 on change in the composition of the Court and the particular positions of various Burger Court justices on administrative due process requirements.

72. See e.g., *Smith v. Organization of Foster Families,* 431 U.S. 816 (1977).

73. One of the leaders in this discussion of administrative due process was Henry J. Friendly, "Some Kind of a Hearing," 123 *U. Pennsylvania L. Rev.* 1267 (1975).

74. Laurence Tribe, *American Constitutional Law* (Mineola, NY: Foundation Press, 1978), §10-7.

75. *Board of Regents v. Roth, supra* note 70.

76. 424 U.S. 319 (1976).

77. *Id.,* at pp. 569–70.

78. *Id.,* at pp. 571–72.

79. *Id.,* at p. 573.

80. *Id.*

81. *Id.,* at pp. 577–78.

82. William Van Alstyne, "Cracks in 'The New Property': Adjudicative Due Process in the Administrative State," 62 *Cornell L. Rev.* 445, 489–90 (1977).

83. *Weinberger v. Salfi,* 422 U.S. 749, 771-72 (1975).

84. *Bishop v. Wood,* 426 U.S. 341 (1976).

85. *Id.,* at p. 689.

86. *Wisconsin v. Constantineau, supra* note 69.

87. *Id.,* at p. 437.

88. *Paul v. Davis,* 424 U.S. 693 (1976).

89. *Id.,* at p. 701.

90. *Bishop v. Wood, supra* note 84, at p. 353 n. 4, Justice Brennan dissenting.

91. *Siegert v. Gilley,* 500 U.S. 226, 233-234 (1991).

92. *Id.,* at p. 247.

93. *Dixon v. Love,* 431 U.S. 105 (1977).

94. *Board of Curators v. Horowitz,* 435 U.S. 78 (1978).

95. *Ingraham v. Wright,* 430 U.S. 651 (1977).

96. *Meachum v. Fano,* 427 U.S. 215 (1976). See generally *Moody v. Daggett,* 429 U.S. 78 (1976), and *Baxter v. Palmigiano,* 425 U.S. 308 (1976).

97. *Mathews v. Eldridge,* 424 U.S. 319 (1976).

98. *Arnett v. Kennedy,* 416 U.S. 134 (1974) and *Bishop v. Wood, supra* note 84.

99. *Rutan v. Republican Party of Illinois,* 497 U.S. 62, 97 n.2 (1990), Justice Scalia dissenting.

100. He wrote: "[O]ne who avails himself of government entitlements accepts the grant of tenure along with its inherent [procedural] limitations." *Cleveland Bd. of Ed. v. Loudermill,* 470 U.S. 532, 563 (1985), Justice Rehnquist dissenting.

101. *Gonzales v. City of Castle Rock,* 366 F.3d 1093 (10th Cir. Colo., 2004).

102. *Town of Castle Rock, Colorado v. Gonzales,* 125 S. Ct. 2796 (2005).

103. See *Michael H. v. Gerald D.,* 491 U.S. 110 (1989); *Traynor v. Turnage,* 485 U.S. 535 (1988); and circuit court opinions *infra,* n. 104.

104. See *Hamby v. Neel,* 368 F.3d 549 (6th Cir. 2004); *Daugherty v. Thompson,* 322 F.3d 1249 (10th Cir. 2003); *Shipman v. Department of Transportation,* 58 Fed. Appx. 481 (Fed. Cir 2003); *DeLong v. Department of Health and Human Services,* 264 F.3d 1334 (Fed. Cir. 2001).

105. Some treaties contain specific enforcement and adjudication mechanisms within them while others require implementing legislation in each country to clarify adjudication requirements. In addition to treaties, these kinds of processes have also sometimes been mandated by executive agreements or executive orders. See *Dames and Moore v. Regan,* 453 U.S. 654 (1981).

106. *Mathews v. Eldridge, supra* note 97, at p. 335.

107. *Goldberg v. Kelly, supra* note 56, at pp. 262–263.

108. *Board of Regents v. Roth, supra* note 70, at pp. 471, 481.

109. See *supra* note 90.

110. *Stanley v. Illinois,* 405 U.S. 645 (1972).

111. See *Board of Regents v. Roth, supra* note 70, and *Wieman v. Updegraff, supra* note 43. But see *Paul v. Davis, supra* note 88.

112. *Owen v. City of Independence,* 445 U.S. 622, 633 n. 13 (1980). See also *Board of Regents v. Roth, supra* note 70, *Arnett v. Kennedy, supra* note 98, and *Bishop v. Wood, supra* note 84.

113. See Justice Black's dissenting opinions in *Barenblatt v. United States,* 360 U.S. 109 (1959); *Konigsberg v. State Bar of California,* 366 U.S. 36 (1961).

114. *Arnett v. Kennedy, supra* note 98, at p. 157. Despite admonitions that employees were entitled to some pretermination consideration, the Court maintained the same requirements as Arnett in *Cleveland Bd. of Ed. v. Loudermill,* 470 U.S. 532, 546 (1985).

115. *Id.*

116. *Id.,* at pp. 545–546.

117. *Id.,* at p. 547.

118. *Id.,* n. 11.

119. *Id.,* at 547.

120. See e.g., Lisa B. Bingham, "Alternative Dispute Resolution in Public Administration," in Phillip J. Cooper and Chester A. Newland, eds., *Handbook of Public Law and Administration* (San Francisco: Jossey-Bass, 1997).

121. See generally American Bar Association, "Report of Pound Conference Follow-Up Task Force," 74 F.R.D. 159 (1976); Judicial Conference of the United States, Conference of Chief Justices, and American Bar Association, *National Conference on the Causes of Popular Dissatisfaction* (St. Paul, MN: American Bar Association, 1976), pp. 61–97.

122. 5 U.S.C. §554(c).

123. P.L. 104-320, 110 Stat. 3870 (1996).

124. "In rulemaking or determining claims for money or benefits or applications for initial licenses an agency may, when a party will not be prejudiced thereby, adopt procedures for the submission of all or part of the evidence in written form." 5 U.S.C. §556(d).

125. This is a term that was spun off from George Orwell's famous book, *1984* (New York: Harcourt, Brace, Jovanovich, 1949). Orwell wrote an entire appendix to his novel to explain his term "Newspeak," which was the starting point for what has come to be known as Bureauspeak. Describing this fictional language, Orwell, explained: "Newspeak was founded on the English language as we know it, though many Newspeak sentences, even when not containing newly created words, would be barely intelligible to an English-speaker of our own day." *Id.,* at p. 247.

126. See the discussion of the Social Security experiment in the *Eldridge* case study when increased face-to-face processes produced fewer appeals and fewer reversals.

127. *Board of Curators v. Horowitz,* *supra* note 94, at pp. 85–86. See also *Ingraham v. Wright, supra* note 95.

128. See e.g., *Goldberg v. Kelly,* *supra* note 56.

129. *Mulhane v. Central Hanover Trust Co.,* 339 U.S. 306, 314 (1950).

130. 5 U.S.C. §554(b).

131. *Dusenberry v. United States,* 534 U.S. 161, 170 (2002).

132. *Udd v. Massanari,* 245 F.3d 1096, 1102 (9th Cir.2001).

133. *Office of Communications of the United Church of Christ v. Federal Communications Commission,* 359 F. 2d 994 (D.C.Cir. 1966).

134. *Scenic Hudson Preservation Conf. v. Federal Power Comm'n,* 354 F. 2d 608 (2d Cir. 1965).

135. 5 U.S.C. §582(b)(4).

136. 51 *Buffalo L. Rev.* 337 (2003).

137. *Broadfoot v. Diaz,* 245 B.R. 713 (Bankr. N.D. Ga. 2000).

138. *Rio Properties v. Rio Int'l Interlink,* 284 F.3d 1007 (9th Cir. 2002).

139. On the general use of e-mail notice, see *Williams v. Advertising Sex LLC,* 2005 U.S. Dist. LEXIS 25670 (NDVA 2005); *Popular Enterprises v. WEBCOM Media Group,* 225 F.R.D. 560 (EDTN 2004); *Ryan v. Brunswick Corp.,* 2002 U.S. Dist. LEXIS 13837 (WDNY 2002) See also, Jordan S. Ginsberg, "Class Action Notice: The Internet's Time Has Come,"2003 *U. Chicago Legal Forum* 739 (2003).

140. See *Rio Properties, supra* note 138, Colby, *supra* note 136, and Ginsberg, *supra* note 139.

141. 5 U.S.C §554(c)(2).

142. *Id.,* at §554(b).

143. *Id.,* at §555.

144. *Id.*

145. *Lassiter v. Department of Social Services,* 452 U.S. 18 (1981).

146. See *Walters v. National Association of Radiation Supervisors,* 473 U.S. 305 (1985), which upheld a Veterans Administration limit of $10 for the fee that can be paid to a lawyer or representative of a veteran seeking benefits for a service-connected disability.

147. 5 U.S.C. §555(d).

148. The authority that different agencies have to demand evidence or information varies significantly. One of the most dramatic examples of agency subpoena authority backed by statutory authority to impose sanctions is that possessed by the Securities and Exchange Commission. See 15 U.S.C. §77 et seq.

149. 5 U.S.C. §555(d).

150. Kenneth Culp Davis, *Administrative Law: Cases-Test-Problems, 6th ed.* (St. Paul: West, 1977), p. 385.

151. 5 U.S.C. §556(d).

152. *Id.* And see *Schaffer v. Weast,* 2005 U.S. LEXIS 8554 (2005).

153. *Id.*

154. *National Labor Relations Board v. Remington Rand,* 94 F.2d 862, 873 (2d Cir. 1938), cert. denied, 304 U.S. 576 (1938), rev'd on other grounds, 110 F.2d 148 (2d Cir. 1940). See also *American Textile Manufacturers v. Donovan,* 452 U.S. 490, 522 (1981).

155. *Black's Law Dictionary,* 4th ed. (St. Paul: West, 1968), p. 1367.

156. *Richardson v. Perales,* 402 U.S. 389, 401 (1971), and *Consolidated Edison Co. v. NLRB,* 305 U.S. 197, 229 (1938).

157. *Pennaco Energy v. Department of the Interior,* 377 F.3d 1147, 1156 (10th Cir. 2004); *Foust v. Lujan,* 942 F.2d 712, 714 (10th Cir. 1991); and *Hoyl v. Babbitt,* 129 F.3d 1377, 1383 (10th Cir. 1997).

158. 522 U.S. 359, 366 (1998).

159. *Steel Tech Ltd. v. EPA,* 273 F.3d 652, 657 (6th Cir. 2001).

160. *Richardson v. Perales, supra* note 156.

161. *Id.,* at p. 402. The Ninth Circuit recently added that:"[T]he findings of a nontreating nonexamining physician can amount to substantial evidence, so long as other evidence in the record supports those findings." *Saelee v. Chater,* 83 F.3d 322 (9th Cir. 1996).

162. Richardson undermined what is generally referred to as the "residuum rule." This rule was developed in an early state case. "The act may be taken to mean that while the Commission's inquiry is not limited by the common law or statutory rules of evidence or by technical or formal rules of procedure, and it may in its discretion, accept any evidence that is offered, still in the end there must be a residuum of legal evidence to support the claim before an award is made." *Carroll v. Knickerbocker Ice Co.*, 113 N.E. 507, 509 (1916).

163. See generally 5 U.S.C. §§556, 557.

164. 5 U.S.C. §556(d). But see *Air Traffic Controllers Organization v. FLRA*, 685 F.2d 547 (D.C.Cir. 1982).

165. *Professional Air Traffic Controllers Organization v. FLRA*, 685 F.2d 547, 558 (D.C.Cir. 1982).

166. *Id.*, at 559.

167. *Id.*, at 562-63.

168. *Id.*, at 564-65.

169. See e.g., *Maine Care Services v. USDA*, 2001 U.S. Dist. LEXIS 18420 (DME 2001); *Press Broadcasting v. FCC*, 59 F.3d 1365 (D.C.Cir. 1995); *Portland Audubon Society v. Oregon Lands Coalition*, 984 F.2d 1534 (9th Cir. 1993).

170. *Id.*, at §556(e).

171. *Electric Power Supply Association v. Federal Energy Regulatory Commission*, 391 F.3d 1255, 1260 (D.C.Cir. 2004)

172. *Id.*, at 1266.

173. *Association of Administrative Law Judges v. Heckler*, 594 F. Supp. 1132, 1143 (D.D.C. 1984).

174. *Nash v. Bowen*, 869 F.2d 675, 681 (2nd Cir. 1989).

175. *Id.*

176. See *Universal Camera Corp. v. National Labor Relations Board*, 340 U.S. 474 (1951).

177. See e.g., Michael P. Vandenbergh, "The Private Life of Public Law," 105 *Colum. L. Rev.* 2029 (2005); Dru Stevenson, "Privatization of Welfare Services: Delegation by Commercial Contract," 45 *Ariz. L. Rev.* 83 (2003); Sidney A. Shapiro, Outsourcing Government Regulation," 53 *Duke L.J.* 389 (2003); Michele Estrin Gilman, "Legal Accountability in an Era of Privatized Welfare," 89 *Calif. L. Rev.* 569 (2001).

178. P.L. 104-193, 110 Stat. 2161 (1996).

179. 456 U.S. 188 (1982).

180. *McClure v. Harris*, 503 F. Supp. 409 (ND Cal 1998)

181. See Stevenson, *supra* note 177.

182. See e.g., U.S. General Accounting Office, *HMO Complaints and Appeals* (Washington, DC: GAO, 1998).

183. *Id.*, at p. 8.

184. *Id.*

185. *Id.*, at p. 8.

186. *Id.*, at p. 10.

187. The court also ruled that these adjudications by contract insurance firms were not subject to review in the U.S. Court of Claims. *United States v. Erika*, 456 U.S. 201 (1982). The Supreme Court ruled that although there was no specific provision of review, there was also no prohibition on review of Medicare Part B decisions by the agency itself. *Bowen v. Michigan Academy of Family Physicians*, 476 U.S. 667 (1986). Congress later amended the statute to permit judicial review of Medicare Part B decisions. See *Queen City Home Health Care Co. Sullivan*, 978 F.2d 236 (6th Cir. 1992).

188. *Richardson v. McKnight*, 521 U.S. 399 (1997).

189. See generally the Contract Disputes Act of 1978, P.L. 95-563, 92 Stat. 2385. See also Section 6 of the Administrative Dispute Resolution Act of 1996 (see Appendix 3).

190. Robert Pear, "Medicare Change Will Limit Access to Claim Hearing," *New York Times*, April 24, 2005, p. 1.

191. *Id.*

192. P.L. 108-173, 117 Stat. 2066 (2003).

193. GAO, *Medicare: Incomplete Plan to Transfer Appeals Workload from SSA to HHS Threatens Service to Appellants* (Washington, DC: GAO, 2004).

194. *Id.,* at 17.

195. GAO, *Medicare: Concerns Regarding Plans to Transfer the Appeals Workload from SSA to HHS Remain* (Washington: DC: GAO, 2005).

196. *Id.,* at 23.

197. *Id.,* at 33.

198. *Id.,* at 3–4.

199. Department of Health and Human Services, Centers for Medicare & Medicaid Services, "Medicare Program: Changes to the Medicare Claims Appeal Procedures," 70 Fed. Reg. 11420 (2005).

200. See Pear, *supra* note 190.

201. *Citizens Awareness Network v. United States,* 391 F.3d 338 (1st Cir. 2004).

202. *Id.,* at 343-344.

203. 63 Fed. Reg. 41873 (1998).

204. 73 Fed. Reg. 19610, 19611 (2001).

205. 73 Fed. Reg. 19610 (2001).

206. 69 Fed. Reg. 2182 (2004).

207. *Supra* note 201, at 345.

208. *Id.,* at 355.

209. *Id.,* at 355-356.

210. See Heidi Kitrosser, "Secrecy in the Immigration Courts and Beyond: Considering the Right to Know in the Administrative State," 39 *Harvard Civil Rights – Civil Liberties L. Rev.* 95 (2004).

211. *Detroit Free Press v. Ashscroft,* 303 F.3d 681, 707-708 (6th Cir. 2002).

212. Kitosser, *supra* note 210, at 95.

213. David Cole, *Enemy Aliens: Double Standards and Constitutional Freedoms in the War on Terrorism* (New York: The New Press, 2003), p. 5. A abbreviated version was published as "Enemy Aliens," 54 *Stanford L. Rev.* 953 (2002).

214. See Office of the Inspector General, U.S. Department of Justice, *The September 11 Detainees: A Review of the Treatment of Aliens Held on Immigration Charges in Connection with the Investigation of the September 11 Attacks* (Washington, DC: U.S. Department of Justice, 2003), http://www.usdoj.gov/oig/special/03_06/full.pdf, as of November 1, 2003, pp. 158–164.

215. See e.g., *Hamdi v. Rumsfeld,* 124 S. Ct. 2633 (2004).

216. *Detroit Free Press v. Ashcroft,* 195 F. Supp. 2d 937 (EDMI 2002).

217. *Detroit Free Press, supra* note 211, at 683.

218. *Id.,* at 709-710.

219. *Morgan v. United States,* 304 U.S. 1, 14-15 (1938). The *Morgan* quote was also used in striking down an attempt to force a closed hearing on a civil service termination case. *Fitzgerald v. Hampton,* 467 F.2d 755, 766-67 (D.C.Cir. 1972).

220. *Detroit Free Press* , *supra* note 211, at 711.

221. *North Jersey Media Group v. New Jersey Law Journal,* 308 F.3d 198 (3rd Cir. 2002).

222. Hal Rainey, "The 'How Much Process is Due?' Debate: Legal and Managerial Perspectives," in Phillip J. Cooper and Chester A. Newland, eds., *Handbook of Public Law and Administration* (San Francisco: Jossey-Bass, 1997).

7

Judicial Review

Chapters 5 and 6 discussed two of the primary areas of formal administrative law. The third is judicial review of agency decisions. The availability of law courts for appeal and review of administrative actions is one of the central underpinnings of the administrative justice system. (See Chapter 4.) This chapter considers the nature of judicial review, some of the problems in its operation, and several important contemporary trends.

Earlier chapters have approached problems of administrative law from the perspectives of producers and consumers of administrative decisions. Judicial review may perhaps be better understood if the subject is approached from the perspective of the judge. Judges were intentionally made important actors in the administrative justice system. Knowledge of their challenges and responsibilities can help both producers and consumers of administrative decisions appreciate the limitations and importance of judicial review and—what might seem at first to be a rather odd idea—suggest ways in which parties can aid the judges in their tasks. Those tasks arise not only out of the characteristics of modern administrative law cases and the complex contexts in which they develop, but also from the historical demands discussed in Chapter 4. The judges are expected to provide an external check on administrative power, to support the sense of legitimacy of administrative law by ensuring that there is a place where citizens can take their disputes outside the administrative arena for vindication of their rights, and to integrate the law of public administration with the rest of public law and indeed with the rest of our body of law.

At heart, the dilemma judges face in reviewing administrative actions is this: judges ought to presume that government officials act lawfully and should not second-guess the substance of administrative decisions.[1] On the other hand, they perform a vital function in ensuring that administrators obey the law. Unfortunately, there is no clear line between excessive judicial deference to arbitrary or unlawful administration and inappropriate interference with decisions that are properly the province of expert administrators. When a judge affirms an administrator's decision, the challenger will likely claim abdication of judicial responsibility for failure to hold the administrator accountable. Yet, when the same judge reverses or remands an agency judgment, the agency and its supporters will complain about excessive judicial activism and attempts to substitute judicial preference for properly authorized and executed expert administrative judgment.

What students of judicial review can do is examine the purposes of review, the judges' roles, and, in general, the limitations on the review process. Again, it is useful to begin with consideration of a representative example of the problem.

THE PARK AND THE INTERSTATE HIGHWAY

Development of the national system of interstate and defense highways began in the 1950s. In major urban areas federal government assistance was granted to local governments and planning units to construct express highways around the cities as bypasses and through the cities as limited access expressways. Memphis, Tennessee, planned such road construction; among other things, it planned to construct a stretch of I-40 through the city. A group of local residents organized to stop the construction through a central city park.

> Overton Park is a 342-acre, municipally owned park in midtown Memphis used for a zoo, a 9-hole golf course and other recreational purposes. The proposed section of the interstate highway extends in an east-west direction through the Park over the presently existing paved, non-access highway used by diesel buses which is approximately 4800 feet in length. The existing highway is 40 to 50 feet wide. The proposed interstate will consist of six lanes—three running in each direction, separated by a median strip approximately 40 feet wide. The interstate right-of-way will vary from approximately 250 feet in width to approximately 450 feet in width, and will require the use of approximately 26 acres of the Park. The proposed design requires that a large portion of the highway be depressed sufficiently to remove traffic from the sight of users of the Park; however, five or six feet of fill will be required where a creek runs across the right-of-way. A 1200-foot access ramp will be located within the eastern end of the park.[2]

Initial approval was given by the U.S. Bureau of Public Roads (which later became part of the Department of Transportation) in 1956. Following that, hearings and other discussions were conducted on the route of the new highway and various design alternatives.

In the 1960s, while final decisions were pending, a number of provisions were enacted to protect the environment from burgeoning development. Of particular importance to the citizens of Memphis were identical provisions in the Department of Transportation Act of 1966 and the Federal Aid Highway Act of 1968, which conditioned grants of federal funds for highway construction on the satisfaction of environmental requirements:

> After August 23, 1968, the Secretary shall not approve any program or project which requires the use of any publicly owned land fronting a public park, recreation area or wildlife or waterfowl refuge of national, State, or local significance as determined by the Federal, State or local officials having jurisdiction thereof, or any land from an historic site of national, State, or local significance as so determined by such officials unless (1) there is no feasible and prudent alternative to the use of such land, and (2) such program includes all possible planning to minimize harm to such park, recreational area, wildlife and waterfowl refuge, or historic site resulting from such use.[3]

In November 1969, the Secretary of Transportation gave final approval to federal funding of 90 percent of the cost of the Memphis project. A suit was filed by two property owners and taxpayers of Memphis, the Citizens to Preserve Overton Park (a group that had been actively opposing the construction for some time),[4] the Sierra Club, and the National Audubon Society against the Secretary of Transportation and the commissioner of the Tennessee Department of Highways. The plaintiffs asserted that: (1) the Secretary of Transportation had ignored his statutory responsibility since he had issued no findings or statements of reasons or opinions showing, as the statutes require, that there "is no feasible and prudent alternative to the use of such land" and the "program includes all possible planning to minimize harm" to the park; (2) to the degree that these judgments are implicit in approval of the project, the secretary's actions were arbitrary and capricious, not based on fact and reason but on administrative inertia and agreement with local politicians who chose the route through the park as the path of least resistance (so to speak); and (3) the procedures used in the route and design hearings were inadequate and not in compliance with regulations.[5]

The secretary replied that: (1) the suit should be dismissed because those bringing the action did not have standing; (2) if the case were to proceed, it should be decided on summary judgment since the record was adequate for judicial review and there were no material issues of fact; (3) administrative procedures had been observed in substance even if there had been minor technical weaknesses in form; (4) the statute did not require the secretary to make the findings demanded by the plaintiffs; and (5) his actions were not arbitrary and capricious but were exercises of expert discretionary judgment based on a lengthy consideration of the route and design of the highway.

Summary judgment (a decision based on briefs and the record without a trial) was granted to the secretary by the district court. The court found no problem of standing, but neither did it find it necessary to advance beyond summary judgment since many documents and supporting publications were in the record along with the briefs in the case. The court found no material breaches of procedural requirements. Judge Brown found no requirement in the statute that the secretary enter formal findings concerning the existence of feasible alternatives or adequacy of planning. Finally, the court found no cause for concluding that the secretary had acted in an arbitrary and capricious manner. The primary reason advanced in support of this conclusion was that "it was not the intent of Congress to prohibit the building of an expressway through a park if there was any alternative; rather, by providing that such should not be done if there is any feasible and prudent alternative, it was the intent of Congress to avoid the park if, after considering all relevant factors, it is preferable to do so."[6] No systematic investigation was required, but merely a mandate that the secretary consider the relevant factors that together suggest which routes are feasible and prudent, determined with a sensitivity for environmental values.

By the time the case came to the U.S. Court of Appeals for the Sixth Circuit for review of Judge Brown's summary judgment, ten attorneys from seven firms were on the briefs. In a split decision, the appellate court upheld the lower court. Judge Weick, writing for himself and Judge Peck, concluded that documents submitted to the district court provided enough evidence to decide the case and that there were no material issues of fact that would require more than a summary judgment. Specifically, Weick relied on an affidavit prepared for the secretary at the time the suit was decided in the lower court. The affidavit was that of a Mr. Swick, a long-time official in the federal public roads office. Swick's affidavit stated that the route for the highway was selected in 1956 with a concern for avoiding the park, but officials had concluded that too many people would be displaced and the costs would be too high to go around the park. Besides that, by the time Volpe made his final decision, the right of way been purchased and construction had begun on the part of the road that would run to the park. Any change of plans would have meant great expense, further displacement of people and buildings. Press releases and correspondence were also submitted to suggest the damage that would be caused if an alternative was chosen.

Judge Celebreeze dissented, arguing that Mr. Swick's affidavit was not prepared at the time of the decision, but was developed for his superior later at the time of the litigation. He also referred to statements in the record that disputed the affidavit. For example, a former federal highway administrator had testified before a congressional committee "that the decision to build the highway through the park was left 'completely in the hands of the city council' of Memphis." In short, the federal administrators had not taken responsibility for route consideration. Celebreeze further argued that it would have been difficult for the administrator to have considered the statutory environmental requirements, as suggested by Swick, when the statute was enacted 12 years later. Finally, the court, according to Celebreeze, was in no position to know what the secretary had decided because there was no finding by the secretary on the record, nor was there any suggestion as to exactly what the secretary *did* consider when the highway was approved. He would reverse and remand for a full evidentiary hearing.

The Supreme Court agreed with Judge Celebreeze. Justice Marshall wrote for the Court. He agreed that the statute did not require findings by the secretary. However, the secretary was clearly subject to judicial review under the Administrative Procedure Act.[7] In this case the central problem of review appeared to be to determine whether the administrator properly interpreted and applied the statutes that governed his agency's activities. The particular statute under consideration contained "a plain and explicit bar to the use of federal funds for construction of highways through parks—only the most unusual situations are exempted."[8] The only exemption was in cases where there are no feasible alternatives. "For this exemption to apply the Secretary must find that as a matter of sound engineering it would not be feasible to build the highway along any other route."[9] The government argued that the statute implied a general balancing test, but the Court rejected that interpretation.

> They contend that the Secretary should weigh the detriment resulting from the destruction of parkland against the cost of other routes, safety considerations, and other factors, and determine on the basis of the importance that he attaches to these other factors whether, on balance, alternative feasible routes would be "prudent."
>
> But no such wide-ranging endeavor was intended. It is obvious that in most cases considerations of cost, directness of route, and community disruption will indicate that parkland should be used for highway construction whenever possible. Although it may be necessary to transfer funds from one jurisdiction to another, there will always be a smaller outlay required from the public purse when parkland is used since the public already owns the land and there will be no need to pay for right-of-way. And since people do not live or work in parks, if a highway is built on parkland no one will have to leave his home or give up his business. Such factors are common to substantially all highway construction. Thus, if Congress intended these factors to be on an equal footing with preservation of parkland there would have been no need for the statute.
>
> Congress clearly did not intend that cost and disruption of the community were to be ignored by the Secretary. But the very existence of the statutes indicates that protection of parkland was to be given paramount importance.[10]

The Court then summarized its responsibility in reviewing the decision of the secretary to approve the construction. It became a classic statement of the nature and limits of judicial review of agency action which remains valid today, more than three decades after Justice Marshall authored it:

> The Court is first required to decide whether the Secretary acted within the scope of his authority.... This determination naturally begins with a delineation of the scope of the Secretary's authority and discretion.... As has been shown, Congress has specified only a small range of choices that the Secretary can make. Also involved in this initial inquiry is a determination of whether on the facts the Secretary's decision can reasonably be said to be within that range. The reviewing Court must consider whether the Secretary properly construed his authority to approve the use of parkland as limited to situations where there are no feasible alternative routes or where feasible alternative routes involve uniquely difficult problems. And the reviewing Court must be able to find that the Secretary could have reasonably believed that in this case there are no feasible alternatives or that alternatives do involve unique problems.
>
> Scrutiny of the facts does not end, however, with the determination that the Secretary has acted within the scope of his statutory authority. Section 706(2)(A) requires a finding that the actual choice made was not "arbitrary, capricious, an abuse of discretion, or not otherwise in accordance with law."... To make this finding the Court must consider whether the decision was based on a consideration of the relevant factors and whether there has been a clear error of judgment.... Although this inquiry into the facts is to be searching and careful, the ultimate standard of review is a narrow one. The Court is not empowered to substitute its judgment for that of the agency.[11]

The only way to make such a review is to examine the record that was before the administrator at the time the decision was made. But no such record had been submitted in court, merely documentation that tended to support the decision that had already been made and affidavits that were obviously prepared after the fact to support the secretary's decision against the court challenge.

That administrative record is not, however, before us. The lower courts based their review on the litigation affidavits that were presented. These affidavits were merely "post hoc" rationalizations, Burlington Truck Lines v. United States, 371 U.S. 156, 168-160 (1962), which have traditionally been found to be an inadequate basis for review. . . . And they clearly do not constitute the "whole record" compiled by the agency; the basis for review required by §706 of the Administrative Procedure Act.[12]

The Court sent the case back to the district court for a full review, as described in the Court's opinion, of the whole record that was before the secretary when he made his decision giving final approval to the Memphis project. The Court did not reverse the secretary's decision, but it did require the lower court to take a more careful look.[13]

By the time the case was returned to the district court more parties had become involved in the case. The National Wildlife Federation had joined the plaintiffs. Several groups intervened on behalf of the secretary and the commissioner, including the Memphis Chamber of Commerce, Future Memphis, Inc., and the Downtown Association.[14]

Just after the Supreme Court decision was announced, Judge Brown met with the attorneys to discuss future proceedings. Lawyers for the government informed the judge that it would take several weeks to assemble the whole record that had been before the secretary. The fact that it actually took nearly four and one-half months to do so did not encourage observers to believe that such a record had ever actually existed. The court held 25 days of hearings in the fall of 1971, at which some 240 exhibits were taken into evidence. After the hearings, 287 pages of briefs were also submitted.[15] While the government continued to argue that the secretary had made his judgment based on the facts that there were no "feasible and prudent alternative," the judge disagreed. "[W]hether or not we consider the affidavit and deposition as a 'post hoc rationalization,' the evidence is overwhelming that Secretary Volpe did not so consider alternatives."[16] Even if he had considered some alternatives, his interpretation of the requirement of the statute was in error. These two defects in the secretary's decision required that the case be remanded to the secretary to reconsider the facts and the law in light of the judicial rulings.

However, the case was still not over. After the district court decision, Secretary of Transportation Volpe required that the project be restudied in light of the requirements discussed in the judicial opinions. He also noted that he considered the National Environmental Policy Act (NEPA) of 1969 and the noise pollution limitations required by the 1970 Federal Aid Highway Act applicable to the decision. On January 13, 1973, the secretary issued a decision in which he concluded that the project could not be approved. The Memphis I-40 project did not satisfy the requirements of any of the three statutes involved. He ended his opinion as follows:

> Among the possible alternatives which the State of Tennessee may wish to consider are the use
> of the I-240 circumferencial combined with improvements to arterial streets, alternative routes
> such as the L&N Railroad corridor and a broadened use of public transportation facilities
> and services or combinations of the above to meet the transportation needs in and around
> Memphis. . . . Listing these possible alternative should not, of course, be construed either as an
> endorsement of any of them or as an exclusion of any other alternatives that I have not men-
> tioned. Likewise it should not be construed as a finding that the "no build" alternative has
> been rejected.

At this point, the state of Tennessee sued the Secretary of Transportation, arguing that his latest decision was inadequate. In particular, the state asserted that the secretary must find that there were no "feasible and prudent" alternatives, for if there are such alternatives, he must identify them and authorize the state to employ them. The district court agreed and the decision was again remanded to the secretary.

By this time, a new Secretary of Transportation, Claude Brinegar, had been appointed. Represented by a new group of attorneys from the Justice Department, attorneys not involved in earlier stages of the case, and joined by the Citizens to Preserve Overton Park, the secretary appealed the district court decision to the Sixth Circuit Court of Appeals. The case was heard by the same three judges who had originally heard the first appeal in 1970. On April 3, 1974, the court of appeals announced a unanimous decision in favor of the secretary, finding that the secretary had no affirmative obligation to provide the state with an alternative. The secretary's sole job under the statute was to approve or disapprove plans submitted by the state or local governments seeking federal assistance.[17]

MYTH AND REALITY IN JUDICIAL REVIEW

The classic *Overton Park* case illustrates a number of common characteristics of judicial review of administrative action. In addition to demonstrating the kinds of questions that judges ask administrators, the case gives the lie to several more or less widespread myths about the process.

Judicial review is not a simple one-stop gate at which some gatekeeper is charged with deciding whether to allow the administrative decision to go forward or not. As the simple system model of the administrative justice system discussed in Chapter 1 indicated, decisions can exist at several points without going to courts. In fact, only a small percentage of administrative decisions are ever taken to judicial review.[18] If it were otherwise, both the courts and administrative agencies would be in serious trouble. Neither could handle the burden. When cases do go to court, they may be sent back (remanded) for clarification. In a remand, a decision may not be reversed, but the court may find that the decisionmaker needs to supplement the ruling that was made or correct portions of the administrative action that were inadequately supported or decided according to an incorrect interpretation of law. In fact, judicial review has been described as more of a dialogue over the requirements of law between courts and officials in the executive and legislative branches than a dictating of terms in one grand, final decision.[19]

As *Overton Park* indicates, cases that come for review often do not fit the neat rulemaking or adjudication categories. As noted in Chapter 1, administrative decisions can take a variety of forms. Judges who review those decisions, in whatever form they are presented, must ensure that they conform to the requirements of law.

Further, public law cases frequently involve more than two individuals or organizations, particularly where they are public law policy cases as opposed to status cases (see Chapter 1). Part of this dynamic can be explained in terms of the practice of litigation as an interest-group tactic.[20] For the present, it is important to be alert to the fact that while interest group litigation seems like a relatively recent phenomenon and one that has often been tied to what are labeled liberal positions, it has been with us for many decades. Indeed, the seeds of modern interest group litigation can be found in the late nineteenth and early twentieth centuries as conservative groups fought the development of regulatory regimes at the national and state levels. They attracted particular attention when they organized to fight the women's suffrage and child labor amendments.

The more common contemporary picture flows from the work of the National Association for the Advancement of Colored People, Legal Defense and Education Fund (NAACP, LDF), led for many years by Thurgood Marshall, later a justice of the U.S. Supreme Court. Environmental organizations, women's groups, and Native American advocates learned from the strategies and tactics of the NAACP, LDF and used those techniques to affect policy from the 1960s onward. However, the research of scholars such as O'Connor and Epstein demonstrated that, during the decade of the 1970s and into the 1980s, conservative groups became much more active as interest group litigators, such that by the 1980s they were, for example, as active in cases before the U.S. Supreme Court as were liberal groups.[21] (The terms liberal and conservative are used here in their contemporary common meaning.) Since, then, there has been a continued expansion in conservative interest group litigators, with the addition of a host of new organizations such as groups associated with religious causes and what has been termed the property rights movement.[22] In addition to challenging the arguments presented by their political adversaries, these groups on the right also presented issues that were different from those raised by the other groups. Whereas the liberal groups tended to argue social questions, issues of individual freedom, protection for the environment, and inequality, conservative groups have tended to emphasize economic rights, protections against governmental regulation, and majoritarian prerogatives. Both sides have claimed to represent the public interest, merely different conceptions of what that interest is in any given situation.

Quite apart from the particular views of interest groups, however, there is a broader concern. As the members of the Attorney General's Committee on Administrative Procedure noted as long ago as 1941, it is one thing to get agreement between an agency and someone with an interest in an agency decision, but quite another to serve the public interest. For example, it is frequently in the political interests of some regulatory officials to avoid confrontation with the groups they regulate, but, at some point, the failure to confront an individual or business organization for pollution or safety violations is a failure to perform the responsibility assigned to the agency by the legislature. That is especially true during periods of deregulation or times such as these when negotiated alternatives are heavily favored over enforcement. Other parties may become involved in an effort to force administrators to honor their statutory obligations. In *Overton Park,* clearly the local political officials wanted to build through the park and the secretary of transportation had an interest in assisting them. Outside parties intervened to challenge the secretary's cooperation on the ground that it was not in the public interest as declared by congressional enactment. The local chamber of commerce entered on the other side of the case. Then other groups entered as well.

This phenomenon of group convergence around a developing challenge to administrative action is common, particularly once it becomes clear that the case at hand promises to have a significant impact upon public policy. For example, when Judge Frank Johnson ruled for the first time that mental patients who had been committed to state facilities for treatment had a constitutional right to receive that treatment and to be provided with a safe and humane environment, interest groups from around the nation converged on the case in an attempt to affect the remedy that was being developed in the case.[23] It was an opportunity to play a role in shaping the minimum standards of treatment and care, and no serious national interest group could afford to be left out. When the Supreme Court agreed to hear an Ohio case that challenged the practice of double-celling maximum security inmates in state prisons designed to hold one prisoner per cell, all 50 state attorneys general came to the assistance of Ohio in briefs before the Court.[24]

More recently, when the state of Washington sought to add regulations to the operation of oil tankers in the Puget Sound against a backdrop of significant oil spills and failures in the federal regulatory policies, it found itself dealing with an interesting array of parties. The new state regulatory agency and its rules were initially challenged by a group known as INTERTANKO, an acronym for the International Association of Independent Tanker Owners. The members of the group, headquartered in Oslo, Norway, owned about 80 percent of the world's fleet of independently operated tankers. They claimed that Washington's regulatory regime was preempted by federal statutes and international agreements.[25] The state's position was supported by lawyers for Skagit, King, and Snohomish counties, and three environmental interest groups also argued in support of the new rules, including the Washington Environmental Council, National Resource Defense Council, and Ocean Advocates, Inc.

The Clinton administration, which prided itself on a pro-environmental agenda, later became involved as a challenger to the state when 13 counties filed a diplomatic note opposing the state actions and insisting that the U.S. government stop what they regarded as Washington's violations of international accords.[26] Canada both filed a protest and later a friend of the court brief against the state. The federal government then intervened and became the lead challenger in the case as it wound its way to the Supreme Court. Along the way, the Makah Indians also filed in the case. The Makah were in an ongoing fight over their right to hunt a small number of whales as part of their long-standing treaty rights and their relationships with state regulators, the federal government, and international bodies.[27] Twenty states and the Northern Mariana Islands supported Washington. Others filed or joined briefs in the case opposing the state, including the Puget Sound Steamship Operators, the British Columbia Chamber of Shipping, the Baltic and International Maritime Council, the Chamber of Shipping of

America, the Product Liability Advisory Council, the Chamber of Commerce of the United States, the International Chamber of Shipping, and the International Group of Protection and Indemnity Clubs, the Maritime Law Association of the United States, the National Association of Waterfront Employers, Signal Mutual Indemnity Association, the Steamship Association of Southern California, and the conservative interest group litigation organization, the Washington Legal Foundation. The Supreme Court ultimately struck down most of the state's actions and remanded some others for further action.[28]

In addition to the effort by interest groups to intervene, several attorneys may be involved in an administrative case. Some may be from prestigious firms and have a great deal of experience in policy-related adjudications, while others may be from local firms without such experience. On the government side, there may be several government units represented by a number of attorneys. From the judge's perspective, that often means that the quality of arguments provided can be extremely uneven and, in some instances, simply bad. That can be troublesome for the judges who must then craft opinions in the case that not only address the current dispute, but also provide precedents for the future.

In some cases there can be conflict among government units at different levels in different branches or between independent commissions and executive branch agencies.[29] There can also be difficulties in litigation if there is a dispute between the Department of Justice, which generally controls federal government litigation, and agency attorneys, who may legitimately conclude that they have more detailed knowledge in a particular case. The Environmental Protection Agency may argue strongly that agency attorneys who are familiar with the policy and the technical concepts that underpin it know best as compared to Justice Department lawyers who are less experienced in the specifics. On the other hand, the DOJ insists through the Attorney General that it must control litigation policy to ensure a coherent and consistent government position.[30]

As an example of the kind of complexity that a judge may face, consider the cases brought to challenge the use of the legislative veto of agency rulemaking. What follows is a listing of parties and attorneys in one of the most important of the legislative veto cases, *Consumer Energy Council of America v. Federal Energy Regulatory Commission*.[31]

Alan B. Morrison, Washington, D.C., with whom John Cart Sims, Washington, D.C., was on the brief for petitioners.

Larry L. Simms, Acting Asst. Att. Gen., Dept. of Justice, of the bar of the Supreme Court of Vermont, pro hac vice by special leave of Court, Washington, D.C., with whom Harold H. Bruff and Anthony J. Steinmeyer, Attys., Depart. of Justice, Washington, S.C., were on the brief for amicus curiae, U.S.

Jerome M. Feit, Deputy Sol., Federal Energy Regulatoy Comm'n, Washington, D.C., with whom Jerome Nelson, Acting Gen. Counsel, and Stephen R. Melton, Atty., Federal Energy Regulatory Comm'n, Washington, D.C., were on the brief for respondent.

Edward J. Grenier, Jr., Washington, D.C., with whom Michael J. Shea, Glen S. Howard, Marilyn L. Muench, and David A. Gross, Washington, D.C., were on the brief for intervenors, The Process Gas Consumers Group, et al.

C. William Cooper, Falmouth, Mass., with whom Richard M. Merriman, David G. Hanes, L. Peter Farkas, John D. McGrane, Payton G. Bowman, III, and John R. Schaefgen, Jr., Washington, D.C., were on the brief for intervenors, United Distribution Companies.

Michael Davidson, Senate Legal Counsel, Washington, D.C., with whom Elizabeth Culbreth, Deputy Senate Legal Counsel, and Charles Tiefer, Asst. Senate Legal Counsel, Washington, D.C., were on the brief for amicus curiae, U.S. Senate, urging dismissal.

Eugene Gressman, Washington, D.C., for amicus curiae, Speaker of the U.S. House of Representatives, urging dismissal.

John A. Myler, Washington, D.C., was on the brief for intervenor, American Gas Ass'n.

Lawrence V. Robertson, Jr., Washington, D.C., was on the brief for intervenor, Interstate Natural Gas Ass'n of America.

R. Gordon Gooch, B. Donovan Picard, Thomas J. Eastment, and John W. Leslie, Washington, D.C., were on the brief for intervenor, Petrochemical Energy Group.

In this instance the interest groups were well represented, both the gas companies and the consumer groups. A number of the groups were permitted to become "intervenors"—that is, to actually join the case as parties. It would be clear to the experienced observer just from the identity of these groups (and who was representing them) that this was a far more important case than might be otherwise apparent. However, one can also notice that there are a number of different types of attorneys for the government in the case. The Justice Department represented the position of the executive branch, but only as *amicus curiae* (friend of the court). There was separate representation for the Federal Energy Regulatory Commission, using its own attorneys. The reason is that the FERC is an independent regulatory commission, even though it is located in the Department of Energy. What may be even less clear is why there are different attorneys representing the House of Representatives and the Senate, both of which appeared as friends of the court. For some years now, the U.S. Senate has had its own counsel. On the House side, the Clerk of the House has been able to retain counsel to represent the House. Of course, both houses also draw on the American Law Division of the Congressional Research Service to provide assistance.

In one case, the Supreme Court had to appoint an *amicus curiae* to support the position of the Social Security Administration.[32] The case came to the Court because the Court of Appeals had held a disability claimant's challenge unappealable. The Solicitor General, the attorney who represents the U.S. government in the Supreme Court, supported the claimant against the government. Thus, the Court appointed a private attorney to support the decision of the Court of Appeals.

At the state level, the process can be every bit as complex and adds one distinctive dimension. At that level, even more than at the federal level, administrative agencies are dependent on the Attorney General for legal advice as well as for representation in litigation. However, in most states, the Attorney General is independently elected and not appointed by the chief executive as is true at the federal level. Indeed, those who run for state Attorney General are often people who see themselves on a track to run for governor. It can and does happen that an Attorney General of the major party other than the governor's may be elected or the occupant of the Office of Attorney General may sometimes see his or her interest in opposing the positions of the governor or the administration's administrative agencies. Thus, in one state, the Attorney General brought a successful challenge to a state legislative veto statute, naming both houses of the state legislature and the governor.[33] Later, that same office aligned itself with the legislature to bring suit against the governor with respect to who should have control over negotiations under the Indian Gaming Act.

In addition to the controversies over legal representation, it should be clear that cases brought for judicial review of administrative actions often arise in a complex political environment. By the time a decision gets to the judicial review stage, various groups and government agencies may have already invested considerable economic and political resources in the controversy. The intensity of interest and conflict varies, but, whatever the level of political debate, the judge must be aware of the nature of the controversy before him or her and sensitive to the environment in which it arose and is played out.

Finally, *Overton Park* demonstrates that judges who review administrative actions have complex tasks to perform. They certainly do not engage in simplistic mechanical jurisprudence in which only narrow, clean procedural questions are presented for a plain yes or no judgment. The factors discussed in Chapter 3 that make up the law in action come together to frame the responsibilities and opportunities of the judge in administrative law.

JUDGES AND AGENCIES

The various questions that must be dealt with as administrative decisions come for judicial review are conditioned by the legal bases for review, the particular purposes that such review is designed to serve, and the several tasks that together make up the role of the judge in reviewing agency decisions.

The APA on Judicial Review

There are several bases for judicial review, beginning, of course, with the requirements of the Constitution. Statutes and judicial decisions also describe the need for particular types of review of agency action in specific situations. The general underpinning for judicial review in administrative law is the APA, 5 U.S.C. §701 et seq. Section 702 provides that: "A person suffering legal wrong because of agency action, or adversely affected or aggrieved by agency action within the meaning of a relevant statute, is entitled to judicial review thereof." The type of inquiry to be accomplished by the court is set forth in section 706:

> To the extent necessary to decision and when presented, the reviewing court shall decide all relevant questions of law, interpret constitutional and statutory provisions, and determine the meaning or applicability of the terms of an agency action. The reviewing court shall—
>
> (1) compel agency action unlawfully withheld or unreasonably delayed; and
>
> (2) hold unlawful and set aside agency action, findings, and conclusions found to be—
>   (A) arbitrary, capricious, an abuse of discretion, or otherwise not in accordance with law;
>   (B) contrary to constitutional right, power, privilege, or immunity;
>   (C) in excess of statutory jurisdiction, authority, or limitations, or short of statutory right;
>   (D) without observance of procedure required by law;
>   (E) unsupported by substantial evidence in a case subject to section 556 and 557 of this title or otherwise reviewed on the record of an agency hearing provided by statute; or
>   (F) unwarranted by the facts to the extent that the facts are subject to trial de novo by the reviewing court.
>
> In making the foregoing determinations, the court shall review the whole record or those parts of it cited by a party, and due account shall be taken of the rule of prejudicial error.

Functions of Judicial Review

A review such as that prescribed by the APA serves a number of purposes. (1) It establishes the boundaries of administrative authority through interpretation of the Constitution and statutes; (2) it provides feedback to the legislature, agencies, and the public on the meaning of law and the nature of agency authority; (3) it reconciles or at least identifies potentially conflicting federal, state, and local statutes and regulations; (4) it helps agencies develop orderly and regular processes for change and resolution of disputes; (5) it discourages, to some extent at least, abuses of discretion, thereby supporting the legitimacy of administrative decisionmaking; (6) It provides some protection from temporary majoritarian pressures on agencies that might undermine protection of individual rights or interfere with the use of an agency's independent technical expertise; and (7) it forces the development of records for use in later policymaking.

Role of the Public Law Judge

The judge who reviews an administrative action is obligated to accomplish the purposes described above in the manner set forth in the APA, and in accordance with statutory and constitutional law. However, there are also other aspects to the judge's role in such cases.[34]

Judges have an obligation to keep administrators within the law. However, they are able to do so only sporadically, as cases arise, and the way in which cases are structured is largely out of their control. By means of a number of technical jurisdictional and procedural rules, judges can avoid some decisions, but the ability to avoid difficult cases is somewhat limited, particularly in the lower courts. Judges are to some degree captives of the manner in which the advocates cast the case. If the advocates are effective and thorough, the judges have a better case to work with than if the opposite were true.

Second, as a court administrator once said, judges are in a business in which at least half the customers leave dissatisfied. In judicial review of administrative decisions, it is not uncommon for both sides to leave grumbling, one because the court did too much and the other because the court did not do enough. It is important that the judge draft solid, effective opinions. Opinions explain to the winners the judge's reasoning and give guidance for the future. They also explain to the losers why they did not prevail. The judges must—or at least are expected to—craft opinions in such a way that the ruling may be understood, reasonably well accepted, and complied with.

Judges in public law cases must be more than umpires. They must play an often challenging role in managing the cases that come to their courts. In cases where there are 25 or more briefs and 40 or more parties, this may be very difficult.

Part of case management and sometimes of more substantive legal decisionmaking is the task of dealing with multiple and sometimes conflicting units of government or at least agencies that have different missions and agency cultures. These challenges often arise in cases with multiple and diverse organizations challenging the agencies as well. To do this, judges must interpret and relate different statutes that are administered by different agencies that address the same or related issues. Consider the discussion in Chapter 5 concerning the roles of the USDA, FDA, and CDC in dealing with mad cow disease or the interactions of the NRC, DOT, and IAEA in regulating the transportation of nuclear materials. In *Overton Park*, for example, the secretary was obligated by statute to consult with two other cabinet-level departments. The secretary was concerned about three statutes, all of which affected his decision in the case.

In some situations agencies that are very different may be operating in the same policy arena and the same geographic area, but with different roles, and any of these agencies may end up before reviewing courts. The ongoing battle in the Pacific Northwest over the operation of dams on the Columbia and Snake rivers provides one example with a number of agencies involved. Such varied groups as farmers, commercial fishing operators, tribal communities, and electric power providers find themselves involved. When issues such as the amount of water flow over the dams and how it threatens endangered salmon, the judicial review process can be complex indeed. Consider the parties in just one salmon decision rendered by the U.S. Circuit Court of Appeals for the Ninth Circuit in 2005. The decision addressed three companion cases and was styled as follows:

National Wildlife Federation; Idaho Wildlife Federation; Washington Wildlife Federation; Sierra Club; Trout Unlimited; Pacific Coast Federation of Fishermen's Associations; Institute for Fisheries Resources; Idaho Rivers United; Idaho Steelhead and Salmon United; Northwest Sport Fishing Industry Association; Salmon for All; Columbia Riverkeeper; NW Energy Coalition; Federation of Fly Fishers, American Rivers, Inc., Plaintiffs-Appellees, v. National Marine Fisheries Service; United States Army Corps of Engineers; U.S. Bureau of Reclamation, Defendants, Franklin County Farm Bureau Federation; Grant County Farm Board Federation; Washington Farm Bureau Federation; State of Idaho Clarkson Golf & Country Club, Defendants-Intervenors, and Northwest Irrigation Utilities; Public Power Council; Pacific Northwest Generating Cooperative; BPA [Bonneville Power Authority] Customer Group, Defendants-Intervenors-Appellants, v. State of Oregon, Plaintiff-Intervenor-Appellee. National Wildlife Federation; Idaho Wildlife Federation; Washington Wildlife Federation; Sierra Club; Trout Unlimited; Pacific Coast Federation of Fishermen's Association; Institute for Fisheries Resources; Idaho Rivers United; Idaho Steelhead and Salmon United; Northwest Sport Fishing Industry Association, Salmon for all; Columbia Riverkeeper; NW Energy Coalition; Federation of Fly Fishers; American Rivers, Inc., Plaintiffs-Appellees, v. National Marine Fisheries Service; United States Army Corps of Engineers; U.S. Bureau of Reclamation, Defendants, Northwest Irrigation Utilities; Public Power Council; Pacific Northwest Generating Cooperative; BPA Customer Group; Franklin County Farm Bureau Federation; Grant County Farm Board Federation; Washington Wildlife Federation; Sierra Club; Trout Unlimited; Pacific Coast Federation of Fishermen's Associations; Institute for Fisheries

Resources; Idaho Rivers United; Idaho Steelhead and Salmon United; Northwest Sport Fishing Industry Association, Salmon for All; Columbia Riverkeeper; NW Energy Coalition; Federation of Fly Fishers; American Rivers, Inc,. Plaintiffs-Appellees, v. National Marine Fisheries Service; United States Army Corps of Engineers; U.S. Bureau of Reclamation, Defendants-Appellants, and Northwest Irrigation Utilities; Public Power Council; Pacific Northwest Generation Cooperative; BPA Customer Group; Franklin County Farm Bureau Federation; Grant Country Farm Board Federation; Washington Farm Bureau Federation; State of Idaho; Clarkson Golf & Country Club, Defendants-Intervenors, v. State of Oregon, Plaintiff-Intervenor-Appellee, No[s]. 05-35569, No. 05-35646, No. 05-35570.[35]

A judge might ask government attorneys to consolidate their positions in the case where that is possible, request written argument on possible areas of conflict in statutes or agency policy, press attorneys at oral argument for clarifications, and draft opinions that attempt to systematically relate the various authorities involved and note points of conflict. Even so, the judge may find it difficult to deal with varied government arguments in addition to the challenges of multiple nongovernmental parties.

The judge must also guard against a preference for what might be termed glamour cases. Former Illinois Congressman Railsback once observed: "I had the experience of representing a couple of social security disability claimants, and . . . I got the distinct feeling that the district court judge could have cared less that I was representing this woman who happened to suffer from emphysema, I was taking up his valuable time."[36] It can be very difficult for judges who have reviewed major government administrative policy decisions to turn next to individual social security cases, freedom of information disputes, and/or small-scale regulatory enforcement cases. Still, there are many more of the latter cases and they are of extreme importance to the parties bringing them. Judges must guard against the temptation to underestimate when the consequences of an unlawful decision may be of no apparent consequence to the nation, yet are of crucial importance to individual citizens.

Finally, the judge must, as the chapter indicated earlier, work on the balance point between careful and thorough review of administrative action and judicial usurpation of administrative authority.

These responsibilities and the manner in which they are performed can be understood in part through considering the questions that are asked as a case comes on for and proceeds through judicial review. Two general questions, each with a number of subsidiary aspects, should be asked: (1) Should the case be allowed to get through the courthouse door for review? (2) If the case is properly presented for review, what kind of review should be provided?

ENTRANCE THROUGH THE COURTHOUSE DOOR: PROCEDURAL ROADBLOCKS TO JUDICIAL REVIEW

Whether a case for judicial review will be allowed to get through the door of the courthouse involves three considerations. First, the case must be presented to a tribunal that has the jurisdiction to decide it. Second, the case must be ready for review and the proper parties must be bringing it. The third question is whether the judges will use the discretion they possess in interpreting procedural rules, what they sometimes refer to as prudential considerations,[37] to block the case.

Jurisdiction

A case can be properly brought only in a court that has jurisdiction—that is, the authority to decide the issues presented in a particular situation and for the specific parties involved. The judicial power is the power to decide cases and controversies.[38] Jurisdiction is the authority to apply that power in a particular case.[39] That authority is provided in broad compass by the Constitution, but more specifically by statute. To obtain judicial review, then, one must show that the court in which the case is brought has jurisdiction to hear it.[40]

More broadly, the judge may be called on to determine whether the rules of judicial self-restraint, discussed in Chapter 3, have been met.[41] Is the case justiciable—in other words, is it the kind of a case the court can hear and do something about?

The Case and the Parties

There are several different questions that judges ask to determine if the suit brought before them is a proper case or controversy. These questions concern the preparation of the case itself and whether the parties bringing the case are properly before the court. The first such question is whether the parties have standing to litigate the case.

At root, the idea of standing to sue is that the party bringing the case must demonstrate that he or she is a proper party to ensure that there is valid case or controversy. The purpose of this Article III requirement is to ensure that the parties to a suit have the "concrete adverseness" that makes for a serious effort to present sharp and clearly defined legal issues to a court.[42] This is to ensure that both parties have good reason to put up their best case so that the adversary system will operate. With both sides fighting hard, the expectation is that they will focus the dispute and cast the core issues in high relief in such a way as to assist the judge in understanding and resolving them.

To have standing, the parties filing the case must demonstrate that they are the right parties to be bringing the matter before the court. As the Supreme Court has explained it:

> The question of standing involves both constitutional limitations on federal-court jurisdiction and prudential limitations on its exercise.... In addition to the immutable requirements of Article III, the federal judiciary has also adhered to a set of prudential principles that bear on the question of standing. Like their constitutional counterparts, these judicial self-imposed limits on the exercise of federal jurisdiction ... are founded in concern about the proper—and properly limited—role of the courts in a democratic society ... but unlike their constitutional counterparts, they can be modified or abrogated by Congress.[43]

The discussion of standing to sue is far more complicated than it used to be. However, it is possible to understand the concept in two parts. First, we can consider the criteria that have been developed and the explanation that has been given to support them. Second, we can consider the judicial politics that have shaped the changes in standing requirements.

In order to demonstrate standing, it is necessary for the party bringing to case to demonstrate that there has been injury in fact to his or her legally protected rights or interests, that the injury was the result of the action or lack of action of the other side, and that the injury is redressable.[44]

> On many occasions, we have reiterated the three requirements that constitute the "irreducible constitutional minimum" of standing.... First, a plaintiff must demonstrate an "injury in fact," which is "concrete," "distinct and palpable," and "actual or imminent."... Second, a plaintiff must establish "a causal connection between the injury and the conduct complained of—the injury has to be 'fairly trace[able] to the challenged action of the defendant, and not ... th[e] result [of] some third party not before the court.'"... Third, a plaintiff must show the "'substantial likelihood' that the requested relief will remedy the alleged injury in fact."[45]

The term "injury in fact" to protected interests implies that one has actually been hurt or stands in imminent danger of being harmed, rather than that one is merely concerned about some hypothetical injury that might or might not occur.[46] The injury must have occurred or be imminent. Thus, when Senator Mitch McConnell (R–KY) led a group challenging various campaign reform policies administered by the Federal Election Commission (FEC), the Court rejected his claim to standing to attack the provisions governing the purchase of advertising time. The Court concluded in 2003 that because the Senator could not be affected by the provision until five years later, the injury was simply too remote to allow him to have standing to sue at the present time.[47]

The frequent reference in commentaries on standing regarding injury to legally protected interests is also important.[48] All citizens are affected in one way or another by most government policies and any number of them may consider themselves to be injured by government action. However, the "generalized undifferentiated injury," that a citizen[49] or even a member of Congress[50] may assert with regard to, say, the operation of U.S. intelligence agencies' activity, is an insufficient basis for a lawsuit challenging official action. Instead, one must point to more specific injury, such as interference with a specific constitutional or statutory right. As the Court noted in the McConnell case, "to satisfy our standing requirements, a plaintiff's alleged injury must be an invasion of a concrete and particularized legally protected interest. . . . Although standing in no way depends on the merits of the plaintiff's contention that particular conduct is illegal, . . . it often turns on the nature and source of the claim asserted."[51]

The Court has also held that the injury must be "fairly traceable" to the actions of the challenged party, which in the case of judicial review means the agency whose decisions are in question. For example, a group representing poor people in the Appalachian coal mining region brought a challenge to a change in the Internal Revenue Service code that reduced the requirements on medical facilities as to the type and amount of free care that had to be provided to the poor. The Court found, *inter alia* (a commonly used legal expression meaning "among other things"), that the parties had not demonstrated that the changes in the tax code actually caused the reduction in the availability of care for the poor.[52]

The final element of redressability requires a showing that there is a "likelihood that the requested relief will redress the alleged injury."[53] Consider two examples. In the first, a citizens' group brought suit to enforce the Right-to-Know statute that requires industries to report their emissions and then calls for various public information and emergency planning activities in the event of an environmental disaster.[54] They notified the company that it was in violation and called upon the Environmental Protection Agency and state authorities to take enforcement action. The company quickly filed its overdue reports and the agencies decided not to take action. The citizens' group sued under so-called citizen suit provisions of the Right-to-Know statute, but the Court found that since the company had already complied, the group had not identified a remedy that would be effective to deal with the past violation.[55]

In another case, a group brought suit against a change in rules by the Department of the Interior. Previously, the rule required that U.S. agencies engaged in projects abroad meet the same kinds of procedural and participation requirements that they would face at home in the United States with respect to the constraints presented by the Endangered Species Act. The Court denied standing among other reasons because it determined that there was little evidence that the relief requested would actually stop the projects that the group said threatened the Nile crocodiles in Egypt or the Asian elephants in Sri Lanka that the group cited as threatened by U.S. projects.[56]

If all this conveys the sense that many potential challenges to administrative action get bogged down in procedural battles far from the merits of the case, that is an accurate perception. But there is more. The Supreme Court, from the 1970s on, has developed what the justices refer to as a set of prudential considerations. These judicially created requirements are not tied to the need to ensure that there is a "case" or "controversy."

> Beyond the constitutional requirements, the federal judiciary has also adhered to a set of prudential principles that bear on the question of standing. Thus, this Court has held that "the plaintiff generally must assert his own legal rights and interests, and cannot rest his claim to relief on the legal rights or interests of third parties." . . . In addition, even when the plaintiff has alleged redressable injury sufficient to meet the requirements of Art III, the Court has refrained from adjudicating "abstract questions of wide public significance" which amount to "generalized grievances," pervasively shared and most appropriately addressed in the representative branches. . . . Finally, the Court has required that the plaintiff's complaint fall within

"the zone of interests to be protected or regulated by the statute or constitutional guarantee in question."[57]

Courts have held that organizations can sue on behalf of the interests of their members.[58] But, in general, neither an individual nor a group may ask for judicial review to protect the interests of a third party not involved in the litigation.[59] Thus, in a case that arose outside of Rochester, New York, the Court held that poor and minority litigants did not have standing to contest a local government's use of restrictive zoning and building codes to prevent developers from constructing low and moderate income housing. The Court would not even allow litigants in that case who were developers and had been denied permits in the past but did not have a project pending currently. If a developer who did have a case pending currently wanted to bring suit, that would be one thing, but the others could not purport to represent the interests of such a third party.[60] This limitation is putatively intended to ensure that the parties before the court are well suited to argue the case.[61] However, the courts have for many years made exceptions where special circumstances exist.[62]

The zone of interest test requires that the grievance "must arguably fall within the zone of interests protected or regulated by the statutory provision or constitutional guarantee invoked in the suit."[63] In its simplest terms, this requirement means that where parties brought the suit under a particular statute, the Court would seek to be certain that the parties and the issues they raised fit within the scope of activities the legislature intended to protect.[64] Since the APA provides a very broad grant of review, its "zone of interests" can be quite wide.[65]

In short, the Supreme Court's development of standing rules has given judges a substantial range of discretion regarding whether someone bringing a case has standing. And unless one can meet the requirements for standing to sue one cannot get through the courthouse door, even though all other procedural requirements have been satisfied.

Of course, in addition to the inquiry whether the parties are appropriate in terms of standing, the Court will also consider carefully whether the case itself is ready for judicial consideration. That includes a determination that the decision to be reviewed is ripe for review and that administrative and lower court remedies have been exhausted. The ripeness concept means that the controversy has reached the point at which it is no longer about hypothetical events, but is concrete.[66] One of most common scenarios in this respect comes about when a new statute is enacted or new regulations are issued. Those who fear that they are likely to be adversely affected may move quickly to court, asking for declaratory and injunctive relief in an effort to block any effort to implement the new mandate. In some exceptional cases, the court may accept such a case, declare the law, and issue an injunction.[67] However, most often the court will tell the challenger to wait until it becomes clear what the responsible agency will do with the new enactment and reject the invitation to speculate about what might or might not happen.[68]

> Without undertaking to survey the intricacies of the ripeness doctrine it is fair to say that its basic rationale is to prevent the courts, through avoidance of premature adjudication, from entangling themselves in abstract disagreements over administrative policies, and also to protect the agencies from judicial interference until an administrative decision has been formalized and its effects felt in a concrete way by the challenging parties. The problem is best seen in a twofold aspect, requiring us to evaluate both the fitness of the issues for judicial decision and the hardship to the parties of withholding court consideration.[69]

With respect to specific decisions, the Court in making a ripeness judgment also looks to ensure that there is finality.[70] According to the Supreme Court: "As a general matter, two conditions must be satisfied for agency action to be 'final': First, the action must mark the 'consummation' of the agency's decisionmaking process . . . —it must not be of a merely tentative or interlocutory nature. And second, the action must be one by which 'rights or obligations have been determined,' or from which 'legal consequences will flow. . . .'"[71] This finality requirement is important because, while many litigants want to get into court and out of what they perceive to be an unfavorable administrative forum, the record needs to be fully developed and the issues clarified before the case is ready to be reviewed. Related to the finality requirement, of course, is the need to ensure that available administrative and lower court remedies have been exhausted.[72]

It might seem as though contemporary governance arrangements would be somewhat easier to deal with in matters of judicial challenge as they are often based upon contracts, which usually contain clauses specifying how and under what conditions disputes are to be addressed. However, a recent case involving concession contracts (contracts to operate hotel, restaurant, and other visitor services) in national parks suggests otherwise. The case arose when the National Park Service (NPS) launched a rulemaking process. Today many of the activities that visitors may assume are operated by the Park Service are in fact provided by private for-profit and in some cases nonprofit firms under contracts with the agency. The use of concession contracts in the parks was further developed and expanded as a result of the National Parks Omnibus Management Act of 1998. The Park Service issued rules implementing the statute, which included a definition of concession contracts: "A concession contract (or contract) means a binding written agreement between the Director and a concessioner. . . . Concession contracts are not contracts within the meaning of . . . (the Contract Disputes Act) and are not service or procurement contracts within the meaning of statutes, regulations or policies that apply only to federal service contracts or other types of federal procurement actions."[73]

The focus of the controversy that ensued was the effort by the Park Service in this definition to remove concession contracts from the coverage of the Contract Disputes Act (CDA), which provides the mechanisms for handling disputes that arise under most federal contracts. The NPS definition was incorporated by reference into its bidding and contract documents. The NPS action followed a long-running disagreement with the Department of the Interior (DOI) Board of Contract Appeals. While the Park Service is a unit within the Department of the Interior, it had disagreed with the position of the board on the applicability of the CDA. The National Park Hospitality Association, a trade association for concession contractors, along with some of its individual members challenged the NPS regulations. The district court and court of appeals substantially upheld the NPS position, but the Supreme Court raised on its own motion the question whether the dispute was ripe for review on grounds that the regulations had not yet actually been applied to any particular dispute.

The NPS case was further complicated by the fact that the rule states a position with respect to the Contract Dispute Act, but the Park Service has no authority to issue rules with respect to the CDA. The federal government's position in the case was that the NPS action was an interpretive rule, setting forth its understanding of the requirements of its legislative mandate and the applicability of the CDA to it.

The Court's majority opinion, written by Justice Thomas, found that the NPS action was nothing more than a policy statement with no binding effect or even clear applicability to any pending disputes. In part because of that determination, the Court concluded that there was no immediate direct effect on anyone's rights or behavior. Therefore, the case was not ripe for adjudication.

However, Justice Breyer, in a dissent joined by Justice O'Connor, disagreed that there was no present effect on the challengers to the regulations. Breyer countered that the association's members are either currently parties to concession contracts or are at one or another stage of the process of bidding for such contracts.

> Those members will likely find that disputes arise under the contracts. And in resolving such disputes, the Park Service, following its regulation, will reject the concessioners' entitlement to the significant protections or financial advantages that the CDA provides. . . . For another thing, the challenged Park Service interpretation causes a present injury. If the CDA does not apply to concession contract disagreements, as the Park Service regulation declares, then some of petitioner's members must plan now for higher contract implementation costs. Given the agency's regulation, bidders will likely be forced to pay more to obtain, or to retain, a concession contract than they believe the contract is worth.[74]

Moreover, he said, it is already clear based on another statute that contractors can bring an action to challenge a policy that threatens the kind of harm that the firms and their trade association are facing.[75]

Therefore, there were harms to the challengers and, since the question presented was a purely legal issue rather than one based in a particular factual context, there was no basis to reject the case for ripeness.

There is an important caveat to the discussion of ripeness in some cases that raises questions of fundamental constitutional rights. Particularly in situations where First Amendment issues are involved, the Supreme Court has crafted exceptions to the normal application of the ripeness doctrine on grounds that even short-term deprivations of such fundamental rights as freedom of speech and of the press are unacceptable. It is in just such situations that a court is more likely to grant a request for an expedited hearing and a possible declaratory judgment even where a new law or regulation has not yet been applied. Indeed, the Supreme Court has indicated that where permitting requirements may affect protected First Amendment rights, an administrative permit process must ensure a prompt judicial review of administrative denial of a permit.[76]

It sometimes happens that a controversy changes while it rises through the levels of the judicial system, either because the parties are no longer in the same situation or because changed behavior or policy appears to eliminate the basis for the controversy.[77] As the Supreme Court defines it: "A case is moot when the issues presented are no longer 'live' or the parties lack a legally cognizable interest in the outcome. The underlying concern is that, when the challenged conduct ceases such that 'there is no reasonable expectation that the wrong will be repeated, . . . then it becomes impossible for the court to grant 'any effectual relief whatever to [the] prevailing party.' . . . In that case, any opinion as to the legality of the challenged action would be advisory."[78]

For example, an Arizona public employee who counseled claimants using both her English and Spanish language skills launched a challenge immediately after the adoption of an initiative that amended the state constitution to require that only English be used in official matters. However, by the time the case worked its way through the legal system, she was no longer a state employee and the case had therefore become moot. "To qualify as a case fit for federal-court adjudication, an actual controversy must be extant at all stages of review, not merely at the time the complaint is filed."[79]

JUDICIAL GATEKEEPING

Most of the procedural rules that control access to judicial review are judicially created.[80] The courts may act as gatekeepers and interpret those rules so as to encourage or block litigation for a variety of reasons, ranging from politics to ideology to judicial philosophy to practical concerns about the posture of particular cases. The clear pattern established in Burger and Rehnquist Court years was to exercise a wider range of discretion as gatekeeper and to restrict access to the courts for judicial review in several kinds of cases. While this continuing trend may sound positive to administrators who would like to avoid judicial review, it poses significant dangers as well.

The procedural rules allow a great deal of flexibility for a court in determining whether a particular case is heard. The judges will usually be called on to exercise that discretion, since technical defenses will almost always be raised to block an appeal of an administrative decision.[81] After all, the surest way to prevent a judgment that overturns a favorable ruling is to prevent the case from getting into court in the first place. There are pressures on judges to deal with cases on these narrow procedural grounds, such as heavy dockets or the desire to avoid particularly complex and politically charged issues. Some judges interpret the procedural rules narrowly to discourage certain types of cases and to encourage others.

In acting as gatekeepers to judicial review, judges fall at points along a continuum even if one keeps ideological considerations out of the calculus. At one extreme is the philosophy that all significant disputes ought to have the fullest possible legal consideration without obstruction by procedural barriers, particularly where governmental decisions are at issue and especially when the decisionmakers are unelected administrators, in order to discourage arbitrariness and encourage fundamental fairness. At the other extreme is the view that the judge's job is to perform a narrow and carefully prescribed error-correction function with respect to cases fully and properly developed according to rigid procedural rules regardless of any consequences of lack of access to the courts. However, most jurists do not operate at these extremes. Most realize that for the judicial process to operate, cases must be presented in a manageable and appropriate form and that rules of judicial self-restraint are also important, especially among judges who do not stand for election and who are frequently protected by life tenure. At the same time, most are also aware that they are often asked to decide issues that cannot be neatly and completely developed within very narrow and rigid guidelines as if they were limited private law disputes without causing substantial injustices—injustices that often have the most severe impact on those least able to endure the hardship.[82] After all, in public law cases, courts are not just umpires for dispute resolution, but represent a separate and coequal branch within the separation of powers scheme and must also play their appropriate role in the system of checks and balances.

Even with that set of tensions in mind and with a fair appreciation for the range of varied judicial perceptions of the proper role of judicial review, it is clear that the Supreme Court during the Burger and Rehnquist years moved toward limitation on access to federal courts for resolution of public law disputes. That pattern had become clear by the mid-1970s.[83]

> Although the pattern is not uniform, it is clear enough: The Supreme Court is making it harder and harder to get a federal court to vindicate federal constitutional and other rights. In some cases, prior decisions have been overruled, either explicitly or silently; in other contexts, restrictive implications in prior cases have been taken up and expanded; in still other situations, new approaches developed by lower courts have been repudiated.... That there is indeed a pattern, and that it is more than accidental, seems clear from the scope and pervasiveness of the phenomenon.[84]

It is a trend that has continued and indeed intensified since then. First, the Court has tightened the rules of standing significantly.[85] Beyond that, it has largely transformed decisions about standing, ripeness, mootness, and other factors that were primarily associated with ensuring an appropriate "case or controversy" into what the Court now terms "prudential considerations," so that even if the case and the parties could properly mount the litigation and ensure a proper case and controversy, the Court will use its discretion to determine whether the case will move forward.[86]

Beyond these more or less direct tools of gatekeeping, the Court has issued a range of other rulings that have been used to discourage lower courts from entertaining cases and potential plaintiffs from bringing them. For example, the Court has substantially reduced the availability of the class action lawsuit,[87] interpreted procedural rules and doctrines so as to discourage federal court activity,[88] restricted the ability of private attorneys general to bring suits that are termed implied private rights of action,[89] and limited the authority of federal district courts to impose remedies such as injunctions that require specific changes in proven cases of maladministration.[90]

One of the results of the hollowing-out of government and the tendency of recent administrations, both Democrat and Republican, to move toward deregulation—or at least alternatives to formal enforcement proceedings—has been a demand by those who consider that they have been harmed to bring action themselves where government either will not or cannot do so. The issue is not one of standing in the sense of injury in fact. Rather, the question is whether there is a basis for a cause of action.

Some statutes, such as the Right-to-Know law mentioned earlier, specifically authorize what are sometimes known as citizen suits or private attorney general actions. In many instances, however, there is no specifically stated basis for a legal action or some question whether what exists is adequate to address the injury. The question then is whether the existing law implies a private right of action. Justice Stevens explained: "Although criminal laws and legislation enacted for the benefit of the public at large were expected to be enforced by public officials, a statute enacted for the benefit of a special class presumptively afforded a remedy for members of that class injured by violations of the statute.... Applying that presumption, our truly conservative federal judges—men like Justice Harlan, Justice Clark, Justice Frankfurter, and Judge Kirkpatrick—readily concluded that it was appropriate to allow private parties who had been injured by a violation of a statute enacted for their special benefit to obtain judicial relief. For rules are meant to be obeyed, and those who violate them should be held responsible for their misdeeds."

The Supreme Court developed a standard that tended to favor such actions in the absence of legislative history to the contrary.[91] However, also beginning in the mid-1970s, the Court moved toward a more restrictive view that shifted the standard to the presumption against an implied right of action unless the legislative history suggested otherwise.[92] More recently, the Court has taken additional steps to limit implied private rights of action. These cases have arisen in a variety of contexts in which many might assume that they had such a right of action. For example, the Court rejected a claim by a college student to an implied right of action to enforce the Family Educational Rights and Privacy Act of 1974 so as to prohibit the unauthorized disclosure of his records.[93] In his opinion for the Court, Chief Justice Rehnquist pursued his desire to reinvigorate the dichotomy between rights and privileges. He wrote:

> Section 1983 provides a remedy only for the deprivation of "rights, privileges, or immunities secured by the Constitution and laws" of the United States. Accordingly, it is rights, not the broader or vaguer "benefits" or "interests," that may be enforced under the authority of that section. This being so, we further reject the notion that our implied right of action cases are separate and distinct from our §1983 cases. To the contrary, our implied right of action cases should guide the determination of whether a statute confers rights enforceable under §1983.[94]

Justice Scalia, the Court's other ardent advocate of a right/privilege dichotomy, pressed the matter still further:

> Our subsequent cases have made clear, however, that §1983 does not provide an avenue for relief every time a state actor violates a federal law. As a threshold matter, the text of §1983 permits the enforcement of "rights, not the broader or vaguer 'benefits' or 'interests.'" [T]to sustain a §1983 action, the plaintiff must demonstrate that the federal statute creates an individually enforceable right in the class of beneficiaries to which he belongs. . . . Even after this showing, "there is only a rebuttable presumption that the right is enforceable under §1983." The defendant may defeat this presumption by demonstrating that Congress did not intend that remedy for a newly created right. . . . Our cases have explained that evidence of such congressional intent may be found directly in the statute creating the right, or inferred from the statute's creation of a 'comprehensive enforcement scheme that is incompatible with individual enforcement under §1983.'[95]

In addition to these areas of limitation, the Supreme Court has reinvigorated the doctrine of nonreviewability that had been thought for most practical purposes to be moribund.[96] The doctrine of nonreviewability holds that certain kinds of administrative decisions are not subject to judicial review. It is true that Section 702 of the APA provides that: "A person suffering legal wrong because of agency action, or adversely affected or aggrieved by agency action within the meaning of a relevant statute, is entitled to judicial review thereof." However, Section 701 explained that: "This chapter applies . . . except to the extent that— (1) statutes preclude judicial review; or (2) agency action is committed to agency discretion by law." Thus, under either of these two conditions, the administrative action in question in nonreviewable. The Supreme Court's opinions in *Abbott Laboratories v. Gardner*[97] and *Citizens to Preserve Overton Park v. Volpe*,[98] appeared to render extremely narrow and weak that clause of the Administrative Procedure Act allowing exceptions to the rule that administrative action is generally reviewable. That interpretation was generally accepted until the mid-1980s.[99] At that point, the Court entertained a series of cases in which the nature and scope of nonreviewability were reconsidered.

Justice O'Connor, writing for the Court in 1984, concluded that "the presumption favoring judicial review of administrative action may be overcome by inferences of intent from the statutory scheme as a whole."[100] Thus, even if the legislature neglected to specify that review was prohibited in a particular situation, the matter might still be nonreviewable if a court found from the broad contours of a statute or from its legislative history that the Congress had not intended to allow review. That was a significant change from the earlier cases that held that review was to be presumed and nonreviewability a narrow exception only to be imposed where Congress had specified its intentions in the clearest possible terms.

In March of 1985, Justice Rehnquist wrote for the Court in *Heckler v. Chaney*,[101] interpreting the second part of the exceptions clause, the barrier to review in cases involving "action committed to agency discretion by law." This has always been a difficult question because, for reasons explained in Chapter 9, there are so many types and levels of discretion that are either explicitly or implicitly available to agencies that this exemption could, if read broadly enough, swallow the general presumption in favor of review. In this case, the question was how to determine whether a refusal to act is or is not reviewable.

The *Heckler* case was the one discussed in Chapter 1 about the prisoner on death row. While Section 706 of the APA calls upon courts to "compel agency action unlawfully withheld or unreasonably delayed," the Court's ruling used the "committed to agency discretion" exception to block review. Writing for the Court, Justice Rehnquist held that: "an agency's decision not to take enforcement action should be presumed immune from judicial review under [section] 701(a)(2). . . . In so stating, we emphasize that the decision is only presumptively unreviewable; the presumption may be rebutted where the substantive statute has provided guidelines for the agency to follow in exercising its powers."[102] However, he warned: "Thus in establishing this presumption in the APA, Congress did not set agencies free to disregard legislative direction in the statutory scheme that the agency administers. Congress may limit an agency's exercise of enforcement power if it wishes, either by setting substantive priorities, or by otherwise circumscribing an agency's power to discriminate among issues or cases it will pursue."[103] Thus, administrative enforcement authority is presumptively nonreviewable.

While these cases clearly indicated a move away from the earlier strong presumption in favor of review, on the same day the Court rendered its decision concerning reviewability of enforcement decisions in *Heckler*, Justice Brennan issued a majority opinion for a sharply divided Court rejecting a nonreviewability claim by the Office of Personnel Management in a case concerning federal civil service disability retirement.[104] In the process, Brennan reminded his colleagues that:

> We have often noted that "only upon a showing of 'clear and convincing evidence' of a contrary legislative intent should the courts restrict access to judicial review." . . . Of course, the . . . question whether a statute precludes judicial review "is determined not only from its express language, but also from the structure of the statutory scheme, its objectives, its legislative history, and the nature of the administrative actions involved."[105]

Then, a year later, an unanimous Court (Justice Rehnquist not participating) issued a strong reaffirmation of the pro-reviewability position. Writing in *Bowen v. Michigan Academy of Family Physicians*,[106] Justice Stevens said:

> We begin with the strong presumption that Congress intends judicial review of administrative action. From the beginning "our cases [have established] that judicial review of a final agency action by an aggrieved person will not be cut off unless there is persuasive reason to believe that such was the purpose of Congress. . . ." In *Marbury v. Madison* [cites], a case itself involving review of executive action, Chief Justice Marshall insisted that "[t]he very essence of civil liberty certainly consists in the right of every individual to claim the protection of the laws." Later, . . . the Chief Justice noted the traditional observance of this right and laid the foundation for the modern presumption of judicial review.
>
> It would excite some surprise if, in a government of laws and of principle, furnished with a department whose appropriate duty it is to decide questions of right, not only between individuals, but between the government and individuals; a ministerial officer might, at his discretion, issue this powerful process . . . leaving to the debtor no remedy, no appeal to the

laws of his country, if he should believe the claim to be unjust. But this anomaly does not exist; this imputation cannot be cast on the legislature of the United States.[107]

The *Bowen* Court went on to reaffirm the principles of *Abbott Laboratories*. However, since then, the composition of the Supreme Court has continued to change and the Court has rendered a number of rulings supporting a wider use of the nonreviewability doctrine.[108] At this point, a decision is not reviewable if: (1) the statute involved specifically prohibits review; (2) if a court determines that even though no prohibition is stated, the statutory scheme or the legislative intent indicates that no review was to be available; or (3) if a court determines that, whether or not the legislation specifies it, the kind of decision involved is committed to agency discretion. That last judgment will be made by seeking to determine whether the legislature has provided standards to control or evaluate the administrative discretion at issue.

WHAT KIND OF REVIEW IS PROVIDED?

If a request for review of an agency decision survives all of these initial challenges, what kind of review will be made? The type of review afforded is conditioned by the applicable statutes and other variables, but, in most cases, the judge examines the record that was before the administrator at the time of the decision, and asks five questions. Increasingly, there may also be two additional questions that are presented either directly or indirectly during judicial review of agency action.

1. Has the administrator acted within his or her proper range of authority?

Deciding this question entails consideration of the enabling act of the agency and any other statutes that the administrator is charged to administer. If the authority the administrator claims is not to be found in the statutes or in an executive order properly issued by the president (in the states by the governor), the administrative action is *ultra vires*, beyond authority, and is by definition illegitimate. The agency must not only have substantive authority, but also jurisdiction to apply it in the situation or to the parties at hand.[109] The court will grant the agency considerable deference in interpreting the statute, but the court remains the arbiter of the meaning of statutes.[110]

2. Were proper procedures followed?

The judge will want evidence to show that the proper procedures were followed by the administrator. Procedural requirements are established by statute, by provisions of the APA, and by agency regulations (see Chapter 5). If an argument is made on the point, the judge might want some indication that the agency procedures were adequate in substance as well as in form. For example, the FCC at one time dealt with license contests by hearing one applicant, deciding the case, and then hearing the other. The second applicant was given a hearing in any event, but this was meaningless if the agency had already decided to award the license to the first party. The Supreme Court required a consolidated hearing procedure in which both parties could participate.[111]

3. Was the decision arbitrary and capricious or an abuse of discretion?

The leading decision by the Supreme Court on the meaning of the term "arbitrary and capricious action" came in a challenge to a long-standing debate in the federal government about whether to impose a requirement that automobile manufacturers install passive restraints, specifically airbags. The case went back to 1966 when Congress created the National Highway Traffic Safety Administration

(NHTSA) and mandated that it issue safety standards. The following year NHTSA developed requirements for seatbelts and, two years after that, proposed passive restraints, devices that did not depend upon the active participation of the driver or passengers. The rule that eventually issued calling for passive restraints for front seat passengers in all vehicles manufactured after August 15, 1975, was upheld against judicial challenge.[112]

President Ford's Secretary of Transportation reopened the rulemaking proceeding and suspended the existing requirements pending the completion of that process, but the Carter administration reversed Coleman's decision and issued the standard that had previously been pending. That standard, which permitted a choice between the use of automatic seatbelts or airbags, was upheld against legal challenge.[113] The Reagan administration reopened the issue and ordered a delay in implementation, pending a consideration whether the passive restraint rule should be rescinded, which is what he ultimately elected to do. This action was challenged and gave rise to the case that ultimately reached the Supreme Court.

The airbags case presented two issues, one of which is relevant at this point. That is whether the rescission of the passive restraint rule was arbitrary and capricious and therefore in violation of the APA. The Court's summary of the requirements of judicial review using the arbitrary and capricious standard remains valid today:

> The scope of review under the arbitrary and capricious standard is narrow and a court is not to substitute its judgment for that of the agency. Nevertheless, the agency must examine the relevant data and articulate a satisfactory explanation for its action including a "rational connection between the facts found and the choice made." . . . In reviewing that explanation, we must "consider whether the decision was based on a consideration of the relevant factors and whether there has been a clear error of judgment." . . . Normally, an agency rule would be arbitrary and capricious if the agency has relied on factors which Congress has not intended it to consider, entirely failed to consider an important aspect of the problem, offered an explanation for its decision that runs counter to the evidence before the agency, or is so implausible that it could not be ascribed to a difference in view or the product of agency expertise. The reviewing court should not attempt itself to make up for such deficiencies: "We may not apply a reasoned basis for the agency's action that the agency itself has not given." . . . "We will, however, uphold a decision of less than ideal clarity if the agency's path may reasonably be discerned." . . . For purposes of this case, it is also relevant that Congress required a record of the rulemaking proceedings to be compiled and submitted to a reviewing court. . . . , and intended that agency findings under the Motor Vehicle Safety Act would be supported by "substantial evidence on the record considered as a whole."[114]

In the case of the passive restraint rule, the Court found that the agency had been arbitrary and capricious because it failed to consider evidence that it had in the record concerning the safety record of airbags and options available with respect to nondetachable seatbelts.

In simplest terms, a finding that the administrator acted arbitrarily or capriciously means that he or she acted without reason or on a whim.[115] The judge begins with the presumption that the administrator acted lawfully, and examines the record to determine the justification for the administrative action advanced when the decision was announced. In most cases that means examining the opinion accompanying an agency order, the publication information accompanying the promulgation of a rule, or other type of agency policy announcement.[116] The judge is not interested in *post hoc* rationalizations of what the administrator might have considered when the decision was made, but rather in what he or she actually took into consideration.[117] If that included considerations that should not have been contemplated, such as race, gender, age, or the like, or failed to consider relevant evidence that was available or other statutory considerations that were omitted,[118] or if there was no clear indication of how the administrator got from the facts found to the conclusion reached, then the decision is arbitrary. That does not mean that the decision must be correct. An administrator may be found to have satisfied the arbitrary and capricious standard of review and still be wrong or have made a less than optimal choice.

4. Was there substantial evidence on the record as a whole to support the conclusion?

Section 706(2)(E) of the APA provides that a court shall "hold unlawful and set aside agency actions, findings, and conclusions found to be . . . unsupported by substantial evidence *in a case subject to section 556 and 557 of this title or otherwise reviewed on the record of an agency hearing provided by statute*" (emphasis added). The point of this language is that judicial review of formal adjudications and formal rulemaking ought to be more formal and more careful than of other kinds of administrative actions. More rigorous judicial review offers greater assurance of the integrity of the record, the adequacy of the record (whether there was a substantial amount of evidence to support the conclusion the administrator reached), and, finally, the proper application of the record (that the administrator considered the whole record and not just those parts of it that supported his or her predispositions). Less formal administrative actions should receive a less formal review than the "substantial evidence" approach. These less formal administrative actions would satisfy the other requirements of §706, with particular attention to the so-called arbitrary and capricious standard noted earlier.

As a practical matter, however, judges usually look to see whether there is substantial evidence in the record as a whole to support an administrative action. The reason that "substantial evidence" becomes a factor centers on the definition of "arbitrary and capricious." When a judge wishes to determine whether an administrative decision was "arbitrary, capricious, an abuse of discretion, or not otherwise in accordance with law" (§706), he or she looks to the record that supports the agency decision. If an arbitrary decision is one that is not based on reason or is a matter of whim, how is the judge to decide whether the record before the court fits that definition? When people say that a decision was without support in reason, they usually mean that there was no evidence to substantiate it. So viewed, one criterion for determining the validity of an administrative decision is whether there is evidence in the record that supports it. Clearly, a decision that relied only on that evidence in the record that supported the agency and not any opposing evidence would be arbitrary and capricious.[119] The only check then is to see whether the administrator relied on substantial evidence in the record as a whole.

The meaning of the word "substantial" in administrative law is extremely vague, and determining whether there was substantial evidence requires judgment. The court wants to know whether there was enough evidence of the kind that reasonable people are accustomed to relying upon in serious matters[120] that the administrator reasonably could have reached the conclusion reached by the agency.[121]

> A court reviewing an agency's adjudicative action should accept the agency's factual findings if those findings are supported by substantial evidence on the record as a whole. See generally *Universal Camera Corp. v. NLRB*, 340 U.S. 474 (1951). The court should not supplant the agency's findings merely by identifying alternative findings that could be supported by substantial evidence.[122]

And as Justice Scalia explained the standard for the majority in *Allentown Mack Sales and Service v. National Labor Relations Board*: "[W]e must decide whether on this record it would have been possible for a reasonable jury to reach the Board's conclusion."[123]

In sum, judges usually look to see whether there is evidence in the record as a whole to support the administrative action. If the case is a formal administrative action, they are aware that the review should be somewhat more probing than in other administrative matters. In any event, administrative records ought to contain some evidence to support the administrator's action.[124]

5. Is there a constitutional violation?

Judges will entertain the argument that the statutes, regulations, or agency practices involved in a particular administrative action are unconstitutional. The claim that an administrator obeyed the requirements of the APA and the enabling act of his agency will, of course, not save an administrative action if there is a constitutional violation.

6. Is there a contractual question?

Although, as previous chapters have indicated, government contract law is distinct from administrative law as defined by the APA, as more and more public administration is accomplished through contracting, it is increasingly common for contractual issues to be important in the review of agency actions. It is becoming increasingly difficult to determine where administrative law ends and government contract law begins. For these and other reasons, it is time to reconsider the relationships among them.

Contract issues may be raised directly under statutes other than the APA according to which contract decisions may be challenged directly or they may be indirectly presented where the decision under review is an agency decision but one that involves contractors in the delivery of services or the operation of regulatory programs. Chapters 5 and 6 provided several examples of such cases, as does the National Park Service concession contracts case discussed earlier in this chapter, which raised the relationship between the Contract Disputes Act and NPS regulations.

7. Is there a supranational issue?

Finally, it is increasingly common to find international issues arising in judicial review of administrative decisions. Some of these are more or less obvious and relatively traditional issues such as decisions by what was formerly known as the Immigration and Naturalization Service (INS)—now called U.S. Citizenship and Immigration Services—or Customs Service rulings about duties on imported goods.[125] However, it is common now to find agencies that are often considered by many Americans to be domestic organizations, such as the U.S. Department of Agriculture, facing complex cases related to globalization in such areas as the supply channels for food and livestock that run across international boundaries. These include recent challenges by U.S. ranchers to obtain USDA permission to resume importation of Canadian cattle following a ban placed on that trade because of the identification of a BSE (mad cow) infected animal.[126]

Then there was the recent case involving actions by the Federal Motor Carrier Safety Administration (FMCSA), part of the U.S. Department of Transportation, that flowed from the loss by the United States of a case brought by Mexico under the North American Free Trade Agreement (NAFTA). The NAFTA case arose because of a U.S. ban on the operation of trucks from Mexico in the United States. After the United States lost the international arbitration decision and the president lifted the ban, Congress sought to block DOT action to facilitate trans-border movement of the trucks. The FMCSA moved to issue rules to deal with the process by which Mexican trucks would receive permits and be inspected. The U.S. agency found itself facing challenges by environmental and public interest groups on grounds that its rulemaking actions did not comply with the National Environmental Policy Act (NEPA) and the Clean Air Act (CAA). Part of the claim had to do with the argument that pollution would increase in association with the agency's processes under the rules because of the dramatic increase in trans-border truck traffic. The circuit court of appeals ruled against the agency. However, a unanimous Supreme Court held that: "FMCSA did not violate NEPA or the relevant CEQ regulations when it did not consider the environmental effect of the increase in cross-border operations of Mexican motor carriers in its [Environmental Assessment]. Nor did FMCSA act improperly by not performing, pursuant to the CAA and relevant regulations, a full conformity review analysis for its proposed regulations."[127] The basis for the Court's ruling was that the agency could not control the decision to allow the increased truck traffic, which was made by the president under compulsion by the NAFTA arbitration.

International issues have also moved well beyond the federal level alone, with challenges brought against administrative agencies or state and local government operations, such as in the case of Washington's effort to improve regulation of oil tanker operations discussed earlier in this chapter. Also at the state level, but in a case based upon contracting, the Commonwealth of Massachusetts was told that, even though it was a participant in the marketplace rather than a regulator of it, the state could not refuse to contract or add burdens to the bids of firms that also did business in one capacity or another with the nation of Myanmar (formerly known as Burma).[128] Other examples include challenges by environmental groups to the City of Nogales, Arizona's operation of a sewage treatment plant that handles waste not only from the city, but also from neighboring Nogales, Sonora, Mexico under the U.S.- Mexico border agreement. The Arizona city was named in the suit because it provides day-to-day operating control of the plant, but the overall control of the facility is vested in a committee of the U.S. Section of the International Boundary and Water Commission. The committee has members from the federal government and the state but not the city. Even so, Nogales, Arizona, found itself facing challenges under the Clean Water Act.[129]

JUDICIAL REVIEW AND THE DEFERENCE QUESTION

This chapter began by noting the tension that judges face in reviewing administrative actions so that they both fulfill the many important functions of judicial review while avoiding the danger of second-guessing the appropriate range of discretion and expertise exercised by administrators. The court cannot ignore the basic requirements for judicial review and simply give an agency carte blanche to exceed the law, abuse its discretion, and act arbitrarily. Nor may it presume to judge the accuracy of an administrator's expert judgments. This is the classic deference problem. Just how much deference should be granted by courts to agencies, under what circumstances, and with what constraints? These issues must be continually faced by judges because, in this day and time, agency actions will be vigorously challenged, especially when they have significant consequences for repeat players. The basic elements of judicial deference are relatively clear and easy to understand. They deal with issues of deference to statutory interpretation, interpretation and application of agency regulations, administrative choice of procedures, and the agency's scientific findings claimed as support for rulemaking and adjudicative decisions. This last question has become an almost constant concern in the past three decades, since this is an era of what Ball has termed "adversarial science."[130]

Deference and the Issue of Legal Interpretation

Chapter 2 discussed the doctrine of contemporaneous administrative construction, which has traditionally held that reviewing courts will grant deference to the contemporaneous interpretation of a statute by the agency charged with its administration. As the Supreme Court has observed on many occasions, "[t]his contemporaneous construction of [the] statute by the men charged with the responsibility of setting its machinery in motion is entitled to particular respect."[131] Historically, three reasons have been advanced to justify the deference. First, the agency has often been the repository of technical expertise and experience in its field.[132] Generalist judges are certainly in no position to second-guess such professionals. Second, the agency is, after all, the institution to which the Congress has delegated authority for implementation of the statute and it therefore possesses both the authority that comes with the legislative delegation and the authority of the executive branch. Third, the importance of the reference to the "contemporaneous" interpretation stems from the fact that it is presumed that the agency was engaged in the conversations that gave rise to the statute in question and many even have participated in the drafting of the law.

The long-running conversations about the deference to statutory interpretation came together in 1984 when the Supreme Court decided *Chevron U.S.A. v. Natural Resources Defense Council.*[133] The ruling in this case set the standard that is still used many years later. The case arose in the context of a challenge to the development by the Environmental Protection Agency (EPA) of something called the "bubble theory" under the Clean Air Act Amendments of 1977. In broad terms, EPA tried to create a vision of measurement and control of air pollution that assumed a bubble over a set of industries and set limits not on individual machines or plants but more broadly to include emissions within the entire bubble. The Supreme Court concluded that the Court of Appeals had failed to exercise the proper deference to agency decisionmaking and reversed it. In the process, the Supreme Court set forth the standard for judicial review:

> When a court reviews an agency's construction of the statute which it administers, it is confronted with two questions. First, always, is the question whether Congress has directly spoken to the precise question at issue. If the intent of Congress is clear, that is the end of the matter for the court, as well as the agency, must give effect to the unambiguously expressed intent of Congress. If, however, the court determined Congress has not directly addressed the precise question at issue, the court does not simply impose its own construction on the statute, as would be necessary in the absence of an administrative interpretation. Rather, if the statute is silent or ambiguous with respect to the specific issue, the question for the court is whether the agency's answer is based on a permissible construction of the statute.
>
> The power of an administrative agency to administer a congressionally created . . . program necessarily requires the formulation of policy and the making of rules to fill any gap left, implicitly or explicitly, by Congress. . . . If Congress has explicitly left a gap for the agency to fill, there is an express delegation of authority to the agency to elucidate a specific provision of the statute by regulation. Such legislative regulations are given controlling weight unless they are arbitrary, capricious, or manifestly contrary to the statute. Sometimes the legislative delegation to an agency on a particular question is implicit rather than explicit. In such a case, a court may not substitute its own construction of a statutory provision for a reasonable interpretation made by the administrator of the an agency.[134]

The Court upheld the agency. In this particular case, it was clear that all of the basic reasons supporting judicial deference were in place. Certainly, it was an area where the agency had greater expertise and experience and in which Congress had delegated authority to EPA. In such a case, deference was due.

> In these cases, the Administrator's interpretation represents a reasonable accommodation of manifestly competing interests and is entitled to deference: the regulatory scheme is technical and complex, the agency considered the matter in a detailed and reasoned fashion, and the decision involved reconciling conflicting policies. . . .
>
> Judges are not experts in the field, and are not part of either political branch of the Government. Courts must, in some cases, reconcile competing political interests, but not on the basis of the judges' personal policy preferences. In contrast, an agency to which Congress has delegated policymaking responsibilities may, within the limits of that delegation, properly rely upon the incumbent administration's views of wise policy to inform its judgments. While agencies are not directly accountable to the people, the Chief Executive is, and it is entirely appropriate for this political branch of the Government to make such policy choices—resolving the competing interest which Congress itself either inadvertently did not resolve, or intentionally left to be resolved by the agency charged with the administration of the statute in light of everyday realities.[135]

Recognizing that courts and agencies may well disagree on what is best or right in any given circumstance, the Court supported the role of the agency. It concluded:

> When a challenge to an agency construction of a statutory provision, fairly conceptualized, really centers on the wisdom of the agency's policy, rather than whether it is a reasonable choice within a gap left open by Congress, the challenge must fail. In such a case, federal judges—who have no constituency—have a duty to respect legitimate policy choices made by those who do. The responsibilities for addressing the wisdom of such policy choices and resolving the struggle between competing views of the public interest are not judicial ones. "Our Constitution vests such responsibilities in the political branches."[136]

Some years later, Justice Rehnquist, who had not participated in the *Chevron* case, wrote for a sharply divided Court in a case testing the so-called abortion "gag rule." The gag rule was a reinterpretation of a statute by the Secretary of Health and Human Services (HHS) during the Reagan administration that resulted in a requirement that federally funded family planning clinics could give information about childbirth and delivery services but could not provide information or referrals concerning abortion services even if the patient specifically asked for that information.[137] Unlike the *Chevron* case, there was no issue of expert knowledge in this case. It was clear that this was a reinterpretation that radically changed a long-standing interpretation of the same statute that had endured in both Republican and Democratic administrations. The Court, citing *Chevron*, concluded that neither of these characteristics mattered. It was enough that HHS was the agency charged with administering the statute.

While it was the case that long-standing interpretations by an agency have generally been afforded great weight, Justice Rehnquist accorded that tradition no importance, concluding that an agency must "be given ample latitude to adapt its rules and policies to the demands of changing circumstances."[138] Justice Stevens, author of the *Chevron* opinion, took Rehnquist to task, charging that the gag rule did not "merely reflect a change in a policy determination that the Secretary had been authorized by Congress to make... [but rather] represented an assumption of policymaking responsibility that Congress had not delegated to the Secretary."[139] There was in the case of the gag rule no issue of contemporaneous construction, nor any question of technical expertise, and a long history of a contradictory interpretation by the agency involved.

> To be sure, agency interpretations that are of long standing come before us with a certain credential of reasonableness, since it is rare that error would long persist. But neither antiquity nor contemporaneity with the statute is a condition of validity. We accord deference to the agencies under *Chevron*, not because of a presumption that they drafted the provisions in question, or were present at the hearings, or spoke to the principal sponsors; but rather because of a presumption that Congress, when it left ambiguity in a statute meant for implementation by an agency, understood that the ambiguity would be resolved, first and foremost, by the agency, and desired the agency (rather than the courts) to possess whatever degrees of discretion the ambiguity allows.[140]

If the legislature has spoken directly to the point in question, "that is the end of the matter," but if the statute is ambiguous and the agency's interpretation is "reasonable in light of the legislature's revealed design, we give the administrator's judgment controlling weight."[141] The point is that the administrator's interpretation must be a permissible one,[142] not necessarily the only one or the wisest choice.[143]

There are similar explanations given as to why courts generally defer to the interpretation of agency regulations by the agency charged with administering the program.[144] The Supreme Court has said that its "task is not to decide which among several competing interpretations best serves the regulatory purpose. Rather, the agency's interpretation must be given 'controlling weight unless it is plainly erroneous or inconsistent with the regulation.' ... In other words, we must defer to the Secretary's interpretation unless an 'alternative reading is compelled by the regulation's plain language or by other indications of the Secretary's intent at the time of the regulation's promulgation.'"[145] The Court noted that this deference is especially warranted if "the regulation concerns 'a complex and highly technical regulatory program,' in which the identification and classification of relevant 'criteria necessarily requires significant expertise and entails the exercise of judgment grounded in policy concerns.'"[146] While the Court acknowledged that an agency interpretation might be due less deference if it conflicts with consistently held prior agency interpretations,[147] an agency must retain the ability to change direction when it considers it necessary and so long as it makes its changes in policy according to proper procedures.[148]

And when it comes to an agency's choice of procedural approaches, where a statute permits alternative strategies, court are expected to grant deference. The same is true with respect to the kinds of remedies agencies choose to apply in any given situation for violations of their regulations and the statutes they administer.[149]

All that having been said, courts do not always grant deference to agency interpretations, nor should they. After all, judges generally regard themselves as experts in the fine art of procedure and legal interpretation. As the Court pointed out in *Chevron,* where the language of a statute unambiguously addresses the particular issue in question, there is no reason for deference. The intentions of Congress may be evident not in specific terms but in the design or clear legislative intent of the statute. In these cases, courts find no reason to defer to agencies.[150] "If the intent of Congress is clear, that is the end of the matter."[151] That is true even where the interpretation by the agency is of long standing.[152] "A regulation's age is no antidote to clear inconsistence with a statute."[153]

Further, no special deference is due where the statute in question is not one that the agency is charged with administering. Thus, no single agency possesses a special competence in interpreting the Administrative Procedure Act as compared to a court.[154] A similar point was made by the Court in the ruling on the National Park Service case discussed earlier, on grounds that the NPS had no authority or special competence with respect to the Contract Disputes Act. It has also been held that no deference is due if "the essential question is one of the interpretation of [a] contract's language, a question of law clearly within the competence of courts."[155] Thus, it would appear that when an agency elects to act by contract rather than by regulation, it is no longer entitled to expect deference should the matter move to a judicial forum.

Similarly, there is no deference due to agency interpretations of its own regulations if they are "plainly erroneous or inconsistent with the regulation."[156] An interpretation would fall into that category if it ran afoul of "the regulation's plain language or by other indications of the Secretary's intent at the time of the regulation's promulgation."[157] Although administrators may reinterpret regulations, interpretations that are inconsistent with long-standing approaches will receive less deference.[158] And clearly, agencies cannot act in a manner that is arbitrary or capricious in the development or application of their regulations.[159]

This deference to interpretation and policy debate took a strange turn in 2001 with the Supreme Court's decision in *United States v. Mead Corp.*[160] This significant case began with what many readers would consider less than significant facts. It began with a dispute over the way that day-planners should be classified for tariff calculation purposes. Along the way, the focus shifted to whether the day-planner case was a situation in which the *Chevron* deference should not apply and, if not, what the appropriate standard of deference, if any, should be. Writing for the majority, Justice Souter said: "We hold that administrative implementation of a particular statutory provision qualifies for *Chevron* deference when it appears that Congress delegated authority to the agency generally to make rules carrying the force of law, and that the agency interpretation claiming deference was promulgated in the exercise of that authority."[161] The use of what was called a Customs letter, however, did not meet that definition and was not, therefore, entitled to *Chevron* deference.

That said, the majority insisted that it was still possible that some deference might be available to the agency's ruling. "The fair measure of deference to an agency administering its own statute has been understood to vary with circumstances, and courts have looked to the degree of the agency's care, its consistency, formality, and relative expertness, and to the persuasiveness of the agency's position, see *Skidmore* [*v. Swift & Co.,* 323 U.S. 134 (1944)]. The approach has produced a spectrum of judicial responses, from great respect at one end to near indifference at the other."[162] Just how much, if any, deference would be due in this case, would depend upon the lower court's application of the *Skidmore* sliding scale to the facts of this case. The Court remanded the case for that determination.

Justice Scalia could barely contain himself in attacking the Court's dramatic change from the Chevron deference approach to judicial review: "What was previously a general presumption of authority in agencies to resolve ambiguity in the statutes they have been authorized to enforce has been changed to a presumption of no such authority, which must be overcome by affirmative legislative intent to the contrary. We will be sorting out the consequences of the *Mead* doctrine, which has today replaced the *Chevron* doctrine, for years to come."[163] He then listed some of most egregious short-comings of the *Mead* ruling:

As for the practical effects of the new rule:

(1) The principal effect will be protracted confusion. . . . It is hard to know what the lower courts are to make of today's guidance.

(2) Another practical effect of today's opinion will be an artificially induced increase in informal rulemaking. Buy stock in the GPO. Since informal rulemaking and formal adjudication are the only more-or-less safe harbors from the storm that the Court has unleashed; and since formal adjudication is not an option but must be mandated by statute or constitutional command; informal rulemaking—which the Court was once careful to make voluntary unless required by statute—will now become a virtual necessity.

(3) Worst of all, the majority's approach will lead to the ossification of large portions of our statutory law. Where *Chevron* applies, statutory ambiguities remain ambiguities subject to the agency's ongoing clarification. . . .

(4) And finally, the majority's approach compounds the confusion it creates by breathing new life into the anachronism of *Skidmore*, which sets forth a sliding scale of deference. . . . [I]n an era when federal statutory law administered by federal agencies is pervasive, and when the ambiguities (intended or unintended) that those statutes contain are innumerable, totality-of-the-circumstances *Skidmore* deference is a recipe for uncertainty, unpredictability, and endless litigation.

[T]oday's decision [is] one of the most significant opinions ever rendered by the Court dealing with the judicial review of administrative action. Its consequences will be enormous, and almost uniformly bad.[164]

It remains to be seen whether Justice Scalia's concerns will be realized, but there is little doubt that the *Mead* standard could produce the results about which he warns, depending upon its application in future cases. The cases that have reached the Supreme Court since then have generally tended to result in a *Chevron* review, but the authors of majority, concurring, and dissenting opinions continue to spar over the likely future of deference.[165]

Deference and the Problem of Agency Expertise

Judicial review and its use of deference to administrative action is perhaps most difficult where the agency administers policies governing scientifically and technologically based activity. Administrative decisions in such areas as air and water pollution[166] and toxic substances control[167] involve difficult and often controversial scientific judgments about which even the recognized experts disagree. Of course, disputes over complex scientific and technological problems arise in cases other than administrative law—for example, in malpractice, personal injury, and infringement of patent suits where there is no authoritative agency with presumed expertise.[168]

In complex cases coming on judicial review from administrative agencies, judges must sometimes work hard simply to understand the language, concepts, and arguments presented. Chief Judge Carl McGowan described the challenge in one such case:

The Clean Water Act of 1977 authorized the Environmental Protection Agency by informal rulemaking to issue regulations imposing effluent limitations for each industry discharging pollutants into the waters of the United States. The statutory standard prescribed for the guidance of EPA was that effluents throughout a five-year period from 1977–1983 should not exceed levels characteristic of plants using "the best practicable control technology currently available." . . . Sixteen different wood and paper companies individually brought petitions to review the regulations applicable to them. . . . The substantive claims made were essentially that in this industry manufacturing techniques vary widely from plant to plant in their scientific and engineering characteristics, and that EPA had been arbitrary and capricious in not providing a sufficient number of groupings to allow for these variations. To the extent that the court turned aside the claims of error made in respect of the hearing procedures followed and the Agency's interpretation of the underlying statute, it was left with the formidable task of acquiring an understanding of sixteen separate plant operations so that it could compare them with one another and with the many more noncomplaining plants and decide whether there had been irrationality in EPA's classifications. This presumably was to be done by the court's mastering the contents of the 140,000 pages of record replete with assertions by chemical engineering reports, assembled in the six-year period of notice and comment.

This task was one to be approached by a court, wholly lacking in expert assistance of its own, with a modest view of its own capabilities in this area, and a firm grasp upon the standards of review properly to be observed by it.[169]

Even with such challenges, however, the court cannot ignore the basic requirements for judicial review and simply give an agency carte blanche to exceed the law, abuse its discretion, and act arbitrarily. Nor may it presume to judge the accuracy of administrators' scientific judgments. In this day and time, agency actions will be vigorously challenged, especially when administrative actions affect repeat players. Scientific data will be presented by all parties.[170]

The court is not generally asked to find that the agency is wrong on a scientific basis. Instead, the scientific arguments are made to show, as in the EPA example cited above, that the administrator acted arbitrarily by refusing to acknowledge competent scientific information or by making gross generalizations that are seen as irrational when viewed in light of the real-world situation as indicated by scientific evidence.

Judges are often painfully aware of their own weaknesses in deciding such matters.[171] In terms of workload, critical political rhetoric, and difficulty in drafting opinions, judges might be tempted to avoid such cases through technical devices or to rubber-stamp administrative decisions. To their credit, judges are aware of the importance of their role in the administrative justice system and understand the need for careful and thorough judicial review.[172] Finally, judges possess an expertise that is not inherently in conflict with the subject matter expertise of the agency:

> If the principal purpose of judicial review of agency action is thought to reside in assuring procedural fair play and reasoned decisionmaking, then we have an expertise to bring to bear that does not derogate from the expertise the agency members should have in their particular fields. The one is expertise that complements, rather than conflicts with the other.[173]

Review in Technical Cases: Present Situation and Future Prospects   Review in these complex cases begins like any other judicial review of administrative action. The judge applies the arbitrary and capricious standard presented earlier in the chapter or with increased scrutiny under the substantial evidence standard where the statute at issue requires it.

That said, the Supreme Court in the Burger and Rehnquist era has indicated a desire to limit the scope of judicial review, particularly where scientific matters are concerned, but even the members of that Court have often differed on whether or how far review should be reduced. The problems and prospects of judicial review can be best understood from a brief examination of two conflicting Supreme Court decisions, *Vermont Yankee Nuclear Power Corporation v. Natural Resources Defense Council*[174] and *Industrial Union Department, AFL-CIO v. American Petroleum Institute*.[175]

Vermont Yankee and the NRC   The *Vermont Yankee* case arose on petitions for judicial review of two actions taken by the Nuclear Regulatory Commission. When the NRC began proceedings to license the Vermont Yankee Nuclear Power Plant, various groups, including the Natural Resources Defense Council, argued that the National Environmental Policy Act (NEPA) required that before a nuclear plant could be licensed, the NRC must consider fully the impact of the nuclear fuel cycle, including problems of transportation, processing, and storage of spent fuel in the cost/benefit analysis.[176] The appeals board of the NRC required the licensing board to report on the impact of the transportation of fuel, but not on processing or storage.[177] The NRC then granted a license to the power facility.

The second NRC action grew out of the first. After the appeals board made its determination about the importance of the impact of the fuel cycle, the NRC, employing a hybrid rulemaking process, began a rulemaking proceeding on that subject. The NRC began with the informal notice and comment procedure and added an oral hearing at which interested parties could present evidence. The commission did not permit cross-examination of witnesses. In the end, the NRC concluded that the impact of the processing and storage of fuel was not of major significance, and such impact as there might be could be accommodated by adding a numerical factor from an impact chart into the cost/benefit analysis for any particular plant license application. These conclusions were apparently based on the testimony of Dr. Frank K. Pittman, director of the Atomic Energy Commission, Division of Waste Management and Transportation. Pittman testified in very general terms that the federal government had the responsibility for planning, constructing, and operating a nuclear fuel processing and storage facility, and that it was ready and able to do so. Pittman indicated that the government had plans for such a facility and studies to support its position that nuclear waste disposal would pose no difficulty.

> Dr. Pittman's description of the new plan—also postponed indefinitely—to build a surface storage facility can only fairly be described as vague but glowing. . . .
>
> In less than two pages, he sets out a very general description of what the facility is supposed to do [cite], accompanied by several schematic drawings. These show the facility will have a cooling system, a transfer area and storage basins, but do not attempt to describe how they will be built and operated, what materials will be used, where such a facility might be located, or what it might cost to build and operate. . . .
>
> No citations are given for these studies; in fact, there are no references to backup materials supporting any of Pittman's statement, or those portions of the Revised Environmental Survey drawn from it.[178]

The environmental groups objected that there was a great deal of evidence contradicting Pittman's testimony and that they should be permitted to cross-examine Pittman on those disputed points. They also argued that the NRC should require careful consideration of nuclear waste management in licensing, since a plant like Vermont Yankee would "produce approximately 160 pounds of plutonium wastes annually during its 40-year life span."[179] The commission rejected those arguments.

The Natural Resources Defense Council sought review of both actions in the U.S. Circuit of Appeals for the District of Columbia Circuit. The Vermont Yankee Nuclear Power Corporation and the Baltimore Gas and Electric Company intervened on behalf of the NRC. Consolidated National Intervenors, Inc., a consortium of some 80 groups and individuals including the Sierra Club and the Union of Concerned Scientists, intervened on the side of the Natural Resources Defense Council. In addition, the state of New York filed an *amicus curiae* urging reversal of the NRC actions, while Commonwealth Edison, Consolidated Edison of New York, Niagara Mohawk Power Corporation, Omaha Public Power District Powers Authority, and Rochester Gas and Electric Corporation filed amicus briefs in support of the NRC.

Chief Judge Bazelon wrote for himself and Judge Edwards. Judge Tamm entered a concurring opinion. On the Vermont Yankee licensing decision based on the appeals board ruling, the court reversed the appeals board interpretation of the requirements of the National Environmental Policy Act. The NEPA requires detailed analyses of the environmental impact of such matters. The court noted that since a plant like Vermont Yankee would produce significant quantities of plutonium that would need to be safeguarded, by the agency's own admission, for some 250,000 years, as well as strontium 90 and cesium 137, which would be dangerous for from 600 to 1,000 years, licensing a plant clearly involved "irreversible and irretrievable commitments of resources."[180] The court remanded the Vermont Yankee licensing decision for further action in light of its ruling on the NRC rulemaking action.

The court then set aside the rulemaking proceeding and remanded it for further action. The basis for this ruling was that the agency's procedure did not demonstrate that there had been consideration of the arguments opposed to Pittman's testimony. Bazelon outlined the court's responsibility in such a review process:

> Absent extraordinary circumstances, it is not proper for a reviewing court to prescribe the procedural format which an agency must use to explore a given set of issues. Unless there are statutory directives to the contrary, an agency has discretion to select procedures which it deems best to compile a record illuminating the issues. Courts are no more expert at fashioning administrative procedures than they are in the substantive areas of responsibility which are left to agency discretion. What a reviewing court can do, however, is scrutinize the record as a whole to insure that genuine opportunities to participate in a meaningful way were provided, and that the agency has taken a good, hard look at the major question before it. . . .
>
> In order to determine whether an agency has lived up to these responsibilities, a reviewing court must examine the record in detail to determine that a real give and take was fostered on the key issues. This does not give a court a license to judge for itself how much weight should be given particular pieces of scientific or technical data, a task for which it is singularly ill-suited. It does require, however, that the court examine the record so that it may satisfy itself that the decision was based "on a consideration of the relevant factors." Where only one side of a controversial issue is developed in any detail, the agency may abuse discretion by deciding the issues on an inadequate record.
>
> A reviewing court must assure itself not only that a diversity of informed opinion was heard but that it was genuinely considered.[181]

The court found that an examination of the record indicated that the procedures had been inadequate to ensure a thorough consideration of the issues. Specifically, the court found that in the absence of opportunities to challenge Dr. Pittman's testimony, the NRC acted arbitrarily.

> The Commission's action in cutting off consideration of waste disposal and reprocessing issues in licensing proceedings based on the cursory development of the facts which occurred in this proceeding was capricious and arbitrary. The portions of the rule pertaining to these matters are set aside and remanded.[182]

The Supreme Court in a unanimous opinion written by Justice Rehnquist (Justices Powell and Blackmun did not participate) reversed and remanded the ruling of the circuit court.[183] The opinion was lengthy, but conveyed one message: Unless a statute required more, agency rulemaking procedures were up to the agency and procedural requirements were not to be increased by the courts. If a reviewing court finds the record insufficient to support a rule, it may vacate the rule and remand it, but it may not add procedures. Referring to the District of Columbia Circuit Court opinion as "Monday morning quarterbacking," the Court chastised the lower court for second-guessing the agency.

The decision in *Vermont Yankee* engendered a great deal of commentary and controversy.[184] The breadth and tenor of the *Vermont Yankee* opinion, coupled with apparent unanimity among the Supreme Court justices, suggested that reviewing courts would be called on to move toward the deference-to-agency action end of the deference-versus-close-scrutiny continuum. However, the clarity and unanimity turned out to be more apparent than real. The review of the Occupational Safety and Health Administration's standard for worker exposure to benzene in 1980 found the Court badly divided and at the other end of the spectrum.

The Benzene Controversy   The Occupational Safety and Health Act of 1970 created the Occupational Safety and Health Administration in the Department of Labor. The act stated:

The Secretary, in promulgating standards dealing with toxic materials or harmful physical agents under this subsection, shall set the standard which most adequately assures, to the extent feasible, on the basis of the best available evidence, that no employee will suffer material impairment of health or functional capacity even if such employee has regular exposure to the hazard dealt with by such standard for the period of his working life. Development of standards under this subsection shall be based upon research, demonstration, experiments, and such other information as may be appropriate. In addition to the attainment of the highest degree of health and safety protection for the employee, other considerations shall be the latest available scientific data in the field, the feasibility of the standards, and experience gained under this and other health and safety laws.[185]

When the agency first began operation it was permitted by Congress to adopt national consensus standards (those generally agreed on) until it conducted OSHA's own investigations with an eye toward setting its own standards.[186] The agency began inquiries into toxic substances with primary research provided by OSHA's research support agency, the National Institute of Occupational Health and Safety (NIOSH). Of immediate interest was worker exposure to vinyl chloride, coke oven emissions, lead, asbestos, cotton dust in cotton mills, and benzene.

Benzene is a toxic substance. Although it could conceivably cause harm to a person who swallowed or touched it, the principal risk of harm comes from inhalation of benzene vapors. When these vapors are inhaled, the benzene diffuses through the lungs and is quickly absorbed into the blood. Exposure to high concentrations produces an almost immediate effect on the central nervous system. Inhalation of concentrations of 20,000 ppm can be fatal within minutes; exposure in the range of 250 to 550 ppm can cause vertigo, nausea, and other symptoms of mild poisoning. . . . Persistent exposures at levels above 25–40 ppm may lead to blood deficiencies and diseases of the blood-forming organs, including aplastic anemia, which is generally fatal.[187]

As early as 1948 benzene-related blood disorders caused Massachusetts to impose a 35-ppm level in work areas. By 1969 the American National Standards Institute recommended an average exposure over a normal workday to no more than 10 ppm. As NIOSH continued its investigation, it found that benzene had been linked to leukemia as early as 1920, and by 1976 a significant amount of data had accumulated showing a definite causal relationship between benzene and leukemia—even at relatively low levels of concentration, although NIOSH was not aware of just how low a level of exposure could lead to the cancer. NIOSH also found significant benzene impact on other nonmalignant blood disorders and chromosome damage, again even at relatively low levels of exposure. NIOSH urged OSHA to substantially reduce allowable worker exposure levels.

The OSHA conducted the hybrid rulemaking process required by its statute, allowing extensive testimony. The record came to 50 volumes. The agency also contracted with a private accounting firm to determine the economic impact of its proposed 1 ppm standard. The statement of basis and purpose in the rule that was finally published was nearly 200 pages in length, and included reasons why the arguments raised during the hearings against the agency standard were rejected.

In this case the Secretary of Labor found, on the basis of substantial evidence, that: (1) exposure to benzene creates a risk of cancer, chromosomal damage, and a variety of nonmalignant but potentially fatal blood disorders, even at the level of 1 ppm; (2) no safe level of exposure has been shown; (3) benefits in the form of saved lives that would be derived from the permanent standard; (4) the number of lives that would be saved could turn out to be either substantial or relatively small; (5) under the present state of scientific knowledge, it is impossible to calculate even in a rough way the number of lives that would be saved, at least without making assumptions that would appear absurd to much of the medical community; and (6) the standard would not materially harm the financial condition of the covered industries.[188]

The American Petroleum Institute sought judicial review in the Fifth Circuit, sitting in Louisiana. The Fifth Circuit struck the OSHA standard, primarily on the ground that the "to the extent feasible" language in the OSHA statute meant that a standard must be both technologically and economically feasible. The court interpreted economic feasibility to mean cost effective where that determination is reached through a cost/benefit analysis showing injury or death prevented per dollar of cost for implementation.[189]

The case went to the Supreme Court, but the cost/benefit analysis question was not reached. The Court was badly divided. The plurality opinion was written by Justice Stevens and was joined by Chief Justice Burger and Justice Stewart. Burger also wrote a separate concurring opinion. Powell joined in some parts of the plurality opinion but not others and entered his own concurring opinion. Justice Rehnquist concurred with the decision, but on entirely different grounds than the others. Justice Marshall wrote the dissent and was joined by Justices Brennan, White, and Blackmun. In short, there were five votes to affirm the lower court decision and set aside the OSHA benzene standard and four votes to uphold the standard, with the dissenters in greater agreement on the basis for their position.

The plurality never actually addressed the cost/benefit question because those justices found the OSHA action invalid on other grounds. The Court determined that the agency must find that existing exposure standards are dangerous, that a new standard is "reasonably necessary or appropriate," and that the new standard will significantly reduce the danger to workers. This threshold finding requirement was developed from a new interpretation of language in a different section of the OSHA act, which defined the term "standard." The Court's imposition of such a threshold finding step in developing a standard was very different from the rulings in *Overton Park* and *Vermont Yankee,* which had ruled that formal administrative findings are not necessary unless the agency enabling act specifically requires them. The plurality then engaged in a long and detailed analysis of the data concerning just how much exposure would lead to what amount of disease.

The Court also assumed that OSHA had based the rule on the carcinogenic effects of benzene and not on other hazards. OSHA's policy was that where a substance was clearly carcinogenic and safe levels had not been determined, it was to be assumed that no exposure level was safe and the standard should be set at the lowest feasible level. The plurality opinion argued that the burden for proving that ambiguity at low levels of exposure was on the agency; but the agency had contended that scientific evidence was not advanced enough to establish lower limits of safety and to make the agency prove minimum dosage levels would place the risk on the workers, contrary to the statute. The plurality disagreed.

The dissenting opinion was written by Justice Marshall for others who had been part of the *Vermont Yankee* ruling. The dissent chastised the plurality for doing in the benzene situation exactly what it had told the lower court in *Vermont Yankee* not to do: second-guessing the administrative policy issues and adding requirements in the decision process not in statute. Recognizing that such scientifically complex rulings pose difficult problems of judicial review, Marshall observed:

> Such decisions were not intended to be unreviewable; they too must be scrutinized to ensure that the Secretary has acted reasonably and within the boundaries set by Congress. But a reviewing court must be mindful of the limited nature of its role. See *Vermont Yankee Nuclear Power Corp. v. NRDC. . . .*[190]
>
> In short, today's decision represents a usurpation of decisionmaking authority that has been exercised by Congress and its authorized representatives. The plurality's construction has no support in the statute's language, structure or legislative history. The threshold finding that the plurality requires is the plurality's own invention.[191]

The dissenters concluded by reminding the others that while the guidelines for judicial review cannot be exact, review must be limited to avoid interference with properly exercised expert administrative judgment. Moreover, the review must be evenhanded. The decision here seemed to violate both principles.

> In the Occupational Safety and Health Act, Congress expressed confidence that the courts would carry out this important responsibility. But in this case the plurality has far exceeded its authority.... *Vermont Yankee*. . . .
>
> Because the approach taken by the plurality is so plainly irreconcilable with the Court's proper institutional role, I am certain that it will not stand the test of time. In all likelihood, today's decision will come to be regarded as an extreme reaction to a regulatory scheme that, as the Members of the plurality perceived it, imposed an unduly harsh burden on regulated industries. But as the Constitution "does not enact Mr. Herbert Spencer's Social Statics," *Lochner v. New York*, 198 U.S. 45, 75 (1905) (Holmes, J., dissenting), so the responsibility to scrutinize federal administrative action does not authorize this Court to strike its own balance between the costs and benefits of occupational safety standards.[192]

The following year, a third case testing the Court's approach to judicial review of such complex cases was decided. This case, *American Textile Manufacturers Institute v. Donovan*,[193] concerned a very different kind of OSHA regulations (those aimed at addressing byssinosis, often called cotton dust disease, faced by those working in the textile industry), but presented issues similar to those raised in the benzene case. In this case, the Court reached the issue they passed in the benzene case, ruling that OSHA was required to perform a feasibility analysis, which did not mean that the agency was obligated to demonstrate a favorable cost/benefit calculation. The Court upheld both the agency's reading of its statutory obligations and sustained, on substantial evidence grounds, its substantive judgments. Justice Brennan wrote for the majority with dissent from Justices Stewart, Rehnquist, and Burger, who had been on the other side in the benzene case. Brennan criticized his conservative colleagues (with quotations taken from two of Burger's own opinions), noting that: "We must measure the validity of the Secretary's actions against the requirements of that Act. For '[t]he judicial function does not extend to substantive revision of regulatory policy. That function lies elsewhere—in congressional and executive oversight or amendatory legislation."[194]

The importance of these cases is not merely that they represent some of the most important opinions on judicial review, but that they indicate why it is so difficult to attain the proper balance between appropriate judicial deference to agency expertise and the need for thorough review in complex cases. Other complicating factors include outdated or poorly drafted statutes and pressures from the executive and legislative branches. Thus, for example, when nationwide publicity focused on parental treatment decisions, the Reagan administration pressured the Department of Health and Human Services to take action to compel hospitals to move to investigate the parents. Whatever the Supreme Court's view of the deference appropriate in the case, it could not ignore the fact that the process that produced the regulations was fundamentally arbitrary and capricious because it was driven by political demands rather than rational decisionmaking supported by an expert process.[195] Finally, the complexities involved in evaluating approaches to judicial review are affected in some cases by the fact that many judges come to the bench with little training or experience in the field of administrative law.

Of course, the dialogue, to use Fisher's term, among courts, administrators, and legislators over the nature and contours of appropriate deference continues. And it is important to be aware of the state of that dialogue at any given point in time. The irony of the conversation in the contemporary era may be that judges talk more about deference now, but may not really exercise it as much, whereas previously they exercised it more but were less concerned about making a public issue of it.

THE IMPORTANCE OF JUDICIAL REVIEW
AND THE DANGER OF PRETENSE

Much has been said in many judicial opinions considered in this chapter about a perceived need to limit access to courts for judicial review and to narrow the type of review that is to be provided for those cases that are accepted. And it is certainly true that many administrators applaud that view on the theory that the less oversight and possible interference by courts, the better. All that having been said, it is not necessarily true that "less is more," as the popular expression goes, even from the perspective of the administrator, who would seem to be the big winner. As was true of changes with respect to rulemaking and adjudication, there is another side to the move to trim judicial review. This is the argument that public managers should be careful what they wish because effective and readily available judicial review offers important contributions to public administration that should not be underappreciated.

For one thing, the efforts by courts to constrain judicial review has sometimes prompted other institutions to take action. Thus, Congress has enacted some statutes to provide access or assist litigants where the Court was unwilling to recognize or permit suits or reward those who prevailed.[196] The lower courts may or may not cooperate in the Supreme Court's effort to trim federal court activity.[197] A few state supreme courts have reacted to the narrowing of some federal doctrines by expanding state rulings, but this creates a very uneven legal fabric and does not apply to federal administrative actions.[198] Judges who oppose limiting access to the courtroom are fond of citing Alexis de Toqueville's observation of almost a century and a half ago: "The American judge is brought into the political arena independent of his own will. He only judges the law because he is obliged to judge a case. The political question which he is called upon to resolve is connected with the interest of the parties and he cannot refuse to decide it without abdicating the duties of his post."[199]

Then there is the fact that the efforts of the Supreme Court to make the procedural barriers to review increasingly complex and discretionary have not in fact resulted in reducing the demand for review. Rather, critics argue that the rulings on standing and the like have not reduced the caseload on the federal courts, but have actually increased the burden because additional space in briefs and hearing time are needed to resolve procedural disputes before the court can proceed to the merits of the case.[200] Given the fact that many courts have come to place limits on the lengths of briefs and oral argument time, the effect is to trade away time and energy from the discussion of the merits of cases and invest that time in arcane debates over procedural issues that may be more tactical than meaningful in a given case. That very much takes the field backward in its development and ignores the many historical reasons (discussed in Chapter 4) that led to a drive for more available and more effective judicial review.

Third, the nature of the move toward restricting review that has been evident since the 1970s has presented serious issues of inequality and inequity. These decisions, which purport to be about constraining judicial review, are not neutral in their effect. They carry a variety of biases. For one thing, the increasing technical procedural intricacies militate in favor of financially well-off, often corporate, litigants who can afford protracted legal battles fought by expensive law firms that have the range of expertise and resources to wage the challenging procedural fights. The rules themselves favor access for regulated industries and are generally more burdensome for efforts by single-shot players or groups. And where the rules do not suffice, some judges have been perfectly willing—having converted what were case and controversy requirements into "prudential" considerations—to ignore what appears to be the clear import of the rules and simply decide which litigants they favor and which they oppose.[201] Thus, some of these rulings can mean that review is not provided where justice, equity, and the historical demands of administrative law development call for it, even though all of the case or controversy requirements are clearly satisfied. On the other hand, they do little or nothing to protect administrators from manifold challenges by those whose cases are no better but who have the ability to wage the battle. These dynamics present the likelihood of uneven patterns of review affecting different policy arenas and increasing levels of complexity, which in turn increase legal workload and costs for government agencies, their legal representatives, and courts.

Fourth, there is the risk of undermining legitimacy. After all, the legislators and even the chief executive who may have demanded action in the first place are often nowhere to be found when it comes time for an agency at the state or local level to take action. Thus, for example, the Equal Employment Opportunity Commission (EEOC) was flying solo when it issued guidelines holding that sexual harassment constituted sex discrimination within the meaning of Title VII of the Civil Rights Act of 1964. However, the ruling in *Meritor Savings Bank v. Vinson*[202] eliminated the debate over the legitimacy of the EEOC policymaking and provided a foundation for the agency to move forward in elaborating and applying the policy.

Beyond that, judicial review can provide a number of benefits. First, it offers feedback on statutory interpretation and tells administrators whether they are correct in their understanding of legislation. When legislators have handed difficult or ambiguous laws to administrative agencies, such feedback can be useful. Among other things, it permits an agency some defense against repeated claims by many legislators that their manifold post hoc interpretations of legislation should govern agency action. Courts also provide feedback on procedural questions. Often these decisions are favorable, providing administrators with an external validation of their actions. Courts also produce interpretations of potentially conflicting legal requirements, helping beleaguered administrators out of difficult situations. Judges can provide instructions that protect agencies against political interference from the executive appointees as well the legislators.

At a more general level, judicial review provides a mechanism for integrating the decisions made by agencies into the existing body of law. Without that, administrative decisions would not operate under the same rule of law as all other elements of American life. With it, rulemaking proceedings and adjudications can be reconciled with the requirements of constitutional law, statutory interpretations, and the rest of American law. Judicial review, then, conveys a sense of administration as a legitimate part of the constitutional whole, as opposed to a picture of disconnected, unaccountable, exotic decisions rendered by unelected elites.

There are even cases in which administrators have been able to use the fact that their agencies have been found in violation of the law to compel political officials to respond to basic needs. Decisions about prisons, mental hospitals, and schools have allowed politicians to provide services they knew were necessary without having to take the politically difficult position of voting expenditures for, say, prison reform outside the context of a judicial mandate.

Finally, judicial review provides an important forum in which to address the complex questions that arise in intergovernmental relations. In an era when there is so much reliance by the national government on the states to implement congressionally enacted programs and when the states in turn rely on local governments or contractors, there are many situations in which there is a need to reconcile varying standards and procedures and to determine the boundaries of authority. There is little evidence from recent history that Congress will seek to resolve these difficulties, and the federal executive agencies, state governments, and local governments or contractors are all parties at interest. Thus, the courts are playing this role more often than ever before.

The point is not that one should make decisions with the hope that they will be overturned, but that judicial review in itself is not necessarily without benefits. It certainly plays an absolutely essential role in supporting the legitimacy of administrative power.

SUMMARY

This chapter has examined judicial review as the third major element of the formal administrative process, noting especially the difficulties encountered by the judge. The judge who is called upon to review decisions of administrative agencies must avoid interference with proper administrative activities and yet ensure thorough review of agency action to prevent or terminate illegal or arbitrary administration. The task is carried out in complex cases that frequently involve many parties who submit intricate and lengthy volumes of argument and evidence. Review serves a number of functions in the administrative process. The nature of the cases and the purposes of review combine to produce a complex role for the judge. The black letter law rules that govern judicial review came primarily from statutes and common law. They govern which cases get into the courthouse for review and the kind of review they receive. Finally, judicial review, which in our time often involves difficult scientific and technological disputes, is a dynamic and continually developing process.

Chapters 5, 6, and 7 have focused on formal administrative law matters. However, many of the tasks and problems of law and administration are not confined to the black letter law and decisions in particular court rulings. We turn to these problems of law and politics in administration in the remaining chapters.

NOTES

1. See *United States v. Armstrong,* 517 U.S. 456, 464 (1996); *United States Postal Service v. Gregory,* 534 U.S. 1, 10 (2001).

2. *Citizens to Preserve Overton Park, Inc. v. Volpe,* 432 F.2d 1307, 1309-10 (6th Cir. 1970).

3. §4(f) of the Department of Transportation Act of 1966, as amended, 49 U.S.C. §1653(f). Cited in *Citizens to Preserve Overton Park v. Volpe,* 401 U.S. 402, 405 n.3 (1971).

4. See e.g., *Nashville 1-40 Steering Committee v. Ellington,* 387 F.2d 179 (6th Cir. 1967) and *South Hill Neighborhood Association Inc. v. Romney,* 421 F.2d 455 (6th Cir. 1969), cited in *Citizens to Preserve Overton Park v. Volpe,* 309 F. Supp. 1189, 1191-92 (WDTN 1970).

5. *Citizens to Preserve Overton Park v. Volpe, Id.,* at p. 1191.

6. *Id.,* at p. 1194.

7. "A threshold question—whether petitioners are entitled to any judicial review—is easily answered. Section 701 of the Administrative Procedure Act . . . provides that the action of 'each authority of the Government of the United States,' which includes the Department of Transportation, 'is subject to judicial review or where agency action is committed to agency discretion by law.' In this case, there is no indication that Congress ought to prohibit judicial review and there is most certainly no 'showing of clear and convincing evidence of a legislative intent' to restrict access to judicial review. *Abbott Laboratories v. Gardner,* 387 U.S. 136, 141 (1967).

    "Similarly, the Secretary's decision does not fall within the exception for action 'committed by law to agency discretion.' This is a very narrow exception." Berger, "Administrative Arbitrariness and Judicial Review," 65 *Columbia L. Rev.* 55 (1965). The legislative history of the Administrative Procedure Act indicates that it is applicable on those rare instances where "statutes are drawn in such broad terms that in a given case there is no law to apply. S. Rep. no. 752, 79th Cong., 1st Sess., 26 (1945)." 401 U.S., at p. 410.

8. *Id.,* at p. 411.

9. *Id.* The Court here refers to Rep. Holifield's comments on that point in the legislative history. 114 Cong. Rec. 19915

10. *Id.,* at pp. 412–13.

11. *Id.,* at pp. 415–16.

12. *Id.,* at p. 419.

13. Justices Black and Brennan would have gone even further. Justice Black, a man not considered an activist judge in most circles, wrote a separate opinion in which Justice Brennan joined: "I agree with the Court that the judgment of the Court of Appeals is wrong and that its action should be reversed. I do not agree that the whole matter should be remanded to the District Court. I think the case should be sent back to the Secretary of Transportation. It is apparent from the Court's opinion today that the Secretary of Transportation completely failed to comply with the duty imposed on him by Congress not to permit a federally financed

public highway to run through a public park 'unless (1) there is no feasible and prudent alternative to the use of the land, and (2) such program includes all possible planning to minimize harm to such park. . . . I regret that I am compelled to conclude for myself that, except for some too late formulations, apparently coming from the Solicitor General's office, this record contains not one word to indicate that the Secretary raised even a finger to comply with the command of Congress." *Id.,* at p. 422.

14. *Citizens to Preserve Overton Park v. Volpe,* 335 F. Supp. 873, 874 (WDTN 1972).

15. *Id.,* at p. 878.

16. *Id.*

17. *Citizens to Preserve Overton Park v. Brinegar,* 494 F.2d 1212 (6th Cir. 1974).

18. The *Eldridge* case study illustrates the point. With an annual caseload in excess of 1,250,000, the government considered the Society Security Administration to be involved in a litigation crisis when the number of cases taken for judicial review exceeded 5,000. See Appendix 1.

19. Louis Fisher, *Constitutional Dialogues* (Princeton, NJ: Princeton University Press, 1988).

20. While much has been published on the subject over the years, this literature can be traced back to Clement E. Vose, *Caucasians Only: The Supreme Court, the NAACP, and the Restrictive Covenant Cases* (Berkeley: University of California Press, 1959).

21. See Karen O'Connor and Lee Epstein, "The Rise of Conservative Interest Group Litigation," 45 *Journal of Politics* 479 (1983); "Amicus Curiae Participation in U.S. Supreme Court Litigation," 16 *Law & Society Review* 311 (1981).

22. See e.g., Jayanth K. Krishnan and Kevin R. den Dulk, "So Help Me God: A Comparative Study of Religious Interest Group Litigation," 30 *Georgia J. Int'l and Comp. L.* 233 (2002); Lee Epstein. "Interest Group Litigation During the Rehnquist Era," 9 *Journal of Law and Politics* 639 (1993); John O. Heinz, "Lawyers for Conservative Causes: Clients, Ideology, and Social Distance," 37 *Law & Society Rev.* 5 (2003).

23. *Wyatt v. Stickney,* 325 F. Supp. 582 (MDAL 1971). See generally, Phillip J. Cooper, *Hard Judicial Choices* (New York: Oxford University Press, 1988), Chapter 7.

24. *Rhodes v. Chapman,* 452 U.S. 337 (1981). See also, Cooper, *Hard Judicial Choices, supra* note 23, Chapter 9.

25. *International Association of Independent Tanker Owners (INTERTANKO) v. Lowry,* 947 F. Supp. 1484 (WDWA 1996).

26. "Note Verbale from the Royal Danish Embassy to the U.S. Department of State 1" (June 14, 1996), quoted in *United States v. Locke,* 529 U.S. 89, 98 (2000).

27. *Anderson v. Evans,* 311 F.3d 1006 (9th Cir. 2002).

28. *United States v. Locke,* 529 U.S. 89 (2000).

29. See e.g., *Board of Governors of the United States Postal Service v. United States Postal Rate Commission,* 654 F.2d 108 (D.C.Cir. 1981).

30. On the politics of representing government before the courts, see Cornell W. Clayton, "Government Lawyers: Who Represents Government and Why Does It Matter?" in Phillip J. Cooper and Chester A. Newland, eds., *Handbook of Public Law and Administration* (San Francisco: Jossey-Bass, 1997).

31. 673 F.2d 425 (D.C.Cir. 1982).

32. *Forney v. Apfel,* 141 L.Ed.2d 269, 273 (1998).

33. *State ex rel. Stephan v. Kansas House of Representatives,* 687 P.2d 622 (Kansas 1984).

34. Professor Abram Chayes wrote an interesting article on this subject entitled "The Role of the Judge in Public Law Litigation," 89 *Harvard L. Rev.* 1281 (1976), which was influential in the debate over judicial roles in the 1970s.

35. 422 F.3d 782 (9th Cir. 2005). Earlier district court rulings may be found at *National Wildlife Federation v. National Marine Fisheries Service,* 2005 U.S. Dist. LEXIS 16658 (D.OR 2005); and 2004 U.S. Dist. LEXIS 15239 (D.OR 2004).

36. U.S. House of Representatives, Hearings Before the Subcommittee on Courts Civil Liberties, and the Administration of Justice of the Committee on the Judiciary, *State of the Judiciary and Access to Justice,* 95th Cong., 1st Sess. 135-36 (1977). Hereafter referred to as *Access to Justice.*

37. *Bennett v. Spear,* 137 L.Ed.2d 281, 295 (1997).

38. U.S. Constitution, Article III.

39. Jurisdiction is particularly important because not all courts have the same characteristics. It is therefore a significant matter which tribunal has jurisdiction over a case. See e.g., David P. Currie and Frank L. Goodman, "Judicial Review of Federal Administrative Action: Quest for the Optimum Forum," 75 *Columbia L. Rev.* 1 (1975). Jurisdiction is particularly important in determining where a case will be initially heard. This is known as primary jurisdiction. Primary jurisdiction is important because the record established in the initial decisionmaking process is the basis for all subsequent appeals. There can also be a qualitative difference in decisions, depending on the tribunal involved. See Burt Neuborne, "The Myth of Parity," 90 *Harvard L. Rev.* 1105 (1977).

40. "Without jurisdiction the court cannot proceed at all in any cause.... On every writ of error or appeal, the first and fundamental question is that of jurisdiction.... The requirement that jurisdiction be established as a threshold matter springs from the nature and limits of the judicial power of the United States and is inflexible and without exception [quotation marks and citations deleted]." *Steel Co. v. Citizens for a Better Environment,* 140 L.Ed.2d 210, 227 (1998).

41. See also Henry Abraham, "The Sixteen Great Maxims," in *The Judicial Process* (New York: Oxford, 1980), pp. 373–400.

42. *Baker v. Carr,* 369 U.S. 186 (1962).

43. *Bennett v. Spear, supra* note 37, at p. 295.

44. *Valley Forge Christian College v. Americans United for Separation of Church and State,* 454 U.S. 464 (1982).

45. *McConnell v. Federal Election Commission,* 540 U.S. 93, 225 (2003), citing *Vermont Agency of Natural Resources v. United States ex rel. Stevens,* 529 U.S. 765, 771 (2000); *Lujan v. Defenders of Wildlife,* 504 U.S. 555 (1992); *Whitmore v. Arkansas,* 495 U.S. 149, 155 (1990); and *Simon v. Eastern Ky. Welfare Rights Organization,* 426 U.S. 26 (1976).

46. *Whitmore v. Arkansas,* 495 U.S. 149, 155 (1990); *Sierra Club v. Morton,* 405 U.S. 727 (1972).

47. *McConnell, supra* note 45, at 226.

48. *Association of Data Processing Service Organizations v. Camp,* 397 U.S. 150, 152-54 (1970); *Barlow v. Collins,* 397 U.S. 159, 164-67 (1970); *Trafficante v. Metropolitan Life Ins. Co.,* 409 U.S. 205 (1972).

49. See *Steel Co. v. Citizens for a Better Environment, supra* note 40. See also *United States v. Richardson,* 418 U.S. 166 (1974) and *Schlesinger v. Reservists Committee to Stop the War,* 418 U.S. 208 (1974).

50. *Byrd v. Raines,* 138 L.Ed.2d 849 (1997).

51. *McConnell, supra* note 45, at 227.

52. *Simon v. Eastern Kentucky Welfare Rights Org.,* 468 U.S. 26, 41 (1976).

53. *Steel Co. v. Citizens for A Better Environment, supra* note 40, at 232.

54. Emergency Planning and Community Right-To-Know Act of 1986, 42 U.S.C. §§11001 et seq.

55. *Steel Co. v. Citizens for a Better Environment, supra* note 40.

56. *Lujan v. Defenders of Wildlife,* 504 U.S. 555, 568-571 (1992).

57. *Valley Forge Christian College v. Americans United for Separation of Church and State,* 454 U.S. 464, 474-475 (1982).

58. *United States v. SCRAP,* 412 U.S. 669 (1973); *NAACP v. Alabama,* 357 U.S. 449 (1958).

59. There are occasional exceptions where it would be difficult or impossible for the third party to defend his or her own interests. See *Singleton v. Wulff,* 428 U.S. 106 (1976) and *Barrows v. Jackson,* 346 U.S. 249 (1953).

60. *Warth v. Seldin,* 422 U.S. 490 (1975).

61. *Id.* See also *Construction Association of Sonoma County v. Petaluma,* 522 F.2d 897 (9th Cir. 1975), cert. denied, 424 U.S. 934 (1976).

62. See *Miller v. Albright,* 140 L.Ed.2d 575, 589 (1998); *Craig v. Boren,* 429 U.S. 190 (1976); *Barrows v. Jackson,* 346 U.S. 249 (1953). See also *National Council for Improved Health v. Shalala,* 122 F.3d 878, 882 (10th Cir. 1997) and *Village of Schaumburg v. Citizens for a Better Environment,* 444 U.S. 620, 634 (1980).

63. *Bennett v. Spear, supra* note 37, at p. 295.

64. *Id.*, at 303.

65. "We have made clear, however, that the breadth of the zone of interests varies according to the provisions of law at issue, so that what comes within the zone of interests of a statute for purposes of obtaining judicial review of administrative action under the 'generous review provisions' of the APA may not do so for other purposes." *Id.*, at p. 296.

66. See *Suitum v. Tahoe Regional Planning Agency*, 137 L.Ed.2d 980 (1997).

67. This is not uncommon in such areas as First Amendment freedoms because of concern that delay might cause people to censor themselves.

68. *Ohio Forestry Association v. Sierra Club*, 140 L.Ed.2d 921 (1998).

69. *Abbott Laboratories v. Gardner*, 387 U.S. 136, 148-149 (1967).

70. "Except where Congress explicitly provides for our correction of the administrative process at a higher level of generality, we intervene in the administration of the laws only when, and to the extent that, a specific 'final agency action' has an actual or immediately threatened effect." *Lujan v. National Wildlife Federation*, 497 U.S. 871, 894 (1990).

71. *Bennett v. Spear*, 137 L.Ed.2d 281, 305 (1997). See also *Alaska Department of Environmental Conservation v. Environmental Protection Agency*, 540 U.S. 461, 483 (2004).

72. There are some exceptions where Congress has determined that a person should be able to go directly to court, but they are indeed exceptions to the general rule. See e.g., *Patsy v. Board of Regents*, 457 U.S. 496 (1982).

73. Quoted in *National Park Hospitality Association v. Department of the Interior*, 538 U.S. 803, 806 (2003).

74. *Id.*, at 817-818.

75. *Id.*, at 820-821.

76. *City of Littleton, Colorado v. Z. J. Gifts D-4*, 541 U.S. 774, 781 (2004).

77. See generally, *Florida General Contractors v. Jacksonville*, 508 U.S. 656 (1993); *City of Mesquite v. Aladdin's Castle, Inc.*, 455 U.S. 283 (1982).

78. *City of Erie v. Pap's A.M.*, 529 U.S. 277, 287 (2000).

79. *Arizonans for Official English v. Arizona*, 137 L.Ed.2d 170, 193-196 (1997).

80. See e.g., *Rescue Army v. Municipal Court*, 331 U.S. 549 (1947), and *Ashwander v. TVA*, 297 U.S. 288 (1936), Justice Brandeis concurring.

81. Kenneth Culp Davis, *Discretionary Justice: A Preliminary Inquiry* (Baton Rouge, LA: Louisiana State University, 1969), at p. 160.

82. See e.g., *Ortwein v. Schwab*, 410 U.S. 656 (1973).

83. Burt Neuborne, "The Procedural Assault on the Warren Legacy: A Study in Repeal by Indirection," 5 *Hofstra L. Rev.* 545 (1977).

84. Board of Governors of the Society of American Law Teachers, "Supreme Court Denial of Citizen Access to Federal Courts to Challenge Unconstitutional or Otherwise Unlawful Actions: The Record of the Burger Court," in *Access to Justice, supra* note 36, at p. 696.

85. *Steel Co. v. Citizens for a Better Environment*, 140 L.Ed.2d 210, 227 (1998); *Bennett v. Spear*, 137 L.Ed.2d 281 (1997); *Byrd v. Raines*, 138 L.Ed.2d 849 (1997); *Lujan v. National Wildlife Federation*, 497 U.S. 871 (1990); *Defenders of Wildlife v. Lujan*, 504 U.S. 555 (1992); *Allen v. Wright*, 468 U.S. 737 (1984); *Valley Forge Christian College v. Americans United for Separation of Church and State*, 454 U.S. 464 (1982); *Gladstone Realtors v. Village of Bellwood*, 441 U.S. 91 (1979); *Simon v. Eastern Kentucky Welfare Rights Org.*, 426 U.S. 26 (1976); *Warth v. Seldin*, 422 U.S. 490 (1975).

86. Thus, in an earlier time, there was only one so-called "prudential standing rule," the stipulation that one could not bring suit to vindicate the rights of a third party, see *Barrows v. Jackson*, 346 U.S. 249 (1953). However, the courts' opinions of the 1980s and 1990s identify three general categories of prudential standing considerations and, in fact, have asserted that there should be a more general prudential consideration beyond the specific categories. See *Valley Forge Christian College v. Americans United for Separation of Church and State*, 454 U.S. 464 (1982). See also *Reno v. Catholic Social Services, Inc.*, 509 U.S. 43, 57, n. 18 (1993).

87. *Amchem Products, Inc. v. Windsor*, 138 L.Ed.2d 689 (1997); *General Telephone Co. of the Southwest v. Falcon*, 457 U.S. 147 (1982); *Eisen v. Carlisle & Jacquelin*, 417 U.S. 156 (1974); and *Zahn v. International Paper Co.*, 414 U.S. 291 (1973).

88. *Moore v. Sims*, 442 U.S. 415 (1979); *Trainor v. Hernandez*, 431 U.S. 434 (1977); *Judice v. Vail*, 430 U.S. 1977); *Doran v. Salem Inn, Inc.*, 422 U.S. 922 (1975); *Hicks v. Miranda*, 422 U.S. 332 (1975); and *Huffman v. Pursue, Ltd.*, 420 U.S. 592 (1975).

89. See *Middlesex County Sewage Authority v. National Sea Clammers Association*, 453 U.S. 1 (1981), which significantly increased the burdens required to sustain an implied private right of action over the standards used before then. See *Cort v. Ash*, 422 U.S. 66 (1975).

90. See *Missouri v. Jenkins*, 495 U.S. 33 (1995); *Freeman v. Pitts*, 503 U.S. 467 (1992); *Wilson v. Seiter*, 501 U.S. 294; *Board of Ed. of Oklahoma City v. Dowell*, 498 U.S. 237 (1991). For the beginnings of this trend during the Burger Court years, see *Rhodes v. Chapman*, 452 U.S. 337 (1981) *Rizzo v. Goode*, 423 U.S. 362 (1976); *Pasadena Bd. of Ed. v. Spangler*, 427 U.S. 424 (1976); *Milliken v. Bradley*, 418 U.S. 717 (1974).

91. See *Cort v. Ash*, 422 U.S. 66 (1975).

92. *Middlesex County Sewage Authority v. National Sea Clammers Association*, 453 U.S. 1 (1981).

93. *Gonzaga University v. Doe*, 536 U.S. 273 (2002).

94. *Id.*, at 283.

95. *City of Rancho Palos Verdes v. Abrams*, 125 S. Ct. 1453, 1458 (2005).

96. See *Abbott Laboratories v. Gardner*, 387 U.S. 136 (1967).

97. 387 U.S. 136 (1967).

98. 401 U.S. 402 (1971).

99. One of the rare exceptions to the presumption of reviewability was the Veterans Administration. Congress did not make review of VA decisions available until 1988, removing it from what the Supreme Court referred to as "splendid isolation." *Brown v. Gardner*, 513 U.S. 115, 122 (1994).

100. *Block v. Community Nutrition Institute*, 467 U.S. 340, 349 (1984).

101. 470 U.S. 821 (1985).

102. *Id.*, at pp. 832–833.

103. *Id.* at p. 833.

104. *Lindahl v. OPM*, 470 U.S. 768 (1985).

105. *Id.*, at pp. 778–779.

106. 476 U.S. 667 (1986).

107. *Id.*, at p. 670.

108. See *Lincoln v. Vigil*, 508 U.S. 182 (1993); *Franklin v. Massachusetts*, 505 U.S. 788 (1992); *Webster v. Doe*, 486 U.S. 592 (1988); *ICC v. Locomotive Engineers*, 482 U.S. 270 (1987);

109. *Food and Drug Administration v. Brown & Williamson Tobacco Corp.*, 529 U.S. 120 (2000).

110. See *International Brotherhood of Teamsters v. Daniel*, 439 U.S. 551, 556 n. 20 (1979); *Udall v. Tallman*, 380 U.S. 1, 4 (1965); and *Power Reactor Co. v. International Union of Electrical Workers*, 367 U.S. 376, 408 (1961). But the Court has the ultimate authority of statutory interpretation. *International Brotherhood, supra*, at pp. 566–67, and *Securities and Exchange Comm'n v. Sloan*, 436 U.S. 103, 117-19 (1978).

111. *Ashbacker v. Federal Communications Commission*, 326 U.S. 327 (1945).

112. *Chrysler v. DOT*, 472 F.2d 659 (6th Cir. 1972).

113. *Pacific Legal Foundation v. DOT*, 593 F.2d 1338 (D.C.Cir. 1979).

114. *Motor Vehicle Manufacturers Association v. State Farm Mutual*, 463 U.S. 29, 43-44 (1983).

115. "Arbitrary action may be colored by improper motivation; it may be action which has an impermissible basis as when Republicans or redheads are denied equal opportunity to do business with the government; or action which is unsupported by evidence, or turns on failure to consider relevant evidence, even in the presence of plenary discretion." Raoul Berger, "Administrative Arbitrariness and Judicial Review," 65 *Columbia L. Rev.* 55, 82-83 (1965).

116. The discussion of *Overton Park* at the beginning of the chapter explains why this is important.

117. *Burlington Truck Lines v. United States,* 371 U.S. 156, 168-69 (1962), and *Citizens to Preserve Overton Park v. Volpe, supra* note 2, at p. 419.

118. There is also a problem if it can be shown that there were related or conflicting statutes that should have been taken into account but were ignored by the administrators. See *Camp v. Pitts,* 411 U.S. 138 (1973), and *Investment Co. Institute v. Camp,* 401 U.S. 617 (1971).

119. *American Textile Manufacturers Institute v. Donovan,* 452 U.S. 490, 523 (1981); *Universal Camera Corp. v. NLRB,* 340 U.S. 474, 487-488 (1961).

120. See e.g., *Richardson v. Perales,* 402 U.S. 389, 402 (1971).

121. *American Textile Manufacturers Institute v. Donovan, supra* note 109, at p. 210.

122. *Arkansas v. Oklahoma,* 503 U.S. 91, 113 (1992).

123. *Allentown Mack Sales and Service v. National Labor Relations Board,* 522 U.S. 359, 366 (1998).

124. There is a continuing discussion about the two dimensions of the term substantial evidence: (1) the amount of evidence necessary to support a decision; and (2) the types of evidence that qualify as substantial.

125. See e.g., *Jama v. Immigration and Customs Enforcement,* 543 U.S. 335 (2005); *Demore v. Hyun Joon Kim,* 538 U.S. 510 (2003); *United States v. Mead Corp.,* 533 U.S. 218 (2001).

126. *Ranchers Cattlemen Action Legal Fund v. USDA,* 2005 U.S. App. LEXIS 17360 (9th Cir. 2005).

127. *DOT v. Public Citizen,* 541 U.S. 752, 773 (2004).

128. *Crosby v. National Foreign Trade Council,* 530 U.S. 363 (2000).

129. *Sierra Club v. Whitman,* 268 F.3d 898 (9th Cir. 2001).

130. Howard Ball, *Justice Downwind* (New York: Oxford University Press, 1986).

131. *Rust v. Sullivan,* 500 U.S. 173, 222 (1991), Justice Stevens dissenting and quoting *Power Reactor Development Co. v. Electrical Workers,* 367 U.S. 396, 408 (1961); *Udall v. Tallman,* 380 U.S. 1 (1965); *Aluminum Co. of America v. Central Lincoln Peoples' Utility District,* 467 U.S. 380. 390 (1984).

132. Of course, it has been argued in the contemporary political context that such expertise is often questioned by the agency's adversaries. See Alfred C. Aman, Jr., *Administrative Law in a Global Era* (Ithaca, NY: Cornell University Press, 1992).

133. 467 U.S. 837 (1984).

134. *Id.,* at 842-844.

135. *Id.,* at 865-866.

136. *Id.*

137. *Rust v. Sullivan, supra* note 131.

138. *Id.,* at pp. 186–187, citing *Motor Vehicle Manufacturers Association. v. State Farm Mutual Ins. Co.,* 463 U.S. 29, 43 (1983).

139. *Rust,* 500 U.S., at p. 222, Justice Stevens dissenting.

140. *Smiley v. Citibank,* 135 L.Ed.2d 25, 31 (1996).

141. *NationsBank v. Variable Annuity,* 513 U.S. 251, 257 (1995).

142. *Auer v. Robbins,* 137 L.Ed.2d 79 (1997).

143. "If the agency's reading fills a gap or defines a term in a reasonable way in light of the legislature's design, we give that reading controlling weight, even if it is not the answer 'the court would have reached if the question initially had arisen in a judicial proceeding.'" *Regions Hospital v. Shalala,* 139 L.Ed.2d 895, 904 (1998).

144. *United States v. O'Hagan,* 138 L.Ed.2d 724 (1997). See also *Martin v. Occupational Safety and Health Review Commission,* 499 U.S. 144, 150-151 (1991); *Lung v. Payne,* 476 U.S. 926, 939 (1986); *Udall v. Tallman,* 380 U.S. 1, 16 (1965).

145. *Thomas Jefferson University v. Shalala,* 512 U.S. 504, 513 (1994).

146. *Id.,* citing *Pauley v. BethEnergy Mines,* 501 U.S. 680, 697 (1991).

147. *Id.,* at 417. See also *INS v. Cardozo-Fonzeca,* 480 U.S. 421, 446 n. 30 (1987).

148. *Smiley v. Citibank,* 135 L.Ed.2d, at pp. 31–32.

149. *ICC v. Transcon Lines,* 513 U.S. 138, 145 (1995).

150. *Dole v. Steelworkers,* 494 U.S. 26, 42 (1990).

151. *Chevron v. Natural Resources Defense Council,* 467 U.S, at pp. 842–843.

152. *Brown v. Garner, supra* note 99, at p. 122.

153. *Id.* See also *Mt. Emmons Mining Company v. Babbitt,* 117 F.3d 1167, 1170 (10th Cir. 1997).

154. *Metropolitan Stevedore Company v. Rambo,* 138 L.Ed.2d 327, 343 (1997).

155. *Burgin v. Office of Personnel Management,* 120 F.3d 494, 497-498 (4th Cir. 1997).

156. *Thomas Jefferson University v. Shalala, supra* note 145, at p. 513.

157. *Id.,* quoting *Gardebring v. Jenkins,* 485 U.S. 415, 430 (1988).

158. *Thomas Jefferson University v. Shalala, supra* note 145, at p. 512. See also *INS v. Cardozo-Fonseca,* 480 U.S. 421, 446 n. 30 (1987).

159. *United States v. O'Hagan,* 138 L.Ed.2d 724, 754 (1997).

160. 533 U.S. 218 (2001).

161. *Id.,* at 221.

162. *Id.,* at 228.

163. *Id.,* at 239.

164. *Id.,* at 245-261.

165. See e.g., *National Cable & Telecommunication Assoc. v. Brand X Internet Services,* 125 S. Ct. 2688 (2005); *Barnhart v. Walton,* 535 U.S. 212 (2002).

166. See e.g., *Alabama Power Co. v. Costle,* 636 F.2d 323 (D.C.Cir. 1980); *Ethyl v. Environmental Protection Agency,* 541 F.2d 1 (D.C.Cir. 1976), cert. denied, 426 U.S. 941 (1976); *International Harvester v. Ruckelshaus,* 478 F.2d 615 (D.C.Cir. 1973); and *Environmental Defense Fund v. Ruckelshaus,* 439 F.2d 584 (D.C.Cir. 1971).

167. See e.g., David Doniger, "Federal Regulation of Vinyl Chloride: A Short Course in the Law and Policy of Toxic Substances Control," 7 *Ecology L. Q.* 501 (1978).

168. This has led to an ongoing debate over the use of scientific evidence in courts. See *Daubert v. Merrell Dow Pharmaceuticals, Inc.,* 509 U.S. 579 (1993).

169. Carl McGowan, "Reflections on Rulemaking Review," 53 *Tulane L. Rev.* 681, 690-91 (1979). The case McGowan was describing was *Weyerhaeuser Co. v. Costle,* 590 F.2d 1011 (D.C.Cir. 1978).

170. Expertise has come to be extremely political. See e.g., Guy Benveniste, *The Politics of Expertise,* 2nd ed., (San Francisco: Boyd & Fraser, 1977), and Mark Green, *The Other Government: Revised Ed.* (New York: Norton, 1978).

171. See e.g., *National Resource Defense Council v. U.S. Nuclear Regulatory Commission,* 547 F.2d 633, 643-44 (D.C.Cir. 1976).

172. See McGowan, *supra* note 169.

173. *Id.,* at p. 686.

174. *Vermont Yankee Nuclear Power Corp. v. Natural Resources Defense Council,* 435 U.S. 519 (1978).

175. *Industrial Union Department, AFL-CIO v. American Petroleum Inst.,* 448 U.S. 607 (1980).

176. 42 U.S.C. §4332(2)(C).

177. *Natural Resources Defense Council v. U.S. Nuclear Regulatory Commission,* 547 F.2d 633, 637 (D.C.Cir. 1976).

178. *Id.,* at pp. 648–49.

179. *Id.,* at p. 638.

180. *Id.,* at pp. 638–39.

181. *Id.,* at pp. 644–46.

182. *Id.,* at p. 655. Judge Tamm concurred in the decision of the court but would simply have remanded the case to the agency on the ground that the record was inadequate to support its findings. He would avoid suggesting that the agency had to modify its procedures.

183. *Supra* note 174.

184. See Chapter 5, note 127.

185. 29 U.S.C. §655 (b)(5), cited in *Industrial Union Department, supra* note 146, at p. 612.

186. 29 U.S.C. §655(a).

187. *Industrial Union Department, supra* note 175.

188. *Id.,* at p. 689, Justice Marshall dissenting.

189. *American Petroleum Inst. v. Occupational Safety and Health Agency,* 581 F.2d 493 (5th Cir. 1978).

190. *Industrial Union Department, supra* note 175, at p. 706.

191. *Id.,* at pp. 712–13.

192. *Id.,* at pp. 723–24.

193. 452 U.S. 490 (1981).

194. *Id.,* pp. 540–541.

195. *Bowen v. American Hospital Ass'n,* 476 U.S. 610 (1986).

196. See e.g., the Civil Rights Attorneys' Fee Act, P.L. 94-559, 90 Stat. 2641, 42 U.S.C. §1988.

197. Chapter 3 discusses the problem of the impact of Supreme Court opinions. See generally, Charles A. Johnson and Bradley Canon, *Judicial Policies: Impact and Implementation,* 2nd Ed. (Washington, DC: CQ, 1995) and Stephen Wasby, *The Impact of the United States Supreme Court* (Homewood, IL: Dorsey, 1970).

198. William J. Brennan, "State Constitutions and the Protection of Individual Rights," 90 *Harvard L. Rev.* 489 (1977), and Donald E. Wilkes, Jr., "The New Federalism in Criminal Procedure: State Court Evasion of the Burger Court," 62 *Kentucky L. J.* 421 (1973). Decisions concerning educational finance in California (*Serrano v. Priest,* 557 P. 2d 929 [Calif. 1976]), Connecticut (*Horton v. Meskill,* 376 A 2d 359 [Conn. 1977]), and New Jersey (*Robinson v. Cahill,* 303 A.2d 273 [NJ 1973]) were clearly rejections by the state courts of the U.S. Supreme Court's ruling in *San Antonio Independent School Dist. v. Rodriguez,* 411 U.S. 1 (1973).

199. Cited in Judge Frank M. Johnson, Jr., "The Other Branches of Government." The John A. Sibley Lecture (University of Georgia School of Law, 1977), in *Access to Justice, supra* note 36 at p. 750, 762. See also Judge A. LeonHigginbotham, Jr., "The Priority of Human Rights in Court Reform," 70 *Federal Rules Decisions* 134 (1976).

200. See the testimony of Father William C. Cunningham, *Access to Justice, supra* note 36, at p. 167.

201. The discussion of the Endangered Species Act cases earlier in the chapter provides a clear example. See *Lujan v. Defenders of Wildlife,* 504 U.S. 555 (1992) and *Bennett v. Spear, supra* note 37.

202. 477 U.S. 57 (1986).

8

Informal Process: "The Lifeblood of the Administrative Process"

As early as 1941, the Attorney General's Committee on Administrative Procedure declared that informal action was "the lifeblood of the administrative process."[1] By the 1960s, Peter Woll had concluded that "requirements of public policy, expertise, and speed have rendered administrative adjudication today primarily informal in nature."[2] By the early 1990s, advocates of reinventing government acted like they had discovered something altogether new when they suggested that the new wave in public administration was to make use of negotiated approaches more widely than formal legal processes and indeed blamed administrative law for much of the difficulty in government.[3] But despite all of the issues about rulemaking, the many administrative adjudications that take place every year, and the thousands of cases brought on judicial review to challenge administrative decisions, the vast majority of administrative actions are taken through informal means.

Indeed, it is very unusual, in terms of the percentage of total business done by administrative agencies, for the producers and consumers of administrative decisions to resolve problems of law and administration or develop policies in a formal way. The attempt is usually made to solve problems short of formal procedures. These informal methods of interaction range from a simple chat on the telephone to full-dress negotiations. This chapter assesses some of the reasons why informal processes are so important, the factors that condition informal administrative action, types of informal approaches to problem resolution, concepts and attitudes that characterize these proceedings, and the opportunities and problems these informal actions present compared to formal processes.

THE REAL-WORLD DECISIONMAKING ENVIRONMENT AND PRESSURES FOR INFORMAL ACTION

Informal processes are employed by all types of agencies and contemporary governance regimes. In the case of single-shot players dealing with social service or other agencies, the consumer of the decision may not fully understand that he or she is involved in an informal administrative proceeding.

Americans are so attuned to a formal due process approach to government action that they tend to ignore notices informing them that administrative action affecting them is in progress. Many think that such notices are really *pro forma* and that, before any real action is taken, they will be personally contacted and accorded a formal means to present their views. It can be difficult to convince them that such an attitude can be dangerous. Failure to acknowledge a letter from the Department of Motor Vehicles, for example, may bring a visit from an officer requesting surrender of one's driver's license. One who ignores a request for information from the Department of Veterans Affairs risks losing educational or other benefits. Sadly, consumers often wait until it is too late to communicate with an agency. In some cases, the failure to respond to opportunities offered for discussion with an agency may permanently foreclose one's chance to contest agency action later.

Today, in the world of governance through collaboration and networks (see Chapter 1), the prevalence and importance of informal processes for making and implementing decisions are more common and significant than ever before. Negotiation and collaboration are pervasive and indeed have been used in some cases to avoid more formal requirements that apply when government agencies make decisions and provide services directly. For all these reasons, it is increasingly important for public managers to be attentive to the role of informal processes and to analyze critically and carefully the informal processes they are required to engage.

The Dynamics of Informal Action and Their Relationships to Formal Processes

In many situations, informal processes are not simply alternatives to formal procedures, but often the two operate in parallel. For example, informal process is often very important even for repeat players dealing with regulatory agencies that will eventually make formal decisions about their business plans. The nuclear power plant licensing process, discussed in Chapter 7, is a useful example of this informal kind of activity.

Suppose Adam Smith, chief executive officer of the Consolidated Utility Company, decides in consultation with his staff to launch a development project for a nuclear power facility to be called Plant Omega. Smith is aware that the licensing process from construction to eventual operation of such a facility is a very long and complex one. His firm cannot wait until it has invested several years in such a project to prepare a licensing package for submission to the appropriate regulatory agencies. Nor is the company likely to purchase land and contract for materials and labor before beginning discussions with those administrators who are in positions to disapprove the project. From the planning stages through construction and application for licensing, a great deal of money will be expended at each stage of the plant development, and that investment must be protected as much as possible.

As an astute business person, Smith will want to begin informal negotiations as early as possible. In this case the appropriate administrative authorities are the Nuclear Regulatory Commission (NRC) and the state public utilities commission (PUC). There are a number of dimensions to the project that Smith will wish to assess. There is the economic dimension, of course, but there are also other dimensions. If, for example, members of the PUC signal that they intend openly and adamantly to oppose the project, the company will understand that it faces an immediate local political battle. If, on the other hand, the company senses that it has allies in the commission, it is well to know that at the outset.

What Smith wishes to acquire is a strong sense of the decision environment within which his firm is operating. He attempts to learn the characteristics of that environment in informal discussions and negotiations with the relevant administrative decisionmakers as early as possible to avoid future problems. This is typical activity when the consumer of the administrative decision is a repeat player, and especially where the decision concerns an expensive project.

From the perspective of the administrators, Mr. Washington of the NRC and Ms. Springfield of the PUC, it is equally important to make informal contact at the earliest opportunity. Plant Omega will be a major work project for the agencies as well as for the company. If the company proceeds with Omega, the administrators will develop a continuing relationship with the company over a period of years. The earlier the agencies become involved, the better administrators can plan to allocate their own resources.

Furthermore, the task of the administrators is not merely to process the papers submitted at various points in the process. Ms. Springfield's agency is charged with providing power that is needed by the community at the best possible cost consistent with a reasonable rate of return on investment for the company that builds and operates the power plants. Her responsibilities include fostering the development of power sources and ensuring that returns are sufficient to permit the power companies to compete for finances needed by the firms. At the same time, her agency is supposed to protect the purchasers of power from overpricing and poor service, problems that can be acute when businesses have a virtual monopoly in their service areas or when market conditions lend themselves to manipulations by venders and brokers, such as in the infamous Enron scandal in which there was deliberate manipulation of supplies and prices.

In an environment in which Ms. Springfield and her colleagues are contemplating new mechanisms for marketing power, there is still much for her officials at the state level to consider. While it may be the case that Illinois power customers will be told to look to the marketplace for many decisions about services and prices, there remain questions about the relationship between governmental units and power companies and the need of the state to address such issues as service to the poor and rules governing termination of service. Ironically, discussions of deregulation in the electric power sector have increased the complexity of the decisionmaking environment.

The relationship between the company and government is clearly not one-sided. The government wants power provided under the proper conditions. The company wants profits and continued financial strength. The initial informal negotiations during the development of the Omega facility will last two years or more. The total lead time for construction and licensing may last from seven to ten years. The process may be represented in this way:

$$T_1 \ldots T_2 \ldots T_3 \ldots T_4 \ldots \ldots T_{10}$$

The parties may begin informal negotiations on Omega at Point T_1. At some point, T_2, the company and the government reach decisions committing themselves to push forward with the project. The actual formal licensing process for construction and later inspection and processing for the operating license occur years after the commitment point. Between T_1, and T_2, both Smith and his counterparts in government continue to assess the decisionmaking environment. The goal is to reduce uncertainty about the future of the project as much as possible before reaching the commitment point.

Once the commitment point is reached, government actors begin to factor the new project into their policy planning. They assume, however informally, that at a certain point in the future, T_{10}, Plant Omega will be operational, on line, and fully productive. The assumptions are made even though administrators know that problems might arise between T_2 and T_{10} that could delay access to power from the new facility. Nevertheless, the plant is now part of the decision environment of both the administrative and business personnel.

Now consider the perspective of Robert Fisher, president of an environmental group opposed to the new nuclear power plant, which does not get involved until T_3 or T_4. Fisher's organization must convince the agencies involved to interpret the applicable statutes and regulations in such a way as to block the construction and licensing. Otherwise, the only real device available is delay through litigation. Even if Fisher's organization has a good argument, it will still be extremely difficult to convince agency personnel. So many human and fiscal resources have been invested by this stage that it becomes very difficult to stop the project. The administrators are no longer neutral actors. They have committed years of work to the project; Omega is part of their policy planning. Asking them to abandon the project now is asking them to admit that their efforts have been wasted. In effect, Washington and Springfield are being asked to tell their supervisors that the project is a white elephant. It is not necessarily bad faith that drives agency personnel forward (again assuming that the argument in opposition to the plant is valid), but sunk costs.

Similarly, it is hard to imagine Mr. Smith going to his board of directors and announcing that, although the firm is five years and $100 million into the project, plans for Plant Omega ought to be discarded.

Informal procedures often develop slowly over a lengthy period. At some point, either before or after action is begun, the producers and consumers make important if unofficial commitments to a course of action. Both the informal relationship and the economic and political factors in the decision environment have important consequences for future decisionmaking. That does not mean that the informal relationship will ensure one particular outcome. The decision environment can change with renewed concerns about nuclear waste storage, security, or even with a dramatic shift in the availability and cost of fossil fuels. Still, the dynamics of the informal interactions are important.

Sensing the Decision Environment

One of the most important dynamics at work in the Plant Omega case is the effort by all of the participants to use the informal signals to help read the decision environment. In fact, this effort to evaluate the context of administrative action is something that most effective public managers do every day. It also explains why experienced people within organizations often come to have importance far beyond their formal position within the agency.

This process involves sampling key features of the decision environment, factors that are present all around the agency, and then translating these disparate indicators into a coherent picture that a manager can use to understand options and predict the consequences of alternative courses of action. It is as if the administrator begins the day by viewing a radar scope. He or she then considers the many returns on the screen and puts together a picture of the environment within which he or she must function that day.

Of course, there are many possible factors in that environment, but there is a relatively small set of items that can serve as a kind of checklist. Think of it this way. Consider these factors as elements of feasibility that must be addressed if plans are to be turned into actions and if consequences are to be anticipated. They include the technical, legal, fiscal, administrative, political, ethical, and cultural dimensions.[4] When applying this or any other useful framework for analyzing the decision environment, it is important to apply all of the elements, though after running the framework it may be clear that only one or a few elements turn out to be critical in any given situation

Technical Feasibility   The first question is whether what is being asked of an agency is technically feasible. While it is true that agencies are often asked to undertake a responsibility precisely because it is considered technically expert and capable of carrying out the task, legislatures often develop technology-forcing policies that seek to push the agency to innovate. In the contemporary context, the technical feasibility question prompts the wise and experienced administrator to consider the technical authority of the agency (its claim to expertise in the field) relative to other players in the decision environment. With the downsizing of agency staffs, contracting out of agency technical work, and increasing competition for technical skills in the marketplace, it is less common to look to an agency as the scientific or technical authority in any given field.

Legal Feasibility   Next, it is necessary to consider the legal feasibility of the action under consideration. Since agencies are the creatures of law, they cannot act beyond their range of authority. Of course, in the contemporary environment, it is necessary not merely to consider such traditional elements as statutes, but also to be alert to executive orders, international authorities such as treaties or executive agreements, as well as contractual obligations.

Even if the agency has the authority to act and the jurisdiction to do so in a particular context, it cannot operate in a manner that violates existing statutes or constitutional provisions. While the government need not operate correctional facilities, once it elects to do so, it must operate them in a lawful manner. The same is true for schools, health facilities, or other programs and services at all levels of government. Similarly, where a government unit contracts with a service provider under conditions that mean that the private organization has become a state actor—as in the case of privately operated prisons—civil rights laws also impose legal feasibility requirements on them (see Chapter 13). That does not, of course, relieve the contracting agency of government of its own legal responsibility.

Fiscal Feasibility   To be sure, a governmental body may have legal authority to act, but without resources, it is little more than a paper tiger. Hence, it is essential to consider fiscal feasibility. In an earlier era, the answer to a question about resources meant looking at the budget appropriated by Congress, the state legislature, or the local governing body, depending upon the kind of organization involved. In the present context, however, public sector organizations deal with assembled budgets, consisting of some appropriated funds along with various other sources such as fees, fines, special funds, grants, or cooperative agreements with other jurisdictions.

A clear understanding of fiscal feasibility can be particularly complex in complex service delivery networks, involving a variety government units at different levels, nonprofit, and for-profit service providers. Additionally, many public bodies now sell various kinds of services—from ambulance to law enforcement to correctional services—as well as purchase them. Whatever the resource base, though, a public manager must consider fiscal feasibility as he or she assesses the decision environment.

Administrative Feasibility   Even if funds are readily available, it is still necessary to be concerned with administrative feasibility. That is, does the agency have the organizational capacity, management capability, operational systems, and trained and experienced people in place to carry out a decision? The classic example of what can happen when there is fiscal feasibility but inadequate administrative capacity occurred following the September 11, 2001, terrorist attacks on the U.S.

Immediately after the shock of what is now simply referred to as 9/11, there were demands from all quarters for action to protect against further terrorist attacks, As has often been true throughout American history, even those who normally challenge proactive government involvement in their business or personal lives demanded coordinated leadership from the federal government. President Bush received immediate assurances from congressional leaders that members on both sides of the aisle and in both houses would support almost any action he wished to undertake, but the White House was unwilling to involve the legislature any more than absolutely necessary. Therefore, the president rejected offers of legislation for a new agency and created by executive order a new Office of Homeland Security in the executive office to be led by the Assistant to the President for Homeland Affairs, former Pennsylvania Governor Tom Ridge.[5] However, Ridge found himself without statutory authority, technical capacity, or appropriations to carry out the mammoth task of bringing order and coordinated operations to the plethora of well-established agencies that had jurisdiction over or another aspect of the field of homeland security elements. Indeed, he had essentially no administrative capacity at all. Unlike Ridge's new office, each of the agencies whose homeland security work he was supposed to coordinate had enabling, program authorization, and appropriations legislation as well as constituencies to support them and resist any outside control, even from the president's designated homeland security chief. By 2002, it was clear that these problems had to be addressed.

The White House then worked with congressional leaders to produce the dramatic legislation known as the Homeland Security Act of 2002.[6] However, that legislation and other statutes, such as the one creating the Transportation Security Administration (TSA), undertook massive challenges with an extremely short time frame for implementation. That was particularly a problem for the newly created Department of Homeland Security, which had to integrate more than 20 existing agencies into the new cabinet department.[7] Congress was prepared to leave no check unsigned in providing funds for the new agency and its programs. That said, DHS had to undertake a host of activities while it was in the process of staffing up and attempting to manage its now large and complex organization.

Among the characteristics of the new department was the expectation that it would make dramatic use of outsourcing for much of its work and that it would manage a wide range of grants and contracts for services around the nation. The attempt to push large amounts of money through a fledgling organization that lacked the capacity even to spend money fast enough and in a manner that was efficient, effective, and accountable produced the inevitable failures, inefficiencies, and simple mistakes.[8] And it came as no surprise when the national news media highlighted serious spending flaws in DHS contracting.[9] The issue was not the resources available to be used for homeland security programs or the legal authority of DHS, but the administrative feasibility of the challenge it was required to undertake. A manager, whether he or she is in a city, state, or federal capacity, must evaluate the decision environment with a sense of his or her organizational capabilities and management systems.

Political Feasibility   There are many times when it may be the case that the technical, legal, fiscal, and administrative elements are present, but the effort is nevertheless doomed to failure. In such circumstances the problem is often one of political feasibility. It is common for the newly minted engineer to come to a situation with what he or she is certain is the correct course of action only to be told that "it won't fly." That expression really means that, at least under the current political realities, the idea will not be accepted by those affected. Thus, an EPA official argued some time back that syringes on the beach should not be a cause for significant public alarm, since his computer check of the published medical literature produced no findings concluding that a child's stepping on a syringe on a beach was any more dangerous than stepping on a tin can. He missed the point. Whether he was or was not correct scientifically, in an era of fear of HIV/AIDS and infectious hepatitis, such a declaration was politically unacceptable. It is often the case that one of the great values inherent in experience, as compared with expertise, is precisely the understanding of the limits of political tolerance.

Ethical Feasibility   There are still two other important dimensions to be considered in a public manager's attempt to understand the decision environment. The first of these is ethical feasibility. This area will be discussed further in Chapter 13, but it is important to note here that ethical feasibility is not limited to issues of concern with corruption or unprofessional behavior in general terms.

It is not uncommon for an administrator to find that a situation presents competing pressures from conflicting value sets. These issues are particularly common in an era when public sector organizations are asked to accomplish more but often with less resources. If, for example, a medical facility is pressed to make cutbacks solely because of financial demands, many of those trained in medical fields will immediately find themselves cross-pressured as they must deal with both with an obligation to obey the political bodies that made the funding decisions and their ethics as medical professionals committed to patients' needs as the primary consideration.

There are also problems of ethical feasibility if an agency has one set of public positions and a possibly contradictory set of internal operating norms. The classic case here is the situation that existed within the Los Angeles Police Department at the time of the Rodney King beating.

Cultural Feasibility   Finally, a public administrator who wishes to be effective will want to ask whether what she or he is attempting to accomplish is culturally feasible. There are two dimensions to this issue: organizational culture and the anthropological sense of culture.

The organizational culture of the agency or city government places clear constraints on the manager's range of possible responses to a given situation. Because organizational cultures are slow to change, the day-to-day work of the organization must function within the limits tolerated by that culture.[10]

Even more important is the recognition that agencies and the contractors who deliver services on their behalf must serve increasingly diverse communities in which culture counts in a variety of important ways. Cultural feasibility in this sense addresses ethno-cultural issues in the anthropological sense. Service delivery programs differ in significant ways in communities with varied ethno-cultural traditions and lifestyles.[11] Whether the challenge is to deliver programs and services in a community with a history of racial discrimination, the need to ensure access to programs for persons with limited English proficiency, responding to the special challenges that have faced Native American communities over many years, meeting the needs of newly arrived refugees with traumatic experiences, or mediating disputes across different religious traditions, it is essential to consider cultural feasibility in public management.[12]

While these factors sound complex, a public manager can develop the skills over time necessary to maintain this continuing evaluation of the decision environment. That is important in all aspects of public administration, but it is especially so when one is operating informally, without the structure imposed by formal procedures. Let us turn from this very general effort to understand the decision environment to a more specific consideration of particular factors that shape informal administrative action.

FACTORS THAT SHAPE INFORMAL ADMINISTRATIVE PROCESSES

As the term "informal process" implies, the types of administrative actions that are informal in nature are very different from one another. It is possible, however, to single out recurring factors that shape and condition informal administration.

Policy Pressures

First, there are numerous policy pressures on administrators to make greater use of informal processes and work with a framework based on negotiation. And once in that mode, it can be politically difficult to change course. Even before the emergence of the reinventing government movement and its implementation as policy during the Clinton administration, bipartisan support for the use of informal procedures, particularly alternative dispute resolution procedures, led in 1990 to the enactment of the Negotiated Rulemaking Act (discussed in Chapter 5) and the Alternative Dispute Resolution Act.[13] Both statutes lapsed for a time when Congress did not complete reauthorization before the deadline, but that problem was remedied in 1996 when the Congress enacted the Administrative Dispute Resolution Act, which made both acts permanent additions to the APA. As Professor Lisa Bingham explained it:

> [The 1996 Act] requires each agency to develop a policy on ADR, in consultation with ACUS and the Federal Mediation and Conciliation Service (FMCS), but it does not set a deadline for adopting the policy. The ADR Act directs the agency to examine ADR in connection with formal and information adjudications, rulemaking, enforcement actions, issuing and revoking licenses or permits, contract administration, litigation brought by or against the agency, and other agency actions. It also requires a agency to appoint a senior official to service as a dispute resolution specialist, with responsibility for implementation of the agency policy.[14]

Clearly, this statute, which passed with bipartisan support from both houses of Congress and the White House, not only provides specific authority for informal mechanisms and removes barriers to their use, but also very clearly encourages their application. Under section 3(a)(2) of the act, each agency is to:

... examine alternative means of resolving disputes in connection with—

(A) formal and informal adjudications;

(B) rulemakings;

(C) enforcement actions;

(D) issuing and revoking licenses or permits;

(E) contract administration;

(F) litigation brought by or against the agency; and

(G) other agency actions.

Moreover, the statute made a decision by an administrator to use such techniques as "settlement negotiations, conciliation, facilitation, mediation, fact finding, minitrials, and arbitration, or any combination thereof" unreviewable in court.[15] Other legislation, such as the Americans with Disabilities Act and the Civil Rights Act of 1991, supported the use of informal disputes resolution processes. Other statutes, such as the Individuals with Disabilities Education Act reauthorization of 1997, have required states to develop alternative dispute resolution processes such as mediation as a condition of receipt of federal grants.[16]

The pressure to employ informal processes came not just from these statutes but also from directives issued by the White House implementing the recommendations of the National Performance Review (NPR) with respect to regulation, administrative enforcement actions, contracting, and service delivery.[17] In its first year evaluation of implementation of NPR recommendations, there were numerous White House references to the use of negotiated enforcement and other informal techniques as compared to the earlier practices referred to as "command and control" procedures.

Many states have implemented statutes encouraging the use of ADR. One of the earliest and most common sets of such acts is in the labor/management relations area, where the use of mediation or various forms of arbitration are authorized in lieu of job actions. Another field at the state level in which informal techniques have been common for many years is in the area of consumer protection, where state ombudspersons or consumer protection bureaus within the offices of state attorneys general often made use of mediation to settle disputes. More recently, many states have adopted a wider range of informal techniques as part of the new public management movement and a number have adopted state-level versions of the Alternative Dispute Resolution Act.

Yet a third source of policy pressure to use informal processes comes from international agreements that set up a host of claims resolution processes for negotiated settlement of disputes.[18] These international devices stem not just from the general trend toward negotiated problem-solving, but also from the very practical problems that arise in the international context where sovereign nations often resist submitting to the jurisdiction of an international tribunal for formal decisions. Although there clearly are authoritative decisionmaking bodies established by many agreements, such as the panel on regulation of the World Trade Organization under the General Agreement on Tariffs and Trade (GATT) and the North American Free Trade Agreement (NAFTA) dispute process, there is a strong preference for negotiated approaches to action. It is also worth noting that at the same time that constitutional courts have become more important in countries that had not previously had a traditional high court like the U.S. Supreme Court,[19] there has been a simultaneous movement to develop more and better informal options.

At all levels, from global to local, contracts very often establish in their terms processes for the resolution of disputes. While there is, at least at the federal government level, a relatively complex set of institutions and processes to resolve contract issues, it is very common these days for the parties to contract to agree to use some form of mediation or arbitration instead.[20] Thus, many contracts provide a legal and a policy pressure to use informal techniques. Federal contracts automatically provide opportunities for ADR, since, unlike the APA, the Alternative Dispute Resolution Act specifically includes contracts. Federal contracting officers often use the informal conference before the formal processing of a contract dispute to consider whether the parties will be willing to undertake an ADR resolution.[21]

Moreover, one of the ideas behind the advocacy of public/private partnerships is to develop more positive and less narrowly legalistic working relationships. In such relationships the effort is not merely to find ways of settling disagreements but to seek to avoid them in the first place.

In the area of procurement and government contracting, many agencies have begun to use a process called partnering. This process is intended to build a strong, collaborative working relationship between contracting parties before disputes arise, and to set up channels of communication that parties will use immediately upon the first sign of a dispute. The chief executive officer or top management of the contractor and the top public administrators responsible for the project go on a retreat, generally lasting for several days, during which they discuss their expectations for the contract and the means through which it will be executed. They set up avenues of communication and processes for handling disputes as soon as they arise. In addition, they simple get to know each other better. After the retreat, they have regular troubleshooting meetings to catch any problem early in its development. The process is one of dispute avoidance.[22]

Even so, there are often disputes over bid processes and contract awards, conflicts over costs associated with change orders (alterations made in specifications or performance terms during the performance of a contract), audit and compliance disputes, disagreements over reimbursable cost calculations, and even in some rare cases debarment proceedings (disciplinary actions brought to penalize a contractor for serious misconduct by removing their eligibility for future contracts). Even if a contract does not specifically set forth alternative dispute resolution techniques, such approaches are commonly used to avoid the costs of formal litigation and the costs to ongoing working relationships that flow from pitched legal battles.

Sunk Costs

In addition to policy, another factor that influences the use and implications of informal processes is the phenomenon of sunk costs. Once the point of commitment is reached by the parties involved in an informal administrative action, changes in policy or in direction are hard to make. Expended effort and fiscal resources provide an inertia that is all but irresistible. Writing of the problem of plant licensing, Justice William O. Douglas once warned:

> Plainly these are not findings that the "safety" standards have been met. They presuppose—contrary to the premise of the Act—that "safety" findings can be made *after construction is finished*. But when that point is reached, when millions have been invested, the momentum is on the side of the applicant, not on the side of the public. The momentum is not only generated by the desire to salvage an investment. No agency wants to be the architect of a "white elephant" [emphasis in original].[23]

This process not only applies in adjudicative-type activities but in other areas as well. Thus, one of the concerns regarding negotiated rulemaking is that while an agency may walk away from the table at any point or ultimately change its position in response to reactions after the consensus position is published as a proposed rule, such steps become more difficult to take the further the process moves along (see Chapter 5).

If, at some point, an agency perceives its investment to be sufficiently large, it may become the advocate for the outside group or individual involved. Taken far enough, administrators may by virtue of perceived sunk costs find themselves co-opted by the party before the agency.

Anticipated Costs

Another factor that influences the informal process is what might be termed "anticipated costs." That is, the costs of pursuing one's objectives through the formal administrative process may be sufficiently high that pressure is created to resolve problems informally and, in effect, to waive the formal options that are supposedly available. Such issues of anticipated cost are complicated by two additional factors. First, while the costs of formal processes are likely to be high, it is often unclear just how high they may be.

For many decisionmakers, it is far better to use an informal process that may yield a compromised resolution and not a victory rather than facing the risk of indeterminate costs. Second, while resources are being used to wage a protracted formal legal battle, they cannot be directed toward other more desirable opportunities. These are often referred to as opportunity costs.

Attorneys commonly see their role as practicing preventive law or fostering alternatives to formal resolution of disputes. The costs of preparation and representation for trial or formal hearings escalate dramatically. In that spirit an attorney might attempt to convince a client who claims that an agency has wrongfully exacted several hundred dollars or more from him or her that it would be much better to settle for a negotiated compromise, and a loss of some of the funds, rather than spend more money for litigation and appeals and perhaps lose in the end anyway.[24]

Power Law

A fourth factor is the significance of what Mark Green has called "power law."[25] For many reasons, political scientists and other academics seem to have particular difficulty with the concept of power.[26] In general, power has negative connotations and taboos. Power is, presumably, something with which nice people do not deal.

Green's study concentrated on the most prestigious Washington law firms, whose primary business is representing repeat players before different branches and departments of government, but his thesis is more broadly applicable. He argued that there are any number of individuals and organizations who use law as a tool to accomplish their ends, to exercise political power.[27] Such clients may say, as J. P. Morgan is reputed to have declared, that they do not want a lawyer who tells them what they cannot do. They want a lawyer who tells them how to do what they want to do.

Unless one goes about it in a corrupt or illegal manner, there is nothing particularly sinister in this. If, for example, one who runs a business decides to pursue a policy and commits resources in pursuit of policy goals, he or she may be unwilling to face the loss, and perhaps the pressure, that comes from changing direction based on a mere prediction that the firm may or may not win in court should a lawsuit develop. One might more likely say something like: "I'm committed to this position. I think I'm right and I'm prepared to use the tools at my disposal to defend my policy."

Green's analysis suggested that power law matters because it affects: (1) the development of statutes; (2) the shaping of cases that will produce important precedents; (3) the adjudication of major public policy related disputes before government agencies; and (4) the development of rules and other types of policy statements issued by agencies. He argued that power law is practiced in both formal and informal ways, and suggests that informal process is by far the preferred mode of operation for these attorneys and their clients.

The practice of power law is based, according to Green, on what he termed the "Ten Commandments of Washington Law." The following is a sketch of his decalogue:

I. *Reputation:* "The impression of power is power." Reputation can come from previous government experience in a particular area, accumulated legal, political and governmental experience, and political contacts.

II. *Intelligence:* It is well to remember that many of those who practice power law came to their position of prominence by virtue of superior intellectual ability and well-developed technical skill and not through some back door to power.

III. *Reconnaissance:* Since information is power, it is at the heart of power law. The power lawyer's job is to be alert for developments that may threaten his clients' interests and to work with the clients to avoid the problems if it is possible to do so.

IV. *Interlocking interests*: Lawyers who begin by representing a firm often become part of the organization. This occurs as partial payment for services. The interrelationships between law firms and client organizations affect the performance of both sides.

V. *Preferential access:* Being well enough known and connected to get opportunities to make one's arguments is important. "Access without brilliance is preferable to brilliance without access."

VI. *Lobbying:* The techniques of lobbying may be far more important than litigation ability from the standpoint of one's client.

VII. *Law-writing:* Participation by an attorney in the drafting of legislation or rules offers obvious advantages of molding policy in favorable terms and less obvious advantages in recognition of prior knowledge in future contests.

VIII. *Inundation:* By sheer dint of volume, legal papers may either exhaust an opponent or else delay the agency to the advantage of one's client.

IX. *Delay:* "For those who seek to avoid regulation, no decision is often a favorable decision." Delaying tactics are frequently used tools in power law.

X. *Corruption:* It is often difficult, when the stakes are high and the ethical problems obscured, to tell when one moves from legitimate advocacy to influence peddling or worse. Some attorneys make it a practice of working close to the line on purpose.[28]

Player Type

Perhaps more than in the formal process, it matters in the informal process whether the players are repeat players or single-shot players. Repeat players have many more options than do single-shot players. In many cases they are able to argue technical procedural legal points as well as or better than agency personnel or attorney general representatives, and they may have more financial and scientific resources at their disposal. Small-business people or individuals who have little expertise and are not financially able to acquire the services of first-rate administrative law attorneys may have few options in their interactions with the social service, regulatory, or second-generation regulatory agencies they encounter.

In the contemporary environment, there are some interesting twists on this dynamic. For one thing, many nonprofit organizations have become so important to state and local institutions that they have become very effective repeat players. Unlike for-profit firms, the effectiveness of nonprofits often stems not so much from their ability to mobilize financial and legal resources as from their political importance and from the fact that governments often become dependent upon such NGOs to deliver services under contract that government no longer has the capacity to deliver directly.

The increasing range of international participants in administrative decisions has also become significant. Consider one example. Many state and local governments have become very active and entrepreneurial in their economic development efforts. However, a foreign government might allege before the World Trade Organization that a state or one of its subdivisions has engaged in prohibited trade practices such as creating preferences for local products or barriers to trade using excessively burdensome or arbitrary regulations. In such cases, the state or locality cannot defend itself before the WTO but must depend upon the U.S. federal government to do so whether in formal action or informal negotiations. There are similar complexities associated with issues arising under the North American Free Trade Agreement (NAFTA). Of course, these increasingly important roles for international players are arising around the world, particularly where there are efforts at regional integration as in the case of the European Union.

Felt Need for Individualized Justice

One of the factors that pushes administrators toward informal process and away from rule-oriented formal administrative activity is a strongly felt need for individualized treatment by those before the agency. It is one of the great problems of public administration that Weberian theories of bureaucracy dictate rule-oriented behavior, standard operating procedures for getting work done, and a dispassionate approach to that work. It is a difficulty because those who come before an agency are likely to interpret those characteristics as rule-bound, rigid, and unfeeling bureaucratic behavior. Most of us have seen or felt this reaction to bureaucracy. An administrator explains to a client that a rule precludes granting the client's request. The client says, "But you don't understand! The rule doesn't apply in my case!" and walks away shaking his or her head and complaining, not about the rule but about the callous bureaucrat who applied the rule. Hence, it comes as no surprise that the National Performance Review pointed with pride to the initiative of Occupational Safety and Health Administration (OSHA) officials in Maine who worked to negotiate inspections and enforcement issues with local businesses to avoid blanket application of national rules without noting that the ability to be flexible in one case means the freedom not to be flexible in another situation.

Jerome Frank, a member of the Securities and Exchange Commission and later a judge on the Second Circuit Court of Appeals, once wrote that discretionary decisionmaking by administrators is often prompted not by the administrator's desire for discretion and informality, but because those before agencies demand individualized consideration outside of normal procedures.[29]

The Power of the Raised Eyebrow

The perceptions of those dealing with an agency are important in another more coercive sense. The power of the raised eyebrow is the ability to cause an individual to act not by positive directive or by sanction but voluntarily, out of concern that an administrator might employ a sanction at some time in the future. Two examples are tax audits and broadcast licensing. Most people fear tax audits not because of what the Internal Revenue Service is going to do to them, but because of what the agency might possibly do. The threat of an audit may be enough to deter some taxpayers from cutting corners. A broadcaster might be concerned about FCC suggestions on adult programming or public service, not because the commission is likely to commence a formal disciplinary proceeding against the station, but because lack of cooperation might be remembered by those at the commission when it comes time for station license renewal.

One of the most effective of the raised eyebrow agencies is the Securities and Exchange Commission (SEC). Even if one thought it likely that one's case would prevail in a formal administrative proceeding, it would be dangerous to ignore SEC suggestions concerning a new securities issue. A mere hint that one is under special scrutiny by the commission could destroy the marketability of the new issue.[30] The power of the raised eyebrow is important not because of what an agency can or will do, but because of what the party before the agency believes the agency could or would do.

The significance of this power varies depending on who is involved. Obviously, repeat players are not likely to be overawed by agency authority. They are likely to know exactly what an agency can and cannot do, and are not as likely as single-shot players to be frightened by the mere possibility that an agency may institute a formal proceeding against them. In fact, the raised eyebrow can work in reverse. Administrators may be loath to take certain actions because they know that the repeat players affected might have sufficient legal, economic, and political resources to block or weaken the agency.

The Due Process, Efficiency, and Dispute Resolution Models

Finally, the pressure on agencies to process their workloads—often extremely large workloads—also has an effect. Many years ago, Herbert Packer made a study of the criminal justice system that is somewhat analogous to the administrative justice system. Packer found that there are two models of how the system works, or ought to work, which he called the "due process" and "crime control" models.[31] The due process model is based on the proposition that the task of the criminal justice system is to investigate allegations of breaches of law and enforce the law. The party involved should be accorded all due process protections beginning with the presumption of innocence. The ultimate goal is to discover the truth and achieve justice. Packer suggested that most citizens, including participants in the criminal justice system, would agree with those ideals. On the other hand, Packer argued that what an impartial observer of the actual operation of the system sees is less like the due process model than the crime control or efficiency model, which is based on the assumption that the task of the criminal justice system is to control crime. Crime is controlled by processing cases and achieving convictions. Given limited resources, accomplishing these goals requires efforts to improve the efficiency of case processing. In the criminal justice context, this means emphasizing informal processes such as plea bargaining.[32]

Ideally, an administrative agency's or a local government organization's goal is to implement and administer a policy or law. It has a formal process for doing so. In reality, agencies can be overloaded, regardless of what kind of agency is involved. The efficiency model may more accurately describe the operation of such an agency. The short-term goal may be to maximize efficient processing of the docket, and pressures to use informal processes for clearing cases become intense. The *Eldridge* case study in Appendix 1 illustrates the problem as does the discussion of Medicare claims processing in Chapter 6.

More recently, ADR advocates and critics alike have concluded that dispute resolution is a third model, though exactly how it is to be characterized is a matter of ongoing debate. Carrie Menkel-Meadow has argued that there are three variations. There are those who focus on ADR as (1) "speedy, less costly, and therefore more efficient case processing. This strand of the movement has been called the quantitative, caseload-reducing, or case management side of ADR;" (2) "the qualitative argument that both dispute processes and their outcomes can be improved with alternatives to full-scale trial;" and (3) those who define ADR as some combination of the quantitative and qualitative approaches."[33] However defined, the emphasis is on the resolution of the dispute.

✳ ADR and the Contract Model ✳

As this and earlier chapters have explained at some length, one of most important developments in the field in recent decades is the increasingly important contract model. The fact that contracts often contain requirements for informal processes was noted above, but two other factors are important influences. The first is that public managers often deal not with one or two contracts but often with several or perhaps many contracts of several different kinds. A common example is the city manager who may have half a dozen or more bargaining units within the city organization, all represented by different unions, each of which has its own contract. It is normal for such collective bargaining agreements to contain a set of informal processes to be used for personnel actions and other decisionmaking. While it is certainly the desire of managers to avoid the problem, it is not at all uncommon for several contracts in one organization to require different kinds of informal processes for different purposes. The same is true for other kinds of contracts. In an earlier time, there were efforts at the federal and state levels to try to impose boilerplate language (standard language that is more or less automatically included) in all contracts mandating a particular type of process. However, in an effort to improve public/private partnerships and to enhance flexibility, the effort has been made to open contract processes to negotiation. The number and variations among contract dispute resolution processes is now an important fact of life for managers, particularly those at the state and local levels.

There is another factor that has become more important as the amount of contracting and dependence of government units on contractors have increased. In the contemporary context, most informal processes involve some kind of negotiation. Lloyd Burton has observed that from the moment that negotiations begin, another factor comes into play, what he terms negotiating culture.[34] In particular, he points out that there is often a mismatch of negotiating cultures within which administrative agencies operate. This problem begins from the fact that there are usually informal rules that operate at the negotiating table that not only govern how the sides relate to each other but also have to do with the internal cultures that govern each side's internal operations. The private sector side generally operates according to standard business assumptions in which they have no responsibilities to anyone except their organization and, if it is a for-profit firm, its officers and stockholders. However, the government representatives begin from a much more complex position and must operate according to what has been called the public sector negotiating culture. Clearly, the public sector representatives must negotiate for ends and by means that are consistent with law, within the authority that has been delegated to them, within the policies of the sitting government, and with a concern for the public interest. That can create what Burton has referred to as ethical discontinuities at the bargaining table. Those ethical constraints affect virtually all aspects of the negotiating process even if the members of the public sector team never acknowledge their role.

There can also be such discontinuities for not-for-profit organizations, though their negotiating cultures may be many and varied. Some are membership organizations with established boards of directors and see their role in ways that are not all that different from for-profit firms except that they may not be seeking a profit in the traditional sense. Others are volunteer-based organizations that are driven by strongly held religious, political, or social commitments. They often come to the table with strong advocacy tendencies, seeking to get the most for their cause and to win more than just money. Still others may represent coalitions of NGOs, an increasingly popular arrangement. They must be concerned both about the causes their coalition champions, the needs of the coalition leadership, and the problems of holding the coalition together. It is not at all unusual to have coalition representatives negotiate with government, only to have members of the coalition later challenge the agreement on grounds that the coalition officers misrepresented the commitments of the groups to the government or the government's positions to the groups.[35]

Some or all of these factors may be present in the decision whether to employ informal administrative processes and can very clearly shape the operation of such procedures if they are pursued. For all these reasons, it is dangerous to assume that informal processes are always simple or to ignore the fact that they carry their own potential motive forces and tendencies.

THE NATURE OF INFORMAL PROCESSES

Informal processes are just that informal. Therefore, one cannot establish a concise and specific taxonomy of informal processes in administrative law. One can describe a few of the more common types of informal mechanisms and the general attitudes that guide the use of these and other informal techniques. The informal devices may generally be classified as preformal, filtering, or opting-out procedures.

Preformal processes attempt to resolve problems early in the administrative process and avoid having to resort to the formal stages. The two most common approaches are informal negotiations and early settlements and preclearance procedures. Almost all agencies use the first of these approaches to problem solving. Informal negotiated settlements have the obvious benefit of resolving problems congenially, which allows for continued good relationships between agency clients and administrators. Preclearance procedures take different forms in different agencies. Examples are Federal Trade Commission preclearance of proposed corporate mergers where antitrust laws could be a problem, and Securities and Exchange Commission deficiency letter procedures where the SEC reviews a prospectus for a security and notes deficiencies so that they may be corrected before formal registration and marketing of the securities issue. Another type of preclearance process is the issuance of advisory opinions, which were discussed briefly in earlier chapters. Advisory opinions are an agency's general views about how it expects to deal with certain situations that may arise. While agencies are not bound by such commentaries, it is in the interest of all concerned for the administrators to issue accurate advisory opinions and to follow them. Doing so may reduce the likelihood of formal procedures. The third type of preformal processes are diversion programs. These devices try to move a dispute out of the track that might lead toward more formal action. The early efforts in this direction came with what was termed "court annexed arbitration."[36] The idea was that several federal district courts established local rules that required parties in some kinds of cases to submit to an alternative dispute resolution process and, however indirectly, placed pressure on the parties to use these procedures to settle their disputes and keep them out of the court.[37] Strictly speaking, most of these programs involved mediation rather than arbitration and were mandatory rather than completely voluntary.[38]

Another more recent type of diversion process is the minitrial in which the parties bring key decisionmakers to a forum in which representatives for both sides present major elements of their evidence and arguments as if advocating in court though without the constraints of judicial proceedings. The decisionmakers can then decide whether they think it worthwhile to move toward a settlement or to take the more formal route and proceed with an adversarial process. Keyes provides an example of the process used by the U.S. Army Corps of Engineers in which the contract officer gave the contractor just over three hours to present the firm's core case, then allowed for cross-examination and redirect, and then facilitated a discussion, all of which were observed by an impartial attorney who provided a summary of his findings. Based upon that process, the parties undertook negotiations the next day, which were completed in one session.[39] Again, the object is to push potential parties off the track that would otherwise lead to more formal disputes and into an early settlement.

The second major type of informal action is what can be termed "filtering action." Filtering procedures serve two purposes: (1) they attempt to eliminate unnecessary formal procedures through a fairly structured negotiating process; and (2) where cases are going to move to formal action, efforts are made to simplify those procedures by reducing the number of issues in dispute and obtaining as much agreement as those involved are willing to provide. The predominant example of a filtering procedure is the prehearing conference. Prehearing conferences in administrative law are patterned after the pretrial conference model established in the Federal Rules of Civil Procedure[40] and authorized by the Administrative Procedure Act.[41] The ALJ can call a prehearing conference to ask the parties to limit the issues to be argued, the number of witnesses to be presented, and stipulate to as many of the pertinent facts as possible. The conference is also an opportunity to reach a settlement before the formal process gets under way. If no settlement can be obtained, at least the scope of the formal proceeding can be narrowed and the issues properly defined.

Finally, there are opting-out techniques, which are procedures that are often employed after a formal proceeding has begun or when it is imminent aimed at resolving the difficulty short of completing the formal process. One of the reasons for the use of the term opting-out is because it is not at all uncommon for the regulatory agencies to start a formal process or even to file a suit and then to consider ADR options. It is a technique for placing pressure on those at the negotiating table. These opting-out techniques are often characterized as falling on a continuum from least to most binding, and more than one technique may be used if the parties decide, or are required by contract, to move down the continuum.[42] They include negotiation, mediation, and arbitration and variations of those techniques.

The difference between negotiation and the other approaches is that negotiation involves the parties directly, but the other techniques employ a neutral third party either to facilitate negotiations or to issue findings and make some kind of award. In mediation, the neutral third party usually does not have the power to make decisions in the dispute but is there to help the parties engage with one another in a constructive manner, even if at arm's length, or to assist the process of negotiation with the hope of achieving a settlement. The term "facilitator" is used to describe a person who serves these kinds of functions in a negotiated rulemaking proceeding because he or she facilitates the sessions of the committee (see Chapter 5).[43] The mediator is a person mutually selected by the parties, often from lists maintained by the American Arbitration Association or the Federal Mediation and Conciliation Service. Wise mediators call upon the parties to provide a contract that sets forth their responsibilities, protects the mediator from being sued or called as a party in the event of later litigation, and ensures that information produced during settlement will be privileged and cannot be introduced later in court.

The difference between mediation and arbitration is that it is normally the case that an arbitrator issues a binding decision. There are variations on arbitration that are really intended to act like diversion processes and that produce nonbinding decisions that should encourage the parties to seek settlement.[44] However, the more common form is that the parties enter into a contract with an arbitrator, present the case to him or her, and agree to be bound by the arbitrator's decision. The parties agree to the choice of the arbitrator and may establish boundaries in their agreement. The outside party normally ensures that the agreement provides protection for the arbitrator should one side or the other litigate later.

At the end of the day, the results of settlement are often turned into a consent decree. A consent decree is an agreement to cease a certain type of conduct that an agency asserts is illegal without admitting any guilt or liability or to take a specified set of actions in the future. One of the reasons that some regulated parties will enter into a consent decree it that it does not automatically make the party involved vulnerable to damage claims in private suits brought against the firm. The agency gets the result it seeks, namely, a cessation of some unacceptable practices. The organization may be able to settle on terms that are less harsh than might have been imposed if the administrative process had run its course. Finally, the organization preserves all its legal options in the event that it faces future suits. In addition to these types of settlements entered into by parties in an administrative proceeding, some settlements are entered in court.

Consent decrees take their name from the fact that they are court orders entered on consent of the parties. That is, the parties ask a judge to enter a decree so that the settlement becomes an order of the court that can later be enforced using the power of the court to hold an offending party in contempt. In some cases, of course, it is the state or federal agency that is charged with a legal violation and that ultimately settles the dispute with a consent decree.

In the end, while there is a growing range of sophisticated ADR techniques, informal processes are very often extremely simple and flexible. In some respects it is better to think of these procedures in terms of the attitudes that characterize them rather than in terms of specific classes of procedure. In informal processes, administrators often appear to be acting in a consultative or supervisory mode rather than in the more aggressive watchdog mode. They often settle for giving guidance to those before the agency rather than mandating specific types of conduct. Negotiation is preferred to adjudication. The informal approach works particularly well where both sides are more interested in conciliation than in confrontation.

ADVANTAGES AND DISADVANTAGES OF INFORMAL PROCESSES

As in any area of public policy or administration, there are significant pluses and minuses associated with the use of informal administrative processes to resolve problems. The following is a brief summary of some of the most obvious costs and benefits. Chapter 9, on administrative discretion, and Chapter 10, on regulation, will deal in some detail with specific implications of the use of informal processes.

Advantages

The first obvious advantage to informal processes is speed. It is much easier and faster to resolve problems with a telephone call or a visit and a confirming letter than it is to proceed to formal methods. Given the number of problems on an average agency docket and the fact that formal processes can last for months and sometimes years, it is in the agency's (or city's) best interest to do things the easy way. Depending on the type of player involved (consider, for example, the Social Security disability claimants' difficulties discussed in the *Eldridge* case study), delay can be a major concern for both the administrator and also for the citizen, community group, or business that needs a decision in order to move on to their own next steps.

A related advantage is low-cost resolution of problems. As soon as a case becomes a formal proceeding, costs escalate rapidly. Many single-shot players are particularly hard-hit by legal fees and delayed benefit payments. The costs are also difficult for agencies and some repeat players to carry. Expense is a particular problem where there are lengthy administrative hearings that involve many parties and a large number of expert witnesses. Informal procedures are not without cost, but they can be quite inexpensive relative to formal approaches to problem solving. In fact, a Government Accountability Office (GAO) study found that in both the public and private sectors, the effort to reduce costs and save time was a leading reason why organizations moved to create ADR programs.[45]

Related to these concerns has been a need to resolve an increasing number of disputes. Thus, GAO found, for example, that:

> In the private sector, the number of discrimination complaints filed with EEOC grew by 43 percent between fiscal years 1991 and 1994—from 63,898 to 91,189—before beginning to decline. In the federal sector, the increase in the number of discrimination complaints filed with federal agencies was also substantial, rising by 55 percent between fiscal years 1991 and 1995—from 17,696 to 27,472.[46]

And when it is considered that in fiscal 1995 discrimination claims that involved a hearing and a subsequent appeal to EEOC took an average of 801 days to process,[47] the problem becomes obvious.

A fourth presumed advantage is that informal processes may take place in a more congenial atmosphere than might be present in a formal adversary-type proceeding. And perhaps in part because of that kind of environment, the available data seem to suggest a higher level of participant satisfaction with informal processes.[48]

Related to this issue of environment and attitude is the tendency for informal processes to enhance the willingness of parties to settle. Thus, the GAO study calculated the percentage of cases resolved by ADR in the Department of Air Force at 73 percent, Postal Service (North Florida) at 74 percent, Postal Service (Southern California) at 94 percent, and Walter Reed Army Medical Center at 68 percent. In the Seattle Interagency ADR Consortium, a group of organizations that share ADR programs and resources reported an 89 percent settlement rate between May 1993 and February 1997.[49]

Another strength of informal processes cited as a factor in this higher clearance rate is that ADR techniques seek to move participants away from positions and toward a recognition of interests.

> Simply stated, each disputant stakes out a position—such as a complaint of discrimination or a defense against a complaint—and hopes to win the case. But interest-based dispute resolution, which is the basis for some ADR techniques, focuses on determining the disputants' underlying interests and working to resolve their conflict at a more basic level, perhaps even bringing about a change in the work environment in which their conflicts developed.[50]

There are often more than two sides to an administrative disagreement or policy and exploration of the facets of a problem may be more relaxed and flexible in the informal setting.

A related advantage may be described in terms of game theory.[51] The use of informal processes allows those involved to more easily play a non–zero sum game. This conceptual framework assumes that interactions among political, economic, and social actors may be thought of as contests in which all the actors attempt to pursue their own best interests.[52] There are basically two kinds of games: zero sum games and non–zero sum games. In the first, there is one winner and one loser. The winnings of the winner equal the losses to the loser. In the non–zero sum game there is no absolute winner or loser. The informal process, since it is not cast in rigid adversary terms, encourages non–zero sum games. In the real world, such games are easier to play and the results are often more acceptable to all concerned than the zero sum type.

Informal processes often make it possible to resolve problems without disrupting ongoing projects or lifestyles. While negotiations are underway, it is often possible for those involved to continue in existing routines rather than face an immediate shutdown of an industrial plant or an immediate loss of income from benefits. The absence of the threat of traumatic disruption may allow for a less crisis-ridden and more reasoned approach to problems.

Finally, informal processes permit administrative discretion. Agencies can be more flexible in the informal environment than is possible once a formal procedure has been instituted. There is more room for judgment and individual consideration in the decision process.

Challenges and Disadvantages

Between the obvious advantages described above and the intense efforts of ADR advocates to encourage in the most enthusiastic terms—and where possible to mandate—informal processes, the picture that emerges is that the pluses are so obvious that only a crazy person would opt for more formal alternatives, and certainly not litigation! Of course, whenever something seems so obvious, a wise public administrator would do well to look closely and carefully. After all, if it sounds too good to be true, as the saying goes, it probably is. Or, more accurately, while it may be true that there are many advantages to informal processes, it is important to pay attention to the challenges and possible disadvantages that may be involved as well.

In an effort to ensure a more balanced picture than is often presented, the discussion to follow will deliberately emphasize these challenges and caution the reader to keep the intentional emphasis in mind. Consider the problems that may be and often are presented by informal processes, the challenges of administering under ADR settlements, and issues arising in negotiated enforcement.

The Downsides of Informal Processes   One danger is that the ability of an administrator to be particularly sensitive to one individual or group before the agency implies the ability to discriminate against another.[53] The possibility of falling victim to discrimination is somewhat higher in informal proceedings than in formal proceedings because there is often little record of informal understandings or negotiations, especially where the outcome is a decision by an agency not to take action or not to enforce. It was, after all, in part in an effort to prevent or check arbitrariness that formal administrative procedures were initially instituted.

These risks grow in those settings where the use of informal techniques is not voluntary but mandated. Thus, the GAO study found that it was common in the private sector organizations studied to require employees to submit to binding arbitration as a condition of employment. That also meant that their chances on an appeal if they were dissatisfied were considerably reduced since any legal challenge was limited to a review of the arbitration, a much narrower process than would otherwise have been available in a normal lawsuit.[54] The same situation obtains in some public sector employment situations.

Second, and related to differences between the parties before the agencies, is the danger that the distinction between repeat players and single-shot players can be extremely important in the informal process. This can be true in what are termed ADR processes but can be even more of an issue in other types of informal processes that lack the structure and guidelines of ADR tools. If an administrator's concern about a repeat player's power is strong enough, the vigor with which the administrator pursues the wider public interest may be jeopardized.

Steven Marchese provided a useful analysis of these issues in a piece on the expanding use of mediation in disputes between parents of children with special needs and school administrators under the Individuals with Disabilities Education Act.[55] He pointed out that:

> Power imbalances between families and districts, information inequities between the parties, lack of guaranteed parental access to paid advocacy, and the absence of uniform mediator training and qualifications are all significant concerns left unanswered by the statute. As a result, the statute formally introduces voluntary mediation into the special education dispute resolution process without providing sufficient guidance to parents, school districts, and state agencies as to how it can be used in furtherance of the statute's goals. The danger is that the rush to resolve conflict may yield results that are unfair to the very people the IDEA was designed to empower.[56]

Above all, he warned, the parents in such a situation are often not aware that, once they have entered into the mediation process and have reached a settlement, they may have waived other protections that may be available to them and that, henceforth, any challenges to their child's situation may be expected to focus on what is in the agreement and probably not the actual standards of the IDEA. While parents with sufficient resources and knowledge may work well on their child's behalf with school officials in the ADR process, there is a danger that for others the circumstances and consequences may be very different.

Because of these dangers, Marchese and others have placed a premium on training mediators and other facilitators or decisionmakers and also on educating single-shot players who are making a decision to enter into an ADR process.[57] Further, the challenge is to ensure that they receive necessary additional information and clarifications as they move through the process. While an administrative law judge would be expected to provide that educational function in formal adjudications, that function is not always assured by mediators or other third-party participants.

Marchese also argued that these issues call for a different approach that looks beyond the traditionally limited and contract-oriented approach to examining settlements in cases such as these. Shin Imai, writing in the very different context of negotiations between governments and First Nations People (Native Canadians), has suggested that, where a court is involved at all in a dispute, "there are three ways in which courts could enhance negotiation...: by establishing a negotiation framework and...parameters...; by determining the relationship between negotiation and adjudication using principles of dispute system design...; and by ensuring the integrity of the negotiation process...."[58] In sum, he said, it is better to avoid the dichotomy that is common today in which some ADR advocates argue for a clear separation between the courts and alternative dispute resolution processes and to consider more of a continuum—at one end of which is a formal adjudicative process before a judge and at the other a completely separate and independent process with gradations between.

Third, for reasons already established, the effects of sunk costs may subvert the objectivity of the decisionmaker and foster a combative attitude to latecomers to a particular policy discussion. The point is not that sunk costs always rule the day, because there are many examples to the contrary.[59] However, the push is strong to stay with explicit or even tacit negotiated understandings.

Fourth, also related to the problem of sunk costs, is the fact that, particularly in informal processes, intra- or interorganizational politics may play a disproportionate role in the decision process. Bureaucratic politics and organization theory and behavior variables are almost always important in decision-making, but informal processes may permit these factors to play more of a role than they should.[60] And even if they do not really make a critical difference, it is common for those affected by a decision to believe they did.

Fifth, access to the formal process may be deterred. Woll and others have observed that parties with matters pending before agencies may not really be able to move the dispute to a formal proceeding even if that option is technically available. Given the expense and the time required to pursue a formal remedy, there is sometimes no practical alternative to resolving a problem through the informal channel. When that happens, the spirit of free negotiation mutually conducted may give way to a more coercive atmosphere without the protections afforded in the formal setting. And recall the discussion of mandatory arbitration found by the GAO study noted above. The mere availability of access to the formal process may serve as an important check.

Sixth, the informal process provides no guarantee of openness. Closed or private proceedings may allow for more candid discussions, but they do not permit the check available in open proceedings where good records are kept and the forum is available to outsiders. Suspicions that there were back-room games can be exacerbated where negotiations are conducted in secret and where records are not available as is common in informal processes. Much of the discussion of ADR processes focuses on employment disputes or individual discrimination claims, which are often handled in protected settings, but informal processes are used across the spectrum of administrative decisions where the interests at stake are not those of a few parties but concern the broad public interest. Noel Keyes cites one experienced agency representative who expressed concern with the lack of knowledge of or access to settlements and settlement processes and added: "He also found this particularly troubling given the number of experienced agency counsel that express their belief that their agencies today willingly pay out larger settlements to comply with the 'spirit' of their agency's ADR initiatives and mandates."[61]

Seventh, many types of informal processes provide no guidance or protection for the future for those who deal with an agency. Many agencies favor advisory opinions and agency interpretive rules in part because they are not binding. Similarly, settlements are often not binding in or even applicable to future situations or cases. (The caveat here, of course, is that consent decrees and formal settlement agreements are binding at least to the organizations that are specifically parties to them.) In fact, one of the attractive features of informal procedures is to treat individual problems on an ad hoc basis that provides no restrictions on future decisionmaking. Unlike formal proceedings, informal processes often do not result in any kind of formal written decision that can be referred to or treated as precedent by others in the future. It is true that the binding effect of precedent in administrative law is more limited than in some other areas of jurisprudence. Still, such opinions are available and can be studied with some likelihood that an agency will honor its precedents. That option is not available from many informal decision processes. Even in the case of more structured ADR procedures, while there may be a written decision, there is often no record in the common usage of that term, and an agreement at the outset that a decision in the case will not mean an admission of guilt or set a precedent for other cases.

The arguments in favor of confidentiality and against the development of complete and open records often have to do with the effort to keep costs down, processes less burdensome, and relationships among the parties relatively simple and as congenial as possible. However, as ADR techniques have developed and as the use of various informal techniques has been routinized, these assumptions about costs and relationships have come to be open to some question. First, some of these negotiated processes have themselves becomes relatively complex and quite expensive. Many involve third parties as facilitators, mediators, or arbitrators. Lawyers are more and more common in these settings. While negotiated processes can apparently be quite efficient for certain kinds of relatively limited problems, there really is very little systematic analysis in the public sector demonstrating how much resource savings there is in the expanded use of informal processes.[62] The cost calculation gets particularly murky if it turns out that agencies must address many individual problem resolutions for the same type of issue and still end up having to litigate for policy reasons. It was with just such problems in mind that the Congress warned in the Dispute Resolution Act that:

An agency shall consider not using a dispute resolution proceeding if—

(1) a definitive or authoritative resolution of the matter is required for precedential value, and such a proceeding is not likely to be accepted generally as an authoritative precedent;

(2) the matter involves or may bear upon significant questions of Government policy that require additional procedures before a final resolution may be made, and such a proceeding would not likely serve to develop a recommended policy for the agency;

(3) maintaining established policies is of special importance, so that variations among individual decisions are not increased and such a proceeding would not likely reach consistent results among individual decision;

(4) the matter significantly affects persons or organizations who are not parties to the proceeding;

(5) a full public record of the proceeding is important, and a dispute resolution proceeding cannot provide such a record; and

(6) the agency must maintain continuing jurisdiction over the matter with authority to alter the disposition of the matter in the light of changed circumstances, and a dispute resolution proceeding would interfere with the agency's fulfilling that requirement.[63]

Similarly, it is not always true that the use of informal techniques prevents conflict-oriented behavior. The fact is that negotiated proceedings can range across the spectrum from very cooperative processes aimed at so-called win/win solutions to extremely adversarial interactions in which the parties want as much of a zero sum win as they can get. Thus, the available evidence suggests that it is important in ADR proceedings to seek to get a dispute into settlement negotiations early before the level of conflict rises too much and before the parties have hardened their positions, making them less willing to shift from position bargaining to interest bargaining.

Further, even if it is possible to establish a cooperative working relationship among some of the parties, the fact is that many of the disputes facing public managers involve multiple parties and multidimensional collections of issues. Among other things, that can mean that the problem is not resolved merely because a set of parties came to an agreement with an agency. Consider the case of a discrimination dispute in Memphis, Tennessee, that appeared to have been settled only to end up in the United States Supreme Court. African-American firefighters in Memphis sued the city, alleging discrimination in hiring and promotion practices. The parties settled with no admission by the city of discrimination but several commitments with respect to both hiring and promotion of minority firefighters. A year later the city announced that budget deficits required a reduction in force. The district court concluded that a last hired/first fired process would result in undermining the consent decree and ordered modifications in the city's layoff procedure to accommodate the agreement. The Supreme Court overturned the lower courts and ruled in favor of the firefighters' union. Among other reasons, the Court found that the union had not been a party to the earlier suit or settlement.[64] The city had no authority to bargain away the rights or contract provisions of the union or its members.

Even assuming that it is possible to get to agreement among the key parties, settlements can still require the participation of others who are not willing to cooperate. It may require judicial cooperation in the development of a consent agreement. The courts may refuse that cooperation as in the refusal of the Third Circuit Court of Appeals to accept certification of a class for purposes of a settlement in the landmark asbestos claims cases, a decision ultimately upheld by the U.S. Supreme Court.[65]

Managing Under Settlements   As these last two examples suggest, there are complexities associated with both the effort to get to informal settlements, and also to administer under those agreements. The tendency by ADR advocates has been to focus on getting an agreement and too seldom to discuss what happens afterwards.[66] Consider just a few of the more common problems.

It is sometimes not clear just who will be responsible for what aspects of implementation and enforcement of decrees. Judges have often found that the attorneys who were so active in negotiating agreements vanished after the decree was entered, leaving the judge and sometimes others involved wondering who is responsible for what. And if that is a problem early in the implementation period of an settlement, it can become much more complex as time passes.

For one thing, administrators now must be very alert when entering a new position to determine whether the organization is operating any informal agreements, particularly judicially enforceable consent decrees. Consider the example of Minnesota State Prison at Stillwater. A 1977 consent decree had included a wide range of provisions covering, among other things, medical care issues.[67] In 1989 a case was brought, claiming that the prison administration was seriously in violation of that decree with the result that there were significant problems with tuberculosis among the inmates that could and should have been prevented.[68] A prisoner who was seriously ill with tuberculosis sought help but was not even tested for six months. In the interim his cell-mates and others complained that this inmate was a danger to them. The authorities moved the prisoner around from cell to cell and these other cell-mates ultimately contracted the disease. When the case was litigated, it became clear that prison employees were not even aware of the requirements of the consent decree, including the prison officer legally charged with its administration. The prison administrators thought that the prison physician was responsible for all medical care issues, but the physician was only a part-time employee who regarded himself as responsible only for acute and emergency care. No one had generated standards for the implementation of the decree, or at least no one was aware of any such policies. The medical case had been provided under state contracts, but the administrators responsible for the prison's operations were not aware of the contents of those contracts. The state official in charge of the state's tuberculosis program maintained that she had no responsibility for what happened at the prison. It should be clear that apart from whatever other problems there were in the operation of the prison, some of them stemmed from a failure adequately to implement a consent decree and from a failure to ensure that responsible officials were educated as to the requirements of the decree and a failure to manage its provisions.

This need to be alert to agreements of various sorts also extends to other kinds of agreements apart from settlements. Indeed, many local governments as well as state and federal agencies participate in governance regimes that operate on the basis of different kinds of agreements, many of which are termed memorandum of understanding or memorandum of agreement. At the state and local level, such agreements are often termed intergovernmental agreements, interagency agreements, or inter-jurisdictional agreements. These agreements are often entered to avoid formal conflicts as well as to initiate cooperative programs and processes. They are generally problem-solving devices. As is true of settlements, these are agreements in the nature of contracts, but their legal authority and terms may be anything but clear. It is not enough to be alert to statutes, regulations, city charters, and ordinances in the contemporary world of governance.

But even if the on-scene managers undertake to learn about and fulfill agency or city obligations under various kinds of settlements, there can be challenges. Specifically, it is not at all uncommon for legislative or executive branch officials to refuse to support consent decrees. Thus, a New York legislature once told the governor that although the executive branch had negotiated a consent decree covering conditions at a state facility for developmentally disabled children, that did not mean the legislature was obligated to support it! In other jurisdictions, legislatures have refused to support the results of arbitration on grounds that the constitutional power of appropriations rests with the legislature and cannot be delegated away to an arbitrator. Chief executives have been known to be less than sympathetic to requests from department heads for resources to implement settlements with which they disagree and to which they had not personally been a party.

Sometimes the reluctance of these key political leaders can stem from political pique, but they arise from other kinds of causes as well. Thus, it is a common belief that third parties who aid settlements or render arbitration judgments begin from a "split the difference" mentality for the simple reason that they are hired by the parties and have an incentive, should they wish to be hired again, not to anger one side or the other more than necessary. Another common frustration is the belief that the parties to settlements often use them to, as the expression goes, game the system, packing far more into a consent decree than they could ever get in appropriations bills and then insisting that the whole thing was mandated by the judge and they were powerless to stop him.

The situation can be even more troublesome. This arises when there are what amount to false negotiations. That can occur when, for example, the state negotiates an agreement and promptly repudiates it after it is issued. This is precisely what happened in Alabama when the governor authorized a settlement and later disavowed the agreement, claimed that the attorneys representing the state had no authority to agree to the provisions involved, and went back to court seeking a stay of the decree pending an attempt to vacate it.[69] Then there is the problem that there are almost always clauses included in the agreements that permit escape from its obligations under various contingencies. Consent decrees are, after all, treated like contracts. One attorney interviewed for research on a book on remedial decrees explained that he was perfectly happy to agree to many things in a settlement so long as he was able to draft the escape clause.

Negotiated Enforcement   One of the most important decisions that administrators make is whether, when, and under what conditions to take enforcement action. That is true whether it is a matter of enforcing existing statutes and regulations or the terms of a settlement agreement.

The Dispute Resolution Act and various executive orders encourage the use of flexible enforcement that is tailored to particular circumstances. However, as noted above, the discretion to be lenient and to tailor enforcement action to special needs in one case is also the discretion to not to be flexible elsewhere. That kind of lack of consistency and uniformity can lead—and in many cases has led—to significant issues of equality and equity. That was one of the strong historical arguments in favor of standard setting by rulemaking. And since enforcement discretion is presumptively unreviewable,[70] the consequences of arbitrariness can be very important and difficult to detect. Beyond that, of course, an agreement—as between an inspector and a regulated firm—may be mutually satisfactory but not at all in the public interest.

There is another dimension of enforcement, but of a different type. Rather than an issue of negotiating about whether or how to enforce, this is an issue of enforcement of a negotiated agreement because of limiting terms in the agreement itself. It has become increasingly common for the parties to a settlement to include in the agreement commitments to keep the specific terms of the settlement confidential as well as to agree not to reveal any evidence about the dispute or even to discuss the case at all. That has even become common in cases that were settled during the course of litigation.[71] These types of secrecy commitments can create very real difficulties for managers who must administer in the wake of settlements. Consider the case of sexual harassment resolutions. It is common for both the person bringing the complaint and the party accused to agree to enter into informal processes in search of a settlement in order to avoid public disclosure of potentially embarrassing information. It is common for settlement agreements in such circumstances to include prohibitions against disclosure of any information about the matter and to allow no formal statement of guilt or innocence. It is also common for the party accused to request that the record be expunged at a certain point in the future or upon completion of any actions required by the agreement to be completed, such as counseling or a probationary period. Clearly, these kinds of restrictions inhibit the ability of the administrator to communicate fully and effectively about an important management concern. It may also make it difficult to take formal action in the future in the event that it becomes necessary. And, not incidentally, it can make it appear as if the administrator is a party to some kind of cover-up.

There is one other complex area that has become more significant in recent years. It arises because of the expanding use of contractors not only to provide services but actually to administer programs on behalf of governmental units at all levels. One of the most common of these arrangements is where a not-for-profit administers a state program operated under federal grant support. In that situation, the program management contractor is frequently charged with purchasing goods and services and then ensuring compliance with the contracts. In effect, the management contractor makes enforcement decisions about compliance with contract terms and also about whether program participants will face some kind of adverse action for failure to meet program guidelines, whether they are generated at the federal or state level. The more levels and parties that are involved, the more complex and potentially problematic are the issues of enforcement under contract. This is an area that has received very little public attention despite the fact that it is increasingly pervasive.

This discussion of the challenges of using informal decision processes, including what are termed alternative dispute resolution techniques, is not intended to discourage their use. They are, as the Attorney General's Committee said many years before the contemporary ADR movement developed, absolutely essential to effective management. However, it would not do to approach these tools as some of their advocates present them and to ignore the many important administrative issues that arise in their use and in the implementation of the decisions they produce. Clearly, the more these techniques are used by public managers, the more sophisticated administrators must be in integrating the issues of economy, effectiveness, efficiency, equity, responsiveness, and responsibility.[72]

SUMMARY

Clearly, then, despite the preoccupation of the administrative law literature with the formal administrative process, most of the activity is informal rather than formal in nature. Many factors encourage the use of the informal process. A number of these factors, such as power law and sunk costs, also condition the operation of those informal processes.

In this chapter we noted that while it is not possible to categorize all the various forms of informal processes, they can generally be thought of in terms of preformal processes (which involve negotiation), filtering processes (used in connection with formal proceedings to simplify and shorten the process), and opting-out mechanisms for resolving disputes short of the full run of formal process.

There are several important advantages in using informal as against formal administrative process, but there are also a number of dangers or shortcomings that can attend their use. The role of administrative discretion, which is so important in informal processes, is both one of the major advantages and, because of the danger of arbitrariness, one of the great disadvantages. It is to this double-edged concept, administrative discretion, that we turn in Chapter 9.

NOTES

1. U.S. Senate, Report of the Attorney General's Committee on Administrative Procedure, *Administrative Procedure in Government Agencies,* Sen. Doc. no. 8, 77th Cong., 1st Sess. (1941), p. 35.

2. Peter Woll, *Administrative Law: The Informal Process* (Los Angeles: University of California Press, 1963), p. 3. For a short summary of Woll's findings, see "Informal Administrative Adjudication: Summary of Findings," 7 *UCLA Law Review* 436 (1960).

3. See Al Gore, Report of the National Performance Review, *From Red Tape to Results: Creating a Government that Works Better & Costs Less* (Washington, DC: Government Printing Office, 1993), and David Osborne and Ted Gaebler, *Reinventing Government* (New York: Penguin, 1992).

4. This feasibility framework, the research basis for it, and a more complete development of each of the dimensions are presented in Phillip J. Cooper and Claudia María Vargas, *Implementing Sustainable Development: From Global Policy to Local Action* (Lanham, MD: Rowman & Littlefield, 2004).

5. Executive Order 13228, 66 Fed. Reg. 51812 (2001).

6. P.L. 107-296, 116 Stat. 2135 (2005).

7. See Donald F. Kettl, *System Under Stress: Homeland Security and American Politics* (Washington, DC: CQ Press, 2004), Ch. 3.

8. Office of the Inspector General, Department of Homeland Security, *Major Management Challenges Facing the Department of Homeland Security* (Washington, DC: Department of Homeland Security Office of Inspector General, 2004); U.S. General Accounting Office, *Homeland Security: Overview of Department of Homeland Security Management Challenges* (Washington, DC: GAO, 2005); GAO, *Homeland Security: Further Action Needed to Promote Successful Use of Special DHS Acquisition Authority* (Washington, DC : GAO 2004).

9. Scott Higham and Robert O'Harrow, Jr., "The High Cost of a Rush to Security: TSA Lost Control of Over $300 Million Spent by Contractor to Hire Airport Screeners After 9/11," *Washington Post,* June 30, 2005, A01; Higham and O'Harrow, "Contracting Rush for Security Led to Waste, Abuse," *Washington Post,* May 22, 2005, p. A01.

10. Edgar Schein, *Organizational Culture and Leadership,* 2nd ed. (San Francisco: Jossey-Bass, 1992); J. Steven Ott, *The Organizational Culture Perspective* (Belmont, CA: Wadsworth, 1989).

11. See Claudia María Vargas, ed., "Symposium: Bridging Solitudes—Partnership Challenges in Canadian Refugee Service Delivery," 18 *Refuge* 1 (2000); Vargas, "Cultural Mediation for Refugee Children: A Comparative Derived Model." 12 *Journal of Refugee Studies* 284 (1999).

12. See e.g., Lloyd Burton, *Worship and Wilderness: Culture, Religion, and Law in Public Lands Management* (Madison, WI: University of Wisconsin Press, 2002); Carol Locust, "Walking in Two Worlds: Native Americans and the VR System," 22 *American Rehabilitation,* 2 (1996); "The Impact of Differing Belief Systems between Native Americans and Their Rehabilitation Service Providers," 9 *Rehabilitation Education* 205 (1995).

13. Lisa Bingham, "Alternative Dispute Resolution in Public Administration," in Phillip J. Cooper and Chester A. Newland, eds., *Handbook of Public Law and Administration* (San Francisco: Jossey-Bass, 1997), pp. 548–549.

14. *Id.*

15. *Id.*

16. See Steven Marchese, "Putting Square Pegs into Round Holes: Mediation and the Rights of Children with Disabilities under the IDEA," 53 *Rutgers L. Rev.* 333 (2001).

17. See e.g., Executive Order 12866, "Regulatory Planning and Review," 58 Fed. Reg. 51735 (1993); "Presidential Memorandum, Negotiated Rulemaking," September 30, 1993, at http://govinfo.library.unt.edu/npr/library/direct/memos/2682.html, as of December 28, 2005.

18. See e.g., *Dames & Moore v. Regan,* 453 U.S. 654 (1981).

19. See generally C. Neal Tate and Torbjorn Vallinder, eds., *The Global Expansion of Judicial Power* (New York: New York University Press, 1995).

20. See W. Noel Keyes, *Government Contracts,* 2nd ed. (St. Paul: West Publishing, 1996), pp. 736–58.

21. W. Noel Keyes, *Government Contracts in a Nutshell,* 4th ed. (St. Paul: Thomson-West, 2004), pp. 397–400.

22. Bingham, *supra* note 13, at p. 552.

23. *Power Reactor Development Co. v. International Union of Electrical, Radio and Machine Workers,* 367 U.S. 396, 417 (1961), Justice Douglas dissenting.

24. See e.g., Kenneth Culp Davis, *Discretionary Justice* (Baton Rouge: Louisiana State University Press, 1969), p. 158. See also *United Gas Pipeline Co. v. Ideal Cement Co.,* 369 U.S. 134, 136-37 (1962), Justice Douglas dissenting.

25. Mark Green, *The Other Government: The Unseen Power of Washington Lawyers* (New York: Norton, 1978).

26. One of the more interesting efforts to deal with the concept of power is described in James MacGregor Burns, *Leadership* (New York: Harper & Row, 1978), Part 1.

27. Burns's definition of power is a useful one for thinking about the nature and significance of power law. "On these assumptions, I view the power process as one in which power holders (P), possessing certain motives and goals, have the capacity to secure changes in the behavior of a respondent (R), human or animal, and in the environment, by utilizing resources in their power base, including factors of skill, relative to the targets of their power wielding and necessary to secure such changes. This view of power deals with three elements in the process: the motives and resources of power holders; the motives and resources of power recipients; and the relationship among all these." *Id.*, at p. 13.

28. Green, *supra* note 25, at pp. 12–16.

29. Jerome Frank, *If Men Were Angels: Some Aspects of Government in a Democracy* (New York: Harper & Brothers, 1942), Ch. 10.

30. Precisely for this reason, SEC personnel are prohibited from discussing such matters. That does not mean word of an investigation will not get out. The risk that someone might learn of SEC concern is a rather powerful deterrent.

31. Herbert L. Packer, "Two Models of the Criminal justice Process," in George F. Cole, ed., *Criminal Justice: Law and Politics* (Belmont, CA: Duxbury Press, 1972), pp. 35–52.

32. Milton Heumann, *Plea Bargaining* (Chicago: University of Chicago Press, 1977).

33. Carrie Menkel-Meadow, "When Dispute Resolution Begets Disputes of Its Own: Conflicts Among Dispute Professionals," 44 *UCLA L. Rev.* 1871, 1871-1873 (1997).

34. Lloyd Burton, "Ethical Discontinuities in Public-Private Sector Negotiation," 9 *Journal of Policy Analysis and Management* 23 (1990).

35. Author interview with Hassan Kahn, director, Fiji Council of Social Services, January 8, 1996.

36. See A. Leo Levin, "Court Annexed Arbitration," 16 *Journal of Law Reform* 537 (1983); Paul Nejelski and Andrew S. Zeldin, "Court Annexed Arbitration in the Federal Courts: The Philadelphia Story," 42 *Maryland Law Review* 787 (1983).

37. Joe S. Cecil, "Report on the Mediation Program in the Eastern District of Michigan," Federal Judicial Center, April 1983, p. 1.

38. See Karl Tegland, *Mediation in the Western District of Washington,* (Washington, DC: Federal Judicial Center, 1984).

39. Keyes, *supra* note 21, at p. 399.

40. Rule 16, Federal Rules of Civil Procedure, 1 *Moore's Rule Pamphlet* 134 (1981).

41. 5 U.S.C. §554(c)(1).

42. See Bingham, *supra* note 13, at pp. 550–562.

43. 5 U.S.C. 562 (4). See Bingham, *supra* note 13, at pp. 552–553.

44. See Brigham, *supra* note 13, at p. 557.

45. U.S. General Accounting Office, *Alternative Dispute Resolution: Employers' Experiences with ADR in the Workplace* (Washington, DC: GAO, 1997).

46. *Id.*, at p. 4.3.

47. *Id.*

48. "The Postal Service surveys found, for example, that 90 percent of the mediation users believed that the process was fair, compared with 41 percent of the participants in the traditional EEO process. Further, 72 percent of mediation users were satisfied with the outcomes of their disputes, compared with 40 percent of the participants in the traditional process." *Id.*, at p. 6.3.

49. *Id.*, at p. 6.1.

50. *Id.*, at p. 4.4. See also Brigham, *supra* note 13.

51. Robert Lineberry provides a very useful introductory discussion of this subject in his *American Public Policy: What Government Does and What Difference It Makes* (New York: Harper & Row, 1977), pp. 30–36.

52. Lineberry summarizes "The Prisoner's Dilemma" and "The Tragedy of the Commons," two stories that explain why it may often be difficult to know what is in one's best interest. *Id.*

53. "The discretionary power to be lenient is an impossibility without a concomitant power not to be lenient, and injustice from the discretionary power not to be is especially frequent; the power to be lenient is the power to discriminate." Davis, *supra* note 24, at p. 170.

54. *Id.*, at p. 72.

55. *Supra* note 16.

56. *Id.*, at pp. 350–351.

57. See also Naomi Karp and Erica Wood, J.D., "Health Plan Internal Consumer Dispute Resolution Practices: Highlights from a National Study," 5 *Journal of Health Care Law & Policy* 283 (2002).

58. Shin Imai, "Sound Science, Careful Policy Analysis, and Ongoing Relationships. Integrating Litigation and Negotiation in Aboriginal Lands and Resources Disputes," 41 *Osgoode Hall L.J.* 587, pp. 589–590 (2003).

59. Thus, for example, Louisiana Energy Services withdrew its application to build a nuclear fuel enrichment facility in April 1998, seven years and $34 million into the project. Roland J. Jensen to U.S. Nuclear Regulatory Commission, April 22, 1998. See also Christopher H. Foreman, Jr., *The Promise and Peril of Environmental Justice* (Washington, DC: Brookings Institution, 1998), pp. 128–29.

60. See generally Graham Allison, *Essence of Decision* (Boston: Little, Brown, 1971); and Francis Rourke, *Bureaucracy, Politics and Public Policy* (Boston: Little, Brown, 1969).

61. Keyes, *supra* note 21, at p. 400.

62. "Cost savings were difficult to establish. Only one company and one federal agency had performed evaluations that produced data regarding cost savings . . . The agency that gathered data on cost savings found that, when the cost of settlement was factored in, it was unclear whether its ADR process was less costly than the traditional equal employment opportunity (EEO) complaint process." GAO report, *supra* note 45, at p. 1.

63. 5 U.S.C. §582(b).

64. *Firefighters v. Stotts,* 467 U.S. 561 (1984).

65. *Amchem Products, Inc. v. Windsor,* 521 U.S. 591 (1997).

66. This issue is addressed in greater detail in Phillip J. Cooper, *Hard Judicial Choices* (New York: Oxford University Press, 1988).

67. See *Hines v. Anderson,* 439 F.Supp. 12 (DMN 1977).

68. *DeGidio v. Pung,* 704 F.Supp. 922 (DMN 1989).

69. See Cooper, *Hard Judicial Choices, supra* note 66, at pp. 193–194.

70. *Heckler v. Chaney,* 470 U.S. 821 (1985).

71. See Brian T. Fitzgerald, "Sealed v. Dealed: A Public Court System Going Secretly Private," 6 *Journal of Law and Politics* 381 (1990).

72. This challenge is presented in greater detail in Phillip J. Cooper, *Governing by Contract* (Washington, DC: CQ Press, 2002), Ch. 1.

9

Administrative Discretion: Uses, Abuses, Controversies, and Remedies

This chapter focuses on the nature, sources, uses, abuses, and perceptions of administrative discretion. Like "informal process," administrative discretion is a rather difficult concept with which to deal because it takes so many forms and may exist in varying levels or degrees.[1] There are few situations in which an administrator can be accurately described as having no discretion.[2] However, because we operate in a constitutional framework, no administrator has complete discretion either.

Most citizens are ambivalent about just how much discretion unelected public officials ought to possess. When they come to an agency for a permit or service, they want the people they encounter to have enough discretion to give them the decisions they seek, and they hate being told either that the agency spokespersons have to ask someone else in the agency for permission or that they would love to be helpful but they do not have the authority to depart from the standard operating procedures and agency rules. In fact, the National Performance Review pointed to exactly that kind of situation as a core criticism of contemporary government.[3] At the same time, many people both inside government and out are convinced that they have at some point been victims of the arbitrary use of discretionary authority.

Ernst Freund defined administrative discretion as follows: "When we speak of administrative discretion, we mean that a determination may be reached, in part at least, on the basis of considerations not entirely susceptible of proof or disproof."[4] Indeed, there are any number of possible ways to define the term. For present purposes we shall define administrative discretion to mean the power of an administrator to make significant decisions that have the force of law, directly or indirectly, and that are not specifically mandated by the Constitution, statutes, or other sources of black letter law. Before exploring the critical elements of the issue, consider the following case study of a problem of discretion.

"DISCRETIONARY CLEMENCY"[5]

The United States Attorney for the District of Utah died in fall 1974. William J. Lockhart accepted an interim appointment to fill the vacancy. Lockhart assumed the office on November 22, a particularly difficult time. On September 16, President Ford had announced his clemency program for Vietnam draft evaders, to be administered primarily by the United States Attorney offices throughout the country.[6] Amnesty was promised to those liable for prosecution for draft evasion on condition that they come forward and accept alternative service in public or charitable institutions for a period of up to two years.

Such a program would have been difficult to administer under the best of conditions, but administrative problems were exacerbated by the time limit for entry into the program imposed by the president. United States Attorneys were directed by the Department of Justice to prepare a list by January 13, 1975, of those cases that "retained prosecutive merit." Individuals whose cases "lack[ed] prosecutive merit" were to be cleared and told that they need not participate in the alternative service program to avoid future legal difficulties. The others were to be notified that they must report to U.S. Attorneys for consideration of alternative service or face possible prosecution.

As he began work on administering the clemency program in Utah, Lockhart established a set of basic operating principles. However he implemented the program, Lockhart considered himself constrained by "an obligation of reasoned decision" to be able first to explain logically and in writing his policy and findings.[7] Second, he observed that the administrator of the program had a "moral, legal, and constitutional obligation to make a reasonable effort to assure consistency in the exercise of prosecutorial discretion, and violates the requirements of equal protection if [h]e fails to make that reasonable effort."[8] Third, the administration of the program "should not have the effect of encouraging or causing prosecutions or other punitive action which would not have been initiated in the absence of clemency."[9]

After studying the program, Lockhart concluded that the vesting of unlimited discretion in U.S. Attorneys to deal with draft evaders more or less as each official saw fit led to arbitrary and inconsistent administration. He also found that the program was structured so that the individuals were open to more punishment than they might have been if the program had not been instituted.

The directive that required U.S. Attorneys to develop a list of individuals whose cases "retained prosecutive merit" did not define that language. Lockhart assumed that an assessment of prosecutive merit required that two judgments be made in each case. First, his office had to determine whether there was enough evidence and sufficiently strong circumstances in the file to assume that a prosecution, if instituted, would have some chance of success. Since U.S. Attorney staffs lacked sufficient personpower to investigate cases thoroughly, and because draft evasion cases had had very low priority compared with other cases, many of the files had to be rejected for weak evidentiary and factual case development. Second, in Lockhart's view, the U.S. Attorney's office had to determine that the defendant could have a fair trial if a prosecution were actually undertaken. The age or weak preparation of case files suggested that a number of defendants might be unable to locate witnesses or that other speedy trial–related rights might constitutionally bar prosecution.

Finally, Lockhart concluded that, when individuals whose cases were found to have prosecutive merit came in to negotiate alternative service, he and other U.S. Attorneys would have "an unreviewed power to impose a sentence, in the form of a period of two years' alternative service, without trial or other adequate processes for establishing the facts, and without any understandable or meaningful standards, either for determining the kind of violation or circumstances constituting 'prosecutive merit,' or for determining appropriate periods of alternative service."[10]

Several specific aspects of the program gave Lockhart concern that some alleged violators could be dealt with more harshly under the clemency program than they would otherwise have been. First, the requirement of a complete review of all case files would force some U.S. Attorney offices that had generally ignored the evader cases up to 1972–1973 to consider prosecutions. The case files might be selected as prosecutable or nonprosecutable simply because the cases that were poorly investigated offered little chance of successful prosecution, and not because one case was more or less deserving of prosecution than another. Unlike the usual situation in which a prosecutor could negotiate a case with a defendant, the clemency program permitted the U.S. Attorney to be prosecutor, jury, and sentencing judge without the check of a possible hearing before a judge at which the attorney would be made to explain his or her actions. After examining problems in his own and other districts, Lockhart determined that the structure and vagueness of the program might encourage prosecutors to avoid hard decisions in favor of a split-the-difference mentality in which alternative service would be required in questionable cases.

> Thus, ambiguity in program guidelines created a serious probability that alternative service would be imposed as a "lesser alternative" in many situations where exercise of prosecutorial discretion would have rendered prosecution unlikely.[11]

Lockhart examined the program, the problems, and his case files and concluded: "The final decision of the District of Utah, however, determined that none of the persons who had remained in the United States, and hence accessible for prosecution, would be required to render alternative service, thus exempting all Utah applicants from the Clemency Program."[12] Based on the lack of guidance in program administration and his assessment of the lack of justifiable decision criteria, Lockhart had decided that he could not recommend any cases as having prosecutive merit and requiring alternative service.

Lockhart's difficulties and his ultimate assessment of the clemency program exemplify the problems and opportunities that are presented when administrators are granted considerable authority and a great deal of discretion in exercising that authority. In his attempts to administer the program, Lockhart quickly saw that the same discretion that permitted him to be sensitive to the individual problems and circumstances of one person seeking clemency also allowed him, if he chose, to be arbitrary or abusive toward another. It is not always the case that administrators exhibit such self-awareness and concern for the double-edged nature of the discretion they exercise.

WHY IS ADMINISTRATIVE DISCRETION NECESSARY?

Administrative discretion is both necessary and, to some degree, desirable. It is necessary in part because, as scholars from Goodnow to Davis agree, it is not possible for a legislature to draft statutes clearly and specifically enough to dictate every action to be taken in the administration of a program at all points in the future.[13] Even if it were possible to draft extraordinarily specific legislation, it would be extremely difficult to get agreement in the legislature over all the minutiae in such a bill.[14] Jerome Frank once observed that those who argue for the elimination of all discretion by enactment of rigid statutes ignore the fundamental fact that administration is human behavior, and human behavior is not analogous to the operation of machinery.

> It is imperative that in a democracy it should never be forgotten that public office is, of necessity, held by mere men who have human frailties . . . . To pretend, then, that government, in any of its phases, is a machine; that it is not a human affair; that the language of statutes—if only they are adequately worded—plus appeals to the upper courts, will alone do away with the effect of human weaknesses in government is to worship illusion. And it is a dangerous illusion . . . .
>
> Yet curiously, it often happens that the very men who one day stress that truth [that public officers are human], the next day help to obscure it, by distorting the real truth contained in the phrase "a government of laws, and not of men." As a consequence, sometimes, hypnotized by those words, we picture as an existing reality—or at least as a completely achievable ideal— a government so contrived that it matters not at all what men, at any given moment, constitute government. Such an idea is a narcotic. It is bad medicine. It does not protect us from bad government. On the contrary, it invites bad government.[15]

In addition to the structural and behavioral reasons why discretion is necessary, there are functional arguments. A primary reason for the rise in administrative activity was the desire to improve the effectiveness and efficiency of administration through increased flexibility in management of administrative problems.[16] Therefore, it is important to remember that "flexibility, especially at early stages in an agency's development of its program, may facilitate the ultimate advancement of the legislative purpose, while standards and controls may tend to obscure . . . the purposes behind a statute."[17] Flexibility is needed both for management effectiveness and also to allow the law to evolve as agencies develop.[18] In fact, when the first Hoover Commission examined the problems of administering the government, one of its criticisms was not that government had excessive discretion, but that it was excessively rigid. "Many of the statutes and regulations that control the administrative practices and procedures of the Government are unduly detailed and rigid. It is impossible to secure enough authority and discretion to seize opportunities for economic and effective operations."[19]

Finally, administrative discretion is necessary because the technical expertise that is the basis for a good deal of administrative activity is constantly changing. Agency structures and authorizations that are not flexible enough to permit the agency or local government organization to keep pace are counterproductive.

On another level, discretion is desirable because it permits individualized consideration and treatment of those before an agency. As Freund put it: "The plausible argument in favor of administrative discretion is that it individualizes the exercise of public power over private interests, permitting its adjustment to varying circumstances and avoiding an undesirable standardization of restraints, disqualifications, and particularity of requirements."[20] The demand for individualized attention, discussed in Chapter 8, is never ending. Eliminating the discretion to make individual assessments could wreak havoc on those who must deal with agencies. Judge J. Skelly Wright, in a review of Davis's *Discretionary Justice,* summarized his own and Davis's view on this point.

> This is not to say that he (Davis) argues for complete elimination of discretionary decisionmaking. He would not exchange Lewis Carroll's fantasy for Franz Kafka's nightmare. A tyranny of petty bureaucrats who lack power to change the rules even an iota in order to do justice is at least as bad as a tyranny of petty bureaucrats who make up the rules as they go along.[21]

Law and Administrative Discretion: In Search of the Optimum Combination

The fact that administrative discretion is necessary and relatively useful does not mean that the more discretion administrators have the better off we are. Lockhart's experience with the clemency program suggests a number of reasons why excessive discretion can be a problem. Recognizing the dangers, Davis observed: "Discretion is a tool when properly used; like an axe, it can be a weapon for mayhem or murder."[22] The language is a bit strong, but the point is well taken. There is no absolute positive or negative correlation between discretion and just and equitable decisions.

If one were to depict graphically the relationship between discretion and just decisionmaking, the ardent antibureaucratic position might be represented by straight line A in Figure 9.1. A more realistic presentation of the relationship is curved line B, which suggests that complete discretion and no discretion can both result in unfair, arbitrary, and inconsistent decisions. The curve indicates that there is some point at which adequate and appropriate discretion meets useful guidance by rules and standards to provide an optimum mix.

The relationship between discretion and flexibility to promote efficient administration can be similarly viewed. One of the major arguments for discretion is that it permits an agency to develop and apply its expertise in a flexible manner with a likelihood of more efficient administration than if the agency were required to operate in a rule-bound manner. Again, it is tempting to think in terms of a straight-line relationship; many administrators seem to think that the more discretion they have the more efficient they are likely to be. As a study conducted by Abraham Sofaer suggests, however, that assumption is wishful thinking.[23]

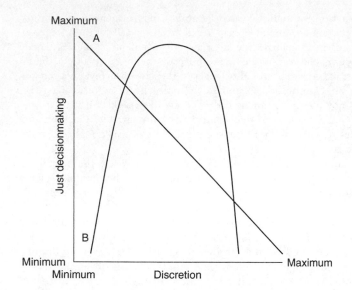

FIGURE 9.1 The Relationship of Discretion to Just Decisions

Sofaer studied what was then called the United States Immigration and Naturalization Service (INS), now known as Citizenship and Immigration Services since the reorganization that placed immigration into the Department of Homeland Security. The INS has historically held one of the broadest grants of discretion in its decisionmaking processes of any agency government at any level.[24] Sofaer examined cases involving so-called "change of status" requests in which resident aliens sought to have their status changed from temporary resident to permanent resident. The effect is the same as if the alien had obtained immigrant status from a U.S. embassy in the home country. Sofaer characterized the level of discretion in such proceedings as follows:

> Numerous discretionary decisions are made. The Examiner's initial determination to grant or deny an eligible alien's application on the basis of "discretion" is virtually ungoverned by standards. Several grounds for denying discretionary relief are identifiable; but adjudicators are given little guidance in applying them, and virtually no limits exist on their authority to decide any individual application one way or the other. The statutory prerequisites for eligibility incorporate many discretionary provisions that allow INS to waive ineligibility. In addition, aspects of the processes of administrative review and enforcement are highly discretionary.[25]

The results of the study did not support the argument that the more discretion is granted, the better administration will be.

> First, the evidence seemed to confirm the hypothesis that relatively undefined grounds of decision more frequently cause inconsistent results than well-defined grounds. We found that Examiners applied different standards in exercising discretion on the merits; that the Service's view of discretion has changed periodically; that extensive and successful political intervention on the merits strongly correlates with the presence of discretionary power; that official Service policy on the meaning of discretion permits inconsistent results; and that there are striking variations among INS districts in their rates of denial of section 245 cases that do not appear explainable in terms of the character of the districts involved. Many of the applications, initially denied, were granted on motions to reopen (by Examiners) or at deportation hearings (by SIO's [Special Inquiry Officers]). We found that, in cases where the facts had not changed upon "appeal," denials based on relatively undefined "discretionary" grounds were far more

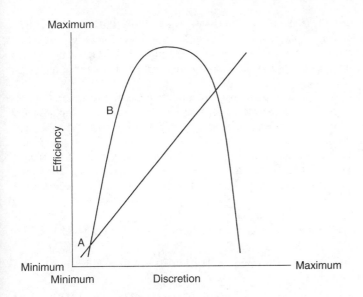

FIGURE 9.2 The Relationship of Efficiency to Discretion

frequently reversed than denials based on the relatively well-defined "statutory" grounds, Moreover, this correlation resulted from inconsistent decision making, rather than from any other cause. Examiner reversals of discretionary decisions on the same record were over-whelmingly due to political intervention . . . .

On the other hand, the evidence seemed to refute the hypothesis that discretion results in less costly, speedier administration . . . . The presence of discretionary power seemed throughout the administrative process, disproportionately to attract political intervention. Intervention on the merits of the denied applications we studied took place exclusively in connection with denials based on discretion . . . . Significantly, "appeals" of denials based on discretionary grounds were relatively more frequent than "appeals" of denials based on the more well defined statutory grounds. Discretionary power to "reverse" decisions and to delay or suspend enforcement led to changed results in 55% of the random sample denials we examined; most of the other cases were either pending or involved aliens who departed the United States voluntarily.[26]

As was true of the discretion-to-justice relationship, the discretion-to-efficiency relationship is better represented by a curve rather than a straight line (see Figure 9.2). From his examination of the INS, which operates at the high-discretion end of the spectrum, Sofaer concluded: "Broad discretion in adjudication and enforcement at INS causes inconsistency, arbitrariness, and inefficiency."[27] The task of the administrator in any given situation is to operate as close to the optimum portion of the curve as possible.

The story of INS since Sofaer's critical analysis would not lead one to change from the conclusions that he reached. The tendency of an agency with such broad discretion to attract political intervention has been a continuing problem. Beyond that obvious difficulty, signals from the public that they ought to take a hard approach to their decisions and a lack of regular oversight and accountability reinforce the tendency toward abuse. The reaction of Congress, even in face of occasional revelations of abuse, has ironically been to increase the discretion of the agency in key areas in large part because the issue of immigration continues to be a hot-button issue with many of their constituents.

While one of the most commonly mentioned immigration issues of the past two decades has been illegal immigration, one of the most important has been the way the nation responds to refugees seeking asylum. The warnings of things to come emerged during the late 1970s when the United States adopted an approach in which applicants for asylum from Cuba were essentially automatically accepted while refugees from Haiti found it nearly impossible to qualify. Given the regime in Haiti, the claims of many refugees that they faced "a well founded fear of persecution" (the legal requirement for asylum) if they were returned to their home country were at least as credible as the arguments by Cubans seeking admission to the United States. The difference was that U.S. policy opposed the Cuban regime and supported Haiti's ruler.

During the 1980s, the United States was an active participant in conflict in Central America.[28] The United States supported right-wing regimes in El Salvador, Guatemala, and Honduras and just as actively supplied and supported the "Contra" insurgents in their attempt to overturn the Sandinista government in Nicaragua. In the process, the United States violated the neutrality of such longtime friends as Costa Rica and engaged in a range of nefarious activities to support the Contras, including the now infamous Iran/Contra affair in which U.S. weapons were promised in exchange for assistance in money laundering in the effort to get resources to the Contras.[29] The Special Counsel investigating Iran/Contra found that:

- the sale of arms to Iran contravened United States Government policy and may have violated the Arms Export Control Act;

- the provision and coordination of support to the contras violated the Boland Amendment ban on aid to military activities in Nicaragua;

- the policies behind both the Iran and contra operations were fully reviewed and developed at the highest levels of the Reagan Administration;

- although there was little evidence of National Security Council level knowledge of most of the actual contra-support operations, there was no evidence than any NSC member dissented from the underlying policy—keeping the contras alive despite congressional limitations on contra support;

- the Iran operations were carried out with the knowledge of, among others, President Ronald Reagan, Vice President George Bush, Secretary of Defense Caspar W. Weinberger, Director of Central Intelligence William J. Casey, and national security advisers Robert C. McFarlane and John M. Poindexter; of these officials, only Weinberger and Shultz dissented from the policy decision, and Weinberger eventually acquiesced by ordering the Department of Defense to provide the necessary arms; and

- large volumes of highly relevant, contemporaneously created documents were systematically and willfully withheld from investigation by several Reagan Administration officials.

- Following the revelation of these operations in October and November 1986, Reagan Administration officials deliberately deceived the Congress and the public about the level and extent of official knowledge of and support for these operations.[30]

The devastation in Central America with the war itself and the terror of death squads sent hundreds of thousands of refugees into exile. When they arrived in the United States, it became increasingly clear that the broad discretion of the INS was being used to treat asylum seekers from Nicaragua positively, but to systematically exclude applicants from El Salvador and Guatemala.[31] The Senate Judiciary Committee concluded in 1987 that "an estimated 62,000 innocent civilians have been killed since the start of the current civil war in El Salvador."[32] Even so, "In the first half of FY 1987, the Immigration and Naturalization Service granted asylum to 3 percent of those Salvadoran asylum applications adjudicated and 88 percent of those by Nicaraguans."[33] During this same period, it was later determined, applicants from Poland and Iran were being approved at rates of 49 percent and 66 percent respectively, even though there was no evidence of the kind of systematic assassination of civilians evident in the Salvadoran or, for that matter, Guatemalan cases.[34] Eventually the claim of arbitrary and discriminatory decisionmaking made its way to federal court where it was obvious that the abuses would become clear. In the face of that, the U.S. government entered into a consent decree in the case of *American Baptist Churches v. Thornburgh*,[35] effectively admitting the discrimination and agreeing to reconsider virtually all Salvadoran and Guatemalan asylum applicants during the period. In the process, the government recognized that:

> ...foreign policy and border enforcement considerations are not relevant to the determination of whether an applicant for asylum has a well-founded fear of prosecution; the fact than an individual is from a country whose government the United States supports or with which it has favorable relations is not relevant to the determination of whether an application for asylum has a well-founded fear of persecution; whether or not the United States Government agrees with the political or ideological beliefs of the individual is not relevant to the determination of whether an applicant for asylum has a well-founded fear of persecution....[36]

At the time, the INS plainly did not have the personnel to provide all of the required hearings and other processes, leaving many applicants at risk for having identified themselves but unlikely to be able to get a final resolution of their cases during the required period. When the impossible nature of this situation became clear, the government tacitly admitted that there would be ten of thousands of asylum seekers utterly adrift in the United States, caught between undocumented status and the inability of the government to make up for what had admittedly been an arbitrary, discriminatory, and illegal use of discretion in the first instance.

Ironically, with all of these recognitions of abuse of discretion in the asylum determination process and despite the recognition of the inadequate resources of the INS, pressure was increased on the INS to deal with expanded border control processes and programs aimed at seeking out and excluding illegal immigrants. The additional irony was that the evidence of abuses did not result in a limitation of INS discretion, a move that would in fact have been a kind of protection for the agency against the continuing pattern of political intervention, but instead became part of a change in immigration process in 1996 that gave the agency even more discretion than before.[37] The INS agents at entry points were granted by this legislation authority to conduct what are termed expedited removals with very limited review available from those decisions.[38]

Then came September 11, 2001, and with it a raft of draconian measures related to both immigration and asylum, some of which have been detailed in earlier chapters (see for example Chapter 6 on closed INS hearings). The Justice Department began making deliberate and routine use of the most technical violations of the now extraordinarily complex immigration laws as the basis for deportation, exclusion, or to detain and hold persons for extended periods in lieu of making substantive charges for terrorist activities or any other criminal offense.[39] Congress pushed the situation still further by expanding discretionary authority for the agency,[40] now part of the Department of Homeland Security, when it passed legislation known as the Real ID Act. In the process, the new legislation exempted some of the increased discretionary authority from provisions of the APA and from standard judicial review practices.

Another agency that was traditionally granted wide discretion was the Internal Revenue Service. Here again, during hearings held in 1997 and 1998, it became clear that the broad discretion granted to the agency had produced neither efficiency nor justice. In fact, the numerous stories of abuse of discretion led to significant changes in the agency as well as creation of outside oversight mechanisms intended to block such behavior in the future.

TYPES OF DISCRETIONARY DECISIONS

Recognizing the ambiguity in the nature and purposes of discretionary administration, let us turn more specifically to the types and sources of discretion. For analytical and practical purposes, it is possible to classify discretionary decisions into three general types: substantive, procedural, and complex. A substantive discretionary determination is a decision in which the administrator by discretion determines a right, duty, or obligation, or promulgates a rule on particular questions of policy. Lockhart had the substantive discretion to determine whether any individual on whom he was holding a draft evader case file would be required to render alternative service and for what length of time up to two years.

A procedural discretionary decision is selection of a procedure to be used to gather facts or make policy decisions. Agency enabling acts and state or federal administrative procedures acts mandate a variety of processes, but administrators may nevertheless exercise considerable discretion on the means they use to deal with a problem. For example, an agency may elect to develop information by the use of consultants, through staff investigations, or hearings of varying types and levels of formality.

Finally, a complex discretionary decision is both substantive and procedural. For example, an administrator may opt for an information-gathering technique that will bias the substantive decision—such as when a regulatory agency seeks information and advice primarily from task forces made up predominantly of representatives of the regulated industry.[41] One of the most important and least understood complex discretionary decisions is the decision "not to decide or not to act at this time."[42] A serious problem in government is, on the one hand, to discourage administrators from inflicting harm through excessively zealous administration, and on the other, to get administrators to pursue their tasks aggressively. A decision not to act may mean that an agency will not adopt a fact-finding process to better understand a controversy and that the agency's current policy is to maintain the status quo. These are not neutral or trivial decisions.

Lockhart was making a complex discretionary decision when he established an informal set of criteria for determining whether to recommend any of his pending cases for alternative service. His assessment of the proper action to take was based upon an analysis of the operational weaknesses involved in implementing the clemency program and on consideration of the strengths and weaknesses of the case files. The decision rules he adopted and the procedure he used to establish them constituted a complex discretionary determination. In this situation, the result was that none of those who might have been confronted with alternative service or prosecution had to face those options.

SOURCES OF DISCRETIONARY AUTHORITY

The characteristics of discretionary decisionmaking and the limits on it are to some extent functions of the sources from which the authority to exercise discretion emanates. Some of the more common of these sources are: (1) broad legislative or executive delegations of authority to administrators; (2) expertise in a particular field; (3) experience in a specific area of activity; (4) political support from groups and individuals both in and out of government; (5) the intergovernmental factor; (6) the move to entrepreneurial government; and (7) emergency conditions.

Broad Delegations of Authority

For several reasons, some of which were noted earlier, legislatures frequently draft statutes containing language that is relatively vague or open to rather wide interpretation. Some of the worst of these statutes were referred to by some commentators as "skeleton legislation."[43] Such legislative delegations of authority to administrative agencies provide the most basic source of discretion.

> First, the legislature may endow an agency with plenary responsibilities in an area and plainly indicate that within that area its range of choice is entirely free. Second, the legislature may issue directives that are intended to control the agency's choice among alternatives but that, because of their generality, ambiguity, or vagueness, do not clearly determine choices in particular cases.[44]

According to Freund:

> A statute confers discretion when it refers an official for the use of his powers to beliefs, expectations, or tendencies instead of facts, or to such terms as "adequate," "advisable," "appropriate," "beneficial" ... "competent," "convenient," "detrimental," "expedient," "equitable," "fair," "fit," "necessary," "practicable," "proper," "reasonable," "reputable," "safe," "sufficient," "wholesome," or their opposites.[45]

Judge Henry J. Friendly listed other commonly used statutory terms that, either accidentally or by design, confer discretion on administrators:

> There are numerous examples; just and reasonable rates, undue preference or prejudice, public convenience and necessity, discrimination in membership in a labor organization, bargaining in good faith, unfair methods of competition, are a sufficient sampling.[46]

There are indications that legislatures, and particularly the U.S. Congress, are attempting to draw statutory language more tightly to limit delegation of broad discretionary authority to executive agencies.[47] Even assuming that legislators understand the need for precision, significant factors remain that limit their ability to draft such legislation.[48] For example, state legislators rarely have the time and staff support necessary to develop detailed knowledge in special areas of administration.

The literature on administrative law seldom acknowledges the fact, but broad grants of authority from the chief executive are also important sources of discretion. The clemency program for draft evaders created by President Ford through an executive order, discussed earlier, is a prime example. Another important executive delegation was President Johnson's affirmative action in contracting program (later called the Philadelphia Plan), also created by an executive order.[49] More recent examples include executive orders issued by presidents Reagan and Clinton on regulatory activity, discussed in Chapter 5, which vested considerable authority in the Office of Management and Budget to block rules proposed by various executive agencies. In addition to executive orders, presidents have employed presidential memoranda, national security directives, and presidential signing statements, among other devices, to issue orders and delegate discretion to administrators.[50]

Expertise and Discretion

One of the most important sources of administrative discretion is a *de facto* matter rather than a black letter law authority. It is the expertise (or "expertness"—both terms are employed in the literature of administrative law) that administrators possess in a particular field. Years before administrators were concerned with worker exposure to asbestos or disposal of nuclear and toxic chemical wastes, observers of the changing administrative environment noted: "The administration of general legislation by technical experts, skilled and trained in specialized fields, is 'the contemporary answer to the challenge to bridge the gap between popular government and scientific government.'"[51] Scientific and technological knowledge confers a certain amount of authority on those who have it.[52] Agencies that have developed research staffs have learned where to find technical information in the government and how to use outside consultants to have more flexibility and options in decisionmaking.

While agency claims to expertise will continue to be an important source of discretionary authority, the administrative environment has become more complex in recent years. Particularly in the regulatory area, claims to expertise by administrative agencies are now, and will continue to be, regularly challenged. In a sense, this willingness to challenge agency claims to expertise has long been with us. In the early years of the Environmental Protection Agency (EPA), agency rules and enforcement actions frequently met with challenges from regulated industries and environmental groups. In one case, environmental groups argued that administrative judgments about the danger of some pesticides were arbitrary because they ignored a significant body of scientific evidence.[53] In another now-famous case, automotive manufacturers challenged an EPA determination that it was technologically feasible for the manufacturers to meet Clean Air Act standards even though a National Academy of Sciences report raised serious doubts about their capabilities.[54]

At that point, it seemed clear that: (1) agencies needed to develop a respectable level of expertness in their field to have any flexibility or effectiveness; and (2) beyond that threshold level, superior expertise by administrators in their field relative to other actors in the administrative process promises increased discretionary authority. However, many agencies have suffered cutbacks in resources as well as challenges from political appointees chosen to rein in regulators. Moreover, the competition to hire scientists and technical professionals has become intense and government has often lost out in that contest. In this kind of setting, it was not surprising that agencies such as the EPA found themselves hiring, for example, a host of young engineers just out of school. These engineers gained valuable training and experience with the agency in such areas as cleanup efforts on abandoned toxic waste sites under the Superfund program, only to then take positions at major firms with great improvements in salary and working conditions.

Another result of these dynamics is that agencies frequently contract for expertise. In such a setting, agency claims that it is a repository of knowledge are more difficult to sustain and others are less willing simply to grant the agency discretion. Additionally, there have been a number of high visibility cases in which agencies either refused to provide the bases for their conclusion or were found to have had political interference with expert judgments within the agency, such as forced changes in congressional testimony. These issues will be discussed further in Chapter 10.

It is still true that expertise is an important basis for discretion and, as Chapter 7 explained, judges are to start with a presumption in favor of agency claims. However, it is more accurate to start from the premise that agencies derive discretion if and when they can claim special types of comparatively greater amounts of expertise than their challengers and where they have well-established reputations for professional independence from political interference.

The Experience Factor

Discussions of administrative "expertise" often mask the important difference in the quality of administration between expertness and experience. As Chapter 8 explained in the discussion of key factors in the decision environment, one may have a great deal of technical knowledge, yet no experience in the use of that knowledge. The experienced administrator, according to Gellhorn, usually has a sense of the continuity of agency activity and is sensitive to the impact of agency decisions on those before the agency.[55] Experience, like technical expertise, indirectly affords administrators discretion in judgment; it permits flexibility because it enables an administrator to understand what is workable as well as what may objectively be correct. Experience also enables an administrator to assess the political costs that may arise from a particular course of action.

Political Support from Groups and Individuals
Both In and Out of Government

Another *de facto* source of administrative discretion is the political support for its action that an agency can marshal from other levels and units within government, or from clientele groups outside the government.[56] When agencies take major actions, initiatives that affect more than just a small number of single-shot players, they attract political support or opposition from groups and organizations that perceive themselves to be helped or injured. Examples of agency options altered by the vagaries of changing patterns of political support include the experiences of the Defense Department (DOD) and the Federal Trade Commission (FTC).

Support for DOD initiatives has, of course, fluctuated with changes in public opinion. Sentiment against the Vietnam War during the early 1970s translated into relatively low levels of support for DOD plans and projects. Since then, however, the DOD has enjoyed a resurgence of support in public opinion and in the legislative arena. More specifically, the Defense Department has enjoyed some independence, quite apart from general public opinion, because of its ability to mobilize political support in important constituencies. Relationships between DOD and defense production and research and development industries is one source of such support. Thus, for example, the televised presentation of U.S. air attacks on Iraqi targets in the first Gulf War provided support for continued development of expensive sophisticated weapons systems even in a time of general efforts to cutback overall defense spending. The closing of a major defense installation or the loss of jobs dependent on government contracts can mobilize constituent groups quickly.[57] In fact, the base-closure efforts of the 1990s were so volatile that a special process was created, based upon appointment of a commission to recommend base closures in such a way that members of Congress could individually vote to support bases in their districts even though they knew that the process would result in their closure in the end. Another round of base-closing efforts even under the new policy saw DOD recommendation lose to the political efforts of a number of states and communities during 2005.

The Federal Trade Commission's ability to exercise options has varied considerably over the years. A. Lee Fritschler and James M. Hoefler's well-known case study, *Smoking and Politics: Policy Making and the Federal Bureaucracy,*[58] shows how the FTC was able to build support in other units of government for its attempt to limit cigarette advertising. But Fritschler also noted the opposition engendered by the FTC antismoking effort. Later, the FTC found itself embroiled in major political controversies over its attempt to regulate advertising directed at small children and the merchandising activities of the funeral industry. In 1980, the opponents of the commission secured passage of the Federal Trade Commission Improvement Act, which specifically limited FTC action in some areas and reduced agency discretion by including a legislative veto option for Congress.[59] Since then, during an extended period of deregulation and declining pressure for strong enforcement efforts, the agency has faded as a key player relative to others.

The Intergovernmental Factor

One of the other factors affecting relative levels of discretion is the changing character of intergovernmental relations (an issue that will be addressed in greater detail in Chapter 10). The increasing reliance on state or local governments to carry out federal policies in most policy fields has meant a continuing debate over which administrators at which level should possess what types and amounts of discretion. On the one hand, the fact that state or local agencies sometimes operate with both federal and state authority behind them in the environment or safety fields, for example, clearly means that those administrators can exercise substantial discretion. And to that base of discretionary authority are added the claims made by state or local officials to have special expertise as to how these policies look in their particular jurisdiction. However, there are two key limiting factors.

First, there is often a tension between federal agencies and their state or local counterparts as to just how much discretion is retained by the federal government. This often takes the form of an argument about how much of the field has been preempted by congressional legislation or federal regulations.[60] And even if the Washington (or federal regional) offices do not contest discretion exercised by state or local agencies, regulated organizations may bring that kind of challenge on grounds that state or local action violates the commerce clause of Article I, Section 8 of the Constitution by placing burdens on or discriminating against interstate commerce.[61] Similarly, states are often in tension with local governments with respect to just who possesses what authority and what discretion in its use.[62] Second, there is the problem of the unfunded mandate discussed in earlier chapters. If states or localities are overloaded by delegations of authority and responsibility without adequate resources, they are often unable to effectively exercise discretion.

Notwithstanding these limiting factors, the dynamics of contemporary intergovernmental relations provide sources of administrative discretion for state and local governments. At the local level, that is particularly true if the community is located in a home rule state in which local governments have general ordinance authority.

The Move to Entrepreneurial Government

Finally, the contemporary movement toward entrepreneurial government has sought to provide additional discretion to public managers. There are at least three themes that call for greater administrative discretion within what is sometimes referred to as the new public management or reinventing government. They include the customer orientation, the "competition prescription," and contracting out.

As Chapter 4 explained, the Clinton administration's National Performance Review took as a point of departure the idea that:

> The federal government is filled with good people trapped in bad systems.... When we blame the people and impose more controls, we make the system worse.... We assume that we can't trust employees to make decisions, so we spell out in precise detail how they must do virtually everything, then audit them to ensure that they have obeyed every rule.[63]

Then, borrowing from Osborne and Gaebler's *Reinventing Government* and the private sector Total Quality Management literature, the NPR called upon government to view those who come to agencies for action as customers.[64] The problem with this lack of discretion based on a view of government as rife with fraud abuse and waste is that it produces poor customer service. "The result is a culture of fear and resignation. To survive, employees keep a low profile. They decide that the safest answer in any given situation is a firm 'maybe.' They follow the rules, pass the buck, and keep their heads down."[65]

The response was an attempt to "create a culture of public entrepreneurship."[66] One of the key ways to achieve that culture was the call by the NPR to the effect that: "Put simply, all federal agencies will delegate, decentralize, and empower employees to make decisions. This will let front-line and front-office workers use their creative judgments as they offer service to customers and solve problems."[67]

Another of the core assumptions of the entrepreneurial approach is that government ought to make constructive use of the dynamics of the marketplace to achieve better performance and greater efficiency, something Donald Kettl has referred to as "the competition prescription."[68] This concept serves as a support for discretion for two reasons. First, it argues that there needs to be sufficient flexibility in how modes of implementation and service delivery are selected to take advantage of competition, both among units of government and between government and private sector organizations. Second, in order to compete, public managers must have sufficient flexibility to innovate for greater efficiency and effectiveness and in order to make rapid changes in response to evolving market trends.

Of course, the expanded use of contracting out of services and program management is related to the market dynamic, but is even broader in scope. On the one hand, the assumption is that for-profit or not-for-profit organizations can save money in large part because they are not freighted with the kind of constraints under which government organizations operate and also because large amounts of work are shed by those agencies to be accomplished by the contractor. What that means, however, is that often the agencies are in truth delegating large amounts of discretion to the contractor. Thus, contracting out supports expansion of administrative discretion, but within the contractor as compared to the agency. In fact, for reasons that are discussed elsewhere in this volume, government agencies often lose discretion to the contractor while a contract is in force. Put in its most favorable light, contractors become partners in administrative discretion.

Emergencies as Sources of Discretion

Recent events have underscored the long-standing practice of conferring on chief executives and administrative agencies large amounts of discretion to deal with emergencies such as wars or natural disasters.

The dramatic grants of discretion to the president and administrative agencies in the wake of the September 11, 2001, attacks provide an obvious example. Wars and other international emergencies have often triggered broad delegations of discretion. In most instances, the Congress has quickly passed something like a war powers act that granted broad discretion to the president and ratified actions that may have been taken to meet the emergency conditions before the legislation was enacted. In the post-9/11 context, Congress quickly enacted a use of force resolution, the USA Patriot Act, and, later, the Homeland Security Act, along with massive defense spending bills, containing wide-ranging discretion as well as appropriations and supplemental spending bills. These pieces of legislation not only used broad language in granting discretion, but contained many exemptions from contracting and administrative procedure requirements that are otherwise applicable to administrative agencies.

These grants of discretion are not limited to federal officials. One need only consider the range of actions at the state and city level in New York following the 9/11 attacks. Some who were unaware that mayors in some strong-mayor cities can issue executive orders learned quickly from Mayor Rudolph W. Giuliani's orders that such authority exists. Governors and mayors, in turn, often subdelegate considerable discretion to members of their senior managers team, and so on. More recently, New York's Governor George E. Pitaki responded to the terrorist attack on the London transport system in 2005 by issuing an executive order authorizing increased discretion for Connecticut and New Jersey law enforcement officers to take actions with respect to the New York commuter transport systems.[69]

Hurricane Katrina provides an example not only of broad grants of discretion but also demands by the public and legislators that elected executives and agency officials use their discretion to the maximum to meet emergency conditions arising from natural disasters. Louisiana governor Kathleen Blanco issued executive orders lifting a variety of standard limitations on the discretion of both state and local officials following the disastrous hurricane and the system failures that became so obvious in its aftermath. Indeed, after issuing Proclamation 48 KBB 2005, declaring an emergency for the hurricane, she issued 77 executive orders between August 26 and December 20, 2005, dealing with the storm and its impact, suspending a wide variety of otherwise applicable legal constraints on officials at all levels.[70]

The fact that emergency situations produce expanded administrative discretion appears intuitively obvious. One might assume that legislatures would, of course, sanction expanded executive discretion as needed to address particular situations and that authority would then be terminated once the emergency had passed. However, the situation is more complex than it first appears.

First, many executives are happy to have executive support but are quite willing to assert that they have inherent discretionary authority to address such situations that derives from the Constitution (federal or state) or the city charter at the local government level and gives them sufficient powers above and beyond whatever a legislature may support. Hence, the Bush administration has asserted that it had constitutional power to authorize domestic surveillance whether the Foreign Intelligence Surveillance Act or the congressional use of force resolution provided for it or not.[71]

Second, the fact that legislatures are willing to pass broad legislation quickly to support discretionary authority in emergency situations, without the usual committee examination and detailed legislative debates that are standard procedures, makes it tempting for the executive to press for wider powers than those specifically associated with the particular problems presented by an emergency. For example, the White House was able to get a section on human capital management inserted into the Homeland Security Act which applies to all executive branch agencies and was also able to have the Department of Homeland Security and the Defense Department exempted from the standard civil service system. These agencies were allowed to create their own human resources systems (which have since been developed), with the idea that these would be opening wedges to dramatically change all executive branch agency HR systems.[72] While the language of the special HR system discussion was framed in terms of the special needs of DHS and DOD for systems responsive to flexibility and management discretion, the generally applicable provisions when read in light of the President's Management Agenda (discussed in Chapter 4) make clear that this was a wedge opportunity rather than something specifically required by the emergency.

Third, it has historically been the case that emergency discretion often does not end when most observers consider that the specific conditions have changed, and indeed, emergency powers have emerged years later in surprising circumstances. The Supreme Court has held, for example, that war-related emergency powers do not necessarily end when a peace treaty is signed, arguing that the effects of the war can linger for some time thereafter.[73] Further, the step of suspending provisions of law such as contracting requirements—frequently suspended in emergencies—often leaves in its wake a host of problems that must be addressed after the emergency conditions have passed.

Beyond these factors, it is surprising to many Americans to realize that the United States has operated under a state of emergency for many years at a time—in fact, continuously from 1933 to 1976—which is why Congress ultimately enacted the National Emergencies Act (NEA) to end emergency declarations automatically after two years.[74] Even so, it has been common for presidents simply to issue a renewed declaration of emergency for situations that are reaching the two-year limit imposed by the NEA. Finally, for the reasons indicated in the discussion of emergency rulemaking in Chapter 5, it is tempting for governors or presidents to claim emergency conditions that demand expanded discretion in circumstances that may not really warrant that action.

CONFLICTING VALUES AND PERCEPTIONS ON ADMINISTRATIVE DISCRETION

Whatever its source, administrative discretion is often understood and addressed by different people in very different ways. Various actors in the administrative justice system operate from different sets of values, acquired during the professional development process. Administrators and judicial officials (both lawyers and judges) share many values—for example, the importance of the democratic process and the principle of the rule of law—but their priorities are often quite different. And when officials with differing values or priorities approach basic problems (such as how to provide administrators sufficient discretion to accomplish the manifold purposes for which their agencies were created, and at the same time ensure against arbitrariness and abuse of discretion), the value conflicts can and do have important consequences. To understand how administrative discretion is used and how abuses are checked, it is important to be aware of the value conflicts between administratively oriented officials and those with legal orientations.

Administrative Imperatives: Expertise, Flexibility, and Efficiency

In tracing the history of public administration, one soon comes across the scholarly debates over whether the field of public administration should be dominated by managerial rather than legalistic values. This extremely important and long-standing dispute had significant consequences for the training, thought, and practice of public administrators. When Frank Goodnow, often referred to as the father of modern public administration, dealt with the problem of ensuring adequate discretion while protecting against abuses, he established a set of priorities.[75] The first interest was governmental efficiency, then the preservation of individual rights and liberties, and, finally, the promotion of social welfare.[76] It is not surprising that someone writing in the early years of the twentieth century focused on administrative expertise and efficiency as the goal of administrative activity. It was the age of the efficiency expert, when Taylorism was popular and the industrial managers of large enterprises were applauded for their skills. Nor is it surprising that lawyers and judicial scholars such as Elihu Root and John Dickinson, writing during this same period, were so adamant in insisting that protection of individual rights was prior to efficiency and managerial values.[77]

That tension was carried over to the newly developing academic and professional field of public administration. Leonard D. White, in his famous text *Introduction to the Study of Public Administration,* called for the public administration community to turn from the emphasis on legal aspects of the field to the managerial aspects. He asserted that "the study of administration should start from the base of management rather than the foundation of law."[78] His admonition was taken so seriously that in 1968 Dwight Waldo observed that it was his "opinion that we now suffer from lack of attention to constitutional-legal matters. Our early anti-legal and anti-lawyer bias is understandable and forgivable, but it is dangerously obsolete and self-defeating."[79]

At some point, one can observe the argument over priorities changing to a new kind of relationship between legal officers and administrators. Several factors suggest that administrators may consider, or be tempted to consider, judicial review and other legal aspects of administration as unfortunate and unwise constraints on administrative discretion. First, very few administration programs require the study of legal aspects of administration, and in fewer programs still are such courses taught by faculty whose primary area of research is law and administration. Second, an emphasis on management technique may lead an administrator to conclude that anything that constrains his or her flexibility to select management options is to be dealt with if necessary, to be avoided if possible. Sofaer's study of the Immigration and Naturalization Service, discussed earlier, provides an example.

One of the least painful alternatives for the administrator is to make rules governing his or her own conduct. In 1971, the Administrative Conference of the United States recommended that the INS publish rules as to how it intended to exercise its discretion. The rules would, of course, be subject to change as the agency saw fit, but they would give those who must deal with the INS some idea how the agency would interact with them. The INS chose to respond to the Administrative Conference request by memorandum. Sofaer commented:

> The Service's official response to the Conference recommendation is hardly calculated to cause me to pause before accepting the need for mandatory rulemaking. Its comments, in total, consisted of these three sentences: "Exercise of discretion inherently requires flexibility in assessing diverse factual patterns. Decisions must necessarily be made on a case by case basis utilizing criteria set forth in published precedents. Formulation of standards for the exercising of discretion is self-defeating since standards would impair flexibility."[80]

The argument that greater discretion allows increased flexibility to take advantage of management opportunities, which will increase agency effectiveness and result in the most efficient performance of the people's business, is intuitively satisfying, but it does not come to grips with the legal and political elements of the modern administrative environment. This approach to administration lends itself to an impatient if not openly hostile view, toward the relationship between courts and agencies.

Administrators with a strong antilegal and promanagement penchant may fail to bring agency counsel into decision processes until too late, and then only with the expectation that the lawyers will ward off perceived challenges to the agency. Some lawyers sense that there is an unwritten law of administration: attorneys should not be called in until the administrator is in so much difficulty that it is too late to do anything about the situation. If an administrator does adopt the posture that judicial interactions with his or her agency are threatening or hostile and not justifiable in terms of management effectiveness, the instructions to agency attorneys may be to employ technical defenses against appeal or any other ethically acceptable devices to win for the agency. Kenneth Culp Davis has suggested that winning through discouraging full judicial review of agency actions is not necessarily supportive of the overall purpose of the agency:

> The needed escape, I think, has to be from the tendency of government lawyers, like any other lawyers, to use all available tricks to win for their client. That government lawyers use all legal ethical means to win their cases is, of course, only natural. But I think they can and should rise to a slightly higher degree of sophistication. Uncle Sam is not an ordinary client. Uncle Sam always wins when justice is done. This means that he may lose when judgment is entered for him, and he may win when judgment is entered against him. That this is so is not merely an idealist's dream but a hard-headed reality. It has *sometimes* been the basis on which government lawyers have exercised their important discretionary power [emphasis in original].[81]

Finally, some administrators respond to the possibility of interaction with legal actors with anxiety as well as annoyance. Whether from lack of knowledge of judicial/administrative interactions or from horror stories (apocryphal or real) about judicial interference in agency activity, many administrators' efforts are hampered by the fear of becoming embroiled in a lawsuit. Taken far enough, such anxiety can lead to the kind of paralysis about which the National Performance Review complained, in which the administrator is afraid to depart in any way from proven standard operating procedures.

In sum, the perspectives that administrators have of judicial actors, institutions, and values affect how they perceive and use their discretion. If the legal actors and elements in the administrative environment are believed to be opponents of the managers, dysfunctional types of administrative behavior may result. Values and perceptions are, of course, also important to judicial actors.

Judicial Imperatives: Due Process, Equal Protection, and Substantial Justice

If the watchwords of public administration are expertise, flexibility, and efficiency, the terms that guide the judiciary in reviewing governmental actions have traditionally been protection of the concept of due process of law, prevention of violations of equal protection of the laws, and general concern that government actions ought to be characterized by substantial justice or fundamental fairness. Two recurring themes in post–New Deal judicial opinions and articles by members of the judiciary are important to an understanding of administrative discretion. First, the judges sitting in various courts have found it difficult to define the role of the courts in reviewing administrative actions. Second, although judges recognize the need for judicial deference to administrative initiatives, they have been uncomfortable with the argument that administrative expertise, flexibility, and efficiency are always adequate to justify broad discretionary action. These concerns about the loss of core legal norms to contemporary political and administrative tensions remain even though some members of the U.S. Supreme Court and U.S. Circuit Courts of Appeals have sought to afford administrators greater discretion with less procedural constraints than has been the case in many years.

Toward the end of the New Deal, momentum grew in the judiciary to support administrative exercises of discretion. At the same time, however, there was a countertrend based on growing fear of administrative arbitrariness.[82] In the Supreme Court, these divergent themes emerge rather clearly, with the majority most often holding in support of administrative expertise and experience and the dissenters warning of "administrative authoritarianism."[83] For example, in *Securities and Exchange Commission v. Chenery,* a classic case defining the nature of judicial review of administrative action decided just at the time of the enactment of the APA, the Court stated:

> The scope of our review of an administrative order wherein a new principle is announced and applied is no different from that which pertains to ordinary administrative action. The wisdom of the principle adopted is none of our concern . . . . Our duty is at an end when it becomes evident that the Commission's action is based upon substantial evidence and is consistent with the authority granted by Congress . . . . The facts being undisputed, we are not free to disturb the Commission's judgment save where it has plainly abused its discretion in these matters . . . .
>
> The Commission's conclusion here rests squarely in that area where administrative judgments are entitled to the greatest amount of weight by the appellate courts. It is the product of administrative experience, appreciation of the complexities of the problem, realization of the statutory policies, and responsible treatment of the uncontested facts. It is the type of judgment which administrative agencies are best equipped to make and which justifies the use of the administrative process . . . . Whether we agree or disagree with the results reached, it is an allowable judgment which we cannot disturb.[84]

The basis for deference was the Court's acceptance of the need for flexibility for an agency to exercise its capacity in the public interest. But not everyone was convinced. Dissenting in *Chenery,* Justice Jackson wrote:

I suggest that administrative experience is of weight in judicial review only to this point—it is a persuasive reason for deference to the Commission in the exercise of its discretionary powers under and within the law. It cannot be invoked to support action outside the law. And what action is and what is not within the law must be determined by the courts, when authorized to review, no matter how much deference is due to the agencies' fact finding. Surely an administrative agency is not a law unto itself, but the Court does not really face up to the fact that this is the justification it is offering for sustaining the Commission action.[85]

By the time of the decision in *Universal Camera Corporation v. National Labor Relations Board,* the APA had come into its own.[86] The Court was busy applying the new statute and working out its own role in the administrative justice system:

Our power to review the correctness of application of the present standard ought seldom to be called into action. Whether on the record as a whole there is substantial evidence to support agency findings is a question which Congress has placed in the keeping of the Courts of Appeals. This Court will intervene only in what ought to be the rare instance when the standard appears to have been misapprehended or grossly misapplied.[87]

The Court was insisting that courts should not be in the business of judging the wisdom of agency decisions. They were to defer to the expertise of the administrator as long as the decision itself was within the legal power granted to the agency and as long as there was substantial evidence in the record as a whole to support the decision.

However, the more that deference to agency discretion was granted, the more fear grew that broad grants of power would inevitably lead to arbitrariness. Justice Douglas, who had himself spent a considerable time on the SEC, wrote:

Unless we make the requirements for administrative action strict and demanding expertise, the strength of modern government can become a monster which rules with no practical limits on its discretion. Absolute discretion, like corruption, marks the beginning of the end of liberty. This case is perhaps insignificant in the annals. But the standard set for men of good will is even more useful to the venal.[88]

It was one thing for that debate to take place between the majority and minority members of the Supreme Court. It was quite another in the many courts below, where some judges maintained strict deference and others saw themselves as guardians against excess power in the hands of bureaucratic officials.[89] The latter group frequently reminded their judicial colleagues and administrators that, "absent any evidence to the contrary, Congress may rather be presumed to have intended that the courts shall fulfill their traditional role of defining and maintaining the proper bounds of administrative discretion and safeguarding the rights of the individual."[90] For the contemporary administrator, the immediate impact may be conflicting interpretations of one's statutory authority or review of particular decisions by different judges sitting in different jurisdictions.[91]

The process of defining the judicial role continues as the administrative environment changes and new judges come to the bench. On the whole, there is a fair measure of judicial discretion in the review of administrative discretion. Like administrators, different judges may exercise their discretion in different ways. Also like administrators, judges are socialized into their profession with a set of values that affects their actions. The fundamental priorities of due process, equal protection of the laws, and substantial justice necessarily often conflict with the administrative managerial emphasis on expertise, flexibility, and efficiency.

Judges do respect expertise in administration, but it is a cautious respect, which "does not eliminate the need for judicial review of agency actions, and inherent in that albeit limited power of review is the need for an agency to spell out its reasons."[92] This antipathy toward claims of expertise suggests general agreement with Justice Douglas's warning that expertise can become a monster that rules with no limits on its discretion,[93] and with Justice Jackson's fear of administrative authoritarianism justified by claims of expertise and experience.[94]

Judges are often skeptical of administrative action justified on the ground of administrative flexibility. "To permit flexibility under the APA does not, however, mean that agencies are granted carte blanche to proceed in any way they see fit. Flexibility is not synonymous with uncontrolled discretion."[95] Judges understand the advantages of flexibility, but prefer to have clear standards available where there is a good chance that someone may suffer a serious loss of property or liberty.[96]

If judges tend to be skeptical of expertise and claimed requirements for flexibility, many tend to be openly hostile to administrative efficiency and convenience when these are claimed to justify discretionary administrative action, unless the need for it is clearly demonstrated. "We must not play fast and loose with basic constitutional guarantees in the interest of administrative efficiency."[97]

This distrust stems in part from a fundamental tension built into the framework of government. The Supreme Court has often reminded administrators that:

> The establishment of prompt efficacious procedures to achieve legitimate state ends is a proper state interest worthy of cognizance in constitutional adjudication. But the Constitution recognizes higher values than speed and efficiency. Indeed, one might fairly say of the Bill of Rights in general, and the Due Process Clause in particular, that they were designed to protect the fragile values of a vulnerable citizenry from the overbearing concern for efficiency and efficacy that may characterize praiseworthy government officials no less, and perhaps more, than mediocre ones.[98]

The Constitution was designed to ensure just but not efficient government, and judges often see their duty as ensuring against the natural tendency of officials to arrogate power to themselves, using the need for efficiency as justification.

Judges have also had long experience with repeated administrative rationalizations based on efficiency used to justify agency actions, many of which turned out to be arbitrary or actually violative of the constitutional or statutory rights of people before the agency. Administrative convenience and necessity were used in each case to support the administrator and urge judicial deference. In cases relying on irrebuttable presumptions, the Supreme Court observed: "The State's interest in administrative ease and certainty cannot, in and of itself, save the conclusive presumption from invalidity."[99] In cases challenging residency requirements for receipt of public services and benefits, the Court held: "The argument that the waiting period serves as an administratively efficient rule of thumb for determining residency will not withstand scrutiny."[100] The same arguments have been used by agencies to treat women employees and citizens differently from similarly situated males.[101]

Clearly, these differing values and perspectives are held to different degrees by different decision-makers. Progress can and should be made in understanding and dealing with the inherent conflicts between those who exercise administrative discretion and those who must ensure against abuses of discretionary authority. Administrators who become more familiar with the law will be better able to anticipate judicial concerns and deal with them. They will also understand that judicial interaction with the agency, much more than an annoying interference, is inevitable and necessary to the successful operation of the administrative justice system. Judges have shown themselves to be increasingly sensitive to some aspects of agency activity.

That said, concerns about the loss of core legal norms to contemporary political and administrative tensions remain even though some members of the U.S. Supreme Court and U.S. Circuit Courts of Appeals have sought to afford administrators greater discretion with less procedural constraints than has been the case in many years. Even Chief Justice Rehnquist observed: "But the fact that the implementation of a program capable of providing individualized consideration might present administrative challenges does not render constitutional an otherwise problematic system."[102] Justice O'Connor reminded her colleagues that: "We have repeatedly rejected efforts to justify sex-based classifications on the ground of administrative convenience."[103] Judge Posner's and Judge Fuentes's rebukes of the

Citizenship and Immigration Service made the point in unmistakable terms, and Judge Sack of the Second Circuit has insisted that: "[R]endering State officials secure in the knowledge that they can act quickly and decisively in urgent situations and that the law will protect them when they do, there is a critical difference between necessary latitude and infinite license. As the Supreme Court stated in *Stanley v. Illinois:* 'The establishment of prompt efficacious procedures to achieve legitimate state ends is a proper state interest worthy of cognizance in constitutional adjudication. But the Constitution recognizes higher values than speed and efficiency.' "[104]

Governance Imperatives: Creativity, Flexibility, Results-Oriented, and Independence

The increasing tendency to employ various governance mechanisms, involving both governmental and nongovernmental organizations, whether driven by deliberate design or resulting from the hollowing-out of government, has added a third set of values into the mix. For reasons noted earlier in the chapter, the press for entrepreneurial government and rise of governance regimes has fed the tendency to expand discretion, including providing what is often thought to be government discretion to nongovernmental organizations (also discussed earlier in the chapter). But these governance regimes often carry their own set of values that are not necessarily the same as those of either a government agency or the courts. They are the values that have supported the rise of the governance model, including creativity, flexibility, a results-oriented drive, and independence.

Governance regimes are commonly created as problem-solving mechanisms. They are often constructed on the assumption that existing governmental institutions are too rigid or that the authority necessary to address pressing problems is fragmented and allotted among too many agencies that contest for control rather than collaborate for problem solving. Hence, the ability to create mechanisms outside normal jurisdictional boundaries, free from standard procedural constraints, is a central dynamic of contemporary governance.

Related to that dynamic is the argument for governance arrangements that are seen as functioning outside and independent of existing institutional, elective, and partisan politics. Indeed, nonprofit organizations and for-profit firms are attractive partners in such collaborative creations precisely because they can operate free from the procedural and substantive policy constraints facing federal or state administrative agencies and local governments.[105]

Finally, governance regimes are generally constructed by contractual mechanisms with disputes to be resolved through alternatives to standard judicial processes. Where these governance arrangements are in the nature of sophisticated service delivery networks, the issues of the nature, character, and location of discretion become even more complex. It is in part for this reason that such authors as Ronald Moe and Robert Gilmour have expressed such concern about the need for a better understanding of the relationship between the values that drive public law, public administration, and contemporary governance.[106]

REMEDIES FOR ABUSE OF DISCRETION

Clearly, administrative discretion is useful and necessary. It takes many forms, stems from several sources, and is a basic tool for solving problems. These factors make it likely that discretion will be abused intentionally or accidentally and can make it difficult to fix remedies for those abuses. Although Chapters 10, 12, and 13 will discuss the more important remedies in more detail, it is useful to summarize here the most frequently used remedies for abuse of discretion.

Self-Help

The most obvious way for the public manager to protect against abuses is to take action to prevent it in the first place. Many scholars and study groups have long advocated that the best way for administrators to do this is to place all agency standards, policy positions, and procedures in rules promulgated so that they may be read and understood by all who must deal with the agency.[107] If an agency action is challenged and the administrator can show that the action was based on standards made known in published rules before the fact, the likelihood of judicial support and deference increases. A judge who thinks that an administrator is making up the rules as he or she goes along is very likely to overturn an agency action. Agencies can change standards as the need arises, but the fact that standards are set and changed in an orderly, rational process is a sign of well-used authority.

A second mechanism for self-help is to develop a proper and complete record of each agency action. The record must be made while the agency action is in progress. Another trigger of judicial disfavor is the perception that a record was made up after the fact, as a *post hoc* rationalization of agency action.

Finally, administrators can assure adequate procedures to resolve administrative disputes, whether they are formal (such as administrative appeals processes) or informal (such as agency ombudsmen), to convince clients, the legislature, and the courts that the agency makes every effort to deal with such unfortunate instances of abuse of discretion as may arise.

Unfortunately, for many reasons, the self-help remedies have not been employed by enough administrators.[108] Moreover, these mechanisms were designed for government agencies and not for many contemporary governance arrangements that reach not only beyond a single agency but outside of government into nonprofit and for-profit organizations. Hence, other approaches to the problem of abuse of discretion have been required.

Oversight by the Legislature and Supervision by the Executive

All agencies are accountable to a higher institutional authority for their actions. Executive branch agencies are responsible both to the chief executive (be it the president, the governor, or the mayor) and to the legislature. Independent commissions are accountable to the legislature even though they need not answer to the executive. Most agencies are required to report and justify their activities both to a subject area committee (a committee concerned with the substantive policy that an agency administers) and to an appropriations committee (a committee that is ostensibly concerned with ensuring that agency funds are properly expended, but in reality it often considers the substance of agency policy as well.)[109] For reasons that will be discussed in Chapter 10, executive supervision and legislative oversight have not proven to be effective as deterrents or as remedies to abuses of agency discretion. For one thing, neither the legislature (even a committee of the legislature) at the federal or state level nor the chief executive has the time or the staff to pay attention to all the day-to-day activities of even one agency. For another, as Raoul Berger has noted, elections are not likely to be won or lost because a few people suffered from an abuse of administrative discretion.[110]

What the legislature can do is to take care when drafting or revising legislation for an agency to give as much guidance as possible in the statutes.[111] And, as Kenneth Culp Davis pointed out, they can encourage administrators to promulgate rules and guidelines structuring (as Davis put it) their own discretion.[112] Unfortunately, as Chapter 5 explained, legislatures have been moving in the opposite direction.

The problem of executive supervision of agencies that are technically under his or her authority is complex. The *de facto* sources of authority discussed earlier, such as expertise and political support from agency clients, often frustrate executive attempts to control agencies. The executive's primary tools are the budget review process and judicious use of the appointment and dismissal powers. Beyond these mechanisms, executive supervision is more a matter of political acumen and management skill than of institutional checks and legal devices. To the degree that recent presidents of both major political parties have sought to use executive orders and other forms of direct action or have tried to use their White

House staffs to end-run their agencies, the results have often been both poor management and bad policy.

City Managers as a Special Case

It was in part because of the history of political interference with the operation of agencies of local government and because of the limited ability of such political figures to provide professional management supervision that the profession of city management was born.[113] In the classical council/manager form, the manager is hired by the governing body. He or she is then responsible for day-to-day management of the city (or in some parts of the Northeast town) organization. Since the manager is a full time professional manager with the authority to hire and fire department heads, he or she is in a position to supervise subordinates effectively.

However, even in the classic version of the plan, the manager cannot be involved in every day-to-day decision in all departments. And since the manager is ultimately responsible to the council for all aspects of the organization's performance, his or her future is very much tied to the quality of the performance in each of the city's departments. Thus, even in this system there are limits to control over discretion.

In many communities, local variations on the classic plan have evolved in which elected officials have more communication with department heads as opposed to dealing with departments only through the manager's office. Such approaches are intended to increase responsiveness, but they also make the context in which department heads exercise their discretion and the problems of supervision more complex.

County governments are in some respects even more complicated in the issues of discretion that they present. For one thing, they often serve a larger geographical area, with more people, and in more fields of service than cities. But perhaps even more important than all of these concerns is the fact that county departments are often headed by elected officials who cannot be controlled by a county administrator.

For all these reasons, even at the local level, issues of administrative discretion are increasingly complex and mechanisms of control and supervision limited, with the inevitable result that there will be cases of abuse of discretion for which citizens and organizations will seek remedies.

Judicial Remedies

Writers who have considered the problem of remedying abuses of administrative discretion since Goodnow's famous works on the subject have urged that the judiciary should not be the only means for dealing with the problem. The fact is, however, that the judiciary has been one of the most effective remedies for specific abuses by particular administrators. The courts use essentially five approaches to meet allegations of administrative arbitrariness: (1) standard judicial review; (2) judicial intervention in cases of maladministration through the use of injunctions; (3) judgments of money damages awarded to those injured by administrative actions; (4) breach of contract judgments; and (5) criminal convictions where prosecutions are brought for malfeasance or other delicts of law.

Judicial Review   Judicial review of the sort discussed in Chapter 7 may result in several kinds of actions. The judge may reverse or vacate an agency decision. More often, the judge will remand a decision for further proceedings before the agency. Such a disposition delays agency action; repeated remands may have the effect of nullifying a decision. The judge may refuse to enforce agency orders and subpoenas. Agencies like the National Labor Relations Board are virtually powerless without an enforcement order from a court.

Tort Liability Suits   Another alternative through which to address abuse of discretion is that a person injured by maladministration may be afforded an opportunity, under some circumstances, to sue for damages.[114] For reasons that will be discussed in Chapter 13, the opportunity to maintain such suits is limited, and this is particularly true where one is disputing an action in an area involving administrative discretion. The utility of a money damages claim also assumes one can be made whole again by recompense in the form of money damages, which may or may not be true. The Supreme Court has indicated since the late 1970s that it favors remedies for maladministration using money damage suits after the fact rather than injunctions that attempt to alter ongoing administrative patterns.[115] Just how far the Court will take that trend remains to be seen.

Criminal Prosecutions   Another mechanism is that courts, either with or without juries, may render judgments in criminal prosecutions for illegal activities by administrators. Such prosecutions do occur, but they are, fortunately, quite rare. For one thing, criminal laws are normally intended to address only the most extreme of administrative abuses. Furthermore, political realities encourage superiors to take action against suspect employees rather than keep them until criminal prosecutions can be mounted. Although the statement as made in a case short of actual termination of an employee, Justice Scalia recently went so far as to maintain that:

> [T]he State has a significant interest in immediately suspending, when felony charges are filed against them, employees who occupy positions of great public trust and high public visibility, such as police officers . . . . [T]he government does not have to give an employee charged with a felony a paid leave at taxpayer expense. If his services to the government are no longer useful once the felony charge has been filed, the Constitution does not require the government to bear the added expense of hiring a replacement while still paying him.[116]

Contract-Related Actions   Increasingly, the abuses of discretion may be alleged to have been committed not by government employees but by contractors. Depending upon the nature of the contract and the function involved, other kinds of actions may be brought against contractors, though just where the limits are with contracted-out operations is very much an evolving field of law even with our long history of government contracts. One type of action that may sometimes be taken is a suit for breach of contract, generally referred to in public contract law as a contract default. As Chapter 8 indicated, it is increasingly common for contracts to contain a range of options in their terms for addressing alleged problems, usually based upon some kind of ADR process. However, there are sometimes situations in which a problem may be sufficiently severe that an action will be brought to terminate the contract and collect damages from the contractor to remedy the injury caused by its behavior and other costs that may be incurred by government in correcting the difficulty. Other cases may be sometimes be brought where action by a contractor may be said to amount to action by the state (see Chapter). Still other issues may arise involving actions taken by a subcontractor for which both the prime contractor and the government agency remain responsible. Again, this is an area that is very much a developing field, since much of the early case in this regard arose out of purchase agreements rather than contracts for the provision of direct services to the public.[117]

Injunctive Relief   In some situations, a mere judicial declaration that a policy or other action is illegal is not sufficient to solve the problem that gave rise to a lawsuit in the first place. Often the person bringing a suit is asking for a court to end maladministration. Administrators who fail to cease discriminatory actions in schools or housing, or who operate prisons or mental hospitals in what they know (or should know) are unlawful and inhumane conditions, may be told by a court to remedy the situation. For various reasons, generally political, administrators may not respond. In this event a court may use an injunction to force an administrator to do or remain from doing whatever is necessary to remedy the illegal administrative situation that exists.[118] Failure to obey such an order may result in a charge of contempt of court.

Cases in which judges are called on to issue such orders are often no-win situations. The judge is left with two unpalatable choices. He or she can require specific administrative actions from uncooperative or stressed and anxious administrators, and be accused of judicial usurpation and abuse of power, which interferes with the executive and legislative branches of government.[119] Alternatively, the judge can tell people who have proven that they are the victims of maladministration that although the law is on their side, nothing will be done to remedy the situation.

Illustrations of these difficulties have occurred frequently in prison and mental health institutions since the early 1970s. The public has repeatedly shown that it does not support significant expenditures to improve prisons or mental health facilities. Consequently many such facilities are overcrowded (often two or three times more people are housed in them than the institutions were designed for), understaffed, and underfunded. When patients, prisoners, or their families win suits, showing that the conditions of confinement are illegal, the court often requests that the institution develop voluntary plans for change. Unfortunately, the same political forces that prevented adequate support in the first place continue to block solutions, at which point the court is forced to take action. Astute politicians have learned that by forcing the courts to move by injunction to remedy such situations, the blame for increased taxes for improvements in state programs and institutions can be diverted to the judges. The use of such remedies is fraught with all manner of difficulties since, among other things, judges are not trained in the administration of schools, prisons, or mental health facilities. On the other hand, there are often few effective alternatives to ensure compliance with the law. And with all of the problems involved, most mental health or corrections professionals will argue, when they are speaking privately, that much of what has happened in a positive way in their institutions had a great deal to do with the court-ordered reforms and the threat of future suits.

On the other hand, there is often a common misunderstanding about remedial cases to the effect that courts today are still actively supporting intrusive suits and wide-ranging decrees. The fact is that the Supreme Court has issued a lengthy string of decisions warning federal district courts to restrict the types of cases in which they become involved,[120] to limit the scope of the remedies they impose when there is a need for injunctive relief,[121] and to seek to end their supervision of administrative operations as soon as possible given the situation they face.[122] Contrary to what some frustrated officials sometimes assume, most judges want as little as possible to do with remedial decree cases. They often represent major burdens on the court and its limited staff, which, in most jurisdictions, already faces heavy caseloads. More than that, the judges who issue such orders are often the subject of harsh and often unfair criticism. Consider the example of a judge who faced recalcitrant officials in one community.[123]

In 1980, the Civil Rights Division of the U.S. Justice Department brought suit against Yonkers, New York, alleging deliberate discrimination in housing. The case was later joined by the NAACP, which represented all African-American residents of the city who were eligible for public housing. At the same time, the city was facing a school desegregation case caused in part by the residential segregation. The city was found guilty of the charges in 1985.[124] After hearings, the court issued a remedial order in May of 1986 in which the judge essentially ordered the city to do what it had promised to do when it had applied to the federal government for community development block grant (CDBG) funds. The city was required to construct 200 units of public housing with deadlines for initial siting decisions. In addition, the city was given until November to submit a proposal as to how it intended to meet the additional needs that had been identified. The city appealed, but the district court ruling was upheld by the U.S. Circuit Court for the Second Circuit.[125]

In considering what happened next, an appeals court later concluded that the "City totally defaulted" on its obligations under the remedial order. Indeed, when the November deadline arrived, the city informed the district court that it did not intend to comply. Although the plaintiffs asked for a contempt judgment, Judge Sand "patiently endeavored to secure voluntary compliance."[126] Finally, in February 1987, the city council acceded to a first step that would consist of hiring an outside consultant to identify sites for the 200 units the city had promised in its CDBG application and prepare a long-term plan to address the remaining needs.

After the consultant submitted site recommendations, the city council agreed to 12 initial sites provided that the council could select the tenants. That was, of course, not acceptable and the city plainly knew it when it took that position in April 1987. Virtually no progress was made during the rest of the year, but efforts were made to restart negotiations in January of 1988.

Finally, at the end of January, the city council proposed a consent decree. The proposal included deadlines on siting decisions for the initial 200 units, accepted the figures proposed for additional units, and promised to construct them over the next three years. It promised a financing plant to facilitate the other commitments and agreed to enact whatever legislation was needed to assist in the construction of the promised housing, specifically to include any necessary zoning changes.

The plan was immediately accepted, but almost before the ink was dry the city council began resisting its own remedy because of opposition within the community. In March 1988, the city repudiated its earlier promise not to take further legal appeals. It also offered to return the $30 million it had received in CDBG funds rather than comply with the consent decree. The following month "the city announced that it was 'not interested' in completing negotiations on the terms of a long-term plan for the 800 units of subsidized housing."[127]

At this point, in April 1988, the plaintiffs submitted their own proposal to which the city immediately objected. Judge Sand told the city to revise the plan in light of those criticisms. In June, the judge accepted the city's submission. It was clear, however, that progress on construction could not be made until the city council honored its commitment to adopt the promised legislation. There had been no movement on that front until attorneys for the city told the court in late June that the legislation would be enacted at the next council meeting. Instead, the council enacted a moratorium on new public housing in the city. Indeed, at its last meeting in June, the city council rejected a proposed resolution that would have committed the city to compliance with the consent decree as modified.

When Judge Sand asked the city to provide the timetable for action that it had promised, he was informed that the council would not adopt the promised legislation. If he wanted it, they said, the court should impose it. Proposals were offered by plaintiffs to create a housing commission and other steps, but Judge Sand did not want to remove either the legislative or executive functions from the responsibility of the city.

Not surprisingly, the plaintiffs had frequently urged the court to issue contempt citations against the city. Finally, Judge Sand warned the city in late July that he was giving the council until August 1 to pass the promised legislation. (He later said that it would be adequate if they committed the council to passing the legislation in accordance with required procedures in the minimum time.) If they did not do so and were unable to show cause why a finding of contempt should not be imposed, the judge warned that he would fine the recalcitrant legislators $500 per day and that, if they had not complied by August 10, they would be face incarceration. The city would be fined, starting on August 3, beginning with $100 for the first day and doubling each day thereafter. A majority four members of the council refused to comply and, along with the city, were held in contempt. At a hearing a week later, the recalcitrant members indicated that they intended to continue to oppose the court. On September 9, the city ultimately adopted the promised ordinance.

The Second Circuit upheld the judge's contempt actions, but limited the fines on the city to $1 million per day. A sharply divided U.S. Supreme Court upheld the fine against the city but concluded that further efforts to encourage compliance should be taken before fining the individual legislators. Justice Rehnquist wrote for the five-person majority: "Only if that approach failed to produce compliance within a reasonable time should the question of imposing contempt sanctions against petitioners even have been considered."[128]

Writing for the four dissenters, Justice Brennan indicated that the Court's ruling made no sense in light of the overwhelming evidence in the record that sanctions against the city itself would not work. That was particularly clear in light of statements made by the recalcitrant council members, who made it plain that they intended to continue on their course of resistance regardless of the consequences that it brought for the city. But, Brennan warned, in the end the danger of the opinion is that it might render judges timid and unwilling to protect the rule of law and simultaneously embolden law breakers.

The Court's decision today that Judge Sand abused his remedial discretion by imposing personal fines simultaneously with city fines creates no new principle of law; indeed, it invokes no new principle of any sort. But it directs a message to district judges that, despite their repeated and close contact with the various parties and issues, even the most delicate remedial choices by the most conscientious and deliberate judges are subject to being second-guessed by this Court. I hope such a message will not daunt the courage of district courts who, if ever again faced with such protracted defiance, must carefully yet firmly secure compliance with their remedial orders. But I worry that the Court's message will have the unintended effect of emboldening recalcitrant officials continually to test the ultimate reach of the remedial authority of the federal courts, thereby postponing the day when all public officers finally accept that "the responsibility of those who exercise powers in a democratic government is not to reflect inflamed public feeling but to help form its understanding."[129]

For reasons made clear by this and many other stories of the challenges faced by judges in remedial decree cases, it should be obvious why most of them would prefer to avoid such cases.[130] Despite these realities, and the Supreme Court rulings constraining remedial decrees, these kinds of cases continue to be brought in a variety of fields. For example, with increasing jail and prison populations sending large numbers of people to prison for long periods of time and with increasing fiscal stress on corrections organizations in most states, it was virtually a certainty that conditions would become increasingly dangerous and legally unacceptable.[131] That is what has happened in a number of jurisdictions, notwithstanding the Supreme Court's rulings making it more difficult for inmates to demonstrate violations of their rights and its interpretations of federal legislation intended to limit dramatically the circumstances under which inmates can sue and placing constraints on courts that hear such cases.[132] The fact patterns in some of these cases read very much like those of the late 1960s and early 1970s that eventually led to remedial orders issued in dozens of cases. One district court found in a case involving the Morgan County jail, finding that the facility conditions "more nearly resemble the holding units of slave ships during the Middle Passage of the eighteenth century than anything in the twenty-first century."[133] In a 2002 case, Judge Myron Thompson of the Middle District of Alabama said of one of the state's prisons for women: "[T]he . . . plaintiffs are entitled to preliminary-injunctive relief on their claim that they are subject to a substantial risk of serious harm caused by Tutwiler's greatly overcrowded and significantly understaffed open dorms. Indeed, the court is not only convinced that these unsafe conditions have resulted in harm, and the threat of harm, to individual inmates in the immediate past, it is also convinced that they are so severe and widespread today that they are essentially a time bomb ready to explode facility-wide at any unexpected moment in the near future."[134]

These cases are not limited to rulings by federal or state courts about state or local matters, but include federal cases concerning violations by federal agencies. One of the most contentious and visible examples in recent history is a massive class action suit brought by Native Americans against the Secretary of the Interior on grounds that the Department of the Interior and the Treasury had administered Native American trust funds in violation of the government's general trust obligations toward Native Americans and its more specific obligations with respect to the Indian Trust Fund under the General Allotment Act of 1887, the Indian Reorganization Act of 1934, the Indian Self-Determination and Education Assistance Act, and the Indian Trust Fund Management Reform Act.[135] The last of these pieces was enacted in 1994 in response to congressional findings that the federal government had failed in its trust responsibilities over a prolonged period of time, and called for a series of actions to be taken under the oversight of an Office of the Special Trustee for American Indians.

The allotment policy was originally designed as a serious effort to undermine the tribes and nations and make their lands available for non-Indians to develop. As the Supreme Court put it: "The objectives of allotment were simple and clear cut: to extinguish tribal sovereignty, erase reservation boundaries, and force assimilation of Indians into the society at large."[136] Under the allotment program, the federal government allotted parcels of existing Native American lands to individuals and families subject to regulation of its sale. The government would then sell or manage the remaining lands with the proceeds to be held in trust for Native Americans and paid out over time. A class action was brought by small number of Native Americans on behalf of a class, now consisting of approximately 500,000 others, and alleged that the Department of the Interior and the Treasury had not only failed in their historic duties but also had not responded to the 1994 legislation intended to correct the problems that had been the reasons for the Indian Trust Fund Management Reform Act. The plaintiffs charged that the government had failed, *inter alia,* to maintain the records required to determine who was entitled to trust fund money, did not know how much those individuals should receive, and were not protecting confidential information about those Native Americans who had been identified as trust fund beneficiaries. They also claimed that the agency failures were so serious that the court should place the program in receivership under outside control. The government not only rejected the allegations, but also asserted that the court lacked jurisdiction to judge the case or fashion the kind of remedy the plaintiffs sought.

Judge Royce Lamberth of the U.S. District Court for the District of Columbia found that the government was in violation of its trust responsibilities, following a trial in 1999. While he used strong language to describe the government's actions, the remedial steps he ordered were relatively modest. He ordered the government to offer remedial steps, provide regular reports to ensure that corrective steps were implements, and the court retained jurisdiction to provide oversight. The government objected and charged that Lamberth had overstepped his authority, but the D.C. Circuit replied:

> The level of oversight proposed by the district court may well be in excess of that counte-nanced in the typical delay case, but so too is the magnitude of government malfeasance and potential prejudice to the plaintiffs' class. Given the history of destruction of documents and loss of information necessary to conduct an historical accounting, the failure of the government to act could place anything approaching an adequate accounting beyond plaintiffs' reach. This fact, combined with the long-standing inability or unwillingness of government officials to discharge their fiduciary obligations, excuse court oversight that might be excessive in an ordinary case.
>
> The government is correct that the court imposed continual reporting requirements that may be in excess of that which would be minimally required to discharge the government's duties. However, it does not seem that the district court's remedies are disproportionate to the nature of the government's breach.[137]

Lamberth became increasingly frustrated by the government's behavior, first under the Clinton administration and then the Bush administration, observing by 2002 that: "The Department of Interior's administration of the Individual Indian Money (IIM) trust has served as the gold standard for mismanagement by the federal government for more than a century."[138] Although the judge was at the limits of his patience, and despite extremely strong rhetoric, he issued a relatively limited order calling once again for compliance with the court's previous orders:

> In February of 1999, at the end of the first contempt trial in this matter, I stated that "I have never seen more egregious misconduct by the federal government." Now, at the conclusion of the second contempt trial in this action, I stand corrected. The Department of Interior has truly outdone itself this time. The agency has indisputably proven to the Court, Congress, and the individual Indian beneficiaries that it is either unwilling or unable to administer compe-tently the IIM trust. Worse yet, the Department has now undeniably shown that it can no longer be trusted to state accurately the status of its trust reform efforts. In short, there is no longer any doubt that the Secretary of Interior has been and continues to be an unfit trustee-delegate for the United States.
>
> Congress has mandated, the Court has ordered, and the beneficiaries have pleaded for meaningful reform of the IIM trust. This Court need not sit supinely by waiting, hoping that the Department of Interior complies with the orders of this Court and the fiduciary obligations mandated by Congress in the 1994 Act. To do so would be futile. I may have life tenure, but at the rate the Department of Interior is progressing that is not a long enough appointment.[139]

This case is ongoing and complex. It demonstrates that federal courts may be required to fashion remedial decrees to address maladministration with respect to federal agencies as they sometimes must in cases involving state or local agencies.

Negative Discretion and Judicial Responses

Historically, legal challenges to administrators, and sometimes their political superiors as well, have primarily concerned efforts to limit overzealous use of discretion. In the contemporary administrative environment, however, attention has shifted to situations in which administrators either refuse to act at all or withdraw from previously developed policies. Although the need to compel administrative action as well as guard against excessive administrative zeal is rarely discussed these days, it is an important issue that was raised by Carl Friedrich more than 40 years ago:

> Too often it is taken for granted that as long as we can keep government from doing wrong we have made it more responsible. What is more important is to insure effective action of any sort. . . . An official should be as responsible for inaction as for wrong action; certainly the average voter will criticize the government as severely for one as for the other.[140]

The efforts of the Carter, Reagan, Bush, and Clinton administrations to deregulate and generally move administrative agencies to less aggressive approaches to their work, particularly on the regulatory side, have been the focus of controversy. It is important to consider not only limits on the discretion to act but also the legal forces compelling the exercise of discretion. The cases calling for mandatory use of agency authority have been basically of four types: (1) those objecting to an administrative refusal to launch a fact-finding or policymaking process; (2) agency refusal to issue rules; (3) intentional delay in agency action; and (4) rescission of existing or proposed policies.

Controlling the agency agenda is an important element of administrative discretion. Deciding what problems to address and assigning priorities is often more than a question of efficient management. It may involve strategic decisions. Administrators would frankly prefer to avoid some problems. Take the case, described in Chapter 1, in which the involvement of the Food and Drug Administration (FDA) was demanded in the capital punishment controversy. Death row inmates petitioned the FDA to launch an investigation to determine whether the drugs used for execution by lethal injection were safe and effective for the specific applications to which they were put. Drugs could only meet that criteria if they brought about quick and painless death, but the inmates alleged that there was substantial evidence that, in improper dosage and administration, the drugs currently used could "leave a prisoner conscious but paralyzed while dying, a sentient witness of his or her own slow lingering asphyxiation." The FDA refused to investigate on grounds that it lacked jurisdiction to review state-sanctioned uses of drugs for these purposes. The agency did not argue that it lacked the capacity to inquire into the matter, but that it was without jurisdiction in the case. Moreover, the agency claimed that even if it had jurisdiction, it also had complete and unreviewable enforcement discretion concerning whether and when to take administrative action. The FDA refused to act on the basis of that discretion.

The D.C. Circuit Court of Appeals, however, found that the agency did have jurisdiction, which it had previously asserted, for example, in drug experiments involving state prison inmates. The court rejected the claim to unreviewable enforcement discretion and found the FDA refusal to launch an investigation arbitrary and capricious. The court wrote:

> In this case FDA is clearly refusing to exercise enforcement discretion because it does not wish to become embroiled in an issue so morally and emotionally troubling as the death penalty. Yet this action amounts to an abnegation of statutory responsibility by the very agency that Congress charged with the task of ensuring that our people do not suffer harm from mis-branded drugs . . . . As a result of the FDA's inaction, appellants face the risk of cruel execution and are deprived of FDA's expert judgment as to the effectiveness of the drugs used for legal injection . . . .[141]

The court concluded that while it would not dictate the outcome or the particular administrative process to be employed in any given situation, the simple assertion of absolute discretion to refuse to undertake action will be challenged.

The Supreme Court, however, reversed in a decision written by Chief Justice Rehnquist. The opinion assumed that enforcement discretion is presumptively unreviewable under the APA, but acknowledged that it is a rebuttable presumption. Rehnquist contended that the situation is different when an agency refuses to act as opposed to where it actively moves against someone. The Court reached this conclusion notwithstanding the APA's authorization of actions to compel agency action unlawfully withheld as well as for actions taken which are arbitrary, capricious, an abuse of discretion, or not otherwise in accordance with law. In the process, however, Rehnquist warned:

> In so stating, we emphasize that the decision is only presumptively unreviewable; the presumption may be rebutted where the substantive statute has provided guidelines for the agency to follow in exercising its enforcement powers. Thus, in establishing this presumption in the APA, Congress did not set agencies free to disregard legislative direction in the statutory scheme that the agency administers. Congress may limit an agency's exercise of enforcement power if it wishes, either by setting substantive priorities, or by otherwise circumscribing an agency's power to discriminate among issues or cases it will pursue.[142]

Justice Brennan concurred but warned that the decision should be read narrowly, since there are many circumstances under which a decision not to act would be reviewable. Justice Marshall went much further, attacking the presumption of unreviewability (discussed in Chapter 7). He argued that there is no reason to abandon the normal test for reviewability in administrative law. It is enough that any review of agency discretion should be made with a general presumption of validity and deference to expert judgment. He warned: "The problem of agency refusal to act is one of the pressing problems of the modern administrative state, given the enormous powers, for both good and ill, that agency inaction, like agency action, holds over citizens."[143]

Another problem area is the refusal to make rules. The U.S. Circuit Court of Appeals for the Eighth Circuit found that the Secretary of Agriculture had abused his discretion by refusing to issue rules under a statute governing farm loan foreclosure. A family charged that the Department of Agriculture had an obligation under the statute to promulgate rules and provide adequate notice to those affected concerning possible deferments of foreclosures. The government argued that the statute "merely created an additional power to be wielded at the discretion of the agency, or placed in the Secretary's back pocket for safekeeping."[144] The court found the refusal to make rules or institute any kind of process for reasoned decisionmaking a "complete abdication" of responsibility.[145]

In some ways related to the refusal to make rules is the tactic of delaying for as long as possible the issuance of rules required by statute. Here again, courts are willing to draw a line based on the obligations of the statute. Efforts by the EPA to delay implementation of rules required by the Resource Conservation and Recovery Act (RCRA) covering toxic wastes were successfully challenged in a number of lawsuits. Among the remedies sought by the plaintiffs in one of the cases was an award of attorney's fees under the Equal Access to Justice Act. The court awarded the fee, finding that the intentional delaying tactics employed by the agency were "exactly the type of arbitrary governmental behavior that the EAJA was designed to deter."[146]

Finally, a number of challenges have been brought against efforts by administrators to deregulate through rescinding existing agency regulations or withdrawing pending rules. The Federal Communications Commission (FCC) efforts to reduce its regulatory control over broadcasting have prompted several such lawsuits. Another example is the withdrawal of mandatory automobile passive restraint rules by the Department of Transportation. In both cases, administrators claimed that the decision to reduce regulation administratively was not really policymaking and was a purely discretionary matter not subject to judicial examination. The courts rejected that claim and insisted that a change in policy is a policy decision whether it results in promulgation of a new rule or abandonment of an old one. In fact, a panel of the D.C. Circuit Court of Appeals said, "such abrupt shifts in policy do constitute 'danger signals' that the Commission may be acting inconsistently with its statutory mandate.... We will require therefore that the Commission provide a reasoned analysis indicating prior policies and standards are being deliberately changed, not casually ignored."[147] Having said that, however, the court upheld the FCC deregulation. It cautioned the Commission that it was perilously close to violating its statutory responsibility but found enough evidence to say the FCC had met its requirement of reasoned analysis.

The Supreme Court did not find the necessary foundation for the rescission of the automotive passive restraint rule and remanded the matter to the agency. It concluded that an "agency changing its course by rescinding a rule is obligated to supply a reasoned analysis for the change beyond that which may be required when the agency does not act in the first instance."[148] Since a rule was presumably adopted in the first place on the basis of a careful reasoning process using the agency's expertise and available evidence, there is a presumption in favor of the rule. The court concluded:

> In so holding, we fully recognize that "regulatory agencies do not establish rules of conduct to last forever," . . . and that an agency must be given ample latitude to "adapt their rules and policies to the demands of changing circumstances . . . . But the forces of change do not always or necessarily point in the direction of deregulation. In the abstract, there is no more reason to presume that changing circumstances require the rescission of prior action, instead of a revision in or even the extension of current regulation. If Congress established a presumption from which judicial review should start, that presumption—contrary to petitioner's view—is not *against* safety regulation, but against changes in current policy that are not justified by the rulemaking record [emphasis in original].[149]

There is one final problem of what might be termed negative discretion. Administrators often argue that judges should defer to their administrative expertise regardless of the type of policy under consideration. However, judges sometimes doubt that administrators are entitled to such deference when there does not appear to be a policy at all but rather a failure to make any policy or to enforce existing standards. Justice Brennan, for instance, observed that while judges ought to defer to the expertise of correctional administrators, the prison conditions frequently in dispute in court often arise not from a policy decision based upon administrative expertise but from sheer neglect. "There is no reason of comity, judicial restraint, or recognition of expertise for courts to defer to negligent omissions of officials who lack the resources or motivation to operate prisons within the limits of decency."[150]

Federal District Judge Bruce Jenkins of Utah came to a similar conclusion in a case involving claims made against the government by the families of alleged victims of nuclear testing. The court awarded damages to those who demonstrated that their illnesses stemmed from the testing. Jenkins rejected the notion that there should be a deference to administrative discretion in this sort of case. There was, he said, "no official policy of indifference to safety."[151] The "actions taken were negligently insufficient—not as a matter of discretion at all—as a matter of deliberate choice making—but as a matter of negligently failing to warn, to measure and to inform, at a level sufficient to meet the stated goals of the Congress, the executive branch and the Atomic Energy Commission."[152] In sum, administrators may not assume absolute administrative discretion when they refuse to act as compared to cases where they are alleged to have acted too vigorously. The problem of relating administrative discretion and judicial obligations to ensure accountability is all the more difficult when there is no policy for a given action but an actual departure from state policy or simple neglect. This concept of negative discretion is an aspect of the judicial/administrative relationship that is very much a developing matter and worthy of attention.

Special Challenges of Addressing Abuse of Emergency Discretion

There are several special challenges associated with efforts to remedy abuse of discretion in emergency circumstances, several of which were suggested in the earlier discussion in this chapter as to how and why emergencies lead to expanded discretion in the first place. First, the use of legislative grants of authority are often crafted in broad terms that open the door for political executives to push the boundaries. That broad language can make it difficult for courts that must eventually define the outer boundaries of the discretionary actions at issue.[153] Second, the executive is often able to obtain from the legislature statutes that grant agencies exceptions to existing procedural and substantive requirements as was true with the Homeland Security Act and other post-9/11 legislation. Third, the fact that many discretionary activities may be carried out under the secret stamp means that it is difficult to know what is being done, how, and why, even by those who are very directly affected. Thus, those persons who have received security letters issued under the USA Patriot Act were not permitted to challenge them, to complain about them, or to notify anyone else of their existence under pain of criminal prosecution.[154] Since the proceedings of the Foreign Intelligence Surveillance Act (FISA) court are secret and only the government argues before that court, few people even knew of the court's existence, much less were aware of any problems with the behavior of the justice department in both the Clinton and Bush administrations before that court until all of the judges of that body issued a public opinion detailing a series of abuses and pressures to grant the DOJ even greater authority than it had previously exercised.[155] Of course, these issues assume that once an alleged abuse of discretion, a proper party, and a body of law are identified, the matter can proceed, but it is increasingly common for the legislature to make a variety of decisions unreviewable on grounds of the need for discretion to deal with emergency conditions.

Even assuming that one can get an emergency action case into the judiciary, there is a tendency for courts not to want to address executives at the high point of the crisis and to grant the widest possible deference to them when cases do reach appellate tribunals, particularly early in a crisis. Thus, there is the sad history of the Japanese exclusion and internment orders issued at the outset of World War II. It took years for Mr. Greene in the case outlined in Chapter 6, and others like him, to be vindicated in the courts during the red scare of the 1940s and 1950s. More recently, in the wake of 9/11, it took some time before the appellate courts began to draw lines for the Bush administration. However, after a period of time, the courts do tend to come back into the process, but not before a great deal of damage has been done to innocent people and organizations.[156]

Finally, as the earlier discussion noted, that which was undertaken on grounds of emergency often continues, but its presence and origins are forgotten.[157] While the National Emergencies Act limits the time an emergency may be in effect, it does not stop the president from issuing a new emergency declaration when that time limit is reached. The act allows the legislature to attempt to force an end to the situation, but, since a joint resolution is required, the president can veto such a move and an extraordinary majority would be required to override.

SUMMARY

In this chapter we have indicated a number of reasons why administrative discretion is both necessary and desirable. It stems from a variety of sources, which include broad delegations of authority from the legislature and the chief executive, as well as several de facto sources, including expertise, experience, and political support for one's agency, the intergovernmental factor, the move to entrepreneurial government, and the dynamics that flow from emergencies. Problems of allowing constructive use of administrative discretion while limiting abuses are complicated by the fact that administrators and judicial officials come to the problem with different perspectives.

Despite good intentions, historical examples of abuses of administrative discretion are legion. Mechanisms have been developed to remedy such arbitrariness, including self-help, supervision by officials of the legislative and executive branches, and judicial remedies of several types. Chapter 7 considered judicial review in some detail and Chapters 8 and 9 have spoken to the use of injunctions to provide remedies. Chapter 13 will focus on tort liability issues and other aspects of responsibility.

In the present era, the areas to watch with respect to issues of administrative discretion are in the realm of intergovernmental relations, the expanding use of contractors to carry out management functions as well as direct service delivery, the question of negative discretion, and the dramatic increases in discretion that have come as a result of emergency actions. There is a certain irony in the way in which discretion is used today. On the one hand, the importance of negative discretion—the decision to draw back from previous assertions of authority or refusal to use available discretion—is quite unlike most of the historical discussions of the subject, which focused on expanding uses of administrative power. Whether the issue of concern is in the area of social service or regulation, there is far less guidance in administrative law to help with these problems than is needed. On the other hand, the dramatic uses of discretion based on emergency conditions represents a reaching out for far greater discretionary authority than has been permitted in recent decades without the constraints that have generally been imposed by modern administrative law.

Many times more decisions are made by administrators in social services administration than in regulation, but regulation has been the cause of the most vocal debates in administrative law and politics in recent years. The law and politics of regulation are considered in Chapter 10.

NOTES

1. "Generalizations as to the allowable limits of administrative discretion is dangerous, for the field is peculiarly one where differences in degree become differences of substance. It is possible to say, on the one hand, that the responsibility for fashioning a policy, not only of great economic importance but also one that has divided the faiths and loyalties of classes of people, cannot appropriately be entrusted to the administrative; on the other, that the scope of administrative power should not be so narrowly defined as to take away from the administrative its capacity to achieve effectively the purposes of its creation." James M. Landis, *The Administrative Process* (New Haven: Yale University Press, 1938), p. 55.

2. Steve Wexler "Discretion: The Unacknowledged Side of Law," 25 *University of Toronto Law Journal* 120, 122–23 (1972).

3. Al Gore, Report of the National Performance Review, *From Red Tape to Results: Creating a Government that Works Better and Costs Less* (Washington, DC: Government Printing Office, 1993), pp. 2–3.

4. Ernst Freund, *Administrative Powers over Persons and Property: A Comparative Survey* (Chicago: University of Chicago Press, 1928), p. 71.

5. This case study is summarized and interpreted from William J. Lockhart, "Discretionary Clemency: Mercy at the Prosecutor's Option," 1976 *Utah Law Review* 55, 58 (1976). (Hereafter cited as Lockhart.)

6. 10 *Weekly Compilation of Presidential Documents* 1150 (1974).

7. Lockhart, *supra* note 5, at p. 58.

8. *Id.*, at p. 59.

9. *Id.*, at p. 60.

10. *Id.*, at p. 64.

11. *Id.*

12. *Id.*, at p. 57.

13. "There are many duties which the government is called upon to perform in a complex civilization which cannot be performed under a system of unconditional commands. No legislature has such insight or extended vision as to be able to regulate all the details in administrative law, or to put the form of unconditional commands rules which in all cases completely and adequately express the will of the state. It must abandon the system of unconditional commands and resort to conditional commands which vest in the administrative officer large powers of discretionary character." Frank Goodnow, *The Principles of Administrative Law in the United States* (New York: Putnam, 1905), pp. 324–25.

14. "In addition, there appear to be serious institutional constraints on Congress' ability to specify regulatory policy in meaningful detail. Legislative majorities typically represent coalitions of interests that must not only compromise among themselves but also with opponents. Individual politicians often find far more to be lost than gained in taking a readily identifiable stand on a controversial issue of social or economic policy." Richard B. Stewart, "The Reformation of American Administrative Law," 88 *Harvard Law Review* 1667, 1695 (1975). See also Landis, *supra* note 1, at pp. 51–55.

15. Jerome Frank, *If Men Were Angels: Some Aspects of Government in a Democracy* (New York: Harper & Brothers, 1942), pp. 3–7. Landis once noted: "The prime key to the improvement of the administrative process is the selection of qualified personnel. Good men can make poor laws workable; poor men will wreak havoc with good laws." U.S. Senate, *Report on Regulatory Agencies to the President-Elect,* 86th Cong., 2d Sess. (1960), p. 66.

16. "The *raison d'etre* of the administrative process is the increasing need for more flexibility than is provided by either Congress or the courts. Modern regulation requires specialization, expertise, continuity of service, and flexibility for utilization of a variety of skills which would not be possible operating within a strict common-law framework." Peter Woll, *Administrative Law: The Informal Process* (Berkeley: University of California Press, 1963), p. 188. See also Dean Roscoe Pound, *Administrative Law: Its Growth, Procedure and Significance* (Pittsburgh: University of Pittsburgh Press, 1942), p. 28.

17. Abraham D. Sofaer, "Judicial Control of Informal Discretionary Adjudication and Enforcement," 72 *Columbia Law Review* 1293, pp. 1296–97 (1972).

18. "Advocates of discretionary decisionmaking can argue with some force that there is a value in flexible, empirical growth of the law and that the rules for resolving some problems are for one reason or another simply not susceptible of neat codification." J. Skelly Wright, "Beyond Discretionary Justice," 81 *Yale Law Journal* 575, 593 (1972).

19. *The Hoover Commission Report on the Organization of the Executive Branch of Government* (New York: McGraw-Hill, 1949), p. 6.

20. Freund, *supra* note 4, at p. 97.

21. Wright, *supra* note 18, at p. 576.

22. Kenneth Culp Davis, *Discretionary Justice: A Preliminary Inquiry* (Baton Rouge: Louisiana State University Press, 1969), p. 25.

23. Sofaer, *supra* note 17. The details of the study are presented in Abraham Sofaer, "The Change-of-Status Adjudication: A Case Study of the Informal Agency Process," 1 *Journal of Legal Studies* 349 (1972).

24. Sofaer, *Id.,* at p. 1300.

25. *Id.,* at pp. 1300–01.

26. *Id.,* at pp. 1301–02.

27. *Id.,* at pp. 1374.

28. See e.g, Martha Honey, *Hostile Acts: U.S. Policy in Costa Rica in the 1980s* (Gainesville, FL: University Press of Florida, 1994).

29. See Lawrence E. Walsh, *Iran-Contra: The Final Report of the Independent Counsel* (New York: Random House, 1993).

30. *Id.,* pp. xiii–xiv.

31. See e.g., U.S. Senate, Hearing Before the Subcommittee on Immigration and Refugee Affairs of the Committee on the Judiciary, *Central American Migration to the United States,* 101st Cong., 1st Sess. (1989); U.S. House of Representatives, Hearing Before the Subcommittee on Immigration, Refugees, and International Law of the Committee on the Judiciary, *Central American Asylum-Seekers,* 101st Cong., 1st Sess. (1989).

32. U.S. Senate, Report of the Committee on the Judiciary to Accompany S. 332 as Amended, *Providing for a GAO Study on Conditions of Displaced Salvadorans and Nicaraguans, and for Other Purposes,* 100th Cong., 1st Sess. (1987), p. 3.

33. *Id.,* p. 4.

34. U.S. Senate, Hearing Before the Committee on the Judiciary, *Consultation on Refugee Admissions for Fiscal Year 1989,* 100th Cong., 2d Sess. (1989), p. 18.

35. 760 F.Supp. 796 (NDCA 1991).

36. *Id.*, p. 799.

37. Illegal Immigration Reform and Immigrant Responsibility Act of 1996, P.L. 104-208, 110 Stat. 3009, 8 U.S.C. §1101, et seq.

38. See U.S. General Accounting Office, *Illegal Aliens: Changes in the Process of Denying Aliens Entry into the United States* (Washington, DC: GAO, 1998).

39. See David Cole, *Enemy Aliens: Double Standards and Constitutional Freedoms in the War on Terrorism* (New York: The New Press, 2003).

40. Division B of the Emergency Supplemental Appropriations Act for Defense, the Global War on Terror, and Tsunami Relief, 2005, P.L. 109-13, 119 Stat. 231 (2005).

41. This problem and the effort to deal with it through the enactment of the Federal Advisory Committee Act will be addressed in more detail in Chapter 11.

42. Davis, *supra* note 22, at p. 4.

43. Robert M. Cooper, "Administrative Justice and the Role of Discretion," 47 *Yale Law Journal* 577, 582 (1938).

44. Stewart, *supra* note 14, at pp. 1676, n. 25.

45. Freund, *supra* note 4, at p. 71.

46. Henry J. Friendly, *The Federal Administrative Agencies: The Need for Better Definition of Standards* (Cambridge: Harvard University Press, 1962), p. 8.

47. Stephen R. Chitwood, "Legalizing Public Administration," paper presented at the 1978 American Society for Public Administration meeting. The paper discusses the language of the Education for All Handicapped Children Act, Public Law 94-142, as a case in point.

48. "The factors responsible for this lack of specificity are (1) the impossibility of specifying at the outset of new governmental ventures the precise policies to be followed; (2) lack of legislative resources to clarify directives; (3) lack of legislative incentives to clarify directives; (4) legislators' desire to avoid resolution of controversial policy issues; (5) the inherent variability of experience; (6) the limitations of language." Stewart, *supra* note 14, at p. 1677 n. 27.

49. See e.g., Thomas D. Morgan, "Achieving National Goals Through Federal Contracts: Giving Form to an Unconstrained Administrative Process," 1974 *Wisconsin L. Rev.* 301 (1974).

50. Developed further in Phillip J. Cooper, *By Order of the President: The Use & Abuse of Executive Direct Action* (Lawrence, KS: University Press of Kansas, 2002), Kenneth R. Mayer, *With the Stroke of a Pen: Executive Orders and Presidential Power* (Princeton, NJ: Princeton University Press, 2001); William G. Howell, *Power without Persuasion: The Politics of Direct Presidential Action* (Princeton, NJ: Princeton University Press, 2003).

51. Cooper, *supra* note 43, at p. 583. Cooper borrowed the language from John Dickinson, "Judicial Control of Official Discretion," 22 *American Political Science Review* 275, 277 (1928). Jerome Frank expressed a similar sentiment when he wrote: "It has been widely said that the first problem of today is to reconcile the Expert State and the Free State." Frank, *supra* note 15, at p. 18.

52. This is true both of the use of expertise by organizations and the use of expertise by individuals within organizations. Michael Crozier's *The Bureaucratic Phenomenon* (Chicago: University of Chicago Press, 1964) provides a study of how lower-level technicians in an industrial firm can use their technical expertise to their advantage. Managing so-called "knowledge workers" requires more sophisticated techniques than earlier administrative environments precisely because employees understand that their expertise gives them power relative to others in an organization. See Frederick C. Mosher, "The Public Service in the Temporary Society," 31 *Public Administration Review* 47 (1971). See also Peter Drucker, "Productivity and the Knowledge Worker," in *Business and Society in Change* (New York: American Telephone & Telegraph, 1975).

53. *Environmental Defense Fund v. Ruckelshaus,* 439 F.2d 584 (D.C.Cir. 1971).

54. *International Harvester Co. v. Ruckelshaus,* 478 F.2d 615 (D.C.Cir. 1973).

55. See e.g., Walker Gellhorn, *Federal Administrative Proceedings* (Baltimore: Johns Hopkins Press, 1941).

56. Francis Rourke, *Bureaucracy, Politics, and Public Policy* (Boston: Little, Brown, 1969), and Philip Selznick, *TVA and the Grassroots* (New York: Harper & Row, 1949).

57. W. Henry Lambright, *Governing Science and Technology* (New York: Oxford University Press, 1976).

58. A. Lee Fritschler and James M. Hoefler, *Smoking and Politics: Policy Making and the Federal Bureaucracy,* 5th ed. (Upper Saddle River, NJ: Prentice Hall, 1995).

59. Federal Trade Commission Improvement Act of 1980, Public Law 96-252, 94 Stat. 374.

60. See e.g. *American Insurance Association v. Garamendi,* 539 U.S. 396 (2003); *Crosby v. National Foreign Trade Council,* 530 U.S. 363 (2000); *Morales v. TWA,* 504 U.S. 374 (1992).

61. See e.g., *Granholm v. Heald,* 125 S. Ct. 1885 (2005); *Camps Newfound/Owatonna v. Town of Harrison, Maine,* 520 U.S. 564 (1997); *Fulton Corp. v. Faulkner,* 516 U.S. 325 (1996); *Chemical Waste Management v. Hunt,* 504 U.S. 334 (1992).

62. See e.g., *Fort Gratiot Landfill v. Michigan Department of Natural Resources,* 504 U.S. 353 (1992); *Wisconsin Public Intervenor v. Mortier,* 501 U.S. 597 (1991).

63. Gore, *supra* note 3, at pp. 2–3.

64. See B. Guy Peters and Donald J. Savoie, eds., *Governance in a Changing Environment* (Montreal: McGill-Queens University Press, 1995), particularly the pieces by Christopher Pollitt, Patricia W. Ingraham, and Jon Pierre.

65. Gore, *supra* note 3, at p. 5.

66. *Id.,* p. 66.

67. *Id.,* p. 71.

68. Donald F. Kettl, *Sharing Power: Public Governance and Private Markets* (Washington, DC: Brookings Institution, 1993), p. 15.

69. Statement of Governor George E. Pataki, October 6, 2005, at http://www.ny.gov/governor/press/05/oct06_1_05.htm, as of December 24, 2005.

70. Louisiana Executive Orders, at http://gov.louisiana.gov/index.cfm?md=newsroom&tmp=archive&navID=15&catID=5&startIndex=1&numPerPage=25, as of December 24, 2005.

71. President's Radio Address, December 17, 2005, at http://www.whitehouse.gov/news/releases/2005/12/20051217.html, as of December 28, 2005.

72. Homeland Security Act of 2002, 107 P.L. 296; 116 Stat. 2135 (2002), §841.

73. See *Woods v. Cloyd W. Miller,* 333 U.S. 138 (1948); *Fleming v. Mohawk Wrecking & Lumber,* 441 U.S. 111 (1947); *United States Grain Corporation v. Phillips,* 261 U.S. 106 (1923).

74. P.L. 94-412, 90 Stat. 1255 (1976).

75. Oscar Kraines, *The World and Ideas of Ernst Freund: The Search for General Principles of Legislation and Administrative Law* (Tuscaloosa, AL: University of Alabama Press, 1974), pp. 10–11.

76. Frank Goodnow, *Comparative Administrative Law* (New York: Putnam, 1893), pp. 138–40.

77. See Elihu Root, "Public Service by the Bar," an address given April 30, 1916, and published in Robert Bacon and James Broun Scott, eds., *Addresses on Government and Citizenship* (Cambridge: Harvard University Press, 1916), pp. 534–37, and John Dickinson, *Administrative Justice and the Supremacy of Law in the United States* (New York: Russell & Russell, 1927).

   Scholars and practitioners of both law and administration had considerable difficulty dealing with the differences in the legal and managerial perspectives. Probably best known among this group is Woodrow Wilson, who leaned strongly to the managerial perspective in his famous 1887 article "The Study of Administration," and later defined public administration as a subfield of public law. Arthur S. Link, "Woodrow Wilson and the Study of Administration" in Link, ed., *The Higher Realism of Woodrow Wilson and Other Essays* (Nashville: Vanderbilt University Press, 1971), p. 42.

78. Leonard D. White, *Introduction to the Study of Public Administration,* 4th ed. (New York: Macmillan, 1955), p. xvi.

79. Dwight Waldo, "Scope of the Theory of Public Administration," in James C. Charlesworth, ed., *Theory and Practice of Public Administration: Scope, Objectives, and Methods,* Monograph no. 8, Annals of the American Academy of Political and Social Science (1968), pp. 14–15.

80. Sofaer, *supra* note 17, at p. 1313.

81. Davis, *supra* note 22, at p. 160.

82. See e.g., *Ohio Bell Telephone Co. v. Public Utilities Commission,* 301 U.S. 292 (1937), and *St. Joseph Stock Yards Co. v. United States,* 298 U.S. 38 (1936).

83. *Securities and Exchange Commission v. Chenery,* 332 U.S. 194, 216 (1947), Justice Jackson dissenting.

84. *Id.,* at pp. 207–209.

85. *Id.,* at p. 215 (Justice Jackson dissenting).

86. *Universal Camera Corp. v. National Labor Relations Board,* 340 U.S. 474 (1951).

87. *Id.,* at pp. 490–91.

88. *New York v. United States,* 342 U.S. 882, 884 (1951), Justice Douglas dissenting.

89. See e.g., *Klein v. Cohen,* 304 F. Supp. 275, 277 (DCMA 1969), and *Robertson v. Cameron,* 224 F. Supp. 60, 62 (DDC 1063). See also *Jones v. Califano,* 576 F.2d 12, 20 (2d Cir. 1978), and *Appalachian Power Co. v. EPA,* 477 F.2d 495, 507 (4th Cir. 1973).

90. *Capadora v. Celebreeze,* 356 F.2d 1, 6 (2d Cir. 1966). See also *Aquavella v. Richardson,* 437 F. 2d 397, 403 (2d Cir. 1971); *Holmes v. New York City Housing Authority,* 398 F.2d 262 (2d Cir. 1968); *Hornsby v. Allen,* 326 F.2d 605 (5th Cir. 1964); *United States v. Atkins,* 323 F.2d 733 (5th Cir. 1963); and *Shannon v. HUD,* 305 F. Supp. 205, 214 (EDPA 1969).

91. It is a relatively common situation, at least for federal branch administrators, to find themselves facing conflicting interpretations of law. The cases over funding of abortions under Medicaid provide an example of this problem. See *Harris v. McRae,* 448 U.S. 297 (1980). Such conflicts may eventually be resolved by the Supreme Court, as was true of the Medicaid cases, but years can pass between the pronouncements of conflicting decisions and ultimate resolution of the conflict in the Supreme Court.

92. *Citizens Association of Georgetown v. Zoning Commission of Dist. of Columbia,* 477 F.2d 402, 408 (D.C.Cir. 1973). See also *Airline Pilots Association v. Civil Aeronautics Board,* 475 F.2d 900, 906 (D.C.Cir. 1973); *Greater Boston Television Corp. v. Federal Communications Commission,* 444 F.2d 841, 851 (D.C.Cir. 1971); *WAIT Radio v. Federal Communications Commission,* 418 F.2d 1153, 1156 (D.C.Cir. 1969).

93. *Supra* note 88, at p. 884.

94. *Supra* note 83.

95. *Mobil Oil Corp. v. Federal Power Commission,* 483 F.2d 1238, 1254 (D.C.Cir. 1973).

96. *American Iron and Steel Institute v. Environmental Protection Agency,* 526 F.2d 1027, 1046 (3d Cir. 1975).

97. *United States v. Fay,* 247 F.2d 662, 669 (2d Cir. 1957).

98. *Stanley v. Illinois,* 405 U.S. 645, 656 (1972).

99. *Vlandis v. Kline,* 412 U.S. 441, 451 (1973). See also *Stanley v. Illinois, supra* note 89; *Cleveland Board of Education v. LaFleur,* 414 U.S. 632 (1974); *Bell v. Burson,* 402 U.S. 535 (1971).

100. *Shapiro v. Thompson,* 394 U.S. 618, 636 (1969).

101. *Frontiero v. Richardson,* 411 U.S. 677, 688 (1973). See also *Reed v. Reed,* 404 U.S. 71 (1971).

102. *Gratz v. Bollinger,* 539 U.S. 244, 275 (2003).

103. *Tuan Anh Nguyen v. Immigration and Naturalization Service,* 533 U.S. 53, 88 (2001), Justice O'Connor dissenting.

104. *Tenebaum v. Williams,* 193 F.3d 581, 595 (2nd Cir. 1999).

105. See H. George Frederickson, "Whatever Happened to Public Administration? Governance, Governance Everywhere," at http://www.rhul.ac.uk/Management/News-and-Events/seminars/HGeorgeFrederickson11.2.04%20Paper.pdf, as of September 10, 2005, pp. 5–6. Advanced copy provided by author. Forthcoming in Ewan Ferlie, Laurence E. Lynn and Christopher Pollitt, eds. *The Oxford Handbook of Public Management* (London: Oxford University Press, 2006).

106. Ronald C. Moe and Robert S. Gilmour, "Rediscovering Principles of Public Administration: The Neglected Foundation of Public Law," 55 *Public Administration Rev.* 135 (1995); Ronald C. Moe, "'Law' Versus 'Performance' as Objective Standard," 48 *Public Administration Rev.* 675 (1988); "Exploring the Limits of Privatization," 47 *Public Administration Rev.* 453 (1988).

107. U.S. House of Representatives, Task Force on Legal Services and Procedure, *Report on Legal Services and Procedure Prepared for the Commission on Organization of the Executive Branch of the Government,* House Doc. no. 128, 84th Cong., 1st Sess. (1955), p. 24. See also Davis, *supra* note 22.

108. Wright, *supra* note 18, and Sofaer, *supra* note 17. Both argue effectively that voluntary limitation of discretionary authority sounds good, but it does not generally happen.

109. See e.g., Lawrence C. Dodd and Richard L. Schott, *Congress and the Administrative State* (New York: Wiley, 1979).

110. Raoul Berger, "Administrative Arbitrariness and Judicial Review," 65 *Columbia Law Review* 55, 81 (1965).

111. See generally, Gary C. Breyner, *Bureaucratic Discretion: Law and Policy in Federal Regulatory Agencies* (New York: Pergamon Press, 1987).

112. Davis, *supra* note 22.

113. See H. George Frederickson, *Ideal & Practice in Council-Manager Government, Second Edition* (Washington, DC: International City/County Management Association, 1995).

114. See generally Bruce S. Jenkins and Russell C. Kearl, "Problems of Discretion and Responsibility: The Debate Over Tort Liability," in Phillip J. Cooper and Chester A. Newland, eds., *Handbook of Public Law and Administration* (San Francisco: Jossey-Bass, 1997.)

115. See e.g., *Rizzo v. Goode,* 423 U.S. 362 (1976).

116. *Gilbert v. Homar,* 520 U.S. 924, 932-933 (1997).

117. See e.g. F. Trowbridge vom Bauer, "Fifty Years of Government Contract Law," 29 Federal Bar J. 305 (1970).

118. See Robert Wood, ed., *Remedial Law: When Courts Become Administrators* (Amherst, MA: University of Massachusetts Press, 1990) and Phillip J. Cooper, *Hard Judicial Choices* (New York: Oxford University Press, 1988).

119. See e.g., Donald L. Horowitz, *The Courts and Social Policy* (Washington, DC: Brookings Institution, 1977).

120. *Wilson v. Seiter,* 501 U.S. 294 (1991); *Rhodes v. Chapman,* 452 U.S. 337 (1981); *Rizzo v. Goode,* 423 U.S. 362 (1976).

121. See *Missouri v. Jenkins,* 515 U.S. 70 (1995); *Freeman v. Pitts,* 503 U.S. 467 (1992); *Board of Ed. of Oklahoma City v. Dowell,* 498 U.S. 237 (1991); *Milliken v. Bradley,* 418 U.S. 717 (1974).

122. *Board of Ed. of Oklahoma City v. Dowell, supra* note 121; *Pasadena City Bd. of Ed. v. Spangler,* 427 U. S. 424 (1976).

123. *Spallone v. United States,* 493 U.S. 265 (1990).

124. *United States v. Yonkers,* 624 F.Supp. 1276 (SDNY 1985)

125. 837 F.2d 1181 (2d Cir. 1987), cert. denied 100 L.Ed.2d 922 (1988).

126. *United States v. Yonkers,* 865 F.2d 444, 448 (2d Cir. 1988).

127. 856 F.2d, at p. 449.

128. 493 U.S., at p. 280.

129. *Id.,* p. 306, Justice Brennan dissenting.

130. I have dealt with this at length in Phillip J. Cooper, *Hard Judicial Choices, supra* note 118.

131. See the summary figures in *Kane v. Winn,* 319 F. Supp. 2d 162, 181-182 (DMA 2004).

132. See e.g., *Porter v. Nussle,* 534 U.S. 516 (2002); *Sandin v. Conner,* 515 U.S. 472 (1995); *Farmer v. Brennan,* 511 U.S. 825 (1994); *Wilson v. Seiter,* 501 U.S. 294 (1991).

133. *Maynor v. Morgan County,* 147 F.Supp. 1185, 1186 (NDAL 2001).

134. *Laube v. Haley,* 234 F. Supp. 2d 1227, 1253 (MDAL 2002).

135. On the broad trust obligations, see *United States v. Mitchell,* 463 U.S. 206, 225 (1983); *Seminole Nation v. United States,* 316 U.S. 286, 297 (1942).

136. *Yakima v. Yakima Indian Nation,* 502 U.S. 251, 254 (1992).

137. *Cobell v. Norton,* 240 F.3d 1081, 1109 (D.C.Cir. 2001).

138. *Cobell v. Norton,* 226 F. Supp. 2d 1 (D.D.C. 2002).

139. *Id.,* at pp. 160–161.

140. Carl Friedrich, "Public Policy and the Nature of Administrative Responsibility," in Friedrich and E. S. Mason (eds.) *Public Policy* (Cambridge: Harvard, 1940), p. 4.

141. *Chaney v. Heckler,* 718 F.2d 1174 (D.C.Cir. 1983).

142. *Heckler v. Chaney,* 470 U.S. 821, 832–833 (1985).

143. *Id.,* p. 855, Justice Marshall concurring.

144. *Allison v. Block,* 723 F.2d 631, 633 (8th Cir. 1983).

145. *Id.,* at p. 638.

146. *Environmental Defense Fund v. EPA,* 716 F.2d 915, 921 (D.C.Cir. 1983). Another key case compelling production of rules was *Illinois v. Gorsuch,* 530 F. Supp. 340 (D.D.C. 1981).

147. *Office of Communications of the United Church of Christ v. F.C.C.,* 707 F.2d 1413, 1425 (D.C.Cir. 1983).

148. *Motor Vehicle Manufacturers' Association v. State Farm Mutual,* 463 U.S. 29, 42 (1983).

149. *Id.*

150. *Rhodes v. Chapman,* 452 U.S. 337, 362 (1981), Justice Brennan concurring in part, dissenting in part.

151. *Irene Allen v. United States,* 588 F. Supp. 247, 337 (D.Utah 1984).

152. *Id.,* at p. 338.

153. See e.g., the post-9/11 use of force resolution, P.L. 107-40, 115 Stat. 224 (2001).

154. See *Doe v. Gonzales,* 386 F. Supp. 2d 66 (D.CT 2005); *Doe v. Ashcroft,* 334 F. Supp. 2d 471 (SDNY 2004); *Doe v. Ashcroft,* 317 F. Supp. 2d 488 (SDNY 2004).

155. See *In re all Matters Submitted to the Foreign Intelligence Surveillance Court,* 218 F. Supp. 2d 611 (FISC 2002).

156. See e.g., *Hamdi v. Rumsfeld,* 542 U.S. 507 (2004); *Rasul v. Bush,* 542 U.S. 466 (2004); *Padilla v. Hanft,* 2005 U.S. App. LEXIS 28229 (4th Cir. 2005).

157. See U.S. Senate, Report of the Special Committee on National Emergencies and Delegated Emergency Powers, *Executive Orders in Times of War and National Emergency,* 93rd Cong., 2d Sess. (1974).

10

Politics and Regulatory Agencies: Law and Politics in Administration

When the first edition of this volume was written, and in the years since then, there was a broad debate—widespread condemnation, really—concerning regulatory policies and the agencies charged with enforcing them.[1] It seemed that the era of the creation of regulatory programs in fields from occupational health and safety to the environment to control over airlines routes and rates was about to disappear into the dustbin of history. Voices around the world, in developing as well as developed countries, including the United States, increasingly called upon governments to unleash the forces of the marketplace to solve pressing problems that had hitherto been dealt with through regulatory regimes.[2] In fact, the call was not merely to deregulate but for governments to divest themselves of many of their activities through privatization or at least by contracting out if the functions could not be completely shed by the public sector.[3] These demands were made by the U.S. government and international institutions like the World Bank and the International Monetary Fund as conditions of assistance to developing countries.[4] Those with strong ideological views issued increasingly adamant calls for a public choice orientation, a blend of decentralization, deregulation, and increasing options for citizens to express their preferences for services through voucher systems and other market oriented techniques.[5] Others even questioned the idea that there is a distinctive public sector with organizations that have unique characteristics.[6] These calls came from Democratic as well as Republican party spokespersons and others of similar orientation in other countries.[7] Not surprisingly, these movements came during a period when economists (or analysts with a strong economics orientation) were assuming a prominent, some might say dominant role, in policymaking.[8] Speaking of this wave of deregulation rhetoric and policy, none other than Nobel Prize–winning economist and Chairman of the Council of Economic Advisers in the Clinton Administration Joseph Stiglitz wrote, "'We are all Berliners' was the sentiment of President Kennedy's declaration. Thirty years later, we were all deregulators. The distinction between the parties lay only in the degree of their enthusiasm. . . ."[9]

But a funny thing happened on the way to the twenty-first century. Even while the condemnation of regulation was becoming a chorus of virtually all political parties and the public, there were simultaneous demands for more, different, and increasingly complex regulatory programs. From the Love Canal toxic waste battle to the Lockerbee Scotland terrorist bombing of Pan Am Flight 103 to the Chernobyl nuclear disaster to the savings and loan collapse to the ValuJet crash in the Florida Everglades to the food contamination crises of the late 1990s to Enron's scandalous manipulation of electricity prices to the corporate governance debacles of Enron, Global Crossing, and WorldCom, to name only a few, to mad cow to 9/11 to Katrina to parental reaction against violent video games and predatory behavior on the Internet to issues of indecency on television (exemplified by the Super Bowl halftime issue discussed in Chapter 1),[10] there have been repeated calls to develop new regulatory programs, to improve existing regulatory operations, and even to reconsider some of the deregulation efforts that had previously been undertaken.

Today public administrators find themselves operating in a realm of parallel systems management in which new market-based programs must be implemented alongside more traditional regulatory policies, often in the same agency or ministry.[11] This chapter examines the forces that shape regulatory policies and their administration. First, it examines the paradoxical continued use of regulation as a policy instrument at the same time that antiregulatory sentiment is at a high point. Second, it considers the primary actors and institutions in the politics of regulatory agencies. Finally, the chapter addresses three increasingly complex and important issues in regulatory administration: intergovernmental complexity, international forces, and participation questions.

REGULATION AFTER DEREGULATION: OR "I HATE ALL OF BIG GOVERNMENT EXCEPT THE PART THAT I THINK IS NEEDED!"

Few people will say that they like being regulated. At a broad political level, there is no doubt that the general sentiment in favor of deregulation, different regulation, or perhaps better regulation has been and continues to be strong. In fact, there have been new varieties of arguments advanced in recent years in opposition to regulatory activities at all levels of government and not just those carried out from Washington. At the same time, there have been demands for new regulatory programs and, in some case, second thoughts about some of the deregulation that has already been carried out.

The Attack on Regulation

As Chapter 4 explained, President Jimmy Carter, like other candidates of the past three decades of both major political parties, ran against Washington. And he made no secret of his interest in challenging the regulatory regime that operated from there. Carter led successful efforts to deregulate significant portions of airline operations,[12] rail service,[13] and trucking.[14] President Carter told Congress that: "We must work together to review the laws that established the regulatory programs. Those that needlessly restrict competition, impose rigidity, or are otherwise out of date must be revised or eliminated."[15] Natural gas deregulation legislation was adopted in 1978 and Carter immediately announced his intention to roll back price constraints on oil with effective deregulation to be completed by mid-1981.[16]

Looking back on it from today's perspective, there is a tendency to assume that contemporary market-oriented approaches to regulation were creatures of the 1980s or even the 1990s, but virtually all of the techniques now in use were advocated by Carter.

> The Administration's reform program emphasizes the use of innovative regulatory techniques as an alternative to traditional command-and-control regulation; there techniques are generally less likely to interfere with competition. Many work by structuring incentives that will resolve regulatory problems through market mechanisms. These innovative regulatory techniques

move away from centralized decisionmaking and allow industry and consumers more freedom of choice.[17]

The arguments against various types of regulation ranged from a general dislike of having one's activities regulated to calculations that regulation costs too much, to a more moderate but still strongly held view that regulation must be modified in response to demonstrated problems in administering it.

President Carter went beyond support for deregulation legislation to call upon regulatory agencies to reexamine their decisionmaking processes, both to improve their existing operations and also to consider alternative approaches to regulation that made greater use of market-oriented tools.[18] Carter insisted that: "We provide common sense management for the regulatory process."[19] He championed what became known as the Paperwork Reduction Act (PRA), intended to reduce the paperwork burdens often encountered in regulatory enforcement. He created the Regulatory Analysis Review Group (RARG), made up of representatives of regulatory agencies to consider agency efforts, and developed a Regulatory Council to contemplate innovative techniques of regulation that avoided what was increasingly referred to as traditional "command and control" approaches—characterized, according to criticism, by detailed, burdensome, and rigid regulations adopted by closed and arrogant agencies and administered in a harsh, insensitive, and punitive manner. The administration asked executive branch agencies to consider the following eight techniques as alternatives to traditional regulatory strategies.

Marketable rights—The distribution of a limited amount of rights to or permits for scarce resources that parties can then buy, sell, or trade as market dynamics dictate as in the case of emissions permit trading.

Economic incentives—The use of user fees, subsidies, or tax credits (rather than government-enforced standards) to encourage private sector achievement of regulatory goals to reduce direct regulatory enforcement costs and stimulate desirable behavior.

Compliance reform—The practice of replacing or supplementing strict governmental monitoring and enforcement with market-oriented mechanisms, including third-party compliance and supervised self-certification in order to enhance compliance cooperation and reduce enforcement costs to the government.

Enhanced competition—Removal of barriers to market entry or limits on the services that may be provided by those already in the market in order to reduce costs and improve the quality and diversity of products and services.

Performance standards—The effort to replace regulations based on engineering standards that specify the exact means of compliance with specified targets that the regulated organizations to meet in the manner they think best.

Information disclosure—Provides users of a product or service with relevant information about the nature of the product and the consequences of using it, such as in the case of nutrition labeling, in order to substitute consumer choice in the marketplace for centralized decision-making by an agency as to controlled conditions of distribution.

Voluntary standards—Relies, within limits, on regulatory standards developed by third parties (often nonprofit trade associations) or the regulated industries themselves in order to simplify and reduce the costs of standard setting and enforcement with the hope that reduced conflict and costs will increase compliance.

Tiering—The focus is on tailoring regulatory requirements (often record keeping and reporting requirements, compliance responsibilities, and the meeting of highly specific eligibility requirements for funding programs) to fit the size or nature of the regulated entity with particular concern for small businesses, relatively small local government units, and nonprofit organizations.

(The above list and descriptions were assembled from U.S. Regulatory Council documents on the innovative techniques program.[20])

President Reagan followed suit, but his administration was even more intense in criticizing regulatory practice. Chapter 5 explained how he employed executive orders and presidential memoranda to constrain even those agencies charged by Congress with implementation of new complex regulatory programs, such as the Environmental Protection Agency (EPA). He also directed his political appointees to trim back on regulatory activity. Thus, agencies like the Federal Communications Commission (FCC) undertook to deregulate by administrative proceedings.[21]

George H. W. Bush went so far as to declare a 90-day moratorium on the issuance of regulations, which was later extended. He then created the Quayle Council on Competitiveness that provided a mechanism for those targeted by agency regulations to take political appeals directly to the White House around the agencies and off the record.[22] As he moved toward a run for reelection, the Bush administration elevated the visibility of the antiregulatory effort.[23]

While Clinton ran against what he argued were abuses of the regulatory system by his predecessors, as Chapter 5 indicated, he continued a number of the existing constraints on regulatory agencies and added his own, partly as a result of the condemnation of regulation by Vice President Al Gore's National Performance Review (NPR).[24] The reinvented approach to regulation in the Clinton years sought to employ virtually all of what the Carter administration had advanced in its innovative techniques initiative. Above all, in the Clinton years, the theme was to use a negotiated approach rather than a legal enforcement approach to the greatest degree possible. The administration signaled its intentions in a number of highly publicized national conferences such as the "timber summit," a gathering organized to address tensions surrounding regulation of timber operations sparked by controversies over logging in old growth forests of the Northwest and the enforcement of the Endangered Species Act. This issue became known around the country as the Spotted Owl controversy.

The George W. Bush administration made use of all of the tools developed by its predecessors and has left no doubt as to its antiregulatory credentials. The Bush White House pursued that agenda with somewhat less fanfare but, in some respects at least, with more sophistication than did previous administrations. The administration moved quickly to block Clinton administration rules that the Bush White House contended were pushed out to get them into force before the new administration could consider them. It also moved to delay issuance of rules that the new administration argued required further consideration such as the very controversial action to delay and reconsider rules governing arsenic in drinking water. These actions originated with a memorandum prepared by White House Chief of Staff Andrew H. Card on January 20, 2001.[25] The president also participated in the first use of the Congressional Review Act (discussed in Chapter 5) when he signed the congressional resolution overturning the Occupational Health and Safety Administration (OSHA) ergonomics rules in March of 2001.[26]

Unlike the Reagan, George H. W. Bush, and Clinton administrations, however, the George W. Bush White House did not assign the battle against regulation to the vice president. In fact, George W. Bush kept the Clinton regulatory review executive order in force and modified it only to remove references to the role of the vice president and focus the activities in the Office of Management and Budget (OMB), specifically the Office of Information and Regulatory Affairs.[27] Instead of presidential pronouncements issued with great fanfare like those of previous administrations, the George W. Bush White House chose to develop its policies to constrain or block new regulation and trim back where possible using policies issued in the form of bulletins, circulars, and other procedural requirements issued by the OMB. These policies included a guidance document for administrative agencies conducting regulatory analyses under existing statutes and executive orders issued in 2003 (expanding upon the requirements of the executive orders on regulatory analysis),[28] a peer-review process that applies to the foundations of reasoning presented by regulatory agencies in 2004 (as compared to the traditional deference to agency expertise),[29] a set of guidance for the issuance of administrative interpretative rules and guidance documents in 2005 (to require regulatory analysis and review requirements in situations other than substantive or legislative rules),[30] and an OMB bulletin on how risk assessments are to be conducted in conjunction with regulatory decisions (to expand upon the elements of risk assessment already part of Executive Order 12866).[31]

The message that has come through from all of these administrations has been a set of principles accepted by Democrats and Republicans alike: First, regulation should not be imposed unless it is truly necessary. Second, regulation is not truly necessary if there is some less intrusive mechanism for obtaining the same results. Third, there are market-oriented tools that rely upon incentives, information, and market choice that avoid the need for traditional command and control regulation. Fourth, if regulation does appear to be needed, it is essential to ensure that the potential impacts of those programs are carefully analyzed before they are imposed. Finally, if they are imposed, they should be as flexible as possible and oriented toward a risk-assessment approach to determine how much action is truly needed given enforcement costs.

New Attacks on Regulatory Activity

At the same time, new attacks on the regulatory programs were emerging around the nation. Some of these challenges were focused on the argument that even if some regulatory programs were necessary, there were far too many cases in which agencies were taking rigid and insensitive approaches to enforcement.[32] The NPR accepted that criticism and called for a shift from an enforcement attitude to a negotiated approach emphasizing sensitivity to the costs and burdens of compliance and a willingness to consider unique circumstances.[33]

Other challenges went beyond the rules or even the agencies that administered them to constitutional attacks on the regulatory statutes themselves. State and local officials brought a number of successful suits against programs like the Brady gun control bill that struck all or portions of congressional regulatory policies.[34] The Supreme Court also sought to draw boundaries not only on the basis of the reserve powers of the states under the Tenth Amendment but also by restricting the scope of the congressional power to regulate interstate commerce as it struck down the Gun-Free School Zones Act[35] and the Violence Against Women Act.[36] These disputes emerged as the intergovernmental complexities of regulatory policy increased significantly (a subject that will be considered at length later in this chapter).

Individuals and interest groups also went on the attack. There have been specific issues like First Amendment complaints that have succeeded against policies such as the Communications Decency Act that sought to control adult-oriented material on the Internet.[37] Other issues such as state controls on physician-assisted suicide[38] and the national effort to deal with clashes over the relationship of church and state in the Religious Freedom Restoration Act[39] have engendered challenges as well.

There have also been more general movements, asserting that there should be a reexamination of the constitutional underpinnings of some regulatory policies. Probably the most dramatic example is what has come to be known as the movement against regulatory takings.[40] Traditionally, the theory has been that while the Fifth Amendment requires just compensation in the event that the government takes one's private property for public use, regulation is usually not considered to be a taking. As Justice Douglas put it, the costs of regulation are the price that we pay for civilization.[41] That has generally been the controlling theory even in those cases in which regulations had significant impacts on businesses or private property.

However, this long-established principle was challenged by a coalition of political activists with strong ideological views and a group of more moderate citizens who simply think that some regulations go so far that they exceed limited impact on one's property and actually convert it to the use of the government. Thus, they contend that that conversion represents a taking. It is an argument that regulation and taking are not separate categories but ends of a single continuum. Thus, property holders in California concluded that the Pacific Coastal Initiative that sought to control the development of private property along the coast so as to preserve the environment went so far as to be a taking, and the Supreme Court agreed.[42] Similarly, the Court rejected a South Carolina limitation on coastal development. In the process, the Court rejected the idea that regulatory programs could survive as long as they were rationally related to a legitimate state purpose. Rather, the Court found that in order to justify serious constraints there had to be a problem present that was the equivalent of a nuisance or some inherent danger in the activity itself.[43]

In *Dolan v. City of Tigard*,[44] the Supreme Court even struck down what most administrators saw as an enforcement of traditional zoning restrictions. In the process, the Supreme Court shifted the burden to communities to justify denials of permit requests in order to avoid a claim that what purported to be regulation was in fact a taking of property. These victories fueled efforts, particularly in some of the western states, to attack federal government controls on land, an effort known as the "sagebrush rebellion."[45]

All of these attacks have sent the message that it can no longer be assumed that Congress or state legislatures have the authority to adopt whatever regulatory programs that they choose to enact. In the process, the Supreme Court has indicated a willingness to reopen issues that many observers thought had long since been resolved in favor of federal and state authority. The Court has not consistently ruled against government in takings claims, but there remains uncertainty as to just where the takings cases will go in the future as a constraint on regulation.[46]

The Demand for New Regulation

Even as reactions against regulations increased, politicians who advocated deregulation were rewarded at the polls, and courts were entertaining new challenges to long-standing regulatory policies, new demands surfaced that government should provide more and better regulation in a variety of fields. Consider the case of environmental regulation.

By the late 1970s, it was increasingly common for political candidates to attack environmental regulation (often along with health and safety regulations) as the primary example of governmental intrusiveness and regulatory burdens on the economy. However, even as Americans and citizens of other countries around the world expressed resentment at the polls by electing candidates who promised deregulation, they were demanding that government—particularly the national government—do something about the growing problems on what are now called the green and brown agendas of environmental protection.[47] The green issues included questions of conservation and environmental protection. The brown agenda concerned the management of hazardous materials, such as toxic chemicals and nuclear waste, and the cleanup of previously polluted sites.

Notwithstanding their general opposition to regulatory programs, Americans maintained a solid support for environmental legislation throughout the 1970s. And indeed, in the early years, these were bipartisan concerns. In 1971 the Council on Environmental Quality of the Nixon administration produced its report on the hazard to citizens and the environment from the inherent danger, misuse, or lack of proper waste treatment of the over 1,000 new chemical compounds marketed each year.[48] In its investigations of toxic chemicals, Congress found brain damage was caused by exposure to Kepone, lead, mercury, and other heavy metals.[49] Products used to manufacture or refine items for commercial and retail markets, such as vinyl chloride, arsenic, asbestos, myrex, fluorocarbons, and polychlorinated biphenyls (PCBs), were also found to be dangerous. In stating the need for the Toxic Substance Control Act,[50] the legislature noted that in 1975 as many Americans died of cancer as in all the battle deaths in Vietnam, Korea, and World War II combined.[51] Congress also observed that the National Cancer Institute had found that 60 to 90 percent of those deaths could be attributed to environmental contaminants.[52] Most people have forgotten that it was Richard Nixon who created the Environmental Protection Agency (EPA) through a reorganization order. Nixon warned that the work of the agency was so important that the EPA needed to maintain independence from political interference.

These frightening reports began to attract public attention when studies found that significant medical problems were caused by low-level exposure to widely used substances such as asbestos and benzene.[53] Over time public opinion seemed to become more resistant to the barrage of reports that rats exposed to large doses of some chemical contracted cancer. However, such news as the fact that a worker who has been exposed to asbestos and is a smoker has a likelihood of contracting cancer that is 92 times greater than average had a great impact on public opinion.[54]

And there were very immediate forces that demanded attention. The 1978 accident at the Three Mile Island nuclear power station caused intense anxiety, not only in the east but wherever nuclear power stations were located. The discovery of the Love Canal chemical dump site was one of a series of events that fueled demands for new and more intense environmental regulation even in an era of deregulation.[55] Panic set in when the community realized that there were abnormally high incidences of cancer, especially among children who lived on or near the buried disposal site. Beyond that, it was learned that containers of nuclear wastes that had been dumped at sea in years past were leaking. The proverbial last straw was the realization, confirmed by private and governmental organizations, that illegally disposed of chemicals and materials from unsafe dump sites were rapidly filtering into streams and underground aquifers from which communities draw drinking water. Hearings conducted in 1980 by a congressional subcommittee determined that there were some 200 unprotected dump sites within one mile of the supply points for municipal water companies.[56] The subcommittee warned that the situation was actually worse, but inadequate or nonexistent monitoring facilities in various states and localities made it impossible to accurately assess the scope of the problem. The discovery that there were gaps in regulatory legislation that made it difficult to address these issues brought cries for legislative action.

Of course, 1980 was also a presidential election year, and environmental regulation was a target even while Congress and environmental agencies were formulating responses to public fear and anger. When the Reagan administration moved to curb EPA rulemaking and enforcement, Congress reacted strongly, eventually enacting amended legislation that mandated more extensive action. Then there was Times Beach. In 1981 it was discovered that used oil that contained toxic chemicals had been spread on the roads of Times Beach, Missouri, to keep down dust. Eventually, the entire town was evacuated. Then, in 1984, there was the Bhopal Disaster in which 5,000 people died or became seriously ill from a chemical release in India. When Americans discovered that a plant of the same type was being operated by the same company in West Virginia, there were calls for action. There was hardly time to react to Bhopal when, in 1986, a nuclear power facility in Chernobyl in the Ukraine became one of the most extensive environmental disasters in history—as the nuclear pollution from the plant spread not only to neighboring communities but quite literally around the world. By this point, Americans were learning that there were serious nuclear problems in the United States at facilities operated by the military and the Department of Energy in such places as Rocky Flats, Colorado, and the Hanford Nuclear Reservation in Washington. The problem of where to put nuclear waste still had not been resolved and trust that those involved would do the right thing vanished as Utah citizens learned that they had been intentionally deceived by the federal government in the 1950s and 1960s when they were exposed to nuclear fallout from testing at the Nevada test site.[57] It was becoming clear that the U.S. government was one of the most extensive polluters in American history, but existing legislation provided no vehicle by which to force federal agencies to comply with the same requirements imposed on everyone else in the nation, in government or out. And if all that were not enough, there came the night in 1990 when the oil tanker Exxon Valdez ran aground in Prince William's sound, Alaska, sending millions of gallons of crude oil into one of the most beautiful and sensitive ecosystems in North America.

Each of these events triggered demands for action, often in the form of calls for new or strengthened policies and for a tightening of regulatory controls and enforcement in those areas where environmental laws were already in place. A partial list of the legislation includes:

The Resource Conservation and Recovery Act 1976

Toxic Substances Control Act 1976

Comprehensive Environmental Response, Compensation, and Liability Act (Superfund) 1980

Alaska National Interest Conservation Act 1980

Hazardous and Solid Waste Amendments 1984

Superfund Amendments and Reauthorization Act (SARA) 1986

Asbestos Hazard Emergency Response Act 1986

Safe Drinking Water Amendments of 1986

Emergency Planning and Community Right to Know Act of 1986

Federal Water Quality Act 1987

Federal Insecticide, Fungicide, and Rodenticide Act Amendments 1988

Ocean Pollution Act 1990

Oil Pollution Prevention Act 1990

Clean Air Act Amendments of 1990

Residential Lead-Based Paint Hazard Reduction Act 1992

Federal Facilities Compliance Act 1992

California Desert Protection Act 1994

More broadly, the global community embarked on a new era of efforts to respond to environmental problems while simultaneously addressing the pressing need for economic development in many countries around the world. Beginning with the first major global conference in Stockholm in 1972, the United States was involved in an ongoing effort to fashion both international environmental policies and domestic efforts to implement global accords.[58] As was true at home, the international community continued to develop these new regulatory programs during the same years that there was a clarion call in international bodies and many national governments for deregulation. Consider the following partial list from the late 1970s on:

London Convention on Civil Liability for Oil Pollution Damage Resulting from Exploration for and Exploitation of Seabed Mineral Resources 1977

Convention on Long-Range Transboundary Air Pollution 1979

Bonn Convention on the Conservation of Migratory Species of Wild Animals 1989

Convention of the Conservation of Antarctic Marine Living Resources 1980

UN Convention on the Law of the Sea 1982

Vienna Convention to Protect the Ozone Layer 1985

Convention on Early Notification of a Nuclear Accident 1986

Convention on Assistance in the Case of a Nuclear Accident or Radiological Emergency 1986

Montreal Protocol 1987

Convention on the Regulation of Antarctic Mineral Resources Activities 1988

Protocol Concerning the Control of Emissions of Nitrogen Oxides 1988

Basel Convention on the Control of Transboundary Movements of Hazardous Wastes and Their Disposal 1989

Protocol on the Reduction of Volatile Organic Compounds 1991

Espoo Convention on Environmental Impact Assessment in a Transboundary Context 1991

Bamako Convention on the Ban of the Import into Africa and the Control of Transboundary Movements and Management of Hazardous Wastes Within Africa 1991

Biodiversity Convention 1992

Kyoto Protocol on Climate Change 1997

In addition, the global community, throughout the 1990s, entered into a series of nonbinding statements of commitment and programs of action on various aspects of sustainable development, beginning with the Rio Declaration and Agenda 21 at the Earth Summit in 1992.[59] These agreements were reinforced at the ten year anniversary conference of Agenda 21 in Johannesburg in 2002.

Even though the United States was not committed to all of these accords, the EPA alone faced more than 100 sets of international obligations along with the many new domestic programs developed during this period. On top of that, U.S. presidents have added requirements by executive orders and memoranda outlined in previous chapters. Additionally, there were ongoing efforts to reduce personnel and budgets in the agencies involved.

While all of this was going on, agencies were called upon to implement the innovative techniques developed as alternatives to traditional command and control regulation. Some of these are simply alternative modes or regulation, while others seek to shift more directly to market-based, incentive-oriented mechanisms to encourage desirable behavior by businesses, governments, and consumers and to discourage dangerous or inappropriate behavior.

Traditional regulatory programs often and for many years involved the use of engineering standards or performance standards to set limits for certain kinds of pollution or extraction of resources. Most are designed medium-by-medium to address air, water, or toxic pollution, for example. The difference is that engineering standards control both the ends to be achieved and the means to be used for their attainment, whereas performance standards set the goals but leave the choice of means to the regulated party. An increasingly popular approach is what can be called a tracking or manifest system under which regulated parties are required to establish what amounts to a paper trail of their activities such that any resulting environmental damage can be traced to the door of the responsible party where restitution may be obtained. This is a standard approach, for example, in dealing with toxic chemicals. Related to these techniques are liability policies that make regulated parties liable for damage claims brought by the government or, in some instances private parties, in a court.

In addition to these more or less traditional tools, there are a number of other devices that can be termed process policies which are intended to avoid prejudgment of particular questions but to provide ways to achieve sound decisions.[60] Commonly used examples include environmental impact assessment requirements, mandatory risk assessments, contingency planning requirements, obligatory cost-benefit analyses, and environmental dispute resolution (EDR), which is a set of ADR techniques adapted for use in environmental settings.

Finally, there are a variety of market-oriented mechanisms. Typical techniques include the use of permits, marketable rights, environmental funds or trusts, eco-pricing, eco-labeling, debt for nature swaps, extraction taxes, carbon taxes, special taxes on hazardous industries, user fees, loans or subsidies conditioned on desirable behavior, license fees, and insurance obligations (or other forms of indemnification) for those engaged in potentially dangerous or damaging activity. While a number of these are more or less self-explanatory, the others require some consideration.

Marketable rights assume a system in which regulators set a ceiling on emissions for a geographic area. Within that, emissions permits are granted to firms operating in that zone. A market is then created within which permit holders may buy or sell their permits. Presumably, more efficient firms will develop cleaner technologies and will then have excess permit capacity that they can sell to others for needed cash. Other firms operating at industry standard may expand their operations, but would be required to pay to obtain additional emissions capacity in the marketplace. To this point, marketable rights have been used in the United States in connection with air emissions.[61]

Environmental funds or trusts have become popular in a number of jurisdictions. The basic idea is to take some portion of the financing of environmental management out of the traditional politics of the budgetary process and permit resources acquired through permits, fees, special taxes, and foreign aid to be managed in the manner of a trust. Trusts may be managed by environmental agencies or independent boards of directors.

Indemnification and loan policies use the costs of insurance and the availability of mortgages and other capital funds to pressure firms to avoid dangerous situations as well as to correct any harm they might cause. At root, the Polluter Pays Principle (PPP) is intended not only to ensure that the people or firms responsible for environmental degradation bear the cost of fixing the problem, but also to provide a deterrent effect such that potential polluters will think twice. In order to avoid sophisticated techniques of evasion of responsibility, some governments have instituted liability schemes that follow the pollution. Thus, a firm that acquires a polluter, in effect, buys responsibility for fixing the problems of the target firm. That deterrent has caused firms, insurance companies, and lenders to require inspections of properties and indemnification for any environmental liabilities traceable to a previous owner that are discovered in a property in the future.

Eco-pricing is based on the idea that the price structure of a product ought to incorporate environmental costs in order to reflect what is termed the true cost.[62] That includes such issues as funds for reforestation, restoration projects, and cleanup or reprocessing of byproducts. In some instances, the increment is used directly by the firm or paid to NGOs or indigenous groups, but often the idea is that the increment is paid to the government as if it were a use tax. The government then becomes responsible to undertake the appropriate restoration projects.

Eco-labeling is a process that discloses the ecological impact and character of a product. Most often, it has some form of positive message that links the product or service to some beneficial environmental outcome. While eco-labeling is sometimes advanced as an educational or disclosure device, its principal purpose is to market the product. Thus, there have been considerable disputes about the accuracy of environmental claims and there is virtually no one to respond to those charges.

Behind all of these options is the claim that the marketplace and associated business taxes and fees are often more effective than traditional government regulation, are more cost effective, and do not depend upon active policing or simple moral suasion to achieve their ends. Of course, critics of the economic approach contend that the marketplace will never adequately offset environmental degradation, nor will it provide incentives strong enough to protect against abuses.

Discussions of some of the newer tools sometimes imply that they are replacements for existing mechanisms of environmental management that will reduce the scope and character of administrative burdens and costs. Indeed, in some cases the expectation is that the market will handle most of the work. That is simply not true. The more accurate representation is that the array of new tools and techniques is being layered onto existing structures and processes. They are not self-operating and they do pose new institutional and management challenges.

Even those tools that are market-based require administration. Marketable rights can operate only if someone sets the limits for emissions and monitors them to ensure that the total does not exceed the ceiling. That monitoring task, if it is to be precise enough to be useful, is made increasingly difficult the larger the geographic area involved because, among other things, nonpoint source pollution confounds measurements of outputs from firms with permits. Moreover, markets for marketable rights must be built, maintained, and controlled.

The concept that permitting processes are effective controls is true only to the degree that some agency designs the processes effectively, ensures adequate data collection and evaluation to determine eligibility for permits, and has means available to monitor compliance with the permit requirements with an effective means available to revoke the permit in the event that the conditions are violated. Moreover, that capacity must include the ability to evaluate renewal requests and competing claims where the number of available permits is limited.

Fees and taxes do not eliminate the need for complex administrative systems, just different types of systems. Funds must be audited, collected, and expended for intended purposes.[63] Indeed, the idea of environmental taxes and eco-pricing represents a subtle shifting of work for environmental cleanup and preservation to the government. The idea is that by paying a fee in the form of a charge included in the final price of a product, or a simple tax, firms are freed from responsibility for cleanup and conservation. They simply include the cost as an expense and press forward. That makes environmental preservation and cleanup a public works project, leaving the government carrying all of the uncertainties and burdens and removing the incentives from commercial entities to avoid liabilities by doing the environmental job themselves. In such circumstances, the taxes or fees would never be large enough to cover the real costs of cleanup and would significantly reduce the incentives to avoid pollution in the first place. It is much less expensive to take that precautionary action than it is to do the cleanup later. Moreover, that system would require dramatic increases in the size of government environmental operations with increased administrative costs.

If eco-labeling is to have any significant function beyond promoting products, it will require some kind of monitoring and enforcement. Since the products involved are often imported and since technical information is not readily available even on domestic materials, the use of deceptive advertising laws to ensure effectiveness is of little help. Furthermore, the tendency of firms to employ "greenspeak" (environmental language) in their marketing claims whether or not it is justified is already well known.[64]

Environmental dispute resolution, while an attractive alternative in some settings, remains a limited option. It has produced successes, but there is no evidence to believe that it will be more than a partial answer to some environmental problems in certain settings. The stakes are often simply too high and the disputes often too complex with too many parties to get the kind of focus and boundaries that cause players to regard new EDR techniques as attractive. The use of these tools requires trained personnel to achieve the settlements but also the tools necessary to ensure compliance and to take action in the event of a default.

Risk assessment, while useful in some respects, can only be part of the regulatory process. On the other hand, it certainly can be and has been used in a very different way to block or place increased burden on regulatory programs. Used as a tool of regulation, the idea has been that questionable products or practices should be subjected to a careful risk assessment of sufficient scope and depth to protect the environment and the public against dangers of many types. Used as a constraint on regulation, risk assessment is employed to ensure that the costs and burdens of regulation are proportionate to the nature and level of risk that regulatory policy is designed to address. Through the 1970s, the focus was on the former idea of risk assessment, but at least since the 1990s the emphasis has been on the use of risk assessments as constraints on regulation.

The 2005 OMB Proposed Risk Assessment Bulletin looked back to the National Academy of Sciences (NAS) report of 1983 on Risk Assessment in the Federal Government to make the case for the need for expanded and more systematic use of the process in regulation. The OMB requires that risk assessments "meet the three key attributes of utility, objectivity, and integrity." However, there is inevitably a significant element in subjectivity in the design, conduct, and application of risk assessments. That same 1983 NAS report observed: "A single risk management decision is often based on an assessment that, itself, comprises many discrete decisions—choices among assumptions, interpretations, relatively weighing of conflicting of evidence—that analysts must make if useful overall conclusions are to be reached...."[65] The more recent 1994 National Academy study found that these uncertainties remained notwithstanding the developments in risk assessment methodology.[66] In fact, the 1994 provided 27 pages of discussion about these uncertainties. The OMB proposal called upon agencies to characterize the nature and amount of uncertainty and said that, in the end: "Influential risk assessments should, to the extent possible, provide a discussion regarding the nature, difficulty, feasibility, cost and time associated with undertaking research to resolve a report's key scientific limitations and uncertainties."[67]

While there continues to be considerable debate over the problems of methodology and premises of risk assessment, one of the most fundamental challenges is the one pointed out by Aldo Leopold nearly half a century ago.[68] Notwithstanding the formulaic reference to health, safety, and the environment in risk assessment policies, the tendency has been to focus on and calculate risk to human health and safety. If harm to environment itself is considered, the calculations may become very murky because it is virtually impossible to calculate, for example, species loss in a situation where the species has no commercial value.

Moreover, risk assessment requires more—not less—administration. Among other things, an era of adversarial science has meant that, like environmental impact statements, risk assessments will be challenged by those who represent competing interests.[69] Someone must evaluate the assessment and then determine limits to action. The assumption is sometimes made that risk assessment yields binary decisions, i.e., that a project should or should not be permitted to proceed. But risk assessments are not designed that way. They produce measures in terms of probabilities on the basis of which someone must make further judgments. There is a tendency to point to the scientific power of risk assessments, but risk assessments are only tools, devices with their own limitations the importance of which depends upon how they are employed and what actions are taken as a result of their application in any given context.

At the end of the day, then, despite the move to deregulate, there is in many respects more regulation now than before. In many instances, what were advocated as alternatives to regulation turn out to be alternative types of regulation. And all of these policy instruments, whether traditional or market-oriented approaches, require administration.

REGULATION AS A POLICY OPTION

While the brief story in the previous section speaks to environmental regulation, the same kinds of issues arise in a host of other areas as well. Certainly, the effort to address the dramatic financial abuses of what Stiglitz called "The Roaring Nineties" and after provides another set of examples and produced such legislation as the Sarbanes-Oxley Act of 2002. Political rhetoric notwithstanding, most regulatory programs continue not because anyone likes regulation or for ideological reasons but because they are responses to important problems on the public agenda. Regulation is one of several possible types of policy that the legislature may choose to employ.

Decisions about which approach should be pursued come from what is generally referred to as the public policy process. While the leading authors on public policy have varied approaches to the field, most generally agree that it consists of several stages, including agenda setting, policy formulation, adoption, implementation, evaluation, and termination.[70]

Agenda Setting

An issue is a problem on the public policy agenda. In its simplest terms, a policy is an answer to that problem. The first step is to identify and articulate the issue, one of the most difficult and often underappreciated aspects of policymaking.[71] The next question is whether the problem belongs on the public agenda or ought to be resolved privately.[72] Assuming that the issue gets to the agenda, the problem is to determine what priority it should have relative to other pending issues.

Often issues rise to top priority not because they are in some scientific sense the most critical, but because they achieve sufficient political support. Thus, events and media coverage can come together to bring about pressure for action. When that happens, as Kingdon has argued, the circumstances can create an open window through which advocates can push a policy.[73] Using the environmental examples noted earlier, there is no question that the publicity surrounding the Love Canal battle and the furor that arose in connection with the Bhopal disaster opened windows that allowed advocates to push through Congress the Superfund program and the "Right To Know" law, respectively. More recently, certainly the Enron revelations and other well-publicized stories of financial misdeeds open a policy window for strengthened market regulation.

Policy Formulation

The next stage is policy formulation. Before designing specific responses to a problem a decision must be made as to what type of policy is to be employed. Frohock, relying heavily on Lowi's work, developed a five-part typology describing the major types of policy options that the legislature might consider, including regulatory policies, distributive, redistributive, capitalization, and ethical policies.[74]

The first category is *regulatory policy*. Regulatory programs place limits on various forms of activity. Regulatory bodies may, for example, limit access to business or the professions, as in the licensing of physicians and attorneys. They may set routes and rates, as for utility or taxi cab companies. Regulators may be charged with ensuring fair trade practices, or health, safety, or other aspects of business activity.

Regulatory administrators may use a carrot-and-stick approach in dealing with regulated parties or develop innovative techniques of regulations,[75] but at its core, regulation is, to one degree or another, coercive.[76] The extent of coerciveness varies. One agency can threaten only bad publicity, while in another officials have substantial coercive power, "like a shotgun behind the door" as Securities and Exchange Commission Chair (and later Supreme Court Justice) William O. Douglas put it, but try in particular to avoid using available sanctions. Some regulatory programs have authority to impose many sanctions, up to and including criminal prosecutions. Regulatory programs that rely heavily on the use of coercive authority are those that have generally come to be known as command-and-control regulation.

A second category of policy option is *distributive policy*. "Distributive policies grant goods and services to specific segments of the population."[77] Such programs as veterans' benefits are intended to dispense assistance to those who qualify. The difficulty for the legislature, and later for administrators, is to properly define the eligible members of the target group and then to select the agencies and procedures by which to disburse the funds.

A third type of policy is *redistributive policy*, which is "aim[ed] at rearranging one or more of the basic schedules of social and economic rewards."[78] The most frequently cited example of a redistributive policy was, for many years, the progressive income tax, which attempted to ease the burdens on the poorer members of the society by placing the major burden for support of social programs and governmental expenditures on the wealthier citizens. However, changes in tax policy have made the income tax much less redistributive in character. Another example is the Food Stamp program under which lower income persons get a subsidy in the form of food stamps that enables them to leverage their own limited food budget into an amount of food more likely to meet the needs of the family.

A fourth type is what Frohock calls a *capitalization policy*. In some respects similar to distributive policies, capitalization policies provide subsidies, tax credits, tax abatements, contracts, or grants to aid in capital formation. The purpose is to provide incentives for the private sector to develop or expand industries in needed areas of the economy or to aid beleaguered, but valued, businesses such as the family farm. There is some degree of irony, and not a little hypocrisy, in our tendency to speak of redistributive assistance as entitlement programs that burden the society but to ignore the scope and significance of capitalization policies, which may also be entitlement programs and even more costly.

Finally, some responses to public problems come in the form of *ethical policies*[79] of which the Ethics in Government Act[80] as it was originally enacted is an example. Although it now has a variety of regulatory aspects, the Ethics in Government Act was designed to encourage public servants to note and act to avoid possible conflicts of interest, and attempts to promote public support for civil servants by publicizing their efforts to prevent unethical practices. Another example is President Clinton's executive order on environmental justice that calls upon agencies to pay attention to possible inequitable impacts of environmental actions on minority communities.[81] The order itself provided no sanctions, but encouraged consideration of environmental equity issues in decisionmaking.

After the policymaking body has selected a type of policy and surveyed the specific options available within that policy area, it must consider which means will likely work best. Traditionally, we tend to think of this process as focused on a variety of decision support tools like cost/benefit analysis. We seek to determine the costs and benefits for each option as far as they can be analyzed?

The problems encountered in discussing costs and benefits of regulatory programs are central to policy formulation, adoption, and evaluation. As Chapter 5 explained, agencies face demands not only to provide such analyses for rules that have significant impacts, but also to demonstrate that the cost/benefit calculus meets several criteria. It is worth repeating here the pertinent provisions of President Clinton's Executive Order 12866.

Section 1. Statement of Regulatory Philosophy and Principles.

(a) …. In deciding whether and how to regulate, agencies should assess all costs and benefits of available regulatory alternatives, including the alternative of not regulating. Costs and benefits shall be understood to include both quantifiable measures (to the fullest extent that these can be usefully estimated) and qualitative measures of costs and benefits that are difficult to quantify, but nevertheless essential to consider. Further, in choosing among alternative regulatory approaches, agencies should select those approaches that maximize net benefits (including potential economic, environmental, public health and safety, and other advantages, distributive impacts; and equity), unless a statute requires another regulatory approach.

(b) ...To ensure that the agencies' regulatory programs are consistent with the philosophy set forth above, agencies should adhere to the following principles, to the extent permitted by law and where applicable.

(1) .... Each agency shall identify the problem that it intends to address (including, where applicable, the failures of private markets or public institutions that warrant new agency action) as well as assess the significance of that problem. ...

(3) Each agency shall identify and assess available alternatives to direct regulation, including providing economic incentives to encourage the desired behavior, such as user fees or marketable permits, or providing information upon which choices can be made by the public.

(4) In setting regulatory priorities, each agency shall consider, to the extent reasonable, the degree and nature of the risks posed by various substances or activities within its jurisdiction.

(5) When an agency determines that a regulation is the best available method of achieving the regulatory objective, it shall design its regulations in the most cost-effective manner to achieve the regulatory objectives. In doing so, each agency shall consider incentives for innovation, consistency, predictability, the costs of enforcement and compliance (to the government, regulated entities, and the public), flexibility, distributive impacts, and equity.

(6) Each agency shall assess both the costs and the benefits of the intended regulation and, recognizing that some costs and benefits are difficult to quantify, propose or adopt a regulation only upon a reasoned determination that the benefits of the intended regulation justify its costs.

(7) Each agency shall base its decisions on the best reasonably obtainable scientific, technical, economic, and other information concerning the need for, and consequences of, the intended regulation. ...

(9) ...Each agency shall assess the effects of Federal regulations on State, local, and tribal governments, including specifically the availability of resources to carry out those mandates, and seek to minimize those burdens that uniquely or significantly affect such governmental entities, consistent with achieving regulatory objectives. ...

(11) Each agency shall tailor its regulations to impose the least burden on society, including individuals, businesses of differing sizes, and other entities (including small communities and governmental entities), consistent with obtaining the regulatory objectives, taking into account, among other things, and to the extent practicable, the costs of cumulative regulations. (See full text of E.O. 12866 in Appendix 4.)

The idea that there ought to be a relationship between costs and benefits is intuitively appealing. After all, the common assumption is that rational policymakers consider all options, analyze each alternative, and select the best proposal. Presumably, techniques like cost/benefit analysis is one way of undertaking those analyses.

However, on reflection, this effort to assess costs and benefits turns out to be considerably more complex than is readily apparent. And when all of the demands in the executive order above are added to that seemingly reasonable expectation, the result can be paralysis.[82] For present purposes, two problems are particularly important: (1) economic versus political perspectives on regulatory policy, and (2) technical difficulties in computing costs and benefits.

James Q. Wilson has addressed the important differences between economic and political perspectives on regulatory policy. He observed that one need not give up all concern about making rational and effective public policies to understand that the attempt to apply hard economic analysis techniques to the public policy process frequently will not explain behavior, and often will not lead to better policies.[83] He based his conclusion on three differences in the economic and political perspectives on policy.

> First, politics concerns preferences that do not always have a common market measuring rod. In an economic market, we seek to maximize our "utility," a goal that substantively can be almost anything but in practice involves things that have, or can easily be given, money values....
>
> In nonmarket relationships, such as in voluntary associations or in legislatures, we may also behave in a rationally self-interested manner—but we do so in a setting that does not usually permit monetary (or quantitative) values to be assigned to our competing preferences in any nonarbitrary way....
>
> Second, political action requires assembling majority coalitions to make decisions that bind everyone whether or not he belongs to that coalition. When we make purchases in a market, we commit only ourselves, and we consume as much or as little of a given product as we wish. When we participate in making decisions in the political arena, we are implicitly committing others as well as ourselves, and we are "consuming" not only a known product (such as the candidate for whom we vote) but also a large number of unknown products (all the policies the winning candidate will help enact)....
>
> The third and most important difference between economics and politics is that whereas economics is based on the assumption that preferences are given, politics must take into account the efforts made to change preferences.[84]

What problems ought to be on the public agenda, what priority to assign a particular problem, what policy options are available, who will benefit from alternative policy choices, and who will pay are political decisions shaped by a variety of forces and factors, only some of which are amenable to economic analysis. They are historically not about questions of efficiency. "Politics differs from economics in that it manages conflict by forming heterogenous coalitions out of persons with changeable and incommensurable preferences in order to make binding decisions for everyone."[85]

There are several basic issues associated with the failure to understand the important distinctions between these perspectives. The first problem can be summed up by the statement: "Americans love numbers."[86] When offered what appears to be a scientific analysis of a problem and possible solutions, it is tempting to let the numbers, whether or not the data are valid or the analysis appropriate, dominate the debate.[87] A Report of the House Subcommittee on Oversight and Investigations gave an example of excessive reliance on cost-benefit economic-efficiency-oriented models of public policy analysis and decisionmaking:

> Let's examine...the variables which would have been involved if the government of Abraham Lincoln had been required to perform a cost-benefit analysis on a proposed Emancipation Proclamation.
>
> Some of the non-trivial variables on the cost side would have been the loss of equity (property value) to the slaveholders; the effect on economic production of a complete alteration of the system of production and distribution in the Southern States; the direct and indirect costs of introducing a wage system in those states; the impact on the war effort (increased Southern resistance); the extent and timing of a migration of unskilled Blacks into the North with resulting employment impacts and demands on private charities; and the additional costs of maintaining public order in the Southern military districts.
>
> Each of these costs would have had to have been estimated for a variety of industries and regions and then generalized into a single accounting system. Inasmuch as the impacts would not have occurred simultaneously, each one would have had to have been estimated for a given period of time.

On the benefits side, some of the easier variables to estimate would have been essentially offsets to the cost, such as the potential long-run increase in productivity resulting from a switch to a wage system, the additional manpower available to the Northern Army, and the additional labor to be employed in post-war industrialization and to settle the West. The most difficult quantification problem would have been in assigning a dollar value to human dignity and freedom. Again, each one would have to have been estimated for a given time to make the comparisons meaningful.

Inasmuch as economic historians tell us that slavery was a profitable system, the cost benefit analysis, at least in the short run, probably would have deemed that Lincoln not free the slaves unless a substantial dollar value was assigned to human dignity and freedom.[88]

As President Roosevelt is reputed to have said to one of his policy analysts, the logic is one thing, but the conclusion is absolutely wrong![89]

The second concern in considering costs versus benefits is that there are a host of specific technical problems. A House subcommittee report mentioned several. First, computations of costs of particular regulatory programs are often very weak.[90] The source of data for estimating costs is often the industry that is now, or is about to be, regulated. Such data have proven over the years to be fraught with problems of bias.[91] Second, it found that such analyses rarely take account of technological change (the learning curve) as a factor that reduces costs of programs over time.[92] Third, the subcommittee found that it is extremely difficult to deal with incremental costs; that is, to determine which costs are attributable to a particular government policy.[93] The subcommittee observed that techniques for calculating benefits are "primitive."[94] To calculate the benefits of a particular program, one must be able to anticipate the specific effects of a given policy decision.[95] This means forecasting accurately and at a level of specificity that in many instances exceeds our capacity for calculation. Another problem is "applying dollar values to items that lack a market price."[96] Nor are costs and benefits always distributed fairly, hence the costs and benefits of a given type of activity, and the policies created to deal with it, may not allow comparability in analysis.[97] In the nearly 30 years since the subcommittee report first issued these criticisms, and despite a great deal of work to improve not merely cost/benefit calculations but also risk analysis and a variety of other decision tools, many of the same problems remain.

The fact that these continuing issues are largely dealt with through a series of complex assumptions, along with the rise of consulting firms providing contradictory analyses of the same issues and proposals, have encouraged considerable skepticism as to the reality of claims to the objectivity and scientific stature of these techniques. Indeed, these doubts in many legislators have sometimes led to tendency by some to reject technical analyses out of hand, a reaction that is just as dangerous as its opposite.

Another major problem, quite apart from technical issues, is the ethical complexity and significance of the choices that are made. The response is that, although no one likes to place a dollar value on human life, the loss of a limb, or pain and suffering from an illness or injury, it is done all the time. Courts assign values in wrongful death suits and insurance companies evaluate costs and risks in actuarial judgments every day. But courts are acting after the fact, and insurance companies are merely making knowledgeable predictions about events over which they have little or no control. Policymakers have choices in which ethical considerations are involved, and they must bear the responsibility for those decisions. The common contemporary practice of attempting to create quasi-markets to assist in policy analyses by surveying to determine what dollar-value people place on something does not resolve the ethical problem and presents a range of methodological difficulties.

Yet another difficulty has been the tendency to transform important political decisions into what appear to be questions for resolution by experts. And by not just subject matter experts, but rather by a particular type of experts—economists. In such circumstances, what are in reality political decisions that affect a wide variety of values can get transformed into a situation in which it appears that the range of choices is limited to those deemed to be acceptable to groups of elite analysts with their own sets of biases.

One of the most important of those biases is the tendency to use the concept of efficiency as one of the most critical factors in assessing regulatory policies. In fact, Meier, Garman, and Keiser have referred to the difficulties that have arisen with the growth of the myth that "the goal of regulation is efficiency," the tendency to focus much of the criticism of regulatory policies on arguments that they are ineffi-cient.[98] The plain fact is that regulatory policies have been and will continue to be developed for political reasons and will rarely ever have a claim to efficiency as one of their primary purposes.

> Arguing that efficiency is the goal of regulation is essentially a normative argument; it is an argument that efficiency should be the goal of regulation. To be sure, agencies can have more than one goal, and regulatory objectives should be accomplished in the most efficient way possible. But when efficiency conflicts with other goals, efficiency is often a second priority.[99]

Whatever the source and mode of decision, a policy is developed for consideration. In truth, what often emerges from the policy process is not one answer but several related responses that come together into a package referred to as a policy mix. In the environmental examples described earlier, a legislative response might include regulations governing the handling of toxic waste, a permitting and tracking system for monitoring compliance with those regulations, a potential liability for toxic waste handlers who violate the law that is both an enforcement tool and an incentive for possible violators to bring themselves into compliance, and it may even include the opportunity for grants to improve the handling and disposal of wastes. While we would often speak of this as a policy because it came from a single piece of legislation, it is in truth a mix of policy tools, all of which are related but each of which is intended to achieve a different specific purpose.

Policy mixes are constructed from a variety of policy tools. These tools include the full range of possible responses that a government can take to a problem.[100] They could involve legal prohibitions, regulation, taxation, a system of fees or fines, grants-in-aid, incentive systems, information disclosure and monitoring, direct government action such as the provision of services, or the use of government contracts to leverage action.

Of course, there are many different tools that can be combined in any number of policy mixes. Which seem most popular vary from problem to problem and over time. Thus, while the contemporary policy world frowns on the use of regulation and encourages the use of market-oriented tools such as incentive systems, the plain fact is that regulation remains one of a host of frequently selected options.

Policy Adoption

After a policy is formulated, it must be adopted. An understanding of this dimension of the policy process requires an awareness of which institutions must approve proposals and the variety of stake-holders who participate in the debate. There are a variety of institutions, groups, and individuals who have interests in policies that affect them. They tend to remain involved with the policy process in that policy space (a particular field of policy—also known as a policy domain) over time. Thus, in the health care arena, there are state government organizations, the U.S. Department of Health and Human Services, state health agencies, associations of physicians and other health care professionals, managed care organizations, insurance companies, and health committees of Congress, all of whom have an ongoing interest in health care policy. We refer to this set of stakeholders as a policy community (also sometimes as policy networks, policy subsystems, or advocacy coalitions).[101] These organizations remain active in the health care policy space over time, are considerably more attentive to policymaking in that field than the public at large or even other players in the general public policy arena, and consequently tend to be more knowledgeable about activities in the field. Interest groups in a given policy community often come together to form coalitions to develop and advocate policy proposals.[102]

It is also crucial to consider the institutions that must actually enact the policy. Despite the tendency of many scholars and practitioners, particularly politicians, to emphasize process over institutions for much of the past three decades, there has been a resurgence of awareness of the importance of insti-tutions in regulatory or any other kind of policy.[103] As Michael Sandel put it, "Political institutions are not simply instruments that implement ideas independently conceived; they are themselves embodiments of ideas."[104]

In an institution as complex as Congress, or some state legislatures, the committees are organizations within a larger institution and often have their own institutional character. The determination of which congressional committees will consider a proposed policy can make all the difference to the success or failure of the policy. Advocates must determine where the money will come from to administer the program. Also extremely important are decisions as to which organization will administer the program and who will provide oversight to ensure the proper administration of the policy. Few legislators wish to be accused of creating more bureaucracy by adding a new agency to administer a new policy, but there are drawbacks to assigning a new program to an existing agency. An old agency has an existing agenda of problems and responsibilities and a limited amount of resources to do its job. The new program, particularly if it is not adequately funded, may not receive the attention it would in a new agency whose existence revolves around administering the new program.

Implementation

Once a policy is adopted, it must be implemented. That is, it must be translated into action, operated, and maintained or reformed to meet new challenges. In fact, much of the public policy scholarship of the past three decades has concerned efforts to understand why policy on the ground often looks so different from the original design as it was written at the time a statute was adopted.[105]

The determinations as to the best strategies and tactics for executing the provisions of a new law are complex. The institutional mechanisms and processes to administer the program must be designed and constructed. If no new organization is to be developed and the policy is to be assigned for implementation to an existing agency, how will the host organizations be modified to meet the new obligation and what precautions will be created to ensure that the new policy is not lost once it is dropped into an organization already involved in meeting a variety of other responsibilities? Whatever the organizational setting, priorities for resource allocation must be developed and put into operation.

These tasks can be particularly difficult if the legislation was poorly crafted, the agency must immediately resolve a crisis, or if statutory time limits were placed on the development of rules or guidelines for the program. It is not uncommon for those charged with implementing a policy to face all three of these challenges simultaneously. As Chapter 5 explained, these are among the factors that had led many agencies at the federal and state levels to employ emergency rules, interim final rules, or interpretative rules.

These factors are still present even if a policy is created with the expectations that its actual operation will be contracted out to a nonprofit or a for-profit firm. In some respects, it can even be more complex for reasons explained in earlier chapters.

Evaluation

Policy evaluation is, or should be, an ongoing process that determines how well the program in operation meets the objectives defined in the formulation and adoption stages. Evaluators must determine whether unexpected costs have arisen in administering the program, e.g., increased acid rain and health and safety risks to miners have come from encouraging the power industry to use more coal. The actual operating costs must be compared with the costs that were anticipated at the time of adoption.

Of course, the task of evaluation is both complex and often controversial. How do we know what success means? Who determines success? Is the purpose of evaluation to fix blame or to fix problems so that the policy will work better in the future? Are the evaluators intended to be advisors and consultants, advocates, or hired guns? These are among the most common and difficult questions presented in evaluation efforts.

Increasingly, the challenge has been to focus evaluation on performance at the point of service. That is, there should be some kind of involvement of those who are the intended beneficiaries of a program in the determination of its successes and shortcomings. Moreover, the object is not merely to determine whether the targets of a policy are happy with it, since, for example, in regulatory settings it is rarely the case that regulated firms or individuals have positive reactions to the policy. The challenge is to determine whether the outcomes that the policy was designed to achieve have in fact resulted. The other challenge is to avoid the danger that an evaluation comes as a kind of snapshot of the policy at one moment in time as compared to an ongoing process that helps an organization achieve what is commonly referred to as continuous improvement.

The George W. Bush administration announced its intentions to take performance evaluation seriously and to do it systematically in an effort to avoid some of the most common criticisms.[106] In addition, the administration made it clear that it would tie those evaluations to the budget process far more directly than had been done before, thus addressing another common criticism of policy evaluation efforts in the past.[107] The administration focused that effort on the use by the Office of Management and Budget of a device called the Program Assessment Rating Tool (PART). The PART provides a questionnaire for each program in each agency by policy type that not only addresses standard performance questions as to how the agency was doing with a program in a given year, but even raises questions as to whether the program is justified. In the first three years, the administration focused on the development and use of the PART, but thereafter the White House moved to integrate the results of the assessments into the president's budget proposal. For example, when the White House moved to eliminate or make deep cuts in 154 programs in the president's fiscal year 2006 budget proposal, the administration offered the results of its PART assessment process as a key element of its justifications for the funding changes.[108] That said, there are still questions about the degree to which the PART represents a return to top-down policy evaluation and the question whether the OMB analyses are more political than analytic.

Policy Termination or Transformation

Finally, and occasionally, the policy process comes to a stage known as policy termination. The problem is to determine how to bring an end to an outdated or ineffective program or how to transform such a policy into an updated and more functional operation. Termination is difficult because of the loss of jobs to those involved in the program and because over the years agencies build strong relationships with client organizations.[109] Interest groups may mobilize in support of the program. It is also made more difficult by the tendency of talented public managers to avoid involvement in programs or offices that seemed destined to be terminated. There are few career incentives for the best and the brightest to invest their time and energy on what can be one of the most important functions of public administration.

REGULATION BY CONTRACTING

One of the policy tools that is usually thought of as virtually the antithesis of regulation is contracting. In fact, the call to privatize, or more accurately to contract out, has often been justified on the grounds that this approach to accomplishing public purposes will free the organizations involved of regulations and permit flexible and efficient responses to problem solving and service needs. However, as it was noted in Chapter 5, contracting is a tool that is sometimes used to accomplish regulatory purposes. In an era when all levels of government are increasingly relying on contractors to perform public functions, it is important to be alert to this regulatory character. It arises from the nature of contracts itself, the system of regulations that govern government contracting, the use of accounting rules and expenditure controls as regulatory instruments, the use of grants and contracts as mechanisms of inter-governmental regulation, and the common requirements that government contracts meet what are often termed national (or state) goals clauses.

Contracts Are in Their Nature Regulatory

Indeed, contracts are themselves systems of rules governing relationships, often even including the rules governing how disputes that might arise under the contract will be resolved. They are based on a model of negotiation among parties who are supposedly equal (although it is clear that this is often a legal fiction rather than any kind of description of the real situation). Even so, the assumption is that so long as they have the capacity to contract, that is, they are adult individuals or officers of organizations with the authority to enter into legally binding agreements, and who are neither mentally incapable of such an agreement or acting under duress, parties, including governments, entering into contracts are under-stood to be binding themselves to an enforceable set of rules of behavior and performance. Either party may enforce the provisions of the contract and the rules that apply remain in force until the contract is terminated. If the agreement is terminated through what is termed a fundamental breach, a breaking of the terms of the agreement that is so significant as to end the relationship, the party responsible for the breach is accountable to the other party for damages that may result. In the case of government contracts, unacceptable behavior by a contractor may also trigger a range of possible punitive sanctions up to and including debarment. Debarment prohibits the organization from bidding on future contracts and could, for some firms or nonprofits be a death knell.[110]

In the current environment in which contracts are not simple purchasing agreements but involve complex and sometimes ongoing relationships for delivery of services or for participation in regulatory programs, the contracts establish quite complex systems of rules. The fact that jurisdictions often have a variety of contractual relationships in force at any given time means that several sets of regulations apply to agency operations from the contracts in addition to whatever standard regulations have been promulgated by that agency through normal administrative law processes and any applicable statutory constraints.

Regulations Attach to Virtually All Government Contracting

In fact, there are many statutes and regulations that govern contract relationships in addition to the terms of the contracts themselves. At the federal government level, the Federal Property and Admin-istrative Services Act of 1949 and its defense-oriented equivalent, the Armed Forces Procurement Act of 1947, as amended, have governed contracting since the late 1940s. These statutes have been implemented through the Federal Acquisition Regulation (FAR) under a process now under the supervision of the Office of Federal Procurement Policy in the Executive Office of the President along with representatives of some of the federal agencies.[111] To these rules are added agency supplements to the FAR covering unique issues that apply to particular fields of contracting.[112]

As Chapter 4 explained in the discussion of the National Performance Review during the Clinton administration, there was a flurry of legislation, executive orders, and memoranda in the 1990s, ostensibly seeking to simplify and unburden the contracting process led by the Federal Acquisitions Streamlining Act of 1994.[113] While there has been some progress in the effort to streamline the process, the FAR is—at the time of this writing—lengthy, complex, and ongoing. In fact, Congress finally recognized the level and complexity of regulations associated with government contracting and required agencies generating such rules to adopt procedures that mirror those required for other agency rule-making in the APA.[114]

Perhaps ironically, the effort to encourage (or force, depending upon one's point of view) federal agencies to engage in more outsourcing during the Clinton and George W. Bush administrations has actually increased the body of controls exerted by the legislature and the president on those agencies. For example, the 1998 Federal Activities Inventory Reform Act (FAIR) requires that federal agencies prepare a list each year of activities performed by their organizations that are not "inherently government functions" and that might be made available for competitive bidding and must then make decisions whether to offer those activities for bid.[115] The legislation also gives business persons a right to challenge the omission of particular agency functions from that list.

State and local governments operate under their own legal systems, including both statutes and regulations for contracting. And while efforts have been made to develop greater uniformity across states and local governments[116] and even internationally,[117] there is a long way to go.

Expenditure and Accounting Controls as Regulation

In addition to the general structure of rules governing contractual relationships, the issue of control of behavior under contracts has often come down to the use of accounting controls on spending and reimbursements of costs. Indeed, until relatively recently, much of the discussion of contract administration has focused on audit and control issues, with particular attention to cost accounting and determinations about what kinds of contractor costs are allowable.[118] In a very real way, these decisions as to the kinds of costs that may be reimbursed and the kinds of business practices that may be included in direct and indirect cost calculations under contracts are regulations.

The more complex contractual relationships, particularly in the service delivery area, often lead to policy decisions that may not be called regulations but plainly have precisely the same effect. As contractors have undertaken a wide variety of tasks that were previously not thought of as contracted functions these decisions have called for new and imaginative forms of control.

Intergovernmental Regulation through Grants and Contracts

One of the areas in which there have been new types of contracting is the intergovernmental arena. Indeed, grants and contracts have been used as tools of regulation in intergovernmental activities. While the federal government has been able in some fields to regulate the states and activities within the states directly through the commerce clause of the Constitution, there are certain areas that it must regulate indirectly, if at all, through the taxing and spending powers. These are fields such as health, safety, and education that have traditionally been matters for the states (and by delegation from the states to local governments) under the reserve powers clause of the Tenth Amendment. And since the Supreme Court has been more willing in recent years than in the past to press this distinction in defense of state autonomy,[119] there have been a variety of efforts to use grants and contracts to obtain compliance with federal regulatory efforts and even to enlist the states and localities to implement the national programs. The standard way that this is done is to condition receipt of, for example, federal education or health care dollars on compliance with a host of regulations. Thus, for example, the federal government required states to adopt a 21-year-old drinking age and made that action a condition for the receipt of federal highway funds.[120]

While grants are legally distinct from contracts,[121] the relationships among granting agencies and recipients, whether they are other government units or nongovernmental organizations, have come to look more and more like contracts.[122] Moreover, many states, and in some instances localities, operate programs under federal grants by the use of contracts. As long ago as the 1972 Federal Procurement Commission Report, this field of "contracting under grants" was recognized as a special species of government contract, and one that carries a variety of complexities.[123] Chief among these is the fact that the contracts must meet both the requirements of the federal government that provided the initial funds and also those of the state government. These operations have an obvious and intricate regulatory character to them.

The increased reliance on governance arrangements that involve not only more or less traditional government contract providers, but also sets of nonprofit organizations, for-profit firms, and government units has presented problems leading some to call for new forms of regulation. For example, in the wake of Hurricane Katrina the Red Cross mobilized to address the calamitous conditions in which the storm's victims found themselves. Given its earlier experiences after the 9/11 attacks and the response to the tsunami in Asia a year earlier, this leading nonprofit organization was aware that it lacked the capacity to manage the disbursement of assistance funds to victims who had been relocated to sites around the nation. The Red Cross entered into a contract with a firm that operated call centers which, in turn, subcontracted with another firm, Spherion Corp., which was to hire large numbers of temp employees to work call centers in three parts of the nation. The *Washington Post* broke the story that all was not going well in this well-intended program.[124] One of those centers, located in Bakersfield, California, had some Red Cross volunteers but also more than 400 Spherion workers responding to as many as 16,000 calls a day. Once a disbursement was approved through the call center, a check would be made available at Western Union offices where they could be picked up by storm victims. However, some of the subcontractors' employees engaged in a scheme to divert funds to themselves and their families. The Red Cross discovered an unusually large number of disbursements from one particular Western Union office and alerted authorities who moved in to investigate and, ultimately, to make arrests. Even so, in light of the previous bad publicity that the Red Cross had received in the aftermath of 9/11, the organization knew that there was a serious danger that millions of donors might react badly, and issued a statement acknowledging the fraud and promising to work with authorities to deal with the problem.[125] Indeed, a special task force had to be created in the U.S. Department of Justice to address fraud associated with Hurricane Katrina.[126] Serious problems of fraud had also arisen in connection with various tsunami relief efforts. Just what kinds of laws or regulatory units will be required to support some of these governance arrangements and maintain the integrity of their programs and processes is at this point unclear, but new mechanisms are clearly needed, not only to protect donors and aid recipients, but also to protect the humanitarian agencies and government organizations involved in assistance efforts.

National Goals Clauses

Both federal and state governments have developed another mechanism by which to use contracts as regulatory instruments. They are referred to as national (or state) goals clauses. These are provisions that are required to be included in contracts to ensure that organizations with which the government contracts are not violating existing laws and are responding to policy initiatives that seek to achieve the public interest even though they are not directly related to the subject of the contract at issue. These are of two types. The first are mandatory obligations that may originate in statute or in executive orders. In these situations, contractors are required to provide certifications that they are in compliance with the policies, such as civil rights laws, and may face compliance audits to ensure that they are living up to the terms of those certifications.

Some of these clauses are intended to ensure that government is not engaged in practices indirectly that would be problematic if it engaged in them directly. For example, one of the tensions in contracting has to do with the fact that private sector organizations may pay lower wages to their employees, may not provide some of the benefits enjoyed by public sector workers, and may not meet the same workplace standards as are required for civil servants.[127] But where government is indirectly the employer by virtue of its contractual relationships with private firms, it cannot escape responsibility for the conditions of the workers.[128]

The other category includes items that are not mandated by law but are merely policy positions that government seeks to pursue. They may give preference to would-be contractors who promise compliance or provide bonus payments or other incentives to those who meet goals statements. For example, it is common to find goals clauses at all levels of government that state a preference for recycled goods and for contractors that operate in ways that are considered environmentally friendly. In fact, the EPA published a study of such practices at the state and local level to explore possible techniques for incorporating environmental considerations in contracting.[129] It is perhaps interesting, though not particularly surprising, that the EPA document was actually prepared by a contractor.

It should be clear by this point that anyone who suggests that the increased use of government contracts to accomplish public purposes is an alternative to regulation does not understand the law of contracts and most assuredly is not familiar with the law of government contracts. Indeed, contracts are tools that are often used as instruments of regulation. And whether they are intended to do so or not, they are regulatory in character.

WHY HAVE POLICYMAKERS OPTED FOR REGULATION?

By this point, it should be clear that regulation is neither right nor wrong, good nor bad, in the abstract. Regulatory programs are policy choices selected from among available alternatives during the give and take of the policy process to deal with a problem that found its way onto the public policy agenda. Public policies are political choices that may or may not be reconcilable with economic efficiency criteria. In some situations, regulatory programs may be appropriate, while other contexts might be better suited to alternative strategies. Ultimately, the choice is not based on economics or on the views of policy analysts, but is a political judgment.

Monographs and articles are filled with explanations of why policymakers have chosen regulation in various policy contexts. In the late 1970s, as the deregulation movement was gathering steam, a Senate investigation of problems in regulation, the Ribicoff Committee's *Study on Federal Regulation*, found a number of recurring themes in the creation of regulatory programs that remain true today.[130] What follows is a summary, based on the Ribicoff study, of the more frequently cited reasons. The point is not to make a normative argument here, but to describe the factors that have led policymakers to opt for regulation over time.

1. The Need to Regulate Natural Monopoly

Utility services such as natural gas, electricity, and, more recently, cable television are often monopolies within a particular service area. Theoretically, a purchaser has some choices in this area, but as a practical matter homeowners and apartment dwellers have little choice in where to buy most of their utilities. Regulation is used to substitute for the market forces that would not be present in a monopoly.

Notwithstanding many initiatives undertaken to deregulate such fields as electric utilities and telecommunications, it is still the case that monopolies or near monopolies are critically important in most areas. And even when there are more markets in these fields, there will be many important issues to address that will not be settled in the marketplace. Thus, equity issues associated with providing essential services to the poor, the elderly, or those with special health needs such as basic telephone connection or supports for winter heating in cold climate areas, and complex questions associated with the processes and conditions associated with disconnecting utility services mean that in these areas, as in others, there will be a parallel system operating in which there are markets and regulation working side by side.

2. Efforts to Encourage Proper Use of Natural Resources

As the earlier discussion of trends in environmental regulation explained, there are a host of environmental fields in which there continues to be strong demand for regulatory action on both the green and brown agendas.[131] Though it is in everyone's long-run best interest to use natural resources wisely, near-term market pressures and incentives, carelessness, or ignorance often cause abuse of those resources and demands for access to previously protected areas for exploration.[132] Regulatory programs often seek to curb such abuses. Similarly, the marketplace does not provide incentives to clean up the effects of past behavior or disincentives to continue with that kind of behavior in the absence of regulation. As the earlier discussion in this chapter explained, whether the tools used are more or less traditional regulation or less direct strategies like liability schemes and the like, the policy mixes developed to address these issues are and will continue to be regulatory whatever they may be called.

3. The Need to Ensure That Participants in the Marketplace Take Account of Externalities or "Spillover" Effects of Their Actions

Frequently, actions have unanticipated consequences that market forces will not resolve. For example, the burning of fossil fuels in power facilities and industrial plants produces chemicals that are carried long distances on air currents. When these chemicals mix with atmospheric moisture and fall as precipitation, they become acid rain. By 1980, a subcommittee of the House Committee on Interstate and Foreign Commerce found that 100 of 214 Adirondack (upstate New York) lakes were acidified to the point that fish and most organic life were unable to survive.[133] In a sample of 350 of its many lakes, Wisconsin officials found that 47 had been acidified and that most lakes tested had a level of acidity ten times higher than normal.[134] More than 75 percent of the sulfur pollution falling in New England comes from outside that region.[135] The people who burn the fuels have economic incentives to burn the cheapest fuel available, such as high sulfur coal, and to resist requests to install costly air pollution control equipment. They are not the people who experience the acid rain effects. On the other hand, those who have the acid rain and therefore the incentive to do something about the air pollution are not in a position to take such action. Regulation is used to force producers and consumers to take account of the external effects of their actions.

This problem has increasingly important international dimensions. The U.S. government had to be pressed hard by Canada to recognize the impact of problems like acid rain coming from the United States that affected Canadians even more than Americans. However, when air pollution and water pollution in the Southwestern United States from industrial facilities on the Mexican side of the border fouled the air in several states and closed beaches in Southern California, at least some Americans began to get the message, demanding special commitments associated with the North American Free Trade Agreement to address such issues. Since then, as the list of international agreements cited earlier demonstrates, there have been attempts to create international regulatory regimes to address greenhouse gases, chlorofluorocarbons (CFCs), and transboundary shipments of hazardous wastes. While efforts have been made to develop some kind of comprehensive regulatory mechanism to address global warming, the United States has not yet accepted the Kyoto requirements.

4. Problems of Unavailability, Inadequacy, or Fraudulent Information about Health, Safety, Financial Services, or Other Concerns

A free market system assumes that one can choose among competing alternatives in the marketplace and that one can acquire information about those alternatives on which to base decisions. In a complex scientific world, it is often difficult or impossible for consumers to acquire information they need. Regulation can force sellers to provide labeling information on the contents or safety features of their products to enable the consumer to make rational market choices.

Indeed, it became clear during the 1980s and 1990s as more fields were deregulated, yielding more and more complex market choices in fields from nutritional supplements to retirement investment programs, that there was a greater need than before to pay attention to the availability and use of information in the marketplace. In addition to the need to deal with the availability of information, the concern to address deceptive or even fraudulent claims has also been an important problem leading to calls for greater regulation in areas such as financial services.

5. Prevention of Destructive Competition

If price competition becomes active enough or various kinds of predatory market practices are employed, there may be destructive consequences that may not be apparent until far enough into the future that consumers would not take the negative factors into consideration in their initial market choices.[136] Such competition can also destabilize the marketplace as it did during the depression of the 1930s.

The financial frenzy of the 1980s domestically and the 1990s internationally and the sheer market power of the merged and reorganized corporations have renewed these concerns. Moreover, the existence of 7-day and 24-hour trading around the world by computer, has meant that impacts can be experienced so rapidly that normal market decisionmaking that might ameliorate difficulties cannot always be brought to bear before a great deal of damage has been done. Regulation seeks to moderate the negative effects.

In some sense, this kind of motivation for regulation is what politically active economists refer to with the pejorative term "protectionism." However, international agreements in many areas have only been possible because safeguards in the form of regulation have been built into the process. Thus, the United States has worked hard to open markets in Asia, but has simultaneously created policies like the Chip Protection Act and enhanced copyright protection efforts to prevent international firms or other countries from taking advantage by dumping products on the U.S. market at artificially low costs to drive out competition.[137]

Another aspect of this motivation in an increasingly open trade environment has been the attempt to protect domestic social and environmental standards from undermining the viability of U.S. firms. Hence, efforts by the United States to restrain importation of goods manufactured by child labor and merchandise produced in ways or using materials that would violate American environmental laws seek to prevent destructive competition that would drive out more responsible local firms or force them to abandon basic domestic policies in order to compete.

6. Protection of Consumers from Sharply Rising Prices and Windfall Profits

Dramatic shifts in market conditions such as gasoline and diesel, and fuel oil price increases first during the 1970s and again in later years have had devastating impacts on the national economy in general. They also resulted in particularly harsh effects on those who live in cold climates or in areas with no public transportation systems, and on those living on fixed incomes. Price limits have been used to mitigate the effects of such dramatic market forces.

7. Dangers of Price Discrimination

Regulation historically has been used to curb attempts to control markets by using discriminatory pricing policies, for example, the battle in the late 1800s between the railroads and farmers, who asserted that the carriers were using price discrimination to force farmers to do business on railroad terms. Another example is the allegation that major oil companies have used discriminatory wholesale prices and supply policies to drive independent gasoline retailers out of business. This fear reemerged during the 1980s and 1990s with waves of mergers of very large firms in such fields as airlines, banking, health maintenance organizations (HMOs), oil, and telecommunications. Then there were the price manipulations of Enron and other energy providers.

8. Efforts to Promote or Preserve Key Industries

Regulation has been used to promote, protect, and guide (or drive, depending on one's ideological orientation) new or desired industries. The Civil Aeronautics Board was created to promote air transport using various kinds of regulations. Establishment of minimum rates by regulation insulates the industry from price competition and permits some of the costs of innovation and the development of management techniques to be passed through in pricing without penalties from other firms that might choose to undercut prices.

Such issues have been particularly sensitive when what are considered basic infrastructure is at stake. Thus, critics of the now defunct Interstate Commerce Commission (ICC) berated it for using rate setting to protect inefficient modes of transport such as freight rail and barges from the price competition available from truck lines. However, when the oil crisis of the 1970s hit with effects that have been felt ever since, even in periods of price declines, both rail and barge transport that had been preserved through regulation became not only viable and profitable, but essential to the national transportation infrastructure.

9. Decisions to Provide Service to Special Groups through the Use of Cross-Subsidies

Market forces provide incentives for certain industries to limit service to particularly lucrative markets and abandon service to smaller communities. But national policy may favor continued service to ensure complete networks of services to all parts of the country. Regulation was used for many years along with subsidies to permit, for example, air carriers to argue for higher air fares on all routes to subsidize continued service to smaller communities.

Deregulation has led to a practice known as "creaming" in which airlines or other service providers have been able to opt out of all but the most lucrative markets. The development of commuter airlines and other regional start-up airlines brought a variety of complex challenges, including much higher rate tickets and less service and poorer quality service in many markets, particularly since most of the commuter airlines are owned by or affiliated with major carriers. The result has been that many medium-sized and smaller communities have little or no meaningful competition in the contemporary setting. The difficulties of regulating some of these smaller or newer operations without the kind of organizational infrastructure of traditional carriers had led to growing concerns about safety.[138] While many pleasure travelers have been able to take advantage of much reduced fares on certain limited routes, the normal business traveler has been required to cross-subsidize those discounts and to contribute to carriers making record profits in a period of declining service. Hence there have been calls for renewed regulation.

10. Control of Competing Industries

It is sometimes considered to be in the national interest to have coherent national policies for particular fields. The legislature may charge an agency with responsibility to coordinate in that area so as to preserve the maximum number of options. For example, the Department of Energy has an obligation to assist in developing and maintaining a variety of energy options for the future.

11. Preservation of Established Property Rights

A television station license issued by the Federal Communications Commission is what makes the difference between a collection of electronics equipment and a prosperous business. Protecting this kind of asserted property right is a complex problem. It may seem ironic, but at the same time that some critics of regulation are claiming that the government is guilty of taking their property without just compensation by imposing regulations, others are charging that deregulation has resulted in a taking of their property because of a failure to protect vested rights previously recognized by government.[139]

Contrary to much contemporary rhetoric, the history of regulatory policies shows that decisions to impose regulation are most often intensely pragmatic reactions to particular problems and not theoretical judgments about market deficiencies. Many times policies were adopted because individuals or firms had abused others by manipulations of the market system, or because certain problems were becoming increasingly unacceptable to the public. The Securities and Exchange Commission (SEC) was created to administer a variety of regulatory programs because of massive repeated proven abuses of the securities markets by private individuals and business firms.[140] The Food and Drug Administration (FDA) was created in response to wretched conditions in the food and drug industries that produced adulterated food and impure, unsafe, and ineffective drugs.[141] The National Labor Relations Board (NLRB) came into existence, and was later strengthened, to ensure fair labor standards at a time when the nation was rocked by violent labor-management confrontations. Similarly, the newer agencies created in the 1960s and 1970s came about through pragmatic political judgments. Congress created the highway safety regulatory programs because 50,000 Americans were killed annually in traffic accidents and automobile manufacturers seemed unwilling to improve safety features.[142] The history of the Consumer Product Safety Commission (CPSC) legislation indicates that this body was created because Congress determined that 20 million people were injured each year in product-related accidents; of this number 110,000 resulted in permanent disability and 30,000 died.[143] The legislative history of the Occupational Safety and Health Administration (OSHA) shows that more workers were killed in job-related accidents in the four years prior to the act than had died in Vietnam in the same period.[144] The Federal Elections Commission (FEC) was created because the Watergate debacle had demonstrated gross abuses of campaign financing.[145] Similar findings can be found in most regulatory legislative histories.[146]

INSTITUTIONS FOR THE TWENTY-FIRST CENTURY: ORGANIZATIONAL ASPECTS OF REGULATORY ADMINISTRATION

Whatever gave rise to a regulatory program, the policies are assigned to an agency or an independent commission for administration. And despite the tendency in recent decades to focus on process and not on institutions, there is a renewed recognition of the need to pay attention to the institutions designed to carry out regulatory and other governmental functions.[147] This is true internationally as well as in the domestic arena.[148] Those who work in or deal with regulatory agencies should be alert to the opportunities and dangers that their organizations face in the political environment in which they operate.

Consider the classic view of the behavior of regulatory bodies, the more contemporary view of the political environment in which such organizations operate, the conflict model of life in contemporary regulatory settings, and the issue of parallel systems management in this context.

Bernstein's Life Cycle of a Regulatory Commission

One of the most traditional sets of critiques of traditional regulatory agencies, and in particular of independent regulatory commissions, is embodied in Marver Bernstein's classic work *Regulating Business by Independent Commission*.[149] Bernstein used a conceptual framework to describe the operation of regulatory commissions, which he called "The Life Cycle of a Regulatory Commission."[150] "Despite variations in time sequence and the particular circumstances surrounding the creation of each one," he wrote, "the national independent commissions have experienced roughly similar growth, maturity, and decline."[151] Bernstein's work has itself been criticized because not all commissions have suffered the fate he described and because the pitfalls he ascribed to independent commissions may afflict other organizations. Moreover, many regulatory organizations are not independent regulatory commissions but executive branch agencies. Nevertheless, Bernstein's model can illustrate some of the opportunities and problems that an administrator in a regulatory agency might see. His life cycle consists of four phases: "gestation," "youth," "maturity," and "old age."

The gestation of regulatory bodies begins, according to Bernstein, when a major problem appears. An example would be the OPEC oil embargo in the 1970s. As the situation degenerates (e.g., when the gas lines formed), distress increases. Interest groups emerge and demand that the legislature act to resolve the problem. For many reasons, wrote Bernstein, the legislature enacts a compromise bill that may very well be "out of date by the time it is enacted."

In its youth, the regulatory agency is at a disadvantage relative to the regulated industry in terms of expertise and experience, but it does have a relatively high level of zeal.[152] Bernstein noted that new regulatory bodies have a relatively high level of political support in their first few years, which the administrators may not be able to exploit. Even so, they may take a relatively bold and expansive view of their opportunities and responsibilities in the initial months of the agency's life.

Once the regulated groups realize that the regulatory program will indeed be implemented, they will attempt to influence appointments to key positions in the agency. "Most commissions have tried initially to achieve independence from regulated groups. They have embarked on the regulatory task with some exuberance with a desire to clarify goals and mark out basic policies. But the characteristics of youth have only a transitory existence and soon fade away."[153]

Bernstein added: "In the period of maturity, regulation usually becomes more positive in its approach. Its functions are less those of a policeman and more like that of a manager of an industry."[154] At this point, the agency may become less an outside umpire of regulated activity and behave more like a facilitator. The ICC and the Civil Aeronautics Board (CAB) were both examples of agencies that were seen in this light for many years. In this period of operation, Bernstein held, homeostasis takes over. Routine is comfortable, and therefore important. Neither organizational life nor the policy it produces maintains vitality. The agency does not actively press issues that have not been forced on it. Existing rules, precedents, and court opinions tend to increase court-like formality in agency proceedings.

> The close of the period of maturity is marked by the commission's surrender to the regulated. Politically isolated, lacking a firm basis of public support, lethargic in attitude and approach and bogged down by precedents and backlogs, unsupported in its demand for more staff and money, the commission finally becomes a captive of the regulated group.[155]

Finally, the agency slips into old age, the period Bernstein described as "debility and decline." The agency is without sufficient power or initiative to take any significant action against those it is charged with regulating.[156] Many of the better people have left the agency and those who remain no longer have a strong sense of purpose. Both operations and the quality of management decisions decline.

Organizational Pressures, the Capture Thesis, and Political Styles

Those who disagree with Bernstein acknowledge that all agencies, including regulatory commissions, are vulnerable to the failings he described, but add that not all agencies, not even all independent commissions, actually succumb to them. James Q. Wilson pointed out that while some regulatory agencies may fall victim to the capture thesis, others do not.[157] Kenneth Meier went so far as to count agency capture as one of a list of myths about regulation.[158] While he acknowledged that there have been cases of agency capture, he contended that regulators "vary a great deal in their relationship with the regulated; some are close, and some are distant."[159] In fact, in many instances agencies have made important policy decisions that adversely affect very powerful interests, contrary to Bernstein's captive agency theory.

Wilson argued that regulatory agency behavior may be primarily conditioned by the style of political interactions that characterize an agency's political environment. Specifically, the political climate in which an agency operates is determined by the manner in which the costs and benefits of the policy administered by the agency are distributed.[160] But he warned that costs and benefits, in this context, refer to beliefs and values as well as to economic interests.

Wilson contended that where the public policy administered by an agency distributes benefits and costs widely across the population, what he called "majoritarian politics" will prevail. (See Figure 10.1, which is a two-dimensional representation of Wilson's framework.) "Interest groups have little incentive to form around such issues because no small, definable segment of society (an industry, an occupation, a locality) can expect to capture a disproportionate share of the benefits or avoid a disproportionate share of the burdens."[161] Antitrust legislation is an example of a regulatory program born and operated in majoritarian politics.

Distribution of benefits \ Distribution of costs	Wide	Narrow
Wide	Majoritarian	Entrepreneurial
Narrow	Client	Interest group

FIGURE 10.1 Wilson's Framework: Political Styles and Regulatory Environments

SOURCE: Derived from James Q. Wilson, *The Politics of Regulation* (New York: Basic Books, 1980).

Where the distribution of costs and benefits is narrow, Wilson says "interest group politics" predominate. In such situations, the general public may not become aroused, but the interest groups that stand to gain or lose from administration of the policy have a "strong incentive to organize and exercise political influence."[162] Wilson cited various labor-management relations regulations as situations in which interest groups compete but the conflict remains relatively narrow.

"Client politics" characterize situations in which costs are widely distributed and benefits narrowly concentrated.

> Some small, easily organized group will benefit and thus has a powerful incentive to organize and lobby; the costs of the benefit are distributed at a low per capita over a large number of people, and hence they have little incentive to organize in opposition—if, indeed, they even hear of the policy. . .. Absent. . .watchdog organizations, however, client politics produces regulatory legislation that most nearly approximates the producer-dominance [or capture] model.[163]

Finally, Wilson termed as "entrepreneurial politics" policy activity in areas in which costs are rather narrowly concentrated but benefits are widely distributed. Much of the health and safety regulatory activity of the past two decades involved entrepreneurial politics as a major factor in its origins and operation. Ralph Nader has often been seen as one of the leading examples of policy entrepreneurs over the past four decades.[164]

Wilson's typology of political styles that affect the development and implementation of regulatory politics is descriptive of some aspects of regulatory activity. As a theoretical device it is vulnerable to several significant criticisms.[165] But Wilson's work does indicate that those who would understand regulatory politics solely from the premise that agencies behave as they do because they are captured by the regulated organizations vastly oversimplify the situation. Over time, different agencies that administer regulatory programs face a variety of political styles from changing interest groups.

Along with Wilson's political styles perspective, it is also useful to understand the importance of regulatory administration within a conflict model of political relationships. The 1980s and 1990s witnessed the growth of two seemingly contradictory forms of behavior both within and outside regulatory agencies. On the one hand, for reasons discussed at length in Chapter 8, this was a period in which the tendency to settle issues by negotiation and the effort to achieve non–zero sum solutions was matched by a very different proclivity of many participants in the regulatory arena to emphasize conflict in search of victories instead. In some cases this was a reflection of a swing to more intense ideological politics, particularly on the right. In other cases, it was the tendency to fight harder over declining resources. At the same time, to the degree that people were encouraged to adopt a competitive and entrepreneurial attitude, conflict has been fostered.[166] Moreover, E. E. Schattschneider argued long ago that when decisions concern very important issues, political behavior is more often characterized by conflict than by polite efforts at consensus building through bargaining.[167] Interestingly, in some cases the battles are not simply between the regulators and the regulated or between for-profit firms and advocacy groups demanding that the firms be more tightly regulated, but between for-profit firms with competing claims. For example, it was insurance companies that pressed government to move forward with enforcement of rules mandating that manufacturers install airbags in automobiles.[168]

The management trends described in Chapter 4 that have led to what has been termed hollow government; that is, the tendency to downsize and deregulate significantly, has meant that agencies must often buy through contract the expertise that they formerly sought to recruit in the form of full-time staff. In addition, the regulated organizations are often able to field not only comparable or superior expertise but also to call upon substantial legal resources to make their case.

Internal Dynamics and Regulatory Organizations

In addition to an understanding of their political environment and black letter law requirements applicable to their agencies, it is important for administrators to be sensitive to the internal dynamics of regulatory agencies.

As Graham Allison has argued, everyone wants to believe that his or her agency is a rational policymaker, but, in fact, much agency decisionmaking can be better understood by examining patterns of interaction within an organization than by considering careful calculations about costs and benefits of all available policy options.[169] Subunits and departments within organizations shape routines and develop channels of communication. These organizational routines, communications links, and informal relationships among units have important effects on decisionmaking.

Second, the people who operate organizations are often not stable management teams. James Thompson observed many years ago that organizations are frequently directed by shifting coalitions of individuals and that situation has become even more significant in contemporary organizations.[170] The coalitions change as individuals within the organization perceive themselves to be affected by changing patterns of professional and personal rewards or risks. Those who expect regulatory agencies to operate consistently over an extended period of time may understand the importance of organizational routines, but may not be aware of changing patterns of influence among key agency personnel.

Individual bureaucratic politics also matter.[171] Personalities come and go, particularly in regulatory agencies, and each administrator comes to the agency with differing capabilities and skills for playing bureaucratic politics. Even experienced administrators vary in how well they can perform in a particular organization. Administrators also differ in terms of their skill in interacting with important elements in the political environment. This can have a significant effect on the overall ability of the organization to maximize its goals and to avoid or neutralize threats. Bureaucratic politics skills are particularly important internally in regulatory agencies that employ experts from different scientific disciplines or professions, e.g., law or medicine. Effective working relations between technical experts and administrative generalists are often difficult to maintain.

There is also the important reality of parallel systems management described earlier. It is increasingly necessary for regulatory agencies to operate both traditional enforcement-oriented regulatory operations with the requisite personnel for that function and also implement market based, incentive-oriented policy tools that emphasize negotiated approaches to ensuring compliance with the different types of professionals required to carry out those assignments. Normally, those who discuss the differences between what they term command and control regulation and market alternatives focus on the relationship between the regulated organizations and the regulatory agency. However, part of the demands of organizing and staffing for many of the newer tasks that agencies must carry out under regulatory innovations is the need to include interest groups and community representatives in some of the negotiation tools. Thus, negotiated rulemaking panels are generally expected to include at least some representatives of groups that are considered representatives of important interests in the field. The need to operate these quite different approaches can add stress to management.

Extensive consideration is often given to the size and structure of an agency. However, because regulatory agencies are created during different historical periods to deal with special problems in particular ways, they vary dramatically in both size and form. For example, the Ribicoff Committee asked:

What is the optimal size of a regulatory Commission? As Professor Cushman has pointed out, "There is no ideal size. When Lincoln was asked how long a soldier's legs ought to be, he replied that they should be long enough to reach from his body to the ground; and so a commission ought to be big enough or small enough to perform efficiently the task assigned to it."[172]

While there have been discussions about the growth in regulatory agencies since the 1960s, the use of general numbers is not particularly helpful. The number of mandates enacted by Congress, from treaty obligations or from executive orders, has escalated dramatically as explained earlier in this chapter and in Chapter 5. Thus, President Reagan's Executive Order 12291, dramatically increasing cost/benefit analyses, was referred to euphemistically around Washington as the Economists' Full Employment Act of 1981. Staff added to address increased analytic and interbranch relations responsibilities had virtually no effect on the availability of people in the field to carry out the requirements of the programs. In fact, in some instances, the growing complexity of the Washington headquarters offices of federal agencies has led some of the field personnel operating out of regional offices to see a greater disconnect between the rulemaking side of the house and the enforcement side.

A good deal has been written suggesting that regulatory agencies be standardized into single-administrator-headed executive branch agencies. Much of this commentary was prepared by people who worked for the chief executive and, not surprisingly, were interested in making regulatory agencies more manageable by and politically responsive to the president who is, after all, the chief executive officer of government.[173]

This reorganization-standardization approach to regulatory agencies has not necessarily met many of the expectations that supported the trend. There have been specific problems, such as the criticism of the Federal Aviation Administration (FAA). Supposedly, the Nixon-era reorganizations that folded independent agencies into executive branch departments would leave the regulators' independence intact. However, it became clear to FAA watchers during the Reagan, Bush, and Clinton years that there was considerable political involvement varying from pressure to support general deregulation and alternative regulation trends to budget pressures to outright White House involvement in specific cases, as in the instance of the strike by the Professional Air Traffic Controllers (PATCO) union.[174] It is noteworthy that a good deal of that criticism has come from a truly independent body, the National Transportation Safety Board (NTSB).[175]

At the state level, there are some commissions, most notably public utilities commissions, established either by constitution or statute, and these have generally remained independent. There was a wave of attempts by governors, particularly during the 1970s, to consolidate individual agencies into super departments, generally pursued on grounds of efficiency and accountability. While President Carter used his reorganization record in Georgia as a major claim to success as he ran for the presidency, the results of the state level reorganizations seem to have been mixed.

With respect to multimember commissions, the need for balanced commission membership, collegial decisionmaking, and varying degrees of independence from pressure from current political demands are still of concern to many legislators.[176] Many of the multiheaded commissions' statutes at the national level permit the president to designate the chair and vest in that person management authority for the basic administration of agency operations, as opposed to substantive policymaking, which remains with the entire commission. Thus, the politics surrounding appointments to chair the Securities and Exchange Commission (SEC) following the public awareness of the numerous financial scandals of late 1990s and first few years of the new century. The Bush administration appointed a chair who was seen to be a strong leader, but then, once the furor over misdeeds in the marketplace began to subside, there were pressures from the financial community because of allegations that the SEC's aggressive approach was interfering in economic growth.

This chapter has considered the laws and institutions that shape regulatory activities. It has also considered some of the problems and prospects faced by those who administer the agencies, the regulated parties, and the judges who review agency regulations or adjudications brought under regulations. We turn now to the other participants in the regulatory process: the president, the Congress, state and local governments, and the public.

THE PRESIDENT AND THE REGULATORY PROCESS

The president is an important figure in regulatory administration. However, the chief executive's opportunities and resources are more complex than many recognize. The key elements necessary to an understanding of the president's role are: (1) an assessment of the actual power the chief executive possesses; (2) presidential controls on regulatory bodies; and (3) a critical assessment of presidential consultation and coordination of regulatory activity.

Presidential Power: Real and Imagined

Presidents have several more or less formal sources of authority at their disposal to deal with regulatory agencies, including appointment and removal powers, budgetary authority, rulemaking clearance power, and coordination and control authority. However, the power of the chief executive over the regulatory agencies may, in some cases, be more apparent than real. There are several reasons for this disparity.

First, there are limits to the president's formal powers. For example, legal doctrines prohibit the chief executive from firing members of independent regulatory commissions who perform adjudicatory functions unless good cause is shown. In addition, there are checks by other branches. For example, the president has the power to make appointments, but the appointments are usually subject to the Senate confirmation process.[177]

Second, the constitutional obligation to "take care that the Laws be faithfully executed"[178] requires the chief executive to respect properly enacted laws.[179] Since most agencies operate on the basis of an enabling act and administer several additional statutes, and because each agency is different from the others, the president's authority is limited by a maze of statutes.

In recent years there has been considerable controversy over arguments by the George W. Bush administration concerning a very broad interpretation of executive authority referred to as the unitary executive theory.[180] There are variations on the unitary executive theme that represent a continuum, from the argument that the president is the head of the executive branch of the federal government and therefore must protect his or her constitutional authority to carry out those responsibilities, to the other end of the spectrum at which the White House argues that it holds the power under Article II of the Constitution to control all the administrative activity of the federal government and that authority carries with it a host of inherent powers that preclude interference by Congress even through properly enacted statutes. The Bush White House has taken a position on that dramatic end of the spectrum, which it has used to justify the issuance of a host of presidential signing statements that do not veto new statutes to be returned to the legislature for further consideration, but make declarations as to what the White House sees as unconstitutional provisions of the new laws that intrude upon the president's power to control the unitary executive.[181] In the first term, the assertion of the unitary executive power was asserted some 82 times as a justification to effectively nullify specific statutory provisions.[182] However, notwithstanding energetic support for the doctrine by Justice Scalia, the Supreme Court has not supported presidential claims to this unitary executive authority.[183] As the Court explained in *Hamdi v. Rumsfeld* in 2004, such wide-ranging claims to executive power will not stand even in times of war and national emergency: "We have long since made clear that a state of war is not a blank check for the President when it comes to the rights of the Nation's citizens."[184]

Whatever the formal claims to legal authority may be, the sheer diversity and complexity of the agencies exceeds the capacity of any one individual for personal control or management. Even the management of the White House is complex. As Stephen Hess has said, the presidency is not one person, but is itself an organization.[185] Aware that technological expertise and interest group support have given agencies some degree of independence from presidential direction, presidents have built an impressive counterbureaucracy in the Executive Office of the President. The Executive Office consists of financial and technical advisers who help the president administer the executive branch. Hess points out that the managerial complexity of the administrative arm of government is exacerbated by political diversity in the agencies and in the regulated clientele. He observes that what a president can do is to organize the White House as effectively as possible and staff it with the right personnel. The staffing problem is a continuing one because of high turnover and because some political executives are co-opted ("go native," in political parlance) by the agencies or their interest groups.[186]

Presidential Control and Constraints on Regulatory Bodies

Many presidents, at least as far back as Franklin Delano Roosevelt, have considered greater presidential control necessary to challenge what they perceived to be contentious, unresponsive, and even unbridled agencies. However, several more recent chief executives have gone beyond the level of frustration to see agencies and civil servants as adversaries who are to be fought through every available means. President Nixon was for many years characterized as the leading example of a president who saw his relationship to the regulatory bureaucracy as adversarial,[187] but Ronald Reagan clearly took the title when he came to office. And, as Chapter 4 explained, despite their rhetoric, presidents whose rhetoric may have been less confrontational, like Carter, George H. W. Bush, and Clinton, turned out to be in practice relatively adversarial in their own right and in a variety of ways both obvious and subtle.

Among the tactics used by presidents who wish to gain control of the bureaucracy have been: (1) reorganization; (2) counterstaffing; (3) direct legislative or administrative attack; and (4) indirect administrative attack.

Reorganization   Presidents generally justify large-scale executive branch reorganizations on the ground of managerial efficiency. However, reorganizations frequently do not save money and often do not result in increased efficiency. Instead, reorganization is accomplished to move opponents out of key positions in the bureaucracy and to maneuver more amenable officials into important posts.[188] Reorganizations are often slow, low-key operations. In some cases, like the Carter administration, the reorganization goes hand-in-hand with a stated desire for cabinet government.[189] James Pfiffner explained that when Carter took office, he proclaimed that: "I believe in Cabinet administration of our government. There will never be an instance while I am President when the members of the White House staff dominate or act in a superior position to the members of our Cabinet."[190] However, just over two years later, he fired five of his cabinet secretaries and appointed a White House chief of staff.[191] For one thing, he learned that some of his department heads, most notably Joseph Califano, could play the control-through-reorganization game better than he could. For another, he came to realize, as many presidents do, that simply managing the White House itself is a difficult challenge.

Counterstaffing and the Appointment Power   Counterstaffing is a strategy in which key positions in an agency are filled by officials who are known to hold policy positions and practice management styles contrary to prevailing agency attitudes and practices. President Reagan carefully counterstaffed key positions across the executive branch, including in such important regulatory agencies as the Environmental Protection Agency, the Department of the Interior, the Department of Energy, the Federal Communications Commission, and the Occupational Safety and Health Administration. In the case of the Department of Energy and the Department of Education, the administration went so far as to charge the new appointees with the mission of eliminating their agencies. Not only did the administration employ this approach in the top spots, but it also worked to penetrate as deeply as possible into agencies.[192]

In counterstaffing, one assumes a conflict mode of interaction with the bureaucracy in the hope that such a move will make dramatic changes in agency operation. Thus, while Ann Gorsuch Burford and James Watt took intense political heat for their dramatic (some would say draconian) efforts to turn, respectively, the EPA and the Department of the Interior on their heads, there is no doubt that they were doing precisely what they were put in those positions to accomplish. They both fought to recreate their agencies in the administration's image while fighting off the protestations of Congress.[193] The George W. Bush administration adopted the counterstaffing strategy in a variety of key positions. One of the most obvious and dramatic was the appointment of Interior Secretary Gale Norton who, like her former colleague James Watt, had been a lawyer for the Mountain States Legal Foundation and who came to Interior with a clear change in direction from her Clinton-era predecessors.

One of the advantages of counterstaffing from the White House point of view is that this process reaches independent regulatory bodies, in which the President can appoint the chair, as well as the executive branch agencies. Thus, even though it was technically independent, the FCC underwent a dramatic transformation under the chairmanship of Reagan appointee Mark Fowler. This counterstaffing approach is particularly attractive if the purpose is to block action or undue policy as was true in the regulatory policies of both the Reagan and Bush administrations, but much more difficult if the president seeks to push through new programs or initiatives.

The irony is that while the lessons of counterstaffing have been learned, most presidents are not thought to have done very well on the positive side of the appointment authority. In fact, scholars who have examined the matter over the years have concluded that chief executives often either are indifferent to the use of appointments except in the most general sense,[194] or that they have been too busy trying to organize their presidency and staff the top positions as well as key White House jobs to pay attention to the many important regulatory posts that are available.[195] Few administrations have established systematic appointments procedures that include close personal consideration by the president of the qualifications of potential appointees beyond their political credentials. Drawing on interviews with those responsible for screening appointments over several administrations, the Ribicoff Committee in its pathbreaking study, noted that appointments were often made by the BOGSAT method ("Bunch Of Guys Sitting Around a Table").[196]

Even assuming presidents had the time and knowledge to become active and effective in the area, a number of disincentives discourage them from personally selecting highly qualified regulators. Glenn Robinson observed that: "Neither the patronage value that the president attaches to individual appointments in particular nor the public importance he attaches to agency appointments in general outweighs the substantial political costs incurred by selecting an appointee who is too controversial."[197] The political costs for selecting individuals with established records in their fields (and hence with established friends and opponents) can be high. Of course, Robinson's generalization does not hold if a president deliberately selects counterstaffing as a strategy for dealing with the bureaucracy. In that event, the president is accepting conflict and gambling that he or she will win. At least two tactics are available to implement counterstaffing. First, the president can select someone with a well-documented, but not necessarily widely known, record whose approach is dramatically different from current agency policy and wager that, given traditional deference to presidential regulatory appointments, opposing groups inside or outside the agency will not be able to block the appointment or win the public relations contest in the media. President Reagan's selection of James Watt to head the Department of the Interior was a prime example.[198] In the Watt appointment, the fact that the president's party was the Senate majority party helped. Second, the president can select a highly visible candidate with a strongly held and advocated philosophical position, but without a well-known, detailed record. An example is the Reagan appointment of former South Carolina Governor Edwards to the position of energy secretary.

Another major difficulty in the appointments process can be avoiding conflicts of interest. There are several facets to this problem. First, the president must avoid appointing people who will face opposition in confirmation proceedings or attract negative public opinion because they are so intimately tied to the industry they will regulate that they are, in general terms, in a conflict of interest. Second, the president is required to enforce conflict-of-interest rules among those who have been appointed to an agency. By the late 1980s there were already complaints that the restrictions of the Ethics in Government Act as implemented was already an onerous burden and a deterrent to well-qualified professionals who might otherwise be willing to serve for a time. However, when President Clinton came to office in early 1993, his first action after taking the oath of office was to sign Executive Order 12832 entitled "Ethics Commitments by Executive Branch Appointees," which added another 11 pages worth of restrictions to the existing requirements. Critics suggested that these burdens were part of the problems that meant that "Clinton has taken longer than any president since 1960 and probably was the slowest in history" to staff the administration's key positions.[199] While it is true that there is always the risk that a president will be accused of maintaining a revolving-door syndrome, that is, that those who serve come from the regulated industry and return to that industry when they leave office, there is some question whether the pendulum has swung too far in the other direction.

Indirect Administrative Attack   There are a number of indirect devices the president can employ among the most common of which are budget authority and creation of a counterbureaucracy.

The most widely recognized means the president may use in dealing with regulators are the budget preparation process and White House negotiating strength in the congressional appropriations process. However, although the budgetary power of the president is important, certain factors limit even this power.

First, most regulatory agencies are quite small compared to other agencies.

> Most of the important influences at work upon a regulatory agency are the White House, on one hand, and Congress, on the other. . ... In fact, government regulatory agencies are step-children whose custody is contested by both Congress and the Executive but without very much affection from either one. Furthermore, as stepchildren they are often starvelings receiving only crumbs in the federal budget.[200]

Regulatory bodies are small in size, and in fiscal terms, contrary to all the political rhetoric and particularly when their budgets are compared to their legislative mandates. Many of the expenditures are mandated by statutes and, of these, substantial sums are not available to the agency for its own operation but go to grantees or contractors. Therefore, it may be rather difficult to get much leverage through the budget preparation process. Additionally, there is always a chance that an agency will be able to mobilize interest group support in the congressional appropriations process (what has been referred to as an "end run around the White House"). Thus, when the Clinton administration sought to make significant cuts in the EPA budget in its early budget cutting efforts, Congress promptly restored the cuts.

Nevertheless, the president can use the budget process either to help or hinder an agency, particularly if the agency wants to undertake a new project. The president's budget preparation power can be used in a variety of ways, including manipulations of the numbers and types of agency personnel.[201]

The creation of a counterbureaucracy has involved the use of OMB and other offices as political tools. There is no question that counterbureaucracy has been used often in modern history even by presidents who loudly protested their commitment to cabinet government.[202] This subject was first discussed during the Nixon years when the Executive Office of the President underwent significant growth in size and importance. Theoretically, at least the change from what had been the Bureau of the Budget to what became the Office of Management and Budget was supposed to underscore the growing importance of management as a matter for White House interest and leadership. In truth, however, because of Nixon's strongly held view that the bureaucracy was not sufficiently willing to bend to his will and that civil servants were in many respects an adversarial force to be conquered, management took a back seat and OMB became the focal point of counterbureaucracy warfare.[203]

Direct Legislative or Administrative Attack   Of course, efforts to get control often have been undertaken through legislation or by executive orders in addition to more subtle means. For example, the Carter administration made passage of the Civil Service Reform Act of 1978 (CSRA) an important priority. On the one hand, CSRA was intended to rationalize and modernize the civil service as well as to integrate a plethora of varying enactments such as civil rights laws that had accumulated over time. On the other hand, it was also very much about control. Jimmy Carter came out of nowhere to win the White House largely by running against Washington. When he won the presidency, he was concerned that the civil service system had become unmanageable and specifically that good people could not be rewarded for superior performance and problem employees could not be disciplined. Moreover, senior civil servants seemed to be barriers to change. The CSRA sought to implement a pay for performance scheme (though it was never fully funded), authorize management experiments at various sites, alter the process of disciplinary actions and appeals, and move senior managers into something called the Senior Executive Service (SES). The SES officials could be moved from agency to agency and enjoyed less protections against political direction than traditional civil servants. The object was ostensibly to make it possible to use their expertise wherever in government it was required and to provide more flexibility for managers to employ them where and how they were needed. It was also to make them more responsive. While some senior personnel embraced the concept, many had to be pushed—and pushed hard—to enter the SES in part at least because they saw the control aspects of the legislation.

In addition to such general, government wide efforts, Carter focused a good deal of attention on regulatory agencies. As Chapters 4 and 5 explained, his administration boasted passage of more deregulatory legislation than any other in recent history, whether Republican or Democrat. Beyond simple deregulation, he also championed policies that sought to constrain regulatory agencies such as the Regulatory Flexibility Act.

As Chapter 4 explained, the Clinton administration's National Performance Review suggested that the president avoid the politically complex and time-consuming legislative process and proceed with efforts to get control of the system through executive orders. And the administration did precisely that. Many of the regulatory agencies were regarded as outmoded, insensitive, and excessively confrontational. The administration moved to address those issues primarily through executive orders.

Presidential Consultation and Coordination of Regulatory Policymaking and Enforcement

Theoretically, at least, some of these measures, such as the executive clearance processes, were supposed to serve the rational and desirable interest in better coordination and management of the executive. After all, the president is charged with responsibility for the executive branch of the federal government and is obligated by the Constitution's duty-to-take-care clause to ensure agencies faithfully execute the law. In carrying out these responsibilities, the president is expected to coordinate and direct executive branch operations and to generate, and later to accept responsibility for, executive branch policies. On the other hand, most agencies are created by statute (and their appropriations are drawn from the Treasury) to be operated according to their technical expertise, not to act as extensions of political parties. The APA and other statutes require that policymaking through rulemaking will not be upheld if it is arbitrary, capricious, or not in accord with statutory authority. Similarly, agency adjudications are quasi-judicial actions that determine important questions of legal status or obligation. They are also government actions that affect important individual interests. Partisan or political intervention in agency adjudications and some rulemaking processes, known as *ex parte* communication, is generally prohibited by the APA.[204] There can be, and frequently has been, conflict between the need for governmental accountability to the electorate through the president's office and some degree of neutral competence to be exercised by professional administrators in agencies free of political pressure from the White House.[205] The distinction between quasi-legislative and quasi-judicial activities by agencies is easily blurred.[206] Presidential efforts to control or coordinate policy in the former are permissible, but presidential intervention in the latter may not be. There are some means that presidents may clearly employ, but the debate over the extent of permissible presidential involvement in agency operations is unresolved.

The White House likes to picture these matters as efforts at consultation and coordination, while people in the regulatory agencies and many supporters of regulatory programs term it simply as intervention in an attempt to control the agencies and their policies. This is a very broad set of issues, but it can be made more understandable if we seek to view the process from both internal and external perspectives.

To the degree that presidents are seen to be seeking to improve economy, efficiency, effectiveness, responsiveness, responsibility, and equity, there usually is support for presidential efforts to coordinate and consult with regulatory bodies. In fact, the pledge to do precisely that has been a commitment of virtually every candidate of both major parties for years. Hence, passage of the Paperwork Reduction Act[207] during the Carter years and the Unfunded Mandate Reform Act of 1995,[208] which promised to place limits on the ability of Congress and federal agencies to add new burdens without resources to state and local governments brought nothing but praise.[209] And there really is not much concern with whether that goal is achieved through direct or indirect means. Indeed, even Congress said little when the Clinton administration issued a barrage of executive orders directing change. For example, the NPR argued that among the most problematic areas of regulation is the way that government regulates its own internal operations.

There is no control over the controls.

- One agency requires 23 signatures to purchase a single personal computer.

- Another agency routes routine responses to congressional inquiries through nearly two dozen officers for approval.

- Nearly 890 laws govern the Defense Department's efforts to purchase items.

- The Agricultural Department uses over 1,088 pounds of federal personnel laws, regulations, directives, case laws, and departmental guidance to make personnel decisions.

- In one Interior Department regional office, over 33,000 pages of internal regulations and handbooks are used to govern fewer than 200 employees.

- For one mid-size agency—the National Aeronautics and Space Administration—over 130 audits of the agency were performed this past year by outside groups such as the General Accounting Office and the Merit System Protection Board.[210]

Therefore, it came as no surprise and counted for little more than a sound bite on the evening news when the president promptly issued Executive Order 12861 requiring that: "Each executive department and agency shall undertake to eliminate not less than 50 percent of its civilian internal management regulations that are not required by law within 3 years of the effective date of this order." Despite the fact that there was no rational basis for the 50 percent figure, that such an arbitrary action might potentially pose as many problems as it solved, or that the White House did not take the simultaneous opportunity to eliminate the many existing executive orders that imposed burdens on the effectiveness and efficiency of the agencies, no one particularly cared.

It also comes as no surprise when the president seeks to press for particular kinds of policy change or development by administrative agencies. After all, the president does have the executive power under Article II of the Constitution and is elected, among other reasons, to lead the executive branch of government. While there may certainly be disagreement with an administration's policy positions, so long as they are expressed openly and carried out through normal processes, the debate usually remains focused on the policies themselves rather than on accusations of unwarranted presidential intervention.

Thus, for example, when the Clinton administration came to office, the president issued a memorandum to the Secretary of Health and Human Services asking her to open a rulemaking proceeding to consider elimination of the so-called gag rule (discussed in Chapter 7) prohibiting federally funded family planning clinics from providing information concerning abortion-related services. While there certainly was criticism about the policy, the president's action was accepted and indeed expected. Neither does it come as a surprise when a new cabinet officer appointed by an incoming president moves to implement the administration's policy preferences. The story of the swings in the development of the rules on automobile airbags detailed in Chapter 7 provides a classic example.

In the contemporary era, presidential involvement has become more controversial when it is perceived to be an effort to intervene in the normal operation of regulatory agencies for ideological or partisan reasons or on behalf of influential political supporters or campaign contributors. However, tensions have grown where a president is seen to be seeking to win through intervention in regulatory processes what he or she did not win in Congress. Controversy has also emerged where the intervention is seen to undermine the administrative law processes.

The debate over presidential intervention is certainly not new. Some modern advocates have urged that presidents not only have the authority to intervene but ought to do so.[211] Others have answered, in the words of Judge Henry J. Friendly: "Quite simply, I find it hard to think of worse."[212] Still others, who have had experiences at the upper levels of regulatory agencies have noted that for much of modern history, the problem has been to get presidents to pay any attention at all to regulatory bodies.[213]

As Chapters 4 and 5 explained, President Carter was one who did pay attention. Of course, Carter went to Congress for deregulation, one of the few truly bipartisan efforts in modern Washington history. He also created two bodies in the White House, the Regulatory Council and the Regulatory Analysis Review Group in part at least to address the lack of coordination between competing agencies and conflicting regulations. The Regulatory Council, consisting of representatives of some 36 executive branch and independent regulatory agencies, brought regulators together with representatives from the Executive Office of the President to give broad consideration to regulatory programs and procedures.[214] The Regulatory Analysis Review Group (RARG) was created to perform regulatory analyses on particular regulations. In both cases, members of the group were primarily drawn from the agencies involved. While proponents applauded the attempt to get coordinated regulatory action and some sense of the impact of regulation, opponents denounced the effort as "an unwarranted presidential intrusion into the regulatory process."[215]

The level of conflict over presidential intervention grew dramatically during the Reagan and Bush years. Four types of criticism were pressed during this period, with shifting emphasis but a common thread. Those challenges included the claim that: (1) people were appointed to lead the regulatory agencies who never intended to carry out the policies assigned to their offices; (2) deliberate actions were taken by the White House on grounds of extreme ideology to delay or obstruct implementation of duly enacted statutes; (3) mechanisms of political appeal were created to circumvent existing administrative law procedures; and (4) that, at their worst, these administrations created tools to manipulate the regulatory system to protect particular political supporters. The common theme behind these criticisms was the view that what made these behaviors especially dangerous is that they were based not on an open dialogue with the Congress but pursued through administrative means that in some instances relied on subterfuge.

Soon after Reagan took office, it was clear that his political appointees were moving to block, if possible, or at least to delay, the issuance of new regulations, even those required by legislation (see discussion earlier in this chapter and in Chapter 5). Almost immediately, the new administration issued its Executive Order 12291, which was clearly intended not to improve rulemaking but to block regulation. While the details were explained in earlier chapters, certain elements drew fire immediately. First, it was clear that the Office of Information and Regulatory Affairs (OIRA) created by the Paperwork Reduction Act within the Office of Management and Budget was rapidly becoming the headquarters of the antiregulatory operation in the White House. Second, it became obvious that OIRA was deliberately delaying the rulemaking process; so much so, that agencies like EPA were only able to defend their inability to meet statutory rulemaking deadlines by keeping logs showing delays in clearance processes at OIRA. It was also clear that the vice president was to head a group known as the Task Force on Regulatory Relief that would have final authority over disputes with OIRA on compliance with White House policy. That group was staffed by the director of OIRA, so there was little likelihood that appeals from OIRA to the Task Force would succeed. That was true even in some cases where all sides in a rulemaking process were in agreement except the White House.[216]

With the issuance of other executive orders, OIRA's authority was expanded and more hurdles were placed upon agencies to constrain the regulatory work. When agencies began to use interim rules to accomplish their obligations while waiting for OMB cooperation, the OIRA Administrator admonished them for seeking to "end run" the process.[217] Meanwhile, there was a pitched battle raging between congressional oversight committees, agencies, and the White House over OIRA's intervention.

When the George H. W. Bush administration came to office, the Reagan policies remained in place and the conflict they had created intensified. Congress had threatened drastic action if the White House did not stop using its OIRA review processes under the executive orders as a back door effort to defeat statutory regulation obligations. At that point, OIRA found that it could use the Paperwork Reduction Act (PRA) itself as a tool by refusing to allow agencies to gather information that they needed to develop rules or take all but very limited enforcement actions. The battle that emerged over the use of the executive order and PRA review processes led to a standoff when the White House reneged on a side-bar agreement between OMB and the House Government Operations Committee under which the PRA would be reauthorized. The agreement, entitled "Administrative Agreement: Procedures Governing OIRA Review of Regulations Under Executive Order Nos. 12291 and 12498," would have assured Congress that OIRA would disclose contacts with parties from outside government and critical communications between OMB and regulatory agencies concerning pending rulemaking matters. However, White House Counsel, C. Boyden Gray not only repudiated the agreement that had already been approved by OMB Director Richard Darman, but threatened that the White House would impose sweeping executive privilege claims to withhold information that was already being disclosed.[218] The PRA was ultimately not reauthorized until well into President Clinton's first term after an agreement was reached with Clinton's new OIRA director to address the problems raised during the Reagan and Bush years.[219]

But that was only one aspect of the battle over White House intervention. The task force headed by Bush was replaced by Vice President Quayle's Council on Competitiveness. There was no new statutory authority for this group or even an executive order. Rather, its creation was announced in a White House press release in April 1989 and direction was finally given to agencies in a memorandum from the office of the Cabinet Secretary more than a year later in June 1990.[220] Where the previous task force had exercised an essentially reactive function, taking appeals from OIRA decisions, Quayle's council took a much more proactive role, participating in OIRA meetings, and taking other decisions totally outside the public eye.[221] Not only did the Council demand that agencies put forward deregulation proposals,[222] but it also defined its scope of authority in the broadest possible terms, indicating that it claimed the power to review a wide range of materials prepared by agencies that extended well beyond what was authorized by Executive Order 12291. The Council insisted that it could review: "strategy statements, guidelines, policy manuals, grant and loan procedures, Advance Notices of Proposed Rulemaking, press releases, and other documents announcing or implementing regulatory policy that affects the public."[223]

There were strong accusations that Quayle's Council was acting as an advocacy body for regulated organizations who had lost their fights in Congress and in the administrative agencies involved. Critics charged that: "The Council has become an off-the-record, no-fingerprints operation for subverting necessary and appropriate regulatory activity of the Federal Government."[224] House Subcommittee on Health and the Environment Chairman, Henry Waxman (D-CA) stated flatly that: "There is unmistakable evidence that White House officials, spearheaded by Vice President Dan Quayle...are working with industry to undermine implementation of the new clean air law....This is not only horrible policy, it is clearly illegal."[225]

When Congress sought disclosure of who was talking with the Council and what the Council was doing, the administration responded with a blanket claim of executive privilege. The White House speaking through the EPA, informed John Dingell, chair of the House Subcommittee on Oversight and Investigations, that:

[I]t is the Administration's position that written communications involving the President's Council on Competitiveness are deliberative materials within the Executive office of the President, and there is concern that disclosure of these documents would inhibit the candor that is necessary to the deliberative process within the Executive office of the President and Executive branch.[226]

The documents detailing pressure tactics by the Council, particularly with respect to EPA, but also in health regulation areas as well, were regularly leaked to reporters. Congressional committees acquired copies of revisions in agency proposed rules demanded by the Council. Congress not only refused to reauthorize the PRA, but, when the Quayle Commission expanded its interventions and made good on the threatened executive privilege claims, the legislature moved to prohibit the use of any appropriations to support the Council in the FY93.

Despite growing criticism the Bush administration pressed the attack. The president announced in his State of the Union Address that he intended to impose a 90-day moratorium on the issuance of new rules and a call for review and, where possible, repeal of existing rules. While he explained his dramatic action in terms of the need for better coordination in the executive branch, he did not hide his intention to challenge the Congress. "Although the Congress has created the regulatory schemes within which we must operate, I am confident that, with your help, the executive branch can do much to create conditions conducive to a healthy and robust economy."[227] It was also clear that despite the growing criticism of the Quayle Council, he would stay with that approach. Hence, in his moratorium memorandum, Bush directed agencies to work with the Council and, with its assistance, designate "a senior official to serve as your agency's permanent regulatory oversight official."[228]

Quayle lost no time in asserting his leadership and indeed control in the effort, issuing his own memorandum to department heads almost immediately after Bush's announcement.[229] Only a few months later, the debate over the Quayle Council went international as information became public about the role of the Council in constraining EPA director William Reilly's flexibility as the U.S. representative at the Rio Earth Summit. The administration's attempt to salvage what had become an international embarrassment was not aided by the president's last-minute decision to attend the summit. The international criticism of the U.S. refusal to support the biodiversity treaty joined domestic outrage at Quayle Council manipulation of wetlands and clean air policy.

Indeed, the Clinton/Gore Democratic presidential ticket made criticism of the Reagan/Bush era attack on environmental, health, and safety agencies an important part of the campaign. In fact, Gore's outspoken positions on environmental issues were reportedly an important factor in his selection for the second spot on the ticket. However, once in office, as noted earlier, the administration added to—rather than subtracted from—the burdens placed on regulatory agencies and developed its own reputation for doing end runs around its own agencies through the issuance of presidential directives, though nothing matched the interventions of Reagan's OMB or Bush's Quayle Council.

As this chapter and the discussion of rulemaking in Chapter 5 noted, the George W. Bush administration has used a variety of tools to constrain regulation, but it has often done so with less public fanfare. The administration was quick to focus on performance and accountability rather than a battle against regulation, avoiding the use of the vice president in this arena and focusing activity in the Office of Information and Regulatory Affairs of the Office of Management and Budget. Then, using the system of regulatory analysis and review policies discussed earlier in this chapter, the administration has quietly but effectively returned significant numbers of proposed regulations to agencies without OMB approval (what are termed "return" letters) and had indicated to agencies difficulties with their existing regulatory programs that ought to be addressed ("prompt" letters).[230] While some high-visibility matters such as the arsenic levels in water supplies and endangered species rules controversies have drawn criticism, most of the issues have attracted relatively little public attention.

While these tactics are available to presidents, there are many forces that constrain the ability of most chief executives to have the kind of control over regulatory agencies that they would like to possess. Richard Neustadt long ago asserted that the real power of the presidency is the power to persuade.[231]

One need not go quite that far to accept the proposition that the exercise of formal power is in itself insufficient to establish and maintain effective working relations with agencies.[232] The evidence from several administrations that have sought to move beyond general coordination and seeking intervention and control is that successes may be limited relative to the political costs involved and, at worst, can be disastrous to the integrity of both the agencies and the administration.[233]

CONGRESS IN THE REGULATORY PROCESS

The role of Congress in the regulatory process has become relatively unfocused and the future uncertain because of a variety of contemporary political and institutional dynamics. Like recent presidents, recent legislatures have responded to antiregulation political sentiment that makes it politically profitable for members of Congress to be seen as leaders in what is termed, often inappropriately,[234] as the regulatory reform movement. Others who are of the view that some administrative agencies have too much discretionary authority may consider themselves compelled to deal with the problems created by the political handoff of policy problems to agencies, when the Congress was unable to resolve particularly difficult dimensions of a problem. Some legislators who have decided that the pendulum has swung too far in the direction of presidential dominance (particularly if it happens to be a president of the other party) appear to wish to reassert congressional power. In some instances this was a general reaction,[235] while in others it came as a response to presidential abuses of power as in the case of Watergate or Iran/Contra.[236] At the time of this writing, there is considerable attention to the question whether Congress has paid sufficient attention to Bush administration policies in the period since the 9/11 attacks, brought on by expanding executive branch claims to authority and disclosure of domestic surveillance.

Three other forces that have been of critical importance in the past two decades must be added to these recurring factors shaping legislative/executive relations. First, there has been a relatively dramatic ideological swing to the right, not only in the United States but in many countries around the world.[237] Ideologically driven conflict has had and continues to produce increased stresses between legislators and regulatory agencies that are administering laws often adopted by very different legislatures in earlier years. Second, the growing importance of political money, specifically of campaign contributions, has given single issue groups and others affected by regulatory policy an importance that has clearly shaped the way politics, and therefore institutional relations, are conducted. Finally, and very much affected by the previous two, is the breakdown of some of the traditional informal rules and understandings for relationships among members of Congress and between legislative bodies and administrative agencies.

Louis Fisher has pointed out an important truth that was well understood by professionals of both major parties for years. Nonstatutory elements of the relationships between the branches have always been important, but, he notes, they are as fragile as they are critical. "Much depends on a 'keep the faith' attitude among agency officials."[238] Fisher reminds us that "violations of trust" can have serious consequences. Unfortunately, many of the traditional informal sets of understandings and expected norms of conduct, for many years known informally as "Washington Rules" have broken down, not only between legislative staff and administrative agencies, but even among members.[239] In part because of this fact a number legislators have decided in the past several years not to run for reelection.

All of these factors affect the nature and conduct of the relationships among the branches. Of particular importance to the relationships between the legislature and regulatory agencies are oversight, the budgetary factor, and the varying quality of legislation.

Legislative Oversight

Many interesting studies have been made over the years of legislative efforts to oversee the activities of regulatory agencies to ensure that they do what they were designed to do, and in the manner intended.[240]

Even so, it is still the case that one of the most informative studies of oversight emerged from the Ribicoff Committee report.[241] In fact, much of the most interesting work on the subject has come from within government, particularly from the Congressional Research Service and the General Accounting Office.[242]

As Dodd and Schott have observed, oversight

> involves the attempts by Congress to view and control policy implementation by the agencies and officials of the executive branch. As an all-pervasive process, it can read Congress into every facet of administration; precisely for this reason, oversight is a slippery and ephemeral process that is difficult to identify, measure, or study in a precise manner.[243]

Oversight can indeed be a "slippery and ephemeral process." In part, the complexity arises from problems similar to those faced by the president. Legislators have an obligation to ensure the accountability of administrators but should not interfere for narrow partisan purposes with ongoing efforts by professional administrators. In providing the kinds of checks envisioned by the framers of the Constitution, they must respect the concept of the separation of powers.

Two examples highlight the difficulty of understanding the legislative role with respect to agencies. First, there is an ongoing long-standing conflict over whether the legislature should merely review past and existing agency practices or attempt to control present or future actions.[244] Members of Congress, not surprisingly, see themselves doing both.

> This report is grounded in the idea that oversight is not simply hindsight: oversight involves a wide range of congressional efforts to review and control policy implementation by the regulatory agencies. Thus, oversight includes study, review, and investigations, but it also involves an active concern with the administration of policy during implementation. Congressional oversight thus includes both participation before agency action and review after the fact.[245]

If "control" simply means "active concern," there is no conflict. If, however, control is taken to mean attempts to coerce agency action or inaction in a particular case, there may be legal difficulties.[246] Overly intrusive legislative actions may also have a detrimental impact apart from whatever legal questions might be involved.

> Legislative controls which are unduly detailed stifle initiative; make for inflexibility and inefficiency in the conduct of governmental programs; sometimes result in imposing the will of individual legislators, or small groups, in matters in which they do not speak for the entire legislature and which are best left to executive officials; and end in frustrating the basic will of the legislative body.[247]

A second example of the "slippery" nature of oversight is the concern with ensuring that an agency administers policy as Congress intended, when it enacted the statute. The intent behind a statute is the consensus that existed at the precise moment the law was enacted. Members of Congress who discuss a statute after its passage are in no position to insist that their understanding of legislative intent is the correct understanding. After all, no one legislator embodies the intentions of the entire Congress at any one time, much less across time. Members conducting oversight efforts can indicate what they thought the intent of the law originally was and what many members now think it should be, but the significance of such a claim is difficult to interpret.

> Unfortunately, it is not always easy to know what Congress' intent was with respect to a particular law. In many instances even supporters of a measure have quite different views of the purpose of that law. Sometimes the same statute will reflect conflicting goals, e.g., regulation and promotion. In those cases where congressional intent is unclear, oversight operates to indicate to the agencies what the current Congress thinks was the intent of the Congress that passed the law. The regulatory agencies are not legally bound by the interpretation.[248]

For present purposes, constituent casework by individual members of the legislature is not considered oversight.[249] When a legislator responds to a complaint from an individual or an organization in his or her home district, the expectation is not that the legislator will check to ensure that the bureaucracy is operating properly, but that the legislator will act as a personal political advocate. Complaints from constituents can and occasionally do lead to investigations and other forms of oversight, but there is no evidence to suggest that a concern for legislative oversight is what motivates legislators to hire caseworkers or to become involved in the process themselves. Indeed, a strong case could be made for the proposition that constituent casework is often detrimental to broader oversight efforts. Thus, for example, there has been a developing frustration with the dramatic growth in what are termed "earmarks," which are special budget items often added at the last moment in the appropriations process. While some of these come from the Washington corps of lobbyists, many earmarks come from business, institutions, or governmental organizations in a legislator's home district or state and are viewed as a kind of constituent casework.

Several purposes are served by oversight. Senator Ribicoff developed one of the best summaries of those purposes in an article entitled "Congressional Oversight and Regulatory Reform."

> The primary purpose of oversight is to ensure that agencies administer the laws enacted by Congress in accordance with congressional intent. Oversight also serves to promote a constant interchange with the regulatory agencies to see that the general concerns of the public are brought to the attention of the agencies and reflected in their policies. Oversight serves, too, to prevent dishonesty, waste, and abuse of the administrative process. Finally, and importantly, effective congressional oversight should prevent the agencies from making decisions that are properly left to the political process. In sum, legislative oversight of the regulatory agencies should ensure the accountability of non-elected representatives of the people.[250]

Ribicoff omitted one important purpose of oversight. Oversight should not merely be an adversarial interaction between the legislature and agencies to ensure that the latter perform properly. It should also be a cooperative effort to determine whether programs enacted by the legislature are effective in accomplishing their intended goals.[251]

A much later Congressional Research Study summarized the purposes of oversight as a means to:

- improve the efficiency, economy, and effectiveness of governmental operations;
- evaluate programs and performance;
- detect and prevent poor administration, waste, abuse, arbitrary and capricious behavior, or illegal and unconstitutional conduct;
- protect civil liberties and constitutional rights;
- inform the general public and ensure that executive policies reflect the public interest;
- gather information to develop new legislative proposals or to amend existing statutes;
- ensure administrative compliance with legislative intent; and
- prevent executive encroachment on legislative authority and prerogatives.

In sum, oversight is a way for Congress to check on, and check, the executive.[252]

Congressional oversight is conducted through the committee system, most often in subcommittees. To replace the earlier special investigating committee approach to oversight,[253] Congress mandated in the Legislative Reorganization Act of 1946 that standing committees are responsible for oversight of agencies.[254] Basically, there are three kinds of oversight, conducted by three types of committees. Attempts in the mid- and late 1970s to centralize control over oversight were rejected.[255]

Within each house oversight of regulatory agencies is shared primarily by the appropriations, authorization, and government operations committees. This tripartite structure was reaffirmed by the Legislative Reorganization Act of 1946. Under that Act appropriations committees had the responsibility for "fiscal" oversight, the spending of funds by Federal agencies. The authorizing committees were primarily responsible for "legislative" oversight of agencies within their jurisdiction. The authorizing committees were to determine whether a particular program was working and to propose remedies to problems they uncovered. The government operations committees were primarily responsible for "investigative oversight," a type of oversight which is often wider ranging than "fiscal" or "legislative" oversight.[256]

Authorization committees, also known as subject matter committees, create programs and, in theory at least, assess their effectiveness with an eye toward new or amended legislation. These committees consider the substantive authority on which legislation depends, and their bills authorize the Congress to appropriate funds for the program. Appropriations committees must meet to consider the budget requests for each fiscal year. Theoretically, they evaluate how agencies have guarded previously appropriated funds against fraud, abuse, and waste. In practice, many members of appropriations committees give substantive consideration to agency operations from a financial audit justification. For example, emphasis by regulators on a strong enforcement program that adversely affects a particular industry may lead an appropriations committee member to suggest that the program is an inappropriate use of agency resources. Government operations committees often carry out cross-agency investigations of administrative procedures.

Oversight can be conducted both formally and informally. Legislative proposals for change in administrative operations or full-scale hearings to produce such evidence as is needed to make the legislative changes are, of course, formal processes. Informal methods include special hearings, preparation and publication of reports on the performance of an agency or policy,[257] references to agency performance in floor debates or speeches in Congress, and informal contacts by committee members or staff with an agency.[258]

> Our interviews with congressional staff members also show high levels of informal oversight activity. Communications between Members and the agencies are very frequent. In fact, the Commission-Committee study found that staff communication with agency personnel was the most frequently used oversight technique. Some staff members claimed to be in daily contact with the agency they oversee.[259]

Informal techniques may be quite effective because informal studies or inquiries can easily become formal legislative action, with important consequences for administrators. The power of the raised eyebrow is a most effective tool for legislative oversight.[260]

The availability of resources that legislative committees can call on in support of oversight efforts is a continuing problem. Much of the oversight work is done by small subcommittees. The members of those committees often have particular interests in subjects in their own jurisdictions, but their schedules are crowded. They are often serving on several committees and subcommittees at the same time. Neither the legislators nor the members of their staffs have sufficient time to do in-depth analysis of agency activities.

For years one of the issues was that, if the committees were truly meeting their oversight responsibilities, there would be a great deal of time and staff resource invested in the effort. Drawing on a study by James P. McGrath of the Congressional Research Service, the Ribicoff Committee concluded that the 93rd and 94th Congresses held 1,077 hearings on major agencies. In the days when Congress was doing a good deal of oversight, the agendas published by committees and subcommittees for their oversight tasks were quite extensive. Figure 10.2 depicts the number of oversight proceedings for just one subcommittee of a single committee in the U.S. House of Representatives in the 105th Congress.

However, at the time of this writing, one of the tensions in Congress is a serious lack of attention to oversight and the partisan and ideological tensions that have come to be such a problem in setting the oversight agenda for committees and administrative agencies that are to come before the legislature as

DAN BURTON, INDIANA
CHAIRMAN

HENRY A. WAXMAN, CALIFORNIA
RANKING MINORITY MEMBER

ONE HUNDRED FIFTH CONGRESS

Congress of the United States

House of Representatives

COMMITTEE ON GOVERNMENT REFORM AND OVERSIGHT

2157 RAYBURN HOUSE OFFICE BUILDING

WASHINGTON, DC 20515–6143

(202) 225–5074

SUBCOMMITTEE ON GOVERNMENT MANAGEMENT,
INFORMATION, AND TECHNOLOGY

PROPOSED AGENDA FOR THE 105TH CONGRESS

1. Oversight of the Government Performance and Results Act
2. Oversight of the Year 2000 Computer Software Conversion
3. Travel Abuse by Senior Executive Branch Officials
4. Oversight of the Federal Elections Commission
5. Oversight of Federal Information Policies
6. Health Information Privacy Protection proposal
7. Federal Statistics proposal
8. Office of Inspector General for the White House
9. Chief Financial Officer for the White House
10. Oversight of the Chief Financial Officers Act
11. Oversight of the Inspector Generals Act
12. Oversight of the U.S. Information Agency
13. Oversight of the Federal Communications Commission
14. Oversight of the Replacement Process for Comptroller General
15. Oversight of the Debt Collection Improvement Act
16. IRS coverage under the Debt Collection Improvement Act
17. Oversight of the INS'Operation Gatekeeper
18. Oversight of the aftermath of the Northridge Earthquake
19. Oversight of Information Technology Policy
20. Oversight of Management Practices at the U.S. Forest Service
21. Oversight of Management Practices at the U.S. Customs Service
22. Oversight of the Federal Workers Compensation System
23. Oversight of Government Corporations/Performance-Based Organizations
24. Oversight of the GSA's Personal Property Program
25. Oversight of Federal Procurement Policy
26. Oversight of Financial Management Practices at the Department of Defense
27. Oversight of Financial Management Practices at the IRS

FIGURE 10.2 A Sample Oversight Agenda for a Single Congressional Subcommittee

well as in the conduct of hearings and decision processes. In a check of House of Representative committee oversight plans, which committees are required to prepare and publish under House rules,[261] one committee listed only its plan for the 108th Congress and that was as of December 2005, which was halfway through the 109th Congress.[262]

The House Committee on Veterans' Affairs is charged with addressing a wide range of issues that are particularly challenging in the contemporary environment, with troops in the field in Iraq and Afghanistan, and record numbers of them returning home with serious long-term injuries. Yet the oversight agenda for the Subcommittee on Disability Assistance and Memorial Affairs contained only 6 items for the two-year session, the Subcommittee on Economic Opportunity had 9, the Subcommittee on Health 13, and the Subcommittee on Oversight and Investigations 18.[263]

The minority Democrats in both the House and Senate have complained about the lack of oversight and alleged that the selection of the oversight subjects that are chosen are based more on partisan and ideological criteria than on the need to address serious issues or problems. They also charge that the majority has not treated minority requests for oversight with the comity that had previously been expected in committee operations even in the midst of serious partisan differences. For example, Congressman Henry Waxman (D-CA), Ranking Member, wrote to the Chairman of the House Committee on Government Reform, Representative Tom Davis (R-VA), just after Davis released the proposed agenda for the 109th Congress, with the following concerns:

Dear Mr. Chairman:
. . .I am writing to describe 12 additional topics and four previously requested topics that should be incorporated into the oversight plan and examined by our Committee this year. . ..

One of your predecessors, Chairman William Clinger, argued that control of our Committee should belong to a member of a different political party than the President so as to ensure that our oversight responsibilities are performed independently. I am not proposing such a dramatic change. I am suggesting, however, that our oversight plan should be developed on a bipartisan basis and reflect the views of all members of the Committee.

The oversight plan you propose lists over 140 topics for full committee and subcommittee oversight. Among these topics are "diploma mills," "the activities of the Bureau of Economic Analysis," "the redundant nature of GSA's structure for its Federal Supply Service," and "the federal government's migration to Internet Protocol version IPv6." I don't dispute the value of these topics. But as the primary oversight committee in the House, our Committee has a constitutional responsibility to provide a check on the abuses of the executive branch. We cannot fulfill this responsibility unless we are willing to take on difficult and politically controversial issues and follow the facts where they lead. . ..[264]

Committee staffs shoulder the primary burden of oversight detail work, but staffs are often too small to analyze the complex and very large agencies they are asked to study. To handle the workload and to add to the capacity for independent analysis, members of Congress expanded their in-house staff capability in a fashion similar to the enhancement of the Executive Office of the President. In the wake of Watergate, Congress created some new support bodies, such as the Office of Technology Assessment and the Congressional Budget Office, and built upon others already in existence, like the Congressional Research Service and the General Accounting Office (since renamed the Government Accountability Office), to assist the Congress as a whole, its committees, and its individual members.

Some of the sense of distrust that caused Congress to expand its staff and research support capabilities in the wake of the Nixon administration emerged again during the Reagan years, particularly after evidence surfaced that the administration had altered testimony by various agency personnel and admission by OMB director David Stockman that he had regularly misled Congress in his testimony on the Hill.[265] However, Congress eliminated the Office of Technology Assessment and reduced resource support for the other bodies after the previous build-up. To the degree that this move signals less distrust by legislators of the information they receive from the executive branch, that could be considered a positive turn. If, and to the extent that, it signals a declining interest in expert analysis relative to emphasis on ideology, it is most assuredly a move backwards.

In addition to the fact that the legislature is doing less oversight now than before, Congress continues to receive low marks for the quality of its oversight efforts as it has for many years. The Ribicoff Committee concluded that "Congress oversees in an episodic, erratic manner."[266] More than a decade later, critics continued to charge that oversight is:

"Congress's neglected function," that is, oversight is not done, or when done that it is uncoordinated, unsystematic, sporadic, and usually informal, with members of Congress. . .

seeking particularistic influence or publicity for purposes or reelection. ... And when members of Congress do oversee, they do it sporadically, for the quick payoff, usually with little long-term significance.[267]

More recently, in testimony in late 2005, the GAO concluded that presidential influence over the regulatory process has increased while Congress has shown little effective influence.[268]

For some time, appropriations committees got higher marks than other committees for oversight in that their efforts are more systematic and regular.[269] Of course, part of the reason was that, in theory at least, the annual appropriations process automatically triggers periodic hearings. However, for some years now, appropriations processes have been anything but regular with frequent use of continuing resolutions and extremely large and complex consolidated appropriations acts passed well after the beginning of the fiscal year. Often many of the provisions that have been built into these large bills have not been considered in full committee processes. Even so, the annual appropriations process at least should provide a regular context for exploration of the performance of programs and the agencies that administer them.

By contrast, unless regulatory agency statutes have reauthorization requirements, often referred to as "sunset" provisions, there is no regular requirement for other committees to conduct oversight proceedings. Because of the press of business, oversight tends to be haphazard and in response to some particular problem that has drawn public attention.

> Oversight tends to be done on a crisis basis only. The crisis may be local, involving a constituent, or national in scope. The oversight effort is usually initiated not in accordance with any preplanned set of priorities, but rather in response to a newspaper article, a complaint from a constituent or special interest group, or information from a disgruntled agency employee. "The regulatory agencies are generally left unsupervised until one of their policies or actions stirs up disapproval loud enough to reach congressional ears."[270]

Thus, immediately after two accidents in separate mines that happened in rapid succession killed West Virginia coal miners in early January 2006, oversight hearings were convened by the Subcommittee on Labor, HHS and Education of the Senate Appropriations Committee into the performance of the Mine Safety and Health Administration (MSHA) located in the U.S. Department of Labor.[271]

In addition to the shortage of time, staff, information, and lack of regular procedures, legislative oversight suffers from a lack of generally agreed-on standards for agency performance. To determine whether an agency is performing properly, it is necessary to define what "properly" means. Proper agency performance might be defined as faithfully executing the provisions of law that the agency is charged to administer. However, poorly drafted or excessively broad statutes can make it difficult to know what an agency is supposed to do, let alone whether it is doing it well or badly. Another problem is that legislative oversight is conducted through a legislative committee structure that is badly fragmented.[272] The members of different committees often refuse to cooperate with each other.[273] Committee chairs in particular guard their prerogatives and their political turf.

Finally, there are relatively few political incentives for representatives to shift their time and resources from other activities to concentrate on conducting oversight in any positive way.[274] There may be political mileage in leading an attack on regulatory agencies in general, or on one agency in particular, but, on the whole, oversight is long, involved, and tedious. It rarely draws press coverage unless some particularly egregious agency error is uncovered. Few interest groups will make a special effort to aid a legislator's reelection bid in the home district because he or she found after a lengthy hearing that a particular agency was doing a good job. (Casework, on the other hand, has a rather direct, if occasionally small, payoff. The person for whom a congressman prodded the Social Security Administration to process a check will remember that service and tell others about it.) Constituents rarely know or care about oversight. Improving oversight requires a serious incentive to make it worth the legislator's time.

There can be a number of negative consequences of oversight. For one thing, it can be extremely burdensome to the agencies. Oversight hearings may more often be pursued for political notoriety or to score ideological debating points than to make careful analyses of agency performance. Hearings can also be used to punish or ridicule administrators in difficult positions who are attempting to do a good job. Then there is the well-understood fact that the concentration of the oversight function in small subcommittees can allow a few individuals to wield tremendous power. Finally, there is the persistent criticism in recent decades that oversight has provided a platform for attempts to micromanage the executive.[275] While that complaint is not new, there have been concerns that Congress was increasingly moved not merely to involve itself in particular agency actions, but in the wider decision processes.[276]

More recently, there have been two factors that have further discouraged oversight. There may be partisan disincentives for a legislature dominated by one party to conduct aggressive oversight of agencies under the control of a president from that same party. Additionally, the White House may constrain information Congress needs to carry out its oversight duties. For example, the theory of the unified executive has been asserted by the George W. Bush administration to block efforts by Congress to compel regular reports on important programs or agencies.[277] Executive privilege is another mechanism that is used to limit disclosure. In the George W. Bush and previous administrations, the use of classified devices such as national security directives has been another barrier that limited the ability of Congress to monitor the activities of the executive branch or to obtain key documents.[278]

During the mid-1990s, attention shifted for many members of Congress away from traditional modes of oversight toward efforts to impose process constraints on all administrative agencies. The newly elected Republican majority in the 104th Congress referred to these as bills growing out of their "Contract with America," a theme central to their electoral victory. Critics both within Congress and outside of it argued that these bills were nothing less than efforts to paralyze regulatory bodies. Senator Leahy (D-VT) wrote:

> The committee was never given an opportunity to vote on whether or [not] it supported this legislation. There are many reasons the committee should have rejected and the Senate should reject this legislation.
>
> First, this legislation claims to be a regulatory reform bill. It is not. It is a regulatory policy bill. Unfortunately the policy assumptions of this legislation are contrary to both historic and contemporary American values.
>
> Second, it does not make regulation more efficient. It is a "monkey wrench" bill that makes better regulations nearly impossible.
>
> Third, this is not a bill that benefits the public or the middle class. The corporate clients of the big Washington law firms and beltway consultants, not the middle class, will be its beneficiaries. They will employ the scientists and attorneys to contest cost/benefit analyses, risk assessments, or file petitions for review of regulations.
>
> Fourth, this bill does not protect the public from government. It is, instead, a profoundly anti-democratic, elitist bill.[279]

The advocates of these new legislative programs began from existing notions of hybrid rulemaking, preclearance, regulatory flexibility analysis, regulatory impact analyses, and risk analysis to create far more extensive procedural requirements in each of these areas. To make the point about just how complex and impossible the procedural requirements of one of these bills (H.R. 9) would have been, the flow chart in Figure 10.3 was published in the *New York Times*.

These packages did not pass as such. However, the majority did manage to enact a number of the elements of these larger packages as riders on the critical debt limit extension legislation. Title II of Public Law 104-121 was entitled the Small Business Regulatory Fairness Act of 1996. It contained within it subtitles on "regulatory compliance simplification," "regulatory enforcement reforms," "Equal Access to Justice Act amendments," "Regulatory Flexibility Act amendments," and "congressional review." (Chapter 5 discussed the regulatory flexibility and congressional review requirements.) Not only did Congress add substantially to regulatory requirements, but it added other levers that allowed

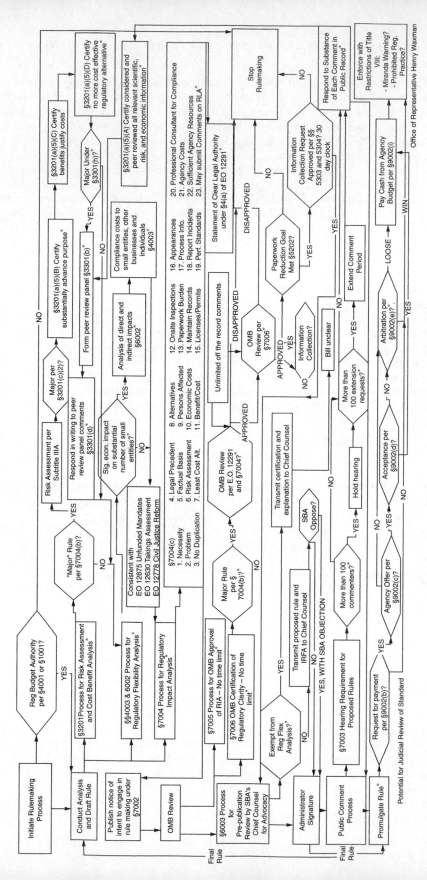

FIGURE 10.3 The Threat of a Rulemaking Nightmare: What Proposed Legislation Might Have Done

SOURCE: Office of Representative Henry Waxman.

regulated bodies and the Congress itself to avoid normal oversight procedures in favor of more definitive forms of intervention. First, it subjected more of the regulatory analysis and review processes carried out by agencies to judicial review under the APA. Second, with respect to enforcement actions brought by the federal government, the amendments to the Equal Access to Justice Act provided that a regulated firm can recover its litigation costs even if it ultimately loses its case if there is an excessive difference between the sanction demanded by the enforcement officials and the final sanction imposed after adjudication.[280] And then Congress moved to insulate its own decisions under the congressional review process from judicial review. The new section 805 of the APA provides that: "No determination, finding, action, or omission under this [congressional review] chapter shall be subject to judicial review."

The most recent efforts in Congress have been to take the George W. Bush administration's Program Assessment Review Tool approach to policy, program, and agency evaluation and attempt to apply it legislatively to all regulatory agencies. The House Government Reform Committee voted out what it called the Program Assessment and Results Act with a favorable recommendation to the full House in the spring of 2005. The bill would in essence mandate by legislation the use of the PART process by OMB.[281] It would be permanent, with no sunset provision, and would not involve any notice or participation opportunities. The minority of the subcommittee, while agreeing that program assessment is certainly a worthwhile activity in general terms, warned that the OMB had demonstrated a willingness to politicize its PART appraisals and attack congressional enactments in the first few years of the use of that tool rather than ensuring a professional and nonpartisan assessment of actual performance.[282] The Senate Subcommittee on Federal Financial Management, Government Information, and International Security of the Committee on Homeland Security and Government Affairs held hearings on the PART process in June 2005 with ideas in mind similar to those pending in the House. Professor Beryl Radin testified in the Senate hearings warning that while there are clearly positive aspects to performance assessment, there are also risks in adopting the approach used by the Bush OMB PART process. She made six key points:

(1) Many federal programs have multiple and conflicting goals.

(2) Not all federal programs are alike [and the PART process is not sufficiently sensitive to those differences].

(3) OMB budget examiners and OMB itself have a limited perspective on programs.

(4) There are many different types of information that are useful to those who are charged with running or assessing programs.

(5) OMB calls for new data sources but does not acknowledge that agencies are not able to collect this data.

(6) PART focuses on an executive branch perspective and is not easily transferred to the congressional branch.[283]

Thus, Radin concludes there are areas of concern about the existing use of the PART by OMB and even more questions that would arise if Congress were to attempt a similar process.

It remains to be seen whether Congress will rely on these process changes or will reconsider its own oversight responsibilities. Ironically, to this point at least, the addition of new provisions of law that have made life difficult for regulatory agencies have also added to the legislature's own oversight burdens, at least if that body intends to monitor the implementation of the new requirements on the agencies, much less to add new ones.[284]

The Budget Process

The budget process is also important because (1) it is a lever to force agency responsiveness to Congress and (2) it is the means by which government establishes priorities. As to the former, Congress can set levels and limits for funding certain regulatory programs, establish purposes for which funds will be spent, and include "limitations provisions" that specify activities for which agency funds may not be expended.[285] On the matter of priority setting, regulatory agencies can find themselves in a very difficult position between the president's budget recommendations and the budget actually produced by Congress. Agency needs and expectations for funding may run afoul of executive branch budget-cutting pressures, which is what happened when President Clinton tried to cut EPA funding only to have Congress insist on increasing the agency's budget. The fragile relationships with both the Hill and the White House can be difficult to maintain. That is particularly true in a setting where individual appropriations changes must be reconciled with overall budget deals set between congressional leaders and the White House.

The potential effectiveness of budgetary controls as oversight tools has been influenced by the economic and political environment. First, in budget cutting periods there may be relatively few resources that can be used as incentives to obtain agency compliance with legislative wishes. Moreover, even if there had been resources, the political mood has been such that neither the White House nor Congress has been interested in budget growth, except in limited areas. The same sorts of forces have affected many state agencies, both because of the involvement of state agencies in federal programs and because the political climate had a similar impact in many states and localities.

The issues of a balanced budget and the national debt are once again becoming so critical that they have produced pressure and political opportunity for across-the-board constraints on government spending. The importance of government-wide budget deals or across the board cut strategies is that they are blunt instruments that do not permit the kind of focused action needed to address the performance of particular agencies. There is some degree of irony in that fact, given the call within the context of the Government Performance and Results Act and other Clinton- and George W. Bush–era management shifts that emphasize performance-driven agency behavior.[286]

The Problem of the Political Handoff

The pressures legislators face can tempt them to deal with policy problems by a political handoff. That is, it is easier to pass a law making an agency responsible for solving a problem than to resolve fundamental policy conflicts before assigning a statute to an agency for implementation. Broad grants of authority and discretion may permit an agency to be innovative, but if there is not regular, conscientious oversight, there are dangers for those who are regulated by the agency and for agency administrators. The danger of abuse of discretion is obvious. The danger for the administrator can be that a lack of regular interaction between Congress and the agency may lead to a campaign against the agency by a congressional newcomer or an incumbent who needs an issue around which to build a reelection campaign.

In sum, there is great attractiveness to the idea that regulatory agencies should be the servants of Congress because the members of Congress are accountable to the electorate. But a host of political opportunities and incentives impinge on legislative performance apart from the substance or quality of regulatory programs. The framers of the Constitution were concerned that actions by the executive branch might automatically seem suspect to Americans, and those of the legislative branch might appear presumptively proper. It was for this reason that Madison warned in Federalist Paper No. 48:

> The legislative department is everywhere extending the sphere of its activity and drawing all power into its impetuous vortex. . . . [I]t is against the enterprising ambition of this department that the people ought to indulge all their jealousy and exhaust all their precautions.
>
> The legislative department derives a superiority in our governments from other circumstances. Its constitutional powers being at once more extensive, and less susceptible of precise limits, it can, with greater facility, mask, under complicated and indirect measures, the encroachments which it makes on coordinate departments.[287]

This debate over delegation of unresolved issues is the traditional version of the political handoff.[288] And, as earlier chapters have pointed out, things have changed considerably such that:

> Congress began to curtail or withdraw its sweeping, open-ended grants of unchecked exec- utive authority—over national health care, environmental protection, consumer and trans- portation safety, occupational health, foreign aid, and military weapons acquisitions, to name a few. Many congressional requirements of executive agencies were made more detailed and precise.[289]

However, what purported to be regulatory reform efforts in the past two decades have, in reality, created new versions of the political handoff problem. Examples include the excessive reliance on sunset provisions, the theory that market-oriented policies will handle complex problems, and the effort to work around the bureaucracy by opting for government corporations or other governance devices.

The Ribicoff Committee supported the use of sunset provisions in legislation authorizing regu- latory activity. These provisions state that unless a policy embodied in statute receives a new authori- zation within a given period, usually five years, the sun will set (so to speak) on the program and it will cease to exist. In theory, this control should force periodic and presumably comprehensive reassessment of agency performance. In time sunset reviews would, in theory at least, become systematized. After more than three decades of experience with the widespread use of this tool, though, it cannot be said that a sunset provision will guarantee a careful, thoughtful, or systematic assessment of the performance of a regulatory program or agency. Sometimes that has indeed happened while in other cases—even those cases involving large and complex policies—it has not. The sunset review may simply provide an opportunity to score political points and give a great deal of leverage to committee chairs. It has also been the case that some major reauthorization deadlines have come when Congress was enmeshed in a variety of other obligations, including other reauthorization efforts. That was the case in the 1980s and 1990s with respect to a variety of environmental laws. Then there is the problem of interest group imbalance. It is much easier to defeat legislation than it is to enact it. Some legislation came into being through a momentous effort to develop an interest group coalition around an issue, e.g., civil rights statutes. That kind of coalition generally breaks down after the law is enacted. The same is true of consumer-oriented legislation. Periodic reauthorization gives an advantage to smaller but better organized and financed interest groups over loose coalitions of public interest groups unless those groups can organize effectively and have the resources to support strong interest group coalitions.[290]

Where political forces have been powerful enough to do so, they have made efforts in recent years to remove sunset provisions from authorizations so that the legislative authority becomes permanent. One important example of this tendency is the move at the first reauthorization of the USA Patriot Act to make that controversial legislation permanent. While there was broad support for some form of a reauthorized Patriot Act, critics of the legislation, both Democrats and Republicans, were driven to ensure that problems with the law as written and as applied were remedied before the authorization was made permanent.

Another form of handoff is the effort to shift policies toward the marketplace through systems of incentives or by contracting out—discussed earlier in this chapter and in other parts of this volume. But seeking to move much of the day-to-day decisionmaking out of government agencies and into the market means shedding decisionmaking authority from government agencies. It also means altering decision processes and substantive policy choices for which agencies were generally held accountable in oversight activities. That, in turn, has meant that the legislature needs to find new ways to set standards and conduct oversight in contracting and market-oriented regulatory programs, challenges which, to this point at least, have not been met. In order to do that, Congress will be required to develop new approaches to oversight and enhance staff resources to develop the kind of information needed to support that activity. Comptroller General Bowsher tried to highlight this reality for Congress even as he testified about his plans to meet legislative requests for significant cuts in GAO staff and expenditures.[291]

Finally, after Congress and chief executives had piled layers of obligations, both procedural and substantive, on many administrative agencies, increased the ratio of political appointees at the top of agencies and at headquarters relative to the people available for enforcement and operations in the field, and then cut operating budgets, members reached the apparently surprising conclusion that some agencies simply could not do the jobs they were asked to perform. However, rather than rebuilding and streamlining the agencies, the decision has been made in several circumstances to create government corporations as alternatives on the theory that they would be more business-like, more efficient, and less enmeshed in what is often referred to by critics as the red tape that burdens government agencies.

While the idea of government corporations is certainly not new, their numbers and uses have definitely undergone significant increases since the 1970s when President Carter turned to the ill-fated Synthetic Fuels Corporation as an answer to the energy crisis. In order to have the flexibility that was supposed to produce enhanced results, these corporations have often been exempted from pay caps, administrative procedure laws, and a variety of other standard accountability mechanisms applied to agencies. However, the performance of these agencies as regulators and market protectors, among other functions, has been very controversial.[292] They have been a kind of mechanism for political handoffs to address difficult issues outside of the normal governmental agency and the effort to devise appropriate devices to maintain their accountability is very much a work in progress. At root these kinds of political handoffs represent challenges to the public law framework supporting public administration and, as Robert Gilmour, Ronald Moe, and Thomas Stanton have explained, as such they present serious problems.[293]

The other great issue associated with these corporations is that instead of being protective or service-oriented, they may become mechanisms that create perverse incentives that can undermine regulatory regimes. One recent example involves the Pension Benefit Guaranty Corporation (PBGC). The PBGC was created to assist workers whose employers had collapsed leaving them without pension benefits. However, it is increasingly being seen as a mechanism that firms can use to rid themselves of expensive pension obligations. The agreement by the PBGC to accept the pension obligations of United Airlines in 2005 suggested a way to use the public corporation to benefit the firm. United used this mechanism as a vehicle to help bring it out of bankruptcy by transferring its underfunded obligations to the public agency. As the PBGC explained it,

> Collectively, United's pension plans are underfunded by $9.8 billion on a termination basis, $6.6 billion of which is guaranteed, according to the PBGC. The four plans are: the UA Pilot Defined Benefit Plan, which covers 14,100 participants and has $2.8 billion in assets to pay $5.7 billion in promised benefits; the United Airlines Ground Employees Retirement Plan, which covers 36,100 participants and has $1.3 billion in assets to pay $4.0 billion in promised benefits; the UA Flight Attendant Defined Benefit Pension Plan, which covers 28,600 participants and has $1.4 billion in assets to pay $3.3 billion in promised benefits; and the Management, Administrative and Public Contact Defined Benefit Pension Plan, which covers 42,700 participants and has $1.5 billion in assets to pay $3.8 billion in promised benefits..[294]

Unfortunately, at the time the corporation undertook this responsibility, the PBGC was itself already in significant financial difficulty. As the corporation explained: "As of September 30, 2004, the PBGC's own balance sheet showed a $23.3 billion deficit, with $39 billion in assets to pay $62.3 billion in guaranteed pension benefits to more than 1 million workers and retirees. By law, the PBGC is required to keep premiums as low as possible and has no call on the U.S. Treasury beyond a $100 million line of credit."[295]

To the degree that efforts are made to avoid traditional regulatory devices through other kinds of governance arrangements of the sort described in earlier chapters—often involving not only different types of government agencies at various levels of government, but also nonprofit or for-profit organizations—the situation may entail another type of political handoff. As debates over timber and endangered species act problems in the Pacific Northwest have demonstrated, the fact that there may be a negotiated resolution in the near term does not mean the parties will refrain from moving the regulatory issues into the courts over time. If control over problems that are in their nature regulatory are handed over to governance regimes that are networks of agencies and nongovernmental organizations, there is the additional problem referred to in the networking literature as "leakage of accountability."[296] The nature and focus of authority in such governance arrangements are often unclear and fragmented making accountability even more challenging than it would otherwise be if a standard regulatory regime were to be employed.[297]

Similarly, the decision to develop through international agreements various bodies to resolve regulatory problems involving firms or groups from several nations presents all of those difficulties of the political handoff and more. For one thing, there are serious questions as to how bodies like the regulatory panels established under the General Agreement on Tariffs and Trade (GATT) or the North American Free Trade Agreement (NAFTA) will themselves be held to account. There is not a clear line of sovereignty in such situations, not to mention the complexities that arise when subnational units of government are involved in the disputes. Indeed, these dynamics have helped to redefine intergovernmental relations such that it extends from supranational organizations to local governments.

INTERGOVERNMENTAL DIMENSIONS OF REGULATION

As in all other aspects of American public life, intergovernmental relations are crucial to regulation, and that significance has only increased in recent years. Of particular importance to public managers—both those who administer regulatory programs and those who are consumers of regulatory decisions—are the contemporary context of intergovernmental relations, the concepts of preemption and partial preemption, state challenge to reduced federal regulatory protections, state retention of control over their own regulatory authority, state immunity from federal regulation, state and local governments as market participants and as regulators, and federal government efforts to address federalism concerns in regulatory policy.

The Contemporary Intergovernmental Context
and the Challenges That Flow from It

There are several factors noted at various points in this volume that are important to recall when contemplating the intergovernmental dimension of regulation in the contemporary context. First, there is the problem of unfunded mandates, both in the form of statutory obligations and also those imposed by federal agencies through rulemaking or as conditions of the receipt of federal funds. For reasons noted earlier, the plain fact is that there is little evidence to date that the Unfunded Mandates Reform Act has resulted in any significant reductions of burdens on states or localities. For one thing, it was not made retroactive and therefore did not affect an entire body of mandates. Moreover, it has not been shown to have reduced mandates imposed by federal agencies.[298] Beyond all that, burdens that have been imposed to accompany federal grants or contracts are presumably "funded" mandates, when in reality the states and localities are required to do more and in many cases receive less than they did before. Certainly the bipartisan criticisms by governors and state legislators around the nation in response to the No Child Left Behind Act is an obvious example of the problem. Even programs for which there is broad public and political support, such as the Individuals with Disabilities Education Act (IDEA), have become subjects of controversy because of the ongoing unwillingness of the federal government to fully fund that legislation.

At the same time, state and local governments have been in competition with each other for economic development opportunities. That competition has made it particularly important for these units to try to enhance efficiency and service delivery at the same time that they are asked to carry out complex regulatory challenges from zoning laws to nationally imposed environmental regulations like the Right-to-Know law. This also must be done in the context of varying state mandates. At the street level, that can mean that local government officials, both elected members of the governing body and professional managers must compete to get and keep jobs and maintain the tax base while addressing a complex set of regulatory burdens.[299]

These dynamics can also lead to competitions among state regulatory systems. Thus, when Ben & Jerry's ice cream company headquartered in Vermont announced on its packaging that it was made from milk produced in dairies that did not use bovine growth hormone, Illinois moved against the company. The complaint was not that there was anything wrong with the company's position on the hormone, but that the process for ensuring that the claim was accurate was inadequate. In the Vermont case, farmers were permitted to sign a statement attesting that their products were free of the substance, but Illinois insisted that a simple assurance by the producer was insufficient to guarantee that the product truly was free of growth hormone-affected milk.

At the same time, states have been engaged in a similar dispute over claims that farm products are organically grown. The U.S. Department of Agriculture found itself in considerable controversy when it was considering whether to impose national standards because different states have standards that vary widely and are, in some cases, enforced—if at all—by nongovernmental organizations rather than by an agency of the state. Since the ability to label products as organic permits producers to gain competitive advantages in some markets and to reap higher profits as well, this is a debate of consequence. On the other hand, voluntary standard-setting organizations in those states with very high standards worry that national regulations would eliminate their ability to use their state's traditional reputation for the highest standards and to keep out of their markets products that may be acceptable to USDA as organic but are not in particular parts of the country. These standard-setting debates can be as complex as they are economically important. Consider the argument about whether hydroponically grown tomatoes, which are grown in a liquid medium and not in soil, can qualify as organically grown. Ultimately, a decision on that point at USDA was a political debate, not a scientific judgment.

Of course, in an attempt to deal with their complex environment, many communities and states have been active in the attempt to form intergovernmental partnerships ranging from simple contracts between local governments for the provision of recreational services to politically important interstate compacts that must be approved by Congress such as the New England Dairy Compact, that governed for some years the prices and conditions of sale of milk products in the New England states. Some even involve the federal government or federal facilities within states. These bodies not only require that local governments and states dedicate considerable energy to representation and coordination, but may have important powers and make important regulatory-type decisions that carry considerable complexity. Thus, when Congress worked with the District of Columbia and the Commonwealth of Virginia to create the Metropolitan Washington Airport Authority (MWAA), governing operations at Reagan/ National and Dulles airports, it left itself options by mandating a review board made up of members of Congress that could veto MWAA decisions. The board and the authority tried to argue that a citizen group challenging decisions about the level of air traffic was barred from bringing the action, but the Supreme Court ruled:

> Petitioners lay great stress on the fact that the Board of Review was established by the bylaws of MWAA, which was created by legislation enacted by the Commonwealth of Virginia and the District of Columbia. Putting aside the unsettled question whether the District of Columbia acts as a State or as an agency of the Federal Government for separation-of-powers purposes, we believe the fact that the Board of Review was created by state enactments is not enough to immunize it from separation-of-powers review.[300]

Preemption and Partial Preemption

Of course, what does and does not happen at the state and local level is often determined in Washington under the doctrine of preemption. The preemption doctrine flows from the Supremacy Clause of the

Constitution found in Article VI, which states: "This Constitution and the laws which shall be made in pursuance thereof shall be the supreme Law of the Land; and the judges in the several states shall be bound thereby, any Thing in the Constitution or Laws of any state to the Contrary notwithstanding." Hence, regulatory statutes enacted by Congress, so long as they are issued within the authority of Article I of the Constitution, trump state and local laws or ordinances and render them void.[301] If Congress made clear when it enacted legislation whether it intended to preempt state law, the issue would be simple. Unfortunately, it often does not specify those intentions.

Given these basics, the Supreme Court has explained that there are three ways that preemption can occur.

> Pre-emption may be either expressed or implied, and "is compelled whether Congress' command is explicitly stated in the statute's language or implicitly contained in its structure and purpose."...Absent explicit preemptive language, we have recognized at least two types of implied pre-emption: field pre-emption, where the scheme of federal regulation is "so pervasive as to make reasonable the inference that Congress left no room for the States to supplement it," and conflict pre-emption, where "compliance with both federal and state regulations is a physical impossibility,"...or where state law "stands as an obstacle to the accomplishment and execution of the full purposes and objectives of Congress."[302]

Often, the problem for state officials and for courts is to determine whether any of these types of implied preemption is present. For reasons discussed at several points earlier in this volume, it is often not a simple task to determine precisely what Congress intended.

In an era of deregulation, when the national government has sought to step back from involvement, one of the questions of preemption arises when states or even localities seek to act where the federal government has left the field. Thus, following airline deregulation, a group of state attorneys general sought to address consumer complaints about false and misleading ticket pricing through state consumer-protection actions. Their efforts were blocked when the Supreme Court concluded that the federal deregulation statute had preempted any attempt by states to take action in that arena.[303]

These well-established positions do not, however, mean that any time a state or even a locality tries to act in a field where Congress has legislated that a court will find preemption. Thus, in an important case concerning regulation of nuclear power, a California intervention was permitted against claims that the Nuclear Regulatory Commission had preempted the field. Intervention was also permitted when a Wisconsin community developed its own regulation of spraying of insecticides on area farm fields in the absence of state or federal action under the Federal Insecticide, Fungicide, and Rodenticide Act.[304]

State Challenge to Reduced or Inadequate Federal Regulatory Protections

Quite apart from the issue of preemption many states and state officials have been challenging decisions by federal regulatory agencies to relax existing standards, block or delay more rigorous new standards that had been in development, or simply failing to exercise existing regulatory authority in clearly egregious circumstances. In some instances, the challenge has been direct, with state legal action against federal agencies, in such areas as air pollution standards, while in others the states or individual officials have simply sought alternative means to do themselves what the federal government appeared unwilling to do. Thus, state attorneys general launched and ultimately settled a dramatic set of suits against tobacco companies. Rhode Island's attorney general used a variety of state law causes of action to go after the manufacturers of lead-based paint.[305] New York Attorney General Eliot L. Spitzer took on ten major investment banking institutions because the Securities and Exchange Commission seemed unwilling to act until revelations of serious abuses and conflicts of interest were demonstrated by Spitzer's investigations. Connecticut Attorney General Richard Blumenthal put the matter bluntly in a media interview:

There is a clear dramatic trend of Republican and Democratic attorneys general expanding the scope of their law enforcement efforts in a more aggressive and proactive way to fill gaps left at the federal level or to address unmet needs.... The climate is now very similar to the Reagan years, where there was a retreat at the federal level in many of these areas and in some instances actually a complete abrogation of authority.[306]

For many state officials, since the federal government has the authority to act and even to preempt the state action, it should take the lead and also work with the states in the process.

State Retention of Control over Their Own Regulatory Authority

Indeed, to some observers it seemed as though, given the rulings issued by the U.S. Supreme Court from 1937 through the 1960s, there appeared to be little question that the federal government, using the commerce clause of the Constitution, could regulate a wide variety of activities and that, once Congress had chosen to act in a given policy area, states were preempted from any involvement. But a number of trends have developed that have demonstrated quite clearly that no such automatic federal dominance is to be assumed.

First, the 1970s saw an effort by Congress to break the image of federal authorities invading states and localities to regulate those targets identified by national decisionmakers. Increasingly, the legislature adopted a three-option approach to regulatory policy. Statutes permitted states to develop and administer their own regulatory standards, provided they were at least as stringent as the federal version and approved by the relevant federal agency. This option allowed states to tailor regulatory programs to local needs. Alternatively, states could choose to accept responsibility for administration of federal standards. This approach allowed states to use the technical expertise and the investment of resources committed by the federal government to develop standards, while avoiding the problem of two sets of regulators interested in similar questions. Presumably, state officials would apply the federal standards with greater sensitivity to local problems. Both of these options permitted federal agencies with relatively small field staffs and limited resources to concentrate on policymaking and targeted enforcement efforts. In the final scenario, federal authorities would step in if the state was unable or unwilling to provide either standards or enforcement. This model has been upheld by the Supreme Court and has been used consistently since the 1970s.[307]

The other trend has seen state and local officials who have challenged what many had thought was firmly established federal dominance, ultimately receiving support from the U.S. Supreme Court. These were in the areas of limitation on federal assertion of regulatory power, state retention of control over regulation by their officials, and intergovernmental immunity. As to the first, the Court struck down the Gun Free School Zones Act of 1990 that made it illegal to possess firearms in a school zone on grounds that this was not a subject that Congress could reach under the commerce clause.[308] In so doing, the Court began an effort to reinterpret the reach of the commerce clause when that seemed to be a settled area of law.[309] Just how far the court will take that significantly revised interpretation of the commerce clause is not clear.

However, the Court has taken a similarly constraining view with respect to efforts to press states for cooperation in regulatory programs. The problem of developing and locating low-level nuclear waste disposal facilities plagued the federal government and the states for years. While many urged Congress simply to require a federal agency to take over regulation in the field, others argued in favor of facilitating an intergovernmental solution in which the states would play a more central role and the federal government would provide support. A compromise was suggested by several states that urged Congress to adopt a statute requiring states either to join with other states in regional compacts that would establish acceptable disposal facilities or accept responsibility to establish a state's own regulatory program if it failed to enter into a regional agreement by a set deadline. Congress adopted that statute, but, not surprisingly, many states were not able to join in the regional compacts within the deadline. When it came time for the trigger date for state programs, New York objected on grounds that while the Congress had authority to regulate nuclear waste disposal by the federal government, that authority did not include the power to force the state to use its regulatory capabilities. The Supreme Court agreed with the state.[310] On the basis of that ruling, local law enforcement officials in two states challenged the Brady gun control law, claiming that it forced local officials to participate in federal regulatory programs in violation of the Tenth Amendment reserve powers clause. Again, the Supreme Court agreed.[311]

Finally, the Court issued a ruling finding that Florida was immune from a suit brought under the Indian Gaming Act.[312] Chief Justice Rehnquist, writing for a badly divided Court, began to construct a kind of intergovernmental immunity under the Eleventh Amendment that was a dramatic change from the Court's prior rulings. He had once before been able to get a majority for a Tenth Amendment–based immunity from federal control,[313] but that ruling was later overturned.[314] Justice Stevens in dissent pointed out that the importance of this ruling reaches far beyond the Indian gaming issue. "Rather, it prevents Congress from providing a federal forum for a broad range of actions against States, from those sounding in copyright and patent law, to those concerning bankruptcy, environmental law, and the regulation of our vast national economy."[315] This new form of immunity has been used, for example, to strike down the application of portions of the Americans with Disabilities Act and the Age Discrimination in Employment Act to state governments.[316] It has also been used, as Justice Stevens predicted, with respect to regulatory agencies.

In another instance, a company was denied permission to bring its vessels into port in Charleston, South Carolina. The firm complained to the Federal Maritime Commission (FMC), alleging that the South Carolina State Ports Authority action violated the Shipping Act. The FMC assigned the complaint to an administrative law judge but the state answered that it was immune from FMC adjudication of the complaint, and a sharply divided Supreme Court agreed in an opinion by Justice Thomas.[317] Justice Breyer replied for the four dissenters:

> The Court holds that a private person cannot bring a complaint against a State to a federal administrative agency where the agency (1) will use an internal adjudicative process to decide if the complaint is well founded, and (2) if so, proceed to court to enforce the law. Where does the Constitution contain the principle of law that the Court enunciates? I cannot find the answer to this question in any text, in any tradition, or in any relevant purpose.[318]

Here again, it is not clear just how far the states or the U.S. Supreme Court will wish to push this line of cases.

State and Local Governments as Market Participants and as Regulators

Finally, this set of questions about state and local governments in the future is made more complex because these governments are increasingly acting not merely as regulators of the marketplace but also as market participants. Relatively little consideration has been given to this growing phenomenon, but we have some indications of the kinds of questions that can be anticipated.

The Supreme Court has recognized a difference for some purposes between situations in which government units act as market participants rather than market regulators. In a Massachusetts case, the Court rejected a challenge under the interstate commerce clause to a city requirement that 50 percent of all employees on city construction projects had to be hired locally. The Court wrote: "when a state or local government enters the market as a participant, it is not subject to the restraints of the commerce clause. If the city is a market participant, then the Commerce Clause establishes no barrier to conditions such as those which the city demands for participation.... Insofar as the city expended its own funds in entering into construction projects it was a market participant."[319] Well, that would seem to settle the matter, but there is more. Camden, New Jersey, adopted a policy similar to the Boston requirement and was promptly challenged, but on different grounds. The Supreme Court, in that case, decided only a year after the Massachusetts matter, found that while the local hiring requirement did not violate the interstate commerce clause, it did violate the privileges and immunities clause.[320]

States have found themselves in similar quandaries. The state of South Dakota operated a cement plant and gave preference to in-state buyers. The Supreme Court rejected a challenge by an out-of-state firm brought on commerce clause grounds. Justice Blackmun wrote: "Here the state acts as market participant rather than as market regulator. Such policies, while perhaps protectionist in a loose sense, reflect the essential and patently unobjectionable purpose of state government—to serve the citizens of the State."[321] However, the Court put boundaries around that broad language in a later ruling. The case involved a challenge to an Alaska requirement, placed into timber contracts, that called for the initial processing of the raw lumber in Alaska before it could be removed from the state. The Court found that the Alaska contract requirement did violate the commerce clause.[322] The Court agreed that the state could attach some normal business conditions to the contract and yet remain a market participant outside the constraints of the commerce clause. However, the state may not disguise attempts at market regulation with the claim of market participation.

More recently, two novel aspects of this problem have arisen, concerning the development of contemporary service networks, in one case, and questions of supranational considerations on the other. In the latter situation, the Antilles Cement Corporation sued, challenging Puerto Rico legislation that required use of "'construction materials manufactured in Puerto Rico' in all construction works financed with public funds"[323] and an additional statute that required "all bags of cement manufactured outside of Puerto Rico to carry a warning label, in both Spanish and English, stating that. . .this cement shall not be used in construction works of the governments of the United States and of Puerto Rico nor in works financed with funds. . . ."[324] The district court struck down the two legislative provisions on grounds that they violated the commerce clause, rejecting in the process the argument by Puerto Rico that the exemption from commerce clause barriers for market participants should apply. The U.S. Court of Appeals for the First Circuit vacated that decision, finding that there were alternative statutory grounds that might have been considered to avoid the constitutional question. However, the appeals court made it quite clear that it was working to avoid the question of the applicability of the market participant exception to the foreign commerce clause. Recognizing that the commerce clause does apply in foreign commerce as it does in interstate commerce, the panel observed: "It is uncertain whether the market participant doctrine applies at all in the context of the dormant Foreign Commerce Clause. The Supreme Court has never breached this frontier. . . . The issue has arisen sporadically in other courts, and what little case law there is appears to be in some disarray."[325] As examples of this disarray, the court pointed to a California state court decision striking down the state's "Buy American" law on grounds that it violated federal power over foreign affairs,[326] while a U.S. Circuit Court of Appeals for the Third Circuit ruling upheld Pennsylvania "Buy American" legislation using the market participant exemption in the context of the foreign commerce clause.[327]

The other case raises issues about how state or local governments are to be viewed when they use complex governing devices. A 2004 decision by the Third Circuit suggests some of the kinds of complexities that can arise. In this case, the City of Pittsburgh and its Urban Redevelopment Authority responded to a hotel firm's request to assist in the development of a piece of property by creating a tax increment financing (TIF) arrangement. Under this kind of arrangement, an area is designated as a TIF district. Then the difference between the current tax revenue from the existing land is compared to the anticipated revenue from the property after development, creating a tax increment that is then used to obtain financing for the development. Under the TIF arrangement, the company would get support for the development of the property of $3.56 million, 60 percent of the new tax increment would be used to repay the bonds, and the remaining 40 percent would be divided among the City, the School District, and the County.[328] In this case, the city required that, as a condition of the TIF, the firm accept a labor neutrality agreement that entailed organizing and collective bargaining elements. The short story is that there later arose a disagreement over the labor provisions of the agreement and the company challenged the requirements on grounds that they were preempted by federal labor law. The Third Circuit found the city was acting in this instance as a market participant and its agreement was therefore exempt from preemption under the federal law.

Given the increasing pressures on governments to be more actively involved as participants in the marketplace and the continuing pressures on governments to regulate in important areas of modern life, this question of relationship between market participants and market regulators is likely to grow in importance and complexity.

Federal Government Responses to Intergovernmental Tension

All of these forces have led to increased tension across intergovernmental relations and it is well known that many national politicians have attempted to capitalize on it. Four of five recent presidents have been former governors, all of whom ran as outsiders against a Washington establishment that they insisted did not understand the real world beyond the Washington Beltway. All insisted that, once elected, they would ensure that the regulatory agencies would be more sensitive to state and local concerns. However, all of them also had national agendas and all wanted to use the nationwide powers of their office—both formal legal power and informal political authority—to accomplish their goals. And all of them inherited large bodies of congressional enactments that establish most of the dynamics of intergovernmental relations, both structural and fiscal.

President Carter issued executive orders and supported Regulatory Flexibility Act legislation that called for greater central government sensitivity to impacts on states and local governments and other statutes that continued the three-tier regulatory framework discussed above. At the same time, however, there was little real change in response to state and local demands. The Reagan administration talked the same story but sent two very different messages. On the one hand, the administration issued an executive order mandating that federal agencies take into account in rulemaking proceedings the impact of their actions on state and local governments. On the other hand, it eliminated revenue sharing, increased unfunded mandates, decreased federal assistance (in real terms), and used federal mandates on deregulation and the opening of federal lands and resources to commercial exploitation without protections that states demanded for resource royalties and environmental concerns. The Clinton administration issued its own executive orders on federalism and intergovernmental partnerships, but, like their predecessors, these seemed in practice to be more rhetoric than significant policy change. While it expanded the requirements for consultations with states, Indian tribal governments, and local governments in rulemaking, and supported unfunded mandate legislation, none of these have been shown to have significantly affected Washington-imposed burdens or the state or local government resources needed to meet them.

In fact, in 1998 the Clinton administration walked into two firestorms of protest in the intergovernmental arena. The first arose when the EPA issued a policy document on environmental justice issues, authorizing appeals from state and local permit decisions for siting, construction, or operation of commercial operations that were alleged to have a disproportionate impact on minority communities (see Appendix 2).[329] State and local governments were upset with an entirely new opportunity for federal government intervention in what had been traditionally regarded as state and local functions. While there was no objection to the desire to protect predominantly minority communities from becoming the home for all of the businesses that no one else wanted in their neighborhoods, the means chosen raised serious conflict. Not only that, but the spark burst into a blaze when it was learned that the EPA deliberately did not consult with state governments and their representatives before issuing the policy. The EPA spent considerable energies for the rest of 1998 seeking to put out the fire. At about the same time, the Clinton administration issued a revised executive order on federalism in which it again admonished federal agencies to consider the impacts of their actions on states and localities and avoid ill-considered preemption of their authority.[330] However, the pronouncement brought an outcry from state and local governments when they found that the order also contained a list of cases in which it was acceptable for federal agencies to preempt. Indeed, some critics read this as an instruction for agencies as to how to intrude even further into state and local matters. There was so much protest in response that the administration suspended that order only months after it was initially issued.[331]

The George W. Bush administration has had more than its own share of similar difficulties, again notwithstanding the president declared concern with the protections of state authority and discretion. First, there was the beginning of an ongoing clash with governors over the unfunded and underfunded mandates from the No Child Left Behind Act discussed earlier. Although it is a grant-based program (since education is a field committed to state control under the Tenth Amendment to the Constitution), it was very clearly designed to regulate state and local educational decisions, using key federal funding as a lever to coerce compliance. Second, there has been the range of demands on state and local governments under the general rubric of homeland security. States, regional governments, and local agencies face a variety of federal demands for action across a range of operating areas. The funding systems established to address some—but by no means all—of these obligations have been fragmented and uneven in terms of their effectiveness at delivering the required level of resources to the subnational governments that need them most.[332] Third, the wars in Afghanistan and Iraq have relied heavily on mobilized units of the Reserve and National Guard. However, governors have complained that the management of National Guard personnel and resources must be done in coordination with the states, since the Guard has domestic roles in everything from forest fire responses, to high-risk rescues, and to flood recovery, to name but a few of many obligations. The issue here is not merely that the units were called into active duty, but that there has not been sufficient coordination with the states in the management of Guard units and operations.

Congress has, of course, significantly expanded the Regulatory Flexibility Act. However, although the statutory language includes small units of government in its list of groups to be considered in terms of rulemaking impact, it is equally clear that the focus is on small business and nonprofit organizations. To date there is little indication that this statute has had any significant effect in the intergovernmental arena. It has also been suggested that congressional and presidential efforts to constrain rulemaking have been intended in part at least to address the intergovernmental burdens. The problem is that there is little evidence that that result has in fact occurred and these policies may have made it more difficult for agencies to issue some of the rules that state and local governments would like to see issued for clarification and policy improvement.

INTERNATIONAL ISSUES IN REGULATION

While it is true that most of the nations of the world have unitary governments, rather than a system of federalism such as that found in the United States, many of the intergovernmental issues noted above have related variations in countries around the world, particular in an era when decentralization is widely advocated.[333] Beyond that, as other chapters and earlier discussions in this chapter have explained, contemporary intergovernmental relations deal not only with relationships between national and subnational governments, but also with supranational relationships, whether they are bilateral agreements among nations, regional integration agreements like the European Union, or global arrangements. Unfortunately, there is little evidence to date that many in the United States are even alert to the importance of the international dimension of regulatory policy and administration, much less taking concerted steps to address the many critical issues that these developments present.

Obviously, those countries that have been involved in regional integration efforts, like the nations of the European Union, and developing countries that must comply with a wide variety of regulations imposed by international funding organizations like the World Bank or the International Monetary Fund, as well as donor nations like the United States, are paying considerable attention both to what is being done in other national regulatory systems and in the international bodies in which they must participate. Indeed, even before the Maastricht Treaty formally moved Europe into the age of the European Union, it was clear that European community law was supreme over most of the domestic law of member states and that judges in those countries were bound to apply that law.[334] At the same time, many countries, in Europe and elsewhere, were significantly altering their legal systems, in many cases by creating new constitutional courts or sanctioning the expansion of jurisdiction and powers of existing national tribunals.[335] With particular attention to regulation, many other countries in the world were committed to deregulation, privatization, performance-based management, and other elements of what we called in the 1990s the "New Public Management" before the United States moved significantly in that direction.[336] Part of that trend had to do with a generally conservative shift in elections for parliament or president in several countries, while other factors were born of economic and managerial concerns.[337] Thus, there has been a good deal of information sharing about regulatory practices in other countries,[338] but very little in the United States.

In its recommendation 91-1 issued as long ago as 1991, the Administrative Conference of the United States (ACUS) warned:

> If American administrative agencies could ever afford to engage in regulatory activities without regard to the policies and practices of administrative agencies abroad, the character and pace of world developments suggest that that era has come to a close. The substantive problems facing agencies have parallels, to a greater or lesser extent, in the problems facing those agencies' counterparts in foreign countries. The policies and procedures developed by governments abroad are likely to be of interest and benefit to American regulators, and those developed here may be of utility abroad.[339]

In addition to the fact that there is much to be learned from the experience of other countries, there are more specific reasons why American administrators must come to be more attentive to the international arena. First, the United States is signatory to literally hundreds of treaties, protocols, and nonbinding sets of commitments that have direct impacts on agency operations. The discussion of environmental policy earlier in the chapter provides a variety of examples. Since 1972 "the number of such agreements in which the United States participates or in which it has a significant interest has grown from fewer than 50 to more than 170."[340] Second, the United States expends substantial amounts of appropriated funds each year to support international organizations such as the World Health Organization, Pan American Health Organization, International Labor Organization, UN Conference on Trade and Development, and UN Population Fund, which frequently interact with U.S. institutions.[341] Third, in addition to more focused bilateral agreements or specific policy-oriented treaties, it is increasingly common to find regional or global agreements that require that disputes concerning national or subnational systems of regulation to be resolved in international bodies. For instance, the North American Free Trade Agreement (NAFTA) established a panel for the resolution of complaints of unfair trade practices, challenges based on investor protection provisions, and general demands for authoritative interpretations of the treaty and created two other mechanisms for dealing with disputes under the supplemental agreements to NAFTA having to do with environmental and labor issues.[342] The United States faces a variety of challenges before the panel on regulation of the World Trade Organization established by the General Agreement on Tariffs and Trade.

George A. Bermann prepared a very useful report that provided the base for the Administrative Conference recommendations on cooperation with foreign government regulators. It was based on a study of the issues and problems encountered over time by the Federal Aviation Administration, one of the U.S. regulators that for obvious reasons has had a history of working with international agencies and counterparts in other countries. In the report Bermann raised a number of important problems involved in integrating international regulatory policies with rulemaking on the domestic side.[343] It is necessary to understand the agency's statutory authority to engage in government-to-government consultations and coordination. The administrators involved need to decide whether the situation at hand is one that fits the foreign policy exemption under the APA or must satisfy normal APA requirements. If the APA does apply, then it is important to consider how notice and record materials will be prepared to take into account material received from international sources as well as the degree to which the agency is exercising discretion and compared simply to compliance with previous negotiated international obligations. It is also necessary to assess the degree to which requirements under the Federal Advisory Committee Act and Sunshine Act (both of which are discussed in Chapter 11) are implicated.

The ACUS recommendations that came from the discussion sparked by Bermann's report included a range of additional issues that agencies should address:

Recommendation

1. Each agency should inform itself of the existence of foreign (including regional and international) regulatory bodies whose activities may relate to the mission of that agency.

2. Each agency should determine whether and to what extent regulatory cooperation with one or more foreign regulatory bodies is appropriate. Desirable forms of cooperation may include the simple exchange of information, coordination of regulatory objectives, consultation in advance of rulemaking, and reciprocal participation in rulemaking processes. Apart from general considerations of cost and staffing, factors to be considered in deciding the importance and intensity of the cooperative effort to be made, the forms of cooperation to adopt, and the geographic range of foreign regulatory bodies with which to cooperate, include:

   a. the extent to which the participating regulatory agencies share common regulatory objectives;
   b. the importance of commonality, and therefore international harmonization, in the development of regulatory policy in the particular field;
   c. the extent to which the capabilities of foreign regulatory bodies justify the agency's reliance on their technical, regulatory, and administrative resources;
   d. the opportunities that international regulatory cooperation presents for improvement in the enforcement and administration of the agency's program (as, for example, through mutual recognition of tests, inspections, and certifications or through mutual assistance in information gathering and other forms of assistance);
   e. the presence of existing bilateral or multilateral frameworks for addressing common regulatory concerns;
   f. the receptivity of a given foreign regulatory body to meaningful participation by American regulatory and private interests in its policymaking processes; and
   g. in appropriate consultation with the Department of State, the foreign policy of the United States.

3. Even when an agency concludes that the factors set out in paragraph 2 do not counsel substantial regulatory cooperation with foreign governments, it should nevertheless explore the possibilities of international cooperation in enforcement, including mutual assistance in information gathering and, where appropriate, reliance upon foreign tests, inspections, and certifications.

4. When an agency concludes that it has a pronounced interest in cooperation with foreign regulatory bodies, it should consider adopting various modes of cooperation with those agencies, including:

   a. the establishment of common regulatory agendas;
   b. the systematic exchange of information about present and proposed foreign regulation;
   c. concerted efforts to reduce differences between the agency's rules and those adopted by foreign government regulators where those differences are not justified;
   d. the creation of joint technical or working groups to conduct joint research and development and to identify common solutions to regulatory problems (for example, through parallel notices of proposed rulemaking);
   e. the establishment of joint administrative teams to draft common procedures and enforcement policies;
   f. the mutual recognition of foreign agency tests, inspections and certification, to the extent that the American agency is satisfied that foreign regulatory bodies have sufficient expertise and employ comparable standards; and
   g. the holding of periodic bilateral or multilateral meetings to assess the effectiveness of past cooperative efforts and to chart future ones.

5. a. When engaging in international regulatory cooperation, an agency should ensure that it does so in a manner consistent with national statutes and international engagements.
   b. An agency engaging in international regulatory cooperation should also be alert to the possibility that foreign regulatory bodies may have different regulatory objectives, particularly where a government-owned or controlled enterprise is involved.

6. To promote acceptance of and compliance with the measures that result from its cooperation with foreign regulatory bodies, an agency should enlist the support and participation of other affected agencies, regulated interests, public interest groups, and other affected domestic interests, as follows:

   a. Where appropriate, agencies should, so far as considerations of time and international relations permit, afford affected private and public interests timely notice of any formal system of collaboration with

Recommendation (*Continued*)

   foreign regulatory bodies that exists and an opportunity where reasonable to participate and comment on decisionmaking under such system.

   b. The agency should, where appropriate, also encourage the establishment of working relations between domestic interests and their foreign counterparts, including manufacturers, other trade and industry interests, and consumer and other public interest groups.

   c. The agency should assemble an interagency advisory group, consisting of the Department of State and other affected agencies such as the Departments of Commerce and Defense and the U.S. Trade Representative's Office, if one does not exist. Each member agency of an advisory group should, without prejudice to its independent decisionmaking, both inform that group about the nature and extent of its concerted activities with foreign regulatory bodies relevant to the purposes of the group and seek that group's advice. In addition, the Chairman of the Administrative Conference should convene a meeting of the heads of interested agencies to discuss the need for establishing a permanent, government-wide mechanism for organizing, promoting, and monitoring international regulatory cooperation on the part of American agencies.

7. Agencies should, consistent with their statutory mandate and the public interest, give sympathetic consideration to petitions by private and public interest groups for proposed rulemaking that contemplate the reduction of differences between agency rules and the rules adopted by foreign government regulators, where those differences are not justified.

8. a. Once an agency has a program of international regulatory cooperation with a foreign regulatory body, it should routinely advise that body before initiating proposed rulemaking, and should seek to engage that body's participation in the rulemaking process.

   b. Conversely, the agency should see to it that it is informed of initiatives by those foreign regulatory bodies and ensure that its views are considered by those bodies early in the conduct of their rulemaking procedures.

   c. Where, following joint rule development efforts, an agency ultimately proposes a rule that differs from the rule proposed by the foreign counterpart, it should specify the difference in its notice of proposed rulemaking and request that it be specified in any corresponding foreign notice.

9. An agency should adopt reasonable measures to facilitate communication of views by foreign regulatory bodies on proposed rules.

10. While international consultations of the sort described in this recommendation do not appear to necessitate any radical departure from an agency's ordinary practices in compliance with applicable procedural statutes, an agency engaged in such consultations should make reasonable efforts to ensure that affected interests are aware of them. For example, when an agency substantially relies on those consultations in its rulemaking (or where foreign government rules, practices, or views have otherwise substantially influenced the agency's proposals), it should describe both the fact and the substance of those consultations in its notices of proposed rulemaking, rulemaking records, and statements of basis and purpose under the Administrative Procedure Act. Where the objective of harmonizing American and foreign agency rules has had a significant influence on the shape of the rule, that fact also should be acknowledged.

11. An agency that engages in systematic exchanges of information and consultations with foreign regulatory bodies should seek to ensure that domestic interests do not suffer competitive disadvantage from the release of valuable information by those bodies to foreign private interests. This may require that the agency seek to reach agreement with its foreign counterparts concerning the conditions under which information will be disclosed.

12. While harmonization of standards with foreign regulatory bodies may be a legitimate objective of any agency whose activities affect transnational interests or transactions (and therefore may appropriately influence the rulemaking outcome), it should be pursued within the overall framework of the agency's statutory mandate and with due regard for the interests that Congress intended the agency to promote. Accordingly, agencies should ensure that any accord informally reached through international regulatory cooperation is genuinely subject to reexamination and reconsideration in the course of the rulemaking process.[344]

Thus, it is clear that the forces of globalization have already come to the regulatory arena. The need now is to adapt to it and explore both the lessons to be learned from other regulatory regimes around the world and to build on the work of ACUS and its collaborators to better understand how to regulate in an intergovernmental environment that includes supranational obligations and relationships. Of course, as the ACUS recommendations noted above indicate, one of the important aspects of this international aspect of regulation will be to address the need to protect the opportunities for participation in the regulatory process.

PUBLIC PARTICIPATION IN THE REGULATORY PROCESS

As this chapter has noted, most aspects of law and regulatory administration are highly controversial. Surprisingly, in one area there seems to be relatively little disagreement. The need both to increase the amount and improve the quality of public participation in regulatory activities has been supported by a wide range of individuals and groups in the past two decades. Although some differences of opinion on a few of the suggested remedies remain, there is even considerable consensus on the elements of the problem. In fact, one can practically overlay the outlines of the several articles and study reports on the subject, tracing back to the early 1970s.[345] Consider the difficulties individuals and public interest groups face in participating and the points in the regulatory process where such interest groups or individuals do intervene and how.

The Problem of Participation

Several factors merged in the 1970s as it became clear that the level of public participation, as opposed to participation by the regulated organizations, was low and that there were substantial burdens discouraging increased public involvement. Groups that wanted to participate in particular regulatory proceedings pressed the claim that the law does and ought to require agencies to permit public participation.[346] They made essentially two arguments. First, rulemaking proceedings should be open to all who have a serious interest in the proposed rule and who have something to contribute to the deliberations on whether to promulgate the rule. Second, even where an agency is conducting a regulatory adjudication for a licensing proceeding (which is a species of adjudication), there should be an opportunity for meaningful participation by those who can demonstrate a substantial interest (which is not necessarily the equivalent of legal standing) in the matter. The rationale for involvement in rulemaking is clear, but involvement in quasi-judicial actions is more troublesome. The argument is that there are at least three possible decisions that can be reached in, for example, a power plant licensing case: (1) a decision in the regulated firm's interest; (2) a decision that serves the agency's interest; and (3) a decision that serves the public interest. A decision can serve the interests of both the agency and the regulated industry, but may or may not be in the public interest. Public participation, even if it is not equal to that of the regulated group, may infuse outside ideas into what could be, and sometimes is, a too-congenial proceeding between an agency and its client organizations (see Chapter 8).

At the same time, some scholars and administrators, in evaluating what had happened during the 1960s, began to look for ways to open the processes of government, both to improve those processes and to restore a greater sense of legitimacy to government. Civil rights, environmental, and consumer interest groups were also learning that they could be effective by using litigation or the threat of it as an interest group tactic.[347]

Finally, scholars and reformers in government had come to the conclusion that one need not look for sinister scenarios or accept power elite theories of decisionmaking to recognize that there was much truth in the assertion that regulatory agencies were often either dependent on or biased toward the groups and organizations they regulated.

We do not need to subscribe to the theory of regulatory "capture". . .to explain this tendency toward industry domination. Rather, the reason appears to be simply in the fact that regulatory agencies respond to the inputs they receive in the same fashion as any other decisionmaking body. And, until the recent past, the source of almost all input to the agencies was the regulated industries. As the Landis report noted, ". . .it is the daily machine-gun like impact on both agency and its staff of industry representation that makes for industry orientation on the part of many honest and capable agency members as well as agency staffs."[348]

Indeed, there have been some rather dramatic instances of real or potential conflicts of interest. For example, it was just that kind of problem that ensured the demise of the Federal Power Commission and had a great deal to do with the enactment of the Federal Advisory Committee Act.[349] At the request of then California Congressman John Moss, the General Accounting Office did a study of the Federal Power Commission, which at that time regulated natural gas. When financial disclosure statements of 125 FPC executives were filed or brought up to date, GAO learned that "19 officials owned prohibited securities of the following companies: Exxon Corporation, Union Oil Company, Standard Oil of Indiana, Texaco Corporation, Pacific Power and Light Company, Tenneco Oil Company, Central Telephone and Utility Company, Cities Service, Commonwealth Edison, Northern Illinois Gas, Occidental Petroleum, Monsanto Company, Washington Gas Light Company, Atlantic Richfield Company, and Potomac Electric Power Company."[350] The appearance of industry-mindedness in an agency charged with regulation of natural gas was obvious and unacceptable.

But, in general, potential conflict of interest is not so much the problem as the fact that outside input to regulatory bodies is unsystematic, while industry interaction with the agency is ongoing, well financed, and expertly prepared. Administrators want to believe that they can remain unaffected and stand as neutral arbiters of the public interest, but there are limits. Those limits are particularly tested when a regulatory body has both a regulatory and a promotional responsibility, like the historic difficulties of the Federal Aviation Administration (FAA), the Federal Communications Commission (FCC), and bodies that regulate utilities. Indeed, critics have charged that the problem of potentially conflicting missions at the FAA contributed to such tragedies as the ValuJet crash.[351] Such an agency is often expected to help an industry prosper and simultaneously to act as its watchdog. Those who have studied this problem have encouraged Congress and the agencies to expand opportunities for participation, and to a degree this has been done.

Methods of Participation

Public interest groups participate in agency proceedings in several different forums and by a number of means. They may serve on task forces or advisory groups maintained by the agency. They may submit comments on notice-and-comment rulemaking processes. If a statute requires a hearing in connection with rulemaking (either a formal or a hybrid rulemaking proceeding), groups that can demonstrate a substantial interest may participate if the agency enabling act requires the opportunity to intervene or if agency rules permit it. They are expected to be represented on negotiated rulemaking committees if that option is selected by an agency (see Chapter 5). Many agencies permit intervention in licensing or ratemaking proceedings, but this is often limited to nonrepetitive presentation of evidence and views. Adjudications are difficult to deal with because of the due process rights of the regulated party. Participation by third parties can create due process difficulties in terms of notice and in cross-examining those who give adverse evidence.[352] Whether, and in what manner, would-be private attorneys general will be permitted to participate in such proceedings depends on agency rules and judicial interpretations of statutory requirements.[353]

Public interest groups often participate in congressional oversight hearings, but what type of participation is permitted is up to the committee involved. It is certainly true, as explained earlier in this chapter, that the policy community surrounding any particular regulatory activity will be active and that public interest groups make every effort to play an active role, but effort and access are not always the same thing. And, as the discussion of congressional activity and some of the tactics of the White House like the use of the Quayle Council indicated, participation in the political forum is not protected in the same way in those political arenas as it is assured by the APA in agency proceedings. Of course, even agency-level participation has become more complex as agencies have increasingly contracted out various kinds of activities, ranging from the drafting of possible rules to arranging for meetings during rulemaking efforts.

Finally, as Chapter 7 explained, groups may seek to participate in regulatory proceedings before the courts.[354] In certain situations, they may be able to obtain standing to bring an agency ruling up for judicial review. That may also require that they demonstrate that the legislation involved implies a private right of action as explained in Chapter 7. At other times, they may ask permission to intervene in proceedings brought by some other party.[355]

Roadblocks to Participation

Limitations on public participation may be defined as falling into several general categories: (1) lack of notice; (2) lack of organization; (3) lack of funds; (4) lack of expertise; (5) procedural bars to participation; and (6) intergovernmental complexity.

It is extremely difficult for most citizens to get word of agency action, even if they are part of what is known as the informed public and that remains true despite the Internet revolution. Few know what the *Federal Register* is, much less how to read it. Fewer still are aware of Regulation.gov. In fact, many students of administrative law are either unaware the new e-government techniques (described in Chapter 5) or still attempting to learn how to use the new tools. For the vast majority of people who rely on television news or local newspapers for their information, there is little coverage of regulatory matters except in very general terms and then usually after important decisions have already been made. The increasing dominance of what is termed "infotainment" in an era when the FCC requires less public service programming and exercises even less control over cable channels is only exacerbating these difficulties.

Lack of organization is also important. Many people may be interested in a particular regulatory action, but they can have no effect unless they know of a group that will advance their cause or have the time and the skills to develop an organization from the ground up. In many cases, groups that wish to be effective must establish offices in the capital where they can develop communication with agencies and congressional committees. The lack of a firm and ongoing connection to the policy community in a given domain often stands as a bar to effective and timely knowledge and participation in the regulatory process. After many years of experience with fax machines, microcomputers, cell phones, and the recent addition of hand-held Internet equipment like the increasingly ubiquitous Blackberry℗, few knowledgeable political players would argue that these devices are any substitute for being there.

For all these reasons, effective participation in agency proceedings tends to be expensive. Filing fees, copying costs, and transcript charges alone can be staggering, the Internet notwithstanding. Few groups can afford the expense if proceedings go on very long. After surveying the dockets of several major agencies and analyzing participation in those cases, the Ribicoff Committee summarized important challenges to participation that remain even three decades after that report was written:

> In all of the preceding examples comparing public interest groups costs to industry costs is like
> comparing David and Goliath. Effective participation in regulatory proceeding does indeed
> depend on the quality and extent of one's legal counsel. It also depends upon the quality
> and extent of expert testimony and technical submissions. It requires ample administrative
> and clerical resources, costs which are frequently taken for granted. Yet time after time,
> industry is able to spend 10, or 50, or 100 times as much money on participation as public
> interest groups. The persistence and ingenuity of the public interest groups in their efforts to

participate effectively is laudable, but the lack of resources to insure adequate representation is lamentable.[356]

Effective participation in complex regulatory proceedings requires expertise. First, one must have a lawyer skilled in administrative law—preferably someone who knows the law, politics, and procedures of the agency. Technical experts are needed both to make one's case and to interpret the submissions of others in the proceedings. Such expertise is expensive and not easy to find. For one thing, it is often difficult to get experts to volunteer their services because they may want to be hired later by the firms against whom the public interest groups are proceeding! Government experts may not wish to serve because of possible conflict within their agencies, or between agencies if the expert is perceived to be making statements against the government's interests in a proceeding.

Finally, there are procedural roadblocks to participation both in agencies and in courts. Many regulatory agencies have not formulated clear rules on when and to what extent intervenors will be allowed to participate. It is frequently a matter of discretion with the administrative law judge conducting a proceeding to decide whether, and in what manner, a group will be heard. In the courts, there was for several years a strong movement to relax rules of standing and other procedural bars to review. But, as Chapter 7 indicated, many of these doctrines have been reinterpreted since the early 1970s and are again formidable barriers to many groups that would like to appeal administrative rulings.[357]

As this and earlier chapters have explained, regulatory problems increasingly are affected by globalization, and when supranational issues are in play there can be mismatches between the ability effectively to participate between multinational firms and global interest groups, local businesses, or public interest groups. Thus, international environmental groups have clashed with local environmental groups in some developing countries, each with different agendas seeking to influence policymakers and administrators. Then, of course, there are the questions about which parties may be able to have their voices heard in international institutions such as the World Trade Organizations.

This supranational complexity is often also connected to the new intergovernmental complexity that operates within nations. When regulatory regimes involve national agencies, state regulators acting on national or enhanced state level standards, and even with the addition of local participants in the process or the substantial use of contractors at all levels, the maze can be difficult even for well-educated and interested would-be participants to navigate.

Finally, there are the opportunities and challenges of electronic participation with an emphasis on the use of the Internet to drive down cost and enhance access. A focus on the Internet as a provider of public information—while it may ultimately enhance access as prices for technology decline and education in its use improve—presently involves a socioeconomic bias. It is the problem popularly known as the digital divide. The Internet may help smaller public interest groups that are part of the policy community and can use relatively modest investments in technology to enhance participation, but many people still lack the combination of knowledge of the regulatory policy system and access to and skill in the use of microcomputer and Internet technology. As Chapter 5 explained, it is not enough to know how to use a computer and connect to the Internet. One must understand where to go on the Internet and what kinds of information one must have to engage a particular regulatory process.

There is another problem with modern computer and telecommunications technology that runs in parallel with the more commonly understood aspects of the digital divide. It is the assumption about how much everyone else knows about the technological innovations that are being incorporated into contemporary service and regulatory systems. Thus, Chapter 6 explained some of the difficulties with the modified procedures for the adjudication of Medicare cases, involving teleconferencing and online processing of disputes and appeals. Chapter 5 explained some of the difficulties of acquiring the information needed to participate in online regulatory dockets. Some agencies have made it nearly impossible to contact a person directly and direct lost and confused individuals to so-called "help" pages on websites that leave even experienced computer and Internet users hopelessly lost and frustrated. And even when it is possible to contact a real person, there is the problem that some agencies engage call centers by contract to handle service contacts or take information.

The best that can be said of efforts to use the Internet to address problems of participation in the regulatory process is that they are still very much in the formative stages and have perhaps opened as many questions and challenges as they have solved. Apart from the several varieties of digital divide and access problems noted above, there remain questions about what the impacts of efforts to make greater use of the Internet in regulation might be. As has been true for alternative dispute resolution (see Chapter 8), the fact that so much that is written about the increased use of e-government is promotional in character means that there has not yet developed a sufficient critical literature that addresses what some of the longer term issues might be.

Professor Cary Coglianese has provided a useful set of questions that might fruitfully be considered both by scholars and by those who seek to design enhanced online participation mechanisms.

Mobilization. Do more people get involved in the rulemaking process?
Distribution. Is there any change in the kinds of people who participate?. . .
Frequency. Do specific individuals and organizations participate more frequently?. . .
Knowledge. Is learning enhanced or inhibited?. . .
Tone. Does the tone, style, emphasis, or sophistication of expression change?
Ideas. Do the ideas generated by the public, or the views that they express, change?. . .
Conflict. Are conflicts mitigated or exacerbated?. . .
Perceptions. How do people feel about their participation. . .?
Spillovers. Are there any effects that spill over into other policy forums. . .?
Organization. How, if at all, do the roles of political organizations like trade associations, unions, or public advocacy groups change?. . .[358]

For all these reasons, participation is in many respects more complex and challenging than ever. The excessive reliance on the Internet to address these difficulties has, in some respects at least, added to rather than resolved some of those difficulties.

SUMMARY

This chapter has presented an overview of the problems and new directions in regulatory law and administration. It has sought to distinguish between, on the one hand, careful, detailed consideration of particular problems of improving regulation as a policy technique chosen by the legislature to advance particular purposes, and, on the other, the macro-level debate over the inherent goodness or badness of regulation. Regulation is one of a number of policy options; it is selected most often not because it is particularly favored but because specific circumstances of problems seem more amenable to regulation than to other available solutions. The decisions as to which policy mechanism ought to be employed is a political decision, not an economic judgment.

Those interested in regulatory reform can learn a great deal about possible directions for change by examining the institutions and actors involved in the regulatory process. In particular, this chapter has considered: regulatory agencies as organizations; the role of the president in the regulatory process; the congressional task in regulatory activity; the intergovernmental institutions and relationships that affect regulation; the increasingly important international dimension; and the problems and prospects of public participation. For the president, the key aspects of regulatory administration appear to be improvements in the appointments process and the desire to improve control and coordination within the executive branch. Unfortunately, the evidence from both the Congress and the White House in recent decades is that there has been insufficient attention to improving regulatory administration and far too much attention to ideologically driven policies and agency bashing. Sadly, the political treatment of regulation and its reality on the ground have grown further apart at a time when attention to the real challenges of making critically important policies work is more important than ever before. At a minimum, it must be clear to any careful student of the subject or practitioner in the field, that public managers must deal with parallel systems management in which more or less traditional techniques or regulation will continue to operate side by side with more recent attempts at market-oriented policies. That reality requires more attention to regulation, not less.

The debate over regulatory politics and administration cuts across government and seems likely to be a focal point for discussion and action for the foreseeable future. Another such cross-cutting area of public law and public administration is the acquisition, use, and dissemination of information by government. Chapter 11 addresses that subject.

NOTES

1. The shrillest critics have been such people as Friedrich von Hayek, *The Road to Serfdom* (Chicago: University of Chicago Press, 1944), and Murray Weidenbaum, whose ideas appear in U.S. Senate, Hearings Before the Subcommittee on Administrative Practices and Procedure, *Administrative Procedure Reform Act of 1978,* 95th Cong., 2nd Sess. (1978), pp. 425–28.

2. See B. Guy Peters and Donald Savoie, *Governance in a Changing Environment* (Montreal: McGill/Queens University Press, 1995). See also Organization for Economic Cooperation and Development (OECD), *The OECD Report on Regulatory Reform* (Paris: OECD, 1997); Management Advisory Board and Management Improvement Advisory Committee (1993) *Accountability in the Public Sector.* Canberra: Australian Government Publishing Service; OECD *Economic Instruments for Environmental Protection* (Paris: OECD, 1989).

3. E. S. Savas, *Privatizing the Public Sector* (Chatham, NJ: Chatham House, 1982) and John E. Chubb and Terry M. Moe, *Politics, Markets, and America's Schools* (Washington, DC: Brookings Institution, 1990). See also Donald J. Savoie, *Thatcher, Reagan, Mulrooney: In Search of a New Bureaucracy* (Toronto: University of Toronto Press, 1994).

4. See U.S. House, Hearing before the Subcommittees on Human Rights and International Organizations, Western Hemisphere Affairs, and International Economic Policy and Trade of the Committee on Foreign Affair, *The Enterprise for the Americas Initiative,* 101st Cong., 2nd Sess. (1990).

5. David Osborne and Ted Gaebler, *Reinventing Government* (New York: Penguin, 1993); Ostrom, Vincent, *The Intellectual Crisis in American Public Administration,* 2nd ed. (Tuscaloosa: University of Alabama, 1989).

6. See Barry Bozeman, *All Organizations Are Public* (San Francisco: Jossey-Bass, 1987) and "Exploring the Limits of Public and Private Sectors: Sector Boundaries as Maginot Line," 48 *Public Administration Review* 672 (1988).

7. Al Gore, Report of the National Performance Review, *From Red Tape to Results: Creating a Government That Works Better & Costs Less* (Washington, DC: Government Printing Office, 1993). See also Will Marshall and Martin Schram, eds., *Mandate for Change* (New York: The Progressive Policy Institute, 1993).

8. See the discussion and critique offered by Nobel Prize–winning economist Joseph E. Stiglitz, *The Roaring Nineties* (New York: W. W. Norton, 2003).

9. *Id.,* at p. 91.

10. See e.g., Federal Trade Commission, *Marketing Violent Entertainment to Children: A Review of Self-Regulation and Industry Practices in the Motion Picture, Music Recording, & Electronic Game Industries* (Washington, DC: Federal Trade Commission, 2000).

11. I have addressed this argument in greater detail in "Toward the Hybrid State: The Case of Environmental Management in a Deregulated and Reengineered State," 61 *International Review of Administrative Sciences* 185 (1995).

12. Airline Deregulation Act of 1978, P.L. 95-504, 92 Stat. 1705.

13. Staggers Rail Act of 1980, P.L. 96-448, 94 Stat. 1895.

14. Motor Carrier Act of 1980, P.L. 96-296, 94 Stat. 793.

15. United States Regulatory Council, *Regulatory Reform Highlights: An Inventory of Initiatives, 1978–1980* (Washington, DC: U.S. Regulatory Council, 1980), p. 1.

16. *Id.,* at pp. 2–3.

17. *Id.,* at p. 9.

18. See e.g., U.S. Regulatory Council, *Regulating with Common Sense: A Progress Report on Innovative Regulatory Techniques* (Washington, DC: U.S. Regulatory Council, 1980), and U.S. Regulatory Council Conference, *Innovative Techniques in Theory and Practice, Proceedings* (Washington, DC: U.S. Regulatory Council, 1980).

19. *Id.,* p. 4.

20. See Regulatory Council documents, *supra* notes 15 and 18.

21. See e.g., *F.C.C. v. WNCN Listeners Guild,* 450 U.S. 582 (1981); *Motor Vehicle Manufacturers Association v. State Farm Mutual,* 463 U.S. 29 (1983).

22. Memorandum for the Secretary of the Interior,. . .Agriculture, Energy, Administrator of the Environmental Protection Agency, Chairman of the Federal Energy Regulatory Commission, Chairman of the Nuclear Regulatory Commission, January 28, 1992.

23. See George H. W. Bush, "Remarks on Regulatory Reform," 28 *Weekly Compilation of Presidential Documents* 726 (1992).

24. Report of the National Performance Review, *Improving Regulatory Systems* (Washington, DC: National Performance Review, 1993).

25. Andrew H. Card, "Memorandum for the Heads and Acting Heads of Executive Departments and Agencies," January 20, 2001, with a follow-on memorandum from OMB Director Mitchell E. Daniels, Jr., "Memorandum for the Heads and Acting Heads of Executive Departments and Agencies: Effective Regulatory Review," January 26, 2001.

26. The rules were issued in November 2000, 65 Fed. Reg. 68262 (2000).

27. Executive Order 13258, 67 Fed. Reg. 9385 (2002).

28. OMB, "OMB Regulatory Review: Principles and Procedures," September 20, 2001, followed later by OMBCircular, A-4, "Regulatory Analysis," September 17, 2003, at http://www.whitehouse.gov/omb/inforeg/regpol-agency_review.html, as of January 10, 2006.

29. OMB, "Final Information Quality Bulletin for Peer Review," December 15, 2004, at http://www.whitehouse.gov/omb/memoranda/fy2005/m05-03.pdf, as of January 10, 2006.

30. OMB, "Draft Office of Management and Budget Good Guidance Practices Bulletin and Request for Comment," November 23, 2005, at http://www.whitehouse.gov/omb/inforeg/regpol.html, as of January 10, 2006.

31. OMB, "Proposed Risk Assessment Bulletin," January 9, 2006 at http://www.whitehouse.gov/omb/inforeg/proposed_risk_assessment_bulletin_010906.pdf, as of January 10, 2006.

32. Eugene Bardach and Robert A. Kagan, *Going By the Book: The Problem of Regulatory Unreasonableness* (Philadelphia: Temple University Press, 1982).

33. See note 24 *supra.*

34. *Printz v. United States,* 521 U.S. 898 (1997).

35. *United States v. Lopez,* 514 U.S. 549 (1995).

36. *United States v. Morrison,* 529 U.S. 598 (2000).

37. *Ashcroft v. ACLU,* 542 U.S. 656 (2004); *Reno v. American Civil Liberties Union,* 521 U.S. 844 (1997).

38. *Washington v. Glucksberg,* 521 U.S. 702 (1997).

39. *City of Boerne v. Flores,* 521 U.S. 507 (1997).

40. See William A. Fischel, *Regulatory Takings: Law, Economics, and Politics* (Cambridge: Harvard University Press, 1995).

41. *Day-Brite Lighting v. Missouri,* 342 U.S. 421 (1952).

42. *Nolan v. California Coastal Commission,* 483 U.S. 825 (1987).

43. *Lucas v. South Carolina Coastal Council,* 505 U.S. 1003 (1992).

44. 512 U.S. 374 (1994).

45. See Walter A. Rosenbaum, *Environmental Politics and Policy,* 4th ed. (Washington, DC: Congressional Quarterly Press, 1998), pp. 114–115.

46. Notable contemporary cases in which the Court did not support takings claims included *Tahoe-Sierra Preservation Council v. Tahoe Regional Planning Agency,* 535 U.S. 302 (2002); *Palazzolo v. Rhode Island,* 533 U.S. 606 (2001).

47. Walter A. Rosenbaum, *Environmental Politics and Policy,* 6th ed., (Washington, DC: CQ Press, 2005).

48. Council on Environmental Quality, "Toxic Substances," in U.S. House of Representatives, Environment and Natural Resources Policy Division of the Library of Congress for the House Committee on Interstate and Foreign Commerce, *Legislative History of the Toxic Substances Control Act* (Committee Print, 1976). (Hereafter referred to as Toxic Substances Act History.)

49. *Id.,* at p. 4.

50. *Id.,* at pp. 3–6.

51. *Id.,* at p. 4.

52. *Id.*

53. The story of the growing awareness of low level toxicity of such substances as benzene is summarized in *Industrial Union Department, AFL-CIO v. American Petroleum Institute,* 448 U.S. 607, 615-27 (1980).

54. History of Toxic Substances Control Act, *supra* note 48, at p. 4.

55. See e.g., E. J. Dionne, Jr., "The Love Canal Legacy: Lawsuits and Bitterness," *New York Times,* September 7, 1981, p. 11.

56. Irving Molotsky, "House Panel Lists Toxic Sites Threatening Water Supplies in U.S.," *New York Times,* September 28, 1980, p. 45.

57. Howard Ball, *Justice Downwind* (New York: Oxford University Press, 1986).

58. See e.g., United Nations, *Report of the United Nations Conference on the Human Environment* (New York: United Nations, 1972); World Commission on Environment and Development, *Our Common Future* (New York: Oxford, 1987).

59. United Nations, *Agenda 21 The United Nations Programme of Action from Rio* (New York: United Nations, 1992).

60. Richard B. Stewart, "Regulation, Innovation, and Administrative Law: A Conceptual Framework," 69 *California Law Review* 1263 (1981).

61. U.S. General Accounting Office, *Air Pollution: Overview and Issues on Emissions Allowance Trading Programs* (Washington, DC: General Accounting Office, 1997).

62. Stephan Schmidheiny, et al. *Changing Course* (Cambridge: Massachusetts Institute of Technology Press, 1992), pp. 14–33.

63. See U.S. House of Representatives, Hearings Before the Committee on Ways and Means, *The Environment,* 101st Cong., 2nd Sess., (1990).

64. M. Jimmie Killingsworth and Jacqueline S. Palmer, *Ecospeak: Rhetoric and Environmental Politics in America* (Carbondale: University of Southern Illinois, 1992).

65. National Research Council, *Risk Assessment in the Federal Government: Managing the Process* (Washington, DC: National Academy Press, 1983), p. 83.

66. National Research Council, *Science and Judgment in Risk Assessment* (Washington, DC: National Academy Press, 1994), p. 160. Also at http://fermat.nap.edu/books/030904894X/html/index.html, as of February 8, 2006.

67. OMB, "Proposed Risk Assessment Bulletin," *supra* note 31, at 20.

68. Aldo Leopold, *A Sand County Almanac* (New York: Ballantine Books, 1966) (originally published in 1949).

69. Ball, *supra* note 57.

70. See e.g., James E. Anderson, *Public Policymaking* (Boston: Houghton Mifflin, 1990); Charles O. Jones, *An Introduction to the Study of Public Policy,* 3rd ed. (Monterey: Brooks/Cole, 1984); Robert L. Lineberry, *American Public Policy* (New York: Harper & Row, 1977).

71. See David Dery, *Problem Definition in Policy Analysis* (Lawrence, KS: University Press of Kansas, 1984).

72. On agenda setting generally, see David A. Rochefort and Roger W. Cobb, "Problem Definition, Agenda Access, and Policy Choice," 21 *Policy Studies Journal* 56 (1993); Roger W. Cobb and C. Elder, eds.,

Participation in American Politics: The Dynamics of Agenda-Building (Baltimore, MD: Johns Hopkins University Press, 1983).

73. John W. Kingdon, *Agendas, Alternatives, and Public Policies* (New York: Harper Collins, 1984).

74. Fred M. Frohock, *Public Policy: Scope and Logic* (Englewood Cliffs, NJ: Prentice Hall, 1979), pp. 11–15.

75. See note 18 *supra*.

76. Theodore J. Lowi, "Four Systems of Policy, Politics and Choice," *Public Administration Review* 298, 299–300 (1972).

77. Frohock, *supra* note 74, at p. 13.

78. *Id.*

79. I should note in passing that I disagree with some of the classifications as applied by Frohock to specific policies. *Id.*, at p. 14.

80. On the Ethics in Government Act, see Chapter 13.

81. Executive Order 12898, "Environmental Justice for Minority Populations." See generally, Robert D. Bullard, *Dumping on Dixie* (Boulder: Westview Press, 1990).

82. U.S. House of Representatives, Report of the Subcommittee on Oversight and Investigation of the Committee on Interstate and Foreign Commerce, *Cost-Benefit Analysis: Wonder Tool or Mirage?* 96th Cong., 2d Sess. (1980), p. 5.

83. James Q. Wilson, "The Politics of Regulation," in Wilson, ed., *The Politics of Regulation* (New York: Basic Books, 1980), pp. 358–63.

84. *Id.,* at pp. 362–63.

85. *Id.*, at p. 363.

86. Subcommittee Report, *supra* note 82, at p. 7.

87. Also from the Subcommittee Report, p. 7: "While it is not nearly as easy to quantify the costs and benefits of a proposed regulation as it is to quantify baseball statistics, whenever some quantification is done—no matter how speculative or limited—the number tends to get into the public domain and the qualifications tend to get forgotten. When important elements are not quantified or are quantified inadequately or unfairly, the quantification can have a pernicious effect. Dr. Lester Lave commented upon this phenomenon in this testimony before the Subcommittee:

> "'There is a Gresham's law of decision making: quantified effects tend to dominate consideration, even if the unquantified effects are believed to be more important. Thus, quantification is likely to be pernicious if important aspects are left unquantified, if the quantification isn't even handed for benefits and costs, or if the quantification is inadequate.'"

88. *Id.,* at p. 6.

89. Luther Gulick, "The Twenty-fifth Anniversary of the American Society for Public Administration," *25 Public Administration Review* 1, 3 (1965).

90. Subcommittee Report, *supra* note 82, at p. 10.

91. *Id.,* at p. 11.

92. *Id.,* at p. 16.

93. *Id.*

94. *Id.,* at p. 17.

95. *Id.*

96. *Id.,* at p. 20. Green has asked: "What is the value of avoiding pain and suffering to an auto crash victim, or the loss of consortium to the victim's spouse? Can a dollar figure be put on the benefit of a six-year-old not disfigured from flammable sleepwear? How do we calculate the environmental benefits of seeing across the Grand Canyon, of utilizing recreational areas, of avoiding property depreciation due to pollution? What is the dollar value of investor confidence in safe food and drugs?" Statement of Mark Green and Nancy Diabble of Public Citizens Congress Watch before the Senate Governmental Affairs Committee, "Regulatory Reform Act," May 1, 1979 (mimeographed), at p. 4.

97. Subcommittee Report, *supra* note 82, at p. 25.

98. Kenneth J. Meier, E. Thomas Garman, and Lael R. Keiser, *Regulation and Consumer Protection: Politics, Bureaucracy, and Economics,* 3rd ed. (Houston, TX: DAME Publications, Inc., 1998), pp. 6–7.

99. *Id.*

100. Lester Salamon, *The Tools of Government* (New York: Oxford University Press, 2002). Frederick C. Mosher, "The Changing Responsibilities and Tactics of the Federal Government," 40 *Public Administration Review* 541 (1980); Lester M. Salamon, ed., *Beyond Privatization: The Tools of Government Action* (Washington, DC: Urban Institute, 1989).

101. Paul A. Sabatier and Hanj C. Jenkins-Smith, eds., *Policy Change: An Advocacy Coalition Approach* (Boulder, CO: Westview Publishing, 1993), pp. 16–38; A Lee Fritschler and James M. Hoefler, *Smoking and Politics: Politics and the Federal Bureaucracy,* 3rd ed. (Upper Saddle River, NJ: Prentice Hall, 1995); Randall B. Ripley and Grace A. Franklin, *Congress, the Bureaucracy, and Public Policy,* 4th ed. (Englewood Cliffs. NJ: Prentice Hall, 1987).

102. See Sabatier and Jenkins-Smith, *Id.*

103. James G. March and Johan P. Olsen, *Rediscovering Institutions* (New York: Free Press, 1989), pp. 2–3.

104. Michael J. Sandel, *Democracy's Discontent* (Cambridge: Harvard University Press, 1996), p. ix.

105. See e.g., Jeffrey L. Pressman and Aaron B. Wildavsky, *Implementation,* 3rd Ed. (Berkeley: University of California Press, 1984); Donald Van Meter Donald and Carl Van Horn "The Policy Implementation Process: A Conceptual Framework," *Administration & Society* 6 (Feb): 445–488 (1975); Robert T. Nakamura and Frank Smallwood, *The Politics of Policy Implementation* (New York: St. Martins, 1980); Daniel A. Mazmanian and Paul A. Sabatier, *Effective Policy Implementation* (Lexington, MS: D.C. Heath, 1981).

106. OMB, *The President's Management Agenda* (Washington, DC: Office of Management and Budget, 2002).

107. *Id.,* at pp. 27–30.

108. Office of Management and Budget, *Major Savings and Reforms in the President's 2006 Budget* (Washington, DC: OMB, 2005), also at http://www.whitehouse.gov/omb/budget/fy2006/pdf/savings.pdf, as of January 28, 2006.

109. See Janet E. Frantz, "Political Resources for Policy Termination," 30 *Policy Studies Journal* 11 (2002); Peter deLeon, "Commentary," 30 *Policy Studies Journal* 47 (2002); Mark Daniels, "Implementing Policy Termination," 14 *Policy Studies Review,* 353 (1995/1996); Peter deLeon, "Policy Evaluation and Program Termination," 2 *Policy Studies Review* 631 (1983); Peter deLeon, "Public Policy Termination: An End and a Beginning," 4 *Policy Analysis* 369 (1978).

110. See generally, W. Noel Keyes, *Government Contracts,* 2nd ed. (St. Paul, MN: West Publishing Co., 1996).

111. See generally, Keyes, *Id.,* at pp. 34–46. See also the Office of Federal Procurement Policy Reauthorization Act of 1988, P.L. 100–679, 102 Stat. 4055.

112. *Id.,* at pp. 45–46.

113. P.L. 103-355. See also Executive Order 12931, "Federal Procurement Reform" and Executive Order 12954, "Ensuring the Economical and Efficient Administration and Completion of Federal Government Contracts."

114. Amendments to the Office of Federal Procurement Policy Act of 1984, P.L. 98-577, 98 Stat. 3076.

115. P.L. 105-270; 112 Stat. 2382 (1998).

116. For example, Keyes has argued that "Just as we have a Uniform Commercial Code for private transactions, there should be a Uniform Code for procurements by states and the larger municipalities." *Supra* note 110, at p. 19.

117. Thus, there has been an effort to develop an International Procurement Code under the General Agreement on Tariffs and Trade in the World Trade Organization.

118. See e.g., U.S. Office of Management and Budget, *Summary Report of the SWAT Team on Civilian Agency Contracting* (Washington, DC: Office of Management and Budget, 1992).

119. See *Printz v. United States, supra* note 34; *Seminole Tribe v. Florida,* 134 L.Ed.2d 252 (1996); *New York v. United States,* 505 U.S. 144 (1992).

120. *South Dakota v. Dole,* 483 U.S. 203 (1987).

121. *Bennett v. Kentucky,* 470 U.S. 656, 669 (1985).

122. Discussed further in Phillip J. Cooper, *Governing by Contract: Challenges and Opportunities for Public Managers* (Washington, DC: CQ Press, 2003), pp. 72–74.

123. U.S. Commission on Government Procurement, *Report of the Commission on Government Procurement* (Washington, DC: Government Printing Office, 1972).

124. Jacqueline L. Salmon, "Fraud Alleged at Red Cross Call Centers Contract Workers in Calif. Stole From Katrina Aid Program, Indictments Say," *Washington Post,* December 27, 2005, p. A-2.

125. American Red Cross, "Red Cross Statement on Fraud on the Bakersfield Call Center," December 27, 2005, at http://www.redcross.org/pressrelease/0,1077,0_314_5029,00.html, as of January 19, 2006.

126. U.S. Department of Justice, Hurricane Katrina Fraud Task Force, at http://www.usdoj.gov/katrina/Katrina_Fraud/index.html, as of January 21, 2006.

127. See Donald F. Kettl, *Sharing Power* (Washington, DC: Brookings Institution, 1993).

128. See U.S. General Accounting Office, *Worker Protection: Federal Contractors and Violations of Labor Law* (Washington, DC: GAO, 1995).

129. U.S. Environmental Protection Agency, *A Study of State and Local Government Procurement Practices That Consider Environmental Performance of Goods and Services* (Washington, DC: Environmental Protection Agency, 1996).

130. U.S. Senate, Committee on Governmental Affairs, *Study on Federal Regulation,* 95th Cong., 2d Sess. (1978), vol. 6, chap. 2.

131. See Rosenbaum, *supra* note 45.

132. This problem is epitomized by the "tragedy of the commons." See Lineberry, *supra* note 70, at pp. 31–32.

133. U.S. House of Representatives, Hearings Before the Subcommittee on Oversight and Investigations of the Committee on Interstate and Foreign Commerce, *Acid Rain,* 96th Cong., 2d Sess. (1980), p. 14.

134. *Id.,* at pp. 25–26.

135. *Id.,* at p. 2.

136. Eddy, Potter, and Paige argue, based upon their analysis from trial records and other data, that the dramatic competition among aircraft manufacturers for orders for airbuses resulted in unsafe technical changes in design to save enough weight to allow one more seat in the aircraft. The design ultimately failed, resulting in the loss of a fully loaded airliner. Paul Eddy, Elaine Potter, and Bruce Paige, *Destination Disaster* (New York: Ballantine, 1976). See also Mary Schiavo, *Flying Blind, Flying Safe* (New York: Avon Books, 1997).

137. See C.R. McManis, "International Protection for Semiconductor Chip Designs and the Standard of Judicial Review of Presidential Proclamations Issued Pursuant to the Semiconductor Chip Protection Act of 1984." 22 *George Washington Journal of International Law & Economics* 331 (1988).

138. See Schiavo, *supra* note 136.

139. See e.g., J. Gregory Sidak and Daniel F. Spulber, *Deregulatory Takings and the Regulatory Contract: The Competitive Transformation of Network Industries in the United States* (Cambridge: Cambridge University Press, 1997).

140. See Louis D. Brandeis, *Other People's Money* (New York: Harper & Row, 1967); John Kenneth Galbraith, *The Great Crash* (Boston: Houghton Mifflin, 1961); Ralph DeBedts, *The New Deal's SEC: The Formative Years* (New York: Columbia University Press, 1964); William O. Douglas, *Democracy and Finance* (Port Washington, NY: Kennikat Press, 1940).

141. The sad state of affairs that led to the creation of the Food and Drug Administration was presented in Upton Sinclair's classic *The Jungle* (New York: Airmont, 1965). The enabling legislation has been reconsidered on at least three occasions since the 1930s, but each time a major incident involving food, drugs, or cosmetics caused legislators to strengthen the agency's authority.

142. See the legislative histories of the National Traffic and Motor Vehicle Safety Act of 1966, P.L. 89-563, 80 Stat. 718, and the Highway Safety Act of 1966, P.. 89-564, 80 Stat. 731, in 1966 *U.S. Code Congressional and Administrative News* 2709, 2741 (1966).

143. These are results of the study by the National Commission on Product Safety, cited in Kenneth Culp Davis, *Administrative Law: Cases—Text—Problems,* 6th ed. (St. Paul: West, 1977), p. 9.

POLITICS AND REGULATORY AGENCIES: LAW AND POLITICS IN ADMINISTRATION**   **423**

144. U.S. Senate, Subcommittee on Labor of the Committee on Labor and Public Welfare, *Legislative History of the Occupational Safety and Health Act of 1970,* 92nd Cong., 1st Sess. (1971), p. 142.

145. See e.g., Federal Election Commission, *Legislative History of Federal Election Campaign Act Amendment of 1974* (Washington, DC: Government Printing Office, 1977).

146. See e.g., U.S. Senate, Subcommittee on Labor of the Committee on Human Resources, *Legislative History of the Federal Mine Safety and Health Act of 1977,* 95th Cong., 2d Sess. (1978).

147. See March and Olsen, *supra* note 103.

148. World Bank, *World Development Report 1997* (New York: Oxford University Press, 1997).

149. Marver Bernstein, *Regulating Business by Independent Commission* (Princeton, NJ: Princeton University Press, 1955).

150. *Id.,* Ch. 3. Bernstein was not alone in his life-cycle approach to regulatory agencies. See Galbraith, *supra* note 140, at p. 96.

151. *Id.,* at p. 74.

152. *Id.,* at p. 79.

153. *Id.,* at p. 84.

154. *Id.,* at p. 87.

155. *Id.,* at p. 90.

156. *Id.,* at p. 92.

157. Wilson, *supra* note 83.

158. Meier, Garman, and Keiser, *supra* note 98, p. 6.

159. *Id.*

160. *Id.,* at p. 366.

161. *Id.,* at p. 367.

162. *Id.,* at p. 368.

163. *Id.,* at p. 369.

164. *Id.,* at pp. 370–72.

165. Wilson's essay does not explain many anomalous cases. Additionally, Wilson suggests that Bernstein's capture thesis does not come to grips with the fact that agencies do make decisions contrary to the regulated interests. He also argues that his own characterization of the politics that give rise to regulatory programs and guide their operations explains behavior better. Bernstein might answer that he did not say that agencies were not born in a variety of political environments. They did not come into existence as captives of the regulated interests; in fact, the captive process does not begin until a regulated interest recognizes that it has lost the battle to prevent regulation. Second, Bernstein might answer that agencies may decide against the wishes of regulated interests in their early years, but such decisions become more unusual over time. Finally, he might argue that it is an oversimplification to assume that the "captive" thesis means that agencies will never act against the regulated group. A more sophisticated analysis might suggest that at least during what he describes as the years of maturity, the regulated party may have come to be in a superior debating position relative to outsiders who wish to affect agency policy.

166. Patricia Ingraham has examined the competing values involved in advocacy of quality management principles that advocate cooperation, innovation, and mutual support and some of the new public management approaches that emphasize a cutback approach in which risk taking is dangerous and a market mentality that emphasizes competition over cooperation. "Quality Management in Public Organizations: Prospects and Dilemmas," Peters and Savoie, *supra* note 2.

167. E.E. Schattschneider, *The Semi-Sovereign People* (New York: Holt, Rinehart, and Winston, 1960).

168. See *Motor Vehicle Manufacturers Association. v. State Farm Mutual Insurance Co.,* 463 U.S. 29, 43 (1983).

169. Graham T. Allison, *Essence of Decision* (Boston: Little, Brown, 1971), Ch. 3.

170. James D. Thompson, *Organizations in Action* (New York: McGraw-Hill, 1967), Chs. 9–10.

171. See generally, Francis Rourke, *Bureaucracy, Politics, and Policy* (Boston: Little, Brown, 1969), and W. Henry Lambright, *Governing Science and Technology* (New York: Oxford University Press, 1976).

172. *Study on Federal Regulation, supra* note 130, vol. 1, p. 26.

173. See e.g., President's Advisory Council on Executive Organization (Ash Council), *A New Regulatory Framework: Report on Selected Independent Regulatory Agencies* (Washington, DC: Government Printing Office, 1971).

174. *Air Traffic Controllers Organization v. Federal Labor Relations Authority,* 685 F.2d 547 (D.C.Cir. 1982).

175. See generally, Schiavo, *supra* note 136.

176. See e.g., *Study on Federal Regulation, supra* note 61, vol. 1, p. 23, and Roger G. Noll, *Reforming Regulation: An Evaluation of the Ash Council Proposals* (Washington, DC: Brookings Institution, 1971).

177. U.S. Constitution, Article II, §2, cl. 2.

178. *Id.,* Article II, §3.

179. See *Lear Siegler, Inc. Energy Products Division v. Lehman,* 842 F.2d 1102, 1124 (9th Cir. 1988) and *Kendall v. United States,* 37 U.S. (12 Pet.) 524 (1838).

180. See Christopher Yoo, Steven G. Calabresi, and Laurence D. Nee, "The Unitary Executive During the Third Half-Century, 1889–1945," 80 *Notre Dame Law Review* 1 (2004); Steven G. Calabresi, "The Virtues of Presidential Government," 18 *Constitutional Commentary* 51 (2001); Lawrence Lessig and Cass Sunstein, "The President and the Administration," 94 *Columbia Law Review* 2 (1994).

181. "George W. Bush, Edgar Allan Poe, and the Use and Abuse of Presidential Signing Statements," 35 *Presidential Studies Quarterly* 515 (2005).

182. *Id.,* at p. 552.

183. See *Morrison v. Olson,* 487 U.S. 654 (1988); *Humphrey's Executor v. United States,* 295 U.S. 602 (1935); and *Wiener v. United States,* 357 U.S. 349 (1958). The Court has rejected the idea that *Myers v. United States,* 272 U.S. 5 (1926) could support such a broad assertion. In the Wiener ruling, reiterated in Morrison, the Court observed: "The assumption was short-lived that the Myers case recognized the President's inherent constitutional power to remove officials no matter what the relation of the executive to the discharge of their duties and no matter what restrictions Congress may have imposed regarding the nature of their tenure." 357 U.S., at 352.

184. *Hamdi v. Rumsfeld,* 542 U.S. 507, 536 (2004), citing *Youngstown Sheet & Tube v. Sawyer,* 343 U.S. 579, 587 (1952).

185. Stephen Hess, *Organizing the Presidency* (Washington, DC: Brookings Institution, 1976).

186. On the general debate over relationships between political appointees, the presidents who appointed them, and the agencies in which they serve, see Patricia Ingraham, "Building Bridges or Burning Them? The President, the Appointees and the Bureaucracy." 47 *Public Administration Review* 425 (1987); Carolyn Ban and Patricia Ingraham, "Short-Timers: Political Appointee Mobility and Its Impact on Political/Career Relations in the Reagan Administration," 22 *Administration & Society* 106 (1990); Hugh Heclo, *A Government of Strangers* (Washington, DC: Brookings Institution, 1977).

187. See e.g., Richard Nation, *The Plot That Failed* (New York: Wiley, 1975).

188. Harold Seidman, *Politics, Position, and Power,* 2nd ed. (New York: Oxford University Press, 1976). See also Nathan, *supra* note 187.

189. See Stephen Hess, *Presidents & the Presidency* (Washington, DC: Brookings Institution, 1996) and Hess, *Organizing the Presidency,* 2nd ed. (Washington, DC: Brookings Institution, 1988).

190. Quoted in James P. Pfiffner, *The Strategic Presidency,* 2nd ed., Revised (Lawrence, KS: University Press of Kansas, 1996), p. 45.

191. *Id.,* at p. 25.

192. See e.g., Robert F. Durant, *The Administrative Presidency Revisited* (Albany, NY: State University of New York Press, 1992).

193. *Id.*

194. See Glenn O. Robinson, "The Federal Communications Commission: An Essay on Regulatory Watchdogs," 64 *Virginia Law Review* 169, 183–85 (1978) and Henry J. Friendly, *The Federal Administrative Agencies* (Cambridge: Harvard University Press, 1962), pp. 142–43.

195. See Pfiffner, *supra* note 190.

196. *Study on Federal Regulation, supra* note 130, Vol. 1, p. 6.

197. Robinson, *supra* note 194, at p. 188.

198. See generally, Durant, *supra* note 192.

199. Pfiffner, *supra* note 190, at p. 169.

200. William Cary, *Politics and the Regulatory Agencies* (New York: McGraw-Hill, 1967), p. 4.

201. Where an agency is in need of special varieties and levels of personnel such as scientists, lawyers, or high-level administrators, that presidential discretion can be extremely important.

202. See Pfiffner, *supra* note 190.

203. See Larry Berman, *The Office of Management and Budget and the Presidency, 1921–1979* (Princeton: Princeton University Press, 1979) and Nathan, *supra* note 187.

204. 5 U.S.C. §§554(d), 557(d). See Appendix 3.

205. See Hugh Heclo, "OMB and the Presidency: The Problem of Neutral Competence," 38 *Public Interest* 80 (1975); Berman, *supra* note 203.

206. See the discussion of the Overton Park case in Chapter 7.

207. P.L. 96-511, 94 Stat. 2812.

208. P.L. 104-4, 109 Stat. 48 (1996).

209. This is true whether they actually have the result they promise. See U.S. General Accounting Office, *Unfunded Mandates: Reform Act Has Had Little Effect on Agencies' Rulemaking Actions* (Washington, DC: General Accounting Office, 1998).

210. National Performance Review, *Streamlining Management Control* (Washington, DC: National Performance Review, 1993), p. 1.

211. See e.g., Emmette Redford, "The President and the Regulatory Commissions," 44 *Tulane L. Rev.* 288 (1965).

212. Henry J. Friendly, *The Federal Administrative Agencies: The Need for Better Definition of Standards* (Cambridge: Harvard University Press, 1962), p. 153.

213. William Cary, *Politics and Regulatory Agencies* (New York: McGraw-Hill, 1967), pp. 7–8.

214. U.S. Regulatory Council, *Regulatory Reform Highlights, 1978–80* (Washington, DC: U.S. Regulatory Council, 1980), p. 8.

215. Martin Tolchin, "Battle Intensifies Over Authority of President to Control Agencies," *New York Times,* January 17, 1979, p. 1. See also, *Sierra Club v. Costle,* 657 F.2d 298 (D.C.Cir. 1981).

216. See Howard Ball, *Controlling Regulatory Sprawl* (Westport, CT: Greenwood Press, 1984).

217. Memorandum, Christopher DeMuth, Administrator, OIRA, to Department and Agency Regulatory Contacts, September 22, 1983.

218. C. Boyden Gray, Counsel to the President, to John Conyers, Chairman, Committee on Government Operations, April 30, 1990.

219. Paperwork Reduction Act of 1995, P.L. 104-13, 109 Stat. 163, 44 U.S.C. §3501 et seq.

220. Christine Triano and Nancy Watzman, *All the Vice President's Men* (Washington, DC: OMB Watch, 1991), p. i.

221. See Malcolm D. Woolf, "Clean Air or Hot Air?: Lessons From the Quayle Competitiveness Council's Oversight of EPA," 10 *J. Law & Public Policy* 97 (1993).

222. This was done in an October 1990 memorandum to cabinet secretaries and agency heads. See *Id.,* at p. 7.

223. Memorandum from the Vice President to all heads of executive departments and agencies, March 22, 1991, quoted in Triano and Watzman, *supra* note 220, at p. 7.

224. Congressman David E. Skaggs (D-CO), quoted in Keith Schneider, "Prominence Proves Perilous for Bush's Rule Slayer," Washington Post, June 30, 1992.

225. Christine Triana, "Quayle and Co.," *Government Information Insider,* June 1991, p. 8.

226. Don R. Clay, Assistant Administrator, Environmental Protection Agency, to John D. Dingell, Chair, Subcommittee on Oversight and Investigations, September 1991.

227. See note 22 *supra.*

228. Memorandum for Certain Department and Agency Heads, "Reducing the Burden of Government Regulation," January 28, 1992, p. 2.

229. Vice President Dan Quayle, Memorandum for Certain Department and Agency Heads, "Reducing the Burden of Government Regulations," February 4, 1992.

230. Office of Management and Budget, Office of Information and Regulatory Affairs, "Regulatory Matters," at http://www.whitehouse.gov/omb/inforeg/regpol.html, as of January 22, 2006.

231. Richard Neustadt, *Presidential Power* (New York: Wiley, 1960).

232. See James McGregor Burns, *Leadership* (New York: Harper & Row, 1978), Ch. 1.

233. On the limits of impact from presidential directives, see U.S. General Accounting Office, *Regulatory Reform: Implementation of the Regulatory Review Executive Order* (Washington, DC: GAO, 1996).

234. This comment stems from the fact that most of the efforts have not been aimed at ensuring more effective or better quality regulation but to eliminating it. Indeed, the term reform has suffered such devaluation in recent decades as to be to all intents and purposes meaningless. I have addressed this issue in greater detail in Phillip J. Cooper, et al., *Public Administration for the Twenty-First Century* (Fort Worth, TX: Harcourt Brace, 1997), pp. 10–15.

235. James L. Sundquist, *The Decline and Resurgence of Congress* (Washington, DC: Brookings Institution, 1981).

236. See generally, Louis Fisher, *Constitutional Conflicts Between Congress and the President,* 4th Ed., Revised (Lawrence, KS: Kansas University Press, 1997).

237. "These structural tendencies toward disagreement are generally exacerbated by the phenomenon of divided government—one party in control of the presidency and the other dominant in either one or both houses of Congress—and by an unusually high level of ideological tension between the two branches." Robert S. Gilmour and Alexis A. Halley, eds., *Who Makes Public Policy? The Struggle for Control between Congress and the Executive* (Chatham, NJ: Chatham House Publishers, 1994), p. 4.

238. *Id.,* p. 103.

239. See generally, Phillip J. Cooper, *By Order of the President: The Use & Abuse of Executive Direct Action* (Lawrence, KS: University Press of Kansas, 2002), Ch. 8.

240. See Gilmour and Halley, *supra* note 237; Joel D. Aberbach, *Keeping a Watchful Eye: The Politics of Congressional Oversight* (Washington, DC: Brookings Institution, 1990); Christopher H. Foreman, Jr., *Signals from the Hill: Congressional Oversight and the Challenge of Social Regulation* (New Haven: Yale University Press, 1988); Lawrence S. Dodd and Richard L. Schott, *Congress and the Administrative State* (New York: Wiley, 1979); Morris Ogul, *Congress Oversees the Bureaucracy* (Pittsburgh: Pittsburgh University Press, 1976); and Joseph P. Harris, *Congressional Control of Administration* (Garden City, NJ: Doubleday, 1964).

241. *Congressional Oversight of Regulatory Agencies,* Study on Federal Regulation, *supra* note 130, vol. 2. Another very useful older study of oversight is U.S. Senate, Congressional Research Service and General Accounting Office for the Subcommittee on Oversight Procedures of the Committee on Government Operations, *Congressional Oversight: Methods and Techniques,* 94th Cong., 2nd Sess. (1976).

242. See e.g., Morton Rosenberg, *Investigative Oversight: An Introduction to the Law, Practice and Procedure of Congressional Inquiry* (Washington, DC: Congressional Research Service, 1995).

243. Dodd and Schott, *supra* note 240, at p. 156; Harris, *supra* note 240, at p. 1. *Study on Federal Regulation, supra* note 130, vol. 2, p. 4.

244. Harris, *supra* note 240, at p. 9.

245. *Study on Federal Regulation, supra* note 130, vol. 2, p. 4.

246. See e.g., *Chadha v. Immigration and Naturalization Service,* 634 F.2d 409 (9th Cir. 1981).

247. Harris, *supra* note 240, at p. 2.

248. *Study on Federal Regulation, supra* note 130, vol. 2, at p. 4.

249. On casework generally, see *Congressional Oversight, supra* note 241, Ch. 13, "Casework and Projects: Oversight in the Member's Office," pp. 67–70.

250. Abraham Ribicoff, "Congressional Oversight and Regulatory Reform," 28 *Administrative L. Rev.* 415, 418 (1976).

251. *Study on Federal Regulation, supra* note 130, vol. 2, at p. 4.

252. Frederick M. Kaiser, CRS Report for Congress, "Congressional Oversight" (Washington, DC: Congressional Research Service, 2001), p. 2.

253. *Id.*, at pp. 16–17.

254. The 1946 Legislative Reorganization Act was the first statute requiring congressional committees to oversee federal agencies. Section 136 of the act stated that: "Each standing committee of the Senate and the House of Representatives shall exercise continuous watchfulness of the execution by the administrative agencies concerned of any laws, the subject matter of which is within the jurisdiction of such committees." *Id.*, at p. 16.

255. Gilmour and Halley, *supra* note 237, at p. 9.

256. *Id.*, at p. 15.

257. Examples of each of these are provided in Congressional Oversight, *supra* note 241.

258. *Study on Federal Regulation, supra* note 130, vol. 2, p. 31.

259. *Id.*, at p. 81.

260. See Chapter 8.

261. At the time of this writing, the agenda setting and publication is required under clause 2(d)(1) of Rule X of the House of Representatives.

262. "House Science Committee Oversight Agenda—108th Congress," at http://www.house.gov/science/committeeinfo/PDFs/oversight.pdf, as of January 28, 2006.

263. U.S. House of Representatives, Committee on Veterans' Affairs, "Oversight Plan for 109th Congress," at http://veterans.house.gov/about/plan109.html, as of January 28, 2006.

264. Henry A. Waxman to Tom Davis, February 8, 2005, at http://www.democrats.reform.house.gov/story.asp?ID=787&Issue=Open+Government, as of January 28, 2006.

265. See David A. Stockman, *The Triumph of Politics: Why the Reagan Revolution Failed* (New York: Harper & Row, 1986).

266. *Study on Federal Regulation, supra* note 130, vol. 2, p. 94.

267. Aberbach, *supra* note 240, at pp. 187–188.

268. "Federal Rulemaking: Past Reviews and Emerging Trends Suggest Issues That Merit Congressional Attention," Testimony of J. Christopher Mihm, Managing Director, Strategic Issues, Government Accountability Office, before the Subcommittee on Commercial and Administrative Law, Committee on the Judiciary, House of Representatives, November 1, 2005, p. 6.

269. *Study on Federal Regulation, supra* note 130, vol. 2, p. 66.

270. *Id.,* at pp. 66–67.

271. "Mine Safety: MSHA's Programs for Ensuring the Safety and Health of Coal Miners Could be Strengthened," Testimony by Robert E. Robertson, Director Education, Workforce, and Income Security Issues, Government Accountability Office, before the Subcommittee on Labor, HHS and Education, Committee on Appropriations, U.S. Senate, January 23, 2006.

272. *Id.,* at p. 94.

273. *Id.,* at p. 156.

274. See Aberbach, *supra* note 240, at pp. 187–193.

275. See Gilmour and Halley, *supra* note 237, at pp. 9–11.

276. James Q. Wilson, *Bureaucracy: What Government Agencies Do and Why They Do It* (New York: Basic Books, 1989), pp. 241–242.

277. The barriers imposed in such situations are discussed in Cooper, "George W. Bush, Edgar Allan Poe, and the Use of Presidential Signing Statements," *supra* note 181.

278. Discussed in greater detail in Cooper, *By Order of the President, supra* note 239, Ch. 6.

279. U.S. Senate, Report of the Committee on the Judiciary together with Additional and Supplemental Views, *The Comprehensive Regulatory Reform Act of 1995—S. 343,* 104th Cong., 1st Sess. (1995), p. 151.

280. P.L. 104-121, Sec. 231, 232.

281. U.S. House of Representatives, Committee on Government Reform, *Program Assessment and Results Act,* H-Rpt. 109-26, 109th Cong., 1st Sess. (2005).

282. *Id.,* pp. 20–21.

283. Beryl A. Radin, Testimony to the Senate Homeland Security and Government Affairs Subcommittee on Federal Financial Management, Government Information, and International Security, June 14, 2005, pp. 2–4.

284. See e.g, "Effect of an Agency's Failure to Report to Congress the Promulgation of a Rule Covered Under the Congressional Review Act," Memorandum, American Law Division, Congressional Research Service to House Subcommittee on National Economic Growth, Natural Resources, and Regulatory Affairs, Committee on Government Reform and Oversight, March 25, 1998; U.S. General Accounting Office, *Regulatory Reform: Implementation of the Small Business Advocacy Review Panel Requirements* (Washington, DC: General Accounting Office, 1998); U.S. General Accounting Office, Testimony Before the Subcommittees on Government Programs and Oversight and Regulatory Reform and Paperwork Reduction, Committee on Small Business, House of Representative, *Regulatory Flexibility Act: Implementation of the Small Business Advocacy Review Panel Requirements* (Washington, DC: General Accounting Office, 1998).

285. *Study on Federal Regulation, supra* note 130, vol. 2, at pp. 30–32.

286. See Government Performance and Results Act, Public Law 103-62, August 3, 1993 and U.S. General Accounting Office, *Managing for Results: Regulatory Agencies Identified Significant Barriers to Focusing on Results* (Washington, DC: General Accounting Office, 1997); National Academy of Public Administration, *Congressional Oversight of Regulatory Agencies: The Need to Strike a Balance and Focus on Performance* (Washington, DC: National Academy of Public Administration, 1988).

287. Alexander Hamilton, James Madison, and John Jay, *The Federalist Papers* (New York: Mentor, 1961), pp. 309–310.

288. Theodore Lowi, *The End of Liberalism* (New York: Norton, 1969).

289. Gilmour and Halley, *supra* note 237, p. 8.

290. Paul A. Sabatier and Hank C. Jenkins-Smith, *Policy Change and Learning: An Advocacy Coalition Approach* (Boulder, CO: Westview Press, 1993); Jon Bennett, *Meeting Needs: NGO Coordination in Practice* (London: Earthscan Publications, 1995); Thomas Princen and Matthias Finger, *Environmental NGOs in World Politics* (London: Routledge, 1994).

291. Charles A. Bowsher, Testimony Before the Committee on Governmental Affairs, United States Senate, *Congressional Oversight: The General Accounting Office* (Washington, DC: General Accounting Office, 1995).

292. Thomas H. Stanton, *A State of Risk: Will Government-Sponsored Enterprises Be the Next Financial Crisis?* (New York: Harper Business, 1991); Stanton, "Increasing the Accountability of Government-Sponsored Enterprises: Next Steps," 51 *Public Administration Review* 572 (1991); Stanton, "Increasing the Accountability of Government-Sponsored Enterprises: First Steps," 50 *Public Administration Review* 590 (1990); Ronald C. Moe and Thomas H. Stanton, "Government-Sponsored Enterprises as Federal Instrumentalities: Reconciling Private Management with Public Accountability," 49 *Public Administration Review* 321 (1989).

293. Ronald C. Moe and Robert S. Gilmour, "Rediscovering Principles of Public Administration: The Neglected Foundation of Public Law," 55 *Public Administration Review* 135 (1995).

294. Pension Benefit Guaranty Corporation, Press Release, April 22, 2005, "PBGC Reaches Pension Settlement with United Airlines," at http://www.pbgc.gov/media/news-archive/2005/pr05-36.html, as of February 3, 2006.

295. *Id.*

296. H. Brinton Milward, "The Changing Character of the Public Sector," in James Perry, ed., *Handbook of Public Administration,* Second Edition (San Francisco: Jossey-Bass, 1996), p. 87. See also Eugene Bardach and Cara Lesser, "Accountability in Human Service Collaboratives—For What? And to Whom?" 6 *Journal of Public Administration Research and Theory* 197 (1996).

297. The problem of focused responsibility and accountability arises even in networks defined just in terms of government agencies. Thus, the Government Accountability Office issued a study recently that counted some 11 federal agencies and 13 Native American tribes or nations involved in regulation of fish and wildlife

issues in the Columbia River Basin, and that does not count the state, local, interstate, nonprofit, or for-profit organizations. See U.S. Government Accountability Office, *Columbia River Basin: A Multilayered Collection of Directives and Plans Guide Federal Fish and Wildlife Activities* (Washington, DC: GAO, 2004).

298. U.S. General Accounting Office, *Unfunded Mandates: Reform Act Has Had Little Effect on Agencies' Rulemaking Actions* (Washington, DC: General Accounting Office, 1998).

299. See e.g., General Accounting Officer, *Business Regulation: California Manufacturers Use Multiple Strategies to Comply with Laws* (Washington, DC: GAO, 1998).

300. *Metropolitan Washington Airports Authority v. Citizens for the Abatement of Aircraft Noise,* 501 U.S. 252, 266 (1991).

301. See *Cipollone v. Liggett Group,* 505 U.S. 504, 516 (1992).

302. *Gade v. National Solid Wastes Management Association,* 505 U.S. 88, 98 (1992).

303. *Morales v. TWA,* 504 U.S. 374 (1992).

304. *Pacific Gas & Electric v. Energy Resources Conservation and Development Commission,* 461 U.S. 190 (1983); *Wisconsin Public Intervenor v. Mortier,* 501 U.S. 597 (1991).

305. *State of Rhode Island v. Lead Industries Association,* 2001 R.I. Super. LEXIS 31 (RISuperCt 2001).

306. Stephen Labaton, "States Seek to Counter U.S. Deregulation," *New York Times,* January 13, 2002, p. 21.

307. *Hodel v. Virginia Surface Mining Association,* 452 U.S. 264 (1981).

308. *United States v. Lopez,* 514 U.S. 549 (1995).

309. See the dissents by Justices Souter and Breyer in *Id.*

310. *New York v. United States,* 505 U.S. 144 (1992).

311. *Printz v. United States, supra* note 34.

312. *Seminole Tribe of Florida v. Florida,* 517 U.S. 44 (1996).

313. *National League of Cities v. Usery,* 426 U.S. 833 (1976).

314. *Garcia v. San Antonio Metropolitan Transit Authority,* 469 U.S. 528 (1985).

315. *Id.,* at p. 280.

316. *Bd. of Trustees of the University of Alabama v. Garrett,* 531 U.S. 356 (2001); *Kimel v. Florida Bd. of Regents,* 528 U.S. 62 (2000). See also *College Savings Bank v. Florida Prepaid Postsecondary Education Expense Board,* 527 U.S. 666 (1999).

317. *Federal Maritime Commission v. South Carolina State Ports Authority,* 535 U.S. 743 (2002).

318. *Id.,* at p. 772.

319. *White v. Massachusetts Council of Construction Workers,* 460 U.S. 204 (1983).

320. *United Building Trades Council v. Camden,* 465 U.S. 208 (1984).

321. *Reeves v. Stake,* 447 U.S. 429 (1980).

322. *South Central Timber Development v. Wunnicke,* 467 U.S. 82 (1984).

323. 3 P.R. Laws Ann. §§ 927-927h.

324. 10 P.R. Laws Ann. § 167e(a)(4).

325. *Antilles Cement Corp. v. Acevedo,* 408 F.3d 41, 47 (1st Cir. 2005).

326. *Bethlehem Steel Corp. v. Bd. of Comm'rs,* 276 Cal. App. 2d 221, 228-29, 80 Cal. Rptr. 800 (1969).

327. *Trojan Techs., Inc. v. Pennsylvania,* 916 F.2d 903, 910 (3d Cir. 1990).

328. *Hotel Employees & Restaurant Employees Union, Local 57 v. Sage Hospitality Resources,* 390 F.3d 206, 208 (3rd Cir. 2004).

329. Environmental Protection Agency, "Interim Guidance for Investigating Title VI Administrative Complaints Challenging Permits," February 1998.

330. Executive Order 13083, 63 Fed. Reg. 27651 (1998).

331. Executive Order 13095, 63 Fed. Reg. 42565 (1998). See David S. Broder, "Executive Order Urged Consulting, but Didn't," *Washington Post,* July 16, 1998, p. A15.

332. See e.g., U.S. Government Accountability Office, *Homeland Security: Reforming Federal Grants to Better Meet Outstanding Needs* (Washington, DC: GAO, 2003).

333. See Organization for Economic Co-operation and Development, *Managing Across Levels of Government* (Paris: OECD, 1997).

334. See International Institute of Administrative Sciences, Preliminary Report of Working Group I, "European Community and Law," prepared for presentation at the IIAS International Conference, Madrid, Spain, November 1990.

335. C. Neal Tate and Torbjorn Vallinder, eds., *The Global Expansion of Judicial Power* (New York: New York University Press, 1995).

336. See Peters and Savoie, *supra* note 2, and the other works cited in that note.

337. Donald J. Savoie, *Thatcher, Reagan, Mulrooney: In Search of a New Bureaucracy* (Toronto: University of Toronto Press, 1994).

338. See e.g., OECD, *Regulatory Impact Analysis: Best Practices in OECD Countries* (Paris: OECD, 1997); OECD, *Putting Markets to Work: The Design and Use of Marketable Permits and Obligations* (Paris: OECD, 1997).

339. Administrative Conference of the United States, Recommendation 91-1, "Federal Agency Cooperation with Foreign Government Regulators," June 13, 1991, 1 CFR §305.91-1.

340. U.S. General Accounting Office, *International Environment: U.S. Funding of Environmental Programs and Activities* (Washington, DC: General Accounting Office, 1996), p. 1.

341. U.S. General Accounting Office, *United Nations: U.S. Participation in Five Affiliated International Organizations* (Washington, DC: General Accounting Office, 1997).

342. U.S. General Accounting Office, *North American Free Trade Agreement: Impacts and Implementation* (Washington, DC: General Accounting Office, 1997).

343. George A. Bermann, *Regulatory Cooperation With Counterpart Agencies Abroad: The FAA's Aircraft Certification Experience* (Washington, DC: Administrative Conference of the United States, 1991), pp. 47–68.

344. *Id.*, pp. 2–5.

345. See generally, *Study on Federal Regulation, supra* note 130, vol. 3, *Public Participation in Regulatory Agency Proceedings*; Ernest Gellhorn, "Public Participation in Administrative Agency Proceedings," 81 *Yale L. Journal* 359 (1972); Roger C. Cramton, "The Why, Where and How of Broadened Public Participation in the Administrative Process," 60 *Georgetown L. J.* 525 (1972).

346. The cases most often cited as the classics in this are include *National Welfare Rights Organization v. Finch,* 429 F.2d 725 (D.C.Cir. 1970); *Office of Communication of the United Church of Christ v. Federal Communications Commission,* 359 F.2d 994 (D.C.Cir. 1966); and *Scenic Hudson Preservation Conference v. Federal Power Commission,* 354 F.2d 608 (2nd Cir. 1965).

347. The classic treatment of interest group litigation in the civil rights battle, see Clement Vose, *Caucasians Only: The Supreme Court, the NAACP, and the Restrictive Covenant Cases* (Berkeley: University of California, 1959).

348. *Study on Federal Regulation, supra* note 130, vol. 3, p. 2.

349. 5 U.S.C. App. 1, see Appendix 3 of this volume.

350. U.S. General Accounting Office, *Need for Improving the Regulation of the Natural Gas Industry and Management of Internal Operations* (Washington, DC: General Accounting Office, 1974), pp. 35–36.

351. See Schiavo, *supra* note 136.

352. See Cramton, *supra* note 345, at pp. 428–432, and Gelhorn, *supra* note 345, at p. 388.

353. See *United Church of Christ v. F.C.C., supra* note 246.

354. See e.g., Rosemary O'Leary, *Environmental Change: Federal Courts and the EPA* (Philadelphia: Temple University Press, 1993).

355. See the discussion of the Overton Park case in Chapter 7.

356. *Study on Federal Regulation, supra* note 130, vol. 3, p. 22.

357. *Id.*, part II.

358. Cary Coglianese, "The Internet and Citizen Participation in Rulemaking," 1 *II/S: Journal of Law and Policy* 33, 48 (2004).

11

Acquisition, Use, and Dissemination of Information: A System of Information Policy

Government is information. Its employees are nearly all information workers, its raw material is information inputs, its product is those inputs transformed into policies, which are simply an authoritative form of information."[1] Harlan Cleveland was overstating the point with this observation, but not by much. Government is clearly one of the most important collectors, custodians, users, and sources of information in our society. One scholar's evaluation of Freedom of Information Act requests per year as far back as the 1980s gives some indication of the scope of government information management activities. She found that: "The Department of Defense processed 83,173 FOIA requests in 1985; Health and Human Services had 105,687 requests, with 45,953 to the Food and Drug Administration; Treasury had 23,217 and the Department of Energy, 5,723."[2] Many agency Chief Information Officers (CIOs) would look back nostalgically on such light demand, for the situation has expanded dramatically. At that time, the personal computer was only beginning to be used widely, few organizations were fully networked (or "wired" as we would put it in more contemporary terms), and the Internet and its World Wide Web, as we know it today, did not yet exist. Ten years later, in the mid-1990s, the Department of Defense computer systems experienced an estimated 250,000 attacks by computer hackers and others, "about 64 percent of attacks were successful at gaining access, and that only a small percentage of these attacks were detected."[3] Just that one department of the federal government in the mid-1990s operated some 2.1 million computers and more than 10,000 computer networks.[4] During the first half of the 1990s alone, agencies at the national level committed more than $145 billion to purchase and maintain information systems.[5]

Today, laptop and handheld computers with cellular modems can be used virtually anywhere in the world to access huge volumes of information, to communicate voice, data, and images, and to perform complex tasks, drawing upon the capabilities of various other computers located around the globe through computer languages capable of enlisting multiple computer resources and integrating them into single problem-solving (and sometimes problem-creating[6]) networks. The sheer volume of information that must be managed, protected, or accessed is quite literally overwhelming. Indeed, trying to obtain information from cyberspace has often been compared to the attempt to take a drink from a fire hose. The torrent of information that comes onto a computer screen from a relatively simple inquiry is startling.

However, dramatically increased opportunities often bring with them a host of real and potential problems. When the first edition of this text was published, many of the concerns discussed with respect to information policy were relatively primitive as compared with today's challenges. Consider the fact that one study found that all 24 federal agencies examined between 1996 and 1998 had significant security weaknesses, the most common of which was "poor control over access to sensitive data and systems."[7] And then there was the development of what came to be known as the Y2K problem or the "millennium bug." Because of the simple decision years ago to save computer memory space and processing time by coding years with two digits instead of four, thousands of organizations around the world invested billions of dollars seeking to correct their hardware and software so as to recognize the correct century and avoid paralysis of critical systems. Then there was the decision by state and federal legislators to make use of the fact that it is nearly impossible to escape having information about one's life and activities show up in numerous computer systems, by allowing governmental agencies to match records across databases for the purpose of tracking down parents who had not paid child support, fraudulent welfare applications, and numerous other kinds of possible legal violations. And once there is access to cross-network and cross-database information sharing, society is presented with a range of questions about personal privacy that it has not yet begun to consider seriously. More recently, this concept has been labeled data-mining, which has become a serious matter of debate because it has been done by both government and private sector organizations. To all of these developments is added the very important fact that all of this has taken place in the context of globalization and dramatically expanded contracting-out of government services in which the range of people who can gain access to information, and who can therefore use it for well or ill, has grown exponentially.

Our political and social norms recognize that information is personally, financially, and politically valuable. It is also potentially dangerous if it is misused or if it falls into the wrong hands. We continue to learn just how useful and threatening information can be as we develop new technologies which make it possible to collect, organize, access, and disseminate unbelievable quantities of data about every imaginable subject. The rapid rise and spread of the crime of identity theft is only one of the most obvious of these challenges.

In sum, unlike the days when many of our information policies were created in which the focus was on who had a file folder full of information and what he or should could or would do with it, in today's environment the problems are at least as much about information systems—the rapidly changing technologies that make up those systems—and the effort to manage both the information and the systems as they are about the information itself. The effort to meet these difficulties is made all the more difficult because the technology is changing so rapidly that there are serious questions whether information policy is keeping pace with the challenges.

Administrative agencies—together with the contractors or grantees working with or for them—are the bodies asked to acquire information for policymaking, enforcement, and adjudication across the wide range of public sector activities. Naturally, the law of public administration must come to grips with information practices. This chapter examines the system of information law for public management, both in terms of its basic elements and a variety of additions that have been adopted over time. It also considers some of the contemporary challenges facing those who must administer within this system, including the significance of the global dimension and issues raised by expanded uses of contracting and other contemporary governance devices used to deliver services.

DEVELOPING INFORMATION POLICY
IN A CHANGING ENVIRONMENT

As has most of the law governing public administration, the system of information law has accumulated in an ad hoc fashion over time. And, as we have seen in several other areas, this process of legal development has occurred in a complex and rapidly changing environment. Several factors shape our efforts to ensure adequate authority for agencies to obtain the information they need to carry out assigned tasks while simultaneously protecting the citizenry against abuses. They include a growing record of abuses, changing technology, increasing intergovernmental complexity, and misunderstandings about the current state of the law. These are associated with what is best termed the "information paradox." It is also important to approach information law and policy with an awareness of the confusing concept of information.

The Information Paradox and Associated Problems

James Madison wrote: "A popular Government, without popular information, or the means of acquiring it, is but a Prologue to a Farce or a Tragedy; or, perhaps both. Knowledge will forever govern ignorance: And a people who mean to be their own Governors, must arm themselves with the power knowledge gives."[8] In a society that depends upon administrative experts for the implementation of its policy judgments, much of the information needed to govern must be acquired, digested, and used by administrative agencies.

Yet liberty is impossible where there is no privacy. In fact, even the organizations we require to advance our personal and professional interests in a modern society must have a modicum of privacy to survive and be effective, a contention supported by the U.S. Supreme Court.[9] Therefore, the constitutional framers, legislators, judges, and, yes, administrators have developed a variety of rules limiting what kind of information government may acquire, how it may be obtained, and what may be done with it. Clearly then, the nature of our political order dictates that all efforts to fashion information policy must be worked out within the constraints of a paradox; call it the information paradox. Not surprisingly, it turns out that some of the legal provisions crafted to achieve effective government and protect personal freedom conflict.[10] Indeed, each measure taken to enhance privacy is a possible problem for administrators, who need information to implement policy, and for the public, who must elect the representatives to enact it.

It is tempting to dismiss as paranoia much of the anxiety expressed by those who constantly raise the image of Orwell's *1984*.[11] In reality, though, we do have a history of troublesome information practices that would in a number of respects surprise even Orwell. The revelations of the Watergate era startled the nation and prompted a host of new information laws. Certainly the contemporary revelations of the G. W. Bush administration's National Security Agency's program of intercepting communications within the United States prompted challenges from both major parties and from conservatives as well as liberals, particularly since Congress stood ready to work with the White House on modifications that might be necessary to the Foreign Intelligence Surveillance Act in order to pursue national security threats while preserving essential privacy guarantees.[12] In fact, as in so many areas of law and administration, much of the law governing information acquisition, use, and dissemination came not from theoretical debates or predictions of a harmful future, but in response to particular problems that have emerged over time.

Some of the difficulties developed without any intention to injure, but they caused great harm nevertheless. For example, an incident in 1970 demonstrated the dangers of the misuse of information from screening programs that seem at first benign. Four soldiers who died during a military exercise were reported to have had the sickle cell trait. The likelihood of having the trait, but not the disease, is quite high among some portions of the population. There is no evidence that the trait has any direct effect. Even so, after the incident involving the four soldiers, some hypothesized that those with the trait might have difficulties under stress.

> Although these hypotheses have never been proven, the concern raised by them caused temporary employment discrimination against persons with the sickle cell trait by the New York Fire Department and the Transit Authority of New York, the New York Telephone Company, and several major airlines. The Secretary of the Army stated in 1972 that applicants for certain positions must be screened for the sickle cell trait and that carriers are ineligible. In addition, a number of life insurance companies, without any actuarial support, for a time charged extra-high premiums to, or dropped their coverage of, sickle cell carriers. It was only after a dramatic political attack by black physicians and business leaders that this genetic discrimination ceased.[13]

Despite the fact that discrimination against persons with disabilities was recognized as an important issue and partially addressed with the passage of Americans with Disabilities Act,[14] that effort did not stop the kind of problem exemplified in the sickle cell trait example. In fact, it did not even help to prevent the manifold forms of abuse visited upon those who are known to have tested positive for HIV as well as those who have been afflicted by full-blown AIDS. Indeed, people with HIV infection were only recognized by the Supreme Court to qualify for protection under the ADA in 1998.[15]

Other policy issues came from more systemic causes. The Privacy Protection Study Commission found a number of facts of modern life emerging around the nation:

> First, while an organization makes and keeps records about individuals to facilitate relationships with them, it also makes and keeps records about individuals for other programs, such as documenting the record-keeping organization's own actions and making it possible for other organizations—government agencies for example—to monitor the actions of individuals.
>
> Second, there is an accelerating trend, most obvious in the credit and financial areas, toward the accumulation in records of more and more personal details about an individual.
>
> Third, more and more records about an individual are collected, maintained, and disclosed by organizations with which the individual has no direct relationship but whose records help to shape his life.
>
> Fourth, most record-keeping organizations consult the records of other organizations to verify the information they obtain from an individual and thus pay as much or more attention to what other organizations report about him than they pay to what he reports about himself; and
>
> Fifth, neither law nor technology now gives an individual the tools he needs to protect his legitimate interest in the records organizations keep about him.[16]

Probably the greatest catalyst for first major round of information law development were the abuses that became apparent in the Watergate debacle.[17] The withholding of information from those outside government and from the Congress as well as the discovery of inappropriate uses of files for political purposes produced demands for change. The Freedom of Information amendments and the Right to Privacy Act stemmed from these events. By contrast, one of the most dramatic events that resulted in actions to carve out exceptions to information practices laws and expand both the acquisition and use of information was 9/11.

Changing technology has also created dramatic new ways of obtaining information, like chemical and genetic screening and so-called DNA fingerprinting from the testing of normal bodily fluids submitted in connection with standard physical examinations. Recent concern about drug testing and AIDS screening has suggested some of the questions that arise in the acquisition of personal information by medical testing. Genetic screening poses many more possibilities and questions.[18] In addition to the issues associated with DNA identification techniques, the current efforts to employ various kinds of personal data are now grouped under the heading of "biometrics" such as "facial recognition, finger-print recognition, hand geometry, and iris recognition."[19]

Yet another feature of the environment within which information policies are developed and implemented is that the intergovernmental complexity of the administrative world requires a great deal of information sharing. State, local, and federal agencies may need to exchange data in situations ranging from social service delivery to regulatory enforcement to national security and emergency preparedness. However, federal and state information statutes differ, as do agency regulations within a given level of government.[20] Information can also cross public sector/private sector lines under some circumstances, as in the situation in which federal authorities acquire bank records directly from financial institutions. That kind of sharing happens regularly in the contracting out of public services to for-profit or nonprofit firms. While the Supreme Court tried to stop the practice, private organi-zations have continued to try to use public information access laws to obtain information about their competitors.[21]

Finally, the fragmentation and diversity of information practice laws makes this an area in which both producers and consumers of administrative decisions often lack knowledge of applicable rules. It is not a field like, say, due process in which most of us have been socialized into an awareness of rudimentary concepts and constraints. Hence, particular patience is required in ensuring that all parties to a discussion of an information practice begin with a common understanding of the claim at issue and the legal authority appropriate to its resolution.

Information, Data, Evidence, Property, or Free Speech?

One of the critical factors that has affected our ability to produce comprehensive, effective, and workable information policies derives from the fact that the target keeps moving. The language of a number of information laws is drawn from a time when most information could be understood to be some tangible item, such as a document that became part of a file stored in a file folder that could be possessed exclusively by one person or office. It was possible to distinguish such a document from a formal notice of agency action which was, in turn, a document that was made publicly available through such means as publication in the federal or state register. Individual information was often thought to be material provided to the agency involved by the person about whom a file was constructed. These rather simplistic ideas continued even into the formative years of the computer era. After all, infor-mation was often collected on index cards. That information was made machine readable by key punching onto what were known as IBM cards (after the computer firm) and much of what was then called data processing was little more than sorting of punched cards according to characteristics such as age, gender, income, test scores, addresses, or some combination. Today we would recognize that activity not so much as the processing of information but as the sorting of data, discrete descriptions of people, places, things, or events. Information is generally understood today as interpretations of those data into more fully developed descriptions or analyses.

As computer memory systems developed and grew into both working and storage memory, these data cards were read into stored databases. Microcomputer systems even took the visual symbols of files and the documents as icons in software. The spreadsheet provided a computer version of the accounting ledger sheet for financial work, and more sophisticated software packages made it possible to read data directly from databases into spreadsheets. Spreadsheet and database programs were made relational, such that an entry into one spreadsheet or database would automatically be fed into other related databases, spreadsheets, and report formats to eliminate the need for multiple entries and calculations. The ease of data entry, calculation, and retrieval meant that while the terms may remain similar to traditional terminology, the true nature and power of information systems had changed radically.

In the contemporary environment, however, that same changing computer technology makes it possible to collect, handle, and distribute incredible amounts of information very quickly, not only within systems but across systems as well. Using databases available from third parties, it is possible to acquire substantial amounts of information without asking the subject for anything and in a form that bears little relationship to the old idea of information as tangible property, discussed above. With these capabilities, it is common to program computer systems to acquire large amounts of data and to transform it into information that can be abused as well as used. The hardware and software barriers that used to provide some protection against inappropriate uses or distribution of information have now become far less significant than before. There are still computer systems in government that do not, as the expression goes, talk to each other, leading to the post-9/11 problem of connecting the dots, but many other communicate with each other—and with systems outside of government—far too easily.

At the same time, different types of material have different status in law, and the corresponding policies governing their collection, management, use, and dissemination vary as well. When parties seek to bring information into a dispute as evidence, there are rules governing its introduction, use, maintenance, release, and destruction. Of course, it is often not clear to those who create potential evidence that they are doing so. And then there is the fact that it is not always clear in advance just what kind of material will be sought as evidence at some point in the future.

One of the most obvious examples of this kind of problem has arisen with respect to the rapidly growing and now pervasive use of e-mail. Matthew Bester has noted that what began as a Department of Defense creation called the Advanced Research Projects Agency Network (ARPAnet) and grew into an electronic mail system in which it was estimated that "some 2.6 trillion e-mail messages passed through U.S.-based computer networks" in 1997 alone.[22] Today no one really knows how many e-mails are handled on a daily, let alone an annual, basis. Many people thought—and some still suffer under the mistaken view—that when they delete messages from their e-mail systems, that information is destroyed. However, some, including Oliver North, were educated on that score during the Iran/Contra scandal when they learned that it was possible to retrieve e-mail messages from a computer system after the users had thought they had been destroyed.[23]

It is now commonplace for attorneys to request significant amounts of information from computer systems as they conduct the discovery phase of a case, seeking potential evidence. "According to one report during the U.S. Justice Department's investigation into the merger of Microsoft Corp. with Intuit Corp., Intuit was served with an electronic data request totaling 76 pages. Intuit met the request by searching 15,000,000 pages of text and more than 80,000 e-mail messages."[24] While it is acceptable for organizations to use regular information management plans to eliminate excess material in their computer systems, it is not acceptable to deliberately destroy potential evidence.[25] Doing so can lead to civil or even criminal sanctions.[26] In the case of governments, there are evolving conversations about which organizations and what kinds of computerized records fall within records preservation statutes.[27]

Then there is the problem of just what kind of information is considered worthy to be used as evidence, whatever its source may be. For the most part, arguments about admission of evidence historically had to do with protecting juries made up of lay persons from the attempted use of deceptive, irrelevant, redundant, unreliable, or unchallengeable information in court cases. However, as both public law and private law disputes have become more complex, the issue has expanded to include debates over whether and how certain types of information should be used even by trained decisionmakers such as judges. The contemporary debate over what is sometimes termed "junk science," is a classic example.[28] In an era of what has been referred to earlier chapters as "adversarial science," and where so many expert witnesses are paid large amounts of money to provide scientific support for all sides in legal controversies, the debate over what qualifies as scientific evidence is important.

The U.S. Supreme Court addressed that topic in a 1993 case, *Daubert v. Merrell Dow Pharmaceuticals*.[29] The case went back to 1971 when Joyce Daubert learned that she was pregnant. Her OB/GYN prescribed Bendectin to treat the nausea and vomiting associated with her pregnancy. She was also receiving Bendectin a year later from her family physician. When she first started taking the drug she was about 34–41 days into her pregnancy. Her son Jason was born in July of 1973 with limb reduction in his arm and hand. The Dauberts brought suit in 1983 against Merrell Dow and Dow Chemical on grounds of strict liability, breach of warranty, and negligence. They argued that by 1973 the defendants had received word of 96 cases of limb deformities in people who had been taking the drug. They contended that two studies, one animal and one human, should have given the company reason to know of the risks and that it failed to warn doctors and consumers.

The U.S. District Court for the Southern District of California therefore dismissed the company motion for summary judgment and held "drug manufacturers may be held strictly liable for failure to warn of known or reasonably knowable side effects."[30] In December of 1989, however, another judge granted Merrell Dow's motion for summary judgment on grounds that Rule 703 of the Federal Rules of Evidence—which requires that scientific evidence "must be sufficiently established to have general acceptance in the field to which it belongs"—was not met. Specifically, the court found that "Absent a scientific understanding of the cause of the birth defects at issue in Bendectin cases, causation may be shown only through reliance upon epidemiological evidence."[31] The Dauberts did not have epidemiological evidence, but they did offer test tube and live birth studies, pharmacological studies, and expert reevaluation of published epidemiological studies. That evidence did not meet the required test.

Prior to the *Daubert* decision by the Supreme Court, the standard that had been cited came from a case decided by a Court of Appeals in 1923.[32] Of course, a great deal had happened since then in science and in law, including revision of the rules of evidence. The Supreme Court opinion did not decide whether the evidence offered by the Dauberts was adequate. Rather, it assigned trial court judges the task of evaluating proffered evidence and purported to tell them how to do it. Unfortunately, while it made the judges gatekeepers, it provided them with little real guidance on how to perform the task.

> Faced with a proffer of expert scientific testimony, then, the trial judge must determine at the outset . . . whether the expert is proposing to testify to (1) scientific knowledge that (2) will assist the trier of fact to understand or determine a fact in issue. This entails a preliminary assessment of whether the reasoning or methodology underlying the testimony is scientifically valid and of whether that reasoning or methodology properly can be applied to the facts in issue. We are confident that federal judges possess the capacity to undertake this review.[33]

Of course, confidence in their ability is one thing, and criteria as to how to exercise that judgment quite another. The Court wrote:

> Many factors will bear on the inquiry, and we do not presume to set out a definitive checklist or test. But some general observations are appropriate.
>
> Ordinarily, a key question to be answered in determining whether a theory or technique is scientific knowledge that will assist the trier of fact will be whether it can be (and has been) tested. . . . "[T]he criterion of the scientific status of a theory is its falsifiability, or refutability, or testability."
>
> Another pertinent consideration is whether the theory or technique has been subjected to peer review and publication. Publication . . . is not a sine qua non of admissibility; it does not necessarily correlate with reliability . . . and in some instances well-grounded but innovative theories will not have been published. . . . But submission to the scrutiny of the scientific community is a component of "good science," in part because it increases the likelihood that substantive flaws in methodology will be detected. . . . The fact of publication (or lack thereof) in a peer-reviewed journal thus will be a relevant, though not dispositive, consideration in assessing the scientific validity of a particular technique or methodology on which an opinion is premised.
>
> Additionally, in the case of a particular scientific technique, the court ordinarily should consider the known or potential rate of error . . . .

Finally, "general acceptance" can yet have a bearing on the inquiry. A "reliability assessment does not require, although it does permit, explicit identification of a relevant scientific community and an express determination of a particular degree of acceptance within that community."[34]

To be sure, the status of scientific evidence in a court and its character in scientific discourse can be two quite different things, owing to the radically different nature of the respective tasks of judges and scientists. Judge Bruce Jenkins (borrowing substantially from Chief Judge Howard Markey) explored this tension in his ruling on the liability of the federal government for exposure of Utah citizens to fallout from nuclear tests at the Nevada test site.

> This court has attempted to formulate an ordered theory of decision. While the effort lacks the mathematical purity of physical theory, it is the judicial resolution of the questions raised by this case with which the court is concerned. The theory of decision melds the method of science with principles of law and public policy.
>
> "The differences between the judicial and the scientific-technological processes are profound and pervasive. Failure to recognize that difference has led to judicial expressions of frustration and an unfortunate tendency to rest judicial decisions on current, and often transient, 'truths' and 'facts' of science and technology. The purpose and function of science is to learn physical facts . . . .
>
> "The purpose and unction of law is to resolve disputes and to facilitate a structure for the organization of a just society—in a word, to provide justice.
>
> "Science normally evolves a new, general physical principle from hypotheses proven by numerous specific experiments. The normal judicial process is precisely the reverse, for, when properly conducted, it applies an existing, generally accepted moral or social value—an ethical principle—a rule of law—to a specific problem . . . ."
>
> In the law, as in science, one always faces uncertainty. This court, faced with the duty of judgment in this case, does not have the luxury of the zealous absolutists who "know beyond doubt" that each and every cancer in the Great Basin is the result of open air atomic testing, or of their absolutist counterparts who "know beyond doubt" that none resulted. The court is disciplined by the record and the application of rules of law.
>
> The court's findings of fact have a certainty that is relative to the evidence presented to the court by others. They are not fixed in absolute terms . . . . In the pragmatic world of "fact" the court passes judgment on the probable. Dispute resolution demands rational decision, not perfect knowledge.[35]

What happens with information that is or might be offered as evidence matters for a variety of obvious reasons, but also for reasons that might not be readily apparent. To take one example, public managers can very well find themselves facing demands for information that they cannot reveal because of a legal settlement that included in its terms a ban against disclosure. This kind of problem can occur, for example, in sexual harassment cases where a variety of people with obvious concerns become angry at an administrator who cannot provide information about a person or event because there was a settlement in which the organization and parties agreed not to disclose. As Chapter 8 indicated, such nondisclosure agreements are increasingly common and are one of the attractive features of alternative dispute resolution techniques. They do, however, raise difficult questions from a public access to information perspective since there is often a suspicion that the parties were deliberately burying information that should be available to the public. Similarly, so-called SLAPP suits (Strategic Lawsuits Against Public Participation), brought by powerful organizations against citizens who complain about such activities as private commercial developments and their potential impact on the environment and community life can coerce citizen commentators into settlements that bar future speech, even if it would be protected from governmental censorship by the First Amendment.[36] At the same time, there is increasing concern that evidentiary processes are being used to acquire vast amounts of detailed information about people's private lives that is then spread across television screens around the world.

Another issue of status important to public managers concerns whether the information qualifies as private property, since property is protected by patent and copyright laws as well as constitutionally secured against a taking by government for public use without just compensation.[37] In addition to the information stored in information systems, the software they employ and even the algorithms on which that software is constructed can become property. The creative materials produced for computers or for use on the Internet fall into the category of intellectual property.[38] Much of the law that affects that kind of property is unclear and continually under development. Indeed, an entirely new field known as Internet law is currently evolving. But these issues are not simply exotic curiosities to be resolved in esoteric lawyerly debates. They manage to find their way into public administration.

Consider, for example, the debate over the regulation of encryption technology during the 1990s. Encryption programs are devices used to provide security for computer transmissions and management of Internet commerce. Such programs are also used to protect data within systems and the systems themselves against attack by hackers, thieves, or saboteurs. Because they perform such vital tasks, the encryption programs are valuable commodities that are sold around the world. The U.S. government has had two concerns. First, law enforcement and intelligence services do not want software developers selling products that will help criminals and terrorists hide their activities more effectively than they already do. There is evidence that they have already done precisely that.[39] Hence, there have been efforts to require software developers to provide so-called keys to the encryption systems to be held in safe hands unless a situation arises in which government can meet requirements roughly equivalent to those needed for a telephone wire tap. Officials could then use the keys to access the information. Without the keys, the firms could not sell their products domestically or receive an export license to market them abroad. Manufacturers counter that companies around the world are already marketing such programs without giving keys to the government, and to place such requirements on American firms will simply drive them out of a market in which they have every right to participate.

Finally, whatever its form or origins, it is always important for public managers to be alert to whether a particular information policy issue presents questions of freedom of expression, search and seizure issues, or threats to the right to privacy that fall within the protections afforded by the U.S. Constitution. Indeed, these protections against government intrusion lie at the very core of the system of information policy.

THE SYSTEM OF INFORMATION POLICY

Precisely because our information practice laws are diverse and fragmented, it is useful to think of them as elements in a system of information policy.[40] It is a system with a number of constitutional and statutory elements. These provisions are interrelated and overlap. Unfortunately they also sometimes conflict.

It is an open system that is continually affected by a wide range of changes in the environment. The national system is described below, but states have similar systems about which more will be said later in the chapter. The system can be envisaged as a set of concentric circles at the center of which are its constitutional elements (see Figure 11.1).

Constitutional Elements

At the heart of the system are constitutional elements drawn from the language of the Constitution and Supreme Court interpretations of its articles and amendments. These elements include provisions that ensure a representative and deliberative form of government with specifically protected rights of

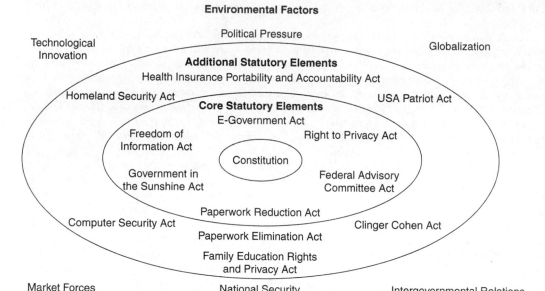

FIGURE 11.1   The System of Information Policy

expression and political action. Also included are the constitutional protection of privacy and prohibitions against unreasonable searches and seizures. This Fourth Amendment protection is afforded to private citizens and organizations, both commercial and political, in administrative as well as in criminal contexts. While the language of the Bill of Rights speaks principally of limitations on the powers of the federal government, the restrictions apply to the states and local governments under the Fourteenth Amendment.

The Constitution contains a number of clauses supporting the deliberative processes essential to our governance. The state of the union requirement, the congressional journal mandate, and the audits and accounts clause all support that process. It is, however, clearly the First Amendment that provides the most direct protection for democratic exchange. Indeed, some scholars of freedom of expression, led by Alexander Meiklejohn, have regarded freedom of speech as a means to the end of self-government and not as an end in itself. Meiklejohn wrote: "The principle of freedom of speech springs from the necessities of the program of self-government. It is not a Law of Nature or of Reason in the abstract. It is a deduction from the basic American agreement that public issues shall be decided by universal suffrage."[41] For him, the speaker was far less important than the message and the need of listeners to hear it. "Now, in the method of political self-government, the point of ultimate interest is not the words of the speakers, but the minds of the hearers . . . . What is essential is not that everyone shall speak, but that everything worth saying shall be said."[42]

From those premises flow two sets of concerns. The first is that government may not interfere with the efforts of individual citizens to exercise their freedom of expression. The Supreme Court has held that the same logic requires protection of freedom of association and the maintenance of privacy in those associations.[43] Those premises supported a range of decisions precluding wide-ranging information collection efforts concerning public employees. They also set limits on the scope of investigations that government may undertake into political groups. Furthermore, the Court has read those guarantees as protecting the expenditure of funds to advance political beliefs and limiting government to regulate them.[44]

Second, some First Amendment scholars have gone so far as to contend that government has an affirmative obligation to enhance free expression. Emerson insisted that government must "undertake positively to promote and encourage freedom of expression, as by furnishing facilities, eliminate the media of communication, or making information available."[45] In reality, the Supreme Court has not gone quite that far, but has fashioned what it has termed a free-flow theory of the First Amendment. The principal elements of this doctrine include the expectation that the First Amendment: (1) guarantees the rights of listeners as well as speakers; (2) protects the message itself regardless of its source as well as the process by which it is conveyed; (3) bars government from attempting to limit the stock of information available to the public by efforts to block communications; and (4) requires some assurance of access to information.

There are several caveats that have a significant impact upon day-to-day administration. The first is that there is a distinction between speech and action. Action may be limited where simple speech would be protected. For example, the First Amendment supports criticism of government programs, but it does not protect people who destroy records they are required by statute or valid agency rules to maintain.[46] The second concerns the so-called public forum doctrine. Under this line of cases, the Court has held that not all government offices and channels are presumptively open. The Court has, for example, upheld prohibitions of the practice by a community association of distributing its newsletters to neighbors by placing them in residents' mailboxes; a ban on union circulars to teachers in school mailboxes; and limitations on access by certain groups to participation in the benefits of contributions developed under the Combined Federal Campaign.[47] While the Court has recognized some claims under the First Amendment for access to information, it has rejected the idea that this constitutional provision is a kind of freedom of information act.

Third, the Court has traditionally allowed more flexibility for regulation where children might be involved.[48] Thus, while broadcasting is protected by the First Amendment, it has been treated differently from print journalism such that greater regulation has been permitted.[49] At the same time, the arrival of the Internet—and the fact that children have both the skills and the access to travel around the world to websites that their parents and the community would prefer that they not see—has raised new issues. Congress attempted to control what it referred to as indecent materials on the Internet that could reach children. However, the Supreme Court struck down that portion of the Communications Decency Act of 1996 as vague and overly broad.[50] In so doing, Justice Stevens, writing for the majority observed:

> In order to deny minors access to potentially harmful speech, the CDA effectively suppresses a large amount of speech that adults have a constitutional right to receive and to address to one another. That burden on adult speech is unacceptable if less restrictive alternatives would be at least as effective in achieving the legitimate purpose that the statute was enact to serve.[51]

Congress then worked to tailor the policy to address those concerns when it enacted the Child Online Protection Act (COPA). The Court rejected a challenge to the law on its face insofar as it allowed the use of community standards as a basis for a determination that material was harmful to children and therefore violated the act.[52] However, the Court then upheld a preliminary injunction against the COPA because Congress failed to use the least restrictive alternative. The lower court found that the use of blocking and filtering software would have allowed more carefully tailored protection for children while censoring less material for adults.[53]

The Supreme Court has also carved out exceptions from some of these protections where the government lays restrictions on organizations or programs receiving government funds. It upheld government restrictions that prohibited federally funded family planning programs from providing any information regarding abortion services, even if it was requested by a patient, while allowing the clinics to provide information on full-term delivery services.[54] It also upheld controversial restrictions on funding for the National Endowment for the Arts that prohibit support for exhibits considered indecent.[55] And, returning to the Internet issue, the Court rejected a challenge to the Children's Internet Protection Act that removed federal funding for Internet access from libraries that failed to install filtering software on their computers.[56]

Rulings in the field of search and seizure are of great interest on a day-to-day basis to many public managers. The statutes administered by agencies and the ordinances of local communities frequently require businesses or individuals to maintain files for examination or make their premises available for inspection or both. To assist administrators in their enforcement activities, agencies are often given investigatory power by the same statutes. As in all areas of administrative law, the power of an agency is circumscribed by the statutes governing its operations. There are numerous situations in which these statutory inspection duties present possible constitutional issues concerning the Fourth Amendment prohibition of unreasonable searches and seizures.

Debates about administrative inspection powers developed during World War II when agencies were called upon to monitor rigorous domestic rationing programs and economic controls. From that time through the 1950s arguments continued as to whether the Fourth Amendment search and seizure protections applied to administrative as well as to criminal matters. Indeed, the Supreme Court ruled in *Franks v. Maryland,* in 1959, that administrative searches were not covered by the constitutional provision.[57]

The commonly accepted view was that the Fourth and Fifth Amendments were designed to protect criminal defendants. The history turns out to be considerably more complex than that and not particularly helpful at this point in our national development. Moreover, if we assume that the major premise behind the Bill of Rights is to protect citizens from intrusion into their ideas, papers, possessions, and homes, then the violation is the same whether it is a police officer or an administrative inspector who knocks on the door.

In 1967, the Supreme Court rejected the narrower conception and reversed its *Franks v. Maryland* decision in *Camara v. Municipal Court,* holding that the Fourth Amendment does apply in administrative contexts.[58] In a companion case, *See v. Seattle*, the Court ruled that the search and seizure provisions apply to commercial property as well as private residences.[59] While the federal courts have sought to maintain the basic Fourth Amendment protections against unreasonable searches and seizures, they have authorized a variety of exceptions based on a rule of reasonableness that seek to accommodate the information gathering efforts required to carry out regulatory programs.

Examples of permissible searches include situations in which "no-notice" inspections are a central part of a program that is not punitive in nature and cases involving inspections of businesses that are traditionally closely regulated. The latter include such activities as weapons or liquor sales or the operation of automobile junkyards.[60] The question of no-notice inspections and nonpunitive purpose arose in *Wyman v. James*.[61] This case challenged no-notice visits by social workers to the homes of families receiving Aid to Families with Dependent Children (since amended and now known as Temporary Assistance to Needy Families [TANF]). Refusal to permit such visits meant an end to the benefits. The Court found that this kind of visit was not punitive but rehabilitative and necessary to ensure the welfare of the children. Moreover, the parent could refuse the visit and forfeit the benefits, so the visit was not a search against the will of the resident. Critics promptly challenged the Court on grounds that it was violating the doctrine of unconstitutional conditions by making receipt of public benefits contingent upon the surrender of constitutional rights.

In general, the Fourth Amendment prohibits unreasonable searches and seizures, where unreasonable is defined as lacking a valid search warrant. The Supreme Court has indicated, however, that the standard of probable cause needed for administrative officials to obtain a warrant may be substantially less rigorous than those employed in criminal cases.[62] It is enough, for example, that an agency demonstrates that a firm is scheduled for inspection as part of a regular program of monitoring and demonstrates that the inspection program has safeguards to ensure against arbitrariness and harassment. For instance, the Occupational Safety and Health Administration argued that it should be permitted to make warrantless surprise inspections because effective regulatory enforcement would be stifled if it was necessary to delay action until a warrant could be obtained. For one thing, firms in violation may temporarily clean up problem situations if they know inspectors are coming, only to let the violations develop again once the inspector leaves. The Supreme Court struck down the OSHA inspection program because the agency's enabling act had not clearly indicated a legislative recognition of a need for warrantless surprise inspections, nor did it provide adequate guidelines to protect against abuses.[63] However, the Court upheld an inspection program under the Federal Mine Safety and Health Act, concluding that the legislative history demonstrated specific congressional insistence that a surprise inspection system was essential to the specific enforcement needs of the mine safety program. Moreover, the Court found the inspection program provided sufficient certainty and regularity to avoid arbitrariness.[64]

The Court expanded the range of options available to agencies in its decision in *Dow Chemical v. United States*.[65] In *Dow,* the Court held that aerial photography of an industrial facility conducted without a warrant is not a violation of the Fourth Amendment prohibition of unreasonable searches and seizures. The Court concluded:

> When Congress invests an agency with enforcement and investigatory authority, it is not necessary to identify explicitly each and every technique that may be used in the course of executing the statutory mission . . . .
> Regulatory or enforcement authority generally carries with it all the modes of inquiry and investigation traditionally employed or useful to execute the authority granted . . . .[66]

The controlling standard for warrantless administrative search and seizure cases involving businesses that are traditionally closely regulated was set forth in *New York v. Burger,* a case concerning a search of a junkyard by local officers routinely assigned to monitor the records and facilities of auto recyclers to discourage handling of stolen property.

> This warrantless inspection, however, even in the context of a pervasively regulated business, will be deemed to be reasonable only so long as three criteria are met. First, there must be a "substantial" government interest that informs the regulatory scheme pursuant to which the inspection is made . . . .
> Second, the warrantless inspections must be "necessary to further [the] regulatory scheme." . . . For example, in *Dewey* we recognized that forcing mine inspectors to obtain a warrant before every inspection might alert mine owners or operators to the impending inspection, thereby frustrating the purposes of the . . . Act . . . .
> Finally, "the statute's inspection program, in terms of the certainty and regularity of its application, [must] provid[e] a constitutionally adequate substitute for a warrant." . . . In other words, the regulatory statute must perform the two basic functions of a warrant: it must advise the owner of the commercial premises that the search is being made pursuant to the law and has a properly defined scope, and it must limit the discretion of the inspecting officers. To perform this first function, the statute must be "sufficiently comprehensive and defined that the owner of commercial property cannot help but be aware that his property will be subject to periodic inspections undertaken for specific purposes." . . . In addition, in defining how a statute limits the discretion of the inspectors, we have observed that it must be "carefully limited in time, place, and scope."[67]

These rules apply not only to searches but also in some cases to seizures, such as a seizure by the Food and Drug Administration of veterinary medicines from a manufacturer.[68] That approach has been held to apply even in some cases in which a person is seized, as in the case coming from Lynn, Massachusetts, in which police kicked in a door and assisted in the seizure of a woman under an involuntary commitment order.[69] These actions may be bolstered where there is an emergency situation.[70]

One of a growing variety of challenges to administrative searches and seizures has involved airport passenger screening. While there are likely to continue to be cases brought to test the specific procedures used, to this point at least, the general position in the federal courts that have considered the issue is that these screening processes are valid administrative searches.[71]

However, there are two sets of circumstances that have become increasingly common where judicial responses have been less permissive. If a judge is of the view that the real purpose of an administrative search is to serve as a cover for criminal investigations or, more generally, if it appears that otherwise standard building and health code inspections are being used for other purposes, lines will be drawn.[72] Thus, for example, it has become an attractive tactic for communities seeking to clear out so-called "crack houses" or gang meeting places to attempt to use emergency inspections and condemnations. However, if the circumstances are such that it has employed readily obtainable administrative search warrants and ensured minimum due process requirements, a local government may find itself in difficulties.

Another major means of obtaining information is the use of subpoenas. Unlike the search warrant, the subpoena calls upon the person who is the object of the order to produce evidence rather than permitting the official to take it. Even assuming that an agency is granted subpoena power by its enabling act, it must go to court to obtain compliance since the subpoena is enforced through the contempt power.

> The requirements for enforcement of an administrative subpoena are not onerous. In order to obtain judicial backing the agency must prove that (1) the subpoena is issued a congressionally authorized purpose, the information sought is (2) relevant to the authorized purpose and (3) adequately described, and (4) proper procedures have been employed in issuing the subpoena.[73]

The fact that subpoenas require judicial enforcement emphasizes an important distinction between the subpoena and the search warrant. The warrant can be obtained in an *ex parte* proceeding (without the intended target of the warrant present) and, once issued, can be enforced over the objection of the subject of the warrant. By contrast, the target of a subpoena may ask a court to quash the order on grounds that the request is beyond the authority of the issuing agency or that the evidence called for is not relevant to the purpose of the investigation. The principal reason for using the warrant as opposed to the subpoena is to catch someone off guard and prevent them from moving or destroying evidence.[74]

The availability of subpoenas has raised an interesting question. Can subpoenas be used to obtain material about an organization or a person that is in someone else's possession? In one such case, the Supreme Court permitted the acquisition of records in the custody of an accountant over objections that the real target of the investigation was effectively self-incriminated in violation of the Fifth Amendment.[75] Another case produced an even better picture of how important a third-party subpoena power can be.

In *United States v. Miller*, the Court held constitutional the practice of obtaining records through a subpoena issued to a bank instead of by acquiring a warrant, and without giving the individual involved either notice or an opportunity to object.[76] Under the provisions of the inappropriately entitled Bank Secrecy Act of 1970, banks are required to develop and maintain microform records of deposits, withdrawals, canceled checks, and bank drafts, as well as account information on anyone with access to a bank account. Congress justified the record-keeping statute as useful in criminal, tax, and regulatory investigations.[77]

Mr. Miller was arrested for producing liquor without a proper license and for violation of tax laws. It seems that the local fire department arrived at a warehouse fire only to find that the blaze came from a distillery that had exploded. The authorities found Miller, the burning still, and gallons of whiskey with no tax stamp. The authorities, seeking more evidence to demonstrate that Miller had been selling the liquor, subpoenaed records from the banks in which Miller maintained accounts. Following his conviction, Miller's attorney appealed, arguing that the records were held in confidence by the bank for the account holder. Removing the records without a warrant and without notice or an opportunity to object was, he asserted, an unreasonable search and seizure within the meaning of the Fourth Amendment.

The Court ruled against Miller. In so doing, it went far beyond merely upholding the particular government action involved. It held that there is no expectation of privacy in financial records such as bank statements or canceled checks. "Even if we direct our attention to the original checks and deposit slips, rather than to the microfilm copies actually viewed and obtained by means of the subpoena, we perceive no legitimate expectation of privacy in their contents."[78]

In addition to the other provisions discussed above, the due process clause has also been asserted as an element of the system of information law protecting individuals against certain kinds of uses of information in the government's possession. It has been alleged that release of unproven allegations of damaging information can harm one's reputation. For example, the Court found a due process violation where county authorities had a woman's picture and name posted at liquor outlets with instructions not to sell to her even though she had never had a hearing finding her an alcohol abuser.[79]

However, in a later case, the Court decided a quite similar situation in a very different way, with significant consequences for government information policy.[80] In this case, Louisville police circulated bulletins to businesses in the area identifying several individuals as "active shoplifters." Mr. Davis sued on grounds that he was not a shoplifter and had never been convicted of shoplifting. He further asserted that this "designation would inhibit him from entering business establishments for fear of being suspected of shoplifting and possibly apprehended, and would seriously impair his future employment opportunities."[81] He sought damages and an injunction to prevent police from further distribution of the bulletins. Justice Rehnquist, writing for the Court, held:

> While we have in a number of our prior cases pointed out the frequently drastic effect of the "stigma" which may result from defamation by the government in a variety of contexts, this line of cases does not establish the proposition that reputation alone, apart from some more tangible interests such as employment, is either "liberty" or "property" by itself sufficient to invoke the procedural protections of the Due Process Clause.[82]

The breadth of the opinion worried dissenters in the case, seemingly encouraging irresponsible use of damaging information.

There is a constitutional right to privacy, most often presented in cases involving the family, procreation, and abortion.[83] Although that right could potentially be asserted as a limitation on government's power to acquire some types of information, particularly in the area of marriage or procreation, it has not figured prominently in information policy debates to date. Rather, protection of privacy has been largely left to statutes.

The Statutory Elements

In addition to the constitutional elements of the system of information law, legislatures have developed a variety of statutory elements. Like the constitutional features, the statutes are principally intended to support the deliberative processes of government and to protect privacy.

There are in truth two rings of fair information practices statutes (see Figure 11.1). The inner ring can be viewed as a core set of relatively general protections for appropriate information practices. The outer ring is consists of an ad hoc collection of laws adopted more recently that were designed to plug holes in the system of information policy and bring it up to date. While the history of several of these enactments can be traced further back, most of the inner ring elements were adopted or strengthened during the 1970s in the aftermath of Watergate and other instances of information abuse, while the outer ring enactments came about primarily in the 1980s and 1990s.

The Inner Ring of Fair Information Policy   The inner ring includes the Freedom of Information, the Right to Privacy Act, the Government in the Sunshine Act, the Paperwork Reduction Act, the Federal Advisory Committee Act, and the E-Government Act. Together, these statutes, and their state level equivalents, provide the essential fabric of fair information policy.

The Privacy Act of 1974 developed in the wake of Watergate-era disclosures about abuses of agency information collection and dissemination practices.[84] Like the federal law, the state privacy acts were often adopted as amendments to the state administrative procedure acts. The essential principles shaping the sections of the Privacy Act of 1974 were summarized by the President's Commission on Privacy:

1. There shall be no personal-data record-keeping system whose very existence is secret and there shall be a policy of openness about an organization's personal data record-keeping policies, practices and systems. (The Openness Principle)

2. An individual about whom information is maintained by a record-keeping organization in individually identified form shall have a right to see and copy that information. (The Individual Access Principle)

3. An individual about whom information is maintained by a record-keeping organization shall have a right to correct or amend the substance of that information. (The Individual Participation Principle)

4. There shall be limits on the types of information an organization may collect about an individual, as well as certain requirements with respect to the manner in which it collects such information. (The Collection Limitation Principle)

5. There shall be limits on the internal uses of information about an individual within a record-keeping organization. (The Use Limitation Principle)

6. There shall be limits on the external disclosures of information about an individual a record-keeping organization may make. (The Disclosure Limitation Principle)

7. A record-keeping organization shall bear an affirmative responsibility for establishing reasonable and proper information management policies and practices which assure its collection, maintenance, use, and dissemination of information about an individual is necessary and lawful and the information itself is current and accurate. (The Information Management Principle)

8. A record-keeping organization shall be accountable for its personal-data record-keeping policies, practices, and systems. (The Accountability Principle)[85]

The principal statutory devices for supporting public debate about government performance and substantive policy questions are the Freedom of Information Act (FOIA),[86] the Government in the Sunshine Act,[87] and the Federal Advisory Committee Act (FACA).[88] Following enactment of the original version of the FOIA, the U.S. Attorney General summarized the policy goals of the act as follows:

1. that disclosure be the general rule, not the exception;

2. that all individuals have equal rights of access;

3. that the burden should be on government to justify the withholding of a document, not on the person requesting it;

4. that individuals improperly denied access to a document should have a right to seek injunctive relief in the courts; and

5. that there should be a fundamental shift in the attitudes and policies regarding government information of those in positions of responsibility.[89]

The FOIA has been the subject of considerable debate since it was strengthened in 1974. Its supporters point to a variety of cases in which reporters and others were able to uncover important evidence concerning government abuses or to obtain information important to pending public policy debates. However, they have been critical of the issuance of complex procedures for identifying documents and processing requests by various agencies. Finally, there have been criticisms that the courts have granted too much deference to administrative agencies in interpreting the various exemptions from disclosure listed in the act. Indeed, one examination in the mid-1980s demonstrated that a decade after it had been strengthened the Supreme Court had ruled in favor of disclosure in only two of the nineteen FOIA cases it has decided.[90] Critics charge that the situation did not improve even after that in spite of the fact that a number of amendments have been enacted which were intended to make the FOIA process less burdensome and more effective.[91]

The issues surfaced because of concerns about the costs and complexities that can arise when one submits an FOIA request and the tendency of some agencies to rely often on the exemptions in the statute that permit them to withhold information. One of the most important of the exemptions concerns national security–related information. The standards for determining what information should be classified are prescribed by the president through an executive order. And once an agency, domestic or otherwise, attaches a classification to documents, the FOIA is unlikely to be useful in obtaining the information even if it is improperly classified. A Department of Justice survey concluded in the 1980s found that "in no instance has an appellate court upheld, on the substantive merits of the case, a decision to reject an agency's classification claim."[92]

Professor Lotte Feinberg has explained that the way that security classifications are controlled and the general attitude of particular administrations toward disclosure of information have affected the utility of the FOIA over time.[93] The Carter administration was of the view that too much had been held in secret, undermining public confidence and supporting the suspicion that the secret stamp was often used not to protect national security but to protect people in government. After a participative process later praised by Congress, the administration issued Executive Order 12065, providing for more information release and shifting the presumption in favor of disclosure of information as an administration-wide policy. The Reagan administration not only took the position that the Carter move was a bad idea, but that, if anything, classification controls needed to be tightened. It did just that in Executive Order 12356, which most assuredly was not developed in a participative process.[94] Feinberg points out that the FOIA amendments of 1986 were implemented amidst all of this activity. While these provisions appeared to relax requirements, overall "more categories of records could now be exempted, and it became easier to meet the exemption standard."[95] Not only that, but the Justice Department was instructed to vigorously defend agencies facing FOIA litigation.[96] The George H. W. Bush administration continued those policies and, as Chapter 10 indicated, asserted executive privilege in such high visibility areas as the Quayle Commission activities.

The Clinton administration switched course again, issuing a Executive Order 12958, which once more shifted the presumption in favor of declassification and disclosure. However, Feinberg points out that terrorist incidents at home and abroad, such as the Oklahoma City bombing, brought a tightening in some areas as law enforcement and investigative powers were expanded. Such activities also fit within FOIA exemptions. Moreover, the Clinton administration's first White House counsel took an aggressive approach to demands on the administration for access to information and interposed significant executive privilege claims in such areas as the operations of the health care task force dispute that also involved First Lady Hillary Rodham Clinton.

The George W. Bush administration moved dramatically to control information flow in a variety of ways. While criticisms of the effort to maintain an extremely tight control over information by Congress, the news media, and others have often been met with references to the post-9/11 world, the fact is that many of the information constraints had nothing to do with national security and reach far beyond it to what the administration referred to as its power to "control the unitary executive." The administration has been very direct about its refusal to provide information, at least to those who read the administration statements carefully. Thus, the administration issued a host of presidential signing statements that signed legislation into law, but rejected on constitutional grounds the language and requirements contained in the new law. In these statements, the president made it clear that the administration would decide for itself when and what information it would provide in virtually any area of public policy. During the administration's first four years in office, the president asserted the power to supervise the unitary executive 82 times, a claim to exclusive power over foreign affairs 77 times, sole control over the authority to make recommendations to Congress 54 times, the claimed authority to determine and impose national security classification and withhold information 48 times, the claimed power to keep secret deliberate processes of the executive branch 39 times, the commander-in-chief powers 37 times, rejection of mandatory report or approval from Congress 22 times, and unimpeded authority to conduct negotiations for foreign affairs 15 times. In all, the White House rejected some 505 legislative provisions. The president rejected those parts of the legislation but signed the files into law nonetheless.[97] Many of the reasons stated in this list were employed to reject or interpret (as the administrative decided was appropriate) provisions of the new statutes requiring that information be provided by the administration, including formal requirements for the issuance of reports. The following is fairly typical of the statements used to warn that the administration would control information as it wished, statutory language to the contrary notwithstanding:

> The executive branch does not construe this provision to impose any independent or affirmative requirement to share such information with the Congress or the Comptroller General and shall construe it in any event in a manner consistent with the constitutional authorities of the President to supervise the unitary executive branch and to withhold information the disclosure of which could impair foreign relations, the national security, the deliberative processes of the Executive, or the performance of the Executive's constitutional duties.[98]

It was for these reasons that Republicans as well as Democrats have expressed frustration with the G. W. Bush administration's overall approach to the release of information.[99]

One of the things that has happened during the G. W. Bush years, perhaps not surprisingly, is a dramatic increase in FOIA information demands. The GAO reported in 2005 that: "In fiscal year 2004, the 25 agencies we reviewed [which handled 97 percent of all federal FOIA requests] reported receiving and processing about 4 million requests, an increase of 25 percent compared to 2003. From 2002 to 2004, the number of requests received increased by 71 percent, and the number of requests processed increased by 68 percent."[100]

As in so many things, the Internet has played a role in how the FOIA operates and who requests and obtains what kinds of information. The 1996 amendments to the FOIA, common known as the "e-FOIA Act," sought to reduce the need for individualized requests by making more information more readily available on agency websites through what are termed "electronic reading rooms" that post information that has been disclosed through the FOIA process and that has frequently been requested. Agencies were also to make available information of various types, including material about how the agency processes FOIA requests and the requirements for making such requests.[101]

In fact, the U.S. Department of Justice now reports on FOIA cases and practices in online postings. The DOJ points out that one of the most important changes in recent years in FOIA administration has been the use of contractors by agencies to do the work of processing FOIA claims.

> [D]epartments and agencies that make use of contractors in their FOIA operations give them a significant share of their total FOIA work. At the newly created Department of Homeland Security, for example, contractors perform approximately one-third of all headquarters FOIA work. The same is true at the Department of State, where contractors likewise undertake a wide range of FOIA activities. Similarly, at the PBGC, a much smaller agency, the ideal staff consists of two contractor employees out of a total of five or six FOIA personnel, and at the Justice Department's Executive Office for United States Attorneys, eight out of twenty-six FOIA personnel are contractor employees. At the main FOIA office, both of the Department of the Interior and of one of its sub-agencies, the Bureau of Land Management ("BLM"), contractors perform approximately half of the overall work. Surprisingly, one agency where contractor personnel play no direct role in the actual processing of FOIA requests is the Department of Energy—an agency heavily laden with contractors elsewhere—where contractors perform strictly clerical duties in support of FOIA processing.
>
> Indeed, at most agencies that now use contractors to support their FOIA operations, the scope of FOIA duties performed by contractors is nearly as broad as of those performed by government employees....[102]

"Thus," according to DOJ, "for a variety of reasons, perhaps most especially due to recent movements toward privatizing the work of government in general, the use of contractors in the processes of FOIA administration now has become a large part of the FOIA landscape and is likely to remain so for some time to come."[103]

Of course, the FOIA is not the only statute intended to facilitate the free flow of information. Another of the open-government statutes is the Government in the Sunshine Act of 1976.

The Sunshine Act has the goal of opening meetings of collegial bodies "composed of two or more individual members, a majority of whom are appointed to such positions by the President with the advice and consent of the Senate, and any subdivision thereof authorized to act on behalf of the agency."[104] Clearly, that definition automatically excludes many important meetings from the requirements of the statute. For those meetings that are covered, the act requires published announcements of meetings, prior justification for conducting closed sessions, preparation and maintenance of complete records of meetings held, whether open or closed, and an annual reporting of compliance.

State sunshine acts vary widely, from those modeled on the federal version to others that are much broader and are not limited to collegial bodies. States actually developed the so-called sunshine laws before the federal government, with Florida providing particularly aggressive policies in the area. Some of the state statutes apply the same rules to local government bodies as they do to state agencies, with sometimes complex results. If the requirements at the state level are not sensitive to the small size of local governing bodies, they can produce traps for local officials in which an informal conversation can suddenly qualify as a meeting within the meaning of sunshine requirements. Of course, the difficulty is that sunshine laws were intended, in some states at least, to cut off what may have appeared to be friendly conversations but were in fact the settings in which key decisions were made outside the public eye. This tension can be avoided, but it is a sensitive area.

The Federal Advisory Committee Act (FACA) recognizes the importance of advisory committees in government decisionmaking. Advisory committees are collections of experts, interest group representatives, or other interested parties assembled by the administrative agencies or the chief executive to provide advice either on an ad hoc basis or as a continuing body. The FACA is intended to foster fairness and openness in the operation of those groups that provide government with vital information.[105] Henry Steck summarized the purposes of the act as follows:

> First, the Act is a committee management law designed to create an orderly set of standards and uniform procedures for regulating the establishment, operation, administration, and duration of advisory committees . . . . Second, the Act is a "sunshine law" requiring that "Congress and the public should be kept informed with respect to the number, purpose, membership, activities, and cost of advisory committees . . . ." Third, the Act is a fair balance law. It requires that the membership of advisory committees be "fairly balanced in terms of points of view represented and the functions to be performed."[106]

The United States Circuit Court of Appeals for the D.C. Circuit provided a slightly more detailed explanation in a case challenging operations of the Health Care Task Force (headed by then First Lady, now Senator, Hillary Rodham Clinton), one of the few FACA cases that has become widely known.

> Congress passed FACA in 1972 to control the growth and operation of the "numerous committees, boards, commissions, councils, and similar groups which have been established to advise officers, and agencies in the executive branch of the Federal Government." . . . As Congress put it, FACA's purpose was: to eliminate unnecessary advisory committees; to limit the formation of new committees to the minimum number necessary; to keep the functions of the committees advisory in nature; to hold the committees to uniform standards and procedures; and to keep Congress and the public informed of their activities . . . . The statute orders agency heads to promulgate guidelines and regulations to govern the administration and operations of advisory committees.
>
> FACA places a number of restrictions on the advisory committees themselves. Before it can meet or take any action a committee first must file a detailed charter . . . . The committee must give advance notice in the Federal Register of any meetings . . . ; and it must hold all meetings in public . . . . Under section 10, the committee must keep detailed minutes of each meeting, . . . and make the records available—along with any reports, records, or other documents used by the committee—to the public, provided they do not fall within the exemptions of the Freedom of Information Act (FOIA) . . . . Under section 5, an advisory

committee established by the President or by legislation must be "fairly balanced in terms of the point of view represented." . . . The Act also requires that precautions be taken to ensure that the advice and recommendations of the committee "will not be inappropriately influenced by the appointing authority or by any special interest.[107]

Even more controversial than the Clinton health task force case was the adamant refusal of the George W. Bush administration to provide information on the so-called energy task force, formally known as the National Energy Policy Development Group (NEPDG), convened under the leadership of Vice President Cheney to develop energy policy proposals. Given massive profits and revelations of serious misdeeds by various players in the energy marketplace, there was increasing pressure to obtain information about the membership and activities of the NEPDG and any subcommittees or task forces associated with it that involved participants from outside the federal government. However, the resolution of the litigation that grew out of the controversy produced opinions that raise serious questions about the effectiveness of the FACA in cases involving high-level advisory group operations.

Judicial Watch and the Sierra Club, two groups usually identified as being from opposite ends of the political spectrum, sued Vice President Cheney and others to obtain information concerning the NEPDG. While the groups acknowledged that President Bush had not specifically appointed any nongovernmental members to the group, they indicated that they had reason to believe that energy company officials were involved in various informal subgroups that were consulted by staff in support of the work of the NEPDG. While the district court dismissed portions of the complaint, the court concluded that it would reserve judgment on other issues pending discovery and issued orders for the production of information, indicating that the administration was, of course, free to make a formal claim of executive privilege with regard to any specific types of information that would properly limit the discovery process. The administration promptly moved to the U.S. Circuit Court of Appeals, seeking a mandamus order (an order compelling a lower court or other public official to obey the limits of the law) to prohibit the district court from compelling release of information and requiring the court to dismiss the case entirely. A panel of the D.C. Circuit refused to issue such an order. However, the Supreme Court issued an opinion that, while it did not specifically order the Court of Appeals to issue the mandamus to block further action by the district court, came very close to doing so. In the process it used language calling for considerable deference in the application of FACA claims to advisory groups set up to assist the president or vice president:

> Were the Vice President not a party in the case, the argument . . . might present different considerations. Here, however, the Vice President and his comembers on the NEPDG are the subjects of the discovery orders. The mandamus petition alleges that the orders threaten "substantial intrusions on the process by which those in closest operational proximity to the President advise the President." . . . It is well established that "a President's communications and activities encompass a vastly wider range of sensitive material than would be true of any 'ordinary individual.'" . . . As *United States v. Nixon* explained, these principles do not mean that the "President is above the law." . . . Rather, they simply acknowledge that the public interest requires that a coequal branch of Government "afford Presidential confidentiality the greatest protection consistent with the fair administration of justice," . . . and give recognition to the paramount necessity of protecting the Executive Branch from vexatious litigation that might distract it from the energetic performance of its constitutional duties.[108]

When the D.C. Circuit received the case on remand from the Supreme Court, it was heard *en banc* (by the full court). That court determined that, in light of the Supreme Court opinion, it would interpret the FACA narrowly. "We therefore hold that such a committee is composed wholly of federal officials if the President has given no one other than a federal official a vote in or, if the committee acts by consensus, a veto over the committee's decisions." Since the so-called "stakeholders" whose views were provided through staff to the NEPDG did not have either a vote or a veto, there was no FACA issue and the court ordered the district court to dismiss the Judicial Watch and Sierra Club complaints.[109]

This and future administrations now have relatively clear instructions on how to avoid the FACA if they are willing to take the steps necessary to do so.

For this and other reasons, what had been designed to be a relatively simple committee management and accountability process has turned out in practice to be one that can be complex and occasionally quite controversial. On one level, there are few difficulties when interagency committees are created to discuss complex issues, since, among other things, the members are government officials who are accountable through a variety of statutes for their actions. On the other hand, when it enacted the FACA Congress faced a long and complex history in which it was clear that there were many groups, most of whose members were not government officials and not otherwise accountable, who played key roles in the shaping of important policies—in many cases policies that would affect the members of those advisory groups directly. Thus, it should come as no surprise that negotiated rulemaking committees are designated by statute as advisory committee within the meaning of the FACA.[110]

Difficulties arise, however, where there is a desire to bring in people from the outside and avoid the burdens of disclosure, open meeting, records, and accountability requirements. Another common approach is to ask a committee of a professional group for input.[111] Similarly, governance arrangements that bring together a wide range of federal agencies, state and local government units, nonprofit organizations, and for-profit firms raise a number of potential issues for the FACA where the task of the working group is to resolve policy issues. As the discussion of negotiated rulemaking committees in Chapter 5 indicates, such arrangements can be useful, they must be managed with care if they are to avoid difficulties. While there is a natural attractiveness to these practices, the dangers of backdoor deals, undemocratic processes, and a lack of accountability are obvious.

After a thorough analysis of the operation of the FACA, consideration of challenges to it, and assessment of the impacts of the statute, Croly and Funk concluded:

> The act, however, is not only an economic bargain. It also seems to promote openness, participation, and accountability in regulatory decisionmaking, thus enhancing the political legitimacy of the administrative state. Additionally, the act helps to ensure that such participation is unbiased and evenhanded, thereby minimizing the danger of illicit influence on agency decisionmaking. These virtues are interdependent. Because self-serving advice, however cheap, is no bargain, it is crucial that balance, even-handedness, and openness continue to be promoted in advisory-committee activities.[112]

The next piece of the inner circle of information policy is the Paperwork Reduction Act (PRA). When it was originally enacted during the Carter administration, the act was named for its purpose. It was designed to constrain, and even to reduce, the seemingly insatiable demands by federal agencies for data and reports. Too often these demands seemed to pay little heed to the burdens placed upon small business, local governments, nonprofit organizations, and tribal governments. And while the PRA has had a rocky history since then, its purposes remain essentially the same:

1. Reaffirm the fundamental purpose of the Paperwork Reduction Act of 1980—to minimize the Federal paperwork burdens imposed on the public by Government;

2. Clarify that the Act applies to all Government-sponsored collections of information (including disclosure requirements), eliminating any confusion over the coverage of third-party paperwork burdens (those imposed by one private party due to a Federal regulatory mandate), caused by the U.S. Supreme Court's 1990 decision in *Dole v. United Steelworkers of America;*

3. Emphasize the fundamental responsibilities of each Federal agency to minimize paperwork burdens and foster paperwork reduction, by requiring a thorough review of each proposed collection of information for need and practical utility, the Act's fundamental standards, agency planning to maximize the use of information already available within Government or already collected by the public, and improved opportunity for public comment on a proposed paperwork requirement;

4. Seek to reduce the paperwork burdens imposed on the public through better implementation of the annual Government-wide paperwork reduction goal of 5 percent;

5. Reauthorize appropriations for the Office of Information and Regulatory Affairs (OIRA) within the Office of Management and Budget (OMB) . . . ;

6. Enhance opportunities for public participation in government decisions regarding paperwork burdens;

7. Establish policies to promote the dissemination of public information on a timely and equitable basis, and in useful forms and formats;

8. Strengthen agency accountability for managing information resources in support of efficient and effective accomplishment of agency missions and programs; and

9. Improve OIRA and other central management agency oversight of agency information resources management (IRM) policies and practices.[113]

As Chapter 10 explained, the Office of Information and Regulatory Affairs became the focus of controversy during the Reagan and Bush administrations when it was used as the headquarters of the attack on regulation and when it became the working partner of the Quayle Commission. After Congress drew a line in the sand about the OIRA use of Executive Orders 12291 and 12498 to block agency action, the office moved to use its authority under the PRA to place barriers in the way of agency rulemaking and enforcement efforts. In all of this, OIRA withheld information that Congress demanded in oversight proceedings. Part of this information had to do with contacts by regulated industries and their associations that played a part in OIRA efforts to block regulatory action. As Chapter 10 also indicated, all of these actions, and the broken deal made between OMB and Congress, meant that the PRA lapsed until well into the Clinton administration.

While all of that was pending, the Supreme Court issued a ruling in the *Dole v. Steelworkers*[114] case that read agency requirements for disclosure through product labeling so as not to fit within PRA requirements. The case was significant for a number of reasons, but most important here because in it the Court limited the reach of the act so as not to apply to such practices as requiring regulated firms to disclose product contents or provide other warnings. While the Congress was unwilling to permit the White House to continue the kinds of practices in which OIRA had been engaged in the past, neither was it any more favorably disposed toward regulation. Hence, it deliberately overturned the Supreme Court ruling and applied the paperwork constraints even to disclosure requirements. That is no small bit of irony, considering the fact that many of the same legislators who insisted that agencies move away from command and control type regulations and toward disclosure through labeling as one of the market-based alternative regulatory techniques, then promptly placed burdens in the way of implementing those very steps through the application of OIRA control under the PRA.

The Paperwork Reduction Act had an indirect effect on privacy in that it counseled reduction of data collection and provided mechanisms for the Office of Management and Budget to influence agency data collection and management practices.[115] The OIRA must approve agency requests to require submission of data in many circumstances, seeks to discourage agencies from acquiring more information than is absolutely needed, and calls for better use and management of the information that agencies already have on hand.

Like the FOIA, the PRA has seen legislation adopted to address the Internet age and the rise of e-government, about which more will be said below. The Paperwork Reduction Act has been joined by a 1998 statute entitled the Government Paperwork Elimination Act, which was included as part of the omnibus appropriations bill for FY1999.[116] This short piece of legislation encouraged the acquisition of the hardware and software systems needed for "the acquisition and use of information technology, including alternative information technologies that provide for electronic submission, maintenance, or disclosure of information as a substitute for paper and for the use and acceptance of electronic signatures."[117] It required OMB to develop procedures to facilitate electronic filing of information about employment and employees. The new law also gave these electronic records full legal force and effect.

Finally, a new key element has been added to the inner ring. It is the E-Government Act of 2002.[118] Congress announced the purposes of the act:

1. To provide effective leadership of Federal Government efforts to develop and promote electronic Government services and processes by establishing an Administrator of a new Office of Electronic Government within the Office of Management and Budget.

2. To promote use of the Internet and other information technologies to provide increased opportunities for citizen participation in Government.

3. To promote interagency collaboration in providing electronic Government services, where this collaboration would improve the service to citizens by integrating related functions, and in the use of internal electronic Government processes, where this collaboration would improve the efficiency and effectiveness of the processes.

4. To improve the ability of the Government to achieve agency missions and program performance goals.

5. To promote the use of the Internet and emerging technologies within and across Government agencies to provide citizen-centric Government information and services.

6. To reduce costs and burdens for businesses and other Government entities.

7. To promote better informed decisionmaking by policy makers.

8. To promote access to high quality Government information and services across multiple channels.

9. To make the Federal Government more transparent and accountable.

10. To transform agency operations by utilizing, where appropriate, best practices from public and private sector organizations.

11. To provide enhanced access to Government information and services in a manner consistent with laws regarding protection of personal privacy, national security, records retention, access for persons with disabilities, and other relevant laws.

The E-Government Act has four major elements. The legislation includes a framework for the management of e-government efforts, actions to promote e-government, information security elements, and consideration of issues of privacy and information sharing with regard to statistics and business data. The management structure is based on the creation of an Office of Electronic Government within OMB, a Chief Information Officer (CIO) in each agency, and a CIO Council that brings together agency CIOs with the OMB's Administrator of the Office of Electronic Government. The act seeks to draw on the private sector as a source of innovation and requires the director of OEG to "issue announcements seeking unique and innovative solutions to facilitate the development and enhancement of electronic Government services and processes." Then OEG was required to create "a multiagency technical assistance team to assist in screening proposals submitted to the Administrator to provide unique and innovative solutions to facilitate the development and enhancement of electronic Government services and processes. The team shall be composed of employees of the agencies represented on the Council who have expertise in scientific and technical disciplines that would facilitate the assessment of the feasibility of the proposals."[119] Agencies are expected to work with the OMB efforts and also to be innovative and active in their own programs to enhance the use of Internet-based information programs and services and address those efforts in their performance measurements.

Sections 202 (c) and (d) of the act require agencies to address the digital divide (discussed in several earlier chapters) in two important ways. They are to avoid diminished access. "When promulgating policies and implementing programs regarding the provision of Government information and services over the Internet, agency heads shall consider the impact on persons without access to the Internet, and shall, to the extent practicable—(1) ensure that the availability of Government information and services has not been diminished for individuals who lack access to the Internet; and (2) pursue alternate modes of delivery that make Government information and services more accessible to individuals who do not own computers or lack access to the Internet." Second, they are to ensure accessibility to people with disabilities. "All actions taken by Federal departments and agencies under this Act shall be in compliance with section 508 of the Rehabilitation Act of 1973 (29 U.S.C. 794d)." At the time of this writing, there are many issues about both diminished access and access for persons with disabilities, some of which were discussed in Chapter 5.

In addition, the act seeks to remove barriers to increased use of e-government and enhance coordination and interoperability (the ability to connect, integrate, or work across information technology systems) of federal agency websites and information systems. The act gives the General Services Administration (GSA) responsibility for working with agencies to develop online portals for government and assisting in ensuring that interoperability. In addition to this broad effort at government-wide and cross-agency access and integration, the E-Government Act addresses two specific areas for effort. It mandates Internet-based information for the federal courts and requires the opportunity for online filings of legal materials. As Chapter 5 explained in some detail, Section 206 puts the federal rulemaking process online with requirements for the rulemaking portals or Regulation.gov and RegInfo.gov as well as requiring individual agencies to establish their online dockets for rulemaking such that comments can be offered through the Internet.

Also in the area of promotion of e-government, the legislation calls for development of an e-capable federal workforce through training and establishes an "information technology exchange" program under which federal and private sector employees can be exchanged for various periods between three months and a year. It also calls for "share-in-savings" contracts for the Department of Defense for information technology contracts in which the contractor's suggestions result in cost savings and encourages the use of such contracts in other executive branch agencies. This process, commonly known in contracting circles as gain-sharing, is intended to provide an incentive for contractors to propose cost-saving measures with the savings to be split between the contractor and the government agency for which the work is being done.[120] State and local governments are authorized under the act to use the federal supply schedule to purchase IT equipment.

Section 208 of the act attempts to address some of the many privacy concerns raised about e-government and insists that "agencies implement citizen centered electronic Government." Toward that end, this portion of the act requires agencies to perform a "privacy impact assessment" before "developing or procuring information technology that collects, maintains, or disseminates information that is in an identifiable form; or (ii) initiating a new collection of information that—(I) will be collected, maintained, or disseminated using information technology; and (II) includes any information in an identifiable form permitting the physical or online contacting of a specific individual, if identical questions have been posed to, or identical reporting requirements." This assessment is to be reviewed by the agency's Chief Information Officer and, "if practicable," that assessment is to be made available to the public. The impact assessment is to explain:

I. what information is to be collected;

II. why the information is being collected;

III. the intended use of the agency for the information;

IV. with whom the information will be shared;

V. what notice or opportunities for consent would be provided to individuals regarding what information is collected and how that information is shared;

VI. how the information will be secured; and

VII. whether a system of records is being created under section 552a of title 5, United States Code, (commonly referred to as the "Privacy Act").[121]

In addition to this aspect of security, Title III of the E-Government Act is the Federal Information Security Management Act of 2002 (FISMA).[122] The FISMA defines information security as the effort to protect:

> ... information and information systems from unauthorized access, use, disclosure, disruption, modification, or destruction in order to provide—
>
> (A) integrity, which means guarding against improper information modification or destruction, and includes ensuring information nonrepudiation and authenticity;
>
> (B) confidentiality, which means preserving authorized restrictions on access and disclosure, including means for protecting personal privacy and proprietary information; and
>
> (C) availability, which means ensuring timely and reliable access to and use of information.[123]

Each agency is required to create a security program, to train and supervise its people in the implementation of the plan, and to have those security systems and procedures evaluated annually by the Inspector General or other independent auditor with reports on all of these activities to the OMB. The OMB, in turn, is required to report to the Congress annually on the state of information security in the agencies.[124]

Finally, Title V of the legislation, the Confidential Information Protection and Statistical Efficiency Act, is intended to facilitate a complex tension. On the one hand, it seeks to ensure that agencies and contractors do not disclose or use improperly information submitted to government with a promise of confidentiality, while at the same time facilitating information sharing among agencies to avoid multiple overlapping data collection efforts and to allow greater comparability across agencies. Given the history of the tensions between information sharing and privacy and the additional difficulties presented by the growing intergovernmental complexity of information systems and the expanded use of contractors in social service delivery, this aspect of e-government is likely to be an ongoing and serious challenge for the future. Those tensions are only likely to grow because at the same time that there is increasing concern about the vulnerability of sensitive information and public sector information systems, there is growing pressure in the post-9/11 environment to reduce or eliminate barriers that were created to prevent personal information to flow across systems that were intended to be separate. One clear example of this tension was the removal by the USA Patriot Act of what had been termed "the firewall" between acquisition and use of information collected in connection with international intelligence and the use of information acquired for those purposes in domestic police and prosecutorial efforts for standard criminal investigations.[125]

The Outer Ring: The Effort to Knit a Stronger Fabric of Information Policy   These general fair information practices statutes have been supplemented by a host of more focused statutory requirements. While this collection of legislation contains too many provisions to present here, the following examples give a flavor of the kinds of efforts that have been evolving in an attempt to keep pace with the rapidly changing information management field.

The Family Educational Rights and Privacy Act of 1974 extended most of the privacy protections available to adults under the Privacy Act to schoolchildren and their parents, using the threat of deprivation of federal aid to education as the sanction to enforce compliance by state and local officials.[126] However, the Supreme Court's ruling that this statute does not provide a private right of action raises serious questions about its effectiveness, particularly in light of the political difficulties that make it unlikely that the federal government would really make good on the threat to cut off federal education dollars.[127] Two other statutes, the Fair Credit Reporting Act[128] and the Right to Financial Privacy Act[129] add limited protections against abuses of information in the marketplace. The Right to Financial Privacy Act was adopted as Title XI of the Financial Institutions Regulatory and Interest Rate Control Act of 1978 in response to the Supreme Court's holding in the *United States v. Miller* case discussed earlier. The bill that was ultimately adopted is a much weaker version of the legislation that was introduced, and merely provides for notice and a limited opportunity to object to government efforts to obtain bank records.[130]

Other additions to the complex of statutes supporting privacy were adopted in response to feared and actual computer abuses discussed earlier. Among the many provisions of the Comprehensive Crime Control Act of 1984 is a section entitled the "Counterfeit Access Device and Computer Fraud and Abuse Act of 1984 (P.L. 98-473, 98 Stat. 2190)." The chapter defines three types of computer-related criminal offenses:

(a) Whoever—

(1) knowingly accesses a computer without authorization, or having accessed a computer with authorization, uses the opportunity such access provides for purposes to which such authorization does not extend, and by means of such conduct obtains information that has been determined by the United States Government pursuant to an Executive Order or statute to require protection against unauthorized disclosure for reasons of national defense or foreign relations, or any restricted data, as defined in paragraph r section 11 of the Atomic Energy Act of 1954, with the intent or reason to believe that such information so obtained is to be used in the injury of the United States, or to the advantage of any foreign nation;

(2) knowingly accesses a computer without authorization, or having accessed a computer with authorization, uses the opportunity such access provides for purposes to which such authorization does not extend, and thereby obtains information contained in a financial record or a financial institution, as such terms are defined in the Right to Privacy Act of 1978 (12 U.S.C. 3401 et seq.), or contained in a file of a consumer reporting agency on a consumer, as such terms are defined in the Fair Credit Reporting Act (15 U.S.C. 1681 et seq.); or

(3) knowingly accesses a computer without authorization, or having accessed a computer with authorization, uses the opportunity such access provides for purposes to which such authorization does not extend, and by means of such conduct knowingly uses, modifies, destroys, or discloses information in, or prevents authorized use of such computer, if such computer is operated for or on behalf of the Government of the United States and such conduct affects such operation shall be punished as provided in subsection (c) of this section . . . .

Another effort, called the Computer Security Act of 1987, required that "any information, the loss, misuse, or unauthorized access to or modification of which could adversely affect the national interest or the conduct of which could adversely affect the national interest or the conduct of Federal programs, or the privacy to which individuals are entitled under the Privacy Act, but which has not been specifically authorized under criteria established by an Executive Order or an Act of Congress to be kept secret in the interest of national defense or foreign policy." It was becoming increasingly clear that the common reliance on executive orders to define not only what fits within more or less traditional notions of classified information but also what is sensitive was inadequate.

Another major issue that elicited important legislation had to do with the growing use and sharing of health care information. Health care records contain perhaps more specifically identified personal information than any other body of information. Such records contain specific information about that person's health, employer, insurance companies, personal identifier account information (both public and private), and records of care by providers. Yet this information is demanded by insurance companies, health care providers, and government organizations on a regular basis and is frequently shared across sectoral and jurisdictional boundaries, including international boundaries over the Internet. Consider a simple example.

A patient goes to a physician for treatment in a New England state. Records are updated and recordings are provided to a firm for transcription and presentation in the correct formats. That transcription service (or its subcontractors) may operate anywhere, including in another country. The patient then indicates that she is about to move across the country for a new job. The physician's office informs the patient that she may obtain a full or a partial copy of her medical records to take with her, but that it will be necessary to complete a request that will be filled by a copying service that maintains and ships medical records. The order copy will not come from the physician's office, but from the records firm.

The patient arrives in her new home on the West Coast and processes into her new state position. She receives a bill from a Southern California firm that handled the request for her records from her former physician's office. In the meantime, she is informed that to obtain insurance over a very limited amount, she will need to have a minor physical examination in her own home by a representative of the insurance company. Concerned about her privacy and her health as well as her desire to obtain insurance to protect her family, she inquires of the customer service representatives at the insurance company about the credentials of the person who will come to her home and also, for security reasons, asks whether he or she will have a specific kind of identification to present upon arrival. The insurance company representatives apologize, but indicate that they really do not know because the examinations are handled by a contractor that operates out of Texas. The new employee calls the Texas firm, which indicates that it also does not know the answers to all of her questions because the people who provide those services in each community are individual subcontractors, some of whom are nurses and other clinical people who do this work on the side.

This real example illustrates just some of the reasons why Congress considered it necessary to enact the Health Insurance Portability and Accountability Act (HIPAA), which contains policies aimed at protecting the privacy of medical information.[131] It also shows why it has been so challenging to develop implementing regulations and procedures as well as to train all of the various people involved in the handling of this information.

But there was more at issue in a time of such dramatic technological change than just a set of specific problems in particular policy domains. That reality led Congress to enact the Electronic Freedom of Information Act Amendments of 1996 and a counterpart update for the Privacy Act known as the Computer Matching and Privacy Protection Act of 1988. The provisions of both statutes are included in the updated APA in Appendix 3. While these statutes sought to address some of the difficulties posed by the language of the FOIA and Privacy Acts, this language was becoming rapidly outdated. There was a need to describe information that ought to be disclosed but that did not fit in form or content with the traditional physical file–based conceptualization of the FOIA, and to begin to contemplate the ability to match great quantities of personal information across a variety of government databases.

It became increasingly clear, however, that attempts to deal with particular information problems could not succeed unless attention was paid to system management issues. That was all the more important because virtually all studies done on the subject indicated that there were a host of systems problems, ranging from outdated processes for acquiring and updating information technology (IT) systems to a lack of attention to information resources management (IRM), despite the fact that efforts had been underway for years to improve contracting processes and that the Paperwork Reduction Act specifically called for development of effective IRM practices. That led to a flurry of activity, at the center of which was the Information Technology Management Reform Act (ITMRA) of 1996. This statute, later termed the Clinger-Cohen Act, sought to address both the IT acquisition and IRM aspects. This effort was underway as efforts were being made in the Federal Acquisition Reform Act (FARA) and the Federal Acquisition Streamlining Act (FASA) to simplify contracting.[132] On the executive side, President Clinton issued Executive Order 13011 on Federal Information Technology and OMB revised its Circular A-130 on Management of Federal Information Resources.

Extensive reliance was placed in all of these developments on the creation of an effective cadre of Chief Information Officers (CIOs) modeled on the Chief Financial Officers (CFO) Act. These officials are brought together in a Chief Information Officers Council intended to work with OMB to develop executive branch policies and solve problems that arise across government systems. There was also created a Government Information Technology Services Board to implement National Performance Review recommendations in the IT and IRM area and an Information Technology Resources Board to seek out new problems and recommend solutions.

Many of the Clinton-era actions were altered or included in modified form in the E-Government Act described earlier. To these actions were added the changes brought about in the wake of 9/11 in the USA Patriot Act of 2001 and the Homeland Security Act of 2002, about which more will be said shortly.

Private Law Problems in the System of Information Law

Long before any of the present cluster of statutes and regulations governing information policy were developed, and well before the courts had begun to interpret constitutional provisions as a part of a loose set of information policies, private parties were discussing such issues as privacy. There are, for example, repeated references in much that has been written about privacy law in the past three decades to a seminal article by Samuel Warren and Louis Brandeis published in 1890 and entitled "The Right to Privacy."[133] At the time, the authors had a relatively narrow concern. They were interested in the use of private tort suits against those who would invade one's private life, threaten one's reputation, or snatch one's creative efforts.

Moreover, one of the tools that has been widely used to acquire information from both public and private sources is the process of discovery, carried out in connection with trials, in which private parties can invoke the power of the court to elicit data they might not otherwise obtain. Despite the considerable history of private litigation in information policy, it remains unclear just what influence these private law–based elements of the system of information law will have in the future. There is considerable distress about abuses of the discovery process, requests for excessive and often unnecessary quantities of evidence.

At some point this growing and evolving body of fair information practices laws will mature to a point at which the Congress, and state legislatures at their level, will be able to return to efforts to take a more comprehensive view. Such an effort would aim to consolidate the large number of very specific laws and reconcile their conflicting elements. It would attempt to relate the public and private sector elements, the information management aspects, and interagency and intergovernmental dimensions. In the past, such efforts at synthesis and rationalization have taken place when the key policymakers judge that the pace of change has slowed and policy can be made to catch up with it. In the information policy arena, it will be necessary to address this need for comprehensive reconsideration on the fly, as it were, since there is no realistic expectation that the technological and market-based forces that have driven the dramatic changes of recent decades are likely to slow any time soon.

WORKING WITH THE SYSTEM

As this survey of the pieces that together comprise the system of information law indicates, this is a complex and growing aspect of law and administration. It also suggests a general approach to information practices. In order to answer specific questions regarding information policy, it is essential to tie the particular provisions governing administrative activity to the more general premises of the system. If we think first about the system and the purposes it is intended to serve, determine whether the problem at hand implicates a constitutional, statutory, or private authority, retain a sense of the interrelatedness of the statutory elements, and then turn to the particular sections at issue, the whole complex picture becomes much more comprehensible. The key is not merely in interpreting the exemptions of the FOIA or the Right to Privacy Act but in making the linkages among the fragmented but interconnected pieces that make up the system.

It is also essential to bear in mind the contradictions that have evolved in the system over time. The problem is not merely the ongoing stresses created by the information paradox addressed earlier, but also the fact that the growing complexity of the system in operation is such that many public administrators, let alone private citizens, find it overwhelming. Thus, a system that was expected to both protect citizens against abuses by government as well as the private sector and to provide useful mechanisms to hold public agencies to account has become in some respects less protective and more forbidding as a tool for citizen inquiry.

CHALLENGES TO THE SYSTEM

For the present, it is clear that there will continue to be a variety of challenges to the system. Among those that are already before us, and likely will be for the foreseeable future, are the new technical environment of information policy, the global context of U.S. information management, problems of security, issues of intergovernmental complexity, the use of alternative tools of public management, and the contract factor.

The Contemporary Technical Environment of Information Policy

Technological changes have, in many important respects, rendered many information policies obsolete. There are certain elements of technological change in the information field that are likely to continue to be critical factors for such new policies as they are developed. They include issues of capacity, speed, compatibility, complexity, intrusiveness, and control.

First, there is the issue of capacity. For a long time, the sheer problem of storing information and retrieving it set constraints on just how much information could be acquired and used. File folders, filing cabinets, and bookshelves used to define an office. Three major developments have changed that. Obviously, one of the major changes is that room-sized computers gave way to desktop and even notebook personal computers and handheld devices. That brought the creation of large numbers of standalone information storage systems, the very existence of which may not be known by responsible agency officials. Even in offices that are networked, such that most software and information is shared, there are literally hundreds of individual hard drives, CD-ROMs, backup copies, and data sticks that are not on the network and are under the control of individuals. The people who may be on a networked system for official purposes have their own computers on which they can store anything they wish, whether it is legal or not. The dramatic growth in the amount of information that can be easily and inexpensively stored is not merely a quantitative difference but a qualitative change in many important respects. But beyond that, contemporary software keyed to Internet applications allows computers to call upon the memory and processing capacity of other computers, dramatically reducing the need to think in terms of storage capacity in any one computer. That same kind of capability also dramatically increases the speed at which the data can be accessed and processed.

Ironically, one of the important technological developments that has dramatically altered problems of information management is one that was intended to simplify the process. Increased compatibility across hardware and software systems was intended to created seamless systems that took advantage of state-of-the-art operations at minimum prices. However, the fact that more aspects of many systems are now compatible means that the physical and system isolation that used to protect information has rapidly disappeared. Computers attached to networks are now more vulnerable in a variety of ways than standalone systems. Networks can be monitored, backup systems accessed, and hard drives read through network capabilities.

Another feature of modern administration, the paperless office, has had similarly complex effects. For the first several years, new computers that were supposed to reduce the paper generated in offices had precisely the opposite effect. Out of fear of system crashes, staffs maintained both paper and computer records. Now that the amount of information has grown dramatically, and there is greater (indeed sometimes excessive) confidence in systems and their backup technology, paper records are being eliminated. Organizations increasingly refuse to distribute hard copy of reports, documents, and records. It was in part the elimination of alternative systems that created such panic with respect to the so-called Y2K problem. However, it also means that organizations are more vulnerable than ever to breaches of computer security.

The Security Challenge

Security has now been redefined into two very different concepts—national security and information systems as critical infrastructure subject to attack or intrusion, and personal security in the sense of protection of critical personal information. As indicated at the beginning of this chapter, despite repeated claims to the contrary, there is overwhelming empirical evidence in study after study that computer security systems simply have not kept pace with the need to simultaneously permit easy access for working with information and provide protection from abuse of those systems. Whole new kinds of information problems have emerged, such as identity theft, the now common criminal practice of using limited amounts of identification information to steal a person's identity and use it for fraudulent purposes such as false applications for benefits or access to credit. Less extreme, but, in some respects at least, just as problematic is the temptation for those with access to information about others for which they have no legitimate need to obtain and retain more information than is needed for an otherwise legitimate official function.

It is true that attempts have been made to address security problems, particularly by major federal agencies:

> In May 1996, we reported that attacks on Defense computer systems were a serious and growing threat. The exact number of attacks could not be readily determined because tests showed that only a small portion were actually detected and reported. However, the Defense Information Systems Agency estimated that attacks numbered in the hundreds of thousands per year, were successful 65 percent of the time, and that the number of attacks was doubling each year. At a minimum, these attacks are a multimillion dollar nuisance to Defense. At worst, they are a serious threat to national security. According to Defense officials, attackers have obtained and corrupted sensitive information—they have stolen, modified, and destroyed both data and software. They have installed unwanted files and "back doors" which circumvent normal system protection and allow attackers unauthorized access in the future. They have shut down and crashed entire systems and networks, denying service to users who depend on automated systems to help meet critical missions. Numerous Defense functions have been adversely affected, including weapons and supercomputer research, logistics, finance, procurement, personnel management, military health, and payroll. In March 1998, DOD announced that it had recently identified a series of organized intrusions, indicating that such events continue to be a problem.[134]

Indeed, President Clinton issued Presidential Decision Directive (PDD) 63 in 1998, terming the computer security issue a national security risk. The Directive created a National Coordinator for Security, Infrastructure Protection, and Counter-Terrorism, a Critical Infrastructure Coordination Group; and a Critical Infrastructure Assurance Office, which is housed in the Department of Commerce.

> The Directive outlines planned actions pertaining to federal information security, which include:
>
> (1) requiring each federal department and agency to develop a plan for protecting its own critical infrastructure, including its cyber-based systems;

(2) reviewing existing federal, state, and local entities charged with information assurance tasks;

(3) enhancing collection and analysis of information on the foreign information warfare threat to our critical infrastructures;

(4) establishing a National Infrastructure Protection Center within the Federal Bureau of Investigation to facilitate and coordinate the federal government's investigation and response to attacks on its critical infrastructures;

(5) assessing U.S. Government systems' vulnerability to interception and exploitation; and

(6) incorporating agency infrastructure assurance functions in agency strategic planning and performance measurement frameworks.[135]

These initiatives are primarily intended to protect against intrusions from external threats. Unfortunately, some of the most troublesome problems may arise from within in terms of abuses by those with otherwise legitimate authority to access systems. For example, while a General Accounting Office study found weaknesses in controlling unauthorized access to important personal information from the "Internal Revenue Service, the Health Care Financing Administration, the Social Security Administration, and the Department of Veterans Affairs [that] place sensitive tax, medical, and other personal records at risk of disclosure,"[136] there was only limited information regarding protections against abuses by employees of those agencies. Even so, the Social Security Administration's Inspector General reported that "29 criminal convictions involving SSA employees were obtained during fiscal year 1997, most of which involved creating fictitious identifies, fraudulently selling SSA cards, mis-appropriating refunds, or abusing access to confidential information."[137] Some private sector organizations have paid attention to these internal issues because of a concern with industrial espionage.

Since these issues that evolved in the 1990s, there have been new and expanding risks and threats. The GAO pointed out the following risks in computer systems resources, such as:

- federal payments and collections could be lost or stolen;

- computer resources could be used for unauthorized purposes or to launch attacks on others;

- sensitive information, such as taxpayer data, social security records, medical records, and proprietary business information could be inappropriately disclosed, browsed, or copied for purposes of industrial espionage or other types of crime;

- critical operations, such as those supporting national defense and emergency services, could be disrupted;

- data could be modified or destroyed for purposes of fraud, identity theft, or disruption; and

- agency missions could be undermined by embarrassing incidents that result in diminished confidence in their ability to conduct operations and fulfill their fiduciary responsibilities.[138]

Not only have the risks been expanding, there has also been evolutionary—some might say revolutionary—development of the types of threats to information systems. At present, these threats include terrorists, criminal groups, foreign intelligence services, spyware/malware authors, hackers, insider threats, botnet operators, phishers, and spammers. The GAO prepared a useful table for understanding these different threats (see Table 11.1).

The GAO has provided a continuing stream of analyses for Congress on these issues, and Congress has attempted to address some of those problems as in the passage of Controlling the Assault of Non-Solicited Pornography and Marketing (CAN-SPAM) Act of 2003.[139]

However, the threats and risks have sometimes merged, as when hackers sell their services to carry out attacks on businesses or provide software to others who intend to use it to steal identities. Terrorists can develop their own cyberforces or purchase technology of many kinds to launch attacks. Nations now use a combination of techniques to probe potential adversaries' cyber-weaknesses much in the

T A B L E 11.1 Sources of Emerging Cybersecurity Threats

Threat	Description
Terrorists	Terrorists may use phishing scams or spyware/malware in order to generate funds or gather sensitive information.
Criminal Groups	There is an increased use of cyber intrusions by criminal groups that attack systems for monetary gain; further, organized crime groups are using spam, phishing, and spyware/malware to commit identity theft and online fraud.
Foreign Intelligence Services	Foreign intelligence services use cyber tools as part of their information-gathering and espionage activities.
Spyware/Malware Authors	Individuals or organizations with malicious intent carry out attacks against users by producing and distributing spyware and malware.
Hackers	Hackers sometimes break into networks for the thrill of the challenge or for bragging rights in the hacker community. While remote cracking once required a fair amount of skill or computer knowledge, hacker scan now download attack scripts and protocols from the Internet and launch them against victim sites. Thus, while attack tools have become more sophisticated, they have also become easier to use.
Insider Threat	The disgruntled organization insider is a principal source of computer crimes. Insiders may not need a great deal of knowledge about computer intrusions because their knowledge of a target system often allows them to gain unrestricted access to cause damage to the system or to steal system data. The insider threat also includes outsourcing vendors. Employees who accidentally introduce malware into systems also fall into this category.
Botnet Operators	Botnet operators are hackers; however, instead of breaking into systems for the challenge or bragging rights, they take over multiple systems to enable them to coordinate attacks and distribute malware, spam, and phishing scams. The services of these networks are sometimes made available on underground markets (e.g., purchasing a denial-of-service attack, servers to relay spam or phishing scams, etc.).
Phishers	Individuals or small groups that execute phishing scams in an attempt to steal identities or information for monetary gain. Phishers may also use spam and spyware/malware to accomplish their objectives.
Spammers	Individuals or organizations that distribute unsolicited e-mail with hidden or false information in order to sell products, conduct phishing scams, distribute spyware/malware, or attack organizations (i.e., denial-of-service).

SOURCE: This table is reproduced from U.S. Government Accountability Office, Information Security: Emerging Cybersecurity Issues Threaten Federal Information Systems (Washington DC: GAO, 2005), Table 1, p. 13.

manner in which they used to use aircraft or ships to test for gaps in a nation's early warning radar systems.

Certainly, nothing was more significant in bringing these challenges to public awareness than the attacks on September 11, 2001. On one level, the policy actions taken in the wake of the attacks included the USA Patriot Act, Homeland Security Act, and a variety of executive direct actions taken through what the Bush administration has termed Homeland Security Directives. On another level, many of the restrictions on government agencies' acquisition of information have been either formally or informally relaxed.[140] The boundaries of intelligence gathering, both domestically and internationally, have been expanded. The Department of Homeland Security now has an important role under its legislation along with the OMB's responsibilities under the FISMA (discussed earlier). The DHS has been working through a difficult period of development and it remains to be seen just how the responsibilities for information policy will be organized.

In addition to these high visibility responses to cyberwarfare and terrorism threats, there are two particular areas of domestic policy that continue to attract policy attention because they contain such valuable and dangerous information and have had repeated difficulties in ensuring its security. The first of these issue areas is the problem of protecting tax records from intrusion by outsiders or misuse within government. Here again, studies by the Government Accountability Office have been flowing to various committees of Congress. With regard to the Internal Revenue Service, the GAO found that:

> IRS has not effectively implemented information security controls to properly protect the confidentiality, integrity, and availability of data processed by the facility's computers and networks. In addition to the 21 previously reported weaknesses that remain uncorrected, we identified 39 new information security weaknesses during this review. Serious weaknesses related to electronic access to computing resources from sources located on IRS's internal computer network place sensitive taxpayer and Bank Secrecy Act data—including information related to financial crimes, terrorist financing, money laundering, and other illicit activities—at significant risk of unauthorized disclosure, modification, or destruction. In addition, information security weaknesses that exist in other control areas, such as physical security, segregation of duties, and service continuity, further increase risk to the computing environment . . . .
>
> Electronic access controls were not effectively implemented to prevent, limit, and detect unauthorized access to the facility's computer systems and data. Numerous vulnerabilities existed in IRS's computing environment because of the cumulative effects of control weaknesses in the areas of user accounts and passwords, access rights and permissions, network services and security, and audit and monitoring of security-related events.[141]

The other major area of concern has to do with the use and abuse of Social Security numbers (SSNs). In this case, the problem is not only with government agencies, but also with the sale of information among private firms.

> Agencies at all levels of government frequently collect and use SSNs to administer their programs, verify applicants' eligibility for services and benefits, and perform research and evaluations of their programs. Although some government agencies are taking steps to limit the use and display of SSNs, these numbers are still available in a variety of public records held by states, local jurisdictions, and courts.
>
> Certain private sector entities that we have reviewed, such as information resellers, credit reporting agencies (CRAs), and health care organizations, also routinely obtain and use SSNs. These entities often obtain SSNs from various public sources or their clients wishing to use their services. We found that these entities used SSNs for various purposes, such as to build tools that verify an individual's identity or match existing records.[142]

At the same time that the federal government has been attempting to protect against inappropriate use of tax records or SSNs, there has been just as much effort to make information available to homeland security efforts and the agencies responsible for them.

The Global Context of U.S. Information Management

It is, of course, true that cyberwarfare, as it is called, is now a very real national security threat. It is also true that information warfare can operate in the private sector as well as in the public arena. However, there are many other dimensions of the global reality in the information age.

One of the issues is the constraint on the ability of national governments to exercise the same level of control over their domestic situation. Global markets trade around the clock every day of the year.

While national governments can exercise some degree of control over their own domestic markets, they cannot control markets located elsewhere, nor can they reach secondary instruments that exchange not stocks themselves but other instruments keyed to stock prices or market indexes. Automated trading happens so rapidly that it is extremely difficult to regulate it. Despite much-touted tools said to be able to halt trading in the event of unusual activity, recent years have seen increasingly dramatic market swings at very large volumes. It has also witnessed dramatic ripple effects in one country's markets based upon action elsewhere in the globe. The 1998 example of swings in parts of Asia dramatically altering first other Asian markets and then those in Europe and the U.S. is an obvious example. Similarly, trading in currencies and in strategic materials or other commodities can have profound effects on domestic realities. For all but the largest economies, the other frightening reality is the ability to use global computer networks to move huge amounts of capital very rapidly from one part of the world to another.

Finally, the rise of easily accessible global networking also raises serious questions about the ability of governments and agencies at all levels to control and coordinate their employees and subordinate units. The concept of picket fence federalism—developed some three decades ago to describe the process by which officials in any given policy space have tended to pay less attention to their nominal superiors and to form networks with other officials and agencies in that policy arena—now has entirely new meaning. At one time, picket fence federalism meant the willingness of local health officials to communicate directly with the Centers for Disease Control (CDC) or the National Institutes of Health (NIH) rather than state health departments or local legislatures. Now, picket fence intergovernmental relations operates globally. Officials at any level, NGOs, or for-profit firms can place questions in listservs read daily by thousands of people around the globe and receive significant amounts of material without ever consulting with colleagues, much less superiors.

Issues of Intergovernmental Complexity

This issue of seeking to manage efficiently and effectively across levels of government and with NGOs means that intergovernmental relations is more complex than ever. But there is more at stake than the picket fence problem. There is also the concern that comes with increased national level delegation of responsibility for policy implementation to state and local governments.

For one thing, in the regulatory arena, the intergovernmental framework for regulation (discussed in Chapter 10) means that states, and in some cases local officials, are carrying out federally mandated inspection programs. That means that administrative search and seizure questions become more complex and the law must be developed to address them.[143] It also means that there is a growing issue of the relationships among federal and state freedom of information and privacy act issues.

First, many states and localities have large numbers of computers and systems with very limited security or management systems, if they exist at all. There is great variation among subnational governments, not only terms of sophistication of systems but also in terms of resources to support information-policy problem solving. The need for the management of systems and large bodies of information at these levels has far outpaced the resources available.

It also means that states and localities are more responsible for the day-to-day administration of more policies involving a wider array of people and organizations, both public and private. And certainly the new intergovernmental demands coupled with reductions in personnel and budget cuts at the state and local levels has meant an increase in the amount of contract work.

Finally, the current dynamics also mean that state and local governments are being pressed to take active roles and responsibilities for homeland security. Thus, for example, Congress enacted the Real I.D. Act, which pressures states to provide increased verification and record-keeping when it issues driver's licenses.[144] At the same time, some states have been concerned about the lack of protection of personal data by the federal government and have adopted their own measures aimed at doing so.[145] At this point it is not at all clear what directions these intergovernmental conflicts will take and what law they will produce on information policy.

The Contract Factor

The increasing importance of contracting out has raised a variety of relatively obvious concerns, but it has also presented some issues that are relatively novel as well. For example, in an attempt to improve the efficiency of contracting, there has been a desire to allow more contracting procedures to be done through the Internet. Such electronic practices as advertising, preclearing bidders, and even bidding itself are now commonplace. It is also relatively common now for contract providers of services at the national and state level to be able to access numerous governmental data systems in performing their duties under their agreements. For example, one study showed that by the late 1990s the Health Care Finance Administration (HCFA) had some 60 contractors who use shared systems that contain information about medical condition, health care history, and finances of more than 850 million Medicare claims processed each year.[146] The HCFA Inspector General reported that these contractors were not providing acceptable levels of protection for this confidential information and in fact, "contractor employees could potentially browse data on individuals, search out information on acquaintances or others, and, possibly, sell or otherwise use this information for personal gain or malicious purposes."[147]

On the other hand, the information access process is often not a two-way street. Contractors seek to protect their own records and often argue that access to their systems, except for standard auditing procedures, jeopardizes their proprietary information. That issue of governmental, or even public, access to contractor records can become quite complex.[148] For many contractors, the argument is that since government can maintain as protected those documents that are classified as internal memoranda, the same protections should apply to many kinds of materials within the firm.

Of course, other firms frequently seek to obtain information concerning their competitors' contracting processes, and contracting firms often try to convince agencies not to disclose contract information. Thus, when McDonnell Douglas Corporation learned that the National Aeronautics and Space Administration (NASA) had received a FOIA request to disclose a variety of information about its contract with McDonnell Douglas for Med-Lite launch vehicles, the company protested. It claimed that disclosure of such information as the pricing, incentive arrangements, and billing mechanisms would cause damage both to NASA and to the firm itself and should be withheld under exemption four of the FOIA, which applies to trade secrets and other confidential financial information. The District Court for the District of Columbia disagreed, concluding that that exemption applied only "if disclosure is likely to (1) impair the Government's ability to obtain necessary information in the future, or (2) cause substantial harm to the competitive position of the person from whom the information was obtained."[149] It found in this case that there was insufficient evidence of damage from potential competitors and, moreover, that the fact that disclosure may make the bidding on future contracts more competitive "does not qualify as a substantial competitive injury and should be viewed as the cost of doing business with the government."[150] Of course, such so-called "costs of doing business" with the government are among the reasons that bidders sometimes seek to charge governments higher prices.

The tensions over what information is to be considered proprietary and what belongs to government, as well as which information within the control of the government will be released, is likely to become increasingly important as more governmental functions are performed by contractors and as more bidders—not just for-profit firms but also not-for-profits—seek to compete for contracts. The answers to those questions matter not only among the competitors for contracts but also have a great deal to do with the government's and the general public's ability to maintain accountability of contract processes and the organizations that operate them.[151]

Another aspect of information policy relative to contracting that has been evolving goes well beyond access to information systems or control over particular types of information and down to basic constitutional questions. Consider two examples. The first involved a man who had held a contract with Wabaunsee County, Kansas, for trash collection services. The man was, in the Supreme Court's words, a constant outspoken critic of the county board and its members. He even ran unsuccessfully for the board himself.[152] After nine years of contracting with him, the board voted to terminate his contract.

However, the cities in the county retained the authority to opt out of the county contract and five of the six municipalities did just that, executing contracts with their long-time trash hauler. Even so, he brought suit against the county, claiming a violation of his First Amendment protected free speech rights. The county argued that a contractor is not like a public employee and does not have the same kinds of First Amendment protections. The Court recognized that: "[T]he Board exercised contractual power, and its interests as a public service provider, including its interest in being free from intensive judicial supervision of its daily management functions, are potentially implicated. Deference is therefore due to the government's reasonable assessments of its interests as contractor."[153] However, it added that while contractors are not exactly in same position as public employees with respect to their free speech protections, it was necessary to "recognize the right of independent government contractors exercising their First Amendment rights."[154]

A case originating in Northlake, Illinois, involved a list of towing companies used by the city. After one company's owner refused to make a campaign contribution to the mayor's reelection campaign, as requested by the campaign committee, his firm was removed from the list. He had also displayed a campaign poster for the opposition candidate. Although this case also raised a First Amendment issue, it was unlike the Kansas case in that it presented a case of freedom of association. Here again, the Court concluded that the First Amendment does apply. While it noted that the case-by-case evaluation that it called for "will allow the courts to consider the necessity of according to the government the discretion it requires in the administration and awarding of contracts over the whole range of public works and the delivery of governmental services,"[155] the Court warned that "[W]e fail to see a difference of constitutional magnitude between the threat of job loss to an employee of the State, and a threat of loss of contracts to a contractor."[156] The Court's ambiguous position on the relationship between the way that constitutional protections will apply to contractors and the way they apply to government employees is a problem for contract administrators. On the one hand, it recognizes that governments have particular interests in maintaining flexible authority with respect to their management of contracts. At the same time, the Court recognized the obvious realities that constitutional strictures do apply. And given that the facts of these two cases are relatively extreme, it is revealing that the Court itself had difficulty explaining how the conflicts should be resolved.

Does this mean that unsuccessful bidders will now frequently challenge government on grounds that actions were based upon previous disputes between the contractor and the agency or criticism of existing contracts by would-be competitors? What if a contractor associated with a particular religious groups should be denied a contract?[157] If the Court was unwilling to provide a standard but is calling instead for a case-by-case consideration of the government's action, how are public managers to shape their behavior?

Governance Regimes: Alternative Tools of Public Management and Their Consequences

Of course, contracting out is one of a host of contemporary techniques employed by government these days in an effort to improve efficiency, cut costs, and achieve greater flexibility. Many of the problems noted above also apply when government employs government corporations, advisory groups, negotiating committees, or other alternatives to standard administrative agency operations to achieve its ends. As earlier chapters have indicated, there is considerable ambiguity in each of these approaches, and indeed that lack of clarity is endemic in the effort to use whatever techniques appear promising rather than using traditional institutions and more common administrative law procedures. On the one hand, the object is often to avoid what are considered to be excessively burdensome, rigid, and constraining organizational forms or processes. On the other hand, many of those structures and procedures were developed precisely to deal with the kinds of difficulties discussed in this chapter. It is a commonplace too often ignored in contemporary public policy and public management discussions that one person's red tape is another person's accountability and protection against abuse.

SUMMARY

This chapter has investigated the issues raised by our growing dependence upon large quantities of information for the operation of public programs and the changing technology and mechanisms used to manage that information. It suggested that the development and application of legal authorities for the resolutions of these problems are difficult because the environmental factors influencing information practices change faster than the laws have been able to adapt. Nevertheless, we do recognize the information paradox that requires access to more information at precisely the same time that we are attempting to find better ways to insure privacy.

There are a variety of constitutional, statutory, and private law authorities that together make up a system of information law. Both the constitutional and statutory elements respond to the need to ensure accountability and support the deliberative processes necessary for a republic such as ours to survive as well as the effort to insure privacy. The task is to integrate the many pieces of the system into a comprehensible picture in a time when the dynamism of information management is greater than ever before.

In the end, of course, the critical factor in all of this is not just the policies that are crafted in an attempt to render the system workable or the elected officials at the top of governments at all levels who approve those policies. Rather, many of the most important decisions about information rest on a day-to-day basis with the people who deliver public services and operate important regulatory programs. It is to these public servants that we turn in Chapter 12.

NOTES

1. Harlan Cleveland, "Government Is Information (But Not Vice Versa)," 46 *Public Administration Review* 605, 605 (1986).

2. Lotte Feinberg, "Managing the Freedom of Information Act and Federal Information Policy," 46 *Public Administration Review* 615, 615 (1986).

3. U.S. General Accounting Office, *High Risk Series: Information Management and Technology* (Washington, DC: General Accounting Office, 1997), p. 34 (hereafter cited as High Risk Report).

4. U.S. General Accounting Office, *Information Security Management: Learning from Leading Organizations* (Washington, DC: General Accounting Office, 1998), pp. 6–7.

5. *Id.,* at p. 6.

6. As in the case of so-called "Botnets." These are networks set up by hackers who create networks from computers that they can break into and then connect over the Internet into a network. These robot networks can then be used to launch attacks or their services can be sold to others for nefarious purposes. See U.S. Government Accountability Office, *Information Security: Emerging Cybersecurity Issues Threaten Federal Information Systems* (Washington, DC: GAO, 2005), p. 13.

7. U.S. General Accounting Office, *Information Security: Serious Weaknesses Place Critical Federal Operations and Assets at Risk* (Washington, DC: General Accounting Office, 1998), p. 5.

8. Letter to W. T. Barry, August 4, 1822, cited in *Environmental Protection Agency v. Mink,* 410 U.S. 73, 110-111 (1973), Justice Douglas dissenting.

9. *NAACP v. Alabama ex rel. Patterson,* 357 U.S. 449 (1958). See also Alan F. Westin, *Privacy and Freedom* (New York: Atheneum, 1967), p. 51.

10. Much is made of the supposedly complementary nature of the Freedom of Information Act and the Right to Privacy Act, but there is evidence that the sponsors of the two bills and the groups participating in the legislative battle over their passage were not particularly concerned with the fit of the legislation. Senator Kennedy noted: "With the need to enact the Freedom of Information Act amendments over the veto of President Ford, and with the need to complete work on the Privacy Act in the closing days of the 93rd

Congress, the two laws do not appear to mesh as easily as might have been desired. Two different committees in the Senate worked on the different bills; and while the Office of Management and Budget was pressing hard for enactment of privacy legislation, the Justice Department was pressing equally hard to defeat the Freedom of Information legislation." U.S. Congress, Joint Committee Print of the Senate Committee on Government Operations and the Subcommittee on Government Information and Individual Rights of the House Committee on Government Operations, *Legislative History of the Privacy Act of 1974, Source Book on Privacy,* 94th Cong., 2d Sess. (1976) (hereafter cited as Source Book on Privacy), pp. 1173.

The legislative history of the Freedom of Information Act is to be found in U.S. Congress, Joint Committee Print of the Subcommittee on Government Information and Individual Rights and the Subcommittee on Administrative Practice and Procedure of the Senate Committee on the Judiciary, Freedom of Information Act Amendments of 1974, *Source Book, Legislative History, Text, and Other Documents,* 94th Cong., 1st Sess. (1975) (hereafter cited as the Source Book on FOIA).

11. The reference is to George Orwell's *Nineteen Eighty-Four: A Novel* (1949). One finds frequent reference in literature on information policy to Orwell, Aldous Huxley's *Brave New World* (1932), and Franz Kafka's *The Trial* (1925).

12. On the core issues in this debate, see Elizabeth B. Bazan and Jennifer K. Elsea, American Law Division, Congressional Research Service, "Presidential Authority to Conduct Warrantless Electronic Surveillance to Gather Foreign Intelligence Information Memorandum," January 5, 2006, at http://www.fas.org/sgp/crs/intel/m010506.pdf, as of February 12, 2006; U.S. Department of Justice, "Legal Authorities Supporting the Activities of the National Security Agency Described by the President," January 19, 2006, at http://www.usdoj.gov/opa/whitepaperonnsalegalauthorities.pdf, as of February 12, 2006.

13. Leonard L. Riskin and Philip P. Reilly, "Remedies for Improper Disclosure of Genetic Data," 8 *Rutgers-Camden L. J.* 480, 489 (1977).

14. 42 U.S.C. §12101 et seq.

15. *Bragdon v. Abbott,* 524 U.S. 624 (1998).

16. Privacy Protection Study Commission, *Personal Privacy in an Information Society* (Washington, DC: Government Printing Office, 1977), p. 8.

17. While the 1930s efforts that resulted in the Federal Register Act were important and the initial version of the Freedom of Information Act was adopted a decade before Watergate, these two steps were too narrow to be considered a full-scale effort at the development of fair information policy.

18. Aubrey Milunsky and Philip Reilly, "The New Genetics: Emerging Medicolegal Issues in the Prenatal Diagnosis of Hereditary Disorders," 1 *American Journal of Law & Medicine* 71, 78 (1975).

19. See e.g., U.S. General Accounting Office, *Aviation Security Challenges in Using Biometric Technologies* (Washington, DC: GAO, 2004), p. 2.

20. Comment, "OSHA Records and Privacy: Competing Interests in the Workplace," 27 *American University Law Review* 953 (1978).

21. *Chrysler v. Brown,* 441 U.S. 281 (1979).

22. Matthew J. Bester, Comment: "A Wreck on the Info-Bahn: Electronic Mail and the Destruction of Evidence," 6 *Communications Law Conspectus* 75, 75 n. 1, 2 (1998).

23. *Id.,* at p. 77.

24. *Id.,* at pp. 77–78.

25. This is a complex issue. See the U.S. Supreme Court's ruling in the Arthur Andersen case involving destruction of Enron documents, *Arthur Andersen LLP v. United States,* 161 L. Ed. 2d 1008 (2005).

26. See generally, Bester, *supra* note 22.

27. See e.g., *Armstrong v. Executive Office of the President,* 90 F.3d 553 (D.C.Cir. 1996).

28. See Sheila Jasanoff, *Science at the Bar: Law, Science, and Technology in America* (Cambridge: Harvard University Press, 1995).

29. 509 U.S. 579 (1993).

30. 711 F.Supp. 546, 548 (SDCA 1989).

31. 727 F.Supp., at p. 572.

32. *Frye v. United States,* 293 F. 1013, 1014 (D.C.Cir. 1923).

33. 509 U.S., at pp. 592–593.

34. *Id.,* at pp. 593–594.

35. *Allen v. United States,* 588 F.Supp. 247, 259-260 (D.Utah 1984).

36. Comment, "When Rights Collide: Reconciling the First Amendment Rights of Opposing Parties in Civil Litigation," 52 *University of Miami L. Rev.* 587 (1998).

37. See U.S. Constitution, Amendments 5 and 14.

38. See e.g., Henry H. Perritt, Jr., "Property and Innovation in the Global Information Infrastructure," 1996 *University of Chicago Legal Forum* 261 (1996).

39. See generally, Joel C. Mandelman, "Lest We Walk into the Well: Guarding the Keys—Encrypting the Constitution: To Speak, Search & Seize in Cyberspace," 8 *Albany Law Journal of Science & Technology* 227 (1998).

40. The idea of a system of information law is taken from Thomas I. Emerson, *The System of Free Expression* (New York: Vintage Books, 1970).

41. Alexander Meiklejohn, *Political Freedom* (New York: Oxford, 1965), p. 27.

42. *Id.,* at p. 26.

43. *NAACP v. Alabama,* 357 U.S. 449 (1958).

44. See e.g., *First National Bank v. Bellotti,* 435 U.S. 765 (1978).

45. Emerson, *supra* note 40, at p. 4.

46. *United States v. O'Brien,* 391 U.S. 367 (1968).

47. *Postal Service Commission v. Council of Greenburgh Civic Assn.,* 453 U.S. 114 (1981); *Perry Education Assn. v. Perry Local Education Assn.,* 460 U.S. 37 (1983); and *Cornelius v. NAACP Legal Defense and Education Fund,* 87 L.Ed 2d 567 (1985).

48. See *Ginsberg v. New York,* 390 U.S. 629 (1968).

49. *F.C.C. v. Pacifica,* 438 U.S. 726 (1978).

50. *Reno v. ACLU,* 521 U.S. 844 (1997).

51. *Id.,* at p. 874.

52. *Ashcroft v. ACLU,* 535 U.S. 564 (2002).

53. *Ashcroft v. ACLU,* 542 U.S. 656 (2004).

54. *Rust v. Sullivan,* 500 U.S. 173 (1991).

55. *National Endowment for the Arts v. Finley,* 524 U.S. 569 (1998).

56. *United States v. American Library Association,* 539 U.S. 194 (2003).

57. *Frank v. Maryland,* 359 U.S. 360 (1959).

58. *Camara v. Municipal Court,* 387 U.S. 523 (1967).

59. *See v. Seattle,* 387 U.S. 541 (1967).

60. See e.g., *United States v. Biswell,* 406 U.S. 31 1 (1972); and *Colonnade Catering v. United States,* 397 U.S. 73 (1970).

61. *Wyman v. James,* 400 U.S. 309 (1971).

62. See *National Engineering & Contracting Co. v. Occupational Safety and Health Review Commission,* 45 F.3d 476 (D.C.Cir. 1995).

63. *Marshall v. Barlows,* 436 U.S. 307 (1978).

64. *Donovan v. Dewey,* 452 U.S. 594 (1981).

65. *Dow Chemical v. United States,* 476 U.S. 227 (1986).

66. *Id.,* at p. 233.

67. *New York v. Burger,* 482 U.S. 691, 702-703 (1987). See also *United States v. V-1 Oil Co.,* 63 F.3d 909 (9th Cir. 1995); *LSR Industries, Inc. v. Espy,* 34 F.3d 1301 (7th Cir. 1994);

68. *United States v. Agent Chemical Laboratories,* 93 F.3d 572, 577 (9th Cir. 1997).

69. *McCabe v. Life-Line Ambulance Service,* 77 F.3d 540 (1st Cir. 1996).

70. *Id.,* at pp. 549–550.

71. See e.g., *United States v. Hartwell,* 2006 U.S. App. LEXIS 2319 (3rd Cir. 2006); *United States v. Marquez,* 2005 U.S. App. LEXIS 14442 (9th Cir. 2005).

72. *United States v. Bulacan,* 156 F.3d 963 (9th Cir. 1998); *United States v. Davis,* 482 F.2d 893 (9th Cir. 1973).

73. *United States v. Sturm, Ruger & Co.,* 84 F.3d 1, 4 (1996). See also *Reich v. Montana Sulphur & Chemical Co.,* 32 F.3d 440 (1994).

74. The Court has, however, held that warrants can be chosen over subpoenas even where the target of the search is not a probable defendant. *Zurcher v. Stanford Daily,* 436 U.S. 547 (1978).

75. *Couch v. United States,* 409 U.S. 322 (1973).

76. *United States v. Miller,* 425 U.S. 435 (1976).

77. 12 U.S.C. Section 189b.

78. 425 U.S., at p. 443.

79. *Wisconsin v. Constantineau,* 400 U.S. 433 (1971).

80. *Paul v. Davis,* 424 U.S. 693 (1976).

81. *Id.,* at p. 697.

82. *Id.,* at p. 701.

83. *Griswold v. Connecticut,* 381 U.S. 479 (1965).

84. 5 U.S.C. Section 552a. In addition to the *Source Book on Privacy, supra* note 10, students of the Privacy Act should examine U.S. Senate, Joint Hearings Before the Ad Hoc Subcommittee on Privacy and Information Systems of the Committee on Government Operations and the Subcommittee on Constitutional Rights of the Committee on the Judiciary, *Privacy: The Collection, Use, and Computerization of Personal Data,* 93rd Congress, 2d Session, 1974.

85. Privacy Protection Study Commission, *The Privacy Act of 1974: An Assessment* (Washington, DC: Government Printing Office, 1977), pp. 76–77.

86. 5 U.S.C. Section 552.

87. 5 U.S.C. Section 552b.

88. 5 U.S.C. App. 2.

89. Cited in Bernard Schwartz, *Administrative Law* (Boston: Little, Brown, 1976), p. 128.

90. I have discussed this question of deferential interpretation of FOIA exemptions in slightly greater detail in Cooper, "The Supreme Court, the First Amendment, and Freedom of Information," 46 *Public Administration Rev.* 622 (1986). This article is part of a symposium edited by Lotte Feinberg and Harold Relyea entitled "Toward a Government Information Policy—FOIA at 20," which summarizes many of the successes and problems experienced under FOIA since its enactment in 1966.

91. See "Note: The Freedom of Information Act in 1990: More Freedom for the Government; Less Information for the Public," 1991 *Duke L. J.* 753 (1991).

92. U.S. Department of Justice, *Freedom of Information Case List, September 1985 Edition* (Washington, DC: GPO, 1985), p. 274.

93. Lotte E. Feinberg, "Open Government and Freedom of Information: Fishbowl Accountability?" in Phillip J. Cooper and Chester A. Newland, eds., *Handbook of Public Law and Administration* (San Francisco: Jossey-Bass, 1997).

94. See U.S. House of Representatives, Hearings Before a Subcommittee of the Committee on Government Operations, *Executive Order on Security Classification,* 97th Cong., 2nd Sess. (1982).

95. *Id.,* at p. 389.

96. Feinberg, *supra* note 93, at pp. 380–381.

97. I have explained these actions in Phillip J. Cooper, "George W. Bush, Edgar Allan Poe, and the Use and Abuse of Presidential Signing Statements," 35 *Presidential Studies Quarterly* 515 (2005).

98. 38 *Weekly Compilation of Presidential Documents* 2092–2093 (2002).

99. U.S. Senate, Hearings before the Committee on the Judiciary. *Department of Justice Oversight: Preserving Our Freedoms while Defending Against Terrorism,* 107th Cong., 1st Sess. (2001).

100. U.S. Government Accountability Office, *Information Management: Implementation of the Freedom of Information Act* (Washington, DC: GAO, 2005), p. 13.

101. See U.S. Government Accountability Office, *Information Management: Progress in Implementing the 1996 Electronic Freedom of Information Act Amendments* (Washington, DC: GAO, 2001).

102. U.S. Department of Justice, Office of Information and Privacy, "FOIA Post: The Use of Contractors in FOIA Administration," at http://www.usdoj.gov/oip/foiapost/2004foiapost27.htm, as of February 17, 2006.

103. *Id.*

104. 5 U.S.C. Section 552b(a)(1). On the Sunshine Act generally, see U.S. Congress, Joint Committee Print of the Senate Committee on Government Operations and the House Committee on Government Operations, *Government in the Sunshine Act, S.5 (Pub. L. No. 94-409); Source Book, Legislative History, Texts, and Other Documents,* 94th Congress, 2d Session, (1976).

105. The best summary and analysis of the FACA to date is Steven P. Croly and William F. Funk, "The Federal Advisory Committee Act and Good Government," 14 *Yale Journal on Regulation* 451 (1997).

106. Henry J. Steck, "Private Influence on Environmental Policy: The Case of the National Industrial Pollution Control Council," 5 *Environmental Law* 241, 248–249 (1975). See also Jerry W. Markham, "The Federal Advisory Committee Act," 35 *U. Pittsburgh L. Rev.* 557 (1974).

107. *Association of American Physicians and Surgeons v. Clinton,* 997 F.2d 898, 902-903 (D.C.Cir. 1993).

108. *Chaney v. United States District Court,* 542 U.S. 367, 381-382 (2004).

109. *In re Cheney,* 406 F.3d 723 (D.C.Cir. 2005).

110. 5 U.S.C. §562(7).

111. *Public Citizen v. Department of Justice,* 491 U.S. 440 (1989).

112. Croly and Funk, *supra* note 105, at p. 527.

113. U.S. Senate, Committee on Governmental Affairs, *Paperwork Reduction Act of 1995,* Report 104-8, 104th Cong., 1st Sess. (1995), pp. 1–2.

114. 494 U.S. 26 (1990).

115. See generally, Feinberg, *supra* note 2, at p. 614.

116. P.L. 105-277, 112 Stat. 2681 (1998), §§1701 et seq.

117. *Id.,* at §1702.

118. P.L. 107-347, 116 Stat. 2899 (2002)

119. *Id.,* Section 101a.

120. I have explained this concept further in Phillip J. Cooper, *Governing by Contract: Challenges and Opportunities for Public Managers* (Washington, DC: CQ Press, 2003), pp. 98–100.

121. Supra note 188, Section 208(b)(2)(B)(ii).

122. *Id.,* Section 301 et seq.

123. *Id.*

124. See e.g., Office of Management and Budget, *Federal Information Security Management Act (FISMA) 2004 Report to Congress* (Washington, DC: OMB, 2005).

125. See *In re: Sealed Cases,* 310 F.3d 717 (US For. Intel. Surveillance Court of Rev. 2002).

126. P.L. 93-380, 88 Stat. 484, Section 513 (1974), 20 U.S.C. Section 1232g.

127. *Gonzaga University v. Doe,* 536 U.S. 273 (2002).

128. P.L. 91-508, 84 Stat. 1114, Title 6 (1970), 15 U.S.C. Section 1681 et seq.

129. P.L. 95-630, 92 Stat. 3641 (1978), 12 U.S.C. Section 3401 et seq.

130. See the discussion of this history at 1978 *U.S. Code Congressional and Administrative News* 9306 (1978).

131. P.L. 104-191, 110 Stat. 1936 (1996).

132. See e.g., U.S. General Accounting Office, *Information Management Reform: Effective Implementation Is Essential for Improving Federal Performance* (Washington, DC: General Accounting Office, 1996).

133. 4 *Harvard L. Rev.* 193 (1890).

134. U.S. General Accounting Office, *Information Security: Serious Weaknesses Place Critical Federal Operations and Assets at Risk,* (Washington, DC: General Accounting Office, 1998), p. 26.

135. *Id.,* at p. 8.

136. *Id.,* at p. 5.

137. *Id.,* at p. 29.

138. U.S. Government Accountability Office, *Information Security: Continued Efforts Needed to Sustain Progress in Implementing Statutory Requirement,* (Washington, DC: GAO, 2005), pp. 4–5.

139. P.L. 108-187, 117 Stat. 2699 (2003).

140. U.S. Government Accountability Office, *Information Security: Emerging Cybersecurity Issues Threaten Federal Information Systems* (Washington, DC: GAO, 2005).

141. U.S. Government Accountability Office, *Information Security: Internal Revenue Service Needs to Remedy Serious Weaknesses over Taxpayer and Bank Secrecy Act Data* (Washington, DC: GAO, 2005), pp. 9–10.

142. U.S. Government Accountability Office, *Social Security Numbers: Federal and State Laws Restrict Use of SSNs, Yet Gaps Remain* (Washington, DC: GOA 2005), p. 2.

143. *Beverly California Corp. v. Shalala,* 78 F.3d 403 (8th Cir. 1996).

144. P.L. 109-13; 119 Stat. 231 (2005).

145. GAO, *Social Security Numbers: Federal and State Laws Restrict Use of SSNs, Yet Gaps Remain, supra* note 142.

146. *Supra* note 7, at p. 27.

147. *Id.,* at pp. 27–28.

148. "Furthering the Accountability Principle in Privatizing Federal Corrections: The Need for Access to Private Prison Records," 28 *U. Michigan L. J.* 249 (1995)

149. *McDonnell Douglas Corp. v. National Aeronautics & Space Administration,* 981 F.Supp. 12, 15 (D.D.C. 1997).

150. *Id.,* at p. 16.

151. See generally, *Forsham v. Harris,* 445 U.S. 169 (1980).

152. *Board of County Commissioners, Wabaunsee County v. Umbehr,* 518 U.S. 668 (1996).

153. *Id.,* at pp. 678-679.

154. *Id.,* at p. 685.

155. *O'Hare Truck Service v. Northlake,* 518 U.S. 712, 718-719 (1996).

156. *Id.,* at p. 722.

157. See e.g., *Rosenberger v. University of Virginia,* 515 U.S. 819 (1995).

12

The Law and Public Employees

Chapters 8 through 11 have addressed problems of law, politics, and administration that have raised important and difficult issues for administrators, the public, and the courts. In this chapter we turn to another challenging area: legal controversies that arise in connection with government employment. As the nation neared the turn of the twenty-first century, the U.S. Merit System Protection Board (MSPB) study reported that there were 1.7 million full-time permanent members of the civil service.[1] A Center for the Study of the States found that in that same year there were "nearly 17 million jobs in state and local government . . . , adding up to about one in seven jobs in the United States nonfarm total."[2] The U.S. Department of Labor reported that state and local government, "excluding education and hospitals, employed about 7.9 million people in 2004. Seven out of 10 of these workers were employed in local government."[3] Despite the effort by the federal government to cut over a quarter million civil servants and the downsizing efforts at the state and local levels, it is clear that civil servants represent a very important segment of the economy, delivering a wide range of services not only in the United States but around the world. They are responsible for critical programs that affect everyone. Beyond all that, they represent a large number of the nation's citizens. Obviously, then, the rules that concern public employees affect the lives of a significant portion of the American community, its workforce and their families.

The truth is that the actual size of the body of people who deliver public services is unknown.[4] For one thing, all levels of government rely on large numbers of contractors to carry out many public functions. The ambiguity is not really an accident. There is no question that politicians at all levels have bragged to their constituents about reducing the size of government. What they did not say is that there were often just as many people involved, but they now work for contractors and therefore are not counted on civil service rolls.

However those who provide government services are counted—or for that matter, not counted— the public sector is a very large employer. Moreover, government, whether it functions directly— through federal, state, or local agencies—or indirectly—through nongovernmental organizations—is a special employer.[5] Among other things, it represents all the people within its jurisdiction and is expected to be responsive and responsible to the citizenry.[6] Government agencies are also special employers because they have only those powers granted to them by law, and even those powers are limited by the rights and liberties of citizens and employees granted by the Constitution and statutes.

For supervisors, the real and perceived constraints on their ability to engage, manage, discipline, or even terminate their employees is a major and continuing frustration. An MSPB survey found that supervisors cited a variety of reasons for not taking action when they believed it was appropriate, ranging from the time and resources that it would take to pursue the matter to the costs to the agency if the employee pressed an appeal.[7] As one respondent put it to MSPB researchers, "If any employee's conduct and/or performance is unacceptable, make it easier to terminate them. The time and effort needed to terminate an unacceptable non-probationary employee is tremendous.... Supervisors quickly learn that it's not worth the hassle. Thus, mediocre employees are allowed to scrape by, and the good performers get dumped on."[8]

At the same time, employees who have paid attention to major Supreme Court rulings over the past two decades and who have probed statutory developments affecting the civil service beyond the press releases, worry that the law has moved backwards, providing less protection for public employees than existed before.[9] They also worry about whole new classes of issues that are providing the basis for constraints on their liberties and adverse actions on the job, ranging from their smoking habits[10] to their sexual preferences.[11] And they also see, layered on top of these issues, new or developing issues such as the damage of agency efficiency and effectiveness from downsizing and outsourcing as well as increasing stresses associated with what MSPB calls "work-life balance."[12]

The fact is that both managers and employees have legitimate bases for their respective concerns. However, one of the critical starting points for a more positive working relationship is a more accurate assessment of the public law affecting public service. To understand how these tensions between employees and their government employers are managed, it is necessary to consider the setting within which such conflicts arise and the interests affected by their resolution, the changing nature of public service, the constitutional protections afforded to public servants, and the statutory requirements that govern public employment.

THE SETTING AND THE INTERESTS

One of the great difficulties in legal and political discussions of public employees is that civil servants are popularly assumed to be part of a more or less homogeneous group, a monolith unaffectionately known as "the bureaucracy." Actually, the public sector is exceedingly rich in talent and training as well as diverse in backgrounds and political perspectives. Unfortunately, so is the body of law that governs how these officials function and protects them from abuse.

A Complex Legal Environment in Which to Address Stressful Challenges

Two examples of public employee disputes demonstrate the complexity of this area of administration. They should be considered along with the discussion of the Kansas and Illinois contracting cases discussed in Chapter 11.

Bessie Givhan was a junior high school teacher in the Western Line Consolidated School District in Mississippi. She was terminated and filed suit for reinstatement.[13] At the time, the school district was under a desegregation order issued by the U.S. District Court for the Northern District of Mississippi.[14] Though the school district later advanced a number of alleged incidents that supported its decision to fire Givhan, the primary reason for her dismissal was a number of altercations between the school principal and Ms. Givhan:

> In an effort to show that its decision was justified, respondent School District introduced
> evidence of, among other things, a series of private encounters between petitioner and the

school principal in which petitioner allegedly made "petty and unreasonable demands" in a manner variously described by the principal as "insulting," "hostile," "loud," and "arrogant." . . . Finding that petitioner had made "demands" on but two occasions and that those demands "were neither 'petty' nor 'unreasonable,' insomuch as all the complaints in question involved employment policies and practices at [the] school which [petitioner] conceived to be racially discriminatory in purpose or effect," the District Court concluded that the primary reason for the school district's failure to renew petitioner's contract was her criticism of the policies and practices of the school district, especially the school to which she was assigned to teach.[15]

Givhan asserted that her termination was a reprisal by the principal for having the temerity to challenge his administrative practices, which she considered illegal and unjust. She claimed interference with her First Amendment right to freedom of speech. Givhan argued that the other charges leveled against her after the dismissal were attempts to rationalize this unconstitutional reprisal.

The school board insisted that her constitutional rights had not been involved, arguing that she was fired because of "an antagonistic and hostile attitude to the administration."[16] The board insisted that Givhan's private encounters with the principal represented not free speech but insubordinate behavior that would cause disharmony in the school and disrupt administration of education. In any case, it asserted, Givhan had done a number of other things that would have justified her termination quite apart from the difficulties with the principal.[17]

The district court found a First Amendment violation and ordered reinstatement, but the Circuit Court of Appeals reversed. The Supreme Court vacated the lower court decision and sent the case back to the district court for a determination whether Givhan would or would not have been terminated "but for" the arguments with the principal, which it ruled were protected by the First Amendment.[18]

Another example of a law and personnel conflict (more fully presented in an article by Mark Coven[19]) was the dismissal of a high-level New Hampshire executive.[20] Mr. Bennett was director of the New Hampshire Department of Resources and Economic Development. He was appointed by the governor and reported to the commissioner of the department. The governor and the commissioner promoted development of a pulp mill in the state, but Bennett disagreed and let his superiors know of his disapproval. They replied that while they would not force him to promote the project publicly, he should refrain from openly opposing the plan.[21] The plan was very controversial. Everyone wanted economic progress, but many feared environmental damage from the proposed plant. The community that was the prospective site of the mill was planning a referendum that the company involved agreed would determine whether the mill would be constructed.[22] While all this was in progress, Mr. Bennett found himself in a difficult spot. Following a speech to a Chamber of Commerce group, he was asked a direct question about his opinion of the pulp mill proposal. He answered:

> I'll be short and sweet on that one. The official policy of the Administration because Governor Thomson unilaterally announced that the pulp mill will locate in the Connecticut River Valley, his official policy is that we are pro pulp mill . . . . I think that the idea of a pulp mill stinks. It contravenes everything that the state, everything that we are trying to do, that I've talked to you about, about quality it would be a catastrophe in my judgment. Don't quote me on that.[23]

Bennett was fired for insubordination, and his dismissal was upheld by the state supreme court against claims that his termination violated his First and Fourteenth Amendment rights.

Both cases were complex disputes involving constitutional, statutory, and, to some degree, procedural dimensions. The two contract cases discussed in Chapter 11 raised that additional dimension. In both of the present cases, state or local government employees asserted federally protected rights. In the contract cases, contractors claimed the kinds of protections normally available to regular government employees.

More broadly, there are several general factors that complicate public personnel disputes. Since nearly 90 percent of all civilian public employees are state and local workers, contests involving them are frequently complex intergovernmental disputes implicating a variety of local, state, and federal legal questions.[24] Moreover, given that a substantial portion of public employees are covered by some form of collective bargaining arrangements,[25] additional contractual issues must be considered beyond the constitutional and statutory authorities. "Whereas previously to understand the personnel policies and procedures of a jurisdiction one had only to consult the civil service law and rules, now one must also study the content of collective agreements entered into by the public employer with a union or unions."[26]

In addition, the tasks performed by government employees are manifold, complex, and often extremely important.[27] They require high quality people who are properly trained and experienced. Therefore, human resource management difficulties must be dealt with in a manner that encourages professionalism and career development, not merely as a unilateral demand for obedience to the public employer. Finally, because of the lack of privacy in the society, a tightly interconnected employment market, and the close connection (and, in some cases, overlap) between the public and private sectors, an adverse action taken by government against a government employee or job applicant can have a profound and lasting impact on the person's life and career. The stakes are often very high. It is against this backdrop that controversies involving public employees arise and must be resolved.

Producer and Consumer Perspectives Are Different, and the Differences Matter

The differences between producer and consumer perspectives on problems of law and administration, discussed at several points in this book, are particularly important and difficult to deal with in human resources management controversies. A public service professional is a producer of administrative decisions for those outside government who must deal with the agency, for those at other levels of government who are affected by his or her actions, for those in other agencies at the same level, and for subordinates within his or her agency whose careers are at stake. An employee is simultaneously a consumer as a citizen generally interested in the use of governmental authority and tax dollars, a client who makes demands on other agencies for services or law enforcement, an officer of an agency whose work is affected by decisions of other agencies and other levels of government, and an employee who is the consumer of decisions made by superiors and co-workers. The problems that arose in *Bennett* and *Givhan* can be properly understood only if one remains aware of these varying perspectives and their implications. Furthermore, there are occasions—for example, "whistleblowing"—in which apparent conflicts in the public servant's role can complicate his or her position.[28]

The Changing Nature of Public Employment: Varied Types of Employees

Because there are so many different kinds of jobs and titles in public service, it is difficult to generalize about employee rights and responsibilities. Indeed, that challenge is increasing as the George W. Bush administration has moved, with the support of Congress, to develop models of human resource management outside the traditional civil service framework, using the Department of Defense and the Department of Homeland Security as test cases. The first round of these alternative systems came in the Homeland Security Act of 2002, Section 841 of which provided in part that: "[T]he Secretary of Homeland Security may, in regulations prescribed jointly with the Director of the Office of Personnel Management, establish, and from time to time adjust, a human resources management system for some or all of the organizational units of the Department of Homeland Security."[29] And indeed DHS did just that in 2005.[30] Congress also allowed the U.S. Department of Defense to do essentially the same thing in the National Defense Authorization Act for FY 2004.[31] The DOD has done so and has published regulations for what it calls the National Security Personnel System (NSPS).[32] The National Aeronautics and Space Administration (NASA) and the Government Accountability Office (GAO) have also moved to use flexibility accorded to them to implement innovative systems.[33]

These new programs are part of an overall effort to reframe what was once called personnel management and was later reconceptualized and developed into human resources management. Now called human capital management, this is an approach to hiring and supervising public service professionals that is intended to be "results oriented, customer focused, and collaborative in nature," and that emphasizes flexibility in order to drive organizations toward high performance.[34] In fact, the Homeland Security Act became the vehicle to adopt a broad-based human capital management program. Title XIII of that legislation was entitled the Chief Human Capital Officers Act of 2002. It created a Chief Human Capital Officer in each executive branch agency and a Chief Human Capital Officers Council to be chaired by the Director of the Office of Personnel Management (OPM). The act charged them with responsibility to implement human capital management systems with flexibility provided in the legislation to do that.

Of course, all of this flexibility and agency-by-agency innovation effort took many different parts of the federal public service off in their own individual directions, to the point where the GAO complained:

> We are fast approaching the point where "standard governmentwide" human capital policies and processes are neither standard nor governmentwide. We believe that human capital reform should avoid further fragmentation within the civil service, ensure reasonable consistency within the overall civilian workforce, and help maintain a reasonably level playing field among federal agencies in competing for talent.

In addition to these broad efforts, the intense emphasis on outsourcing and increased use of contract providers has been another important driver for change in public service. This outsourcing drive has meant that many of the people doing public work are actually employees of private nonprofit or for-profit organizations. In addition, there has been a tendency for many government units to hire individual contractors for a variety of functions. Many of them operate in a no-person's-land between the private world and what has traditionally been referred to as the civil service.

Even so, it is necessary in order to make sense of all this complexity to develop a simple typology as a basis for discussion, recognizing that these categories represent starting points and not a complete set of definitions as to types or conditions of public service. Most public servants can be described as general civil service employees, political officers, special employees, or contract employees. Indeed, the case law often draws these distinctions.

Civil Servants   General civil service employees are employed and managed in accordance with the merit principle.

> The merit concept [holds] that appointments, promotions, and other personnel actions should be made on the basis of relative ability. For appointments and promotions, this has usually meant the administration of competitive examinations, scores on which have been believed to distinguish between the candidates according to capacity to perform satisfactorily on the job. For other personnel actions such as salary increases, reduction-in-force, and dismissals, the assumption has also been that the employee's "merit" could be determined and he or she should be treated accordingly.[35]

Above all, the merit principle requires skill and professionalism to be preferred over political connections. In fact, general civil servants are those who possess the skills and experience to do the day-to-day work of most agencies, at least those portions of it that have not been contracted out.

Political Officials   Political officials are, generally speaking, those who can be considered policy-making or confidential employees. Ranging from cabinet-level appointees to press aides, policymaking officials are those for whom partisan affiliation or political loyalty is an appropriate employment consideration.[36] The chief executive is elected to govern on the basis of law and a political platform. Political officers are the appointed officials who help the elected officer implement that policy agenda;

they are employed and managed by elected or highly placed appointees. Just which public positions are, in their nature, or ought to be political as opposed to general civil service posts is a matter of continuing conflict, at least in the courts.[37] However, elected officials at both the national and state levels of both political parties have for many years argued for more political and fewer general civil service employees. Patricia Ingraham pointed out, for example, that while the Clinton administration moved to eliminate more than 270,000 civil service positions, it expressed no interest whatever in cutting the number of political appointees and that, in fact, the number of political jobs has increased ever since the Johnson administration under both Democratic and Republican presidents.[38] The same is true in many states. She noted that the old argument based in simple patronage has given way to more contemporary justifications grounded in the view that careerists will not be sufficiently responsive to political directions.

Contract Employees   Beyond that, many elected officials have expressed doubts about whether a significant portion of the remaining general civil service positions ought to be exclusively governmental positions or should be filled by contract employees or contracting firms who hire private sector employees to carry out public functions. The basis for this argument is the assertion that contractors will be less expensive than government employees. It has the added advantage of allowing the politicians to claim that they have reduced the size of government because they have reduced the number of civil servants, even if the reality is that the same numbers of people are employed by government, albeit through contracts rather than standard civil service positions.

While claims about contract cost savings are often made, the reality is more complex and in some cases simply not accurate.[39] First, accounting techniques are often inadequate to determine precisely what the governmental costs for a particular service were at the outset and there is, therefore, little accurate foundation for cost comparisons.[40] Second, the full range of actual costs of contract administration are rarely included in such calculations, and effective contract administration requires an adequate number of sophisticated government staff quite apart from the expenses involved in such critical work as market analysis and forecasting. Third, as many public servants point out, the competition is often not carried out on truly comparable terms. While the economic explanation is virtually always cited, studies indicate that political decisions often explain more than cost.[41] And that has indeed been part of the criticism of the pressure for new policies developed by the OMB under President George W. Bush's competitive sourcing initiatives.[42] There is also evidence to believe that these other motivations may include efforts at public sector union-busting.[43]

Contract employees may either be employed directly by government on individual service contracts or indirectly work for government as employees of contractors who deliver government services to citizens. These employees may work on what are termed public sites, as in the case of those who work in correctional or health facilities. They may also work off-site, but deal directly with citizens, as in the case of health care finance contractors who handle claims but work out of corporate offices. They may also be both off-site and indirect service personnel in the sense that they deal with agencies and not with citizens who make claims on or have disputes with government agencies.

Special Employees   Special employees are public servants holding particularly sensitive posts that serve special government requirements. More will be said about special employees later, but, for the moment, administrative law judges and officials who deal in national security affairs are examples. Security-sensitive positions have expanded dramatically in the years since the 9/11 attacks in 2001. These employees may or may not be covered by general civil service requirements, but there are usually additional rules that apply to their specific tasks. The two most common types of special rules are provisions guaranteeing independence from certain kinds of interference, special guidelines to ensure accountability in addition to normal performance evaluations, and, increasingly, special clearance requirements for security-related jobs.

The category into which one's position is placed can be extremely important in establishing the type and amount of legal protections that are available against adverse actions by the government.

Modes of Adverse Action: Regulation, Prohibition, and Sanctions

There are three basic ways in which the government as an employer can legally affect or limit one's exercise of perceived rights or liberties. First, it can regulate certain activities by employees. For example, government may regulate the time, place, and manner of such recognized rights as union participation or peaceful picketing.[44] Citizens have the right to use peaceful picketing as a form of protected political expression, but they may not block access to public buildings or otherwise interfere with the normal functioning of government.[45]

Second, government may act by prohibition. Government units may bar the exercise of claimed employee rights, such as statutes and regulations that prohibit certain kinds of partisan political activities. Another common prohibition on public employees is the general ban on public employee strikes. The firing of air traffic controllers who struck against the FAA was a dramatic case in point.

Less dramatic, but increasingly common are situations in which public employers are moving to prohibit the use of agency computers, data systems, and Internet connections for various purposes. This practice is now standard throughout public agencies at all levels of government. That said, there is surprisingly little case law on the subject, at least at the level of federal courts, but to this point at least it appears that such limitations, if carefully drawn, will stand.[46]

Finally, government may punish employees who violate agency rules or statutes. Standard adverse personnel actions include reduction in pay grade, reductions in responsibility, suspension, and, if the case warrants, termination of employment.[47] If such an adverse action is taken or an employee brings a grievance, dispute resolution procedures are triggered. Normally, at the federal level, a general civil service employee is entitled to proceed either through the dispute resolution procedure specified in the collective bargaining agreement or through the agency standard procedure, with the possibility of a review by the Merit System Protection Board in some instances.[48] If a constitutional question is raised, there may be recourse to litigation in court in the event of adverse action.[49]

When Illinois Governor James Thompson argued that these controls are inadequate and that greater political control was needed, the Supreme Court overturned his actions. In so doing, the Court said:

> A government's interest in securing effective employees can be met by discharging, demoting or transferring staff members whose work is deficient. A government's interest in securing employees who will loyally implement its policies can be adequately served by choosing or dismissing certain high-level employees on the basis of their political views .... Likewise, the preservation of the democratic process is no more furthered by the patronage promotions, transfers, and rehires at issue here than it is by patronage dismissals.[50]

A Multiplicity of Interests Involved in Many Conflicts

Recognizing that cases of adverse action by government against employees frequently present strong arguments for both the protection of the worker and the needs of the employer, courts often use a balancing test to resolve difficult cases.[51] The balance is usually struck by weighing the interests of the employee as a worker and as a citizen against "the interest of the State as an employer in the efficiency of the public services it performs through its employees."[52] In fact, however, disputes between public servants and government units raise a multiplicity of interests.[53]

Employees, of course, do have an important personal interest in job security and advancement. They also often have a professional interest in effective and evenhanded performance of their duties. The career civil service is based on the premise that it is possible to develop a cadre of government employees who are professionals in the business of operating government and who have something approaching "neutral competence."[54] Neutral competence can be roughly defined as nonpartisan professionalism in administration of government programs and services. It has often been argued that there is really no such thing as neutral competence and that one does not find this characteristic in practice. However, city managers argue that they represent a large body of professionals who operate as close to this ideal as can reasonably be expected, regardless of the political affiliations of the council members, and that it is their responsibility to ensure that their subordinates in local government are insulated from political pressures to the extent possible in order to support neutral competence.

Additionally, for many public servants, public administration is a second profession.[55] That is, many of those in administrative posts entered government as lawyers, doctors, and engineers, and they brought their professional standards with them. It is a fact of life that public servants are, on occasion, forced to deal with conflicts between their personal and professional interests (see Chapter 13 for more discussion of this issue). Finally, government workers are also part owners of the institutions in which they are employed and have a citizenship interest in how those institutions perform.

Employers (supervisors) also have important interests. Like any manager, a government supervisor has a managerial interest in effective, efficient, and harmonious organizational operations. On the other side, a government supervisor has a responsiveness interest in maintaining an organization that is responsive to public needs. As a public organization, an agency may have to respond to acute needs for which there is, under the circumstances, no alternative but service by that agency. Employee demands that interfere with this responsiveness jeopardize the agency and run counter to the interests of its clients. The supervisor also has a responsibility interest in implementing public policy choices made by the political process, which may engender conflict with subordinates who think the new policies incorrect. Finally, supervisors are also employees and share employee interests.

The public also has interests in employee performance. First, there is a service interest in the effective, efficient, and fundamentally fair operation of government agencies and employees. Second, the public has a fiduciary interest or expectation of public office in all forms as authority held in trust for the benefit of the public. Third, the citizenry has a deliberative interest in being informed on public problems and administrative difficulties, in order to make political decisions through the democratic process. This interest may clash with the asserted interests of government supervisors.

> More importantly, the question whether a school system requires additional funds is a matter of legitimate public concern on which the judgment of the school administration, including the School Board, cannot, in a society that leaves such questions to popular vote, be taken as conclusive. On such a question free and open debate is vital to informed decision-making by the electorate. Teachers are, as a class, the members of a community most likely to have informed and definite opinions as to how funds allotted to the operation of the schools should be spent. Accordingly, it is essential that they be able to speak out freely on such questions without fear of retaliatory dismissal.[56]

The *Bennett* case presents this problem in rather clear terms. The governor had an employer's interests in blocking adverse commentary on the pulp mill project, Bennett had a variety of employee interests in making his views known, and the public, in particular the community that was to vote in the referendum, had interests in hearing an informed public servant speak on a subject within the jurisdiction of his office.[57]

In sum, because the legal environment of public employment is so complex and because the problems encountered by public servants implicate such a wide range of essential interests, they give rise to a considerable amount of litigation. In much of that litigation employees assert their constitutional rights, and it is to a summary of major developments in the constitutional law of public employment that we turn next.

CONSTITUTIONAL ISSUES IN PUBLIC SERVICE

Among the most commonly presented constitutional issues in public employee controversies are the rights to expression and association (First Amendment), to due process of law (Fifth and Fourteenth Amendments), to equal protection of the law (Fifth and Fourteenth Amendments), and to privacy

(Fourth, Ninth, and Fourteenth Amendments). Since Chapter 6 dealt with due process in some detail, those matters will not be repeated here.

The Doctrine of Unconstitutional Conditions

The cornerstone of constitutional protection for public employees is the doctrine of unconstitutional conditions, a rule of law created by the Supreme Court in a number of cases from the 1950s on. This doctrine holds that although there may be no constitutional right to hold a public job or receive a government benefit, government may not condition a job or a benefit on an agreement to forfeit constitutional rights.[58]

> For at least a quarter-century, this Court has made clear that even though a person has no "right" to a valuable governmental benefit and even though the government may deny him the benefit for any number of reasons, there are some reasons upon which the government may not rely. It may not deny a benefit to a person on a basis that infringes his constitutionally protected interests—especially, his interest in freedom of speech....
>
> We have applied this general principle to denials of tax exemptions, *Speiser v. Randall*...; unemployment benefits, *Sherbert v. Verner*...; and welfare payments, *Shapiro v. Thompson*...; *Graham v. Richardson*... But, most often, we have applied the principle to denials of public employment. *United Public Workers v. Mitchell*...; *Wieman v. Updegraff*...; *Shelton v. Tucker*...; *Torcaso v. Watkins*...; *Cafeteria Workers v. McElroy*...; *Cramp v. Board of Public Instruction*...; *Baggett v. Bullitt*...; *Elfbrandt v. Russell*...; *Keyishian v. Board of Regents*...; *Whitehill v. Elkins*...; *United States v. Robel*...; *Pickering v. Board of Education*.... We have applied the principle regardless of the public employee's contractual or other claim to a job.[59]

Public employees may challenge actions by their superiors that interfere with their fundamental constitutional rights. The traditional view when the doctrine of unconstitutional conditions was created was that government actions that infringe on these rights must cease unless the government can demonstrate a compelling state interest, an interest so vital that it justifies the interference with the employee's freedom, and the means chosen to achieve those ends must be narrowly tailored so as to produce no greater infringement on protected freedoms than is truly necessary.

Unfortunately, there has been a reemergence of the right/privilege dichotomy that predated the doctrine of unconstitutional conditions in a string of cases from the 1970s through the 1990s. Thus, in 1990, Justice Scalia wrote:

> I am not sure, in any event, that the right-privilege distinction has been as unequivocally rejected as Justice Stevens supposes. It certainly has been recognized that the fact that the government need not confer a certain benefit does not mean that it can attach any conditions whatever to the conferral of that benefit. But it remains true that certain conditions can be attached to benefits that cannot be imposed as prescriptions upon the public at large. If Justice Stevens chooses to call this something other than a right-privilege distinction, that is fine and good—but it is in any case what explains the nonpatronage restrictions upon federal employees that the Court continues to approve."[60]

If Justice Scalia is not sure what the status of the so-called right/privilege dichotomy is, then public employees and their supervisors must also be permitted at least as much uncertainty. If it has been so clear for so long that public employment is not simply a privilege to which any conditions an employer chooses may be attached, and if it is equally clear that government may not force someone to surrender his or her constitutional rights and liberties in order to obtain a government job or benefit, then why is there so much confusion? Put in slightly different terms, why are both employees and supervisors so insecure about their actions and their decisions? In order to answer those questions, it is necessary to examine several varieties of disputes that arise concerning assertions of public employee rights and supervisory prerogatives.

First Amendment Freedoms: Speech and Association

Government has over the years engaged in a variety of activities that have been held to violate employees' First Amendment freedoms. The Court has struck down any number of loyalty oaths for employees as a condition of employment.[61] Most of the oaths required an employee to swear that he or she was not at the time and had not been a member of or associated with any organization that was considered subversive. In most cases, the oaths were struck because they were extremely vague.[62] As Chapter 6 indicated, many groups were placed on lists of subversive organizations that clearly were not out to overthrow the government. (The NAACP was a prime example.) Not only was it difficult to know whether one had at some point been even loosely associated with a group that might turn up on someone's list, but the words used in the oaths were often subject to differing interpretations. In one case, the Court struck down a state civil service law under which a teacher who assigned readings from Marx or Engels could find that he or she had violated state loyalty oath requirements forbidding seditious conduct.[63] The reason that some government requirements are declared void for vagueness is that one who cannot understand what speech is permitted or which organizations are acceptable is likely to engage in self-censorship for fear of inadvertently committing some breach of law. Such uncertainty has a "chilling effect" on the exercise of fundamental rights. The Court has not ruled out oaths in which employees are asked to promise to properly perform the duties of their office and to enforce the law. Indeed, the Constitution contains some oath requirements.[64] Where oaths are prospective rather than retrospective and do not force surrender of beliefs or associations, they have been upheld.[65]

A number of government restrictions on employment have been struck down because they violate the First Amendment right to freedom of association and the right to privacy in those associations. The Supreme Court first announced that freedom of association was protected by the First Amendment in 1958.[66] The Court has held that there are very few instances in which it is the government's business to know to which organizations one belongs. Such information would be relevant to a Democratic president who does not want a Republican press representative, but these considerations certainly do not apply to general civil servants. Given the fact that guilt by association was so widely used in U.S. history to deprive people of jobs, the Court has required that only knowing-membership—that is, membership in which one knew of the unlawful aims of an organization and actively pursued those aims—could be relevant to public employment in all but the most unusual circumstances.[67] A major problem with government requirements that employees disclose all of their organizational affiliations is what is termed "over-breadth." The Supreme Court has ruled that even if the government has a compelling enough reason to justify interference with fundamental freedoms, such as the right to association, its method of accomplishing its goals should be narrowly tailored to that task and should not be overly broad.[68] Again, the concern is that broad requirements for disclosure may intimidate citizens from exercising their basic freedoms.

In a general sense, the Court has held that public employees may not be fired merely for exercising their right to freedom of expression.[69] That is true whether one is a tenured employee or not.[70] However, the Court's rulings indicate that more limits may be placed on political[71] and special employees.[72] And, although the Court has repeatedly held that employees may not be terminated merely for making statements that criticize the current administration in matters of public concern,[73] that is not the end of the matter. The Court has recognized the problem of balancing employee rights against employer concerns in maintaining effective and efficient operation of public organizations.[74] Where the employer is able to show that the comments made by the employee were knowingly false or resulted in severe damage to the effective operation of the agency, the employee may yet be in trouble.[75] In several cases employers claimed that an employee was dismissed for other reasons, not because he or she exercised protected First Amendment freedoms.[76] Two of the most common charges are conduct unbecoming an officer and insubordination. Against this, the employee must prove that he or she was fired because of the exercise of the free speech right.

Earlier U.S. Supreme Court opinions suggested that if the exercise of freedom of speech was a significant factor in one's dismissal, reinstatement was required.[77] But later cases made it more difficult for the employee to prevail. In *Mt. Healthy Board of Education v. Doyle*, the Court held:

Initially, in this case, the burden was properly placed upon respondent to show that his conduct was constitutionally protected, and that this conduct was a "substantial factor"—or, to put it in other words, that it was a "motivating factor" in the board's decision not to rehire him. Respondent having carried that burden, however, the District Court should have gone on to determine whether the Board had shown by a preponderance of the evidence that it would have reached the same decision as to respondent's reemployment even in the absence of the protected conduct.[78]

In *Givhan,* the Court wrote: "And while the District Court found that petitioner's criticism was the 'primary' reason for the School District's failure to rehire her, it did not find that she would have been rehired *but for* her criticism."[79] (Emphasis in original.)

The most direct statement of the Court's willingness to defer to management interests in First Amendment disputes came in *Connick v. Myers.*[80] This case arose when Myers, a deputy district attorney in Orleans Parish, Louisiana, got into a disagreement with her supervisor regarding a job transfer. She had been offered an internal transfer and promotion, but she resisted the step up because it would have required her to prosecute cases in the court of a judge with whom she had been working on an offender diversion program. She saw the move as a conflict of interest. When her supervisor insisted she accept, she charged that this was another example of his poor administration of the office. Her criticism alleged a range of administrative problems, including attempts to coerce employees into participating in partisan political activities. The supervisor indicated that her views were not widely shared within the office. At that, Myers went home and prepared a questionnaire which she circulated to other employees. Her supervisor summoned Myers and summarily dismissed her. The district court awarded damages on grounds that there was no question that she had been fired because of her First Amendment–protected speech, and there was no showing of significant impairment of organizational operations as defined by previous case law that justified the termination.[81]

The Supreme Court reversed, finding that Myers had not adequately demonstrated the public significance of her speech. In so doing, the Court added a new requirement to the existing burden an employee must carry in defending his or her speech against reprisal. It was not, however, merely the Court's change of this test regarding when an employee can be disciplined that made the case so important, but Justice White's insistence upon broad deference to management discretion in such matters:

> When employee expression cannot fairly be considered as relating to any matter of political, social, or other concern of the community, government officials should enjoy wide latitude in managing their officers, without intrusive oversight by the judiciary in the name of the First Amendment. Perhaps the government employer's dismissal of the worker may not be fair, but ordinary dismissals from government service which violate no fixed tenure or applicable statute or regulation are not subject to judicial review even if the reasons for the dismissal are alleged to be mistaken or unreasonable.[82] . . .
>
> We hold only that where a public employee speaks not as a citizen upon matters of public concern, but instead as an employee upon matters only of personal interest, absent the most unusual circumstances, a federal court is not the appropriate forum in which to review the wisdom of a personnel decision taken by a public agency allegedly in reaction to the employee's behavior . . . . When close working relationships are essential to fulfilling public responsibilities, a wide degree of deference to employers' judgment is appropriate. Furthermore, we do not see the necessity for an employer to allow events to unfold to the extent that the disruption of the office and the destruction of working relationships is manifest before taking action.[83]

The Court's language in *Connick,* coupled with its cautions against extensive judicially imposed due process requirements (see Chapter 6), indicated a significant shift toward deference to administrative interests.

While managers may applaud this move, the situation may not really be so positive as it seems, even from their perspective. There are two continuing problems that have dogged both employees and their supervisors since the *Connick* ruling. At the level of specifics, it continues to be difficult to determine precisely what speech will be considered speech of public concern and what will be regarded as private, and therefore unprotected. After all, the Court in *Connick* rejected the claim that the management of a public organization fit the class of speech on matters of public concern. More generally, the difficulty is with the use of balancing tests. First, Justice Black long ago challenged the use of balancing tests with respect to constitutionally protected liberties because, in operation, they tend to balance the good of the many against the claims of the one which in reality most often means little protection for unpopular expression or association.[84] On the other hand, notwithstanding that strong bias, decisionmakers can never have real confidence in their actions because balancing tests mean case-by-case determinations, the results of which will not be known until after the case is litigated.

For example, four years after *Connick,* the Supreme Court overturned the dismissal of a probationary data entry clerk. The case arose on the day that President Reagan was shot when co-workers overheard the young woman say, "If they go for him again, I hope they get him."[85] The plurality ruled that her statement was speech of public concern and that the employer could not prevail on the balancing test. On the other hand, three years after the *Rankin* case, the Court struck down challenges to the abortion gag rule issued by HHS, prohibiting employees at federally funded family planning clinics from answering patients' questions about abortion services. The Court concluded in *Rust v. Sullivan* that employees could talk about abortion elsewhere but not in connection with their federally funded activities.[86] It is difficult to see how the *Rust* case represents anything other than a return to the right/privilege dichotomy since it squarely conditioned receipt of jobs and programs on the surrender of free speech.

A decade after *Connick,* the Court announced its decision in *Waters v. Churchill,* which dramatically undercut what limited freedom of speech existed for public employees.[87] Ironically, in so doing, the Court provided no more clarity or certainty for supervisors. The *Waters* case began when Cheryl Churchill, a nurse in the obstetrics department at McDonough District Hospital in Macomb, Illinois, had a conversation in the cafeteria during the dinner break with another nurse, Melanie Perkins-Graham, who was then contemplating a transfer to that department. Their conversation was overheard by Mary Lou Ballew, another obstetrics nurse, and two colleagues—Jean Welty, another nurse, and Dr. Thomas Koch, who was then clinical head of obstetrics. Ballew, who was not on the best of terms with Churchill, reported her version of the conversation to Cynthia Waters, Churchill's supervisor. Ballew told Waters that Churchill was "knocking the department,"[88] making critical comments about Waters to Perkins-Graham, and reported that she also had harsh words for Kathleen Davis, the vice president of nursing at the hospital. Specifically, she argued that the cross-training policy put in place at the hospital was not designed to enhance the competence of the employees but to allow the hospital to deal with staff shortages and that patient care was being jeopardized in the process. When called in by Waters, Perkins-Graham also indicated that Churchill had made critical remarks.

Churchill denied the characterizations of the conversation provided by Ballew and Perkins-Graham, contending that Ballew had had it in for her ever since an incident in which she, Churchill, had covered for Ballew when she made an error.[89] Moreover, Churchill claimed that while she had been critical of Davis and the cross-training policy, she had actually made comments in defense of Waters and suggested that Perkins-Graham should transfer to the department. When Dr. Koch and the other nurse who overheard the conversation were later questioned, after Churchill had been fired, they confirmed her version of the conversation.[90] However, they were never questioned by Waters or Davis before disciplinary action was taken and Churchill was terminated.[91] The Seventh Circuit Court of Appeals ruled in favor of Churchill on grounds that her speech was of the sort protected under *Connick* and that the decision whether to terminate had to be based on what was actually said, determined by some reasonable process and not merely the employer's impression of what the employee was alleged to have said. And in this case, at least two key witnesses were not even consulted.

The Supreme Court reversed, though it refused to go as far as Justice Scalia and two other members of the Court would have gone in deferring to the employer. Justice O'Connor, writing for the plurality, observed that: "Though the First Amendment creates a strong presumption against punishing protected speech even inadvertently, the balance need not always be struck in that direction."[92] That having been said, however, the Court refused to provide a standard by which to determine how to decide such cases and warned that: "We must therefore reconcile ourselves to answering the question on a case-by-case basis."[93]

> Accordingly, all we say today is that the propriety of a proposed procedure must turn on the particular context in which the question arises—on the cost of the procedure and the relative magnitude and constitutional significance of the risks it would decrease and increase.[94]

Justice O'Connor clearly did not wish to admit openly that she had dramatically undercut the ability of public employees to discuss issues of public concern, but that is the clear import of the ruling. Her language is largely circular and provides cold comfort to anyone seeking to suggest that the First Amendment protections once available to public employees under *Perry v. Sinderman* and *Pickering* still exist in any meaningful sense. The *Waters* Court wrote:

> The government's interest in achieving its goals as effectively and efficiently as possible is elevated from a relatively subordinate interest when it acts as sovereign to a significant one when it acts as employer. The government cannot restrict the speech of the public at large just in the name of efficiency. But where the government is employing someone for the very purpose of effectively achieving its goals, such restrictions may well be appropriate.[95]

> To permit such a shift in approach and simultaneously to permit action to be taken on the basis of hearsay, without efforts to consult readily available witnesses, is to permit not merely a denigration of free speech but also of due process.[96]

The dissenters made these points and reached the obvious conclusion that the Court's "conclusion is erroneous because it provides less protection for a fundamental constitutional right than the law ordinarily provides for less exalted rights, including contractual and statutory rights applicable in the private sector."[97] In other aspects of administrative law, the failure to consider such additional evidence as was available from the two witnesses not consulted by the supervisors would be considered arbitrary and capricious behavior, reversible on that ground alone. At root, the dissenters observed, the Court "underestimates the importance of freedom of speech for the more than 18 million civilian employees of this country's Federal, State, and local Governments, and subordinates that freedom to an abstract interest in bureaucratic efficiency."[98]

A year after *Waters*, the Court took a quite different approach in *United States v. National Treasury Employees Union*.[99] In this case, the Court struck down provisions of the Ethics in Government Act Amendments of 1989 that prohibited federal employees from receiving honoraria. The term *honorarium* was broadly interpreted to include receiving funds for "an appearance, speech or article."[100] Justice Stevens, writing for the Court, began by noting that:

> Federal employees who write for publication in their spare time have made significant contributions to the marketplace of ideas. They include literary giants like Nathaniel Hawthorne and Herman Melville, who were employed by the Customs Service, Walt Whitman, who worked for the Departments of Justice and Interior; and Bret Harte, an employee of the mint. Respondents have yet to make comparable contributions to American culture, but they share with these great artists important characteristics that are relevant to the issue we confront.[101]

The Court began from the fact that the balancing test from *Connick* and *Waters* starts from a determination that the speech in question was delivered "as a citizen upon matters of public concern" and not "as an employee upon matters only of personal interest." The employees in this case included a Postal Service employee who gave lectures on the Quaker religion, an aerospace engineer who lectures on African-American history, a microbiologist who was a dance critic, and an IRS examiner who wrote on the environment. The Court concluded that their activities were covered "within the protected category of citizen comment on matters of public concern." They were "addressed to a public audience, were made outside the workplace, and involved content largely unrelated to their government employment."[102] The majority also added that the ban on honoraria "imposes a significant burden on the public's right to read and hear what the employees would otherwise have written and said."[103] It is interesting that no such argument was offered when the Court concluded in *Connick* and reaffirmed in *Waters* that discussion of the management of a public organization is, in general, not a matter of public concern. Presumably, the public interest in having access to that information, particularly from those best equipped to talk about it, would be even more important.[104]

If the boundaries of First Amendment–protected expression seem unclear in the major Supreme Court rulings on the subject, the situation is even more chaotic in the lower courts. That is to some degree inherent in the use of ad hoc balancing tests and partly due to the internal inconsistencies in the Supreme Court rulings to which the lower courts look for guidance.

The other side of the question whether public employees have freedom of speech is whether anyone, including a public employee, has a right not to speak. Originally, this question emerged in response to the abuse of public servants before congressional and state legislative investigating committees during the McCarthy era.[105] In general, the U.S. Supreme Court decisions held that there is no First Amendment right not to speak as a corollary to the freedom of speech that would allow one to refuse to answer appropriate questions from a properly constituted legislative investigating committee.[106] In a 1977 case, however, the Court held that: "The right to speak and the right to refrain from speaking are complementary concepts for the broader concept of 'individual freedom of mind.'"[107] It is not clear how that right will be accorded, if at all, to public employees. The Court has held that public employees can be required to answer questions about their public duties on pain of dismissal.[108] If the questioning might lead to criminal charges against the employee, he or she may not be compelled to testify or face dismissal unless the employee is granted immunity from prosecution for what he or she might say.[109]

Of course, it is common for those from whom testimony is demanded to seek a grant of immunity. There is a growing wariness on this issue in light of the results of Iran/Contra prosecutions of Lt. Col. Oliver North and Admiral John Poindexter. Both received immunity grants in return for their willingness to testify before the congressional investigating committee, but, in the end, that immunity resulted in reversal of their convictions in the scandal.[110]

Another dimension of free expression is the ability to publish. In an era when so many political appointees write insider books and when the Monica Lewinsky disaster set new lows in public discourse in the broadcast media and in print, it may be surprising to know that there are still complexities involved in decisions by public employees to express their views in print. One of the areas in which conflicts have arisen concerns the desire of public employees to publish in the face of agreements signed on employment that they would submit works for clearance before publication. When recruits agree to such conditions at employment, they obviously do not know what it is that they will learn on the job that might be of great interest to the public. However, in a case that the Supreme Court decided without even accepting briefs on the merits, the Court ruled in a *per curiam* opinion that a broad remedy could be imposed on a former employee of the CIA for breach of contract.[111]

Finally, a continuing First Amendment problem concerns political activity by employees and the imposition of political pressures on employees by their superiors. Many public employees have long argued that the federal government's Hatch Act and the state legislation referred to as "little Hatch Acts," which limit active participation in partisan politics, interfere with their rights to freedom of expression and association. The Supreme Court has upheld the federal act and some state acts on the ground that such interference as exists is justified by the compelling government interest in keeping the civil service free of corruption and the effects of machine politics.[112] That was even before recent amendments intended to support employees.

In the 1970s and 1980s, partisan decisions by officials that affect the careers of civil servants have provided a number of interesting cases. In *Abood v. Detroit*,[113] the Court ruled that employees in unionized government jobs could not be forced to pay those portions of union service fees that were to be used to advance political causes. The Court had decided a year earlier, in *Buckley v. Valeo*,[114] that the expenditure of funds to support a political candidate or issue was a form of free speech protected by the First Amendment. In *Abood* the Court ruled that public employees could not be forced to participate in that expression by means of fees deducted from their salary by their employer and given to the union for purposes not directly related to collective bargaining, contract administration, and grievance adjustment. Potentially more important are several decisions that have directly challenged the entire notion of political patronage hiring and termination of employees.

Writing for the plurality in *Elrod v. Burns,*[115] which challenged the Cook County, Illinois, machine of the late Mayor Richard Daley, Justice Brennan observed that cases alleging interference with protected fundamental rights—in this instance, Republican employees who were fired by a Democratic county administration—involved three determinations. First, the Court had to decide whether there was a substantial infringement of the employees' protected freedom. In this case there was no question but that the employees were being terminated because of their political association. Second, some infringements of liberties may be justified if the government can demonstrate a sufficiently compelling reason. Justice Brennan acknowledged that party affiliation might be appropriate for some jobs in some circumstances. Third, the Court had to decide whether, given that the government action did serve compelling interests, patronage practices as used were overbroad and not sufficiently tailored to achievement of the goals without excessive interference with protected rights. Justice Brennan concluded that the patronage system failed on the third ground. In *Elrod,* a process server and other low-level employees were being fired solely because they belonged to the wrong party. While the criterion of party affiliation may be appropriate and necessary for some high-level policymaking positions, it was not justified as a blanket practice. Justice Stewart wrote the concurring opinion, which along with the three justices in the plurality made up a majority of the Court, but he and his colleague, Justice Blackmun, only went so far as to say that a "nonpolicymaking, nonconfidential government employee" could not be discharged solely because of party affiliation.[116] In 1980, however, the Court held:

> In sum, the ultimate inquiry is not whether the label "policymaker" or "confidential" fits a particular position; rather, the question is whether the hiring authority can demonstrate that party affiliation is an appropriate requirement for the effective performance of the public office involved.[117]

The 1980s were a period when partisanship and ideological pressures were sufficiently powerful that the issue of patronage again went to the Court. This time it came when a governor mandated that all hiring promotions and transfers would be screened by a party-dominated committee. The Court struck down this bold attack.[118] It created no small stir in the public law community, however, when Justice Scalia, dissenting in the *Rutan* case, announced that he saw absolutely nothing wrong with patronage as a basis for public sector personnel decisions.

Fourth Amendment Searches and Seizures

The First Amendment has, of course, been only one of the arenas of constitutional conflict over public employment in the contemporary era. Another set of issues that has been of concern to both managers and employees relates to Fourth Amendment questions about searches and seizures. As Chapter 11 explained, searches and seizures under the Fourth Amendment normally require a warrant, specifying the person or things sought and, in order to obtain the warrant, providing probable cause to justify the search. That discussion also explained that administrative searches require less rigorous probable cause, but must nevertheless withstand Fourth Amendment scrutiny.

Three types of warrantless searches have been of increasing concern with respect to public employees. They are physical searches of one's office, mandatory drug testing, and monitoring of e-mail. Starting in the late 1980s, a variety of rulings began to emerge suggesting that employers had substantial authority with respect to employee searches and seizures. The Supreme Court's 1987 ruling in *O'Connor v. Ortega*[119] opened the door to broad searches of employee offices and files. That decision was in some respects even more important, though, because of the basis of the ruling, which, like the opinions in the First Amendment area described earlier, employed a case-by-case balancing approach but put a thumb on the scales on the side of employers. And, like the other cases, the *Ortega* ruling provided no clear standard, leaving both employers and employees quite rightly feeling very uncertain.

The *Ortega* case arose from an investigation that eventuated in the termination of a psychiatrist who headed a residency program at a state hospital. Hospital officials decided that the psychiatrist should be investigated, though no formal charges had been brought against him. He was asked to take a paid leave of absence during the investigation, but elected to take vacation time. While still on vacation, he was informed that he was being placed on paid leave and was to stay away from the hospital until the investigation was completed. The investigative team was made up of hospital staff. On several occasions they entered his office and searched it, including his files and desk, seizing a variety of items, including his personal property. Among other things, they seized a Valentine's card, a photograph, and a book of poetry. No effort was made to distinguish between what was personal and what was state property. As one of the members of the investigating team later put it: "trying to sort State from non-State, it was too much to do, so I gave it up and boxed it up."[120]

There was no warrant sought, and it is unclear that anyone ever established a formal basis for the search before it was conducted. When challenged, the state argued that the searches were conducted "pursuant to a Hospital policy of conducting a routine inventory of state property in the office of a terminated employee."[121] The problem with that claim was that, at the time the searches were conducted, no formal charges had been made against the employee, much less had he been "terminated." It was admitted that there was no policy of searching the offices of employees who were on administrative leave, which was his status at the time. Ortega argued quite convincingly that they only searched the office to try to find evidence against him.

After he was terminated, Ortega brought suit on Fourth Amendment grounds. While the district court dismissed his suit without a hearing as to the nature or circumstances of the searches and seizures, the Ninth Circuit Court of Appeals reversed, finding that Ortega had "a reasonable expectation of privacy in his office"[122] and that the search violated the Fourth Amendment. However, the Supreme Court reversed and remanded with a plurality opinion written by Justice O'Connor. The fifth vote for a majority came from Justice Scalia, who would have gone even further than the plurality and would simply have concluded that public employees have no Fourth Amendment protection against searches by their employers.[123]

However, the plurality began by asserting that: "Searches and seizures by government employers or supervisors of the private property of their employees, therefore, are subject to the restraints of the Fourth Amendment."[124] Moreover, O'Connor wrote, "[i]ndividuals do not lose Fourth Amendment rights merely because they work for the government instead of a private employer."[125] Even so, the Court did not grant that as a general principle public employees have a reasonable expectation of privacy in their offices, desks, or files. Indeed, the plurality avoided stating any principle by which to assess such cases and threw the whole issue wide open, declaring that "the question of whether an employee has a reasonable expectation of privacy must be addressed on a case-by-case basis" in a process that would "balance the invasion of the employees' legitimate expectations of privacy against the government's need for supervision, control and the efficient operation of the workplace."[126] But the process was not to be a straight balance between employee interests and employer concerns for an efficient and properly operating workplace. Rather, the Court put a thumb on the scale, concluding that in the case of public employees there are "special needs, beyond the normal need for law enforcement [that] make the ... probable-cause requirement impracticable," for legitimate work-related, noninvestigatory intrusions as well as investigations of work-related misconduct.[127] In the end, the Court held that whether the employee did have some expectation of privacy would be determined not by a requirement for an administrative warrant (discussed in Chapter 11) or even for probable cause, but rather on a decision as to the reasonableness of the intrusion under all the circumstances.

If that sounds confusing, it is. Indeed, Justice Scalia attacked O'Connor's opinion in his concurrence. He based his criticism on the range of problems that he saw would be caused "by an ad hoc, case-by-case definition of the Fourth Amendment standards to be applied in differing factual circumstances" and objecting "to the formulation of a standard so devoid of content that it produces rather than eliminates uncertainty in this field."[128]

The four dissenters, led by Justice Blackmun, were even more critical. They pointed out that the Court had effectively undermined the Fourth Amendment protections available to public employees. For one thing, Blackmun noted, in prior cases the warrant and probable cause requirements were abandoned and a balancing test was used only where it was impracticable under the circumstances to employ the more stringent standards. That would occur where there was no time to obtain a warrant or where there was a threat that evidence might be destroyed or removed. None of those conditions existed in the Ortega case. And, Blackmun said, the Court took the situation from bad to worse by basing its evasion of this standard on a 1985 ruling involving searches of high school students.[129]

That was not the end of the story. The worst predictions of both sets of critics of the Court's *Ortega* ruling proved to be accurate. Following on the dissenters' predictions, the *Ortega* ruling was cited in a variety of important opinions in the lower courts and was significant to the Court's 1989 ruling in the drug testing case, *National Treasury Employees v. Von Raab.*[130] For many public employees, the *Ortega* case meant a serious loss protections previously available to them.[131]

On the other hand, Justice Scalia's fear that the *Ortega* opinion did not provide enough certainty for employers was borne out when the case was sent back to the district court for further action. The Supreme Court plurality opinion remanded the *Ortega* case to the lower courts because there had been no proceeding to make findings about the precise justification for the searches and seizures and whether they were reasonable in nature and scope.[132] That was in 1987. The case was not ultimately resolved until 1998, some 16 years after Dr. Ortega's battle with his employer began, when the Circuit Court of Appeals affirmed the results of a trial in the district court. The jury had rendered a verdict against the two hospital supervisors in the amount of $376,000 in compensatory damages and an additional $25,000 against O'Connor and $35,000 against Friday in punitive damages. The Supreme Court plurality's decision ultimately meant a reduction in protections for both sides, with juries now able to determine "reasonableness" for themselves on a case-by-case basis, assuming that an employee can mount a challenge and sustain it for years.

While the strange tale of Dr. Ortega was unfolding, the Supreme Court decided its first cases on the subject of warrantless drug testing, *Skinner v. Railway Labor Executives' Association*[133] and *National Treasury Employees v. Von Raab.*[134] The *Von Raab* Court employed the same kind of "special needs" approach as in *Ortega* to reduce the employees' reasonable expectation of privacy and called for each drug-testing program to be subjected to a balancing test. The Court itself was uncertain as to how the balancing test would work with respect to all of the employees in the Customs Service and sent portions of the case back for further consideration.

In the years since, courts have upheld a variety of drug-testing programs for police and other public safety employees as well as persons with security clearances.[135] However, there continued to be challenges to a variety of programs for other types of employees.[136] These courts have generally applied the basic balancing approach from *Skinner* and *Von Raab.*

> Our cases establish that where a Fourth Amendment intrusion serves special government needs, beyond the normal need for law enforcement, it is necessary to balance the individuals' privacy expectations against the Government's interests to determine whether it is impractical to require a warrant or some level of individualized suspicion in the particular context.[137]

The Supreme Court elaborated on that standard in a case concerning drug testing of student athletes. Writing for the Court this time, Justice Scalia said:

> The first factor to be considered is the nature of the privacy interest upon which the search here at issue intrudes. The Fourth Amendment does not protect all subject expectations of privacy, but only those that society recognizes as legitimate . . . .

Having considered the scope of the legitimate expectation of privacy at issue here, we turn next to the character of the intrusion that is complained of. . . .

Finally, we turn to consider the nature and immediacy of the governmental concern at issue here, and the efficacy of this means for meeting it.[138]

It is sad, and not a little ironic, that many of the incidents that gave rise to the case law governing such testing for public employees involved drug searches in high schools,[139] monitoring of those on probation,[140] and investigations of train wrecks.[141] It was largely on the basis of these cases, plus the foundation ruling of *Ortega,* that courts have upheld such programs as direct observation of the provision of urine samples by public employees.[142] Interestingly, that very intrusive part of the Wilmington, Delaware employee testing program was actually suggested by the contractor and had not originally been a part of the city's invitation for bids.[143]

On the other hand, in a Georgia case decided in 1997, the Supreme Court struck down a requirement that those wishing to be candidates for elected office in the state had to take drug tests.[144] In concluding that no "special needs" had been demonstrated in the case because no specific problem of drug use among elected officials had been demonstrated, the Court warned that it was not accepted to "diminis[h] personal privacy for a symbol's sake."[145]

While this debate over drug testing was in progress, another and in many ways more controversial issue involving testing has evolved. It is the testing of employees for Human Immunodeficiency Virus (HIV) and Acquired Immunodeficiency Syndrome (AIDS). As is true in drug testing, the wide-open, case-by-case approach to decisions based upon the special needs doctrine has led to conflicting opinions in various courts. Thus, a federal district court in Ohio upheld mandatory testing for firefighters and paramedics,[146] but an Eighth Circuit panel overturned a program requiring testing for employees of a state agency dealing with mentally retarded clients.[147] It will likely be some time before these ambiguities will be reduced given the Supreme Court's approach to date.

A third set of issues has drawn increasing interest in recent years, though not a significant body of case law as yet. These are situations in which employees object to controls and surveillance on computer use, including Internet access and e-mail. These cases arose first in private sector employment settings as firms sought to deal with employees who appeared to be spending more time on personal e-mail or Internet activities than on their duties. Another issue is the use of office systems to access and distribute materials that disturb other employees, sometimes rising to the level of engendering harassment claims based on the assertion that permitting sexually explicit displays on office computers and sexist or racist e-mail constitutes a hostile work environment (a legal prohibition discussed later in this chapter) in violation of Title VII of the Civil Rights Act of 1964.[148] In order to enforce policies created to address these issues, a number of firms have installed software that is used to monitor e-mail and Internet sites visited by employees as well as filters that allow the organization to block e-mail from undesirable sources or unsolicited bulk e-mail (generally referred to as "spam").

> Something is happening in the U.S. workplace, and it is depriving American workers of their privacy rights and companies of their international competitiveness. Workplace privacy has become a matter of great consequence, particularly because American workers are falling victim to e-mail spying, which is occurring without any protection against such abuse. Electronic monitoring software sales are expected to swell nearly five times from $139 million in 2001 to $662 million by 2006. A 2004 survey of employer monitoring verified that "70% of responding employers have implemented a written e-mail policy governing use and content, 74% monitor employee outgoing and incoming e-mail, and 60% monitor employee Internet connections."[149]

As noted earlier, public sector organizations have generally not exercised the degree of control used in many private sector organizations, but they do have similar concerns and can run checks on machines and systems in the event of alleged violations of computer use policies.

The case law is only beginning to develop in this area. Thus far, for example, the Fifth Circuit has upheld a University of Texas decision to block as spam e-mails from an online dating service.[150] The Fourth Circuit has upheld a Virginia computer-use policy that prohibited the use of state-owned computers to access Internet sites that contained "sexually explicit content" without explicit permission, in a case brought by university faculty members whose fields required that they access materials that might be regarded as falling within the state's prohibition.[151] One of the challenges in dealing with Internet sites, of course, is the definitions that are used to identify banned material. In the Fourth Circuit case, Judge Murnaghan, for example, noted that:

> The Act restricts over 101,000 state employees, including university professors, librarians, museum workers, and physicians and social workers at state hospitals, from researching, discussing, and writing about sexually explicit material. As the district court noted, "the Act's broad definition of 'sexually explicit' content would include research and debate on sexual themes in art, literature, history and the law, speech and research by medical and mental health professionals concerning sexual disease, sexual dysfunction, and sexually related mental disorders, and the routine exchange of information among social workers on sexual assault and child abuse." *Urofsky v. Allen,* 995 F. Supp. 634, 636 (E.D. Va. 1998).[152]

Although the state modified its definition following the early portion of the litigation, Judge Murnaghan contended that the problem remained. These two cases were launched in part on First Amendment grounds, but the question remains about enforcement and the issue of monitoring of Internet use. It will be interesting to watch how employers and the courts work through some of these issues over time.

There are several complicating factors presenting by technological changes. For example, it is increasingly common today for employees to use laptop computers that travel with them rather than office machines physically connected to an organization's central IT system. Laptops and handheld computing devices with Internet capabilities also use so-called hot-spots, free Internet access portals accessed via wireless technology at various locations. For these and other reasons it will likely be some time before it is clear just what kinds of policies will be implemented as well as the specific mechanisms of enforcement and dispute resolution that will be developed to enforce those policies.

Constitutional Conflict over Privacy and Lifestyle: Not Minor Matters at All

Of course, while the debates over drug and HIV testing are fought out on the basis of the Fourth Amendment (as applied to the states through the Fourteenth), they also relate to concepts of privacy protected by other provisions, including the Ninth Amendment. Indeed, they are often discussed as part of a set of concerns about lifestyle, questions about residence, appearance, off-the-job associations, smoking, eating or drinking habits, and relationships with families or sexual partners. Obviously, these disputes relate not only to job performance, but also to demands that public servants must adjust their lifestyles and off-duty conduct to conform to the public image of the government.

From the employer's perspective, employees with colorful lifestyles may harm public confidence in the professionalism or integrity of the public service. From the employees' perspective, as long as their conduct does not endanger others or affect their actual performance on the job, their lives should be their own.

These issues implicate a variety of constitutional provisions. Some challenges by employees to rules of public employment are based on the constitutionally protected right to privacy. Of course, there is no specifically articulated right to privacy in the Constitution, but, as was true of the right to association, the Supreme Court has determined that this right is implied by other provisions of the Bill of Rights.[153] In one case, local school boards required pregnant teachers to take maternity leave five months before their projected delivery date. The Court ruled that this restriction unduly interfered with the woman's protected rights concerning family life and the decision to bear children.[154]

Similar arguments have been made by government employees who object to restrictions on their sexual conduct or lifestyle. Some lower federal courts have supported the employees,[155] but the Supreme Court has carefully avoided several cases that raised questions about prohibitions against homosexuality or firings of public employees who underwent sex change operations. However, in *Lawrence v. Texas,* decided in 2003, the Supreme Court said:

> Liberty protects the person from unwarranted government intrusions into a dwelling or other private places. In our tradition the State is not omnipresent in the home. And there are other spheres of our lives and existence, outside the home, where the State should not be a dominant presence. Freedom extends beyond spatial bounds. Liberty presumes an autonomy of self that includes freedom of thought, belief, expression, and certain intimate conduct. The instant case involves liberty of the person both in its spatial and more transcendent dimensions.[156]

In the *Lawrence* case, the Court struck down a "Texas statute making it a crime for two persons of the same sex to engage in certain intimate sexual conduct."[157] The Court concluded that the Texas statute violated liberty protections within the meaning of the due process clause of the Fourteenth Amendment and, in so doing, reversed its own ruling in a 1986 case that had upheld a Georgia law prohibiting homosexual behavior.[158] The majority in *Lawrence* based its ruling on substantive due process protections and therefore indicated that it was unnecessary to address any equal protection questions. Justice O'Connor concurred with the majority decision, but would have struck down the Texas legislation on equal protection grounds. She wrote:

> Moral disapproval of a group cannot be a legitimate governmental interest under the Equal Protection Clause because legal classifications must not be "drawn for the purpose of disadvantaging the group burdened by the law.". . . Texas' invocation of moral disapproval as a legitimate state interest proves nothing more than Texas' desire to criminalize homosexual sodomy. But the Equal Protection Clause prevents a State from creating "a classification of persons undertaken for its own sake."[159]

However, O'Connor was plainly taking that approach with the intention of avoiding providing a foundation for an attack on state laws that prohibited gay marriage. She wrote: "Unlike the moral disapproval of same-sex relations—the asserted state interest in this case—other reasons exist to promote the institution of marriage beyond mere moral disapproval of an excluded group."[160]

It is as yet uncertain just what kind of impact the *Lawrence* case will have in public employment cases, though the majority's approach would appear to raise serious doubts about the ability simply to attack a public employee because, as a homosexual, they would be engaged in a lifestyle that could be prohibited. To this point, the military "Don't Ask, Don't Tell" policy initiated during the Clinton administration has not produced a definitive ruling and the Supreme Court has not taken any related cases.

That said, both before and after the *Lawrence* decision, some federal district courts have allowed employees to bring cases asserting punishment or termination based on what was termed a gay or lesbian lifestyle.[161] A Utah case preceded *Lawrence* and was addressed on equal protection grounds. A veteran teacher who also happened to be a very successful volleyball coach found herself in the midst of a difficult situation. She had been away from the school for a year while completing a graduate degree program. Upon her return, a volleyball player called her and asked her if she was gay. The coach answered that she was. Calls were made to the school administration in an attempt to block her return as coach. Her ex-husband allegedly spoke with school officials about her as well. She was not rehired as a coach, notwithstanding the fact that she had never had any negative information on her record and had led the team to four state championships. She was also served with a letter from the school that read in part:

> The District has received reports that you have made public and expressed to students your homosexual orientation and lifestyle. If these reports are true, we are concerned about the potential disruption in the school community and advise you of the following:

– You are not to make any comments, announcements or statements to students, staff members, or parents of students regarding your homosexual orientation or lifestyle.

– If students, staff members, or parents of students ask about your sexual orientation or anything concerning the subject, you shall tell them that the subject is private and personal and inappropriate to discuss with them.

This memo is to place you on notice of the expectations the school district has for you concerning this matter. A violation of these requirements may jeopardize your job and be cause for termination.[162]

Anticipating Justice O'Connor's arguments in *Lawrence,* Judge Bruce Jenkins of the U.S. District Court in Utah wrote: "Despite mounting evidence that gay males and lesbians suffer from employment discrimination and, as recent events in Wyoming remind us, other more life-threatening expressions of bias, courts, including the Supreme Court, have not yet recognized a person's sexual orientation as a status that deserves heightened protection."[163] However, he concluded, any class-based discrimination must nevertheless be rationally related to some legitimate state purpose, and the school district's actions were not. "Although the Constitution cannot control prejudices, neither this court nor any other court should, directly or indirectly, legitimize them."[164]

In addition to these issues, challenges have also been brought by public servants who asserted that restrictions on dress or personal appearance interfered with their freedom of expression. However, the Supreme Court ruled that regulations limiting the style and length of, for example, a police officer's hair are not unconstitutional violations of the employee's liberty.[165] In fact, the Court has gone beyond that to rule that the military could bar an officer who was a rabbi from wearing his yarmulke in the hospital to which he was assigned.[166] In this case, the Court rejected a free exercise of religion claim under the First Amendment to uphold the Air Force action.

An important lifestyle consideration that has prompted constitutional litigation, particularly given contemporary residential markets and living patterns in much of the country, is the frequently imposed requirement that one live within the government jurisdiction in which one is employed. Police officers, firefighters, and teachers have brought suits challenging such rules. In *McCarthy v. Philadelphia Civil Service Commission,* the Supreme Court held that a requirement that city employees reside in the city did not violate the employee's right to travel or his liberty under the Constitution.[167] The Court did not even bother to hear argument in the *McCarthy* case in which six members of the Court joined a *per curiam* opinion permitting a 16-year veteran of the Philadelphia Fire Department to be fired because he did not live in the city. Relying on that weak foundation, lower courts have upheld residency requirements even where supervisors supported the employee and stated on the record that their residency would have no bearing on their ability to perform their duties.[168]

Employees have found themselves under pressure to avoid certain off-the-job associations and even smoking, eating, or drinking habits. For example, some Connecticut corrections officers argued that the state had violated their constitutional rights when it took action against them because they were members of the "Outlaws Motorcycle Club," but a federal district court rejected the challenge.[169] With respect to smoking, the Florida Supreme Court upheld a City of North Miami regulation that required persons seeking jobs in the city to submit an affidavit attesting that they had not used tobacco products for one year.[170] Another antismoking requirement was upheld in Oklahoma.[171] These are requirements that are to be distinguished from rules governing conduct on the job.[172] The argument in support of these rules is that "employers experience higher costs from smoking employees through higher absenteeism, lower productivity, and higher life insurance costs."[173] Of course, critics contend that if employers are justified on those grounds, then presumably a public employer might also be able to deal with such serious health risks as high cholesterol, obesity, or "genetic predisposition to medical conditions and diseases."[174] And if these are acceptable, could the employer also prohibit risky recreational activities?

As many as half the states have adopted some form of legal protection against interference by employers in lifestyle matters.[175] However, this is still very much a developing area of the law with many ambiguities. And it is also unclear whether public employees will enjoy the benefits of some of the efforts to protect off-the-job behavior.

Equal Protection: The Problem of Discrimination
and the Attempt to Remedy It

Historically, the effort to address discrimination against women and minority groups has been a difficult battle waged under the Fourteenth Amendment (where state or local governments are involved) and the Fifth Amendment (for federal government questions).[176] In particular, the attempt to deal with discrimination in public employment based on race, sex, and alienage has been most complex. But before reaching cases that address these particular problems, it is necessary to outline the premises and assumptions on which courts depend in handling claims of unconstitutional discrimination.

The Basic Framework for Equal Protection Analysis   Almost all laws and regulations classify people, things, or actions. Laws are directed at particular groups of people, such as residents of a community, business persons, doctors, minors, or pension recipients. But not all laws that classify or treat different groups of people differently can be said to involve unconstitutional, or invidious, discrimination in violation of the equal protection clause of the Fourteenth Amendment. The problem for courts is to determine what kinds of unequal treatment violate the Constitution. That problem is complicated by the fact that some laws that appear to be fair and nondiscriminatory as written are administered in a discriminatory manner.[177] The Supreme Court has developed a general framework for dealing with such cases.

In most instances, the courts will assume that government officials act lawfully.[178] Therefore, one who asserts that government officials have unconstitutionally discriminated in law (that is, in the manner in which a law is written) or under color of law (the manner in which law or policy is administered by people authorized to act) carries the burden of proving that those officials have acted unlawfully. All the government need do is demonstrate that its actions are rationally related to a legitimate government interest. For example, suppose a group of 15-year-olds challenge a state law requiring mandatory school attendance until the age of 16. True, the law classifies and treats people differently based on age, but the state will merely claim that mandatory attendance until approximately 16 years of age is rationally related to the legitimate state purpose of ensuring a minimum level of education for all its citizens. The law would stand.

The Supreme Court has found over the years that certain criteria used to treat people differently are inherently suspicious because they have historically been used to discriminate unconstitutionally. They are referred to as "suspect classifications," the best example being government action that treats people differently on the basis of race.[179] Where the person charging discrimination shows that the government treats citizens differently on the basis of a suspect classification or discriminates in providing opportunities to exercise fundamental rights (e.g., when the right to due process, in a criminal case, the right to marry, or the right to travel are made to depend on one's ability to pay), the Court becomes more vigilant and imposes strict judicial scrutiny. At the point where the Court is convinced that government is treating people differently on the basis of a suspect classification or with respect to their fundamental rights, the burden of proof shifts to the government to justify the discrimination. The government must do more than merely show that its actions are rationally related to some legitimate state purpose. It must demonstrate a compelling interest, sufficiently grave to overcome the harm done to those who were discriminated against, and the means used must be narrowly tailored to achieve that goal.[180] The Court has ruled that suspect classifications are those that involve a "discrete and insular minority," which has suffered a history of discrimination, has been "relegated to such a position of powerlessness as to command extraordinary protection from the majoritarian political process,"[181] and may possess the characteristic that distinguishes them from others as an accident of birth.[182] Race, illegitimacy, and alienage have all been treated as suspect classifications at one time or another.[183] Obviously, it is, and should be, extremely difficult to justify discrimination and stand the test of strict judicial scrutiny.

There is another element to the problem. The equal protection clause prohibits discrimination in law or under color of law (*de jure*), but it does not prohibit accidental differentials—differences in conditions not deliberately created either overtly or covertly—(*de facto*). This is important because those who practiced discrimination long ago became sophisticated enough to avoid using words or writing policies that actually stated the intention to discriminate. For that reason, the courts have generally looked to the effect of the government action to decide whether there was *de jure* discrimination, rather than attempting to determine what was in the minds of the officials when they acted or wrote a law.[184]

If the action complained of had the effect of treating, for example, African Americans differently from others, strict scrutiny would be triggered and the government would be required to justify the differential treatment. In *Washington v. Davis*, a 1976 case, the Supreme Court held that it is necessary to demonstrate both discriminatory effect and discriminatory intent to trigger strict judicial scrutiny in a constitutional claim.[185] Those who claimed that they were being subjected to discrimination had to prove that the discrimination was intentional. In later cases, the Court gave examples of guidelines to prove intent, including an examination of the impact or effect of the government action, the "historical background of the decision," the "specific sequence of events leading up to the challenged decision," a determination whether there had been "departures from the normal procedural sequence," and the "legislative or administrative history" of the action, including records, minutes, or hearing transcripts.[186]

In 1979, a woman brought a suit against the personnel administrator of Massachusetts, arguing that the state's veterans preference law was unconstitutional discrimination on the basis of sex.[187] She argued that, until relatively recently, U.S. military guidelines limited the number of women who could serve in the military to roughly 2 percent of the members of the armed services, hence limiting the number of women who could qualify for veterans preference. The challengers proved that, at the time the law was extended during the Vietnam years, the legislature had been told that its program—which provided a lifetime absolute preference over all nonveterans—would make it all but impossible for most women to break out of the lowest-paid clerical positions into better paying government jobs that would offer career advancement. The women produced figures to show that the number of women who were able to get beyond the minimal civil service levels was indeed very low and that a variety of men had been hired over women who had higher scores on civil service examinations. They argued that some form of preference to help returning veterans or to encourage others to serve might be justified, but that the lifelong absolute preference enacted in the face of an awareness of its impact on women was unconstitutional. The Supreme Court disagreed, holding that the program was not intentional gender-based discrimination. "Discriminatory purpose, however, implies more than intent as volition or intent as awareness of consequences. It implies that the decisionmaker, in this case a state legislature, selected or reaffirmed a particular course of action at least in part 'because of,' not merely 'in spite of,' its adverse effects upon an identifiable group."[188]

In sum, developments in equal protection law since the 1970s pose significant difficulties for those who wish to pursue constitutional claims under the equal protection clause. Currently, the Supreme Court generally regards race as the only classification that is treated as a "suspect class."

Given that we are a nation of immigrants, it is embarrassing for Americans to be reminded of the discrimination against aliens in our history, particularly since World War I. A volatile economy and a more competitive job market, along with a major increase in the number of refugees, immigrants, and permanent resident aliens have increased tensions. In the 1960s and 1970s a number of cases were brought by aliens who permanently reside in this country, some with the expectation of becoming citizens, all paying taxes, and also living subject to all other laws (including compulsory military service if required), who would like to work for government at all levels in jobs ranging from clerk typist, to teacher, police officer, or engineer. For a time, the Supreme Court treated classifications based on alienage as suspect. It struck laws that barred professionals from practicing,[189] prevented persons from receiving benefits from public programs,[190] or precluded resident aliens from public employment.[191] However, even during that period, the Court granted considerably more deference to the federal government because of the relationship between immigration and naturalization policy and foreign policy.[192]

In the late 1970s, however, the Supreme Court handed down rulings permitting state governments considerably more latitude in restricting certain kinds of jobs to citizens only. The Court held that where the nature of a government job is such that it is of particular importance and involves a considerable amount of discretion, a state may be able to justify a limitation.[193] Specifically, the Court upheld a New York restriction on the certification of teachers[194] and a state restriction that citizens only be hired as state troopers.[195] To this point at least, that increased deference to public employers has continued, though courts will look to see if the requisite connection is shown for requiring citizenship in a given context.[196]

Gender, while not a suspect classification, is treated with what has been termed an intermediate level of scrutiny. That is, classifications based on gender must be more than merely rationally related to a legitimate state object. "Classifications by gender must serve important governmental objectives and must be substantially related to achievement of those objectives."[197] While it is difficult to understand the distinction, the idea is that while courts should not impose strict judicial scrutiny on gender classifications with its compelling interest standard, they should require more than a mere showing that a policy has some rational basis. After the court settled on its intermediate level of scrutiny approach to gender cases, there were a number of additional cases.[198] In a highly publicized case in which the Court struck down single-sex education at the Virginia Military Institute, the Court said that: "Parties who seek to defend gender-based government action must demonstrate an 'exceedingly persuasive justification' for that action."[199] However, the requirements to prove intentional discrimination are very difficult to meet in the contemporary world of sophisticated discrimination. And while it may be the case that current conditions are in truth the effects of prior discrimination, that is an extremely difficult contention to prove under current constitutional law.

Therefore, most of the litigation brought in federal courts alleging racial or gender discrimination in government employment since the 1970s has been launched under Title VII of the Civil Rights Act of 1964, as amended over the years.[200] That legislation and the Civil Service Reform Act of 1978[201] (CSRA) have made most legislation barring discrimination in employment practices applicable to the government as an employer, or else provided a government equivalent. The fact that the litigation patterns have changed has not, however, meant that the continuing conversation over discrimination has become any less heated or complex. We will return for a closer look at these statutory issues shortly, but there is one other area of constitutional argument that is important to the public employment context. It is the debate over affirmative action.

The Affirmative Action Debate   One area in which there have continued to be a substantial number of constitutional equal protection arguments litigated is in the form of challenges to affirmative action programs. Those who have launched these challenges have argued that programs implemented to bring more women and minority employees into government service or private employment, to increase diversity of the student body in universities as well as graduate and professional programs, to encourage the growth of minority business enterprises, and to eliminate the effects of past discrimination are forms of reverse racial or gender discrimination.

Like other disputes in the law and public management field, the judicial reaction to these cases differed sharply in different periods. First, in the years following *Brown v. Board of Education*,[202] it became excruciatingly clear that everything from silent but forceful delaying tactics to "massive resistance" would be used to frustrate the desegregation rulings.[203] Finally, by the late 1960s, the Court had had enough. It ordered that remedial action needed to be taken immediately to eliminate segregated systems "root and branch," and to drop references to the infamous "all deliberate speed" language that had been interpreted to support delays.[204]

The Court signaled that it was time to use remedial orders to force action, even if it was unpopular. It was against that backdrop that the Court issued its famous ruling in *Swann v. Charlotte Mechlenburg Bd. of Ed.*,[205] which upheld the use of transportation plans to move students as needed to eliminate segregated schools. Hence, there was no serious question by the early 1970s that a court could order a race or gender conscious remedy that imposed an affirmative obligation on an agency or unit of government where there was a proven case of segregation in violation of the Constitution or civil rights statutes. The emerging debate concerned what level of proof was needed to sustain a finding of discrimination and invoke an affirmative remedy, what the scope of that remedy could be, and under what conditions such a remedy would be terminated.[206]

Second, by the mid- to late 1970s the focus and the nature of the affirmative action debate shifted, as did the context within which it was waged. The question was what happens if the decision is made voluntarily to undertake an affirmative action program in order to remedy a lack of diversity and the effects of past discrimination, even though no formal legal finding of discrimination had been rendered. Some of those cases arose when a particular organization simply decided to undertake a diversity effort. Others were voluntary in the sense that no finding of discrimination had been issued, but the program was developed in large part because federal authorities warned schools or firms that they would be the subject of legal action if they did not elect to do something about their situation.

The irony that emerged was in the form of a Catch-22 demonstrated by the ruling in *Board of Regents v. Bakke.*[207] There was no question that if the university had been found guilty of discrimination in its admissions practices in violation of Title VI of the Civil Rights Act (which prohibits discrimination by any organization or program receiving federal funds), it could have been ordered by a court to undertake a race-conscious enrollment policy as a remedy for the violation. If it lost such a case, however, millions of dollars of federal funding would have been placed at risk and the university could have been subject to other sanctions. However, if it undertook a voluntary program, there were questions whether it could be found guilty of reverse discrimination in violation of the Fourteenth Amendment to the Constitution. A badly fragmented Supreme Court was unable to achieve a majority opinion, but struck down the U.C. Davis program because it set aside seats for minority students. On the other hand, the Court did not rule out the possibility that race could be one factor in considering the overall qualifications of a student. The following year, another badly fragmented Supreme Court ruling upheld a voluntary affirmative action program developed by a company for employee training against a challenge under Title VII.[208] Here again, the firm created the program in the face of a threat of prosecution for discrimination that it would clearly have lost. Justices Marshall and Brennan argued that racial discrimination has been pervasive in American society for generations, and individuals in the job market and those attempting to obtain professional educations have been, and continued to be, disadvantaged by that discrimination, both directly and indirectly.[209]

With new members appointed by Presidents Reagan and Bush, the Supreme Court began a difficult reconsideration of the very idea of voluntary affirmative action. Where there was a proven case of discrimination, even that Court continued to uphold race-conscious remedies,[210] albeit with greater limitations on the lower courts than before. In one case at least, the Court found that even though there had not been a formal finding of discrimination, there was sufficient evidence that there had been such discrimination that the Court upheld a voluntary program to increase the number of women in previously male-dominated positions.[211] The Court upheld two affirmative action programs launched by the federal government; the first concerned with contract set asides for minority business enterprises[212] and the second involving a Federal Communications Commission affirmative action process for increasing the number of broadcasting licenses held by minority firms.[213]

Beginning in the mid-1980s and extending throughout the 1990s, however, there was an intense and growing attack on voluntary affirmative action and on the nature, scope, and duration of affirmative remedies, even those issued in cases where prior discrimination had been proven. Financial stresses of the early 1980s added fuel to disagreements over affirmative action. To that difficult situation was added a shift by the Justice Department under the Reagan administration. It moved away from a consistent position in favor of affirmative action for more than a decade, to opposition to programs which challenged seniority systems or which provided classwide relief to individuals who may not personally have been victims of direct discrimination by a particular employer. Indeed, some federal district judges found themselves confronted by the federal authorities switching sides within a single case.[214]

These complexities came together in *Memphis Firefighters v. Stotts*[215] and *Wygant v. Jackson Board of Education*.[216] The Court struck down efforts in two communities to preserve diversity gains in the face of pending layoffs, one by a board of education and the other by a judge acting to modify a consent decree.

However, the case that really signaled the degree of change was the *City of Richmond v. Croson*.[217] In *Croson* the Court struck down a contract set-aside program instituted by the City of Richmond, Virginia, using the previously upheld federal program as a model. Justice O'Connor wrote for the Court, justifying the decision to strike the Richmond plan while preserving the federal government plan on the argument that the Congress had special powers not possessed by the states and its actions in the area of civil rights stood in a different posture from those undertaken in the states. However, while insisting that voluntary affirmative action programs would have to withstand "strict judicial scrutiny," the heaviest burden possible, in order to survive review, the Court would not absolutely foreclose the possibility that there may be some situation in which a voluntary program may be acceptable.

Justice Antonin Scalia concurred, but roundly chastised O'Connor for creating a situation where the Court said affirmative action was not *per se* unconstitutional but establishing a set of rules for review that made it all but impossible to satisfy her demands for justification. While his method was crude, he had a strong case for his criticism of O'Connor's reasoning. On the other hand, O'Connor held the crucial fifth vote in the area of affirmative action, which means that she was in a position to set the terms, not Scalia.

And, indeed, O'Connor weighed in heavily in 1995, taking another step in the direction of eliminating voluntary affirmative action. Writing for the Court in *Adarand Construction Assn. v. Pena*,[218] O'Connor struck down a federal program that gave incentives to prime contractors who hired minority subcontractors. Of course, now she had to come to grips with the obvious contradiction between the *Adarand* ruling and the two prior cases upholding federal affirmative action programs. Acting as though she had never made her argument about differences in the *Richmond* case, O'Connor wrote that it was absurd to have equal protection mean one thing for the states and something else for the federal government. She therefore overturned the broadcast licensing case directly.

In the end, O'Connor concluded: "We hold today that all racial classifications, imposed by whatever federal, state, or local governmental actor, must be analyzed by a reviewing court under strict scrutiny. In other words, such classifications are constitutional only if they are narrowly tailored measures that further compelling governmental interests. To the extent that Metro Broadcasting is inconsistent with that holding, it is overruled."[219] While arguing that her opinion really followed the preceding cases, she added that "our decision today alters the playing field in some important respects."

Scalia concurred, noting that he was simply opposed to affirmative action even as a remedy. Thomas concurred as well, suggesting that any other position amounts to "a racial paternalism exception to the principle of equal protection."[220]

The dissenters, led by Justice Stevens, insisted that the Court had inappropriately equated an action by the majority "to impose a special burden on a minority race and a decision by the majority to provide a benefit to certain members of that minority notwithstanding its incidental burden on some members of the majority."[221] He also pointed out O'Connor's inconsistencies with respect to the federal versus state or local programs in *Croson*.[222]

Life after *Adarand* has been complex. The Clinton administration launched a yearlong study in an effort to retain affirmative action programs while bringing federal contracting processes into compliance with *Adarand*.[223] The First Circuit upheld the promotion of an African-American police officer, though he scored one point lower than white officers, on affirmative action grounds.[224]

On the other hand, it appeared for a time that the Supreme Court might take the next step and ban affirmative action altogether[225] and cases were launched by anti–affirmative action forces in several parts of the country to push the Court in that direction. Thus, the Fifth Circuit rendered a dramatic decision in 1996, *Hopwood v. State of Texas*,[226] warning that any further effort by the University of Texas either "disguised or overt" to use racial classifications would not only violate the constitution but would subject state officials to claims for both actual and punitive damages.[227] The Fourth Circuit issued a ruling striking down minority fellowships.[228] The First Circuit reversed a district court ruling and struck down a Boston school affirmative action program for admission to its three competitive admission schools.[229]

Dade County, Florida's Black Business Enterprise program, its Hispanic Business Enterprise program, and its Women Business Enterprise program were all struck down,[230] even though the Black Enterprise program (later used as the model for the Hispanic and Women's programs) had been upheld more than a decade earlier.[231] The United District Court for the District of Minnesota stuck down the Disadvantaged Business Enterprise program operated by Minnesota under the Intermodal Surface Transportation Act of 1991 (ISTEA).[232] The Dallas, Texas, Fire Department affirmative action promotion policy was rejected both as to its race-based and gender-based elements.[233]

In California, then-Governor Pete Wilson supported Proposition 209, a measure adopted by the voters that effectively bars voluntary affirmative action in that state. He also issued an executive order requiring state agencies not to employ race or gender conscious policies. Challenges to Proposition 209 were unsuccessful.[234] Florida Governor Jeb Bush took similar actions by executive order to block affirmative action in state government.[235]

However, the Supreme Court finally accepted two affirmative action cases, this time returning to the arena of university admissions. These two cases, *Gratz v. Bollinger*[236] and *Grutter v. Bollinger*,[237] came in the form of challenges to undergraduate and law school admissions at the University of Michigan. Once again the justices were not only sharply divided on whether to uphold the policies, but they were also fragmented as to the appropriate reasoning for their respective positions. There was a majority to uphold the law school admissions program. Those justices applied the strict scrutiny test, but found that diversity in the student body was a compelling interest and that the process which considered race as one factor, but not a definitive factor, was sufficiently narrowly tailored to meet the constitutional test. While the *Bollinger* cases put to rest the idea that the Court was prepared to outlaw affirmative action altogether, it did not settle the question of what other affirmative action programs, and in which fields, would be able to survive the strict scrutiny test. And to make the situation even more uncertain, Justice Sandra Day O'Connor, the author of the *Grutter v. Bollinger* opinion, has since been replaced by Justice Samuel Alito, and Chief Justice William Rehnquist, author of the *Gratz v. Bollinger* opinion, has been replaced by Chief Justice Johns Roberts. It remains to be seen how they will respond to future cases.

STATUTORY PROTECTIONS FOR PUBLIC EMPLOYEES

In addition to the body of constitutional law protecting the rights of public employees, there are a number of statutory developments about which public employers and employees should be aware, even if they are not familiar with the details of each. These are statutes that govern employee political activity (discussed earlier in the chapter), protection against discrimination, and the general operation of the civil service system.

Statutory Antidiscrimination Programs

The statutes enacted by the federal government to eliminate discrimination fall into three general categories: (1) broad attacks on discriminatory practices in employment; (2) specific attempts to deal with sex discrimination; and (3) attempts to deal with special problems of discrimination and accommodation.

The Civil Rights Act of 1964   For decades now, the primary mechanism for dealing with discrimination in employment has been the Civil Rights Act of 1964.[238] The act prohibited discrimination on the basis of race, sex, religion, and national origin, and established the Equal Employment Opportunity Commission (EEOC). But that act was passed during a period of severe conflict over federal enforcement of fair employment practices, and the bill that was eventually enacted contained many compromises and changes from the one that was originally introduced. For one thing, the EEOC had extremely limited powers, serving primarily as a clearinghouse for complaints by employees. The 1964 act was amended and substantially strengthened by the Equal Employment Opportunity Act of 1972.[239] Among other things, the amendments extended the coverage of the Title VII antidiscrimination provisions to most federal, state, and local employees. Second, EEOC was given substantial enforcement authority, including the power to prosecute cases in court. The basic antidiscrimination provisions of the act were strengthened again in the Civil Rights Act of 1991.[240]

Under contemporary provisions, an employee or applicant may assert that the employer's actions constituted disparate treatment, that they resulted in disparate impact, or involved racial harassment. "The plaintiff's burden in a Title VII disparate impact case is to prove that a particular employment practice has caused a significant adverse effect on a protected group.... Once the plaintiff establishes the adverse effect, the burden shifts to the employer to produce evidence that the challenged practice is a business necessity."[241] Racial harassment can be based upon the creation by the employer of a hostile work environment. "A racially hostile work environment exists when an employer 'creates or condones an environment at the work place which significantly and adversely affects the psychological well-being of an employee because of his or her race.'"[242]

An important aspect of the 1972 amendments to the Civil Rights Act is that they were designed with a concern for the need to deal with sex discrimination. The original 1964 act was primarily designed to deal with racial discrimination in employment and places of public accommodation. The women's movement was not yet a central factor in American politics when it was passed, but by the early 1970s more women were politically active and more were employed in a wider variety of positions than ever before. The EEOC has since attempted to deal with such matters through issuance of guidelines and dispute resolution procedures.[243] Other important statutory developments on sex discrimination include the Equal Pay Act[244] and the pregnancy discrimination amendments to the Civil Rights Act.[245] The Equal Pay Act was intended to eliminate widespread pay disparities between males and females doing the same kind of work.

Another important set of developments affecting the pay and benefits of women arose from Supreme Court interpretations of Title VII. The Court refused to permit women to be charged more for their retirement annuities or to be paid less per month after retirement. Although employers and their annuity contractors argued that such rulings would undermine the actuarial soundness of the plans, the Court answered that the act was not designed to permit assumptions to be made about the life expectancy of an individual woman because of the statistics of the class as a whole. Title VII, the Court held, "requires employers to treat their employees as individuals, not 'as simply components of a racial, religious, sexual, or national class.'"[246] The pregnancy discrimination amendments were designed as a response to a Supreme Court ruling that employers need not consider pregnancy-related problems as medical disabilities in insurance plans or other benefit programs.[247]

Sexual Harassment: A Complex and Important Issue   One of the most important gender-related issues that has come to the fore in the contemporary era is the matter of sexual harassment. This insidious practice of conditioning employment or promotions on compliance with demands for sexual favors has been with us for a long time,[248] but has drawn more attention as more women entered the workforce in virtually all fields. It came to particular prominence with the confirmation debate over the nomination of Associate Justice Clarence Thomas, following charges by former EEOC employee Anita Hill that he had harassed her. Whatever the events and forces were that brought this issue into the light of public debate, it was an extremely important development for any organization, for public as well as private managers, and for the well-being of employees.

The Supreme Court has determined that sexual harassment does qualify as sex discrimination under Title VII, finding that a valid claim may arise either from direct "[u]nwelcome sexual advances, requests for sexual favors, and other verbal or physical conduct of a sexual nature" or from a situation in which "discrimination based on sex has created a hostile or abusive work environment."[249] In some states, action was taken even before the Supreme Court ruling. Thus, Governor Mario Cuomo of New York issued Executive Order 19 in 1983, requiring each agency of state government to create a policy to combat sexual harassment and a process for entertaining and processing complaints:

> WHEREAS, sexual harassment in the workplace is not merely offensive but is a form of discrimination in violation of Federal and State law; and
>
> WHEREAS, every State employee is entitled to a working environment free from sexual harassment and its deleterious economic, psychological and physical effects; and
>
> WHEREAS, the cost to the State is considerable in both human and financial terms including the replacement of personnel who leave their job, increased use of health benefit plans due to emotional and physical stress, absenteeism, and decline in individual and workgroup productivity;
>
> NOW, THEREFORE, I, Mario M. Cuomo, Governor of the State of New York, by virtue of the authority vested in me by the Constitution and Laws of the State of New York, do hereby establish a New York State Policy Statement on Sexual Harassment in the Workplace.

While all professional public managers agree that sexual harassment is wrong, the complexity arises from the fact that harassment can be very subtle and very difficult to define and demonstrate. The Equal Employment Opportunity Commission first issued guidelines defining sexual harassment and judging it to be sex discrimination within the meaning of Title VII in 1980. Those guidelines provided that harassment could occur either in the quid pro quo form in which a direct demand was made for sexual favors, or from a finding that there was behavior by superiors such that "such conduct has the purpose or effect of unreasonably interfering with an individual's work performance or creating an intimidating, hostile, or offensive working environment."[250] The basic theory is that while no specific demand is made, conditions are created in which the employee receives the message that she or he had better comply with expectations or face retribution. This is what is known as "hostile environment" harassment. When the Supreme Court rendered its first ruling on sexual harassment in 1986, it accepted the not only the Commission's conclusions that harassment was sex discrimination, but also its definition of quid pro quo and hostile environment as the two actionable forms of harassment.[251]

However, the Court was not prepared in that ruling to explain what the standards would be according to which decisions would be made about employer liability. Neither was it necessary in that case for the Court to articulate precisely what an employee would have to prove to demonstrate hostile environment harassment. The facts in the *Meritor Savings Bank*[252] case were so extreme that it was not necessary to consider subtleties to decide the case. However, with the flurry of cases brought in the lower federal courts, it was clear that the justices would be called upon to address both the standards of proof and liability issues.

In *Harris v. Forklift Systems,* the Court was faced with a situation involving allegations of harassment by the president of the company. The woman who brought the charges had complained about his behavior and he had promised to stop but did not. She did not complain of quid pro quo harassment, but asserted that the president had created a hostile environment. The lower courts had ruled that it was necessary for a victim to prove psychological injury in order to maintain a hostile environment case, but the Supreme Court disagreed. The Court found that: "When the workplace is permeated with discriminatory intimidation, ridicule, and insult, ... that is sufficiently severe or pervasive to alter the conditions of the victim's employment and create an abusive working environment, ... Title VII is violated."[253] That required the employee to demonstrate that it was the kind of hostile or abusive environment that a "reasonable person would find hostile or abusive."[254] But the Court warned that this was not a narrow assessment:

> [W]hether an environment is "hostile" or "abusive" can be determined only by looking at all the circumstances. These may include the frequency of the discriminatory conduct; its severity; whether it is physically threatening or humiliating, or a mere offensive utterance and whether it unreasonably interferes with an employee's work performance."[255]

Harassment cases can also stem from behavior by supervisors of the same sex as the victim.[256]

In 1992, the Court also found that Title IX of the Civil Rights Act, which prohibits discrimination on the basis of sex in educational programs supported by federal funds, provides a vehicle for students to file suit against teachers, administrators, and the school district for sexual harassment.[257] And as is true with respect to the employment cases, harassment by someone of the same sex can give rise to a claim under Title IX.[258]

Following the early decisions in lower courts and the Supreme Court rulings, many supervisors became fearful that innocent things they or their subordinates might say or do could be construed as harassment. Sadly, some women may not have received the opportunities and career development support they should have had because of concern by their supervisors about false, but nevertheless damaging, allegations of unacceptable relationships.

Some employees who determined that inappropriate relationships between superiors and co-workers were driving decisions in their workplace launched sexual harassment suits. In these cases, an employee alleged that others in the organization had engaged in sexual behavior and were rewarded for it, sending the message to the rest that they should do likewise, and creating a hostile work environment for those who chose not to participate.

The Supreme Court has attempted to address both the fears of what constitutes harassment and the liability standards that apply if harassment is found. The effort to stop harassment, the Court said, "requires neither asexuality nor androgyny in the workplace."[259] In another case, the Court cautioned that "Title VII does not prohibit 'genuine but innocuous differences in the ways men and women routinely interact with members of the same sex and of the opposite sex.' . . . [O]ffhand comments, and isolated incidents (unless extremely serious) will not amount to discriminatory changes in the "terms and conditions of employment."[260]

A significant part of the ambiguity about the organization's liability really concerns one area of responsibility. Clearly, if superiors are aware of harassing behavior and deliberately refuse to take action or if they take retribution against a victim who complains of harassment, their liability is obvious. The anxiety arises, however, from the concern that subordinates may harass those under their authority but that superiors may not be aware of the lower-level official's behavior and yet face suits against themselves and their organizations. Indeed, there have been cases brought in which an employee did not report harassment above the level of the immediate supervisor, resigned, and then brought suit seeking damages from the organization. In one such situation, a former lifeguard sued the City of Boca Raton, Florida, after a lengthy period of hostile environment harassment by two lower-level supervisors. While the city had an antiharassment policy, which it revised and strengthened in 1986, it never circulated that policy to the lifeguards or their immediate supervisors. The woman who ultimately quit and then brought suit had never complained about the behavior to anyone above the two alleged harassers. When another lifeguard contacted the city personnel director, the two problem supervisors were reprimanded and given a choice of a suspension or loss of vacation time. The question was whether the city was liable under the circumstances, particularly where no personnel action had been taken against the employee who suffered harassment. In another case, an employee resigned after suffering an ongoing pattern of hostile environment harassment, but also had not brought a complaint to higher-level officials. The Supreme Court issued the following standard:

> An employer is subject to vicarious liability to a victimized employee for an actionable hostile environment created by a supervisor with immediate (or successively higher) authority over the employee. When no tangible employment action is taken, a defending employer may raise an affirmative defense to liability or damages, subject to proof by a preponderance of the evidence . . . . The defense comprises two necessary elements: (a) that the employer exercised reasonable care to prevent and correct promptly any sexually harassing behavior, and (b) that the plaintiff employee unreasonably failed to take advantage of any preventive or corrective opportunities provided by the employer or to avoid harm otherwise. While proof that an employer had promulgated an anti-harassment policy with complaint procedure is not necessary in every instance as a matter of law, the need for a stated policy suitable to the employment

circumstances may appropriately be addressed in any case when litigating the first element of the defense. And while proof than an employee failed to fulfill the corresponding obligation of reasonable care to avoid harm is not limited to showing an unreasonable failure to use any complaint procedure provided by the employer, a demonstration of such failure will normally suffice to satisfy the employer's burden under the second element of the defense. No affirmative defense is available, however, when the supervisor's harassment culminates in a tangible employment action, such as discharge, demotion, or undesirable reassignment.[261]

Since it is now possible for victims of harassment to seek punitive as well as compensatory damages under certain circumstances,[262] and it is clear that organizations can be held responsible whether top-level officials had specific knowledge of harassing behavior or not, it is likely that more attention will be paid to this very important issue. Fairly common suggestions for managers to address the problem of harassment include the following:

1. Develop a firm, clear policy statement on harassment. While the policy must be present by the highest levels of the administration, it is useful to provide for review and participation by others at line levels of the organization.

2. Disseminate the policy to everyone in the organization with the personal endorsement of each major level of administrative authority, emphasizing the administration's commitment to serious implementation. It should be made absolutely clear that violation of the policy will not be tolerated, and that sanctions will be taken and will be severe.

3. Develop a process for the handling of sexual harassment complaints. Such a process does not relieve supervisors of their ongoing responsibility to combat sexual harassment. Rather, the process operates in parallel with regular management efforts.

    To be effective such a process must be well known to everyone within the organization, accessible, and regarded as credible. Procedures that intimidate victims or discourage complaints exacerbate the damage caused by harassment and jeopardize the organization. In order to accomplish this goal, the process must be—and be understood to be—confidential, fair, and sensitive. That means, among other things, that it should not require the alleged victim to go through his or her immediate supervisor.

4. All supervisors at all levels of the organization should be oriented and regularly updated on issues of sexual harassment, its prevention, and remedies.

5. If it becomes necessary to invoke the sexual harassment policy to address an existing problem, it should be clear that those within the organization will watch the outcome for an indication of the administration's seriousness with respect to sexual harassment concerns.

The Age Discrimination in Employment Act   The Age Discrimination in Employment Act of 1967[263] (ADEA) was enacted to deal with major problems faced by workers over age 40 as a flood of younger workers entered the workforce. The statute simply states that employers should not discriminate in hiring, promotions, or other personnel decisions on the basis of age unless there is some *bona fide* job-related reason for doing so. Many governmental units were not covered by this act, and, following a decision in which the Supreme Court held that there was no constitutional ground for claiming protection against age-based discrimination,[264] Congress amended the ADEA to make it applicable to most government employees.[265]

That was, however, but the beginning of the story. Several developments in the economy and in management approaches have changed the context within which ADEA issues arise. First, the 1980s saw the rise of a wave of mergers in the private sector based largely on the idea that profits were to be increased based on productivity gains. However, those gains were not to be achieved principally by producing more or better quality goods and services but primarily by cutting costs. And, in most instances, that meant reducing the costs of the workforce. That, in turn, led to a tendency to seek ways to eliminate more senior employees for the simple reason that they cost substantially more in salaries and fringe benefits than newer employees. Second, those costs prompted governments to launch major early retirement buy-out programs in which employees were essentially told to take a buy-out or face termination. Another feature of this wave of new management approaches was to shed portions of an organization's infrastructure and simply contract for as much work as possible, leaving the costs of employees with the contractor. These dynamics, in turn, altered the traditional notion that one could expect to be employed by the same organization through to retirement years. Indeed, increasingly large numbers of employees, highly skilled as well as unskilled, found themselves unemployed just as they neared the point of retirement, making it very clear that these were not all simply individual cases of problematic employees but an intentional practice among some employers.[266] Then there were the dramatic increases in health care costs that have far outpaced inflation faced by both public and private sector employers. It is much cheaper to insure a younger workforce than an aging one, not to mention the retirement packages that contain health care obligations. These factors provided additional incentives for employers to discriminate against employees based on age.

The irony is that the economic instability, the inadequacy of many retirement programs, and the growing costs of living have meant that many retirees had to go back to work just to survive. All of these forces have added an immediacy to ADEA claims and dramatic increases in the number of such cases brought over the years.

While many of these trends developed first in the private sector, they have long since come to public employment as well. Thus, the 1980s saw significant reductions in force at the federal and state levels.[267] In the 1990s, the reinventing government effort championed a reduction of more than 270,000 federal employees. Numerous states have followed the private sector model, offering early retirement packages to senior employees. Much of the privatization movement has been aimed at the simple theory that contracting out government functions will save costs because it means that public employers can avoid personnel lines and fringe benefit expenses.[268]

Ironically, it is not at all clear how much is really being saved. For one thing, the retirement of senior people usually means a loss of knowledge and experience. Agencies often find themselves hiring back those employees as contractors at greater cost than they would have expended had the person remained in the agency. In many situations, this trend has meant the hiring of numerous contract employees who function in the agency as if they were civil servants but are not covered by the same laws or policies. One other reason why the claims of savings are dubious is the fact noted earlier in the chapter that the full and actual costs of contract administration are virtually never included in the calculation.

All of these dynamics have meant that challenges under the ADEA have burgeoned. However, apart from the broad policy goal of seeking to discourage discrimination on the basis of age, this statute has presented a host of ambiguities. The employee bears the burden of demonstrating a *prima facie* case that the action was based on age discrimination. In general, an employee must show that he or she was over 40 and performing in a satisfactory manner at the time that the employer took action. It was only in 2005 that the Supreme Court indicated that plaintiffs could employ the same kind of disparate impact standard for establishing the foundation case of discrimination in the same manner as the rules for Title VII explained earlier. Assuming that one is able to make the *prima facie* case, the employer then is permitted to provide "reasonable factors other than age" (RFOA) for the action.[269] If that is done, then the employee has the burden of demonstrating that the employer's stated reason was in truth a pretext and the real motive was age discrimination. For example, the Supreme Court rejected the argument by more-senior employees of the City of Jackson, Mississippi, that larger raises directed at lower-level employees was age discrimination. The city was able to demonstrate that the reason for the difference was an effort to deal with pay equity issues and to meet the competition provided by other local jurisdiction for the same kinds of workers.[270]

Some of these complexities arise from the decision to use a civil rights–type statute to fight age discrimination as opposed to focusing responsibility for implementation in a single agency. That model is attractive because there is an opportunity for individuals to seek to protect themselves against discrimination. They need not wait for or depend upon the resources of an agency to act.

However, this kind of approach depends upon literally hundreds of individuals bringing cases around the country. These cases frequently produce conflicting interpretations in the lower courts, which must then be filtered through the appellate process, with many important rulings ultimately awaiting resolution by the U.S. Supreme Court. There is the added problem that has arisen from the series of opinions issued by the Court since 1996, which have developed a very different approach to state immunity from money damage suits even where the Congress has made clear its collective intention to abrogate (eliminate) state immunity. This line of cases will be discussed further in Chapter 13, but, for example, the Court has held that individuals may not bring suits for damages against state government under the ADEA.[271]

Americans with Disabilities Act   A hybrid model was used when Congress in 1990 adopted the Americans with Disabilities Act (ADA).[272] While Congress had previously adopted the Rehabilitation Act of 1973,[273] the effort during the 1980s was to obtain passage of a much more comprehensive piece of legislation that would be to persons with disabilities what the Civil Rights Act of 1964 was to others. The Congress concluded:

(1) some 43,000,000 Americans have one or more physical or mental disabilities, and this number is increasing as the population as a whole is growing older;

(2) historically, society has tended to isolate and segregate individuals with disabilities, and, despite some improvements, such forms of discrimination against individuals with disabilities continue to be a serious and pervasive social problem;

(3) discrimination against individuals with disabilities persists in such critical areas as employment, housing, public accommodations, education, transportation, communication, recreation, institutionalization, health services, voting, and access to public services;

(4) unlike individuals who have experienced discrimination the basis of race, color, sex, national origin, religion, or age, individuals who have experienced discrimination on the basis of disability have often had no legal recourse to redress such discrimination;

(5) individuals with disabilities continually encounter various forms of discrimination, including outright intentional exclusion, the discriminatory effects of architectural, transportation, and communication barriers, overprotective rules and policies, failure to make modification to existing facilities and practices, exclusionary qualification standards and criteria, segregation and relegation to lesser services, programs, activities, benefits, jobs, or other opportunities; . . .[274]

And, indeed, the ADA seeks to eliminate discrimination in employment, public services (including contract services), transportation, communications, and places of public accommodation.

In the area of employment, the ADA has both a positive and a negative element. It prohibits discrimination in hiring, promotion, job training, or other terms and conditions of employment. It affirmatively obligates employers to make "reasonable accommodations" to disabled applicants and employees. "Reasonable accommodations" is defined to mean:

(A) making existing facilities used by employees readily accessible to and usable by individuals with disabilities; and

(B) job restructuring, part-time or modified work schedules, reassignment to a vacant position, acquisition or modification of equipment or devices, appropriate adjustment or modification of examinations, training materials or policies, the provision of qualified readers or interpreters, and other similar accommodations for individuals with disabilities.[275]

The primary vehicle for enforcement is a provision giving persons who suffer the discrimination the same options as other employees covered by Title VII. The Department of Justice is authorized to issue implementing regulations, conduct investigations and bring suit, however, much of the responsibility assigned to the Justice Department and other agencies is to provide assistance in planning for compliance by affected organizations and ensuring that their own operations and processes (including contract operations) are in compliance. It is, thus, a hybrid design in which agencies have important roles but individuals carry the primary responsibility for implementation. And, indeed, there are, at the time of this writing, many cases working their way up through the judicial system, seeking to clarify as well as to enforce provisions of the statute. That process does take time. Thus, it was only in 1998 that the Supreme Court for the first time addressed the question whether a person with asymptomatic HIV qualified for protection under the ADA.[276]

In addition, the claimants under the ADA have faced some of the same difficulties before the Supreme Court with respect to state immunity from suit as those bringing ADEA actions. In 2001, the Court blocked damage suits for enforcement of the ADA by state employees against the state government on Eleventh Amendment grounds. In that case, a nurse who had left her supervisory position for breast cancer treatment was denied her position when she returned a brief time later. She sued, but the Court concluded that Congress had failed to demonstrate sufficient history of employment discrimination by state governments to justify suits against the state under Title I of the ADA.[277] The dissenters chastised the Court for blatant second-guessing of the legislature on a matter that was properly within the judgment of legislators. However, in 2004, the Court upheld congressional abrogation of immunity under Title II of the act in a case presenting challenges to inaccessible judicial buildings and proceedings[278] and in 2006 upheld abrogation in a case involving alleged inability to access programs and services in a corrections setting.[279] There is some irony in the fact that the Court left local governments subject to damages suits as well as private employers even as it blocked suits against state governments.

The Family Medical Leave Act   There is one more health-related policy that has become very important to employers and employees. It is the Family Medical Leave Act of 1993.[280] "Under the FMLA, either spouse may be provided twelve weeks of unpaid leave in order to care for a newborn child, an adopted infant, or a seriously ill family member, while preserving job security and medical benefits."[281] States have also adopted family leave statutes. This is very much an emerging field at present and it will be important for both employers and employees as it develops. However, given the comments concerning the ADA and ADEA above, it is worth noting that the Supreme Court has upheld the congressional abrogation of state government immunity for this statute.[282]

The Civil Service Reform Act

The Civil Service Reform Act, enacted during the Carter years, is a long and complex statute that fundamentally restructured the civil service. In general terms, it divided the former Civil Service Commission into two basic parts, according to their functions. The Office of Personnel Management (OPM) is charged with general administration of the civil service system, particularly including efforts to improve governmental personnel management techniques and performance evaluations. The Merit System Protection Board (MSPB) was created as an independent organization designed to resolve civil disputes of several kinds. Where the dispute involves allegations of discrimination, the CSRA contains provisions under which the EEOC can be called on to review the board's rulings. A reconciliation process is available should the two agencies disagree.

Although there are a number of constitutional law protections for employees, statutes to govern public personnel matters, and a new organizational structure for the management at least of the federal civil service, two major problems remain. First, there are gaps or ambiguities in the law on the problems encountered by special employees and the supervisors who manage those employees. Second, the black letter law and public policy pronouncements may offer several options for public servants who encounter problems in employment, but the informal interactions within the bureaucracy can make it difficult for the civil servant to use the formal protections. Indeed, the pressures can force public servants into moral dilemmas.

Special Employees in the Public Service

Several kinds of public service jobs are sufficiently special as to require exceptions to some of the standard rules that govern general civil service personnel. However, many special employees are not primarily political employees in a patronage sense, and consequently they have not traditionally been deprived of all the usual protections afforded to civil servants. In fact, some positions require added independence and security. Regulatory decisionmakers are one such group. Chapter 10 noted the conflict between the need of regulatory officials to maintain independence and the president's attempts to coordinate regulatory policy. The courts have held that executives may not fire regulatory commissioners who make quasi-judicial decisions without good cause.

For similar reasons, the Administrative Procedure Act established administrative law judges as officers protected by civil service procedures and rules, but it gave them additional protections. Specifically, ALJs may not be assigned to tasks other than normal ALJ duties. The APA insulates their pay and promotion decisions from attempts at retribution by agency employers. However, providing such extraordinary protections to ALJs means that few mechanisms are available by which to evaluate ALJ performance or to provide the ALJs with incentives to improve their productivity. A number of studies have been done to find ways to preserve needed protections for ALJs and at the same time allow agencies to:

- identify unsatisfactory administrative law judges and take personnel action,
- make effective use of administrative law judges to assure maximum productivity,
- plan adequately for administrative law judge requirements to meet workload,
- provide the Civil Service Commission (OPM) with information to determine the adequacy of its administrative law judges certifying practices
- develop administrative law judges to their maximum potential through training or diversity of experience, and
- establish appropriate management feedback mechanisms to determine the effectiveness of an administrative law judge personnel management system.[283]

Another group of special employees for whom the conflict between civil service protections and accountability remains a problem is the Senior Executive Service. However, in the case of the SES, the employees are somewhat more vulnerable than they were before the establishment of this category, rather than more protected. Indeed, the Senior Executive Service was created by the Civil Service Reform Act precisely to develop a body of senior executives who could be rewarded for outstanding performance through such devices as merit pay, could be used more flexibly in varying jobs as the need presented itself, and could be removed from important positions if they failed to perform effectively without the necessity of satisfying standard civil service adverse personnel action procedures. But, as Bernard Rosen pointed out in an article, the removal of standard protections can make it difficult for senior career executives to perform one of their important traditional roles—that is, to aid new administrations or inexperienced political appointees to understand all aspects of their various problems and opportunities without fear of reprisal for failing to be sufficiently responsive to political agendas.

> The mythology about political executives having to overcome resistant career executives originates largely in the tensions of an administration's first year and are subsequently publicized in the "war stories" of a few departed officials. There is no persuasive evidence, however, that the alleged resistance goes beyond the responsible action of making sure that the political decision makers see all aspects of an issue before they decide.[284]

Given the frequent turnover in political executives and the complexity of agencies and their problems, there is a danger that high-level civil servants with valuable experience and knowledge may not be available to advise new administrations or may be unwilling to risk "speaking truth to power."[285]

One group of special employees that has been expanding dramatically since 2001 can be classified under the rubric of national security professionals. There are two problems for these employees. First, courts traditionally grant a considerable amount of deference to the military and the president in matters of national security or military administration. Second, many of the statutes designed to protect civil servants and private citizens have generally contained exemptions for national security affairs. Because of the reluctance of the courts to interfere in such matters, military and security workers have been subjected to serious abuses in the name of national security. In addition to intrusive and sometimes biased psychological testing, there are well-documented abuses of polygraph or "lie detector" testing.[286] Interestingly, while Congress adopted legislation aimed at protecting private sector employees from abusive and intrusive polygraph practices, public employees were not included.[287] A third area of frequently reported abuses for military and security affairs workers is wiretapping of telephones of current and past employees.[288]

As the discussion earlier in this chapter indicated, there is a dramatic change in progress for employees of the Department of Homeland Security and the Department of Defense under entirely new human resource management systems that are completely outside the standard civil service system. Just what the future issues will be under these new systems is not as yet clear. Neither is it certain whether these will remain special systems or become the leading edge of change across the federal government. Historically, at least, many of the changes at the federal level have led to changes at the state level as well.

CONTRACT EMPLOYEES AND THEIR BOSSES

Of course, it is inappropriate for public employers to seek to evade the law by contracting out. Besides, such tactics often do not work. Notice that a variety of issues raised in this chapter to this point arose in connection with contracting procedures or contract operations (see the discussion of affirmative action above).

Another group that might, with qualifications, be referred to as special employees are not direct government employees, but are employed by firms that depend to a large extent on government contracts. Contracting is much more than an agreement to acquire goods and services for government at the best price possible, consistent with a fair rate of return for the business. It is also a policy tool that can be used as a lever to accomplish a variety of purposes.[289] In a general sense, government contractors are required to conform to a host of approved personnel practices, such as affirmative action, as a condition of receiving their contracts. Their progress in meeting those personnel requirements is monitored by the Office of Federal Contract Compliance (OFCCP) and the EEOC, among other government agencies. In a very real sense, the conditions of employment for those employed by government contractors are heavily influenced by federal personnel policies. On the other hand, they do not enjoy civil service protections.[290] Just what directions the law and politics of the contract process will take in the near term is unclear, and so is the environment of the contract worker and his or her supervisor.

SUMMARY

This chapter has presented problems and developments that have emerged in the area of public law and public administration, which is concerned with the relationship between public employees and their supervisors. The problems may vary considerably, depending on whether one speaks of general civil service employees, political executives, special employees, or contract employees. Many disputes center on adverse actions of several types taken against employees by their supervisors. It is true that there simply may be a conflict between the needs and rights of the individual as against the concerns of the organization, but many conflicts involve a multiplicity of interests that are associated with the goals of the employees, their employers, and the general public for whose benefit the public organizations exist.

Aware of some of these conflicting interests, the courts have over the years issued a variety of rulings that enable public employees to receive protection for their constitutional rights under the Bill of Rights and the Fourteenth Amendment. The Supreme Court, though, has drawn back from the tendency to expand protections for public employees in recent decades. Ironically, the fact that it has done this by subjecting most claims to ad hoc balancing tests, though with presumptions in favor of the employer, has frustrated both employers and employees. Employees know that they have less likelihood of vindication in many areas, but, on the other hand, employers have little certainty about their own decisions.

However, legislatures have gone much further, developing a set of statutory protections for public employees and obligations for employers. Given the modern administrative context within which these rights are exercised, a variety of problems are still in need of resolution so that employees may feel both protected and responsible. At the same time, there is the fear that public managers might be overcome with the host of statutes, regulations, and judicial pronouncements, limiting their ability to carry out their agencies' responsibilities in an efficient and effective manner.

This tension between the need to protect employees while simultaneously ensuring accountability has been at the heart of ongoing discussions of administrative responsibility. These discussions have ranged widely from commentaries on ethical behavior in the public sector to the technicalities of tort suits for money damages against employees and units of government. That broad concern is the subject of Chapter 13.

NOTES

1. U.S. Merit System Protection Board, *The Changing Federal Workplace: Employee Perspectives* (Washington, DC: Merit System Protection Board, 1998), p. v. A more recent MSPB survey reports the number at just over 1.5 million. See U.S. Merit System Protection Board, *The Federal Workforce for the 21st Century: Results of the Merit Principles Survey 2000* (Washington, DC: Merit System Protection Board, 2003), p. 1.

2. Samuel M. Ehrenhalt, Center for the Study of the States, Government Employment Report, *The New Geography of Government Jobs: Hiring in State and Local Government Shifts to South and West, and to Medium and Small States* (Albany, NY: Nelson A. Rockefeller Institute of Government, 1997), p. 2.

3. U.S. Department of Labor, Bureau of Labor Statistics, "State and Local Government, Excluding Education and Hospitals," at http://www.bls.gov/oco/cg/cgs042.htm, as of March 3, 2006.

4. For a discussion of the complexities of understanding the number and nature of public employees, see Paul C. Light, *The True Size of Government* (Washington, DC: Brookings Institution Press, 1999).

5. Robert D. Lee, Jr., *Public Personnel Systems* (Baltimore: University Park Press, 1979), pp. 1–4.

6. See generally Frederick Mosher, Jr., *Democracy and the Public Service* (New York: Oxford University Press, 1968); Thomas I. Emerson, *The System of Freedom of Expression* (New York: Vintage Books, 1970), Ch. 15; and Paul Appleby, *Big Democracy* (New York: Knopf, 1949).

7. U.S. Merit System Protection Board, *Federal Supervisors and Strategic Human Resources Management* (Washington, DC: Merit System Protection Board, 1998), pp. 4–5.

8. U.S. Merit System Protection Board, Office of Policy and Evaluation, *What's on the Minds of Federal Human Capital Stakeholders* (Washington, DC: Merit System Protection Board, 2004), p. 15.

9. See e.g., Charles W. Hemingway, "A Closer Look at *Waters v. Churchill* and *United States v. National Treasury Employees Union:* Constitutional Tensions Between the Government as Employer and the Citizen as Federal Employee," 44 *American University Law Review* 2231 (1995).

10. Note: "*City of North Miami v. Kurtz*: Is Sacrificing Employee Privacy Rights the Cost of Health Care Reform," 27 *University of Toledo L. Rev.* 545 (1996).

11. Sharon G. Portwood, "Employment Discrimination in the Public Sector Based on Sexual Orientation: Conflicts Between Research Evidence and the Law," 19 *Law & Psychology Rev.* 113 (1995).

12. MSPB, *What's on the Minds, supra* note 8, at p. 19.

13. The case eventually went to the U.S. Supreme Court as *Givhan v. Western Line Consolidated School Dist.,* 439 U.S. 410 (1979).

14. Givhan brought her action against the school district as an intervenor in the pending desegregation case. *Id.,* at pp. 411–412.

15. *Id.,* at pp. 412-413.

16. *Id.,* at p. 412 n. 1.

17. On the other allegations, the court of appeals found: "Appellants also sought to establish these other bases for the decision not to rehire: (1) that Givhan 'downgraded' the papers of white students; (2) that she was one of a number of teachers who walked out of a meeting about desegregation in the fall of 1969 and attempted to disrupt it by blowing automobile horns outside the gymnasium; (3) that the school district had received a threat by Givhan and other teachers not to return to work when schools reopened on a unitary basis in February, 1970; and (4) that Givhan had protected a student during a weapons shakedown at Riverside, in March, 1970, by concealing a student's knife until completion of a search. The evidence on the first three of these points was inconclusive and the district judge did not clearly err in rejecting or ignoring it. Givhan admitted the fourth incident, but the district judge properly rejected that as a justification for her not being rehired, as there was no evidence that (the principal] relied on it in making his decision [cites]." *Id.,* at p. 412 n. 2.

18. *Id.,* at p. 417.

19. Mark Coven, "The First Amendment Rights of Policymaking Public Employees," 12 *Harvard Civil Rights-Civil Liberties L. Rev.* 559 (1977).

20. The case was *Bennett v. Thompson,* 363 A.2d 187 (N.H. 1976), appeal dismissed, 429 U.S. 1082 (1977).

21. Coven, *supra* note 19, at pp. 560–61.

22. *Id.,* at p. 562.

23. *Bennett v. Thomson,* quoted in Coven, *supra* note 19, at p. 561.

24. See Lee, *supra* note 5, at p. 5.

25. Felix A. Nigro and Lloyd G. Nigro, *The New Public Personnel Administration,* 2nd ed. (Itasca, IL: Peacock, 1981), p. 12.

26. *Id.,* at p. 13.

27. See generally, Carolyn Ban and Norma Riccucci, eds., *Public Personnel Management: Current Concerns, Future Challenges,* 2nd ed. (New York: Longman, 1997).

28. See e.g., Congressional Research Service, *National Security Whistleblowers* (Washington, DC: CRS, 2005).

29. P.L. 107-396, 116 Stat. 2135 (2002).

30. 70 Fed. Reg. 5272 (2005).

31. 5 U.S.C. §9902.

32. 70 Fed. Reg. 66116 (2005).

33. See e.g., GAO Human Capital Reform Act, Public Law 108-271, 118 Stat. 811 (2004).

34. U.S. Government Accountability Office, *Human Capital: Building on the Current Momentum to Transform the Federal Government* (Washington, DC: GAO, 2004), p. 1.

35. Ban and Riccucci, *supra* note 27, at p. 2.

36. See *Rutan v. Republican Party of Illinois,* 497 U.S. 62 (1990); *Branti v. Finkel,* 445 U.S. 507 (1980).

37. "No clear line can be drawn between policymaking and nonpolicymaking positions. While nonpolicymaking individuals usually have limited responsibility, that is not to say that one with a number of responsibilities may have only limited objectives. An employee with responsibilities that are not well defined or are of broad scope more likely functions in a policymaking position. In determining whether an employee occupies a

policymaking position, consideration should also be given to whether the employee acts as an adviser or formulates plans for the implementation of broad goals. Thus, the political loyalty justification is a matter of proof, or at least argument, directed at particular kinds of jobs.'" *Elrod v. Burns,* 427 U.S. 347, 367-68 (1976).

"Under some circumstances, a position may be appropriately considered political even though it is neither confidential nor policymaking in character. As one obvious example, if a State's election laws require that precincts be supervised by two election judges of different parties, a Republican judge could be legitimately discharged solely for changing his party registration. That conclusion would not depend on any finding that the job involved participation in policy decisions or access to confidential information. Rather, it would simply rest on the fact that party membership was essential to the discharge of the employee's governmental responsibilities.

"It is equally clear that party affiliation is not necessarily relevant to every policymaking or confidential position. The coach of a state university's football team formulates policy, but no one could seriously claim that Republicans make better coaches than Democrats, or vice versa, no matter which party is in control of the state government. On the other hand, it is equally clear that the Governor of a State may appropriately believe that the official duties of various assistants who help write speeches, explain his views to the press, or communicate with the legislature cannot be performed effectively unless those persons share his political beliefs and party commitments." *Branti v. Finkel, supra* note 36, at p. 518.

38. Patricia W. Ingraham, "Political/Career Relationships in Public Management: The Good, the Bad, and the Possibilities, in Ban and Riccucci," *supra* note 27, at p. 317.

39. See e.g., U.S. General Accounting Office, *Private and Public Prisons: Studies Comparing Operational Costs and/or Quality of Service* (Washington, DC: General Accounting Office, 1996).

40. For a discussion of these complexities, see Craig E. Richards, Rima Shore, and Max B. Sawicky, *Risky Business: Private Management of Public Schools* (Washington, DC: Economic Policy Institute, 1996).

41. See e.g., Ruth Hoogland DeHoog, *Contracting Out for Human Services* (Albany, NY; State University of New York, 1984).

42. On these changes, see Clay Johnson, Deputy Director of OMB for Management, Memorandum: Implementing Strategic Sourcing, May 20, 2005; Office of Management and Budget, Circular No. A-76 (Revised), Performance of Commercial Activities, May 29, 2005.

43. See Don Kettl, "Privatization: Implications for the Public Work Force," in Ban and Riccucci, *supra* note 27, at p. 298.

44. See e.g., *United States v. O'Brien,* 391 U.S. 367 (1968), and *Grayned v. Rockford,* 408 U.S. 104 (1972). But see *Carey v. Brown,* 447 U.S. 455 (1980), and *Chicago Police Dept. v. Mosely,* 408 U.S. 92 (1972).

45. *Adderley v. Florida,* 385 U.S. 39 (1966).

46. See e.g., *Urofsky v. Gilmore,* 216 F.3d 401 (4th Cir. 2000).

47. See e.g., Nigro and Nigro, *supra* note 25, Chap. 14, "Justice for the Worker Grievances and Appeals."

48. U.S. Office of Personnel Management, *Manager's Handbook* (Washington, DC: Government Printing Office, 1981), pp. 197–204.

49. See e.g., *Perry v. Sindermann,* 408 U.S. 593 (1972), and *Pickering v. Board of Education,* 391 U.S. 563 (1968).

50. *Rutan v. Republican Party of Illinois,* 497 U.S. 62, 74 (1990).

51. *Pickering,* 391 U.S., at p. 568.

52. *Mt. Healthy Board of Education v. Doyle,* 429 U.S. 274, 284 (1977).

53. Coven, *supra* note 19, at p. 559. Coven's discussion of the public's deliberative interest is particularly interesting.

54. See e.g., Hugh Heclo, "OMB and the Presidency: The Problem of Neutral Competence," 38 *Public Interest* 80 (1975), and Larry Berman, *The Office of Management and Budget and the Presidency, 1921–1979* (Princeton, NJ: Princeton University Press, 1978).

55. Frederick C. Mosher, ed., *American Public Administration: Past, Present, Future* (Tuscaloosa: University of Alabama Press, 1975), p. 7.

56. *Pickering, supra* note 49, at pp. 571–72.

57. Coven, *supra* note 19, at pp. 573–75.

58. *Keyishian v. Board of Regents,* 385 U.S. 589 (1967).

59. *Perry, supra* note 49, at p. 577.

60. *Rutan, supra* note 50, at p. 97 n. 2, Justice Scalia dissenting.

61. With the exception of three cases decided in 1951 and 1952 (*Adler v. Board of Education,* 342 U.S. 485 [1952]; *Garner v. Board of Public Works,* 341 U.S. 716 [1951]; *Gerende v. Board of Supervisors,* 341 U.S. 56 [1951]) and nullified by later decisions, the Court has struck down virtually every retrospective loyalty oath or association disclosure statement to come before it. See e.g., *Wieman v. Updegraff,* 344 U.S. 183 (1952); *Speiser v. Randall,* 357 U.S. 513 (1958); *Shelton v. Tucker,* 364 U.S. 479 (1960); *Cramp v. Board of Public Instruction,* 368 U.S. 278 (1961); *Baggett v. Bullitt,* 377 U.S. 360 (1964); *Elfbrandt v. Russell,* 384 U.S. 11 (1966); and *Keyishian v. Board of Regents, supra* note 58. See also *Baird v. State Bar,* 401 U.S. 1 (1971): *In re Stolar,* 401 U.S. 23 (1971); and *Law Student Civil Rights Research Council v. Wadmond,* 401 U.S. 154 (1971).

62. An excellent example of how vague and sweeping the language of such oaths has been is the Oklahoma oath at issue in *Wieman v. Updegraff, supra* note 61, at p. 184 n.1.

63. *Keyishian, supra* note 58.

64. See e.g., U.S. Constitution, Article 11, §1, cl. 8, and Article VI, §3.

65. *Cole v. Richardson,* 405 U.S. 676 (1972).

66. *NAACP v. Alabama,* 357 U.S. 449 (1958). See also *Bates v. Little Rock,* 361 U.S. 516 (1960).

67. *Yates v. United States,* 354 U.S. 298 (1957); *Scales v. United States,* 367 U.S. 203 (1961); *Noto v. United States,* 367 U.S. 290 (1961); *Aptheker v. Secretary of State,* 378 U.S. 500 (1964); *Keyishian v. Board of Regents, supra* note 48; *United States v. Robel,* 389 U.S. 258 (1967); and *Communist Party of Indiana v. Whitcomb,* 414 U.S. 441 (1974).

68. *Buckley v. Valeo,* 424 U.S. 1, 25 (1976); *Kusper v. Pontikes,* 414 U.S. 51, 57 (1973); and *Shelton v. Tucker,* 364 U.S. 479 (1960).

69. *Pickering, supra* note 49, at p. 568.

70. *Perry, supra* note 49, at p. 596.

71. See generally, *Elrod v. Burns, supra* note 37 and *Branti v. Finkel, supra* note 36.

72. See *Snepp v. United States,* 444 U.S. 507 (1980); and *United States v. Marchetti,* 466 F. 2d 1309 (4th Cir. 1972), cert. denied, 409 U.S. 1063 (1972).

73. *Pickering, supra* note 49, at p. 570.

74. *Id.,* at p. 568.

75. *Id.,* at pp. 569–570. See also *Givhan v. Western Line Consolidated School Dist., supra* note 13, at pp. 414–415.

76. That was the case in *Givhan, supra* note 13, and *Mt. Healthy Board of Education v. Doyle, supra* note 52.

77. That is precisely the manner in which the district courts in *Mt. Healthy* and *Givhan* had interpreted *Pickering* and *Perry v. Sindermann.*

78. *Supra* note 52, at p. 287.

79. *Supra* note 13, at p. 417.

80. 461 U.S. 138 (1983).

81. *Myers v. Connick,* 507 F.Supp. 752 (EDLA 1981), aff'd 654 F.2d 719 (5th Cir. 1981).

82. *Connick,* 461 U.S., at p. 146.

83. *Id.,* at pp. 147–152.

84. See Justice Black's dissenting opinions criticizing balancing tests in *Barenblatt v. United States,* 360 U.S. 109 (1958) and *Konigsberg v. State Bar,* 366 U.S. 36 (1961).

85. *Rankin v. McPherson,* 483 U.S. 378, 381 (1987).

86. *Rust v. Sullivan,* 500 U.S. 173 (1991). I have addressed this case in greater length in "Rusty Pipes: The Rust Decision and the Supreme Court's Free Flow Theory of the First Amendment," 6 *Notre Dame Journal of Law, Ethics, & Policy* 359 (1992).

87. *Waters v. Churchill,* 511 U.S. 661 (1994).

88. *Id.,* at p. 666.

89. *Id.*

90. *Id.*

91. *Id.*

92. *Id.*, at p. 670.

93. *Id.*, at p. 671.

94. *Id.*

95. *Id.*, at 675.

96. The Court observed: "But employers, public and private, often do rely on hearsay, on past similar conduct, on their personal knowledge of people's credibility, and on other factors that the judicial process ignores. Such reliance may sometimes be the most effective way for the employer to avoid future recurrences of improper and disruptive conduct. What works best in a judicial proceeding may not be appropriate in the employment context." *Id.* at 676.

97. *Id.*, at 695, Justice Stevens dissenting.

98. *Id.*, at 696.

99. 513 U.S. 454 (1995).

100. *Id.*, at pp. 459–460.

101. *Id.*, at pp. 464–465.

102. *Id.*, at p. 466.

103. *Id.*, at p. 470.

104. See generally, Charles W. Hemmingway, "A Closer Look at *Waters v. Churchill* and *United States v. National Treasury Employees Union*: Constitutional Tensions Between the Government as Employer and the Citizen as Federal Employee," 44 *American U.L. Rev.* 2231 (1995).

105. See e.g., *Watkins v. United States*, 354 U.S. 178 (1957); *Sweezey v. New Hampshire*, 354 U.S. 234 (1957); *NAACP V. Alabama*, *supra* note 66; *Uphaus v. Wyman*, 360 U.S. 72 (1959); and *Barenblatt v. United States*, 360 U.S. 109 (1959).

106. *Barenblatt*, *supra* note 105, and *Gibson v. Florida Legislative Investigating Comm.*, 372 U.S. 539 (1963).

107. *Wooley v. Maynard*, 430 U.S. 705 (1977).

108. *Gardner v. Broderick*, 392 U.S. 273 (1968).

109. *Lefkowitz v. Cunningham*, 431 U.S. 801 (1977); *Lefkowitz v. Turley*, 414 U.S. 70 (1973); and *Garrity v. New Jersey*, 385 U.S. 493 (1967).

110. *United States v. North*, 910 F.2d 843 (D.C.Cir. 1990); *United States v. Poindexter*, 951 F.2d 369 (D.C.Cir. 1991). See generally, Lawrence E. Walsh, *Iran-Contra: The Final Report* (New York: Random House, 1994), Part IV, Chapters 2–3.

111. *Snepp v. United States*, 444 U.S. 507 (1980).

112. *National Assn of Letter Carriers v. Civil Service Comm'n*, 413 U.S. 548 (1973); *Broadrick v. Oklahoma*, 413 U.S. 601 (1973); and *United Public Workers v. Mitchell*, 330 U.S. 75 (1947).

113. *Abood v. Detroit*, 431 U.S. 209 (1977).

114. *Buckley*, *supra* note 68.

115. *Elrod*, *supra* note 37.

116. *Id.*, at pp. 374–75.

117. *Branti*, *supra* note 36, at p. 518.

118. *Rutan*, *supra* note 50.

119. 480 U.S. 709 (1987).

120. *Id.*, at pp. 713–714.

121. *Id.*, at p. 713.

122. *Id.*, at p. 714.

123. *Id.*, at pp. 729–732, Justice Scalia concurring.

124. *Id.,* at p. 715.

125. *Id.,* at 717.

126. *Id.,* at pp. 719–720.

127. *Id.,* at p. 725.

128. *Id.,* at 730.

129. *New Jersey v. T.L.O.,* 469 U.S. 325 (1985).

130. 489 U.S. 532 (1989).

131. See generally, Martin Wald and Jeffrey D. Kahn, "Privacy Rights of Public Employees," 6 *The Labor Lawyer* 301 (1990).

132. *O'Connor v. Ortega, supra* note 119, at pp. 728–729.

133. 489 U.S. 602 (1989).

134. 489 U.S. 656 (1989).

135. See e.g., *Anonymous Firemen v. City of Willoughby,* 779 F.Supp. 402 (NDOH 1991); *Taylor v. O'Grady,* 888 F.2d 1189 (7th Cir. 1989); *Hartness v. Bush,* 919 F.2d 170 (D.C.Cir. 1990).

136. See Comment: "Individual Privacy Interest and the 'Special Needs' Analysis for Involuntary Drug and HIV Tests," 86 *California L. Rev.* 119 (1998).

137. *National Treasury Employees v. Von Raab, supra* note 134, at pp. 665–666.

138. *Veronia School District 47J v. Action,* 515 U.S. 646, 654-661 (1995).

139. *Id.,* and *New Jersey v. T.L.O.,* 469 U.S. 325 (1985). Both cases relied in no small measure on the special authority of schools to supervise minors.

140. *Griffin v. Wisconsin,* 483 U.S. 868 (1987).

141. *Skinner, supra* note 133.

142. See e.g., *Wilcher v. City of Wilmington,* 139 F.3d 366 (3rd Cir. 1998).

143. *Id.,* at 371.

144. *Chandler v. Miller,* 520 U.S. 305 (1997).

145. *Id.,* p. 322.

146. *Anonymous Fireman v. City of Willoughby,* 779 F.Supp. 402 (NDOH 1991).

147. *Glover v. Eastern Nebraska Community Office of Retardation,* 867 F.2d 461 (8th Cir. 1989).

148. 42 U.S.C. §2000e et seq. On risks to the employer, see e.g., Mark E. Schreiber, "Employer E-Mail and Internet Risks, Policy Guidelines and Investigations," 85 *Massachusetts L. Rev.* 74 (2000).

149. Michael L. Rustad and Sandra R. Paulsson, "Monitoring Employee E-mail and Internet Usage: Avoiding the Omniscient Electronic Sweatshop: Insights from Europe," 7 *U. Pennsylvania. J. Labor & Employment Law* 829, 829–830 (2005).

150. *White Buffalo Ventures v. University of Texas at Austin,* 420 F.3d 366 (5th Cir. 2005).

151. *Urofsky v. Gilmore, supra* note 46.

152. *Id.,* at p. 438.

153. *Griswold v. Connecticut,* 381 U.S. 479 (1965).

154. *Cleveland Board of Education v. La Fleur,* 414 U.S. 632 (1974).

155. See e.g., Nigro and Nigro, *supra* note 25, at pp. 418–20.

156. 539 U.S. 558, 562 (2003).

157. *Id.*

158. *Bowers v. Hardwick,* 478 U.S. 186 (1986).

159. 538 U.S. at 583, Justice O'Connor concurring.

160. *Id.,* at p. 585.

161. *Dier v. City of Hillsboro,* 2004 U.S. Dist. LEXIS 10783 (D.OR 2004).

162. *Weaver v. Nebo School District,* 29 F. Supp. 2d 1279, 1281-1282 (D.UT 1998).

163. *Id.*, at pp. 1287.

164. *Id.*, at pp. 1289.

165. *Kelley v. Johnson,* 425 U.S. 238 (1976).

166. *Goldman v. Weinberger,* 475 U.S. 503 (1986).

167. *McCarthy v. Philadelphia Civil Service Commission,* 424 U.S. 645 (1976).

168. See e.g., *Clinton Police Department Bargaining Unit v. City of Clinton,* 464 N.W.2d 875 (Iowa 1991).

169. *Piscottano v. Murphy,* 2005 U.S. Dist. LEXIS 17140 (D.CT 2005).

170. *City of North Miami v. Kurtz,* 653 So.2d 1025 (Fla. 1995).

171. *Grusendorf v. City of Oklahoma City,* 816 F.2d 539 (10th Cir. 1987).

172. Thus, for example, since the Supreme Court has held that prisoners have a right under certain conditions to be free of forced exposure to smoke, *Helling v. McKinney,* 509 U.S. 25 (1993), prison guards can be regulated in their use of tobacco products on the job.

173. Note: "*City of North Miami v. Kurtz*: Is Sacrificing Employee Privacy Rights the Cost of Health Care Reform?" 27 *University of Toledo L. Rev.* 545, 547–548 (1996).

174. *Id.*, at p. 546.

175. See Terry Morehead Dworkin, "It's My Life—Leave Me Alone: Off the Job Employee Associational Privacy Rights," 35 *American Business L. J.* 47 (1997).

176. See e.g., *Weinberger v. Weisenfeld,* 420 U.S. 636 (1975); *Frontiero v. Richardson,* 411 U.S. 677 (1973); and *Bolling v. Sharpe,* 347 U.S. 497 (1954).

177. The classic example is *Yick Wo v. Hopkins,* 118 U.S. 356 (1886).

178. This two-tier framework for equal protection analysis is found in *San Antonio Independent School Dist. v. Rodriguez,* 411 U.S. 1 (1973).

179. See e.g., *Loving v. Virginia,* 388 U.S. 1 (1967), and *Strauder v. West Virginia,* 100 U.S. 303 (1880).

180. One of the few examples in which the Court has upheld a clear race-based classification was itself problematic, since it was the Japanese exclusion order case, *Korematsu v. United States,* 323 U.S. 214 (1944).

181. *San Antonio, supra* note 178, at p. 28.

182. *Frontiero v. Richardson,* 411 U.S. 677, 686 (1973).

183. On alienage, see *Nyquist v. Mauclet,* 432 U.S. 1 (1977), and *Graham v. Richardson,* 403 U.S. 365 (1971). On illegitimacy, see *Levy v. Louisiana,* 391 U.S. 68 (1968), *Glona v. American Guarantee & Liability Ins. Co.,* 391 U.S. 73 (1968). In later cases, however, the Court backed away from treating all classifications based on legitimacy (*Mathews v. Lucas,* 427 U.S. 495 [1976] and *Lalli v. Lalli,* 439 U.S. 259 [1978]) or alienage (*Foley v. Connelie,* 435 U.S. 291 [1978] and *Ambach v. Norwick,* 441 U.S. 68 [1979]) as inherently suspect.

184. Justice Black was particularly concerned that the courts should focus on the effect of government action and not on guesses about the intent of government officials. He wrote: "It is difficult or impossible for any court to determine the 'sole' or 'dominant' motivation behind the choices of a group of legislators. Furthermore, there is an element of futility in a judicial attempt to invalidate a law because of the bad motives of its supporters. If the law is struck down for this reason, rather than because of its facial content or effect, it would presumably be valid as soon as the legislature or relevant governing body repassed it for different reasons."

185. *Washington v. Davis,* 426 U.S. 229 (1976).

186. *Village of Arlington Heights v. Metropolitan Housing Development Corp.,* 429 U.S. 252, 267-68 (1977).

187. *Personnel Administrator v. Feeney,* 442 U.S. 256 (1979).

188. *Id.*, at p. 279.

189. *In re Griffiths,* 413 U.S. 717 (1973) and *Examining Board v. Flores de Otero,* 426 U.S. 572 (1976).

190. *Graham v. Richardson,* 403 U.S. 365 (1971) and *Nyquist v. Mauclet, supra* note 183.

191. *Sugarman v. Dougall,* 413 U.S. 634 (1973) and *Hampton v. Mow Sun Wong,* 426 U.S. 88 (1976).

192. See e.g., *Mathews v. Diaz,* 426 U.S. 67 (1976).

193. *Amback v. Norwick,* 441 U.S. 68, 75-80 (1979).

194. *Id.*

195. *Foley v. Connelie,* 435 U.S. 291 (1978).

196. These are requirements drawn from the *Foley, Id.,* and *Ambach, supra* note 193, cases. See e.g., *Cabell v. Chavez-Salido,* 454 U.S. 432 (1982). See also *Quintero de Quintero v. Aponte-Roque,* 974 F.2d 226 (1st Cir. 1992). The Supreme Court did make an exception in the case of a notary public, *Bernal v. Fainter,* 467 U.S. 216 (1984).

197. *Craig v. Boren,* 429 U.S. 190 (1976).

198. See *J.E.B. v. Alabama,* 511 U.S. 127 (1994) (striking preemptory jury challenges based on gender); *Mississippi University for Women v. Hogan,* 458 U.S. 718 (1982) (overturning women-only admissions to a state university); and *United States v. Virginia,* 135 L.Ed.2d 735 (1996) (overturning gender-segregated education at the Virginia Military Institute).

199. *United States v. Virginia,* 135 L.Ed.2d, at p. 750.

200. 42 U.S.C. §2000e et seq.

201. Civil Service Reform Act of 1978, Public Law 95-454, 92 Stat. 1111 (1978). The CSRA provided that:

    (a) Any employee who has authority to take, direct others to take, recommend, or approve any personnel action, shall not, with respect to such authority—

        (1) discriminate for or against any employee or applicant employment—

            (A) on the basis of race, color, religion, sex, or national origin, as prohibited under section 717 of the Civil Rights Act of 1964 (42 U.S.C. 2000e-16);

            (B) on the basis of age, as prohibited under sections 12 and 15 of the Age Discrimination in Employment Act of 1967 (29 U.S.C. 631, 633a);

            (C) on the basis of sex, as prohibited under section 6(d) of the Fair Labor Standards Act of 1938 (29 U.S.C. 206 (d));

            (D) on the basis of handicapping condition, as prohibited under section 501 of the Rehabilitation Act of 1973 (29 U.S.C. 791); or

            (E) on the basis of marital status or political affiliation, as prohibited under any law, rule, or regulations.

202. 347 U.S. 483 (1954) and *Brown II,* 349 U.S. 294 (1955).

203. See e.g., *Cooper v. Aaron,* 358 U.S. 1 (1958); *Green v. County School Board,* 391 U.S. 430 (1968).

204. See *Alexander v. Holmes County, Mississippi,* 396 U.S. 1218 (1969).

205. 402 U.S. 1 (1970).

206. See e.g., *Missouri v. Jenkins,* 515 U.S. 70 (1995); *Board of Ed. of Oklahoma City v. Dowell,* 498 U.S. 237 (1991); *Freeman v. Pitts,* 503 U.S. 467 (1992); *Milliken v. Bradley,* 418 U.S. 717 (1974).

207. 438 U.S. 265 (1978).

208. *United Steelworkers of American v. Weber,* 443 U.S. 193 (1979).

209. See *Regents v. Bakke,* 438 U.S. 265, 395-96 (1978), Justice Marshall in a separate opinion.

210. See *United States v. Paradise,* 480 U.S. 149 (1987).

211. See *Johnson v. Santa Clara County Transportation Agency,* 480 U.S. 616 (1987).

212. *Fullilove v. Klutznick,* 448 U.S. 448 (1980).

213. *Metropolitan Broadcasting v. FCC,* 497 U.S. 547 (1990).

214. See *Boston Chapter NAACP v. Beecher,* 679 F.2d 965 (1st Cir. 1982); *Castro v. Beecher,* 522 F. Supp. 873 (D. Mass 1981).

215. *Firefighters v. Stotts,* 467 U.S. 561 (1984).

216. *Wygant v. Jackson Bd. of Ed.,* 476 U.S. 267 (1986).

217. 488 U.S. 469 (1989).

218. 515 U.S. 200 (1995).

219. *Id.,* at p. 227.

220. *Id.,* at p. 240, Justice Thomas concurring in part.

221. *Id.,* at p. 243, Justice Stevens dissenting.

222. *Id.,* at pp. 250–251.

223. See e.g., Department of Defense, General Services Administration, National Aeronautics and Space Administration, "Federal Acquisition Regulation: Reform of Affirmative Action in Federal Procurement, 63 *Fed. Reg.* 35719 (1998).

224. *Boston Police Superior Officers Federation v. City of Boston,* 147 F.3d 13 (1st Cir. 1998).

225. In the spring of 1996, O'Connor issued another ruling striking down a diversity effort under the strict scrutiny test, this time in a case involving a Texas redistricting plan that created majority African-American and Hispanic voting districts. *Bush v. Vera,* 135 L.Ed.2d 248 (1996). On the same day, Chief Justice Rehnquist wrote for the Court in a related case from North Carolina, striking down their redistricting plan. In the process, he warned that the Court would strike down race-conscious actions where "race becomes the dominant and controlling consideration" and promised that decisions based on race would be treated as constitutionally suspect "whether or not the reason for the racial classification is benign or the purpose remedial." *Shaw v. Hunt,* 517 U.S. 899, 905, 218 (1996).

226. 78 F.3d 932 (5th Cir. 1996).

227. *Id.* at 19.

228. *Podberesky v. Kirwan,* 38 F.3d 147 (4th Cir. 1994), cert. denied, 115 S.Ct. 2001 (1995).

229. *Wessmann v. Gittens,* 160 F.3d 790 (1st Cir. 1998).

230. *Engineering Contractors Association v. Metropolitan Dade County,* 943 F.Supp. 1546 (S.D.Fla 1996), aff'd 122 F.3d 895 (11th Cir. 1997).

231. *South Florida Chapter of Associated General Contractors v. Metropolitan Dade County,* 723 F.2d 846 (11th Cir. 1984).

232. *In re Sherbrooke Sodding,* 17 F.Supp.2d 1026 (D.MN 1998).

233. *Dallas Firefighters Association v. City of Dallas, Texas,* 150 F.3d 438 (5th Cir. 1998).

234. See *Coalition for Economic Equity v. Wilson,* 122 F.3d 692 (9th Cir. 1997).

235. Florida Governor Jeb Bush, Executive Order 99-281, http://www.state.fl.us/eog/executive_orders/1999/November/eo99-281, July 30, 2001.

236. 539 U.S. 244 (2003).

237. 539 U.S. 306 (2003).

238. P.L. 88-352, 78 Stat. 241 (1964), 42 U.S.C. §2000e.

239. P.L. 92-261, 86 Stat. 103 (1972), 42 U.S.C. §2000e.

240. P.L. 102-166, 105 Stat. 1071 (1991).

241. *United States v. City of Warren, Michigan,* 138 F.3d 1083, 1091-1092 (6th Cir. 1998).

242. *Moss v. Advance Circuits,* 981 F.3d 1239, 1247 (D.MN 1997).

243. See 45 Fed. Reg. 74676, November 10, 1980, and 45 Fed. Reg. 25024, April 11, 1980. See *Meritor Savings Bank v. Vinson,* 477 U.S. 57 (1986).

244. P.L. 88-38, 77 Stat. 56 (1963), 29 U.S.C. §203 and 206(d).

245. P.L. 95-555, 92 Stat. 2076 (1978), 42 U.S.C. §2000e.

246. *Los Angeles Dept. of Water & Power v. Manhart,* 435 U.S. 702, 708 (1978); *Arizona Governing Committee v. Norris,* 463 U.S. 1073, 1083 (1983).

247. *General Electric Co. v. Gilbert,* 429 U.S. 125 (1976). But see *Nashville Gas Co. v. Satty,* 434 U.S. 136 (1977).

248. See generally, *Barnes v. Costle,* 561 F.2d 983 (D.C.Cir. 1977).

249. *Meritor Savings Bank v. Vinson, supra* note 243, at pp. 65.

250. 29 C.F.R. 1604.11(a)(3).

251. *Meritor Savings Bank, FSB v. Vinson, supra* note 243, at pp. 65–67.

252. *Supra* note 243.

253. 510 U.S. 17, 21 (1993).

254. *Id.,* at p. 22.

255. *Id.,* at p. 23.

256. *Oncale v. Sundowner Offshore Service,* 523 U.S. 75 (1998).

257. *Franklin v. Gwinnett County Public Schools,* 503 U.S. 60 (1992).

258. *Alida Star v. Lago Vista Independent School District,* 525 U.S. 274 (1998).

259. *Oncale v. Sundowner Offshore Service, supra* note 256, at p. 81.

260. *Faragher v. City of Boca Raton,* 524 U.S. 775, 788 (1998).

261. *Id.,* at pp. 807–808. See also *Burlington Industries v. Ellerth,* 524 U.S. 742, 761 (1998).

262. *Deters v. Equifax Credit Information Services,* 981 F.Supp. 1381 (DKS 1997).

263. P.L. 90-202, 81 Stat. 602 (1967), 29 U.S.C. §621 et seq.

264. *Massachusetts v. Murgia,* 427 U.S. 307 (1976).

265. Public Law 95-256, 92 Stat. 189 (1978), 5 U.S.C. §§3322, 8335, 8339; 29 U.S.C. §§623, 624, 626, 631, 633a, 634.

266. See e.g., *Hazen Paper Co. v. Biggins,* 507 U.S. 604 (1993).

267. See e.g., *Mete v. New York State O.M.R.D.D.,* 984 F.Supp. 125 (NDNY 1997).

268. See Donald F. Kettl, "Privatization: Implications for the Public Workforce," in Ban and Riccuci, *supra* note 27.

269. See e.g., *Smith v. City of Jackson, Mississippi,* 544 U.S. 228 (2005).

270. *Id.*

271. *Kimel v. Florida Bd. of Regents,* 528 U.S. 62 (2000).

272. P.L. 101-336, 104 Stat. 327 (1990).

273. P.L. 93-112, 87 Stat. 355 (1973), 29 U.S.C. §701 et seq.

274. *Id.,* at Sec. 2(a).

275. *Id.,* at Sec. 101(9).

276. *Bragdon v. Abbott,* 524 U.S. 624 (1998)

277. *Board of Trustees of the University of Alabama v. Garrett,* 531 U.S. 356 (2001).

278. *Tennessee v. Lane,* 541 U.S. 509 (2004).

279. *United States v. Georgia,* 163 L. Ed. 2d 650 (2006).

280. P.L. 103-3, 107 Stat. 6, (1993), 29 U.S.C. 2601 et seq.

281. Maureen Porette and Brian Gunn, "The Family and Medical Leave Act of 1993: The Time Has Finally Come for Governmental Recognition of True 'Family Values,'" 8 *St. John's Journal of Legal Commentary* 587 (1993).

282. *Nevada Department of Human Resources v. Hibbs,* 538 U.S. 721 (2003).

283. *Administrative Law Process: Better Management Is Needed* (Washington, DC: General Accounting Office, 1978), p. iv. In May 1979, the GAO issued another report, *Management Improvements in the Administrative Law Process: Much Remains to Be Done,* in which it concluded that very little had been done by agencies to improve the problems noted in the earlier report and called for an effort to achieve the same goals advanced earlier. *Id.,* at pp. 1–2. See also U.S. House of Representatives, Hearings Before the Committee on Post Office and Civil Service, *Selection and Oversight of Administrative Law Judges,* 96th Cong., 2d Sess., 1980, and Hearings Before the Subcommittee on Investigations of the Committee on Post Office and Civil Service, *Administrative Law Judge Program of the Federal Trade Commission,* 96th Cong., 2d Sess. (1980).

    Unfortunately, the efforts to make real management improvements were preempted by political efforts to interfere with the adjudicative process in order to force a reduction in Social Security disability roles, discussed in Chapter 4.

284. Bernard Rosen, "Uncertainty in the Senior Executive Service," 41 *Public Administration Rev.* 203, 204 (1981).

285. Aaron Wildavsky, *Speaking Truth to Power* (Boston: Little, Brown, 1979), p. 12.

286. U.S. House of Representatives, Legislative History of the Privacy Act of 1974, *Source Book on Privacy,* 94th Cong., 2nd Sess (1976), pp. 558–59.

287. Employee Polygraph Protection Act of 1988, P.L. 100-347, 102 Stat. 646 (1988), 29 U.S.C. §2001 et seq. The Congress did eventually include White House and Capitol Hill employees in its coverage when they made a variety of existing civil rights and other human resources laws applicable to the president's staff and congressional employees. See P.L. 104-1, 109 Stat. 10 (1995) and P.L. 104-331, 110 Stat. 4058 (1996).

288. See e.g., *Halperin v. Kissinger,* 606 F.2d 1192 (D.C.Cir. 1979), aff'd by an equally divided court, 452 U.S. 713 (1981).

289. This has been true for many years, see Phillip J. Cooper, "Government Contracts in Public Administration: The Role and Environment of the Contracting Office," 40 *Public Administration Rev.* 459 (1980).

290. See e.g., *Becker v. Philco Corp.,* 389 U.S. 979 (1967), Justice Douglas dissenting from denial of cert.

13

Administrative Responsibility

The recent decades have been hard years for the public service, and in no small measure that has been because of the loss of faith in government and the belief that its political leaders, its institutions, and the people who operate and manage them are not responsible.[1] Despite the fact that the indictment, at least insofar as it has been directed toward professional public servants, is grossly unfair and often misdirected, it is a view too widely shared to be seen as anything but a major problem. And besides, there is a very real record of serious scandals, starting with Watergate in the Nixon years that drove a president from office, Iran-Contra that demonstrated gross illegality and double-dealing during the Reagan and Bush administrations, the impeachment of William Jefferson Clinton following disclosure of misbehavior and deception of the American public, and a variety of significant issues arising during the G. W. Bush years, including among others the prosecution of Vice President Cheney's chief of staff, I. "Scooter" Libby, the indictment of the head of the contracting agency in the White House, the Abramoff lobbying scandal as well as the confession of former Representative Randy "Duke" Cunningham (R-CA) to bribery charges. What is worse, many of the presidents in recent decades from both political parties have been only too willing to attack professional public servants and the institutions in which they serve when it suited their political interests.

These behaviors have been mirrored in other countries around the globe, from Panama to Columbia, to Paraguay, to Brazil in the western hemisphere, to abuses by officials in Africa, Europe, and Asia. The last three decades have seen numerous administrations around the globe fall from scandal. So serious and pervasive were some of these problems that the World Bank felt moved to make the effort to build competent and effective public institutions and the elimination of corruption an important priority.[2]

On the other hand, the fact is that most of these scandals came from the behavior not of career public servants, but of political appointees or elected officials. Still, there is no question that many good, honest, dedicated, and already underappreciated public service professionals have been victimized by these political leaders and by the destructive and sometimes unethical behavior of media representatives. Some, far too many in fact, have even faced violence at the hands of crude and misinformed citizens. While the Oklahoma City bombing was a particularly heinous example, there are many other smaller and less extreme, but still frightening, cases.

At the same time, many of those citizens came of age in an era that has celebrated materialism more than ever before. The United Nations Development Programme observed that: "'Keeping up with the Joneses,' has shifted from striving to match the consumption of a next-door neighbor to pursuing the life styles of the rich and famous depicted in movies and television shows."[3] The idea that salary level and lifestyle are the critical measures of the value of people has once again become commonplace and was demonstrated in extreme form in the case of the Enron mess and other corporate scandals.

It has been a period in which elected officials around the globe have celebrated the marketplace and have sought to privatize, or at least to contract out, as many services as possible that were formerly provided by public agencies. Based in part on these premises, these have been years in which many have seen public policy as a fee-for-service arrangement, implying that if they are not satisfied with what they personally receive, then they ought not to support government. Thus, the issue of government responsibility is too often seen in egocentric ways, rather than being understood in terms of the public interest. For many, indeed, there is no belief in the concept of the public interest at all, just a multiplicity of private interests (see Chapter 4). In such an era, it is not surprising that many people assume that professionals in government are operating from the same motives that drive their own behavior and find it difficult to comprehend a group of people who willingly often forego so much of what is regularly enjoyed by the people whom they serve and who so often criticize and even caricature public servants.

Whether the condemnations and tensions are civil or fair, the issue of ensuring administrative responsibility continues to be extremely important, not only in fact, but also in the perception of the citizens we serve. Indeed, the newly elected president of what is now the Czech Republic, Vaclav Havel, made it the subject of his first speech to the people of his country. Speaking of the emergence of his country from years of authoritarian rule, he warned: "The worst thing is that we live in a contaminated moral environment. We fell morally ill because we got used to saying something different from what we thought. We learned not to believe in anything, to ignore each other, to care only for ourselves."[4] He called for a politics and a government based upon "morality in practice." Not by any stretch a naive man, having spent time as a political prisoner, Havel recognized the counterintuitive nature of what he was saying. Even so, he said:

> Let us teach ourselves and others that politics can be not only the art of the possible, especially if "the possible" includes the art of speculation, calculation, intrigue, secret deals, and pragmatic maneuvering, but that it can also be the art of the impossible, namely the art of improving ourselves and the world.[5]

Despite its importance, however, administrative responsibility is one of the most difficult goals to achieve, or even to discuss comprehensively. The fundamental concern is that those who govern ought to act responsibly, judged by appropriate standards, and be held to account if they do not meet that criteria. But in a republic that depends for its governance upon many officials who are not elected, ensuring responsibility on the part of public administrators is a complex problem. Accomplishing that task without adding excessive additional burdens to the already substantial obligations facing administrators makes the challenge that much more difficult.

This chapter surveys a variety of critical elements of administrative responsibility. An understanding of the contemporary complexities of administrative responsibility requires consideration of the theoretical foundations of the subject, the debate over suits against governments and officials, the liabilities and immunities of public officers, and the risks facing administrators in this environment. It considers both internal and external mechanisms that are employed in an effort to ensure responsible behavior and to remedy abuses. In that context, the chapter addresses the difficulties that come with the confusion of law and ethics. It also examines the changing character of the debates over administrative responsibility as market values have become increasingly important in the public as well as the private sector.

INTERNAL VERSUS EXTERNAL APPROACHES: A CLASSIC FRAMEWORK AND ITS CONTEMPORARY VARIANTS

The concept of responsibility can be understood by posing a number of important questions: (1) Responsibility in what form? (2) Responsibility to what or whom? and (3) Responsibility for what? Let us consider some possible responses. Figure 13.1 is a guide to this analysis.

Carl Friedrich and Herman Finer, the leading early participants in debates over how to ensure administrative responsibility, provided us with two classic alternative approaches. Finer insisted that: "It is most important clearly to distinguish a 'sense of duty' or 'a sense of responsibility' from the fact of responsibility, that is, effective answerability."[6] That "sense of duty" or responsibility means that an administrator feels or understands an obligation. It is a subjective form of responsibility as opposed to legal answerability for one's conduct. The former is an internal check on those who govern, while the latter is an external constraint on administrative behavior. Friedrich rejected the external control approach, insisting that: "Responsible conduct of administrative functions is not so much enforced as it is elicited."[7] He argued that there is no effective way to ensure objective responsibility in public officials through the use of external constraints in a complex modern government and, further, that the record shows that most administrators, most of the time, do in fact obey a subjective ethic of responsibility. The subjective check comes as a result of proper recruitment procedures (which produce people with a clear sense of public service), correct training, and effective professional socialization processes for those who enter government service.

The core of the debate centered on whether one ensures responsibility through external means or by developing internal checks. Finer summarized it as follows:

> My chief difference with Professor Friedrich was and is my insistence upon distinguishing responsibility as an arrangement of correction and punishment even up to dismissal both of politicians and officials, while he believed and believes in reliance upon responsibility as a sense of responsibility, largely unsanctioned, except by loyalty to professional standards.[8]

Most observers have concluded that both internal and external mechanisms are needed to ensure official accountability.

INTERNAL FORMS OF RESPONSIBILITY

Internal forms of administrative responsibility include at least the role of professionalism, the significance of representation, and, ultimately, ethical considerations.

Administrators often feel constrained to obey professional norms, but what does that entail? At a minimum, professionalism for public officials requires mastery of and continued competency in the technical expertise needed to operate public organizations and administer public policy. This is sometimes referred to as the responsibility which comes from membership in the "fellowship of science."[9] But professionalism in the public service implies more than an obligation to be a "respectable technician" and do no harm.[10] It includes responsibility for statesmanship where that concept implies a recognition that administrators are involved in the public policy process, have a positive duty to govern,

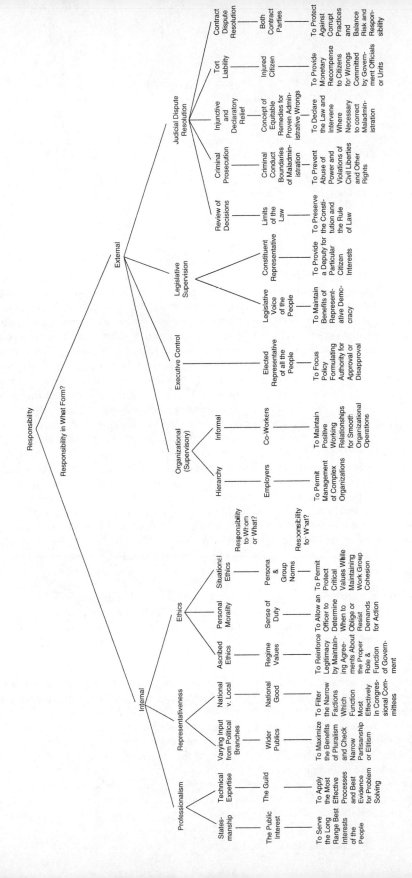

FIGURE 13.1 Modes, Types, and Directions of Responsibility

have an obligation to tell the majority and its elected representatives when they are wrong, and to be generally concerned about the ends of administration as well as the means of achieving these ends. As an aspect of responsibility, then, professionalism means more than mere technical proficiency and faithfulness to the majority will.[11]

Another aspect of the internal form of responsibility is the fact of and need for representativeness among public officials. Norton Long wrote that:

> Responsibility is a product of responsible institutions; and with all their deficiencies—which are many indeed—the departments of administration come closer than any other organs of government to achieving responsible behavior by virtue of the breadth and depth of their consideration of the relevant facts and because of the representative character of their personnel.[12]

While there has been considerable debate on the question whether professional public administrators are more representative of the American people than, say, members of Congress in terms of socioeconomic background, education, race, gender, and income characteristics,[13] administrators are, and must be, concerned with representativeness in at least two ways. First, careerists can provide inputs to the policy process that differ from the contributions of elected officials. Those inputs may take the form of special knowledge passed to elected officials in a particular policy area. They may also involve representation of concerns to elected decisionmakers on behalf of interest groups, which—though their views are important and their stake in the controversy is great—might not be heard in the normal pull and haul of interest group politics. That may occur either because the groups lack resources to convey their message effectively or because they are too small to pose a significant political threat at election time. Second, public officials can and should have a broad view of the problems of governance. Nationwide, statewide, and comprehensive community perspectives are luxuries that many elected officials with relatively limited electoral constituencies may think they cannot afford politically.

A third aspect of internal responsibility is the commitment to ethical considerations.[14] Ethical problems may vary considerably but often concern one or more of three elements. At one level, there are questions of ascribed ethics, situations in which we discuss the demands that stem from our notions of civil virtue. John Rohr has argued, for example, that the Constitution, if properly and carefully considered, provides a variety of regime values that should guide administrative behavior.[15] A second set of questions concerns the issue of personal morality and emphasizes the concept of obligation or duty as the central factor in evaluating administrative action.[16] Stephen Bailey has written that "personal ethics in the public service is compounded of mental attitudes and moral qualities," both of which are necessary.[17]

> The three essential attitudes are: (1) a recognition of the moral ambiguity of all men and of all public policies, (2) a recognition of the contextual forces which condition moral priorities in the public service, and (3) a recognition of the paradoxes of procedures. The essential moral qualities of the ethical public servant are: (1) optimism, (2) courage, and (3) fairness tempered by charity.[18]

The third common consideration is generally referred to as situational ethics, which involves the day-to-day problem of adjusting civic virtue–based expectations and personal moral presumptions with varying but immediate problems that most often arise in organizations rather than in isolated individual situations.[19] Hence, it is common to speak of organizational ethics. Of course, ethical dilemmas often arise for public managers precisely because there may be occasions in which regime values, personal ethics, and organizational ethics clash. We will return to this theme later in the chapter, in a discussion of the relationship between law and ethics.

One aspect of the definition of the term responsibility is answerability. That is, it is possible to understand responsible conduct in part by asking to whom or what responsibility is owed. We can posit such a focus of responsibility for each of the internal forms noted above. That part of professionalism concerned with technical expertise implies answerability to the guild—other professional public servants. The more that the professional is a specialist, the more that the sense of guild membership becomes a factor. It is often said that public administration is a second profession precisely because people are often socialized in a specific field, such as forestry, nursing, agriculture, or law enforcement and then come to the wider practice of public management as their careers develop and they assume management responsibilities.[20] The standards they learned with respect to how to be a good engineer, social worker, or street cop remain within them. Indeed, Nalbandian has argued persuasively that one of the critically important tasks of city managers is to be interpreters of the specialists in the departments of city government to the governing body and of the political officials on the governing body to the department heads and their subordinates.[21]

That aspect of internal responsibility that focuses upon statesmanship implies a somewhat different obligation: this time to the concept of the public interest for which ends are as important as means. The concept of the public interest is one which is a perennial focus of debate.[22] And it is a debate in which public administrators participate along with citizens and their elected representatives, even if the roles in the discussion vary among the participants. However, with all of that, the suggestion that the "public interest" lacks utility and critical value in political and administrative theory because of vagueness is about as convincing a suggestion as the idea that we should reject "liberty," "equality," or "democracy" on similar grounds.

That aspect of representativeness which is concerned with inputs to be added to the perspectives of elected branch officials suggests a responsibility to wider publics. The other dimension of representativeness involves an obligation to the good of the nation as a whole as opposed to smaller constituencies. These two obligations have become even more important in an era of single-issue politics, when the kinds of policy communities described in Chapter 10 have come to play such a dominant role in policymaking. In such situations, the professional public manager may be among the few participants in the policy conversation who can take a wider view.

The nature of various forms of responsibility is also disclosed by the purposes served. The puroses of these internal forms might be summarized as follows. One attempts to meet the challenge of statesmanship to serve the long-range best interests of the people. The concern with technical expertise communicated and evaluated by guild standards seeks to apply the most effective procedures and the best evidence for problem solving. The effort to add inputs to the policy process that may vary from elected officials' views serves to maximize the benefits of pluralism and check narrow partisanship or elitism. The attempt to remind oneself of the need for an interest in the national good can help to filter the narrow and contentious factions that play such a critical role in legislatures and particularly in legislative committees.[23] The attempt to observe regime values reinforces legitimacy by maintaining fundamental agreements on the proper role and function of government. The effort to develop the sense of duty presents a translation of the personal moral sense associated with the attempt to become one's noblest self into the context of a public service career such that a public officer can determine when to oblige and when to resist demands for action.[24] Situational ethics is a vehicle for applying critical values in such a way as to maintain cohesion in work groups.

Of course, the classical discussions of internal responsibility, from Friedrich on, assumed that those doing the people's business were government employees. Much of that literature started from Friedrich's idea that the critical task was to recruit the right kind of people, which meant those with the values and education that suited them well to work as government professionals. He then advocated a careful socialization process that would imbue those government professionals with the mission and values of the organizations they served as well as those of the public service. Then these public servants would undergo a career development process that would integrate their perspectives into the larger body of governmental obligations and norms.

In modern governance arrangements, there are many kinds of individuals and organizations involved from the nonprofit and for-profit sectors operating under contracts or grants as well as varied levels and types of governmental agencies. Government does not recruit and hire all or even necessarily most of the people doing the work, nor does it socialize or train them as professionals. Many of these individuals are not supervised by government managers, but work for their own organizations. That does not mean that the individuals who come from nonprofit or for-profit organizations are less expert or dedicated than a government employee, but that their orientations and responsibilities as well as the criteria by which they are evaluated are often very different one from another. These differences can often lead to what Lloyd Burton has termed ethical discontinuities in public sector negotiating cultures.[25]

Nonprofit employees may be paid, but many of those who participate in public service programs operated by nonprofits under grants or contracts are volunteers and are in a very different position in terms of responsibility than paid workers. Nonprofit managers often have a more focused set of people to whom they are responsible than a government official, since the nonprofit executives must focus first on their obligations to their board of directors or trustees. For-profit managers, of course, must operate from a very different foundation and purpose than either the nonprofit or governmental managers, though Lester Salamon has argued quite persuasively that there are forces of convergence that make the differences more complex and subtle and increase some of the similarities across sectors in the contemporary market-driven context.[26] For all these reasons, the increasing use of governance arrangements that cross sectors and jurisdictions poses a range of issues for further scholarly and practitioner development with respect to internal as well as external aspects of responsibility.

EXTERNAL MECHANISMS OF RESPONSIBILITY

External forms of responsibility include at least organizational or supervisory obligations, executive control, legislative supervision, and judicial dispute resolution.

It has been said that government organizations do nothing except through the work of individual public officials. On the other hand, officials—particularly unelected administrative officers—have no authority to act except for that which is given them by virtue of their office or position within a government organization.

There are at least two aspects of organizational responsibility, and violation of either can result in immediate, and more or less severe, sanctions. Hierarchy is the formal variety of organizational check. Indeed, Max Weber's theory of bureaucracy asserts that complex problems in the modern world are dealt with through large bureaucratic organizations that operate upon rational-legal authority in a hierarchical arrangement of responsibility that functions through the efforts of officials who exercise judgment within a range of delegated authority.[27] While modern management techniques have sought to move away from strict hierarchies and toward flatter organizations, including the use of networks of several smaller organizations in place of unified organizations that look like the classic pyramid shape, or by creating partnerships of public and nongovernmental organizations, either for-profit or not-for-profit, through contracts, the reality of authority remains. At certain key points in organizations, networks, and contractual relationships lie decision authority over both people and mission performance. Indeed, while the public sector followed the private sector in the late 1980s and 1990s in many of the management techniques that challenged hierarchy, more recent years have seen a move in the private sector toward massive mergers and consolidations and the use of more traditional hierarchy. As Chapter 1 explained, one of the great challenges in the growth of contracting out has been the need to reconcile the essentially horizontal character of contractual relationships with the vertical system of political power that governs public contracting, provides it with funds, and can call contracting agencies and officers to task for their performance.[28]

The other organizational form of accountability is the ability of informal work groups within formal organizations to prescribe unofficial guidelines and to administer a range of sanctions, one of the most potent of which is ostracism, to those who breach the informal group's norms.[29] In fact, one of the common elements of many of the management trends of recent decades has been aimed at tapping these forces at the point-of-service level in organizations and using it to move not only individuals, but the organization as a whole toward improved performance to the agency's clientele.

Executive control and legislative supervision are two of the best-known forms of external responsibility. Unlike the organizational and judicial forms, the direction of public officials by the chief executive (be it the president, the governor, or the mayor) and legislative oversight differ because both forms are based upon actions by officials who must periodically face the electorate. Given the fact that these elected officials represent different constituencies, operate under varying institutional constraints, and work from rather different functional perspectives, efforts by legislators and elected executives to ensure responsible behavior by subordinate officials are often contradictory and frequently conflict laden.[30] Officials who consider themselves responsible to the president (or the governor or mayor) may face rough going in the legislative appropriations process or in subject matter committee oversight investigations. In addition to the crosscutting pressures between these two forms of responsibility, each has particular difficulties.[31] The literature is replete with studies on the problems of maintaining executive control[32] and conducting legislative oversight of the bureaucracy.[33]

Variations on these themes exist in local governments with the council/manager form and in counties where many department heads are elected rather than appointed by the county administrator. In such situations, there is a blending of legislative and executive powers, at least at the level of elected officials. Similar complexities exist in regional governmental bodies or in the operation of interjurisdictional agreements, whether at the local level or in regional bodies created by interstate compacts. And, of course, these arrangements vary in international accords as well. Even less formal cooperative relationships among different countries pose complex issues, since they often involve working relationships between countries that have a separation of powers form of government and others that have one or another variation of the parliamentary form. Finally, complex contractual arrangements for service delivery, like all of these examples, raise interesting and sometimes contentious debates over the relative importance of executive and legislative responsibility.

The judicial form of responsibility also has a number of aspects, each of which responds to particular problems in constitutional, statutory, contractual, and common law that have developed over the nation's history. The plethora of legal tools for maintenance of responsible government conducted by accountable officials rests upon at least two premises. First, despite the many shortcomings of our legal system, the rule of law does in fact operate here. The Supreme Court has, on more than one occasion, reminded us that: "No man in this country is so high that he is above the law. No officer of the law may set that law at defiance with impunity. All the officers of government, from the highest to the lowest, are creatures of the law, and are bound to obey it."[34] And Chief Justice Marshall was quick to observe that: "The very essence of civil liberty certainly consists in the right of every individual to claim the protection of the laws, whenever he receives an injury. One of the first duties of government is to afford that protection."[35] The fact that officials choose to act through contractual arrangements rather than deliver services directly does not eliminate those facts of public law.

As previous chapters have indicated, there are several types of judicial protection that are quite different in their operation. They include: (1) judicial review of administrative decisions (considered in Chapter 7); (2) criminal prosecution of officials for violation of state or federal criminal statutes; (3) suits for injunctive or declaratory relief in which a court is asked to declare the law and stop an official from doing something illegal or to compel an official to take action (see Chapter 9); (4) suits seeking money damages from individual officials or units of government for injuries suffered by citizens; and (5) contractual challenges in which agencies seek to invoke the power of the courts to manage operations and maintain accountability or in which contractors seek the help of courts to hold agencies to the agreement.

As was true of the internal forms of responsibility, the external forms are best understood if considered in light of the responsibility to whom and for what questions. Organizational responsibility in its hierarchical aspect involves responsibility of an individual to the employer in order to permit effective management of complex organizations. The informal aspect concerns answerability to one's coworkers for the purpose of maintaining positive working relationships, allowing smooth organizational operations.

Executive or presidential responsibility makes one answerable to the elected representative of all the people (or as close as the United States comes to having a representative of all the people), which allows the society to focus policy formulating and implementation authority for nationwide (or, in the case of governors, statewide) approval or disapproval. That is, the executive uses the authority of the office to move the administration in a general direction toward the accomplishment of a series of goals that the chief executive considers to be the public agenda. While the electorate may or may not be able or willing to respond to particular policy judgments, it can and, in theory at least, does react to the agenda the executive has identified and the order of priority given the items on that agenda.

This form (and legislative responsibility) has a special variant on the council/manager form of local government. In this arrangement, the city manager is made answerable on behalf of the city administrative organization. Although he or she is not elected, neither does the manager enjoy any protection against immediate removal by the governing body. In turn, city department heads are hired and fired by the manager. In the classic version of the plan, the manager is to be responsible for the city organization to the politically elected governing body while simultaneously insulating the city departments from political intervention.[36] In the contemporary context, however, many communities have chosen hybrid versions in which elected officials expect that they can have some degree of more direct answerability from city departments. In other cases, independently elected mayors hire and fire city administrators, in an arrangement that looks more like the classic type of executive responsibility.

Legislative responsibility occurs in at least two forms. The administrative official is responsible to legislators as members of the organization, which is the legislative voice of the people, and also as representatives of particular constituencies or interests. One dimension of legislative supervision is oversight that attempts to ensure that agencies effectively and efficiently perform the obligations assigned to them by statute (see Chapter 10). The other element is constituent casework in which the legislators are not so much interested in ensuring that the administrative structure functions properly as they are with moving agencies to comply with their constituents' special needs or wishes.[37] The purpose of the broader of these two is, of course, the maintenance of the benefits of representative democracy, while the latter provides a deputy for particular communities and interests.

Judicial forms of responsibility also involve a number of directions and purposes. The process of judicial review of decisions ensures responsibility to the substantive and procedural limits of the law, beyond which no official has any authority (see Chapter 7). This serves to preserve the Constitution and the idea of the supremacy of law.[38] Criminal prosecution keeps the official responsible to observe the criminal conduct boundaries of administration in order to prevent abuses of power and violations of civil liberties or other protected rights. Injunctive and declaratory relief makes administrators amenable to equitable remedies for proven administrative wrongs. This serves to provide a declaration of the meaning of the law and permits judicial intervention in administrative activity where necessary to correct maladministration, particularly where money damages awarded after the fact of the injury will not serve to protect the citizenry (see Chapter 9). Tort liability provides official responsibility to the injured citizen directly in order to provide monetary recompense for wrongs committed by government officials or units.[39] Finally, contract dispute resolution provides responsibility to both parties in what we have come to call public/private partnerships against breaches of contract by the other, and to statutory and regulatory limits established to govern contract policy. It seeks to protect the public treasury against corrupt practices and to provide a balance of risk and financial responsibility for the performance of agreements between the government and the contractor.

THE LAW AND ETHICS CONFUSION

It is important to address, even if only briefly, an important distinction that is often confused both in policy and in literature about the responsibility of public officials.[40] There is a tendency to treat law and ethics interchangeably. They are not the same, and indeed, the failure to distinguish between the two can create both legal and conceptual difficulties while undermining the effort to achieve a higher ethical standard in public service.

It was no surprise to see people react to many of the serious problems of the 1970s, 1980s, and 1990s with calls for more of an emphasis on ethics in public service. Neither was it unexpected that laws would be passed such as the Office of Independent Counsel statute[41] to investigate abuses of power or the Inspector General Act[42] to look into possible cases of fraud, abuse, and waste. Nor was it surprising when Congress passed the Ethics in Government Act, seeking to stop the so-called revolving door phenomenon in which people working in government left the public payroll only to take positions with the firms with which they had interacted while in office, often representing those same organizations before the agencies the former public employees had only recently left. State governments followed with an array of so-called ethics laws aimed primarily at potential conflicts of interest between public officers or their families and other organizations.

But even if many of these statutes were referred to as (or justified on the basis of) ethics considerations, they were about law rather than ethics. Law and ethics are not synonymous, and the tendency to meld the two in public administration scholarship and practice can be detrimental to our understanding and use of both. It is important to be alert to the distinctions between the two even if their ultimate goals may be to produce similar results—that is, responsible behavior in public officials.

There are many kinds of behavior that most people would consider to be immoral or unethical, but they are not illegal. People in and out of public life may be less than truthful, but while that may be unethical, it is only illegal under certain conditions. And there are many technical legal violations that few people would regard as unethical even if they are plainly breaking the law. Hence, few people think themselves, or anyone else, unethical because they drive a few miles over the speed limit. Public servants have been known to push the legal limits of agency regulations to the breaking point in order to serve a needy citizen. That kind of behavior may very well exceed the law, but, in close cases at least, many may be tempted to regard it as ethical nevertheless.

As the framework discussed earlier explained, law is an external check that seeks to be as objective as possible and is not dependent upon the feelings or beliefs of the people involved. Ethics, on the other hand, is principally a force, often highly subjective in nature, directed by the individual involved. It is an internal, and largely voluntary, check. When the individual's ability to choose is significantly constrained, ethics fades and law emerges as the dominant factor. While it is true that many laws are adopted in an effort to enshrine principles of behavior that are thought to be right and just, once adopted they are law whether they are right in some moral sense or not.

There is also a tendency to think that the codification and enforcement of ethics principles will solve ethical problems. Once the code is given legal authority and enforced, it is a body of law. The process of adopting such a law is no substitute for the more subtle and complex need for ethical development and education. There is no evidence that any of these so-called ethics laws have led to a higher level of moral discussion and development. Indeed, the tendency to confuse law and ethics can produce circular arguments that really avoid the most difficult ethical dilemmas. It is no small bit of irony that President Clinton's first act in office after taking the oath was to sign an executive order aimed at elevating the level of ethical behavior in his administration.[43] Despite the fact that, when it was originally passed, the Ethics in Government Act was expected by Congress not to be a burden, but really to support ethical behavior in the public service. Yet there is little doubt that the statute has now become a burden both for administrations seeking to qualify appointees for office and for many civil servants who fear tripping across provisions of the law. Thus, Chapter 12 provided examples of ordinary civil servants who were in trouble because they accepted modest honoraria for lectures or publications that no one could seriously have argued impaired their job performance or created real conflicts of interest. Indeed, it is clear that many people who might otherwise consider public service are simply unwilling to accept the implications about the character of public servants that one is likely to take from these laws.

At the state level, many ethics laws have been passed that the governments involved simply do not have the capacity to implement and administer effectively. That has led public servants to be unable to comply where proper reporting materials or compliance guidance are not readily available. Technically, they are breaking the law. One could hardly conclude that such laws have enhanced ethical conduct or encouraged public service professionals to engage in more frequent and thorough ethical considerations of their performance.

On the more positive front, there has been a growing literature over the past three decades on public sector ethics.[44] It has sought to reengage not only contemporary discussions of the subject, but also to link current ethical considerations to their historical foundations.[45] And there have been increasing numbers of texts and courses on ethics offered in public administration programs.[46] It is in fact interesting that one is more likely today to find some kind of requirement to study ethics in a public administration curriculum than one is to find a requirement for exposure to administrative law. As the comments earlier in this chapter on ethics as an internal check indicated, much of the work in the area of ethics focuses on regime values, situational or organizational ethics, and personal ethics.

It is, of course, very positive to find this reemergence of public sector ethics. However, it is important to keep in mind that ethics and law serve different purposes and operate in different ways. It is precisely why the founders, while committed to the importance of honorable behavior by those in office, insisted on what they termed "auxiliary precautions." In the modern context, one of the more common auxiliary measures is the ability to sue public officials or units of government for damages if, by breaking the law, they cause damages to the citizen involved.

THE SUPREME COURT AND THE DEBATE
OVER LIABILITY AND IMMUNITY

Indeed, the topic that has occupied the most attention among those debating the problems of external administrative responsibility in the contemporary context has been the range of suits brought against administrators and government units seeking monetary damages. For contemporary administrators, there are two levels of knowledge that are of importance. At the technical level, it is useful to have some basic understanding about: (1) the historical emergence of liability and immunity rules; (2) the contemporary debate over damage suits; and (3) issue of congressional abrogation of state immunity. At the more general level, however, it is useful to be aware that there has been a developing trend of rulings from the Supreme Court that seem to suggest greater protections from damage suits for public managers, and to some extent for units of government. However, as is true in so many other areas of administrative law, the Court has left a good deal of confusion in its wake and created a lack of certainty and predictability for everyone concerned.

Let us turn first to some of the issues that arise from the historical development of the liability and immunity issue. As with most areas of the law of public administration, the contemporary picture is more the product of practice and political reality than of overarching theory.

On reading a sample of the considerable literature on the subject of suits against officers and governmental units (and indeed many opinions written by various justices of the Supreme Court), one would likely come away with the impression that the development of official liability suits is a relatively recent phenomenon, or at least that until recently the law governing whether an official or a government unit could be sued was fairly well settled. That seemingly established law appeared to hold that claims for damages were generally barred by the doctrine of sovereign immunity (in the case of government units) and official immunity (in the instance of public officials). There are, we are told, some exceptions, where, for example, statutes had been enacted, permitting specific kinds of suits with stringent limitations. Suits against public officers appeared to be limited to ministerial activities (those in which the official had no discretion). Suits against government units, where they were allowed at all, were apparently limited to instances where the local government unit was performing a proprietary, as opposed to a governmental, function and where the task involved was basically ministerial, as opposed to discretionary.

However, a wider analysis suggests that: (1) it is very difficult to identify any historically consistent, clearly defined and applied doctrine showing when government units or officials are immune and when they are liable; (2) when all Supreme Court cases on the subject extending back to the earliest years of the republic are considered, the Court often permitted suits in the face of immunity claims; and (3) of the cases that did result in significant rulings in favor of immunity, until relatively recently most came in a narrow range of fact patterns.

Early Confusion: From One Extreme to the Other

A brief consideration of two nineteenth-century Supreme Court rulings suggests how much approaches to liability claims varied. In examining the two cases, it is important to think of them from the perspectives of both the officials involved and the plaintiffs. Captain Little commanded the American frigate *Boston,* in which capacity he came to be involved in a most complex regulatory problem. In February 1799, the Congress cut off American trade with France and her possessions. A section of the act directed the president to order American naval vessels to enforce the trade ban. Little received the following orders from the president:

> Sir—Herewith you will receive an act of Congress, further to suspend the commercial intercourse between the United States and France, and the dependencies thereof, the whole of which requires your attention. But it is the command of the President, that you consider particularly, the fifth section as part of your instructions, and govern yourself accordingly.
>
> A proper discharge of the important duties enjoined on you, arising out of this act, will require the exercise of a sound and impartial judgment. You are not only to do all that in you lies to prevent all intercourse, whether direct or circuitous, between the ports of the United States and those of France and her dependencies, in cases where the vessels or cargoes are apparently, as well as really, American and protected by American papers only; but you are to be vigilant that vessels or cargoes really American, but covered by Danish or other foreign papers, and bound to, or from, French ports, do not escape you.
>
> Whenever, on just suspicion, you send a vessel into port to be dealt with according to the aforementioned law, besides sending with her all her papers, send all the evidence you can obtain to support your suspicions, and effect her condemnation.
>
> At the same time that you are thus attentive to fulfill the objects of the law, you are to be extremely careful not to harass, or injure the trade of foreign nations with whom we are at peace, nor the fair trade of our own citizens.[47]

On December 2, 1799, Little sighted the Danish brigantine *Flying Fish* and, believing it might be an American vessel flying false colors, gave chase. During the chase, the master of the *Flying Fish* threw the ship's log and papers over the side. Upon boarding her, Little determined (after catching the master in a lie about the vessel's ports of call) that the ship had delivered goods from St. Thomas, a Danish island, to Jeremie, a French port, and was returning with a load of coffee. Little seized the vessel and returned it to Boston for legal process. The vessel was not an American ship and therefore not subject to seizure. The ship's owner, a German who lived in St. Thomas, sued Little.

Captain Little claimed that he should be immune from the suit, given that he was a military officer obeying the orders issued to him by the president, and alternatively, he should not be found liable for the seizure of the ship because he had probable cause to believe the vessel was in violation of a statute that he was obligated to enforce. Little was found personally liable in the amount of $8,504. The basis for the liability was that, although the president's orders charged commanders to halt shipping to or from French ports, the statute itself only stated that he should intervene if "it shall appear that such a ship or vessel is bound or sailing *to* any port or place within the territory of the French republic, or her dependencies" [emphasis added]. The president's order was, then, in excess of the authority granted by statute and Little's actions taken under that directive amounted to a plain trespass.[48]

Following *Little* and a number of other early nineteenth-century cases, the availability of a suit for personal damages against administrative officials seemed clear. However, matters became a great deal more confused following later decisions, particularly those occurring in the second half of the nineteenth century. Consider the difference in approach to ensuring responsibility through liability suits for money damages exhibited in the case of *In re Ayers*.[49]

Ayers was partially based on facts that led to an earlier Supreme Court decision, *Poindexter v. Greenhow*.[50] Virginia, like so many other states in the South at the time, had issued a great many bonds— the obligations of which it was ultimately unable to meet. The state, in 1871, enacted a law that resulted in a two-thirds reduction of bond and interest value, but it made the bond coupons receivable at standard value for taxes and other payments due the state. The state continued to default and the bonds became practically valueless except for their use in paying obligations to the state. Virginia later passed a law requiring those who wished to pay tax obligations with the bond coupons to pay both coupons and specie and then permitted the taxpayer to file suit to establish the legitimacy of the bond coupons.

Thomas Poindexter paid a tax collector $12 in coupons and $0.45 in specie; whereupon the tax collector seized a desk valued at $30 in satisfaction of the tax debt. Poindexter sued Samuel Greenhow, the treasurer of the City of Richmond, to recover his desk on the grounds that the later Virginia bond laws impaired the obligations of the state bond agreement, a contract, in violation of the Constitution. The treasurer defended on grounds that the suit was in truth a case in which the state was the real party being sued and the action was therefore barred by sovereign immunity. Second, he asserted that his own actions were justified as he was only carrying out statutory obligations imposed by the state to collect specie or execute a levy on property. The Supreme Court held that the suit was not barred by sovereign immunity and that the state action was an impairment of the obligation of contract in violation of the Constitution.

A number of individuals and firms purchased large quantities of Virginia bonds after the *Poindexter* decision, believing them to be valid. The state then passed a series of laws making it practically impossible to show that bond coupons used to pay state debts were valid and not counterfeit. The Virginia Attorney General, Ayers, was instructed to institute suits to collect taxes previously paid with bond coupons. He was held in contempt by the federal district court for violation of the Constitution— specifically, enforcement of a public policy that violated a contract when he had been previously ordered to desist. The attorney general argued that he should be protected because the suit was really against the state and therefore barred by the Eleventh Amendment. The Supreme Court agreed.

Clearly, the *Ayers* and *Little* cases represent very different views of the vulnerability of officials and units of government to suit. There is no straight-line development of doctrine from a rigorous application of liability to officials—even when they thought they were acting properly under orders from superiors—to an insulation of officials from suits for their action, even when the official should have known the orders were unconstitutional.

We could hazard several possible explanations for the differences in the cases in the post–Civil War period. *Ayers* and kindred decisions came very late in the nineteenth century and were contemporaneous with such rulings as the *Slaughter-House* and *Civil Rights Cases*.[51] These opinions suggested concern on the part of the justices of the Court that the states were in jeopardy as viable political institutions. Broad immunity might have been perceived as a form of protection. Most of the cases that provided a restrictive reading of liability were Civil War economic recovery cases, focusing on defaults on state bonds and the like, responsibility for which may have been viewed in terms of later nineteenth century *laissez faire* economic jurisprudence. Another factor may have been the effect of British common law on official immunity, which was still developing and provided broad protections against suits.[52] The decisions may have been the result of varying perceptions of the background of the Eleventh Amendment. What the late nineteenth-century cases did not represent was a carefully drawn development of doctrine that came to grips with the problem of keeping administrators responsible, while preserving the effectiveness of government operations.

An examination of the 28 major cases on official and governmental liability and immunity issued by the U.S. Supreme Court during the nineteenth century reveals 17 opinions in which suits were allowed to proceed against claims of immunity.[53] One case decided before the Marshall Court years and four decisions rendered during the Marshall period rejected claims of immunity. Three cases in the 1840s and 1850s saw rulings in favor of claimed immunities.[54] Of the total of 11 cases in which the immunity claim was granted—most of which occurred after the Civil War—five involved claims for impairment of contract against southern states for various types of default or alterations of terms on state bond; two were suits against the postmaster general of the United States; one was against a ship's captain by a member of the crew; one was against the federal government on a land claim; and one was against a trial judge. On the other hand, the 17 cases in which immunity claims did not stand as a bar to the suit stretched from 1793 to 1896 and concerned the State of Georgia, the governor and railroad commissioner of Texas, two vessels owned by the federal government, two state treasurers, five local government units, a collector of fines for a militia court, two military commanders, federal custodians of the Arlington National Cemetery, and one state judge who was in charge of jury selection in his jurisdiction.

In almost all the cases, the Court acknowledged that there is such a thing as sovereign immunity, though that did not stop the Court from rejecting claims to immunity. It is possible by processes of analogy and differentiation to make generalizations about possible directions of doctrinal development, but we cannot trace any relatively steady pattern of development extending back to the founders of the government. An examination of cases extending back to the early years of the republic supports the Supreme Court's later rulings, suggesting a richer history of suits against government than is generally acknowledged.[55]

The Dramatic Twentieth-Century Increase in Suits against Government

There were several significant cases decided between the turn of the twentieth century and the 1930s.[56] The *Ex parte Young* (1908) opinion—holding that the Eleventh Amendment sovereign immunity does not bar federal suits seeking injunctive relief against state officials for conduct violating federal rights—was the most significant of these. But it was after World War II that the dramatic mid-twentieth-century surge of cases against official and government units began. Between the opinion in *Tenney v. Brandhove* in 1951 and 1980, the Supreme Court rendered more than 30 major opinions in this area, most of which were decided after 1970.[57] Additionally, by the late 1970s, the Supreme Court began to warn that it intended to trim the availability of injunctive relief in the form of remedial decrees and that the better course was for aggrieved citizens to bring suit for damages against the offending official.[58] That message was clearly received, as the number and range of tort liability cases against officials and units in federal and state courts shot rapidly upward. A variety of other factors appear to have contributed to this increase: (1) the growing importance of government at all levels in the daily lives of citizens and operations of business; (2) an increasing awareness of the harm that a governmental official or unit can inflict;[59] (3) judicial reactions to continuous and widespread criticisms of sovereign and official immunity; (4) developing legal and political sophistication on the part of individuals and groups; (5) expanding availability of legal resources to those who wish to litigate; (6) proven cases of officials' dramatic abuse of office that involved the victimization of citizens;[60] (7) the presence of justices on the Court who seemed determined to develop some kind of doctrine to guide judicial forms of government responsibility; and (8) enactment of a host of statutes that used a civil rights model of implementation (see Chapter 12) and authorized the use of compensatory and even in some case punitive damage suits as the basis for action.

Whatever the causes, the Supreme Court has faced continuing requests to deal clearly and directly with the need for judicial remedies while simultaneously addressing the need to protect public officers and agencies from the fear and the burdens not only of money damage judgments but also of numerous, often groundless litigation. In order to comprehend the contemporary debate, it is necessary to consider the nature of sovereign and official immunity, the reasons given in support of the doctrine, and the arguments advanced in opposition to the idea of insulating public officers from accountability for their actions.

THE NEED FOR RESPONSIBLE AND EFFECTIVE GOVERNMENT: THE CORE OF THE SOVEREIGN AND OFFICIAL IMMUNITY DEBATE

There have been two doctrines employed to prevent suits against government units or officials. The first is sovereign immunity of government units from suit. The second is referred to as official immunity. Both doctrines have been under attack for years by legal scholars, state courts, and members of the United States Supreme Court. Both doctrines have been limited over time by statute and by judicial decisions in both federal and state courts.[61] And while it appeared for a time that these protections against suit were on the wane, a host of rulings from late 1980s on revived and strengthened them.

The Sovereign Immunity Concept

Based upon a simplistic repetition of the British maxim that "the king can do no wrong," and that the crown was the highest authority for the decision of legal controversies, sovereign immunity traditionally held that the sovereign could not be taken before a court without its permission. Since the government is treated as the sovereign, it may not be sued without its permission. The common law concept of immunity can be traced back to feudal England. Under the feudal system no lord could be called to answer before a vassal, and given that the king was the highest lord in the realm, it was not possible to order him to answer to any tribunal.[62] The king was sovereign and the courts acted in his name and under his authority. The subordinate courts could not call the crown into court unless he agreed to the proceeding. Additionally, as the king was perceived to be the embodiment of perfect justice, it would be rather awkward to compel him to answer for his actions. Of course, we have no king and the government is not the sovereign. The Constitution is the ultimate statement of authority. And if the government, or its officials, act in violation of that Constitution they could hardly be said to be acting as sovereign. Even so, using the concept in much too loose a sense, that doctrine remains and the government is treated as sovereign.

Although there is nothing in the Constitution to support the conclusion, the Supreme Court found that sovereign immunity did bar suits against the federal government or the state governments unless those units voluntarily submitted to the litigation.[63] Initially, the Court rejected the claim to sovereign immunity by the states where federal courts were involved, since the states were not sovereign in such matters and perhaps also because the members of the Court were uncomfortable with the doctrine of sovereign immunity itself. In fact, Article III of the Constitution had clearly contemplated cases brought by citizens of one state against another state.[64]

Following the Court's rejection of the state defenses, the Eleventh Amendment was added to the Constitution providing that "the judicial power of the United States shall not be construed to extend to any suit in law or equity, commenced or prosecuted against on the United States by Citizens of another State, or by Citizens or Subjects of any Foreign State." As the Supreme Court has indicated on many occasions:

> While the Amendment by its term does not bar suits against a State by its own citizens, this Court has consistently held that an unconsenting State is immune from suits brought in federal courts by her own citizens as well as by citizens of another State.[65]

In other words, the Eleventh Amendment is to be read as the constitutional basis of state sovereign immunity, barring suits against the state either by its own citizens or by citizens of another state. Indeed, the Court has gone so far as to hold that: "[The significance of this [Eleventh] Amendment 'lies in its affirmation that the fundamental principle of sovereign immunity limits the grant of judicial authority in Article III of the Constitution.'"[66]

Official and Sovereign Immunity

Even so, the amendment does not speak directly to suits against federal or state officials executing government policy. In the earlier cases decided in the nineteenth century on a claim of official immunity, the Court rejected the argument that suits such as this were really suits against the government in which the individual officer was only a "nominal party."[67] If an officer was sued, it was up to the official to show that his or her conduct was justified by a valid grant of authority from the government. As the discussion of the *Little* case demonstrated, officials who claimed to be performing a duty required by a statute or order that was later shown to be illegal were not protected from personal liability for their official acts. However, later cases read the nominal party idea much more favorably to the officials.[68] The Court held in *Edelman v. Jordan* that: "It is also well established that even though a State is not named a party to the action, the suit may nonetheless be barred by the Eleventh Amendment."[69] Who is the real defendant as compared with the actual party named in the suit? If it is the state and its policies, and not the individual official, then the Eleventh Amendment sovereign immunity may protect both the official and government.

Claims were also made in the nineteenth century by local government officials that counties, cities, and other municipal corporations should have sovereign immunity like the state, which would protect them from suit in federal court. The Supreme Court did not agree.[70] The grounds were simply that local governments are municipal corporations and, as such, may sue and be sued like other corporate bodies. The local governments exist at the pleasure of the state governments and have never been sovereign in their own right.

The development of official immunity, protecting government office holders or employees, is the second area in which immunity has grown over time. Later in this chapter we shall turn to just how different types of officials came to have protections against suit and where the limits of that protection are today. For the moment, consider the official immunity matter as a part of the debate over whether they should be protected at all.

There was significant resistance to providing public officers with immunity that would require the law to treat them more favorably than ordinary citizens. Chief Justice Holt maintained in a 1703 British case that "if public officers will infringe men's rights, they ought to pay greater damages than other men, to deter and hinder other officials from like offenses."[71] In another early British case, Lord Mansfield wrote: "Therefore to lay down in an English court of justice such a monstrous proposition, as that a governor, acting by virtue of letters patent under the great seal, is accountable only to God and his own conscience; that he is absolutely despotic, and can spoil, plunder, and affect his Majesty's subjects, both in their liberty and property, with impunity, is a doctrine that cannot be maintained."[72] Early claims of official immunity did not fare well in the United States Supreme Court.[73]

Three lines of doctrinal development provided more protections as the years passed. One type of protection was the development, already noted, of the nominal party doctrine, barring suits against an official when the government was the real target of the litigation. Second, the Court created common law protections for officers performing discretionary functions. In *Kendall v. Stokes,* Chief Justice Taney wrote:

> But a public officer is not liable to an action if he falls into error in a case where the act to be done is not merely a ministerial one, but is one in relation to which it is his duty to exercise judgment and discretion; even though an individual may suffer by his mistake.[74]

The idea was that some functions are ministerial in that they involve no exercise of judgment by the official and the duty to perform the function is clear. But where an official has discretion, judgment is called for and the official should not be punished if, in reaching such a decision, he or she errs without malicious intent. The third type of protection was announced by the Court in a series of decisions, beginning in 1872, in which the Court found certain public functions so dangerous that the officials performing those duties should have absolute immunity from suit, while granting others a limited form of immunity.[75] That is the origin of the modern concept of qualified immunity for public officials in use in modified form today and discussed further later in this chapter.

The Arguments in Support of Immunities

Generally, three types of justifications are advanced to support the existence of sovereign and official immunity in the United States.[76] They include conceptual, historical, and public policy arguments.[77] Justice Holmes is frequently cited as a leading advocate of the argument that sovereign immunity is defensible as a concept apart from history or desirable public policy. Holmes observed:

> Some doubts have been expressed as to the source of the immunity of a sovereign power from suit without its own permission, but the answer has been public property since before the days of Hobbes. (*Leviathan,* c. 26, 2.) A sovereign is exempt from suit, not because of any formal conception or obsolete theory, but on the logical and practical ground that there can be no legal right as against the authority that makes the law on which the right depends.[78]

The argument from history is essentially a negative argument that runs roughly as follows:[79] Sovereign and official immunity were part of the British common law that we inherited and that neither the Supreme Court nor the state courts formally rejected until recently. In fact, the doctrines have been cited repeatedly and elaborated upon over the decades. Therefore, both doctrines are supported by the principle of *stare decisis* and ought to stand, unless clear and convincing arguments are made to the contrary.

Clearly the most important, and most often repeated, argument in support of these doctrines of immunity is the public policy argument. The Supreme Court's opinions over the years have recognized a variety of public policy concerns as reasons for permitting the continued use of immunity from suit.[80] Included among these considerations are fears that if suits are permitted: (1) officials will have less independence (or feel they have less independence, amounting to the same thing) in performing their duties;[81] (2) that unfair judgments will result where officials were acting in good faith and made honest errors resulting in substantial damage awards being rendered against them;[82] (3) officials will not be willing to perform their duties aggressively and creatively for fear that they will be sued;[83] (4) that officials and government units will waste time defending against frivolous claims or suits filed to harass the defendants; and (5) that unless officials are made to carry legal burdens personally (this of course will exacerbate other untoward consequences noted above), the costs for defense and satisfaction of successful claims will sap the public coffers and consume funds that would otherwise be employed to provide public services.

Chief Justice Burger emphasized these concerns in *Scheuer v. Rhodes*.[84] Beginning from Justice Jackson's admonition that "it is not a tort for government to govern,"[85] Burger wrote that:

> Public officials, whether governors, mayors, or police, legislators or judges, who fail to make decisions . . . do not fully and faithfully perform the duties of their offices. Implicit in the idea that officials have some immunity—absolute or qualified—for their acts, is a recognition that they may err. The concept of immunity assumes this and goes on to assume that it is better to risk some error and possible injury from such error than not to decide or act at all.[86]

On a number of occasions, the Court has recognized that it is involved in what it terms a weighing process that judges the injury to individual citizens without possibility of recovery against the harm to be done by suing the officials and units.[87] Frequently, it has opted for the protection of the latter.[88]

The Critique of the Immunity Doctrine

But the immunity doctrines have been roundly criticized over the years.[89] The conceptual and historical arguments in support of the doctrines have been effectively refuted and the public policy argument has been challenged by suggested alternatives to complete immunity. Moreover, the arguments in favor of immunity do not fully come to grips with the larger issue of the need to ensure responsibility.

The criticisms have been leveled by scholars and judges at both the state and federal level. William Olson was not overstating the case when he wrote that "perhaps no other rule of law has been subjected to a more protracted or caustic challenge."[90] Olson observed that the abrogation of immunity (the legal terminology for nullification of the doctrine) in the 1960s and 1970s can be traced to attacks on immunity that go back to the 1920s. The criticism, in his view, correctly charged that immunity is "inequitable, outmoded, unduly harsh, and antithetical to concepts of American justice."[91]

Judicial criticism of immunity is not new. Though the public policy argument survives, the historical and conceptual underpinnings have long since been undermined. In *United States v. Lee,* Justice Miller, writing for the Court, noted that there are at least two major difficulties in attempts to employ sovereign and official immunity in America. In the first place, it was indeed possible to obtain redress even in England against the crown for violation of rights, so that simplistic representations about absolute immunity being our heritage from England are exaggerations.[92] Second, assuming that we had in fact inherited an absolute protection for officials and units of government from England, there were good reasons why that immunity should not apply in America. Miller stressed the difference between the status of a citizen and that of a subject. A citizen need not defer to a government official as a vassal would to a lord. Therefore there is no reason why a citizen individually or the people collectively cannot call officials to answer for their actions before a court.[93] The judiciary exists under the Constitution in part to protect citizens from abuse by those in government. Those who accept positions of public trust must understand that fact and respect the limits of their authority. Allowing officials immunity, wrote Miller, "sanctions a tyranny which has no existence in the monarchies of Europe, nor in any other government which has a just claim to well-regulated liberty. . . ."[94]

The argument also concerned whether and to what degree the United States at the turn of the twenty-first century should be basing its decisions about the responsibility of public officials and government units on the common law heritage from England. The fact that officials in the United States operate in a positive law state under a written constitution in a government based upon separation of powers, including a coequal judiciary, and a system of federalism seems to a number of justices to be out of character with the idea that the legal accountability of public officials should rest on precedents borrowed from centuries past drawn from a country that is a parliamentary system with a constitutional monarchy, a system of noblemen known as peers, no separation of powers, a subordinate judiciary, no federalism, and no written constitution. That debate continues to the present.[95]

Another of the major judicial challenges to the doctrines arose when Justice Matthews confronted another aspect of the pro-immunity argument in the *Virginia Coupon Cases.*[96] The argument in favor of immunity ran as follows. Assuming there is an identifiable sovereign in the United States, by definition that sovereign could not be responsible to any higher authority. Sovereignty, after all, entails freedom from responsibility to anyone. The second premise underlying the sovereign immunity doctrine is that the government is the sovereign, or acts for the sovereign, which amounts to the same thing. If both premises are correct, it follows that governments and government officials are immune from suit unless they give consent to be sued. But Matthews demonstrated that the second premise was faulty. There is, indeed, a sovereign. It is a collective sovereign we refer to as the state. But the government acts only on behalf of the state when it obeys the rules of the state. If the government exceeds its authority or abuses its discretion, it has no claim to sovereignty. In this country, the Constitution is the fundamental order issued by the sovereign to the government.[97] It is for the courts to determine whether the government has exceeded the command of the sovereign. In sum, sovereign and official immunity is not historically or conceptually justifiable.

Another group of judges who have criticized immunity is the state judiciary. Although federal law provided no sovereign immunity to state or local government units, state law in many states did grant such protections against most suits that were brought in state courts. In time, a number of state judges rejected immunity. In so doing, several of the state judges saw themselves as doing little that was innovative. Instead, they often noted that they were taking a "final step that carries to its conclusion an established legislative and judicial trend."[98]

Judges and commentators have advanced similar criticisms of the immunity accorded to public officials. Justice Strong wrote that: "We do not perceive how holding an office under a State, and claiming to act for the State, can relieve the holder from obligation to obey the Constitution of the United States, or take away the power of Congress to punish his disobedience."[99] The proposition that officials should be liable for ministerial acts, but not for functions involving discretion, has been criticized both because it is unworkable and because it shields all official activities of any importance, no matter how much harm results from those actions.[100]

Finally, critics have maintained that the danger of frivolous lawsuits can be dealt with by proper judicial management of cases.[101] Such policy problems as remain can be managed by according officials a limited immunity, protecting them from action for mistakes innocently made in judgment or legal interpretation.[102] Clarification of the limited immunity concept and restrictions on such burdensome litigation elements has further substantiated the critics' assertions.[103]

The debate continues over whether there should be any immunity and, if so, what type ought to be available. In order to function in the contemporary administrative environment, though, it is necessary to move beyond the wider debate to more specific questions about what types of immunity are presently available. Consider first the current state of liability rules governing units of government.

WAIVERS OF IMMUNITY AND STATUTORY RIGHTS
TO SUE MEAN DAMAGE SUITS CONTINUE

The caveat in the whole concept of sovereign or official immunity is that government may waive immunity and allow suits to be brought.[104] That is true of both the federal and state governments.[105] The federal government has enacted a general waiver that allows some claims to be brought, with a number of exceptions, under the Federal Tort Claims Act (also frequently referred to as the Tucker Act) in the United States Court of Federal Claims.[106] The class of federal actions that are exempt from suits under that legislation is substantial. For example, the act does not allow suits that challenge the performance by the government of discretionary functions[107] or cases brought by former members of the armed services for injuries suffered while on active duty.[108] As Chief Justice Rehnquist observed in a recent case: "Congress created the Claims Court to permit 'a special and limited class of cases' to proceed against the United States, . . . and the court 'can take cognizance only of those [claims] which by the terms of some act of Congress are committed to it.'"[109] Cases involving contracts with the U.S. government or other matters in which Congress has authorized suit are brought in this way.

Many states have waived their immunity by open-ended statutes that allow normal legal claims that could be brought against an individual to be brought against the state or its agencies with some exceptions. Other states have closed-ended statutes that permit only certain types of suits and retain immunity against all others. Of course, since local governments are creatures of the state, state laws may grant certain forms of immunity or deny it to local jurisdictions with respect to state law issues.

The areas that have become the subjects of debate more recently are the degree to which the Congress can waive the immunity of states from suit and the kind of showing that is needed to demonstrate that a state has waived its own immunity, rendering it vulnerable to suit. Until 1996, there was little question of the ability of the federal government to make states and their officials subject to suits. Indeed, the Congress had adopted a variety of laws that made states, their officials, local governments, and local officers subject to suits for damages or injunctive relief since shortly after the Civil War. However, in 1996, the Supreme Court issued an extremely broad and very dramatic ruling in *Seminole Tribe of Florida v. Florida*[110] that imposed a dramatic limit on federal ability to subject states to suit. (This case was discussed briefly in Chapter 10.) The case arose out of the Indian Gaming in Act in which Congress prescribed a process for states and tribal governments to negotiate the conditions under which gambling operations could be conducted on Native American lands. The Seminole Tribe sued the state for failing to negotiate in good faith as required under the statute.

Congress is given the authority under Article I, Section 8 to "regulate Commerce with foreign Nations, and among the several States, and with the Indian tribes." And, of course, the supremacy clause of Article VI states that: "This Constitution, and the Laws of the United States which shall be made in Pursuance thereof; and all Treaties made, or which shall be made, under the Authority of the United States, shall be the supreme Law of the Land; and the Judges in every State shall be bound thereby, any Thing in the Constitution or Laws of any State to the Contrary notwithstanding." It was on these grounds that Congress adopted the legislation and expected that it would be enforceable in federal court. It was manifestly clear that Congress intended to abrogate the states' immunity.

This case was fought both outside and within the Court at two different levels. There was, to be sure, the relatively technical legal argument concerning constitutionally acceptable processes for addressing disputes between Native American groups and states that has long been the subject complex litigation. However, at a different level, it was a chance for Chief Justice Rehnquist to render a broad and really quite extreme set of claims limiting the powers of the federal government over the states. In the process, he held that Congress did not have power under the commerce clause, and indeed under no provision of the Constitution other than the Fourteenth Amendment, to abrogate state immunity. The Fourteenth Amendment, he noted, specifically authorized Congress to take enforcement actions against the states and spoke to limitations on the states. Of course, he did not explain why only the Fourteenth Amendment could serve as a basis when both the Thirteenth and Fifteenth Amendments contain exactly the same language with respect to enforcement authority.

Justice Stevens warned that the importance of the ruling went well beyond the Indian gaming questions at issue. "Rather, it prevents Congress from providing a federal forum for a broad range of actions against States, from those sounding in copyright and patent law, to those concerning bankruptcy, environmental law, and the regulation of our vast national economy."[111] Justice Souter wrote for three dissenters, forcefully explaining the problems and dangers of Rehnquist's opinion. He began by observing that "the Court today holds for the first time since the founding of the Republic that Congress has no authority to subject a State to the jurisdiction of a federal court at the behest of an individual asserting a federal right."[112] After explaining that Rehnquist had ignored and abused precedents, and overturned the one he could not seem to avoid, Souter concluded by noting that the *Seminole* ruling contradicts not only the clear intentions of the constitutional framers but also is contrary to a string of Supreme Court rulings reaching at least as far back as *Cohens v. Virginia* rendered in 1821.[113]

The fears of the dissenters turned out to have merit, with a string of cases continuing a conversation, but not necessarily adding clarity as to the limits of the congressional authority to render states subject to liability by abrogating immunity. Consider just some of the cases. A nursing supervisor at the University of Alabama at Birmingham brought an Americans with Disabilities Act (ADA) suit against the university when her previous position was not restored to her after completing a course of treatment for breast cancer. In 2001, a sharply divided Court in an opinion by Chief Justice Rehnquist struck down the application of Title I of the ADA, regarding employment discrimination, as applied liability actions against the states, but indicated that local governments and private employers would continue to be liable.[114] The majority applied a test which had the Court second-guessing the quantity and quality of evidence Congress had before it at the time the legislation was passed. The dissenters pointed out that there was a profusion of evidence of discrimination before the Congress at that time and appended page after page of citations to support the point. The Court took a similar action against the Age Discrimination in Employment Act.[115] However, in 2003 it upheld congressional abrogation of state immunity for the Family Medical Leave Act.[116] Then in 2004, it upheld abrogation with regard to Title II of the ADA (though not for Title I) in a case involving access to courthouses by a court reporter and a person hailed before a court who could not get up the stairs and into the courtroom.[117]

A number of states were emboldened to challenge well-established liability situations as a result of the Court's rulings. Texas, following the *Seminole* ruling, even went so far as to attempt to assert immunity against enforcement of a consent decree that it had entered with strong publicly stated commitment not long before, concerning a program for children under Medicaid. The Supreme Court rejected that extreme reach.[118] In 2006, the Court reversed an 11th Circuit ruling supporting a challenge by Georgia to the application of Title II of the ADA to prison inmates.[119]

The rejection of abrogation authority has also been extended to regulatory actions, just as the dissenters in *Seminole* warned that it might. A cruise ship firm that offered gambling cruises sought to operate out of the Port of Charleston, South Carolina, and applied to the South Carolina State Ports Authority for permission. The state refused the company's request on grounds that it would not support gambling cruises out of Charleston, but the company responded that the port already supported cruise lines that had gambling on its vessels. When the state stood firm, the company claimed that the state was in violation of the Shipping Act and asked the Federal Maritime Commission (FMC) to take enforcement action. Again acting by a 5–4 majority, this time in an opinion by Justice Thomas, the Court held that "state sovereign immunity bars such an adjudicative proceeding."[120]

It is, at this writing, not clear what the future holds in this arena, but the consequences have already begun to match the warnings offered by the dissenters in *Seminole*. Dissenting in the FMC case, Justice Breyer wrote:

> The Court holds that a private person cannot bring a complaint against a State to a federal administrative agency where the agency (1) will use an internal adjudicative process to decide if the complaint is well founded, and (2) if so, proceed to court to enforce the law. Where does the Constitution contain the principle of law that the Court enunciates? I cannot find the answer to this question in any text, in any tradition, or in any relevant purpose. In saying this, I do not simply reiterate the dissenting views set forth in many of the Court's recent sovereign immunity decisions. . . . . For even were I to believe that those decisions properly stated the law—which I do not—I still could not accept the Court's conclusion here.[121]

One of the more commonly asked question is whether a state, in adopting various types of legislation, has voluntarily waived its immunity and permitted suit. In a dramatic ruling, in 1985, another sharply divided Court, this time led by Justice O'Connor, said that even if a state had issued a general statement of immunity that did not mean that it consented to be sued in federal court. The California Constitution states that "Suits may be brought against the State in such manner and in such courts as shall be directed by law." Even so, the Court warned that:

> Although a State's general waiver of sovereign immunity may subject it to suit in state court, it is not enough to waive the immunity guaranteed by the Eleventh Amendment. . . . Thus, in order for a state statute or constitutional provision to constitute a waiver of Eleventh Amendment immunity, it must specify the State's intention to subject itself to suit in federal court.[122]

Rehnquist and O'Connor, like a number of the justices in the late nineteenth century, have long feared that the states were being overwhelmed by the federal government and have fought a running battle to roll back rulings they see as responsible for permitting that trend.

If some of these discussions about immunity from suit seem to have become increasingly complex and unclear, that is only because that is precisely the situation. Indeed, during the past three decades, about half the members of the Court have repeatedly complained about that trend. Dissenting in the California waiver case, Justice Brennan wrote: "The Court's sovereign immunity doctrine has other unfortunate results. Because the doctrine is inconsistent with the essential function of the federal courts—to provide a fair and impartial forum for the uniform interpretation and enforcement of the supreme law of the land—it has led to the development of a complex body of technical rules made necessary by the need to circumvent the intolerable constriction of federal jurisdiction that would otherwise occur."[123] What he meant is that the Court's rulings on sovereign immunity have not stopped liability suits. What they have done is to force injured parties to target individual officials rather than the state, with a variety of attendant problems. Speaking of the California case and an earlier one arising out of egregious conditions at a state mental hospital, Brennan insisted that in the rush to insulate states from suit, those who had been wronged by the state were being denied an opportunity to be made whole.

> I might tolerate all of these results—the unprecedented intrusion on Congress' lawmaking power and consequent increase in the power of the courts, the development of a complex set of rules to circumvent the obviously untenable results that would otherwise ensue, the lack of respect for precedent and the lessons of the past . . . if the Court's sovereign immunity doctrine derived from essential constitutional values protecting the freedom of our people or the structure of our federal system. But that is sadly not the case. Instead, the paradoxical effect of the Court's doctrine is to require the federal courts to protect States that violate federal law from the legal consequences of their conduct.[124]

At the end of the day, there are a variety of waivers of immunity, both federal and state. There are also a variety of statutes discussed in earlier chapters (see, e.g., Chapter 12) that recognize rights and authorize suits for damages. While the suits have been rendered more complex and, in many cases, ambiguous by the debates over the types of immunity that might be available, the rise in litigation continues.

CITIES, COUNTIES, AND OTHER POLITICAL SUBDIVISIONS AND THE IMMUNITY DEBATE

One of the most important aspects of the continuing debate over liability suits against officials and government concerns the vulnerability of municipalities and counties to suit in federal court, along with the related question whether these political subdivisions have any immunity in the federal forum. Historically, cities and counties have been subject to suit in both federal and state courts on a variety of legal claims.

> Since colonial times, a distinct feature of our Nation's system of governance has been the conferral of political power upon public and municipal corporations for the management of local concern. As Monell recounted, by 1871, municipalities, like private corporations, were treated as natural persons for virtually all purposes of constitutional statutory analysis. In particular, they were routinely sued in both federal and state courts. . . . Local government units were regularly held to answer violations as well as for common-law actions for breach of contract.[125]

Moreover, state sovereign immunity from suit under the Eleventh Amendment does not apply to local governments.[126]

Is a Local Government a Person?

Still, the question whether political subdivisions of states could be sued under the Civil Rights Act of 1871 (42 U.S.C. §1983)—which allows one to sue "any person" who under color of state law violates federally protected rights—is important.[127] If so, then it would be relatively easy to get a local unit of government into federal court to enforce federal rights. The question was whether the term "person" referred to in the statute included artificial persons such as municipal corporations. The Court in *Monroe v. Pape,* decided in 1961, concluded that it did not.[128] However, the debate over the applicability of Section 1983 to municipalities had not yet ended. An important piece of *Monroe* was overruled by the Supreme Court in 1978 in *Monell v. Department of Social Services.*[129]

Jane Monell and a number of other women who were employed by the New York City Board of Education and Department of Social Services sued those organizations, several city officials, and the

City of New York, claiming that the agencies forced women to take unpaid maternity leave before it was medically necessary for them to do so. While the case was pending, the city and its agencies changed their policies, making the case moot except for the claim to back pay lost by the women due to early maternity leave. The district court concluded that Monroe had conferred upon municipalities immunity from suits for money damages.

The Supreme Court rejected the idea that *Monroe* had provided a broad immunity from liability to government units and overturned it on the question whether a municipality was a "person" within the meaning of Section 1983, but upheld the conclusion of *Monroe* that municipalities may not "be sued under Section 1983 for an injury inflicted solely by its employees or agents."[130] This latter point goes to the doctrine known as *respondeat superior,* which makes private employers responsible for the actions of their agents under certain conditions. On reviewing the legislative history and the state of the case law at the time the 1871 act was under consideration, the Court concluded that the *Monroe's* reading of the legislative history was wrong. Second, *Monell* found that the members of Congress knew and should have known from existing case law that the statute would be read as a broad protection for legal rights that would apply to local governments.[131]

The remaining major question about §1983 liability for municipalities was whether local government units, like public officials, would be permitted some limited form of immunity. That problem, not dealt with in *Monell,* came to the court in *Owen v. City of Independence.*[132] This case began in 1972 when a disagreement arose between George Owen, then chief of police for the City of Independence, Missouri, and the city manager over police department management practices, particularly those involving the police property room. One of the incidents that precipitated the dispute was a report that a gun that had supposedly been disposed of properly was found in the possession of a felon in Kansas City.[133] The controversy escalated and received considerable publicity. The city legal department investigated and found no violations of law. The city manager continued the investigation, but, on the basis of preliminary information, members of the city council pressed for Owen's dismissal. He was fired without a hearing. Owen sued under §1983 on grounds that his termination had held him up to public scorn and ridicule without an opportunity for a hearing in violation of due process requirements of the Fourteenth Amendment.

The district court dismissed the case, finding no right to have been violated, and held that, in any case, the members of the city council were not aware that a hearing was required under recent Supreme Court rulings.[134] The court of appeals reversed and the city sought review in the Supreme Court.[135] The Court accepted the case, but remanded it for further consideration in light of *Monell.* On remand, the court of appeals concluded that Owen's right had been violated, but decided that the city had a limited good faith immunity to protect it from damages since it could not reasonably have known of the Supreme Court's requirement that Owen be accorded a hearing.[136] The Supreme Court reversed, finding that municipalities do not have a limited good faith immunity to protect them against liability.

In order to understand the *Owen* decision, it is necessary to be aware of the types of immunity that have been afforded local government units at common law in state courts over the years. Two approaches have been important, but both have been roundly criticized and neither has previously been found by the Supreme Court to control federal suits. The first is the so-called governmental-versus-proprietary distinction.

> The governmental-proprietary distinction owed its existence to the dual nature of the municipal corporation. On the one hand, the municipality was a corporate body, capable of performing the same "proprietary" functions as any private corporation, and liable for its torts in the same manner and to the same extent, as well. On the other hand, the municipality was an arm of the State, and when acting in that "governmental" or "public" capacity, it shared the immunity traditionally accorded the sovereign. But the principle of sovereign immunity—itself a somewhat arid fountainhead for municipal immunity—is necessarily nullified when the State expressly or impliedly allows itself, or its creations to be sued. Municipalities were therefore liable not only for their "proprietary" acts, but also for those

"governmental" functions as to which the State has withdrawn their immunity. And, by the end of the 19th century, courts regularly held that in imposing a specific duty on the municipality either in its charter or by statute, the State had impliedly withdrawn the city's immunity from liability for the nonperformance of its obligations.[137]

But which government actions are "governmental" and which are "proprietary"? And what happens if, in any situation, governmental and proprietary functions become intertwined?[138] Those who have studied the problem variously termed the governmental/proprietary distinction a "quagmire,"[139] "an anachronism without a rational base,"[140] and "a legalistic crazy quilt."[141] The Court itself once announced that:

> A comparative study of the cases in the forty-eight States will disclose an irreconcilable conflict. More than that, the decisions in each of the States are disharmonious and disclose the inevitable chaos when courts try to apply a rule of law that is inherently unsound.[142]

The second approach to immunity is its so-called ministerial-versus-discretionary action distinction. Justice Brennan summarized this concept well in *Owen*:

> The second common-law distinction between municipal functions—that protecting the city from suits challenging "discretionary" decisions—was grounded not on the principle of sovereign immunity, but on concern for separation of powers. A large part of the municipality's responsibilities involved broad discretionary decisions on issues of public policy decisions that affected large numbers of persons and called for a delicate balancing of competing considerations. For a court or jury, in the guise of a tort suit, to review the reasonableness of the city's judgment on these matters would be an infringement upon the powers properly vested in a coordinate and coequal branch of government.[143]

But, again, this distinction is very difficult to apply since almost any decision by a local government may be held to involve discretion.

The *Owen* Court concluded that: "By its terms, Section 1983 creates a species of tort liability that on its face admits of no immunities."[144] While the Court has recognized that the statute did not eliminate all forms of common law immunity from suit, it has generally examined the basis and purpose of various immunities claimed in any particular case before determining the effect of §1983.[145] In the case of the immunities claimed by the City of Independence, the Court concluded that the proprietary-versus-governmental concept was neither well founded nor consistently developed as a bar to liability suits in federal courts. As to the discretionary-versus-ministerial distinctions, the purpose of the claimed immunity would not be served since there is no branch involved to which deference is due when a federal court hears a suit against a local government unit that is alleged to have violated the United States Constitution.[146]

The *Owen* Court further asserted that the existence of such suits should not frighten individual officials out of aggressively pursuing their duties since these cases do not involve personal damages. To the degree that municipal authorities are deterred from taking actions that would result in an award against the city, the purposes of the statute will be served.[147] However, while the Court has refused to recognize various forms of immunity for government units, it has done so for government officials.

Liability for Policy, Not for Individual Officials' Actions

Of course, while *Monell* made local governments liable to suit, it specifically refused to make them answerable in damages for anything that local officials might do. Arguments over just what it is that the city or county can be called to answer for in recent years have focused on the question of where the dividing line is between what can be said to be only the actions of individual local government officials and what is an action by the community. This is not a small thing, since juries often hesitate to return substantial verdicts against individual city employees, but are much less troubled at levying large judgments against the municipality. And besides, citizens who are victimized by misconduct often rightly claim that while they may actually have suffered at the hands of, for example, a particular police officer, the real cause of the problem were the policies of the department that condoned or perhaps even encouraged the kind of behaviors in evidence. Collecting damages against the officer, in such circumstances, would neither fully compensate the victim nor would it change the root causes that brought about the illegal conduct. This was, of course, the argument made in the Rodney King beating episode in Los Angeles and years earlier in the police/community relations battles involving Mayor Rizzo in Philadelphia.[148] Obviously, no city government or department would formally announce that it had a policy of using excessive violence or intimidation to police the community. And there have historically been many cases in which local governments (and states for that matter) had unwritten but deliberate policies that applied to a variety of people and situations. Therefore, what is policy may sometimes be a matter of custom, sometimes referred to as a pattern and practice, of a certain type of behavior.

The other situation that may occur is that cities, school districts, or counties may make what amount to policy decisions not in the form of ordinances to apply to a broad class of cases in the future but in the form of individual decisions made by officials vested with the authority to speak for the unit of government. These may be policy choices whether they come in the particular or the general form. Hence, the continuing debate is over when it can be said that a community has taken action as a matter of policy, whether it is done in the form of a collective decision by a governing body or as an individual edict from an official empowered to make such decisions.

Since the mid-1980s, however, there has been a string of decisions that have limited the types of actions that will be treated as policy. To begin, the Court has said that "the word policy generally implies a course of action consciously chosen from among various alternatives."[149] While a single decision by municipal policymaker can be the basis for such a claim, "Municipal liability attaches only where the decisionmaker possesses final authority to establish municipal policy with respect to the action ordered."[150] In 1988, the Court attempted to summarize the basic principles for determining when the city could be sued for individual acts based on its decisions to that time:

> First, a majority of the Court agreed that municipalities may be held liable under §1983 only for acts for which the municipality itself is actually responsible.... Second, only those municipal officials who have "final policymaking authority" may by their actions subject the government to §1983 liability.... Third, whether a particular official has "final policymaking authority" is a question of state law.... Fourth, the challenged action must have been taken pursuant to a policy adopted by the official or officials responsible under state law for making policy in that area of the city's business.[151]

There were still cases that arose concerning whether a failure to act could be the basis for a suit. These suits often emerged where a citizen alleged that a failure to train city employees resulted in injury to them. The Court found that there "are limited circumstances in which an allegation of a 'failure to train' can be the basis for liability under 1983."[152]

> [I]t may happen that in light of the duties assigned to specific officers or employees the need for more or different training is so obvious, and the inadequacy so likely to result in the violation of constitutional rights, that the policymakers of the city can reasonably be said to have been deliberately indifferent to the need. In that event, the failure to provide proper training may fairly be said to represent a policy for which the city is responsible, and for which the city may be held liable if it actually causes injury.[153]

However, in a 1997 case, the Court expressed a desire to narrow this opportunity for suit as much as possible. The case grew out of a situation in which a couple was stopped after a police pursuit and the woman was assaulted by a reserve sheriff's deputy, causing serious injuries. It turned out that the officer involved—a nephew of the sheriff—had been hired even though he had a history of misdemeanor violations, including assault. The jury found that the county hiring policy and training policy were "so inadequate as to amount to deliberate indifference to the constitutional needs of the plaintiff."[154] However, the Supreme Court concluded that that was not sufficient. "The plaintiff must also demonstrate that, through its deliberate conduct, the municipality was the 'moving force' behind the injury alleged. That is, a plaintiff must show that the municipal action was taken with the requisite degree of culpability and must demonstrate a direct causal link between the municipal action and the deprivation of federal rights."[155] At this point, four members of the Court dissented sharply, warning that the Court was pretending to make available an avenue for redress but had constructed such a complex set of requirements and constraints that the law had become very difficult to apply.[156]

There is no doubt that the Court, in claiming to preserve the basic ruling from *Monell,* while simultaneously moving to curtail the availability of such suits against municipalities, has created an extremely complex and difficult situation. It is yet another example in which the trend tends to suggest movement in favor of local managers, but the reality is far from predictable or clear. Indeed, the tendency may very well be to move back in the direction of suits against individual officers that really have to do with behavior of the government unit. And since the units usually indemnify their employees for injuries committed in the line of duty, the community will still be required to pay the costs.

THE LIABILITY OF PUBLIC OFFICERS

The Court has fashioned two forms of immunity from suit for particular types of government officials based not upon the office held, but upon the functions they perform. Some officers enjoy an absolute immunity while others are accorded a limited immunity. These protections can be traced to the decisions recognizing judicial immunity, which, in turn, relied heavily upon British precedents.[157] The nature and operation of the immunities vary for judicial, legislative, and executive officials.

Judicial Immunity

The absolute immunity of judges from civil suits was established in *Bradley v. Fisher,* decided by the Supreme Court in 1872.[158] The absolute immunity was held to apply unless the judge acted in "clear absence of all jurisdiction over the subject matter,"[159] even if the judge acted maliciously.[160] Years later, the Court held that the same immunity applied to cases brought under the Civil Rights Act of 1871 (§1983).[161]

Just how absolute the immunity for judges can be was tested in *Stump v. Sparkmun,* decided in 1978.[162] The case alleged that some actions taken by judges cannot realistically be viewed as judicial and, further, there is a point at which judicial conduct results in such egregious violations of constitutional liberties that it is not protected. Linda Sparkmun's mother asked Judge Stump to issue an order authorizing her to have Linda sterilized and granting immunity from any suit that might arise against the mother, the doctors, and the hospital involved. She claimed that Linda was 15 years old, borderline mentally retarded, and was spending too much time with men.[163] She asserted that Linda's conduct might lead to "unfortunate circumstances." The order was issued. Linda was told that she was to have an appendectomy. She did not learn what had been done to her until after she was married and found that she could not become pregnant. The district court found immunity, but the court of appeals reversed. The Supreme Court reversed finding immunity because there was no clear absence of jurisdiction.

The same immunity that protects judges also shields other actors in the adjudicatory process. *Imbler v. Pachtman* concluded that prosecutors are immune even if they knowingly use false or misleading testimony in prosecuting a case.[164] That immunity does not, however, apply to court-appointed defense counsel[165] or other court employees such as a court reporter.[166]

Legislative Immunity

Judicial immunity rests heavily upon public policy arguments and the availability of review of the decision on appeal. Similarly, the Court has concluded, again primarily on public policy grounds, that those performing legislative functions ought to have immunity from damages liability, with account-ability left to the electorate. Unlike judicial immunity, however, legislative immunity does have the speech or debate clause of the Constitution as a base.[167]

The Court first found legislative immunity in *Tenney v. Brandhove,* decided in 1951.[168] Brandhove sued a fellow member of the California legislature under §1983. Tenney chaired a sort of California HUAC (House Un-American Activities) body that made a number of accusations against Brandhove and had him prosecuted unsuccessfully for contempt for refusal to appear before the committee. The Court concluded that §1983 had not abrogated common law legislative immunity.[169]

But two more contemporary rulings suggest that the shield of immunity might have one or two weak points. In one case, a woman sued former Representative Otto Passman for damages, alleging sex discrimination in violation of the Fifth Amendment due process clause.[170] Passman sent her a letter terminating her employment as his aide, stating that while he had found her to be "able, energetic and a very hard worker," he had "concluded that it was essential that the understudy to my Administrative Assistant be a male."[171] The district court dismissed Davis's claim, but a panel of the court of appeals reversed, concluding that the suit could proceed.[172] Further, if her allegations were proven, the con-gressman's "conduct violated the Fifth Amendment; and his conduct was not shielded by the Speech or Debate Clause of the Constitution, Art. 1, Section 6, cl 1."[173] The Supreme Court reversed and re-manded the en banc ruling, agreeing instead with the earlier three-judge panel's decision.[174]

Another case involved Senator Proxmire's "Golden Fleece Award" for wasteful expenditure of public funds.[175] It seems that the senator had allegedly named Ronald Hutchinson, director of research at a state mental hospital and an adjunct professor at a Michigan university, as a recipient of the award. It was the senator's view that Hutchinson's federally supported research on aggressive behavior in primates was not worthwhile. In addition to making a speech accusing the researcher of making a "monkey out of the American taxpayer,"[176] the senator distributed press releases containing the same allegations, had an aide contact the various agencies providing grant funds to the scientist, and published portions of his speech in a newsletter that was widely distributed. Hutchinson produced clear evidence of the *bona fides* of his research and sued the senator for defamation. Proxmire claimed immunity under the speech or debate clause, but the Supreme Court held that the protection of that clause, while broad, did not extend to extensive dissemination of such allegations away from the legislature.[177]

In sum, there is a constitutionally based and common law developed legislative immunity that extends to both national and state legislators for legislative functions which is absolute at least as long as the actions involved can be considered protected by the speech or debate clause. That immunity was also extended by the Court to local governing bodies in 1998.[178]

Executive Immunity

The executive immunity cases treat officials differently depending upon whether they are performing executive functions or are involved with adjudicatory processes. This line of Supreme Court decisions establishing limited immunity for executive officials is traceable to *Spalding v. Vilas,* decided in 1896.[179] Relying on *Bradley v. Fisher* and a series of British opinions (most of which had to do with military officers), the Court found immunity for the executive.[180]

Spalding involved the head of a department, but how would the Court respond to suits against lower level executive officials? The answer to that question did not come until the decision in *Barr v. Matteo* was rendered in 1959.[181] *Barr* was a very important decision in part because, after that opinion, it would be erroneously assumed that questions about official liability and immunity had been settled. The fact is that the *Barr* Court itself was unsettled. The decision was based on four votes in favor of immunity and four against, with one concurring vote by Justice Black. Black's vote resulted in a sufficient total in favor of the officials, but his opinion was based not on immunity grounds, but on the First Amendment freedom of expression. Justice Brennan's dissent in *Barr* would eventually become the controlling law.

Barr was a suit by former employees against two officers of the Office of Rent Stabilization for libel. In press releases, Matteo and others allegedly maliciously insinuated that several employees had attempted to defraud the government in a pay scheme. Writing for himself and Justices Frankfurter, Clark, and Whittaker, Justice Harlan sustained the claim of absolute privilege for these lower-level employees.[182] Harlan relied upon the opinions in *Spalding* and *Tenney* along with public policy justifications for his opinion.

The Court recognized that there may be differences between the kind of duties and the type of policy interests involved depending upon whether the official sued is a cabinet-level officer or one of lesser rank, but it gave no guidance on how that problem ought to be dealt with. "It is not the title of his office but the duties with which the particular officer sought to be made to respond to damages is entrusted ... which must provide the guide in delineating the scope of the rule which clothes the official acts of the executive officer with immunity from civil defamation suits."[183] The reference to the relationship between the types of duties involved and the immunity granted would be important in later cases.

There were several sharp dissents, the most important of which for the development of executive immunity was that written by Justice Brennan.[184] He concluded that a qualified privilege would protect the officer and yet make it possible to deal with malicious injuries to citizens.[185] Brennan asserted that a limited good faith immunity would not be unworkable and burdensome since summary judgment procedures would be used to dispose of unmeritorious claims without requiring the burden of a trial.[186] In the final analysis, he warned:

> [T]he courts should be wary of any argument based on the fear that subjecting government officers to the nuisance of litigation and the uncertainties of its outcomes may put an undue burden on the conduct of public business. Such a burden is hardly one peculiar to public officers: citizens generally go through life subject to litigation and the possibility of a miscarriage of justice.[187]

There are ways of dealing with the problem of the burden of litigation, but, Brennan argued, solving that difficulty by declaring officials absolutely immune "has too much of the flavor of throwing out the baby with the bath."[188]

In a later case, Chief Justice Warren wrote for the Court finding that police officers accused of false arrest did have a limited immunity available to them.[189] The Court further decided that, although §1983 did not abrogate all common law immunities of public officials, police officers had never enjoyed an absolute immunity from liability. Even under §1983, the Court held, the police officers should have a "defense of good faith and probable cause."[190]

The *Bivens v. Six Unknown Named Agents of the Federal Bureau of Narcotics* decision, rendered in 1971, was not concerned with the degree of immunity of executive branch officials from suits, but whether federal officials could be sued under the general federal question jurisdiction of the federal courts for claimed violation of constitutional rights.[191] The Court concluded that federal officials could be brought to court even though there is no statute analogous to §1983 (covering state officials) specifically authorizing such suits.[192] No statutory grounds need be asserted when a citizen sues a federal administrator for a violation of a particular constitutional right. Since then, the effort has been first to define the degree of immunity from liability available to executive officers and second to seek ways to reduce the burdens of litigation on those officials even though they would ultimately be able to successfully defend themselves.

Scheuer v. Rhodes[193] was a suit filed under Section 1983 by the families of the students killed during demonstrations at Kent State University against the governor and other Ohio officials. In a unanimous opinion, the Court held that these officials had no absolute immunity. The Court found that if such an absolute immunity were granted "Section 1983 would be drained of meaning."[194] After all, what is the point of a statute enacted to provide for suits against officials who violate citizens' rights if all of the officials are then carefully insulated from suit by absolute immunities? Instead, the Court held that executive officials are generally entitled to a qualified immunity."[195]

Just what that qualified immunity entailed remained to be determined in *Wood v. Strickland*.[196] The Court noted that there was a great deal of confusion regarding the meaning of the qualified good faith immunity recognized in *Scheuer*[197] and attempted a clarification. It recognized the difficulty of drafting language to assure administrators that they need not fear accidentally walking into a lawsuit in the course of their normal duties while ensuring some basic level of responsible conduct. It concluded that a two-part standard was required. Referred to as a test consisting of an objective and a subjective standard, the *Wood* decision focused both on what the administrator intended by his or her actions and what that administrator should reasonably have been expected to know about the actual state of the law.

> Therefore, in the specific context of school discipline, we hold that a school board member is not immune from liability for damages under Section 1983 if he knew or reasonably should have known that the action he took within his sphere of official responsibility would violate the constitutional rights of the student affected, or if he took the action with the malicious intention to cause a deprivation of constitutional rights or other injury to the student. That is not to say that school board members are "charged with predicting the future course of constitutional law." . . . A compensatory award will be appropriate only if the school board member has acted with such an impermissible motivation or with such disregard of the student's clearly established constitutional rights that his action cannot reasonably be characterized as being in good faith.[198]

The *Wood* Court's remark that administrators need not predict the future course of constitutional law did not assuage the fears of officials around the country. The ruling in *Procunier v. Navarette*[199] gave those administrators some sense of what the Court's objective standard meant. *Procunier* was a suit under §1983 against California prison officials alleging that policies and practices restricting mail sent by inmates was an unconstitutional infringement of freedom of expression under the First Amendment. The Court did not rule on whether prison communications were protected until 1974, at which time it did find them covered by the First Amendment.[200] But the instances involved in the *Procunier* case took place in 1971 and 1972. Repeating its earlier language from *Wood,* the Court held that the officials would have no immunity "if the constitutional right allegedly infringed by them was clearly established at the time of the challenged conduct, if they knew or reasonably should have known that their conduct violated the constitutional norm."[201] Since the right involved in this case was not clearly established at the time of the incident, there could be no liability. There was no allegation that the actions of the officials were malicious.

These executive immunity cases evidence a concern for the warnings voiced in the *Barr v. Matteo* dissents by Warren and Brennan that complete immunity does not balance the needs of the officials with the rights of citizens who seek to hold them legally responsible since only one pan of the scales was loaded. The qualified immunity doctrine is an attempt to even the balance. The *Butz v. Economou*[202] opinion was in part a recital of the development of that doctrine.

The *Butz* case arose when an official of a firm which had been licensed to trade in commodity futures brought a liability action in federal court. He alleged that his constitutional rights were violated when, after he had criticized the agency, an administrative proceeding was commenced against his firm. He charged that the Secretary of Agriculture, the agency attorney in the case against him, and the administrative law judge should all be held liable. The government's answer was simple. Although the *Bivens* case had permitted suits to be filed against federal officials under the Constitution, it had not overruled *Barr's* recognition of absolute immunity for federal officers. Therefore, these officials were absolutely immune for actions taken within their authority. The Court gave neither side in the case what it sought.

The Court made an attempt to differentiate *Barr,* but its primary effort was a comprehensive evaluation of Supreme Court decisions on official immunity. The *Butz* Court concluded: "None of these decisions with respect to state officials furnishes any support for the submission of the United

States that federal officials are absolutely immune from liability for their constitutional transgressions."[203] It would, said the Court, "amount to standing the Constitution on its head to say that the Bill of Rights imposed more responsibility on state officials than it does on federal officers."[204] Federal officials who violate the Constitution are, by definition, not acting within their proper range of authority. Consequently, they are entitled only to the same limited good faith immunity that governs state officials.[205]

However, the Court recognized that not all executives perform executive functions.[206] Judges had been granted immunity because of their function as had other adjudicatory officials such as prosecutors. "We think that adjudication within a federal administrative agency shares enough of the characteristics of the judicial process that those who participate in such adjudications should also be immune from suits for damages."[207] On this basis, the *Butz* Court found that all the officials involved in deciding "to initiate or continue a proceeding subject to agency adjudication are entitled to absolute immunity from damages liability for their parts in that decision."[208]

Further clarification of the status of executive branch officials came in two decisions rendered in 1982 that continue to provide the basic rules for immunity today. In *Harlow v. Fitzgerald,*[209] Justice Powell, writing for an 8–1 majority, rejected claims by Bryce Harlow and Alexander Butterfield that their positions and functions as presidential assistants required absolute immunity from liability suits.[210] In the other case, *Nixon v. Fitzgerald,* the Court found that the president does enjoy absolute immunity for injuries growing out of his official acts. Of course, the Court has more recently refused to protect President Clinton against litigation concerning events that took place before he came to office.[211]

The Court was primarily concerned in *Harlow* with clarification of the qualified immunity standard announced in *Wood.* It also sought to answer complaints by officials that permitting extensive pretrial proceedings results in significant interference with the administrative process regardless of whether the official actually was found to be liable in a trial.

Specifically, the Supreme Court was responding to some degree of confusion among officials and lower courts regarding the Court's use of "subjective" and "objective" aspects of good faith immunity. Further, since an official claiming immunity bears the burden of establishing his or her eligibility for the protection, how should the official avoid spending substantial amounts of time and money in the pleading and discovery stages of a suit, when the Court has urged lower courts to dispose of frivolous legal actions by summary judgments (without trials)? The *Harlow* Court's response to the first problem was to eliminated the so-called subjective aspects of good faith immunity. Its reaction to the second concern was to limit discovery and instruct judges to protect officials in the pretrial process to avoid excessive burdens in cases likely to be dismissed in summary judgments proceedings. Justice Powell wrote:

> Qualified or "good faith" immunity is an affirmative defense that must be pleaded by a defendant official. . . . Decisions of this Court have established that the "good faith" defense has both an "objective" and a "subjective" aspect. The objective element involves a presumptive knowledge of and respect for "basic unquestioned constitutional rights. . . ." The subjective component refers to "permissible intentions. . . ." Characteristically, the Court has defined these elements by identifying the circumstances in which qualified immunity would not be available. Referring both to the objective and subjective elements, we have held that qualified immunity would be defeated if an official "knew or reasonably should have known that the action he took within his sphere of official responsibility would violate the constitutional rights of the [plaintiff], or if he took the action with malicious intention to cause a deprivation of constitutional rights or other injury. . . ."
>
> The subjective element of the good faith defense frequently has proved incompatible with our admonition in *Butz* that insubstantial claims should not proceed to trial. . . .
>
> Consistently with the balance at which we aimed in *Butz,* we conclude today that bare allegations of malice should not suffice to subject government officials either to the costs of trial or to the burdens of broad-reaching discovery. We therefore hold that *government officials performing discretionary functions generally are shielded from liability for civil damages insofar as their conduct does not violate clearly established statutory or constitutional rights of which a reasonable person would have known.* . . .

Reliance on the objective reasonableness of an official's conduct, as measured by reference to clearly established law, should avoid excessive disruption of government and permit the resolution of many insubstantial claims on summary judgment. On summary judgment, the judge appropriately may determine, not only the currently applicable law, but whether that law was clearly established at the time an action occurred. If the law at that time was not clearly established, an official could not fairly be said to "know" that the law forbade conduct not previously identified as unlawful. Until this threshold immunity question is resolved, discovery should not be allowed. *If the law was clearly established, the immunity defense ordinarily should fail, since a reasonably competent public official should know the law governing his conduct.* Nevertheless, if the official pleading the defense claims extraordinary circumstances and can prove that he neither knew nor should have known of the relevant legal standard, the defense should be sustained. But again, the defense would turn primarily on objective factors.

By defining the limits of qualified immunity in objective terms, we provide no license to lawless conduct. The public interest in deterrence of unlawful conduct and in compensation of victims remains protected by a test that focuses on the objective legal reasonableness of an official's acts. Where an official could be expected to know that certain conduct would violate statutory or constitutional rights, he should be made to hesitate; and a person who suffers injury caused by such conduct may have a cause of action. But where an official's duties legitimately require action in which clearly established rights are not implicated, the public interest may be better served by action taken "with independence and without fear of consequences."[212] [Emphasis added.]

The *Harlow* ruling was a strong admonition to trial court judges not only to employ summary judgment to stop groundless suits, but also to prevent the use of discovery procedures to attempt to try the case on paper before a summary judgment. The obvious difficulty is that someone injured by an official may be caught in a Catch-22, unable to acquire evidence regarding the objective nature of the facts surrounding official action because of limitations on discovery processes.

In the years since *Harlow,* the common practice has been for officials who are sued to ask the court at the earliest possible point to determine whether the suit should be barred because of qualified immunity. The idea is to avoid the burdens that come in the pretrial process. And if the judge refuses, the official can appeal. In one such case in which the lower court sought to limit an official's appeal, Justice Scalia, for the Supreme Court majority, wrote: "*Harlow* and *Mitchell* make clear that the defense is meant to give government officials a right, not merely to avoid 'standing trial,' but also to avoid the burdens of 'such pretrial matters as discovery' . . . , as '[i]nquiries of this kind can be peculiarly disruptive of effective government.'"[213]

In sum, neither state nor federal officials are absolutely immune from suit. They do enjoy a qualified immunity based upon objective determinations as to the state of the law at the time of their actions. Simple mistakes will not subject them to federal liability. They need not predict the future of constitutional development since they will not be called to answer for a constitutional violation unless the right involved was clearly established at the time of the incident alleged to be unlawful and the official should reasonably have been expected to know of the right and that his or her conduct violated the right. There is absolute immunity available to executive branch employees engaged in agency adjudication, including those who decide to launch or pursue an administrative adjudication.

VULNERABILITY: REAL AND PERCEIVED

The level of anxiety felt by administrators both for their personal vulnerability to damages liability and for problems in their management of units of government is high, but just how real is the threat as opposed to the perception? As the discussion to this point in the chapter has indicated, there is uncertainty, but there are a number of factors that should cause competent and reasonably cautious public officials not to let their anxiety get the better of them.

First, suits against officials are usually not easy to prosecute. For example, Section 1983 suits require the plaintiff to show injury to a protected right by an official acting under color of law that was clearly established at the time of the action. But the Supreme Court has been rather generous to administrators in its reading of what constitutes such a violation. The Court has given strong warnings to lower courts to protect officials from suits for mere mistakes in judgment and reject claims that fail to state a compensable claim or which appear intended to harass the officials.[214]

Second, the more recent rulings of the Court direct lower courts to make judgments about whether a suit is barred by qualified immunity as early in the process as possible and provide an opportunity to appeal that ruling if it goes against the official.

Where a suit is allowed to move to a judgment, most jurisdictions indemnify officials for damage claims arising out of the performance of their duty. There are, however, two common exceptions. The first is where punitive damages are involved. In those situations, many states allow the public employer to choose whether to indemnify the official or not. The second is in the event of damages growing out of criminal conduct by a public employee. In either of those two instances, the employee may be in serious trouble, but obtaining punitive damages usually requires a very rigorous proof and high standards. Clearly, it is important for officials to know the policy of their employer with regard to indemnification. It may also be is advisable to determine whether one's professional association offers malpractice insurance.

Another important question is who will represent the employee in a suit. Many (though by no means all) jurisdictions, including the federal government, will represent an employee sued for conduct in the line of duty, though the employee may choose to be represented by private counsel at his or her own expense. However, in most instances the employee must request government representation in writing. It is not automatic. Also, government attorneys are usually required to tell the employee that while they will be represented, the attorney must do so with the interests of the government unit in mind, and may not take positions adverse to the best interests of the unit involved. In any case, it is good to know what the rules are in one's organization well before the situation arises in which it is necessary to trigger them.

There clearly are areas of uncertainty that rightly concern knowledgeable public officials. For one thing, there is always a set of questions concerning how the state and local governments will choose to implement state liability laws. That may be the real danger area for many officials since the kind of claim often lodged may not be a federal civil rights matter, but litigation brought in state courts under state law. The current state of many state liability and immunity statutes is uncertain because the legislation is often not updated frequently enough to take into account changes in federal law and state court rulings. This is an important area for in-service training at both the state and local levels. In some instances, local governments obtain assistance in this effort from the League of Cities in their state, while state agencies may call on the Office of the Attorney General.

Another area of concern is changing federal legislation, though the general trend has been for Congress to seek to limit damage suits. Thus, in 1988 Congress adopted the Federal Employee Liability Reform and Tort Compensation Action.[215] Under this statute, when a tort action is brought against a federal employee acting in the line of duty, the federal government is allowed to substitute itself as a party and convert the litigation to a claim under the Federal Tort Claims Act with all of the limitations and immunities that entails.[216] However, that statute does not operate to block a *Bivens* suit claiming a constitutional violation or a suit brought under a statute that specifically authorizes recovery against a government employee.[217]

In 1996, Congress enacted the Prison Litigation Reform Act.[218] This statute seeks to address one of the areas that has produced the greatest volume of suits against government officials. It sets a variety of limits on the kind and even the number of federal court actions that can be brought by prisoners in an effort to prevent administrators from having even to respond to a host of frivolous lawsuits.[219]

In other instances, Congress has in fact created expanded opportunities for damage claims against government units or officials. Chapter 12 summarized a variety of civil rights–related statutes that all authorize such suits. In some instances, these damage claims may come in the form of suits to recover expenses that grew out of a failure by a community to comply with federal law. One example is the ability of families who remove their children with special health needs from local public schools in disputes over accommodations to be provided to them under the Individuals with Disabilities Education Act (IDEA). The Supreme Court has ruled that, if they ultimately win in a judicial appeal, they can recover the cost of sending the child to a private school.[220]

One of the statutes that has created a good deal of uncertainty is the Civil Rights Act of 1991, which authorizes not only compensatory damages intended to make the victim whole again, but also punitive damages intended to punish those guilty of discrimination and deter others from similar conduct. Punitive damages are a much more powerful weapon because they are much larger in amount than compensatory awards and because many jurisdictions can choose not to indemnify their employees. However, there is a fear that plaintiffs will regularly seek punitive damage awards, raising the anxiety level of both officials and units of government and the complexity of the litigation.

Another problem is that because many of the Supreme Court's rulings set forth complex and sometimes ambiguous positions, lower courts, both federal and state, may render a wide variety of rulings based upon the same precedents. That will, in turn, require appellate clarification.

CONTRACTS AND RESPONSIBILITY

It should be clear from the discussions of the historical evolution of legal doctrines associated with administrative responsibility that disputes over contracts of various kinds have been at the heart of many of the cases that have shaped the field. Of course, the increasing tendency to use contracts to perform a wider array of services than ever before has resulted in an variety of administrative responsibility issues. As some of the discussions of contracting in earlier chapters have indicated, there are far more questions than proposed solutions.[221]

For the most part, however, these cases have historically tended to focus on disputes between the government and a contracting party. As wider use is made of contracts for the delivery of services and as the concept of "public/private partnerships" has been expanded to have contractors performing a wider array of functions, the level of complexity of contract disputes has increased significantly. Increasingly, in recent years, more questions are being raised about whether contractors that perform functions traditionally performed by public agencies can be made responsible and what types of vehicles are available for doing that. While this is an extremely complex topic that can take up a great deal of page space, there are three critical points that are important in the context of the present discussion.

First, traditionally, for reasons discussed in earlier chapters, the law of government contracts has been kept separate from administrative law. The primary focus in the contract area has been with respect to the bid processes, since much of the history of the development of government contracting has concerned the effort to stop corruption in the awarding of public program funds at all levels of government. There are three other areas that have consumed a great deal of time in government contract law. These are: (1) various debates over cost reimbursement and payments; (2) disputes over breach of contract and the resulting financial obligations of the parties; and (3) various kinds of disciplinary actions that may be taken against contractors by the government and the contractors' rights in such processes.[222] Because these two bodies of law have been treated separately and given the limited terms in which contract responsibility issues have been understood, there has not been an effective effort either in policy or in the academic literature of public administration to integrate the two sets of legal responsibility concerns.

Second, we have moved through a period in which the argument has repeatedly been made that law should not be a major focus, but rather public officials should focus on results and take such innovative steps as are needed to achieve those results. Indeed, arguments have often been made that in the modern context the lines between public and private organizations are increasingly artificial and ought not to stand in the way of solving problems. In earlier chapters, reference was made to the debate between Ronald Moe and Barry Bozeman on this point.[223] However, Moe, Robert Gilmour, Louis Fisher, Francis Leazes, Donald Kettl, and Thomas Stanton, among others, have written a good deal, making a solid case that, particularly when it comes to issues of responsibility, the distinctions are very important and so is the public law based on which public agencies act and are called to account.[224] To this point, unfortunately, the tendency continues to be on the "anything that works" side, and the problems raised by the public law critics have not been given the attention they deserve. Hence, statutes at the federal and state levels have not been adequately strengthened and adapted to meet the increasing array of novel approaches to public services and regulation.

Third, many of the new types of contractor issues are now bubbling up through the courts, and the Supreme Court has only begun to address the range of legal responsibility for contract-related disputes that we have before us, let alone the new ones that are emerging virtually every day in the contemporary context. Several of these have been raised in earlier chapters (see, e.g., Chapters 11 and 12). In addition to those issues already discussed there are three other areas that are important to mention and to monitor over the coming years.

The first question has to do with when a contractor can be held responsible (when acting in the name of the state) such that the contractor may be sued under the statutes discussed earlier in this chapter that are used to address administrative responsibility for government officials and agencies. While the Supreme Court has provided some guidance in this area,[225] there is a long way to go before we will be able to predict with confidence what types of so-called partnerships will render the nongovernmental partners subject to standard responsibility tools.

Consider three examples. At one end of the spectrum is a case in which a doctor was working as a prison physician under contract to the state. In that instance, there was little difficulty finding that he was a state actor.[226] However, at the other end the Court decided in two cases concerning the National Collegiate Athletic Association (NCAA) that it is not a state actor even with respect to actions taken by universities pursuant to NCAA rules and disciplinary procedures. In the first case, a state university removed a coach of a major national basketball program under threat of sanctions by the NCAA. Although the Court agreed that the action by the state school were subject to suit under the §1983, the NCAA was not—even though the school took the action at the direction of and under the threat of sanctions by that organization.[227] In a 1999 case, the Court was asked to address the question from a different angle when a student brought a challenge under Title IX of the Civil Rights Act concerning the applicability of NCAA eligibility rules. In this case, the student charged that the NCAA receives a great deal of federal money in the form of dues it collects from member institutions. Here again, the Court concluded that the NCAA remains private, whatever the member institutions may choose to do on the basis of their affiliation with the organization.[228] Between these two ends of the spectrum lie a host of other situations. For example, the Supreme Court has concluded that a Pennsylvania worker's compensation statute that permits the insurers under the state program to refuse payment, pending a utilization review by another private program participant without notice or an opportunity for the claimant, is neither action under "color of law" within the meaning of §1983 nor a deprivation of due process under the Fourteenth Amendment.[229] In this case, the Court held that, although the insurer acted "with knowledge of and pursuant to the state statute," that does not make them a state action.[230]

> The actor will not be held to constitutional standards unless there is a sufficiently close nexus between the State and the challenged action of the regulated entity so that the latter may be fairly treated as that of the State itself. . . . Whether such a close nexus exists . . . depends on whether the State has expressed coercive power or has provided such significant

encouragement, either overt or covert, that the choice must in law be deemed to be that of the state.[231]

And it should be obvious that if the Supreme Court is a long way from providing clear resolutions of these questions, the lower courts, literally hundreds of them, are even less certain. For example, one appeals court found that a not-for-profit corporation that was responsible for designing, operating, and promoting a municipal festival was not a state actor.[232] However, another court determined that a volunteer fire department is a state actor.[233]

Second, once it is determined that such an action can be brought against a contract service provider, what, if any, immunities will be applied and on what grounds? Chapter 1 set forth a brief description of *Richardson v. McKnight,* concerning a suit brought by a Tennessee prisoner against guards employed by the Corrections Corporation of America, which operates facilities under contract with the state. The Court found that the privately employed prison guards, despite the fact that they are performing virtually the same functions as guards employed by the state, are not entitled to the same kinds of immunity. In an interesting argument (that drove the dissenters around the bend) Justice Breyer argued that the very forces of the marketplace that were at the heart of the reason for contracting provided alternatives to the immunity normally accorded to public servants.

> First, the most important special government immunity producing concern—unwarranted timidity—is less likely present, or at least is not special, when a private company subject to competitive market pressures mean not only that a firm whose guards are too aggressive will face damages that raise costs, thereby threatening its replacement, but also that a firm whose guards are too timid will face threats of replacement by other firms with records that demonstrate their ability to do both a safer and a more effective job....
>
> Second, "privatization" helps to meet the immunity-related need "to ensure that talented candidates" are "not deterred by the threat of damages suits from entering public service."... It does so in part because of the comprehensive insurance-coverage requirements just mentioned. The insurance increases the likelihood of employee indemnification and to that extent reduces the employment-discouraging fear of unwarranted liability potential applicants face. Because privatization law also frees the private prison-management firm from many civil service law restraints, ... it permits the private firm, unlike a government department, to offset any increased employee liability risk with higher pay or extra benefits. In respect to this second government-immunity-related purpose then, it is difficult to find a special need for immunity, for the guards' employer can operate like other private firms; it need not operate like a typical government department.
>
> Third, lawsuits may well distract these employees from their duties... , but the risk of distraction alone cannot be sufficient grounds for an immunity. Our qualified immunity cases do not contemplate the complete elimination of lawsuit-based distractions.[234]

Although the majority was at pains to argue that its opinion was to be read narrowly, its arguments were quite broad in character. Buried within the discussion was an important assertion:

> This is not to say that government employees, in their efforts to act within constitutional limits, will always, or often, sacrifice the otherwise effective performance of their duties. Rather, it is to say that government employees typically act within a *different* system. They work within a system that is responsible through elected officials to voters who, when they vote, rarely consider the performance of individual subdepartments or civil service rules that, while providing employee security, may limit the incentives or the ability of individual departments or supervisors flexibly to reward, or to punish, individual employees.[235]

If that is true, then there are interesting issues to be addressed about the sets of assumptions that are made about the similarities and differences present when services are contracted out as compared to delivered by public agencies.

Following *McKnight,* the Ninth Circuit rendered an interesting opinion concerning the contracting out the management of certain city functions. In this case, Los Angeles contracted with Lockheed Information Management Services to process parking tickets for the city, including, among other functions, setting disputes over tickets for trial. Several operators of fleets of commercial vehicles, including a vending machine company, hired a law firm to challenge tickets. The firm began going to court to fight every ticket, hundreds of them. Lockheed allegedly retaliated by tightening the documentation requirements needed to have a ticket scheduled for trial. The firm sued Lockheed under §1983. In the process, the company sought to impose the standard qualified immunity. The court, citing *McKnight,* denied Lockheed that immunity. However, the court said that when the case went to trial, the firm might be able to present a defense based on "good faith or probable cause."[236] Here again, it is not at all clear how similar to or different from the standard approaches the contractor cases will be.

It might seem from the *McKnight* case that some degree of clarity might be emerging about contractor liability when acting on behalf of government, but that is far from the case. In a case involving a federal correctional facility in New York, a narrow 5–4 majority of the Court took things in a very different direction. In this case, a contractor had made a decision not to allow inmates in a halfway house operated under contract for the federal government to use the elevator below the sixth floor. An inmate with a heart condition alleged that he was not provided with the medication that he needed and that he was also prevented from using the elevator, even though he should have been able to do so because of his condition. He was injured as a result of the situation. Since this was a federally operated facility, he sued the corporate contractor under a *Bivens* type action. Chief Justice Rehnquist wrote for the majority, finding that, because he could not have brought suit against a federal agency, he could not bring suit against a corporation contracted with the agency.[237] However, the dissenters pointed out that there was no legal basis for equating a private contractor with a federal agency in terms of immunity. Further, corporations are treated as persons in the law, whether they are commercial corporations or municipal corporations. And, of course, the logic of this opinion runs completely counter to that of *McKnight,* which contended that the purposes of immunity and role of liabilities for contractors and their employees are entirely different from that of agencies and public employees, leaving a great deal of ambiguity in our understanding of these concepts and the law that covers them. "Indeed," Justice Stevens wrote for the four dissenters, "a tragic consequence of today's decision is the clear incentive it gives to corporate managers of privately operated custodial institutions to adopt cost-saving policies that jeopardize the constitutional rights of the tens of thousands of inmates in their custody."[238]

Third, there are many unanswered questions about the approaches that will be taken to the resolution of disputes brought by citizens adversely affected by government performance under inter-jurisdictional agreements. There is a plethora of agreements among different levels of government and among governments at the same level. The liability and immunity situation under many of these is very unclear. Consider one example that made it to the Supreme Court. A physicist was hired by Lawrence Livermore Laboratories in California, which is operated by the University of California for the federal government under contract. The physicist charged that the laboratory management had violated his contract. The Regents of the University of California asserted Eleventh Amendment sovereign immunity against the claim. The Court of Appeals rejected that argument on grounds that the federal contract provided that the Department of Energy "and not the State of California, is liable for any judgment rendered against the University in its performance of the Contract."[239] The Supreme Court reversed, finding that sovereign immunity applied notwithstanding the federal government's willingness to indemnify the state.

Of course, there are other kinds of immunities or protections that are sometimes available. One other argument that has been used to defeat claims against contractors comes in the form of the so-called "government contractor defense." As long ago as 1918, the Court held that "if the contractor is bound to build according to plans and specifications prepared by [the government], the contractor will not be responsible for the consequences of defects in the plans and specifications."[240] This issue reemerged at the Supreme Court level in the 1990s, when companies that lost money in the settlement of suits brought by veterans who had been exposed to the defoliant Agent Orange in Vietnam attempted to recover their losses from the government. The companies settled the case with the veterans, but later sued the government on grounds that the government should indemnify them. The Court held that the government contractor defense would have been available to protect the companies if they had taken the case to court. However, the defense entitled them to immunity from damages, not to indemnification when they chose to settle.[241]

It should be clear from this very brief summary of government contract–related responsibility issues that many governments have waded into very deep waters well before they understood their situation, that of the contractors, or the ability of citizens to ensure responsible behavior. This area of public law will be an extremely important field for development in the years to come unless there is a dramatic reversal in the tendency to contract out more and more functions. At the time of this writing, there is no evidence of such a dramatic change in course.

POLITICS, MARKETS, AND LAW: COMPETING CONCEPTS OF RESPONSIBILITY

This discussion of the fit, or lack of it, between issues arising out of the increased use of contracting and legal responsibility is only one part of a much larger issue that has been influencing the way we think about administrative responsibility in the contemporary context. The reinventing-government movement, the National Performance Review on which it was based, and the reaction against "red tape"—which is a repeated theme in this entire conversation of public management in the 1990s—speak to a broad tendency in the United States and elsewhere to move away from a traditional approach to responsibility. And, of course, despite its many differences with its predecessor in the White House, the George W. Bush administration's Presidential Management Agenda is squarely in that same New Public Management approach to governance. It is an effort, first, to move away from the legal conception of administrative responsibility toward a more political approach, and, second, to shift to a market-based idea of responsibility.

Ironically, a number of countries with parliamentary governments have been moving in the other direction. Traditionally, parliamentary systems, particularly those based on the British (or Westminister) model, employ something known as ministerial responsibility in place of the American legal approach.[242] The idea is that cabinet ministers are individually responsible for the behavior of their ministry and collectively responsible for the actions of the government as a whole. "The concentration of responsibility in the hands of Ministers reflects the fundamental democratic principle that the power of the state be exercised under the authority of elected officials accountable to the representatives of the electorate."[243] In this approach, the ministers shield the careerists from public challenge and take the heat themselves during ministers' question period. In that setting, the opposition will challenge the minister to explain what has happened and what has been done to correct the problem. The idea is not so much to fix blame on individual public servants or to obtain redress for particular citizens injured by the ministry but to identify administrative problems and fix them in the interest of the society as a whole. Obviously, the minister then deals with whatever discipline or other corrections are required internally and without the glare of publicity.

When they learn of this tradition, many American administrators envy their counterparts in Canada or Great Britain and wish their political superiors would stand up in that way instead of scapegoating or running for cover when the television cameras start. However, the reality is that a number of countries with this kind of political approach to responsibility have been moving more in the direction of the kind of legal and individually oriented form more traditional in the United States.[244] In part, this has to do with the rise of a rights orientation in many of those countries and the development of constitutional courts with much wider powers than were historically available.[245] In some cases, traditional cabinet privilege that was recognized as a kind of veil over the internal workings of the government in power has been eliminated to allow pursuit of wrongdoers.[246]

While this convergence between the legal and the political approaches has been underway, a third approach to responsibility has gained in importance—a market-oriented conception. The core value in the market perspective is efficiency. It has a number of dimensions.

First, there is a simple assumption that cost is a critical component: That which costs less is more responsible. (Of course, that is in reality an economy judgment, but that distinction is often missed.[247]) Then there is a cost/benefit view. Responsible public action requires a positive cost/benefit calculation. Such a view ignores the fact that, despite all of the continuing work that has been done to make such analyses more sophisticated, major difficulties remain (see Chapter 10). Such approaches rarely acknowledge that many of actions that agencies must take which may not be regarded as cost effective are mandated by legislation. In such circumstances the administrator is responsible for action whether that task is appropriate or not.

Third, there are performance standards. In theory, contemporary performance management argues that the focus should not be on the inputs to agencies, such as the numbers of people or dollars committed to a program, or to outputs, as in the number of cases processed, but to outcomes in the sense of actual improvements in the problematic situations that brought about new policies in the first place. In practice, the emphasis is usually on outputs since they are much easier to measure than outcomes. Ironically, in practice, performance standards work a good deal like regulations. They establish norms for behavior and reward or discipline administrators based upon whether those standards are met.

Fourth, there is often an effort to define responsibility in terms of customer satisfaction. The assumption is that if the clients receive adequate levels of quality service at a good price, then the agency is acting responsibly. This approach views citizens or subjects as consumers or customers. One variation on this customer satisfaction approach is the market-choice perspective typified by voucher programs. The idea is that, if given choices, consumers will select the better services and those organizations, whether public or private. The service providers that win those customers will prosper and poor performers will fade away. This is very much based on the idea discussed earlier of public policy as a fee-for-service operation. If the direct customers of an organization's services are satisfied, then presumably the organization is properly behaving responsibly. There are many problems with this approach, discussed in earlier chapters, starting with the assumption that, for example, the entire society should be bound by the choices of parents who happen to have children in school at a particular moment in time as compared to considering the views of all those who support public education. This is a confusion between clients and constituents.

Apart from its other limitations, the market approach ignores the fact that people have legal rights and legislation imposes legally enforceable obligations on administrators and their agencies. And there is no question that the larger issues of political responsibility are continuously present. The central concern here is that there are potentially significant tensions among these three approaches to administrative responsibility, which are too rarely considered by the advocates of the three perspectives, and particularly by those who advocate the market approach. The fact is that all three—the legal, the political, and the market—have some elements that are useful and, in any case, they must operate together since neither the political nor the legal approach can be ignored or eliminated in our system. The assumption by some advocates that the market approach can be used in place of the other two—and particularly that it can eliminate the "red tape" that grows out of the legal approach—has created many problems and solved few. Indeed, if it is uncritically accepted by public managers, they may find themselves in serious difficulties in the legal system of the sort discussed throughout this chapter.

SUMMARY

The problem of responsibility will continue to be one of the most difficult challenges that administrators and their elected superiors will be called upon to address. Excessive external checks may threaten the initiative and creativity that careerists can bring to their tasks. Yet there is no way that the presence of external mechanisms of accountability can be abandoned in a nation that operates on the supremacy of law and distrusts the possession of power by unelected officials. Still, the external checks should be understood as part of a larger framework for the maintenance of responsibility. The internal elements are equally critical to that structure and may not be dismissed as wishful thinking. The recent reemergence of discourse on such matters as ethics in the public service is a positive sign.

Even so, administrators must function in the same world as other citizens, a world in which lawsuits are, for good or ill, common. The debate over the degree to which public administrators should face suits for money damages continues. Despite the obvious anxiety the subject brings to every administrator, vulnerability to tort liability suits is not in reality as severe as the picture so often painted. There are areas of uncertainty and risk. The question of municipal liability has indeed presented serious problems. Nevertheless, the application of the principles of administrative law in day-to-day administration is the best protection.

NOTES

1. Joseph S. Nye, Jr., Philip D. Zelinkow, and David C. King, eds., *Why People Don't Trust Government* (Cambridge: Harvard University Press, 1997).

2. See World Bank, *World Development Report 1997: The State in a Changing World* (New York: Oxford University Press, 1997).

3. United Nations Development Programme, *Human Development Report 1998* (New York: Oxford University Press, 1998), p. 6

4. Vaclav Havel, *The Art of the Impossible: Politics as Morality in Practice* (New York: Alfred A. Knopf, 1994), p. 4.

5. *Id.*, pp. 7–8.

6. Herman Finer, "Better Government Personnel: America's Next Frontier," 51 *Political Science Quarterly* 569, 582 (1936).

7. Carl Friedrich, "Public Policy and the Nature of Administrative Responsibility," in C. J. Friedrich and E. S. Mason, eds., *Public Policy* (Cambridge: Harvard, 1940), p. 19.

8. Herman Finer, "Administrative Responsibility in Democratic Government," 1 *Public Administration Rev.* 335, 335 (1941).

9. See Friedrich, *supra* note 7, at p. 12 and Finer, *supra* note 8, at p. 340.

10. The term "respectable technician" is taken from Herbert Storing, "American Statesmanship: Old and New," in R. Goldwin, ed., *Bureaucrats, Policy Analysts, Statesmen: Who Leads?* (Washington, DC: American Enterprise Institute, 1980), p. 113.

11. On the importance of a wider understanding of statesmanship for those who govern, Storing wrote: "My beginning point is the observation that there is a strong tendency to resolve the role of the public official into two simple elements: populism, or radical democracy, and scientific management." *Id.*, at p. 88. Properly developed, Storing contended, statesmanship could go a good way toward helping those in government understand their roles.

    Despite the fact that Friedrich understood the complexity of the administrative task, he ultimately defined responsibility quite narrowly. His criteria were "technical knowledge and popular sentiment." *Supra* note 7, at p. 12.

12. Norton Long, "Bureaucracy and Constitutionalism," 46 *American Political Science Rev.* 808, 815 (1952).

13. See generally, Kenneth Meier, "Representative Bureaucracy: An Empirical Analysis," 69 *American Political Science Rev.* 526 (1975); Samuel Krislov, *Representative Bureaucracy* (Englewood Cliffs, NJ: Prentice Hall, 1974).

14. See generally, John Rohr, *Ethics for Bureaucrats*, 2nd ed. (New York: Marcel Dekker, 1989).

15. *Id.*

16. See e.g., Joel L. Fleishman, et al., *Public Duties. The Moral Obligations of Government Officials* (Cambridge: Harvard, 1981) and John P. Burke, *Bureaucratic Responsibility* (Baltimore: Johns Hopkins, 1986).

17. Stephen Bailey, "Ethics and the Public Service," in R. Martin, ed., *Public Administration and Democracy: Essays in Honor of Paul Appleby* (Syracuse, NY: Syracuse University, 1965).

18. *Id.,* at pp. 285–286.

19. Terry Cooper, *The Responsible Administrator* (Port Washington, NY: Kennikat, 1982).

20. While it is now dated, Herbert Kaufman's *The Forest Ranger: A Study in Administrative Behavior* (Baltimore: Johns Hopkins University Press, 1960) is still the classic work on this phenomenon.

21. John Nalbandian's book, *Professionalism in Local Government: Transformations in Roles, Responsibilities and Values of City Managers* (San Francisco: Jossey-Bass, 1991).

22. Some, like Glendon Schubert, "The Public Interest in Administrative Decision Making: Theorem, Theosophy, or Theory," 51 *American Political Science Rev.* 346 (1957), would abandon the concept as a weak construction since it cannot be easily operationalized. But others, including Storing, "The Crucial Link: Public Administration, Responsibility and the Public Interest, 24 *Public Administration Rev.* 39 (1964); Paul Appleby, *Big Democracy* (New York: Alfred A. Knopf, 1949); E. Pendleton Herring, *Public Administration and the Public Interest* (New York: McGraw Hill, 1936); and Emmette Redford, *Ideal and Practice in Public Administration* (Tuscaloosa: University of Alabama, 1958), Ch. 5, clearly have the better of the argument.

23. See Long, *supra* note 12, at p. 814, and Eugene Dvorin and Robert Simmons, *From Amoral to Humane Bureaucracy* (San Francisco: Canfield, 1972), p. 39.

24. This approach regards individual morality as a positive concept and not a series of "thou shalt nots" to be observed as a matter of tradition or solely because of theological considerations. Stephen Bailey used such an approach when he wrote that optimism is one of the three essential moral qualities of the ethical public servant. "Optimism is an inadequate term. . . . But optimism is a better word than realism, for the latter dampens the fires of possibility. . . . It is the quality which enables man to face ambiguity and paradox without becoming immobilized." Bailey, *supra* note 17, at p. 293.

25. Lloyd Burton, "Ethical Discontinuities in Public–Private Sector Negotiation," 9 *Journal of Policy Analysis and Management* 23 (1990).

26. Lester M. Salamon, *The Resilient Sector: The State of Nonprofit America* (Washington, DC: Brookings Institution Press, 2003).

27. H. Gerth and C. Wright Mills, *From Max Weber: Essays in Sociology* (New York: Oxford, 1946).

28. For one of the most interesting and revealing accounts of the clashes that can emerge in this setting, see Barbara S. Romzek and Melvin Dubnick, "Accountability in the Public Sector: Lessons from the Challenger Tragedy," 47 *Public Administration Rev.* 227 (1987).

29. See e.g., Herbert Simon, *Administrative Behavior,* 3rd ed. (New York: Free Press, 1976), pp. 148–149. See also Chester Barnard, *The Functions of the Executive* (Cambridge: Harvard, 1938), and Michael Crozier, *The Bureaucratic Phenomenon* (Chicago: University of Chicago, 1946).

30. One of the best examples of this continuing controversy is the debate over the legislative veto. See Barbara Craig, *The Legislative Veto* (Boulder, CO: Westview, 1983); Robert Dixon, "The Congressional Veto and Separation of Powers: The Executive on a Leash," 56 *N. Carolina L. Rev.* 423 (1978); Bernard Schwartz, "The Legislative Veto and the Constitution—A Reexamination," 46 *Geo. Wash. L. Rev.* 351 (1978); Harold Bruff and Walter Gellhorn, "Congressional Control of Administrative Regulation: A Study of the Legislative Veto," 90 *Harvard L. Rev.* 1369 (1977).

31. Probably the greatest weakness in the discussion of administrative responsibility conducted by Friedrich, Finer, and Levitan was the failure to acknowledge the tension among the branches. These scholars assumed legislative supremacy as the cornerstone of administrative responsibility. See Finer, *supra* 6, at p. 338; Friedrich, *supra* note 7, at pp. 12–14; David Levitan, "The Responsibility of Administrative Officials in a Democratic Society," 61 *Political Science Quarterly* 562, 571–573 (1946). While that assumption may have merit in a parliamentary government such as Great Britain's, our framers did not intend legislative supremacy and, indeed, were quite clear in their concern for the dangers of legislative usurpation of power. James Madison, Alexander Hamilton, and John Jay, *The Federalist Papers* (New York: Mentor, 1961), pp. 308–311.

32. See the discussion of this subject in Chapters 10. For the classic arguments in this area, see generally, Richard Nathan, *The Plot That Failed* (New York: John Wiley, 1975); Harold Seidman, *Politics, Position, and Power,*

2nd ed. (New York: Oxford, 1976); and Stephen Hess, *Organizing the Presidency* (Washington, DC: Brookings, 1976). More recent commentaries include James P. Pfiffner, *The Strategic Presidency*, 2nd ed. Revised.(Lawrence, KS: University Press of Kansas, 1996); Stephen Hess, *Presidents & the Presidency* (Washington, DC: Brookings Institution, 1996); Robert F. Durant, *The Administrative Presidency Revisited* (Albany, NY: State University of New York Press, 1992); and Hess, *Organizing the Presidency*, 2nd ed. (Washington, DC: Brookings Institution, 1988).

33. See the discussion of oversight difficulties in Chapter 10. Lawrence Dodd and Richard Schott, *Congress and the Administrative State* (New York: John Wiley, 1979); U.S. Senate, Committee on Operations, *Study on Federal Regulation: Congressional Oversight of Regulatory Agencies,* 95th Cong., 1st Sess., (Comm. Print 1977), Vol. 2; Harold Bruff and Ernest Gellhorn, *supra* note 28; Morris Ogul, *Congress Oversees the Bureaucracy* (Pittsburgh: University of Pittsburgh, 1976); and Joseph Harris, *Congressional Control of Administration* (Garden City, NY: Doubleday, 1964).

34. *United States v. Lee,* 106 U.S. 196, 220 (1882) and *Butz v. Economou,* 438 U.S. 478, 506 (1978).

35. *Marbury v. Madison,* 1 Cranch 137, 163 (1803) and *Davis v. Passman,* 442 U.S. 228, 242 (1979).

36. See H. George Frederickson, ed., *Ideal & Practice in Council-Manager Government,* 2nd ed. (Washington, DC: ICMA, 1995).

37. While some commentators, such as Morris Ogul, *Congress Oversees the Bureaucracy* (Pittsburgh: University of Pittsburgh Press, 1976), consider casework part of oversight, it really is quite different in purpose and effect. Casework may prompt oversight, but it is usually not concerned with improving administration and may indeed undermine effective administration by burdening agencies with special pleaders while the larger clientele receive less attention.

38. One of the better observations on this point was made by Leon Jaworski in the oral argument on *United States v. Nixon,* 418 U.S. 638 (1974). "Now, the President may be right in how he reads the Constitution. But he may also be wrong. And if he is wrong, who is there to tell him so? And if there is no one, then the President, of course, is free to pursue his course of erroneous interpretations. What then becomes of our constitutional form of government?" Leon Friedman, ed., *United States v. Nixon: The President Before the Supreme Court* (New York: Chelsea House, 1974), pp. 528–29.

39. See David Rosenbloom, "Public Administrators, Official Immunity, and the Supreme Court: Developments During the 1970s," 40 *Public Administration Rev.* 166, 168 (1980).

40. I have written about this at greater length in Phillip J. Cooper, Linda P. Brady, Olivia Hidalgo-Hardeman, Albert Hyde, Katherine C. Naff, J. Steven Ott, and Harvey White, *Public Administration for the Twenty-First Century* (Fort Worth: Harcourt Brace, 1998), Ch. 3.

41. Katy J. Harriger, *Independent Justice: The Federal Special Prosecutor in American Politics* (Lawrence, KS: University Press of Kansas, 1992).

42. See Inspector General Act of 1978, P.L. 95-452, 92 Stat. 1101, 5 U.S.C. Appx. §1 et seq.

43. E.O. 12834 "Ethics Commitments by Executive Branch Appointees".

44. Led by John Rohr, *supra* note 14.

45. See William D. Richardson, *Democracy, Bureaucracy, & Character* (Lawrence, KS: University of Kansas Press, 1997); Joel L. Fleishman, Lance Liebman, and Mark H. Moore, eds., *Public Duties: The Moral Obligations of Government Officials* (Cambridge: Harvard, 1981); William Richardson and Lloyd Nigro, "Administrative Ethics and Founding Thought: Constitutional Correctives, Honor, and Education," 47 *Public Administration Rev.* 367 (1987).

46. See e.g., James Bowman and Donald Menzel, *Teaching Ethics and Values in Public Administration Programs: Innovations, Strategies, and Issues* (Albany, NY: State University of New York Press, 1998); H. George Frederickson, *Ethics and Public Adminsitration* (Armonk, NY: M.E. Sharpe, 1993); Terry L. Cooper and N. Dale Wright, eds., *Exemplary Public Adminsitrators: Character and Leadership in Government* (San Francisco: Jossey-Bass, 1992); Carol W. Lewis, *The Ethics Challenge in Public Service* (San Francisco: Jossey-Bass, 1991); James S. Bowman, ed., *Ethical Frontiers in Public Management* (San Francisco: Jossey-Bass, 1991).

47. *Little v. Barreme,* 6 U.S. (2 Cr.) 170, 171–172 (1804).

48. *Id.,* at p. 179.

49. *In re Ayers,* 123 U.S. 443 (1887).

50. *Poindexter v. Greenhow,* 114 U.S. 270 (1885).

51. *Slaughter-House Cases*, 83 U.S. 36 (1883); *Civil Rights Cases*, 109 U.S. 3 (1873).

52. This was certainly true for the two major cases in this period that recognized immunity in certain types of government officials, *Bradley v. Fisher*, 80 U.S. (13 Wall.) 335 (1872) and *Spalding v. Vilas*, 161 U.S. 483 (1896). Chief Justice Warren explained the impact of the British common law development on these cases in his dissent in *Barr v. Matteo*, 360 U.S. 564, 579–582 (1959), Justice Warren dissenting.

53. These cases allowing suits against claimed immunity included: *Chisholm v. Georgia*, 2 U.S. (2 Dall.) 419 (1793); *Little v. Barreme, supra* note 47; *United States v. Judge Peters*, 9 U.S. (5 Cr.) 115 (1809); *Wise v. Withers*, 7 U.S. (3 Cr.) 331 (1806); *Osborne v. President and Directors and Company of the Bank of the United States*, 22 U.S. (9 Wheat.) 738 (1824); *City of Providence v. Clapp*, 58 U.S. (17 How.) 161 (1855); *Weightman v. Corporation of Washington*, 66 U.S. (1 Black) 39 (1862); *Levy Court of Washington County v. Woodward*, 69 U.S. (2 Wall.) 501 (1864); *Board of Supervisors of Mercer County v. Cowles*, 74 U.S. (7 Wall.) II 8 (1869); *The Davis*, 77 U.S. 15 (1870); *Davis v. Gray*, 83 U.S. 203 (1873); *Bates v. Clark*, 95 U.S. 204 (1877); *Ex Parte Virginia*, 100 U.S. 339 (1880); *United States v. Lee, supra* note 34; *Poindexter v. Greenhow, supra* note 50; and *Lincoln County v. Luning*, 133 U.S. 529 (1896).

54. The cases include: *Kendall v. Stokes*, 44 U.S. (3 How.) 878 (1845); *Wilkes v. Kinsman*, 48 U.S. (7 How.) 89 (1849); and *Hill v. United States*, 9 Howard 386 (1850). The other cases where the claim for some kind of immunity from suit was upheld included: *Bradley v. Fisher, supra* note 52; *Louisiana v. Gamble*, 107 U.S. 711 (1882); *Cunningham v. Macon and Brunswick RR Co.*, 109 U.S. 446 (1883); *Hedged v. Southern*, 17 U.S. 52 (1886); *Ex Parte Ayers, supra* note 30; *Hans v. Louisiana*, 134 U.S. 1 (1890); *Belknap v. Schild*, 161 U.S. 10 (1896); and *Spalding v. Vilas, supra* note 52.

55. *Owen v. City of Independence*, 445 U.S. 622 (1980) and *Butz v. Economou*, 438 U.S. 478 (1978). See also Clyde Jacobs, *The Eleventh Amendment and Sovereign Immunity* (Westport, CN: Greenwood, 1972), p. 150.

56. See e.g., *Giles v. Harris*, 189 U.S. 475 (1903); *Barney v. City of New York*, 193 U.S. 430 (1904); *Devine v. Los Angeles*, 202 U.S. 313 (1906); *Ex Parte Young*, 209 U.S. 123 (1908); *Myers v. Anderson*, 238 U.S. 368 (1915); and *Yaselli v. Goff*, 12 F.2d 396 (2d Cir. 1926), aff'd 275 U.S. 503.

57. *Tenney v. Brandhove*, 341 U.S. 367 (1951).

58. *Rizzo v. Goode*, 423 U.S. 362 (1976). These restrictions are discussed in Chapter 9.

59. *Bivens v. Six Unknown Named Agents of the Federal Bureau of Narcotics*, 403 U.S. 388, 391–394 (1971).

60. See e.g., *Kissinger v. Halperin*, 606 F.2d 1192 (D.C.Cir. 1979), aff'd 452 U.S. 713 (1981).

61. William Olson, "Governmental Immunity from Tort Liability: Two Decades of Decline," 31 *Baylor Law Rev.* 485 (1979).

62. *Hall v. Nevada*, 440 U.S. 410 (1979).

63. Walter Gellhorn et al., *Administrative Law: Cases and Comments*, 7th ed. (Mineola, NY: Foundation Press, 1979), pp. 1055–56.

64. *Chisholm v. Georgia, supra* note 53. See also Jacobs, *supra* note 55, at pp. 46–57.

65. *Edelman v. Jordan*, 415 U.S. 651, 662 (1974).

66. *Atascadero State Hospital v. Scanlon*, 473 U.S. 234, 238 (1985).

67. Examples include *Little v. Barreme, supra* note 47; *United States v. Judge Peters, supra* note 51; *Osborn v. Bank of the United States*, 22 U.S. (9 Wheat.) 738 (1824); *United States v. Lee, supra* note 34; *Davis v. Gray, supra* note 53; and *Poindexter v. Greenhow, supra* note 50.

68. *Cunningham v. Macon and Brunswick RR Co., supra* note 54; *In re Ayers, supra* note 49; and *Belknap v. Schild, supra* note 54.

69. *Edelman v. Jordan, supra* note 65, at p. 663. See also *Scheuer v. Rhodes*, 416 U.S. 232 (1974).

70. The Court rejected the proposition in a number of cases. *City of Providence v. Clapp, supra* note 53; *Weightman v. Washington, supra* note 53; *Levy Court v. Woodward, supra* note 53; *Board of Supervisors of Mercer County v. Cowles, supra* note 53; and *Lincoln County v. Luning, supra* note 53. See Justice Brennan's commentary in *Owen v. City of Independence, supra* note 55.

71. *Ashby v. White*, 2 Ld.Raym.Rpt. 938, 956 (1703).

72. *Mostyn v. Fabrigas*, 1 Cowp. 161, 175 (1744).

73. See e.g., *Little v. Barreme, supra* note 47; and *Wise v. Withers, supra* note 53.

74. *Kendall v. Stokes, supra* note 54, at p. 98. See also *Wilkes v. Dinsman, supra* note 54, at pp. 129–31.

75. *Bradley v. Fisher, supra* note 52. This functional immunity was developed in a series of cases described later in this chapter.

76. See *Jacobs, supra* note 55, and Charles Rhyne, William Rhyne, and Stephen Elmendorf, *Tort Liability and Immunity of Municipal Officers* (Washington, DC: National Institute of Municipal Law Officers, 1976), pp. 1–2.

77. *Jacobs, supra* note 55, at p. 150.

78. *Kawananakoa v. Polybank,* 205 U.S. 349, 353 (1907).

79. Jacobs, *supra* note 55.

80. *Id.,* at pp. 153–54.

81. See e.g., *Tenney v. Brandhove, supra* note 57, and *Bradley v. Fisher, supra* note 52.

82. *Butz v. Economou, supra* note 55, at pp. 496–97.

83. See *Spalding v. Vilas, supra* note 52; *Barr v. Matteo,* supra note 52, at pp. 572–73; *Wood v. Strickland,* 420 U.S. 308, 319-320 (1975); and *Imbler v. Pachtman,* 424 U.S. 409 (1976).

84. *Scheuer v. Rhodes, supra* note 69.

85. *Dalehite v. United States,* 346 U.S. 15, 57 (1953).

86. *Scheuer v. Rhodes, supra* note 69, at pp. 241–42.

87. *Barr v. Matteo, supra* note 52, at pp. 564–65.

88. One of the most often cited rationales for electing the official's side of the balance noted above, even to the point of permitting some absolute immunity for particular officials, is presented in Judge Learned Hand's opinion in *Gregoire v. Biddle,* 177 F.2d 579, 580-581 (2d Cir. 1949).

89. See e.g., Gellhorn et al., *supra* note 63, and Kenneth Culp Davis, *Administrative Law Treatise* (St.Paul, MN: West, 1959), p. 451.

90. Olson, *supra* note 61, at p. 485.

91. *Id.,* at p. 487.

92. *United States v. Lee, supra* note 34, at pp. 205–206.

93. *Id.,* pp. 208–209.

94. *Id.,* at p. 221.

95. See the clash over this subject between the majority and dissenters in *Seminole Tribe of Florida v. Florida,* 134 L.Ed.2d 252 (1996) and *Atascadero State Hospital v. Scanlon,* 473 U.S. 234 (1985).

96. *Poindexter v. Greenhow, supra* note 50.

97. *Id.,* at pp. 290–91.

98. *Muskopf v. Corning Hospital District,* 359 P.2d 457, 463 (Cal. 1961). On the state abrogation of immunity and its aftermath, see *Hicks v. State,* 544 P.2d 1153, 1155 (NM 1976); *Spanel v. Mounds View School District no. 621,* 118 N.W.2d 795, 799 (MN 1962); National League of Cities, *The New World of Municipal Liability: Current City Trends and Legislative Actions in the Fifty States* (Washington, DC: National League of Cities, 1978); Rhyne et al. and John Lichty, *Redress Against Sovereignty: A Study of the Increasing Liability of Municipalities in Tort* (Grand Forks, ND: Bureau of Government Affairs, 1972).

99. *Ex Parte Virginia,* 100 U.S. 339, 348 (1880).

100. *Gellhorn et al., supra* note 63, at p. 923.

101. See e.g., *Butz v. Economou, supra* note 34, at pp. 505–508 and *Davis v. Passman, supra* note 35, at p. 248.

102. *Barr v. Matteo,* supra note 52, at p. 586 (Justice Brennan dissenting).

103. *Harlow v. Fitzgerald,* 457 U.S. 800 (1982).

104. *Hercules v. United States,* 516 U.S. 417, 422 (1996).

105. *Atascadero State Hospital v. Scanlon,* 473 U.S. 234 (1985).

106. Before this process was created, claims of recompense from the federal government were often handled by what are termed private laws, legislation introduced on behalf of particular individuals, or firms who had suffered losses at the hands of the government.

107. See generally, Howard Ball, *Justice Downwind* (New York: Oxford University Press, 1986).

108. *Feres v. United States*, 340 U.S. 135 (1950).

109. *Hercules v. United States, supra* note 104, at p. 423.

110. *Supra* note 95.

111. *Id.,* at 280, Justice Stevens dissenting.

112. *Id.,* at 294, Justice Souter dissenting.

113. *Id.,* at p. 346.

114. *Board of Trustees of the University of Alabama v. Garrett,* 531 U.S. 356 (2001).

115. *Kimel v. Florida Bd. of Regents,* 528 U.S. 62 (2000).

116. *Nevada Department of Human Resources v. Hibbs,* 538 U.S. 721 (2003).

117. *Tennessee v. Lane,* 541 U.S. 509 (2004).

118. *Frew v. Hawkins,* 540 U.S. 431 (2004).

119. *United States v. Georgia,* 126 S. Ct. 877 (2006).

120. *Federal Maritime Commission v. South Carolina State Ports Authority,* 535 U.S. 743, (2002).

121. *Id.,* at p. 773.

122. *Atascadero State Hospital v. Scanlon, supra* note 105, at p. 241.

123. *Id.,* at 188, Justice Brennan dissenting.

124. *Id.,* at 190.

125. *Owen v. City of Independence, supra* note 55, at pp. 638–39.

126. See e.g., *Moore v. County of Alameda,* 411 U.S. 693, 717 (1973).

127. 42 U.S.C. §1983.

128. 365 U.S. 167 (1961).

129. 436 U.S. 658, 663 (1978).

130. *Owen v. City of Independence, supra* note 55, at p. 633. This is a quick summary of the respondeat superior notion. The Court rejected liability for municipalities solely on the basis of the actions of employees in *Monell, supra* note 129, at p. 663, fn 7 and reiterated its view in *Owen.*

131. *Supra* note 129 at, pp. 690–91.

132. *Supra* note 55.

133. *Id.,* at p. 625.

134. *Owen v. City of Independence,* 421 F.Supp. 1110, 1123 (WDMO 1976).

135. *Owen v. City of Independence,* 560 F. 2d 925 (8th Cir. 1977).

136. *Owen v. City of Independence,* 589 F.2d 335 (8th Cir. 1978).

137. *Owen v. City of Independence, supra* note 55, at pp. 644–46.

138. See Lichty, *supra* note 98. Olson has highlighted the problem nicely, *supra* note 61.

139. Lichty, *supra* note 98, at p. 1.

140. Walter Gellhorn and Clark Byse, *Administrative Law,* 5th ed. (Mineola, NY: Foundation Press, 1970), p. 323, cited in Lichty, *Id.,* at p. 2.

141. Olson, *supra* note 61, at p. 487.

142. *Indian Towing Co. v. United States,* 350 U.S. 61, 65 (1955).

143. *Owen v. City of Independence, supra* note 55, at p. 648.

144. *Id.,* at p. 635.

145. *Id.,* at pp. 637–38.

146. *Id.,* at pp. 648–49.

147. "Moreover, [Section] 1983 was intended not only to provide compensation to the victims of past abuses, but to serve as a deterrent against future constitutional deprivations as well. [cites] The knowledge that a municipality will be liable for all of its injurious conduct, whether committed in good faith or not, should create an incentive for officials who may harbor doubts about the lawfulness of their intended actions to err

on the side of protecting citizens' constitutional rights. Furthermore, the threat that damages might be levied against the city may encourage those in a policymaking position to institute internal rules and programs designed to minimize the likelihood of unintentional infringements on constitutional rights. Such procedures are particularly beneficial in preventing those 'systematic' injuries that result not so much from the conduct of any single individual, but from the interactive behavior of several government officials, each of whom may be acting in good faith." *Id.,* at pp. 651–52.

148. See Phillip J. Cooper, *Hard Judicial Choices* (New York: Oxford University Press, 1988), Ch. 11.

149. *Oklahoma City v. Tuttle,* 471 U.S. 808, 823 (1985).

150. *Pembaur v. Cincinnati,* 475 U.S. 469, 482 (1986).

151. *St. Louis v. Praprotnik,* 485 U.S. 112, 124 (1988).

152. *Canton v. Harris,* 489 U.S. 378, 387 (1989).

153. *Id.,* at p. 390.

154. *Board of Commissioners of Bryan Cty. v. Brown,* 137 L.Ed.2d 626, 638 (1997).

155. *Id.,* at 639.

156. See e.g., the dissent by Justice Breyer, *Id.,* at p. 656.

157. *Barr v. Matteo, supra* note 52, Chief Justice Warren dissenting.

158. *Supra* note 52. Bradley wasn't the first such case against judges. See *Wise v. Withers, supra* note 51. In a case decided not long after Bradley, *Ex Parte Virginia,* 100 U.S. 339 (1880), a Virginia judge was found guilty of a violation of a federal law and held against a claim of immunity. He had excluded blacks from consideration as jurors in the county in which he sat. The Court found that: "Whether the act done by him was judicial or not is to be determined by its character, and not by the character of the agent. Whether he was a county judge or not is of no importance." *Id.,* at p. 348. Jury selection was considered a judicial act.

159. *Id.,* at p. 351.

160. *Id.,* at p. 347.

161. *Pierson v. Ray,* 386 U.S. 547 (1967).

162. 435 U.S. 349 (1978).

163. The opinion, which provides a facsimile of the mother's affidavit, contains no evidence of mental retardation or illness and indicates that Linda had been making satisfactory progress in public schools. *Id.,* at pp. 336–37.

164. *Imbler v. Pachtman,* 424 U.S. 409 (1976). However, the Court has also held that while the absolute immunity applied to a prosecutor who represented the government in a probable cause hearing, it did not apply to that same prosecutor when he was advising police in the case. *Burns v. Reed,* 500 U.S. 478 (1991).

165. *Ferry v. Ackerman,* 444 U.S. 193 (1980).

166. *Antoine v. Byers & Anderson, Inc.,* 508 U.S. 429 (1993).

167. Article 1, Section 6, clause I provides in pertinent part: "The Senators and Representatives . . . shall in all Cases except Treason, Felony and Breach of the Peace, be privileged from Arrest during their attendance at the Session of their respective Houses, and in going to and returning from the same; and for any Speech or Debate in either House, they shall not be questioned in any other Place."

168. *Tenney v. Brandhove, supra* note 57.

169. *Lake Country Estates v. Tahoe Regional Planning Agency,* 440 U.S. 391, 403 (1979). For a discussion of the public policy arguments with respect to legislative immunity, see *Eastland v. United States Servicemen's Fund,* 421 U.S. 491, 503 (1975); *Supreme Court of Virginia v. Consumers Union,* 446 U.S. 719, 733 (1980); and *Dombrowski v. Eastland,* 387 U.S. 82 (1967).

170. *Davis v. Passman,* 442 U.S. 228 (1979).

171. His letter to her is reproduced in the opinion. *Id.,* at p. 230 n. 3.

172. Whether these types of cases may in the future be brought under Title VII of the Civil Rights Act of 1964 remains to be seen since the Congress has moved to make itself responsible for statutory obligations from which it had been previously exempt.

173. *Supra* note 170, p. 232.

174. *Id.,* at p. 246.

175. *Hutchinson v. Proxmire*, 443 U.S. 111 (1979).

176. *Id.*, at p. 116.

177. *Id.*, at pp. 126–130.

178. *Bogan v. Scott-Harris*, 140 L.Ed.2d 79 (1998).

179. 161 U.S. 483 (1896).

180. See generally, *Barr v. Matteo*, 360 U.S. 563 (1959), Chief Justice Warren dissenting, and *Spalding v. Vilas*, 161 U.S., at p. 498.

181. 360 U.S. 564 (1959).

182. *Id.*, at pp. 572–573.

183. *Id.*, at pp. 573–574.

184. Chief Justice Warren's dissent was extremely strong. His answer to the public policy argument was as follows: "The principal opinion in this case purports to launch the Court on a balancing process in order to reconcile the interest of the public in obtaining fearless executive performance and the interest of the individual in having redress for defamation. Even accepting for the moment that these are the proper interests to be balanced, the ultimate disposition is not the result of a balance. On the one hand, the principal opinion sets up a vague standard under which no government employee can tell with any certainty whether he will receive absolute immunity for his acts. On the other hand, it has not given the slightest consideration to the interest of the individual who is defamed. It is a complete annihilation of his interest." *Id.*, at p. 578, Chief Justice Warren dissenting.

185. *Id.*, at pp. 586–587, Justice Brennan dissenting.

186. *Id.*, at pp. 588–589.

187. *Id.*

188. *Id.*

189. *Pierson v. Ray, supra* note 161.

190. "The common law has never granted police officers an absolute and unqualified immunity, and the officers in this case do not claim that they are entitled to one. Their claim is rather that they should not be liable if they acted in good faith and with probable cause in making an arrest under statutory authority that they believed to be valid. . . . A policeman's lot is not so unhappy that he must choose between being charged with dereliction of duty if he does not arrest when he has probable cause, and being mulcted in damages if he does." *Id.*, at p. 555.

191. 403 U.S. 388 (1971).

192. *Id.*, at p. 389.

193. *Scheuer v. Rhodes, supra* note 69.

194. *Id.*, at p. 248.

195. "These conditions suggest that, in varying scope, a qualified immunity is available to officers of the executive branch of government, the variation being dependent upon the scope of discretion and responsibilities of the office and all the circumstances as they reasonably appeared at the time of the action on which liability is sought to be based. It is the existence of reasonable grounds for the belief formed at the time and in light of all the circumstances, coupled with good faith belief, that affords a basis for qualified immunity to executive officers for acts performed in the course of official conduct." *Id.*, at pp. 247–248.

196. *Wood v. Strickland*, 420 U.S. 308 (1975).

197. *Id.*, at p. 315.

198. *Id.*, at pp. 321–322.

199. *Procunier v. Navarette*, 434 U.S. 555 (1978).

200. *Procunier v. Martinez*, 416 U.S. 396 (1974).

201. *Procunier v. Navarette*, 434 U.S., at p. 562.

202. *Butz v. Economou, supra* note 55.

203. *Id.*, p. 498.

204. *Id.*, at p. 504.

205. However, the Court has refused to treat federal agencies like officials and make them subject to *Bivens* type actions. *FDIC v. Meyer,* 510 U.S. 471 (1994).

206. *Id.*, at p. 508.

207. *Id.*, at p. 512.

208. *Id.*, at p. 516.

209. *Nixon v. Fitzgerald,* 457 U.S. 731 (1982).

210. *Supra* note 101.

211. *Clinton v. Jones,* 137 L.Ed.2d 945 (1997).

212. *Id.*, at pp. 815–19.

213. *Behrens v. Pelletier,* 133 L.Ed.2d 773, 785 (1996). See also *John v. Fankell,* 138 L.Ed.2d 108, 114 (1997) and *Crawford-El v. Britton,* 140 L.Ed.2d 759, 774 (1998).

214. "Federal officials will not be liable for mere mistakes in judgment, whether the mistake is one of fact or law.... Insubstantial lawsuits can be quickly terminated by federal courts alert to the possibilities of artful pleading. Unless the complaint states a compensable claim for relief under the Federal Constitution, it should not survive a motion to dismiss. Moreover, the Court recognized in Scheuer that damage suits concerning constitutional violations need not proceed to trial, but can be terminated on a properly supported motion for summary judgment based on the defense of immunity.... In responding to such a motion, plaintiffs may not play dog in the manager; and firm application of the Federal Rules of Civil Procedure will ensure that federal officials are not harassed by frivolous lawsuits." *Butz v. Economou,* 438 U.S., at pp. 507–508.

215. P.L. 100-694, 102 Stat. 4563 (1988), 28 U.S.C. 2671 et seq. See e.g., D.A. Morris, "Federal Employees' Liability since the Federal Employees Liability Reform & Tort Compensation Act of 1988," 25 *Creighton L. Rev.* 73 (1991); "Torts—Personal Liability of Government Employees—Federal Employee Liability Reform and Tort Compensation Act. *United States v. Smith,* 111 S.Ct. 1180," 59 *Tenn. L. Rev.* 173 (1991).

216. See *United States v. Smith,* 499 U.S. 160 (1991).

217. *Id.*, at 166–167.

218. P.L. 104-134, 110 Stat. 1321 (1996).

219. See the discussion of the statute's intent and operation in *Crawford-El v. Britton,* 140 L.Ed.2d 759, 778 (1998).

220. *Florence County School Dist. Four v. Carter,* 510 U.S. 7 (1993).

221. See Craig Richards, Rima Shore, and Max B. Sawicky, *Ricky Business: Private Management of Public Schools* (Washington, DC: Economic Policy Institute, 1996), and Donald F. Kettl, *Sharing Power* (Washington, DC: Brookings, 1993).

222. W. Noel Keyes, *Government Contracts, Second Edition* (St. Paul, MN: West Publishing Co., 1996).

223. See Barry Bozeman, *All Organizations Are Public.* (San Francisco: Jossey-Bass, 1987); "Exploring the Limits of Public and Private Sectors: Sector Boundaries as Maginot Line," 48 *Public Administration Review* 672 (1988).

224. See Ronald C. Moe and Robert S. Gilmour, "Rediscovering Principles of Public Administration: The Neglected Foundation of Public Law," 55 *Public Administration Review* 135 (1995); Ronald C. Moe and Thomas H. Stanton, "Government-Sponsored Enterprises as Federal Instrumentalities: Reconciling Private Management with Public Accountability," 49 *Public Administration Rev.* 321 (1989); Ronald Moe, "'Law' Versus 'Performance' as Objective Standard," 48 *Public Administration Rev.* 675 (1988); "Exploring the Limits of Privatization," 47 *Public Administration Rev.* 453 (1987).

225. See generally, *Lugar v. Edmondson Oil Co.,* 457 U.S. 922 (1982); *Blum v. Yaretsky,* 457 U.S. 991 (1982); *Rendell-Baker v. Kohn,* 457 U.S. 830 (1982).

226. *West v. Atkins,* 487 U.S. 42 (1988).

227. *National Collegiate Athletic Association v. Tarkanian,* 488 U.S. 179 (1988).

228. *National Collegiate Athletic Association v. Smith,* 142 L.Ed.2d 929 (1999).

229. *American Mfrs. Ins. Co. v. Sullivan,* 119 S.Ct. 977 (1999).

230. *Id.*, at p. 987.

231. *Id.*, at p. 986.

232. *United Auto Workers v. Gaston Festivals, Inc.,* 43 F.3d 902 (4th Cir. 1995).

233. *Goldstein v. Chestnut Ridge Volunteer Fire Co.,* 984 F.Supp. 367 (DNMD 1997).

234. *Id.,* at 550–552.

235. *Id.,* at 551.

236. *Ace Beverage Co. v. Lockheed Information Management Services,* 144 F.3d 1218, 1220 (9th Cir. 1998).

237. *Correctional Services Corporation v. Malesko,* 534 U.S. 61 (2001).

238. *Id.,* at p. 81.

239. *Regents of the University of California v. Department of Energy,* 137 L.Ed.2d 55, 60 (1997).

240. *United States v. Sperin,* 248 U.S. 132 (1918), quoted in *Hercules Incorporated v. United States,* 516 U.S. 417, 424 (1996).

241. *Hercules,* supra note 104.

242. Donald Savoie, ed., *Restoring Accountability: Research Studies, Volumes 1, 2, and 3,* in Commission of Inquiry into the Sponsorship Program & Advertising Activities (Ottawa: Public Works and Government Services Canada, 2006).

243. Paul M. Tellier, *Public Service 2000: A Report on Progress.* (Ottawa: Ministry of Supply and Services, 1992), pp. 94–99.

244. See e.g., S. L. Sutherland, "The Al-Mashat affair," 34 *Canadian Public Administration* 573 (1992).

245. C. Neal Tate and Torbjorn Vallinder, eds., *The Global Expansion of Judicial Power* (New York: New York University Press, 1995).

246. Consider the Australian examples *Sankey v. Whitlam,* 142 CLR 1 (1978), and *Commonwealth v. Northern Land Council,* 30 FCR 1 (1991). On the British experience, see Sunkin in Tate and Vallinder, *supra* note 231.

247. See Henry Mintzberg, "A Note on that Dirty Word 'Efficiency'," 5 *Interfaces* 101 (1982).

14

Law and Administration for the Twenty-First Century

For all of the twists and turns, criticisms and innovations, management trends and technological developments, public law remains and will continue to be a central fact of public administration life. Indeed, for reasons explained in the preceding chapters, whole new areas of public law have had to be developed to come to grips with the changing nature of the field and the intersectoral, intergovernmental, and international context within which public administration operates.

For some, particularly those who always saw law as a nettlesome aspect of public administration and hoped that the legacy of post-Reagan era politics and the coming of new public management meant an end to its significance, its enduring and even growing role may come as a surprise. Indeed, one of the most common reactions of students who take a course in public law and public administration (whatever it may be called in the catalog) is that they had no idea that law was such a pervasive part of public life and that it seems to be expanding even in an age of deregulation. To public law scholars and to thoughtful and experienced practitioners, however, this comes as no surprise at all. Indeed, it is clear to these observers that new, more sophisticated, and more effective legal tools are needed to address the kinds of policies and problems modern public managers are called upon to face daily. And they are equally convinced that, if anything, the events of recent decades have proven that those who govern, the institutions through which they operate, and the people they serve need the fundamental values that public law has long embodied. This chapter considers briefly the backdrop for change in the law of public administration, the importance of renewed attention to public institutions created and managed with public law instruments, and the new directions that public law appears destined to take in the years to come.

THE POST-REAGAN POLITICS AND NEW PUBLIC MANAGEMENT MYTHS AND REALITIES

No one has been willing to come out publicly against the rule of law. No public official has attacked the Constitution or suggested that it should be eliminated because it is responsible for inefficiencies in government. No newly elected chief executives or legislators of any party have been willing to argue that they should be able simply to ignore the statutes adopted by previous governments. None have been willing to announce that they should be able to order administrators to act in a manner that is "arbitrary, capricious, and abuse of discretion or not otherwise in accordance with law."[1] None have openly suggested that agencies should make rules in ways that fail to be open, orderly, and participative or that citizens should not be entitled to the basic requisites of due process of law and fundamental fairness in their individual disputes with the government. Yet, in a host of ways since the 1980s, many officials (unfortunately including a number of judges and even a few justices of the U.S. Supreme Court) have lambasted public law requirements and processes in ways that conveyed all of these messages that none of them would ever dare to state openly and directly. In other cases, these critics simply sought to ignore legal obligations or create back-door mechanisms to evade administrative law requirements. On still other occasions, officials sat quietly and refused to defend principles and modes of operation that they knew very well to be central to the practice and the study of the practice of public administration when they were under both direct and indirect attack. These active or passive aggressive reactions against public law in public administration have extended not only to elected and some career officials, but also to a number of their academic counterparts.

While most of the earlier chapters in this volume have detailed these attacks on public law in public administration, it is useful to note some of them here and to suggest some difficulties with those positions from both a practical and theoretical perspective. It is possible to identify several fundamental myths and the realities that actually confront public managers.

Myth 1: Law Is an Obstacle and the Courts Are Making It More So

It is interesting how many people in public life operate on the assumption that law and courts represent obstacles that interfere with effective management. Moreover, many seem to think that every day in every way judges are making it easier to sue officials and are actively seeking to insinuate themselves into the operation of public agencies. While there certainly have been cases in which such things have happened, the fact is that the general trends have been in the other direction for a long time now.

At a city managers' meeting not long ago, a number of those present were complaining about how the courts had imposed extremely burdensome new record-keeping and compliance requirements on them—a new unfunded mandate. It turned out that the reality was quite different. It seems that a couple contracted to build a new home in an area where a septic system was required. They were told that the site was not conducive to installation of a large enough septic system to handle to size of the home they wanted to build. They were to reconcile the mismatch and have the system inspected prior to occupancy. They did neither of those things. They later sold the home, but the purchasers learned to their chagrin that they had to make major repairs of more than $30,000 to bring their property into compliance. They sued and recovered the money from the seller.[2] Real estate organizations, mortgage lenders, and other interest groups prevailed upon the state legislature to pass a law making local governments responsible for maintaining large amounts of detailed records over long periods of time and ensuring inspections, all to protect purchasers and lenders. The burdens were not placed on the local officials by the court. All the court did was to make the seller of one property pay the purchaser for the repair of defects about which the seller knew at the time of sale. Still, many local officials are convinced that the judge did them in.

As the preceding chapters demonstrated, led by the Supreme Court, judges have raised increased burdens on citizens who seek expanded due process protections in adjudications, increased the standing requirements to get cases into court for judicial review, granted increasingly broad standards for deference to administrative decisions, and restricted the use, scope, and duration of remedial orders. They have granted wider discretionary authority to supervisory officials, reduced the opportunities in which employees can bring formal challenges by restricting the scope of liberties of public employees, reduced adjudicative rights when adverse action is taken, and placed more stringent restrictions on the ability of an employee or a citizen outside an agency even to get a tort liability case to a trial. These, and many other examples, have been provided throughout this text.

However, as these pages also demonstrated, there have been difficulties in these trends, such as the ability of administrators to get prompt resolution of important legal questions and creation of greater uncertainty in a variety of contexts because of the use of balancing tests intended to provide more consideration to administrators. After all, the mechanisms of public law were created both to help provide tools to carry out the often difficulty and frequently very controversial tasks assigned to public administrators and also to help address issues of legitimacy. As this volume has explained throughout, it is important always to evaluate changes in the field in light of both sets of questions. Public managers are, after all, unelected officials who exercise a wide range of important powers over citizens outside of government and employees within it. Our positions and those powers are created by law and our ability to act is inherently tied to that body of public law that supports public authority and defines, both procedurally and substantively, its outer boundaries.

Myth 2: Deregulation and Privatization Will Put an End to Judicial Interference in Officials' Lives

Another myth addressed throughout this book is the idea that the deregulation and privatization trends should mean an end to the complexities and challenges that result from legal procedures and constraints. Virtually all of the previous chapters have explained the many ways in which these two benchmarks of policy change have had quite the opposite effect.

The first irony, of course, is that during a period in which many elected officials and citizens have demanded deregulation, a variety of ongoing problems and new circumstances have led to simultaneous calls for more, better, or newer types of regulation. This trend has been strong at virtually all levels of governments, including the regional and international levels. All of this has meant a variety of legal challenges that require resolution and inevitably call for courts to become involved.

The expanded use of contracts, both in terms of the numbers of contracts and also the expanding scope of activities now managed through contract processes, adds to regulatory complexity and to opportunities for litigation. As Chapters 5 and 10 explained in detail, every contract is a regulatory regime. It establishes a host of rules according to which the contract will be operated. And, as pressures are placed for greater responsiveness, responsibility, and equity in contracting, the rules governing the overall contracting process have intensified the complexity of the law governing the overall contracting process.

It is, of course, completely appropriate for elected officials regularly to evaluate and reconsider the regulatory programs that they have created to determine whether individual policies or overall procedures should be changed. As the Supreme Court explained in the airbags case (see Chapter 7), such reexaminations may sometimes, but not always, lead to deregulation. As Chapter 10 explained, these evaluations may, and often do, lead to expanded policies. There is also no reason why officials should not consider the most effective use of contracting tools to accomplish important purposes. However, it is a myth to think that doing so means a reduction in or even an end to the importance of public law issues, processes, and actors.

Myth 3: Law Is the Problem and New Public Management Is the Solution

Another troublesome myth is the tendency of those advocating various recent management techniques to suggest that law and legal process equals "red tape" and red tape is the problem of modern governance. There is always much to be learned from innovative approaches that are offered in the hope of improving public administration. The field has a long history of considering new programs of change, plunging in at the outset, and then later sifting out those elements that seem to have lasting value and discarding the parts that were little more than hyperbole used by management consultants to peddle their wares. So it should be and will be with waves such as reinventing government and the new public management. Contributions such as efforts to focus more on performance at the point of service, the desire to enhance communications between those who serve and those directly affected, the desire to spark innovation throughout the organization, and the interest in understanding how dynamic environments force managers and indeed their organizations to continuously seek to improve and learn are all useful.

All that having been said, it was not helpful that the approach to selling some of these techniques has been to blame law, regulation, legal process, and courts for the problems of governance and to suggest that if only that red tape (read legal aspects of public administration) could be eliminated, all would be well. First, as the preceding pages have explained (See Chapters 6, 8, and 9), the absence of formal procedures and the maximization of administrative discretion have at various times and ways created a host of difficulties, problems that administrative law was brought into existence to address (See Chapter 4). The discretion to be creative and responsive in one situation can also be the opportunity to be arbitrary and capricious or to discriminate in another. While as public administrators we desire to have as few burdens and constraints as possible, as employees and as consumers of administrative decisions we continue to demand all the protections we can get. Moreover, there is no indication whatever that the body politic is prepared to abandon any of its tools of accountability. They want enhanced performance at the point of service delivery, but they also want to be able to get due process in a dispute with that same agency and to be able to seek judicial review at the end of the day.

Ironically, some of those who have been the most vocal advocates of the new public management, of both major political parties, have used complex and burdensome executive orders and memoranda to impose far more red tape requirements than ever existed before (See Chapters 4 and 5).

As several chapters have explained, the need is to become more sophisticated than ever before. If contemporary lessons about new management techniques are to be used most effectively, the requirement is for parallel systems management. As Chapter 10 explained, that means that new programs and delivery systems based upon expanded contracting or network management must often be operated alongside existing, more traditional regulatory and service systems. This reality requires a refinement and innovation in the law of public administration that will allow managers to administer both sets of activities simultaneously. Thus, for example, it means that the traditional tendency to have statutes that seek to distinguish sharply between contract law and administrative law is outmoded and troublesome. The need is not to get law out of the way but to work to understand the law that governs and to work toward modernization of the law such that it both facilitates effective administration and at the same time serves ongoing fundamental values and purposes.

There is also a need to recognize that the directions in which contemporary public management trends have moved the field and changing employment patterns mean that the law of public administration must recognize a multiplicity of factors. For example, there is no small amount of hypocrisy involved in arguing that public employees are special and that there are therefore special needs that justify a wide range of constraints on them, while simultaneously arguing that they must be more like private sector employees. The decisions of the Supreme Court have moved public employees backward in terms of protections even as the demands on them have dramatically increased. Contemporary advocates should not expect to recruit and retain top quality people and demand more creativity and risk from them while simultaneously seeking to provide them with fewer protections in an environment that offers few new rewards.

Myth 4: If We Could Just Design the Right Policies, There Wouldn't Be a Problem

One of the other myths that has emerged has come with the tendency to think that policy tools could be designed so as to be less dependent upon public law techniques and mechanisms. There is no doubt that the reemergence of public policy work in the past three decades has made important contributions. On the other hand, there has also been an element in that field that suggests that market tools could be used to avoid some of the burdens or even some of the "implementation games," to use Bardach's term (See Chapter 4), that get in the way of policy success.

As several chapters have explained, policy tools are virtually never self-operating, and that includes the techniques that were created to take advantage of the dynamics of the marketplace. Whether the effort is to establish markets for trading emissions permits or the effort to use food nutrition labeling to enhance health and safety, there are a host of important public law issues and processes involved. Here again, the object must be to find ways to make certain that the law of public administration is properly crafted and updated to address the special problems created by the new techniques and also to make certain that the new policy tools are utilized in such a way that they fit into the overall legal regime of the nation.

TOWARD A PUBLIC LAW FOR FUTURE PUBLIC ADMINISTRATION

As in all areas of public life, then, the challenge is to move forward, not backward, but to do so in a way that comprehends the fundamental role of public law in public administration and yet addresses the need for innovation. That law for future public administration requires an effort to rediscover public law, a focus on administrative law as the law of connections, and pursuit of a more effective study of public law in public administration.

Rediscovering Administrative Law

The first requirement to move forward in this field is to rediscover it. That means it is necessary to remind ourselves about how critical elements of the law of public administration have evolved and what its contemporary dynamics are. When it comes to administrative law, it is clear that Justice Holmes was correct that the "life of the law is experience." As these chapters have explained, there has been a great deal of change in the field in recent decades. The number of statutes and executive orders that have altered both substance and process required a very substantial update of this book even from its last edition.

This rediscovery process means not only renewed attention by policymakers and scholars but also by students of public administration, most of whom also happen to be practitioners. Some four decades ago, Dwight Waldo expressed his view that the antilaw bias in public administration had gone on far too long and had been counterproductive for the field.[3] And indeed, there appeared for a decade or more thereafter to be a resurgence of public law scholarship and instruction in public administration programs. Unfortunately, it seems as though the political attacks on public administration, the myths noted above, and demands for change in the field have led to a tendency to exhibit less concern that students entering the field be literate in the law at least to the degree essential to an effective and responsible public sector professional.

There are several dimensions of public law to which students, whether they are newcomers to public administration or practitioners returning to upgrade skills, need to be exposed. And if they are to be effective and keep their organizations and people operating at peak levels, public managers must continually update their knowledge of key public law issues relevant to their work. While there has been progress in ensuring that students are exposed to ethical issues in public administration, that is not the same thing as public law knowledge. Indeed, for reasons explained in Chapter 13, there can be tensions between the requirements of law and of ethics. Neither is it sufficient to say that public law is "covered" because someone in an introduction to the field talks about the fact that it is important to be aware that public administration operates in a constitutional context. The courts presume that public administrators know the law relevant to our field and will hold us liable for violations of it. Yet the plain fact is that many of our programs do not provide the students with that knowledge, or, in some cases, even with the tools to obtain it on their own.

Second, it is important even as all of us rediscover public law in public administration to address the changing nature of fundamental concepts behind some of the contemporary changes in the field. For example, while the Constitution was very much about the business of creating a national infrastructure at the time that it was first created, the tendency in the past several decades has been to focus less on that aspect and more on either officials' powers and limits or, even more commonly, attention to constitutional rights and liberties. In an era when, for example, taxation and spending and the role of government as market regulator and market participant has been changing so rapidly in the context of a global market and new communication and commercial relationships, it becomes important to pay renewed attention to the constitutional infrastructure issues.

Another example of an area of change that requires a return to fundamentals is the shift from power to contract as a basis for action in the public sector. This is not merely a restatement of the growing number of contracts in service delivery. Rather, there are wide areas in which the approach to governing is not to identify authority and act but to negotiate various types of relations and then operate under those negotiated agreements in the form of what we often call governance regimes. There was a time before the development of modern administrative law in which this kind of behavior caused the concern that the public interest was not always an important factor in agreements between government and others about the resolution of conflicts or the shaping of new actions. Even within government, there has been an increasing tendency to work out interjurisdictional agreements—negotiated solutions between branches to do things that raised judicial issues—and to circumvent existing rulemaking and adjudication practices in favor negotiated arrangements.

For reasons pointed out in discussions throughout this volume, the dynamics of contract relationships and related governance regimes are different in many important respects from traditional power-based action by government. There has been surprisingly little attention to existing law regarding public contracts or contractual mechanisms in existing relationships among governmental units, much less has there been attention to understanding some of the tensions between the use of private concepts of contract in the public context. Neither has there been sufficient attention to the relationship between the vertical, authority-based, positive law–grounded model of administrative action on contracts and the horizontal, negotiated, common law–originated model (See Chapter 1).

Administrative Law as the Law of Connections

Of course, there is also the need to consider the future directions of the field. One way to view administrative law in the twenty-first century is to conceptualize it as the law of connections. It will be increasingly important to focus on the way in which public law facilitates the many relationships that make up the modern fabric of governance and also the ways in which that law can and should place boundaries around them so as to conform to the Constitution, individual rights and liberties, and the rule of law.

Among the critically important connections to be addressed are the relationships between the Constitution and administrative agencies (including the newer forms of organizations created to carry out policy), connections among organizations at the same level and between units at different levels involved in various types of governance activities, and the connections between domestic actions and those of regional or global international bodies. Among the many important connections that it must be able to address effectively is that between government and the market, since public institutions will continue to act both as regulator and as market participant.

One of the connections that will require further attention is that between the law of public management and public policy. As preceding chapters have noted, the tendency has been for there to be a wide gulf between administrative law and public policy analyses. Even the basic concepts used in each are significantly different. Hence, the term *issue* has a very different meaning in public policy than it does in public law. There is the additional problem that public policy has often assumed the classic model in which a legislature adopts a statute, the executive implements it, and the judiciary interprets it. The problem in the present and for the future is that change has been occurring so rapidly that that traditional model of policymaking is often significantly modified in practice. Thus, it is now common for a problem to emerge that requires a response, for the parties to the issue to take the matter to court, for the judge to have to decide in the absence of a directly applicable policy statement by a legislature or agency, and to render a decision that is often understood by all involved to be a significant act of policymaking. The law involving surrogate parenting or genetic engineering activities are classic examples.[4] Legislatures often come in after the fact to write statutes based in no small part on the rulings already rendered by courts. The executive may either respond to that legislature or seek to preempt it by the use of executive orders. Of course, courts at the state level have often been more willing to give public policy explanations for their actions or using public policy as a basis for decision than their federal counterparts.[5] Some of this has to do with the common law character of much of the work of state courts. This area of connection is critical.

Toward a More Effective Study of Public Law and Public Administration

Of course, the development of a law of connections will require more and more effective study of public law and public administration. A serious study in this field must be more than the study of the Constitution. Clearly, constitutional issues represent one fundamental set of issues in the law of public administration, but there are many others as well.

Just as clearly, while the U.S. Supreme Court's rulings are extremely important in all areas of public law, they are by no means the only judicial decisions. As the processes of public administration are more decentralized and rely on multiple working relationships among different types of organizations in different locations, the number of disputes and the range of opinions across lower federal and state courts will likely increase. We are already seeing evidence of this in the area of contracting issues, discussed in several chapters of this volume. Moreover, as the federal government has developed a wide variety of policies to be administered through a civil rights model (See Chapter 12), it actually invites a wider range of participation by courts in a variety of jurisdictions.

A serious public law scholarship requires more attention to statutes and to finding frameworks by which to integrate them into a more coherent picture. The fact is that with the exception of certain provisions such as Title VII of the 1964 Civil Rights Act, public law literature to date has tended to deal with statutes in relatively narrow areas (if at all), and there has been little attempt to address the relationship between the dramatic range of statutes and the broad changes in public administration. This volume has sought to provide some of that integration, but much more work is needed.

Our new scholarship must comprehend both the methods of legal authority and of contract. This volume has demonstrated many of the problem areas in which public contract law is inadequate and in which the rest of public law deals with the subject not at all. When so much of what government does is done by contract, this lacuna in the scholarship of public law cannot continue.

Finally, while there have been some improvements, it will be increasingly necessary to ensure that public law scholarship does not focus solely on the national level or the domestic picture. This volume has sought to employ examples across the levels of government as well as across sectors and to consider supranational dimensions. That does not mean scholarship should aim solely at state or local levels or at international activities, though for comparative purposes studies across local governments, states, or countries will be very helpful. It also requires studies that integrate these levels because the connections will be increasingly common and intricate. For example, the discussion of international dimensions of domestic rulemaking activities demonstrates that we are already at a point where the porous nature of national boundaries has already affected administrative action.

INSTITUTIONS, PROCESSES, AND THE FUTURE
OF PUBLIC ADMINISTRATION

While there is much that is new that is shaping public administration and the law that is central to it, there are two fundamental factors that remain. The first has already been addressed. It is the reality that public administration will continue to operate on a basis of public law.[6] The second is that it operates in an institutional context, albeit one that is constantly evolving.

Ironically, one of the problems that plagued administrative law for decades and prevented it from playing its proper role in public administration has now come to dominate public management itself. That is the tendency to celebrate process as the central concern. It is based in part on the idea that public institutions have been rendered obsolete by the rise of process democracy and technique-oriented management. Indeed, some critics suggest that it is those governmental institutions, and the legal/constitutional structure on which they are constructed, that stand in the way of progress.[7]

The assumption of process democracy is that the business of government in a democratic state is to set up processes for citizen participation, representation, and protection of individual rights.[8] Then citizens associate with others who have similar interests to voice their concerns. The groups are necessary because, in a complex society with many voices and a great deal of noise, organization is required to marshal political power and to clearly and forcefully articulate a policy position. These groups, variously called special interest groups, lobbying organizations, or just nongovernmental organizations (NGOs), negotiate with one another and with the leaders of government to arrive at a decision on the best course of action for the society in any given area.[9] This model of governance has been referred to as a "procedural republic" in which government is relatively neutral about the ends to be pursued and the means by which they are to be achieved but ensures that the process for decision exists and is open.[10] At one end of this spectrum is the more or less traditional model of pluralism. At the other end are market choice advocates, who would rely even more on process—in this case market-oriented processes.

Taken together, these contemporary perspectives on the role of government and the nature and purposes of public institutions have suggested that what matters is process, not institutions.[11] They emphasize a utilitarian attitude that assumes that choices are discrete and often at the level of the individual or the special interest group. It is not surprising that, in a period dominated by these attitudes and by governments that advocate them as well, institutions have not been given the kind of attention that is necessary if there is to be an infrastructure adequate to support sustainable development in the years to come.

Institutions Matter

However, none of the changes that have been discussed in this volume eliminate the need for properly designed, professionally staffed, well-managed, and strong public institutions regardless of which party happens to be in power at any given time. Indeed, there is no small amount of irony in the fact that in an era of growing social and technological complexity, increasingly sophisticated market behavior, and greater calls for accountability, attacks on institutions have intensified. Certainly the debacle that is the Department of Homeland Security is exhibit A for the lack of attention to the meaning and importance of institutions.

First, while contemporary management literature explains many reasons why the elements of Max Weber's bureaucracy concept are problematic, no one has effectively refuted his argument that complex societies require complex economies, legal systems, and mechanisms to ensure security.[12] The governing structure is essential to ensure a workable infrastructure, not only to allow those in positions of authority to govern, but also to allow private individuals to undertake the many business and personal tasks they seek to achieve. Given those historical realities, institutions are needed to support governmental and social efforts. As Joseph Shumpeter put it, in complex societies, "bureaucracy is not an obstacle to democracy but an inevitable complement to it."[13] While we may not approve of the bureaucratic model,

Shumpeter's basic point stands unchallenged. The marketplace itself requires a host of institutions for its creation, maintenance, and protection.

Hence, both developed and developing countries are encountering the seemingly ironic fact that the more sophisticated they become economically, the more they require larger, better-trained, and more capable legal institutions along with the statutes, courts, regulatory bodies, and judges needed to respond to the many requests for action just from the private sector, let alone the demands from public sector activity. Privatization requires the development of sophisticated government contract laws that have not traditionally existed in many jurisdictions. The more that trade and financial investment are globalized, the more complex and intense are the demands to provide the institutional infrastructure needed to support those economic activities. And if such developments are needed to support the private sector, they are even more essential as governments have been called upon to take on more complex tasks. That is exactly why the World Bank focused a World Development Report on the need for the development of stronger institutions.[14] Second, notwithstanding the fashions of recent years and the many efforts at deregulation and privatization that they have produced, it is clear the many existing government regulatory and social service programs are simply not going to be replaced by market alternatives.

> A primary distinction between public administration and other endeavors is that officers of government are created by and act within the authority of law. Thus the legal framework offers the basis of public administration. It also ensures rights, security, and stability. It is both the means by which governments regulate and provide services to citizens and the means by which those citizens may protect their rights. It is also a vehicle with which to address problems of corruption or abuse of power. . . . It provides means for controlling the public sector in the sense of providing mechanisms of accountability and responsibility.[15]

Privatization, like the other elements of the new public management, does not mean an end to institutions. What it does mean is that there is a need to create an institutional capability for contract management and to ensure accountability. Most governments lack that capacity presently, and their administrative tools for that purpose are often inadequate or out of date.

The other major demand that outstrips existing institutional capacity in contemporary governance is the demand for government to become a provider, analyst, and distributor of unprecedented amounts of information of all types. For reasons addressed in Chapter 11, the increased complexity of the modern environment demands far more analytic capability than ever before. We have advanced into the e-government era before establishing even adequate responses to what existed before, let alone what has come with e-government. Not only that, but governments no longer have the kind of advantage over others in terms of access to information that they once possessed. Indeed, private firms may send their negotiating teams to the bargaining table with far more data and analysis than their public sector counterparts. At the same time, government is increasingly expected to get the maximum amount of information out onto the Internet and down to the community level as quickly and inexpensively as possible. In a world in which nations as well as private sector firms compete, one of the great institutional challenges for the future is in information management.

These are just a few of many areas in which institutional capacity-building is absolutely critical. But capacity-building, using the term more broadly, is not something that the marketplace provides. In a competitive environment, the market tends to buy capacity rather than build it. Thus, another of the ironies of the growing orientation to the market is the need for governments to build their own capacity to compete and to govern even while they are under increasing cost pressures to limit expenditures. The fact is that investors wish to benefit from modern infrastructure and well-educated and highly skilled employees, but they often do not wish to pay the levels of taxes needed to produce those desirable characteristics. And when economic times are good, the demand is for tax cuts rather than a recognition that that is a time for investment in essential institutional infrastructure.

If institutions are so important, what are the premises that should be considered in constructing an institutional framework for the twenty-first century? While there are, of course, a variety of standard questions that are usually posed about organizational design, these are not the items that are the most critical for institution building. Rather, the central problem is the need to consider the relationships among institutions, culture, public morality, and the clash of competing values.

Institutions Are Not Just Functional Mechanisms

In one sense, it is quite possible to design a set of institutions for modern governance by determining the functions to be performed and matching those with existing institutions. Judgments can then be made about whether to add new institutions, modify existing agencies, or to create ad hoc problem-solving groups. But, of course, institutions are about more than how to carry out a task in a given political and economic environment. They are not merely mechanisms.

Institutions are instruments for achieving goals and maintaining values. Even institutions in the private sector manifest values. Indeed, it is often said that it is as important to design organizations for values as it is for functions.[16] Thus, if the critical purpose of an institution is expertise, then the design that will likely come to the fore is one that may not emphasize participation. If a critical value is participation, then an organizational design may result in which efficiency is not a primary consideration. If responsibility is the critical value, then experts may have to give ground to political officials and public opinion.[17]

Public institutions are very much about achieving broad public goals and manifesting the values that are fundamentally important in the society. They are, it is true, means to ends, but of course means and ends are often very much interrelated. Michael Sandel's observation, noted briefly in Chapter 13, is worth repeating. "Political institutions are not simply instruments that implement ideas independently conceived; they are themselves embodiments of ideas."[18]

Whatever values may be behind the creation of public institutions, it would be a rare case in which it could be said that nations create their institutions primarily for the purpose of achieving instrumental rationality judged according to efficiency criteria. That may be the driving force behind market choices, but, as Chapter 10 explained, it is not the same as political and social judgment. Indeed, in many instances, political institutions exist to do what markets cannot and should not be expected to do, such as addressing issues of equity or the unanticipated social consequences of economic development.[19]

Similarly, the process models do not get at the fact that the values on which political institutions are built are not simply relative, to be determined when next a public opinion poll is taken. Indeed, majorities and their representatives at any moment in time may make decisions that are not in keeping with the basic constitutional, cultural, ethical, environmental, or economic foundations of the society. Too much emphasis on process democracy and not enough on the substantive and fundamental values that a particular society seeks to advance and for which its institutions are designed leads to two cornerstones of the contemporary problem that Sandel has termed "democracy's discontent."

> One is the fear that, individually and collectively, we are losing control of the forces that govern our lives. The other is the sense that, from family to neighborhood to nation, the moral fabric of community is unraveling around us. These two fears—for the loss of self-government and the erosion of community—together define the anxiety of the age.[20]

Institutions Are Not Fixed in Concrete, nor Do They Stand Alone

The effort to be clear about the fundamental relationship between the design of an institutional framework and the fundamental values it reflects is not meant to suggest that institutions are unchangeable any more than the societies that they are designed to serve are. Institutions, like societies, evolve over time and indeed they must sometimes adapt rather rapidly to emergencies or newly emerging challenges.

And it would be equally erroneous to assume that well-designed institutions can eliminate the need for good, honest, effective, and efficient officials. Good institutions have failed under weak leadership in virtually every country at some time or other. As earlier chapters have explained in several ways, contemporary public officials must be able to manage within their own agency or unit of government, work effectively across units, and operate effectively outside government, linking their organizations to nonprofit and even for-profit firms.

On the other hand, well-designed institutions can provide correctives for the temporary occupants of public offices who may be popular but may not possess the requisite aptitudes or training for a task. The structure of organizations is constraining as are the accountability mechanisms, but they serve to remind temporary occupants of office that they are part of the government and should not get lost in their own egos.

Institutions Reflect Culture and Morality

While it is true that institutions evolve, one of the characteristics of what we call institutions is that they have an enduring quality. While ad hoc groups or temporary agencies come and go over time, institutions are not intended to function only during one presidential administration. Indeed, one of the great difficulties in designing institutions is that there is so much pressure for short-term decisionmaking and so little incentive to take a longer view, particularly if doing so entails costs in the present for benefits in an indefinite future. Internally, there is an impatience to make good things happen quickly during the incumbency of the sitting administration and put off unfortunate consequences until some future time. But one of the roles of institutions is to embody longer-term values that are structured into the decisionmaking process in such a way as to try to make us slow down and consider the match of what we seek to do in the short term with what we value in the long run. Thus, institutions are in some sense about the maintenance of fundamental values and moral premises in the face of day-to-day challenges.

From a public law perspective, institutions are the product of law, they participate in developing the law, and they are actively engaged in its implementation and enforcement. Even beyond that, however, they represent a framework of operating government within which public law is both a central driving force and a restraining influence.

CONCLUSION

At a time when everyone is so certain of their normative positions—that they know what is right and that the way to govern is to employ more or less raw political power to get to what is right—we are well advised as public servants, citizens, and scholars to recall the line from Robert Bolt's play *A Man for All Seasons*. In it, Sir Thomas More, then Lord High Chancellor of England, warns us about the importance of the law in times when some are too sure of their own rectitude. Responding to the claim that he was engaged in "piling sophistication on sophistication," More answered: "No sheer simplicity. . . . I know what is legal, not what is right. And I'll stick to what is legal . . . . The currents and eddies of right and wrong, which you find such plain sailing, I can't navigate. I'm no voyager. But in the thickets of the law, oh, there I'm a forester." As public administrators, scholars, and students of public management, we must navigate the shoals of what is right, but we must also be foresters in the law.

NOTES

1. 5 U.S.C. §706.

2. *Bianchi v. Lorenz,* 701 A.2d 1037 (VT 1997).

3. Dwight Waldo, "Scope of the Theory of Public Administration" in James C. Charlesworth, ed., *Theory and Practice of Public Administration: Scope, Objectives, and Methods, monograph no. 8, Annals of the American Academy of Political and Social Science* (1968), pp. 14–15.

4. See e.g., *In re Baby M.*, 525 A.2d 1128 (NJ 1987), rev'd 537 A.2d 1227 (NJ 1988); *Stiver v. Parker*, 975 F.2d 261 (6th Cir. 1992).

5. See e.g., *Moore v. Regents*, 271 Cal. Rptr. 146 (Cal. 1990).

6. See Ronald C. Moe and Robert S. Gilmour, "Rediscovering Principles of Public Administration: The Neglected Foundation of Public Law," 55 *Public Administration Review* 135 (1995); Ronald C. Moe and Thomas H. Stanton, "Government-Sponsored Enterprises as Federal Instrumentalities: Reconciling Private Management with Public Accountability," 49 *Public Administration Review* 321 (1989); Ronald Moe, "'Law' Versus 'Performance' as Objective Standard," 48 *Public Administration Review* 675 (1988); "Exploring the Limits of Privatization," 47 *Public Administration Review* 453 (1987).

7. See e.g., David Osborne and Ted Gaebler, *Reinventing Government* (New York: Penguin, 1992).

8. Michael J. Sandel, *Democracy's Discontent* (Cambridge: Harvard University Press, 1996), p. 4.

9. One of the classic formulations of pluralism is that provided by Robert Dahl, *Who Governs* (New Haven: Yale University Press, 1961).

10. Sandel, *supra* note 8, at p. 4.

11. James G. March and Johan P. Olsen, *Rediscovering Institutions* (New York: Free Press, 1989), pp. 2–3.

12. H. H. Gerth and C. Wright Mills, eds., *From Max Weber: Essays in Sociology* (New York: Oxford, 1946).

13. *Capitalism, Socialism, and Democracy*, 3rd ed. (New York: Harper & Row, 1950), p. 206.

14. World Bank, *World Development Report 1997: The State in a Changing World* (New York: Oxford University Press, 1997).

15. United Nations Experts Group on Public Administration and Finance, "Draft Report of the Twelfth Meeting of Experts on the United Nations Programme in Public Administration and Finance to the Resumed 50th General Assembly Session on Public Administration and Development," August 11, 1995, p. 48.

16. See Edgar Schein, *Organizational Culture and Leadership*, 2nd ed. (San Francisco: Jossey-Bass, 1992).

17. See John Nalbandian, *Professionalism in Local Government: Transformations in Roles, Responsibilities and Values of City Managers* (San Francisco: Jossey-Bass, 1991).

18. Sandel, *supra* note 8, at p. ix.

19. This is, for example, why the nations gathered at the Copenhagen Social Summit felt it necessary to say under Commitment 8 that nations obligated themselves to "review the impact of structural adjustment programmes on social development, including, where appropriate, by means of gender-sensitive social impact assessments and other relevant methods, in order to develop policies to reduce their negative effects and improve their positive impact; the cooperation of international financial institutions in the review could be requested by interested countries." United Nations, *Copenhagen Declaration and Program of Action* (New York: United Nations, 1995), pp. 27–28.

20. Sandel, *supra* note 8, at p. 3

Appendix 1

Mathews v. Eldridge

The Anatomy of an
Administrative Law Case

NOTE

This case study is an independent piece to be used with several portions of this book. The reader should be aware that a variety of changes, some good and some bad, have been made in the administrative and political operations of the program that is the focus of this study. The HEW has long since been re-created as the Department of Health and Human Services (HHS). Efforts have been made to restructure the Social Security Administration (SSA) to provide it with independence sufficient to protect it from political interference in claims administration.[1] There have been changes in the Social Security statutes and regulations concerning the substantive standards and procedural protections available in claims disputes.[2] However, many of the types of problems that one encounters in the story of George Eldridge's odyssey through the Social Security system persist, though perhaps in different forms and contexts in this and other social service programs.[3] The terrible problems with summary denials and terminations of Supplementary Security Income benefits during 1997 and 1998 provide but a few examples.[4]

However, this case study is not intended as a commentary on the Social Security Administration, nor is it meant to explain the current state of disability policy process. It is a study of a major administrative law case in the modern administrative environment and, as such, it reveals some of the many difficulties involved in operating the administrative justice system. Further, it is an example not from the regulatory side that has more commonly been the focus of such case studies, but from the social service domain, the area that affects more people on a daily basis than the regulatory agencies' activities.

This is also the story of the U.S. Supreme Court ruling that has defined the requirements of administrative due process since it was rendered in the mid-1970s.

For all these reasons, it is both a very special case study and simultaneously a useful exemplar of a host of issues important to public administration. It is for all these reasons that the story was left as it was originally written. The reader should bear that in mind and take the story on its own terms, and in its own time frame—the mid-1970s.

INTRODUCTION

The SSA, headquartered in Baltimore, handles more legal disputes in a year than all of the federal courts in the United States combined. Its cases are substantial, with the average Social Security disability claim running approximately $25,000. These decisions are complex determinations made through an intergovernmental decisionmaking system that involves federal officials and state departments of vocational rehabilitation. Most citizens are much more likely to find themselves in this type of legal controversy—a benefit claim dispute—than they are to face criminal prosecution, or even to defend against or maintain a substantial civil suit in local courts. The stakes can be very high. One might begin the struggle with a home, furniture, and a fair standard of existence and end it a decade later with no home, little furniture, and substantial debts.

This article investigates one such case, *Mathews v. Eldridge*.[5] This is a useful case to study, for it is in some ways typical. It demonstrates how a contest over benefits arises and is conducted. At the same time, it is a particularly important and unique case that, unlike the thousands of other contested benefit cases raised each year, found its way to the U.S. Supreme Court and resulted in the resolution of an extremely important controversy in a far-reaching decision from the Court. In *Eldridge,* the Court held that there is no constitutional right to an oral hearing prior to the termination of Social Security disability benefits. Since that opinion was delivered in 1976, the Supreme Court has applied the *Eldridge* ruling to a wide range of administrative law controversies. Just how the case got to the Court and the significance of its result are the subjects of this study.[6] In particular, this investigation will present commentary on the perspective of George Eldridge, the claimant. Eldridge, and all those who make such claims, was the ultimate consumer of the administrative decision and the legal judgment produced by the administrative justice system. That consumer perspective is an important one for other consumers of administrative decisions and for the producers of those determinations.

From an analytic perspective, the study of this case reveals a number of interesting factors that may inform the study of administrative law.[7] These phenomena include: (1) the significance of the interaction of the several levels and units of government involved; (2) the special problems that arise in social service claims as opposed to the more publicized and more frequently analyzed regulatory cases; (3) the essential meaning and complexity of the concept of due process of law in theory and in practice; (4) the presence of what appears to be a conflict between the essential values of the administrative process and the judicial process; (5) the basic distinctions between administrative and judicial proceedings; (6) the relationship of precedent to policy; (7) the significance of judicial politics with the change from the Warren to Burger Court; and (8) the relationship of law to the policy process.

GEORGE ELDRIDGE ENTERS THE SYSTEM

George Eldridge lived in Norton, Virginia, a small coal mining city of approximately 5,500 citizens in the southwestern corner of the state. His disagreement with the Social Security Administration and the Virginia Department of Vocational Rehabilitation began in 1967 and continued off and on until March of 1978. Before it was over, "George Eldridge had his home foreclosed. He and his six children were sleeping in one bed because all of their furniture had been repossessed." How did this happen?

Mr. Eldridge: The Person and the Predicament

Eldridge was born in Lee County, Virginia. He was removed from school in the fifth grade by a bout with pneumonia. While he was recovering from this illness in 1936, the family moved to the mountain community of Norton in connection with the father's transfer. He was employed by the L & N Railroad, the same company that would later employ George.

When he was able to do so, George took a job doing section labor for the L & N. Section labor involved laying new track, cross ties, making repairs, and installing and maintaining rail lines and switches at mine entrances and near the coal tipples where trucks loaded the coal through chutes into waiting rail cars. It was hard work and, as he now adds with some pride, the tasks were performed by hand as opposed to the more recently developed mechanical means.

> The biggest snow we had come in March of '41 or '42. It measured 46 inches here at the bus station. I walked from Endover, that's up in the hollow from Appalachia tool house, two miles and a half in that snow to sweep switches so the trainmen could get to the switches to throw them and pick up their loads.
>
> And I walked back—there was no way to ride. When I got back home, it was so cold, I pulled off my pants and stood them up against the wall.[8]

Eldridge worked for the L & N for almost three years before he was drafted into the army. Upon his discharge, he went back to work on the railroad as an employee of the Interstate Railroad before it was acquired by the Southern Railroad Company.

After about nine years with that rail line, Eldridge switched jobs. He became a soft drink distributor for Royal Crown Cola, and it was during his work for RC that Eldridge became totally disabled. He had been diagnosed as having spinal arthritis in the 1940's, but, since he lacked educational prerequisites, Eldridge saw no alternative to the strenuous delivery job. His health degenerated, but, by this time, he had a house and a large family to consider. Finally, after eight years at the delivery job, his working days came to an end.

> I was working in the town of Coeburn. I got down from the truck and then I couldn't raise my legs to get up on the running board of the truck to get back into the truck. They had to come and get me. . . . I laid thirty-one days in the hospital unable to move my legs.[9]

Some time after he became disabled, Eldridge began to suffer from diabetes. He found himself learning to deal with a multiplicity of medications for the arthritis and diabetes, including insulin injections and a new diet.

Gaining Entrance to the Program: The First Round

In 1967 Eldridge applied at the local Social Security office in Norton for complete disability benefits under the Social Security Act. His application for benefits was initially rejected and that decision was upheld in an administrative review routinely conducted by the Social Security headquarters office in Baltimore. His case was reconsidered at his request by the state agency. A decision against him was rendered in late 1967. Eldridge requested and received a hearing before a hearing examiner (these examiners have since been designated as administrative law judges),[10] in spring 1968. One June 2, the hearing examiner announced his decision in Eldridge's favor. Shortly thereafter, Eldridge was placed in the disability program and was informed, though he does not remember ever having been notified, that his condition would be periodically reevaluated to determine his continued eligibility for benefits.

In June 1969 he was contacted and asked to submit information showing that he was still disabled.[11] He filled out the forms, which included comments about treatment that he had been receiving from physicians along with the names and addresses of the doctors. He was not physically examined by government doctors.

In February 1970 Eldridge was notified that the state agency had concluded that his disability had ended as of January and that his benefits would be terminated the next month. To understand what happened to Eldridge from this point on, it is necessary to investigate briefly the procedures involved in the termination of benefits.[12]

Disability Benefit Terminations

Under the regulations issued by HEW, which has overall responsibility for the SSA, and the legislation that provides for the disability program, there are several stages of review to which one has recourse when a decision is made by the state vocational rehabilitation agency to terminate bene fits.[13] The rehabilitation agencies act for the SSA in the initial stage of decisionmaking. They moni tor recipients of benefits on a regular basis to ensure their continued disability. They do not usually actually examine the recipients. Instead, a staff doctor and a case worker evaluate the papers sent in by people like Eldridge. They request medical reports from the recipient's physician and have access to vocational specialists and psychiatrists for advice. It is a process of paper review.

If the state agency staff workers conclude that the recipient is no longer eligible because he or she is physically able to be employed at some substantial gainful employment existing in the national economy, whether there would be a specific position for the claimant or not, they notify the indi vidual and indicate in general terms why they believe the disability no longer exists. The recipient is told that he or she has ten days to submit additional reports or other pertinent evidence and that it might be possible to obtain an extension of the time limit if it is necessary to obtain further evi dence of continued eligibility. Claimants are told that termination normally occurs two months from the date that the person was determined to be no longer eligible.

If no additional evidence is submitted to the state agency, the entire record is sent to the Balti more office of the SSA for review and final determination. The headquarters may not reverse an unfavorable decision to the claimant, but it may return a determination by the state agency in favor of the benefit recipient.[14] If the SSA headquarters determines that the benefits are to be terminated, the recipient is told of that decision and of the termination date. The claimant is also advised that it is possible to have the case reconsidered by the state agency. If reconsideration is requested, a differ ent team of reviewers should be chosen in the state agency to review the file again. If they agree with the earlier determination, the recipient may request further proceedings. Benefits do not con tinue through the reconsideration process or later administrative review. Benefits cease as of the date indicated by the SSA headquarters. If the claimant wins at some point in the process, back benefits are paid.

The next stage in the process of review is an oral hearing conducted before an administrative law judge at which the claimant may appear with an attorney, although most do not,[15] or someone else to speak on his or her behalf. Representation is permitted, but it is neither required nor provid ed by the government. Further, the amount of compensation that an attorney may receive for representing a client in such a hearing is limited by law.[16] The standard fee in such a case, assuming that there is no special problem in computation or payment, is 25 percent of the back benefit pay ments recovered. The purpose of the hearing is to determine whether the individual meets the requirements of the program.

In the event that the claimant is dissatisfied with the decision of the administrative law judge, an appeal may be taken to the Appeals Council of the Social Security Administration. This is a paper appeal.

If the claimant is still unhappy, the case may be taken to a federal district court for judicial review of the administrative record.[17] Here, of course, testimony is taken before a federal district judge, although the review is limited to examination of the record to determine whether there was substantial evidence on which the agency could have reached its final determination. Finally, if one alleges a federal legal question, it might be possible to appeal the decision of the district court, but such cases are rare.

MR. ELDRIDGE AND THE APPEALS PROCESS

As things stood in February 1970, Eldridge had lost his 1969 review. He and his family faced an immediate loss of the disability benefits. It was a frightening prospect for a man with six children, a home to pay for, and a wife who was dying of cancer.

The Second Round: 1969–1971

But the terse letter informing him of the termination decision evoked anger and frustration as well as fear. Eldridge could not understand how the officials could determine that he was no longer disabled without having seen him or performing any sort of medical tests. As he saw it, nothing had changed in the eighteen months since he had won his dispute before the administrative law judge.

Perhaps most upsetting to Eldridge was the manner in which the decision was made. Eldridge argued that he was not asking for charity. He had paid premiums into the program while he was able to work. He had proven in his hearing in 1968 that he was completely disabled within the meaning of the applicable statute and regulations. Now, without an opportunity to be heard, the benefits would end.

But of course there was an opportunity to fight the decision after the payments were stopped. Eldridge had fought the 1968 eligibility decision by himself, but this time he felt that he needed help despite the cost. His concern and his anger prompted Eldridge to respond to the notice from SSA in two ways.

First, he began his administrative appeals process by requesting that the agency reconsider his case. On April 11 and again on April 23 he contacted the local office requesting a prompt decision. But Eldridge knew that he was unlikely to get through the reconsideration process and on to a hearing without a lengthy delay. He'd been through it before. It would probably be months before his benefits were restored. In fact, the mean time from termination to eventual reinstatement for successful claimants was then just over eighteen months.

An Attempt to Challenge SSA

In addition to his administrative efforts, Eldridge's anger at what he felt was an unfair and arbitrary process of decisionmaking prompted him to challenge the Social Security Administration on constitutional grounds in court. On April 27, 1970, Mr. McAfee of Cline, McAfee, Adkins & Gillenwater, a Norton law firm, filed suit for Eldridge in the U.S. District Court for the Western District of Virginia. The legal issue that the court was to decide can be easily stated, but a decision either way would have profound implications both for those receiving benefits—the consumers of administrative decisions—and for the administrators of the program—the producers of administrative judgments.

Eldridge's attorney argued that it was a violation of due process of law protected by the Fifth Amendment of the Constitution of the United States for the Secretary of HEW, responsible for SSA, to terminate a disability recipient's benefits without first providing the person with an oral hearing. Such a hearing would permit a claimant to appear in person, to present evidence in his behalf, to question witnesses, and to respond to adverse evidence that had been placed in his disability file. The hearing, it was argued, should be held before an administrative law judge who has independence from those who administer the program. In short, Eldridge wanted the same kind of hearing that he would be entitled to later in the process to be provided before his benefit checks were stopped.

In June, the district court ordered the government to resume the benefit payments pending the outcome of the litigation. In that same month, Eldridge's wife died. His total income until that point had consisted of a VA payment of $136 per month. Eldridge remembered with bitter feelings the fact that discontinuance of benefits prevented him from providing his wife with the few things that she had requested.

While the constitutional case was pending before the court, the administrative appeal continued. The reconsideration decision was unfavorable. Eldridge's attorney immediately filed requesting a hearing, which did not occur until March 17, 1971. The administrative law judge, a different examiner than the one Eldridge had faced in 1968, concluded that he was still completely disabled and ordered that payments be resumed with back payments to be paid for the several months during which the benefits had been interrupted. Had it not been for the intervention of the court, Eldridge would have faced a financial nightmare. As it was, he had to pay medical bills for himself and his family as well as attorney fees.

When the administrative appeal was resolved in Eldridge's favor, the district court dismissed the constitutional suit as moot. That is, Eldridge no longer had an actual live case or controversy with the government. To be sure, he disagreed with the government's policy, but the law requires more than general disagreement. It demands that an individual have standing to sue. He must be substantially injured or stand in imminent danger of being injured by the party he is suing.[18] Further, the dispute must be a continuing disagreement or the suit will be dismissed for mootness.[19]

ONCE MORE INTO THE BREACH

It was not long, though, before Eldridge was again engaged in a controversy with the SSA. A year after his second victory in a hearing, Eldridge received another set of forms from the state agency. He frowned as he read the same form letter that had started his last year-long battle.

> When your disability payments began, you were notified by the Social Security Administration that your condition might improve and your claim was scheduled for review. The Social Security Administration has requested us . . . to develop current evidence as to whether your condition still prevents you from working.[20]

Round Three: One More Time

Once again Eldridge filled out the forms. He indicated that his situation had not changed. He answered the questions about the kinds of medical treatment he was receiving and when he had last seen his physician. With the hope that things would go better this time, he mailed the package.

In May 1972, Eldridge received another letter from the Social Security Administration:

> Although you indicated in the report you recently completed for us that you do not feel your condition has improved so that you are able to return to work, the other information and evidence in your case shows that you are able to work and have been since May 1972. You were initially found to be disabled due to chronic anxiety and back strain. In addition you have been found to have diabetes. Medical evidence shows no significant motion limitations of your back which would impose severe functional restrictions. Diabetes is under control and no complications have been noted, secondary to this. Although you remain somewhat anxious, there is no indications [sic] of your continued emotional problems of sufficient severity to preclude all work for which you are qualified.
>
> Therefore, disability benefits being paid on your Social Security number may be stopped unless additional evidence is submitted which shows that you are still unable to work because of your impairments.[21]

Now Eldridge was really furious. Twice he had proven his case in person. Stacks of medical reports had been submitted. He had yet to be examined by a physician who worked for the government.[22] For the third time, he prepared to fight the state agency. He wrote back to the agency:

> In regards to your letter of May 1972 asking for more evidence to prove my disability, I think you should already have enough evidence in my files to prove the disability already. Besides if I was able to work I would have worked because if I was able to work I could

make more money than social security paid me. Another thing, if you will check my reports a little closer I think that you will find that I have arthritis of the spine rather than a strained back as you stated in your letter. The people at the disability section in Richmond have never made a yes decision in my case. I have always had to have a hearing in order to get the decision made properly. Even at the last hearing that was held in my case I had to employ an attorney, and the examiner made his decision wholly in my favor and stated in his decision for me for my checks to continue without interruption. So go ahead and make your own decision in the case. I know I'm not able to work, if I ever get able to work I will, I will get by some way without the social security even though I've paid into it while I was able to work.[23]

It was false bravado. Eldridge knew full well that he could not do without the benefits. He just could not understand why he was being treated in what he perceived to be an inhumane fashion. Even more than seven years after he wrote that letter, his blue eyes flashed with indignation when he discussed the episode.

The state agency entered a determination against him and forwarded the findings to Baltimore for final decision. The SSA wrote Eldridge again on June 12, confirming the earlier judgment of the state agency and informing him that his benefits would end in July. He could, of course, file for reconsideration any time within six months after termination.

He was already exhausted. The cost of the proceedings and the breaks in payments over the several years of dealing with SSA meant that by the time this round of adjudication ended, Eldridge would lose his home, a mobile home, his automobile, and his furniture.

The Journey to the Supreme Court Begins

Eldridge again followed the dual strategy. He turned to the courts, represented this time by a different attorney, Mr. Donald Earls, then with Cline, McAfee et al., later with Earls, Wolfe and Farmer, also of Norton, Virginia. He filed suit in the district court in Abingdon, Virginia, in August 1972. The issue was the same due process claim that Eldridge's attorney had raised a year earlier in that same court, but this time the judge did not order continuation of payments pending the outcome of the litigation.

The case was not a review of an administrative decision as such. Under other circumstances, Eldridge might have battled his way through reconsideration, hearing, and Appeals Council stages to get to the district court. This process is known as exhaustion of administrative remedies. The so-called exhaustion doctrine is intended to reduce court review of individual administrative decisions. If he had pursued this route, his case would have been reviewed by a district court judge. The judge in such a case would have examined the decision of the agency to terminate benefits in light of what is known as the "substantial evidence rule."[24] He or she would have examined the record to determine whether on the record as a whole there was substantial evidence to support the decision of the agency.[25]

But Eldridge was *not* seeking judicial review of a substantive agency decision. Speaking for Eldridge, Earls argued that they were willing to concede that the agency had examined the benefit termination in the manner prescribed by statute and regulations. The complaint was that the regulations and other guidelines, insofar as they provided no pretermination hearing, were themselves unconstitutional. That sort of case was brought as a civil suit naming the then Secretary of Health, Education, and Welfare, Caspar Weinberger.

His case came on for argument before Judge Turk, a judge whose docket frequently contained Social Security disability cases. On April 9, 1973, the judge announced his ruling for Eldridge. Before analyzing his opinion, it is necessary to understand the background of the constitutional problem that Eldridge had raised.

WHY DID GEORGE ELDRIDGE INSIST ON A CONSTITUTIONAL REMEDY?

Eldridge sued because he was convinced that he had been treated in a manner that was patently unfair. In more formal terms than he would use, he thought that the several decisions made in his case by unseen and unnamed administrators who, on three separate occasions, had withdrawn his benefits, had been made arbitrarily and capriciously. In fact, his argument was even more basic. His attorney, Mr. Earls, asserted that the procedure employed by the HEW violated the long-standing principle that administrators should not be able to seriously injure a citizen's liberty or property interests without giving an opportunity for a hearing.

The Fear of Administrative Arbitrariness

Ever since administrative agencies have been in use, there has been fear of abuse of authority by administrators.[26] Years before administrative law was recognized as a major branch of American law, the Supreme Court noted that there exist dangers of possible arbitrary administration of an otherwise useful law.

> When we consider the nature and theory of our institutions of government, the principles upon which they are supposed to rest, and review the history of their development, we are constrained to conclude that they do not mean to leave room for the play and action of purely personal and arbitrary power. Sovereignty itself is, of course, not subject to law, for it is the author and source of law, but in our system, while sovereign powers are delegated to the agencies of government, sovereignty itself remains with the people, by whom and for whom all government exists and acts. And the law is the definition and limitation of power.... For the very idea that one man may be compelled to hold his life, or the means of living, or any material right essential to the employment of life, at the mere will of another seems to be intolerable in any country where freedom prevails, as being the essence of slavery itself.[27]

As this country entered the twentieth century and faced the social, economic, and political changes that were on the horizon, serious questions were asked about the manner in which administrative agencies would be dealt with, particularly where they were charged with making decisions in individual cases.[28] In such situations, the agencies were acting like courts.[29] The generally accepted solution was to require the agencies to provide some basic elements of due process of law.[30] Fair procedure and the possibility of review by a court of law would serve as a sufficient check, or so it was thought.[31]

Due process includes, at least, notice to those to be affected by the agency, an opportunity to be heard, decision by an impartial decisionmaker, and the availability of review of the initial decision.[32] In the *Eldridge* case, this discussion of procedural due process raises at least three questions: (1) What kind of problems are presented by the increases in social service benefit cases? (2) What is the significance of the so-called right/privilege dichotomy, which is mentioned in discussions of benefit claims adjudications? (3) At what point in a dispute between the government and a citizen is a hearing required?

The major regulatory commissions such as the Interstate Commerce Commission deal primarily with business rather than individual citizens. With increased social service demands brought on by the growth of urban areas, the Great Depression, World War II, and the postwar need for education and other services has come an increase in disputes involving individual claimants for disability, retirement, welfare, medical aid, educational support, and veterans' benefits. These individuals are relatively less able than organizations to wage legal battles with government. In particular, they suffer immediately and personally from delays in the administrative law processes. They frequently do not understand the complex legal issues at stake, are not represented by attorneys, and are unable to understand all the "red tape" that stands between them and what they perceive to be benefits they are entitled to receive. An additional complication is the fact that several of these programs are administered by federal, state, and, in some cases, local officials.

The benefit cases also focus attention on what was earlier known as the right/privilege dichotomy, which doctrine held that due process requires hearings and other procedural protections where an individual faces an injury to a liberty or property right, but not where a mere privilege is at stake. Such benefit programs as Aid to Families with Dependent Children were considered matters of privilege, hence not protected by due process.[33] The Supreme Court rejected this view and, in *Sherbert v. Verner,* held:

> Nor may the South Carolina court's construction of the statute be saved from constitutional infirmity on the ground that employment compensation benefits are appellant's "right" but merely a "privilege." ... For example, the Court recognized with respect to Federal social security benefits that the interest of a covered employee under the Act is of sufficient substance to fall within the protection from arbitrary governmental action afforded by the Due Process Clause.[34]

Students of due process such as Judge J. Skelly Wright observed that social benefit programs are essential parts of modern life, and cannot be relegated to the status of mere privilege.[35]

Finally, assuming that some process is due in a particular case, at what point in the interaction between the government and the claimant is the hearing required? Before this question can be answered, one must understand a number of cases that were to be at the heart of George Eldridge's case.

Development of Administrative Due Process:
Goldberg v. Kelly and Related Cases

The Court had ruled that before a final tax assessment decision, citizens must be afforded an opportunity for a hearing that is more than a mere chance to complain. "A hearing in its very essence demands that he who is entitled to it shall have a right to support his allegations by argument however brief, and, if need be, by proof, however informal."[36] After all, "the fundamental requisite of due process is the opportunity to be heard."[37]

Of course, not every administrative action requires a hearing, but:

> In administrative proceedings of a quasi-judicial character, the liberty and property of the citizen shall be protected by the rudimentary requirements of fair play. These demand a fair and open hearing.[38]

And "whether any procedural protections are due depends upon the extent to which an individual will be condemned to suffer grievous loss."[39] The court has found such "grievous loss" where an organization's name was placed on the attorney general's list of subversive organizations without a hearing,[40] where dismissal from government employment will bring public opprobrium and cause a mark on the character of the individual,[41] where an individual faced forfeiture of unemployment benefits for refusal to work on Saturdays for religious reasons,[42] and where garnishment of wages is undertaken without due process,[43] all require some form of due process hearing protection.

In 1970 came the landmark case of *Goldberg v. Kelly,*[44] in which the court concluded that the due process clause required that recipients of Aid to Families with Dependent Children (AFDC) be afforded an evidentiary hearing, though not a full trial in the traditional sense, prior to termination of their benefits. New York and other states had employed a procedure by which the claimants could object to termination, but would not actually receive a "fair hearing" before a state hearing officer until after termination. If the claimant succeeded at that hearing, back benefits would be paid.

Justice Brennan wrote for the seven-to-two majority in *Goldberg*. Justices Black and Burger dissented. Justice Brennan wrote: "Appellant does not contend that procedural due process is not applicable to the termination of welfare benefits. Such benefits are a matter of statutory entitlement for persons qualified to receive them."[45] Brennan then made reference to a significant footnote:

It may be realistic today to regard welfare entitlements as more like "property" than a "gratuity." Much of the existing wealth in this country takes the form of rights that do not fall within traditional common-law concepts of property. It has been aptly noted that "[s]ociety today is built around entitlement. The automobile dealer has his franchise, the doctor and lawyer their professional licenses, the worker his union membership, contract, and pension rights, the executive his contract and stock options: all are devices to aid security and independence. Many of the most important of these entitlements flow from government: subsidies to farmers and businessmen, routes for airlines and channels for television stations; long term contracts for defense, space, and education; social security pensions for individuals. Such sources of security, whether private or public, are no longer regarded as luxuries or gratuities; to the recipients they are essentials, fully deserved, and in no sense a form of charity. It is only the poor whose entitlements, although recognized by public policy, have not been effectively enforced." Reich, "Individual Rights and Social Welfare: The Emerging Legal Issues," 74 *Yale L.J.* 1245, 1255 (1965). See also Reich, "The New Property," 73 *Yale L.J.* 733 (1964).[46]

The majority opinion continued as follows:

Their [benefit payments] termination involves state action that adjudicates important rights. The constitutional challenge cannot be answered by an argument that public assistance benefits are "a privilege and not a right." *Shapiro v. Thompson,* 394 U.S. 618.[47]

Brennan observed that qualified recipients were in no position to fight a post-termination proceeding. "Since he lacks independent resources, his situation becomes immediately desperate. His need to concentrate upon finding the means for daily subsistence, in turn, adversely affects his ability to seek redress from the welfare bureaucracy."[48]

The government argued that administrative due process is a flexible concept that should not be read to require the increased administrative burden and financial costs involved, which outweighed, in its view, possible injury to claimants. Brennan rejected that notion. "Thus, the interest of the eligible recipient in uninterrupted receipt of public assistance, coupled with the State's interest that his payments not be erroneously terminated, clearly outweighs the State's competing concern to prevent any increase in its fiscal and administrative burdens."[49] Brennan's due process calculation was not a simple balance. He discussed the role of the constitutional principle at stake as well as the societal interest in fair administration of public policy.

The majority opinion, however, did not read the concept of "welfare" or social benefit narrowly. Neither did it limit the requirement of pretermination hearing to AFDC. A companion case to *Goldberg, Wheeler v. Montgomery,*[50] indicated that the Court did not intend to have its opinion read so narrowly. The case involved a challenge to old-age benefits procedures, which required some notice and related procedures prior to termination. The Court struck the decision as violative of due process under *Goldberg* since "the procedure does not, however, afford the recipient an evidentiary hearing at which he may appear and offer oral evidence and confront and cross-examine witnesses against him."[51]

Following the *Goldberg* decision, the right to a hearing before adverse action was recognized in parole revocation (*Morrissey v. Brewer*[52]), in probation revocation (*Gagnon v. Scarpelli*[53]), in prison disciplinary procedures (*Wolff v. McDonnel*[54]), in suspension of driver's licenses (*Bell v. Burson*[55]), in opportunity to demonstrate bona fides as a state resident for tuition purposes (*Vlandis v. Kline*[56]), in suspension from secondary school for more than ten days (*Goss v. Lopez*[57]), in various forms of attachment of goods or bank accounts (*Fuentes v. Shevin*[58]), and in removal without hearing from public housing projects (*Caulder v. Durham*[59]).

Richardson v. Wright: One Direct Challenge Avoided

Of course, by the time of the *Goldberg* ruling, Eldridge was well into the second round of his contest with the Social Security Administration. A number of other disability recipients who were in predicaments similar to Eldridge's launched litigation aimed at obtaining a clear application by the Supreme Court of *Goldberg* to the disability program.[60]

The Court noted probable jurisdiction in *Richardson v. Wright*.[61] But while that case was pending, HEW issued new regulations for termination that were only slightly different from the existing procedures. The justices vacated the lower court judgment and remanded the case for consideration in light of the new rules. It was clearly an attempt by HEW to avoid a ruling, and it worked.[62] Justice Brennan, author of the *Goldberg* decision, filed a dissent for himself and justice Marshall in the *Richardson* case that asserted that the same maneuver had been attempted unsuccessfully in *Goldberg*. In his view, *Goldberg* was clearly applicable and the delay in declaring that fact would only cause hardship for wrongfully terminated claimants.

THE DISTRICT COURT ACTS

It was against this developing body of law on administrative due process that Judge Turk of the District Court for the Western District of Virginia dealt with the case of *Eldridge v. Weinberger*.[63] In addition to an obvious facility with the due process cases, Judge Turk's opinion in Eldridge indicated a familiarity with the stages and problems of disability decisionmaking.

Judge Turk and the Due Process Cases

Given the location in which Judge Turk sits and his reference to Haviland and Glomb's study, "The Disability Insurance Program and Low Income Claimants in Appalachia,"[64] it is also clear that Judge Turk understood the particular problems faced by people like Eldridge in proving their disability.[65] The comments of administrative law judges and experienced attorneys indicate that the special difficulties in shouldering the requisite burden of proof are what make the availability of hearings a significant issue.[66]

Haviland and Glomb, who had studied a series of cases drawn from a sample over time of their practice in disability claims in Appalachia, argued as follows:

> The hypothesis of this article is that the Disability Insurance Benefits program is not geared to the pattern of cases described herein and, accordingly, will not work well for a predictably significant group of claimants throughout the nation who suffer from chronic diseases or injuries of a non-traumatic nature. Rather, the program is geared to the more middle-class claimant who has worked on a regular basis all of his life until some traumatic event robbed him of his ability to work. This person would usually have little difficulty with the medical evidence requirement in establishing that he is suffering from a physical or mental impairment— this could be documented by the trauma itself and his subsequent medical treatment for that trauma.

Since the onset of his disability can be pin-pointed, he will have very little difficulty with the current insurance requirement. The pre-existing skills and residual capacity for retraining of our hypothetical middle-class worker make him more suited for rehabilitation for jobs which actually exist in the "national economy." For the middle class worker, the "national employability tests" may be a realistic standard of employment, but for the type of person described in this study, it is not a realistic test, since his age, existing skills, and lack of trainability severely limit the likelihood of his rehabilitation.

The hypothesis, that the persons studied herein do not fit the programmed image of the Disability Insurance Benefit program, should alert the advocate to the fact that in presenting the cases of claimants who fit into the factual pattern discussed they will be "swimming against the current" of the programmed image.[67]

Some explanation is needed to indicate why there might be difficulty in proving disability.

"The idea of the disability benefit program is simple. If a worker or one of his surviving dependents, who normally would not qualify for social security benefits until achieving retirement age, becomes disabled, he may begin to receive his retirement benefits at once and need not wait until retirement age is reached."[68] But it may not be as simple as it sounds. An experienced administrative law judge explains:

The most common misconceptions of entitlement for disability benefits are the following: the claimant paid into the Society Security fund for many years, and he is, therefore, entitled to his money; the claimant has been found disabled by some other unit of government, i.e., the Veterans' Administration or state compensation board and he is, therefore, automatically entitled to benefits; and the claimant has an attending physician's medical report that confirms the disability. Of course, the opinions of attending physicians cannot be ignored, but such conclusions are valid only if they are supported by objective medical findings and if the physician follows the specific definition of disability in the Social Security Act. Usually, when doctors identify a patient as "disabled," they mean that the patient is unable to perform his regular job.[69]

The first problem for the claimant is to prove that he is eligible to receive benefits in terms of timing. That is, he must show that he was insured at the time that the disability began. Specifically, he must show that he had been insured for twenty quarters out of the forty quarters prior to the beginning of his injury, roughly five out of the previous ten years. If the injury was a traumatic accident such as an on-the-job incident, the beginning of the disability is easy to determine and prove. If, on the other hand, one is dealing with something like chronic serious arthritis or progressive lung disorders, it may be nearly impossible to pinpoint precisely the onset of the disease. Assuming that one can make such a showing, the next problem is to show eligibility at that time. In a number of cases cited by Haviland and Glomb, proving insured status is difficult because unskilled or semi-skilled workers often worked in marginal operations that did not maintain adequate records.

The second problem is proving total disability. The Social Security Disability program is an all-or-nothing arrangement that covers only total disability as demonstrated by medical evidence. That requirement contains two different adjudicatory problems. (1) What is meant by total disability? (2) What type and level of proof is needed?

The regulations defining the methods of proving disability under section 223 (d) (1) provide two basic methods of proof. The first method provides for proof of disability by medical evidence showing the existence of certain specified pathologies which is apparently presumed to be disabling without any actual showing that the pathology has any relationship to the claimed inability to work. The second method provides that the claimant must prove that a physical condition, regardless of the severity of the condition as contrasted to section 1502 (a), in fact prevents him from functioning in jobs theoretically available to him in the national economy.

The claimant's burden of producing the medical evidence required by either method of proof of disability is usually met by the submission of written reports signed by licensed physician reflecting an examination and a course of treatment.[70]

The specific pathologies are frequently dealt with in terms of a list of disabling conditions provided in the regulations. The burden of proof for showing such disability and for demonstrating its continued existence, should the claimant be placed on the program, rests with the claimant. Additionally, in cases where chronic disorders in skeletal conditions or cardiovascular systems are complicated by age and long exposure to chemicals and the like, the evidence needed may be exceedingly hard to gather. Simple laboratory tests may not detect or properly portray the actual condition of the claimant. Beyond that, a number of the tests are not absolutely reliable because they may be improperly administered or because they test for specific disorders rather than the synergistic effects of more than one medical malady.[71]

Finally, assuming that one can develop a complete set of medical evidence and the necessary data proving the eligibility of the claimant at the time of the onset of the disabling injury or disease, the problem of the national employability standard must be dealt with.

Proof of disability under the functional method of 1502 (b) requires proof not only that the claimant's impairment precludes him from engaging in his "previous employment" or any equivalent employment, but also that he cannot, "considering his age, educational, and work experience, engage in any other kind of substantial gainful work which exists in the national economy, regardless of whether such work exists in the immediate area in which he lives, or whether a specific job vacancy exists for him or whether he would be hired if he applied for work."[72]

In short, the determination of eligibility and disability is a complex fact-finding process involving data on medical diagnoses and treatment, vocational possibilities, and legal interpretation. The evidence submitted in the form of medical reports does not necessarily speak for itself. In fact, studies of the hearing process have found that a major aspect of the hearing examiner's task is to complete the often inadequate record that gets through the initial and reconsideration stages to the hearing stage.[73] Most claimants, particularly those who are poorly educated and lack independent financial means, do not have attorneys to aid them in preparing and asserting their claims.[74] Finally, there are complex problems of proof in cases where, like the one in which Eldridge was a claimant, the person seeking benefits is an older, unskilled, poorly educated person who suffers from nontraumatic interacting diseases rather than a traumatic injury.

The Decision and the Court of Appeals Affirmance

On April 9, 1973, Judge Turk announced his decision in favor of Eldridge, holding specifically that *Goldberg v. Kelly* and other related cases clearly mandated that the government provide a pretermination hearing for those receiving disability benefits under Title II of the Social Security Act, just as the Supreme Court had required pretermination hearings for those receiving benefits under Title I, old age survivors benefits (*Wheeler v. Montgomery*), and under Title IV, Aid to Families with Dependent Children (*Goldberg v. Kelly*).[75]

The government argued that recipients of Title II benefits are to be distinguished from those involved in programs under the other titles. In particular, those receiving benefits under AFDC are by definition destitute, while benefit claimants under the disability program are not made eligible for the program by proof of poverty. Beyond that, the federal government attorneys argued, the nature of the evidence and the kind of questions dealt with in a disability case are unlike those at issue in a welfare termination hearing. In the latter case, there might be hearsay and possibly even rumors involved, which require complex fact-finding processes to sort out and verify. Disability claims, on the other hand, are decided on the basis of scientific evidence submitted by doctors and vocational experts. The evidence in the disability cases is, in legal terms, more accurate and proba-tive than some of the material presented in welfare cases. Finally, the government attorneys con-tended that a decision in favor of Eldridge would result in an intolerable financial and administrative burden on the federal government because of the funds required to provide the increased number of hearings and the likely increases and continued benefit costs for ineligible recipients who would continue to receive benefits while their cases dragged through the hearing process. Certainly, they said, such a burden is not justified to provide a relatively minor increase in the accuracy of the fact-finding process beyond the existing procedural protections available to clai-mants. After all, those who lost payments, but later succeeded with their claims in a hearing would be entitled to receive back benefits.

Judge Turk rejected each of these contentions. From a doctrinal viewpoint, he found that the cases in the area of administrative due process clearly required a hearing before termination.[76] As for government claims about administrative overload, he observed that the Supreme Court had specifi-cally rejected the increased costs and administrative burdens argument in both *Goldberg* and *Wheeler.* Moreover, he observed that the experience under *Goldberg* requirements had not produced any evi-dence of the anticipated administrative and financial overburden.

Judge Turk began by noting that it seemed strange to assert that it is constitutionally necessary to provide hearings in cases of Titles I and IV of a statute while rejecting the same requirement from Title II of that law. He recited the holding of *Goldberg* and its companion case, *Wheeler v. Montgomery.* He also noted that a case regarding the application of the prehearing requirement to disability clai-mants had been taken to the Supreme Court, in *Wright v. Richardson.*[77] While the *Wright* case was en route to the Court, the Social Security Administration added a requirement to its termination regulations that required the agency to notify the claimant of the reasons for termination and permit the claimant to submit within ten days additional written information relating to his claim. The Court remanded the case for reconsideration in light of the new regulations. Justices Brennan, Douglas, and Marshall would have decided the case at that time and in favor of the application of Goldberg evidentiary hearing rule.[78]

Following these more or less introductory remarks, Judge Turk moved to the core of his opin-ion. He began by recognizing the fact that procedural due process is a somewhat flexible concept.

> In deciding whether the requirements of due process have been satisfied in this case, it is important first to recognize that due process safeguards vary with the rights sought to be protected. In *Cafeteria Workers v. McElroy,* 367 U.S. 886, 895 . . . the Supreme Court stated:
>
>> "The very nature of due process negates any concept of inflexible procedures universally applicable to every imaginable situation . . . what procedures due process may require under any given set of circumstances must begin with a determination of the precise nature of the government function involved as well as of the private interest that has been affected by government action."

The court in *Goldberg* presented the issue in a similar manner as follows:

> "The extent to which procedural due process must be afforded to the recipient is influenced by the extent to which he may be 'condemned to suffer grievous loss.' *Joint Anti-Fascist Refugee Committee v. McGrath,* 341 U.S. 123, 168 (1951) (Frankfurter, J., concurring), and depends upon whether the recipient's interest in avoiding that loss outweighs the governmental interest in summary adjudication. 397 U.S. 254 at 262263 (1970)."[79]

The government's attempt to draw a distinction between the "grievous loss" to be suffered by the welfare recipient and the problems faced by the disability claimant "is not persuasive for purposes of due process."[80]

> Although disability beneficiaries are not by definition dependent on benefit payments for their livelihood, they are by definition unable to engage in substantial gainful activity, and to cut off

payments erroneously may create a loss as "grievous" as that which concerned the Supreme Court in the cases of welfare and old age beneficiaries.[81]

But, argued Judge Turk, this decision does not hinge alone on the narrow issue of the similarity of welfare recipients and disability claimants. The due process question is more basic than that, and the answer to it requires an examination of these more fundamental concerns.

Turk's consideration then turned to a demonstration of the fact that the Supreme Court had clearly applied a prior hearing requirement to diverse cases of government decisions respecting individuals in which the loss would quite plainly be "less grievous" than that suffered by George Eldridge and others like him. He focused on *Sniadach v. Family Finance Corporation,*[82] *Bell v. Burson,*[83] and *Fuentes v. Shevin.*[84] These cases were decided both before and after the *Goldberg v. Kelly* decision. In *Sniadach,* the Supreme Court had struck down as violative of due process a Wisconsin wage garnishment statute that permitted creditors to "freeze of the wages due an employee without notice or a prior hearing."[85] In *Fuentes,* the Court voided Florida and Pennsylvania repossession laws that did not provide prior due process safeguards. Finally, the Court in *Bell v. Burson* struck down a Georgia law that contained an irrebuttable presumption. While the Reverend Bell was having Sunday dinner with parishioners of his circuit ministry, his parked car was struck by a young girl who rode her bicycle into the car. The law, based on insurance requirements, would have resulted in the revocation of Bell's license or posting of a bond, neither of which the minister could afford. The statute held that since he was uninsured he was presumed to have been at fault. He argued, and the Supreme Court concurred, that to deprive him of his license without a prior hearing to prove that he could not possibly be found liable was a violation of due process.

Turk concluded that these cases rejected the government's insistence on a narrow meaning of procedural due process.

> In *Fuentes* it was argued that Sniadach and Goldberg should be narrowly read as limited to cases involving absolute necessities. In rejecting a narrow reading of those cases the court states:
>
>> "Both decisions were in the mainstream of past cases, having little or nothing to do with the absolute 'necessities' of life but establishing that due process requires an opportunity for a hearing before a deprivation of property takes effect.... While Sniadach and Goldberg emphasized the special importance of wages and welfare benefits, they did not convert that emphasis into a new and more limited constitutional doctrine."
>>
>> "Nor did they carve out a rule of 'necessity' for the sort of nonfinal deprivations of property that they involved. 407 U.S. at 88."
>
> The court in *Fuentes* also made reference to the case of *Bell v. Burson,* ... in which the court had held that there must be an opportunity for a hearing on the issue of fault before the license of an uninsured motorist could be suspended. The court in *Fuentes* noted that the driver's license involved in *Bell* did not rise to the level of a "necessity" as in the cases of wages or welfare benefits but was nevertheless an important interest entitled to the protection of procedural due process. From the above cases it is thus apparent that *Goldberg* is not distinguishable from the case at bar in terms of the criterion for benefits.[86]

Having disposed of the need for a hearing argument, Turk turned to the two remaining government contentions on the nature of evidence in disability claims and the burden on government resources.

The government contention that the evidence involved in disability cases is easily understood and well suited to a clear interpretation is, according to Turk, incorrect. First, the facts of the *Eldridge* case refute such a simplistic assumption. On several occasions Eldridge's paper record had been reviewed and reconsidered with a decision against his claim. Yet on each occasion where his case was heard before a hearing examiner, the decision was in his favor.

Second, disability evidentiary problems fall within the *Goldberg v. Kelly* ruling:

> It is true that the court in *Goldberg* stated that "[p]articularly where credibility and veracity are at issue, as they must be in many termination proceedings, written submissions are a wholly unsatisfactory basis for decision. . . ." But the court also characterized the pretermination hearing as important "where recipients have challenged proposed terminations as resting on incorrect or misleading factual premises or on the misapplication of rules or policies to the facts of particular cases." . . . There is no doubt that medical evidence may be conflicting, *Richardson v. Perales,* 402 U.S. 389 (1971), and the Secretary must exercise judgment in resolving the conflicting medical evidence, 20 C.F.R. 404.1526. Thus there will be a resolution of factual issues in disability cases, and the exercise of subjective judgement to resolve conflicting evidence of a factual nature makes the value of a hearing self-evident. But in addition, it is noteworthy that determinations of total disability are not exclusively a function of medical evidence. The four elements of proof required for the establishment of a disability claim were set forth in *Underwood v. Ribicoff,* 298 F.2d 850, 851 (4th Cir. 1962) as follows:
>
> (1) the objective medical facts . . . ,
> (2) the diagnosis . . . of . . . treating and examining physicians on subsidiary questions of fact,
> (3) the subjective evidence of pain and disability testified to by Claimant, and corroborated by his wife and . . . neighbors, [and]
> (4) claimant's educational background, work history, and present age.
>
> There is no requirement that a disability under the Social Security Act be proven by "objective" medical evidence. *Flake v. Gardner,* 399 F.2d 532, 540 (9th Cir. 1968); *Whitt v. Gardner,* 389 F.2d 906, 909 (6th Cir. 1968). The testimony of the claimant or witnesses in his behalf may be crucial in establishing a disability. See *Page v. Celebreeze,* 311 F.2d 757 (5th Cir. 1963).[87]

Finally, even if the evidence were clearer, the right to due process protections prior to deprivation of liberty or property interests is not dependent on the fact that the claimant is likely to win the case.

In response to the contention that defendants could repossess goods without first affording plaintiffs a Hearing in the case of a default in payments on a conditional sales contract, the court [in *Fuentes*] stated:

> "The right to be heard does not depend on an advance showing that **one** will surely prevail at the hearing. To one who protests against the taking of his property without due process of law, it is no answer to say that in his particular case due process of law would have led to the same result because he had no adequate defense on the merits." *Coe v. Armour Fertilizer Works* . . . . It is enough to invoke the procedural safeguards of the Fourteenth Amendment that a significant property interest is at stake. . . ."

The Court also stated:

> "The issues decisive of the ultimate right of continued possession, of course, may be quite simple. The simplicity of the issues might be relevant to the formality or scheduling of a prior hearing." See *Lindsey v. Normet.* . . . But it certainly cannot undercut the right to a prior hearing of some kind.[88]

The arguments concerning the catastrophic impact of a pretermination hearing requirement were presented, said Turk, in almost exactly the same terms in *Goldberg,* in which the Supreme Court responded that the right to due process was not to be forfeited to possible increases in administrative inconvenience. Beyond that, Justice Brennan, writing for the *Goldberg* court, indicated that the rearranging of existing agency procedures could result in a substantial savings.[89]

The government advanced the same argument in *Richardson v. Wright*. Brennan wrote for the dissenters in *Richardson*, arguing that the figures advanced by HEW were inflated and misleading. Judge Turk summarized Brennan's critique.

> He there noted that the Secretary had assumed that all beneficiaries will demand a prior hearing. The Secretary's own figures show that of the 39,078 cases in which determinations of cessation of disability were rendered in 1972 only 2,801 post-termination hearings were held. It is certainly likely that even a smaller percentage of disability beneficiaries would demand pre-termination hearings due to the fact that the new regulations provide for notice and an opportunity to respond in writing before termination.
>
> Justice Brennan also noted that the Secretary assumes that all of those demanding hearings will lose, and that the Secretary will be unable to recover any of the benefits paid to the beneficiaries pending the hearing. Both of these assumptions are unwarranted. Not only do a substantial number of persons demanding a hearing prevail, but the Secretary is directed to require a refund from the beneficiary or decrease future benefits in the case of an overpayment. 20 C.F.R. 404.501-404.502. The Secretary also assumes that a pretermination hearing would entail a two-month delay in the termination of disability benefits. But under current procedures benefits are paid for two months after a disability ceases, and it is hard to believe that it would take an additional two months (four months after an initial determination that disability had ceased) to have a hearings.[90]

Turk concluded by indicating that procedural due process does not exist to minimize costs and maximize administrative efficiency.

> What the Supreme Court said in a related area is worth repeating here in light of the Secretary's argument.
>
> A prior hearing always imposes some costs in time, effort, and expense, and it is often more efficient to dispense with the opportunity for such a hearing. But these rather ordinary costs cannot outweigh the constitutional right. See *Bell v. Burson,* supra 402 U.S. at 540541 . . .; *Goldberg v. Kelly,* supra 397 U.S. at 261. . . . Procedural due process is not intended to promote efficiency or accommodate all possible interests; it is intended to protect the particular interests of the person whose possessions are about to be taken.
>
> The establishment of prompt efficacious procedures to achieve legitimate state ends is a proper state interest worthy of cognizance in constitutional adjudication. But the Constitution recognizes higher values than speed and efficiency. Indeed, one might fairly say of the Bill of Rights in general, and the Due Process Clause in particular, that they were designed to protect the fragile values of a vulnerable citizenry from the overbearing concern for efficiency and efficacy that may characterize praiseworthy government officials no less, and perhaps more, than mediocre ones." *Stanley v. Illinois,* 405 U.S. 645, 656 . . . *Fuentes v. Shevin.* . . .
>
> In *Bell v. Burson,* . . . the court rejected the argument that the additional cost of an expanded hearing was sufficient to forego a hearing as to fault prior to the revocation of a drivers license. The court there stated:
>
> > "[I]t is fundamental that except in emergency situations (and this is not one) due process requires that when a State seeks to terminate an interest such as that here involved, it must afford 'notice and opportunity for hearing appropriate to the nature of the case before the termination becomes effective. . . .' "
>
> In *Fuentes,* supra . . . , the court stated:
>
> > "There are extraordinary situations that justify postponing notice and opportunity for a hearing. . . . These situations, however, must be truly unusual. Only in a few limited situations has this Court allowed outright seizure without opportunity for a prior hearing."[91]

The government promptly appealed Judge Turk's decision to the U.S. Circuit Court of Appeals for the Fourth Circuit. The case came on for hearing nearly a year after the district court ruling in February 1974. The appeals court affirmed that ruling in a *per curiam* opinion (an unsigned opinion for the court) on April 1, 1974. The terse opinion merely held that the affirmance was predicated on the opinion as presented by Judge Turk. Again the government appealed, this time to the U.S. Supreme Court.

POLICY CRISIS: LAW AND THE POLICY PROCESS

Judge Turk's decision in the *Eldridge* case was a shock to the Social Security policy system. It was not the only such challenge to the existing pattern of administration, but it was a significant one. It was all the more important because it came at a time when the Social Security Administration was facing a number of serious problems, many of which were related to the disability program.

Shocking the System

The *Eldridge* case was a shock because it meant that the policy system that operated the disability program would be forced from its routine, if problematic, day-to-day administrative mode into a more active phase of the policy process. The Social Security Administration had begun life with responsibility only for the Old Age and Survivor's Insurance program. That responsibility was significantly expanded with the creation of the Disability Program as part of Title II of the Social Security Act.[92]

A problem had been recognized as early as the 1940s. Clearly, there were a number of people who, to use the bureaucratic parlance, fell between the cracks in existing social insurance policies. Some could not qualify for retirement benefits because of age. Others could not be retrained because they were completely disabled. These people were not covered by private plans, because many of them were unskilled or semiskilled workers whose previous work experiences had not included major benefit packages. Finally, they were not covered by unemployment compensation programs of other types.

A policy was formulated. With a recognition by the government that disability insurance programs are the most difficult of all such plans to administer, and with an understanding of the ideological and emotional concerns over the status of this program as welfare or as social insurance, the plan was drafted.[93] The policy intentionally set up a complex intergovernmental mechanism for administering the program through the use of state vocational rehabilitation agencies. The purpose, of course, was to identify those who were in a position to benefit from rehabilitation and to get them into the system for treatment. Additionally, since the program was designed to be a total disability program as opposed to an unemployment compensation plan, the state agencies would provide expert vocational counselors to evaluate claimants with regard to the entire spectrum of possible employment, rather than from a concern for whether the claimant was able to return to his or her previous area of employment.

Congress adopted the policy as part of Title II of the Social Security Act. Amendments were added in 1967 to maintain the program as a total disability program rather than permitting it to lean toward an unemployment compensation activity.[94]

The plan was implemented and has been extremely active, processing more than 1.2 million claims in 1974 alone. The Bureau of Disability Insurance and the Bureau of Hearings and Appeals grew. The SSA developed a reputation for self-examination and evaluation.[95] It contracted for several major evaluation projects conducted by independent researchers.[96]

Still, the agency had settled into a more or less routine mode of operation until the 1970s. Then things began to deteriorate. The black lung and SSI programs were implemented without additional staff. Delays increased, congressional concern over problems of administration grew, hearing demands increased, and the reversal rate at the hearing stage exceeded 50 percent.[97] Not only were these problems serious, they promised to worsen. The number of cases appealed from the agency to the federal district courts increased significantly. What is perhaps more significant is the fact that the government was losing a major portion of the cases taken to the federal courts. It faced not only losses through individual claims, but also significant challenges to the entire administrative mechanism used to manage the disability system. It became clear that the Social Security Administration would have to take a hard look at its program with a view toward implementation of the many suggestions and, in some cases, mandates given with regard to the disability program. Insider and critic alike could agree on at least two things: (1) the program was serving a vital need for many people; and (2) there were major weaknesses in the program that were inherent in programs of this type, regardless of the effectiveness of the administrative efforts focused on the program.

There is a temptation to look at cases like Mr. Eldridge's with great sympathy for the claimant and a predictable indignation about the individual hardship inflicted by what appears to be an uncaring bureaucracy. Unfortunately, such reaction is myopic since it ignores the many pressures that affect an agency, especially a social service agency that has a tremendous responsibility in times of economic difficulty in the national economy. Let us examine briefly a few of the more significant shocks to the administrative system of the Social Security disability program during the time that Eldridge's case was winding its way to a decision in the Supreme Court. In particular, the agency was concerned by an increased procedural caseload, a high reversal rate at the hearing stage, increasing appeals of agency decisions to federal courts, along with a corresponding increase in agency losses in those judicial challenges, a recognition of weaknesses in the existing Social Security disability program appeals process, and the growing awareness of the impact of intergovernmental relations on the administration of the program.

Growing Caseload

The problem that administrators saw was the growing caseload coming from state agencies for hearing. As the caseload grew, so did the length of time necessary to process cases.

> The reasons for this increase in median processing time are not difficult to identify: 52,000 hearing requests were received in 1971; 155,000 hearing requests were received in 1975, and while the work load increased 300 percent, personnel (presiding officers and supporting staff) increased by only 200 percent. Unless dramatic increases in efficiency were achieved, increases in processing times and backlogs were certain to develop.
>
> Constant consideration has been given to increasing the productivity of each presiding officer. As a consequence, average case dispositions per year were up from 227 per experienced ALJ (administrative law judge) in 1975 to 302 per ALJ in 1976. With hearing requests holding relatively constant, the backlog of pending cases plummeted from 111,000 to 90,000 in 1976 alone.[98]

An examination of case flow in one year in the mid-1970s illustrates the magnitude of the problem. In calendar 1974 1,250,400 initial claims for disability were made and processed in the state agencies of which 60 percent were disallowed. Of that 60 percent, 29 percent, or 215,000 cases, were dealt with on reconsideration in the state agencies with 69 percent disallowed. Of that 69 percent, 35 percent were taken to hearing stage. Administrative law judges, at the federal level, delivered 51,900 decisions of which approximately 51 percent were disallowed. About half of those cases disapproved at hearing stage were taken for an administrative appeal to the Social Security Appeals Council. Of these 13,300 decisions, 86 percent were against the claimant. Finally, roughly 2,500 of the denials by the Appeals Council were taken to judicial review in federal district courts where some 28 percent were allowed.[99]

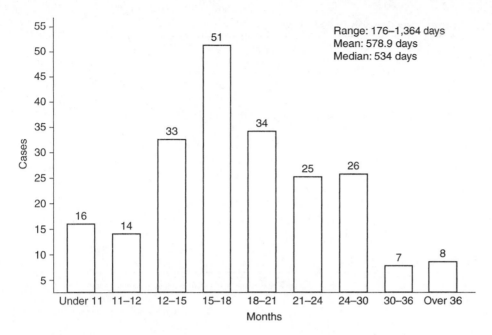

FIGURE 1.1 214 Cases: Time from the Date an Application was filed to the Date of Award Notice[100]

One of the significant aspects of this caseload is the length of time needed by a claimant to get through the various levels of administrative process to a hearing and eventually to a final award decision by the Bureau of Disability of the SSA. Figure 1.1 shows the time 214 cases took, from date of application for benefits to award, from a study done by the staff of the Social Security Subcommittee of the House Ways and Means Committee, published just a month before Eldridge's case went to oral argument before the Supreme Court.

These time figures must be understood in light of the case load figures. Table 1.1 presents the hearing demand on the agency.

TABLE 1.1 Requests for Hearing: Receipts, Processed, and Pending.[101]

Fiscal Year	Receipts	Processed	Pending
1970	42,573	38,480	13,747
1971	52,427	45,301	20,873
1972	103,691	61,030	63,534
1973	72,202	68,356[a]	36,780
1974	121,504	80,783[b]	72,233
1975	154,945	121,009	111,169

[a]Excludes 30,000 black lung cases transferred back to BDI.
[b]Excludes 268 black lung cases transferred back to BDI.

TABLE 1.2 End-of-Year Growth in Pending Cases[102]

Calendar Year	Total Social Security Cases	Disability Cases
1960	337	
1968	1,751	1,307
1969	2,370	1,748
1970	2,769	2,001
1971	3,148	2,251
1972	3,775	2,676
1973	4,033	3,018
1974 (June 17)	5,092[a]	4,187
1974	6,191[a]	4,301
1975 (August 31)	9,226[a]	4,723

[a]Including black lung cases. On June 17, 1974, 384 black lung cases were pending; 1,200 were pending on January 1, 1975, and 3,338 were pending on August 31, 1975.

Reversals at Hearing

Not only were there more hearings, but the rate of decisions in those hearings, contrary to the initial findings of the state agencies, increased rather dramatically. In 1960, the rate of reversals at hearings was approximately 30 percent. This figure increased to roughly 39 percent by 1966. By 1974, however, the rate was approximately 50 percent reversal.

A number of reasons were advanced to explain the high rate of reversal. For example, it was suggested that only those with borderline cases took cases to appeal, meaning that it is not unlikely that borderline cases would have an approximately equal chance for success on appeal.[103] However, that does not account for the dramatic increase in the rate of reversal. Critics suggested that there were other reasons, one of which was that many meritorious claims could only be satisfactorily resolved by a face-to-face meeting between government officials and the claimant.[104]

Increasing Losses

In addition to having more proceedings that resulted in reversals in administrative hearings, the Social Security Administration noticed a significant increase in the number of cases being taken to federal district courts on appeal. Table 1.2 gives an indication of the magnitude of the problem. The extent of the caseload in the federal courts can be understood in some measure by reference to the fact that, for example, in August 1975 the office of legal counsel prepared 502 briefs for Social Security and black lung cases.[105] Roughly 75 to 80 percent of the total Social Security caseload is made up of disability cases.[106]

Another problem was that the court activity was unevenly distributed across the nation, suggesting some difficulty with the manner in which the program was administered in certain locations.[107]

More claimants seem to apply for benefits and to appeal denials with more frequency in certain parts of the country than in others. For instance of the 2,595 pending social security cases at the end of fiscal 1973, 887 (34 percent) [arose in]

Puerto Rico	252
South Carolina	182
West Virginia-Southern	111
Kentucky-Eastern	297

The jurisdictions noted account for considerably less than 10 percent of the disabled workers receiving benefits, even though they have an extremely high incidence of disability to the national average.

In terms of court workload by circuit the same disparity existed. The fourth and fifth circuits have had 47 percent of all the disability court cases. The fourth, fifth, and sixth circuits taken together have had 69 percent of the cases and they will be even harder hit when the black lung cases mature. On the other hand, New York and California which have roughly 20 percent of the disability caseload have had only 6 percent of the court cases. . . .

Obviously, the impact of the social security disability caseload on various courts in the country is uneven and, undoubtedly, will be of crisis proportions in certain judicial districts in the next few years. For instance, in the second and tenth circuits social security cases constituted only 1 percent of civil caseloads; but in the fourth circuit they made up 5 percent. In the District Court for Eastern Kentucky they were 22 percent of the civil caseload.[108]

This growing caseload in the courts, of course, is burdensome to the administration in that it requires time and personnel costs. But more had been at issue than numbers. There had been a growing qualitative difference in the manner in which the district courts addressed the cases coming to them from the Social Security Administration. As judges became more dissatisfied with agency decisionmaking in individual cases, their decisionmaking tended to range somewhat further than in former years. The reversal rate at the district court level reached nearly 30 percent during the time when Eldridge's case was winding its way through the federal courts. The courts were also dealing losses on substantial constitutional issues to the administration. The *Eldridge* case was one such loss.[109]

Criticism in the Literature

Literature generated during the early 1970s added insight to the problems already apparent to those in Social Security policy. Four generalizations emerged in articles and books during these years. First, most commentators in and out of government agreed that some form of oral hearing, whether or not a full evidentiary hearing, at which the claimant could appear and obtain full explanation of the agency ruling in his case, is needed.[110] Second, with the exception of one or two major authors, most writers agreed at least implicitly that the *Goldberg v. Kelly* pretermination fair hearing requirements would apply to disability claimants.[111] Third, they were nearly unanimous in concluding that the preparation of the record at the initial determination and reconsideration stages was in many cases inadequate.[112] Finally, they were virtually unanimous in concluding that the ones victimized by the weaknesses in the process and most severely affected by the existing decision structure of the disability program were the claimants, who were in no position to bear such burdens.[113]

Experiments were conducted to determine whether some form of early conference would improve the quality of decisionmaking. The results of the program were promising. Table 1.3 indicates some of the results.

Investigators and those in the agencies acknowledged that such a program would, if applied to all disability appeals, result in a higher rate of allowances of claims. On the other hand, it would probably mean a reduction in the number of hearing requests and ultimate reversals. In monetary terms, most observers felt that the program would still result in slightly higher costs. On the other hand, delays might be reduced.

Moreover, there was a general recognition that the claimants were much more satisfied if they were afforded a fair hearing even if it was not a formal trial-type proceeding. Unless they obtain a

TABLE 1.3 Results of SSA Hearing Experiment

	Interview Cases		Noninterview Cases	
	Number	*Percent*	*Number*	*Percent*
Denials changed to allowances	132	19.6	8	1.3
Denials upheld	539	–	576	–
Total number of denials	671	–	584	–
Requested hearing	214	39.7	241	41.8
Decision changed at hearing	46	22.2	73	37.2
Decision changed: total cases, reconsideration and hearing	178	26.0	81	14.0

SOURCE: Staff Report, "Background Material on Social Security Hearings and Appeals."[114]

hearing, claimants do not see the evidence that the agency has on hand when it makes its initial determination nor do they get more than a terse general statement in the agency termination letter explaining why they are no longer considered disabled.[115] Month after month they wait, with no more indication of their fate than an occasional form letter from either the state agency or the Baltimore office indicating the status of the claim as each milestone in the appeals process occurs.

There seemed to be little doubt in the minds of those writing on the subject that the *Goldberg* fair hearing requirement would be imposed on the Social Security disability program. That small amount of doubt rested on the likely impact of the changes in personnel on the Supreme Court rather than on the appropriate doctrinal evaluation.[116] There was, on the other hand, some question as to just how formal such a fair hearing must be. Just what kind of process was due was the central theme of a seminal article authored in 1975 by Judge Henry J. Friendly.[117] Judge Friendly was interested in the confusion surrounding the nature and extent of procedural due process required in administrative proceedings. Among other conclusions, Judge Friendly was concerned that the due process requirements had been extended too far and had cast administrative proceedings in an adversary model, which was not appropriate in some situations. The question before those considering changes in the Social Security process was whether such a change would pass constitutional muster. Most observers agreed that the Court's decision in the *Eldridge* case would be the key to those inquiries.[118]

At least among those who had studied the hearings process, there was a great deal of agreement that one of the reasons for the high rate of reversal of early decisions and for delays at the hearing stage was that the records sent up to the administrative law judge from the state agencies were woefully inadequate.[119] Consider the following story recounted by Representative B. F. Sisk of California.

> Another of my constituents, Miss F., had her disability claim twice denied before her doctors' reports were even obtained and reviewed. Her case appears to be a prime example of the many cases that are being denied without adequate review and then appealed. The backlog of cases awaiting hearings, according to many hearing judges with whom I've been in contact and as evidenced in the many complaints I receive from claimants, could be alleviated if claims were properly developed and reviewed at the initial and reconsideration stages of processing.
>
> Miss F., who is going blind from uncontrollable diabetes and who suffers from other diabetes complications, applied for disability benefits in November of 1974 at which time she

signed permission slips for Social Security officials to contact her physicians to obtain information about her condition. Her claim was denied in April of this year (1975) and she immediately requested reconsideration of the claim. She talked with her doctors and they advised her that they had not been contacted by the Social Security Administration at the time she received the first denial. Miss F.'s claim was denied again after reconsideration in May. Interestingly, at the time she was notified of the second denial, one of her doctors had just submitted his report two days before she received the denial notice and the other doctor had not yet submitted his report. In May she requested a hearing on the claim and she has not yet been notified [as of October] of the hearing date.

In this case, it appears to me, if Social Security personnel were not going to contact the physicians as indicated to the claimant when she signed the consent forms at the Social Security office, then she should have been instructed to submit the medical reports herself. At any rate, the obvious problem here is that this claim was never properly developed prior to the issuance of the initial and reconsideration decisions.[120]

This weakness in record preparation is a recurring theme that is especially highlighted in the writing of administrative law judges, who know that the record will have to be properly supplemented or it will surely be overturned on judicial review for lack of substantial evidence to support the administrative determination.[121]

Finally, observers of the Social Security system were very much concerned that, given the existing procedures, the claimants were forced to bear the costs of the weaknesses and inequities of the system since benefits were withheld or terminated pending the outcome of an excessively lengthy administrative process. "Understandably, the Social Security Administration, like all government agencies, has been under heavy pressure to cut costs. Unfortunately, this has happened at the expense of their program beneficiaries."[122] Representative Claude Pepper of Florida put it this way:

In *Goldberg* the Court recognized that: "Termination of aid pending resolution of a controversy over eligibility may deprive an eligible recipient of the very means to live while he waits. Since he lacks independent resources, his situation becomes immediately desperate." These same considerations that the *Goldberg* Court deemed so important in requiring the Government to continue making Uninterrupted payments until an evidentiary hearing has been held, are equally compelling in the case of disability applicants and should require that the Government provide an appeals process designed to resolve the claims of the applicants with reasonable promptness.[123]

After describing a particularly maddening case involving one of his constituents, Representative John Heinz III of Pennsylvania said: "Personally, I think that the Social Security Administration has treated Mr. S and his parents with the consideration that one would expect of George Orwell's Big Brother in his novel *1984,* and the rationality of the investigator in Kafka's *The Trial.* This case would truly make for theater of the absurd."[124] One case recounted by Congressman Sisk presented the problem in stark terms.

One of my constituents, Mr. H., a man terminally ill with cancer, filed his claim for disability benefits in December of 1973, and after having his claim denied at the initial and reconsideration levels, he requested a hearing on July 15, 1974. The claim was not scheduled for a hearing until February 21, 1975, 7 months later, and by that time my constituent was hospitalized for the last time.

The hearing decision reversed the two earlier denials, approving a period of disability for this man back to October of 1973. Unfortunately, however, the claimant died before benefit payments were made to him, and his poor widow suffered further frustration after the benefits which were due her late husband were erroneously issued to her in his name; and a delay of 4 months occurred before the proper payments were issued to the widow. The family had no other financial resources on which to depend during this time.[125]

The Intergovernmental Process

Given the description of the process for determining disability claims, it should be clear that the fact that both state and federal agencies are continuously interacting both in the administration of the Social Security Disability program and in decisions in specific claims is of major importance. Initially, Congress sought to involve state agencies in such a way that vocational rehabilitation organizations with existing connections with the medical community and an understanding of local needs would be the most effective mechanism for ensuring success of the program.[126] While the *Eldridge* case was en route to the court, that concept was facing substantial criticism from two different perspectives.

On the one hand, experienced state and federal administrators as well as members of Congress were greatly concerned about the inconsistency among various state agencies. An example of the disparity is found in the staff report done in 1975 for the Subcommittee on Social Security of the House Ways and Means Committee.

> The percent of reversals by the State agencies on reconsideration over the years have been relatively stable—between 30 and 40 percent. The variation in rates between State agencies—like that on initial determinations—was quite substantial in calendar 1974, varying from a low of 19.5 percent in Kentucky to 45.9 percent in New Jersey with a national average of 30.5.[127]

Marie Clark, supervisor of Disability Determination Services of Cheyenne, Wyoming, described the plight of the claimant in the following graphic terms: "I think the claims become involved in an incredible administrative ping-pong game when they are filed. They are kicked back and forth between State and Federal Offices until the claimants don't know where to go for help in pursuing their claims."[128]

Second, the intergovernmental significance of the process relates to the problems of administering a highly decentralized system without clear standards.[129] The original idea was to provide a basic insurance manual to the states and to supplement that document with letters until revisions of the basic manual could be prepared and distributed. Additionally, a series of precedents were to be developed that would focus on court decisions and rulings of the Appeals Council. Problems emerged because the precedents that were prepared had to be "sanitized" to ensure privacy for the claimants.[130] That meant that the cases were generalized beyond usefulness as precedents, and the idea soon faded.[131] During hearings in 1975, Congressmen Pickle of Texas and Steiger of Wisconsin questioned a panel of state directors of Disability Determination Services:

MR. PICKLE: Let me ask you, are the directives which come from the social security offices, regional or national, are they clear and concise, or is there confusion on the kind of federal instruction that you get?

MR. BROWN: The most recent one is a very good example of a very confused one. I have not been through it. Some of the staff have, and it is most difficult to decipher.
Interestingly enough, we got it the same day that our regional offices in Atlanta did. They had no more advance notice than we did, and the next day we had to implement it.

MR. GAUGHAN: Needless to say, some of us have not implemented it yet.

MR. PICKLE: Have you understood it yet?

MR. GAUGHAN: No, sir.

MR. PICKLE: Is this average or normal?

MRS. CLARK: Over the years, the instructions from BDI have been very good until the advent of the SSI program. When we got SSI instructions, there was confusion in the whole system due to a number of reasons, and this was reflected in the instructions.

MR. PICKLE: I am primarily talking about the advent of the SSI.

MRS. CLARK: All right. I think that lately we have noticed a strong effort by BDI to upgrade the DISM, to clarify instructions and to bring order, clarity and ease of reference into the manual.

MR. STEIGER: Hold on a minute, Jake! You talk about confusion. What is the "DISM"?

MRS. CLARK: It is the Disability Insurance State Model.

MR. STEIGER: All right. There also is a BDI, which I assume is the Bureau of Disability Insurance, and there is DIL. What is the DIL?

MR. SORENSON: Disability Insurance Letter.

MR. GAUGHAN: They put it out in letter form until they get the printing completed.

MR. STEIGER: I appreciate that clarification. That is DIL?

MR. PICKLE: I thought that was a pickle. [Laughter]

MR. STEIGER: Did I ever open myself up for that one![132]

The testimony of these and other state officials showed concern over the problems of information flow between their offices and the federal government. Particularly troublesome was the problem of inadequate lead time to implement new policy decisions emanating from the Bureau of Disability Insurance in Baltimore, which has overall federal responsibility for the program. The state officers also pointed out that while much of the discussion of the disability program has centered on the hearing process, approximately 96 percent of disability decisions are made in the state agencies by people who make less money than their federal counterparts and who have inadequate support staffs and training programs.[133]

In summer 1975, the Subcommittee on Social Security of the Ways and Means Committee published its "Staff Survey of State Disability Agencies Under Social Security and SSI Programs."[134] This document provided responses by all the state disability agencies to questions posed to the committee staff relating to the intergovernmental problems involved in the administration of the disability program and the Supplemental Security Income program. The responses reveal general dissatisfaction with communication, coordination, and training activities by the federal offices.[135] Many states called for outright federalization of the programs.[136] Half of the state agencies indicated that the reasons advanced by the Ways and Means Committee in 1954 for dividing the program administration among state and federal agencies no longer existed or were not being realized under the existing organization. Most of the states did, however, have positive comments about the work of the regional Social Security offices.

ELDRIDGE ON THE CONGRESSIONAL AGENDA

In April 1974, the Circuit Court of Appeals affirmed Eldridge's victory in the district court; the case would not be heard before the U.S. Supreme Court until October 1975. In the interim, Congress focused its attention on problems in the Social Security disability program. The forthcoming decision in the *Eldridge* case figured prominently in all its deliberations.

The Committee Staff Reports

The congressional activity took place mainly in the Social Security Subcommittee of the House Ways and Means Committee. Two factors were particularly noteworthy in connection with the committee's work. First, the subcommittee had a very thorough staff that provided clear and succinct background data on the particularly significant aspects of this policy problem. Second, Social Security problems hit home for each member of Congress because a large part of the case work done by members' staffs is related to chasing down claims for frightened or unhappy constituents.[137] The subcommittee, in turn, felt the pressure from colleagues from both houses of Congress and from both sides of the aisle to do something about the problems of administering the disability program.

Those involved were nearly unanimous in support of the role performed by the Social Security Disability Program and, in general, by the administrators involved in the program. Their concern was with improving the system in terms of both equity and cost effectiveness. The fact that these concepts are in some senses contradictory was a significant factor in the discussions.

The first signal of forthcoming congressional activity came with the publication in 1974 of the "Committee Report on the Disability Insurance Program," which has become known in the literature of the field as the "Staff Report." That report highlighted a number of significant problems in the program, and was reinforced when more than seventy members of Congress addressed letters to the Subcommittee on Social Security requesting that some action be taken to deal with the "appeals crisis" in Social Security in particular and with the delays in Social Security disability proceedings in general.

Social Security Subcommittee Hearings on the Appeals Crisis

In 1975, plans were made to conduct hearings in the fall before the subcommittee to deal with the problem of delays and other subjects. Meanwhile, at the Social Security Administration, Commissioner Caldwell was working to make what improvements he could.[138] He reported his efforts to the subcommittee staff in July of that year, just as the staff was preparing its important report, "Background Materials on Social Security Hearings and Appeals." This document summarized the hearings process, the problems noted earlier in the discussion of the policy area, impending significant decisions like the *Eldridge* case, which promised to seriously challenge the administration of the program, and a summary of data on problems of time delay and variance in decisionmaking among administrative law judges and state agencies. The report was prepared for the hearings scheduled in September and October.

Also published in summer 1975 was the "Staff Survey of State Disability Agencies Under Social Security and SSI Programs." This report highlighted the intergovernmental problems in the programs.[139]

Hearings were conducted by the subcommittee on September 19, 26, and October 3 and 20, 1975. Those called included several prominent scholars of Social Security law, the head of administrative law judge activities for the Civil Service Commission, a panel of state administrators, and a number of members of Congress who recited case after case of damage they attributed to the delays and inaccurate decisions that they felt harmed their constituents. The *Eldridge* case popped up in each of these panels and the statements submitted to support the testimony.

On Friday, October 3, just three days before the case was to be heard in the Supreme Court, John Rhinelander, former general counsel of HEW, appeared before the subcommittee along with Donald Gonya, deputy assistant general counsel for the Social Security Division, and Frank Dell Aqua, head of the Litigation Branch. Rhinelander led the testimony in which the *Eldridge* case was a focal point. He felt that the case was significant enough to submit into the hearing record all 140 pages of the briefs filed for the government and Eldridge.

The proceedings of the hearings were published in December while the *Eldridge* case was pending before the Court. The subcommittee also published another important document during December, "Recent Studies Relevant to the Disability Hearings and Appeals Crisis." This report contained the so-called Boyd Report of the Social Security Task Force on the Disability Claims Process, Edwin Yourman's "Report on a Study of Social Security Benefit Hearings, Appeals and Judicial Review," and Professor Victor Rosenblum's study, "The Administrative Law Judge in the Administrative Process: Interrelationships of Case Law with Statutory and Pragmatic Factors in Determining ALJ Roles."[140]

BEFORE THE BURGER COURT

It was within this complex political and administrative context that the *Eldridge* case came to the Supreme Court of the United States.

Preparations for the Judicial Confrontation

Of the thousands of cases brought to the Supreme Court every year, only a few will receive a full oral argument and result in a full signed opinion. Most of the cases that merit such treatment are almost by definition major questions of law and public policy. As such, the policy impact of a decision in this type of case is a matter of concern to the justices. On the other hand, the Court does operate under decision rules that are set by norms of constitutional interpretation, statutory interpretation, and *stare decisis* or common law principles. The *Eldridge* case was presented from two quite different perspectives. The government argued the case primarily—almost exclusively—as a public policy problem set in cost-benefit terms. Counsel for Eldridge argued the case as a constitutional claim based on a specific line of precedents, particularly *Goldberg v. Kelly* and associated rulings.

Mr. Eldridge was very surprised to learn that his case was being appealed by the government to the Supreme Court.

QUESTION: What did you think when you heard that the government was going to appeal your case to the Supreme Court of the United States?

ANSWER: Well, I thought that by them carrying it that far, that they was really out to try to beat me, because that was the first case that I'd ever heard of them taking to the Supreme Court.

QUESTION: How did you find out about that? Did Mr. Earls call you and tell you "Mr. Eldridge, we're going to have to go to the Supreme Court?" What did you think then?

ANSWER: Well, I thought that if they was going to spend money to carry it that far, that they were just out to finish it off. That's what I thought.

QUESTION: Did you ever understand why they were taking your case to the Supreme Court?

ANSWER: No, I didn't understand it. I knowed I couldn't work.

QUESTION: And you've never understood why the government, the Solicitor General, and the Supreme Court were tied up with your case?

ANSWER: No, I don't guess I ever will.[141]

Despite the fact that Mr. Earls explained the case to him, Eldridge just could not understand why this was happening.

QUESTION: All of this time, you felt that they were out to get you for winning—is that it?

ANSWER: Well, from the way they done me, I never knowed of them doing anybody else that way.

QUESTION: You mean you think because you won somebody got angry at you because you beat them? They just didn't care?

ANSWER: No, I've always thought that there was somebody in there that was handling my claim that really didn't understand the whole situation, or didn't care or something![142]

When the Supreme Court granted the writ of certiorari, Mr. Earls acquired some unanticipated assistance from attorneys for two different legal aid societies. David Webster from Atlanta Legal Aid Society and an attorney from California Rural Legal Assistance contacted Earls and volunteered their services to do research and help in preparing for the oral argument to come.

The Briefs

Earls and his colleagues were rather surprised by the tack taken by the government in their brief. In fact, he believed that the attorneys for the government had "missed the case."

The brief for the government was fifty-six pages in length with an appendix of sixty-seven pages. Only about five pages of this document were given to the constitutional doctrine of due process.

The statement of facts in the government's brief was somewhat deceptive, for it gave the impression that Eldridge had not really been reasonable and patient in his dealings with the government.

> Respondent, a resident of Virginia, applied for disability benefits under the Social Security Act, which were awarded by the Secretary, acting through the Social Security Administration, effective in June 1968. Respondent was informed that his claim would be reexamined due to the possibility of his medical recovery, and that his benefits would be terminated if the review demonstrated that he was no longer disabled.
>
> The Virginia state agency scheduled respondent's case for review in 1972 and in March 1972 sent him a questionnaire. The letter requested respondent to complete and return the questionnaire within ten days, and also informed him that if he required assistance or had any questions he could visit or telephone any Social Security office. . . .
>
> The state agency asked respondent to furnish within ten days any further evidence relating to the reasons it gave or to request further time to obtain such evidence. In response he disputed one characterization of his claim made in the state agency's statement of reasons and stated that the agency already had "enough evidence" in the file upon which to base a decision.
>
> Upon the basis of this information, the state agency determined that respondent had ceased to be disabled in May of 1972 and forwarded that determination to the Social Security Administration. . . . Social Security notified respondent in writing of this determination and of his right to request reconsideration within six months.
>
> Respondent did not seek reconsideration. Rather, on August 3, 1972, he filed this complaint in this case.[143]

Conveniently relegated to footnotes were the comments about the battle for the initial benefit decision before the hearing examiner in 1968 and the battle through the process that had lasted from February 1970 through the spring of 1971, less than a year before the immediate decision that led to this suit.

There were essentially four parts to the government's brief. First, it argued that the existing procedures were fair, but Eldridge was just not patient enough to avail himself of the alternatives available.[144] Second, the government asserted that the interests of the government in "avoiding unneeded administrative burdens and costs" outweighed the "worker's interest in continued receipt of disability insurance benefits assessed in light of the reliability of the existing procedures."[145] Third, a point related to the second line of argument, it was suggested that "because the statute did not require proof of indigency, disability recipients were not as needy as welfare recipients."[146] Fourth, and this was the core of the argument, the government argued that a pretermination hearing requirement would pose unacceptable administrative and economic burdens on the agency. In short, the government could not afford to provide pretermination hearings.

The government did not get to the discussion of the constitutional point until page 35 of the brief. Several cases were cited for the proposition that procedural due process is a flexible concept. All but one of the cases, it should be noted, had actually resulted in decisions for the aggrieved party demanding a hearing before the adverse action to which they objected.

The only major Social Security disability case cited by the government was *Richardson v. Perales,*[147] used to support the proposition that the medical reports were good evidence of disability and provided sufficient certainty to protect the claimant. *Richardson,* of course, had only been concerned with whether such reports, absent the presence in the hearing room of their authors, could be admitted in a hearing at all since they were clearly of a hearsay character. Again, that case concerned admissibility in a hearing of reports. The Court was not talking about a situation in which the report was considered outside the hearing context and that, after all, was all that Eldridge wanted. On two other occasions he had succeeded against the reports in hearings while the paper review of the record prior to the hearing stage had worked against his claim. It was also what was at the heart of the decision in *Underwood v. Ribicoff,* cited by the district court in *Eldridge* and accepted by the court of appeals.[148] *Underwood* rejected the proposition that there was nothing more involved in a disability determination than an examination of medical reports of physicians.[149] That case was not mentioned at all by the government.

The government brief quickly moved away from the constitutional issue and back to the cost argument. Using figures that the solicitor general admitted during the oral argument were "a little misleading," the government argued that to require pretermination hearings would result in as many as 1,000 additional hearings at a total cost, given possible wrongful benefit payments, of some $25 million dollars. What it failed to say was that even at that outside estimate the total cost would have been less than one-tenth of 1 percent of the cost of the entire program on an annual basis. "Moreover, some beneficiaries who now accept an adverse initial determination would be likely to request a pretermination hearing if the effect would be to prolong the payment of benefits."[150] The appendix was given over to a continuation of the statistical analysis and copies of the forms and letters used in the termination process.

In sum, except for the comment that the statute did not require that the claimant be destitute by definition, it was the same argument that the government had advanced in *Goldberg v. Kelly* and again in *Richardson v. Wright*.

The brief for respondents was terse by comparison, totaling a mere eleven pages. Eldridge's counsel felt that since it was essentially the same argument that had been rejected in the earlier cases and not materially affected by the barrage of statistics, the Court would cut through the bulk and reject the differentiation from *Goldberg* on the merits attempted by the government.[151]

The brief for Eldridge made a brief supplementary comment on the statement of facts presented by the government. The argument was in three parts. First, George Eldridge had been through the administrative process completely twice and was now into his third foray. On each of the earlier occasions, he had lost in the paper reviews and had prevailed in the hearing because of the complexity of judging disability under the *Underwood v. Ribicoff* standard. The second round had stretched some eighteen months between the decision that disability had ceased and the judgment by the hearing examiner awarding the benefits. Second, Earls argued that the welfare option was not a viable one because:

(1) Qualification for welfare benefits may require more stringent standards than qualifications for Social Security disability benefits; (2) A welfare recipient may submit his property to a lien for the amount of assistance received; (and) (3) Welfare benefits do not commence spontaneously but rather start after a sometimes lengthy investigation.[152]

Finally, he argued,

George Eldridge is as much entitled to an opportunity for an evidentiary hearing concerning his termination of disability benefits as: (1) A welfare recipient concerning his welfare check, *Goldberg v. Kelly,* supra; (2) A wage earner concerning his paycheck, *Sniadach v. Family Finance Corp.,* 395 U.S. 337 (1969); (3) A parolee concerning his freedom, *Morrisey v. Brewer,* 408 U.S. 471 (1972); (4) A prison inmate concerning his good time credits, *Wolff v. McDonnell,* supra; (5) A consumer concerning his old stove, *Fuentes v. Shevin,* 407 U.S. 67 (1972); (6) An uninsured motorist concerning his license, *Bell v. Burson,* 402 U.S. 535 (1971); (7) An elderly person concerning his Medicare benefits, *Martinez v. Richardson,* 472 F.2d. 421 (10 Cir. 1973); (8) A student concerning his suspension from school, *Goss v. Lopez,* 43 L.W. 4181 (1975).[153]

In each of these cases, some prior hearing was required.

Strategy and Tactics

Given the existing string of precedents, the support in journals, and the narrow four-to-three decision conflict on the same legal question in *Richardson v. Wright,* what prompted the government to risk what many observers felt would be a major loss in a significant case? There were at least two reasons that an analyst of this case might highlight.

One force compelling the government to fight was fear. Reversal rates were climbing, losses in district courts were increasing, and pressure, both economic and political, seemed to be mounting on all sides. In short, the government fought because there seemed to be no alternative.

But there was a more positive reason to take on the challenge. Since *Goldberg* and *Richardson,* the composition of the Court had changed. By the mid-1970s, the Court had clearly established an identity as the Burger Court. Of the original Warren Court, only Justices Brennan, Marshall, and Douglas remained.

Given Justice Douglas's uphill battle to recover from a stroke suffered a year before, it seemed unlikely that he would be able to participate fully in the consideration and decision in *Eldridge.* As it happened, while he was able to be on the bench at the time of the oral argument, Douglas was seriously weakened by his illness and was forced to resign while *Eldridge* was pending.

Chief Justice Burger and Justice Blackmun voted to dismiss in *Richardson v. Wright* along with Justice Stewart and White. Since then, Justices Powell and Rehnquist had joined the Court. There was little doubt that the latter two members would join the Chief Justice and Justice Blackmun on this kind of case.

One of the major themes of the Burger Court had been the Chief Justice's concern for reducing the use of judicial mechanisms for problem resolutions.[154] In his speeches he urged the courts to resist the temptation to engage in activities beyond the traditional bounds of courts.[155] He urged reduction in federal court jurisdiction, streamlined administration, and deference to state courts.[156] Fear of increased dockets and judicialization of government were central themes in his comments and opinions.[157]

Finally, by fall 1975 there were signals in at least two major decisions rendered by the Court that its members were about to reverse the direction of doctrinal development in the area of procedural due process in administrative proceedings. In a 1974 decision, *Arnett v. Kennedy,*[158] the Court faced a request by a nonprobationary federal civil servant that he be given a hearing prior to the termination of his employment under *Goldberg, Fuentes,*[159] *Sniadach,*[160] *Bell,*[161] and *Board of Regents v. Roth.*[162] The civil servant had made allegations of corrupt practices in the ill-fated Office of Economic Opportunity. Under existing statutes and regulations, he was given written notice of the reasons for his dismissal and could appear before the person who fired him, in this case the person he had accused of malfeasance, to object to his discharge. After termination, he could ask for an administrative appeal, which would eventually (the average was more than eleven months) result in a later hearing. If he succeeded at that hearing, he could be reinstated with back pay.

Justice Rehnquist wrote the plurality opinion that was joined by Chief Justice Burger and Justice Stewart. Rehnquist dismissed the precedents advanced, holding that all that was required was that the employee get a chance at some point to clear his name.[163] Rehnquist chose the one major case in the past two decades that gave him the takeoff point he needed: *Cafeteria Workers v. McElroy.*[164] Because this case figured prominently in *Eldridge,* it deserves comment here.

Cafeteria Workers was a 1961 case in which a pretermination hearing was denied to Rachael Brawner. Mrs. Brawner had been employed at a cafeteria on a naval installation. When she arrived for work one morning, she was denied access to the facility for alleged security reasons that were never revealed. She was employed by the concessionaire who operated the cafeteria, but lost her job because she was not permitted access to her place of employment. She demanded a hearing to learn on what grounds she had been marked as a security risk. The Court held: "What procedural due process may require under any given set of circumstances must begin with a determination of the precise nature of the government function involved as well as the public interest that has been affected by government action."[165] That decision was written by Justice Stewart. It stood as an exception, an exception justified by the particular defense and national security environment in that case.[166]

Justices Powell and Blackmun concurred in the *Arnett v. Kennedy,* but not on the grounds of *McElroy.* In fact, Justice Powell observed that the plurality opinion was "incompatible with the principles laid down in *Roth* and *Sindermann*" and "misconceives the origin of the right to procedural due process. That right is conferred not by legislative grace but by constitutional guarantee."[167] Nevertheless, Powell and Blackmun concurred on grounds that just when the hearing must be afforded depends on a balancing process in which the government's interest in expeditious removal of an unsatisfactory employee is weighed against the interest of the affected employee. . . .

[Since the employee] would be reinstated and awarded back pay if he prevails on the merits [any] actual injury would consist of a temporary interruption of his income during the interim. [That] could constitute a serious loss in many cases. But the possible deprivation is considerably less severe than that involved in *Goldberg*.[168]

The dissent, written by Justice Marshall and joined by Justices Douglas and Brennan, was a powerful statement.

During the period of delay, the employee is off the government payroll. His ability to secure other employment to tide himself over may be significantly hindered by the outstanding charges against him. Even aside from the stigma that attends a dismissal for cause, few employers will be willing to hire and train a new employee knowing that he will return to a former Government position as soon as an appeal is successful. And in many states, including Illinois, where appellee resides, a worker discharged for cause is not even eligible for employment compensation.

Many workers, particularly those at the bottom of the pay scale, will suffer severe and painful economic dislocations from even a temporary loss of wages. Few public employees earn more than enough to pay their expenses from month to month. . . . Like many of us, they may be required to meet substantial fixed costs on a regular basis and lack substantial savings to meet those expenses while not receiving a salary. The loss of income for even a few weeks may well impair their ability to provide the essentials of life to buy food, meet mortgage or rent payments, or procure medical services. . . . The plight of the discharged employee may not be far different from that of the welfare recipient in *Goldberg* who, "pending resolution of a controversy . . . may [be] deprived . . . of the very means by which he waits." Appellee, although earning an annual salary of $16,000 before his dismissal, far above the mean salary for federal employees, was nonetheless driven to the brink of financial ruin while he waited. He had to borrow money to support his family, his debts went unpaid, his family lost the protection of his health insurance and, finally, he was forced to apply for public assistance. In this context justice delayed may well be justice denied.

To argue that dismissal from tenured Government employment is not a serious enough deprivation to require a prior hearing because the discharged employee may draw on the welfare system in the interim is to exhibit a gross insensitivity to the plight of these employees. First, it assumes that the discharged employee will be eligible for welfare. Often welfare applicants must be all but stripped of their worldly goods before being admitted to the welfare rolls, hence it is likely that the employee will suffer considerable hardship before becoming eligible. . . . He may have to give up his home or cherished personal possessions in order to become eligible. The argument also assumes all but instant eligibility which is, sadly, far from likely even when all the employee's other sources of support have been depleted.[169]

The government received another favorable sign in June 1975 when the Court decided *Weinberger v. Salfi*.[170] The facts were these. Mrs. Salfi married Londo Salfi in May 1972. Approximately a month later, he was hospitalized following a heart attack. He died the following November. She promptly applied for survivors' benefits under the Social Security Act for herself and children's benefits for her daughter by a previous marriage. The Social Security Administration disapproved her claim on the ground that the statute presumes that those married less than nine months prior to the death of the insured wage earner were married for the purpose of taking advantage of Social Security benefits.

Mrs. Salfi sued claiming that such an irrebuttable presumption was a violation of the due process clause in the same sense as the presumption that a father of a child born out of wedlock was an unfit parent, held unconstitutional by the Court in 1972 in *Stanley v. Illinois*, or the assumption of nonresidence for tuition purposes, struck down in 1974 in *Vlandis v. Kline*. What Mrs. Salfi wanted was a hearing to show that since her husband was in good health at the time of their wedding with no history of serious illness, let alone coronary disease, she could not possibly have married him to take advantage of survivors' benefits.

In the opinion written for the Court by Justice Rehnquist, equal protection arguments raised in earlier cases such as *Dandridge v. Williams,*[171] *Fleming v. Nestor,*[172] and *Richardson v. Belcher*[173] were used to say that Congress could make such classifications. It is true that these cases claimed a violation of the due process clause of the Fifth Amendment, but this is a deceptive generalization. Each of these cases claimed discriminatory action in violation of the concept of equal protection. But since there is no equal protection clause in the Fifth Amendment, the Court has frequently said that that amendment includes within its due process clause equal protection guarantees against discrimination by the federal government paralleling those of the Fourteenth Amendment regarding state government actions.[174] In sum, the cases cited by those disagreeing with the government in *Dandridge* etc. objected to unequal treatment and to denial of a hearing. In the irrebuttable presumption cases, all of which had gone against the government in the last decade, it was indeed a claim for a hearing that was at issue.

What was at the heart of Rehnquist's concern did not appear until relatively late in the opinion.

> Large numbers of people are eligible for these programs and are potentially subject to inquiry as to the validity of their relationship to wage earners. . . . Not only does the prophylactic approach thus obviate the necessity for large numbers of individualized determinations, but it also protects large numbers of claimants who satisfy the rule from the uncertainties and delays of administrative inquiry into the circumstances of their marriage. Nor is it at all clear that individual determinations could effectively filter out sham arrangements, since neither marital intent, life expectancy, nor knowledge of terminal illness has been shown by appellees to be reliably determinable.[175]

The Rehnquist opinion also sought to resurrect the right-privilege dichotomy that had been buried years before.[176] He observed: "We hold that these cases [*Stanley* and *Vlandis*] are not controlling on the issue before us now. Unlike the claims involved in *Stanley* and *LaFleur,* a noncontractual claim to receive funds from the public treasury enjoys no constitutionally protected status."[177]

Justice Brennan rebutted the argument on the merits. Brennan demonstrated that *Stanley, LaFleur, Vlandis,* and the other irrebuttable presumption cases were exactly on point and could not be differentiated. On the nature of the presumption in *Salfi,* Brennan wrote:

> We have been presented with no evidence at all that the problem of collusive marriages is one which exists at all. Indeed, the very fact that Congress has continually moved back the amount of time required to avoid the rebuttable presumption . . . suggests that it found, for each time period set, that it was depriving people of benefits without alleviating any real problem of collusion. There is no reason to believe that the nine-month period is any more likely to discard any high proportion of collusive marriages than the five-year, three-year, or one-year periods employed earlier.
>
> The Court says: "The Administrative difficulties of individual eligibility determinations are without doubt matters which Congress may consider when determining whether to rely on rules which sweep more broadly than the evils with which they seek to deal." . . .
>
> But, as we said in *Stanley v. Illinois,* . . . "The Constitution recognizes higher values than speed and efficiency."[178]

The changes in Court personnel and the two decisions considered augured well for the government. The signals were not lost on Solicitor General Bork, who was to present the oral argument in the Supreme Court. He would couch much of the language of his argument in *Arnett* and *Salfi* terms and references to judicial administration, efficiency, and increasing caseloads.[179]

Still, no one seemed ready to predict victory for the government in the *Eldridge* case. In fact, implicit in most of the reports and testimony issued in the year before the case was heard was an expectation that the precedents were strong and more likely than not to result in a loss for HEW, particularly in light of the documented injustices to claimants in their battles with the SSA.

There had also been doubts at the time of *Richardson v. Wright* and the government diverted the litigation. The amended regulations obtained a remand for further consideration from the Court. A similar ploy had been attempted by New York in *Goldberg* without success.

In *Eldridge,* a last ditch effort was made to stave off the Supreme Court decision by interposing a jurisdictional question. The decision in *Salfi* had been rendered in late June, but it was not until two days before the oral argument in the Court, October 4, 1975, that Mr. Earls was served with typescript of a supplemental brief by the government. In that brief, the government argued that there was no jurisdiction for the district court to have heard *Eldridge* since the decision was not final. That is, George Eldridge had not taken the case all the way through the administrative process. It was very nearly the same argument that the government had made and lost in *Salfi*. After all, this case did not present a matter of judicial review of an agency decision in a particular case. It was a constitutional claim against the constitutionality of agency regulations. Further, the government had brought the case on appeal and had never before raised any question of the jurisdiction of the federal courts to hear the case. Why now?

There were at least two possibilities, either of which might benefit the government. First, one may ask whether the government hoped that the Court might take the out afforded and once again avoid dealing directly with the constitutional question. Such a jurisdictional decision would blunt the effect of the decision of the lower courts in *Eldridge*. It would also give the government an opportunity to select a case for Supreme Court review that would have facts that were not clearly adverse to the government's case. Second, this tactic, if indeed it was a tactic, permitted attorneys for the government to get *Salfi* into the Eldridge litigation even though the legal question involved was not the same. *Salfi* was a very recent decision in which the Court had treated a Social Security claim in a manner quite unlike other recent due process claims for hearing.

Preparation for Eldridge's presentation was quite different from that of the Solicitor General. For Mr. Earls, it was "quite a weekend." This would be Earls's first appearance before the Supreme Court of the United States. Mr. Earls is a native of Norton, Virginia. Educated at the University of Virginia and the Washington and Lee School of Law, he had clerked in a federal district court after law school. He returned to Norton where he married and began practice with a local firm. He had been in practice just long enough to qualify for admission to the Supreme Court bar when the *Eldridge* case arose.

Earls and his colleagues met at Earls's hotel room and worked through the weekend before the argument. Earls had not been particularly moved by the fact that Mr. Bork was personally handling the *Eldridge* case and would present the argument. He did take note when his colleagues informed him that Bork did not usually play such a personal role unless the case was a matter of top priority.[180]

Counsel for Eldridge wanted to approach the case in straightforward constitutional due process terms. The oral argument would be in two parts. First, there would be an analysis of the relationship of *Eldridge* to *Goldberg v. Kelly* and associated cases. Second, the facts of the *Eldridge* case would be recounted to illustrate in graphic terms what happens to people who face delays and the physical and monetary costs associated with terminations without hearings. Such an analysis, Earls was certain, would clearly demonstrate the correctness of Judge Turk's opinion in the district court. It would also refute the government's contention that harm from a lack of pretermination proceedings is unlikely and, in any case, would probably not impose severe hardship like that of the welfare recipient in *Goldberg*.

It was crucial, from Earls's point of view, that the Court understand Judge Turk's opinion. Turk had clearly delineated the confusing pattern of facts in the *Eldridge* case as the claim and appeals moved through the complex procedures involved in disability determination. Turk had carefully, through consideration of both precedent and policy problems, placed that adjudicatory process as it affected Eldridge into the stream of constitutional doctrine on procedural due process. That melding of substance and process was, for Earls, the crux of the case. The argument before the Court would not, however, work out as planned. It was instead characterized by procedural confusion and conceptual complexity.

The Oral Argument: A Survey and Analysis

The oral argument presented by Mr. Bork continued with the fiction that this case began in 1972. Bork began as follows:

> Here the secretary of HEW terminated the respondent's disability payments in 1972 on the basis of medical reports and the respondent was given a summary of that evidence; (and) given an opportunity to submit additional evidence in a written rebuttal. There were post-termination procedures available to him, including a full evidentiary hearing which I shall describe in a moment, but he brought this suit instead of availing himself of those procedures, claiming a constitutional right to pretermination oral hearing.[181]

Again, Bork later said: "He was entitled to administrative reconsideration, to an evidentiary hearing and so forth. He availed himself of none of this, but brought suit before the Secretary had made a final decision after a hearing."[182] No mention is made of the fact that Eldridge had gone through the entire process two and one-half times before the case ever got to the courts. The government's effort clearly was to cast the case in terms of judicial review rather than as a constitutional challenge.

As he turned to the merits, Bork used *McElroy* as a takeoff point and then took up the "balance" argument that has become popular to an extreme.

> We are, in effect, dealing with a cost benefit judgment; and so viewed the question becomes really how many? The decision of this case will have a heavy impact upon the decision of how many decisional processes of government must be conformed to a judicial model rather than to an administrative model. I think that is important and clearly there has to be a stopping point somewhere to the imposition of, judicial models upon governmental decision-making because it is very expensive; and in some circumstances, which I would contend this is one, adds little or nothing to the alternative procedures provided.

Bork sharpened the point a short time later:

> It would be nice to say, I suppose, that the system must be perfect. Nobody must ever be terminated no matter how temporarily, but indeed I don't think any legal process, any chemical a process or any industrial process ever can afford to remove the last bit of impurities in that process. It gets extraordinarily expensive. Indeed, it begins to defeat the ends of the process. *I can put an approximate dollar value on both sides of this due process equation.* (Emphasis added.)

He then equated what would be paid out in eventually denied claims and the costs of the program with the interest at 8 percent on claims withheld from rightful claimants for a year on the claim. The total figure that he computed for increased government costs of an adverse decision in the case was $25,000,000, which is less than one-tenth of 1 percent of the program expenditures per year.[183] Bork neglected to inform the Court that, unlike the case of welfare recipients, the Secretary can recover from wrongful payments and there is no such thing as being judgment proof in such a proceeding because the common practice is to wait until the claimant applies for any other Social Security benefits, including old-age benefits, and then subtract a base 25 percent per month until the wrongful payment is recouped. His cost/benefit calculus also neglected the fact that the standard attorney fee for a disability benefit case is 25 percent of the back payments.

The government used figures not given by SSA in any of the hearings nor found by the studies conducted by independent researchers or by the staff of the Social Security subcommittee of the House Ways and Means Committee during their continuing efforts to deal with the problems of the program. Beyond that, as the brief showed, welfare is not available to many disability claimants.

Speaking for Eldridge, Earls asked where the figure was that accounted for the loss of Eldridge's house during the last delay, the nights his children went hungry, and the pain suffered because he could not give his dying wife food she requested? Earls contended that Bork's argument was an abstraction based on little or no case law, an apocryphal cost-benefit analysis, and a studied ignorance of the full record and lower court ruling in the case.

The success of the government's diversionary tactic was immediately apparent as Earls began his oral argument. Earls managed to get out just two sentences before the questions started. Justice Rehnquist, author of the *Salfi* opinion, immediately attempted to cast the case as one involving only judicial review. In addition, he accepted the fact pattern as presented by the government and asked a stream of questions about finality and the assertion that Eldridge did not take advantage of procedures available to him. Finally, he was joined by Justice White. They asked:

What is your case or controversy? Have they terminated you or not?

MR. EARLS: The Secretary did terminate Mr. Eldridge's benefits. The district court reinstated his benefits until such time as he was afforded an evidentiary hearing.

JUSTICE WHITE: The government challenged the district court order. The Secretary terminated you, right? The district court reinstated you, right?

MR. EARLS: That's correct.

JUSTICE WHITE: Now the government is challenging the district court order reinstating those benefits?

MR. EARLS: Challenging the district court order and the Fourth Circuit Court of Appeals order upholding the district court.

JUSTICE WHITE: You never exhausted your administrative remedies.

MR. EARLS: Your honor, what we're . . .

JUSTICE WHITE: Well, did you? You did not exhaust them. And you might have won.

MR. EARLS: That is the government's argument, Mr. Justice White. Our contention is this, that by benefits being terminated prior to being afforded an evidentiary hearing, we were denied due process. We went twice, Mr. Eldridge, factually speaking, went twice through an administrative hearing.

That was one of the few lengthy passages that Earls managed until the end of his argument. From this point on it appeared that either the government had successfully cast the case as one in which Eldridge just gave up too soon or they had not fully read and understood Judge Turk's decision. Earls and his colleagues saw at once what was happening. So did Justice Brennan.

Brennan attempted to lead Earls step by step out of the procedural quagmire, but by then it was too late. Time was passing rapidly and there was to be another tangential line of discussion before Earls could get back to the constitutional argument that he had planned to make.

As soon as Justice Brennan had assisted Earls in straightening out the fact pattern of the case, Justices White and Rehnquist began asking questions about the procedural adequacy of the evidentiary hearing, such as whether Earls was satisfied with the subpoena and cross-examination provisions of the regulations. Earls tried to indicate that all he wanted was to move the existing hearing up to pretermination and not to change or expand the provisions of the hearing itself.[184]

He did respond briefly to the cold medical record argument made by Bork. The idea was to suggest that the medical records were enough. That view had been rejected in Judge Turk's opinion, but Bork had carefully avoided any reference to that decision. Earls saw an opportunity and interjected:

Your honor, in the case of *Underwood v. Ribicoff,* the Fourth Circuit held that the main element in determining benefits is not only the objective cold medical record as the Secretary says. They said that subjective evidence such as the claimant's appearance before an administrative law judge, and the testimony of the claimant, his wife and neighbors as to his ability to work and in many of these cases, and George Eldridge is a good example, you can look at him and tell he is disabled.

Earls was trying to indicate the significance of the fact that he had three times been denied benefits during paper reviews but had won twice at hearings.

Earls tried to return to his argument that the hypothesis advanced by the government that a claimant would not suffer because of the benefits was wrong. At least it was certainly wrong with respect to Eldridge.

> The Secretary's figures point out that 90 percent of the total [Social Security] benefit population earn nothing, so I would say that as opposed to *Goldberg v. Kelly* and need, they are indistinguishable. I feel in the George Eldridge case, where Mr. Eldridge was required to sleep in one bed with five children, lost his home that he had worked all his life for, as a laborer on the railroad and then as a soda distributor, driving a truck and carrying cases of soda: there certainly he lost everything which could not be recouped. . . . This is what happened in the George Eldridge case, and this is what happens in many of the cases.[185]

As Earls and his colleagues walked the length of the great marble halls from the courtroom and down the front staircase into the afternoon, everyone knew what had happened. The alignment on the Court seemed clear. The government had framed the case as it had wished and successfully diverted the argument from a constitutional matter to a narrow procedural discussion.

"A DOLLAR VALUE ON BOTH SIDES OF THIS DUE PROCESS EQUATION": THE GOVERNMENT'S BALANCING FORMULA SUCCEEDS

The government succeeded beyond its most optimistic expectations. The opinion of the Court was to be little more than an amalgamation of the government's brief, its argument, and the Court's language from *Arnett v. Kennedy* and *Salfi*. Perhaps more significant was the fact that the government had managed to get a clear mandate for a straight balance between administrative efficiency and due process requirements, something that was unprecedented except for *Cafeteria Workers v. McElroy*, which was a special case involving defense and security claims.

Justice Powell's Balancing Test

The alignment of the Court was predictable. Powell wrote for Burger, White, Blackmun, and Rehnquist. Brennan wrote for himself and Justice Marshall. By this time, February 1976, Justice Douglas had retired and had been replaced by Justice John Paul Stevens who, of course, did not take part in *Eldridge*.

Justice Powell accepted the facts as stated by the government.[186] The only facts noted were that Eldridge was placed on benefits in 1968, and when in 1972 he was declared ineligible, he ignored his administrative alternatives and ran directly to the district court.[187] Not so much as a footnote indicates that he had been through the entire process two and a half times. Nor was there any indication of the fact that he had lost in paper proceedings and had won on each opportunity for a hearing. Neither was there any reference to the loss of his house, his car, or his furniture. The name Smith could have been substituted for Eldridge without changing a thing. The government had presented the case as an abstract policy issue and that is how the Court treated it. Justice Powell disposed of Judge Turk's complex decision in one paragraph.[188] The government did not win its jurisdiction argument on *Salfi*, but then, from a tactical point of view, winning on the issue was quite insignificant.

On the merits, Powell developed a balancing test by reading *Goldberg* as though it had set forth a simple balance test.

More precisely, our prior decisions indicate that identification of the specific dictates of due process generally requires consideration of three distinct factors; first, the private interest that will be affected by the official action; second, the risk of an erroneous deprivation of such interest through the procedures used, and the probable value, if any, of additional or substitute procedural safeguards; and finally, the government's interest, including the function involved and the fiscal and administrative burdens that the additional or substitute procedural requirement would entail.

But when Justice Brennan, who wrote the *Goldberg* opinion, discussed the fact that due process must not be inflexible, he clearly did not imply that a straight balance test was at issue. To the degree that he was concerned with examining the burdens on government, he was adamant in rejecting simple dollar calculations and on including what appear to be intangibles.

Moreover, important governmental interests are promoted by affording recipients a pretermination evidentiary hearing. From its foundation the Nation's basic commitment has been to foster the dignity and well-being of all persons within its borders. We have come to recognize that forces not within the control of the poor contribute to their poverty. This perception, against the background of our traditions, has significantly influenced the development of the contemporary public assistance system. Welfare, by meeting the basic demands of subsistence, can help bring within the reach of the poor the same opportunities that are available to others to participate meaningfully in the life of the community. At the same time, welfare guards against the societal malaise that may flow from a widespread sense of unjustified frustration and insecurity. Public assistance, then, is not mere charity, but a "means to promote the general Welfare, and to secure the Blessings of Liberty to ourselves and our Posterity." The same governmental interests that counsel the provision to those eligible to receive it; pretermination evidentiary hearings are indispensable to that end.

Appellant does not challenge the force of these considerations but argues that they are outweighed by countervailing governmental interests in conserving fiscal and administrative resources. These interests, the argument goes, justify the delay of any evidentiary hearing until after discontinuance of grants. Summary adjudication protects the public fisc by stopping payments promptly upon discovery of reason to believe that a recipient is no longer eligible. Since most terminations are accepted without challenge, summary adjudication also conserves both the fisc and administrative time and energy by reducing the number of evidentiary hearings held. We agree with the District Court, however, that these governmental interests are not overriding in the welfare context. The requirement of a prior hearing doubtless involves some greater expense, and the benefits paid to ineligible recipients pending decision at the hearing probably cannot be recouped [unlike Social Security], since these recipients are likely to be judgment-proof. But the State is not without weapons to minimize these costs.

Justice Powell applied his balance test to Social Security disability benefits. Following the lead of the government's argument, Justice Powell reasoned from the premise that the statute does not require a demonstration of financial need to the conclusion that disability claimants are not needy, though he referred to no supporting data. He concluded:

In view of the torpidity of this administrative review process, . . . and the typically modest resources of the family unit of the physically disabled worker, the hardship imposed on the erroneously terminated disability recipient may be significant. Still, the disabled worker's need is likely to be less than that of a welfare recipient. In addition to the possibility of access to private resources, other forms of government assistance will become available where the termination of disability benefits places a worker or his family at or below the subsistence level.[189]

The only evidence in this case on the matter is to the contrary.

Powell then turned to the question of the quality of adjudication. Again, he adopted the government's theoretical position that it is probably relatively easy to prove disability from medical reports, hence hearings are not especially necessary. That does not address the fact that hearings result in reversal in more than 50 percent of the cases brought on appeal, or that Eldridge had won twice in hearings but had lost three times in paper reviews. Nor does it come to grips with the problems noted in the congressional hearings of claimants whose claims were rejected even before medical records were obtained.

Powell's acceptance of the government theory is all the more surprising in light of the fact that two law review articles were cited in the record, one in the brief in the Supreme Court and the other by Judge Turk in his opinion, which demonstrate conclusively why medical reports alone, as a cold paper record, so frequently result in incorrect or unjust decisions.[190] In particular, Turk referred to the Haviland and Glomb study, which focused on Appalachia and demonstrated empirically just why people like Eldridge have a particularly difficult time winning a paper review but do much better in hearings. Also ignored was the controlling law on proof of disability, *Underwood v. Ribicoff,* cited both in Supreme Court and in the lower court briefs.

Finally, Powell arrived at the crux of his argument, the question of cost and administrative burden.

> In striking the appropriate due process balance the final factor to be assessed is the public interest. This includes the administrative burden and other societal costs that would be associated with requiring, as a matter of constitutional right, an evidentiary hearing upon demand in all cases prior to the termination of disability benefits. The most visible burden would be the incremental cost resulting from the increased number of hearings and the expense of providing benefits to ineligible recipients pending decision. No one can predict the extent of the increase, but the fact that full benefits would continue until after such hearings would assure the exhaustion in most cases of this attractive option. Nor would the theoretical right of the Secretary to recover undeserved benefits result, as a practical matter, in any substantial offset to the added outlay of public funds. The parties submit widely varying estimates of the probable additional financial cost. We only need say that experience with the constitutionalizing of government procedures suggests that the ultimate additional cost in terms of money and administrative burden would not be insubstantial.[191]

However, as mentioned earlier, the ability of the Secretary to recover is very real, since the government need not sue for back payments. The agency is authorized to withhold overpayment from future benefits and does so at the rate of approximately 25 percent per month until the bill is paid. After his initial discussion on costs versus benefits, Justice Powell drops, almost in passing, his comment about constitutionalizing government. His comment presumes that everyone knows and agrees that "constitutionalizing of government procedures" is bad. Students of constitutional law would respond that this government's actions are legitimate because they are "constitutionalized."

Justice Powell then continued with his assessment of costs.

> Financial cost alone is not a controlling weight in determining whether due process requires a particular procedural safeguard prior to some administrative decisions. But the Government's interest, and hence that of the public, in conserving scarce fiscal and administrative resources, is a factor that must be weighed. At some point the benefit of an additional safeguard to the individual affected by the administrative action and to society in terms of increased assurance that the action is just, may be outweighed by the cost. . . .
>
>   But more is implicated in cases of this type than ad hoc weighing of fiscal and administrative burdens against the interests of a particular category of claimants. The ultimate balance involves a determination as to when, under our constitutional system, judicial type procedures must be imposed upon administrative action to assure fairness. . . . In assessing what process is due in this

case, substantial weight must be given to the good faith judgments of the individuals charged by Congress with the administration of the social welfare system that the procedures they have provided assure fair consideration of the entitlement claims of individuals.[192]

The majority opinion, for obvious reasons, does not in any way refer to the proposition advanced by the lower court or to the precedents called forth in the previous *Eldridge* decision that the Bill of Rights was added to the Constitution precisely because the citizenry and a number of the framers of that document were not prepared to yield to the "good-faith judgments"[193] of any government officials.

Dissenters Fear Debased Constitutional Currency

Justice Brennan's brief dissent expresses the utter disdain that, as the author of the decision in *Goldberg v. Kelly,* he felt in examining this opinion. He was joined by Justice Marshall. There is no doubt that they would have been joined by Justice Douglas had he remained with the Court. Brennan's dissent had two parts. First, he responded to the merits of the *Eldridge* case itself and manner in which the Court dealt with it.

> I would add that the Court's consideration that a discontinuance of disability benefits may cause the recipient to suffer only a limited deprivation is no argument. It is speculative. Moreover, the very legislative determination of need in fact, presumes a need by the recipient which is not this Court's to denigrate. Indeed, in the present case, it is indicated that because disability benefits were terminated there was a foreclosure upon the Eldridge home and the family's furniture was repossessed, forcing Eldridge, his wife and children to sleep in one bed. . . . Finally, it is no argument that a worker who has been placed in the untenable position of having been denied disability benefits may still seek other forms of public assistance.[194]

(Brennan's comment was inaccurate with regard to Eldridge's wife, who had died of cancer shortly before he lost the house.) Second, Brennan referred to his dissenting opinion in *Richardson v. Wright* for comments on the precedents and discussion of specific policy matters relevant to Social Security disability claims in general. Dissenting in *Richardson,* Brennan had argued as follows: "The Secretary does not contend that disability beneficiaries differ from welfare and old age recipients with respect to their entitlements to benefits or the drastic consequences that may befall them if their benefits are erroneously discontinued."[195]

Of course, the government changed its position on whether the disability claimant faced the same degree of harm when it presented its arguments in *Eldridge.* Brennan continued:

> The only distinctions urged are that the evidence ordinarily adduced to support suspension and termination of disability benefits differ markedly from that relied upon to cut off welfare benefits and that an undue monetary and administrative burden would result if prior hearings were required. Neither distinction withstands analysis. . . . Hence, the Secretary concludes, while procedural due process requires a pretermination evidentiary hearing for welfare and old age recipients, for disability beneficiaries a written presentation will suffice.
>
> The Secretary seriously misconstrues the holding in *Goldberg.* The Court there said that "the pretermination hearing has one function only: to produce an initial determination of the validity of the welfare department's grounds for discontinuance of payments in order to protect a recipient against an erroneous termination of his benefits." . . . The Secretary does not deny that due process safeguards fulfill the same function in disability cases. In *Goldberg,* the Court held that welfare recipients were entitled to hearings because decisions to discontinue benefits were challenged "as resting on incorrect or misleading factual premises or on misapplication of rules or policies to the facts of particular cases." Id., at 268 the Court expressly put aside consideration of situations "where there are no factual issues in dispute or where the

application of the rule of law is not intertwined with factual issues." However reliable the evidence upon which a disability determination is normally based, and however rarely it involves questions of credibility and veracity, it is plain that, as with welfare and old-age determinations, the determination that an individual is or is not "disabled" will frequently depend upon the resolution of factual issues and the application of legal rules to the facts found. It is precisely for that reason that a hearing must be held.[196]

Brennan was particularly upset by the attempt to narrow the language of *Goldberg* to make issues of credibility and veracity the touchstone of pretermination hearings.

[The Secretary] first quotes the statement that "particularly where credibility and veracity are at issue, as they must be in many termination proceedings, written submissions are a wholly unsatisfactory basis for decisions." . . . Apart from the obvious fact that that was not an absolute statement intended to limit hearings solely to those instances, it was but one of three reasons given to demonstrate that written submissions are insufficient. The Court also said that written submissions "are an unrealistic option for most recipients, who lack the educational attainment necessary to write effectively and who cannot obtain professional assistance" and that they "do not afford the flexibility of oral presentations; they do not permit the recipient to mold his argument to the issues the decision maker appears to regard as important." Significantly, the Secretary does not deny that those reasons are as fully applicable to disability beneficiaries as to welfare recipients.[197]

He then turned to a recitation of the specific regulations involved in disability termination and a consideration of how each fits in the hearing debate.

Brennan did not accept the cost argument. He concluded the Richardson dissent on that note.

I do not deny that prior hearings will entail some additional administrative burdens and expense. Administrative fairness usually does. Despite the Secretary's protestations to the contrary, I believe that in the disability, as in the welfare, area "much of the drain on fiscal and administrative resources can be reduced by developing procedures for prompt pretermination hearings and by skillful use of personnel and facilities." . . . The Court's conclusion on this point in *Goldberg* is fully applicable here:

"... Thus the interest of the eligible recipient in uninterrupted receipt of public assistance, coupled with the State's interest that his payments not be erroneously terminated, clearly outweighs the State's competing concern to prevent any increase in its fiscal and administrative burdens."[198]

THE COURT HAD SPOKEN

The decision of the Court in the *Eldridge* case was significant for several reasons. For administrators, the opinion signaled a major shift in how much process is due and just what agencies will be expected to provide. To legal scholars, the decision set forth in the new controlling law on the test for procedural due process, which would be broadly applied to processes as diverse as commitment of juveniles to mental health facilities and removal of drivers' licenses.[199] Some of the concerns about this doctrinal development will be recounted shortly. But Eldridge and his counsel had not thought of the case in policy terms. For them, the question was what was to happen to Eldridge and his family.

George Eldridge Responds

Earls called Eldridge as soon as the decision was announced to give him the news. Eldridge could not understand how it had happened, but his more immediate concern was how to deal with his impending loss of disability benefits again. After all, the Supreme Court decision overturning Judge Turk and the Fourth Circuit meant that the *Eldridge* case was back to where it had been in 1973. His benefits had been terminated.

Eldridge requested reconsideration by the Virginia office. He did not receive a response until October 1977, approximately eighteen months after the Supreme Court decision. Earls promptly requested another hearing for Eldridge. In March 1978, two full years after the decision against him in the Supreme Court and ten years after his initial victory in his first hearing, Eldridge was found by an administrative law judge, the third such judge, to be eligible for benefits. It is reported that when the records arrived for consideration by the administrative law judge, it was delivered in two cartons.[200]

Eldridge still does not understand what happened. He does feel strongly that the off-and-on status with continuing controversy has harmed him irreparably. He is tired of asking the local Social Security official to call the local power company to ask them not to turn off the electricity while administrative decisions come and go.

> I think somebody is responsible for the things I've lost. They're responsible for making my health worse. They're responsible for the hardships that they've caused me and my children.
>
> I don't want to lay up no big treasures in this world. But if I get disabled to work and they've got a program to take care of me, then I want it. I don't want to beat around no bush about it after paying into it when I was able to work.
>
> All I want out of life is something to eat, wear and a place to stay. Well, hell, they won't let you have a place to stay.[201]

It is insecurity as to his dwelling that particularly upsets George Eldridge. "When it boils down to where, after a man working hard all of his life that he's able to work, they won't let him have a home to live in by stopping his money and causing his little kids to go to the table and find nothing on it, well. . . ."[202]

Eldridge's unending problem was that he would take money from his back payments to attempt to start anew, but would soon find himself pressed again. Back payments less fees never were quite what they were expected to be. That is how he lost his home, his mobile home, and other items. "I've lost a lot of money. In fact, the money what they've given me, two thirds of it has been lost trying to have a home. Just trying to have a home."[203]

For George Eldridge this case continues since his claim can be reevaluated in the future. Given his past experiences, that is not a comforting prospect.

Scholarly Criticisms of the Simplistic Balancing Test

Several law reviews noted the delivery of the *Eldridge* decision[204] although the full significance of the balancing test set forth in Justice Powell's opinion only later came to light.[205] In an early critique of the decision, Jerry Mashaw[206] concluded: "The *Eldridge* approach is unsatisfactory both as employed in that case and as a general formulation of due process review of administrative procedures. The failing of *Eldridge* is its focus on technique rather than questions of value. That focus, it is argued, generates an inquiry that is incomplete because unresponsive to the full range of concerns embodied in the due process clause."[207]

The decision was not justified by precedent. It was not an example of judicial self-restraint, but was instead judicial activism in a conservative political and economic direction. The opinion in *Eldridge,* particularly when it is considered in light of the rationale of *Weinberger v. Salfi*[208] and *Arnett v. Kennedy,*[209] moves due process doctrine backward toward a reemergence of the right-privilege dichotomy, which most commentators had thought died more than a decade earlier.[210]

It is no argument to maintain that some kind of hearing at some point is due process of law. Where citizens suffer significant injury at the hands of government officials, such as was endured by

George Eldridge, and repeated studies indicate that his is not an unusual set of circumstances, justice delayed is in a very real and tangible way justice denied.

SUMMARY

An examination of Eldridge's journey through the Social Security disability process is a lesson in the anatomy of an administrative law case. It demonstrates the complexity of due process of law in theory and practice. His case illustrates the interaction of state and federal agencies in social service claims as well as the relationship between those agencies and the federal courts.

Cases like *Eldridge* do not arise and are not resolved in a policy vacuum. The process of policymaking is ongoing. In the case of social service programs, there are constant tensions between administrative problems and judicial values. These programs continually present the dilemma of administering a massive program efficiently while simultaneously demonstrating a concern for individual problems and peculiar circumstances.

The manner in which the Supreme Court dealt with the case is illustrative of the significance of judicial policymaking. It demonstrates the significance of personnel changes on the Court. When the judicial process is considered from the vantage point of the administrator with an eye toward a particular policy area, one can see the relationship of law to the process of policy implementation. The decision in *Eldridge* highlights the relationship, whether properly or improperly evaluated, between policy and precedent in Supreme Court decisionmaking.

One of the goals of this piece has been to view a complex administrative problem from a number of relevant perspectives, emphasizing the view of the claimant, who is the ultimate consumer of the decisions that issue from the administrative justice system. It is important that the claimant's feelings and concerns be understood. One is reminded of Justice Douglas's comments in dissent in another Social Security disability case. "This case is minuscule in relation to the staggering problems of the Nation. But when a grave injustice is wreaked on an individual by the presently powerful federal and state bureaucracy, it is a matter of concern to everyone, for these days the average man can say 'There but for the grace of God go I.'"[211]

NOTES

1. Social Security Independence and Program Improvements Act of 1994, P.L. 103-296, 108 Stat. 1464.

2. See U.S. General Accounting Office, *Social Security Disability: SSA Actions to Reduce Backlogs and Achieve More Consistent Decisions Deserve High Priority* (Washington, DC: GAO, 1997); U.S. General Accounting Office, *Social Security Disability: SSA Making Progress in Conducting Continuing Disability Reviews* (Washington, DC: GAO, 1998).

3. On the continuing debates over SSA reviews, see Martha Derthick, *Agency Under Stress: The Social Security Administration in American Government* (Washington, DC: Brookings Institution, 1990).

4. The draconian processes that led to these results came in part from poorly crafted legislation and from criticism of failures to exercise sufficiently strong enforcement practices in the past. See U.S. General Accounting Office, *Supplemental Security Income: Action Needed on Long-Standing Problems Affecting Program Integrity* (Washington, DC: GAO, 1998). At the same time, there was a history of arbitrariness, *Sullivan v. Zebley,* 493 U.S. 521 (1990).

5. 424 U.S. 319 (1976).

6. This study has, from an instructional perspective at least, a clear debt to Anthony Lewis's *'Gideon's Trumpet* (New York: Random House, 1964) and Alan F. Westin''s *The Anatomy of a Constitutional Law Case* (New York: Macmillan, 1958).

7. The substantive analysis of Social Security disability issues employs Haviland and Glomb's "The Disability Insurance Benefits Program and Low Income Claimants in Appalachia," 73 *W. Virginia L. Rev.* 109 (1971), as a conceptual base.

8. Interview with Mr. George Eldridge by the author in Norton, Virginia, August 27, 1979.

9. *Id.*

10. 5 C.F.R. §903.203a (1980).

11. A copy of the form letter is shown in Brief for Petitioner, *Mathews v. Eldridge,* p. 32a.

12. See generally Fred Davis and James Reynolds, "Profile of a Social Security Disability," 42 *Missouri L. Rev.* 541 (1977). There continue to be changes in regulations, but most of the procedures remain roughly like those that existed during the ten-year period covered by this study.

13. U.S. House of Representatives Subcommittee on Social Security of the Committee on Ways and Means, *Background Materials on Social Security Hearings and Appeals,* 94th Cong., 1st Sess. (1975), p. 2.

14. Davis and Reynolds, *supra* note 12, at p. 548.

15. Jerome Smith, "Social Security Appeals in Disability Cases," 28 *Administrative L. Rev.* 13, 14 (1976). See also Jerry L. Mashaw et al., *Social Security Hearings and Appeals: A Study of the Social Security Administrative Hearing System* (Lexington, MA: Heath, 1978), pp. 66–69.

16. Davis and Reynolds, *supra* note 12, at p. 543.

17. See generally Mashaw et al., *supra* note 15, chap. 5.

18. *Simon v. Eastern Kentucky Welfare Rights Organization,* 426 U.S. 26 (1976). See also *Warth v. Seldin,* 422 U.S. 490 (1975).

19. *DeFunis v. Odegaard,* 416 U.S. 312 (1974).

20. Brief for Petitioner, *supra* note 11, p. 32A.

21. *Id.,* at p. 7 n. 5.

22. He was seen at one point in this process, but not physically examined, by a consulting psychiatrist.

23. Reproduced in Jerry L. Mashaw, "The Supreme Court''s Due Process Calculus for Administrative Adjudication in *Mathews v. Eldridge*: Three Factors in Search of a Theory of Value," 44 *U. Chicago L. Rev.* 28, 35 (1976).

24. The substantial evidence rule, though it is a fairly complex rule in particular cases, is based on the relatively simple notion that since the administrator is considered to be expert, there should be no major burden of proof in administrative cases. Instead, the administrator must have relied on some evidence and not have merely acted arbitrarily.

25. See e.g., *Richardson v. Perales,* 402 U.S. 389 (1971).

26. See *Rooke''s Case,* 5 Co. Rep. 996, 77 Eng. Rep. 209 (1599).

27. *Yick Wo v. Hopkins,* 118 U.S. 356, 359-60 (1886).

28. See generally John Dickinson, *Administrative Justice and the Supremacy of Law in the United States* (New York: Russell & Russell, 1927).

29. *Id.,* at pp. 35–36.

30. Walter Gellhorn,*Federal Administrative Proceedings* (Baltimore: Johns Hopkins Press, 1941) and James M. Landis,*The Administrative Process* (New Haven: Yale University Press, 1938).

31. U.S. Senate, Report of the Attorney General''s Committee on Administrative Procedure, *Administrative Procedure in Government Agencies,* Sen. Doc. no. 8, 77th Cong., 1st Sess. (1941).

32. Albert H. Meyerhoff and Jeffrey A. Mishkin, "Application of *Goldberg v. Kelly* Hearing Requirements to Termination of Social Security Benefits," 26 *Stanford L. Rev.* 549, 549–50 (1974).

33. See e.g., William W. Van Alstyne, "The Demise of the Right-Privilege Distinction in Constitutional Law," 81 *Harvard L. Rev.* 1439 (1968).

34. *Sherbert v. Verner,* 374 U.S. 398, 404-405 (1963).

35. J. Skelly Wright, "Poverty, Minorities and Respect for Law," 1970 *Duke L. J.* 425 (1970). See also Charles Reich, "The New Property, " 78 *Yale L. J.* 733 (1964).

36. *Londoner v. Denver*, 210 U.S. 373 (1908).

37. *Grannis v. Ordean*, 234 U.S. 385, 394 (1913); *Dent v. West Virginia*, 129 U.S. 114, 124-25 (1889); and *Armstrong v. Manzo*, 380 U.S. 545, 552 (1965).

38. *Morgan v. United States*, 304 U.S. 1, 14-15 (1938).

39. *Joint Anti-Fascist Refugee Committee v. McGrath*, 341 U.S. 123, 168 (1951).

40. *McGrath, Id.; Greene v. McElroy*, 360 U.S. 474 (1959).

41. *Wieman v. Updegraff*, 344 U.S. 183 (1952).

42. *Sherbert v. Verner, supra* note 34.

43. *Sniadach v. Family Finance Corp.*, 395 U.S. 337 (1969).

44. 397 U.S. 254 (1970).

45. *Id.,* at pp. 261–62.

46. *Id.,* at p. 262 n. 8.

47. *Id.,* at p. 262.

48. *Id.,* at p. 264.

49. *Id.,* at p. 266.

50. 397 U.S. 280 (1970).

51. *Id.,* at pp. 281–282.

52. 408 U.S. 471 (1972).

53. 411 U.S. 778 (1973).

54. 418 U.S. 539 (1974).

55. 402 U.S. 535 (1971).

56. 412 U.S. 441 (1973).

57. 419 U.S. 565 (1975).

58. 407 U.S. 67 (1972). See also *Mitchell v. W.T. Grant*, 416 U.S. 600 (1974) and *North Georgia Finishing v. Di-Chem*, 419 U.S. 601 (1975).

59. 433 F. 2d 998 (4th Cir., 1970), *certiorari* denied 401 U.S. 1003 (1971). See also *Escalera v. New York City Housing Authority*, 425 F. 2d 853 (2d Cir. 1970), *certiorari* denied 400 U.S. 853 (1970).

60. See e.g., *Messer v. Finch*, 314 F. Supp. 511 (E.D. Ky 1970), and *Wright v. Finch*, 321 F. Supp. 383 (D. D.C. 1971).

61. 405 U.S. 208 (1972).

62. *Id.,* at p. 212.

63. 361 F. Supp. 520 (W.D.Va. 1973).

64. James M. Haviland and Michael B. Glomb, "The Disability Insurance Benefits Program and Low Income Claimants in Appalachia," 73 *W. Virginia L. Rev.* 109 (1971).

65. Until relatively recently there were few judges hearing Social Security disability cases in the mining areas of Virginia.

66. See Gerald Hayes, "Profile of a Social Security Disability and the Administrative Law Judge," 1975 *Air Force L. Rev.* 73 (1975). See also Smith, *supra* note 15, and Davis and Reynolds, *supra* note 12.

67. Haviland and Glomb, *supra* note 64, at pp. 113–14.

68. Davis and Reynolds, *supra* note 12, at p. 542.

69. Hayes, *supra* note 66, at p. 75.

70. Haviland and Glomb, *supra* note 64, at pp. 115–116.

71. *Id.,* at pp. 126–27.

72. *Id.,* at p. 128.

73. Mashaw et at., *supra* note 15, at pp. 50–51.

74. Jerome Smith, *supra* note 15, at p. 14.

75. *Eldridge v. Weinberger, supra* note 63.

76. *Id.,* at pp. 525–26.

77. 405 U.S. 208 (1972).

78. *Id.,* at pp. 209–27.

79. Eldridge v. Weinberger, *supra* note 63, at p. 523.

80. *Id.*

81. *Id.*

82. *Supra* note 43.

83. *Supra* note 55.

84. *Supra* note 58.

85. *Eldridge v. Weinberger, supra* note 63, at p. 524.

86. *Id.*

87. *Id.,* at pp. 524–25.

88. *Id.,* at p. 525.

89. *Id.,* at pp. 525–26.

90. *Id.,* at p. 526.

91. *Id.,* at p. 527.

92. See generally Robert G. Dixon, *Social Security Disability and Mass Justice: A Problem in Welfare Adjudication* (New York: Praeger, 1973).

93. This debate over the insurance or social welfare base for the disability program will remain a significant dispute for the foreseeable future.

94. See generally Dixon, *supra* note 92.

95. Such investigations as U.S. House of Representatives, Hearings Before the Subcommittee on Social Security of the Committee on Ways and Means, *Delays in Social Security Appeals,* 94th Cong., 1st Sess. (1975) contain a great deal of criticism, but they also acknowledge SSA efforts to improve performance.

96. See e.g., Mashaw et al., *supra* note 15. See also "Report of the Disability Claims Process Task Force;" Edwin Yourman, "Report on a Study of Social Security Benefit Hearings;" and Victor G. Rosenblum, "The Administrative Law Judge in the Administrative Process," all in U.S., House of Representatives, Subcommittee on Social Security of the House Ways and Means Committee, *Recent Studies Relevant to the Disability Hearings and Appeals Crisis,* 94th Cong., 1st Sess. (1975).

97. For a presentation of reversal rates, see Background Materials, *supra* note 13, at p. 25.

98. Mashaw et al., *supra* note 15, at pp. 1–2.

99. Background Materials, *supra* note 13, at p. 28.

100. *Id.,* at p. 21.

101. *Id.,* at p. 23.

102. *Id.*

103. Mashaw et al., *supra* note 15, at p. 24.

104. See generally Haviland and Glomb, *supra* note 64.

105. Background Materials, *supra* note 13, at p. 13.

106. *Id.*

107. *Id.*

108. *Id.*

109. See the statement of John B. Rhinelander, *in Delays in Social Security Appeals, supra* note 95, at p. 267 et seq.

110. See generally *Delays in Social Security Appeals, supra* note 95.

111. See e.g., Meyerhoff and Mishkin, *supra* note 32.

112. Mashaw et al., *supra* note 15, at pp. 46–64.

113. *Id.,* at p. 30.

114. *Background Materials, supra* note 13, at p. 10.

115. Transcript of oral argument in *Mathews v. Eldridge,*p. 10.

116. Meyerhoff and Mishkin, *supra* note 32.

117. Henry J. Friendly, "Some Kind of a Hearing," 123 *U. Pennsylvania L. Rev.* 267 (1965).

118. See the testimony of John Rhinelander, in *Delays in Social Security Appeals, supra* note 95.

119. Mashaw et al., *supra* note 15, at pp. 49–64.

120. *Delays in Social Security Appeals, supra* note 95, at p. 231.

121. See e.g., Smith, *supra* note 15.

122. Testimony of Representative John A. Siberling, in *Delays in Social Security Appeals, supra* note 95, at p. 247.

123. *Id.,* at p. 236.

124. *Id.,* at p. 242.

125. *Id.,* at p. 231.

126. U.S. House of Representatives, Subcommittee on Social Security of the Committee on Ways and Means, *Staff Survey of State Disability Agencies Under Social Security and SSI Program,* 94th Cong., 1st Sess (1975), pp. 1–3 (Hereafter cited as *Staff Survey*).

127. *Background Materials, supra* note 13, at p. 12.

128. *Delays in Social Security Appeals, supra* note 95 at p. 445.

129. See generally Dixon, *supra* note 92. See also Dixon's testimony in *Delays in Social Security Appeals, supra* note 95, at pp. 111–20.

130. Dixon, in *Delays in Social Security Appeals, supra* note 95, at p. 154.

131. Yourman, in *Id.,* at pp. 148–49.

132. *Delays in Social Security Appeals, supra* note 95, at p. 471.

133. *Id.,* at pp. 442, 469–70.

134. See *Staff Survey, supra* note 126.

135. *Id.,* at pp. 8–10.

136. *Id.,* at p. 4. See also the comments of Marie A. Clark, in *Delays in Social Security Appeals, supra* note 95, at p. 445.

137. *Id.,* at pp. 227–66.

138. See Caldwell's testimony, in *Id.,* at pp. 35–45.

139. "Twenty-four State agencies believe that the reasons given by the Committee on Ways and Means in 1954 for having State agencies under the vocational rehabilitation agency make disability determinations are no longer valid." *Staff Survey, supra* note 126, at p. 2.

140. U.S. House of Representatives, Subcommittee on Social Security of the Committee on Ways and Means, *Recent Studies Relevant to the Disability Hearings and Appeals Crisis,* 94th Cong., 1st Sess. (1975).

141. Eldridge interview, *supra* note 8.

142. *Id.*

143. Brief for Petitioner, *Mathews v. Eldridge,* pp. 5–6 and pp. 1–2.

144. *Id.,* at p. 11.

145. *Id.*

146. *Id.,* at p. 12.

147. 402 U.S. 389 (1971).

148. *Eldridge v. Weinberger, supra* note 63, at pp. 524–25.

149. *Underwood v. Ribicoff,* 298 F.2d 850 (4th Cir. 1962).

150. Brief for Petitioner, *supra* note 143, at p. 51.

151. Interview with Donald Earls, August 27, 1979.

152. Brief for Respondent, *Mathews v. Eldridge,* at pp. 9–10.

153. *Id.,* at p. 11.

154. Warren E. Burger, "The State of the Federal Judiciary," in Walter F. Murphy and C. Herman Pritchett, *Courts, Judges, and Politics* (New York: Random House, 1974). See also Warren E. Burger, "1976 Annual Report of the State of the Judiciary," in *National Conference on the Causes of Popular Dissatisfaction with the Administration of Justice* (St. Paul, MN: Judicial Conference of the United States, 1976).

155. *Id.* See also Warren E. Burger, "Annual Report on the State of the Judiciary," 1979.

156. Tom Goldstein, "Burger Asks Judges to Help Preserve Role of State Courts," *New York Times,* March 20, 1970, p. B12.

157. See e.g., *Santobello v. New York,* 404 U.S. 257 (1971), and *Stone v. Powell,* 428 U.S. 465 (1976), Chief Justice Burger concurring.

158. 416 U.S. 134 (1974).

159. *Fuentes v. Shevin, supra* note 58.

160. *Sniadach v. Family Finance Corp., supra* note 43.

161. *Bell v. Burson, supra* note 55.

162. *Board of Regents v. Roth,* 408 U.S. 564 (1972).

163. *Arnett v. Kennedy, supra* note 158, at p. 157.

164. *Cafeteria Workers v. McElroy,* 367 U.S. 886 (1961).

165. *Id.,* at pp. 895–96.

166. Compare *United States v. Robel,* 389 U.S. 258 (1967).

167. *Arnett v. Kennedy, supra* note 158, Justice Powell concurring.

168. *Id.,* at pp. 166–69.

169. *Id.,* at pp. 219–21.

170. 422 U.S. 749 (1975).

171. 397 U.S. 471 (1970).

172. 363 U.S. 603 (1960).

173. 404 U.S. 78 (1971).

174. See e.g., *Frontiero v. Richardson,* 411 U.S. 677 (1973) and *Weinberger v. Wiesenfeld,* 420 U.S. 636 (1975).

175. *Weinberger v. Salfi, supra* note 170, at pp. 781–82.

176. Van Alstyne, *supra* note 33.

177. *Weinberger v. Salfi, supra* note 170, at pp. 77–72.

178. *Id.,* at pp. 803–4, Justice Brennan dissenting.

179. Transcript of oral argument in *Mathews v. Eldridge,* pp. 3–4.

180. Interview with Donald Earls.

181. Transcript of oral argument, in *Mathews v. Eldridge,* p. 1.

182. *Id.,* at p. 3.

183. Brief for Petitioner, *supra* note 143, at p. 66A.

184. Transcript of oral argument, in *Matthews v. Eldridge,* p. 24.

185. *Id.,* at pp. 24–26.

186. *Mathews v. Eldridge, supra* note 5, at pp. 323–26.

187. *Id.*

188. *Id.,* at pp. 325–26.

189. *Id.,* at p. 342.

190. Haviland and Glomb, *supra* note 64; and Meyerhoff and Mishkin, *supra* note 32.

191. 424 U.S, at p. 347.

192. *Id.,* at pp. 348–49.

193. See generally Robert A. Rutland, *The Birth of the Bill of Rights, 1776–1791* (Chapel Hill: University of North Carolina Press, 1955).

194. *Mathews v. Eldridge, supra* note 5, Justice Brennan dissenting.

195. *Richardson v. Wright, supra* note 61, at p. 215.

196. *Id.,* at pp. 215–17.

197. *Id.,* at p. 218.

198. *Id.,* at p. 227.

199. See e.g., *Parham v. J.R.,* 442 U.S. 584, 599-600 (1979), and *Mackey v. Montrym,* 443 U.S. 1, 10-11 (1979).

200. Interview with Donald Earls.

201. Interview with George Eldridge.

202. *Id.*

203. *Id.*

204. Jerry L. Mashaw, "The Supreme Court"'s Due Process Calculus for Administrative Adjudication in *Mathews v. Eldridge*: Three Factors in Search of a Theory of Value," 44 *U. Chicago L. Rev.* 28 (1976).

205. See note 199, *supra.*

206. Recently Mashaw served as project director on the social security process conducted under the auspices of the National Center for Administrative Justice. See note 15, *supra.*

207. See e.g., Mashaw, *supra* note 204, p. 30.

208. *Weinberger v. Salfi, supra* note 170.

209. *Arnett v. Kennedy, supra* note 158.

210. Van Alstyne, *supra* note 33.

211. *Richardson v. Perales, supra* note 25, at p. 413, Justice Douglas dissenting.

Appendix 2

The EPA and Environmental Justice

New Regulation, Social Policy, in the Context of Sustainable Development

NOTE

Like the Eldridge case study in Appendix 1, the EPA and environmental justice case study that follows is to be used with several portions of the text. As was true of the other case study, this is a story of an administrative process and legal process, but it also presents a political, economic, and social context. In addition to providing a useful exemplar of what can happen in complex regulatory processes that arise in a politically charged setting, it also presents other important issues and themes that arose as this regulatory process evolved. In particular, it addresses the concept of equity, issues of diversity, and the importance of the international context within which domestic regulatory problems arise and by which they are affected. It is also a useful case study by which to see what can happen when administrators decide to abandon normal administrative law processes in a headlong rush to produce a policy without a sensitivity for the legal context of public administration.

Finally, it must be remembered that, like any case study, this is a story during a fixed period of time. Just as Social Security processes have changed since the Eldridge case emerged, so too the environmental justice efforts continue as this is being written. Even so, it is a revealing story about many aspects of regulation. It also explores critically important issues of equity that arise across the spectrum of public law in public administration.

INTRODUCTION

The preamble to *Agenda 21,* the product of the Rio Earth Summit, begins as follows:

> Humanity stands at a defining moment in history. We are confronted with a perpetuation of disparities between and within nations, a worsening of poverty, hunger, ill health and illiteracy, and the continuing deterioration of the ecosystems on which we depend for our well-being. However, integration of environment and development concerns and greater attention to them will lead to the fulfillment of basic needs, improved living standards for all, better

protected and managed ecosystems and a safer, more prosperous future. No nation can achieve this on its own, but together we can—in a global partnership for sustainable development.[1]

In this short paragraph more than 175 governments agreed to a statement of a great challenge and to an approach to its solution—sustainable development. But it is clear that there are significant issues of equity in this commitment. Principle 7 of the Rio Declaration adds: "In view of the different contributions to global environmental degradation, States have common but differentiated responsibilities."[2] The World Commission on Environment and Development, better known as the Brundtland Commission, added: "Sustainable development is development that meets the needs of the present without compromising the ability of future generations to meet their own needs."[3] This presents a different kind of equity issue, equity across generations. Finally, 117 heads of government in Copenhagen underscored the Brundtland Commission's core argument that "economic development, social development and environmental protection are interdependent and mutually reinforcing components of sustainable development."[4] Central to these interwoven foundations for change is a recognition that there are serious social issues as well as critical problems of environmental protection and economic development that must be addressed if the global community is to enter the new century on a sustainable path. And at the core of many of these issues in all three realms are extreme and worsening crises of inequity. The problem of equity must be addressed if the goal of sustainable development to which virtually all of the world's nations have committed themselves is to be achieved.

However, the evidence to date suggests that, for all of its rhetoric, the global community has not adequately committed itself to the development of the balance among the economic, social, and environmental elements of sustainable development. In fact, the evidence is that while some progress has been made, "the overall trends for sustainable development are worse today than they were in 1992."[5] The United Nations Environmental Programme's *Global Environmental Outlook* report (GEO-1) concluded in 1997 that "Progress towards a global sustainable future is just too slow. A sense of urgency is lacking. Internationally and nationally, the funds and political will are insufficient to halt further global environmental degradation and to address the most pressing environmental issues—even though technology and knowledge are available to do so."[6] The evidence is strong that economic growth predominates over concern with the environment in most places around the globe.[7] Financial support has not been produced in the manner or in the amounts committed at Rio or Copenhagen. While the signatories to the Rio Declaration and *Agenda 21* accepted their special responsibility to provide financial support for the sustainable development effort and to focus on assisting the most desperate people immediately, the Rio+5 report found that: "Regrettably, on average ODA [official development assistance] as a percentage of GNP of developed counties has drastically declined in the post-UNCED period, from 0.34 per cent in 1992 to 0.27 per cent in 1995."[8] In fact, official development assistance actually fell in both constant dollar and even in absolute dollar terms.[9] Despite the continued focus on growth and the lack of investment in sustainable development, the global economy has been and remains volatile and fragile, with serious dangers on the horizon and significant impacts already present in Latin American and Asia. And if the economic and environmental situation is volatile and troubled, the social development situation is far worse. The Rio+5 report found that: "Too many countries have seen economic conditions worsen and public services deteriorate; the total number of people in the world living in poverty has increased."[10] The 1997 UNDP Human Development Report put it bluntly:

> Although poverty has been dramatically reduced in many parts of the world, a quarter of the world's people remain in severe poverty. In a global economy of $25 trillion, this is a scandal—reflecting shameful inequalities and inexcusable failures of national and international policy.[11]

More specifically, the Human Development Report states that: (1) some 1.3 billion people "live on incomes of less than $1 a day;" (2) current estimates indicate that by 2000 "half the people in Sub-Saharan

Africa will be in income poverty;" (3) in Latin America some 110 million people are currently estimated to be poor by standard income measures, and the figures continue to grow despite some progress during the early 1990s; (4) "some 160 million children are moderately or severely malnourished;" and in fact the Human Development Index (HDI) has actually declined in 30 countries (3 of those in Latin America) during the past year.[12]

In the United States, progress on the environmental front has been uneven. And, indeed to advocates of the emerging environmental justice movement, to use the term "uneven" is a dramatic understatement. As will become clear in the pages that follow, they argue that while many communities applaud their environmentally friendly attitudes, others carry an undue weight that comes from the rest of society's demands for rapid economic growth and from a standard of living that represents the highest level of consumption of resources and production of pollution in the world.

This case study is about the response of the U.S. government to calls for new efforts at regulation intended to achieve environmental justice. It teaches a variety of lessons about regulation in the modern context. To be sure, it speaks to the law and politics of regulation in post-deregulation era world. It also addresses what happens when regulatory efforts are undertaken that seek to avoid traditional techniques. It is instructive to pay attention to the importance of intergovernmental relations here, to the significance of the blend of government policymaking and market dynamics, and to complex political relationships among interest groups in the process. This is a battle that takes place in the context of contemporary efforts to achieve sustainable development in a competitive domestic and international economic context. That is the reality for virtually all conversations of regulation now and in the foreseeable future. Finally, this case study also explores debates about concepts of equity, a critically important concept in modern public life.

This story begins with a consideration of the concept of equity in sustainable development. It turns next to the effort to move from general rhetorical commitments to environmental justice to policy action by the EPA. It concludes with an analysis of some of the problems that emerged from this new regulatory effort and a consideration of lessons concerning the complexities of the environmental justice concept. It also offers a new framework for addressing issues of environmental equity in cases raising environmental equity concerns.

THE PROBLEM OF EQUITY IN SUSTAINABLE DEVELOPMENT

What made the global move toward sustainable development different from the environmental efforts that preceded it was a recognition of the interrelationship among the critical elements of economic development, social policy, and environmental protection. It was a growing recognition that in a world with a rapidly expanding population, a history of excessive and wasteful use of resources in developed countries, and a huge population in developing, often very poor nations, something had to change. There were and are very large issues about who had benefited from the use and abuse of the world's resources and who had paid. It was clear that the developed countries had built their high standard of living on the extraction of resources not only from their own lands but from less developed nations at bargain basement prices, if they were not simply taken at the point of a gun, and in ways that left devastating impacts not only on their natural resources but also on their people and their cultures. At the same time, these nations were not prepared to give up their own dreams for a better life and the enjoyment of the advantages that come with economic development just because environmentalists in rich western capitals called for conservation. That development, in turn, entailed the use of yet more resources. There were serious issues of both inequality and equity to be addressed if sustainable development was to be achieved. To meet that challenge, it is necessary to understand the relationship between equality and equity, to better understand the nature and uses of the concept of equity, and to relate the intergenerational and intragenerational aspects of equity in sustainable development. This complex set of issues set the stage for the regulatory battle to follow.

Equality and Equity in Sustainable Development

The several agreements and sets of commitments reached during the 1990s, from Rio's Earth Summit through Istanbul's City Summit, establish a set of principles that provide the framework against which the discussion of equality and equity in sustainable development takes place.[13] The beginning of the discussion at the Rio Earth Summit concerned the environmental protection principle, the commitment that protection of the global commons is required for the preservation of life itself and is essential to both social and economic development. The commitments associated with this principle consider both what is commonly referred to as the green agenda, which is primarily associated with conservation and with the management of natural resources, and the brown agenda, which emphasizes issues of pollution control with respect to current activities and cleanup of environmental damage already done. However, there is also the principle of integration and balance which emphasizes the fact that, despite the obvious tensions among environmental activists, neoliberal economists, and social policy advocates, the only hope for humankind is an effective working balance among these elements. Gro Harlem Brundtland put the matter bluntly in her foreword to the report of the World Commission on Environment and Development:

> When the terms of reference of our Commission were originally being discussed in 1982, there were those who wanted its considerations to be limited to "environmental issues" only. This would have been a grave mistake. The environment does not exist as a sphere separate from human actions, ambitions, and needs, and attempts to defend it in isolation from human concerns have given the very word "environment" a connotation of naivety in some political circles. The word "development" has also been narrowed by some into a very limited focus, along the lines of "what poor nations should do to become richer," and thus again is automatically dismissed by many in the international arena as being a concern of specialists, of those involved in questions of "development assistance."[14]

Against this backdrop, the common commitments recognize a right to development, but with an obligation of mutual respect. The international conferences have consistently accepted the basic right of sovereign nations "to exploit their own resources pursuant to their own environmental and developmental policies" since the 1972 Stockholm Conference. However, that same principle also calls upon the states to accept "responsibility to ensure that activities within their jurisdiction or control do not cause damage to the environment of other States or of areas beyond the limits of national jurisdiction."[15] This concern for transboundary issues extends not only to deliberate actions, as in the transboundary shipment of hazardous waste, but also to responsibility for what appear to be domestic actions that nevertheless plainly have transboundary effects.

There is an equality principle and an equity principle. The equality principle starts from the premise that all people are valuable, regardless of their race, gender, religion, cultural heritage, physical condition, or age. There are two subordinate principles embodied in the equality commitment. First, there is a nondiscrimination principle that bars deliberate discriminatory treatment. Second, there is a participation principle that calls upon governments to empower all persons within the society, and particularly women, to participate fully in the economy, the public policy process, and social action as they affect all aspects of life, including environmental issues.

The equity principle has two dimensions. The intergenerational principle begins from the commitment to "meet the needs of the present without compromising the ability of future generations to meet their own needs." However, beyond those general admonitions that emphasize the environmental dimensions of sustainable development, there are numerous other elements to the intergenerational equity commitment that speak specifically to children and the elderly. These began with the recognition of the importance of the involvement of youth in the Rio Declaration and reached a much wider scope in the Copenhagen Declaration and Commitments. Beyond these factors, there are numerous commitments with respect to intragenerational equity. These commitments stress the need to address the special concerns of women, indigenous persons, and persons with disabilities, all groups that have historically been excluded from key decisions that have had significant environmental, social, and economic consequences on their lives, and to include them in decisionmaking. The intragenerational equity dimension also has numerous specific recognitions that developing nations have been specifically disadvantaged by the actions of developed countries and international institutions which now have an obligation not only to accord them the dignity that they deserve as sovereign states with proud cultural traditions but also to undertake differential burdens in sustainable development efforts to assist these countries, in part to make up for past abuses.

The Nature of Uses of Equity

Of course, what these principles indicate is that equality and equity are not the same. It is important to consider what equity is, how it differs from equality, and why it matters in terms of its inter- and intragenerational dimensions. This effort to take equity seriously is all the more important because the concept is used so loosely and inappropriately in public administration, in public policy debates, in the general discourse on sustainable development, and specifically with respect to the term *environmental equity.*

The concept of equity goes back to Aristotle.[16] It arises from the fact that while decisions of those who govern should be just, justice is not always served by treating everyone in the same way. This seemingly contradictory idea stems from two different problems. First, laws and other official decisions are meant to apply to a broad range of persons and situations. It is clear that policies will be made that have unintended harsh effects on unintended targets. Thus, it would be considered unjust to treat the poor mother who steals to feed her starving child with the same degree of harshness as we would the professional criminal. She would be guilty of the same crime but equity would be invoked to conclude that she should be treated differently in the interest of justice. Second, there is a corrective sense of equity in which we conclude that it is necessary to provide special consideration for someone who suffered because of the inappropriate behavior of another. In either case, equity is about a deliberately unequal treatment in the interest of justice.

The legal community has spent centuries developing the concept of equity. At first, when lands that became nations were governed by kings or queens—or for that matter, tribal chieftains—the issue of equity was addressed by an appeal to the ruler. Since the ruler was presumed to be ordained by God (or in some societies by the gods), he or she was anointed under divine authority with the power to exercise perfect truth and perfect justice. However, when the ruler's subordinates issued decisions, they were not so endowed. They could make mistakes and do injustices. Thus, in many countries, the ruler appointed a particular person to hear appeals from these other officials and to do justice in the name of the monarch to parties who may have been injured. In Britain, for example, the king (or queen) appointed the Lord High Chancellor (known as My Lord Keeper for his role as keeper of the King's conscience) to hear cases in equity.

In the modern manifestation, courts are often given jurisdiction to decide cases in law and equity.[17] For example, when courts are told to issue remedial orders to correct an injustice in the past, they are instructed to take into account the special circumstances of the case and provide a remedy designed to make the victim of past conduct whole again where a simple award of damages would not be sufficient. Thus, judges issue injunctions that require government to cease illegal behavior and take remedial steps.[18] In countries that have traditionally functioned on a civil code system with distinct limits on the discretion of courts, there has nevertheless been a move toward according a wider scope. It is not clear just now how this trend will evolve.[19]

The discussion and development of the meaning and uses of equity in international law continues to date. Edith Brown Weiss has been a leading voice in this conversation. She notes that:

> Today we regard equity as serving several functions: filling gaps in the law (*praeter legem*), providing the basis for the most just interpretation (*infra legem*), providing a moral basis for making an exception to the normal application of a rule of international law (*contra legem*), and as providing a basis for deciding a case in a way that disregards existing law (*ex aequo et bono*).[20]

Thus, this more appropriate use of equity as a deliberate departure from standard or equal treatment in the interest of justice is well established both within many countries and among nations.

This use of the concept was also well understood by the drafters of *Agenda 21,* the Copenhagen accords, and other sets of critical commitments. Unfortunately, it has become very common, particularly in the realm of social policy, to treat the term *equity* as if it meant equality and *inequity* as if it meant only inequality. That is in some sense understandable, since something that is inequitable is unjust and that which is unequal would seem to be unjust and therefore wrong. However, an action at equity is a deliberate decision to single out some people or even some nations for special treatment because they have been or may be subject to injustices. Hence, the special commitments of *Agenda 21* and the Copenhagen accords recognize that special solicitude is required for the least developed nations and for groups of people such as women, indigenous persons, ethnic or religious minorities, the disabled, and children because they have been so disadvantaged by past behavior by the developed countries, sometimes by those in power within the developing world, and often within their own nations.

This is not to say that equity is only a legal concept. It is and should be a social, political, and economic concept as well. However, it would be a serious misuse of the term, and jeopardize the effort to do justice for developing nations and people who have suffered in the past and continue to be at a disadvantage today, if equity were not properly understood. In this perspective, equity in sustainable development is a specific response to issues presented by the marketplace, either because it can be used to address problems the market is not designed to consider or because of market failures that produce injuries to the weak and the poor. It is political as well in that it is a justification for relief for groups that have been either intentionally or unintentionally harmed by past political decisions. In both the social and juridical uses, equity calls for a process of careful consideration of context and the unique facts of the specific problem presented for remediation and recognizes that blunt instruments will not suffice to redress injustice. In the end, the more we focus on the concept of equity in its various manifestations, the more we see the natural way in which it links the pieces of sustainable development.

Intergenerational and Intragenerational Equity Issues

There is one other aspect of equity in which there is need for an effort to bring together the different perspectives that form the basis for sustainable development. It is important to recognize the critical syntheses called for in the common commitments and articulated most clearly in the Brundtland report. First, of course, is the foundation principle of sustainable development, which holds that only by bringing together the social, economic, and environmental perspectives can there be a sustainable future. Notwithstanding the fundamental character of this commitment, it remains one of the most difficult tasks both within nations and in the international arena to keep advocates in each of these fields from seeking to pull policymaking off in one dimension. Policy entrepreneurs who enjoy dominance in their particular field are loathe to engage with those who seem to speak a different language and who have goals that seem to be in competition with, if not in opposition to, their own priorities. Moreover, in certain countries or regions, one or more of these groups tend to enjoy substantial political support. Hence, there is no serious doubt that economic development forces are dominant in Asia whereas environmental interests are much stronger at least in relative terms in North America and Western Europe. In much of Latin America, by contrast, there is a good deal of support for social development, perhaps in part because economic values were so dominant for so long.

Second, the Brundtland Commission pressed the argument that the global community must continually address issues of both intergenerational and intragenerational equity. As noted above, the Social Summit and Habitat II, in particular, have emphasized that intergenerational equity means not merely generations in the distant future, but also just relationships in terms of who benefits and who pays within the groups of children, adults, and older persons who are seeking "a healthy and productive life in harmony with the environment" as called for in Principle 8 of the *Copenhagen Declaration*.[21] Indeed, the very young and the elderly live at the intersection between inter- and intragenerational equity concerns. Thus, the concern is not merely with who pays and benefits, or with whose range of choices for satisfying needs shall be dominant, but also about the treatment of the aged, children, and other groups who are either vulnerable or who have traditionally suffered most from social, economic, or environmental problems. Beyond that, intragenerational equity issues may be presented in sustainable development literature in the language of capacity building, providing the essential capabilities for groups or nations to meet their own sustainable development needs by ensuring that they have the tools and resources despite issues of inequality or worse.

Many of these issues and forces have given rise to what is a rapidly growing environmental justice movement. Indeed, environmental justice provides a vehicle for thinking about how we might better bring the three dimensions of sustainable development closer together and also a context for considering more carefully how to use the concept of equity in the sustainable development effort. However, there are also potentially problematic elements to the environmental justice debate as it is currently evolving both domestically and internationally. In that regard, it is useful to use the rise of environmental justice in the United States as a case study with particular attention to lessons about the problems that have arisen on all sides in the debate.

ENVIRONMENTAL JUSTICE IN THE UNITED STATES: A DEMONSTRATION OF PROBLEMS

The environmental justice movement arose out of the efforts of civil rights leaders during the 1980s and 1990s, though its roots can be traced even further back. It proceeds from the premise that some people in the society and their communities have been called upon to pay a disproportionate cost for the economic gains of the wider society. It has become a matter of considerable interest and activity in the past several years, but has unfortunately turned into a battleground that has produced little for the people in whose name the battle has been fought. Indeed, it has seen many of those people turn against each other as well as against the advocates on all sides of the effort. Its story can be understood in four parts. First, there was the rise of environmental justice as environmental racism. Second, there evolved an inadequate policy developed essentially around, rather than through, the normal policy process. Third, as conflict emerged over that policy, the level of anger grew with members of the minority communities pitted against each other and organizations that needed to be part of a joint effort locked in battle. Finally, in the wake of these battles, efforts to save the policy have still failed to understand the real problem and address it.

Environmental Justice as Environmental Racism: The Rise of a Political Movement in the United States

The early 1980s were clearly years of tremendous dynamism around the world, and that was certainly true in the United States. On the environmental front, the battle by local residents at Love Canal in upstate New York brought the risks of abandoned hazardous waste sites to national and even international attention. The political energy that flowed from that battle helped to ensure passage of the Superfund program in Congress. However, President Reagan was elected in 1980, and his administration insisted that environmental regulation was too aggressive and too intrusive, resulting in undue burdens on economic growth. On the international level, the Reagan administration dramatically changed the U.S. positions on a variety of issues, leading to major confrontations in 1982 at the United Nations Environmental Programme conference in Nairobi at the ten-year point after Stockholm. This was also a difficult period for the civil rights movement in the United States as the old coalition that had been responsible for so much success earlier found it difficult to attract young members and had difficulty identifying an agenda that would engage their imagination.

It was in this context that many Americans began saying firmly "Not in My Backyard" (NIMBY) to any hint that environmentally undesirable businesses might be located in their area.[22] It was also when African-Americans, Latinos, and Native Americans began asking in response "Why Always in My Backyard?" (WAMBY).[23] And when efforts were made to locate a disposal site for soil mixed with PCB-contaminated oil in a largely African-American area in Warren County, North Carolina, the civil rights community reacted strongly with protests joined by a number of leaders. One of those involved in mounting the protests was Benjamin Chavis, then head of the United Church of Christ Commission for Racial Justice and later head of the National Association for the Advancement of Colored People (NAACP). It was Chavis who coined the term *environmental racism,* which he later defined as follows:

> Environmental racism is defined as racial discrimination in environmental policy making and the unequal enforcement of environment laws and regulations. It is the deliberate targeting of people of color communities for toxic waste facilities and the official sanctioning of a life threatening presence of poisons and pollutants in people of color communities. It is also manifested in the history of excluding people of color from the leadership of the environmental movement.[24]

His United Church of Christ Commission for Racial Justice then undertook a study, published in 1987, which found not only that there was a pattern of siting various kinds of waste facilities and other undesirable industries in predominantly minority communities, but that race, rather than class, was the best predictor of this pattern.[25]

Another of those participating in the North Carolina demonstrations was Walter Fauntroy, who represented the District of Columbia in the U.S. House of Representatives. Fauntroy called upon the U.S. General Accounting Office (GAO), the investigatory arm of the Congress, to explore the environmental racism question.[26] The GAO produced its report in 1983 and its findings were consistent with those of the Church of Christ Commission report.[27]

Even before the Warren County episode set all of this in motion, Robert Bullard, who would become the leading advocate for what was coming to be known as the environmental justice movement, had begun research on the issue. In 1979, Bullard was a sociology professor at Texas Southern University in Houston when his wife, attorney Linda McKeever, asked his help with a case. She was suing the city, the state, and Browning Ferris Industries on behalf of home owners against the siting of a solid waste facility in their neighborhood.[28] Bullard and his students found that waste facilities in the area were overwhelmingly concentrated in minority neighborhoods.

Bullard went on to publish his research on the environmental justice problems in the American South[29] and other collections that included cases affecting Latino and Native American communities in other parts of the country.[30]

By 1990 efforts were underway to get a better understanding of this emerging phenomenon. In that year the University of Michigan hosted a conference on "The Incidence of Environmental Hazards," which brought together a variety of those doing research in this new field.[31] In 1991 some 650 such activists gathered in Washington for what was termed the "First National Environmental Leadership Summit." Shortly thereafter, the *National Law Journal* published a special study on environmental justice, concluding that: (1) there was unequal treatment of communities of color as compared to white communities even taking income into account; (2) enforcement actions by federal authorities on pollution problems were slower to come in minority communities; (3) cleanups in those communities were less thorough than in white communities; and (4) enforcement penalties were lower than in white communities.[32]

These events were followed by a wave of similar gatherings and studies. Each produced a new collection of research and commentary, a kind of running chronicle of the rise of a social/political movement.[33] However, even as the movement was gaining momentum, its internal and external tensions were beginning to surface. One of the first such tensions was the fact that the meetings and the movement itself quite deliberately did not include mainline environmentalist leaders or their organizations. Indeed, the advocates of environmental justice began from the premise that those groups and their spokespersons were part of the problem rather than allies in possible solutions. Bullard put it bluntly:

> Historically, the mainstream environmental movement in the United States has developed agendas that focus on such goals as wilderness and wildlife preservation, wise resource management, pollution abatement, and population control. It has been primarily supported by middle- and upper-middle-class whites. . . .
>
> Not surprisingly, mainstream groups were slow in broadening their base to include poor and working-class whites, let alone African Americans and other people of color. Moreover, they were ill-equipped to deal with the environmental, economic, and social concerns of these communities.[34]

Of course, it came as no surprise that mainstream environmentalists were not pleased at the characterization that had been painted of them and a number were fully prepared to point out that the environmental justice movement could have been supported by some of those with well-established scientific expertise in a number of critical areas. After all, it was becoming increasingly clear that while the leaders of what was coming to be called the EJ movement had certainly raised the consciences of many and had placed an important set of problems on the policy agenda, there was much work to be done to develop effective methodologies and launch important research to support the policy development process to come.[35] The response from Bullard, Bunyan Bryant, and other EJ leaders was that scientific debates had for too long tied up the effort to bring environmental justice. Indeed, there was a clear sense of frustration in some of their writings, which charged, in essence, that debates over just what level of causation had to be proven to show harm from hazardous chemical exposure was little more than a cover to maintain the status quo.[36]

It was also becoming increasingly clear that Native Americans and Latinos felt strongly that each group had special problems quite different from those of African-Americans or others.[37] That was one of the reasons why some Native Americans refused to participate in a proposed World Council of Churches–sponsored conference. Jace Weaver, who ultimately organized the North American Native Workshop on Environmental Justice, wrote:

> Both George [Tinker] and I previously had spoken and participated at conferences planned by one or another of the organizations making up the loose-knit movement. We had experienced

firsthand the marginalization of indigenous concerns at such meetings, and we had no desire to once again be token presences at largely non-Native gatherings. Instead, we proposed an all-Native workshop, which would assemble some of the people working on the grassroots, national, and international levels, to address the wide range of environmental problems facing Native communities.[38]

Among other things, Native Americans were concerned about issues that related the spiritual elements of their cultures to questions of land and resource use as in the debate over placement of nuclear wastes in Ward Valley, California. On the other hand, they were frustrated by stereotypes about the relationships between indigenous peoples and the environment that went from naive on the one hand to malevolent on the other extreme. Then there was the fact that it was learned in the 1980s that, during the 1950s and 1960s, federal officials had knowingly and deliberately permitted Navajo uranium miners to be exposed to radioactive gases destined to cause them serious illness and death while withholding knowledge of the situation from the miners.[39]

Latinos also argued that they had special issues for which they needed to advocate. It was with no small bit of irony that Chairman John Conyers had to announce that Congressman Estaban Torres was unable to be present at hearings on environmental justice in early 1993 because he was attending the funeral of Cesar Chavez, who had fought against the exposure of farm workers to toxic pesticides and herbicides and worked to improve their health and sanitation conditions. There were also numerous issues relating to communities in the West and Southwest that involved mining and other environmental concerns that were quite different from the issues most often identified by African-American leaders in the East and Southeast. The civil rights movement had not always seen a strong alliance between African-American and Latino leaders.

Even with these concerns and tensions, however, it was clear that the EJ movement was gaining force. Its leaders were being heard and, thanks to their diligent efforts, the momentum was building toward some kind of environmental justice policy.

Government Produces Inadequate Policy Via an Unusual Route

The Bush administration was having a difficult time on the environmental front as the 1992 presidential election approached. The policies and tactics of the Reagan administration in the environmental field as well as in the field of civil rights were widely attacked, not only in the United States but around the world. President Bush insisted that he wanted to be known as "the Environmental President," and that he would take such unusual actions to achieve that goal as appointing well-known environmentalist William Reilly to head the effort at the Environmental Protection Agency (EPA). And in fact, in 1990, Reilly began conversations with leaders of the EJ movement, eventually creating the Office of Environmental Equity and establishing an Environmental Equity Work Group. However, the administration got into serious trouble in the run-up to the Rio Earth Summit. Bush opposed a number of agreements pending for the Summit. To make matters worse, the president ran hot and cold on whether and how he would participate. He sent EPA Administrator Reilly, who found himself left high and dry as the administration changed its public line, concluding with a late decision by Bush to attend the conference himself. Reilly was quoted as saying that "he felt like he was 'bungee jumping where someone else might cut the cord.'"[40]

The Clinton administration came to office campaigning on a strong commitment to the environment. Indeed, one of the reasons for including Al Gore on the ticket was his environmentalist reputation. Bullard and Chavis participated in the presidential transition process in the natural resources cluster in early 1993. Their efforts were rewarded in 1994 when President Clinton issued Executive Order 12898 entitled "Environmental Justice for Minority Populations." The order called upon executive branch agencies to develop processes for including environmental justice considerations in their decisionmaking. It also established an interagency working group on EJ. Unfortunately, it did not add resources to the agencies for the purpose of implementing the policy.

There was also activity in Congress. In March of 1993, the Civil and Constitutional Rights Subcommittee of the House Judiciary Committee held hearings under its Chair, long-time civil rights advocate Don Edwards of California. The following month, Edwards appeared before a subcommittee of the Government Operations Committee in hearings on environmental justice and called for the use of civil rights laws to address EJ issues:

> I call on the EPA to enforce Title VI by requiring the recipients of federal pollution control funds to show that they are being used in a non-discriminatory way. Racial minority groups must be proportionately represented among the beneficiaries of federal funds.
>
> Furthermore, the EPA must establish and enforce siting and permitting guidelines that will take into consideration the existing environmental burden of a community. Communities of color must not continue to be the dumping grounds for our nation's wastes because the politically powerful say "Not in My Backyard."[41]

The Title VI to which Congressman Edwards referred is a part of the Civil Rights Act of 1964 that prohibits discrimination in any activities receiving funds from the national government.[42] The idea was to have the Environmental Protection Agency threaten to cut off federal funds if state or local officials, or any other entity receiving federal dollars, engaged in environmental racism. This was a position promoted by several of the legal advocacy groups that had joined the discussion. And, in fact, it was in 1993 that the first petition was presented to EPA on Title VI grounds, asking the agency to take action.

Indeed, the discussion was shifting to focus debate on a number of specific environmental justice battles emerging around the country. One of the centers of this conflict was the state of Louisiana, and an area in that state known as "Cancer Alley." This stretch of land along the Mississippi River between Baton Rouge and New Orleans is lined with one chemical- or petroleum-based industry after another. In 1993, the Louisiana Advisory Committee to the U.S. Commission on Civil Rights issued its report entitled *The Battle for Environmental Justice in Louisiana: Government, Industry, and the People.*[43]

> At least 38 major chemical companies and 112 industrial sites are located in the industrial corridor. Discharges are calculated upwards to 400 million pounds of waste into the environment each year. At last count, there are approximately 800 suspected and confirmed hazardous waste sites in Louisiana and 12 Superfund sites.[44]

The Advisory Committee pointed out that most of the residents of the area were relatively poor and mostly African-American. The committee called for action by both state and federal environmental regulatory authorities. The U.S. Commission on Civil Rights concurred in those recommendations and, in a letter to EPA Administrator Carol Browner, Commission Chairman Arthur Fletcher specifically called upon the agency to develop strategies "which will target environmental equity enforcement under the civil rights statutes and regulations administered by the U.S. Environmental Protection Agencies."[45]

In fact, EPA was already giving consideration to that approach, but the process slowed as controversy grew. In its early budget request, the Clinton administration had actually suggested a budget cut for EPA, but Congress rejected that plan. Moreover, the administration in general and EPA in particular was emphasizing a new approach to regulation that called for less formal legal enforcement and more negotiation. Moreover, differences of opinion began to surface within EPA over what kind of policy to pursue, what the data were that supported it, and what the process should be by which the policy was to be generated. Even as more interest groups were launching lawsuits as private attorneys general (private parties claiming to represent the public interest), studies were beginning to emerge from several sources that challenged earlier claims about the causes and patterns of environmental justice problems. Thus, the General Accounting Office, which had formerly supported the claim that race was the dominant indicator in explaining the siting of hazardous facilities, issued a new report in 1995 raising doubts about the primacy of race as an explanation.[46] New York University Law Professor Vicki Been published an influential article that found that in some cases permits had been issued when a community was majority white but that after industrial facilities came into the area, the properties declined in value.[47] Poorer families, many of which were minority families, then moved in because those were the homes they could afford. Thus, attention to permitting processes and assumptions about race-based decisions might miss the point entirely. It could be, she argued, that the more important emphasis needed to be on housing discrimination or other kinds of policy issues. At a minimum, she said, studies that simply correlated current demographics with numbers of facilities really did not explain what had happened to cause the situation or why it had occurred, and really could not do so. On top of these studies, rumors surfaced that some within EPA had the same kinds of views.

The EPA had a variety of other concerns at the time. It had been facing a range of issues around the country, including several sets of legislative debates over reauthorization of environmental laws like the Superfund statute. The agency had been very much involved in the administration's effort to move away from a legal enforcement approach to regulation and toward market tools, like establishing a market for the trading of emission permits. When it was necessary to move in a particular case, pressures were strong within the administration to negotiate rather than enforce. The Congress and the administration moved to put more burdens on regulatory agencies that sought to issue new rules. Ironically, although Clinton had run against Bush in part on grounds that burdens on rule-making had prevented vigorous environmental action, Clinton issued Executive Order 12866 that was in some respects even more burdensome than what had existed before. Specifically, agencies like EPA were now responsible not only to do extensive cost/benefit analyses to justify action, but were also required to provide risk analyses and tie the level of regulatory action to the level of risk in any given situation. Both environmental activists and environmental justice advocates saw this as a vehicle to avoid serious regulatory requirements and a move undermining efforts to really clean up existing polluted sites.

There was also growing frustration with the Clinton administration in general. Despite its rhetoric, it was clear that the administration had chosen economic development as its primary focus. It seemed to many that the administration was abandoning its Democratic allies in Congress as it negotiated budget deals with Republican leaders and brought the Democrats in only after the fact. Indeed, it appeared as though the administration had entered a budget deal that cut the ground out from under its allies on the Hill. Environmentalists and civil rights leaders both, along with their congressional supporters, were fast becoming frustrated. The fact that the Los Angeles riots, in which dozens had been killed and much promised by Washington, actually produced little real policy change or financial support was not a positive sign. Then, on top of everything else, the Democrats lost control of Congress for the first time in decades, which led to pitched battles and resulted in an effort by congressional Republicans to shut down the federal government in order to force administration budget concessions.

There was also growing frustration at the state and local government levels as Washington seemed to continue the trend of the 1980s to push greater responsibility to them without adequate resources. Even so, what funds were coming to the states and local governments seemed to come with more conditions and controls attached even though administration rhetoric ran the other way. This led to passage in 1995 of the Unfunded Mandates Reform Act, but the legislation was not made retroactive and really made little impact at least in the short term.

Against this background, and given the momentum toward the use of civil rights laws to address environmental justice issues, it was not surprising that lawyers would emerge as policy entrepreneurs in the policy development process. California-based attorney Luke Cole of the Center on Race, Poverty, and the Environment wrote EPA Administrator Browner in 1996 demanding action. Environmental justice advocates saw EPA's lack of action itself as a violation of Title VI. The Civil Rights Commission and others kept the pressure on EPA.

However, EJ advocates around the country did not limit themselves to lobbying EPA. Historically, civil rights attorneys have used cases brought under existing laws to push the policy process. Besides, people in many communities were losing hope that Washington would come to their aid. In 1996 a citizens' group in Chester, Pennsylvania—the Chester Residents Concerned for Quality Living—challenged the Pennsylvania Department of Environmental Protection (DEP) on grounds that their permitting processes were discriminatory in violation of Title VI and associated regulations.[48] The case wound its way through the administrative process and into the federal courts where it was initially dismissed by a district court, but that decision was overturned by the U.S. Court of Appeals for the Third Circuit, which recognized the right of the citizens' group to bring the action.[49] At the same time, Robert Kuehn of the Tulane University Environmental Law Clinic in Louisiana was working with citizens' groups there in efforts to block a planned uranium reprocessing plant and a proposed polyvinyl chloride (PVC) production facility. In 1997, they brought formal charges against the Louisiana Department of Environmental Quality for violating Title VI in its permitting processes.

In February of 1998, the Environmental Protection Agency issued what it termed "Interim Guidance for Investigating Title VI Administrative Complaints Challenging Permits,"[50] triggering a firestorm of controversy. The document was presented not as a legally binding rule but as an interim guidance document, what would be termed under the Administrative Procedure Act (APA) as a policy statement.[51] This choice meant that EPA was not required to meet the normal legal requirements for the issuance of regulations, including advanced publication of notice and extensive opportunities for public participation before the agency acted.[52] It also left the agency a great deal of freedom rather than stating a firm rule with which the agency itself would be expected to comply. The document concludes:

> EPA may decide to follow the guidance provided in this document, or to act at variance with the guidance, based on its analysis of the specific facts presented. This guidance may be revised without public notice to reflect changes in EPA's approach to implementing the Small Business Regulatory Enforcement Fairness Act of the Regulatory Flexibility Act, or to clarify and update text.

The guidance document cited Executive Order 12898 and the memorandum issued along with it, relying on Title VI as its authority. The agency asserted jurisdiction over any agency, activity or program at any level of government if any portion of the organization targeted received any funds for any purposes from EPA even if the particular program at issue did not itself receive EPA funds. "Therefore, unless expressly exempted from Title VI by Federal statute, all programs and activities of a department or agency that receives EPA funds are subject to Title VI, including those programs and activities that are not EPA-funded."[53] If the agency found upon review that a state or local government's permitting processes resulted in environmental discrimination, it could move to block EPA funding or refer the case to the Department of Justice for court action.

The Interim Guidance also asserted that: "Moreover, individuals may file a private right of action in court to enforce the nondiscrimination requirements in Title VI or EPA's implementing regulations without exhausting administrative remedies."[54] This was important to EJ advocates for a number of reasons. First, it supported claims by attorneys that they were not required to take their complaints through EPA before bringing a suit in court, known as exhaustion of administrative remedies. Second, it provided support for a claim that these advocates were not required to rely upon EPA or the Department of Justice to bring a case, but could launch one on their own. Given that the U.S. Supreme Court had been moving to limit these so-called implied private rights of action, that was important support.

Interestingly, EPA chose to cite the Court of Appeals ruling in the Chester, Pennsylvania, case as support for its assertion. That was a red flag because the Chester ruling was itself open to debate, which was to be increased as the case was taken on appeal to the United States Supreme Court. Later, in August of 1998, the Supreme Court dismissed the case at the request of the citizens' group on claims that because the permit that was the target of the case was no longer pending, the case was moot. However, state attorneys general, who did not want the Third Circuit ruling to stand, convinced the Supreme Court, even as it dismissed the case, to nullify the appeals court ruling which left EPA without support for that portion of its policy.[55]

Finally, to those who understand civil rights law, the EPA statement was extremely important for another reason. It changed the burden that the advocates would have to meet in court to prove an environmental racism claim. Under existing Supreme Court rulings, in the absence of agency implementing regulations for Title VI, those bringing the case would have to prove both the effect of discrimination and the intent to discriminate. Proving intent to discriminate can be extremely difficult. However, if intent can be inferred from the fact of disparate impact of a particular action (a minority group was disproportionately injured), the burden is much reduced. However, the Court ruled that where an agency had issued regulations aimed at disparate impact, a private party could sue and need demonstrate only discriminatory effect.[56] And EPA specifically indicated that this guidance document applied whether the complaint alleged "either discriminatory intent and/or discriminatory effect in the context of environmental permitting."[57]

The policy then explained that EPA would base its handling of and decision on a complaint on the question whether the permit involved would "create a disparate impact, or add to an existing disparate impact, on a racial or ethnic population." However, the document did not explain how disparate impact was to be defined and what methodology would be used to determine its existence. All that was required was that the EPA Office of Civil Rights should use a "reasonably reliable indicator of disparity."[58] There were similar levels of ambiguity with respect to the process for identifying the affected population.

The Politics of Negativity: Pitting Governments and Communities Against Each Other

Tensions had been building like a dry forest ready to burn and the publication of the EPA "Interim Guidance" provided the lightning strike to set it off. It was a multidimensional conflict that involved a wide range of stakeholders. The clashes came between state and local governments and the EPA, the EPA and the commercial sector and their congressional supporters, between minority environmental racism warriors and economic development advocates in minority communities, and between long-time advocates of environmental justice and emerging critics of that movement. The conflicts were both general as to the nature and contents of the EPA policy and also specific with respect to pending projects.

State and local reaction was swift and strong. Richard Harding, Director of Michigan's Department of Environmental Quality, writing in *Ecostates,* the journal of the Environmental Council of the States (ECOS) (a group made up of heads of state environmental agencies), blasted EPA.

> Anticipating a firestorm of protest, EPA officials circumvented the congressional oversight process by putting this issue in agency guidance. Other than a brief public comment period, EPA has done nothing to encourage a thoughtful discussion of the issue. The April 19, 1998, *Detroit News* reports that EPA documents show State regulators were deliberately shut out of the planning process because they "might slow down the process."[59]

The ECOS organization ultimately took a position opposing the EPA guidance in a letter signed by 34 state environmental commissioners. Other organizations that came out in opposition included the U.S.

Conference of Mayors, the National Association of Counties, the National Governors' Association, and the Western Governor's Association. Apart from their criticisms of the way the policy had been developed, these and other officials worried aloud that the policy could be used by radical environmentalists or others to block efforts to revitalize so-called brownfields areas, formerly polluted sites within urban areas targeted for redevelopment after clean-up. They charged that such moves would cripple efforts to bring jobs and economic growth to minority communities and lead to the use of "green fields" (presently pristine sites) as the locations for new industrial development, adding to existing environmental problems.

Supporters of the EPA policy, including some of the attorneys leading the EJ effort, charged that this was nothing more than evidence that environmental racism was alive and well. They challenged what they regarded as the effort to maintain business as usual in the face of a growing number of cases of communities racked by the effects of pollution from Chicago to Cancer Alley in Louisiana and from Chester, Pennsylvania, to Los Angeles. Robert Bullard warned that there was more on the way because communities were organizing to fight.

> Whether we talk about the miners in New Mexico, or the nuclear dump proposed for California's Ward Valley, which also affect Native Americans, or the Sierra Blanca nuclear dump in Texas, in a mostly Hispanic area, there's clearly a pattern of attacks on communities of color, and they're forming alliances. The Navajos are not alone, and the people of Ward Valley are not alone. It's a signal that the environmental justice movement has matured, and we can tap into each other's resources, experiences and expertise.[60]

And the message was also that this was a movement that was mobilizing people who for too long had not become active in the civil rights movement, including young people who could identify with the environmental issues.

But there were also sharp disputes among different groups who saw themselves as the legitimate spokespersons for minority communities. These disputes came in the form of intergovernmental issues, others emerged around proposed projects, and still others came in scholarly exchanges. Among those groups that responded strongly against the EPA's Interim Guidance were the National Association of Black County Officials, who objected that the new policy preempted the local land use processes. The National Chamber of Commerce also came out in opposition. The president of the organization charged that: "The EPA is pimping the black community to further their own agenda of a pristine earth at the expense of our jobs."[61] The phrase "green racism" emerged to characterize the frustration that elite outsiders, whatever their race or background, were coming in the name of civil rights and interfering in local decisions about development that would provide jobs in minority communities.

A number of these tensions emerged as members of minority communities took opposing views on proposed projects.[62] The clash over the effort by Shintech to open a $700 million PVC plant in St. James Parish, Louisiana, was a very visible symbol of this problem during 1997 and 1998. The Shintech project was challenged on Title VI grounds by Robert Kuehn of the Tulane Environmental Law Clinic and the approval of the project was delayed pending consideration of that complaint. The local and state NAACP chapters took positions in favor of the Shintech plant but the national environmental justice leaders, including the national NAACP, opposed it. In the midst of the Shintech case, another firm, Louisiana Energy Services, announced that after a process lasting more than seven years, and with some $34 million invested, it was terminating its proposal to build the Claiborne Enrichment Center, a uranium enrichment facility.[63] Environment justice advocates celebrated the victory, but opponents saw it as evidence that would-be investors really would pull out rather than face the burdens of lengthy litigation and the delays in the permitting processes that would come with EPA involvement. To EJ advocates, there was nothing new about the claims that civil rights advocates were disruptive outsiders who would cause damage to those they purported to help. On the other hand, that kind of response caused local African-American supporters of the pending projects to become even more frustrated.

In addition to these reactions by minority groups, there was also evidence of differences of opinion within the intellectual community. While a number of debates have appeared in the law review literature in recent years, the most recent round of disputes developed around a book published in the midst of the current battle, during the summer of 1998, by Christopher H. Foreman, Jr., entitled *The Promise and Peril of Environmental Justice.*[64] Foreman had already published pieces critical of the EJ movement, but this volume challenges virtually every aspect of the effort. Foreman, a Senior Fellow in the Governmental Studies Program at the Brookings Institution, described himself as a black, liberal Democrat who voted for Clinton twice, but was more than willing to take on both EPA and EJ advocates, and Robert Bullard in particular. His criticisms of the research on EJ was harsh and unrelenting and his characterization of the movement as it has evolved is that it is in many respects counterproductive.

The battle was also raging at the national level in Washington. The U.S. Chamber of Commerce president wrote President Clinton attacking the EPA policy. Business leaders expressed their frustration on Capital Hill as well. There were two rapid responses. First, in June, the House Appropriations Committee moved to block further action under the EPA policy, adding an amendment to the appropriations bill stating that:

> None of the funds made available in this Act may be used to implement or administer the interim guidance issued February 5, 1998 by the Environmental Protection Agency relating to Title VI of the Civil Rights Act of 1964 and designated as the "Interim Guidance for Investigating Title VI Administrative Complaints Challenging Permits" with respect to complaints filed under such title after the date of enactment of this Act until guidance is finalized. Nothing in this section may be construed to restrict the Environmental Protection Agency from developing or issuing a final guidance relating to Title VI of the Civil Rights Act of 1964.

Second, the House Commerce Committee held oversight hearings in early August on the EPA policy at which the EPA Interim Guidance was harshly criticized. Ann Goode, head of EPA's Office of Civil Rights, was grilled by Congressman John Dingell. The next day, the *Detroit News* featured a story recounting the exchange between Dingell and Goode. It concluded that in response to Dingell's demanding questions, a frustrated Goode replied, "As director of the Office of Civil Rights, local economic development is not something I can help with."[65] The EPA supporters were not surprised by the grilling by the Michigan Congressman, long an EPA critic or by critical articles in the Detroit newspapers, nor were they deterred by them.

Struggling to Recover: A Failure by Most Participants to Address the Real Problem

On the other hand, it was clear to EPA Administrator Carol Browner that EPA was in trouble. She had led the agency's attempt to recover from the wide-ranging attacks it had suffered over much of the 1998. However, the outcome remained very much in doubt.

One of Browner's concerns was to challenge the argument that the policy would block urban redevelopment efforts and particularly the so-called brownfields projects. She wrote the mayor of Detroit, one of the most vocal critics, and officials of the U.S. Conference of Mayors in mid-June calling for EPA and the mayors jointly to host a roundtable discussion of the policy.

The U.S. Conference of Mayors has under consideration whether EPA's recent focus on resolving environmental justice complaints is at odds with accomplishing urban redevelopment. As our brownfields efforts demonstrate, this is not the case. Our experience across the nation has shown that, working in partnerships with communities, we can identify plans for the cleanup and redevelopment of polluted sites that [create] jobs and hope—not division and charges of racism. In fact, none of the currently pending environmental justice complaints registered with EPA concerns a brownfields development. Just the opposite is true— eliminating pollution and restoring hope and jobs is vital to bringing justice to many urban communities.[66]

It was becoming crystal clear to Browner and others that part of the anger was aimed at the EPA policy, but a very significant portion of it was also aimed at the process by which it had been developed. At the time the Interim Guidance was published, EPA called for a 90-day comment period. However, it was equally clear that few of those affected considered that an adequate opportunity to participate in the process. Browner announced that: "We have heard the criticism that EPA's interim guidance for evaluating Title VI complaints was developed without sufficient public input. That is why we have convened a group of highly respected community and business leaders, state and local officials, and community and environmental groups to advise us on these matters."[67] Of course, as soon as EPA began to announce the membership of its 23-person advisory committee, various stakeholders began to criticize the choices and to demand their own representation. The committee met for the first time in July. Before that, federal officials had convened at an environmental justice meeting in Los Angeles where they participated in what was termed a "toxic tour" of largely minority neighborhoods that had been suffering from severe pollution. The advisory committee convened in Philadelphia on July 27–28. As part of the program, the committee toured the now-famous community of Chester. While local officials and some residents felt that the tour was rigged to present the most extreme situations, committee members were still impressed by the severity of what they had seen.

By mid-summer, EPA had 15 active complaints that it was considering under its policy, including the Shintech issue in Louisiana. Disputes within those cases and the public criticism that EPA was receiving led Ann Goode, head of the EPA Office of Civil Rights, to state what EPA saw as the problems to be remedied during her testimony in early August before the Commerce Committee.

The issues identified include the need for:

- substantial involvement from stakeholders
- clear definitions of terms like "disparate impact" and "affected community"
- addressing concerns that the Interim Guidance will not hinder or halt economic re-development in the nation's urban areas and exacerbate urban sprawl
- technical assistance to recipients
- peer reviewed methodologies for the assessment of disparate impact and harm based on sound science[68]

She announced that EPA intended to move on all of those fronts to meet the concerns of the states and local governments and to improve communications with EPA decisionmakers. She noted that the questions about methodologies for evaluating disparate impact were being referred to EPA's Scientific Advisory Board (SAB) for peer review.

The EPA assurances did not satisfy the many critics that who come forward to challenge the interim guidance. A hint of the tenor of things to come came only a week later when Robert Kuehn of the Tulane Environmental Law Clinic responded to a letter from Goode, indicating that a set of questions had been submitted to the SAB for peer review. Kuehn challenged the lack of representativeness of the SAB and his view of biases demonstrated by its performance on other issues. "Therefore, it is crucial that the committee chosen by the SAB to review and answer the OCR's questions be a racially and ethnically diverse as well as one that fully meets the Federal Advisory Committee Act's requirement that it contain a balanced representation of competing views on an issue."[69] That was a not-so-veiled threat that a legal challenge brought under the Federal Advisory Committee Act could very well be in the offing.

The irony is that if EPA had used traditional rulemaking proceedings in the first place, it would not have been subject to this criticism or the accompanying threat. There would have been many issues to address, but the process by which EPA tried to avoid the challenges of rulemaking succeeded in producing not merely the problems that would have been encountered in the normal process, but many more, including serious issues of integrity and credibility.

The situation as 1998 came to an end was, in simple terms, a policy nightmare. Further, there was little likelihood that state and local officials would drop their opposition to more EPA involvement in their land use decisions, an area that is generally regarded in the United States as one of the most important prerogatives of state and local governments. There was no sign that opposition from the private sector would decline or that Congress would be any more favorably disposed toward EPA on this issue in the months to come. The battles within the academic community and indeed within and among minority groups showed no signs of abating. Finally, it seemed as though control of the substantive disputes have slowly been shifting from the original EJ advocates to lawyers.

In the face of all of this, it appeared obvious that EPA would not meet its goal of finalizing its policy by the spring of 1999. And there was every likelihood that some of the 15 pending complaints would land in the courts unless: (1) the complainants dropped their Title VI charges; (2) the firms dropped their permit requests; and (3) the states and localities involved were prepared to accept EPA's verdict on their permitting procedures. None of these seemed likely in the current atmosphere, particularly in light of the positions taken by the various groups involved and the fact that ten state attorneys general had already taken positions in opposition to the EPA guidance. And with the presidential campaign of 2000 heating up, it appeared unlikely that the administration would want to address these issues.

ENVIRONMENTAL JUSTICE, SOCIAL POLICY, AND SUSTAINABLE DEVELOPMENT: LESSONS FROM THE U.S. CASE STUDY

At the end of the day, then, can it be said that the citizens of Chester, Pennsylvania, Louisiana's Cancer Alley, South Chicago, or the pollution-ridden neighborhoods of Los Angeles have had their lives improved as a result of all of the effort and the resources that have been invested in the conflict by the beginning of 1999? It would be very difficult to make that case. Does that mean, however, that the effort to press a commitment to environmental justice is not a fruitful direction for the United States, other countries, or international institutions to pursue? On the contrary. There are lessons from this case, albeit primarily lessons about how not to proceed, that can be learned. At the same time, the international agreements from Rio to Istanbul, commit the global community to sustainable development in which environmental justice can be and must be a useful tool and also an essential element provided that the concept of equity is more adequately developed.

Let us consider first the lessons from the U.S. experience and an alternative approach based on analysis of context, conditions, and responses in equity.

Lessons from the U.S. Case

While most of the lessons from this case study of environmental justice in the United States to date are negative, it would be irresponsible not to recognize three positive features of the EJ effort. First, virtually every international discussion of sustainable development since the Stockholm meeting has resulted in agreement about the importance of building the capability and sense of efficacy of all people, and particularly to attend to those needs for groups who have traditionally been excluded from active participation in critical decisionmaking. The EJ movement seeks to address that need in very real ways and not with mere rhetoric. Second, there is great power in identifying situations of inequity and providing mechanisms to place them in the public eye and on the policy agenda. Third, the EJ movement has served notice that it is not going to be acceptable as, it has been in some places, for decisionmakers to ignore or undervalue the environmental and social dimensions of the sustainable development triangle.

However, there are many serious problems in evidence in the story of environmental justice and the EPA in the United States. These start from very basic issues of conceptual, political, and legal approaches. While it is true that the EJ movement has come to define three basic concepts that provide its foundation, "environmental racism," "environmental equity," and "environmental justice,"[70] in the U.S. case, environmental racism came to predominate and shape the tenor and character of the movement. Thus, the effort to achieve environmental justice came down to an effort to fight environmental racism through a civil rights enforcement model focused almost completely on Title VI of the Civil Rights Act of 1964. Traditionally, this model seeks to find specific past decisions or block current decisions by public officials that are intentionally discriminatory (even if that intent is to be implied from the effects of the discriminatory actions) in violation of law. So framed, it came as no surprise that it was necessary to find an appropriate type of decision to challenge. Hence, virtually the entire effort came to focus on blocking decisions to issue new permits for industrial development or facility siting. There are three sets of decisionmakers who could be targeted in that effort: (1) the federal agency that seems most closely associated with those decisions (even though it usually has little to do with them directly); (2) state environmental protection agencies, which presumably issue rules in the environmental arena; and (3) local governments, which are traditionally the units of government in the U.S. charged with land use planning and the permitting of businesses. While there was a desire to see a new permit/development request in the context of existing environmental problems, this enforcement model did not address the issue in full terms (e.g., relating to poverty alleviation, health improvements, or educational advancement). In fact, there is irony in what has occurred to date. Although environmental justice critics, like Foreman, attacked the movement on grounds that it is unfocused and attempting to resolve all of the social problems under the banner of fighting environmental racism, the actions taken so far have been very narrow, emphasizing an extremely limited aspect of the environment rather than the social or economic issues.

A second irony is that the story of the policy effort through 1998 was not directed toward achieving a positive end state that could be defined as environmental justice. Rather, the effort was negative in the sense of prohibiting action. In its nature the effort tended to move control over the action to the legal community. One of the lessons over the years is that attorneys are better at stopping action or convicting someone of an illegal action than they are at fashioning solutions to the problems they see. Judges tend to suggest in civil rights cases that attorneys often lose interest once the liability finding has been entered and remedies must be fashioned. And once fashioned, there is often no one to help the court ensure implementation.[71]

The other issue that arises in this respect that is quite different from most of the areas in which a civil rights enforcement approach has been taken is that there are significant differences within the affected communities as to what constitutes environmental racism. In general, surveys indicate that communities of color often perceive the presence of racism in the conditions that they find in their communities, but, as this case study demonstrates, there are sharp differences when the issue is a specific decision over a planned facility, particularly if there seems to be a promise of economic development.

In part because of such differences, there continued to be criticism that the process was not bottom-up and based upon participation but often elite and top-down, a criticism often leveled at environmentalists generally who are not seen as bringing positive change to the community.

One of the other sets of lessons that emerges from the U.S. case is that the EJ approach assumed an ability to use a national agency operating in a particular sector to address complex problems in a political, legal, and administrative context that had long since decentralized. The EPA of the 1990s was not the Civil Rights Division of the Department of Justice in the late 1960s and early 1970s.

First, it should have been clear from any examination of the communities most often identified as in need of achieving environmental justice, that no single sectoral agency exercising relatively narrow and limited powers could accomplish the task. Even the critics of the environmental justice movement[72] admitted that there are critical issues of housing, health care, and education as well as environmental concerns to be addressed in these communities. It was not sufficient merely to say that the EJ executive order and EPA policy call for an interagency committee would produce the needed changes. For one thing, it is well understood by practitioners around the world that interministerial committees are notoriously unhelpful. First, unless there are substantial resources to be shared or very significant and direct involvement on a continuing basis by the prime minister or president, these committees are more often a hindrance to policy development and implementation rather than a facilitator of these outcomes.[73]

Second, it was clear that EPA remained, even after almost three decades of operation, a relatively small and very much under-resourced agency. Unlike the Civil Rights Division of the Department of Justice, EPA has traditionally split its legal roles, with counsel for policymaking focused in Washington and lawyers who lead enforcement efforts located in the regional offices around the nation. While the agency has moved to reorganize and rationalize its enforcement operations, it was still a long way from the kind of structure and process that is well suited to civil rights enforcement.

The modest size, limited finances, and broad array of legislative mandates of the EPA are important in this EJ case for another reason. The agency is responsible for a range of very diverse and decentralized programs and operations in which state and local governments are critically important partners. That partnership is largely based upon modest support by EPA. Moreover, the funds available to state and local governments through the EPA have become a small proportion of the overall costs of state and local environmental operations. The days when threatening to withhold federal funding as leverage to coerce state and local compliance with federal agencies are over. A number of the state environmental commissioners in this case study indicated that they were about ready to recommend to their governors that they should tell EPA to keep its money and the mandates that come with it.

Quite about from the financial leverage, the changing character of regulation depends upon the active involvement of the states and local governments. Starting in the 1970s Congress began to use a three-tiered regulatory process. At level one, if states were willing to create their own environmental standards at least as rigorous as the national standards, they would be permitted, upon approval by the national agency, to implement those standards at the state level using their own organizations and people. If the state wanted to use federal standards, it could still do the enforcement itself. Only if the state refused to create rigorous standards or to enforce federal standards would the national agency step in. In truth, many policies now operate completely on the basis of nationally approved state programs, and EPA would not have the capacity to step in if the states did abandon their cooperation. Moreover, programs that affect state and local land use decisions, even if enacted by the Congress, face an uncertain future in the Supreme Court. For example, the Supreme Court struck down a low-level nuclear waste siting law on grounds that it interfered with the constitutional powers of the states because it tried to coerce states into using their regulatory authority.[74] And while it is true that the fact that what is involved here was a federal civil rights claim which gives the national government special authority under the Fourteenth Amendment, there were still a host of constitutional questions that could be litigated if the state and local governments chose to resist EPA rather than to cooperate with it.

Of course, it is clear from this case study that neither the leaders of the EJ movement nor the EPA did anything but antagonize state and local governments, not to mention other NGOs. That is not important solely because such behavior was unlikely to engender the kind of cooperation needed to achieve environmental justice. It also meant that a variety of parties on all sides of the issue had the motivation and the grounds on which to challenge the agency's policy in administrative law. The authority for the Interim Guidance is stated as Section 2-2 of Executive Order 12898, but that executive order does not assert any particular statute or constitutional power as its basis, nor does it specifically refer to Title VI.[75] The fact is that a reviewing court could find that EPA has not clearly established the legal authority on which it is operating. Second, it tried to use a policy statement called "interim guidance" rather than a legislative rule issued pursuant to the Administrative Procedure Act to present what is plainly intended to bind states and localities in their permitting processes. Policy statements and interpretive rules are very ambiguous policy tools in administrative law.[76] While an agency may choose to call a statement a policy statement, a court will decide whether the agency is really issuing something that it means to treat as binding under its authority to issue rules having the force of law.[77] If so, the court would likely find that this is a legislative rule and that it was not issued in accordance with the requirements of the APA. And given the importance of public participation in rulemaking processes, the courts are particularly diligent if they are of the view that an agency is calling a rule a policy statement to avoid the participation requirements of rulemaking.[78] Moreover, having been challenged on its lack of opportunity for participation, the agency created an advisory committee. However, as the case study demonstrated, in choosing that course, the agency has made itself vulnerable to challenge under the Federal Advisory Committee Act. Given its lack of clarity and specificity with respect to the definition of the concept of disparate impact and the lack of clear methodologies for its application, EPA could face due process issues as well as allegations that its decisions are arbitrary and capricious in violation of the APA.[79] And having chosen to accept complaints for resolution under the Interim Guidance, a court could find that there has been "agency action unlawfully withheld," if the agency waits too long to reach decisions in the pending cases. Presumably, the agency would be subject not only to having to respond to a court order in such a situation, but it would also be vulnerable to paying the plaintiffs' costs under the provisions of the Equal Access to Justice Act.

In the end, even if EPA did manage to produce its final guidelines in the near term and even if its policy and the decisions it must make in cases pending under it should survive legal challenge, that will not begin to solve the problems of environmental justice that exist now or are likely to emerge in the future. That is not to say that the long sad history of racial discrimination in the United States has not played a terrible part in bringing about some of the environmental justice tragedies that exist. It has. The point is that the problems are even wider and deeper than EJ advocates have suggested. The records of congressional hearings and other studies cited earlier justify the assertions that there are many communities where people live in terrible environmental conditions with little serious effort at enforcement and no evidence that the residents share in the economic benefits that flow from industries and other commercial activity in their neighborhoods, though they certainly experience the costs. They represent classic examples of the downward spirals that develop when economic development, social conditions, and environmental realities are not seen as mutually interdependent but are allowed to drift. Indeed, in some communities the situations devolve to a point where the EJ advocates' can rightly claim that, by design or by momentum, the areas can be aptly described as "sacrifice zones," areas effectively abandoned to their fate. These communities present serious issues of equity. Markets are not designed to resolve such issues. Neither can they be addressed by efforts to block all development. As Laura Pulido has argued persuasively, it is no answer to tell people who want to make their own decisions about local development that they should set aside the properties for tourism or recreation.[80]

Of course, there are parallel concerns in the international arena notwithstanding the passage of the Basel Convention and the Bamako Convention. To stay with the U.S. case for a moment, there are environmental justice claims being lodged against the U.S. with respect to the impact of pollution at military facilities in Panama and in the border industrial zones in Mexico.[81] And well beyond the U.S. case, there are any number of other examples where some communities' issues of environmental justice represent festering sores. While it is important to understand the forces that brought these situations about and it is very important to stop similar behaviors in the future, a narrow civil rights enforcement orientation of the sort pursued in the United States will not address the conditions that currently exist and is unlikely to help in more than marginal ways in the future.

THE CONTEXT, CONDITIONS, AND RESPONSES IN EQUITY AS A BASIS FOR ENVIRONMENTAL JUSTICE

While the purposes of this case study focused primarily on understanding on a complex regulatory process in the context of contemporary political and social reality, it is necessary to take a step beyond that narrow aspect. Just as in the *Eldridge* case, there was a discussion of options that could have addressed the situation involving Social Security and indeed other social service programs in an environment that calls for due process protections, so it is useful to offer, if only in brief compass, an alternative look at the problem confronted above. For just as the *Eldridge* case concluded with Justice Douglas's warning that "there but for the grace of God go I," we can say of the environmental justice challenge that there but for the grace of God go all of us.

The problem of equity in environmental justice should be addressed within the sustainable development framework. The issue of equity is a concept and area of concern in which all of the players in sustainable development have important interests. Environmental justice can be an area in which to focus conversations about both intergenerational and intragenerational dimensions of equity and to do so in the context of the common commitments that have been reached over a decade of international summits. As Edith Brown Weiss has observed: "Today the traditional definition of equity is eroding. There is a search, though unsystematic, for a new definition. The quest for a consensus on equity in particular contexts will be a major factor affecting international environmental agreements and non-binding legal instruments in the future."[82]

The starting point to address equity issues in environmental justice is a recognition that, for reasons addressed earlier, equity is not a unified concept but one that has several dimensions. Hence, it is necessary to develop not a single answer to the question "What is environmental equity?" but to develop a framework that can be used to engage the many different kinds of equity problems that we find around the world. One possible framework that meets this need considers the context, conditions, and responses in equity as a basis for action.

The Context of Equity Issues

The context of the equity problem in any given situation is both general and particular. At the general level, the context consists of the international commitments and treaties, the regional agreements, the national political and legal institutions and processes, and the culture within which the situation exists. Of the international commitments, those outlined earlier, including the environmental protection principle (with both the green and brown elements), the principle of integration and balance, the right to development with an obligation of mutual respect, the equality principle (including both the nondiscrimination and participation principles), and the equity principle (in both its inter- and intragenerational aspects) are central. These principles set the broad frame and boundaries for consideration of the equity problem, which then must be understood within a set of national institutions and processes. The strengths, weaknesses, and options available must be understood if responses to any given situation are to be effective. Attempts like the EPA and White House approaches discussed throughout this case study to circumvent those institutions and establish administrative law processes are often, as they were in this case, self-defeating. Of course, this need to attend to the existing system also means that it is essential to ensure more adequate and effective institutions and processes.[83] However, that kind of change takes time, and near-term responses to particular problems most often must be sought within the existing context. It is critically important to understand that the context is very much affected by the culture.

At the specific level, the context consists of the institutions, policies, resources, and stakeholders who must be involved to address the problem and the special cultural features that guide their behavior, as well as the proximate and other causes that brought about the current situation, to the degree that they can readily be determined. Even in countries with unified governments, a variety of factors have led ministries to increasingly rely on subnational units at the regional (or state where applicable) or local levels. It should also be said both national and subnational governments are now often dependent upon NGOs performing government functions and services under contract. Environmental equity issues may be problems at the national level, or even issues between nations, but most usually arise in a particular temporal and physical setting. Any attempt to achieve environmental equity that ignores that reality is doomed to failure. If there is any clear lesson that we have gleaned from efforts at sustainable development in addition to the critical interdependence among the economic, social, and environmental dimensions, it is that top-down solutions that do not seek to ensure that policymaking is open, orderly, and participative rarely succeed. It is important to understand the cultural characteristics operating at the local level. Particularly in larger countries or those where the population is racially or ethnically diverse, the differences in local culture can be dramatic. Similarly, differences among the cultures that operate within relevant organizations matter as well.[84] This is true not only of government organizations, but also in NGOs and private firms, and solutions to environmental equity issues usually involve all three.

Finally, the context also includes the causes of the problem to the degree that they can be readily identified. If the situation is focused on the current or recent behavior by one or a few specified actors that threatens a particular population with clearly identifiable harm, the problem-solving challenge is relatively easy. If, as is often true, the problem is more diffuse, with indeterminate impact and causes that are many and spread over a long period of time, as in the Chester, Pennsylvania, case discussed earlier, the situation is very different. There may very well be situations where it is not possible to determine exactly how and why a current problem came into being. That does not mean that it is acceptable to permit the situation to continue. It does mean that the approach to its resolution will be different from other contexts.

The Conditions of Equity

Once the context is understood, it is possible to proceed to identify and then address the particular condition of equity that exists. It is not possible to have a one size fits all response to a problem of environmental equity because there are several quite different conditions that can exist in which judgments as to equity are made. These can be divided into prospective judgments that govern future behavior and present judgments that often consider present conditions caused by past behavior, frequently involving some kind of compensatory response. It is also possible to divide equity judgments between those that involve a comparative assessment (What is equitable as between two or more parties?) and individual determinations (What is an equitable response to one party in a particular circumstance?).

Against that backdrop, it is possible to identify several classes of problems that commonly arise. First, it is common to seek equity in the future allocation of resources and in the distribution of costs. This often arises in treaties or in international contracts, as in discussions of bioprospecting. A second prospective but noncomparative case involves a decision to permit a community or an organization to act in the absence of rules. This is the classic problem of permitting decisions in the absence of clear policy, in which the choice is not between which of two development projects should be allowed to go forward but whether a single proposed project should be authorized and, if so, what burden it should carry for the potential impacts of its action.[85]

Similarly, in present judgments about past conduct, it may be necessary to do equity in the absence of rules. It is common in those jurisdictions where courts have equity powers to conclude that although there is an unacceptable condition for which corrective action must be taken, there is no clear guidance as to what that remedy should be. In such cases, the decisionmaker is called upon to fashion a remedy based upon the unique circumstances of the situation and to make the victim whole again. Where the effort is to provide a remedy for previous conduct, the situation may involve a comparative equity assessment. That is, there must be an allocation of costs among a number of parties responsible for a problem. This is the most common issue presented in the clean-up of abandoned toxic sites such as are addressed by the Superfund program in the United States. There are many complexities in such judgments because there are issues of quantity and quality (What type of harm and how much of it?) as well as ability to pay that must be considered.

Next, there is a condition that may occur in which the court determines that the decisionmaker is asked to make an exception to an existing rule or to ignore a rule completely in the interest of justice. These may occur either in prospective or present equity judgments. For example, a local community group may develop a microenterprise. If government officials apply all of the existing regulations as written, the group will very likely be unable to operate because of the burdens. However, by making an exception, the decisionmaker is in essence making an allocation of risk and cost. With respect to past actions, the decisionmaker may decide not apply the same responsibility to a small organization that gave no indication that its leaders knew they were breaking a rule or in any way intended harm. The group may still be responsible for, say, improper disposal of paint, but equity is used to mitigate the severity of the sanction. This is a classic problem of equity.

Responses in Equity

Once having established the context and the particular condition of equity that is in question, the problem is to select a process for responding to it. That requires both an approach to decision and the means to ensure implementation. The methods of decision usually divide into negotiated resolutions or authoritative institutional decisions.

Negotiated resolutions may either be processes involving equals or they may involve negotiated resolutions among differentially empowered stakeholders. Both of these types negotiations may involve a substantial number of parties, depending upon the equity condition they are designed to address. The obvious example of the first variety is a treaty negotiation in which sovereign nations agree on a method for an allocation of natural resources and costs. These equal negotiating partners may elect to solve their issues through direct negotiation in the event of a disagreement, to use a mediator to aid negotiations, or even to submit disputes to an arbitrator who will make binding decisions.

However, it is obviously the case that many negotiations between developed nations and developing countries are not negotiations among equals, notwithstanding the legal fictions of international law. The same is often true with large states and small ones or major cities and small towns. Indeed, most situations in environmental justice that are to be resolved through negotiations involve attempts at settlement among a substantial number of parties with wide disparities as to their relative resources, expertise, and social, political, or legal power. For negotiation to function as a means to do equity in such cases, it is usually necessary for the negotiations to involve some kind of neutral third-party mediation or facilitation. This is particularly important if community groups are to be able to participate in a serious way. Without challenging the motives of any parties to the negotiation, the imbalances are simply too great in many environmental justice problems for the parties themselves to achieve the balance necessary to do equity without outside help. And even with a third-party neutral, it is still often necessary to provide some kind of resource support for community groups if they are to participate effectively. It is also necessary to address the special concerns raised when one or more of the parties to a negotiation is a government agency. The point here is that if negotiation is to be the tool by which to do equity, the design and support of the process and consideration of the elements necessary to ensure balance and effectiveness are as important as the actual talks about the substantive question at issue.

The alternative to some form of negotiated means for doing equity is to submit the matter to an authoritative institutional decision process. In some cases, the matter may fall under the jurisdiction of a ministry or administrative agency, while in others the issue may be submitted to a judicial tribunal. There are two critical qualifications that must be addressed if it can be said that these processes can achieve environmental justice by doing equity. First, if ministries or local agencies are to make the decision, there must be an accessible opportunity for an appeal to an independent institution, most often a court though there could conceivably be an alternative. The reason quite simply is that the ministry and local agency are very often parties at interest in environmental justice problems and may be accused of wrongdoing. The dangers of bias, conscious or otherwise, can be quite high. That is not to impugn the integrity of the officials involved, but to recognize the realities of institutional life. It also cannot be ignored that, in some cases, part of the problem may be a concern about corruption. Assuming that the decision is to be rendered by a court, there must be assurance of independence. The effort to enhance the credibility of courts in some countries is critically important to sustainable development in general and for environmental justice in particular.[86]

It should also be clear that a decision as to what equity requires in a given situation often requires considerable attention to implementation and monitoring. The fact that the decision is reached through a negotiation process does not, of course, reduce this need. The process for implementation often must include a mechanism for reopening the decision process if, as sometimes happens, new information is uncovered during the process of implementation.

CONCLUSION

A case study of the rise of environmental justice in the United States in the context of sustainable development raises a number of issues and suggests a host of useful lessons, though they are in too many instances lessons about what not to do. To be sure, it is a useful case in understanding the complexities of modern regulation. Certainly, it indicates how many of our most important issues are parts of a larger global policy process, and that action around the world is often taking place simultaneously at many levels of government and society. In addition to that already broad range of common issues in public administration, this case also raises a wide range of issues of diversity that include race, culture, ethnicity, and socioeconomic status. It also demonstrates in the intricate interactions of the public policy process and economic issues in the marketplace.

Finally, the case study raises many elements of problems of equity that are so important in public policy and public management. These issues of equity go to questions of who benefits from public decisions, who pays, and who is compensated for the burdens that may flow from those public choices, both in this country and abroad. It is important to consider new approaches to equity that contemplate both inter- and intragenerational equity.

Of course, this study presents issues of equity in a particular context. Because the need to do equity to achieve environmental justice requires varied responses in many different situations, it will never be possible to issue a simple statement as to what is required by equity. However, it is possible to fashion frameworks to consider how to meet the challenge. This paper provides such a framework based upon the context, conditions, and responses to equity issues. This framework can be applied to much wider range of equity issues that public administrators and their elected superiors confront every day.

NOTES

1. United Nations, *Agenda 21* (New York: United Nations, 1992), p. 15.

2. *Id.,* at p. 10.

3. World Commission on Environment and Development, *Our Common Future* (New York: Oxford University Press, 1987), p. 43.

4. United Nations, *The Copenhagen Declaration and Programme of Action* (New York: United Nations, 1995), p. 3.

5. United Nations, "Programme for the Further Implementation of Agenda 21, United Nations," July 1, 1997, p. 2. (Hereafter *Rio+5 Report*).

6. United Nations Environmental Programme, *Global Environmental Outlook* (New York: Oxford University Press, 1997), p. 3.

7. See e.g., Phillip J. Cooper, *Strengthening Environmental Management and Administration in the Asian and Pacific Region* (New York: United Nations, 1998).

8. *Rio+5 Report*, p. 6.

9. United Nations Division for Sustainable Development, *Financing Sustainable Development* (New York: United Nations, 1997), p. 35.

10. *Rio+5 Report*, p. 3.

11. United Nations Development Programme, *Human Development Report 1997* (New York: Oxford University Press, 1997), p. 2.

12. *Id.,* at pp. 2–3.

13. I developed these principles at some length in two papers. See Cooper, "Maintaining Cultural Integrity Amidst the Global Markets and Within the Global Commons: The Critical Role of the Common International Commitments for Sustainable Development," paper presented at the 1998 Conference of CIES, Buffalo, New York, March 1998; and "Human Centered Sustainable Development at Brundtland Plus-10: Integrating the Social Policy Dimension Through the Common International Commitments," paper presented at the 1997 Conference of CLAD, Isla Margarita, Venezuela, October 1997.

14. *Supra* note 3, at p. xi.

15. Rio Declaration, Principle 2.

16. Aristotle, *Nicomachean Ethics* (Indianapolis: Bobbs-Merrill, 1962), Book 5.

17. See e.g., United States Constitution, Article III.

18. I have addressed these kinds of orders in much greater detail in Phillip J. Cooper, *Hard Judicial Choices* (New York: Oxford University Press, 1988). See also Robert Wood, *Remedial Law* (Amherst, MA: University of Massachusetts Press, 1990).

19. See generally, C. Neal Tate and Torbjorn Vallinder, eds., *The Global Expansion of Judicial Power* (New York: New York University Press, 1995).

20. Edith Brown Weiss, "Environmental Equity and International Law" in Sun Lin, ed., *UNEP's New Way Forward: Environmental Law and Sustainable Development* (Nairobi: United Nations Environmental Programme, 1995), p. 8.

21. *The Copenhagen Declaration and Programme of Action, supra* note 4, at p. 4.

22. See e.g., Barry G. Rabe, *Beyond NIMBY: Hazardous Waste Siting in Canada and the United States* (Washington, DC: Brookings Institution, 1994).

23. Representative Nydia Velazquez, Testimony of Congresswoman Nydia M. Velazquez, U.S. House of Representatives, Hearings before the Legislation and National Security Subcommittee of the Committee on Government Operations, *Environmental Protection Agency Cabinet Elevation—Environmental Equity Issues,* 103rd Cong., 1st Sess. (1993), pp. 11–12.

24. Quoted in Louisiana Advisory Committee to the U.S. Commission on Civil Rights, *The Battle for Environmental Justice in Louisiana: Government, Industry, and the People* (Washington, DC: U.S. Commission on Civil Rights, 1993). See also "Testimony of Dr. Benjamin F. Chavis, Jr., on Behalf of the National Association for the Advancement of Colored People on Environmental Equity and Environmental Justice,"

in U.S. House of Representatives, Hearings Before the Legislation and National Security Subcommittee of the Committee on Government Operations, *Environmental Protection Agency Cabinet Elevation—Environmental Equity Issues,* 103rd Cong., 1st Sess. (1993), p. 28, fn. 2.

25. United Church of Christ, Commission for Racial Justice, *Toxic Wastes and Race in the United States: A National Report on the Racial and Socioeconomic Characteristics of Communities with Hazardous Waste Sites* (New York: United Church of Christ, 1987). See also Bunyan Bryant, ed., *Environmental Justice: Issues, Policies, and Solutions* (Washington, DC: Island Press, 1995), p. 4.

26. Robert D. Bullard, "Environmental Justice for All," in Bullard, ed., *Unequal Protection: Environmental Justice and Communities of Color* (San Francisco: Sierra Club Books, 1994), pp. 5–6.

27. U.S. General Accounting Office, *Siting of Hazardous Waste Landfills and Their Correlation with Racial and Economic Status of Surrounding Communities* (Washington, DC: GAO, 1983).

28. *Bean v. Southwestern Waste Management,* 482 F.Supp. 673 (S.D.Tex. 1979), aff'd, 782 F.2d 1038 (5th Cir. 1986).

29. Robert D. Bullard, *Dumping in Dixie: Race, Class, and Environmental Quality, Second Edition* (Boulder, CO: Westview Press, 1994), original edition published in 1990.

30. See e.g., Robert D. Bullard, ed., *Confronting Environmental Racism: Voices from the Grassroots* (Boston: South End Press, 1993).

31. Bunyan Bryant and Paul Mohai, eds., *Race and the Incidence of Environmental Hazards* (Boulder, CO: Westview Press, 1992).

32. Marianne Lavelle and Marcia Coyle, "Unequal Protection," (Special Supplement) *National Law Journal,* September 21, 1992, reprinted in U.S. House of Representatives, Hearings Before the Legislation and National Security Subcommittee of the Committee on Government Operations, *Environmental Protection Agency Cabinet Elevation—Environmental Equity Issues,* 103rd Cong., 1st Sess. (1993), pp. 169–177.

33. See e.g., Bunyan Bryant, ed. *Environmental Justice: Issues, Policies, and Solutions* (Washington, DC: Island Press, 1995).

34. Bullard, *supra* note 30, at p. 22.

35. The National Institute of Environmental Health Sciences, and the Agency for Toxic Substances and Disease Registry held workshops on environmental justice issues and published the papers in Special Issue, "Equity in Environmental Health: Research Issues and Needs," 9 *Toxicology and Industrial Health* 679 (1993).

36. Bryant, *supra* note 25, at pp. 9–15.

37. See Laura Pulido, "Sustainable Development at Ganados del Valle," in Bullard, *supra* note 30, at pp. 123–25.

38. Jace Weaver, ed., *Defending Mother Earth* (Maryknoll, NY: Orbis Books, 1996). p. xv.

39. See Howard Ball, *Cancer Factories: America's Tragic Quest for Uranium Self-Sufficiency* (Westport, CT: Greenwood Press, 1993).

40. Quoted in Tarla Rai Peterson, *Sharing the Earth: The Rhetoric of Sustainable Development* (Columbia, SC: University of South Carolina Press, 1997), p. 66.

41. House Committee on Government Operations, *supra* note 32, at pp. 100–101.

42. 42 U.S.C. §2000d et seq.

43. Louisiana Advisory Committee to the U.S. Commission on Civil Rights, *The Battle for Environmental Justice in Louisiana: Government, Industry, and the People* (Washington, DC: U.S. Commission on Civil Rights, 1993).

44. *Id.,* at p. 10.

45. Arthur A. Fletcher to Carol M. Browner, September 24, 1993, reprinted in *Id.,* at p. 144.

46. U.S. General Accounting Office, *Hazardous and Nonhazardous Waste: Demographics of People Living Near Waste Facilities* (Washington, DC: GAO, 1995).

47. Vicki L. Been, "Locally Undesirable Land Uses in Minority Neighborhoods: Disproportionate Siting or Market Dynamics," 103 *Yale L. J.* 1406 (1994).

48. See generally, Sheila Foster, "Justice from the Ground Up: Distributive Inequities, Grassroots Resistance, and the Transformative Politics of the Environmental Justice Movement," 86 *California L. Rev.* 775 (1998).

49. *Chester Residents Concerned for Quality of Life v. Seif,* 132 F.3d 925 (3rd Cir. 1997).

50. Cited hereinafter as "Interim Guidance," http://es.epa.gov/oeca/oej.

51. 5 U.S.C. §551 et seq.

52. See Chapter 5. See also Cornelius M. Kerwin, *Rulemaking* (Washington, DC: CQ Press, 1994).

53. "Interim Guidance," p. 3.

54. *Id.,* at p. 4.

55. In terminating No. 97-1620, *Seif v. Chester Residents Concerned,* the Supreme Court ordered: "The judgement is vacated, and the case is remanded to the United States Court of Appeals for the Third Circuit with instructions to dismiss. See *United States v. Munsingwear, Inc.,* 340 U.S. 36 (1950)."

56. *Alexander v. Choate,* 469 U.S. 287, 292-94 (1985).

57. *Id.,* at p. 4.

58. *Id.,* at p. 9.

59. Russell J. Harding, "Environmental Justice: Good Intentions Gone Awry," *Ecostates,* May/June 1998, pp. 11–12.

60. Interview with Robert Bullard, in Jim Motavalli, "People Don't Have 'The Complexion for Protection,' *E Magazine,* July/August 1998.

61. Quoted in editorial, *The Washington Times,* August, 7, 1998.

62. See generally, Colin Crawford, *Uproar at Dancing Rabbit Creek: Battling Over Race, Class, and the Environment* (Reading, MA: Addison-Wesley Publishing, 1996).

63. Roland J. Jensen to the Nuclear Regulatory Commission, April 22, 1998.

64. Christopher H. Foreman, Jr., *The Promise and Peril of Environmental Justice* (Washington, DC: Brookings Institution, 1998).

65. David Mastio, "EPA Exec Concedes to Flaws," *Detroit News,* Washington Bureau, August 7, 1998.

66. Carol M. Browner to Paul Helmke, Dennis Archer, Deedee Corradini, and Patrick McCrory, June 18, 1998.

67. *Id.*

68. Testimony of Ann E. Goode, Director, Office of Civil Rights, U.S. Environmental Protection Agency, Before the Subcommittee on Oversight and Investigations of the Committee on Commerce, U.S. House of Representatives, August 6, 1998.

69. Robert R. Kuehn to Donald Barnes and Dorothy Canter, August 12, 1998.

70. For definitions, see Bryant, *supra* note 25, pp. 5–6, and *Louisiana Advisory Committee, supra* note 43, at p. 3.

71. I have discussed these cases, interviews, and findings in *Hard Judicial Choices, supra* note 18.

72. See Foreman, *supra* note 64 and Bean, *supra* note 47.

73. These findings are based upon on-site interviews with officials and NGOs in six Asian and Pacific Rim nations. Phillip J. Cooper, *Strengthening Environmental Management and Administration in the Asia and Pacific Region* (New York: United Nations, 1998), pp. 51–53.

74. *New York v. United States,* 505 U.S. 144 (1992).

75. In fact, the only reference to Title VI was in a White House memorandum issued the same day. These documents are available on the Internet at http://es.epa.gov/oeca/oej.

76. See *Community Nutrition Institute v. Young,* 818 F.2d 943, 946 (D.C.Cir. 1987); *American Hospital Association v. Bowen,* 834 F.2d 1037, 1046 (D.C.Cir. 1987); *American Bus Association v. United States,* 627 F.2d 525, 529 (D.C.Cir. 1980) (quoting *Pacific Gas & Electric Co. v. FPC,* 506 F.2d 33, 38 [D.C.Cir 1974]).

77. *McLouth Steel Products Corporation v. Thomas,* 838 F.2d 1317, 1320 (D.C.Cir. 1988). See also *General Motors v. Ruckelshaus,* 724 F.2d 979, 985 (D.C.Cir. 1983); *Citizens to Save Spencer County v. United States Environmental Protection Agency,* 600 F.2d 844, 879 n. 171 (D.C.Cir. 1979); *Citizens Communication v. FCC,* 447 F.2d 1201, 1204 n.5 (D.C.Cir. 1971). *Id.,* at 468.

78. *American Hospital Association v. Bowen, supra* note 75, at p. 1044. See also *Alcaraz v. Block,* 746 F.2d 593, 612 (D.C.Cir. 1984).

79. 5 U.S.C. §706.

80. Laura Pulido, "Sustainable Development of Ganados del Valle," in Bullard, *Confronting Environmental Racism, supra* note 30, pp. 132–37.

81. See e.g., Rozelia S. Park, "Note: An Examination of International Environmental Racism Through the Lens of Transboundary Movement of Hazardous Wastes, 5 *Indiana Journal of Global Legal Studies* 659 (1998); Xavier Carlos Vasquez, "The North American Free Trade Agreement and Environmental Racism," 34 *Harvard International L. J.* 357 (1993).

82. Brown Weiss, *supra* note 20, at p. 9.

83. See World Bank, *The State in a Changing World: World Development Report 1997* (New York: Oxford University Press, 1997).

84. Edgar H. Schein, *Organizational Culture and Leadership,* 2nd ed. (San Francisco: Jossey-Bass, 1992).

85. This is the analog of what Weiss refers to in international law as the use of equity to fill in the gaps in existing law or policy. Brown Weis, *supra* note 20, at p. 8.

86. See World Bank, *supra* note 83.

Appendix 3

The Administrative Procedure ACT

(5 U.S.C. §551 et seq.)

§551. Definitions

For the purpose of this subchapter—

(1) "agency" means each authority of the government of the United States, whether or not it is within or subject to review by another agency, but does not include—
   (A) the Congress;
   (B) the courts of the United States;
   (C) the governments of the territories or possessions of the United States;
   (D) the government of the District of Columbia; or except as to the requirements of section 552 of this title;
   (E) agencies composed of representatives of the parties or of representatives of organizations of the parties to the disputes determined by them;
   (F) courts martial and military commissions;
   (G) military authority exercised in the field in time of war or in occupied territory; or
   (H) functions conferred by sections 1738, 1739, 1743, and 1744 of title 12; chapter 2 of title 41; subchapter II of chapter 471 of title 49; or sections 1884, 1891–1902, and former section 1641(b)(2), of title 50, appendix;

(2) "person" includes an individual, partnership, corporation, association, or public or private organization other than an agency;

(3) "party" includes a person or agency named or admitted as a party, or property seeking and entitled as of right to be admitted as a party, in an agency proceeding, and a person or agency admitted by an agency as a party for limited purposes;

(4) "rule" means the whole or a part of an agency statement of general or particular applicability and future effect designed to implement, interpret, or prescribe law or policy or describing the organization, procedure, or practice requirements of an agency and includes the approval or prescription for the future of rates, wages, corporate or financial structures or reorganization thereof, prices, facilities, appliances, services, or allowances therefor or of valuations, costs, or accounting, or practices bearing on any of the foregoing;

(5) "rule making" means agency process for formulating, amending, or repealing a rule;

(6) "order" means the whole or a part of a final disposition, whether affirmative, negative, injunctive, or declaratory in form, of an agency in a matter other than rule making but including licensing;

(7) "adjudication" means agency process for the formulation of an order;

(8) "license" includes the whole or a part of an agency permit, certificate, approval, registration, charter, membership, statutory exemption or other form of permission;

(9) "licensing" includes agency process respecting the grant, renewal, denial, revocation, suspension, annulment, withdrawal, limitation, amendment, modification, or conditioning of a license;

(10) "sanction" includes the whole or a part of an agency—
- (A) prohibition, requirement, limitation, or other condition affecting the freedom of a person;
- (B) withholding of relief;
- (C) imposition of penalty or fine;
- (D) destruction, taking, seizure, or withholding of property;
- (E) assessment of damages, reimbursement, restitution, compensation, costs, charges, or fees;
- (F) requirement, revocation, or suspension of a license; or
- (G) taking other compulsory or restrictive action;

(11) "relief" includes the whole or a part of an agency—
- (A) grant of money, assistance, license, authority, exemption, exception, privilege, or remedy;
- (B) recognition of a claim, right, immunity, privilege, exemption, or exception; or
- (C) taking of other action on the application or petition of, and beneficial to, a person;

(12) "agency proceeding" means an agency process as defined by paragraphs (5), (7), and (9) of this section;

(13) "agency action" includes the whole or a part of an agency rule, order, license, sanction, relief, or the equivalent or denial thereof, or failure to act; and

(14) "ex parte communication" means an oral or written communication not on the public record with respect to which reasonable prior notice to all parties is not given, but it shall not include requests for status reports on any matter or proceeding covered by this subchapter.

§552. Public information; agency rules, opinion, orders, records, and proceedings (Freedom of Information Act)

(a) Each agency shall make available to the public information as follows:
- (1) Each agency shall separately state and currently publish in the Federal Register for the guidance of the public—
  - (A) descriptions of its central and field organization and the established places at which, the employees (and in the case of a uniformed service, the members) from whom, and the methods whereby, the public may obtain information, make submittals or requests, or obtain decisions;
  - (B) statements of the general course and method by which its functions are channeled and determined, including the nature and requirements of all formal and informal procedures available;
  - (C) rules of procedure, descriptions of forms available or the places at which forms may be obtained, and instructions as to the scope and contents of all papers, reports, or examinations;
  - (D) substantive rules of general applicability adopted as authorized by law, and statements of general policy or interpretations of general applicability formulated and adopted by the agency; and
  - (E) each amendment, revision, or repeal of the foregoing. Except to the extent that a person has actual and timely notice of the terms thereof, a person may not in any manner be required to resort to, or be adversely affected by, a matter required to be published in the Federal Register and not so published. For the purpose of this paragraph, matter reasonably available to the class of persons affected thereby is deemed published in the Federal Register when incorporated by reference therein with the approval of the Director of the Federal Register.
- (2) Each agency, in accordance with published rules, shall make available for public inspection and copying—
  - (A) final opinions, including concurring and dissenting opinions, as well as orders, made in the adjudication of cases;
  - (B) those statements of policy and interpretations which have been adopted by the agency and are not published in the Federal Register; and

(C) administrative staff manuals and instructions to staff that affect a member of the public; unless the materials are promptly published and copies offered for sale. To the extent required to prevent a clearly unwarranted invasion of personal privacy, an agency may delete identifying details when it makes available or publishes an opinion, statement of policy, interpretation, or staff manual or instruction. However, in each case the justification for the deletion shall be explained fully in writing. Each agency shall also maintain and make available for public inspection and copying current indexes providing identifying information for the public as to any matter issued, adopted, or promulgated after July 4, 1967, and required by this paragraph to be made available or published. Each agency shall promptly publish, quarterly or more frequently, and distribute (by sale or otherwise) copies of each index or supplements thereto unless it determines by order published in the Federal Register that the publication would be unnecessary and impracticable, in which case the agency shall nonetheless provide copies of such index on request at a cost not to exceed the direct cost of duplication. A final order, opinion, statement of policy, interpretation, or staff manual or instruction that affects a member of the public may be relied on, used, or cited as precedent by an agency against a party other than an agency only if—

    (i) it has been indexed and either made available or published as provided by this paragraph; or

    (ii) the party has actual and timely notice of the terms thereof.

(3) Except with respect to the records made available under paragraphs (1) and (2) of this subsection, each agency, upon any request for records which (A) reasonably describes such records and (B) is made in accordance with published rules stating the time, place, fees (if any), and procedures to be followed, shall make the records promptly available to any person.

(4) (A) (i) In order to carry out the provisions of this section, each agency shall promulgate regulations, pursuant to notice and receipt of public comment, specifying the schedule of fees applicable to the processing of requests under this section and establishing procedures and guidelines for determining when such fees should be waived or reduced. Such schedule shall conform to the guidelines which shall be promulgated, pursuant to notice and receipt of public comment, by the Director of the Office of Management and Budget and which shall provide for a uniform schedule of fees for all agencies.

    (ii) Such agency regulations shall provide that constituent units of such agency—

        (I) fees shall be limited to reasonable standard charges for document search, duplication, and review, when records are requested for commercial use;

        (II) fees shall be limited to reasonable standard charges for document duplication when records are not fought for commercial use and the request is made by an educational or noncommercial scientific institution, whose purpose is scholarly or scientific research or a representative of the news media; and

        (III) for any request not described in (I) or (II), fees shall be limited to reasonable standard charges for document search and duplication.

    (iii) Documents shall be furnished without any charge or at a charge reduced below the fees established under clause (ii) if disclosure of the information is in the public interest because it is likely to contribute significantly to public understanding of the operations or activities of the government and is not primarily in the commercial interest of the requester.

    (iv) Fee schedules shall provide for the recovery of only the direct costs of search, initial examination of a document for the purposes of determining whether the documents must be disclosed under this section and for the purposes of withholding any portions exempt from disclosure under this section. Review costs may not include any costs incurred in resolving issues of law or policy that may be raised in the course of processing a request under this section. No fee may be charged by any agency under this section—

        (I) if the costs of routine collection and processing of the fee are likely to equal or exceed the amount of the fee; or

        (II) for any request described in clause (ii) (II) or (III) of this subparagraph for the first two hours of search time or for the first one hundred pages of duplication.

    (v) No agency may require advance payment of any fee unless the requester has previously failed to pay fees in a timely fashion, or the agency has determined that the fee with exceed $250.

    (vi) Nothing in this subparagraph shall supersede fees chargeable under a statute specifically providing for setting the level of fees for particular types of records.

(vii) In any action by a requester regarding the waiver of fees under this section, the court shall determine the matter de novo: Provided, that the court's review of the matter shall be limited to the record before the agency.

(B) On complaint, the district court of the United States in the district in which the complainant resides, or has his principal place of business, or in which the agency records are situated, or in the District of Columbia, has jurisdiction to enjoin the agency from withholding agency records and to order the production of any agency records improperly withheld from the complainant. In such a case the court shall determine the matter de novo, and may examine the contents of such agency records in camera to determine whether such records or any part thereof shall be withheld under any of the exemptions set forth in subsection (b) of this section, and the burden is on the agency to sustain its action.

(C) Notwithstanding any other provision of law, the defendant shall serve an answer or otherwise plead to any complaint made under this subsection within thirty days after service upon the defendant of the pleading in which such complaint is made, unless the court otherwise directs for good cause shown.

(D) Repealed. Pub. L. 98-620, title IV, Sec 402(2), Nov. 8, 1984, 98 stat 3357.

(E) The court may assess against the United States reasonable attorney fees and other litigation costs reasonably incurred in any case under this section in which the complainant has substantially prevailed.

(F) Whenever the court orders the production of any agency records improperly withheld from the complainant and assesses against the United States reasonable attorney fees and other litigation costs, and the court additionally issues a written finding that the circumstances surrounding the withholding raise questions whether agency personnel acting arbitrarily or capriciously with respect to the withholding, the Special Counsel shall promptly initiate a proceeding to determine whether disciplinary action is warranted against the officer or employee who was primarily responsible for the withholding. The Special Counsel, after investigation and consideration of the evidence submitted, shall submit his findings and recommendations to the administrative authority of the agency concerned and shall send copies of the findings and recommendations to the officer or employee or his representative. The administrative authority shall take the corrective action that the Special Counsel recommends.

(G) In the event of noncompliance with the order of the court, the district court may punish for contempt the responsible employee, and in the case of a uniformed service, the responsible member.

(5) Each agency having more than one member shall maintain and make available for public inspection a record of the final votes of each member in every agency proceeding.

(6) (A) Each agency, upon any request for records made under paragraph (1), (2), or (3) of this subsection, shall—

(i) determine within ten days (excepting Saturdays, Sundays, and legal public holidays) after the receipt of any such request whether to comply with such request and shall immediately notify the person making such request of such determination and the reasons therefor, and of the right of such person to appeal to the head of the agency any adverse determination; and

(ii) make a determination with respect to any appeal within twenty days (excepting Saturdays, Sundays, and legal public holidays) after the receipt of such appeal. If on appeal the denial of the request for records is in whole or in part upheld, the agency shall notify the person making such request of the provisions for judicial review of that determination under paragraph (4) of this subsection.

(B) In unusual circumstances as specified in this subparagraph, the time limits prescribed in either clause (i) or clause (ii) of subparagraph (A) may be extended by written notice to the person making such request setting forth the reasons for such extension and the date on which a determination is expected to be dispatched. No such notice shall specify a date that would result in an extension for more than ten working days. As used in this subparagraph, "unusual circumstances" means, but only to the extent reasonable necessary to the proper processing of the particular request—

(i) the need to search for and collect the requested records from field facilities or other establishments that are separate from the office processing the request;

(ii) the need to search for, collect, and appropriately examine a voluminous amount of separate and distinct records which are demanded in a single request; or

(iii) the need for consultation, which shall be conducted with all practicable speed, with another agency having a substantial interest in the determination of the request or among two or more components of the agency having substantial subject-matter interest therein.

(C) Any person making a request to any agency for records under paragraph (1), (2), or (3) of this subsection shall be deemed to have exhausted his administrative remedies with respect to such request if the agency fails to comply with the applicable time limit provisions of this paragraph. If the Government can show exceptional circumstances exist and that the agency is exercising due diligence in responding to the request, the court may retain jurisdiction and allow the agency additional time to complete its review of the records. Upon any determination by an agency to comply with a request for records, the records shall be made promptly available to such person making such request. Any notification of denial of any request for records under this subsection shall set forth the names and titles or positions of each person responsible for the denial of such request.

(b) This section does not apply to matters that are—

(1) (A) specifically authorized under criteria established by an Executive order to be kept secret in the interest of national defense or foreign policy and

(B) are in fact properly classified pursuant to such Executive order;

(2) related solely to the internal personnel rules and practices of an agency;

(3) specifically exempted from disclosure by statute (other than section 552b of this title), provided that such statute

(A) requires that the matters be withheld from the public in such a manner as to leave no discretion on the issue, or

(B) establishes particular criteria for withholding or refers to particular types of matters to be withheld;

(4) trade secrets and commercial or financial information obtained from a person and privileged or confidential;

(5) inter-agency or intra-agency memorandums or letters which would not be available by law to a party other than an agency in litigation with an agency;

(6) personnel and medical files and similar files the disclosure of which would constitute clearly a unwarranted invasion of personal privacy;

(7) records compiled for law enforcement purposes, but only to the extent that the production of such law enforcement records or information

(A) could reasonably be expected to interfere with enforcement proceedings,

(B) would deprive a person of a right to a fair trial or an impartial adjudication,

(C) could reasonably be expected to constitute an unwarranted invasion of personal privacy,

(D) could reasonably be expected to disclose the identity of a confidential source, including a State, local, or foreign agency or authority or any private institution which furnished information on a confidential basis, and, in the case of a record compiled by a criminal law enforcement authority in the course of a criminal investigation, or by an agency conducting a lawful national security intelligence investigation, information furnished only by the confidential source,

(E) would disclose investigative techniques and procedures for law enforcement investigations or prosecutions if such disclosure could reasonably be expected to risk circumvention of the law, or

(F) could reasonably be expected to endanger the life or physical safety of any individual;

(8) contained in or related to examination, operating, or condition reports prepared by, on behalf of, or for the use of an agency responsible for the regulation or supervision of financial institutions; or

(9) geological and geophysical information and data, including maps, concerning wells. Any reasonably segregable portion of a record shall be provided to any person requesting such record after deletion of the portions which are exempt under this subsection.

(c) (1) Whenever a request is made which involves access to records described in subsection (b)(7)(A) and—

(A) the investigation or proceeding involves a possible violation of criminal law; and

(B) there is reason to believe that
- (i) the subject of the investigation or proceeding is not aware of its pendency, and
- (ii) disclosure of the existence of the records could reasonably be expected to interfere with enforcement proceedings, the agency may, during only such time as that circumstance continues, treat the records as not subject to the requirements of this section.

(2) Whenever informant records maintained by a criminal law enforcement agency under an informant's name or personal identifier are requested by a third party according to the informant's name or personal identified, the agency may treat the records as not subject to the requirements of this section unless the informant's status as an informant has been officially confirmed.

(3) Whenever a request is made which involves access to records maintained by the Federal Bureau of Investigation pertaining to foreign intelligence or counterintelligence, or international terrorism, and the existence of the records is classified information as provided in subsection (b)(1), the Bureau may, as long as the existence of the records remains classified information, treat the records as not subject to the requirements of this section.

(d) This section does not authorize withholding of information or limit the availability of records to the public, except as specifically stated in this section. This section is not authority to withhold information from Congress.

(e) On or before March 1 of each calendar year, each agency shall submit a report covering the preceding calendar year to the Speaker of the House of Representatives and President of the Senate for referral to the appropriate committees of the Congress. The report shall include—
- (1) the number of determinations made by such agency not to comply with requests for records made to such agency under subsection (a) and the reasons for each such determination;
- (2) the number of appeals made by persons under subsection (a) (6), the result of such appeals, and the reason for the action upon each appeal that results in a denial of information;
- (3) the names and titles or positions of each person responsible for the denial of records requested under this section, and the number of instances of participation for each;
- (4) the results of each proceeding conducted pursuant to subsection (a) (4) (F), including a report of the disciplinary action taken against the officer or employee who was primarily responsible for improperly withholding records or an explanation of why disciplinary action was not taken;
- (5) a copy of every rule made by such agency regarding this section;
- (6) a copy of the fee schedule and the total amount of fees collected by the agency for making records available under this section; and
- (7) such other information as indicates efforts to administer fully this section. The Attorney General shall submit an annual report on or before March 1 of each calendar year which shall include for the prior calendar year a listing of the number of cases arising under this section, the exemption involved in each case, the disposition of such case, and the cost, fees, and penalties assessed under subsections (a) (4) (E), (F), and (G). Such report shall also include a description of the efforts undertaken by the Department of Justice to encourage agency compliance with this section.

(f) For purposes of this section, the term "agency" as defined in section 551(1) of this title includes any executive department, military department, Government corporation, Government controlled corporation, or other establishment in the executive branch of the Government (including the Executive Office of the President), or any independent regulatory agency.

§552a. Records maintained on individuals (Right to Privacy Act)

(a) Definitions—For purposes of this section—
- (1) the term "agency" means agency as defined in section 552(e) [should read 552(f)] of this title;
- (2) the term "individual" means a citizen of the United States or an alien lawfully admitted for permanent residence;
- (3) the term "maintain" includes maintain, collect, use, or disseminate;
- (4) the term "record" means any item, collection, or grouping of information about an individual that is maintained by an agency, including, but not limited to, his education, financial transactions,

medical history, and criminal or employment history and that contains his name, or the identifying number, symbol, or other identifying particular assigned to the individual, such as a finger or voice print or a photograph;

(5) the term "system of records" means a group of any records under the control of any agency from which information is retrieved by the name of the individual or by some identifying number, symbol, or other identifying particular assigned to the individual;

(6) the term "statistical record" means a record in a system of records maintained for statistical research or reporting purposes only and not used in whole or in part in making any determination about an identifiable individual, except as provided by section 8 of title 13;

(7) the term "routine use" means, with respect to the disclosure of a record, the use of such record for a purpose which is compatible with the purpose for which it was collected.

(8) the term "matching program"—

(A) means any computerized comparison of—

(i) two or more automated systems of records or a system of records with non-Federal records for the purpose of—

(I) establishing or verifying the eligibility of, or continuing compliance with statutory and regulatory requirements by, applicants for, recipients or beneficiaries of, participants in, or providers of services with respect to, cash or in-kind assistance or payments or delinquent debts under such Federal benefit programs, or

(II) recouping payments or delinquent debts under such Federal benefit programs, or

(ii) two or more automated Federal personnel or payroll systems of records or a system of Federal personnel or payroll records with non-Federal records,

(B) but does not include—

(i) matches performed to produce aggregate statistical data without any personal identifiers;

(ii) matches performed to support any research or statistical project, specific data of which may not be used to make decisions concerning the rights, benefits, or privileges of specific individuals;

(iii) matches performed, by an agency (or component thereof) which performs as its principal function any activity pertaining to the enforcement of criminal laws, subsequent to the initiation of a specific criminal or civil law enforcement investigation of a named person or persons for the purpose of gathering evidence against such person or persons;

(iv) matches of tax information

(I) pursuant to section 6103(d) of the Internal Revenue Code of 1986,

(II) for purposes of tax administration as defined in section 6103(b)(4) of such Code,

(III) for the purpose of intercepting a tax refund due an individual under the authority granted by section 464 or 1137 of the Social Security Act, or

(IV) for the purpose of intercepting a tax refund due an individual under any other tax refund intercept program authorized by statute which has been determined by the Director of the Office of Management and Budget to contain verification, notice, and hearing requirements that are substantially similar to the procedures in section 1137 of the Social Security Act;

(v) matches—

(I) using records predominantly relating to Federal personnel, that are performed for routine administrative purposes (subject to guidance provided by the Director of the Office of Management and Budget pursuant to subsection (v)); or

(II) conducted by an agency using only records from systems of records maintained by that agency; if the purpose of the match is not to take any adverse financial, personnel, disciplinary, or other adverse action against Federal personnel;

(vi) matches performed for foreign counterintelligence purposes or to produce background checks for security clearances of Federal personnel or Federal contractor personnel; or

(vii) matches performed pursuant to section 6103(l)(12) of the Internal Revenue Code of 1986 and section 1144 of the Social Security Act;

(9) the term "recipient agency" means any agency, or contractor thereof, receiving records contained in a system of records from a source agency for use in a matching program;

(10) the term "non-Federal agency" means any State or local government, or agency thereof, which receives records contained in a system of records from a source agency for use in a matching program;

(11) the term "source agency" means any agency which discloses records contained in a system of records to be used in a matching program, or any State or local government, or agency thereof, which discloses records to be used in a matching program;

(12) the term "Federal benefit program" means any program administered or funded by the Federal Government, or by any agent or State on behalf of the Federal Government, providing cash or in-kind assistance in the form of payments, grants, loans, or loan guarantees to individuals; and

(13) the term "Federal personnel" means officers and employees of the Government of the United States, members of the uniformed services (including members of the Reserve Components), individuals entitled to receive immediate or deferred retirement benefits under any retirement program of the Government of the United States (including survivor benefits).

(b) Conditions of Disclosure—No agency shall disclose any record which is contained in a system of records by any means of communication to any person, or to another agency, except pursuant to a written request by, or with the prior written consent of, the individual to whom the record pertains, unless disclosure of the record would be—

(1) to those officers and employees of the agency which maintains the record who have a need for the record in the performance of their duties;

(2) required under section 552 of this title;

(3) for a routine use as defined in subsection (a)(7) of this section and described under subsection (e)(4)(D) of this section;

(4) to the Bureau of the Census for purposes of planning or carrying out a census or survey or related activity pursuant to the provisions of title 13;

(5) to a recipient who has provided the agency with advance adequate written assurance that the record will be used solely as a statistical research or reporting record, and the record is to be transferred in a form that is not individually identifiable;

(6) to the National Archives of the United States as a record which has sufficient historical or other value to warrant its continued preservation by the United States Government, or for evaluation by the Archivist of the United States or the designee of the Archivist to determine whether the record has such value;

(7) to another agency or to an instrumentality of any governmental jurisdiction within or under the control of the United States for a civil or criminal law enforcement activity if the activity is authorized by law, and if the head of the agency or instrumentality has made a written request to the agency which maintains the record specifying the particular portion desired and the law enforcement activity for which the record is sought;

(8) to a person pursuant to a showing of compelling circumstances affecting the health or safety of an individual if upon such disclosure notification is transmitted to the last known address of such individual;

(9) to either House of Congress, or, to the extent of matter within its jurisdiction, any committee or subcommittee thereof, any joint committee of Congress of subcommittee of any such joint committee;

(10) to the Comptroller General, or any of his authorized representatives, in the course of the performance of the duties of the General Accounting Office; or

(11) pursuant to the order of a court of competent jurisdiction; or

(12) to a consumer reporting agency in accordance with section 3711(f) of title 31.

(c) Accounting of Certain Disclosures—Each agency, with respect to each system of records under its control, shall—

(1) except for disclosures made under subsections (b)(1) or (b)(2) of this section, keep an accurate accounting of—

(A) the date, nature, and purpose of each disclosure of a record to any person or to another agency made under subsection (b) of this section; and

(B) the name and address of the person or agency to whom the disclosure is made;

(2) retain the accounting made under paragraph (1) of this subsection for at least five years or the life of the record, whichever is longer, after the disclosure for which the accounting is made;

(3)   except for disclosures made under subsection (b)(7) of this section, make the accounting made under paragraph (1) of this subsection available to the individual named in the record at his request; and

(4)   inform any person or other agency about any correction or notation of dispute made by the agency in accordance with subsection (d) of this section of any record that has been disclosed to the person or agency if an accounting of the disclosure was made.

(d) Access to Records—Each agency that maintains a system of records shall—

(1)   upon request by an individual to gain access to his record or to any information pertaining to him which is contained in the system, permit him and upon his request, a person of his own choosing to accompany him, to review the record and have a copy made of all or any portion thereof in a form comprehensible to him, except that the agency may require the individual to furnish a written statement authorizing discussion of that individual's record in the accompanying person's presence;

(2)   permit the individual to request amendment of a record pertaining to him and—

    (A) not later than 10 days (excluding Saturdays, Sundays, and legal public holidays) after the date or receipt of such request, acknowledge in writing such receipt; and

    (B) promptly, either—

        (i) make any correction of any portion thereof which the individual believes is not accurate, relevant, timely, or complete; or

        (ii) inform the individual of its refusal to amend the record in accordance with his request, the reason for the refusal, the procedures established by the agency for the individual to request a review of that refusal by the head of the agency or an officer designated by the head of the agency, and the name and business address of that official;

(3)   permit the individual who disagrees with the refusal of the agency to amend his record to request a review of such refusal, and not later than 30 days (excluding Saturdays, Sundays, and legal public holidays) from the date on which the individual requests such review, complete such review and make a final determination unless, for good cause shown, the head of the agency extends such 30-day period; and if, after his review, the reviewing official also refuses to amend the record in accordance with the request, permit the individual to file with the agency a concise statement setting forth the reasons for his disagreement with the refusal of the agency, and notify the individual of the provisions for judicial review of the reviewing official's determination under subsection (g)(1)(A) of this section;

(4)   in any disclosure, containing information about which the individual has filed a statement of disagreement, occurring after the filing of the statement under paragraph (3) of this subsection, clearly note any portion of the record which is disputed and provide copies of the statement and, if the agency deems it appropriate, copies of a concise statement of the reasons of the agency for not making the amendments requested, to persons or other agencies to whom the disputed record has been disclosed; and

(5)   nothing in this section shall allow an individual access to any information compiled in reasonable anticipation of a civil action or proceeding.

(e) Agency Requirements—Each agency that maintains a system of records shall—

(1)   maintain in its records only such information about an individual as is relevant and necessary to accomplish a purpose of the agency required to be accomplished by statute or by executive order of the President;

(2)   collect information to the greatest extent practicable directly from the subject individual when the information may result in adverse determinations about an individual's rights, benefits, and privileges under Federal programs;

(3)   inform each individual whom it asks to supply information, on the form which it uses to collect the information or on a separate form that can be retained by the individual—

    (A) the authority (whether granted by statute, or by executive order of the President) which authorizes the solicitation of the information and whether disclosure of such information is mandatory or voluntary;

    (B) the principal purpose or purposes for which the information is intended to be used;

    (C) the routine uses which may be made of the information, as published pursuant to paragraph (4)(D) of this subsection; and

    (D) the effects on him, if any, of not providing all or any part of the requested information;

(4) subject to the provisions of paragraph (11) of this subsection, publish in the Federal Register upon establishment or revision a notice of the existence and character of the system of records, which notice shall include—

   (A) the name and location of the system;

   (B) the categories of individuals on whom records are maintained in the system;

   (C) the categories of records maintained in the system;

   (D) each routine use of the records contained in the system, including the categories of users and the purpose of such use;

   (E) the policies and practices of the agency regarding storage, retrievability, access controls, retention, and disposal of the records;

   (F) the title and business address of the agency official who is responsible for the system of records;

   (G) the agency procedures whereby an individual can be notified at his request if the system of records contains a record pertaining to him;

   (H) the agency procedures whereby an individual can be notified at his request how he can gain access to any record pertaining to him contained in the system of records, and how he can contest its content; and

   (I) the categories of sources of records in the system;

(5) maintain all records which are used by the agency in making any determination about any individual with such accuracy, relevance, timeliness, and completeness as is reasonably necessary to assure fairness to the individual in the determination;

(6) prior to disseminating any record about an individual to any person other than an agency, unless the dissemination is made pursuant to subsection (6)(2) of this section, make reasonable efforts to assure that such records are accurate, complete, timely, and relevant for agency purposes;

(7) maintain no record describing how any individual exercises rights guaranteed by the First Amendment unless expressly authorized by statute or by the individual about whom the record is maintained or unless pertinent to and within the scope of an authorized law enforcement activity;

(8) make reasonable efforts to serve notice on an individual when any record on such individual is made available to any person under compulsory legal process when such process becomes a matter of public record;

(9) establish rules of conduct for persons involved in the design, development, operation, or maintenance of any system of records, or in maintaining any record, and instruct each such person with respect to such rules and the requirements of this section, including any other rules and procedures adopted pursuant to this section and the penalties for noncompliance;

(10) establish appropriate administrative, technical, and physical safeguards to insure the security and confidentiality of records and to protect against any anticipated threats or hazards to their security or integrity which could result in substantial harm, embarrassment, inconvenience, or unfairness to any individual on whom information is maintained; and

(11) at least 30 days prior to publication of information under paragraph (4)(D) of this subsection, publish in the Federal Register notice of any new use or intended use of the information in the system, and provide an opportunity for interested persons to submit written data, views, or arguments to the agency.

(f) Agency Rules—In order to carry out the provisions of this section, each agency that maintains a system of records shall promulgate rules, in accordance with the requirements (including general notice) of section 553 of this title, which shall—

(1) establish procedures whereby an individual can be notified in response to his request if any system of records named by the individual contains a record pertaining to him;

(2) define reasonable times, places, and requirements for identifying an individual who requests his record or information pertaining to him before the agency shall make the record of information available to the individual;

(3) establish procedures for the disclosure to an individual upon his request of his record or information pertaining to him, including special procedure, if deemed necessary, for the disclosure to an individual of medical records, including psychological records, pertaining to him;

(4) establish procedures for reviewing a request from an individual concerning the amendment of any record or information pertaining to the individual, for making a determination on the request, for

an appeal within the agency of an initial adverse agency determination, and for whatever additional means may be necessary for each individual to be able to exercise fully his rights under this section; and

(5) establish fees to be charged, if any, to any individual for making copies of his record, excluding the cost of any search for and review of the record. The Office of the Federal Register shall annually compile and publish the rules promulgated under this subsection and agency notices published under subsection (e)(4) of this section in a form available to the public at low cost.

(g) (1) Civil Remedies—Whenever any agency

(A) makes a determination under subsection (d)(3) of this section not to amend an individual's record in accordance with his request, or fails to make such review in conformity with that subsection;

(B) refuses to comply with an individual request under subsection (d)(1) of this section;

(C) fails to maintain any record concerning any individual with such accuracy, relevance, timeliness, and completeness as is necessary to assure fairness in any determination relating to the qualifications, character, rights, or opportunities of, or benefits to the individual that may be made oil the basis of such record, and consequently a determination is made which is adverse to the individual; or

(D) fails to comply with any other provision of this section, or any rule promulgated thereunder, in such a way as to have an adverse effect on an individual, the individual may bring a civil action against the agency, and the district courts of the United States shall have jurisdiction in the matters under the provisions of this subsection.

(2) (A) In any suit brought under the provisions of subsection (g)(1)(A) of this section, the court may order the agency to amend the individual's record in accordance with his request or in such other way as the court may direct. In such a case the court shall determine the matter de novo.

(B) The court may assess against the United States reasonable attorney fees and other litigation costs reasonably incurred in any case under this paragraph in which the complainant has substantially prevailed.

(3) (A) In any suit brought under the provisions of subsection (g)(1)(B) of this section, the court may enjoin the agency from withholding the records and order the production to the complainant of any agency records improperly withheld from him. In such a case the court shall determine the matter de novo, and may examine the contents of any agency records in camera to determine whether the records or any portion thereof may be withheld under any of the exemptions set forth in subsection (k) of this section, and the burden is on the agency to sustain its action.

(B) The court may assess against the United States reasonable attorney fees and other litigation costs reasonably incurred in any case under this paragraph in which the complainant has substantially prevailed.

(4) In any suit brought under the provisions of subsection (g)(1)(C) or (D) of this section in which the court determines that the agency acted in a manner which was intentional or willful, the United States shall be liable to the individual in an amount equal to the sum of—

(A) actual damages sustained by the individual as a result of the refusal or failure, but in no case shall a person entitled to recovery receive less than the sum of $1,000; and

(B) the costs of the action together with reasonable attorney fees as determined by the court.

(5) An action to enforce any liability created under this section may be brought in the district court of the United States in the district in which the complainant resides, or has his principal place of business, or in which the agency records are situated, or in the District of Columbia, without regard to the amount in controversy, within two years from the date on which the cause of action arises, except that where an agency has materially and willfully misrepresented any information required under this section to be disclosed to an individual and the information so misrepresented is material to establishment of the liability of the agency to the individual under this section, the action may be brought at any time within two years after discovery by the individual of the misrepresentation. Nothing in this section shall be construed to authorize any civil action by reason of any injury sustained as the result of a disclosure of a record prior to September 27, 1975.

(h) Rights of Legal Guardians—For the purposes of this section, the parent of any minor, or the legal guardian of any individual who has been declared to be incompetent due to physical or mental incapacity or age by a court of competent jurisdiction, may act on behalf of the individual.

(i) (1) Criminal Penalties—Any officer or employee of an agency, who by virtue of his employment or official position, has possession of, or access to, agency records which contain individually identifiable information the disclosure of which is prohibited by this section or by rules or regulations established thereunder, and who knowing that disclosure of the specific material is so prohibited, willfully discloses the material in any manner to any person or agency not entitled to receive it, shall be guilty of a misdemeanor and fined not more than $5,000.

(2) Any officer or employee of any agency who willfully maintains a system of records without meeting the notice requirements of subsection (e) (4) of this section shall be guilty of a misdemeanor and fined not more than $5,000.

(3) Any person who knowingly and willfully requests or obtains any record concerning an individual from an agency under false pretenses shall be guilty of a misdemeanor and fined not more than $5,000.

(j) General Exemptions—The head of any agency may promulgate rules, in accordance with the requirements (including general notice) of sections 553(b)(1), (2), and (3), (c), and (e) of this title, to exempt any system of records within the agency from any part of this section except subsections (b), (c)(1) and (2), (e)(4)(A) through (F), (e)(6), (7), (9), (10), and (11), and (i) if the system of records is—

(1) maintained by the Central Intelligence Agency; or

(2) maintained by an agency or component thereof which performs as its principal function any activity pertaining to the enforcement of criminal laws, including police efforts to prevent, control, or reduce crime or to apprehend criminals, and the activities of prosecutors, courts, correctional, probation, pardon, or parole authorities, and which consists of

   (A) information compiled for the purpose of identifying individual criminal offenders and alleged offenders and consisting only of identifying data and notations of arrests, the nature and disposition of criminal charges, sentencing, confinement, release, and parole and probation status;

   (B) information compiled for the purpose of a criminal investigation, including reports of informants and investigators, and associated with an identifiable individual; or

   (C) reports identifiable to an individual compiled at any stage of the process of enforcement of the criminal laws from arrest or indictment through release from supervision. At the time rules are adopted under this subsection, the agency shall include in the statement required under section 553(c) of this title, the reasons why the system of records is to be exempted from a provision of this section.

(k) Specific Exemptions—The head of any agency may promulgate rules, in accordance with the requirements (including general notice) of sections 553(b), (1), (2), and (3)(c) and (e) of this title, to exempt any system of records within the agency from subsections (c), (3)(d), (e)(1), (e)(4), (G), (H), and (1) and (f) of this section if the system of records is—

(1) subject to the provisions of section 552(b)(1) of this title;

(2) investigatory material compiled for law enforcement purposes, other than material within the scope of subsection (j)(2) of this section: Provided, however, that if any individual is denied any right, privilege, or benefit that he would otherwise be entitled by Federal law, or for which he would otherwise be eligible, as a result of the maintenance of such material, such material shall be provided to such individual, except to the extent that the disclosure of such material would reveal the identity of a source who furnished information to the Government under an express promise that the identity of the source would be held in confidence, or prior to the effective date of this section, under an implied promise that the identity of the source would be held in confidence;

(3) maintained in connection with providing protective services to the President of the United States or other individuals pursuant to section 3056 of title 18;

(4) required by statute to be maintained and used solely as statistical records;

(5) investigatory material compiled solely for the purpose of determining suitability, eligibility, or qualifications for Federal civilian employment, military service, Federal contracts, or access to classified information, but only to the extent that the disclosure of such material would reveal the identity of a source who furnished information to the Government under an express promise that the identity

of the source would be held in confidence, or, prior to the effective date of this section, under an implied promise that the identity of the source would be held in confidence;

(6)   testing or examination material used solely to determine individual qualifications for appointment or promotion in the Federal service the disclosure of which would compromise the objectivity or fairness of the testing or examination process; or

(7)   evaluation material used to determine potential for promotion in the armed services, but only to the extent that the disclosure of such material would reveal the identity of a source who furnished information to the Government under an express promise that the identity of the source would be held in confidence, or, prior to the effective date of this section, under an implied promise that the identity of the source would be held in confidence. At the time rules are adopted under this subsection, the agency shall include in the statement required under section 553(c) of this title, the reasons why the system of records is to be exempted from a provision of this section.

(l)   (1)   Archival Records—Each agency record which is accepted by the Archivist of the United States for storage, processing, and servicing in accordance with section 3103 of title 44 shall, for the purposes of this section, be considered to be maintained by the agency which deposited the record and shall be subject to the provisions of this section. The Archivist of the United States shall not disclose the record except to the agency which maintains the record, or under rules established by that agency which are not inconsistent with the provisions of this section.

(2)   Each agency record pertaining to an identifiable individual which was transferred to the National Archives of the United States as a record which has sufficient historical or other value to warrant its continued preservation by the United States Government, prior to the effective date of this section, shall, for the purposes of this section, be considered to be maintained by the National Archives and shall not be subject to the provisions of this section, except that a statement generally describing such records (modeled after the requirements relating to records subject to subsections (e)(4)(A) through (G) of this section) shall be published in the Federal Register.

(3)   Each agency record pertaining to an identifiable individual which is transferred to the National Archives of the United States is a record which has sufficient historical or other value to warrant its continued preservation by the United States Government, on or after the effective date of this section, shall, for the purposes of this section, be considered to be maintained by the National Archives and shall be exempt from the requirements of this section except subsections (e)(4)(A) through (G) and (e)(9) of this section.

(m)   (1)   Government Contractors—When an agency provides by a contract for the operation by or on behalf of the agency of a system of records to accomplish an agency function, the agency shall, consistent with its authority, cause the requirements of this section to be applied to such system. For purposes of subsection (i) of this section any such contractor and any employee of such contractor, if such contract is agreed to on or after the effective date of this section, shall be considered to be an employee of an agency.

(2)   A consumer reporting agency to which a record is disclosed under section 3711(f) of title 31 shall not be considered a contractor for the purposes of this section.

(n)   Mailing Lists—An individual's name and address may not be sold or rented by an agency unless such action is specifically authorized by law. This provision shall not be construed to require the withholding of names and addresses otherwise permitted to be made public.

(o)   Matching Agreements—

(1)   No record which is contained in a system of records may be disclosed to a recipient agency or non-Federal agency for use in a computer matching program except pursuant to a written agreement between the source agency and the recipient agency or non-Federal agency specifying—

(A)   the purpose and legal authority for conducting the program;

(B)   the justification for the program and the anticipated results, including a specific estimate of any savings;

(C)   a description of the records that will be matched, including each data element that will be used, the approximate number of records that will be matched, and the projected starting and completion dates of the matching program;

(D)   procedures for providing individualized notice at the time of application, and notice periodically thereafter as direct by the Data Integrity Board of such agency (subject to guidance provided by the Director of the Office of Management and Budget pursuant to subsection (v), to—

    (i)   applicants for recipients of financial assistance or payments under Federal benefit programs, and

    (ii) applicants for and holders of positions as Federal personnel, that any information provided by such applicants, recipients, holders, and individuals may be subject to verification through matching programs;

(E) procedures for verifying information produced in such matching program as required by subsection (p);

(F) procedures for the retention and timely destruction of identifiable records created by a recipient agency or non-Federal agency in such matching program;

(G) procedures for ensuring the administrative, technical, and physical security of the records matched and the results of such programs;

(H) prohibitions on duplication and redisclosure of records provided by the source agency within or outside the recipient agency or the non-Federal agency, except where required by law or essential to the conduct of the matching program;

(I) procedures governing the use by a recipient agency or non-Federal agency of records provided in a matching program by a source agency, including procedures governing return of the records to the source agency or destruction of records used in such program;

(J) information on assessments that have been made on the accuracy of the records that will be used in such matching program; and

(K) that the Comptroller General may have access to all records of a recipient agency or a non-Federal agency that the Comptroller General deems necessary in order to monitor or verify compliance with the agreement.

(2) (A) A copy of each agreement entered into pursuant to paragraph (1) shall—

    (i)   be transmitted to the Committee on Government Affairs of the Senate and the Committee on Government Operations of the House of Representatives; and

    (ii) be available upon request to the public.

(B) No such agreement shall be effective until 30 days after the date on which such a copy is transmitted pursuant to subparagraph (A)(i).

(C) Such an agreement shall remain in effect only for such period, not to exceed 18 months, as the Data Integrity Board of the agency determines is appropriate in light of the purposes, and length of time necessary for the conduct, of the matching program.

(D) Within 3 months prior to the expiration of such an agreement pursuant to subparagraph (C), the Data Integrity Board of the agency may, without additional review, renew the matching agreement for a current, ongoing matching program for not more than one additional year if—

    (i)   such program will be conducted without any change; and

    (ii) each party to the agreement certifies to the Board in writing that the program has been conducted in compliance with the agreement.

(p) Verification and Opportunity to Contest Findings—

    (1) In order to protect any individual whose records are used in a matching program, no recipient agency, non-Federal agency, or source agency may suspend, terminate, reduce, or make a final denial of any financial assistance or payment under a Federal Benefit program to such individual, or take other adverse action against such individual, as a result of information produced by such matching program, until—

    (A) (i)   the agency has independently verified the information; or

        (ii) the Data Integrity Board of the agency, or in the case of a non-Federal agency the Data Integrity Board of the source agency, determining in accordance with guidance issued by the Director of the Office of Management and Budget that—

           (I) the information is limited to identification and amount of benefits paid by the source agency under a Federal benefit program; and

           (II) there is a high degree of confidence that the information provided to the recipient agency is accurate;

    (B) the individual receives a notice from the agency containing a statement of its findings and informing the individual of the opportunity to contest such findings; and

(C) (i) the expiration of any time period established for the program by statute or regulation for the individual to respond to that notice; or

     (ii) in the case of a program for which no such period is established, the end of the 30-day period beginning on the date on which notice under subparagraph (B) is mailed or otherwise provided to the individual.

(2) Independent verification referred to in paragraph (1) requires investigation and confirmation of specific individual, including where applicable investigation and confirmation of—

    (A) the amount of any asset or income involved;

    (B) whether such individual actually has or had access to such asset or income for such individual's own use; and

    (C) the period or periods when the individual actually had such asset or income.

(3) Notwithstanding paragraph (1), an agency may taken any appropriate action otherwise prohibited by such paragraph if the agency determines that the public health or public safety may be adversely affected or significantly threatened during any notice period required by such paragraph.

(q) Sanctions—

(1) Notwithstanding any other provision of law, no source agency may disclose any record which is contained in a system of records to a recipient agency or non-Federal agency for a matching program if such source agency has reason to believe that the requirements of subsection (p), or any matching agreement entered into pursuant to subsection (o), or both, are not being met by such recipient agency.

(2) No source agency may renew a matching agreement unless—

    (A) the recipient agency or non-Federal agency has certified that it has complied with the provisions of that agreement; and

    (B) the source agency has no reason to believe that the certification is inaccurate.

(r) Report on New Systems and Matching Programs—Each agency that proposes to establish or make a significant change in a system of records or a matching program shall provide adequate advance notice of any such proposal (in duplicate) to the Committee on Government Operations o the House of Representatives, the Committee on Governmental Affairs of the Senate, and the Office of Management and Budget in order to permit an evaluation of the probably or potential effect of such proposal on the privacy or other rights of individuals.

(s) Biennial Report—The President shall biennially submit to the Speaker of the House of Representatives and the President pro tempore of the Senate a report—

(1) describing the actions of the Director of the Office of Management and Budget pursuant to section 6 of the Privacy Act of 1974 during the preceding 2 years;

(2) describing the exercise of individual rights of access and amendment under this section during such years;

(3) identifying changes in or additions to systems of records;

(4) containing such other information concerning administration of this section as may be necessary or useful to the Congress in reviewing the effectiveness of this section in carrying out the purposes of the Privacy Act of 1974.

(t) (1) Effect of Other Laws—No agency shall rely on any exemption contained in section 552 of this title to withhold from an individual any record which is otherwise accessible to such individual under the provisions of this section.

    (2) No agency shall rely on any exemption in this section to withhold from an individual any record which is otherwise accessible to such individual under the provisions of section 552 of this title.

(u) Data Integrity Boards—

(1) Every agency conducting or participating in a matching program shall establish a Data Integrity Board to oversee and coordinate among the various components of such agency the agency's implementation of this sections.

(2) Each Data Integrity Boards shall consist of senior officials designated by the head of the agency, and shall include any senior official designated by the head of the agency as responsible for implementation of this section, and the inspector general of the agency, if any. The inspector general shall not serve as chairman of the Data Integrity Board.

(3)   Each Data Integrity Board—

    (A)   shall review, approve, and maintain all written agreements for receipt or disclosure of agency records for matching programs to ensure compliance with subsection (o), and all relevant statutes, regulations, and guidelines;

    (B)   shall review all matching programs in which the agency has participated during the year, either as a source agency or recipient agency, determine compliance with applicable laws, regulations, guidelines, and agency agreements, and assess the costs and benefits of such programs;

    (C)   shall review all recurring matching programs in which the agency has participated during the year, either as a source agency or recipient agency, for continued justification for such disclosures;

    (D)   shall compile an annual report, which shall be submitted to the head of the agency and the Office of Management and Budget and made available to the public on request, describing the matching activities of the agency, including—

        (i)   matching programs in which the agency has participated as a source agency or recipient agency;

        (ii)   matching agreements proposed under subsection (o) that were disapproved by the Board;

        (iii)   any changes in membership or structure of the Board in the preceding year;

        (iv)   the reasons for any waiver of the requirements in paragraph (4) of this section for completion and submission of a cost-benefit analysis prior to the approval of a matching program;

        (v)   any violations of matching agreements that have been alleged or identified and any corrective action taken; and

        (vi)   any other information required by the Director of the Office of Management and Budget to be included in such report;

    (E)   shall serve as a clearinghouse for receiving and providing information on the accuracy, completeness, and reliability of records used in matching programs;

    (F)   shall provide interpretation and guidance to agency components and personnel on the requirements of this section for matching programs;

    (G)   shall review agency recordkeeping and disposal policies and practices for matching programs to assure compliance with this section; and

    (H)   may review and report on any agency matching activities that are not matching programs.

(4)   (A)   Except as provided in subparagraphs (B) and (C), a Data Integrity Board shall not approve any written agreement for a matching program unless the agency has completed and submitted to such Board a cost-benefit analysis of the proposed program and such analysis demonstrates that the program is likely to be cost effective.

    (B)   The Board may waive the requirements of subparagraph (A) of this paragraph if it determines in writing, in accordance with guidelines prescribed by the Director of the Office of Management and Budget, that a cost-benefit analysis is not required.

    (C)   A cost-benefit analysis shall not be required under subparagraph (A) prior to the initial approval of a written agreement for a matching program that is specifically required by statute. Any subsequent written agreement for such a program shall not be approved by the Data Integrity Board unless the agency has submitted a cost-benefit analysis of the program as conducted under the preceding approval of such agreement.

(5)   (A)   If a matching agreement is disapproved by a Data Integrity Board, any party to such agreement may appeal the disapproval to the Director of the Office of Management and Budget. Timely notice of the filing of such an appeal shall be provided by the Director of the Office of Management and Budget to the Committee on Governmental Affairs of the Senate and the Committee on Government Operations of the House of Representatives.

    (B)   The Director of the Office of Management and Budget may approve a matching agreement notwithstanding the disapproval of a Data Integrity Board if the Director determines that—

        (i)   the matching program will be consistent with all applicable legal, regulatory, and policy requirements;

        (ii)   there is adequate evidence that the matching agreement will be cost-effective; and

        (iii)   the matching program is in the public interest.

(C) The decision of the Director to approve a matching agreements shall not take effect until 30 days after it is reported to committees described in subparagraph (A).

(D) If the Data Integrity Board and the Director of the Office of Management and Budget disapprove a matching program proposed by the inspector general of an agency, the inspector general may report the disapproval to the head of the agency and to the Congress.

(6) The Director of the Office of Management and Budget shall, annually during the first 3 years after the date of enactment of this subsection and biennially thereafter, consolidate in a report to the Congress the information contained in the reports from the various Data Integrity Boards under paragraph (3)(D). Such report shall include detailed information about costs and benefits of matching programs that are conducted during the period covered by such consolidated report, and shall identify each waiver granted by a Data Integrity Board of the requirement for completion and submission of a cost-benefit analysis and the reasons for granting the waiver.

(7) In the reports required by paragraphs (3)(D) and (6), agency matching activities that are not matching programs may be reported on an aggregate basis, if an to the extent necessary to protect ongoing law enforcement or counterintelligence investigations.

(v) Office of Management and Budget Responsibilities—The Director of the Office of Management and Budget shall—

(1) develop and, after notice and opportunity for public comment, prescribe guidelines and regulations for the use of agencies in implementing the provisions of this section; and

(2) provide continuing assistance to and oversight of the implementation of this section by agencies.

§552b. Open meetings (Government in the Sunshine Act)

(a) For purposes of this section—

(1) the term "agency" means any agency, as defined in section 552(e) of this title [should read 552(f)], headed by a collegial body composed of two or more individual members, a majority of whom are appointed to such position by the President with the advice and consent of the Senate, and any subdivisions thereof authorized to act on behalf of the agency;

(2) the term "meeting" means the deliberations of at least the number of individual agency members required to take action on behalf of the agency where such deliberations determine or result in the joint conduct or disposition of official agency business, but does not include deliberations required or permitted by subsection (d) or (e); and

(3) the term "member" means an individual who belongs to a collegial body heading an agency.

(b) Members shall not jointly conduct or dispose of agency business other than in accordance with this section. Except as provided in subsection (c), every portion of every meeting of an agency shall be open to public observation.

(c) Except in a case where the agency finds that the public interest requires otherwise, the second sentence of subsection (b) shall not apply to any portion of an agency meeting, and the requirements of subsections (d) and (e) shall not apply to any information pertaining to such meeting otherwise required by this section to be disclosed to the public, where the agency properly determines that Such portion or portions of its meeting or the disclosure of such information is likely to—

(1) disclose matters that are

(A) specifically authorized under criteria established by an Executive order to be kept secret in the interests of national defense or foreign policy and

(B) in fact properly classified pursuant to such Executive order;

(2) relate solely to the internal personnel rules and practices of an agency;

(3) disclose matters specifically exempted from disclosure by statute (other than section 552 of this title), provided that such statute

(A) requires that the matters be withheld from the public in such a manner as to leave no discretion on the issue, or

(B) establishes particular criteria for withholding or refers to particular types of matters to be withheld;

(4) disclose trade secrets and commercial or financial information obtained from a person and privileged or confidential;

(5) involve accusing any person of a crime, or formally censuring any person;

(6) disclose information of a personal nature where disclosure would constitute a clearly unwarranted invasion of personal privacy;

(7) disclose investigatory records compiled for law enforcement purposes, or information which if written would be contained in such records, but only to the extent that the production of such records or information would

    (A) interfere with enforcement proceedings,

    (B) deprive a person of a eight to a fair trial or an impartial adjudication,

    (C) constitute an unwarranted invasion of personal privacy,

    (D) disclose the identity of a confidential source and, in the case of a record compiled by a criminal law enforcement authority in the course of a criminal investigation, or by an agency conducting a lawful national security intelligence investigation, confidential information furnished only by the confidential source,

    (E) disclose investigative techniques and procedures, or

    (F) endanger the life or physical safety of law enforcement personnel;

(8) disclose information contained in or related to examination, operating, or condition reports prepared by, on behalf of, or for the use of an agency responsible for the regulation or supervision of financial institutions;

(9) disclose information the premature disclosure of which would—

    (A) in the case of an agency which regulates currencies, securities, commodities, or financial institutions, be likely to

        (i) lead to significant financial speculation in currencies, securities, or commodities, or

        (ii) significantly endanger the stability of any financial institution; or

    (B) in the case of any agency, be likely to significantly frustrate implementation of a proposed agency action, except that subparagraph (B) shall not apply in any instance where the agency has already disclosed to the public the content or nature of its proposed action, or where the agency is required by law to make such disclosure on its own initiative prior to taking final agency action on such proposal; or

(10) specifically concern the agency's issuance of a subpoena, or the agency's participation in a civil action or proceeding, an action in a foreign court or international tribunal or an arbitration, or the initiation, conduct, or disposition by the agency of a particular case of formal agency adjudication pursuant to the procedures in section 554 of this title or otherwise involving a determination on the record after opportunity for a hearing.

(d) (1) Action under subsection (c) shall be taken only when a majority of the entire membership of the agency (as defined in subsection (a)(1)) votes to take such action. A separate vote of the agency members shall be taken with respect to each agency meeting a portion or portions of which are proposed to be closed to the public pursuant to subsection (c), or with respect to any information which is proposed to be withheld under subsection (c). A single vote may be taken with respect to a series of meetings, a portion or portions of which are proposed to be closed to the public, or with respect to any information concerning such series of meetings, so long as each meeting in such series involves the same particular matters and is scheduled to be held no more than thirty days after the initial meeting in such series. The vote of each agency member participating in such vote shall be recorded and no proxies shall be allowed.

    (2) Whenever any person whose interests may be directly affected by a portion of a meeting requests that the agency close such portion to the public for any of the reasons referred to in paragraph (5), (6), or (7) of subsection (c), the agency, upon request of any one of its members, shall vote by recorded vote whether to close such meeting.

    (3) Within one day of any vote, taken pursuant to paragraph (1) or (2), the agency shall make publicly available a written copy of such vote reflecting the vote of each member on the question. If a portion of a meeting is to be closed to the public, the agency shall, within one day of the vote taken pursuant to paragraph (1) or (2) of this subsection, make publicly available a full written explanation of its action closing the portion together with a list of all persons expected to attend the meeting and their affiliation.

(4) Any agency, a majority of whose meetings may properly be closed to the public pursuant to paragraph (4), (8), (9)(A), or (10) of subsection (c), or any combination thereof, may provide by regulation for the closing of such meetings or portions thereof in the event that a majority of the members of the agency votes by recorded vote at the beginning of such meeting, or portion thereof, to close the exempt portion or portions of the meeting, and a copy of such vote, reflecting the vote of each member on the question, is made available to the public. The provisions of paragraphs (1), (2), and (3) of this subsection and subsection (e) shall not apply to any portion of a meeting to which such regulations apply: Provided, that the agency shall, except to the extent that such information is exempt in from disclosure under the provisions of subsection (c), provide the public with public announcement of the time, place, and subject matter of the meeting and of each portion thereof at the earliest practicable time.

(e) (1) In the case of each meeting, the agency shall make public announcement, at least one week before the meeting, of the time, place, and subject matter of the meeting, whether it is to be open or closed to the public, and the name and phone number of the official designated by the agency to respond to requests for information about the meeting. Such announcement shall be made unless a majority of the members of the agency determines by a recorded vote that agency business requires that such meeting be called at an earlier date, in which case the agency shall make public announcement of the time, place, and subject matter of such meeting, and whether open or closed to the public, at the earliest practicable time.

(2) The time or place of a meeting may be changed following the public announcement required by paragraph (1) only if the agency publicly announces such change at the earliest practicable time. The subject matter of a meeting, or the determination of the agency to open or close a meeting, or portion of a meeting, to the public, may be changed following the public announcement required by this subsection only if

(A) a majority of the entire membership of the agency determines by a recorded vote that agency business so requires and that no earlier announcement of the change was possible, and

(B) the agency publicly announces such change and the vote of each member upon such change at the earliest practicable time.

(3) Immediately following each public announcement required by this subsection, notice of the time, place, and subject matter of a meeting, whether the meeting is open or closed, any change in one of the preceding, and the name and phone number of the official designated by the agency to respond to requests for information about the meeting, shall also be submitted for publication in the Federal Register.

(f) (1) For every meeting closed pursuant to paragraphs (1) through (10) of subsection (c), the General Counsel or chief legal officer of the agency shall publicly certify that, in his or her opinion, the meeting may be closed to the public and shall state each relevant exemptive provision. A copy of such certification, together with a statement from the presiding officer of the meeting setting forth the time and place of the meeting, and the persons present, shall be retained by the agency. The agency shall maintain a complete transcript or electronic recording adequate to record fully the proceedings of each meeting, or portion of a meeting, closed to the public, except that in the case of a meeting, or portion of a meeting, closed to the public pursuant to paragraph (8), (9)(A), or (10) of subsection (c), the agency shall maintain either such a transcript or recording, or a set of minutes. Such minutes shall fully and clearly describe all matters discussed and shall provide a full and accurate summary of any actions taken, and the reasons therefor, including a description of each of the views expressed on any item and the record of any rollcall vote (reflecting the vote of each member on the question). All documents considered in connection with any action shall be identified in such minutes.

(2) The agency shall make promptly available to the public, in a place easily accessible to the public, the transcript, electronic recording, or minutes (as required by paragraph (1)) of the discussion of any item on the agenda, or of any item of the testimony of any witness received at the meeting, except for such item or items of such discussion or testimony as the agency determines to contain information which have been withheld under subsection (c). Copies of such transcript, or minutes, or a transcription of such recording disclosing the identity of each speaker, shall be furnished to any person at the actual cost of duplication or transcription. The agency shall maintain a complete verbatim copy of the transcript, a complete copy of the minutes, or a complete electronic recording of

each meeting, or portion of a meeting, closed to the public, for a period of at least two years after such meeting, or until one year after the conclusion of any agency proceeding with respect to which the meeting or portion was held, whichever occurs later.

(g) Each agency subject to the requirements of this section shall, within 180 days after the date of enactment of this section, following consultation with the Office of the Chairman of the Administrative Conference of the United States and published notice in the Federal Register of at least thirty days and opportunity for written comment by any person, promulgate regulations to implement the requirements of subsections (b) through (f) of this section. Any person may bring a proceeding in the United States District Court for the District of Columbia to require an agency to promulgate such regulations if such agency has not promulgated such regulations within the time period specified herein. Subject to any limitations of time provided by law, any person may bring a proceeding in the United States Court of Appeals for the District of Columbia to set aside agency regulations issued pursuant to this subsection that are not in accord with the requirements of subsections (b) through (f) of this section and to require the promulgation of regulations that are in accord with such subsections.

(h) (1) The district courts of the United States shall have jurisdiction to enforce the requirements of subsections (b) through (f) of this section by declaratory judgment, injunctive relief, or other relief as may be appropriate. Such actions may be brought by any person against an agency prior to, or within sixty days after, the meeting out of which the violation of this section arises, except that if public announcement of such meeting is not initially provided by the agency in accordance with the requirements of this section, such action may be instituted pursuant to this section at any time prior to sixty days after any public announcement of such meeting. Such actions may be brought in the district court of the United States for the district in which the agency meeting is held or in which the agency in question has its headquarters, or in the District Court for the District of Columbia. In such actions a defendant shall serve his answer within thirty days after the service of the complaint. The burden is on the defendant to sustain his action. In deciding such cases the court may examine in camera any portion of the transcript, electronic recording, or minutes of a meeting closed to the public, and may take such additional evidence as it deems necessary. The court, having due regard for orderly administration and the public interest, as well as the interests of the parties, may grant such equitable relief as it deems appropriate, including granting an injunction against future violations of this section or ordering the agency to make available to the public such portion of the transcript, recording, or minutes of a meeting as is not authorized to be withheld under subsection (c) of this section.

(2) Any Federal court otherwise authorized by law to review agency action may, at the application of any person properly participating in the proceeding pursuant to other applicable law, inquire into violations by the agency of the requirements of this section and afford such relief as it deems appropriate. Nothing in this section authorizes any Federal court having jurisdiction solely on the basis of paragraph (1) to set aside, enjoin, or invalidate any agency action (other than an action to close a meeting or to withhold information under this section) taken or discussed at any agency meeting out of which the violation of this section arose.

(i) The court may assess against any party reasonable attorney fees and other litigation costs reasonably incurred by any other party who substantially prevails in any action brought in accordance with the provisions of subsection (g) or (h) of this section, except that costs may be assessed against the plaintiff only where the court finds that the suit was initiated by the plaintiff primarily for frivolous or dilatory purposes. In the cases of assessment of costs against an agency, the costs may be assessed by the court against the United States.

(j) Each agency subject to the requirements of this section shall annually report to Congress regarding the following:

(1) The changes in the policies and procedures of the agency under this section that have occurred during the preceding 1-year period.

(2) A tabulation of the number of meetings held, the exemptions applied to close meetings, and the days of public notice provided to close meetings.

(3) A brief description of litigation or formal complaints concerning the implementation of this section by the agency.

(4) A brief explanation of any changes in law that have affected the responsibilities of the agency under this section.

(k)   Nothing herein expands or limits the present rights of any person under section 552 of this title, except that the exemptions set forth in subsection (c) of this section shall govern in the case of any request made pursuant to section 552 to copy or inspect the transcripts, recordings, or minutes described in subsection (f) of this section. The requirements of chapter 33 of title 44, United States Code, shall not apply to the transcriptions, recordings, and minutes described in subsection (t) of this section.

(l)   This section does not constitute authority to withhold any information from Congress, and does not authorize the closing of any agency meeting or portion thereof required by any other provision of law to be open.

(m) Nothing in this section authorizes any agency to withhold from any individual any record, including transcripts, recordings, or minutes required by this section, which is otherwise accessible to such individual under section 552a of this title.

§553. Rule making

(a)   This section applies, according to the provisions thereof, except to the extent that there is involved—
   (1)   a military or foreign affairs function of the United States; or
   (2)   a matter relating to agency management or personnel or to public property, loans, grants, benefits, or contracts.

(b)   General notice of proposed rule making shall be published in the Federal Register, unless persons subject thereto are named and either personally served or otherwise have actual notice thereof in accordance with law. The notice shall include—
   (1)   a statement of the time, place, and nature of public rule making proceedings;
   (2)   reference to the legal authority under which the rule is proposed; and
   (3)   either the terms or substance of the proposed rule or a description of the subjects and issues involved. Except when notice or hearing is required by statute, this subsection does not apply—
      (A)   to interpretative rules, general statements of policy, or rules of agency organization, procedure, or practice; or
      (B)   when the agency for good cause finds (and incorporates the finding and a brief statement of reasons therefor in the rules issued) that notice and public procedure thereon are impracticable, unnecessary, or contrary to the public interest.

(c)   After notice required by this section, the agency shall give interested persons an opportunity to participate in the rule making through submission of written data, views, or arguments with or without opportunity for oral presentation. After consideration of the relevant matter presented, the agency shall incorporate in the rules adopted a concise general statement of their basis and purpose. When rules are required by statute to be made on the record after opportunity for an agency hearing, sections 556 and 557 of this title apply instead of this subsection.

(d)   The required publication or service of a substantive rule shall be made not less than 30 days before its effective date, except—
   (1)   a substantive rule which grants or recognizes an exemption or relieves a restriction;
   (2)   interpretative rules and statements of policy; or
   (3)   as otherwise provided by the agency for good cause found and published with the rule.

(e)   Each agency shall give an interested person the right to petition for the issuance, amendment, or repeal of a rule.

§554. Adjudications

(a)   This section applies, according to the provisions thereof, in every case of adjudication required by statute to be determined on the record after opportunity for an agency hearing, except to the extent that there is involved—
   (1)   a matter subject to a subsequent trial of the law and the facts de novo in a court;
   (2)   the selection or tenure of an employee, except an administrative law judge appointed under section 3105 of this title;

(3)   proceedings in which decisions rest solely on inspections, tests, or elections;

(4)   the conduct of military or foreign affairs functions;

(5)   cases in which an agency is acting as an agent for a court; or

(6)   the certification of worker representatives.

(b)   Persons entitled to notice of an agency hearing shall be timely informed of—

(1)   the time, place, and nature of the hearing;

(2)   the legal authority and jurisdiction under which the hearing is to be held; and

(3)   the matters of fact and law asserted. When private persons are the moving parties, other parties to the proceeding shall give prompt notice of issues controverted in fact or law; and in other instances agencies may by rule require responsive pleading. In fixing the time and place for hearings, due regard shall be had for the convenience and necessity of the parties or their representatives.

(c)   The agency shall give all interested parties opportunity for—

(1)   the submission and consideration of facts, arguments, offers of settlement, or proposals of adjustment when time, the nature of the proceeding, and the public interest permit; and

(2)   to the extent that the parties are unable so to determine a controversy by consent, hearing and decision on notice and in accordance with sections 556 and 557 of this title.

(d)   The employee who presides at the reception of evidence pursuant to section 556 of this title shall make the recommended decision or initial decision required by section 557 of this title, unless he becomes unavailable to the agency. Except to the extent required for the disposition of ex parte matters as authorized by law, such as employee may not—

(1)   consult a person or party on a fact in issue, unless on notice and opportunity for all parties to participate; or

(2)   be responsible to or subject to the supervision or direction of an employee or agent engaged in the performance of investigative or prosecuting functions for an agency. An employee or agent engaged in the performance of investigative or prosecuting functions for an agency in a case may not, in that or a factually related case, participate or advise in the decision, recommended decision, or agency review pursuant to section 557 of this title, except as witness or counsel in public proceedings. This subsection does not apply—

(A)   in determining applications for initial licenses;

(B)   to proceedings involving the validity or application of rates, facilities, or practices of public utilities or carriers; or

(C)   to the agency or a member or members of the body comprising the agency.

(e)   The agency, with like effect as in the case of other orders, and in its sound discretion, may issue a declaratory order to terminate a controversy or remove uncertainty.

§555. Ancillary matters

(a)   This section applies, according to the provisions thereof, except as otherwise provided by this subchapter.

(b)   A person compelled to appear in person before an agency or representative thereof is entitled to be accompanied, represented, and advised by counsel or, if permitted by the agency, by other qualified representative. A party is entitled to appear in person or by or with counsel or other duly qualified representative in an agency proceeding. So far as the orderly conduct of public business permits, an interested person may appear before an agency or its responsible employees for the presentation, adjustment, or determination of an issue, request, or controversy in a proceeding, whether interlocutory, summary, or otherwise, or in connection with an agency function. With due regard for the convenience and necessity of the parties or their representatives and within a reasonable time, each agency shall proceed to conclude a matter presented to it. This subsection does not grant or deny a person who is not a lawyer the right to appear for or represent others before an agency or in an agency proceeding.

(c)   Process, requirement of a report, inspection, or other investigative act or demand may not be issued, made, or enforced except as authorized by law. A person compelled to submit data or evidence is entitled to retain or, on payment of lawfully prescribed costs, procure a copy or transcript thereof, except that in a nonpublic investigatory proceeding the witness may for good cause be limited to inspection of the official transcript of his testimony.

(d) Agency subpoenas authorized by law shall be issued to a party on request and, when required by rules of procedure, on a statement or showing of general relevance and reasonable scope of the evidence sought. On contest, the court shall sustain the subpoena or similar process or demand to the extent that it is found to be accordance with law. In a proceeding for enforcement, the court shall issue an order requiring the appearance of the witness or the production of the evidence or data within a reasonable time under penalty of punishment for contempt in cases on contumacious failure to comply.

(e) Prompt notice shall be given of the denial in whole or in part of a written application, petition, or other request of an interested person made in connection with any agency proceeding. Except in affirming a prior denial or when the denial is self-explanatory, the notice shall be accompanied by a brief statement of the grounds for denial.

§556. Hearings; presiding employees; powers and duties; burden of proof; evidence; record as basis of decision

(a) This section applies, according to the provisions thereof, to hearings required by section 553 or 554 of this title to be conducted in accordance with this section.

(b) There shall preside at the taking of evidence—
   (1) the agency;
   (2) one or more members of the body which comprises the agency; or
   (3) one or more administrative law judges appointed under section 3105 of this title. This subchapter does not supersede the conduct of specified classes of proceedings, in whole or in part, by or before boards or other employees specially provided for by or designated under statute. The functions of presiding employees and of employees participating in decisions in accordance with section 557 of this title shall be conducted in an impartial manner. A presiding or participating employee may at any time disqualify himself. On the filing in good faith of a timely and sufficient affidavit of personal bias or other disqualification of a presiding or participating employee, the agency shall determine the matters as a part of the record and decision in the case.

(c) Subject to published rules of the agency and within its powers, employees presiding at hearings may—
   (1) administer oaths and affirmations;
   (2) issue subpoenas authorized by law;
   (3) rule on offers of proof and receive relevant evidence;
   (4) take depositions or have depositions taken when the ends of justice would be served;
   (5) regulate the course of the hearing;
   (6) hold conferences for the settlement or simplification of the issues by consent of the parties or by the use of alternative means of dispute resolution as provided in subchapter IV of this chapter;
   (7) inform the parties as to the availability of one or more alternative means of dispute resolution, and encourage use of such methods;
   (8) require the attendance at any conference held pursuant to paragraph (6) of at least one representative of each party who has authority to negotiate concerning resolution of issues in controversy;
   (9) dispose of procedural requests or similar matters;
   (10) make or recommend decisions in accordance with section 557 of this title; and
   (11) take other action authorized by agency rule consistent with this subchapter.

(d) Except as otherwise provided by statute, the proponent of a rule or order has the burden of proof. Any oral or documentary evidence may be received, but the agency as a matter of policy shall provide for the exclusion of irrelevant, immaterial, or unduly repetitious evidence. A sanction may not be imposed or rule or order issued except on consideration of the whole record or those parts thereof cited by a party and supported by and in accordance with the reliable, probative, and substantial evidence. The agency may, to the extent consistent with the interests of justice and the policy of the underlying statutes administered by the agency, consider a violation of section 557(d) of this title sufficient grounds for a decision adverse to a party who has knowingly committed such violation or knowingly caused such violation to occur. A party is entitled to present his case or defense by oral or documentary evidence, to submit rebuttal evidence, and to conduct such cross-examination as may be required for a full and true disclosure of the facts. In rule making or determining claims for money or benefits or applications for initial licenses an agency may, where a party will not be prejudiced thereby, adopt procedures for the submission of all or part of the evidence in written form.

(e)   The transcript of testimony and exhibits, together with all papers and requests filed in the proceeding, constitutes the exclusive record for decision in accordance with section 557 of this title and, on payment of lawfully prescribed costs, shall be made available to the parties. When an agency decision rests on official notice of a material fact not appearing in the evidence in the record, a party is entitled, on timely request, to an opportunity to show the contrary.

§557. Initial decision; conclusiveness; review by agency; submissions by parties; contents of decisions; record

(a)   This section applies, according to the provisions thereof, when a hearing is required to be conducted in accordance with section 556 of this title.

(b)   When the agency did not preside at the reception of the evidence, the presiding employee or, in cases not subject to section 554(d) of this title, an employee qualified to preside at hearings pursuant to section 556 of this title, shall initially decide the case unless the agency requires, either in specific cases or by general rule, the entire record to be certified to it for decision. When the presiding employee makes an initial decision, that decision then becomes the decision of the agency without further proceedings unless there is an appeal to, or review on motion of, the agency within time provided by rule. On appeal from or review of the initial decision, the agency has all the powers which it would have in making the initial decision except as it may limit the issues on notice or by rule. When the agency makes the decision without having presided at the reception of the evidence, the presiding employee or an employee qualified to preside at hearings pursuant to section 556 of this title shall first recommend a decision, except that in rule making or determining application for initial licenses—

(1)   instead thereof the agency may issue a tentative decision or one of its responsible employees;

(2)   this procedure may be omitted in a case in which the agency finds on the record that due and timely execution of its functions imperatively and unavoidably so requires.

(c)   Before a recommended, initial, or tentative decision, or a decision on agency review of the decision of subordinate employees, the parties are entitled to a reasonable opportunity to submit for the consideration of the employees participating in the decisions—

(1)   proposed findings and conclusions; or

(2)   exceptions to the decisions or recommended decisions of subordinate employees or to tentative agency decisions; and

(3)   supporting reasons for the exceptions or proposed findings or conclusions. The record shall show the ruling on each finding, conclusion or exception presented. All decisions, including initial, recommended, and tentative decisions, are a part of the record and shall include a statement of—

(A)   findings and conclusions, and the reasons or basis therefore, on all the material issues of fact, law, or discretion presented on the record; and

(B)   the appropriate rule, order, sanction, relief, or denial thereof.

(d)   (1)   In any agency which is subject to subsection (a) of this section, except to the extent required for disposition of ex parte matters as authorized by law—

(A)   no interested person outside the agency shall make or knowingly cause to be made to any member of the comprising the agency, administrative law judge, or other employee who is reasonably be expected to, be involved in the decisional process of the proceeding, an ex parte communication relevant to the merits of the proceeding;

(B)   no member of the body comprising the agency, administrative law judge, or other employee who is or may reasonably be expected to be involved in the decisional process of the proceeding, shall make or knowingly cause to be made to any interested person outside the agency an ex parte communication relevant to the merits of the proceeding;

(C)   a member of the body comprising the agency, administrative law judge, or other employee who is or may reasonably be expected to be involved in the decisional process of such proceedings who receives, or who makes or knowingly causes to be made, a communication prohibited by this subsection shall place on the public record of the proceeding:

(i)   all such written communications;

(ii)   memoranda stating the substance of all such oral communications; and

(iii) all written responses, and memoranda stating the substance of all oral responses, to the materials described in clauses (i) and (ii) of this subparagraph;

(D)   upon receipt of a communication knowingly made or knowingly caused to be made by a party in violation of this subsection, the agency, administrative law judge, or other employee presiding at the hearing may, to the extent consistent with the interests of justice and the policy of the underlying statutes, require the party to show cause why his claim or interest in the proceeding should not be dismissed, denied, disregarded, or otherwise adversely affected on account of such violation; and

(E)   the prohibitions of this subsection shall apply beginning at such time as the agency may designate, but in no case shall they begin to apply later an the time at which proceeding is noticed for hearing unless the person responsible for the communication has knowledge that it will be noticed, in which case the prohibitions shall apply beginning at the time of this acquisition of such knowledge.

(2)   This subsection does not constitute authority to withhold information from Congress.

§558. Imposition of sanctions; determination of applications for licenses; suspension, revocation, and expiration of licenses

(a)   This section applies, according to the provisions thereof, to the exercise of a power or authority.

(b)   A sanction may not be imposed or a substantive rule or order issued except within jurisdiction delegated to the agency and as authorized by law.

(c)   When application is made for a license required by law, the agency, with due regard for the rights and privileges of all the interested parties or adversely affected persons and within a reasonable time, shall set and complete proceedings required by law and shall make its decision. Except in cases of willfulness or those in which public health, interest, or safety requires otherwise, the withdrawal, suspension, revocation, or annulment of a license is lawful only if, before the institution of agency proceedings therefor, the licensee has been given—

(1)   notice by the agency in writing of the facts or conduct which may warrant the action; and

(2)   opportunity to demonstrate or achieve compliance with all lawful requirements. When the licensee has made timely and sufficient application for a renewal or a new license in accordance with agency rules, a license with reference to an activity of a continuing nature does not expire until the application has been finally determined by the agency.

§559. Effect on other laws; effect of subsequent statutes

This subchapter, chapter 7, and sections 1305, 3105, 3344, 4301 (2)(E), 5362, and 7521 of this title, and the provisions of section 5335(a)(B) of this title that relate to administrative law judges, do not limit or repeal additional requirements imposed by statute or otherwise recognized by law. Except as otherwise required by law, requirements or privileges relating to evidence or procedure apply equally to agencies and persons. Each agency is granted the authority necessary to comply with the requirements of this subchapter through the issuance of rules or otherwise. Subsequent statutes may not be held to supersede or modify this subchapter, chapter 7, sections 1305, 3105, 3344, 4301(2)(E), 5372, or 7521, or the provisions of section 5335(a)(B) of this title that relate to administrative law judges, except to the extent that it does so expressly.

§561. Purpose (Negotiated Rulemaking Act)

The purpose of this subchapter is to establish a framework for the conduct of negotiated rulemaking, consistent with section 553 of this title, to encourage agencies to use the process when it enhances the informal rulemaking process. Nothing in this subchapter should be construed as an attempt to limit innovation and experimentation with the negotiated rulemaking process or with other innovative rulemaking procedures otherwise authorized by law.

§562. Definitions

For the purposes of this subchapter, the term—

(1) "agency" has the same meaning as in section 551(1) of this title;

(2) "consensus" means unanimous concurrence among the interests represented on a negotiated rulemaking committee established under this subchapter, unless such committee—
   (A) agrees to define such term to mean a general but not unanimous concurrence; or
   (B) agrees upon another specified definition;

(3) "convener" means a person who impartially assists an agency in determining whether establishment of a negotiated rulemaking committee is feasible and appropriate in a particular rulemaking;

(4) "facilitator" means a person who impartially aids in the discussions and negotiations among the members of a negotiated rulemaking committee to develop a proposed rule;

(5) "interest" means, with respect to an issue or matter, multiple parties which have a similar point of view or which are likely to be affected in a similar manner;

(6) "negotiated rulemaking" means rulemaking through the use of a negotiated rulemaking committee;

(7) "negotiated rulemaking committee" or "committee" means an advisory committee established by an agency in accordance with this subchapter and the Federal Advisory Committee Act to consider and discuss issues for the purpose of reaching a consensus in the development of a proposed rule;

(8) "party" has the same meaning as in section 551(3) of this title;

(9) "person" has the same meaning as in section 551(2) of this title;

(10) "rule" has the same meaning as in section 551(4) of this title; and

(11) "rulemaking" means "rule making" as that term is defined in section 551(5) of this title.

§563. Determination of need for negotiated rulemaking committee

(a) Determination of Need by the Agency—An agency may establish a negotiated rulemaking committee to negotiate and develop a proposed rule, if the head of the agency determines that the use of the negotiated rulemaking procedure is in the public interest. In making such a determination, the head of the agency shall consider whether—
   (1) there is a need for a rule;
   (2) there are a limited number of identifiable interests that will be significantly affected by the rule;
   (3) there is a reasonable likelihood that a committee can be convened with a balanced representation of persons who—
      (A) can adequately represent the interests identified under paragraph (2); and
      (B) are willing to negotiate in good faith to reach a consensus on the proposed rule;
   (4) there is a reasonable likelihood that a committee will reach a consensus on the proposed rule within a fixed period of time;
   (5) the negotiated rulemaking procedure will not unreasonably delay the notice of proposed rulemaking and the issuance of the final rule;

(6) the agency has adequate resources and is willing to commit such resources, including technical assistance, to the committee, and

(7) the agency, to the maximum extent possible consistent with the legal obligations of the agency, will use the consensus of the committee with respect to the proposed rule as the basis for the rule proposed by the agency for notice and comment.

(b) Use of Conveners—

    (1) Purposes of conveners—An agency may use the services of a convener to assist the agency in—

        (A) identifying persons who will be significantly affected by a proposed rule, including residents of rural areas; and

        (B) conducting discussions with such persons to identify the issues of concern to such persons, and to ascertain whether the establishment of a negotiated rulemaking committee is feasible and appropriate in the particular rulemaking.

    (2) Duties of conveners—The convener shall report findings and may make recommendations to the agency. Upon request of the agency, the convener shall ascertain the names of persons who are willing and qualified to represent interests that will be significantly affected by the proposed rule, including residents of rural areas. The report and any recommendations of the convener shall be made available to the public upon request.

§564. Publication of notice; applications for membership on committees

(a) Publication of Notice—If, after considering the report of a convener or conducting its own assessment, an agency decides to establish a negotiated rulemaking committee, the agency shall publish in the Federal Register and, as appropriate, in trade or other specialized publications, a notice which shall include—

    (1) an announcement that the agency intends to establish a negotiated rulemaking committee to negotiate and develop a proposed rule;

    (2) a description of the subject and scope of the rule to be developed, and the issues to be considered;

    (3) a list of the interests which are likely to be significantly affected by the rule;

    (4) a list of the persons proposed to represent such interests and the person or persons proposed to represent the agency;

    (5) a proposed agenda and schedule for completing the work of the committee, including a target date for publication by the agency of a proposed rule for notice and comment;

    (6) a description of administrative support for the committee to be provided by the agency, including technical assistance;

    (7) a solicitation for comments on the proposal to establish the committee, and the proposed membership of the negotiated rulemaking committee; and

    (8) an explanation of how a person may apply or nominate another person for membership on the committee, as provided under subsection (b).

(b) Applications for Membership on Committee—Persons who will be significantly affected by a proposed rule and who believe that their interests will not be adequately represented by any person specified in a notice under subsection (a)(4) may apply for, or nominate another person for, membership on the negotiated rulemaking committee to represent such interests with respect to the proposed rule. Each application or nomination shall include—

    (1) the name of the applicant or nominee and a description of the interests such person shall represent;

    (2) evidence that the applicant or nominee is authorized to represent parties related to the interests the person proposed to represent;

    (3) a written commitment that the applicant or nominee shall actively participate in good faith in the development of the rule under consideration; and

    (4) the reasons that the persons specified in the notice under subsection (a)(4) do not adequately represent the interests of the person submitting the application or nomination.

(c) Period for Submission of Comments and Applications—The agency shall provide for a period of at least 30 calendar days for the submission of comments and applications under this section.

§565. Establishment of committee

(a)   Establishment—
   (1)   Determination to establish committee—If after considering comments and applications submitted under section 564, the agency determines that a negotiated rulemaking committee can adequately represent the interests that will be significantly affected by a proposed rule and that it is feasible and appropriate in the particular rulemaking, the agency may establish a negotiated rulemaking committee. In establishing and administering such a committee, the agency shall comply with the Federal Advisory Committee Act with respect to such committee, except as otherwise provided in this subchapter.
   (2)   Determination not to establish committee—If after considering such comments and applications, the agency decides not to establish a negotiated rulemaking committee, the agency shall promptly publish notice of such decision and the reasons therefor in the Federal Register and, as appropriate, in trade or other specified publications, a copy of which shall be sent to any person who applied for, or nominated another person for membership on the negotiated rulemaking committee to represent such interests with respect to the proposed rule.

(b)   Membership—The agency shall limit membership on a negotiated rulemaking committee to 25 members, unless the agency head determines that a greater number of members is necessary for the functioning of the committee or to achieve balanced membership. Each committee shall include at least one person representing the agency.

(c)   Administrative Support—The agency shall provide appropriate administrative support to the negotiated rulemaking committee, including technical assistance.

§566. Conduct of committee activity

(a)   Duties of Committee—Each negotiated rulemaking committee established under this subchapter shall consider the matter proposed by the agency for consideration and shall attempt to reach a consensus concerning a proposed rule with respect to such matter and any other matter the committee determines is relevant to the proposed rule,

(b)   Representatives of Agency on Committee—The person or persons representing the agency on a negotiated rulemaking committee shall participate in the deliberations and activities of the committee with the same rights and responsibilities as other members of the committee, and shall be authorized to fully represent the agency in the discussions and negotiations of the committee.

(c)   Selecting Facilitator—Notwithstanding section 10(e) of the Federal Advisory Committee Act, an agency may nominate either a person from the Federal Government of a person from outside the Federal Government to serve as a facilitator for the negotiations of the committee, subject to the approval of the committee by consensus. If the committee does not approve the nominee of the agency for facilitator, the agency shall submit a substitute nomination. If a committee does not approve any nominee of the agency for facilitator, the committee shall select by consensus a person to serve as facilitator. A person designated to represent the agency in substantive issues may not serve as facilitator or otherwise chair the committee.

(d)   Duties of Facilitator—A facilitator approved or selected by a negotiated rulemaking committee shall—
   (1)   chair the meetings of the committee in an impartial manner;
   (2)   impartially assist the members of the committee in conducting discussions and negotiations; and
   (3)   manage the keeping of minutes and records as required under section 10(b) and (c) of the Federal Advisory Committee Act, except that any personal notes and materials of the facilitator or of the members of a committee shall not be subject to section 552 of this title.

(e)   Committee Procedures—A negotiated rulemaking committee established under this subchapter may adopt procedures for the operation of the committee. No provision of section 553 of this title shall apply to the procedures of a negotiated rulemaking committee.

(f)   Report of Committee—If a committee reaches a consensus on a proposed rule, at the conclusion of negotiations the committee shall transmit to the agency that established the committee a report containing the proposed rule, If the committee does not reach a consensus on a proposed rule, the committee may transmit to the agency a report specifying any areas in which the committee reached a consensus. The committee may include in a report any other information, recommendations, or materials that the committee considers appropriate. Any committee member may include as an addendum to the report additional information, recommendations, or materials.

(g) Records of Committee—In addition to the report required by subsection (f), a committee shall submit to the agency the records required under section 10(b) and (c) of the Federal Advisory Committee Act.

§567. Termination of committee

A negotiated rulemaking committee shall terminate upon promulgation of the final rule under consideration, unless the committee's charter contains an earlier termination date or the agency, after consulting the committee, or the committee itself specifies an earlier termination date.

§568. Services, facilities, and payment of committee member expenses

(a) Services of Conveners and Facilitators—
    (1) In general—An agency may employ or enter into contracts for the services of an individual or organization to serve as a convener or facilitator for a negotiated rulemaking committee under this subchapter, or may use the services of a Government employee to act as a convener or a facilitator for such a committee.
    (2) Determination of conflicting interests—An agency shall determine whether a person under consideration to serve as convener or facilitator of a committee under paragraph (1) has any financial or other interest that would preclude such person from serving in an impartial and independent manner.

(b) Services and Facilities of Other Entities—For purposes of this subchapter, an agency may use the services and facilities of other Federal agencies and public and private agencies and instrumentalities with the consent of such agencies and instrumentalities, and with or without reimbursement to such agencies and instrumentalities, and may accept voluntary and uncompensated services without regard to the provisions of section 1342 of title 31. The Federal Mediation and Conciliation Service may provide services and facilities, with or without reimbursement, to assist agencies under this subchapter, including furnishing conveners, facilitators, and training in negotiated rulemaking.

(c) Expenses of Committee Members—Members of a negotiated rulemaking committee shall be responsible for their own expenses of participation in such committee, except that an agency may, in accordance with section 7(d) of the Federal Advisory Committee Act, pay for a member's reasonable travel and per diem expenses, expenses to obtain technical assistance, and a reasonable rate of compensation, if—
    (1) such member certifies a lack of adequate financial resources to participate in the committee; and
    (2) the agency determines that such member's participation in the committee is necessary to assure an adequate representation of the member's interest.

(d) Status of Member as Federal Employee—A member's receipt of funds under this section or section 569 shall not conclusively determine for purposes of sections 202 through 209 of title 18 whether that member is an employee of the United States Government.

§569. Encouraging negotiated rulemaking

(a) The President shall designate an agency or designate or establish an interagency committee to facilitate and encourage agency use of negotiated rulemaking. An agency that is considering, planning, or conducting a negotiated rulemaking may consult with such agency or committee for information and assistance.

(b) To carry out the purposes of this subchapter, an agency planning or conducting a negotiated rulemaking may accept, hold, administer, and utilize gifts, devises, and bequests of property, both real and personal if that agency's acceptance and use of such gifts, devises, or bequests do not create a conflict of interest. Gifts and bequests of money and proceeds from sales of other property received as gifts, devises, or bequests shall be deposited in the Treasury and shall be disbursed upon the order of the head of such agency. Property accepted pursuant to this section, and the proceeds thereof, shall be used as nearly as possible in accordance with the terms of the gifts, devises, or bequests.

§570. Judicial review

Any agency action relating to establishing, assisting, or terminating a negotiated rulemaking committee under this subchapter shall not be subject to judicial review. Nothing in this section shall bar judicial review of a rule if such judicial review is otherwise provided by law. A rule which is the product of negotiated rulemaking and is subject to judicial review shall not be accorded any greater deference by a court than a rule which is the product of other rulemaking procedures.

§571. Definitions (Administrative Dispute Resolution Act)

For the purposes of this subchapter, the term—

(1) "agency" has the same meaning as in section 551(1) of this title;

(2) "administrative program" includes a Federal function which involves protection of the public interest and the determination of rights, privileges, and obligations of private persons through rule making, adjudication, licensing, or investigation, as those terms are used in subchapter II of this chapter;

(3) "alternative means of dispute resolution" means any procedure that is used to resolve issues in controversy, including, but not limited to, conciliation, facilitation, mediation, factfinding, minitrials, arbitration, and use of ombuds, or any combination thereof;

(4) "award" means any decision by an arbitrator resolving the issues in controversy;

(5) "dispute resolution communication" means any oral or written communication prepared for the purposes of a dispute resolution proceeding, including any memoranda, notes or work product of the neutral, parties or nonparty participant; except that a written agreement to enter into a dispute resolution proceeding, or final written agreement or arbitral award reached as a result of dispute resolution proceeding, is not a dispute resolution communication;

(6) "dispute resolution proceeding" means any process in which an alternative means of dispute resolution is used to resolve an issue in controversy in which a neutral is appointed and specified parties participate;

(7) "in confidence" means, with respect to information, that the information is provided—
   (A) with the expressed intent of the source that it not be disclosed; or
   (B) under circumstances that would create the reasonable expectation on behalf of the source that the information will not be disclosed;

(8) "issue in controversy" means an issue which is material to a decision concerning an administrative program of an agency, and with which there is disagreement—
   (A) between an agency and persons who would be substantially affected by the decision; or
   (B) between persons who would be substantially affected by the decision, except that such term shall not include any matter specified under section 2302 or 7121(c) of this title;

(9) "neutral" means an individual who, with respect to an issue in controversy, functions specifically to aid the parties in resolving the controversy;

(10) "party" means—
    (A) for a proceeding with names parties, the same as in section 551(3) of this title; and
    (B) for a proceeding without names parties, a person who will be significantly affect by the decision in the proceeding as in section 551(2) of this title; and

(11) "person" has the same meaning as in section 551(2) of this title; and

(12) roster means a list of persons qualified to provide services as neutrals.

§572. General authority

(a) An agency may use a dispute resolution proceeding for the resolution of an issue in controversy that relates to an administrative program, if the parties agree to such proceeding.

(b) An agency shall consider not using a dispute resolution proceeding if—
    (1) a definitive or authoritative resolution of the matter is required for precedential value, and such a proceeding is not likely to be accepted generally as an authoritative precedent;
    (2) the matter involves or may bear upon significant questions of Government policy that require additional procedures before a final resolution may be made, and such a proceeding would not likely serve to develop a recommended policy for the agency;
    (3) maintaining established policies is of special importance, so that variations among individual decisions are not increased and such a proceeding would not likely reach consistent results among individual decisions;
    (4) the matter significantly affects person or organizations who are not parties to the proceeding;
    (5) a full public record of the proceeding is important, and a dispute resolution proceeding cannot provide such a record; and
    (6) the agency must maintain continuing jurisdiction over the matter with authority to alter the disposition of the matter in the light of changed circumstances, and a dispute resolution proceeding would interfere with the agency's fulfilling that requirement.

(c) Alternative means of dispute resolution authorized under this subchapter are voluntary procedures which supplement rather than limit other available agency dispute resolution techniques.

§573. Neutrals

(a) A neutral may be a permanent or temporary officer or employee of the Federal Government or any other individual who is acceptable to the parties to a dispute resolution proceeding. A neutral shall have no official, financial, or personal conflict or interest with respect to the issues in controversy, unless such interest is fully disclosed in writing to all parties and all parties agree that the neutral may serve.

(b) A neutral who serves as a conciliator, facilitator, or mediator serves at the will of the parties.

(c) The President shall designate an agency or designate or establish an interagency committee to facilitate and encourage agency use of dispute resolution under this subchapter. Such agency or interagency committee, in consultation with other appropriate Federal agencies and professional organizations experienced in matters concerning dispute resolution, shall—
    (1) encourage and facilitate agency use of alternative means of dispute resolution; and
    (2) develop procedures that permit agencies to obtain the services of neutrals on an expedited basis.

(d) An agency may use the services of one or more employees of other agencies to serve as neutrals in dispute resolution proceedings. The agencies may enter into an interagency agreement that provides for the reimbursement by the user agency or the parties of the full or partial cost of the services of such an employee.

(e) Any agency may enter into a contract with any person for services as a neutral, or for training in connection with alternative means of dispute resolution. The parties in a dispute resolution proceeding shall agree on compensation for the neutral that is fair and reasonable to the Government.

§574. *Confidentiality*

(a) Except as provided in subsection (d) and (e), a neutral in a dispute resolution proceeding shall not voluntarily disclose or through discovery or compulsory process be required to disclose any dispute resolution communication or any communication provided in confidence to the neutral, unless—

    (1) all parties to the dispute resolution proceeding and the neutral consent in writing, and, if the dispute resolution communication was provided by a nonparty participant, that participant also consents in writing;

    (2) the dispute resolution communication has already been made public;

    (3) the dispute resolution communication is required statute to be made public, but a neutral should make such communication public only if no other person is reasonably available to disclose the communication; or

    (4) a court determines that such testimony or disclosure is necessary to—

        (A) prevent a manifest injustice;

        (B) help establish a violation of law; or

        (C) prevent harm to the public health or safety, of sufficient in the particular case to outweigh the integrity of dispute resolution proceedings in general by reducing the confidence of parties in future cases that their communications will remain confidential.

(b) A party to a dispute resolution proceeding shall not voluntarily disclose or through discovery or compulsory process be required to disclose any dispute resolution communication, unless—

    (1) the communication was prepared by the party seeking disclosure;

    (2) all parties to the dispute resolution proceeding consent in writing;

    (3) the dispute resolution communication has already been made public;

    (4) the dispute resolution communication is required by statute to be made public;

    (5) a court determines that such testimony or disclosure is necessary to—

        (A) prevent a manifest injustice;

        (B) help establish a violation of law; or

        (C) prevent harm to the public health and safety, of sufficient magnitude in the particular case to outweigh the integrity of dispute resolution proceedings in general by reducing the confidence of parties in futures cases that their communications will remain confidential;

    (6) the dispute resolution communication is relevant to determining the existence or meaning of an agreement or award that resulted from the dispute resolution proceeding or to the enforcement of such an agreement or award; or

    (7) except for dispute resolution communications generated by the neutral, the dispute resolution communication was provided to or was available to all parties to the dispute resolution proceeding.

(c) Any dispute resolution communication that is disclosed in violation of subsection (a) or (b), shall not be admissible in any proceeding resulting to the issues in controversy with respect to which the communication was made.

(d) (1) The parties may agree to alternative confidential procedures for disclosures by a neutral. Upon such agreement the parties shall inform the neutral before the commencement of the dispute resolution proceeding of any modifications to the provisions of subsection (a) that will govern the confidentiality of the dispute resolution proceeding. If the parties do not so inform the neutral, subsection (a) shall apply.

    (2) To qualify for the exemption established under subsection (j), an alternative confidential procedures under this subsection may not provide for less disclosure than the confidential procedures otherwise provided under this section.

(e) If a demand for disclosure, by way of discovery request or other legal process, is made upon a neutral regarding a dispute resolution communication, the neutral shall make reasonable efforts to notify the parties and any affected nonparty participants of the demand. Any party or affected nonparty participant who received such notice and within 15 calendar days does not offer to defend a refusal of the neutral to disclose the requested information shall have waived any objections to such disclosure.

(f) Nothing in this section shall prevent the discovery or admissibility of any evidence that is otherwise discoverable, merely because the evidence was presented in the course of a dispute resolution proceeding.

(g) Subsections (a) and (b) shall have no effect on the information and data that are necessary to document an agreement reached or order issued pursuant to a dispute resolution proceeding.

(h) Subsections (a) and (b) shall not prevent the gathering of information for research or educational purposes, in cooperation with other agencies, governmental entitles, or dispute resolution programs, so long as the parties and the specific issues in controversy are not identifiable.

(i) Subsections (a) and (b) shall not prevent use of a dispute resolution communication to resolve a dispute between the neutral in a dispute resolution proceeding and a party to or participant in such proceeding, so long as such dispute resolution communication is disclosed only to the extent necessary to resolve such dispute.

(j) A dispute resolution communication which is between a neutral and a party and which may not be disclosed under this section shall also be exempt from disclosure under section 552(b)(3).

§575. Authorization of arbitration

(a) (1) Arbitration may be used as an alternative means of dispute resolution whenever all parties consent. Consent may be obtained either before or after an issue in controversy has arisen. A party may agree to—
   (A) submit only certain issues in controversy to arbitration; or
   (B) arbitration on the condition that the award must be within a range of possible outcomes.
  (2) The arbitration agreement that sets forth the subject matter submitted to the arbitrator shall be in writing. Each such arbitration agreement shall specify a maximum award that may be issued by the arbitrator and may specify other conditions limiting the range of possible outcomes.
  (3) An agency may not require any person to consent to arbitration as a condition of entering into a contract or obtaining a benefit.

(b) An officer or employee of an agency shall not offer to use arbitration for the resolution of issues in controversy unless such officer or employee—
  (1) would otherwise have authority to enter into a settlement concerning the matter; or
  (2) is otherwise specifically authorized by the agency to consent to the use of arbitration.

(c) Prior to using binding arbitration under this subchapter, the head of an agency, in consultation with the Attorney General and after taking into account the factors in section 572(b), shall issue guidance on the appropriate use of binding arbitration and when an officer or employee of the agency has authority to settle an issue in controversy through binding arbitration.

§576. Enforcement of arbitration agreements

An agreement to arbitrate a matter to which this subchapter applies is enforceable pursuant to section 4 of title 9, and no action brought to enforce such an agreement shall be dismissed nor shall relief therein be denied on the grounds that it is against the United States or that the United States is an indispensable party.

§577. Arbitrators

(a) The parties to an arbitration proceeding shall be entitled to participate in the selection of the arbitrator.

(b) The arbitrator shall be neutral who meets the criteria of section 573 of this title.

§578. Authority of the arbitrator

An arbitrator to whom a dispute is referred under this subchapter may—
  (1) regulate the course of and conduct arbitral hearings;

  (2) administer oaths and affirmations;

(3) compel the attendance of witnesses and production of evidence at the hearing under the provisions of section 7 of title 9 only to the extent the agency involved is otherwise authorized by law to do so; and

(4) make awards.

§579. Arbitration proceedings

(a) The arbitrator shall set a time and place for the hearing on the dispute and shall notify the parties not less than 5 days before the hearing.

(b) Any party wishing a record of the hearing shall—
  (1) be responsible for the preparation of such record;
  (2) notify the other parties and the arbitrator of the preparation of such record;
  (3) furnish copies to all identified parties and the arbitrator; and
  (4) pay all costs for such record, unless the parties agree otherwise or the arbitrator determines that the costs should be apportioned.

(c) (1) The parties to the arbitration are entitled to be heard, to present evidence material to the controversy, and to cross-examine witnesses appearing at the hearing.
  (2) The arbitrator may, with the consent of the parties, conduct all or part of the hearing by telephone, television, computer, or other electronic means, if each party has an opportunity to participate.
  (3) The hearing shall be conducted expeditiously and in an informal manner.
  (4) The arbitrator may receive any oral or documentary evidence, except that irrelevant, immaterial, unduly repetitious, or privileged evidence may be excluded by the arbitrator.
  (5) The arbitrator shall interpret and apply relevant statutory and regulatory requirements, legal precedents, and policy directives.

(d) No interested person shall make or knowingly cause to be made to the arbitrator an unauthorized ex part communication relevant to the merits of the proceeding, unless the parties agree otherwise. If a communication is made in violation of this subsection, the arbitrator shall ensure that a memorandum of the communication is prepared and made part of the record, and that an opportunity for rebuttal is allowed. Upon receipt of a communication made in violation of this subsection, the arbitrator may, to the extent consistent with the interests of justice and the policies underlying this subchapter, require the offending party to show cause why the claim of such party should not be resolved against such party as a result of the improper conduct.

(e) The arbitrator shall make the award within 30 days after the close of the hearing, or the date of the filing of any briefs authorized by the arbitrator, whichever date is later, unless—
  (1) the parties agree to some other time limit; or
  (2) the agency provides by rule for some other time limit.

§580. Arbitration awards

(a) (1) Unless the agency provides otherwise by rule, the award in an arbitration proceeding under this subchapter shall include a brief, informal discussion of the factual and legal basis for the award, but formal findings of fact or conclusions of law shall not be required.
  (2) The prevailing parties shall file the award with all relevant agencies, along with proof of service on all parties.

(b) The award in an arbitration proceeding shall become final 30 days after it is served on all parties. Any agency that is a party to the proceeding may extend this 30-day period for an additional 30-day period by serving a notice of such extension on all other parties before the end of the first 30-day period.

(c) A final award is binding on the parties to the arbitration proceeding, and may be enforced pursuant to sections 9 through 13 of title 9. No action brought to enforce such an award shall be dismissed nor shall relief therein be denied on the grounds that it is against the United States or that the United States is an indispensable party.

(d) An award entered under this subchapter in an arbitration proceeding may not serve as an estoppel in any other proceeding for any issue that was resolved in the proceeding. Such an award also may not be used as precedent or otherwise be considered in any factually unrelated proceeding, whether conducted under this subchapter, by an agency, or in a court, or in any other arbitration proceeding.

§581. Judicial review

(a) Notwithstanding any other provision of law, any person adversely affected or aggrieved by an award made in an arbitration proceeding conducted under this subchapter may bring an action for review of such award only pursuant to the provisions of section 9 through 13 of title 9.

(b) (1) A decision by an agency to use or not to use a dispute resolution proceeding under this subchapter shall be committed to the discretion of the agency and shall not be subject to judicial review, except that arbitration shall be subject to judicial review under section 10(b) of title 9.

　　(2) A decision by the head of an agency under section 580 to terminate an arbitration proceeding or vacate an arbitral award shall be committed to the discretion of the agency and shall not be subject to judicial review.

§582. Repealed

§583. Support services

For the purposes of this subchapter, an agency may use (with or without reimbursement) the services and facilities of other Federal agencies, State, local, and tribal governments, public and private organizations and agencies, and individuals, with the consent of such agencies, organization, and individuals. An agency may accept voluntary and uncompensated services for purposes of this subchapter without regard to the provisions of section 1342 of title 31.

§601. Analysis of regulatory functions-definitions. (Regulatory Flexibility Act)

For purposes of this chapter—

(1) the term "agency" means an agency as defined in section 551(1) of this title;

(2) the term "rule" means any rule for which the agency publishes a general notice of proposed rulemaking pursuant to section 553(b) of this title, or any other law, including any rule of general applicability governing Federal grants to State and local governments for which the agency provides an opportunity for notice and public comment, except that the term "rule" does not include a rule of particular applicability relating to rates, wages, corporate or financial structures or reorganizations thereof, prices, facilities, appliances, services, or allowances therefor or to valuations, costs or accounting, or practices relating to such rates, wages, structures, prices, appliances, services, or allowances;

(3) the term "small business" has the same meaning as the term "small business concern" under section 3 of the Small Business Act, unless an agency, after consultation with the Office of Advocacy of the Small Business Administration and after opportunity for public comment establishes one or more definitions of such term which are appropriate to the activities of the agency and publishes such definition(s) in the Federal Register;

(4) the term "small organization" means any not-for-profit enterprise which is independently owned and operated and is not dominant in its field, unless an agency establishes, after opportunity for public comment, one or more definitions of such term which are appropriate to the activities of the agency and publishes such definition(s) in the Federal Register;

(5)   the term "small governmental jurisdiction" means governments of cities, counties, towns, townships, villages, school districts or special districts, with a population of less than fifty thousand, unless an agency establishes, after opportunity for public comment, one or more definitions of such term which are appropriate to the activities of the agency and which are based on such factors as location in rural or sparsely populated areas or limited revenues due to the population of such jurisdiction, and publishes such definition(s); in the Federal Register;

(6)   the term "small entity" shall have the same meaning as the terms "small business," "small organization" and "small governmental jurisdiction" defined in paragraphs (3), (4) and (5) of this section; and

(7)   the term "collection of information"—

(A)   means the obtaining, causing to be obtained, soliciting, or requiring the disclosure to third parties or the public, of facts or opinions by or for an agency, regardless of form or format, calling for either—

(i)   answers to identical questions posed to, or identical reporting or recordkeeping requirements imposed on, 10 or more persons, other than agencies, instrumentalities, or employees of the United States; or

(ii)   answers to questions posed to agencies, instrumentalities, or employees of the United States which are to be used for general statistical purposes; and

(B)   shall not include a collection of information described under section 3518(c) of title 44, United States Code.

(8)   Recordkeeping requirement—The term "recordkeeping requirement" means a requirement imposed by an agency on persons to maintain specified records.

§602. Regulatory agenda

(a)   During the months of October and April of each year, each agency shall publish in the Federal Register a regulatory flexibility agenda which shall contain—

(1)   a brief description of the subject area of any rule which the agency expects to propose or promulgate which is likely to have a significant economic impact on a substantial number of small entities;

(2)   a summary of the nature of any such rule under consideration for each subject area listed in the agenda pursuant to paragraph (1), the objectives and legal basis for the issuance of the rule, and an approximate schedule for completing action on any rule for which the agency has issued a general notice of proposed rulemaking; and

(3)   the name and telephone number of an agency official knowledgeable concerning the items listed in paragraph (1).

(b)   Each regulatory flexibility agenda will be transmitted to the Chief Counsel for Advocacy of the Small Business Administration for comment, if any.

(c)   Each agency shall endeavor to provide notice of each regulatory flexibility agenda to small entities or their representatives through direct notification or publication of the agenda in publications likely to be obtained by such small entities and shall invite comments upon each subject area on the agenda.

(d)   Nothing in this section precludes an agency from considering or acting on any matter not included in a regulatory flexibility agenda, or requires an agency to consider or act on any matter listed in such agenda.

§603. Initial regulatory flexibility analysis

(a)   Whenever an agency is required by section 553 of this title, or any other law, to publish general notice of proposed rulemaking for any proposed rule, or publishes a notice of proposed rulemaking for an interpretative rule involving the internal revenue laws of the United States, the agency shall prepare and make available for public comment an initial regulatory flexibility analysis. Such analysis shall describe the impact of the proposed rule on small entities. The initial regulatory flexibility analysis or a summary shall be published in the Federal Register at the time of the publication of general notice of proposed rulemaking for the rule. The agency shall transmit a copy of the initial regulatory flexibility analysis to the Chief Counsel for Advocacy of the Small Business Administration. In the case of an interpretative rule involving the internal revenue laws of the United States, this chapter applies to interpretative rules published in the Federal Register for codification in the Code of Federal Regulations, but only to the extent that such interpretative rules impose on small entities a collection of information requirement.

(b) Each initial regulatory flexibility analysis required under this section shall contain—
(1) a description of the reasons why action by the agency is being considered;
(2) a succinct statement of the objectives of, and legal basis for, the proposed rule;
(3) a description of and, where feasible, an estimate of the number of small entities to which the proposed rule will apply;
(4) a description of the projected reporting, recordkeeping and other compliance requirements of the proposed rule, including an estimate of the classes of small entities which will be subject to the requirement and the type of professional skills necessary for preparation of the report or record;
(5) an identification, to the extent practicable, of all relevant Federal rules which may duplicate, overlap or conflict with the proposed rule.

(c) Each initial regulatory flexibility analysis shall also contain a description of any significant alternatives to the proposed rule which accomplish the stated objectives of applicable statutes and which minimize any significant economic impact of the proposed rule on small entities. Consistent with the stated objectives of applicable statutes, the analysis shall discuss significant alternatives such as—
(1) the establishment of differing compliance or reporting requirements or timetables that take into account the resources available to small entities;
(2) the clarification, consolidation, or simplification of compliance and reporting requirements under the rule for such small entities;
(3) the use of performance rather than design standards; and
(4) an exemption from coverage of the rule, or any part thereof, for such small entities.

§604. Final regulatory flexibility analysis

(a) When an agency promulgates a final rule under section 553 of this title, after being required by that section or any other law to publish a general notice of proposed rulemaking, or promulgates a final interpretative rule involving the internal revenue laws of the United States as described in section 603(a), the agency shall prepare a final regulatory flexibility analysis. Each final regulatory flexibility analysis shall contain—
(1) a succinct statement of the need for, and the objectives of, the rule;
(2) a summary of the issues raised by the public comments in response to the initial regulatory flexibility analysis, a summary of the assessment of the agency of such issues, and a statement of any changes made in the proposed rule as a result of such comments;
(3) a description of and an estimate of the number of small entities to which the rule will apply or an explanation of why no such estimate is available;
(4) a description of the projected reporting, recordkeeping and other compliance requirements of the rule, including an estimate of the classes of small entities which will be subject to the requirement and the type of professional skills necessary for preparation of the report record; and
(5) a description of the steps the agency has taken to minimize the significant economic impact on small entities consistent with the stated objectives of applicable statutes, including a statement of the factual, policy, and legal reasons for selecting the alternative adopted in the final rule and why each one of the other significant alternatives to the rule considered by the agency which affect the impact on small entities was rejected.

(b) The agency shall make copies of the final regulatory flexibility analysis available to members of the public and shall publish in the Federal Register such analysis or a summary thereof.

§605. Avoidance of duplicative or unnecessary analyses

(a) Any Federal agency may perform the analyses required by sections 602, 603, and 604 of this title in conjunction with or as part of any other agenda or analysis required by any other law if such other analysis satisfies the provisions of such sections.

(b) Sections 603 and 604 of this title shall not apply to any proposed or final rule if the head of the agency certifies that the rule will not, if promulgated, have a significant economic impact on a substantial number of small entities. If the head of the agency makes a certification under the preceding sentence, the agency shall publish such certification in the Federal Register, at the time of publication of general notice of proposed rulemaking for the rule or at the time of publication of the final rule, along with a statement providing the factual basis for such certification. The agency shall provide such certification and statement to the Chief Counsel for Advocacy of the Small Business Administration.

(c) In order to avoid duplicative action, an agency may consider a series of closely related rules as one rule for the purpose of sections 602, 603, 604 and 610 of this title.

§606. Effect on other law

The requirements of sections 603 and 604 of this title do not alter in any manner standards otherwise applicable by law to agency action.

§607. Preparation of analyses

In complying with the provisions of sections 603 and 604 of this title, an agency may provide either a quantifiable or numerical description of the effects of a proposed rule or alternatives to the proposed rule, or more general descriptive statements if quantification is not practicable or reliable.

§608. Procedure for waiver or delay of completion

(a) An agency head may waive or delay the completion of some or all of the requirements of section 603 of this title by publishing in the Federal Register, not later than the date of publication of the final rule, a written finding, with reasons therefor, that the final rule is being promulgated in response to an emergency that makes compliance or timely compliance with the provisions of section 603 of this title impracticable.

(b) Except as provided in section 605(b), an agency head may not waive the requirements of section 604 of this title. An agency head may delay the completion of the requirements of section 604 of this title for a period of not more than one hundred and eighty days after the date of publication in the Federal Register of a final rule by publishing in the Federal Register, not later than such date of publication, a written finding, with reasons therefor, that the final rule is being promulgated in response to an emergency that makes timely compliance with the provisions of section 604 of this title impracticable. If the agency has not prepared a final regulatory flexibility analysis pursuant to section 604 of this title within one hundred and eighty days from the date of publication of the final rule, such rule shall lapse and have no effect. Such a rule shall not be repromulgated until a final regulatory flexibility analysis has been completed by the agency.

§609. Procedures for gathering comments

(a) When any rule is promulgated which will have a significant economic impact on a substantial number of small entities, the head of the agency promulgating the rule of the official of the agency with statutory responsibility for the promulgation of the rule shall assure that small entities have been given an opportunity to participate in the rulemaking for the rule through the reasonable use of techniques such as—

(1) the inclusion in an advanced notice of proposed rulemaking, if issued, of a statement that the proposed rule may have a significant economic effect on a substantial number of small entities;

(2) the publication of general notice of proposed rulemaking in publications likely to be obtained by small entities;

(3) the direct notification of interested small entities;

(4) the conduct of open conferences or public hearings concerning the rule for small entities including soliciting and receiving comments over computer networks; and

(5) the adoption or modification of agency procedural rules to reduce the cost or complexity of participation in the rulemakings by small entities.

(b) Prior to publication of an initial regulatory flexibility analysis which a covered agency is required to conduct by this chapter—

(1) a covered agency shall notify the Chief Counsel for Advocacy of the Small Business Administration and provide the Chief Counsel with information on the potential impacts of the proposed rule on small entities and the type of small entities that might be affected;

(2) not later than 15 days after the date of receipt of the materials described in paragraph (1), the Chief Counsel shall identify individuals representative of affected small entities for the purpose of obtaining advice and recommendations from those individuals about the potential impacts of the proposed rule;

(3) the agency shall convene a review panel for such rule consisting wholly of full time Federal employees of the office within the agency responsible for carrying out the proposed rule, the Office of Information and Regulatory Affairs within the Office of Management and Budget, and the Chief Counsel;

(4) the panel shall review any material the agency has prepared in connection with this chapter, including any draft proposed rule, collect advice and recommendations of each individual small entity representative identified by the agency after consultation with the Chief Counsel, on issues related to subsections 603(b), paragraphs (3), (4) and (5) and 603(c);

(5) not later than 60 days after the date a covered agency convenes a review panel pursuant to paragraph (3), the review panel shall report on the comments of the small entity representatives and its findings as to issues related to subsections 603(b), paragraphs (3), (4) and (5) and 603(c), provided that such report shall be made public as part of the rulemaking record; and

(6) where appropriate, the agency shall modify the proposed rule, the initial regulatory flexibility analysis or the decision on whether an initial regulatory flexibility analysis is required.

(c) An agency may in its discretion apply subsection (b) to rules that the agency intends to certify under subsection 605(b), but the agency believes may have a greater than de minimis impact on a substantial number of small entities.

(d) For purposes of this section, the term "covered agency" means the Environmental Protection Agency and the Occupational Safety and Health Administration of the Department of Labor.

(e) The Chief Counsel for Advocacy, in consultation with the individuals identified in subsection (b)(2), and with the Administrator of the Office of Information and Regulatory Affairs within the Office of Management and Budget, may waive the requirements of subsections (b)(3), (b)(4), and (b)(5) by including in the rulemaking record a written finding, with reasons therefor, that those requirements would not advance the effective participation of small entities in the rulemaking process. For purposes of this subsection, the factors to be considered in making such a finding are as follows:

(1) In developing a proposed rule, the extent to which the covered agency consulted with individuals representative of affected small entities with respect to the potential impacts of the rule and took such concerns into consideration.

(2) Special circumstances requiring prompt issuance of the rule.

(3) Whether the requirements of subsection (b) would provide the individuals identified in subsection (b)(2) with a competitive advantage relative to other small entities.

(f) Small Business Advocacy Chairpersons—
Not later than 30 days after the date of enactment of this Act, the head of each covered agency that has conducted a final regulatory flexibility analysis shall designate a small business advocacy chairperson using

existing personnel to the extent possible, to be responsible for implementing this section and to act as permanent chair of the agency's review panels established pursuant to this section.

§610. Periodic review of rules

(a) Within one hundred and eighty days after the effective date of this chapter, each agency shall publish in the Federal Register a plan for the periodic review of the rules issued by the agency which have or will have a significant economic impact upon a substantial number of small entities. Such plan may be amended by the agency at any time by publishing a revision in the Federal Register. The purpose of the review shall be to determine whether such rules should be continued without change, or should be amended or rescinded, consistent with the stated objectives of applicable statutes, to minimize any significant economic impact of the rules upon a substantial number of such small entities. The plan shall provide for the review of all such agency rules existing on the effective date of this chapter within ten years of that date for the review of such rules adopted after the effective date of this chapter within ten years of the publication of such rules as the final rule. If the head of the agency determines that completion of the review of existing rules is not feasible by the established date, he shall so certify in a statement published in the Federal Register and may extend the completion date by one year at a time for a total of not more than five years.

(b) In reviewing rules to minimize any significant economic impact of the rule on a substantial number of small entities in a manner consistent with the stated objectives of applicable statutes, the agency shall consider the following factors—
   (1) the continued need for the rule;
   (2) the nature of complaints or comments received concerning the rule from the public;
   (3) the complexity of the rule;
   (4) the extent to which the rule overlaps, duplicates or conflicts with other Federal rules, and, to the extent feasible, with State and local governmental rules; and
   (5) the length of time since the rule has been evaluated or the degree to which technology, economic conditions, or other factors have changed in the area affected by the rule.

(c) Each year, each agency shall publish in the Federal Register a list of the rules which have a substantial economic impact on a substantial number of small entities, which are to be reviewed pursuant to this section during the succeeding twelve months. The list shall include a brief description of each rule and the need for and legal basis of such rule and shall invite public comment upon the rule.

§611. Judicial review

(a) (1) For any rule subject to this chapter, a small entity that is adversely affected or aggrieved by final agency action is entitled to judicial review of agency compliance with the requirements of sections 601, 604, 605(b), and 610 in accordance with chapter 7. Agency compliance with sections 607 and 609(a) shall be judicially reviewable in connection with judicial review of section 604.
    (2) Each court having jurisdiction to review such rule for compliance with section 553, or under any other provision of law, shall have jurisdiction to review any claims of noncompliance with sections 601, 604, 605(b), 608(b), and 620 in accordance with chapter 7. Agency noncompliance with sections 607 and 609(a) shall be judicially reviewable in connections with judicial review of section 604.
    (3) (A) A small entity may seek such review during the period beginning on the date of final agency action and ending one year later, except that where a provision of law requires that an action challenging a final agency action be commenced before the expiration of one year, such lesser period shall apply to an action for judicial review under this section.
        (B) In the case where an agency delays the issuance of a final regulatory flexibility analysis pursuant to section 608(b) of this chapter, an action for judicial review under this section shall be filed not later than—
           (i) one year after the date the analysis is made available to the public, or
           (ii) where a provision of law requires that an action challenging a final agency regulation be commenced before the expiration of the 1-year period, the number of days specified in such provision of law that is after the date the analysis is made available to the public.

(4) In granting any relief in an action under this section, the court shall order the agency to take corrective action consistent with this chapter and chapter 7, including, but not limited to—

    (A) remanding the rule to the agency, and

    (B) deferring the enforcement of the rule against small entities unless the court finds that continued enforcement of the rule is in the public interest.

(5) Nothing in this subsection shall be construed to limit the authority of any court to stay the effective date of any rule or provision thereof under any other provision of law or to grant any other relief in addition to the requirements of this section.

(b) In an action for the judicial review of a rule, the regulatory flexibility analysis for such rule, including an analysis prepared or corrected pursuant to paragraph (a)(4), shall constitute part of the entire record of agency action in connection with such review.

(c) Compliance or noncompliance by an agency with the provisions of this chapter shall be subject to judicial review only in accordance with this section.

(d) Nothing in this section bars judicial review of any other impact statement or similar analysis required by any other law if judicial review of such statement or analysis is otherwise permitted by law.

§612. Reports and intervention rights

(a) The Chief Counsel for Advocacy of the Small Business Administration shall monitor agency compliance with this chapter and shall report at least annually thereon to the President and to the Committees on the Committees on the Judiciary and Small Business of the Senate and House of Representatives.

(b) The Chief Counsel for Advocacy of the Small Business Administration is authorized to appear as amicus curiae in any action brought in a court of the United States to review a rule. In any such action, the Chief Counsel is authorized to present his or her views with respect to compliance with this chapter, the adequacy of the rulemaking record with respect to small entities and the effect of the rule on small entities.

(c) A court of the United States shall grant the application of the Chief Counsel for Advocacy of the Small Business Administration to appear in such action for the purposes described in subsection (b).

§701. Application; definitions

(a) This chapter applies, according to the provisions thereof, except to the extent that—

    (1) statutes preclude judicial review; or

    (2) agency action is committed to agency discretion by law.

(b) For the purpose of this chapter—

    (1) "agency" means each authority of the Government of the United States, whether or not it is within or subject to review by another agency, but does not include—

        (A) the Congress;

        (B) the courts of the United States;

        (C) the governments of the territories or possessions of the United States,

        (D) the government of the District of Columbia;

        (E) agencies composed of representatives of the parties or of representatives of organizations of the parties to the disputes determined by them;

        (F) courts martial and military commissions;

        (G) military authority exercised in the field in time of war or in occupied territory; or

        (H) functions conferred by sections 1738, 1739, 1743, and 1744 of title 12; chapter 2 of title 41; or sections 1622, 1884, 1891-1902, and former section 1641 (b) (2), of title 50, appendix; and

    (2) "person," "rule," "order," "license," "sanction," "relief," and "agency action" have the meanings given them by section 551 of this title.

§702. Right of review

A person suffering legal wrong because of agency action, or adversely affected or aggrieved by agency action within the meaning of a relevant statute, is entitled to judicial review thereof. An action in a court of the United States seeking relief other than money damages and stating a claim that an agency or an officer or employee thereof acted or failed to act in an official capacity or under color of legal authority shall not be dismissed nor relief therein be denied on the ground that it is against the United States or that the United States is an indispensable party. The United States may be named as a defendant in any such action, and a judgment or decree may be entered against the United States: Provided, That any mandatory or injunctive decree shall specify the Federal officer or officers (by name or by title), and their successors in office, personally responsible for compliance. Nothing herein (1) affects other limitations on judicial review or the power or duty of the court to dismiss any action or deny relief on any other appropriate legal or equitable ground; or (2) confers authority to grant relief if any other statute that grants consent to suit expressly or impliedly forbids the relief which is sought.

§703. Form and venue of proceeding

The form of proceeding for judicial review is the special statutory review proceeding relevant to the subject matter in a court specified by statute or, in the absence or inadequacy thereof, any applicable form of legal action, including actions for declaratory judgments or writs of prohibitory or mandatory injunction or habeas corpus, in a court of competent jurisdiction. If no special statutory review proceeding is applicable, the action for judicial review may be brought against the United States, the agency by its official title, or the appropriate officer. Except to the extent that prior, adequate, and exclusive opportunity for judicial review is provided by law, agency action is subject to judicial review in civil or criminal proceedings for judicial enforcement.

§704. Actions reviewable

Agency action made reviewable by statute and final agency action for which there is no other adequate remedy in a court are subject to judicial review. A preliminary, procedural, or intermediate agency action or ruling not directly reviewable is subject to review on the review of the final agency action. Except as otherwise expressly required by statute, agency action otherwise final is final for the purposes of this section whether or not there has been presented or determined an application for a declaratory order, for any form of reconsideration, or, unless the agency otherwise requires by rule and provides that the action meanwhile is inoperative, for an appeal to superior agency authority.

§705. Relief pending review

When an agency finds that justice so requires, it may postpone the effective date of action taken by it, pending judicial review. On such conditions as may be required and to the extent necessary to prevent irreparable injury, the reviewing court, including the court to which a case may be taken on appeal from or on application for certiorari or other writ to a reviewing court, may issue all necessary and appropriate process to postpone the effective date of an agency action or to preserve status or rights pending conclusion of the review proceedings.

§706. Scope of review

To the extent necessary to decision and when presented, the reviewing court shall decide all relevant questions of law, interpret constitutional and statutory provisions, and determine the meaning or applicability of the terms of an agency action. The reviewing court shall—

    (1)   compel agency action unlawfully withheld or unreasonably delayed; and

    (2)   hold unlawful and set aside agency action, findings, and conclusions found to be—
        (A)   arbitrary, capricious, an abuse of discretion, or otherwise not in accordance with law;
        (B)   contrary to constitutional right, power, privilege, or immunity;

(C)   in excess of statutory jurisdiction, authority, or limitations, or short of statutory right;

(D)   without observance of procedure required by law;

(E)   unsupported by substantial evidence in a case subject to sections 556 and 557 of this title or otherwise reviewed on the record of an agency hearing provided by statute; or

(F)   unwarranted by the facts to the extent that the facts are subject to trial do novo by the reviewing court. In making the foregoing determinations, the court shall review the whole record of those parts of it cited by a party, and due account shall be taken of the rule of prejudicial error.

§801. Congressional review (Congressional Review Act)

(a)   (1)   (A)   Before a rule can take effect, the Federal agency promulgating such rule shall submit to each House of the Congress and to the Comptroller General a report containing—

(i)   a copy of the rule;

(ii)   a concise general statement relating to the rule, including whether it is a major rule; and

(iii) the proposed effective date of the rule.

(B)   On the date of the submission of the report under subparagraph (A), the Federal agency promulgating the rule shall submit to the Comptroller General and make available to each House of Congress—

(i)   a complete copy of the cost-benefit analysis of the rule, if any;

(ii)   the agency's actions relevant to sections 603, 604, 605, 607, and 609;

(iii) the agency's actions relevant to sections 202, 203, 204, and 205 of the Unfunded Mandates Reform Act of 1995; and

(iv)   any other relevant information or requirements under any other Act and any relevant Executive orders.

(C)   Upon receipt of a report submitted under subparagraph (A), each House shall provide copies of the report to the chairman and ranking member of each standing committee with jurisdiction under the rules of the House of Representatives or the Senate to report a bill to amend the provision of law under which the rule is issued.

(2)   (A)   The Comptroller General shall provide a report on each major rule to the committees of jurisdiction in each House of the Congress by the end of 15 calendar days after the submission or publication date as provided in section 802(b)(2). The report of the Comptroller General shall include an assessment of the agency's compliance with procedural steps required by paragraph (1)(B).

(B)   Federal agencies shall cooperate with the Comptroller General by providing information relevant to the Comptroller General's report under subparagraph (A).

(3)   A major rule relating to a report submitted under paragraph (1) shall take effect on the latest of—

(A)   the later of the date occurring 60 days after the date on which—

(i)   the Congress receives the report submitted under paragraph (1); or

(ii)   the rule is published in the Federal Register, if so published;

(B)   if the Congress passes a joint resolution of disapproval described in section 802 relating to the rule, and the President signs a veto of such resolution, the earlier date—

(i)   on which either House of Congress votes and fails to override the veto of the President; or

(ii)   occurring 30 session days after the date on which the Congress received the veto and objections of the President; or

(C)   the date the rule would have otherwise taken effect, if not for this section (unless a joint resolution of disapproval under section 802 is enacted).

(4)   Except for a major rule, a rule shall take effect as otherwise provided by law after submission to Congress under paragraph (1).

(5)   Notwithstanding paragraph (3), the effective date of a rule shall not be delayed by operation of this chapter beyond the date on which either House of Congress votes to reject a joint resolution of disapproval under section 802.

(b)   (1)   A rule shall not take effect (or continue), if the Congress enacts a joint resolution of disapproval, described under section 802, of the rule.

(2)   A rule that does not take effect (or does not continue) under paragraph (1) may not be reissued in substantially the same form, and a new rule that is substantially the same as such a rule may not be

issued, unless the reissued or new rule is specifically authorized by a law enacted after the date of the joint resolution disapproving the original rule.

(c) (1) Notwithstanding any other provision of this section (except subject to paragraph (3)), a rule that would not take effect by reason of subsection (a)(3) may take effect, if the President makes a determination under paragraph (2) and submits written notice of such determination to the Congress.

(2) Paragraph (1) applies to a determination made by the President by Executive order that the rule should take effect because such rule is—
(A) necessary because of an imminent threat to health or safety or other emergency;
(B) necessary for the enforcement of criminal laws;
(C) necessary for national security; or
(D) issued pursuant to any statute implementing an international trade agreement.

(3) An exercise by the President of the authority under this subsection shall have no effect on the procedures under section 802 or the effect of a joint resolution of disapproval under this section.

(d) (1) In addition to the opportunity for review otherwise provided under this chapter, in the case of any rule for which a report was submitted in accordance with subsection (a)(1)(A) during the period beginning on the date occurring—
(A) in the case of the Senate, 60 session days, or
(B) in the case of the House of Representatives, 60 legislative days, before the date the Congress adjourns a session of Congress through the date on which the same or succeeding Congress first convenes its next session, section 802 shall apply to such rule in the succeeding session of Congress.

(2) (A) In applying section 802 for purposes of such additional review, a rule described under paragraph (1) shall be treated as though—
(i) such rule were published in the Federal Register (as a rule that shall take effect) on—
(I) in the case of the Senate, the 15th session day, or
(II) in the case of the House of Representatives, the 15th legislative day, after the succeeding session of Congress first convenes; and
(ii) a report on such rule were submitted to Congress under subsection (a)(1) on such date.
(B) Nothing in this paragraph shall be construed to affect the requirement under subsection (a)(1) that a report shall be submitted to Congress before a rule can take effect.

(3) A rule described under paragraph (1) shall take effect as otherwise provided by law (including other subsections of this section).

(e) (1) For purposes of this subsection, section 802 shall also apply to any major rule promulgated between March 1, 1996, and the date of the enactment of this chapter.

(2) In applying section 802 for purposes of Congressional review, a rule described under paragraph (1) shall be treated as though—
(A) such rule were published in the Federal Register on the date of enactment of this chapter; and
(B) a report on such rule were submitted to Congress under subsection (a)(1) on such date.

(3) The effectiveness of a rule described under paragraph (1) shall be as otherwise provided by law, unless the rule is made of no force or effect under section 802.

(f) Any rule that takes effect and later is made of no force or effect by enactment of a joint resolution under section 802 shall be treated as though such rule had never taken effect.

(g) If the Congress does not enact a joint resolution of disapproval under section 802 respecting a rule, no court or agency may infer any intent of the Congress from any action or inaction of the Congress with regard to such rule, related statute, or joint resolution of disapproval.

§802. Congressional disapproval procedure

(a) For purposes of this section, the term "joint resolution" means only a joint resolution introduced in the period beginning on the date on which the report referred to in section 801(a)(1)(A) is received by Congress and ending 60 days thereafter (excluding days either House of Congress is adjourned for more than 3 days during a session of Congress), the matter after the resolving clause of which is as follows: "That Congress disapproves the rule submitted by the _____ relating to _____, and such rule shall have no force or effect." (The blank spaces being appropriately filled in).

(b) (1) A joint resolution described in subsection (a) shall be referred to the committees in each House of Congress with jurisdiction.

(2) For purposes of this section, the term "submission or publication date" means the later of the date on which—

(A) the Congress receives the report submitted under section 801(a)(1); or

(B) the rule is published in the Federal Register, if so published.

(c) In the Senate, if the committee to which is referred a joint resolution described in subsection (a) has not reported such joint resolution (or an identical joint resolution) at the end of 20 calendar days after the submission or publication date defined under subsection (b)(2), such committee may be discharged from further consideration of such joint resolution upon a petition supported in writing by 30 Members of the Senate, and such joint resolution shall be placed on the calendar.

(d) (1) In the Senate, when the committee to which a joint resolution is referred has reported, or when a committee is discharged (under subsection (c)) from further consideration of a joint resolution described in subsection (a), it is at any time thereafter in order (even though a previous motion to the same effect has been disagreed to) for a motion to proceed to the consideration of the joint resolution, and all points of order against the joint resolution (and against consideration of the joint resolution) are waived. The motion is not subject to amendment, or to a motion to postpone, or to a motion to proceed to the consideration of other business. A motion to reconsider the vote by which the motion is agreed to or disagreed to shall not be in order. If a motion to proceed to the consideration of the joint resolution is agreed to, the joint resolution shall remain the unfinished business of the Senate until disposed of.

(2) In the Senate, debate on the joint resolution, and on all debatable motions and appeals in connection therewith, shall be limited to not more than 10 hours, which shall be divided equally between those favoring and those opposing the joint resolution. A motion further to limit debate is in order and not debatable. An amendment to, or a motion to postpone, or a motion to proceed to the consideration of other business, or a motion to recommit the joint resolution is not in order.

(3) In the Senate, immediately following the conclusion of the debate on a joint resolution described in subsection (a), and a single quorum call at the conclusion of the debate if requested in accordance with the rules of the Senate, the vote on final passage of the joint resolution shall occur.

(4) Appeals from the decisions of the Chair relating to the application of the rules of the Senate to the procedure relating to a joint resolution described in subsection (a) shall be decided without debate.

(e) In the Senate the procedure specified in subsection (c) or (d) shall not apply to the consideration of a joint resolution respecting a rule—

(1) after the expiration of the 60 session days beginning with the applicable submission or publication date, or

(2) if the report under section 801(a)(1)(A) was submitted during the period referred to in section 801(d)(1), after the expiration of the 60 session days beginning on the 15th session day after the succeeding session of Congress first convenes.

(f) If, before the passage by one House of a joint resolution of that House described in subsection (a), that House receives from the other House a joint resolution described in subsection (a), then the following procedures shall apply:

(1) The joint resolution of the other House shall not be referred to a committee.

(2) With respect to a joint resolution described in subsection (a) of the House receiving the joint resolution—

(A) the procedure in that House shall be the same as if no joint resolution had been received from the other House; but

(B) the vote on final passage shall be on the joint resolution of the other House.

(g) This section is enacted by Congress—

(1) as an exercise of the rulemaking power of the Senate and House of Representatives, respectively, and as such it is deemed a part of the rules of each House, respectively, but applicable only with respect to the procedure to be followed in that House in the case of a joint resolution described in

subsection (a), and it supersedes other rules only to the extent that it is inconsistent with such rules; and

(2)   with full recognition of the constitutional right of either House to change the rules (so far as relating to the procedure of that House) at any time, in the same manner, and to the same extent as in the case of any other rule of that House.

§803. Special rule on statutory, regulatory, and judicial deadlines

(a)   In the case of any deadline for, relating to, or involving any rule which does not take effect (or the effectiveness of which is terminated) because of enactment of a joint resolution under section 802, that deadline is extended until the date 1 year after the date of enactment of the joint resolution. Nothing in this subsection shall be construed to affect a deadline merely by reason of the postponement of a rule's effective date under section 801(a).

(b)   The term "deadline" means any date certain for fulfilling any obligation or exercising any authority established by or under any Federal statute or regulation, or by or under any court order implementing any Federal statute or regulation.

§804. Definitions

For purposes of this chapter

(1)   The term "Federal agency" means any agency as that term is defined in section 551(1).

(2)   The term "major rule" means any rule that the Administrator of the Office of Information and Regulatory Affairs of the Office of Management and Budget finds has resulted in or is likely to result in—

   (A)   an annual effect on the economy of $100,000,000 or more;

   (B)   a major increase in costs or prices for consumers, individual industries, Federal, State, or local government agencies, or geographic regions; or

   (C)   significant adverse effects on competition, employment, investment, productivity, innovation, or on the ability of United States-based enterprises to compete with foreign-based enterprises in domestic and export markets.

   The term does not include any rule promulgated under the Telecommunications Act of 1996 and the amendments made by that Act.

(3)   The term "rule" has the meaning given such term in section 551, except that such term does not include—

   (A)   any rule of particular applicability, including a rule that approves or prescribes for the future rates, wages, prices, services, or allowances therefor, corporate or financial structures, reorganizations, mergers, or acquisitions thereof, or accounting practices or disclosures bearing on any of the foregoing;

   (B)   any rule relating to agency management or personnel; or

   (C)   any rule of agency organization, procedure, or practice that does not substantially affect the rights or obligations of non-agency parties.

§805. Judicial review

No determination, finding, action, or omission under this chapter shall be subject to judicial review.

§806. Applicability; severability

(a)   This chapter shall apply notwithstanding any other provision of law.

(b)   If any provision of this chapter or the application of any provision of this chapter to any person or circumstance, is held invalid, the application of such provision to other persons or circumstances, and the remainder of this chapter, shall not be affected thereby.

§807. Exemption for monetary policy

Nothing in this chapter shall apply to rules that concern monetary policy proposed or implemented by the Board of Governors of the Federal Reserve System or the Federal Open Market Committee.

§808. Effective date of certain rules

Notwithstanding section 801—

(1) any rule that establishes, modifies, opens, closes, or conducts a regulatory program for a commercial, recreational, or subsistence activity related to hunting, fishing, or camping, or

(2) any rule which an agency for good cause finds (and incorporates the finding and a brief statement of reasons therefor in the rule issued) that notice and public procedure thereon are impracticable, unnecessary, or contrary to the public interest, shall take effect at such time as the Federal agency promulgating the rule determines.

§1305. Administrative law judges

For the purposes of sections 3105, 3344, 4301(2)(D), and 5372 of this title and the provisions of section 5335(a)(B) of this title that relate to administrative law judges, the Office of Personnel Management may, and for the purpose of section 7521 of this title the Merit System Protection Board may investigate, require reports by agencies, issue reports, including an annual report to Congress, prescribe regulations, appoint advisory committees as necessary, recommend legislation, subpoena witnesses and records, and pay witness fees as established for the courts of the United States.

§3105. Appointment of administrative law judges

Each agency shall appoint as many administrative law judges as are necessary for proceedings required to be conducted in accordance with sections 556 and 557 of this title. Administrative law judges shall be assigned to cases in rotation so far as practicable, and may not perform duties inconsistent with their duties and responsibilities as administrative law judges.

§3344. Details, administrative law judges

An agency as defined by section 551 of this title which occasionally or temporarily is insufficiently staffed with administrative law judges appointed under section 3105 of this title may use administrative law judges selected by the Office of Personnel Management from and with the consent of other agencies.

§5372. Administrative law judges

(a) (1) There shall be 3 levels of basic pay for administrative law judges . . . .

(2) The Office of Personnel Management shall determine, in accordance with procedures which the Office shall by regulation prescribe, the level in which each administrative law judge position shall be placed and the qualifications to be required for appointment to each level.

(3) (A) Upon appointment to a position in AL-3, an administrative law judge shall be paid at rate A of AL-3, and shall be advanced successively to rates B, C, and D of that level upon completion of 52 weeks of service in the next lower rate, and rates E and F of that level upon completion of 104 weeks of service in the next lower rate.

(B) The Office of Personnel Management may provide for appointment of an administrative law judge in AL-3 at an advanced rate under such circumstances as the Office may determine appropriate.

(b) The Office of Personnel Management shall prescribe regulations necessary to administer this section.

§7521. Actions against administrative law judges

(a) An action may be taken against an administrative law judge appointed under section 3105 of this title by the agency in which the administrative law judge is employed only for good cause established and determined by the Merit System Protection Board on the record after opportunity for hearing before the Board.

(b) The actions covered by this section are—
    (1) a removal;
    (2) a suspension;
    (3) a reduction in grade;
    (4) a reduction in pay; and
    (5) a furlough of 30 days or less; but do not include—
        (A) a suspension or removal under section 7532 of this title;
        (B) a reduction-in-force action under section 3502 of this title; or
        (C) any action initiated under section 1206 of this title.

5 U.S.C. App 1 (1998) Federal Advisory Committee Act

§1. Short Title: This Act may be cited as the "Federal Advisory Committee Act"

§2. Findings and Purpose

(a) The Congress finds that there are numerous committees, boards, commissions, councils, and similar groups which have been established to advise officers and agencies in the executive branch of the Federal Government and that they are frequently a useful and beneficial means of furnishing expert advice, ideas, and diverse opinions to the Federal Government.

(b) The Congress further finds and declares that—
    (1) the need for many existing advisory committees has not been adequately reviewed;
    (2) new advisory committees should be established only when they are determined to be essential and their number should be kept to the minimum necessary;
    (3) advisory committees should be terminated when they are no longer carrying out the purposes for which they were established;
    (4) standards and uniform procedures should govern the establishment, operation, administration, duration of advisory committees;
    (5) the Congress and the public should be kept informed with respect to the number, purpose, membership, activities, and cost of advisory committees; and
    (6) the function of advisory committees should be advisory only, and that all matters under their consideration should be determined, in accordance with law, by the official, agency, or officer involved.

§3. Definitions

For the purpose of this Act—

(1) The term "Director" ["Administrator"] means the Director of the Office of Management and Budget [Administrator of General Services].

(2) The term "advisory committee" means any committee, board, commission, council, conference, panel, task force, or other similar group, or any subcommittee or other subgroup thereof (hereafter in this paragraph referred to as "committee"), which is—
    (A) established by statute or reorganization plan, or
    (B) established or utilized by the President, or

(C) established or utilized by one or more agencies, in the interest of obtaining advice or recommendations for the President or one or more agencies or officers of the Federal Government except that such term excludes

    (i) any committee that is composed wholly of full-time, or permanent part-time, officers or employees of the Federal Government, and

    (ii) any committee that is created by the National Academy of Sciences or the National Academy of Public Administration.

§4. Applicability; restrictions

(a) The provisions of this Act or of any rule, order, or regulation promulgated under this Act shall apply to each advisory committee except to the extent that any Act of Congress establishing any such advisory committee specifically provides otherwise.

(b) Nothing in this Act shall be construed to apply to any advisory committee established or utilized by—

    (1) the Central Intelligence Agency; or

    (2) the Federal Reserve System.

(c) Nothing in this Act shall be construed to apply to any local civic group whose primary function is that of rendering a public service with respect to a Federal program, or any State or local committee, council, board, commission, or similar group established to advise or make recommendations to State or local officials or agencies.

§5. Responsibilities of Congressional committees; review; guidelines

(a) In the exercise of its legislative review function, each standing committee of the Senate and the House of Representatives shall make a continuing review of the activities of each advisory committee under its jurisdiction to determine whether such advisory committee should be abolished or merged with any other advisory committee, whether the responsibilities of such advisory committee should be revised, and whether such advisory committee performs a necessary function not already being performed. Each such standing committee shall take appropriate action to obtain the enactment of legislation necessary to carry out the purpose of this subsection.

(b) In considering legislation establishing, or authorizing the establishment of any advisory committee, each standing committee of the Senate and of the House of Representatives shall determine, and report such determination to the Senate or to the House of Representatives, as the case may be, whether the functions of the proposed advisory committee are being or could be performed by one or more agencies or by an advisory committee already in existence, or by enlarging the mandate of an existing advisory committee. An such legislation shall—

    (1) contain a clearly defined purpose for the advisory committee;

    (2) require the membership of the advisory committee to be fairly balanced in terms of the points of view represented and the functions to be performed by the advisory committee;

    (3) contain appropriate provisions to assure that the advice and recommendations of the advisory committee will not be inappropriately influenced by the appointing authority or by any special interest, but will instead be the result of the advisory committee's independent judgement;

    (4) contain provisions dealing with authorization of appropriations, the date for submission of reports (if any), the duration of the advisory committee, and the publication of reports and other materials, to the extent that the standing committee determines the provisions of section 10 of this Act to be inadequate; and

    (5) contain provisions which will assure that the advisory committee will have adequate staff (either supplied by an agency or employed by it), will be provided adequate quarters, and will have funds available to meet its other necessary expenses.

(c) To the extent they are applicable, the guidelines set out in subsection (b) of this section shall be followed by the President, agency heads, or other Federal officials in creating an advisory committee.

§6. Responsibilities of the President; report to Congress; annual report to Congress; exclusion

(a) The President may delegate responsibility for evaluating and taking action, where appropriate, with respect to all public recommendations made to him by Presidential advisory committees.

(b) Within one year after a Presidential advisory committee has submitted a public report to the President, the President or his delegate shall make a report to the Congress stating either his proposals for action or his reasons for inaction, with respect to the recommendations contained in the public report.

(c) The President shall, not later than December 31 of each year, make an annual report to the Congress on the activities, status, and changes in the composition of advisory committees in existence during the preceding fiscal year. The report shall contain the name of every advisory committee, the date of an authority for its creation, its termination date or the date it is to make a report, its functions, a reference to the reports it has submitted, a statement of whether it is an ad hoc or continuing body, the dates of its meetings, the names and occupations of its current members, and the total estimated annual cost to the United States to fund, service, supply, and maintain such committee. Such report shall include a list of those advisory committees abolished by the President, and in the case of advisory committees established by statute, a list of those advisory committees which the President recommends be abolished together with his reasons therefor. The President shall exclude from this report any information which, in his judgment, should be withheld for reasons of national security, and he shall include in such a report a statement that such information is excluded.

§7. Responsibilities of the Administrator of General Services; Committee Management Secretariat, establishment; review; recommendations to President and Congress; agency cooperation; performance guidelines; uniform pay guidelines; travel expenses; expense recommendations

(a) The Director [Administrator] shall establish and maintain within the Office of Management and Budget [General Services Administration] a Committee Management Secretariat, which shall be responsible for matters relating to advisory committees.

(b) The Director [Administrator] shall, immediately after the enactment of this Act [enacted Oct. 6, 1972], institute a comprehensive review of the activities and responsibilities of each advisory committee to determine—
(1) whether such committee is carrying out its purpose;
(2) whether, consistent with the provisions of applicable statutes, the responsibilities assigned to it should be revised;
(3) whether it should be merged with other advisory committees; or
(4) whether it should be abolished.

The Director [Administrator] may from time to time request such information as he deems necessary to carry out his functions under this subsection. Upon the completion of the Director's [Administrator's] review he shall make recommendations to the President and to either the agency head or the Congress with respect to action he believes should be taken. Thereafter, the Director [Administrator] shall carry out a similar review annually. Agency heads shall cooperate with the Director [Administrator] in making the reviews required by this subsection.

(c) The Director [Administrator] shall prescribe administrative guidelines and management controls applicable to advisory committees, and, to the maximum extent feasible, provide advice, assistance, and guidance to advisory committees to improve their performance. In carrying out his functions under this subsection, the Director [Administrator] shall consider the recommendations of each agency head with respect to means of improving the performance of advisory committees whose duties are related to such agency.

(d) (1) The Director [Administrator], after study and consultation with the Civil Service Commission [Director of the Officer of Personnel Management], shall establish guidelines with respect to uniform fair rates of pay for comparable services of members, staffs, and consultants of advisory committees in a manner which gives appropriate recognition to the responsibilities and qualifications required and other relevant factors. Such regulations shall provide that—

(A) no member of any advisory committee or the staff of any advisory committee shall receive compensation at a rate in excess of the rate specified for GS-18 of the General Schedule under section 5332 of title 5, United States Code;

(B) such members, while engaged in the performance of their duties away from their homes or regular places of business, may be allowed travel expenses, including per diem in lieu of subsistence, as authorized by section 5703 of title 5, United States Code, for persons employed intermittently in the Government service; and

(C) such members—

(i) who are blind or deaf or who otherwise qualify as handicapped individuals (within the meaning of section 501 of the Rehabilitation Act of 1973 (29 U.S.C. 794), and

(ii) who do not otherwise qualify for assistance under section 3102 of title 5, United States Code, by reason of being an employee of an agency (within the meaning of section 3102(a)(1) of such title 5, may be provided services pursuant to section 3102 of such title while in performance of their advisory committee duties.

(2) Nothing in this subsection shall prevent—

(A) an individual who (without regard to his service with an advisory committee) is a full-time employee of the United States, or

(B) an individual who immediately before his service with an advisory committee was such an employee, from receiving compensation at the rate at which he otherwise would be compensated (or was compensated) as a full-time employee of the United States.

(e) The Director [Administrator] shall include in budget recommendations a summary of the amounts he deems necessary for the expenses of advisory committees, including the expenses for publication of reports where appropriate.

§8. Responsibilities of agency heads; Advisory Committee Management Officer, designation

(a) Each agency head shall establish uniform administrative guidelines and management controls for advisory committees established by that agency, which shall be consistent with directives of the Director [Administrator] under section 7 and section 10. Each agency shall maintain systematic information on the nature, functions, and operations of each advisory committee within its jurisdiction.

(b) The head of each agency which has an advisory committee shall designate an Advisory Committee Management Officer who shall—

(1) exercise control and supervision over the establishment, procedures, and accomplishments of advisory committees established by that agency;

(2) assemble and maintain the reports, records, and other papers of any such committee during its existence; and

(3) carry out, on behalf of that agency, the provisions of section 552 of title 5, United States, with respect to such reports, records, and other papers.

§9. Establishment and purpose of advisory committees; publication in Federal Register; charter; filing, contents, copy

(a) No advisory committee shall be established unless such establishment is—

(1) specifically authorized by statute or by the President; or

(2) determined as a matter of formal record, by the head of the agency involved after consultation with the Director [Administrator], with timely notice published in the Federal Register, to be in the public interest in connection with the performance of duties imposed on that agency by law.

(b) Unless otherwise specifically provided by statute or Presidential directive, advisory committees shall be utilized solely for advisory functions. Determinations of action to be taken and policy to be expressed with respect to matters upon which an advisory committee reports or makes recommendations shall be made solely by the President or an officer of the Federal Government.

(c) No advisory committee shall meet or take any action until an advisory committee charter has been filed with

    (1) the Director [Administrator], in the case of Presidential advisory committees, or

    (2) with the head of the agency to whom any advisory committee reports and with the standing committees of the Senate and of the House of Representatives having legislative jurisdiction of such agency. Such charter shall contain the following information:

        (A) the committee's official designation;

        (B) the committee's objectives and scope of its activity;

        (C) the period of time necessary for the committee to carry out its purposes;

        (D) the agency or official to whom the committee reports;

        (E) the agency responsible for providing the necessary support for the committee;

        (F) a description of the duties for which the committee is responsible, and, if such duties are not solely advisory, a specification of the authority for such functions;

        (G) the estimated number and frequency of committee meetings;

        (H) the committee's termination date, if less than two years from the date of the committee's establishment; and

        (I) the date the charter is filed.

A copy of any such charter shall also be furnished to the Library of Congress.

§10. Advisory committee procedures; meetings; notice, publication in Federal Regulations; minutes; certification; annual report; Federal officer or employee, attendance

(a) (1) Each advisory committee meeting shall be open to the public.

    (2) Except when the President determines otherwise for reasons of national security, timely notice of each such meeting shall be published in the Federal Register, and the Director [Administrator] shall prescribe regulations to provide for other types of public notice to insure that all interested persons are notified of such meeting prior thereto.

    (3) Interested persons shall be permitted to attend, appear before, or file statements with any advisory committee, subject to such reasonable rules or regulations as the Director [Administrator] may prescribe.

(b) Subject to section 552 of title, 5, United States Code, the records, reports, transcripts, minutes, appendixes, working papers, drafts, studies, agenda, or other documents which were made available to or prepared for or by each advisory committee shall be available for public inspection and copying at a single location in the offices of the advisory committee or the agency to which the advisory committee reports until the advisory committee ceases to exist.

(c) Detailed minutes of each meeting of each advisory committee shall be kept and shall contain a records of the persons present, a complete and accurate description of matters discussed and conclusion reached, and copies of all reports received, issued, or approved by the advisory committee. The accuracy of all minutes shall be certified to by the chairman of the advisory committee.

(d) Subsections (a)(1) and (a)(3) of this section shall not apply to any portion of an advisory committee meeting where the President, or the head of the agency to which the advisory committee reports, determines that such portion of such meeting may be closed to the public in accordance with subsection (c) of section 552b of title 5, United States Code. Any such determination shall be in writing and shall contain the reasons for such determination. If such a determination is made, the advisory committee shall issue a report at least annually setting forth a summary of its activities and such related matters as would be informative to the public consistent with the policy of section 552(b) of title 5, United States Code.

(e) There shall be designated an officer or employee of the Federal Government to chair or attend each meeting of each advisory committee. The officer or employee so designated is authorized, whenever he determines it to be in the public interest, to adjourn any such meeting. No advisory committee shall conduct any meeting in the absence of that officer or employee.

(f)   Advisory committees shall not hold any meetings except at the call of, or with the advance approval of, a designated officer or employee of the Federal Government, and in the case of advisory committees (other than Presidential advisory committee), with an agenda approved by such officer or employee.

§11. Availability of transcripts; "agency proceeding"

(a)   Except where prohibited by contractual agreements entered into prior to the effective date of this Act [see section 15], agencies and advisory committees shall make available to any person, at actual cost of duplication, copies of transcripts of agency proceedings or advisory committee meetings.

(b)   As used in this section "agency proceeding" means any proceeding as defined in section 551(12) of title 5, United States Code.

§12. Fiscal and administrative provisions; recordkeeping; audit; agency support services

(a)   Each agency shall keep records as will fully disclose the disposition of any funds which may be at the disposal of its advisory committees and the nature and extent of their activities. The General Services Administration, or such other agency as the President may designate, shall maintain financial records with respect to Presidential advisory committees. The Comptroller General of the United States, or any of his authorized representatives, shall have access, for the purpose of audit and examination, to any such records.

(b)   Each agency shall be responsible for providing support services for each advisory committee established by or reporting to it unless the establishing authority provides otherwise. Where any such advisory committee reports to more than one agency, only on agency shall be responsible for support services at any time. In the case of Presidential advisory committee, such services may be provided by the General Services Administration.

§13. Responsibilities of Library of Congress; reports and background papers; depository

Subject to section 552 of title 5, United States Code, the Director [Administrator] shall provide for the filing with the Library of Congress of at least eight copies of each report made by every advisory committee and, where appropriate, background papers prepared by consultants. The Librarian of Congress shall establish a depository for such reports and papers where they shall be available to public inspection and use.

§14. Termination of advisory committees; renewal; continuation

(a)   (1)   Each advisory committee which is in existence on the effective date of this Act [see section 15] shall terminate not later than the expiration of the two-year period following such effective date unless—
  (A)   in the case of an advisory committee established by the President or an officer of the Federal Government, such advisory committee is renewed by the President or that officer by appropriate action prior to the expiration of such two-year period; or
  (B)   in the case of an advisory committee established by an Act of Congress, its duration is otherwise provided for by law.

(2)   Each advisory committee established after such effective date [see section 15] shall terminate not later than the expiration of the two-year period beginning on the date of its establishment unless—
  (A)   in the case of an advisory committee established by the President or an officer of the Federal Government such advisory committee is renewed by the President or such officer by appropriate action prior to the end of such period; or
  (B)   in the case of an advisory committee established by an Act of Congress, its duration is otherwise provided for by law.

(b) (1) Upon the renewal of any advisory committee, such advisory committee shall file a charter in accordance with section 9(c).

(2) Any advisory committee established by an Act of Congress shall file a charter in accordance with such section upon the expiration of each successive two-year period following the date of enactment of the Act establishing such advisory committee.

(3) No advisory committee required under this subsection to file a charter shall take any action (other than preparation and filing of such charter) prior to the date on which such charter is filed.

(c) Any advisory committee which is renewed by the President or any officer of the Federal Government may be continued only for successive two-year periods by appropriate action taken by the President or such officer prior to the date on which such advisory committee would otherwise terminate.

Appendix 4A

Executive Order 12866 (Clinton)

58 Fed. Reg. 51735 (1993)

As Amended by Executive Order 13258 (G. W. Bush)

67 Fed. Reg. 9385 (2002)
(Additions in **bold**)

The American people deserve a regulatory system that works for them, not against them: a regulatory system that protects and improves their health, safety, environment, and well-being and improves the performance of the economy without imposing unacceptable or unreasonable costs on society; regulatory policies that recognize that the private sector and private markets are the best engine for economic growth regulatory approaches that respect the role of State, local, and tribal governments, and regulations that are effective, consistent, sensible, and understandable. We do not have such a regulatory system today.

With this Executive order, the Federal Government begins a program to reform and make more efficient the regulatory process. The objectives of this Executive order are to enhance planning and coordination with respect to both new and existing regulation; to reaffirm the primacy of Federal agencies in the regulatory decision-making process; to restore the integrity and legitimacy of regulatory review and oversight; and to make the process more accessible and open to the public. In pursuing these objectives, the regulatory process shall be conducted so as to meet applicable statutory requirements and with due regard to the direction that has been entrusted to the Federal agencies.

Accordingly, by the authority vested in me as President by the Constitution and laws of the United States of America and the laws of the United States of America, it is hereby ordered as follows:

Section 1. Statement of Regulatory Philosophy and Principles.

(a) The Regulatory Philosophy. Federal agencies should promulgate only such regulations as are required by law, are necessary to interpret the law, or are made necessary by compelling public need, such as material failures of private markets to protect or improve the health and safety of the public, the environment, or the well-being of the American people. In deciding whether and how to regulate, agencies should assess all costs and benefits of available regulatory alternatives, including the alternative of not regulating. Costs and benefits shall be understood to include both quantifiable measures (to the fullest extent that these can be usefully estimated) and qualitative measures of costs and benefits that are difficult to quantify, but nevertheless essential to consider. Further, in choosing among alternative regulatory approaches, agencies should select those approaches that maximize net benefits (including potential economic, environmental, public health and safety, and other advantages, distributive impacts, and equity), unless a statute requires another regulatory approach.

(b) The Principles of Regulation. To ensure that the agencies' regulatory programs are consistent with the philosophy set forth above, agencies should adhere to the following principles, to the extent permitted by law and where applicable:

(1) Each agency shall identify the problem that it intends to address (including, where applicable, the failures of private markets or public institutions that warrant new agency action) as well as assess the significance of that problem.

(2) Each agency shall examine whether existing regulations (or other law) have created, or contributed to, the problem that a new regulation is intended to correct and whether those regulations (or other law) should be modified to achieve the intended goal of regulation more effectively.

(3) Each agency shall identify and assess available alternatives to direct regulation, including providing economic incentives to encourage the desired behavior, such as user fees or marketable permits, or providing information upon which choices can be made by the public.

(4) In setting regulatory priorities, each agency shall consider, to the extent reasonable, the degree and nature of the risks posed by various substances or activities within its jurisdiction.

(5) When an agency determines that a regulation is the best available method of achieving the regulatory objective, it shall design its regulations in the most cost-effective manner to achieve the regulatory objectives. In doing so, each agency shall consider incentives for innovation, consistency, predictability, the costs of enforcement and compliance (to the government, regulated entities, and the public), flexibility, distributive impacts, and equity.

(6) Each agency shall assess both the costs and the benefits of the intended regulation and, recognizing that some costs and benefits are difficult to quantify, propose or adopt a regulation only upon a reasoned determination that the benefits of the intended regulation justify its costs.

(7) Each agency shall base its decisions on the best reasonably obtainable scientific, technical, economic, and other information concerning the need for, and consequences of, the intended regulation.

(8) Each agency shall identify and assess alternative forms of regulation and shall, to the extent feasible, specify performance objectives, rather than specifying the behavior or manner of compliance that regulated entities must adopt.

(9) Wherever feasible, agencies shall seek views of appropriate State, local, and tribal officials before imposing regulatory requirements that might significantly or uniquely affect those governmental entities. Each agency shall assess the effects of Federal regulations on State, local, and tribal governments, including specifically the availability of resources to carry out those mandates, and seek to minimize those burdens that uniquely or significantly affect such governmental entities, consistent with achieving regulatory objectives. In addition, as appropriate, agencies shall seek to harmonize Federal regulatory actions with related State, local, and tribal regulatory and other governmental functions.

(10) Each agency shall avoid regulations that are inconsistent, incompatible, or duplicative with its other regulations or those of other Federal agencies.

(11) Each agency shall tailor its regulations to impose the least burden on society, including individuals, businesses of differing sizes, and other entities (including small communities and governmental entities), consistent with obtaining the regulatory objectives, taking into account, among other things, and to the extent practicable, the costs of cumulative regulations.

(12) Each agency shall draft its regulations to be simple and easy to understand, with the goal of minimizing the potential for uncertainty and litigation arising from such uncertainty.

Section 2. Organization. An efficient regulatory planning and review process is vital to ensure that the Federal Government's regulatory system best serves the American people.

(a) The Agencies. Because Federal agencies are the repositories of significant substantive expertise and experience, they are responsible for developing regulations and assuring that the regulations are consistent with applicable law, the President's priorities, and the principles set forth in this Executive order.

(b) The Office of Management and Budget. Coordinated review of agency rulemaking is necessary to ensure that regulations are consistent with applicable law, the President's priorities, and the principles set forth in this Executive order, and that decisions made by one agency do not conflict with the policies or actions taken or planned by another agency. The Office of Management and Budget (OMB) shall carry out that review function. Within OMB, the Office of Information and Regulatory Affairs (OIRA) is the repository of expertise concerning regulatory issues, including methodologies and procedures that affect more than one agency, this Executive order, and the President's regulatory policies. To the extent permitted by law, OMB shall provide guidance to agencies and assist the President **and regulatory policy advisors** to the President in regulatory planning and shall be the entity that reviews individual regulations, as provided by this Executive order.

(c) **Assistance.** In fulfilling **his** responsibilities under this Executive order, the President and the shall be assisted by the regulatory policy advisors within the Executive Office of the President and by such agency officials and personnel as the President may, from time to time, consult.

Section 3. Definitions. For the purposes of this Order:

(a) "Advisors" refers to such regulatory policy advisors to the President as the President may from time to time consult, including, among others:
  (1) the Director of OMB;
  (2) the Chair (or another member) of the Council of Economic Advisers;
  (3) the Assistant to the President for Economic Policy;
  (4) the Assistant to the President for Domestic Policy;
  (5) the Assistant to the President for National Security Affairs;
  (6) the **Director of the Office of Science and Technology Policy;**
  (7) the **Deputy Assistant to the President and Director for Intergovernmental Affairs;**
  (8) the Assistant to the President and Staff Secretary;
  (9) the Assistant to the President and Chief of Staff to the Vice President;
  (10) the Assistant to the President and Counsel to the President;
  (11) the **Chairman of the Council on Environmental Quality and Director of the Office of Environmental Quality;**
  (12) the **Assistant to the President for Homeland Security; and**
  (13) the Administrator of OIRA, who also shall coordinate communications relating to this Executive order among the agencies, OMB, the other Advisors, and the Office of the Vice President.

(b) "Agency," unless otherwise indicated, means any authority of the United States that is an "agency" under 44 U.S.C. 3502(1), other than those considered to be independent regulatory agencies, as defined in 44 U.S.C. 3502(10).

(c) "Director" means the Director of OMB.

(d) "Regulation" or "rule" means an agency statement of general applicability and future effect, which the agency intends to have the force and effect of law, that is designed to implement, interpret, or prescribe law or policy or to describe the procedure or practice requirements of an agency. It does not, however, include:
  (1) Regulations or rules issues in accordance with the formal rulemaking provisions of 5 U.S.C. 556, 557;
  (2) Regulations or rules that pertain to a military or foreign affairs functions of the United States, other than procurement regulations and regulations involving the import or export of non-defense articles and services;
  (3) Regulations or rules that are limited to agency organizations, management, or personnel matters; or
  (4) Any other category of regulations exempted by the Administrator of OIRA.

(e) "Regulatory action" means any substantive action by an agency (normally published in the Federal Register) that promulgates or is expected to lead to the promulgation of a final rule or regulation, including notices of inquiry, advance notice of proposed rulemaking, and notices of proposed rulemaking.

(f) "Significant regulatory action" means any regulatory action that is likely to result in a rule that may:
  (1) Have an annual effect on the economy of $100 million or more or adversely affect in a material way the economy, a sector of the economy, productivity, competition, jobs, the environment, public health or safety, or State, local, or tribal governments or communities;

(2) Create a serious inconsistency or otherwise interfere with an action taken or planned by another agency;

(3) Materially alter the budgetary impact of entitlements, grants, user fees, or loan programs or the rights and obligations of recipients thereof; or

(4) Raise novel legal or policy issues arising our of legal mandates, the President's priorities, or the principles set forth in this Executive order.

Section 4. Planning Mechanisms. In order to have an effective regulatory program, to provide for coordination of regulations, to maximize consultation and the resolution of potential conflicts at an early stage, to involve the public and its State, local, and tribal officials in regulatory planning, and to ensure that new or revised regulations promote the President's priorities and the principles set forth in this Executive order, these procedures shall to be followed, to the extent permitted by law:

(a) Agencies' Policy Meeting. Early in each year's planning cycle, the **Director** shall convene a meeting of the Advisors and the heads of agencies to seek a common understanding of priorities and to coordinate regulatory efforts to be accomplished in the upcoming year.

(b) Unified Regulatory Agenda. For purposes of this subsection, the term "agency" or "agencies" shall also include those considered to be independent regulatory agencies, as defined in 44 U.S.C. 3502 (10). Each agency shall prepare an agenda of all regulations under development or review, at a time and in a manner specified by the Administrator of OIRA. The description of each regulatory action shall contain, at a minimum, a regulation identifier number, a brief summary of the action, the legal authority for the action, any legal deadline for the action, and the name and telephone number of a knowledgeable agency official. Agencies may incorporate the information required under 5 U.S.C. 602 and 41 U.S.C. 402 into these agendas.

(c) The Regulatory Plan. For purposes of this subsection, the term "agency" or "agencies" shall also include those considered to be independent regulatory agencies, as defined in 44 U.S.C. 3502(10).

(1) As part of the Unified Regulatory Agenda, beginning in 1994, each agency shall prepare a Regulatory Plan (Plan) of the most important significant regulatory actions that the agency reasonably expects to issue in proposed or final form in that fiscal year or thereafter. The Plan shall be approved personally by the agency head and shall contain at a minimum:

(A) A statement of the agency's regulatory objectives and priorities and how they relate to the President's priorities;

(B) A summary of each planned significant regulatory action including, to the extent possible, alternatives to be considered and preliminary estimates of the anticipated costs and benefits;

(C) A summary of the legal basis for each such actions, including whether any aspect of the action is required by statute or court order;

(D) A statement of the need for each such action and, if applicable, how the action will reduce risks to public health, safety, or the environment, as well as how the magnitude of the risk addressed by the action relates to other risks within the jurisdiction of the agency;

(E) The agency's schedule for action, including a statement of any applicable statutory or judicial deadlines; and

(F) The name, address, and telephone number of a person the public may contact for additional information about the planned regulatory action.

(2) Each agency shall forward its Plan to OIRA by June 1st of each year.

(3) Within 10 days calendar days after OIRA has received all agency's Plan, OIRA shall circulate it to other affected agencies **and** the Advisors.

(4) An agency head who believes that a planned regulatory action of another agency may conflict with its own policy or action taken or planned shall promptly notify, in writing, the Administrator of OIRA, who shall forward that communication to the issuing agency, **and** the Advisors.

(5) If the Administrator of OIRA believes that a planned regulatory action of an agency may be inconsistent with the President's priorities or the principles set forth in this Executive order or may be in conflict with any policy or action taken or planned by another agency, the Administrator of OIRA shall promptly notify in writing, the affected agencies, **and** the Advisors.

(6) The **Director** may consult with the heads of agencies with respect to their Plans and, in appropriate instances, request further consideration or inter-agency coordination.

(7) The Plans developed by the issuing agency shall be published annually in the October publication of the Unified Regulatory Agenda. This publication shall be made available to the Congress; State, local, and tribal governments; and the public. Any views on any aspect of any agency Plan, including whether any planned regulatory action might conflict with any other planned or existing regulation, impose any unintended consequences on the public, or confer any unclaimed benefits on the public, should be directed to the issuing agency, with a copy to OIRA.

(d) Regulatory Working Group. Within 30 days of the date of this Executive order, the Administrator of OIRA shall convene a Regulatory Working Group ("Working Group"), which shall consist of representatives of the heads of each agency that the Administrator determines to have significant domestic regulatory responsibility **and** the Advisors. The Administrator of OIRA shall chair the Working Group and shall periodically advise the **Director** on the activities of the Working Group. The Working Group shall serve as a forum to assist agencies in identifying and analyzing important regulatory issues (including, among others (1) the development of innovative regulatory techniques, (2) the methods, efficacy, and utility of comparative risk assessment in regulatory decision-making, and (3) the development of short forms and other streamlined regulatory approaches for small businesses and other entities). The Working Group shall meet at least quarterly and may meet as a whole or in subgroups of agencies with an interest in particular issues or subject areas. To inform its discussions, the Working Group may commission analytical studies and reports by OIRA, the Administrative Conference of the United States, or any other agency.

(e) Conferences. The Administrator of OIRA meet quarterly with representatives of State, local, and tribal governments to identify both existing and proposed regulations that may uniquely or significantly affect those governmental entities. The Administrator of OIRA shall also convene, from time to time, conferences with representatives of businesses, nongovernmental organizations, and the public to discuss regulatory issues of common concern.

Section 5. Existing Regulations. In order to reduce the regulatory burden on the American people, their families, their communities, their State, local, and tribal governments, and their industries; to determine whether regulations promulgated by the executive branch of the Federal Government have become unjustified or unnecessary as a result of changed circumstances; to confirm that regulations are both compatible with each other and not duplicative or inappropriately burdensome in the aggregated; to ensure that all regulations are consistent with the President's priorities and the principles set forth in this Executive order, within applicable law; and to otherwise improve the effectiveness of existing regulations:

(a) Within 90 days of the date of this Executive order, each agency shall submit to OIRA a program, consistent with its resources and regulatory priorities, under which the agency will periodically review its existing significant regulations to determine whether any such regulations should be modified or eliminated so as to make the agency's regulatory program more effective in achieving the regulatory objectives, less burdensome, or in greater alignment with the President's priorities and the principles set forth in this Executive order. Any significant regulations selected for review shall be included in the agency's annual Plan. The agency shall also identify any legislative mandates that require the agency to promulgate or continue to impose regulations that the agency believes are unnecessary or outdated by reason of changed circumstances.

(b) The Administrator of OIRA shall work with the Regulatory Working Group and other interested entities to pursue the objectives of this section. State, local, and tribal governments are specifically encouraged to assist in the identification of regulations that impose significant or unique burdens on those governmental entities and that appear to have outlived their justification or be otherwise inconsistent with the public interest.

(c) The **Director,** in consultation with the Advisors, may identify for review by the appropriate agency or agencies other existing regulations of an agency or groups of regulations of more than one agency that affect a particular group, industry, or sector of the economy, or may identify legislative mandates that may be appropriate for reconsideration by the Congress.

Section 6. Centralized Review of Regulations. The guidelines set forth below shall apply to all regulatory actions, for both new and existing regulations, by agencies other than those agencies specifically exempted by the Administrator of OIRA:

(a) Agency Responsibilities.

    (1) Each agency shall (consistent with its own rules, regulations, or procedures) provide the public with meaningful participation in the regulatory process. In particular, before issuing a notice of proposed rulemaking, each agency should, where appropriate, seek the involvement of those who are intended to benefit from and those expected to be burdened by any regulation (including, specifically, State, local, and tribal officials). In addition, each agency should afford the public a meaningful opportunity to comment on any proposed regulation, which in most cases should include a comment period of not less than 60 days. Each agency also is directed to explore and, where appropriate, use consensual mechanisms for developing regulations, including negotiated rulemaking.

    (2) Within 60 days of the date of this Executive order, each agency head shall designate a Regulatory Policy Officer who shall report to the agency head. The Regulatory Policy Officer shall be involved at each stage of the regulatory process to foster the development of effective, innovative, and least burdensome regulations and to further the principles set forth in this Executive order.

    (3) In addition to adhering to its own rules and procedures and to the requirements of the Administrative Procedure Act, the Regulatory Flexibility Act, the Paperwork Reduction Act, and other applicable law, each agency shall develop its regulatory actions in a timely fashion and adhere to the following procedures with respect to a regulatory action:

    (A) Each agency shall provide OIRA, at such times and in the manner specified by the Administrator of OIRA, with a list of its planned regulatory actions, indicating those which the agency believes are significant regulatory actions within the meaning of this Executive order. Absent a material change in the development of the planned regulatory action, those not designated as significant will not be subject to review under this section unless, within 10 working days of receipt of the list, the Administrator of OIRA notifies the agency that OIRA has determined that a planned regulation is a significant regulatory action within the meaning of this Executive order. The Administrator of OIRA may waive review of any planned regulatory action designated by the agency as significant, in which case the agency need not further comply with subsection (a)(3)(B) or subsection of (a)(3)(C) of this section.

    (B) For each matter identified as, or determined by the Administrator of OIRA to be, a significant regulatory action, the issuing agency shall provide to OIRA:

      (i) The text of the draft regulatory action, together with a reasonably detailed description of the need for the regulatory action and an explanation of how the regulatory action will meet that need; and

      (ii) An assessment of the potential costs and benefits of the regulatory action, including an explanation of the manner in which the regulatory action is consistent with a statutory mandate and, to the extent permitted by law, promotes the President's priorities and avoids undue interference with State, local, and tribal governments in the exercise of their governmental functions.

    (C) For those matters identified as, or determined by the Administrator of OIRA to be, a significant regulatory action within the scope of section 3(f)(1), the agency shall also provide to OIRA the following additional information developed as part of the agency's decision-making process (unless prohibited by law):

      (i) An assessment, including the underlying analysis, of benefits anticipated from the regulatory action (such as, but not limited to, the promotion of the efficient functioning of the economy and private markets, the enhancement of health and safety, the protection of the national environment, and the elimination of reduction of discrimination or bias) together with, to the extent feasible, a quantification of those benefits;

      (ii) An assessment, including the underlying analysis, of costs anticipated from the regulatory action (such as, but not limited to, the direct cost both to the government in administering the regulation and to businesses and others in complying with the regulation, and any adverse effects on the efficient functioning of the economy, private markets (including productivity, employment, and competitiveness), health, safety, and the natural environment), together with, to the extent feasible, a quantification of those costs; and

    (iii)   An assessment, including the underlying analysis, of costs and benefits of potentially effective and reasonably feasible alternatives to the planned regulation, identified by the agencies or the public (including improving the current regulation and reasonably viable nonregulatory actions), and an explanation why the planned regulatory action is preferable to the identified potential alternative.

(D)   In emergency situations or when an agency is obligated by law to act more quickly than normal review procedures allow, the agency shall notify OIRA as soon as possible and, to the extent practicable, comply with subsections (a)(3)(B) and (C) of this section. For those regulatory actions that are governed by a statutory or court-imposed deadline, the agency shall, to the extent practicable, schedule rulemaking proceedings so as to permit sufficient time for OIRA to conduct its review, as set forth below in subsection (b)(2) through (4) of this section.

(E)   After the regulatory action has been published in the Federal Register or otherwise issued to the public, the agency shall:

    (i)   Make available to the public the information set forth in subsections (a)(3)(B) and (C);

    (ii)   Identify for the public, in a complete, clear, and simple manner, the substantive changes between the draft submitted to OIRA for review and the action subsequently announced; and

    (iii)   Identify for the public those changes in the regulatory action that were made at the suggestion or recommendation of OIRA.

(F)   All information provided to the public by the agency shall be in plain, understandable language.

(b)   OIRA Responsibilities. The Administrator of OIRA shall provide meaningful guidance and oversight so that each agency's regulatory actions are consistent with applicable law, the President's priorities, and the principles set forth in this Executive order and do not conflict with the policies or actions of another agency. OIRA shall, to the extent permitted by law, adhere to the following guidelines:

(1)   OIRA may review only actions identified by the agency or by OIRA as significant regulatory actions under subsection (a)(3)(A) of this section.

(2)   OIRA shall waive review or notify the agency in writing of the results of its review within the following time periods:

(A)   For any notices of inquiry, advance notices of proposed rulemaking, or other preliminary regulatory actions prior to a Notice of Proposed Rulemaking, within 10 working days after the date of submission of the draft action to OIRA.

(B)   For all other regulatory actions, within 90 calendar days after the date of submission of the information set forth in subsections (a)(3)(B) and (C) of this section, unless OIRA has previously reviewed this information and, since that review, there has been no material change in the facts and circumstances upon which the regulatory action is based, in which case, OIRA shall complete its review within 45 days; and

(C)   The review process may be extended (1) once by no more than 30 calendar days upon the written approval of the Director and (2) at the request of the agency head.

(3)   For each regulatory action that the Administrator of OIRA returns to an agency for further consideration of some or all of its provisions, the Administrator of OIRA shall provide the issuing agency a written explanation for such return, setting forth the pertinent provision of this Executive order on which OIRA is relying. If the agency head disagrees with some or all of the bases for the return, the agency head shall so inform the Administrator of OIRA in writing.

(4)   Except as otherwise provided by law or required by a Court, in order to ensure greater openness, accessibility, and accountability in the regulatory review process, OIRA shall be governed by the following disclosure requirements:

(A)   Only the Administrator of OIRA (or a particular designee) shall receive oral communications initiated by persons not employed by the executive branch of the Federal Government regarding the substance of a regulatory action under OIRA review;

(B)   All substantive communications between OIRA personnel and persons not employed by the executive branch of the Federal Government regarding a regulatory action under review shall be governed by the following guidelines:

    (i)   A representative from the issuing agency shall be invited to any meeting between OIRA personnel and such persons(s);

(ii)   OIRA shall forward to the issuing agency, within 10 working days of receipt of the communication(s), all written communications, regardless of format, between OIRA personnel and any person who is not employed by the executive branch of the Federal Government, and the dates and names of individuals involved in all substantive oral communications (including meetings to which an agency representative was invited, but did not attend, and telephone conversations between OIRA personnel and any such persons); and

(iii)   OIRA shall publicly disclose relevant information about such communication(s), as set forth below in subsection (b)(4)(C) of this section.

(C)   OIRA shall maintain a publicly available log that shall contain, at a minimum, the following information pertinent to regulatory actions under review:

(i)   The status of all regulatory actions, including if (and if so, when and by whom) Presidential consideration was requested;

(ii)   A notation of all written communications forwarded to an issuing agency under subsection (b)(4)(B)(ii) of this section; and

(iii)   The dates and names of individuals involved in all substantive oral communications, including meetings and telephone conversations, between OIRA personnel and any person not employed by the executive branch of the Federal Government, and the subject matter discussed during such communications.

(D)   After the regulatory action has been published in the Federal Register or otherwise issued to the public, or after the agency has announced its decision not publish or issue the regulatory action, OIRA shall make available to the public all documents exchanged between OIRA and the agency during the review by OIRA under this section.

(5)   All information provided to the public OIRA shall be in plain, understandable language.

Section 7. Resolution of Conflicts.

(a)   To the extent permitted by law, disagreements or conflicts between or among agency heads or between OMB and any agency that cannot be resolved by the Administrator of OIRA shall be resolved by the President, with the assistance of the Chief of Staff to the President ("Chief of Staff") with the relevant agency head (and, as appropriate, other interested government officials). Presidential consideration of such disagreements may be initiated only by the Director, by the head of the issuing agency, or by the head of an agency that has a significant interest in the regulatory action at issue. Such review will not be undertaken at the request of other persons, entities, or their agents.

(b)   Resolution of such conflicts shall be informed by recommendations developed by the Chief of Staff, after consultation with the Advisors (and other executive branch officials or personnel whose responsibilities to the President include the subject matter at issue). The development of these recommendations shall be concluded within 60 days after review has been requested.

(c)   During the Presidential review period, communications with any person not employed by the Federal Government relating to the substance of the regulatory action under review and directed to the Advisors or their staffs or to the staff of the Chief of Staff shall be in writing and shall be forwarded by the recipient to the affected agency(ies) for inclusion in the public docket(s). When the communication is not in writing, such Advisors or staff members shall inform the outside party that the matter is under review and that any comments should be submitted in writing.

(d)   At the end of this review process, the President, or the Chief of Staff acting at the request of the President, shall notify the affected agency and the Administrator of OIRA of the President's decision with respect to the matter.

Section 8. Publication. Except to the extent required by law, an agency shall not publish in the Federal Register or otherwise issue to the public any regulatory action that is subject to review under section 6 of this Executive order until (1) the Administrator of IRA notifies the agency that OIRA has waived its review of the action or has completed its review without any requests for further consideration, or (2) the applicable time period under section 6(b)(2) expires without OIRA having notified the agency that it is returning the regulatory action for further consideration under section 6(b)(3), whichever occurs first. If the terms of the preceding sentence have not been satisfied and an agency wants to publish or otherwise issue a regulatory action, the head of that agency may request Presidential consideration through the Director, as provided under section 7 of this order. Upon receipt of this request, the Director shall notify OIRA and the Advisors. The guidelines and time period set forth in section 7 shall apply to the publication of regulatory actions for which Presidential consideration has been sought.

Section 9. Agency Authority. Nothing in this order shall be construed as displacing the agencies' authority or responsibilities, as authorized by law.

Section 10. Judicial Review. Nothing in this Executive order shall affect any otherwise available judicial review of agency action. This Executive order is intended only to improve the internal management of the Federal Government and does not create any right or benefit, substantive or procedural, enforceable at law or equity by a party against the United States, its agencies or instrumentalities, its officers or employees, or any other person.

Section 11. Revocations. Executive Orders Nos. 12291 and 12498; all amendments to those Executive orders; all guidelines issued under those orders; and any exemptions from those orders heretofore granted for any category of rules are revoked.

Appendix 4B

Executive Order 12291

February 17, 1981
46 Federal Register 13193 (1981)

By the authority vested in me as President by the Constitution and laws of the United States of America, and in order to reduce the burdens of existing and future regulations, increase agency accountability for regulatory actions, provide for presidential oversight of the regulatory process, minimize duplication and conflict of regulations and insure well-reasoned regulations, it is hereby ordered as follows:

Section 1. Definitions. For the purposes of this Order:

(a) "Regulation" or "rule" means an agency statement of general applicability and future effect designed to implement, interpret, or prescribe law or policy or describing the procedure or practice requirements of an agency, but does not include:

    (1) Administrative actions governed by the provisions of Sections 556 and 557 of Title 5 of the United States Code;

    (2) Regulations issued with respect to a military or foreign affairs function of the United States; or

    (3) Regulations related to agency organization, management, or personnel.

(b) "Major rule" means any regulation that is likely to result in:

    (1) An annual effect on the economy of $100 million or more;

    (2) A major increase in costs or prices for consumers, individual industries, Federal, State, or local government agencies, or geographic regions; or

    (3) Significant adverse effects on competition, employment, investment, productivity, innovation, or on the ability of United States–based enterprises to compete with foreign–based enterprises in domestic or export markets.

(c) "Director" means the Director of the Office of Management and Budget.

(d) "Agency" means any authority of the United States that is an "agency" under 44 U.S.C. 3502(l), excluding those agencies specified in 44 U.S.C. 3502(10).

(e) "Task Force" means the Presidential Task Force on Regulatory Relief.

Section 2. General Requirements. In promulgating new regulations, reviewing existing regulations, and developing legislative proposals concerning regulations, all agencies, to the extent permitted by law, shall adhere to the following requirements:

(a) Administrative decisions shall be based on adequate information concerning the need for and consequences of proposed government action;

(b)   Regulatory action shall not be undertaken unless the potential benefits to society for the regulation out-weigh the potential costs to society;

(c)   Regulatory objectives shall be chosen to maximize the net benefits to society;

(d)   Among alternative approaches to any given regulatory objective, the alternative involving the least net cost to society shall be chosen; and

(e)   Agencies shall set regulatory priorities with the aim of maximizing the aggregate net benefits to society, taking into account the condition of the particular industries affected by regulations, the condition of the national economy, and other regulatory actions contemplated for the future.

Section 3. Regulatory Impact Analysis and Review.

(a)   In order to implement Section 2 of this Order, each agency shall, in connection with every major rule, prepare, and to the extent permitted by law consider, a Regulatory Impact Analysis. Such Analyses may be combined with any Regulatory Flexibility Analyses performed under 5 U.S.C. 603 and 604.

(b)   Each agency shall initially determine whether a rule it intends to propose or to issue is a major rule, provided that, the Director, subject to the direction of the Task Force, shall have authority, in accordance with Sections l(b) and 2 of this Order to prescribe criteria for making such determinations, to order a rule to be treated as a major rule, and to require any set of related rules to be considered together as a major rule.

(c)   Except as provided in Section 8 of this Order, agencies shall prepare Regulatory Impact Analyses of major rules and transmit them, along with all notices of proposed rulemaking and all final rules, to the Director as follows:
   (1)   If no notice of proposed rulemaking is to be published for a proposed major rule that is not an emergency rule, the agency shall prepare only a final Regulatory Impact Analysis, which shall be transmitted along with the proposed rule, to the Director at least 60 days prior to the publication of the major rule as a final rule;
   (2)   With respect to all other major rules, the agency shall prepare a preliminary Regulatory Impact Analysis, which shall be transmitted, along with a notice of proposed rulemaking, to the Director at least 60 days prior to the publication of a notice of proposed rulemaking, and a final Regulatory Impact Analysis, which shall be transmitted along with the final rule at least 30 days prior to the publication of the major rule as a final rule;
   (3)   For all rules other than major rules, agencies shall submit to the Director, at least 10 days prior to publication, every notice of proposed rulemaking and final rule.

(d)   To permit each proposed major rule to be analyzed in light of the requirements stated in Section 2 of this Order, each preliminary and final Regulatory Impact Analysis shall contain the following information;
   (1)   A description of the potential benefits of the rule, including any beneficial effects that cannot be quantified in monetary terms, and the identification of those likely to receive the benefits;
   (2)   A description of the potential costs of the rule, including any adverse effects that cannot be quantified in monetary terms, and the identification of those likely to bear the costs;
   (3)   A determination of the potential net benefits of the rule, including an evaluation of effects that cannot be quantified in monetary terms;
   (4)   A description of alternative approaches that could substantially achieve the same regulatory goal at lower cost, together with an analysis of this potential benefit and costs and a brief explanation of the legal reasons why such alternatives, if proposed, could not be adopted; and
   (5)   Unless covered by the description required under paragraph (4) of this subsection, an explanation of any legal reasons why the rule cannot be based on the requirements set forth in Section 2 of this Order.

(e)   (1)   The Director, subject to the direction of the Task Force, which shall resolve any issues raised under this Order or ensure that they are presented to the President, is authorized to review any preliminary or final Regulatory Impact Analysis, notice of proposed rulemaking, or final rule based on the requirements of this Order.
   (2)   The Director shall be deemed to have concluded review unless the Director advises an agency to the contrary under subsection (f) of this Section:

(A) Within 60 days of a submission under subsection (c)(1) or a submission of a preliminary Regulatory Impact Analysis or notice of proposed rulemaking under subsection (c)(2);

(B) Within 30 days of the submission of a final Regulatory Impact Analysis and a final rule under subsection (c)(2); and

(C) Within 10 days of the submission of a notice of proposed rulemaking or final rule under subsection (c)(3).

(f) (1) Upon the request of the Director, an agency shall consult with the Director concerning the review of a preliminary Regulatory Impact Analysis or notice of proposed rulemaking under this Order, and shall, subject to Section 8(a)(2) of this Order, refrain from publishing its preliminary Regulatory Impact Analysis or notice of proposed rulemaking until such review is concluded.

(2) Upon receiving notice that the Director intends to submit views with respect to any final Regulatory Impact Analysis or final rule, the agency shall, subject to Section 8(a)(2) of this Order, refrain from publishing its final Regulatory Impact Analysis or final rule until the agency has responded to the Director's views, and incorporated those views and the agency's response in the rulemaking file.

(3) Nothing in this subsection shall be construed as displacing the agencies' responsibilities delegated by law.

(g) For every rule for which an agency publishes a notice of proposed rulemaking, the agency shall include in its notice:

(1) A brief statement setting forth the agency's initial determination whether the proposed rule is a major rule, together with the reasons underlying that determination; and

(2) For each proposed major rule, a brief summary of the agency's preliminary Regulatory Impact Analysis.

(h) Agencies shall make their preliminary and final Regulatory Impact Analyses available to the public.

(i) Agencies shall initiate reviews of currently effective rules in accordance with the purposes of this Order, and perform Regulatory Impact Analyses of currently effective major rules. The Director, subject to the direction of the Task Force, may designate currently effective rules for review in accordance with this Order, and establish schedules for reviews and Analyses under this Order.

Section 4. Regulatory Review. Before approving any final major rule, each agency shall:

(a) Make a determination that the regulation is clearly within the authority delegated by law and consistent with congressional intent, and include in the Federal Register at the time of promulgation a memorandum of law supporting that determination.

(b) Make a determination that the factual conclusions upon which the rule is based have substantial support in the agency record, viewed as a whole, with full attention to public comments in general and the comments of persons directly affected by the rule in particular.

Section 5. Regulatory Agendas.

(a) Each agency shall publish in October and April of each year, an agenda of proposed regulations that the agency has issued or expects to issue, and currently effective rules that are under agency review pursuant to this Order. These agendas may be incorporated with the agendas published under 5 U.S. §602, and must contain at the minimum:

(1) A summary of the nature of each major rule being considered, the objectives and legal basis for the issuance of the rule, and an approximate schedule for completing action on any major rule for which the agency has issued a notice of proposed rulemaking;

(2) The name and telephone number of a knowledgeable agency official for each item on the agenda; and

(3) A list of existing regulations to be reviewed under the terms of this Order, and a brief discussion of each such regulation.

(b) The Director, subject to the direction of the Task Force, may, to the extent permitted by law:

(1) Require agencies to provide additional information in an agenda; and

(2) Require publication of the agenda in any form.

Section 6. The Task Force and Office of Management and Budget.

(a) To the extent permitted by law, the Director shall have authority, subject to the direction of the Task Force, to:

(1) Designate any proposed or existing rule as a major rule in accordance with Section l(b) of this Order;

(2) Prepare and promulgate uniform standards for the identification of major rules and the development of Regulatory Impact Analyses;

(3) Require an agency to obtain and evaluate, in connection with a regulation, any additional relevant data from any appropriate source;

(4) Waive the requirements of Sections 3, 4, or 7 of this Order with respect to any proposed or existing major rule;

(5) Identify duplicative, overlapping and conflicting rules, existing or proposed, and existing or proposed rules that are inconsistent with the policies underlying statutes governing agencies other than the issuing agency or with the purposes of this Order, and, in each such case, require appropriate inter-agency consultation to minimize or eliminate such duplication, overlap, or conflict;

(6) Develop procedures for estimating the annual benefits and costs of agency regulations, on both an aggregate and economic or industrial sector basis, for purposes of compiling a regulatory budget;

(7) In consultation with interested agencies, prepare for consideration by the President recommendations for changes in the agencies' statutes; and

(8) Monitor agency compliance with the requirements of this Order and advise the President with respect to such compliance.

(b) The Director, subject to the direction of the Task Force, is authorized to establish procedures for the performance of all functions vested in the Director by this Order. The Director shall take appropriate steps to coordinate the implementation of the analysis, transmittal, review, and clearance provisions of this Order with the authorities and requirements provided for or imposed upon the Director and agencies under the Regulatory Flexibility Act, 5 U.S.C. 601 et seq., and the Paperwork Reduction Plan Act of 1980, 44 U.S.C. 3501 et seq.

Section 7. Pending Regulations.

(a) To the extent necessary to permit reconsideration in accordance with this Order, agencies shall, except as provided in Section 8 of this Order, suspend or postpone the effective dates of all major rules that they have promulgated in final form as of the date of this Order, but that have not yet become effective, excluding:

(1) Major rules that cannot legally be postponed or suspended;

(2) Major rules that, for good cause, ought to become effective as final rules without reconsideration. Agencies shall prepare, in accordance with Section 3 of this Order, a final Regulatory Impact Analysis for each major rule that they suspend or postpone.

(b) Agencies shall report to the Director no later than 15 days prior to the effective date of any rule that the agency has promulgated in final form as of the date of this Order, and that has not yet become effective, and that will not be reconsidered under subsection (a) of this Section;

(1) That the rule is excepted from reconsideration under subsection (a), including a brief statement of the legal or other reasons for that determination; or

(2) That the rule is not a major rule.

(c) The Director, subject to the direction of the Task Force, is authorized, to the extent permitted by law, to:

(1) Require reconsideration, in accordance with this Order, of any major rule that an agency has issued in final form as of the date of this Order and that has not become effective; and

(2) Designate a rule that an agency has issued in final form as of the date of this Order and that has not yet become effective as a major rule in accordance with Section l(b) of this Order.

(d) Agencies may, in accordance with the Administrative Procedure Act and other applicable statutes, permit major rules that they have issued in final form as of the date of this Order, and that have not yet become effective, to take effect as interim rules while they are being reconsidered in accordance with this Order, provided that, agencies shall report to the Director, no later than 15 days before any such rule is proposed to take effect as an interim rule, that the rule should appropriately take effect as an interim rule while the rule is under reconsideration.

(e)   Except as provided in Section 8 of this Order, agencies shall, to the extent permitted by law, refrain from promulgating as a final rule any proposed major rule that has been published or issued as of the date of this Order until a final Regulatory Impact Analysis, in accordance with Section 3 of this Order, has been prepared for the proposed major rule.

(f)   Agencies shall report to the Director, no later than 30 days prior to promulgating as a final rule any proposed rule that the agency has published or issued as of the date of this Order and that has not been considered under the terms of this Order:

    (1)   That the rule cannot legally be considered in accordance with this Order, together with a brief explanation of the legal reasons barring such consideration; or

    (2)   That the rule is not a major rule, in which case the agency shall submit to the Director a copy of the proposed rule.

(g)   The Director, subject to the direction of the Task Force, is authorized, to the extent permitted by law, to:

    (1)   Require consideration, in accordance with this Order, of any proposed major rule that the agency has published or issued as of the date of this Order; and

    (2)   Designate a proposed rule that an agency has published or issued as of the date of this Order, as a major rule in accordance with Section 1(b) of this Order.

(h)   The Director shall be deemed to have determined that an agency's report to the Director under subsections (b), (d), or (f) of this Section is consistent with the purposes of this Order, unless the Director advises the agency to the contrary:

    (1)   Within 15 days of its report, in the case of any report under subsections (b) or (d); or

    (2)   Within 30 days of its report, in the case of any report under subsection (i).

(i)   This Section does not supersede the President's Memorandum of January 29, 1981, entitled "Postponement of Pending Regulations," which shall remain in effect until March 30, 1981. In complying with this Section, agencies shall comply with all applicable provisions of the Administrative Procedure Act, and with any other procedural requirements made applicable to the agencies by other statutes.

Section 8. Exemptions.

(a)   The procedures prescribed by this Order shall not apply to:

    (1)   Any regulation that responds to an emergency situation, provided that, any such regulation shall be reported to the Director as soon as is practicable, the agency shall publish in the Federal Register a statement of the reasons why it is impracticable for the agency to follow the procedures of this Order with respect to such a rule, and the agency shall prepare and transmit as soon as is practicable a Regulatory Impact Analysis of any such major rule; and

    (2)   Any regulation for which consideration or reconsideration under the terms of this Order would conflict with deadlines imposed by statute or by judicial order, provided that, any such regulation shall be reported to the Director together with a brief explanation of the conflict, the agency shall publish in the Federal Register a statement of the reasons why it is impracticable for the agency to follow the procedures of this Order with respect to such a rule, and the agency, in consultation with the Director, shall adhere to the requirements of this Order to the extent permitted by statutory or judicial deadlines.

(b)   The Director, subject to the direction of the Task Force, may, in accordance with the purposes of this Order, exempt any class or category of regulations from any or all requirements of this Order.

Section 9. Judicial Review. This Order is intended only to improve the internal management of the Federal government, and is not intended to create any right or benefit, substantive or procedural, enforceable at law by a party against the United States, its agencies, its officers or any person. The determinations made by agencies under Section 4 of this Order, and any Regulatory Impact Analyses for any rule, shall be made part of the whole record of agency action in connection with the rule.

Section 10. Revocations. Executive Orders No. 12044, as amended, and No. 12174 are revoked.

Appendix 4C

Executive Order 12498

January 4, 1985
50 Federal Register 11036 (1986)

By the authority vested in me as President by the Constitution and laws of the United States of America, and in order to create a coordinated process for developing on an annual basis the Administration's Regulatory Program, establish Administration regulatory priorities, increase the accountability of agency heads for the regulatory actions of their agencies, provide for Presidential oversight of the regulatory process, reduce the burdens of existing and future regulations, minimize duplication and conflict of regulations, and enhance public and Congressional understanding of the Administration's regulatory objectives, it is hereby ordered as follows:

Section 1. General Requirements.

(a) There is hereby established a regulatory planning process by which the Administration will develop and publish a Regulatory Program for each year. To implement this process, each Executive agency subject to Executive Order No. 12291 [set out as a note under this section] shall submit to the Director of the Office of Management and Budget (OMB) each year, starting in 1985, a statement of its regulatory policies, goals, and objectives for the coming year and information concerning all significant regulatory actions underway or planned; however, the Director may exempt from this Order such agencies or activities as the Director may deem appropriate in order to achieve the effective implementation of this Order.

(b) The head of each Executive agency subject to this Order shall ensure that all regulatory actions are consistent with the goals of the agency and of the Administration, and will be appropriately implemented.

(c) This program is intended to complement the existing regulatory planning and review procedures of agencies and the Executive branch, including the procedures established by Executive Order No. 12291 [set out as a note under this section].

(d) Absent unusual circumstances, such as new statutory or judicial requirements or unanticipated emergency situations, the Director may, to the extent permitted by law, return for reconsideration any rule submitted for review under Executive Order No. 12291 [set out as a note under this section), that would be subject to Section 2 but was not included in the agency's final Regulatory Program for that year; or any other significant regulatory action that is materially different from those described in the Administration's Regulatory Program for that year.

Section 2. Agency Submission of Draft Regulatory Program.

(a) The head of each agency shall submit to the Director an overview of the agency's regulatory policies, goals, and objectives for the program year and such information concerning all significant regulatory actions of the agency, planned or underway, including actions taken to consider whether to initiate rule-making; requests for public comment; and the development of documents that may influence, anticipate, or could lead to the commencement of rulemaking proceedings at a later date, as the Director deems necessary to develop the Administration's Regulatory Program. This submission shall constitute the agency's draft regulatory program. The draft regulatory program shall be submitted to the Director each year, on a date to be specified by the Director, and shall cover the period from April 1 through March 31 of the following year.

(b) The overview portion of the agency's submission should discuss the agency's broad regulatory purposes, explain how they are consistent with the Administration's regulatory principles, and include a discussion of the significant regulatory actions, as defined by the Director, that it will take. The overview should specifically discuss the significant regulatory actions of the agency to revise or rescind existing rules.

(c) Each agency head shall categorize and describe the regulatory actions described in subsection (a) in such format as the Director shall specify and provide such additional information as the Director may request; however, the Director shall, by Bulletin or Circular, exempt from the requirements of this Order any class or category of regulatory action that the Director determines is not necessary to review in order to achieve the effective implementation of the program.

Section 3. Review, Compilation, and Publication of the Administration's Regulatory Program.

(a) In reviewing each agency's draft regulatory program, the Director shall (i) consider the consistency of the draft regulatory program with the Administration's policies and priorities and the draft regulatory programs submitted by other agencies; and (ii) identify such further regulatory or deregulatory actions as may, in his view, be necessary in order to achieve such consistency. In the event of disagreement over the content of the agency's draft regulatory program, the agency head or the Director may raise issues for further review by the President or by such appropriate Cabinet Council or other forum as the President may designate.

(b) Following the conclusion of the review process established by subsection (a), each agency head shall submit to the Director, by a date to be specified by the Director, the agency's final regulatory plan for compilation and publication as the Administration's Regulatory Program for that year. The Director shall circulate a draft of the Administration's Regulatory Program for agency comment, review, and interagency consideration, if necessary, before publication

(c) After development of the Administration's Regulatory Program for the year, if the agency head proposes to take a regulatory action subject to the provisions of Section 2 and not previously submitted for review under this process, or if the agency head proposes to take a regulatory action that is materially different from the action described in the agency's final Regulatory Program, the agency head shall immediately advise the Director and submit the action to the Director for review in such format as the Director may specify. Except in the case of emergency situations, as defined by the Director, or statutory or judicial deadlines, the agency head shall refrain from taking the proposed regulatory action until the review of this submission by the Director is completed. As to those regulatory actions not also subject to Executive Order No. 12291 [set out as a note under this section], the Director shall be deemed to have concluded that the proposal is consistent with the purposes of this Order, unless he notifies the agency head to the contrary within 10 days of its submission. As to those regulatory actions subject to Executive Order No. 12291, the Director's review shall be governed by the provisions of Section 3(e) of that Order.

(d) To assure consistency with the goals of the Administration, the head of each agency subject to this Order shall adhere to the regulatory principles stated in Section 2 of Executive Order No. 12291 [set out as a note under this section] including those elaborated by the regulatory policy guidelines set forth in the August 11, 1983, Report of the Presidential Task Force on Regulatory Relief, "Reagan Administration Regulatory Achievements."

Section 4. Office of Management and Budget.

The Director of the Office of Management and Budget is authorized, to the extent permitted by law, to take such actions as may be necessary to carry out the provisions of this Order.

Section 5. Judicial Review.

This Order is intended only to improve the internal management of the Federal government, and is not intended to create any right or benefit, substantive or procedural, enforceable at law by a party against the United States, its agencies, its officers or any person.

Appendix 5

Selected Readings on Law
and Administration

Aberbach, Joel D. *Keeping a Watchful Eye: The Politics of Congressional Oversight*. Washington, DC: Brookings Institution, 1990.

Agranoff, Robert, and Michael McGuire. *Collaborative Public Management: New Strategies for Local Governments*. Washington, DC: Georgetown University Press, 2003.

Allison, Graham T. *Essence of Decision*. Boston: Little, Brown, 1971.

Aman, Alfred C., Jr. *Administrative Law in A Global Era*. Ithaca, NY: Cornell University Press, 1992.

Anthony, Robert A. "Interpretative Rules, Policy Statements, Guidances, Manuals, and the Like—Should Federal Agencies Use Them to Bind the Public?" 41 *Duke L. J.* 1311 (1992).

Appleby, Paul. *Big Democracy* New York: Alfred A. Knopf, 1949.

Aristotle. *Nicomachean Ethics*. Indianapolis: Bobbs-Merrill, 1962.

Bailey, Stephen. "Ethics and the Public Service," in R. Martin, ed. *Public Administration and Democracy: Essays in Honor of Paul Appleby*. Syracuse, NY: Syracuse University, 1965.

Bailyn, Bernard. *The Ideological Origins of the American Revolution*. Cambridge: Harvard University Press, 1967.

Ball, Howard. *Cancer Factories: American's Tragic Quest for Uranium Self-Sufficiency*. Westport, CT: Greenwood Press, 1993.

_____. *Controlling Regulatory Sprawl*. Westport, CT: Greenwood Press, 1984.

_____ *Justice Downwind*. New York: Oxford University Press, 1986.

Ban, Carolyn, and Patricia Ingraham. "Short-Timers: Political Appointee Mobility and Its Impact on Political/Career Relations in the Reagan Administration," 22 *Administration & Society* 106 (1990).

Ban, Carolyn, and Norma Riccucci, eds. *Public Personnel Management: Current Concerns, Future Challenges,* 2nd ed. New York: Longman, 1997.

Bardach, Eugene, and Robert A. Kagan. *Going by the Book: The Problem of Regulatory Unreasonableness*. Philadelphia: Temple University Press, 1982.

_____ and Cara Lesser. "Accountability in Human Service Collaboratives—For What? And To Whom?" 6 *Journal of Public Administration Research and Theory* 197 (1996).

Barnard, Chester. *The Functions of the Executive*. Cambridge: Harvard, 1938.

Baum, Lawrence. *American Courts: Process and Policy,* 4th ed. Boston: Houghton Mifflin, 1998.

Bazan, Elizabeth B., and Jennifer K. Elsea. American Law Division, Congressional Research Service, *Presidential Authority to Conduct Warrantless Electronic Surveillance to Gather Foreign Intelligence Information Memorandum*. Washington, DC: Congressional Research Service, 2006.

Bazelon, David. "The Impact of the Courts on Public Administration," 52 *Indiana L. J.* 101 (1976).

Been, Vicki L. "Locally Undesirable Land Uses in Minority Neighborhoods: Disproportionate Siting or Market Dynamics," 103 *Yale L. J.* 1406 (1994).

Becker, Carl L. *The Declaration of Independence: A Study in the History of Political Ideas*. New York: Vintage Books, 1958.

Becker, Theodore L., and Malcolm Feeley. *The Impact of Supreme Court Decisions,* 2nd ed. New York: Oxford, 1973.

Benjamin, Robert. *Administrative Adjudication in the State of New York*. Albany: State of New York, 1942.

Berger, Raoul. "Administrative Arbitrariness – A Reply to Professor Davis," 114 *U. Pennsylvania L. Rev.* 783 (1966).

———. "Administrative Arbitrariness and Judicial Review," 65 *Columbia L. Rev.* 55 (1965).

———. "Rejoinder," 114 *U. Pennsylvania L. Rev.* 816 (1966).

———. "Sequel," 51 *Minnesota L. Rev.* 601 (1967).

———. "Synthesis," 78 *Yale L. J.* 965 (1969).

Berle, Adolph A. *The Three Faces of Power.* New York: Harcourt, Brace & World, 1959.

——— and Gardiner Means, *The Modern Corporation and Private Property.* New York: Macmillan, 1932.

Berman, Larry. *The Office of Management and Budget and the Presidency, 1921–1979.* Princeton: Princeton University Press, 1979.

Bermann, George A. *Regulatory Cooperation with Counterpart Agencies Abroad: The FAA's Aircraft Certification Experience.* Washington, DC: Administrative Conference of the United States, 1991.

Bernstein, Marver. *Regulating Business by Independent Commission.* Princeton: Princeton University Press, 1955.

Bester, Matthew J. "Comment: A Wreck on the Info-Bahn: Electronic Mail and the Destruction of Evidence," 6 *Communications Law Conspectus* 75 (1998).

Beveridge, Albert. *The Life of John Marshall.* Boston: Houghton Mifflin, 1916–1919.

Bickel, Alexander M. *The Least Dangerous Branch.* Indianapolis: Bobbs-Merrill, 1975.

Bingham, Lisa B. "Alternative Dispute Resolution in Public Administration," in Phillip J. Cooper and Chester A. Newland, eds. *Handbook of Public Law and Administration.* San Francisco: Jossey-Bass, 1997.

Bowman, James S., ed. *Ethical Frontiers in Public Management.* San Francisco: Jossey-Bass, 1991.

——— and Donald Menzel. *Teaching Ethics and Values in Public Administration Programs: Innovations, Strategies, and Issues.* Albany, NY: State University of New York Press, 1998.

Bowsher, Charles A. Testimony Before the Committee on Governmental Affairs, United States Senate, *Congressional Oversight: The General Accounting Office.* Washington, DC: GAO, 1995.

Bozeman, Barry. *All Organizations Are Public.* San Francisco: Jossey-Bass, 1987.

———, "Exploring the Limits of Public and Private Sectors: Sector Boundaries as Maginot Line," 48 *Public Administration Review* 672 (1988).

Brandeis, Louis D. *Other People's Money.* New York: Harper & Row, 1967.

Brennan, William J., "State Constitutions and the Protection of Individual Rights," 90 *Harvard L. Rev.* 489 (1977).

Breyer, Stephen. *Regulation and Its Reform.* Cambridge: Harvard University Press, 1982.

———, "Vermont Yankee and the Court's Rule in the Nuclear Energy Controversy," 91 *Harvard L. Rev.* 1833 (1978).

Breyner, Gary C. *Bureaucratic Discretion: Law and Policy in Federal Regulatory Agencies.* New York: Pergamon Press, 1987.

Brownlow Commission. *Report of the President's Committee on Administrative Management* Washington, DC: Government Printing Office, 1937.

Brown Weiss, Edith. "Environmental Equity and International Law" in Sun Lin, ed. *UNEP's New Way Forward: Environmental Law and Sustainable Development.* Nairobi: United Nations Environmental Programme, 1995.

Bruff, Harold. "Presidential Power and Administrative Rulemaking," 88 *Yale L. J.* 451 (1979).

Bruff, Harold H., and Ernest Gellhorn, Congressional Control of Administrative Regulation: A Study of Legislative Vetoes," 90 *Harvard L. Rev.* 1369 (1977).

Bryant, Bunyan, ed. *Environmental Justice: Issues, Policies, and Solutions.* Washington, DC: Island Press, 1995.

——— and Paul Mohai, eds. *Race and the Incidence of Environmental Hazards.* Boulder, CO: Westview Press, 1992.

Bullard, Robert D. *Dumping on Dixie.* Boulder: Westview Press, 1990.

———, ed. *Unequal Protection: Environmental Justice and Communities of Color.* San Francisco: Sierra Club Books, 1994.

Burke, John P. *Bureaucratic Responsibility.* Baltimore: Johns Hopkins, 1986.

Burns, James MacGregor. *Roosevelt: The Lion and the Fox.* New York: Harcourt, Brace & World, 1956.

Burton, Lloyd. "Ethical Discontinuities in Public-Private Sector Negotiation," 9 *Journal of Policy Analysis and Management* 23 (1990).

———. *Worship and Wilderness: Culture, Religion, and Law in Public Lands Management.* Madison, WI: University of Wisconsin Press, 2002.

Calabresi, Steven G. "The Virtues of Presidential Government." 18 *Constitutional Commentary* 51 (2001).

Caldwell, Louis G. "Remarks to the ABA Convention," 58 *Rep. ABA* 197 (1933).

Cameron, Chip, Philip J. Harter, Gail Bingham, and Neil R. Eisner. "Alternative Dispute Resolution with Emphasis on Rulemaking Negotiations," 4 *Administrative Law Journal* 83, 87 (1990).

Cannon, Bradley C. "Reactions of State Supreme Courts to U.S. Supreme Court Civil Liberties Decisions," 8 *Law and Society Rev.* 109 (1973).

Cardozo, Benjamin N. *The Nature of the Judicial Process.* New Haven: Yale University Press, 1921.

Carroll, James D. "Service, Knowledge, and Choice: The Future as Post-Industrial Administration," 35 *Public Administration Rev.* 578 (1975).

Carrow, Milton M. *The Background of Administrative Law.* Newark, NJ: Associated Lawyers, 1948.

Cary, William. *Politics and the Regulatory Agencies.* New York: McGraw-Hill, 1967.

Chayes, Abram. "The Role of the Judge in Public Law Litigation," 89 *Harvard L. Rev.* 1281 (1976).

Chubb, John E., and Terry More, *Politics, Markets, & America's Schools.* Washington, DC: Brookings Institution, 1990.

Clayton, Cornell W. "Government Lawyers: Who Represents Government and Why Does It Matter?" in Phillip J. Cooper and Chester A. Newland, eds. *Handbook of Public Law and Administration.* San Francisco: Jossey-Bass, 1997.

_____, ed. *Government Lawyers: The Federal Legal Bureaucracy and Presidential Politics.* Lawrence, KS: Kansas University Press, 1995.

Cleveland, Harlan. "Government Is Information (But Not Vice Versa)," 46 *Public Administration Review* 605 (1986).

Cobb, Roger W., and C. Elder, eds. *Participation in American Politics: The Dynamics of Agenda-Building.* Baltimore, MD: Johns Hopkins University Press, 1983.

Coffin, Frank M. *On Appeal: Courts, Lawyering, and Judging.* New York: W. W. Norton, 1994.

Coglianese, Cary. "The Internet and Citizen Participation in Rulemaking," 1 *II/S: Journal of Law and Policy* 33 (2004).

Colby, Jeremy. "You've Got Mail: The Modern Trend Towards Universal Electronic Service of Process," 51 *Buffalo L. Rev.* 337 (2003).

Cole, David. *Enemy Aliens: Double Standards and Constitutional Freedoms in the War on Terrorism.* New York: The New Press, 2003.

_____. "Enemy Aliens," 54 *Stanford L. Rev.* 953 (2002).

Comment: "Individual Privacy Interest and the 'Special Needs' Analysis for Involuntary Drug and HIV Tests," 86 *California L. Rev.* 119 (1998).

Comment: "Recombinant DNA: A Case Study in Regulation of Scientific Research," 8 *Ecology L. Q.* 55 (1979).

Commission on Organization of the Executive Branch of Government. *The Hoover Commission Report on the Organization of the Executive Branch of Government.* New York: McGraw-Hill, Inc., 1949.

Cooper, Phillip J. *By Order of the President: The Use and Abuse of Presidential Direct Action.* Lawrence, KS: University Press of Kansas, 2002.

_____. "Canadian Refugee Services: The Challenges of Network Operations," 18 *Refuge* 14 (2000).

_____. "George W. Bush, Edgar Allan Poe, and the Use and Abuse of Presidential Signing Statements," 35 *Presidential Studies Quarterly* 515 (2005).

_____. *Governing by Contract.* Washington, DC: CQ Press, 2002.

_____. "Government Contracts in Public Administration: The Role and Environment of the Contracting Office," 40 *Public Administration Review* 459 (1980).

_____. *Hard Judicial Choices.* New York: Oxford University Press, 1988.

_____. "Rusty Pipes: The Rust Decision and the Supreme Court's Free Flow Theory of the First Amendment," 6 *Notre Dame Journal of Law, Ethics, & Policy* 359 (1992).

_____. "The Supreme Court, the First Amendment, and Freedom of Information," 46 *Public Administration Rev.* 622 (1986).

_____. "Toward the Hybrid State: The Case of Environmental Management in a Deregulated and Reengineered State," 61 *International Review of Administrative Sciences* 185 (1995).

_____ and Howard Ball. *The United States Supreme Court: From the Inside Out.* Englewood Cliffs, NJ: Prentice Hall, 1996.

Cooper, Phillip J., Albert Hyde, J. Steven Ott, Linda Brady, Harvey White, and Olivia Hidalgo-Hardeman, *Public Administration for the Twenty-First Century.* Fort Worth: Harcourt, Brace, 1998.

Cooper, Phillip J., and Chester A. Newland, eds. *Handbook of Public Law and Administration* San Francisco: Jossey-Bass, 1997.

Cooper, Phillip J., and Claudia María Vargas. *Implementing Sustainable Development: From Global Policy to Local Action.* Lanham, MD: Rowman & Littlefield, 2004.

Cooper, Robert M. "Administrative Justice and the Role of Discretion," 47 *Yale Law Journal* 577 (1938).

Cooper, Terry. *The Responsible Administrator.* Port Washington, NY: Kennikat, 1982.

_____ and N. Dale Wright, eds. *Exemplary Public Administrators: Character and Leadership in Government.* San Francisco: Jossey-Bass, 1992.

Corliss, David L. "Ordinances, Statutes, and Democratic Discipline: A Local Perspective on Drafting Laws," in Phillip J. Cooper and Chester A. Newland, eds. *Handbook of Public Law and Administration.* San Francisco: Jossey-Bass, 1997.

Corwin, E. S. "The 'Higher Law' Background of American Constitutional Law," 42 *Harvard L. Rev.* 149 (1928–29).

Coven, Mark. "The First Amendment Rights of Policymaking Public Employees," 12 *Harvard Civil Rights-Civil Liberties L. Rev.* 559 (1977).

Craig, Barbara Hinckson. *The Legislative Veto.* Boulder, CO: Westport, 1983.

Cramton, Roger C. "The Why, Where and How of Broadened Public Participation in the Administrative Process," 60 *Georgetown L. J.* 525 (1972).

Crawford, Colin. *Uproar at Dancing Rabbit Creek: Battling Over Race, Class, and the Environment.* Reading, MA: Addison–Wesley Publishing, 1996.

Croly, Steven P., and William F. Funk, "The Federal Advisory Committee Act and Good Government," 14 *Yale Journal on Regulation* 451 (1997).

Crozier, Michel. *The Bureaucratic Phenomenon.* Chicago: University of Chicago Press, 1964.

Currie, David P., and Frank L. Goodman, "Judicial Review of Federal Administrative Action: Quest for the Optimum Forum," 75 *Columbia L. Rev.* 1 (1975).

Dahl, Robert. *Who Governs.* New Haven: Yale University Press, 1961.

Daniels, Mark. "Implementing Policy Termination," 14 *Policy Studies Review,* 353 (1995/1996).

Davis, Fred, and James Reynolds. "Profile of a Social Security Disability," 42 *Missouri L. Rev.* 541 (1977).

Davis, Kenneth Culp. *Administrative Law.* St. Paul, MN: West Publishing, 1951.

_____. *Administrative Law Treatise.* St. Paul: West, 1958.

_____. *Discretionary Justice: A Preliminary Inquiry.* Baton Rouge: Louisiana State University Press, 1969.

_____. "A Final Word," 14 *U. Pennsylvania L. Rev.* 814 (1966).

_____. "A New Approach to Delegation," 36 *U. Chicago L. Rev.* 713 (1969).

_____. "Not Always," 51 *Minnesota L. Rev.* 643 (1967).

_____. "Postscript," 114 *U. Pennsylvania L. Rev.* 823 (1966).

Davison, J. Forrester, and Nathan D. Grundstein. *Administrative Law: Cases and Readings.* Indianapolis: Bobbs–Merrill, 1952.

De Bedts, Ralph. *The New Deal's SEC: The Formative Years.* New York: Columbia University Press, 1964.

DeHoog, Ruth Hoogland. *Contracting Out for Human Services.* Albany, NY; State University of New York, 1984.

de Leon, Peter "Commentary [on Policy Termination]," 30 *Policy Studies Journal* 47 (2002).

_____. "Policy Evaluation and Program Termination," 2 *Policy Studies Review* 631 (1983).

_____. "Public Policy Termination: An End and a Beginning," 4 *Policy Analysis* 369 (1978).

Deming, W. Edwards. *Out of the Crisis: Quality, Productivity and Competitive Position.* Cambridge, UK: Cambridge University Press, 1988.

Derthick, Martha. *Agency Under Stress: The Social Security Administration in American Government.* Washington, DC: Brookings Institution, 1990.

Dery, David. *Problem Definition in Policy Analysis.* Lawrence, KS: University Press of Kansas, 1984.

Devins, Neal, and Michael Herz, "Velazquez and Beyond: The Uneasy Case for Department of Justice Control of Federal Litigation. 5 *University of Pennsylvania Journal of Constitutional Law* 558 (2003).

Dicey, A. V. *Introduction to the Study of the Law of the Constitution.* London; Macmillan, 1965.

Dickinson, John. *Administrative Justice and the Supremacy of Law in the United States.* New York: Russell & Russell, 1927.

_____. "Judicial Control of Official Discretion," 22 *American Political Science Review* 275 (1928).

Dilulio, John J., Jr., and Donald F. Kettl. *Fine Print: The Contract with America, Devolution, and the Administrative Realities of American Federalism.* Washington, DC: Brookings Institution, 1995.

Dixon, Robert G. "The Congressional Veto and Separation of Powers: The Executive on a Leash," 56 *North Carolina L. Rev.* 423 (1978).

_____. *Social Security Disability and Mass Justice: A Problem in Welfare Adjudication.* New York: Praeger, 1973.

Dodd, Lawrence C., and Richard L. Schott. *Congress and the Administrative State.* New York: Wiley, 1979.

Dolbeare, Kenneth. *Trial Courts in Urban Politics.* New York: Wiley, 1967.

Doniger, David. "Federal Regulation of Vinyl Chloride: A Short Course in the Law and Policy of Toxic Substances Control," 7 *Ecology L. Q.* 501 (1978).

Douglas, William O. *Democracy and Finance.* Port Washington, NY: Kennikat Press, 1940.

Downs, George W., and Patrick D. Larkey. *The Search for Government Efficiency.* New York: Random House, 1986.

Dror, Yehezkel. *The Capacity to Govern.* London: Routledge, 2001.

_____. *Design for the Policy Sciences.* New York: American Elsevier Pub. Co. 1971.

_____. *Public Policymaking Reexamined.* San Francisco: Chandler Pub. Co., 1968.

Drucker, Peter. "Productivity and the Knowledge Worker," in *Business and Society in Change*. New York: American Telephone & Telegraph, 1975.

Durant, Robert F. *The Administrative Presidency Revisited*. Albany, NY: State University of New York Press, 1992.

Dvorin, Eugene, and Robert Simmons. *From Amoral to Humane Bureaucracy*. San Francisco: Canfield, 1972.

Dworkin, Terry Morehead. "It's My Life—Leave Me Alone: Off the Job Employee Associational Privacy Rights," 35 *American Business L. J.* 47 (1997).

Eddy, Paul, Elaine Potter, and Bruce Paige. *Destination Disaster*. New York: Ballantine Books, 1976.

Ehrenhalt, Samuel M., Center for the Study of the States, Government Employment Report, *The New Geography of Government Jobs: Hiring in State and Local Government Shifts to South and West, and to Medium and Small States*. Albany, NY: Nelson A. Rockefeller Institute of Government, 1997.

Eisenstein, James, and Herbert Jacob, *Felony Justice*. Boston: Little, Brown, 1977.

Elliott, Jonathan. *Debates in the Several States on the Adoption of the Federal Constitution as Recommended by the General Convention at Philadelphia in 1787,* 2nd ed. New York: Burt Franklin, 1888.

Emerson, Thomas I. *The System of Free Expression*. New York: Vintage Books, 1970.

Epstein, Lee. *Conservatives in Court*. Knoxville: University of Tennessee Press, 1985.

_____. "Interest Group Litigation During the Rehnquist Era," 9 *Journal of Law and Politics* 639 (1993).

Farrand, Max. *The Framing of the Constitution of the United States*. New Haven: Yale University Press, 1913.

_____, ed., *Records of the Federal Convention of 1787, rev. ed., 4 vols.* New Haven: Yale University Press, 1966.

Feinberg, Lotte. "Managing the Freedom of Information Act and Federal Information Policy," 46 *Public Administration Review* 615 (1986).

_____. "Open Government and Freedom of Information: Fishbowl Accountability?" in Phillip J. Cooper and Chester A. Newland, eds. *Handbook of Public Law and Administration*. San Francisco: Jossey-Bass, 1997.

Fellmeth, Robert. *The Interstate Commerce Commission*. New York: Grossman, 1970

Finer, Herman. "Administrative Responsibility in Democratic Government," 1 *Public Administration Rev.* 335 (1941).

_____. "Better Government Personnel: America's Next Frontier," 51 *Political Science Quarterly* 569 (1936).

Fischel, William A. *Regulatory Takings: Law, Economics, and Politics*. Cambridge: Harvard University Press, 1995.

Fisher, Louis. *The Constitution Between Friends: Congress, the President and the Law*. New York: St. Martin's Press, 1978.

_____. *Constitutional Conflicts Between Congress and the President,* 4th ed., revised. Lawrence, KS: Kansas University Press, 1997.

_____. *Constitutional Dialogues*. Princeton: Princeton University Press, 1988.

_____. "Judicial Misjudgments About the Lawmaking Process: The Legislative Veto Case," 45 *Public Administration Rev.* 705 (1985).

_____. *National Security Whistleblowers*. Washington, DC: Congressional Research Service, 2005.

_____. *One Year After INS v. Chadha: Congressional and Judicial Developments*. Washington, DC: Congressional Research Service, 1984.

Fitzgerald, Brian T. "Sealed v. Dealed: A Public Court System Going Secretly Private," 6 *Journal of Law and Politics* 381 (1990).

Fleishman, Joel L., et al. *Public Duties. The Moral Obligations of Government Officials*. Cambridge: Harvard, 1981.

Foreman, Christopher H., Jr. *The Promise and Peril of Environmental Justice*. Washington, DC: Brookings Institution, 1998.

_____. *Signals from the Hill: Congressional Oversight and the Challenge of Social Regulation*. New Haven: Yale University Press, 1988.

Forkosch, Morris D. *A Treatise on Administrative Law*. Indianapolis: Bobbs-Merrill, 1956.

Foster, Sheila. "Justice from the Ground Up: Distributive Inequities, Grassroots Resistance, and the Transformative Politics of the Environmental Justice Movement," 86 *California L. Rev.* 775 (1998).

Frank, Jerome. *Courts on Trial*. New York: Atheneum, 1971.

_____. *If Men Were Angels: Some Aspects of Government in a Democracy*. New York: Harper & Brothers, 1942.

_____. *Law and the Modern Mind*. New York: Coward-McCann Brentanos, 1930.

Frank, John P. "Political Questions," in Edmund Cahn, ed., *Supreme Court and Supreme Law*. New York: Simon & Schuster, 1971.

Frantz, Janet E. "Political Resources for Policy Termination," 30 *Policy Studies Journal* 11 (2002).

Frederickson, H. George. *Ethics and Public Administration*. Armonk, NY: M. E. Sharpe, 1993.

_____. ed. *Ideal & Practice in Council-Manager Government,* 2nd ed. Washington, DC: International City/County Management Association, 1995.

_____. "Whatever Happened to Public Administration? Governance, Governance Everywhere," Ewan Ferlie, Laurence E. Lynn and Christopher Pollitt, eds. *The Oxford Handbook of Public Management.* London: Oxford University Press, 2006.

_____ and Kevin B. Smith. *The Public Administration Theory Primer.* Boulder, CO: Westview Press, 2002.

Freund, Ernst. *Administrative Powers over Persons and Property: A Comparative Survey.* Chicago: University of Chicago Press, 1928.

_____. *Standards of American Legislation.* Chicago: University of Chicago Press, 1917.

Friedman, Leon, ed. *United States v. Nixon: The President Before the Supreme Court.* New York: Chelsea House, 1974.

Friedrich, Carl J. "Public Policy and the Nature of Administrative Responsibility," in C. J. Friedrich and E. S. Mason, eds. *Public Policy.* Cambridge: Harvard, 1940.

_____. *The Philosophy of Law in Historical Perspective,* 2nd ed. Chicago: University of Chicago Press, 1963.

Friendly, Henry J. *The Federal Administrative Agencies: The Need for Better Definition of Standards.* Cambridge: Harvard University Press, 1962.

_____. "Some Kind of a Hearing," 123 *U. Pennsylvania L. Rev.* 1267 (1975).

Fritschler, A. Lee, and James M. Hoefler. *Smoking and Politics: Politics and the Federal Bureaucracy,* 5th ed. Upper Saddle River, NJ: Prentice Hall, 1995.

Fuchs, Ralph F. "Development and Diversification in Administrative Rule Making," 72 *Northwestern U. L. Rev.* 83 (1977).

Fuller, Lon. "The Case of the Speluncean Explorers," 62 *Harvard L. Rev.* 616 (1949).

_____. *The Morality of Law.* New Haven: Yale University Press, 1969.

Funk, William F., Sidney Shapiro, and Russell L. Weaver, eds. *Administrative Procedure and Practice,* 2nd ed. St. Paul, MN: West Publishing, 2001.

Galanter, Marc. "Why the Haves Come Out Ahead: Speculations on the Limits of Legal Change," 9 *Law & Society Rev.* 95 (1974).

Galbraith, John Kenneth. *The Great Crash of 1929.* Boston: Houghton Mifflin, 1961.

Gellhorn, Ernest. *Administrative Law and Process in a Nutshell.* St. Paul, MN: West Publishing, 1972.

_____. "Public Participation in Administrative Agency Proceedings," 81 *Yale L. Journal* 359 (1972).

_____ and Glen O. Robinson, "Perspectives on Administrative Law," 75 *Columbia L. Rev.* 771 (1975).

_____ and Harold Bruff. "Congressional Control of Administrative Regulation: A Study of Legislative Vetoes," 90 *Harvard L. Rev.* 1369 (1977).

Gellhorn, Walter. *Federal Administrative Proceedings.* Baltimore: John Hopkins, 1941.

_____, Clark Byse, and Peter Strauss. *Administrative Law: Cases and Comments,* 7th ed. Mineola, NY: Foundation Press, 1979.

Gerth, H., and C. Wright Mills. *From Max Weber: Essays in Sociology.* New York: Oxford, 1946.

Gilman, Michele Estrin. "Legal Accountability in an Era of Privatized Welfare," 89 *Calif. L. Rev.* 569 (2001).

Gilmour, Robert S., and Alexis A. Halley, eds. *Who Makes Public Policy? The Struggle for Control between Congress and the Executive.* Chatham, NJ: Chatham House Publishers, 1994.

Ginsberg, Jordan S. "Class Action Notice: The Internet's Time Has Come," 2003 *U. Chicago Legal Forum* 739 (2003).

Goldman, Sheldon, and Thomas P. Jahnige, *The Federal Courts as a Political System,* 2nd ed. New York: Harper & Row, 1976.

Goodman, Frank L. "Judicial Review of Federal Administrative Action: Quest for the Optimum Forum," 75 *Columbia L. Rev.* 1 (1975).

Goodnow, Frank. *Comparative Administrative Law.* New York: Putnam, 1893.

_____. *The Principles of the Administrative Law of the United States.* New York: Putnam, 1905.

Goodsell, Charles. *The Case for Bureaucracy,* 3rd ed. Chatham, NJ: Chatham House, 1994.

_____. "The Grace Commission: Seeking Efficiency for the Whole People," 44 *Public Administration Rev.* 196 (1984).

Gore, Al. *From Red Tape to Results: Creating a Government that Works Better and Costs Less.* Report of the National Performance Review. Washington, DC: Government Printing Office, 1993.

Gray, C. Boyden. "Presidential Involvement in Informal Rulemaking," 47 *Tulane L. Rev.* 863 (1982).

Gray, John Chipman. *The Nature and Sources of Law.* New York: Macmillan, 1927.

Green, Mark J. *The Other Government,* rev. ed. New York: Norton, 1978.

Gulick, Luther. "The Twenty-Fifth Anniversary of the American Society for Public Administration," 25 *Public Administration Review* 1 (1965).

Halberstam, David. *The Best and the Brightest.* New York: Random House, 1972.

Hamilton, Alexander, James Madison, and John Jay. *The Federalist Papers.* New York: Mentor, 1961.

Harrigar, Katy. *Independent Justice: The Federal Special Prosecutor in American Politics.* Lawrence, KS: Kansas University Press, 1992.

Harris, Joseph P. *Congressional Control of Administration.* Garden City, NJ: Doubleday, 1964.

Hart, James. *An Introduction to Administrative Law with Selected Cases.* New York: Crofts, 1940.

Havel, Vaclav. *The Art of the Impossible: Politics as Morality in Practice.* New York: Alfred A. Knopf, 1994.

Haviland, James M., and Michael B. Glomb, "The Disability Insurance Benefits Program and Low Income Claimants in Appalachia," 73 *W. Virginia L. Rev.* 109 (1971).

Hayes, Gerald. "Profile of a Social Security Disability and the Administrative Law Judge," 1975 *Air Force L. Rev.* 73 (1975).

Heclo, Hugh. *A Government of Strangers.* Washington, DC: Brookings Institution, 1977.

_____. "OMB and the Presidency: The Problem of Neutral Competence," 38 *Public Interest* 80 (1975).

Heinz, John O. "Lawyers for Conservative Causes: Clients, Ideology, and Social Distance," 37 *Law & Society Rev.* 5 (2003).

Hemingway, Charles W. "A Closer Look at *Waters v. Churchill* and *United States v. National Treasury Employees Union*: Constitutional Tensions Between the Government as Employer and the Citizen as Federal Employee," 44 *American University L. Rev.* 2231 (1995).

Henderson, Gerald C. *The Federal Trade Commission: A Study in Administrative Law and Procedure.* New Haven: Yale University Press, 1924.

Herring, E. Pendleton. *Public Administration and the Public Interest.* New York: McGraw Hill, 1936.

Hess, Stephen. *Organizing the Presidency.* Washington, DC: Brookings Institution, 1976.

Heumann, Milton. *Plea Bargaining.* Chicago: University of Chicago Press, 1977.

Hofstadter, Richard. *The Age of Reform.* New York: Random House, 1955.

Holmes, Oliver Wendall, Jr. "Natural Law," 32 *Harvard L. Rev.* 40 (1918).

_____. "The Path of the Law," 10 *Harvard L. Rev.* 457 (1918).

Horowitz, Donald L. *The Courts and Social Policy.* Washington, DC: Brookings Institution, 1977.

Howard, J. Woodford. *Mr. Justice Murphy: A Political Biography.* Princeton: Princeton University Press, 1968.

Howell, William G. *Power without Persuasion: The Politics of Direct Presidential Action.* Princeton: Princeton University Press, 2003.

Imai, Shin. "Sound Science, Careful Policy Analysis, and Ongoing Relationships: Integrating Litigation and Negotiation in Aboriginal Lands and Resources Disputes," 41 *Osgoode Hall L. J.* 587 (2003).

Ingraham, Patricia. "Building Bridges or Burning Them? The President, the Appointees and the Bureaucracy." 47 *Public Administration Review* 425 (1987).

Ingraham, Patricia W., and Laurence E. Lynn, Jr., eds. *The Art of Governance: Analyzing Management and Administration.* Washington, DC: Georgetown University Press, 2004.

Jaffe, Louis L. "Book Review (Discretionary Justice)," 14 *Villanova L. Rev.* 773 (1969).

_____. *Judicial Control of Administrative Action.* Boston: Little, Brown, 1965.

_____ and Nathaniel L. Nathanson. *Administrative Law: Cases and Materials.* Boston: Little, Brown, 1976.

Jasanoff, Sheila. *Science at the Bar: Law, Science, and Technology in America.* Cambridge: Harvard University Press, 1995.

Jenkins, Bruce S., and Russell C. Kearl, "Problems of Discretion and Responsibility: The Debate Over Tort Liability," in Phillip J. Cooper and Chester A. Newland, eds. *Handbook of Public Law and Administration.* San Francisco: Jossey-Bass, 1997.

Johnson, Charles A., and Bradley C. Canon. *Judicial Policies: Implementation and Impact,* 2nd ed. Washington, DC: CQ, 1995.

Kaiser, Frederick M. *Congressional Oversight.* Washington, DC: Congressional Research Service, 2001.

Karp, Naomi, and Erica Wood. "Health Plan Internal Consumer Dispute Resolution Practices: Highlights from a National Study," 5 *Journal of Health Care Law & Policy* 283 (2002).

Kaufman, Herbert. *Are Government Organizations Immortal?* Washington, DC: Brookings Institution, 1976.

_____. *The Forest Ranger: A Study in Administrative Behavior.* Baltimore: Johns Hopkins University Press, 1960.

Kerwin, Cornelius M. *Rulemaking,* 3rd ed. Washington, DC: CQ Press, 2005.

Kettl, Donald F. *Sharing Power.* Washington, DC: Brookings Institution, 1993.

_____. *System Under Stress: Homeland Security and American Politics.* Washington, DC: CQ Press, 2004.

Keyes, W. Noel. *Government Contracts,* 4th ed. St. Paul, MN: West Publishing, 2005.

_____. *Government Contracts: Under the Federal Acquisition Regulation,* 2nd ed. St. Paul, MN: West Publishing, 1996.

Kingdon, John W. *Agendas, Alternatives, and Public Policies.* New York: Harper Collins, 1984.

Kitrosser, Heidi. "Secrecy in the Immigration Courts and Beyond: Considering the Right to Know in the Administrative State," 39 *Harvard Civil Rights – Civil Liberties L. Rev.* 95 (2004).

Klonoski, James R., and Robert I. Mendelsohn, *The Politics of Local Justice.* Boston: Little, Brown, 1970.

Kluger, Richard. *Simple Justice.* New York: Knopf, 1976.

Krishnan, Jayanth K., and Kevin R. den Dulk, "So Help Me God: A Comparative Study of Religious Interest Group Litigation," 30 *Georgia J. Int'l & Comp. L.* 233 (2002).

Krislov, Samuel. *Representative Bureaucracy.* Englewood Cliffs, NJ: Prentice Hall, 1974.

Landis, James M. *The Administrative Process.* New Haven: Yale University Press, 1938.

Lasswell, Harold D. *Politics: Who Gets What, When and How.* New York: McGraw-Hill, 1936.

Lessig, Lawrence and Cass Sunstein, "The President and the Administration," 94 *Columbia L. Rev.* 2 (1994).

Leuchtenburg, William. *Franklin D. Roosevelt and the New Deal, 1932–1940.* New York: Harper and Row, 1963.

_____. *The Perils of Prosperity.* Chicago: University of Chicago Press, 1958.

Leventhal, Harold. "Public Contracts and Administrative Law," 52 *ABA J.* 85 (1966).

Levi, Edward. *An Introduction to Legal Reasoning.* Chicago: University of Chicago Press, 1949.

Levin, A. Leo. "Court Annexed Arbitration," 16 *Journal of Law Reform* 537 (1983).

Levitan, David. "The Responsibility of Administrative Officials in a Democratic Society," 61 *Political Science Quarterly* 562 (1946).

Lewis, Anthony. *Gideon's Trumpet.* New York: Random House, 1964.

Lewis, Carol W. *The Ethics Challenge in Public Service.* San Francisco: Jossey-Bass, 1991.

Lichty, John. *Redress Against Sovereignty: A Study of the Increasing Liability of Municipalities in Tort.* Grand Forks, ND: Bureau of Government Affairs, 1972.

Light, Paul C. *The True Size of Government.* Washington, DC: Brookings Institution, 1999.

Lockhart, William J. "Discretionary Clemency: Mercy at the Prosecutor's Option," 1976 *Utah L. Rev.* 55 (1976).

Locust, Carol. "The Impact of Differing Belief Systems between Native Americans and Their Rehabilitation Service Providers," 9 *Rehabilitation Education* 205 (1995).

_____. "Walking in Two Worlds: Native Americans and the VR System," 22 *American Rehabilitation,* 2 (1996).

Loevinger, Lee. "The Administrative Agency as a Paradigm of Government: A Survey of the Administrative Process," 40 *Indiana L. J.* 287 (1965).

Long, Norton. "Bureaucracy and Constitutionalism," 46 *American Political Science Rev.* 808 (1952).

Lorch, Robert S. *Democratic Process and Administrative Law.* Detroit: Wayne State University Press, 1969.

Louisiana Advisory Committee to the U.S. Commission on Civil Rights. *The Battle for Environmental Justice in Louisiana: Government, Industry, and the People.* Washington, DC: U.S. Commission on Civil Rights, 1993.

Lowi, Theodore. *The End of Liberalism.* New York: Norton, 1969.

_____. "Four Systems of Policy, Politics and Choice," *Public Administration Review* 298 (1972).

Lynn, Laurence E., Jr., Carolyn J. Heinrich, and Carolyn J. Hill. *Improving Governance: A New Logic for Empirical Research.* Washington, DC: Georgetown University Press, 2001.

MacNeil, Neil, and Harold W. Metz. *The Hoover Commission Report, 1953–1955: What It Means to You as Citizens and Taxpayers.* New York: Macmillan, 1956.

Madison, James. *Notes on Debates in the Federal Convention of 1787.* Athens: Ohio University Press, 1966.

Maine, Sir Henry. *Ancient Law.* London: Dent, 1972.

Mandelman, Joel C. "Lest We Walk into the Well: Guarding the Keys – Encrypting the Constitution: To Speak, Search and Seize in Cyberspace," 8 *Albany Law Journal of Science & Technology* 227 (1998).

March, James G., and Johan P. Olsen, *Rediscovering Institutions: The Organizational Basis of Politics.* New York: Free Press, 1990.

Marchese, Steven. "Putting Square Pegs into Round Holes: Mediation and the Rights of Children with Disabilities under the Individuals with Disabilities Education Act," 53 *Rutgers L. Rev.* 333 (2001).

Markham, Jerry W. "The Federal Advisory Committee Act," 35 *U. Pittsburgh L. Rev.* 557 (1974).

Mashaw, Jerry L., et al., *Social Security Hearings and Appeals: A Study of the Social Security Administrative Hearing System.* Lexington, MA: D.C. Heath, 1978.

_____. "The Supreme Court's Due Process Calculus for Administrative Adjudication in *Mathews v. Eldridge*: Three Factors in Search of a Theory of Value," 44 *U. Chicago L. Rev.* 28 (1976).

Mayer, Kenneth R. *With the Stroke of a Pen*. Princeton: Princeton University Press, 2001.

Mazmanian, Daniel A., and Paul A. Sabatier. *Effective Policy Implementation*. Lexington, MA: D.C. Heath, 1981.

McCulloch, David. *Truman*. New York: Simon and Schuster, 1992.

McFarland, Carl. "Landis' Report: The Voice of One Crying in the Wilderness," 47 *Virginia L. Rev.* 373 (1961).

McGowan, Carl. "Reflections on Rulemaking Review," 53 *Tulane L. Rev.* 681 (1979).

Meier, Kenneth. "Representative Bureaucracy: An Empirical Analysis," 69 *American Political Science Rev.* 526 (1975).

_____. Thomas Garman, and Lael R. Keiser. *Regulation and Consumer Protection: Politics, Bureaucracy, and Economics,* 3rd ed. Houston: DAME Publications, Inc., 1998.

Meiklejohn, Alexander. *Political Freedom*. New York: Oxford, 1965.

Menkel-Meadow, Carrie. "When Dispute Resolution Begets Disputes of Its Own: Conflicts Among Dispute Professionals," 44 *UCLA L. Rev.* 1871 (1997).

Meyerhoff, Albert H., and Jeffrey A. Mishkin, "Application of *Goldberg v. Kelly* Hearing Requirements to Termination of Social Security Benefits," 26 *Stanford L. Rev.* 549 (1974).

Milunsky, Aubrey, and Philip Reilly. "The New Genetics: Emerging Medicolegal Issues in the Prenatal Diagnosis of Hereditary Disorders," 1 *American Journal of Law & Medicine* 71 (1975).

Milward, H. Brinton. "The Changing Character of the Public Sector," in James Perry, ed. *Handbook of Public Administration,* 2nd ed. San Francisco: Jossey-Bass, 1996.

_____. "Implications of Contracting Out: New Roles for the Hollow State," in Patricia W. Ingraham and Barbara S. Romzek, eds. *New Paradigms for Government*. San Francisco: Jossey-Bass, 1994.

Mintzberg, Henry. "A Note on that Dirty Word 'Efficiency'," 5 *Interfaces* 101 (1982).

Moe, Ronald C. "Exploring the Limits of Privatization," 47 *Public Administration Rev.* 453 (1987).

_____. "'Law' Versus 'Performance' as Objective Standard," 48 *Public Administration Rev.* 675 (1988).

_____ and Robert S. Gilmour, "Rediscovering Principles of Public Administration: The Neglected Foundation of Public Law," 55 *Public Administration Review* 135 (1995).

_____ and Thomas H. Stanton, "Government-Sponsored Enterprises as Federal Instrumentalities: Reconciling Private Management with Public Accountability," 49 *Public Administration Rev.* 321 (1989).

Moe, Terry M. "The Economics of Organization," 26 *American Journal of Political Science* 739 (1984).

Morgan, Thomas D. "Achieving National Goals Through Federal Contracts: Giving Form to an Unconstrained Administrative Process," 1974 *Wisconsin L. Rev.* 301 (1974).

Morris, Clarence, ed. *The Great Legal Philosophers*. Philadelphia: University of Pennsylvania Press, 1971.

Mosher, Frederick C., ed. *American Public Administration: Past, Present, Future*. Tuscaloosa: University of Alabama Press, 1975.

_____. "The Changing Responsibilities and Tactics of the Federal Government," 40 *Public Administration Review* 541 (1980).

_____. *Democracy and the Public Service*. New York: Oxford University Press, 1968.

_____. "The Public Service in the Temporary Society," 31 *Public Administration Review* 47 (1971).

Murphy, Walter F. *Elements of Judicial Strategy*. Chicago: University of Chicago Press, 1964.

_____. "Lower Court Checks on Supreme Court Power," 53 *American Political Science Rev.* 1017 (1959).

Nakamura, Robert T., and Frank Smallwood. *The Politics of Policy Implementation*. New York: St. Martins, 1980.

Nalbandian, John. *Professionalism in Local Government: Transformations in Roles, Responsibilities and Values of City Managers*. San Francisco: Jossey-Bass, 1991.

Nathan, Richard. *The Plot That Failed*. New York: Wiley, 1975.

National Academy of Public Administration. *Congressional Oversight of Regulatory Agencies: The Need to Strike a Balance and Focus on Performance*. Washington, DC: National Academy of Public Administration, 1988.

National Commission on Terrorist Attacks Upon the United States. *The 9/11 Commission Report: Final Report of the National Commission on Terrorist Attacks Upon the United States*. Washington, DC: Government Printing Office, 2003.

National League of Cities. *The New World of Municipal Liability: Current City Trends and Legislative Actions in the Fifty States*. Washington, DC: National League of Cities, 1978.

National Performance Review, *Improving Regulatory Systems*. Washington, DC: National Performance Review, 1993.

National Research Council. *Risk Assessment in the Federal Government: Managing the Process*. Washington, DC: National Academy Press, 1983.

Nejelski, Paul, and Andrew S. Zeldin. "Court Annexed Arbitration in the Federal Courts: The Philadelphia Story," 42 *Maryland L. Rev.* 787 (1983).

Neuborne, Burt. "The Myth of Parity," 90 *Harvard L. Rev.* 1105 (1977).

_____. "The Procedural Assault on the Warren Legacy: A Study in Repeal by Indirection," 5 *Hofstra L. Rev.* 545 (1977).

Neustadt, Richard. *Presidential Power.* New York: Wiley, 1960.

Noll, Roger G. *Reforming Regulation: An Evaluation of the Ash Council Proposals.* Washington, DC: Brookings Institution, 1971.

Note: "*City of North Miami v. Kurtz*: Is Sacrificing Employee Privacy Rights the Cost of Health Care Reform," 27 *University of Toledo L. Rev.* 545 (1996).

_____. "Gubernatorial Executive Orders as Devices for Administrative Direction and Control," 50 *Iowa Law Rev.* 78 (1964).

O'Brien, David. *Storm Center,* 3rd ed. New York: W. W. Norton, 1993.

O'Connor, Karen, and Lee Epstein. "Amicus Curiae Participation in U.S. Supreme Court Litigation," 16 *Law & Society Review* 311 (1981).

_____. "The Rise of Conservative Interest Group Litigation," 45 *Journal of Politics* 479 (1983).

Ogul, Morris. *Congress Oversees the Bureaucracy.* Pittsburgh: Pittsburgh University Press, 1976.

O'Leary, Rosemary. *Environmental Change: Federal Courts and the EPA.* Philadelphia: Temple University Press, 1993.

Olson, William. "Governmental Immunity from Tort Liability: Two Decades of Decline," 31 *Baylor Law Rev.* 485 (1979).

Organization for Economic Cooperation and Development (OECD). *Managing Across Levels of Government.* Paris: OECD, 1997.

_____. *The OECD Report on Regulatory Reform.* Paris: OECD, 1997.

_____. *Putting Markets to Work: The Design and Use of Marketable Permits and Obligations.* Paris: OECD, 1997.

_____. *Regulatory Impact Analysis: Best Practices in OECD Countries.* Paris: OECD, 1997.

Osborne, David, and Ted Gaebler. *Reinventing Government.* New York: Penguin, 1992.

Ostrum, Vincent. *The Intellectual Crisis in American Public Administration,* 2nd ed. Tuscaloosa: University of Alabama Press, 1989.

O'Toole, Lawrence J., Jr., "Different Public Managements? Implications of Structural Context in Hierarchies and Networks," in Jeff Brudney, Laurence J. O'Toole, and Hal Rainey, eds. *Advancing Public Management: New Directions in Theory, Methods, and Practice.* Washington, DC: Georgetown University Press, 2000.

Ott, J. Steven. *The Organizational Culture Perspective.* Belmont, CA: Wadsworth, 1989.

Packer, Herbert L. "Two Models of the Criminal justice Process," in George F. Cole, ed. *Criminal Justice: Law and Politics.* Belmont, CA: Duxbury Press, 1972.

Park, Rozelia S. "An Examination of International Environmental Racism Through the Lens of Transboundary Movement of Hazardous Wastes," 5 *Indiana Journal of Global Legal Studies* 659 (1998).

Paton, George W., and David P. Derham. *A Textbook of Jurisprudence,* 4th ed. London: Oxford University Press, 1972.

Pederson, William. "Formal Records and Informal Rulemaking," 85 *Yale L. J.* 38 (1975).

Peltason, Jack W. *Federal Courts in the Political Process.* Garden City, NY: Doubleday, 1955.

_____. *Fifty-Eight Lonely Men.* Urbana: University of Illinois Press, 1971.

Perritt, Henry H., Jr., "Property and Innovation in the Global Information Infrastructure," 1996 *University of Chicago Legal Forum* 261 (1996).

Perry, James, ed. *The Handbook of Public Administration,* 2nd ed. San Francisco: Jossey-Bass, 1996.

Peters, B. Guy, and Donald Savoie, eds. *Governance in a Changing Environment.* Montreal: McGill-Queens University Press, 1995.

Peterson, Paul E. *The Price of Federalism.* Washington, DC: Brookings, 1995.

Pfifnner, James P. *The Strategic Presidency,* 2nd ed., revised. Lawrence, KS: University Press of Kansas, 1996.

Pierre, Jon. "The Marketization of the State: Citizens, Consumers, and the Emergence of the Public Market," in B. Guy Peters and Donald Savoie, eds., *Governance in a Changing Environment.* Montreal: McGill-Queen's University Press, 1995.

Porette, Maureen, and Brian Gunn. "The Family and Medical Leave Act of 1993: The Time Has Finally Come for Governmental Recognition of True 'Family Values,'" 8 *St. John's Journal of Legal Commentary* 587 (1993).

Portwood, Sharon G. "Employment Discrimination in the Public Sector Based on Sexual Orientation: Conflicts Between Research Evidence and the Law," 19 *Law & Psychology Rev.* 113 (1995).

Post, Charles G. *The Supreme Court and Political Questions.* New York: Da Capo Press, 1969.

Pound, Roscoe. *Administrative Law: Its Growth, Procedure and Significance.* Pittsburgh: University of Pittsburgh Press, 1942.

_____. *An Introduction to the Philosophy of Law.* New Haven: Yale University Press, 1954.

_____. "The Scope and Purpose of Sociological Jurisprudence," 25 *Harvard L. Rev.* 487 (1912).

President's Advisory Council on Executive Organization (Ash Council). *A New Regulatory Framework: Report on Selected Independent Regulatory Agencies.* Washington, DC: Government Printing Office, 1971.

Pressman, Jeffrey L., and Aaron B. Wildavsky. *Implementation,* 3rd ed. Berkeley: University of California Press, 1984.

Pritchett, C. Herman. "Public Law and Judicial Behavior," 30 *Journal of Politics* 480 (1968).

Privacy Protection Study Commission. *Personal Privacy in an Information Society.* Washington, DC: Government Printing Office, 1977.

_____. *The Privacy Act of 1974: An Assessment.* Washington, DC: Government Printing Office, 1977.

Rabe, Barry G. *Beyond NIMBY: Hazardous Waste Siting in Canada and the United States.* Washington, DC: Brookings Institution, 1994.

Rainey, Hal. "The 'How Much Process is Due?' Debate: Legal and Managerial Perspectives," in Phillip J. Cooper and Chester A. Newland, eds. *Handbook of Public Law and Administration.* San Francisco: Jossey-Bass, 1997.

Ramirez, Steven A. "Depoliticizing Financial Regulation," 41 *William & Mary L. Rev.* 503 (2000).

Reagan, Michael D. *The New Federalism.* New York: Oxford University Press, 1972.

Redford, Emmette. *Ideal and Practice in Public Administration.* Tuscaloosa: University of Alabama, 1958.

_____. "The President and the Regulatory Commissions," 44 *Tulane L. Rev.* 288 (1965).

Reich, Charles. "The New Property, " 78 *Yale L. J.* 733 (1964).

Remini, Robert. *Andrew Jackson.* New York: Harper & Row, 1966.

Ribicoff, Abraham. "Congressional Oversight and Regulatory Reform," 28 *Administrative L. Rev.* 415 (1976).

Richards, Craig, Rima Shore, and Max. B. Sawicky. *Risky Business: Private Management of Public Schools.* Washington, DC: Economic Policy Institute, 1996.

Richardson, Richard J., and Kenneth L. Vines, *The Politics of Federal Courts.* Boston: Little, Brown, 1970.

Ripley, Randall B., and Grace A. Franklin. *Congress, the Bureaucracy, and Public Policy,* 4th ed. Chicago Dorsey Press, 1987.

Riskin, Leonard L., and Philip P. Reilly, "Remedies for Improper Disclosure of Genetic Data," 8 *Rutgers-Camden L. J.* 480 (1977).

Rivlin, Alice M. *Reviving the American Dream: The Economy, the States, and the Federal Government.* Washington, DC: Brookings Institution, 1992.

Robinson, Glenn O. "The Federal Communications Commission: An Essay on Regulatory Watchdogs," 64 *Virginia L. Rev.* 169 (1978).

Rochefort, David A., and Roger W. Cobb, "Problem Definition, Agenda Access, and Policy Choice," 21 *Policy Studies Journal* 56 (1993).

Rohr, John. *Ethics for Bureaucrats.* 2nd ed. New York: Marcel Dekker, 1989.

_____. *To Run a Constitution: The Legitimacy of the Administrative State.* Lawrence, KS: Kansas University Press, 1986.

Romzek, Barbara S., and Melvin Dubnick, "Accountability in the Public Sector: Lessons from the Challenger Tragedy," 47 *Public Administration Rev.* 227 (1987).

Root, Elihu. "Public Service by the Bar," in Robert Bacon and James B. Scott, eds., *Elihu Root: Addresses on Government and Citizenship.* Cambridge: Harvard University Press, 1916.

Rosen, Bernard. "Uncertainty in the Senior Executive Service," 41 *Public Administration Rev.* 203 (1981).

Rosenbaum, Walter A. *Environmental Politics and Policy,* 6th ed. Washington, DC: CQ Press, 2005.

Rosenberg, Morton. *Investigative Oversight: An Introduction to the Law, Practice and Procedure of Congressional Inquiry.* Washington, DC: Congressional Research Service, 1995.

Rosenbloom, David. "Public Administrators, Official Immunity, and the Supreme Court: Developments During the 1970s," 40 *Public Administration Rev.* 166 (1980).

Rourke, Francis. *Bureaucracy, Politics, and Public Policy.* Boston: Little, Brown, 1969.

Rumble, Wilfred E., Jr. *American Legal Realism.* Ithaca, NY: Cornell University Press, 1968.

Rustad, Michael L., and Sandra R. Paulsson. "Monitoring Employee E-mail and Internet Usage: Avoiding the Omniscient Electronic Sweatshop: Insights from Europe," 7 *U. Pennsylvania. J. Labor & Employment Law* 829 (2005).

Rutland, Robert A. *The Birth of the Bill of Rights, 1776–1791.* Chapel Hill: University of North Carolina Press, 1955.

Rhyne, Charles, William Rhyne, and Stephen Elmendorf. *Tort Liability and Immunity of Municipal Officers.* Washington, DC: National Institute of Municipal Law Officers, 1976.

Sabatier, Paul A., and Hanj C. Jenkins-Smith, eds. *Policy Change: An Advocacy Coalition Approach*. Boulder, CO: Westview Publishing, 1993.

Salamon, Lester M., ed. *Beyond Privatization: The Tools of Government Action*. Washington, DC: Urban Institute, 1989.

_____. *Partners in Public Service: Government-Nonprofit Relations in the Modern Welfare State*. Baltimore: Johns Hopkins University Press, 1995.

_____. *Resilient Sector: The State of Nonprofit America*. Washington, DC: Brookings Institution Press, 2003.

_____. *The Tools of Government: A Guide to the New Governance*. New York: Oxford University Press, 2002.

Sandel, Michael J. *Democracy's Discontent*. Cambridge: Harvard University Press, 1996.

Savoie, Donald ed. *Restoring Accountability: Research Studies, Volumes 1, 2, & 3*. In Commission of Inquiry into the Sponsorship Program & Advertising Activities. Ottawa: Public Works and Government Services Canada, 2006.

Savoie, Donald J. *Thatcher, Reagan, Mulroney: In Search of a New Bureaucracy*. Toronto: University of Toronto Press, 1994.

Scalia, Antonin. "Vermont Yankee: The APA, the D.C. Circuit, and the Supreme Court," 1979 *Supreme Court Rev.* 345 (1979).

Schattschneider, E. E. *The Semi-Sovereign People*. New York: Holt, Rinehart, and Winston, 1960.

Schein, Edgar. *Organizational Culture and Leadership,* 2nd ed. San Francisco: Jossey-Bass, 1992.

Schivo, Mary. *Flying Blind, Flying Safe*. New York: Avon Books, 1997.

Schlesinger, Arthur M. *The Coming of the New Deal*. Boston: Houghton Mifflin, 1958.

Schmidhauser, John R. *Judges and Justices*. Boston: Little, Brown, 1979.

Schreiber, Mark E. "Employer E-Mail and Internet Risks, Policy Guidelines and Investigations," 85 *Massachusetts L. Rev.* 74 (2000).

Schubert, Glendon. *Judicial Policy Making,* rev. ed. Glenview, IL: Scott, Foresman, 1974.

_____. "The Public Interest in Administrative Decision Making: Theorem, Theosophy, or Theory," 51 *American Political Science Rev.* 346 (1957).

Schuck, Peter. *Agent Orange in Court*. Cambridge: Belknap, 1986.

Schwartz, Bernard. *Administrative Law*. Boston: Little, Brown, 1976.

_____. "The Legislative Veto and the Constitution—A Reexamination," 46 *Geo. Wash. L. Rev.* 351 (1978).

Seidman, Harold. *Politics, Position, and Power,* 2nd ed. New York: Oxford University Press, 1976.

Selznick, Philip. *TVA and the Grassroots*. New York: Harper & Row, 1949.

Sever, Donald W., Jr. *Seabrook and the Nuclear Regulatory Commission: The Licensing of a Nuclear Power Plant*. Hanover, NH: University Press of New England, 1980.

Shapiro, Martin. "Political Jurisprudence," 52 *Kentucky L. J.* 294 (1964).

_____. *The Supreme Court and Administrative Agencies*. New York: Free Press, 1968.

Shapiro, Sidney A. "Outsourcing Government Regulation," 53 *Duke L. J.* 389 (2003).

Sharfman, Isaiah. *The Interstate Commerce Commission*. New York: The Commonwealth Fund, 1937.

Shumpeter, Joseph. *Capitalism, Socialism, and Democracy,* 3rd ed. New York: Harper & Row, 1950.

Sidak, J. Gregory, and Daniel F. Spulber. *Deregulatory Takings and the Regulatory Contract: The Competitive Transformation of Network Industries in the United States*. Cambridge: Cambridge University Press, 1997.

Simon, Herbert. *Administrative Behavior,* 3rd ed. New York: Free Press, 1976.

Simon, James F. *In His Own Image: The Supreme Court in Richard Nixon's Era*. New York: McKay, 1973.

Smith, Jerome. "Social Security Appeals in Disability Cases," 28 *Administrative L. Rev.* 13, 14 (1976).

Sofaer, Abraham. "The Change-of-Status Adjudication: A Case Study of the Informal Agency Process," 1 *Journal of Legal Studies* 349 (1972).

_____. "Judicial Control of Informal Discretionary Adjudication and Enforcement," 72 *Columbia L. Rev.* 1293 (1972).

Stanton, Thomas H. "Increasing the Accountability of Government-Sponsored Enterprises: First Steps," 50 *Public Administration Review* 590 (1990).

_____. "Increasing the Accountability of Government-Sponsored Enterprises: Next Steps," 51 *Public Administration Review* 572 (1991).

_____. *A State of Risk: Will Government-Sponsored Enterprises Be the Next Financial Crisis?* New York: Harper Business, 1991.

Stason, E. Blythe, and Frank E. Cooper. *The Law of Administration Tribunals: A Collection of Judicial Decisions, Statutes, Administrative Rules and Orders and Other Materials,* 3rd ed. Chicago: Callaghan, 1957.

Steck, Henry J. "Private Influence on Environmental Policy: The Case of the National Industrial Pollution Control Council," 5 *Environmental Law* 241 (1975).

Stevenson, Dru. "Privatization of Welfare Services: Delegation by Commercial Contract," 45 *Ariz. L. Rev.* 83 (2003).

Stewart, Richard B. "Regulation, Innovation, and Administrative Law: A Conceptual Framework," 69 *California L. Rev.* 1263 (1981).

_____. "The Reformation of American Administrative Law," 88 *Harvard L. Rev.* 1667 (1975).

_____. "Vermont Yankee and the Evolution of Administrative Procedure," 91 *Harvard L. Rev.* 10 (1978).

Stiglitz, Joseph E. *The Roaring Nineties.* New York: W. W. Norton, 2003.

Stockman, David A. *The Triumph of Politics: Why the Reagan Revolution Failed.* New York: Harper & Row, 1986.

Stone, Julius. *The Province and Function of Law.* Cambridge: Harvard University Press, 1950.

Storing, Herbert. "American Statesmanship: Old and New," in R. Goldwin, ed., *Bureaucrats, Policy Analysts, Statesmen: Who Leads?* Washington, DC: American Enterprise Institute, 1980.

_____. "The Crucial Link: Public Administration, Responsibility and the Public Interest, 24 *Public Administration Rev.* 39 (1964).

Sundquist, James L. *The Decline and Resurgence of Congress.* Washington, DC: Brookings Institution, 1981.

Susskind, Lawrence, and Gerard McMahon, "The Theory and Practice of Negotiated Rulemaking," 3 *Yale Journal on Regulation* 133, 136–37 (1985).

Sutherland, S. L. "The Al-Mashat affair," 34 *Canadian Public Administration* 573 (1992).

Tate, C. Neal, and Torbjorn Vallinder, eds. *The Global Expansion of Judicial Power.* New York: New York University Press, 1995.

Thompson, James D. *Organizations in Action.* New York: McGraw-Hill, 1967.

Tribe, Laurence. *American Constitutional Law.* Mineola, NY: Foundation Press, 1978.

Tucker, Edwin W. *Text-Cases-Problems on Administrative Law, Regulation of Enterprise and Individual Liberties.* St. Paul, MN: West Publishing, 1975.

Ulmer, S. Sidney. *Courts, Law and Judicial Processes.* New York: Free Press, 1981.

United Nations. *Agenda 21 The United Nations Programme of Action from Rio.* New York: United Nations, 1992.

_____. *The Copenhagen Declaration and Programme of Action.* New York: United Nations, 1995.

United Nations Environmental Programme. *Global Environmental Outlook.* New York: Oxford University Press, 1997.

_____. *Report of the United Nations Conference on the Human Environment.* New York: United Nations, 1972.

U.S. Commission on Government Procurement, *Report of the Commission on Government Procurement.* Washington, DC: Government Printing Office, 1972.

U.S. Congress. Joint Committee Print of the Senate Committee on Government Operations and the House Committee on Government Operations, *Government in the Sunshine Act, S.5 (Pub. L. No. 94-409); Source Book, Legislative History, Texts, and Other Documents,* 94th Congress, 2nd Session, (1976).

_____. Joint Committee Print of the Senate Committee on Government Operations and the Subcommittee on Government Information and Individual Rights of the House Committee on Government Operations, *Legislative History of the Privacy Act of 1974, Source Book on Privacy,* 94th Cong., 2nd Sess. (1976).

_____. Joint Committee Print of the Subcommittee on Government Information and Individual Rights and the Subcommittee on Administrative Practice and Procedure of the Senate Committee on the Judiciary, Freedom of Information Act Amendments of 1974, *Source Book, Legislative History, Text, and Other Documents,* 94th Cong., 1st Sess. (1975).

U.S. Department of Homeland Security, Office of the Inspector General. *Department of Homeland Security, Major Management Challenges Facing the Department of Homeland Security.* Washington, DC: Department of Homeland Security Office of Inspector General, 2004.

U.S. Department of Justice. *Legal Authorities Supporting the Activities of the National Security Agency Described by the President.* Washington, DC: Department of Justice, 2006.

_____. Office of the Inspector General. *The September 11 Detainees: A Review of the Treatment of Aliens Held on Immigration Charges in Connection with the Investigation of the September 11 Attacks.* Washington, DC: U.S. Department of Justice, 2003.

U.S. Environmental Protection Agency. *A Study of State and Local Government Procurement Practices that Consider Environmental Performance of Goods and Services.* Washington, DC: Environmental Protection Agency, 1996.

U.S. Federal Election Commission. *Legislative History of Federal Election Campaign Act Amendment of 1974.* Washington, DC: Government Printing Office, 1977.

U.S. Federal Trade Commission. *Marketing Violent Entertainment to Children: A Review of Self-Regulation and Industry Practices in the Motion Picture, Music Recording, & Electronic Game Industries.* Washington, DC: Federal Trade Commission, 2000.

U.S. Government Accountability Office. *Acquisition Reform: Purchase Car Use Cuts Procurement Costs, Improves Efficiency.* Washington, DC: GAO, 1996.

_____. *Administrative Law Process: Better Management Is Needed.* Washington, DC: GAO, 1978.

_____. *Alternative Dispute Resolution: Employers' Experiences with ADR in the Workplace.* Washington, DC: GAO, 1997.

_____. *Aviation Security Challenges in Using Biometric Technologies.* Washington, DC: GAO, 2004.

_____. *Block Grants: Characteristics, Experience, and Lessons Learned.* Washington, DC: GAO, 1995.

_____. *Business Regulation: California Manufacturers Use Multiple Strategies to Comply with Laws.* Washington, DC: GAO, 1998.

_____. *Columbia River Basin: A Multilayered Collection of Directives and Plans Guide Federal Fish and Wildlife Activities.* Washington, DC: GAO, 2004.

_____. *High Risk Series: Information Management and Technology.* Washington, DC: GAO, 1997.

_____. *HMO Complaints and Appeals.* Washington, DC: GAO, 1998.

_____. *Homeland Security: Further Action Needed to Promote Successful Use of Special DHS Acquisition Authority.* Washington, DC : GAO, 2004.

_____. *Homeland Security: Overview of Department of Homeland Security Management Challenges.* Washington, DC: GAO, 2005.

_____. *Homeland Security: Reforming Federal Grants to Better Meet Outstanding Needs.* Washington, DC: GAO, 2003.

_____. *Human Capital: Building on the Current Momentum to Transform the Federal Government.* Washington, DC: GAO, 2004.

_____. *Illegal Aliens: Changes in the Process of Denying Aliens Entry into the United States.* Washington, DC: GAO, 1998.

_____. *Improving the Sourcing Decisions of the Government.* Washington, DC: GAO, 2003.

_____. *Information Management: Implementation of the Freedom of Information Act.* Washington, DC: GAO, 2005.

_____. *Information Management Reform: Effective Implementation Is Essential for Improving Federal Performance.* Washington, DC: GAO, 1996.

_____. *Information Security: Continued Efforts Needed to Sustain Progress in Implementing Statutory Requirement.* Washington, DC: GAO, 2005.

_____. *Information Security: Emerging Cybersecurity Issues Threaten Federal Information Systems.* Washington, DC: GAO, 2005.

_____. *Information Security: Internal Revenue Service Needs to Remedy Serious Weaknesses over Taxpayer and Bank Secrecy Act Data.* Washington, DC: GAO, 2005.

_____. *Information Security Management: Learning from Leading Organizations.* Washington, DC: GAO, 1998.

_____. *Information Security: Serious Weaknesses Place Critical Federal Operations and Assets at Risk.* Washington, DC: GAO, 1998.

_____. *Medicare: Concerns Regarding Plans to Transfer the Appeals Workload from SSA to HHS Remain.* Washington: DC: GAO, 2005.

_____. *Medicare: Incomplete Plan to Transfer Appeals Workload from SSA to HHS Threatens Service to Appellants.* Washington, DC: GAO, 2004.

_____. *North American Free Trade Agreement: Impacts and Implementation.* Washington, DC: GAO, 1997.

_____. *Occupational Safety and Health: Violations of Safety and Health Regulations by Federal Contractors.* Washington, DC: GAO, 1996.

_____. *Private and Public Prisons: Studies Comparing Operational Costs and/or Quality of Service.* Washington, DC: GAO, 1996.

_____. *Regulatory Reform: Implementation of the Regulatory Review Executive Order.* Washington, DC: GAO, 1996.

_____. *Siting of Hazardous Waste Landfills and Their Correlation with Racial and Economic Status of Surrounding Communities.* Washington, DC: GAO, 1983.

_____. *Social Security Disability: SSA Actions to Reduce Backlogs and Achieve More Consistent Decisions Deserve High Priority.* Washington, DC: GAO, 1997.

_____. *Social Security Disability: SSA Making Progress in Conducting Continuing Disability Reviews.* Washington, DC: GAO, 1998.

_____. *Social Security Numbers: Federal and State Laws Restrict Use of SSNs, Yet Gaps Remain.* Washington, DC: GAO, 2005.

_____. *Unfunded Mandates: Reform Act Has Had Little Effect on Agencies' Rulemaking Actions.* Washington, DC: GAO, 1998.

_____. *Worker Protection: Federal Contractors and Violations of Labor Law.* Washington, DC: GAO, 1995.

U.S. House of Representatives. Hearings Before the Committee on Post Office and Civil Service, *Selection and Oversight of Administrative Law Judges,* 96th Cong., 2nd Sess., (1980).

_____. Hearing Before the Subcommittee on Immigration, Refugees, and International Law of the Committee on the Judiciary, *Central American Asylum-Seekers,* 101st Cong., 1st Sess. (1989).

_____. Report of the Subcommittee on Oversight and Investigation of the Committee on Interstate and Foreign Commerce, *Cost-Benefit Analysis: Wonder Tool or Mirage?* 96th Cong., 2nd Sess. (1980).

_____. Subcommittee on Social Security of the Committee on Ways and Means, *Background Materials on Social Security Hearings and Appeals,* 94th Cong., 1st Sess. (1975).

_____. Subcommittee on Social Security of the Committee on Ways and Means, *Delays in Social Security Appeals,* 94th Cong., 1st Sess. (1975).

_____. Subcommittee on Social Security of the Committee on Ways and Means, *Staff Survey of State Disability Agencies Under Social Security and SSI Program,* 94th Cong., 1st Sess. (1975).

_____. Task Force on Legal Services and Procedure, *Report on Legal Services and Procedure Prepared for the Commission on Organization of the Executive Branch,* House Doc. no. 1128, 84th Cong., 1st Sess. (1955).

U.S. Merit System Protection Board. *The Changing Federal Workplace: Employee Perspectives.* Washington, DC: MSPB, 1998.

_____. *Federal Supervisors and Strategic Human Resources Management.* Washington, DC: MSPB, 1998.

_____. *The Federal Workforce for the 21st Century: Results of the Merit Principles Survey 2000.* Washington, DC: MSPB, 2003.

_____. *What's on the Minds of Federal Human Capital Stakeholders.* Washington, DC: MSPB, 2004.

U.S. Office of Management and Budget. *Federal Information Security Management Act (FISMA) 2004 Report to Congress.* Washington, DC: OMB, 2005.

_____. *The President's Management Agenda.* Washington, DC: OMB, 2001.

_____. *Summary Report of the SWAT Team on Civilian Agency Contracting.* Washington, DC: OMB, 1992.

U.S. Regulatory Council. *Innovative Techniques in Theory and Practice, Proceedings.* Washington, DC: U.S. Regulatory Council, 1980.

_____. *Regulating with Common Sense: A Progress Report on Innovative Regulatory Techniques.* Washington, DC: U.S. Regulatory Council, 1980.

_____. *Regulatory Reform Highlights: An Inventory of Initiatives, 1978–1980.* Washington, DC: U.S. Regulatory Council, 1980.

U.S. Senate. Committee on Governmental Affairs, *Study on Federal Regulation,* 95th Cong., 2nd Sess. (1978).

_____. Committee on Governmental Affairs, *Paperwork Reduction Act of 1995,* Report 104-8, 104th Cong., 1st Sess. (1995).

_____. Congressional Research Service and General Accounting Office for the Subcommittee on Oversight Procedures of the Committee on Government Operations, *Congressional Oversight: Methods and Techniques,* 94th Cong., 2nd Sess. (1976).

_____. Hearings Before the Committee on the Judiciary, *Department of Justice Oversight: Preserving Our Freedoms While Defending Against Terrorism,* 107th Cong., 1st Sess. (2001).

_____. Hearing Before the Armed Services Committee, *Security Failures at Los Alamos National Laboratory,* 106th Cong., 2nd Sess. (2000).

_____. Hearing Before the Subcommittee on Immigration and Refugee Affairs of the Committee on the Judiciary, *Central American Migration to the United States,* 101st Cong., 1st Sess. (1989).

_____. Finance Committee, *FDA, Merck, and Vioxx,* 108th Cong., 2nd Sess. (2004).

_____. Report of the Attorney General's Committee on Administrative Procedure, *Administrative Procedure in Government Agencies,* Sen. Doc. no. 8, 77th Cong., 1st Sess. (1941).

_____. Report of the Committee on the Judiciary to Accompany S. 332 as Amended, *Providing for a GAO Study on Conditions of Displaced Salvadorans and Nicaraguans, and for Other Purposes,* 100th Cong., 1st Sess. (1987).

_____. Report of the Special Committee on National Emergencies and Delegated Emergency Powers, *Executive Orders in Times of War and National Emergency,* 93rd Cong., 2nd Sess. (1974).

_____. *Report on Regulatory Agencies to the President-Elect,* 86th Cong., 2nd Sess. (1960).

_____. Subcommittee on Labor of the Committee on Human Resources, *Legislative History of the Federal Mine Safety and Health Act of 1977,* 95th Cong., 2nd Sess. (1978).

_____. Subcommittee on Labor of the Committee on Labor and Public Welfare, *Legislative History of the Occupational Safety and Health Act of 1970,* 92nd Cong., 1st Sess. (1971).

Vandenbergh, Michael P. "The Private Life of Public Law," 105 *Colum. L. Rev.* 2029 (2005).

Van Alstyne, William. "Cracks in 'The New Property': Adjudicative Due Process in the Administrative State," 62 *Cornell L. Rev.* 445 (1977).

_____. "The Demise of the Right-Privilege Distinction in Constitutional Law," 81 *Harvard L. Rev.* 1439 (1968).

Van Meter, Donald, and Carl Van Horn. "The Policy Implementation Process: A Conceptual Framework," 6 *Administration & Society* 445 (1975).

Vargas, Claudia María, ed. "Symposium: Bridging Solitudes—Partnership Challenges in Canadian Refugee Serivce Delivery," 18 *Refuge* 1 (2000).

_____. "Cultural Mediation for Refugee Children: A Comparative Derived Model," 12 *Journal of Refugee Studies* 284 (1999).

Vasquez, Xavier Carlos. "The North American Free Trade Agreement and Environmental Racism," 34 *Harvard International L. J.* 357 (1993).

Vom Bauer, F. Trowbridge. "Fifty Years of Government Contract Law," 29 *Federal Bar Journal* 305 (1970).

von Hayek, Friedrich. *The Road to Serfdom.* Chicago: University of Chicago Press, 1944.

Vose, Clement E. *Caucasians Only: The Supreme Court, the NAACP, and the Restrictive Covenant Cases.* Berkeley: University of California Press, 1959.

Wald, Martin, and Jeffrey D. Kahn. "Privacy Rights of Public Employees," 6 *The Labor Lawyer* 301 (1990).

Waldo, Dwight. *The Administrative State.* New York: Ronald Press, 1948.

_____. *The Enterprise of Public Administration: A Summary View.* Novato, CA: Chandler & Sharp, 1980.

_____. "Scope of the Theory of Public Administration" in James C. Charlesworth, ed., *Theory and Practice of Public Administration: Scope, Objectives, and Methods, monograph no. 8, Annals of the American Academy of Political and Social Science* (1968).

Walsh, Lawrence E. *Iran-Contra: The Final Report of the Independent Counsel.* New York: Random House, 1993.

Wasby, Stephen L. *The Impact of the United States Supreme Court.* Homewood, IL: Dorsey, 1970.

Weisbrod, A. Burton. "The Future of the Nonprofit Sector: Its Entwining with Private Enterprise and Government,"16 *Journal of Policy Analysis and Management* 541 (1997).

Westin, Alan F. *The Anatomy of a Constitutional Law Case.* New York: Macmillan, 1958.

_____. *Privacy and Freedom.* New York: Atheneum, 1967.

Wexler, Steve. "Discretion: The Unacknowledged Side of Law," 25 *University of Toronto Law Journal* 120 (1972).

White, Leonard D. *The Federalists: A Study in Administrative History.* New York: Macmillan, 1959.

_____. *The Jeffersonians: A Study in Administrative History, 1801–1829.* New York: Macmillan, 1959.

_____. *Introduction to the Study of Public Administration,* 4th ed. New York: Macmillan 1955.

Wildavsky, Aaron. *Speaking Truth to Power.* Boston: Little, Brown, 1979.

Williams, Stephen. "'Hybrid Rulemaking' under the Administrative Procedure Act: A Legal and Empirical Analysis," 42 *U. Chicago L. Rev.* 401 (1975).

Wilson, James Q. *Bureaucracy: What Government Agencies Do and Why They Do It.* New York: Basic Books, 1989.

_____. "The Politics of Regulation," in Wilson, ed. *The Politics of Regulation.* New York: Basic Books, 1980.

Woll, Peter. *Administrative Law: The Informal Process.* Berkeley: University of California Press, 1963.

Wood, Robert. *The Creation of the American Republic, 1776–1787.* Chapel Hill: University of North Carolina Press, 1969.

_____, ed. *Remedial Law: When Courts Become Administrators.* Amherst, MA: University of Massachusetts Press, 1990.

Woolf, Malcolm D. "Clean Air or Hot Air?: Lessons from the Quayle Competitiveness Council's Oversight of EPA," 10 *J. Law & Public Policy* 97 (1993).

World Commission on Environment and Development. *Our Common Future.* New York: Oxford, 1987.

Wright, Deil S. *Understanding Intergovernmental Relations,* 3rd ed. Pacific Grove, CA: Brooks/Cole Publishing, 1988.

Wright, J. Skelly. "Beyond Discretionary Justice," 81 *Yale L. J.* 575 (1972).

_____. "Poverty, Minorities and Respect for Law," 1970 *Duke L. J.* 425 (1970).

Yoo, Christopher S., Steven G. Calabresi, and Laurence D. Nee, "The Unitary Executive During the Third Half-Century, 1889–1945," 80 *Notre Dame L. Rev.* 1 (2004).

Judicial Opinions

Index